THE MERITORIOUS SERVICE MEDAL

I

THE IMMEDIATE AWARDS
1916–1928

By the same Author

MERITORIOUS SERVICE MEDALS TO NAVAL FORCES (1983)
MERITORIOUS SERVICE MEDALS TO AERIAL FORCES (1984)
ASHANTI 1895–96 (with M. Fraser) (1987)
A CONTEMPTIBLE LITTLE FLYING CORPS (with J. V. Webb) (1991)

THE
MERITORIOUS SERVICE
MEDAL

I

THE IMMEDIATE AWARDS
1916–1928

Ian McInnes

THE NAVAL & MILITARY PRESS
LIVERPOOL MEDAL Co. Ltd.
MCMXCII

THE MERITORIOUS SERVICE MEDAL

I

THE IMMEDIATE AWARDS

1916–1928

© 1992

Copyright The London Stamp Exchange Ltd.

Published 1992 By

THE NAVAL & MILITARY PRESS

DALLINGTON

EAST SUSSEX

in conjuntion with

LIVERPOOL MEDAL Co. Ltd.

42 BURY BUSINESS CENTRE

KAY STREET

BURY, LANCS.

Contents

Illustrations

SADDLEWORTH 4500

CRIBBSTONES
DELPH
NEAR OLDHAM
OL3 5BZ

THE LORD RHODES, K.G., D.F.C., P.C., D.L.

I am delighted to have the opportunity to commend this
book on the history of the Meritorious Service Medal to
a wide public I hope. It is not a dry as dust history
of an award. It is a human document that brings to light
unselfish service to our community suitably acknowledged
in the awarding of a medal.

Ian McInnes has worked with devotion and dedication on
his human history and we owe him a deep debt of gratitude.
This book plays a signal tribute to the men and women in
our community who have served it so well.

Lord Rhodes of Saddleworth
K.G.

Dedicated to
GEORGE MOSS

Introduction

THE MERITORIOUS SERVICE MEDAL was first awarded in 1847, with an annuity, to reward specially selected long service Non-Commissioned Officers. However, in 1916 it was decided to award this medal to Warrant Officers, Non-Commissioned Officers and Men, irrespective of rank, without annuity, as a reward for valuable and meritorious service, not necessarily in action with the enemy, *i.e.* for standing there and taking it. All these awards, made until 1928, were promulgated in the *London Gazette*.

Originally this compilation of names and numbers was simply my quick reference, to establish the rarity of a particular immediate Meritorious Service Medal of the Great War period. The desirability of any medal (if one is not exclusively a Regimental/Corps collector, or one who judges value only by condition) depends to a large extent on numbers issued to the particular unit or a certain theatre. This work gives the researcher an immediate answer.

The question as to what to concentrate on is one all of us have faced either once or many times in our years of collecting. For me, the articles published in the *O.M.R.S. Journals* from Summer 1973 to Winter 1975, and written mainly by the Journal's editor, Maj. J. M. A. Tamplin, but also by Capt. K. J. Douglas-Morris, R.N., Mr. N. G. Gooding and Dr. F. K. Mitchell sparked off an almost insatiable quest for M.S.M.s and for background information on the medal.

The excellent series of notes by Major N. W. Poulson in Seaby's *'Coin and Medal Bulletin'* of February and March 1967, assisted enormously as did the introduction to Maj. P. E. Abbot's *'Recipients of the Distinguished Conduct Medal 1855–1909,'* and Mr. J. R. Rooke-Matthews's excellent catalogue of M.S.M.s.

My searches carried me to the Public Records Office, to the Manchester Public Library and to many Regimental Museums, all of whom I found very helpful. To all the curators who were kind enough to provide information of medals in their collection I am gratefully indebted.

A résumé of relevant dates, statutes, etc. follows this introduction. This should help the reader understand the changing history of the award. This résumé is followed by the Royal Warrant published in the London Gazette of 19th November, 1920; this should assist still further.

Once having formed a collection of M.S.M.s it was a short step to wanting to analyse the scarcity or otherwise of examples of the medal which came my way. The immediate awards of 1916-28 provided many questions, I found myself asking how many immediate award M.S.M.s were earned in East Africa, how many to A.S.C., how many for gallantry, how many to Yeomanry etc. Having asked the questions I had to find the answers. This work is the result. With approximately 25,670 Meritorious Service Medals awarded between 1916 and 1928 by the Army, 1,022 by the Navy & 859 by the R.A.F., the results are as accurate as is required to show the common and the rare regiments, theatres etc.

What follows is a copy of the indices of the *London Gazettes* (Part IV 1916 to Part II 1928) which contain the alphabetically listed names of the recipients of immediate M.S.M.s for Valuable Service, Gallantry and Devotion to Duty, to the Army, the Royal Navy, the Royal Marines and the Royal Air Force in this period. It also lists the bars, the forfeitures and the cancellations. To find your man you may have to look in almost every index until you succeed, but a short cut is to initially check in part II of 1918, I of 1919 and II of 1919 which contain respectively 4,862, 6,401 and 7,279 recipients of the Field Marshal's bust type, plus the majority of the R.A.F. and R.N. type awards. A small number of recipients' names have been found in the main *Gazettes* which were not indexed. These have been included.

Some *L.G.'s* listing awards for valuable services in the war contain, against a few recipient's names, a theatre, in brackets, *i.e.* (Malta), (Bermuda), etc. All these small and unexpected areas have been included in the footnotes.

Having once established the year and *L.G.* page of award, the second section should be consulted to establish the date, reason and theatre (Appendix J). Because of the confusion of Gallantry and Valuable Service awards on one page, I have indicated separately in the text the gallantry awards by the use of a rosette (❀).

For the R.N. and R.A.F. obverse medals, the separate sections should, of course, be used.

The third tabulation can then be consulted to obtain numbers of M.S.M.s to that Corps. or Regiment both in total and in that particular theatre (Appendix K). Thus:—

> 1310 Pte./A./Sgt. G. Murison 2/Rhod. R. is found on page 1946 of 1919, which in turn is found to contain 129 recipients for valuable service in East Africa in L.G. 7th February 1919.
> The final tabulation shows this as the only award to the Rhodesian Army.

The collector or researcher will then be able to establish from the actual *London Gazette* the particular battalion or unit of any individual, confirming that which is usually impressed on the rim of the medal itself. The only other information the *London Gazette* may reveal is the home town of the man. This is sometimes prefixed with 'E' indicating that he enlisted in that City or Town. It should be noted that in the case of Cavalry and Yeomanry the actual regiment is not always stated in the Gazette, but in these cases extant medals have been traced which do show the details not included in the Gazette.

These indices show the abbreviation of the rank as it appears on the medal, over the years these have varied. For this reason they have not been standardised.

In certain entries, post nominal letters are shown. This practice began in April 1918. A few awards of the M.S.M. would have been made prior to this date to men who had previously won another decoration, and of course many M.S.M. recipients went on to earn other awards, both military and civil, but for interest I have listed here the numbers of combinations found in the indices.

V.C., M.S.M.	2
M.C., M.B.E., D.C.M., M.S.M.	1
M.C., D.C.M. & bar, M.S.M.	1
M.C., M.M., M.S.M.	1
M.C., M.S.M.	21
D.S.C., M.S.M.	1
D.C.M., M.M., M.S.M.	6
D.C.M., M.S.M.	106
D.S.M., M.S.M.	12
M.M., M.S.M.	219
D.F.M., M.S.M.	1
A.F.M., M.S.M.	1

The immediate Meritorious Service Medal was awarded in the main to men of the Royal Artillery (and its component parts, R.G.A., R.F.A. etc.), and the Corps. For a breakdown, see Appendix K.

As mentioned, these lists include M.S.M.s for gallantry. The work of Major J. D. Sainsbury, *'For Gallantry in the Performance of Military Duty'* has been invaluable in confirming my research and especially in revealing many details of previously unpublished citations and recommendations.

The footnotes represent 15 years of culling auction and sale catalogues, answering numberless letters from collectors, scouring the *Gazettes* themselves, and visits to Museums, exhibitions and fairs. They represent the highlights of all those M.S.M. groups seen, identified and researched. I hope they bring as much interest to readers as they have brought to me.

Every man awarded the Meritorious Service Medal earned it. Each award must have a story behind it. I have only traced some of these. I hope that this work encourages many more M.S.M.s to be researched and that many more stories will emerge.

Ian McInnes,
Diggle,
June, 1992.

Acknowledgements

SO MANY people have contributed to my research of the men behind the immediate M.S.M.s that I have found it difficult to recall them all. If I have missed out the name of anyone who has assisted me, I would like to apologise in advance.

However, I have little difficulty in deciding who to name first. I should like to record my sincere thanks to George Moss of New York City for giving me so much encouragement, and especially for giving me complete access to the very significant records which enhance his comprehensive collection of M.S.M. groups, both the annuity and the immediate awards. Readers of this work will note the number of times medals from the Moss collection appear in the footnotes.

Another who gave me whole-hearted encouragement and help was Ian Milroy. His collection of M.S.M.s for services in the many and varied theatres of W.W.I and the post war period provided me with much material.

My interest in this award was initially fired by John Tamplin, and it was his suggestion originally to produce this roll. My thanks therefore go to him, and to Chris Buckland of The Naval & Military Press for publishing it.

Support has come from all over the world. Some overseas contributors are: Cdr. W. M. Bisset *(South Africa)*, Chas. Chamberlain *(New Zealand)*, Doug Honeychurch *(U.S.A.)*, Michael Kavanagh *(Eire)*, Norman Liddell *(Australia)*, Irvin Mortenson *(U.S.A.)*, Alan Polaschek *(New Zealand)*, Jacques Prior *(U.S.A.)*, Joseph Scerri *(Malta)*, Frank Sharpley *(Phillipines)*, Brian Taylor *(Zimbabwe)* and Keith Woods *(Canada)*.

The articles I have written for *Medal News* and the former magazines *Military Chest, Fighting Forces, Coin & Medal News* and *Medals International* have frequently generated information from readers. My thanks go to Diana Birch and David Picton-Philips for accepting and publishing my contributions.

Other names which come to mind, again in strict alphabetical order, are: Mark Abbott, John Arnold, Bernard Austerberry, Chris Bate, Will Bennett, Mike Blackburn, Guy Blanche, Cliff Blood, Dave Boniface, Steve Bradley, Dave Buxton, John Coldron, June Done, Steve Durant, Enid Heard, Brian Higgins, Mike Higgs, Frank Horsefield, Dave Langham, Derek Lister, Llew Lloyd, Peter Loundes, Ken Lovell, Ian Marshall, Mike Minton, Frank Olivant, Roger Perkins, Jim Rooke-Matthews, Peter Sharpe, Jerry Warren and Jack Webb.

My thanks go also to two others without whose work I might never have started—or finished; Miss Fiona McInnes, who typed all the early manuscripts and tabulations, and Jim Balmer of Langlands Edition, whose company styled the book. His help and advice were invaluable.

Pte. J. Pitts, V.C., Manchester Regiment

Condr. H. R. Selby, Indian Ordnance
Department

S.S.M. A. Greenwood, Seaforth Highlanders
(Left)

PLATE II   THE MERITORIOUS SERVICE MEDAL

Q.M.S. R. Scott, V.C.,
Manchester Regiment

Pte. L. J. L. Seigne, 10/Royal Fusiliers

Sjt. (T./Q.M.Sjt.) F. C. Weight,
1/Royal Marines

C.P.O. G. Ambler, R.N.V.R.
South Africa

C.P.O. W. Lamerton, R.N.V.R.
South Africa

Armr. S./Sgt. F. Howard,
Royal Army Ordnance Corps

Sub-Conductor V. D'Auvergne,
Indian Army Ordnance Corps

Résumé of Dates

The terms and conditions under which the Meritorious Service Medal has been issued over the years have been varied many times. Some of the changes are listed below:—

R.W.	Royal Warrant
H.G.	Horse Guards
Q.R.	Queen's Regulations
A.O.	Army Order
L.G.	London Gazette
A.M.Inst.	Air Ministry Instruction
A.F.O.	Admiralty Fleet Order
D.C.I.	Defence Council Instruction

19.12.1845	R.W.	£2,000 available for annuities (increased to £2,250 in 1854, £2,500 in 1855, £4,000 in 1856, £4,400 in 1857, £5,000 in 1868 and £7,500 in 1906.
15.1.1849	R.W.	Introduction of R.M. M.S.M.
5.2.1850	H.G. Memo	No man might wear L.S.G.C. & M.S.M. The first was returned if the second was issued.
4.6.1853	R.W.	By £250 per annum the fund to be increased to £4,000.
13.4.1854	R.W.	Any annuity issued to serving N.C.O.'s to remain in Regt Bank until discharge.
8.2.1855	Order in Council	Award of Gallantry R.M. M.S.M.'s.
1.12.1859	Q.R.	An M.S.M. Annuitant could hold both the M.S.M. and D.C.M.
10.6.1884	R.W.	Amount available confirmed as £5,000 p.a.
31.5.1895	R.W.	Award of M.S.M. to Perm. Mil. forces overseas.
November 1902	A.O. 250	Permission given to wear both L.S.G.C. & M.S.M.
31.8.1906	A.O.	The medal could be awarded to Yeoman of the Guard (without annuity).
12.7.1911	A.O.	It was available for award to Yeomen Warders of the Tower of London (without annuity).
24.10.1914	U. of S.A. Govt. Gazette	Award of U. of S.A. M.S.M.
June 1916	A.O. 183	Ribbon colour changed to crimson with white edges.
4.10.1916	R.W. & A.O. 352	Available to all ranks as an immediately award.
23.11.1916, December 1916	R.W. & A.O. 400	Available as an award for gallantry, not necessarily on active service; a bar was instituted.
3.1.1917	A.O. 45	The medal itself could be awarded for gallantry.

August 1917	A.O. 238	An additional centre white stripe was added.
26.6.1918	L.G. & A.M. Inst.	Adoption of R.A.F. M.S.M.
14.1.1919	Order in Council	Adoption of R.N. M.S.M.
May 1920	A.O. 172	An emblem worn on the ribbon to denote award of bar.
19.11.1920	L.G.	Confirmation of £7,500 for annuities; revision of rules.
7.9.1928	R.W.	Withdrawal of immediate award
1.11.1928	Order in Council	R.N. M.S.M. Discontinued.
28.2.1951	A.O. 29	Only 100 medals per annum were to be awarded. At least 22 years service was required.
1952	(following A.F.O./1794/47)	Final issues of R.M. M.S.M.'s.
1.8.1953	A.O. 98	Those Sgts. & W.O.'s who were on the register before 1.1.51 and had not yet received the annuity or medal, would be issued with the medal but still await the award of the annuity.
11.12.1956	A.O. 166	Qualifying length of service increased to 27 years.
1.12.1977	D.C.I. R.N. J38/78	Re-introduction of M.S.M. to R.N., R.M., Q.A.R.N.N.S. and W.R.N.S. at the rate of 59 per year.
1.12.1977	D.C.I. R.A.F. J19/78	Re-introduction of M.S.M. to R.A.F. at the rate of 70 per year.

Because it is perhaps the most comprehensive, the full details in L.G. Supplement 19th November, 1920 pages 11310–2 are set out in the hope they will answer any questions remaining in the readers mind.

The Royal Warrant

LONDON GAZETTE
19th November, 1920

George, R.I.

George the Fifth by the grace of God of the United Kingdom of Great Britain and Ireland, and of the British Dominions beyond the seas King, Defender of the Faith, Emperor of India, to all to whom these presents shall come Greeting:

Whereas Her late Majesty, Queen Victoria, by a Warrant under Her Sign Manual, dated 19th December, 1845, did ordain (a) that a certain sum of public money (£2,000) should be expended annually in awarding annuities of £20 to Serjeants of the Regular Army as a reward for their good, faithful and efficient service: (b) that the recipients of these annuities should be selected by the Commander-in-Chief of the Army: and (c) that the Serjeants so selected to receive the annuities should also receive the Meritorious Service Medal; and did by Royal Warrant dated 10th June, 1884, apply the conditions of Her previous Royal Warrants regarding these medals and annuities to all soldiers above the rank of Corporal.

And whereas the sum of £2,000 has been increased from time to time.

And whereas by a Warrant under Our Sign Manual dated 4th October, 1916, We did ordain that the grant of the Meritorious Service Medal should be extended to non-commissioned officers and men in Our Military Forces below the rank of Serjeant for valuable and meritorious service; and by our Royal Warrant dated 23rd November, 1916, we did institute a bar or bars which might be awarded to recipients of the Meritorious Service Medal for subsequent approved acts of gallantry in the performance of military duty (not necessarily on active service), or in saving or attempting to save the life of an officer or soldier; and by our Royal Warrant dated 3rd January, 1917, we did still further extend the conditions under which the Meritorious Service Medal might be awarded to soldiers in Our Military Forces who were duly recommended for acts of gallant conduct while performing Military duty otherwise than in action or for devotion to duty in a theatre of war:

And whereas we deem it expedient that all the aforesaid Royal Warrants, as well as all amendments thereto which have been heretofore promulgated, or are not to be promulgated, shall be incorporated in a Warrant under Our Sign Manual:

Now therefore we do hereby declare that the rules and ordinances theretofore in force shall be abrogated, cancelled and annulled, and we are pleased to make, ordain and establish the following rules and ordinances in substitution for the same, which shall from henceforth be inviolably observed and kept:—

Firstly—it is ordained that the medal shall be of silver and designated 'The Meritorious Service Medal,' and shall bear on the obverse the Royal Effigy, and on the reverse the words 'For Meritorious Service' encircled by two laurel leaves and surmounted by the Imperial Crown.

Secondly—it is ordained:—

(a) That a fixed sum of £7,500, part of the Public Monies for the upkeep of Our Army shall be devoted to the purpose of awarding Meritorious Service Annuities of not more than £10 in any one case:

(b) That every Warrant Officer Classes 1 and 2, and every non-commissioned officer above the rank of corporal who has served with the Colours in Our Regular Army for 21 years, or who has been invalided from Our Regular Army after 18 years' Colour Service, shall be eligible to be considered for the grant of a Meritorious Service Annuity provided:

    (i) That he served in or above the rank of Serjeant in a regular unit:

    (ii) That he is in possession of the Medal of long service and good conduct, and has been awarded or is otherwise eligible for, an exemplary character on discharge; and

    (iii) That he is duly recommended for the annuity for good, faithful valuable and meritorious service in respect of the whole period of his Army engagement, by the Commanding Officer of the last Regular Unit with which he served, or by the Officer in Charge of his Records.

(c) That instructions as to procedure in submitting such applications for registration for the medal and annuity shall be laid down in the 'King's Regulations for the Army';

(d) That the names of candidates for the Meritorious Service Annuity who are recommended and accepted shall be entered, in the order in which such acceptance is approved, in a register which shall be kept in the office of Our Principal Secretary of State for War;

(e) That the Military Secretary to our Principal Secretary of State for War shall select from the list of registered candidates the names of those whom he considers to be most deserving to receive any annuities that may fall vacant;

(f) That a Regular Warrant Officer or Non-Commissioned Officer who is thus selected for the grant of a Meritorious Annuity shall also be awarded the Meritorious Service Medal, except that a candidate who is already in possession of the Meritorious Service Medal shall receive the annuity only;

(g) That a Meritorious Service Annuity may be held in addition to ordinary pension, and in conjunction with any additional pension to which the annuitant may be entitled;

(h) That when a Meritorious Service annuitant is promoted to a Commission the annuity shall be surrendered, but he shall receive annually in lieu thereof pay equivalent to such annuity.

Thirdly—it is ordained:—

(a) That the Meritorious Service Medal may be awarded to Warrant Officers Classes I and II, non-commissioned officers and men of Our Military Forces who are duly recommended for the medal by a Commander-in-Chief for gallant conduct in the performance of military duty (not necessarily on active service) or in saving or attempting to save the life of an officer or soldier, or for devotion to duty in a theatre of war.

(b) That a Commander-in-Chief when recommending a soldier of Our Military Forces for the Meritorious Service Medal (or for a bar to the same under (e) of this clause) for gallant conduct shall record his opinion whether the case merits the grant of an additional pension—6d. a day for Europeans and 3d. a day for Non-Europeans—should the soldier be discharged with a pension;

(c) That the additional pension referred to in (b) of this clause may be awarded if the services are duly recommended by a Commander-in-Chief, and deemed to merit the additional pension; provided that this additional pension has not been previously awarded to the soldier;

(d) That in no circumstances shall the award of the Meritorious Service Medal for gallant conduct or devotion to duty carry with it any claim to the annuity granted under the second clause of this Our Royal Warrant;

(e) That should a soldier of any of Our Military Forces who has been awarded the Meritorious Service Medal (either with or without annuity) subsequently perform an approved act of gallantry (not necessarily on active service), in the performance of military duty or in saving or attempting to save the life of an officer or soldier, which, had he not already received the Meritorious Service Medal, would have rendered him eligible for it, may be awarded a Bar; and for every additional such act of gallantry an additional bar may be awarded.

(f) That any soldier of Our Regular Army who is granted the Meritorious Service Medal for gallant conduct or devotion to duty in accordance with the conditions laid down in this clause of this Our Royal Warrant shall, if subsequently recommended and approved for an annuity in accordance with the second clause of this Our Royal Warrant, receive the annuity only. In such case he will receive the annuity as well as any additional pension which may have been awarded him under (c) of this clause.

(g) That soldiers of an Allied or Associated Army, of ranks equivalent to those of Our Military Forces specified in (a) of this clause, who have been associated in operations with Our Military Forces, shall be eligible for the award of the Meritorious Service Medal, but no annuity or additional pension shall accompany such awards: and

(h) That a Register of the Recipients of the Meritorious Service Medal (and bars) awarded under this clause shall be kept in the office of Our Principal Secretary of State for War, but such Register shall be separate and distinct from the Register referred to under (d) of the second clause of this Our Royal Warrant.

The Roll

Awards for Gallantry are denoted by the symbol ✿

Vol. IV, 1916

Abernethy, S.Serjt. W.	10041	Baldwin, Serjt. A. E.	10041
Ackroyd, Serjt. J. W.	10041	— Corpl. F. T.	10934
Adair, By.Serjt.Maj. B.	10041	— Co.Qr.Mr.Serjt. H.	10041
Adams, Qr.Mr.Serjt. (A.S.M.) (A.C.)		Bales, S.Serjt. (A.S.M.) R. J.	10934
H. W.	* 10933	Ballantine, Serjt. C. L.	10934
Ahern, Farrier Serjt. (A.Farrier		Banks, Serjt. R. H.	10041
S.Serjt.) T.	10933	— Serjt. S.	10934
Airey, Lce.Corpl. (A.Q.M.S.) R. C.	† 10041	Bannister, A.Bombr. (A.Corpl.) C. G.	10041
Alder, Shoe Smith H. J. W.	10041	Barber, Driver (A.Corpl.) G. E.	10041
Allanson, S.Serjt. C. R.	10044	Barker, Lce.Corpl. (A.Serjt.) C.	10934
Allen, Serjt. (A.S.S.M.) W. R. P.	10041	Barnden, Serjt. (A.S.S.M.) P.	10041
Allison, S.Serjt. A. W.	10041	Barnes, Serjt. (A.C.S.M.) H. C.	10041
Alsop, Serjt. (A.C.S.M.) E.	10041	— Serjt. W. A.	10041
Andrews, Pte. (A.C.S.M.) H.	10933	Barnett, S.Qr.Mr.Serjt. J. A.	10041
Annear, Serjt. (A.C.) A. H.	10933	Bashford, Lce.Corpl. (A.S.S.M.)	
Archer, Serjt. A.	10041	T. W. H.	10934
Arlett, Farrier Qr.Mr.Serjt. A.	10933	Bateman, Serjt. C. W.	10041
Armstrong, Serjt. (A.C.Q.M.S.) F.	10041	Beardow, A.Qr.Mr.Serjt. A. H.	10041
Ashbee, A.Serjt. C. F.	10441	Beecher, Serjt.Inst. (A.C.S.M.) J.	10041
Aspden, S.Qr.Mr.Serjt. (A.S.S.M.)		Bell, Pte. C. D.	10934
C. R.	10933	— Corpl. G. D.	10934
		— Corpl. N.	10041
Back, Lce.Corpl. (A.S.Serjt.) R. H.	10041	Bennett, S.Qr.Mr.Serjt. (A.S.S.M.)	
Baguley, A.Qr.Mr.Serjt. W. H.	10041	J. C.	10934
Bailey, Lce.Corpl. H.	10933	Benton, Serjt. (A.C.Q.M.S.) H.	10041
Baker, 2nd Corpl. A. G.	10041	Benzevai, Serjt. (A.S.S.M.) W. J.	10934
— Corpl. H. W.	10041	Berryman, Pte. H. T.	10041

---

* 9623, Actg. S.M., H.Q. 29th D.A. Gallipoli, 1915.—For exceptionally good work in the field for the past four months. This N.C.O. is the Artillery Clerk in charge of the 29th D.A.H.Q. office and landed with the 29th D.A. on 25th April, and has performed his duties to the entire satisfaction of the C.R.A., often under shell fire. He has not spared himself and has laboured day and night to ensure the prompt duplication and despatch of artillery orders, returns, and general correspondence, which have been sometimes very heavy. Since the formation of the VIIIth Corps and the withdrawal of the 29th D.A. from the 29th Division for administrative purposes, this N.C.O. has carried out, with the machinery of the 29th D.A.H.Q., the clerical work of the whole of the artillery of the VIIIth Corps on the peninsula, which up till recently comprised 30 batteries of all natures, together with the Ammunition Columns for the same. He is in possession of the medal for Long Service and Good Conduct. (Report dated 28/8/15). (Mention 28/1/16, M.S.M. 11/11/16). Somme, 1916.—For efficiency and high sense of duty. His work has necessitated long hours and constant application and has always merited high praise. (Russian medal of St. George 2nd Class 15/2/17). Arras and Flanders, 1917.—(Mention 14/12/17.)

† South Irish Horse. 1914 Star trio & M.S.M. known.

Betheil, Flight Serjt. H. E.	10934	Cameron, S.Qr.Mr.Serjt. (A.S.S.M.)	
Berwick, Serjt. E. D.	10041	T. G.	10042
Bews, S.Serjt. (A.S.S.M.) J. T.	10934	Campana, Serjt. J. A.	10934
Bilbee, S.Serjt. L. V.	10934	Carr, Fitter T. G.	10042
Birbeck, Serjt. H. J.	10934	Carter, Serjt. T.	10934
Blake, Pte. (actg.Corpl.) J. A.	10934	Caunter, Pnr. (A.L.C.) C. R.	10042
Blyth, Lce.Corpl. (A.Serjt.) A. J.	10041	Cawthorn, S.Qr.Mr.Serjt. J. H.	10042
Blythman, Pnr. G.	10041	Chambers, E.S'kpr.Qr.Mr.Serjt.	
Bolden, Corpl. E.	10934	R. H.	10934
Boswell, Corpl. (actg.Serjt.) S.	10041	Chandler, Co.Serjt. (A.S.M.Supy.	
Bowden, 1st C.S.S.Maj. E. A.	10934	Clerk) A. F.	10042
Bowers, Corpl. (A.C.S.M.) E. J.	10041	Chapman, Pte. (A.S.S.) G. C.	10042
— Wh.S.Serjt. H.	10041	Charlton, Serjt. T. P.	10042
Bowman, Serjt. W.	10934	Checkley, S.Serjt. G.	10042
Boyd, Serjt. J.	10041	Chick, Pte. F. H.	10934
— Staff Serjt. R. W.	10934	Chisholm, Co.Qr.Mr.Serjt. E. A.	10042
Bracey, Lce.Corpl. A. G.	10041	— Lce.Corpl. J.	10042
Braes, Corpl. A.	10041	Chittem, Serjt.Cook D.	10934
Brayton, Pte. J.	10045	Church, Corpl. (A.Serjt.) T. G.	‡ 10042
Brewer, Sadd.S.Serjt. (A.Q.M.S.)		Clark, Co.Qr.Mr.Serjt. J.	10042
E. A.	10041	Clarke, A.Lce.Serjt. A. E.	10042
Brewster, Sub-Condr. W. T.	* 10041	— Pnr.Serjt. J.	10042
Brighton, S.Serjt. R. H.	10045	Classen, Trans.Serjt. A. J.	10042
Brockes, Co.Qr.Mr.Serjt. P. A.	10934	Claydon, Corpl. T. B.	10042
Brooker, B.Qr.Mr.Serjt. H.	10934	Claye, Co.Qr.Mr.Serjt. F. W.	10042
Brooks, Serjt. G.	10041	Clough, S.Serjt. (A.S.M.) J.	10934
Bruce, Armr.Qr.Mr.Serjt. A.	10041	Coachley, Bombr. A.C. (A.S.A.C.)	
— Corpl. (A.S.S.M.) R. W.	10934	J. R. V.	10934
Buchanan, Pte. A. (A.Serjt). C.	10934	Collins, Serjt. D.	10042
Buckeridge, Corpl. C. F.	10042	— Co.Serjt.Maj. H.	10042
Buckingham, Pte. H.	10042	Colville, Serjt. W. H.	10042
Bugler, Mech.S.Serjt. W. T.	10934	Coney, Lce.Corpl. H. R. H.	10042
Bull, 2nd Corpl. A. G. W.	10042	Cook, Wh.Corpl. H.	10042
— S.Serjt. C. E.	10042	— A.Bombr. R.	10042
— Qr.Mr.Serjt. J.	10042	— Serjt. (A.R.S.M.) W.	10934
Bullimore, Lce.Serjt. R. B.	10042	Cooke, Serjt.Maj. W. C.	10934
Burgess, Serjt. C.	10042	Cooper, S.Qr.Mr.Serjt. F. S.	§ 10045
Burns, Serjt. G.	10042	— By.Qr.Mr.Serjt. W.H. S.	10042
Butler, A.Co.Serjt.Maj. A.	10934	Coplin, S.Serjt. (A.S.S.M.) F. I.	10934
Butler, Wh.S.Serjt. W.	10042	Cosier, Pnr.Serjt. J. J.	10042
Butt, S.Serjt. H. G. B.	10045	Cowell, F.of W.Qr.Mr.Serjt. W.	10042
Buxton, Serjt. (A.S.Q.M.S.) M.	† 10934	Cowen, Corpl. J. E.	10042
		Cowley, S.Serjt. T.	10934
Calvert, Corpl. H.	10934	Cox, Pte. (A.Serjt.) F. J.	10042

---

* R.A.O.C. Also M.B.E.

† Commissioned 27 April 1918. 1914 Star (Sgt. 3 Hussars), British War and Victory Medals (2/Lt.), M.S.M. (7 Hussars) known.

‡ K.I.A. 3 December, 1918 aged 31. C.Q.M.S. 7 Field Coy. R.E. From Folkestone.

§ N.Z.F.A., later 2/Lt.

Cox, Serjt.Maj. H.	10934	Dwyer, Corpl. H.	10934
Crawford, Wt.Off. S. H.	10044	Dyas, Serjt. (A.S.Q-M.S.) W. F.	10042
Crick, C.Serjt. (Bde.Supdt.) E. C.	10042	Dye, Serjt. (A.S.S.M.) J.	10934
Crofts, Pte. (actg.Serjt.) J. E.	10042		
Crouch, Serjt. (actg.Sub-Condr.) S. H.	10042	Eager, Serjt. G. L.	10042
Cruickshank, Lce.Corpl. (A.S.S.) A.	10934	Eaton, S.Qr.Mr.Serjt. (A.Sub-Condr.) C.	10042
Cuff, Serjt. E. H.	10042	Edington, Serjt. W. G.	10042
Cusack, E.C.Qr.Mr.Serjt. J. A.	10934	Elliott, Qr.Mr.Serjt. (A.S.M.) (A.C.) F. E.	10042
Damms, Sapper (A.C.Q.M.S.) T. E.	10042	Ellis, Pte. T.	10042
Danby, Serjt. (A.S.S.) C.	10042	— Lce.Corpl. (A.Sub-Condr.) W.	10042
Daniels, 2nd Corpl. (A.Sub-Condr.) T. B.	10934	Elsey, Serjt. P. G.	10042
Dann, Co.Qr.Mr.Serjt. N.	10934	Epsom, S.Serjt. W. E.	10042
Day, Farr.S.Serjt. H.	10042	Evans, Serjt. J.	10042
De Barre, Serjt. S. G.	10934	— Farr.S.Serjt. J. E.	10042
Dealtry, Serjt. W.	* 10042	Exley, Pte. B. E.	10934
Deaville, Bombr. A.	10042		
Dell, Qr.Mr.Serjt. (A.S.M.) A. A.	10042	Fairfull, Serjt. T. B.	10042
Dick, Corpl. J.	10042	Falgate, Farr.Serjt. P. J.	† 10042
Dickson, Armt.S.Serjt. J.	10042	Farthing, Corpl. G. R.	10934
Dixon, Serjt. W. A.	10042	Fellis, Serjt. (A.S.S.) W.	10934
Doak, Pte. (A.S.Q.M.S.) G. G.	10934	Fellows, Pte. E.	10042
Dobson, Serjt. C.	10042	Felstead, Serjt.Maj. G.	10934
Dobson, Lce.Cpl. (A.Sjt.) G. W. H	10042	Fenton, E.C.Qr.Mr.Serjt. J. S.	10934
Dolling, Serjt. F. A.	10042	Findlay, Co.Qr.Mr.Serjt. G.	10042
Domoney, Serjt. (A.C.S.M.) L.	10934	Finlinson, Serjt. H.	10042
Douglas, Serjt. A. R.	10042	Finnegan, Serjt. L. W.	10042
Douglas, Pte. (A.Corpl.) D.	10042	Fiske, Serjt. H. B.	10934
Downie, S.Serjt.Farr J.	10042	Fletcher, Serjt. (A.S.S.) G. E.	10042
Doyne, Driver, F. W.	10042	— Serjt. J. H.	10934
Drewett, Bty.Qr.Mr.Serjt.G. H. A.	10042	Flowers, Serjt. A.	10934
Driver, Corpl. H.	10934	Foinette, Serjt. C. J.	10042
Drumm, E.C.Q.M.S., E. J.	10042	Ford, Farr.S.Serjt. A.	10042
Dunham, Pte. (A.Serjt.) W.	10042	— Farrier S.Serjt. R.	10934
Durbin, A.Serjt. F.	10042	Foster, Flight Serjt. R. G.	10042
Durdan, Serjt. J.	10934	Fox, Serjt. E. W.	10934
		Franklin, Pte. (A.Corpl.) W. J.	10042

* Group was in McInnes collection:— D.C.M. (8028 Sgt. R. Mun. F.) 1914 Star & bar trio (M.I.D. oakleaf), Defence Medal, L.S. & G.C. (Geo. V, 7211089 Sgt. Loyals) and M.S.M. (2–8028 Sgt. R. Mun. F.). Only 23 M.S.M.s to the Regiment, this is the first. He was one of only 200 not killed or captured when 1,000 men of the 2/Munsters were trapped and surrounded when acting as rearguard at Etreux on 27 August, 1914. He fought at Ypres, Festubert, Rue de Bois, Loos, Somme, Passchendaele, Le Catelette, Selle and Forêt de Mormal. He was 51 months in the front line. Of 364 officers and nearly 8,000 men who served in the Royal Munster Fusiliers 179 officers and 4,088 OR's were killed, died of wounds, wounded or taken P.O.W. D.C.M. in *L.G.* 1 January 1917 & 13 February 1917.

† Group Known: D.C.M. (E Batt. 3 Brig. R.H.A.), M.M. (same) British War and Victory Medals (R.A.), L.S. & G.C. (R.A.) & M.S.M.

Franks, Dvr. (A.Farr.Serjt.) P.	10042
Fraser, Serjt. S.	10042
Freer, S.Serjt. G. B.	10044
Fry, Pte. J. W.	10042
Fulton, A.Serjt.Maj. J.	10934
Furniss, Engr.Cl.Corpl. G. S.	10042
Gardiner, Flight Serjt. (A.S.M.) J. R.	* 10934
George, S.Serjt. W. E.	10042
Gibb, Serjt. R.	10042
Gibbons, Co.Qr.Mr.Serjt. H.	10042
Gibson, Serjt. W. E.	10042
Gilchrist, Sapper W.	10042
Gill, Qr.Mr.Serjt. W. J. N.	10045
Gilmour, A.Serjt. W.	10042
Goggin, S.Serjt. A. E.	10934
Golden, Corpl. J. T.	10042
Goldthorpe, Flight Serjt. S. R.	10934
Gooch, Pte. (A.Corpl.) F. S.	10934
Goode, Farr.S.Serjt. J. N.	10042
Gooding, S.Serjt. (A.S.S.M.) W. R. A.	10934
Goodwin, Co.Qr.Mr.Serjt. (A.S.S.M.) J. J.	10042
Gordon, Co.Qr.Mr.Serjt. E.	† 10042
Goslin, Serjt. F. S.	10042
Grainger, Serjt. G. H.	10042
Grant, F.of W.Q.M.Serjt. W.	10042
Green, Corpl. G.	10934
— Flight Serjt. H.	10934
— Lce.Corpl. J. G. L.	10934
Green, Serjt. A.C. (A.S.M., A.C.) R.	10042
Gregory, Serjt. H. W. G.	10042
Gregson, Qr.Mr.Serjt. G. G.	10934
— 2nd Corpl. J.	10042
Griffin, Serjt. F. M.	10042
— Lce.Corpl. W. D.	10042
Griffith, Serjt. (A.Q.M.S.) M.	10042
Griggs, S.Serjt. R. G.	10042
Grimshaw, Serjt. A. L.	10042
Grint, S.Serjt. L. A.	10042
Gunderson, Serjt. O.	10044

Hackney, Pte. (A.Serjt.) C.	10042
Hadingham, S.Serjt. W. K.	10042
Haick, Sub Condr. S. C.	10042
Hale, Armt.S.Serjt. P. F.	‡ 10042
Halewood, Corpl. (A.Serjt.) F.	10042
Hall, S.Serjt. R.	10934
Hallet, Serjt. H. C.	10042
Halsey, Serjt. (A.C.Q.M.S.) F. A.	10042
Hampson, S.Serjt. W. C.	10934
Hanaghan, Mech.S.Serjt. (A.M.S.M.) A. V.	10042
Hancock, Corpl. G. E.	10042
Hankins, Serjt. F. H.	10042
Hanslar, Pte. R. F.	10042
Hanson, Serjt. C. H.	10934
— Eng. Cl., Qr.Mr.Serjt. E.	10042
Hardy, Serjt. E.	10042
— Pte. E. D. P.	10042
— A.Corpl. E. V.	10042
Hargreaves, Corpl. J.	10042
Harker, Serjt. (A.Farr.S.S.) H. M.	10934
Harley, S.Serjt. Wheeler T.	10042
Harlin, E. Skpr. Qr.Mr.Serjt.W. J.	10934
Hart, Pte. (A.Serjt.) H. W.	10934
Hawley, Flight Serjt. A.	10934
Hayes, Driver, A. J.	10042
Hayman, C. Qr.Mr.Serjt. (A.R.S.M.) J. H.	10042
Hazell, Serjt. A.	10043
Healey, Serjt. (A.S.S.Maj.) M.	10043
Hedderwick, Lce.Corpl. (A.Serjt.) R. W.	10934
Hellyer, Flight Serjt. F. J.	10934
Henderson, Lce.Corpl. J. D.	10043
Hennen, Mech.Mach.Qr.Mr.Serjt. E.	10934
Hepple, Serjt. G. W.	§ 10934
Herbert, S.Serjt. R.	10934
Herrington, Co.Serjt.Maj. H.	10043
Hewett, S.Serjt. C. A.	10045
Hibbert, Pte. H.	10934
Higgins, A.R. Serjt. Maj. M.	10043
Hill, Serjt. (A.Suptg.Cl.) C. R.	10934

---

* 1914/15 Star trio, Defence and War Medals and M.S.M. known. No. 178 R.F.C. Born 1886. Enlisted into R.E., to Central Flying School July 1912. R.Ae.C. Aviators Cert. December, 1913. 2/Lieut. January, 1918. Retired Flight Lieut. February. 1931. Recalled and was Wing Commander by June 1942.

† Group known: D.C.M. (4 Sge. Coy. R.M. R.E., *L.G.* 17 April, 1918), 1914/15 Star trio, L.S. & G.C. (Geo. V) and M.S.M. (R.E.)

‡ R.A.O.C., later A./S.M. Also D.C.M.

§ See section IV 1921.

Hill, Serjt. F. F.	10043	Jarvis, Corpl. A.C. (A.S.M.A.C.) C.	10934
— 2nd Corpl. W. A.	10043	Jellen, Pte. (A.S.S.) J.	10043
Hinbest, Farr.Qr.Mr.Serjt.		Jenkins, Dvr. (A.S.) H. W.	10934
F. W. T. H.	10043	Johnson, Serjt. G. E.	10043
Hinson, Serjt. J. A.	10043	Jolliffe, S.Serjt. (A.Armt.S.M.)	
Hinton, S.Serjt. H.	10043	W. G. S. (correction)	10935
Hipperson, S.Serjt. (A.S.Q.M.S.)		Jones, Serjt. (A.C.Q.M.S.) A.	10043
W. A.	10043	— S.Qr.Mr.Serjt. A. F.	10043
Hitchman, Serjt. P. N.	10043	— Pte. (A.Corpl.) F.	10043
Hoare, A.Serjt. H. G.	10043	— Corpl. J.	10934
Hobson, Corpl. T. A.	10043	— Serjt. L.	10043
Hodgkinson, Corpl. (A.Serjt.) T.	10043	— Corpl. W. H.	10043
Hogan, S.Qr.Mr.Serjt. (A.S.S.M.)		Judge, Lce.Corpl. A. A.	10043
F. G.	10043	Justice, Pte. (A.Serjt.) H. S.	10043
Holden, A.Serjt. H. E.	10934		
— Serjt. W.	10043	Kellock, Pte. (A.2nd Corpl) A.	10043
Holmes, Farr.Serjt. J.	10043	Kelly, Sq.S.M. (I.F. and G.) A.	10043
Horn, Serjt. F.	10934	Kemsley, S. Qr.Mr.Serjt. A. N.	10044
Howard, Driver A. A.	10934	Kendall, Corpl. (A.Serjt.) H.	10043
Howell, Bombr. G. J.	10043	— Farr.Serjt. J.	10043
Howley, Shoeing Smith A.	10043	Kilburn, Pte. P.	10043
Hoyten, Serjt. (A.C.S.M.) E. W.	10043	King, Serjt. (A.Q.M.S.) F.	10043
Hughes, Co.Serjt. Maj. H. J.	10043	Kite, Serjt. F. C.	10934
— Corpl. J. H.	10043	Knight, A.Serjt.Maj. A.	10934
— Serjt. (A.C.S.M.) P. R.	10934	— Armt.S.Serjt. (A.Armt.S.M.)	
Hunt, Serjt. H. E.	10934	W. H.	10934
Hunter, S.Serjt. J.	10043	Knott, Co.Qr.Mr.Serjt. W.	10043
— Serjt. M.	10043		
— Pte. T. W.	10934	Lambert, Pte. (A.Corpl.) S. A. N.	10043
Hussey, Serjt. J.	10043	Landamore, 2nd Corpl. E. A.	10043
Hyland, Corpl. T.	10934	Lanman, Serjt. (A.Sub-Condr.) A. H.	10934
Hymers, Gunner J. E.	10043	Larby, S.Serjt. R. W.	10043
Hyson, Pte. W. A.	10043	Lawrence, Pte. F. H.	10043
		Le Feuvre, Farrier S.Serjt.	
Iles, Serjt.Maj. G.	10934	(A.Far. Q.M.S.)	* 10934
— Corpl. T.	10043	Lee, Pte. (A.Serjt.) A.	10934
Ingram, Serjt. J. D.	10043	— Qr.Mr.Serjt. H. W.	10043
Irons, Serjt. P. J.	10043	Leetham, Pte. (A.Serjt.) G. A.	10043
Irwin, Serjt. T. H.	10043	Lehfeldt, S.Serjt. (A.Sqdn. S.M.)	
Itter, Pte. (A.Serjt.) A. E.	10043	F. A.	10045
		Levers, Serjt. W. A.	10934
Jackman, Lce.Corpl. (A.Corpl.) W. J.	10043	Lewarne, Serjt. L. A.	10043
James, Corpl. (A.Serjt.) W.	10043	Lewcock, Serjt. (A.C.S.M.) R.	10043
Jacques, S.Serjt. H.	10934	Lindley, Lce.Corpl. L.	10934

---

* Army Service Corps. Group known: Queen's South Africa Medal (Relief of Kimberley, Paardeberg, Dreifontein, Johannesberg, Diamond Hill, Belfast), King's South Africa Medal (Cpl. Farrier & Carriage Smith), British War Medal (W.O.II) and M.S.M.

Lindsay, Bombr. A.C.		Meikle, Serjt. L. W. G.	10045
(A.Serjt. A.C.) H. V.	* 10934	Mendham, Corpl. (A.C.S.M.) J.	10934
— Serjt. W. T.	10043	Meynell, A.Serjt.Maj. E.	10934
Little, Tpr. G. C.	10045	Miles, Serjt. (A.S.S.M.) H. W.	10934
Livesey, A.S.Qr.Mr.Serjt. M.	10043	Millington, A.Serjt.Maj. E. R.	10934
Llewellyn Armt.S.Serjt.		Mills, C.S.Maj. H.	10043
(A.Armt.S.M.) T. J.	10043	Milner, 2nd Corpl. C.	10043
Loakman, Pte. (A.Serjt.) B. J. P.	10043	Milton, Serjt. F.	10043
Loman, Serjt. (A.S.S.M.) P. G.	10043	Mitchell, Serjt. H. G.	10043
Lort, Serjt. (A.Q.M.S.) A.	10043	— Correction	10935
Lovett, Serjt. (A.S.Q.M.S.) W. E.	10043	Moody, Serjt. H. C.	10934
Low, Lce.Serjt. (A.S.Serjt.) J.	10934	— Qr.Mr.Serjt. H. F.	10045
Lowe, Pte. (A.Corp.) L. W.	10043	Morris, Pte. W. A.	10934
Lugg, Serjt. E. S.	10043	Morrison, Serjt. (A.C.S.M.) H.	10935
Luxton, 2nd Corpl. T.	10043	Mortimer, Lce.Corpl. H. J.	10043
		Moss, S.Qr.Mr.Serjt. T.	10043
McAlister, Lce.Corpl. (A.Serjt.) A.	10043	Mounsey, Corpl. W.	10043
McCann, Serjt. P.	10043	Mulcahy, S.Serjt. G. P.	10044
McCarthy, S.Qr.Mr.Serjt. (A.S.M.) H.	10934	Muncaster, Serjt. T.	10043
— Serjt. (A.S.S.M.) J. P.	10934	Munson, Serjt. C. E.	10043
McCory, Serjt. J.	10043	Musgrave, Qr.Mr.Serjt. (A.S.M.)	
Macdonald Corpl. (A.Serjt.) E.	10043	P. H.	10043
Mace, Lce.Corpl. (A.Mech.S.M.) G. P.	10934	Myatt, Serjt. (A.S.Serjt.) F.	10043
Mackay, Serjt. D.	10934		
— Serjt. (A.Suptg.Cl.) W. N.	10934	Naughton, Serjt. J. P.	10935
Mackesy, E.C. Qr.Mr.Serjt. J.	10934	Newman, Pte. A. W.	10043
McLean, Serjt. A.	10043	Newton, Flight Serjt. D. H.	10935
McMurray, Serjt. W. W.	10043	Nichol, Serjt. (A.C.S.M.) W. A.	10935
McVie, Serjt. J.	10043	Nicholson, S.Serjt. H. P.	10043
Magee, Serjt. E. M.	10043	Niven, S.Serjt. J. K.	10043
Male, S.Serjt. A.	10043	Norman, R. Qr.Mr.Serjt. R. W.	10044
Mallett, Farr.S.Serjt. J. C.	10043	Norris, A.Serjt. T.	10043
Mantell, A.Serjt.Maj. W. G.	10934	Norton, Serjt. A. N.	10043
Margetts, Lce.Corpl. G. D.	10043	Nunn, Serjt. G. H.	† 10043
Marshall, Corpl. (A.S.Sergt.) M.	10934	Nutting, Serjt. A. J.	10043
— C. Sergt.Maj. W.	10043		
Martin, Pte. (A.Corpl.) C.	10043	Oldfield, Corpl. L.	10935
Masters, Tp. Qr.Mr.Serjt. H. W.	10043	O'Leary, Serjt. C. W.	10043
May, Farr.Serjt. P. A.	10934	Orr, Serjt. J.	‡ 10935
Mayoh, Corpl. J.	10043	Owen, S.Qr.Mr.Serjt. P. S.	10043

---

* 56855, A./Sergt., R.G.A. Clerks' Section (attached H.Q. 29th D.A.). Gallipoli, 1915.—
For excellence of work and devotion to duty during the whole period of the occupation.

† Group known: Queen's South Africa Medal (Cape Colony, Orange Free State, Transvaal, South Africa 1901, South Africa 1902, Pte. R.A.M.C.), 1914 Star (Sgt. 2/ H.L.I.) British War and Victory Medals (S. Maj.), L.S. & G.C. (Geo.V, Sgt. H.L.I.) and M.S.M. known. To France in August, 1914. By the end of the war only 50 of them were still with the battalion; he was one.

‡ R.A.M.C. Bar awarded *L.G.* 13 February, 1917.

Oxley, Bombr. A. A.	10043	Roe, Lce.Corpl. (A.S.Serjt.) W. A.	10043
		Rogers, A.2nd Corpl. H. N.	10044
Pace, Serjt. P. W.	10043	Rolle, Qr.Mr.Serjt. (A.C.) (A.S.Maj.	
Parker, Corpl. (A.Serjt.) S. H	10043	A.C.) T. H.	10044
— S.Qr.Mr.Serjt. T.	10935	Rooks, Serjt. T. C.	10044
Parkin, Condr. G.	10935	Rose, Corpl. A. T.	10935
Patrick, Serjt. T.	10043	— A.Corpl. H.	10044
Paul, A.Serjt. C. M.	10045	— Armr. Qr.Mr. Sergt.	
Paull, Pte. W. J.	10935	(A.Armr. S.M.) H. G.	10935
Payne, Corpl. (A.M.S.Serjt.) A.	10935	Roullier, Pte. (A.Serjt.) W.	10935
— Dvr. R.	10043	Rouse, Qr.Mr.Serjt. C. E.	10935
Peachey, By.Qr.Mr.Serjt. H. O.	10043	— Corpl. J.	10044
Peake, Serjt. (A.C.S.M.) A. H.	10043	Rowlands, S.Qr.Mr.Sergt. C. W.	10935
— Farr.Corpl. (A.Serjt.) J.	10043	Rush, Serjt. (A.C.S.M.) W. S.	10044
Pearce, Pte (A.Lce.Serjt) H. W.	10935	Ryan, Lce.Corpl. (A.Sub-Condr.)	
— Serjt. J. E.	10043	H. M.	10044
Perkins, Serjt. F. H.	10935	Ryding, Pte. (A.Serjt.) W.	10044
Peters, Pte. R.	10935		
Picton, Serjt. C.	10043	Samuel, A.Serjt. E. S.	10044
Pierce, S.Qr.Mr.Serjt. F.	10043	Saunders, M.S.Serjt. J. C.	10044
Pinker, Farrier, Qr.Mr.Serjt. W.	10935	— Pte. W. E. G.	10044
Pinney, Pte. C. J.	10935	— Corpl. W. G. F.	10044
Pitman, Dvr. A. G.	10043	Scanlon, Qr.Mr.Serjt. J.J .	10045
Pitt, By.Qr.Mr.Serjt. C.	10043	Schell, A.Qr.Mr.Serjt. J. J.	10045
Porter, Serjt. T.	10043	Scott, Serjt. J. R.	10044
Potter, Corpl. J.	10043	— Serjt. (A.Sub-Condr.) W. C.	10044
Powell, Sapper W. H.	10935	Searle, Serjt. T. G.	10935
Price, Serjt. (A.S.S.M.) F. W.	10935	Self, A.Qr.Mr.Serjt. J. C.	10045
Proctor, Co.Serjt.Maj. J. F.	10045	Sharman, Serjt. F.	10935
Pullen, Farr.S.Serjt. J. W.	10043	Sharp, Serjt. A.	10044
		— Corpl. H.	10044
Quigley, Corpl. W. J.	10043	Shaw, Corpl. T. H.	10044
Quinain, Mech.S.Serjt. (A.M.S.M.)		Shearing, 1st Cl. Air Mech. S.	10935
F. W.	10935	Sheffield, Corpl. (A.L.S.) G. A. C.	10935
		Sheldrake, Corpl. (A.S.S.M.) C. D.	10935
Rabson, Serjt. A.	10043	Shelton, Pte. W. E.	10935
Ralph, Lce.Corpl. (A.Serjt.) J. J.	10043	Sherman, Pte. (A.Serjt.) J.	10044
Randall, Corpl. (A.Serjt.) W.	10935	Sherrod, Serjt. H.	10044
Rapley, A.Serjt.Maj. C.	10935	Shilling, Corpl. (A.Serjt.) L. J.	10045
Rapson, Serjt. (A.Q.M.S.) W.	10043	Shipman, Lce.Serjt. L.	10935
Rees, Serjt. B. M.	10043	Shirt, S.Serjt.Maj. A.J.	10935
Reeve, Dvr. A. N.	10043	Simmonds, Serjt. (A.C.S.M.) F. E.	10044
Renton, C.Qr.Mr.Serjt. J. R.	10043	Simpson, Corpl. H.	10045
Rich, Pte. (A.Serjt.) H.	10935	Simpson, Farrier Qr.Mr.Serjt. R.	10935
Richards, S.Serjt. F. M.	10935	Sims, S.Qr.Mr.Serjt. (A.Sub-	
— Pte. W. C.	10043	Condr.) A.	10044
Rixon, Co.Qr.Mr.Sergt. W.	10043	Slade, S.Serjt. (A.S.M.) F.	10935
Roberts, By.Qr.Mr.Serjt. A. C.	10045	Sloan, Pte. (A.Serjt.) J. W.	10935
— Serjt. F. L. H.	10043	Smart, Serjt. R. H.	10044
— Corpl. F. W. H.	10043	Smart, Serjt. W. G.	10044
Robertson, Serjt. D.	10935	Smeeton, Serjt. F. J.	10044
Rodwell, Serjt. E.	10043	Smith, Farr.Serjt. C. A.	10044

Smith, Pte. (A.M.S.Serjt.) E. H.	10044	Summerson, Pte. T.		10044
— Serjt. (A.S.Q.M.S.) G. E.	10044	Sunter, Serjt. T.		10935
— Bombr. H.	10044	Suters, E.C.S.Serjt. H.		10935
— S. Sergt. (A.S.Q.S.) H. J.	10935	Sutherland, Serjt. (A.S.M.) A.		10935
— A.V.C. Serjt. (A.S.-Serjt.) J.	10044	Sutton, Driver (A.L.C.) A.		10044
— E.C.Qr.Mr.Serjt. (A.Suptg.Cl.)		— A.Serjt. H.		10044
J. P.	10935	— Pte. (A.Serjt.) O.G.		10045
— Serjt. S. J.	10044	Switzer, Serjt. (A.S.S.M.) R.		10044
— Corpl. (A.Serjt.) W. C.	10044			
— Serjt. (A.S.Q.M.S.) W. J.	10044	Taylor, Serjt. A.		10044
— Serjt. W. T.	10044	Telfer, Pte. W.		10935
Snow, Corpl. (A.Serjt.) S.	10044	. Tesch, Serjt. L. R.		10935
Somper, Co.Qr.Mr.Serjt. J.	10044	Thomson, Farr.S.Serjt. A.		10044
Soper, Serjt. G. H.	* 10044	Thurtell, Corpl. (A.Serjt.) C.		10044
Sparshott, Serjt. (A.C.S.M.) G. E.	10044	Tilley, Corpl. (A.Serjt.) W.		10044
Spencer, Serjt. P. J.	10044	Timbers, Farr.Serjt. S.		10935
— Corpl. (A.Sergt.) W. P.	10044	Timoney, Corpl. (A.C.S.M.) A. J.		10044
Stanley, Serjt. P. V.	10044	Tovell, Serjt. (A.S.Q.M.S.) H.	‡ 10044	
Stanton, Serjt. (A.S.M.) A.	10044	Townsend, S.Serjt. H. O.		10044
Staples, Farrier S.Sergt. (A.Farr.		Treadwell, Pte. (A.Serjt.) G. H.		10044
Qr.Mr.S.) J. R.	10935	Tringham, Serjt. W. T.		10044
Stead, Serjt. F.	10044	Troke, Whlr. Corpl. W. H.		10044
Steel, Co.Serjt.Maj. H. W.	10045	Trounce, Serjt. L. J.		10045
Steers, Pte. (A.Serjt.) B.	10044	Tuck, Co.Qr.Mr.Serjt. R. W.		10044
Stevenson, Farrier Serjt. J.	10935	— Serjt. W. G. M.		10044
Steward, Serjt. J.	10935	Tuft, Serjt. (A.C.S.M.) F. A.		10935
Stooke, Serjt. (A.C.S.M.) E.	† 10935	Tunbridge, Pte. (A.L.C.) L. R.		10935
Storrie, Bty.Qr.Mr.Serjt. (A.S.M.)		Turnbull, Serjt. J. R.		10935
W. T.	10044	Turner, S.Serjt. (A.Armt.S.M.) H.		10044
Street, Armt.Qr.Mr.Sergt.		— Correction		10935
(A.Armt.S.M.) H. H.	10044	Tutt, Co.Serjt.Maj. (A.S.S.M.) E.		10044
Strong, Corpl. T. C.	10935	Twohig, Co.Serj.Maj. D.		10935
Studley, Serjt. (A.S.Serjt) R.	10044	Tynan, Co.Qr.Mr.Serjt. W. R.		10044
Styring, Serjt. P. J.	10044			
Suckling, Pte. (A.Serjt.) E. E.	10935			

---

* Group known: Queen's South Africa Medal (Relief of Kimberley, Paardeberg, Dreifontein, Johannesberg, Laing's Nek, Belfast), King's South Africa Medal (both Corpl. R.H.A.), 1914/15 Star trio (Sjt. 2/London Regt.) and M.S.M. (Sgt. 24/London Regt.).

† Group known: B.E.M. (*L.G.* 4, June, 1943), Queen's South Africa Medal (Transvaal, South Africa 1901, South Africa 1902, Sapper, Tel. Bn. R.E.), 1914 Star trio (Sgt./ W.O.2 R.E., M.I.D. oakleaf), Defence Medal, Imperial Service Medal (30 April 1948), L.S. & G.C. (Geo.V, Sgt. R.E.) and M.S.M. ('L' Sig. Co. R.E.).

‡ Group in R.C.T. Museum: Medal of Order of British Empire (Military Ribbon), 1914 Star trio (M.I.D. oakleaf), 1902 Metropolitan Police Coronation Medal, L.S. & G.C. (Geo. V), M.S.M. and French Médaille Militaire.

Unicume, Whr.S.Serjt. H.	10935	Whitmoor, S.Serjt. (A.S.S.M.) E.	10044
Usher, Serjt. F. J.	* 10044	Whittaker, Serjt. T. S.	10044
		Whyte, S.Serjt. W.	10044
Varney, Co.Qr.Mr.Serjt.		Wickham, Co.Qr.Mr.Serjt. A.	10044
(A.M.S.M.) F.	10044	Wigglesworth, A.Serjt. J. T.	10044
Vickery, Qr.Mr.Serjt. A.	10044	Wilkin, Corpl. (A.M.S.Serjt.) J. W.	10044
Vigus, Armt.S.Serjt. (A.Armt.S.M.)		Wilkins, Co.Qr.Mr.Serjt. F.	10935
F. E.	10044	Williams, S.Serjt. A.	10935
Voysey, Serjt. W. A. O.	† 10044	— S.Qr.Mr.Serjt. (A.S.S.M.) A. R.	10935
		— Serjt. G. C.	10044
Wade, S.Qr.Mr.Serjt. J. C.	10045	— Serjt. J. J.	10045
Wadeson, Serjt. (A.Q.M.S.) E.	10044	Wilson, Corpl. E. C.	10044
Waldron, Serjt. E. T.	10044	— Co.Qr.Mr.Serjt. R.	10935
Wales, 2nd Corpl. (A.S.Q.M.S.)		— Pte. (A.Serjt.) W. H.	10935
H. J. H.	10044	Wingrove, Corpl. (A.Serjt.) C. E.	10044
Walkder, Serjt. J. T. H.	10044	Winterbottom, Serjt. A.	10935
Wall, M.S.Serjt. J.	10044	Wood, Flight Serjt. E. R.	10935
Walter, Serjt. (A.S.Q.M.S.) G. T.	10044	— S.Serjt. T.	10044
— S.Serjt. (A.S.Q.M.S.) L. J.	10044	— Serjt. W.	10044
Wansbury, Corpl. V. E.	10935	Woodhead, Co.Qr.Mr.Serjt. C. H.	10935
Ward, Wt.Off. L. A. P.	10044	Woods, Pte. M.	10044
— Eng. Clerk Serjt. G.	10044	Woodward, Serjt. F. T.	10044
— Lce.Corpl. J. W.	10044	— Pte. J. E.	10044
Warner, S.Qr.Mr.Serjt. C. B.	10044	Woolard, S.Qr.Mr.Serjt. (A.S.S.M.) A.	10044
— S.M. F. A.	10045	Wooldridge, Serjt.	
Warner, A.Qr.Mr.Serjt. J.	10045	(A.Sqdn.S.M.) T.	10935
Warry, Co.Serjt.Maj. E.	10935	Woolley, S. Smith Corpl.	
Wassall, Serjt. T. E.	10044	(A.Farr.S.Serjt.) R.	10935
Wassell, Bombr. O. T.	10044	Wray, Armt.St.Serjt. W. G.	10044
Watts, Corpl. A. G.	10044	Wright, Lce.Corpl. G.	10044
Weaver, Corpl. R. S.	10935	— Serjt. (A.C.S.M.) L. G. D.	10044
West, Pte. (A.S.Serjt.) G.	10935	Wrigley, S.Qr.Mr.Serjt. J.	10935
Whelan, By.Qr.Mr.Serjt. F. E.	10044		
Whilton, Serjt.Maj. F.	10935	Yardly, C.S.Maj. D.	10044
Whitbourn, Corpl. E.	10044	Young, A.C.Q.M.Serjt. A.	10044
White, Farr.S.Serjt. H. A.	10044	— Eng.Cl.S.Serjt. F. A. C.	10044
Whiteway, S.Serjt. R.	10044	— By.Qr.Mr.Serjt. G.	10044

---

* Group known: Queen's South Africa Medal (Cape Colony, Orange Free State, Transvaal, South Africa 1901, Cpl. 1/Northumberland Volunteer Artilly.), 1914/15 Star (Sapper R.E.), British War and Victory Medals (2nd Lt), 1911 Coronation (St. John's Ambulance Brigade Reverse, 2nd Amb. Officer), M.S.M. (Postal Section R.E.) and Territorial Force Efficiency Medal (Edw. VII, B.Q.M.S. 1/N.B. R.F.A.).

† 1/4th South Lancs. Regt. France & Flanders from 13 February. 1915 to November, 1918. M.I.D. 25 May 1918 as Lieut. & Q.M. W. A. Okes-Voysey and was later Acting Major.

Vol. I, 1917

Adcock, S.Sjt. (A.S.S.M.) W. J.	52	Bate, L./Cpl. (A.Sjt.) H. J.	52
Alabaster, Coy.S.M. (actg.		Baxter, S.Q.M.S. A. V.	52
R.S.Maj.) G.	2487	— 2nd Cpl. D.	52
Alder, C.S.M. F. H.	52	Beaney, Gunner L. A. ‡ ❀	2487
Aldridge, Cpl. J. E.	52	Beattie, Sjt. J. N.	55
Alexander, Band Sjt. R. D.	1574	Beatton, Pte. H. G.	52
Allen, S.S.M. A.	52	Beckett, S.Q.M.Sjt. (actg.S.Maj.) J.	1574
— Sub-Condr. (actg.Condr.) J. A.	2487	Begley, Pte. T. R.	52
— Pte. R. *	52	Bendall, Sjt. A. W.	52
— Cpl. (A.S.Q.M.S.) S.	52	Bennett, Pte. J. M.	52
Alloway, S.Sjt. H. B.	52	Bent, S.Maj. J. P.	1574
Andress, S.S.M. (A.1st Cl. S.S.M.) P.	52	Bentley, Pte. T. §	52
Andrews, Q.M.S. A. W.	52	Bibby, L.Cpl. E. +	52
— Condr. H. C. †	1574	Bicknell, Sjt. G. H.	52
Archibald, C.S.M. (act. S.M.) G. F.	52	Biddiscombe, B.S.M. G. A.	55
Arnold, S.S.M. E.	52	Billyeald, Cpl. S. ◊	52
Ashby, S.S.Maj. (now 2nd Lt.) W. H.	1574	Bishop, S.M. G. H.	52
Ashton, Staff Sjt. A. E.	2487	— Cpl. (actg.Sjt.) J. H.	1146
Atkins, S.Q.M.S. (A.S.S.M.) C. H.	52	Blackman, B.S.M. G. W.	52
Avery, Cpl. (A.S.M.) A.	52	Bland, S.S. (Mil.F.ofW.) J. W. ¶	2487
Ayres, C.S.M. F. J. D.	52	Blewitt, S.S. (actg.Condr.) H.	2487
		Blunden, Spr. (actg.2nd Cpl) W. C. L.	1574
Bain, S.Maj. J.	2487	Boddington, L.Cpl. W.	52
Bainbridge, Sjt. R. H.	2487	Bond, Q.M.S. E. W.	52
Baker, S.Q.M.S. (act. S.S.M.) E. F.	2487	— Cpl. (actg.Sjt.) L.	2487
Bannester, Sapper S. G. ‡ ❀	2487	Bone, Foreman of Works, S.Sjt. A. E.	52
Barber, S.Sjt. (actg.S.S.M.) J. H. A.	1146	Booth, Q.M.S. (A.S.M.) B.	52
Barkham, Q.M.S. (Art. Clerk)		Bower, Pte. (A.Cpl.) H. R.	52
(A.R.S.M.) J. A.	52	Bowes, Eng. Cl.Sjt. T. W.	52
Bass, Mech.S.Sjt. (A.M.S.M.) G.	52	Bowring, Sjt. J. S.	1574

---

* 2nd Dragoon Gds. Under authority of H.M. the King, awarded by G.O.C.-in-C. 'for attempting to save life from drowning.'

† R.A.O.C. Also Médaille d'Honneur avec Glaives (en Argent).

‡ See Appendix Y.

§ Medal known: 2/R. Mun. Fus. Also awarded M M *L.G.* 29 August, 1918.

+ 2nd Dragoon Gds. (att. M.M.P.). Under authority of H.M. the King, awarded by G.O.C.-in-C. 'for attempting to save life from drowning.'

◊ 2nd Dragoon Gds. Under authority of H.M. the King, awarded by G.O.C.-in-C. 'for attempting to save life from drowning.'

¶ Group known: M.B.E. (2nd type *L.G.* 19 December, 1944. Defence of Malta, for keeping airfields cleared during and after airstrikes), 1914/15 Star trio (S/Sgt. R.E., M.I.D. oakleaf *L.G.* 1 December, 1916 for Egypt) 1939/45 and Africa Stars, Defence and War Medals, L.S. & G.C. (Geo. V Regular Army bar 1851971 W.O.II R.E.) and M.S.M. (15194 R.E.).

Boyd, Pte. (L.Cpl.) W. H.	52	Campbell, Cpl. H.	1574
Bradley, Pte. A.	52	— S.M. J.	52
Brain, S.M. L. J.	52	— Correction	2206
Braine, Cpl. F. A. W.	52	— Q.M.S. W. G.	55
Brand, Sjt. (actg.Sub.Condr.) S.	2487	Canter, B.S.M. C.	52
Brierly, B.S.M. W. T.	52	Cardy, L.Sjt. C. H. A.	1574
Briggs, By.S.Maj. F. W.	1574	Carey, 1st Cl. S.S.M. A. J.	52
Britton, R.Q.M.S. R. E.	1574	Carr, 1st Cl. S.S.M. J. W.	52
— Suptg.Clerk W. P.	52	Cash, C.S.M. T. *	52
Brooke, Q.M.Sjt. J. T.	1574	Castle, S.Sjt. (actg. S.Q.M.S.) E. W.	1146
Brooks, Cpl. (actg.S.S.M.) F.	2487	Catley, Sjt. R.	52
Brown, S.M. G.	1146	Chalmers, Sjt. W.	1146
— Sjt. J. T.	52	Chase, C.S.M. P. C.	1574
— Sjt. W. G.	52	Chavasse, S.S. (A.S.M.) H. L.	52
— Sjt. W. H.	52	Chevalier, Act. Cpl. W. S.	1574
Browne, C.S.M. C. E.	55	Childs, 1.A.M. E. E.	927
Bull, 2nd Cpl. (actg.E.C.S.S.) N. R.	2487	Chymist, A.Sjt. F. † ❀	2488
Bullen, A.C.S.M. Instr. V.	52	Clarke, S.M. (Art.Clerk) P. W.	52
Burchell, Sjt. (tem. Asst.Com.) D.	1146	— S.Q.M.S. W. B.	1146
Burd, 1st Cl. S.S.M. A. V.	52	Clayton, Cpl. (actg.Sjt.) J. W.	2487
— S.Q.M.S. J. G.	2487	Clemons, S.M. (A.Suptg.Cl.) J. W. E.	52
Burdon, Amt S.S. (A.Amt.S.M.) W.	52	Clevey, Pte. (actg.Sjt.) R. J.	1574
Burfitt, Sjt. (actg.C.S.M.) A. E.	52	Coates, B.S.M. H. J.	52
Burns, R.S.M. J.	1574	Cockfield, W.O. N.	55
Burridge, C.S.M. H. J.	52	Cole, Pte. (A.Sjt.) C.	52
Burt, 2nd Cpl. (A.Sjt.E.C.) A. T.	52	— S.S. H. W.	52
Burton, C.S.M. F. J.	52	— Cpl. (A.Sjt.) J.	52
— Correction	1576	Collett, Far.Cpl. (A.Far.Sjt.) B. H.	52
— Cpl. (actg.S.Q.M.S.) J. E.	2487	Collie, Supt.Cl. A.	52
Buss, S.S.M. W. J.	52	Collins, Q.M.S. (actg.Mech.)	
Butler, Eng. Cl. Q.M.S.		(Elec.S.M.) T.	2487
(A.Suptg.Cl.) H.	52	— S.S. Farr. T. C.	52
Byatt, C.S.M. J. W.	52	Condon, R.Q.M.S. J.	1574
Byrom, Amt. S.M. J.	52	Connell, Spr. (A.2nd Cpl.) R. M.	52
		Conole, Sjt. B.	55
Cahill, S.Q.M.S. (actg.S.S.M.) A.	1146	Conway, C.S.M. J.	1574
Cairns, Sjt. M.	52	Cook , Suptg.Clerk F.	1596
— Sjt. T. A.	2487	— Q.M.S. (A.Suptg.Cl.) J.	52
Callander, Pte. (A.Cpl.) W. G.	52	Cooke, S.S. H.	2487
— Correction	1576	Coombes, Q.M.S. (actg.Supt.Clerk) F.	1574
Cameron, Farr.Sjt. J. H.	1146	Coop, Condr. T.	1574

* 14148 C.S.M. Thomas Cash 24/Manchesters (Oldham Pals) *L.G.* 1.1.17 Valuable Service. Details from Regt. Book of Honour: He was repeatedly responsible for work of an important nature in which he always showed conspicuous initiative and skill. During the operations before Ginchy he frequently organised working parties and supervised them under heavy fire.

† L/9566 3/Queen's. Single M.S.M. known: 'During live grenade throwing instruction a bomb was dropped after the fuse had been lighted. Sgt. Chymist at once picked it up and threw it away, probably saving several lives by doing so.' Sittingbourne, Home Forces, 3 June 1916.

Cooper, Sjt. J. C.		52	Dean, S.S.M. (A.1st Cl. S.S.M.) W. H.	52
Copland, Sjt. J. L.		52	Dennis, Ajt. (actg.S.M.) T.	1574
Corbett, Q.M.S. W. H.		52	Dexter, S.M. (Arty. C.) S. H.	52
Cotter, Gunner C. P.	* ❀ 2487		Dible, S.S.M. W.	52
Coulson, Cpl. (A.C.Q.M.S.) S.		52	Dollimore, Cpl. F. E.	1574
Cowland, B.S.M. H. S.		52	Donovan, Sjt. A.C.S.M. F.	1574
Cox, Sjt. (actg.S.S.) A. A.		2487	Dove, E.C.Q.M.S. (actg.Supt.Clerk) J.	1574
— Dvr. (actg.Cpl.) E. V.		52	Dorward, S.S. D. E.	2487
— Sjt. H. G.		1574	Douglas, Farr.Q.M.S. A.	1574
— L.C. (actg.Sjt.) W. S.		1574	Draper, Drvr. J.	52
Coyne, C.S.M. J.		1574	Duff, Farr.Sjt. C.	1574
Crawford, B.S.M. J.		52	Duncan, L.Cpl. A. J.	1574
Crayford, Sjt. (actg.C.S.M.) A. J. V.		1574	Dunham, Pte. (A.Sjt.) A. (correction)	1575
Crocker, actg.S.M. A. T.		2487	Dunlop, Pte. (A.Sjt.) G.	52
— Pte. W. L.		52	Dunn, Cpl. G.	† ❀ 2488
Crooke, R.Q.M.S. C. J.		1574	— Q.M.S. (actg.S.M.) J.	‡ 2487
Crothy, Cpl. (A/Sgt.) W. H.		55	— Sjt. M.	1574
Crow, A.L.Cpl. G.		52	Durman, F.Sjt. C. W.	52
Crusher, Sjt. (actg.C.S.M.) R. B.		1574	Durrant, Eng. Ledger Keeper &	
Crute, Q.M.S. W.		1574	Storeman, Q.M.S. A. M.	52
Cummins, S.M. J. F.		55		
— Pte. W.		1574	Eadie, Sjt. J. J.	1574
Currell, S.S. H.		1574	Eaton, L.Cpl. (A.2nd Cpl.) N. A.	52
Curtis, B.S.M. F. C.		52	Eccles, A.C.S.M. Instr. F. C.	52
			Edington, Supt.Cl. J.	52
Daires, Pte. (A.L.Cpl) W. J.		52	Edmondson, B.Q.M.S. G. R.	52
Dalton, Cpl. (actg.Sjt.) J. B.		1574	Edwards, Gunner (actg. Bombr.)	
Dandy, Cpl. (A.Sjt.) W. R.		52	A. F.	§ ❀ 2487
Davey, Eng. Cl. Q.M.S. F. G. L.		52	— Sjt. T.	2487
Davies, Pte. (A.L.C.) W. J.			Elliott, Sjt. C. B.	55
(correction)		1026	— S.S. (actg.S.Q.M.S.) G. T.	52
Davy, Sjt. N. J. L.		55	— Mech.S.S. S.	52
Dawson, Mec. S.M. G.		52	— Sjt. W. C.	52
Day, C.S.M. G.		2487	Ellis, Sjt. E.	55
De Barre, S.Sjt. S. G. (correction)		1575	— Sjt. H.	55
De la Mare, S.S. J. H.		2487	Elms, 2nd Cpl. (A.C.S.M.) C. J. R.	52

---

  * See Appendix Y.

  † Single in Moss Collection. Only 141 M.S.M.s were awarded to R.F.C. of which only 4 were for gallantry. This was the first. Initially it was a recommendation for the Albert Medal. He was with No. 10 Sqn. on 30 July 1916 at the airfield near Château Warppe, France. A bomb rack was being removed from a plane when a phosphorus bomb fell to the floor and the fuse ignited. Cpl. Dunn seized the bomb and ran around the machine, out of the hanger and into the open, some 30 yds away. As he threw the bomb away it exploded. He prevented a most serious accident and loss of life.

  ‡ Group was in McInnes collection: Queen's Sudan (11059 Pte. R.A.M.C.), British War and Victory Medals (erased), Coronation 1902, L.S. & G.C. (Geo. V. Sgt. R.A.M.C.), M.S.M., Order of St. John, Long Service Medal (one clasp) and Khedive's Sudan (Khartoum). 60 R.A.M.C. officers and 139 O.R.'s were at Omdurman.

  § See Appendix Y. Also awarded Edward Medal, exchanged for George Cross in 1973.

Emerson, Pte. (A.Sjt.) A.		52
Emery, T.S.S.M. A.		2487
Emmerson, Spr. (actg.Sjt.) J. E.		1574
— Sjt. T. W.		52
England, L.Cpl. S.	* ❀	2488
Evans, Pte. (A.Cpl.) W.		52
Evershed, A.Sjt. P.	† ❀	2488
Fairlie, Q.M.S. (Armt.Artr.) G. H.		55
Faulkner, Q.M.S. P. H.		52
Fawcett, Q.M.S. W.		52
Fenn, Sub-Condr. (A.Condr.) S. A.	‡	52
Ferguson, Sjt. W. G.	§ ❀	2488
Feurer, Sjt. (A.S.S.) G. W.		52
Fever, Sapper (actg. L.Cpl.) H. W.	+ ❀	2487
Fillmore, Sjt. (A.S.Q.M.S.) E. W. H.		52
Filtness, Sjt. R. H. G.		52
Finch, S.S. (actg.S.S.M.) G. E.		2487
Finney, Sjt. H.		1574
Fitzgerald, S.M. G.	◊	52
— Correction		2206
Fitzpatrick, Sjt. C. T.		55
Flint, Col.Sjt. R. S.	¶	52
Fowles, S.Sjt. C. D.		52
— Sjt. (A.S.M.) E.		52
Fox, S.M. (Arty. Clerk) J. B.		52
Frankford, Sqn S.M. H. L. A.		2488
Franklin, Eng.Cl.Q.M.S. H. B. J.		52
Franks, S.Q.M.S. W. H.		53
Fraser, Sjt. L.		1574

Freshwater, Eng.Cl. Sjt. C.		53
Frier, Flight Sjt. L.		2487
Fryer, S.Q.M.S. H.		2487
Gaches, Sjt. (A.S.Sjt.) G. R.		53
Gaines, L.Cpl. P.		53
Galbraith, S.Sjt. D.		55
Gales, C.Q.M.S. H.		53
Gallagher, C.S.M. T.		1574
Gardiner, S.M. H. K.		1146
Gerrard, Sjt. (actg.S.S.) P.		2487
Gibson, Sjt. Cook A. G.		55
— Sjt. A. McQ.	**	55
Gilbert, C.S.M. C.		53
Giles, S.Q.M.S. G. W. S.		1574
Glading, R.C.M. W.		53
Godsmark, S.Sjt. C.		53
Goldie, Sjt. (A.C.S.M.) J. H.		53
Golightly, S.S. A.		2487
Goodall, Q.M.S. G. B. W.		55
— L.Cpl. J. W.		2487
Gordon, 1st Cl. S.S.M. J.		1146
— C.S.M. (actg.R.S.M.) J. B.		1575
Goulding, Pte. (actg.S.Sjt.) R. T.		1575
Gower, Pte. S. G.		2487
Grace, C.Q.M.S. W. S. W.		1575
Graham, Sjt. J.		1575
— L.Sjt. (A.S.M.) J. H.		53
Green, Sjt. N.		53
Greenfield, S.S. W. G. H.		1575
Greenslade, Sjt. F. S.		1575

---

* 1/Leics. Regt. Ypres 30 May 1916, 'picked up a smoking bomb in a bomb factory and threw it out of the trench where it burst.'

† 3/R. Sussex Regt. Newhaven 17 October, 1916. 'Threw out a live grenade, dropped by a recruit when acting as instructor.'

‡ R.A.O.C. Also M.B.E.

§ 5/K.O.S.B. 1 June 1916, 'practising throwing Mills bombs and one rolled back, he threw it over the parapet where it immediately exploded.'

+ See Appendix Y.

◊ Group known: Queen's Sudan (L./Sgt. S.D.S.E.A.), British War Medal (W.O.1 N. Staffs.), L.S. & G.C. (Edw. VII, C./Sgt. N. Staffs.), M.S.M. (N. Staffs. R.) Order of the Nile, Khedive's Sudan 1896 (no clasp), Khedive's Sudan 1910 (Nyima 1917-18). Order of the Nile *L.G.* 9 October 1919.

¶ K.R.R.C. entitled to Queen's South Africa Medal and King's South Africa Medal.

** Group known: 1914/15 Star (Pte. 14/Bn. A.I.F.) British War and Victory Medals (A.I.F., Sgt.) and M.S.M. (46 Aust. Inf.).

Greenwood, S.S.M. A	*	53
Grigg, Sjt. J. C.		53
— Correction		2206
Hale, Sub-Cond. W. G.		55
Hales, Sjt. (A.Mech.S.Sjt.) W.		53
Halhett, S.Sjt. (actg.S.S.M.) F. C.		1575
Hall, S.S.M. E. C.		2487
Harris, Cpl. (actg. Sjt.) C. T.	† ❀	2487
Harrison, Amt. S.S. A. T.		1575
— S.S.M. (A.S.S.M.) G.		53
Hatch, B.S.M. F.		53
Hatfield, Sjt. W. W.		53
Hayward, Sjt. (A.S.M.) W. C.		53
Heeley, Tpr. (A.L.C.) J.		53
Heley, actg.Cpl. S.		1575
Hellier, S.S.M. (A.1st Cl. S.S.M.) S.		53
Hemming, Sjt. H. A.		53
Hemus, Sjt. (Arty.Clerk) A. C.		53
Hennessy, Cpl. R. R. J.		53
Herbert, L.Cpl. W.		53
Herdman, S.M. N.		53
Herrington, S.S.M. J. M.		2487
Hetherington, C.S.M. J.		1575
Hickman, Pte. (A.S.S.) J. R.		53
Hickmott, R.Q.M.S. D.		1575
Hill, S.M. F.	‡	53
— S.Sjt. G.		1146
Hills, E.L. and S.Q.M.S. A. C.		53
Hobbs, Sjt. (A.R. Q.M.S.) A.		53
Holborn, A.Cpl. J. S.	§ ❀	2488
Holden, R.S.M. G. W.		1575

Holden, Sjt. W.		53
— — Deletion		1026
Holman, Sjt. W. H.	+ ❀	2488
Holywood, S.Q.M.S. M.		53
Holz, Sjt. H. A.		55
Honey, Sub-Condr. (A.Condr.) N.		53
Hood, L.Cpl. J.		53
Hooper, Flt. Sjt. H. L.		53
Horner, L.Cpl. (actg.Sjt.) H. J.		53
Horton, l.Air Mech. T.		53
Howard, Flt.Sjt. C. J.		53
Howell, L.Sjt. G. W.		53
Hudson, C.S.M. A.		53
Hughes, Sjt. (A.S.S.) R. A.		53
Hulbert, S.S.M. (A.1st Cl. S.S.M.) P.	◊	53
Humbles, Sjt. T.		2487
Humphreys, Q.M.S. J.		53
Hunt, S.S. (A.S.M.) T. H.		53
Hunter, C.S.M. (A.Q.M.S.) M. S.		53
Hurvid, C.S.M. (A.S.M.) R.		53
Hutcheson, C.Q.M.S. S. J.		1575
Huxley, Sjt. (actg.Supt.Clerk) W. H.		1146
Hyett, S.S.M. (A.R.S.M.) T.	¶	53
Hynes, Sjt. M. J.		1575
Iddison, Cpl. G. S.		53
Illing, R.S.M. G. W.		1575
Inglis, L.Cpl. H.		53
— A.Sjt. W. L.		53
James, S.Q.M.S. (actg.S.S.M.) G. C.		1575

---

* Medals on display in Edinburgh Castle: Afghanistan (Kandahar, 72nd Foot), Kabul to Kandahar Star, Queen's Egypt Medal (Tel el Kebir, Seaforths), Queen's Sudan Medal (2/Sea. High.), Queen's South Africa Medal (Cape Colony, South Africa 1902), 1914/15 Star trio (A. & S. High., M.I.D. oakleaf), L.S. & G.C. (Victoria), M.S.M., Khedive's Star 1882, Khedive's Sudan (Khartoum) and R.H.S. Stanhope Gold Medal. Born 1859. Enlisted 1878 and served 20 years. Rejoined for Boer War and W.W.I. Died 1932.

† See Appendix Y. Also awarded Edward Medal.

‡ Group in R.C.T. Museum: M.C., 1914/15 Star trio, R.V.M. (Edw. VII), L.S. & G.C. (Geo. V) and M.S.M. (A.S.C.)

§ 4/S.A. Inf. Borden 23 July 1916. 'During live grenade practice a recruit lodged one on the parapet. Holborn, the instructor, grasped it and threw it out.'

+ 4/R. Sussex R. Broadwater Forest, 30 November, 1916. 'During live grenade practice, threw out a grenade lodged on the parapet.'

◊ Group known: Queen's South Africa Medal (Cape Colony), King's South Africa Medal (both L./Cpl. A.S.C.), 1914 Star & bar trio (C.Q.M.S. & W.O.1 A.S.C.), L.S. & G.C. (Geo. V, S.S.M. A.S.C.) and M.S.M.

¶ Dragoon Gds. P.S.I. to Northampton Yeo.

James, S.S. H.	1575	Kent, C.Q.M.S. N. A.	55
— S.S.M. J. B.	1575	Keyes, Sjt. (actg.A.S.S.M.) J.	53
Jamieson, Sjt. (A.S.S.M.) A. F.	53	— Correction	1576
Jarvis, R.Q.M.S. J.	1575	Kindness, Sjt. G.	53
Jefford, Pte. (actg.Sjt.) W.	1575	King, S.Sjt. F.	55
Jervis, Pte. J.	53	— Pte. F.	53
Johnson, Sapper J. * ❀	2487	Kingston, Pte. (actg.L.Cpl.) F.	1575
Joines, Armr. S.Sjt. W.	53	Knight, S.S. (A.S.S.M.) H. J.	53
Jones, S.S.M. (actg.1st Class S.S.M.)		— Correction	1576
A. C.	2487	Knox, Cpl. (actg.Sjt.) J. ‡	1575
— Sjt. (actg.Condr.) A. E.	2487		
— Sjt. C. F. † ❀	2487	Lammas, A.C.S.M. Instr. A. G. §	53
— E.L. and S.Q.M.S. H. J.	53	Lanchbury, S.Sjt. (actg.S.Q.M.S.)	
— Pte. (actg.L.Cpl.) J. A.	1575	J. J.	1146
		Lane, Mil.Mech.A.A.S. H. W.	53
Keeley, A.L.Cpl. T.	53	Langfield, Flt.Sjt. G. L.	2487
Keenan, 1st Cl. S.S.M. M.	53	Langstone, Cpl. (A.S.Sjt.)	53
Keene, C.S.M. (A.S.M.) J. T.	53	Lawrence, Pte. (Actg. Sjt.) W.	2487
Kendall, C.S.M. H.	53	Layland, Sjt. (A.S.M.) C. T.	53
Kennedy, C.S.M. G. D.	2487	Le Blancq, 1st Cl. S.S.M. E. J.	53

---

* I.W.D., R.E. 'On 23rd August 1916, the tug H.S.7 was on a passage from Hull towing the barges Walker and City to Cardiff for shipment to Mesopotamia. When eight miles E.N.E. of Hartland Point in a heavy sea the tow rope broke. To secure the barges again it proved necessary to approach stern first and to avoid fouling the propeller. When near enough Sapper Johnson jumped aboard at great risk and managed with difficulty to secure a rope. Owing to the high sea running it was almost impossible to keep a footing but he nevertheless persevered with the dangerous task of hauling on board the ten inch tow rope. Whilst he was thus engaged and when the barge was only some ten feet away form the tug, a heavy sea struck her, causing her to list over at such an angle that Sapper Johnson lost his footing and was washed over the side. He saved himself by clutching at a rope but before he could pull himself back on board, another sea flung the barge against the stern of the tug. Sapper Johnson hung between the two and was terribly crushed, his left foot being completely severed above the ankle and his right foot smashed. He was secured and dragged on board the tug and received immediate first aid which in all probability saved his life. The barges had broken adrift twice previously and each time Sapper Johnson had boarded them showing great coolness, courage and pluck in the risky work.'

† 2nd Bn. Worcs. R. 'On 8th December 1916 whilst some men were sitting round a brazier in a hut, one of the men dropped something into the fire. Sergeant Jones saw the article to be a bomb and realising the danger he immediately tried to get it out of the brazier. After two attempts he succeeded in doing so and the bomb, thrown to the ground, immediately exploded. A number of men were slightly wounded but this prompt action probably averted a very serious accident.'

‡ Group known: Queen's South Africa Medal (Cape Colony, Orange Free State, Transvaal, South Africa 1901, South Africa 1902), Africa General Service Medal (Somaliland 1902-04, Jidballi, both Pte. K.R.R.C.), British War and Victory Medals (Cpl. M.F.P.) and M.S.M. (M.F.P.).

§ Awarded M.S.M. Annuity in 1950 (A.O.144, Berkshire Regt.).

Le Petit, Armt.S.S. (A.Armt.S.M.)		
W. J.	*	53
— Deletion	*	356
Leach, R.S.M. F.		2487
Leddon, E.S. Q.M.S. W. E.		53
Lester, S.Q.M.S. H. C.		53
Leverett, Q.M.S. (A.S.M.) F. W.		53
Lewis, Flight Sjt. A. E.		2487
— C.S.M. E. E.		1575
— Pte (A.S.) H. M.		55
Lindley, L.C. G. (Correction)		1575
Lines, Suptg.Clerk A. E.		2488
Lisle, Sjt. (A.S.Sjt.) F. C.		53
Little, S.S. T. F.		2488
Littleton, Armt.S.S.		
(A.Armt.S.M.) G.		53
Longshaw, L.Cpl. E. H.		53
Longstaff, Amt. S.S.		
(actg.Amt. S.M.) J. W.	†	1575
Luce, Pte. (Actg. Cpl.) R.	‡	2488
Ludlow, Pte. (A.L.Cpl.) F. H.		53
Lumb, Sjt. C. A.		55
Lunnis, Sjt. W. R.		55
Lygoe, Pte. H. J. L.	❀	2488
Lynch, 2nd Cpl. (actg.Sjt.) E. W.		1575
— Cpl. J. J.	§	1575
Lyons, Sjt. J. M.		55
— Sjt. (actg.S.S.) W.		2488
McCaffery, Supt.Clerk H. J.		1575
MacEwan, L.C. R.		1575
MacFarlane, L.Cpl. F.		53
McFie, Sqdn. Q.M.S. B. J. S.		53
McInnes, Pte. J.		53

Mackenzie, Farr, Q.M. Cpl. J. K.		53
McKillop, 2nd Cpl. (actg.Cpl.) D.		2488
McLaren, Sjt. D.		2488
McLean, C.S.M. (actg.S.S.M.) A.		1575
McLeod, Sjt. A.	+ ❀	2488
McLoghry, Pte. (actg.Sjt.) J.		2488
McMajon, 1st Class W. O. P.		2488
McMorran, Cpl. J.		53
McNaught, Pte. L.		1575
McNicoll, S.Q.M.S. F.		53
McPherson, A.C.S.M. D. V.		55
McVeigh, B.S.M. T.		53
Mahoney, R.Q.S. (actg.R.S.M.) E.		1575
Maile, Condr. A. C. W.	◊	53
Mallows, C.Q.M.S. H. E.		53
Markey, Armt.S.S. L. E.		53
Martin, Condr. A. W.	¶	53
— L.Cpl. (actg.Cpl.) O.		53
— Sjt. (actg.S.M.) P. J .		1575
Mason, A.C.S.M. (Arty. Clerk) R. P.		53
Mather, Q.M.S. (actg.S.M.) D. G.		2488
Mathie, C.Q.M.S. W. W.		53
Meikeljohn, Pte. E. J.		53
Merrick, Eng. Cl. Q.M.S. F. T.		53
Metherell, Q.M.S. (A.S.M.) (A.C.) T.		53
Metz, A.S.M. L. H.		53
Millard, S.Q.M.S. (actg.S.S.M.) C. J.		2488
Miller, Farr.Sjt. C. G.		53
— Eng. Cl. Sjt. (A.E.C. Q.M.S.)		
P. R. C.		53
— R.S.M. R. W.		2488
Minns, Pte. (actg.Cpl.) A. S.		2488
Minterne, S.Q.M.S. A. H.		2488
Mirams, C.S.M. L. S.		53

---

* R.A.O.C. Awarded D.C.M.

† Group known: 1914 Star trio (M.I.D. oakleaf), General Service Medal (Iraq), L.S. & G.C. (Geo. V), M.S.M. (R.A.O.C.) and Médaille Barbatie si Credinta 2nd class (Roumania); also his diary, various photographs, the certificate accompanying the Roumanian award and his M.I.D. certificate.

‡ Group known: C.B. (Civil, 1947), M.B.E. (Military, 1937), 1914/15 Star trio, Defence Medal, Coronation 1953 and M.S.M. (Middlesex Yeo.). Formerly R.H.A. Commissioner, Schleswig-Holstein 1950–52. Previously held various administrative posts in the Patents Office and Ministry of Labour & National Service. Born 1893.

§ M.S.M. known: 5947 5/R. Irish Fus. This is probably as near as one can get to an M.S.M. for Gallipoli. The Battn. landed there on 7 August, 1915 and then went to Salonika in October, 1915.

+ 3/Seaforth Hldrs. Cromarty, 1 July, 1916. 'During live grenade instruction he picked up and threw out a grenade lodged on the parapet.'

◊ R.A.O.C. Also M.B.E.

¶ R.A.O.C. Also M.B.E.

Mirfin, S.Q.M.S. A. E.		53	Newton, Q.M.S. (A.S.M.) J. E.	54
— Correction		1576	Nicholl, R.Q.M.S. W. E.	2488
Mitchell, A.Sjt. T.	* ❀	2488	Nicholls, Pte. J. J.	55
Mitchinson, Pte. (A.Sjt.) T.		53	Nichols, S.Cpl. (actg.1st Cl. S.S.M.)	
Moon, C.Q.M.S. now Q.M.S. (O.R.S.)			H. A.	2488
J. C.		53	Norton, Cpl. E.	54
Moore, Cpl. P. S.		53		
Morecambe, Mil.Mech.Elec.S.M.			Oakley, Drill Sjt. (A.S.M.) F.	54
W. M. N.		53	O'Brien, Sjt. P.	54
Morris, Fitter, J. F.		53	— S.S. (A.S.S.M.) R.	54
— L.C. (actg.Sjt.) W. J. B.		2488	O'Hanlon, F.of W.Q.M.S. J. W.	54
Moses, Sjt. (actg.C.S.M.) H. J .H.		53	Oliver, Farr.Q.M.S. A. E.	54
Moss, L.Sjt. E.		53	Ormes, Sjt. (actg.S.Sjt.) C. R.	1146
Mott, By.S.M. C. E.		1575	Orton, S.Q.M.S. (actg.S.S.M.) M.	2488
Moulton, Gnr. F. T.		53	Osborn, C.S.M. W. R.	1575
Mount, Sjt. A. E.		1575	Osborne, S.Q.M.S. T.	2488
Muir, S. Condr. A. J.		53	O'Shea, S.S. J. J.	54
Mullholland. R.S.M. P.		1575	Osman, Sub-Condr. (A.Condr.) A.	54
Mullen, A.S.M. C.		53	Owen, Pte. (A.Cpl.) H. A.	† ❀ 2488
— Cpl. (A.Sjt.) M.		53	— Pte. (A.Sjt.) W. N.	‡ ❀ 2488
Mulvany, Sjt. J.		2488		
Murray, Q.M.S. D. A.		53	Padfield, Pte. (A.Sjt.) F. H.	54
— L.Cpl. J.		53	Page, Drvr. (A.Cpl.) T. E.	54
Myhill, Q.M.S. (F.O.W.) F. R.		2488	Palmer, (Sub-Condr.) A. E. J.	2488
			Parker, S.M. C. W.	55
Nash, Cpl. R. E.		53	— C.S.M. J.	1575
Nealon, C.S.M. J. E. B.		53	— Pte. J. T.	1575
— S.M. (F.O.W.) T.		2488	— Sapper (actg. L.Cpl.) S.	§ ❀ 2488
Newman, By.S.M. G.		1575		

---

* 10139 1/Royal Scots Gallantry M.S.M. for Egypt. Single M.S.M. was in McInnes collection. He was a grenade instructor, a man dropped a grenade after igniting the fuse, Sgt. Mitchell made two attempts to recover it, the second after the recruit had knocked it from his hand attempting to get away. The grenade exploded before he could reach it a second time wounding him in the head.

† A.O.C. 'While ammunition was being discharged from S.S. *Megantic* part of a hoist of 13-pr. ammunition fell about forty feet into the bottom of the hold. Simultaneously there was an explosion and a vivid flash from below. Corporal Owen, with great courage, immediately lowered himself into the hold and managed to separate the burning ammunition from the remainder, which consisted of some thirty tons of 13-pr. ammunition, half of which was high explosive. Corporal Owen remained in the hold until all the danger was over, helping to direct the fire hose. But for his courage and promptitude the explosion would have had the most serious consequences for the ship and all on board.' Alexandria, 24th–25th August 1916.

‡ 3rd/1st Bedfordshire Yeo. 'Whilst a party of men were being instructed in live grenade throwing one of the men hit the parapet and the grenade fell back into the trench. Sergeant Owen immediately seized it and managed to throw it over the parapet before it burst, his prompt action averting a very serious accident.' Maresfield Park, 1st August 1916.

§ (Q.M.S.) See Appendix Y.

Parkin, R.S.M. J.	*	54	Pride, E.C.Q.M.S. (actg.Supt.			
Patchell, S.M. H.		1575	Clerk) H.	‡	1575	
Paxton, S.S.M. H.		2488	Prince, S.Sjt. H. M.		54	
Payton, actg.S.M. W. T.		54	Prince-Cox, Sjt. (A.S.S.M.) C.		54	
Pearce, Gunner A.	† ❀	2488	Purchase, Sjt. C. W.		54	
— Q.M.S. (actg.S.M.) G. F.		1146	Pyper, S.S.M. B. L.		1575	
— Amt. S.M. W. R. O.		54				
Pearson, Q.M.S. (A.S.S.M.) E.		54	Rands, S.S.M. R.		54	
Peckham, Pte. (actg.Mch. S.S.) H. M.		2488	Rankine, Sjt. (actg. S.M.) J.		1146	
Pepperell, S.S. (A.S.M.) W. C.		54	Ranson, 1st Cl. S.S.M. W. J.		54	
Pickering, Sjt. J.		54	Redican, Bombr. C.		1575	
— C.S.M. S.		54	Redley, L.Cpl. (A.2nd Cpl.) C.		54	
Pilkington, 1st Cl. S.S.M. F.		54	Rees, actg. Cpl. R. W. G.	† ❀	2488	
Pithers, Q.M.S. C. H.		54	— Coy, Q.M.S. T. J.		54	
Platts, Cpl. A.L.Sjt. J.	‡ ❀	2488	Reid, R.S.M. T.		1575	
Pollock, Sjt. R.		1596	Reimann, S.Q.M.S. (A.S.S.M.) H. E.		54	
Pooley, S.S. R. S.		2488	Reynard, Spr. (A.L. Cpl.) R. W.		54	
Pope, S.S. (A.S.S.M.) W. J.		54	Reynolds, Art.Cpl. R. J.		54	
Popperwell, E.C., Q.M.S.			Richardson, Amt.S.S. G. H.		54	
(A.Suptg.Clerk) W. W.		54	Ricketts, Cpl. J. W.	+ ❀	2488	
Poulton, Cpl. (A.Sjt.) E.		54	— Q.M.S. W. R.		54	
Price, Gunner T.	❀	2488	Riddett, S.S. (actg.S.Q.M.S.) H.		2488	

---

* Group known: (Hon. Wing Commander James Edward Parkin M.B.E., R.A.F.): M.B.E. (1st type, Military Ribbon, *L.G.* 3.6.18, Major R.A.F.), Queen's Sudan Medal (Corpl. 1/Gren. Gds.), 1914 Star and bar (S.M. 1/Gren. Gds.), British War and Victory Medals (M.I.D. oakleaf, W.O.II Gren. Gds.), Defence Medal, Coronation 1911 (Drill Sgt. Gren. Gds.), Coronation 1937, Royal Victorian Medal (Edw. VII, Bronze, Drill Sgt. 1/Gren. Gds.), M.S.M. (Gren. Gds.) and Khedive's Sudan (Khartoum, Corpl. Gren. Gds). Born in 1876, enlisted 1896, was in charge of the Bearer party at the funeral of King Edward VII. Appointed Sergeant Major in 1912 he went to France with the B.E.F. in October, 1914 and was mentioned in despatches in *L.G.* 20 November, 1914. Commissioned in 1915. He transferred to the R.F.C. in August 1915 as Lieutenant and Quarter Master making this in fact a very early award of the M.S.M. for his service prior to commissioning. In the 1951 Air Force List he is shown as Squadron Leader. Hon Wing Commander, Retired. He died in 1963, aged 85.

† See Appendix Y.

‡ 91st Trg. Res. Bn. 'During live grenade throwing instruction a grenade with lighted fuse was dropped. Corporal Platts at once rushed forward and, not having time to reach the bomb, knocked over the man who had dropped it and the officer in charge, falling on the latter and covering him with his body so that his feet covered the officer's head. The bomb exploded and Corporal Platts was wounded in the feet, so that but for his courage and self-sacrifice his officer would have been severely injured if not killed.' Cramlington, 27th September 1916.

§ Group known: Queen's South Africa Medal (Cape Colony, Orange Free State, Transvaal, South Africa 1901, Spr. R.E.), 1914 Star & bar (E.C.Q.M.S.) British War and Victory Medals (W.O.2 R.E., M.I.D. oakleaf), M.S.M. and R.A.F. L.S. & G.C. (Geo. V, S.M.1).

+ 30 Div. Train A.S.C. La Bassée Canal 12 September, 1916. Saved a drowning man.

Ritchie, Pte. (A.Mech.S.S. A.) J. A.	54	Sharpe, Pte. H. E.		54
Rix, Sjt. W.	1575	— L.Cpl. (A.C.S.M.) P.		54
Roberts, Suptg.Clerk F. W.	54	Sheeby, C.Q.M.S. (A.C.S.M.) E. J.		54
Robertson, C.S.M. (A.S.M.) A.	54	Shelley, S.M. E. J.		54
Robinson, Sub-Condr. (A.Condr.)		Shelton, C.S.M. (actg.R.S.M.) G.		1575
C. E. W.	54	Shepherd, Q.M.S. E.		54
Rolfe, Sjt. P. H.	2488	— S.S. (A.Sub-Condr.) S.	† ❀	2488
Rolland, 2nd Cpl. (A.Sub Condr.)		Sherman, Sjt. W.		54
O. D.	54	Short, Sjt. J. J.		1575
Rouse, S.M. W. G. R	54	Siddle, C.S.M. W.		2488
Rowe, Sjt. (A.S.Q.M.S.) W. J.	54	Silver, Pte (A.Sjt.) F.		54
Rushbrook, S.S.M. A.	1575	Simmons, C.S.M. W. H.		55
Rutton, Cpl. B. A.	54	Simons, Arm.S.M. G. H.	‡	2488
Rye, S.S.M. (A.1st Cl. S.S.M.) F.	54	Simpson, S.S. J. W.		2488
		Singleton, Sjt. B,		55
Sagon, Sjt. V. W.	54	— 1st Cl. Air Mech. O. S.		54
Sampson, Pte. (A.Sjt.) J.	54	Slade, C.S.M. (actg.S.M.) H.		2488
Saunders, L. Sjt. (A.S.Q.M.S.) C. J.	54	Smith, Cpl. (A.Sub-Condr.) A. H.		1575
Savage, S.Q.M.S. A. E.	54	— Flt.Sjt. E. F.		54
Schofield, Sqn. Q.M.S. W. H.	2488	— Sjt. E. H.		1575
Schroder, S.S. C. G.	55	— Cpl. (A.C.S.M.) E. S.		54
Scott, Sjt. G.	55	— Sjt. J. H.		1575
— Pte. G. F.	* 54	— L.Cpl. J. H.	§ ❀	2488
Setterfield, C.S.M. F. G.	1575	— 1st Cpl. S.S.M. R. J.		1575
Seyde, Condr. H.	54	— Q.M.S. W.	+	54

---

* 2nd Dragoon Gds. Under authority of H.M. the King, awarded by G.O.C.-in-C. 'for attempting to save life from drowning.'

† A.O.C. 'At Caestres ammunition railhead on 14th August 1916 while ammunition was being unloaded and stacked a shell exploded, setting fire to an adjacent stack of ammunition. At the risk of his life, Staff-Sergeant Shepherd proceeded to stamp out the fire. Failing in this, with the assistance of some other men, he speedily extinguished the fire with buckets of water. The importance of his action can be appreciated from the fact that the cartridges and boxes which were alight were burning right up against the stack on which the accident occurred and in close proximity to other large stacks of ammunition.'

‡ Group known: Queen's South Africa Medal (Cape Colony, Transvaal, Wittebergen), King's South Africa Medal (Arm. Sgt. A.O.C. on both) 1914/15 Star trio (Lieut.), L.S. & G.C. (Edw. VII) and M.S.M.

§ 1st/8th Bn. Middx. R. 'On 21st July 1916 a party of men were unscrewing the cap of a bomb when the firing pin was heard to hit the percussion cap of the detonator. A man threw the bomb into an adjoining passage where 25,000 Mills bombs with detonators fitted were stored. Lance-Corporal Smith was sitting about four yards from the party. He realised the danger and fearing that the bomb would explode rushed up the passage and threw himself on to the bomb. As he did so the bomb exploded—wounding him all over the lower part of the body. He undoubtedly saved the other men from being wounded and the stored bombs from exploding.'

+ Group known: Queen's South Africa Medal (Cape Colony, Orange Free State, Transvaal, South Africa 1902) (L./Cpl. Yorks.), British War Medal (W.O.2 Yorks.), L.S. & G.C. (Geo. V), M.S.M. (No. 6551 attach. Egyptian Army) and Khedive's Sudan 1910 (Nyima 1917–18). Only two 1910 Sudan medals to Green Howards.

Soady, Q.M.S. (A.S.M.) H.	54	Teasdale, L.Cpl. (A.Sjt.) J. W.	54
Soggee, S.S. (A.S.S.M.) V. C.	54	Temple, S.Sjt. A. W.	1575
Soppitt, Eng. Cl. Sjt. (A.Suptg.		Tevelein, L.Cpl. S. R.	55
Cl.Sjt.) C. H.	54	Tew, Sjt. P.	54
Spackman, Q.M.S. A. P.	54	Thomas, L.Cpl. A.	54
Speight, Sjt. A * ❀	2488	— Pnr. Sjt. W.	54
Spraggs, Sjt. H. V.	54	— Pte. (A.Cpl.) W. H.	54
Staines, C.S.M. (A.S.M.) T. J.	54	Thompson, S.M. A. S.	55
Stead, Sapper H.	2488	Tindall, S.S. (A.S.S.M.) R.	54
Stevens, Sjt. J. E. S.	55	Tinton, Cpl. (A.Sjt.) B.	54
Steward, Sjt. H. W.	54	Todd, Pte. A. R. ‡ ❀	2488
— Sjt. S. M.	54	— Cpl. E. E. § ❀	2488
Stewart, Pte. (A.Mech.S.S.) H.	54	— Sjt. J. W.	1575
— A.S.M. J. S. R.	54	Trump, Cpl. (A.C.Q.M.S.) W.	54
Stilton, Gnr. (A.Fitter) P. E.	54	Tubby, C.S.M. T. W.	54
Stokes, Sjt. (A.C.S.M.) F. W.	54	Tucker, S.S.M. (A.1st Cl. S.S.M.)	
— A.Sjt. J. † ❀	2488	A. E.	54
— Q.M.S. (actg.S.M.) W.	1575	Tully, Cpl. (A.Sub-Condr.) M. +	54
Stone, Cpl. A. P.	54	Turner, Sjt. A.	54
Stott, Sjt. L.	54	— S.Sjt. (actg.Q.M.S.) F. F	1575
Stout, L/Sjt. T.	2488	— Cpl. R. R.	2488
Stringer, Sjt. H. B.	54		
Styles, S.S.M. (actg.1st Cl. S.S.M.) G.	1575	Unstead, C.Q.M.S. G. E.	54
Suggate, S.S.M. (actg.Sjt.) A. J.	2488		
Summerfield, Sjt. R. M.	54	Vernon, Cpl. (actg.S.Sjt.) V. H.	1575
Sumner, C.Q.M.S. R.	2488	Viner, Pte. H.	54
Sutherland, Q.M.S. C. H.	2488		
Swain, Cpl. (A.C.S.M.) A. C.	54	Wade, S.M. E.	54
		Walker, Cpl. G.	55
Tallyn, Flt.Sjt. R. J.	54	Walkley, B.S.M. C. E.	54
Taylor, Sapper, H. V.	2488	Walton, Smith-Gnr. (actg.Fitter S.S.)	
— Cpl. (A.S.Sjt.) S. H.	54	P. H.	54
— Sqdn. Sjt.Maj. W.	54	Wardley, Flt.Sjt. L.	54

---

* 11th Bn. York & Lancaster R. 'On 8th August 1916 during live grenade throwing practice a man accidently dropped his grenade after withdrawing the safety pin. Sergeant Speight saw what had occurred and although the fuse was well started picked up the grenade and threw it over the parapet. The party being instructed was composed of men who were throwing grenades for the first time and it is believed that this N.C.O.'s action prevented a panic and saved a serious accident.'

† 57th Trg. Res. Bn. 'During live grenade throwing instruction a badly thrown bomb lodged in the sod revetment on the inside of the throwing pit. With great presence of mind Sergeant Stokes immediately stepped forward, pulled out the bomb and threw it over the parapet, thus averting a serious accident.' Kinmel Park Camp, 22nd November 1916.

‡ Aust. Cyclist Trg. Bn. Chiseldon Camp 3 August, 1916. 'Throwing out a grenade with a lighted fuse which had been dropped.'

§ 63rd Trg. Res. Bn. Kinmel Park Camp, 6 November, 1916. 'Throwing out a live grenade from 5″ of mud where it had stuck in the trench.'

§ R.A.O.C. Also entitled to French Médaille d'Honneur avec Glaives (en Bronze).

Wardrop, Sjt. A. H.		54
Warren, A.Q.M.S. J., Canadian Mounted Rifles Bn., att. Divl. Headquarters (correction)		2994
Waterhouse, Pte. T.		1575
Watkins, F.of W.Q.M.S. A.		54
Watsham, L.Cpl. (A.Sub-cond.) A. V.	*	54
Watson, L.Sjt. F. W.	† ✿	2488
— Bombr. G. C.		55
— Sjt. T.		54
— 1st Class Air Mech. T. P.		2488
Waugh, Gnr. H.		1575
— Sub-Conr. R. T.		54
Webb, S.M. S. G.	‡	55
Webster, S.S.M. J. H.		65
Weeks, Pte. (actg.S.S.M.) P.		1575
— B.S.M. W.		54
Westerman, C.S.M. R. E.		54
White, Cpl. A.		54
— Sqdn. S.M. F.		54
— Sjt. H. J.		54
Whittaker, Sjt. T.		2488
— Cpl. L.S. W. A.		54
Wilkinson, Sjt. E.		2488
— Sapper J. C.		2488

Wiles, S.Condr. H. R.		54
Williams, C.Q.M.S. E. J.		55
— Cpl. (A.S.S.) G.		55
— S.S.M. (actg.1st Cl. S.S.M.) J. A. G.		1575
— Sapper (Actg. 2nd Cpl.) S. M.	§ ✿	2488
— Sjt. W. T.		55
Willsher, S.Sjt. (A.Suptg.Clerk) J. E.		55
Wilson, Fitter Cpl. A. J.		55
— R.Q.M.S. H. J.	+	1575
Woodall, Sjt. F. A.		55
Woodward, Sjt. F.		2488
Woolgar, E.C. Q.M.S. (A.Suptg.Clerk) G. A.		55
Woolner, Cond. H. T.		55
Worsfold, Pte. (A.Sub-Cond.) D.		55
Wyvill, Farr.Q.M.S. J.		55
Yarham, Pte. (A.Cpl.) A. V.		55
Young, S.S.M. (actg.1st Cl. S.S.M.) A.		1146
— L.Cpl. A.	◊ ✿	2488
— S.S. (Actg. S.M.) E. A.		2488

Meritorious Service Medal Bar

Orr, Sjt. J.	¶ ✿	1575

---

* R.A.O.C. Also M.B.E., French Médaille d'Honneur avec Glaives (en Argent) and Russian Silver Medal on the Riband of St. Stanislas.

† 63rd Trg. Res. Bn. Kinmel Park Camp, 13 September, 1916. Similar citation to Todd E.E. *ante.*

‡ Group known: M.B.E. (1st type, military ribbon *L.G.* 1 January, 1919 T./Lieut. Canadian Forces), 1914/15 Star (Cpl. Can. Div. H.Q.), British War and Victory Medals (Captain) and M.S.M. (2/Div. H.Q. Staff Canadian Artillery). Form Quebec Regt.

§ See Appendix Y.

+ K.R.R.C. Also entitled to Queen's South Africa Medal, 4 Bn.

◊ 5/Loyal Regt. Oswestry 17 August, 1916. Similar citation to Todd E.E. *ante.*

¶ R.A.M.C. Medal awarded *L.G.* 11 November, 1916. The first of only seven bars to M.S.M.s.

Vol. II, 1917

Abel, Pte. W. A.	5491
Abrahams, S.M. A. J.	5491
Adams, C.S.M. (A.S.M.) W.	5491
Ahern, Sjt. R.	3949
Airey, Sjt. C. F.	5493
— Pte. (A.S.Q.M.S.) T. H.	5491
Althouse, Dvr. C. S.	5493
Anderson, Sjt. (Actg. Qrmr.S.) R.	3949
— Flt. Sjt. W.	5491
— C.S.M. (A.R.S.M.) W.	5491
Andrews, Pte. E.	3949
Anglesea, C.Q.M.S. T.	5491
Apps, actg. L.Cpl. G.	3949
Armstrong, Sjt. (actg.Co.Sjt.Maj.) C.	6027
Arnall, Sub-Condr. F. T.	5198
Aspinall, F.Sjt. (actg. S.M.) J. A.	5491
Aston, Cpl. (A.Sjt.) W. O.	5491
Astrand, Sjt. E. W.	5491
Atkinson, Mech.S.Sjt. J.	3949
Baikie, R.S.M. S. J. C. *	3949
Bailey, Co.Qrmr.Sjt. A. H.	5197
— 1st Class S.S.M. W. G.	5491
Baker, Pte. W. A.	3949
Baldwin, Mech. S.S. A. G.	5491
Banester, Spr. S. G. (corr.)	3700
Banks, Sjt. G. A.	6027
Barker, Pte. B.	3949
Barnes, S.S.M. W.	5491
Bassett, Sjt. A. O.	3949
Bate, Sjt. R. W.	5491
Bates, Q.M.S. S.	5493
— Cpl. T. A.	5491
Batty, Flt.Sjt. F.	6027
Bawtree, Cpl. (A.Q.M.S.) C. F.	5491
Baxter, Sjt. T. C.	6027
Beaney, Gnr. L. A. (corr.) †	3700
Beckett, Co.Sjt.Maj. H.	6027
Beecroft, Sjt. W. ‡	5197
Beer, Q.M.S. A. J.	5491
Bennett, Sjt. E.	5197
Benson, Cpl. J. A. § ❋	6027
Bethell, Sjt. (Engr. Clerk) S. P.	5491
Bills, S.Sjt. O. E.	3949
Black, Gnr. S.	6027
Blackstock, C.Q.M.S. A.	5491
Blatchford, Dvr. (A.S.S.M.) A.	5493
Bonner, Q.M.S. O.R.S. (A.S.S.M.) F. H.	5491
Bonser, Sjt. R. J. ❋	4602
Boyce, Sgt. T.	5197
Boyde, Co.Sjt.Maj. (actg.Qrmr.Sjt) S. J.	6027
Brain, S.M. H. G.	5493
Branson, Sjt. (actg. C.S.M.) F. O.	3949
Brett, Pte. (A.Sjt.) J.	5491
Brian, Gnr. (A.Bdr.) S. H.	5491
Briscoe, L.Cpl. A.	5493
Broadley, Sjt. (actg. R.S.M.) A. E.	3949
Brodie, S.Sjt. G. L.	5493
Brown, F.Sjt. (A.S.M.) C. W.	5491
— C.S.M. (A.Q.M.S.) H. J.	5491
— Cpl. W.	5491
— Armt. S.Sjt. W. E.	6027
Buck, C.S.M. G. H.	5491
Buckley, S.S. (A.S.Q.M.S.) J.	5491

---

* Shrop. L.I.; lost at sea *en route* to Mudros.

† See *L.G.* 12.3.17 (Valuable Services). A gallantry award for Faversham explosion. See Appendix Y. Group known British War and Victory Medals (1085 Gnr. R.A.) and M.S.M.

‡ K.R.R.C., attached Indian Telegraphs.

§ British War Medal, Victory Medal and M.S.M. with family. Born 1888. Died 1981. Served from 28 September 1915 and went to France in 1916 with 41st D.A.C. At Ouderdom Ammunition Dump, Belgium, on 15 April 1917, a faulty hand grenade fuse began to burn. There being no safe place to throw it, Pte. Benson put it between his legs and localised the explosion but causing him severe abdomen wounds. Twelve men were in the vicinity at the time.

Bullard, Cpl. (A.S.Q.M.S.) G.		5491
Bunting, A.S.M. C. E. H.		5491
Burdekin, S.Sjt. C. B.	*	5493
Burrage, Q.M.S. (A.Supt.Clk.) G. H. D.		5491
Burton, Sjt. F. W.		5491
Butt, Coy.Sjt.Maj. H.		5198
Butterfield, Pte. (A.S.Sjt.) W.		5491
Byart, B.S.M. C.		5491
Caldwell, Pte. F.	† ❀	5197
Callander, Pte. (actg. Cpl.) W. G. (corr.)		3696
Capel, Pte. (actg.Mech.S.Sjt.) J.		3949
Carr, Armr. S.S. L. O.		5491
Catherwood, Pte. F. R.	❀	5197
Cawsey, C.Q.M.S. A. E.		5491
Chamberlain, Sjt. A. S.		5491
Chambers, S.S.M. (A.1st Class S.S.M.) A. E.		5491
Chapman, Sjt. C. H.		6027
Charlesworth, Sjt. (actg.Sjt.Maj.) T.	❀	6027
Charnock, Sjt. (A.S.S.) F.		5491
Chitty, Pte. (A.Sub-Condr.) P. W.		5491
Clark, C.S.M. W.		3949
Clarke, Sjt. (A.S.M.) J. F.		5491
— A.Cpl. S. D.		5491
Clemens, Sjt. V.		6027
Clements, Pte. W. H.		3949
Clifford, A.Sjt. A. B.		5491
Coles, 1st Cl. S.S.M. C.		3949
Collins, Cpl. (A.L.S.) E. W.		5491
— Sjt. J. J.		5491
— S.Sjt. (actg. Sub-Condr.) L. J.		3949
Collum, Regtl. Sjt.Maj. D.		6027
Comfort, S.M. T. W.		5491
Concannon, Pte. (A.C.S.M.) J.		5491
Condon, Bty.S.M. T.		5491
Conn, S.S. (A.S.M.) A.		5491
Cook, Sjt. W. G.		6027
Cooper, Q.M.S. (now temp. Q.M. and Hon. Lt.) F. J.		5491
— Flt.Sjt. H.		5491
Copland, Pte. (A.S.S.) F. E.		5491
Copsey, A./Cpl. T. G.		5491
Corrington, C.Q.M.S. (A.S.S.M.) J. J. A.		5491
Cotter, Gnr. C. P. (corr.)		3700
Cotterell, Cpl. T. E.		5491
Cottey, Q.M.S. (actg.S.M.) R.		3949
Coull, C.S.M. J. J.		5493
Cox, Armr.S.S. C. F.		5491
Crampton, Pte. (actg.S.Sjt.Maj.) H. M.		6027
Crane, By.Sjt.Maj. W. J.		5198
Crawshaw, R.S.M. A.	‡	3949
Creswick, Sjt. (actg.By.Sjt.Maj.) E. P.		6027
Culverhouse, Farr.S.Sjt. W. E.		3949
Currie, Sqdn.Sjt.Maj. D. H.		6027
— Dvr. R.		5197
Darling, Sjt. S. G.		3949
Daunt, S.Q.M.S. A. J. L.		5493
Davidson, Armr.Sjt.M. W.		5493
Davis, Pte. (actg.Lce.Cpl.) G.		3949
— Sgt. (actg.Mech.S.S.) H.		3949
— Sjt. (A.S.Q.M.S.) T. A.		5491
Dawson, B.S.M. (A.R.S.M.) E.		5491
de Bolla, Cpl. J. A.		6027
Deacon, 2nd Cpl. (actg. Sub-Condr.) W. G.	§	6027
Dean, Sjt. D.		5491
— S.Qrmr.Sjt. W. J.		6027
Dear, S.S.M. J. T.		5491
Dempster, Pte. S.		3949
Devlin, Sjt. (A.S.S.) W.		5491
Dick, Cpl. J.		5197
Dickason, Sjt. P.		5198
Dixon, Lce.Cpl. E.	+ ❀	3700

---

 * Group known: O.B.E. (2nd type Civil), M.B.E. (1st type, Military), 1914/15 Star trio (2nd Lieut. N.Z.E.F.), 1937 Coronation, and M.S.M. (Wellington Regt.).

 † Loyal North Lancashire Regt. For conspicuous bravery, presence of mind and promptitude in averting a grenade accident whilst at drill (See Illustration of Army Order of Gen. Sir H. S. Rawlinson, Bart., K.B.E., K.C.V.O., Commanding IV Army).

 ‡ Dragoon Guards. P.S.I. to Yeomanry.

 § R.A.O.C. Also Médaille d'Honneur avec Glaives (en Bronze).

 + 4/Bord. R. Live bombing practice 15 December, 1916.

Dixon, Sqdn. S.M. E. H.		3950	Franklin, Pte. (actg.Sjt.) I. W.		6027
Donnithorne, Gnr. W. J.	* ❀	3700	Fraser, C.S.M. E. R.		5491
Double, Regtl.Qrmr.Sjt. B. H.		5197	— S.M. (now temp. Lt. and Qrmr.) J.		3950
Douglas, Sjt. (A.S.S.) W.		5491	Freemantle, Col.Sjt. (actg. Co.		
Dowling, Cpl. (Sjt.) J.		3950	Sjt.Maj.) A. H.		6028
Downton, Cpl. (A.Q.M.S.) C.		5491	Froggatt, S.S.M. A.		5491
Dunn, C.S.M. (actg. R.S.M.) J. E.		3950	Frost, Regtl. Sjt.Maj. G. F.		6028
Dyke, Regtl.Sjt.Maj. G. H.		6027	Fry, Pte. (actg. Sub-Condr.) E. H.		5197
			Furniss, R.Q.M.S. E. R.		3950
Eaglesfield, Sjt. W. J.	❀	5197			
Eccles, actg. Cpl. S.	❀	4602	Gallagher, Co.Sjt.Maj. R.		6028
Edmonds, S.S. F.		5491	Galley, B.S.M. A. W.		5491
Edwards, Gnr. (Actg. Bomr.)			Gambie, B.Q.M.S. E.		3950
A. F. (corr.)		3700	Gatling, Cpl. (A.S.S.M.) G. E.		5491
— Regtl. Sjt.Maj. G.		6027	Gawthorne, 2nd Cpl. J.		6028
— Dvr. J. B.		5491	Geater, By.Qrmr.Sjt. F. T.		5197
Ellison, Staff Sjt. J. R.		6027	George, Cpl. (A.C.S.M.I.) L.		5491
Elvin, Pte. H.	❀	4602	German, A.Sjt. G. A.		5491
Emans, Sjt. F. J.		6027	Gibson, Sjt. W. J.		5491
Evans, C.S.M. (actg. S.S.M) C. E.		3950	Gledhill, Sjt. T. L.		5491
Evans, Sjt. W.		5491	Godfrey, 2nd Cpl. W. P.		6028
Eycott, C.S.M. (A.S.S.M.) J. J.	†	5491	Golden, Q.M.S. (A.S.M.) J.		5491
Eyre, Sjt. (A.C.Q.M.S.) C.		5491	Gooch, Mech.S.M. A. H.		5491
			Goodyear, Sjt. F. P.		3950
Farra, A.Sjt. R. E.		5491	Grantham, Farr.Sjt. F. R.		6028
Faulkener, Sjt. E.		5491	Gray, Cpl. (A.C.S.M.) F. J.		5492
Fenton, Sjt. R. J.		5491	Grayburn, Cpl. (A.C.S.M.) G.		5492
Fever, Spr. (Actg.Lce.Cpl.) H. W.			Green, Cpl. (A.Q.M.S.) J.		5492
(corr.)		3700	— Sjt. W. Midd'x R.		5492
Finch, Sjt. (Engr. Clk.) W. H.		5491	— Sjt. W. R.A.M.C.		6028
Flemming, Pte. (actg. Cpl.) A. J.		6027	Greenwald, Sjt. (A.Q.M.S.) W. J.		5492
Fletcher, C.Q.M.S. H. J.		3950	Gregory, Sjt. (A.C.S.M.) A. E.		5492
Flint, B.S.M. (A.R.S.M.) E.	‡	5491	Grey, Sjt.Maj. F. W.		5198
Floyd, Cpl. (A.S.S.) R. H.		5491	Griffin, Sjt. S. P.		5492
Foley, Sub-Condr. M.		5198	Griffiths, Cpl. H.		6028
Foster, Pte. (A.Sjt.) C. W.		5491	— R.S.M. P.		3950
Found, C.Q.M.S. (actg. C.S.M.) H.		3950	— C.Q.M.S. W. C.		5492

---

* 57 Siege Bty. R.G.A. 25 December 1916 when an oil store used for heating cartridge dug out caught fire. He extinguished the flames and threw out the stove.

† Staff-Sergt.-Major, R.A.S.C. A serving Soldier since August 1898, he was sent to the Western Front soon after the outbreak of hostilities, and served in many important engagements, including the Battles of Neuve Chapelle, St. Eloi, Festubert, and Cambrai, and in operations in the Retreat and Advance of 1918. After the Armistice he proceeded to Germany with the Army of Occupation, and was stationed on the Rhine until August 1919. He won the Meritorious Service Medal for his consistently good work, and devotion to duty throughout the war, and also held the Queen's and King's South African Medals, the 1914 Star, and the General Service and Victory Medals. In 1920 he was serving in Ireland. 28, Halston Street, Hulme, Manchester.

‡ Awarded M.S.M. Annuity A.O.144 1950 (R.A.).

Griffiths, Actg. Sjt. W. H. T.	* ❀ 3700	
Grimshaw, A.Bombr. A. J.	5493	
Gunn, Q.M.S. (A.Supt.Clk.) J.	5492	
Guyatt, Pte. A. E.	❀ 5197	
Hack, S.S. J. S.	5492	
Hale, Sjt. A.	3950	
Hall, Sjt. G. H.	† 5492	
— S.S. J. W.	5492	
Halse, Sjt. J.	3950	
Hampton, Farr.Sjt. C.	5492	
Hanks, Sjt. J. L.	5492	
Hannah, Sjt. W.	6028	
Hard, Pte. (actg.Cpl.) H.	3950	
Harkness, C.S.M. J.	5493	
Harrington, Cpl. H.	5492	
Harris, Cpl. (Actg. Sjt.) C. T. (corr.)	3700	
— Sjt.Maj. G. R.	6028	
Harrison, Sjt. (A.S.M.) R. W.	5492	
Hart, Cpl. A.	5492	
Harwood, C.S.M. P. J.	5492	
Hately, Cpl. G.	5198	
Hawkes, Pte. H.	‡ ❀ 3700	
Hayball, Q.M.S. E. F.	5492	
Hayday, Sjt. T. W.	5492	
Henderson, S.Q.M.S. D. S.	3950	
Herd, Bty. S.M. D. W.	5492	
Hicks, S.Q.M.S. (A.Sub-Cdr.) A. S.	§ 5492	
Hilton, Fitter, S.Sjt. J.	5492	
Hingle, Cpl. (A.S.S.) J. N.	5492	
Hinman, Sjt. (A.C.S.M.) C. D.	5492	
Hogan, R.S.M. S.	3950	
Hogben, Sjt. (A.C.Q.M.S.) H. O.	5492	
Hooker, Sjt. W. J.	3950	
Hopkins, S.S. (A.S.S.M.) W. E.	5492	

Howe, Mech.S.Sjt. (actg. Mech Sjt.Maj.) D.	3950
Huber, Tech. Sjt.Maj. L. E.	6028
Hughes, Pte. H. H.	3950
— F.S.S. J. E.	5492
Humphrey, Co.Sjt.Maj. F. J.	6028
Humphreys, C.S.M. T. J.	5492
Hunston, Engr.Clk. Q.M.S. B. J.	5492
Hunting, Sjt. J. A.	5493
— C.Q.M.S. W. G.	5492
Hurley, Amt.S.S. J. W.	5492
Hutchison, Pte. T. E.	5492
Huxford, C.S.M. R.	3950
I'Anson, Sjt. (actg. Sjt.Maj.) T.	6028
Illingworth, Lce.Cpl. (actg. Cpl.) A. C.	5197
Illo, Pte. Awudu	❀ 6027
Ireland, Sjt. A.	6028
James, R.S.M. S. E.	3950
Jappe, Flt.Sjt. G.	5492
Jeffers, Pte. W. E.	6028
Jefferson, Sjt. C. H.	5492
Jeffrey, Sjt. F. C.	6028
— Farr. Q.M.S. H. J.	3950
Jelley, Spr. (T.S.S.) H.	5492
Jennings, actg. Regtl. Sjt.Maj. A.	6028
Job, L.C. (Engr.Clk.) W. E. A.	5492
John, act. R. Sjt.Maj. T. J.	6028
Johnson, Sjt. A. W.	6028
— C.Q.M.S. A. W.	5492
— S.S. F. T.	5492
— Spr. J. (corr.)	3700
— Sjt. J.	6028

* 19th Can. Inf. Bn. att. 2nd Can. Entrenching. Bn. Compigny France. A bomb with the pin withdrawn was dropped in an adjoining bay. One second before it exploded Griffiths threw it away.

† 1576 Sgt. G. H. Royal Flying Corps, *L.G.* 5.6.17. Details from *'Sagittarius Rising'* by Lieut. Cecil Lewis: 'Grimly I kept the machine on its course above the trenches, waiting tense and numb, for a shell to get us, while Sgt. Hall worked the old camera handle, changing the plates and made his exposures. At last after an hour I felt a tap on my shoulder. Gratefully I turned for home.' (From PRO/AIR/1/1158/204/5/2488): 'For consistent good work both as an aerial gunner (on photography and patrol work) and as a fitter. By his courage as an aerial gunner and his skill as a fitter he sets an example to all.'

‡ 1st/1st Bn. Herts. R. att. Entrenching Bn. Orillers, France 1 March, 1917. A bomb was fused by a blow from a pickaxe. Hawkes picked it up and threw it into a trench.

§ R.A.O.C. Also M.B.E.

Johnstone, S.M. W.			5492
Jones, Sjt. (A.R.S.M.) A.			5492
— C.S.M. (A.S.M.) A. J.			5492
— Supt. Clerk G. E.			6028
— Sjt. G. F. (corr.)			3700
— S.M. J. H.			3950
— Pte. J. J.			3950
— A.R.S.M. R. J.			5492
— C.Q.M.S. (A.R.S.M.) S. G.			5492
Journeaux, Sjt. (A.Sub-Cdr.) C. G.		*	5492
Joyce, Sqn. S.M. F. J.			3950
Keeling, Sjt. E. S.			5493
Keir, Sjt. (A.C.S.M.) J.			5492
Keirl, By.Q.M.S. A. A.			3950
Keller, S.S.M. (A.1st Class S.S.M.)			
P. E.			5492
Kellett, Flt.Sjt. J. W.			5492
Kempster, Sjt. Z. K.			5198
Kennedy, Co. Sjt.Maj. J.			6028
Kenny, 1st Cl. S.Sjt.Maj. T. C.			6028
Kerss, Sjt. J.		†	3950
— Co. Sjt.Maj. W.			6028
Kilby, Sjt. (Engr. Clk. Draughtsman)			
G. A.			5492
Kilner, Fitter S.S. B.			5492
Kimbell, Sjt. M. L.			5492
King, Sjt. E.		❀	6027
— Sjt. G.			3950
Kippen, Clr.Sjt. (O.R.S.) J. W.			5492
Kissach, Cpl. R.		❀	4602
Knight, Armt.Staff Sjt. (actg.			
Armt. Sjt.Maj.) H. T.			5197
— Farr. Q.M.S. J.			5492
Kortwright, Cpl. J. H.			5493
La Hive, Pte. (A.C.S.M.I.) O.			5492
Lacey, R.S.M. W.			3950

Ladd, Sjt. T. H.			5492
Lamb, S.S.Ftr. J.			5493
Lamont, Sjt. J.			5197
Lancaster, Bry.S.M. W. J.			5492
Lane, Flt.Sjt. E. A.			5492
— Pte. (A.S.Q.M.S.) H. V.			5492
— Pte. J. R.		❀	6027
Langdon, Cpl. (actg. Sjt.) J. E.			6028
Lawrence, Cpl. R.			3950
Lawton, Pte. (L.C.) H.			5492
Le Gresly, Sjt. A. E.			5492
le Marquand, Sjt. (actg. R.S.M.) P. J.			3950
Ledger, Sjt. G. A.			6023
Leigh, Sjt. E. A.			5492
Levet, Cpl. C.			5198
Lewis, Sjt. (A.R.Q.M.S.) H. W.			5492
— Pte. (actg. Qrmr.Sjt.) J. H.			6028
Lidlow, Gnr. C. F.		❀	4602
Lilley, Spr. (actg. Lce.Cpl.) E.			5197
Lindsay, Sjt. G. H.			3950
— Cpl. (A.Sjt.) J.			5492
Little, Sjt. (actg. Sub-Condr.) J. M.			3950
Locke, S.S.M. (A.1st Class S.S.M.) W.			5492
Long, Cpl. G. H.			5492
— A.C.Q.M.S. W. R.E.			5492
— Q.M.S. W. R.Suss.R.			5492
Longhurst, F.Sjt. J.			5492
Lowe, Sjt. (actg. Supt.Clk.) A. B.			6028
Lygoe, Pte. H. J. L. (corr.)			3700
Lynch, Q.M.S. C.			3950
Mabbott, C.S.M. A.	‡ ❀		3949
Maber, Sjt. (A.R.S.M.) C. T. F.			5492
McCormack, B.Q.M.S. W. J.			5492
McCulloch, Sqdn. Sjt.Maj. J. S.			6028
MacDonald, Lce.Sjt. J.		❀	6027
McGill, S.S.M. (actg. 1st Cl.			
S.S.M.) W.			3950

---

* R.A.O.C. Also Croix de Guerre.

† K.R.R.C. Entitled to Queen's South Africa Medal, 4 Bn.

‡ 8th Bn. Notts. and Derby R. 'On 29th January 1917 Sergeant Mabbott was in the observation post of a live grenade throwing range. Lieutenant Rover and Sergeant Ellis were in the throwing bay. Sergeant Ellis pulled out the pin of the bomb he was about to throw and let the lever fly off, retaining the bomb in his hand. Sergeant Mabbott, seeing the bomb was fused, ran round the observation post where he was himself in safety, with the object of getting Sergeant Ellis to throw the bomb. The bomb burst before he could reach Sergeant Ellis killing the latter and wounding Lieutenant Rover and Sergeant Mabbott. By going from the observation post to the throwing bay Sergeant Mabbott showed utter disregard for his own safety, his aim being to take the bomb from Sergeant Ellis in time to avoid a serious accident.'

McGowan, Sjt. (A.C.S.M.I.) W. E. A.	5492	Milne, C.S.M. (A.R.Q.M.S.) W. W.		5492
McGuinness, Sapper (actg.Cpl.) E. N.	3950	Milward, Sjt. (actg. S.M.) E. B.	* ❀	3949
McIntosh, C.S.M. J. S.	3950	Mitchell, Sjt. (A.Q.M.S.) A.		5492
— Q.M.S. (A.S.M.) J. T.	5492	Moore, Pte. F. A.		5492
Mackenzie, Cpl. A.	3950	— Sjt. J. S.		5492
— Sjt. (A.S.Q.M.S.) J.	5492	— Cpl. T. H.		5492
McLeod, Pte. G. S.	5492	Morrison, Farr.Q.M.S. M.		3950
McMurray, Lce.Cpl. W.	3950	— Pte. (actg. Lce.Cpl.) W. J.		3950
McNaught, Cpl. J.	5492	Moscrop, Sjt. J. D.		5492
Maguire, Q.M.S. J.	5492	Mullane, Cpl. (actg. S.Q.M.S.) W. P.		3950
Making, Sjt.Instr. (A.C.S.M.I.) P. R.	5492	Mundy, Sjt. H. W.		5492
Male, Cpl. J. R.	5492			
Malley, Qrmr.Sjt. A. E.	6028	Nairn, Sjt. G.		6028
Marks, Sjt. A. E.	5492	Naylor, L.C. (A.S.) W. L.		5492
Marriage, Sjt. A. C.	3950	Newbury, S.S.M. G.		5492
Marsden, Pte. (A.C.S.M.) H.	5492	Newton, Pte. M.	† ❀	3700
Marsh, Co. Sjt.Maj. A. R.	6028	Nicholls, Cpl. (actg. C.S.M.) G. E.		3950
Marshall, Sjt. W. F.	3950	Nicholson, Bombr. J. M.	❀	5197
Martin, C.S.M. E. J.	5493	Nicol, Sjt.Maj. R. S.		6028
Maskey, Sjt. J.	5197	Nicolson, Sjt. A.	❀	5197
Mason, Sjt.Maj. D.	6028	Noakes, L.Cpl. (A.Sjt.) F.		5492
Masters, Sjt.Maj. J. H.	6028	Noon, Dvr. J. J.		6028
Mellor, S.M. W.	5492	Norrie, Co Sjt.Maj. A.		3950
Menzies, S.S.M. G. B.	5493	Norton, Sjt. S. McL.		5493
Miller, Sjt. C. F.	3950	Nunn, R.Q.M.S. H. F.		3950
— Sjt. J.	5197			
Milne, Cpl. A. P.	5198	O'Connell, 1st Cl. S.Sjt.Maj. W.		6028
— Q.M.S. R.	5492	O'Connor, F.Sjt. (A.S.M.) M		5492
— S.Sjt. W. C.	6028	Ollerenshaw, actg. Lce.Cpl. R.		3950

---

* 54th Can. Inf. Bn. 'During live bombing instruction Lieutenant Bromacombe, Sergeant Milward and a learner were in the throwing bay. The man under instruction hit the parapet with a live bomb and it fell back into the bay. Lieutenant Bromacombe and the man threw themselves flat but Sergeant Milward, who had the easiest means of escape, picked up the bomb and managed to throw it over the parapet just as it exploded, thus averting a serious accident.' France, 23rd February 1917.

† 1st/5th Bn. R. Lancaster R. 'On 14th January whilst on regimental police duty at the guard room of C Camp, 5437 Private M. Newton showed great presence of mind and personal bravery. A fire broke out in the R.S.M.'s hut about fifty yards from the guard room and the hut was ablaze in a few minutes. Private Newton doubled across from the guard room with a fire bucket. On the way he met the provost sergeant whose clothing was on fire. He extinguished it by throwing the contents of the bucket over him and then ran on towards the hut. Here Private Newton found the R.S.M. with his clothing on fire rolling on the ground. He immediately took off his greatcoat and managed to extinguish the flames by wrapping it round the R.S.M. At this moment a shout was raised that there was another man inside the hut. Private Newton at once tried to enter the hut but could not do so immediately owing to the rush of flames coming through the door. He eventually got in and rescued a company sergeant major who was on the floor, dragging him into the open.'

Ovenden, Sjt. A. G.	5493	Reading, Sjt. (A.Q.M.S.) H. W.		5492
Owens, Co. Sjt.Maj. B.	6028	Redwood, Mech.Sjt. M. R.		5493
— Pte. W.	5492	Rees, Actg. Cpl. R. W. G. (corr.)		3700
		Renninson, Pte. J.		3950
Pargeter, S.S.M. E. W.	3950	Richardson, Q.M.S. S. L.		5493
Park, By.Sjt.Maj. W.	5198	— By.Q.M.S. W. J.		5493
Parker, Cpl. (A.Sjt.) H. J.	5492	Riches, Sjt. (A.R.Q.M.S.) W. H.		5493
— Spr. (actg. Lce.Cpl.) S. (corr.)	3700	Richings, Clr.S. (A.R.M.S.) F.		5493
— Q.M.S. (actg. S.M.) W.	3950	Ridge, Sjt. W. H.		6028
Parkinson, S.Sjt. (A.S.M.) J. W.	5492	Ridgeon, Sjt. (A.C.S.M.) A.		5493
Payne, Sjt. C. A.	5198	Ridley, Sjt. H. H.		5493
— Sjt. (Engr.Clk.) A. Supr.Clk. F. A.	5492	Roberts, R.Q.M.S. E. K.		3950
— S.Q.M.S. T. M.	5492	— S.S.M. (A. 1st Class S.S.M.) F. J.		5493
Peace, Sjt. W. J.	6028	Robertson, S.M. (now 2nd Lt.)		
Pearce, Gnr. A. (corr.)	3700	F. McK.		5493
Pearcey, Sjt. (A.C.S.M.) J. W.	5492	Robinson, B.S.M. A. C.		3950
Pearson, Clr. Sjt. (A.C.S.M.I.) H.	5492	— S.M. A. F.		5493
Pearson, By.S.M. T.	3950	Roots, Sjt. E. N.		5493
Peck, Dvr. (actg. Cpl.) E. G.	6028	Rose, L.C. (A.Sub-Condr.) C.		5493
Peters, F.Sjt. H.	5492	— S.Sjt. E. T.		6028
Phillips, Sjt. W. G.	3950	Ross, Sjt. J.		6028
Philpot, L.Sjt. F. R.	5493	— By. Sjt.Maj. J. E.		6028
Phimister, C.S.M. C.	3950	Round, C.Q.M.S. W.		5493
Pickard, Co. Sjt.Maj. F. J.	6028	Rouse, S.Sjt. (actg. S.Sjt.Maj.)		
Piggott, Sjt. W. A.	5197	M. A.		6028
Pike, Sjt. (A.C.S.M.) N.	5492	Ryan, Pte. P.	❀	6027
Pollock, S.Q.M.S. (A.S.S.M.) T.	5492			
Potter, Sjt. R.	3950	Sandy, Pte. (A.L.C.) W.		5493
Pow, Wheeler, S.S. S.	3950	Schoales, Sjt. J.		3950
Powell, Cpl. W. L. L.	5492	Scott, Actg. R.S.M. A.		3950
Prewett, Q.M.S. (A.S.M.) T. C.	5492	— A.Bomdr. W. I.		5493
Price, Cpl. J. F.	6028	Semark, Co. Sjt.Maj. H. J.		6028
— Gnr. T. (corr.)	3700	Seymour, Spr. G.		5493
Purchase, Cpl. (A.Sjt.) F.	5492	Shallcross, Pnr. S. R.		5198
		Sharp, Sjt. A. A.		3950
Quantrill, Q.M.S. H.	5492	Sharpe, C.S.M. W.		5493
Quinn, S.Sjt. (A.S.S.M.) J.	5492	Shaw, Q.M.S. (A.Supt.Clk.) H. G.		5493
Quittenton, Cpl. J. J.	5493	Shawyer, Sjt. (actg. S.S.) C. P.		3950
		Sheen, Sjt. T. L.		6028
Rae, By.Qrmr.Sjt. J.	6028	Shenton, Sjt. A.	* ❀	5197
Rankin, Pte. W.	❀ 6027	Shute, Sjt. S. H.		6028
Rapple, S.Sjt. (actg. Sub-Condr.) R.	6028	Silver, C.S.M. G.	†	5493
Rawle, C.Q.M.S. J. J.	3950	Simmons, R. Sjt.Maj. J. W. T.		6028
Ray, C.Q.M.S. G.	5492	Sinclair, Sjt. W.		3950

* 2/5 Y. & L. France 28 June, 1916. During a bomb throwing practice threw out of the trench a fused bomb which had bounced back. Awarded a bar to his M.S.M. *L.G.* 19 November, 1917.

† Group known: D.C.M. (C.S.M. 14/M.G.C., *L.G.* 3 September 1918), M.M. (Sgt., Manchester Regt.,*L.G.* 14 December, 1916), British War and Victory Medals (W.O. D.C.L.I.), M.S.M. (43/M.G.C.).

Sirman, Pte. (actg. Staff Sjt.) J. J.		6028	Suckling, C.S.M. (A.R.S.M.) R.		5493
Skey, Cpl. A. W.		5493	Sunderland, Pte. E.	✿	6027
Smallman, Sjt. J.		5493	Sutherland, Sjt. A.		5198
Smart, Spr. R. S.		5493	Sutton, Sjt. A. F.	†	5493
Smith, Sjt. A. E.	* ✿	3700	— Staff Sjt. J.	‡	5198
— Driver (actg.Sjt.) E.		3950	Swain, B.Q.M.S. W.		5493
— C.P.O. F. R. (R.N.V.R.)		5493			
— L.C. H.		5493	Tait, Sjt. J.		3950
— C.S.M. (A.M.S.M.) J.		5493	Taylor, C.S.M. F.		3950
— Sjt. W. C.		3950	— 2nd Cpl. F.		6028
— Q.M.S. (A.S.M.) W. F. J.		5493	— Cpl. (Engr. Clk.) L. F.		5493
Snelson, Sjt. R.		5493	Teare, L.Cpl. (A.Cpl.) J. O.		5493
Somerset, Sjt. H. C.		5493	Thomas, S.M. E. B.		5493
Spark, Pte. (A.Sjt.) A. B.		5493	Thomason, F.Sjt. W.		5493
Spencer, Sjt. (A.S.Sjt.) J. R.		5493	Thompson, S.M. C. J.		5493
Stacey, Col. Sjt. (actg.			— Cpl. J.		6028
Sjt.Maj.) C. H.		6028	— A.Q.M.S. S.		5493
Stanley, C.S.M. P. B. W.		5493	Thornton, Cpl. (A.Sjt.) M.		5493
— S.Sjt. S. A.		5493	Tilbury, Cpl. (Actg. Sjt.) M. E.		6028
Stansfield, Spr. J.		5493	Timms, Cpl. G.		6028
Statham, C.S.M. W.		5493	Toal, A.R.S.M. O.		5493
— By. Sjt.Maj. W. H.		6028	Tomkins, Sjt. (A.Clr.Sjt.) B. G.		5493
Stear, B.S.M. E.		5493	Towers, L.Cpl. (A.Sjt.) A.		5493
Sterry, Farr.Q.M.S. D.		3950	Townend, Sjt. (A.Supt.Clk.) W. B.		5493
Stevens, C.S.M. Drill Sjt.			Trant, R.Q.M.S. M.		3950
(A.R.S.M.) F. A.		5493	Trevett, F.Sjt. C.		5493
— S.Sjt. J. T.		5493	Trichard, Condr. C. J.		5198
Stevenson, Tpr. W.		5493	Tucker, A.R.S.M. S.		5493
Stewart, Cpl. J. R.		5493	Tugwell, R. Qrmr.Sjt. G. C. W.		6028
Steyn, Hd.Condr. C. H.		5198	Tull, C.Q.M.S. H. G.		5493
Stock, Gnr. (actg. Bombr.) H.		3950	Turk, L.Cpl. (A.S.Sjt.) C. F.		5493
Stockton, Sjt. H. R.		5198	Turner, L.Sjt. C.		5493
Stone, C.S.M. L. F.		5493	— Sjt. (A.S.S.M.) P. C.		5493
Strachan, C.S.M. G. A.		3950	Tweedie, S.Sjt. L.		5493

---

* 265385 1st/2nd Monmouth R. France 17 Apr. 1917. 'On 5th January 1917 during bombing practice an N.C.O. throwing a live bomb for the first time struck the back of the trench with his hand, thereby losing hold of the bomb which fell to the bottom of the trench. Sergeant Smith, in spite of being obstructed by the thrower, managed to get to the bomb, picked it up and threw it over the parapet where it immediately exploded. Sergeant Smith has served nearly 26 months in France and has been wounded.'

† Capt. & Q.M. Arthur Frank Sutton (No 97864, M.S.M., General List, formerly W.O.1 R.E.), killed 9 August 1945 aged 55. Group known: 1914 Star & bar (2nd Cpl. R.E.) British War and Victory Medals (M.I.D. oakleaf, Sgt. R.E.), Jubilee 1935, L.S. & G.C. (W.O.2 R.E.), M.S.M., French Medal of Honour, silver with swords, and Rumanian Barbatie si Credinta, with miniatures, both groups mounted as worn.

‡ Group known: 1914/15 trio, South African Field Telephone & Postal Corps (bilingual Victory) and M.I.D. oakleaf, M.S.M. (S.A. Staff Sect.) and Belgian Order of Léopold II avec palm.

Tyler, Sjt. F. A.	5493	Wilcox, S.Sjt.Maj. J. A.	6028
		Wiles, Staff Sjt. F.	6028
Vernon, R.Q.M.S. J. W.	3950	Wilkinson, Spr. (A.Cpl.) H.	5493
Vickers, A.Cpl. A.	5493	Willetts, Arm.S.Sjt. A.	5493
		Williams, Spr. (actg. 2nd Cpl.) S.M.	
Walker, Sjt. C. C.	5493	(corr.)	3700
Wallis, Cpl. (A.Sjt.) F. J.	5493	Wilson, Sjt. E. W.	5493
Walsh, R.M.S. J.	3950	— S.S.M. (actg. 1st Cl. S.S.M.) H.	3950
Ward, Pte. H. J.	3950	— C.S.M. O. O.	5493
— B.S.M. J. P.	5493	Wilton, Sjt. H. H.	5493
— Sjt. (actg. S.S.M.) W. (A.S.C.)	3950	Wise, Pte. S. C.	5493
— S.S.M. W.	5493	Wood, Sjt. F. A.	6028
Warren, Sjt. (A.C.S.M.) F.	5493	— Actg. Lce.Cpl. T.	3950
Watson, R.Q.M.S. G. A.	3950	Woodason, S.Sjt. W.	5493
— Pte. (actg. Sjt.) G. R.	6028	Woodbridge, A.Bdr. J. A.	5493
— 1st Cl. Air Mech. T. P.		Woodhouse, Sjt. W.	5198
(Correction)	3700	Woodley, Pte. A. J.	6028
Watts, Amt.S.Sjt. (A.Amt.S.M.)		Wright, Lce.Cpl. (actg. Sjt.) T. C.	5197
H. S.	5493	— Pnr. W.	5198
Weaver, Staff Sjt. (actg. Sjt.Maj.)		Wyatt, Sjt. H. H. E.	3950
A. R.	5197		
Webb, Sub-Cdr. A.	5493	Yates, S.S.M. (A.1st Class S.S.M.)	
West, Coy. Qrmr.Sjt. T. A.	6028	A. J.	5493
Wheeler, C.Q.M.S. R. J. C.	5493	Yeates, Cpl. (actg. Sjt.) A. W.	5197
Whisker, Pte. J. R.	5493	Youngman, S.S. S. J.	5493
White, Cpl. B.	3950		

Vol. III, 1917

Adams, Pte. (Sjt.) E.		8431	Billings, Coy.S.M. R. W.			7771
Addinal, S.Sjt. F. W.		8432	Bird, Cpl. A. C.		❀	8648
Addison, S.Sjt. L. J.		6845	Bishop, S.Sjt. J.			8432
Aldren, Pte. E. B.	❀	10039	— Pte. J. J.			9002
Alexander, A.C.S.M. F. S.		9002	Blackburn, Pte. B.	† ❀		9002
Allcock, Sjt. A.		8432	Bolingbroke, Co.Sjt.Maj.(actg.			
Altham, Co. Qrmr. Sjt. J.		8431	R.S.M.) J. R. H.			8431
Anderson, Sjt. J.		9002	Bonner, actg. Q.M.S. W. H.			9002
Arnold, Armt.S.Sjt. J. J. C.		8431	Bonsor, S.M. C.			7771
Atkins, Pte. J. Q.	* ❀	9615	Booth, Lce.Cpl. W.			8431
Atkinson, Sub-Condr. S.		8432	Bowwgen, Sjt. E. H.		❀	7771
Aylward, S.Sjt. J.		8432	Brett, S.Sjt. V.			8432
			Briant, Sjt. T.			8432
Barber, B.S.M. E.		9002	Bridge, S.Sjt. H.			8432
Barnes, Sjt. H. C.		8431	Bridges, Sjt. A.			8431
— Pte. W.		9002	— R.Q.M.S. J. J.			8431
Barrows, Sub-Condr. J. C. R.		6845	Brigden, Sjt. C. A.			8432
Barter, Sjt. (actg. S.M.) U.		8431	Bright, S.Sjt. L. J.			9002
Bartram, Condr. A.		6845	Brockless, Pte. J.	‡ ❀		9615
Bartrop, Sub-Condr. C. G.		9002	Brodie, S.Sjt. L. G. (corr.)			6824
Barwise, Sub-Condr. A. H. O.		8432	Brookman, S.Sjt. H.			8432
Batt, Pte. A. J.	❀	6845	Brooks, Sjt. L. A. W.		❀	9002
Batterbury, S.Sjt. A.		8432	Browett, Sjt. H. W.			6845
Beaumont, Farr.Qrmr.Sjt. J. A.		8431	Brown, Pte. (actg. Staff Sjt.) L.			8431
Bedwell, Sjt. J. W.		8432	— R.Q.M.S. R.			8431
Bell, Sjt. F.		8431	— S.Sjt. (L.Sub-Condr.) W.			8432
— Armr.Qrmr.Sjt. J.		8431	Brunton, Pte. (actg. S.Q.M.S.) C. S.			8431
Benge, Sjt. (actg. C.S.M.) A. E.		9002	Burdett, S.Sjt. H.			8432
Bennett, Sub-Condr. E.		8432	Burgess, Sjt. S. J.			8431
Benstead, Pte. C. S.		8431	Burrough, Sjt. R. F.			9002
Benwell, Armr. S.Sjt. F. F.		8431	Burton, Armt.S.Sjt. (actg. Armt.			
Best, actg.Sjt. E. R.		9002	S.M.) E.			8431
Bickley, S.S. G. W. A.		9002	— Sjt. G.			8431
Biggs, Pte. (actg. Cpl.) J. A.		9002	Butler, Sjt. O. F.			9002

---

 * Served in Malta, Alexandria, Gallipoli, Egypt and France where he was wounded 16 August 1917. Transferred to Waterways & Docks (R.E.). He was awarded his M.S.M. for throwing a live grenade from a trench.

 † 3rd Garr. Bn. L'pool R. later 3/R.D.C., British War and Victory Medals (Pte. Manchester R.) and M.S.M. known. At Fishguard on 27 April, 1917 when seaplane No. 1033 struck a cliff and burst into flames, he pulled out the pilot before the bombs on the aircraft exploded.

 ‡ See Sidebottom *infra*.

Butterworth, R.S.M. T.	* 8431	Christopher, Co. Q.M.S. W. J.	8431
		Church, Supy. Sub-Condr. F.	8432
Cairns, Spr. W. J.	❀ 9615	Clark, Sub-Condr. A.	8432
Callaghan, Sjt. A. T.	9003	Clarke, Sub-Condr. J.	8432
Cameron, Sjt. (actg. Sub-Condr.) K.	8431	— Sjt. R.	8431
Campbell, Coy. S.M. J. E.	7771	Cleaver, Pte. R. D.	8431
Cargill, Lce. Cpl. R. E.	❀ 7291	Cleveland, Pte. J	8431
Carmody, 2nd Cl. A.M. T. J.	† ❀ 8648	Clubbe, By. S.M. G. A.	8431
Carnegie, L.Sjt. T.	8431	Coates, F.Sjt. W. A. H.	8431
Carrington, C.Q.M.Sjt. (actg. S.S.M.)		Cobner, Sjt. E. L.	8431
J. J. A. (corr.)	7292	Cole, Lce. Cpl. F. T.	8431
— R.Q.M.S. W.	8431	Colwill, Cpl. R.	9002
Castle, S.Sjt. (actg. S.Q.M.S.)		Combes, Lce.Cpl. F. W.	8431
E. W. (Correction)	7292	Conroy, Sjt. M. J.	8431
Cawley, Co. S.M. (actg. R.S.M.) R.	8431	Cook, Sub-Condr. A.	‡ 8432
Chandler, Sjt. H. E.	9002	Coope, Farr.S.Sjt. S.	8432
Chaney, Pte. O	8431	Cooper, Sjt. A.	8431
Chapman, Pte. A.	9002	— Co.S.M. E. (R.W.Surrey R.)	10040
— Sjt. E. C.	8431	— Gnr. E. (R.G.A.)	§ ❀ 9002
Charman, Army Schoolmaster J. L.	8431	— Pte. T.	9002
Cheeseman, Sjt. C.	8431	Cowley, C.S.M. (actg.	
Cherry, actg. Cpl. W. H.	9002	R.S.M.) A. J.	8431
Chignell, C.Q.M.S. (T.S.M.) W. O.	9002	Crotty, Cpl. W. H. (corr.)	6824

---

* Group known: D.C.M. (T./R.S.M. 6 L.N. Lancs.), Queen's South Africa Medal(Cape Colony, Transvaal, South Africa 1902, Cpl), 1914/15 Star (C.S.M.), British War and Victory Medals (M.I.D. oakleaf, W.O.I), L.S. & G.C. (Geo. V, Sgt. L.N.L.R.) and. M.S.M. (for Mesopotamia), D.C.M. *L.G.* 26.8.1918 and 21.10.1918, also for Mesopotamia.

† Awarded bar, also for Gallantry. *L.G.* 17 June 1919.

‡ Medal Group in the Moss collection: M.B.E. (*L.G.* 3 June 1927, Asst. Commissary I.U.L.), India General Service Medal 1895 (Punjab Frontier, Driver 10 F.B.R.A.), China 1900 (Relief of Pekin, Cpl. 12 B/R.F.A.) 1914 Star and bar (Sub Conductor I.O.D.), British War and Victory Medals (Conductor, M.I.D. oakleaf), L.S. & G.C. (Edw. VII, Store Sgt. I.O.D.) and M.S.M. (I.O.D.). Also with the group are six miscellaneous Army Temperance Association Medals. Albert Cook was born in Mile End, London in 1874, enlisted in 1892 and arrived in India two years later. In 1897 took part in the Buner Expedition and other actions north of Peshawar. The main action was at Landakai on 17 August 1897, with 7 Mountain Battery in support of Guides Cavalry and Royal West Kents facing 3,000 tribesmen. He was in China from July 1900 to November 1901 during the Boxer Rebellion, by which time he was a Corporal, having passed a range finders course early in 1900. Promoted Sergeant in 1902, he transferred to the Indian Army in 1906, having married in Bangalore two years previously, when he re-enlisted to complete 21 years. Army L.S. & G.C. in A.O. 172/1911. He embarked from Bombay for Europe 12 November 1914, landing in Marseilles 7 November and remained in France until May 1918 when, *via* Suez, Palestine and Bombay he returned to Karachi. The remainder of his service was at Rawal Pindi and Rangoon. He was commissioned Lieut. in May 1926. He retired in March 1929 a Deputy Commissary and Captain.

§ Gallantry award earned when a P.O.W. in Turkey.

Crowther, S.Sjt. C.	*	8432
Culley, Sjt. B.		8431
Culverhouse, Pte. C. E.		9002
Cunningham, Sjt. R		7771
D'Abreu, 4th Cl.Asst.Sur. A. R.		8432
Dalzell, Sjt. A. G.	† ❀	8648
D'Arcy, 3rd Cl.Asst.Sur. A. F.		8432
Davies, Ty.S.M., C. T.		8431
Davis, By.Qrmr. Sjt. W. C.		8431
Dawson, S.M. H.		9002
De Gruyther, 2nd Cl.Asst.Sur. A. N.		8432
De Knock, S.S. W. C. S.		9002
Deacon, S.S. H.		8431
Dean, Cpl. H.		8431
Dearn, L.C. J. T. V.		9002
Dempster, Sub-Condr. T.		8432
Denness, Pte. S. W.		9002
Dommett, Co.Sjt.Maj. S.		8431
Downes, S.Sjt. E. F. F.		8432
— Cpl. G.		8431
Drake, Co.Sjt.Maj. T. E.		8431
Drennan, Cpl. D.	❀	9002
Drew, C.S.M. O. W.		9002
Dunlop, Sub-Condr. A.		8432
Dunn, 3rd Cl.Asst.Sur. J. J. F.		8432
Dunne, Sub-Condr. (Ty.Condr.) J.		8432
Dyer, S.Sjt. L. C. E.		8432
Dymott, Sjt. G. H.		10040
Eagle, S.Sjt. H.		8432
Eagles, Condr. J.		6845
Earwaker, Staff Sjt. T.		8431
East, actg. R.Q.M.S. F.		8431
Edgerley, Sub-Condr. H. F.		8432
Edwards, Sjt. A. J.		8431
— actg. Sjt. H. J. C.		9002
— Cpl. J.		9002
Elderfield, Lce.Cpl. (Sjt.) P. L.		8431
England, Sjt. (actg. Q.M.S.) R. J. B.		8431
English, Cpl. A. H.		8431
Entwisttle, Pte. W.		8431
Ephgrave, Pte. C. F.	‡ ❀	7771
Ethelston, Cpl. G. W.	❀	8648
Evans, S.M. T. J.		9002
Fagan, actg. C.S.M. A.		9002
Farrelly, S.Sjt. J.		8432
Feakes, Gnr. G.	❀	7771
Fear, Pte. T. N.		8431
Ferrari, Coy.S.M. L. A. F.		7771
Fiddes, C.Q.M.S. A.		8432
Finney, R.S.M. W.		8431
Fitton, Sjt. R.		8431
Floyd, Sjt. T.		8432
Floodgate, Gnr. (actg. Bombr) J. J. ❀		9615
Ford, Pte. (Sjt.) F.		8431
— Condr. H.		9002
Foster, Sadler.Sjt. W.		8431
Fox, 2nd Cl.Asst.Sur. H. A.		8432
Foyle, By.Q.M.S. W. E.		8431
Fraser, Spr. A.		6845
Freeman, Pnr. H.	§ ❀	7291
Fressanges, Condr. G. F.		6845
Frost, By.Qrmr.Sjt. F.	+ ❀	9615
Fulton, Sjt. J.		9002
Gage, Sjt. (actg. C.Q.M.Sjt.) O. H. ❀		7771
Garwood, 1st Class S.S. M. E. J.		9002
Gass, actg. R.S.M. J. J.		8431

* Group known: India General Service Medal (Punjab Frontier, Tirah, L./Cpl. 2/ Yorks.), Africa General Service Medal (Somaliland 1902-04 Sgt. Yorks.), 1914 Star trio (M.I.D. oakleaf Sgt. 1/Yorks.), 1914 Star trio (S. Cond. I.A.S.C.), L.S. & G.C. (Edw. VII Sgt. S. & T.) and M.S.M. (Supply & Transport)
† 69 Sqn. Aust. F.C. Awarded for an attempted rescue of a pilot from a burning aircraft. See Lee and Smith *infra*.
‡ See Gearing *infra*.
§ For Salonika. 1914 Star trio and M.S.M. known. All Pnr. R.E.
+ Group known: D.C.M. (Edw. VII, Cpl. R. Dub. F.), Queen's South Africa Medal, King's South Africa Medal, 1915 Star trio, L.S. & G.C. (Geo. V), M.S.M. (Geo. V, R. Dub. F.) and another M.S.M. (Geo. VI, 2nd type, awarded 1951 with annuity).

Gates, Sub-Condr. T.		8432	Hempstead, S.Sjt. A. A.		6845
Gearing, Pte. D. L.	* ❀	7771	Henderson, Lce.Sjt. J.	❀	6845
George, actg. R.S.M. H.		8431	Henley, Co.S.M. H. T.		8431
Gibson, actg. R.S.M. S.		8431	Hennessey, Sub-Condr. E. P.		8433
Gilleland, Sub-Condr S.		8432	Hicks, Condr. W.		8433
Ginn, Bombr. J.	❀	7771	Hillmer, L.C. (actg.Sjt.) G.		9002
Glenholmes, Pte. W.		8431	Hiscocks, Q.M.S. P. C.		9002
Godden, Sjt. F. J. L.		9002	Hoare, Co. Q.M.S. L.		8431
Goldswain, actg. S.M E.		9002	Hobbs, Spr. C. F.	❀	9615
Goodson, R.Q.M.S. J.		8431	— R.Q.M.S. E.		8431
Goose, Sub-Cpondr. (actg.Condr.)			Holland, Co S.M. J.	❀	7291
J. R.		8431	Hollinshead, Sjt. T.		8431
Gordon, Condr. L. C.	†	8432	Holohan, Co. Qrmr.Sjt. (actg.		
— Cpl. R.		9002	R.Q.M.S.) W.		8431
Grace, Pte. E. A.		9002	Holt, R.Q.M.S. G. E.		8431
Graham, Sjt. A.		9002	— Sjt. J.		8432
— Cpl. (actg. Sjt.) H.		8431	Howe, Sub-Condr. A. J.		8433
Grant, Co. S.M. L.		8431	— S.Sjt. (L.Sub-Condr.) J. D.		8433
Greais, 2nd Cl.Asst.Sur. E. J.		8432	Hubble, S.Sjt. A. C.		8433
Green, S.S.Cook A. J.		9002	Hughes, Sub-Condr. R. W.		6845
Greene, 1st Cl.Asst.Sur. H. A.		8432	— Sub-Condr. W. B.		8433
Griffiths, Sjt. A. C.		8432	Hull, Sub-Condr. A.		8433
Gutridge, S.Sjt. G. W.		8432	Hunt, Pte. S.	❀	9002
			Hurley, S.Sjt. H. A. J.		8433
Haigh, Q.M.S. (O.R.S.) G.		8431	— Sjt. W.		8431
Haiste, actg. Sjt. J. H.		9002	Hurring, Whlr.Sjt. V. G.		9002
Hall, S.Sjt. A. W. R.		8432	Hurst, Cpl. F. W.		9003
— Pte. F.	❀	6845	Hutchinson, By.S.M. A.		8431
— Armt. S.Sjt. W. Q.		8431	Hutton, Pte. R.		9002
Hamilton, Sjt. W.		9002			
Hanmer, actg. Cpl. C.		9002	Immelman, S.Sjt. D. W.		7771
Hare, C.S.M. F. E.		9002	Inglis, Q.M.S. (actg. S.M.) D.		8432
Harris, Sub-Condr. H. G.		8432	Ingram, Sub-Condr. J.		8433
Harvey, Sub-Condr. A. F.		8432	Iredale, Pte. E.	§ ❀	9615
Hay, Sjt. G.		9002			
Hayburn, actg. Sjt. L. C.		9002	Jackson, Sub-Condr. S. B.		8433
Hayes, actg.Co.Qrmr.Sjt. A.	‡	8431	— Pte. W.	§ ❀	9615
Hempsall, S.Sjt. E.		8433	Jacobs, B.Q.M.S. A. F.		9002

---

* M.S.M. known: 32802 7/R. Fus. (originally a Militia Bn.) Home Forces, 'For an act of gallantry in rescuing an officer of the R.F.C. from a burning aeroplane.' See also the awards to Ptes. Ethelston, Taylor and Williams, all 1st (H.S.) Garr. Bn., E. Kent Regt., sharing a joint recommendation.

† Group known: Africa General Service Medal (Somaliland 1902-04, Store Sgt. I.O.D.), 1914 Star (Conductor), British War and Victory Medals (M.I.D. oakleaf, Lieutenant), India General Service Medal (Afghanistan N.W.F. 1919, Conductor I.O.D.), L.S. & G.C. (Edw. VII, Store Sgt.) and M.S.M. (M.I.D. 30 July 1920).

‡ 1914 Star & bar (L./Sgt. Conn. Rangers), British War and Victory Medals (A./W.O.I), Delhi Durbar 1911 (Cpl), L.S. & G.C. (W.O.II Norfolks) and M.S.M. (131 Coy. M.G.C.).

§ See Sidebottom *infra*.

Jacobs, Sjt. W.	❀ 9002	McKenzie, L.C. A.		❀ 9615
James-Moore, Pte. J. H.	8432	McKerlie-Dodds, Lce.Cpl.		
Jeffreys, By.S.M. (actg. R.S.M.)		(actg. Sjt.) J.		8432
A. E. W.	8432	McLaurin, Condr. G. C.		6845
Jenkins, Sjt. H.	8433	MacLeod, S.Sjt. W. G. M.		6845
Johnson, R.S.M. J.	8432	Mair, Pte. (actg. Cpl.) M.		8432
Johnston, Sjt. W. K.	7771	Mannerings, Pte. (Local Sjt.) A. T.		9002
Johnstone, R.S.M. J.	8432	Marchant, Sub-Condr. J. D.		6845
Jolly, Pte. W.	8432	Marriott, Sjt. J. P.		8433
		Marwood, S.S.M. C. T.		10040
Keeble, Pte. C. R.	9002	Matraves, Farr.Qrmr. Sjt. G.		8432
Keogh, actg. Staff Sjt. J.	* 8433	Matson, actg.Sjt. A. E.		9002
King, Pte. A.	8432	Matthews, actg. Cpl. H. J.	❀	9615
Kinnard, Sjt. G. H.	8432	Maxfield, Spr. H.	❀	9615
Knight, Cpl. (actg. Troop/Q.M.S.)		Mayhew, S.S.M. J.		8432
L. S.	9002	Meaking, S.Sjt. E. G.		8433
		Meekcoms, Sjt. A. E.		7771
Lamb, Co. Q.M.S. G. H.	8432	Melling, Sjt. C.		9002
Lanfear, Sjt. J. H.	8433	Merchant, Pte. A. H.		8432
Lang, Cpl. (L.Sjt.) W. J.	8432	Middleton, Armt.S.Sjt. W. C.		8432
Latter, Pte. W. A.	8432	Miller, S.Sjt. (temp. S.S.M.) E.		6845
Lawrence, 2nd Cl.Asst.Sur. G. H.	8433	Mitchell, Sub-Condr. J.		8433
Leahy, Sjt. F. T.	8432	Mitton, Sub-Condr. F.		8433
— actg. Sjt. Cook W.	9002	Moody, S.Sjt. A. E.		6845
Lee, 1st Class Air Mech C. M. T.	† ❀ 8648	Moore, S.Sjt. C.		8433
Leeder, Pte. (Sjt.) H. G.	8432	Moraghan, R.S.M. J. T.		8432
Leigh, R.Q.M.S. J.	8432	Morel, S.Sjt. J. A. C.		8433
Lewis, Sjt. C. P. G.	9002	Morley, S.Sjt. (Sub-Condr.) H.		8433
— Sjt. L. H.	8432	Morris, Sub-Condr. W.		8433
Lockton, S.Sjt. T. P.	8433	Morrison, C.Q.M.S. G.		8432
Long, Sqn.S.M. E. A.	9002			
— Pte. H. A.	8432	Nann, Pte. (local Sjt.) J.		9002
Longton, Pte. R.	9002	Nash, Sjt. P.		7771
— Sjt. W. H. J.	9003	Neal, By. S.M. A.		8432
Loomes, Sjt. F.	‡ ❀ 10039	Nesbitt, Cpl. W. C.		8432
Luff, Sqn.Q.M.S. H.	9002	Newman, S.Sjt. (Spt. Sub-Condr.)		
Luker, actg. Bombr. E.	8432	E. W.		6845
Luxa, 4th Cl.Asst.Sur. H. J.	8433	Newton, actg. Cpl. A.		9002
		Niven, actg. S.M. J. E.		8432
McBean, Co. S.M. A. S.	8432	North, S.Sjt. S. A.		8433
McCartney, S.Sjt. H.	8433	Nugent, Cpl. E.	§	8432
Macey, Sjt. W. C.	8433			
McGlynn, Sjt. J.	8432	Ogg, Spr. (Lce.Cpl.) W.	❀	8648

* M.S.M. known with British War Medal: 29475 Indian Signal Sqn. R.E. Part of Indian Cavalry Div. at the Battle for Baghdad Feb/March 1917.

† See Dalzell *ante.*

‡ 5/K.R.R.C. Home Forces 'For an act of gallantry performed during a grenade throwing instruction 2 June, 1917.'

§ R.A.S.C. att. Supply Depot, Amara, Iraq. Died 13 May, 1918, aged 27. From Old Kent Road, London.

Oliver, Mech.Q.M.S. H. H.	8432	Rankine, Sjt. (actg. S.M.) J.		
— Sjt. R. B.	8432	(Correction)		7292
Olley, Sub-Condr. A. H.	8433	Raphael, 2nd Cl.Asst.Sur. S. C.	⁄	8433
O'Neill, S.Sjt. (Sub-Condr.)		Rawlinson, Gnr. A.		9002
E. M. M.	8433	Rice, Sjt. J. R.		9002
Owen, Army Schoolmaster E.	9002	Richardson, Pte. J. H. S.		9002
		— Sub-Condr. R.		8433
Page, Sjt. H.	* ❀ 10039	Richmond, Cpl. (actg. Sjt.) J.		8432
Palmer, Sdlr. G.	8432	Riley, S.Sjt. (Sub-Condr.) J.		8433
Paradise, Pte. J.	8432	— Pte. W.	❀	8648
Parker, Sjt. C. W.	8433	Robinson, Sjt. A. E. T.		8432
— S.Sjt. F.	6845	Rogers, 3rd Cl.Asst.Sur. J. A.	‡	8433
Parkinson, Cpl. F.	† ❀ 10039	— Sjt. W.		9002
— Dvr. W.	❀ 8648	— S.Sjt. W. S.		8433
Patchett, R.Q.M.S. E.	8432	Rolfe, B.Q.M.S. F. W.		9002
Paterson, S.Sjt. K.	8433	Rossiter, Sub-Condr. B. E.		8433
Pay, S.Sjt. E.	6845	Rowe, Pte. H.	❀ 10039	
Peel, Condr. A. W.	8433	Russell, Cpl. W. H.		9002
Pendridgh, Sjt. T. G.	9002	Ryan, Condr. P. C.		8433
Perkins, B.S.M. W. J.	9002			
Perriton, Sub-Condr. W. L.	8433	Sadler, Sjt. W.		8432
Petchley, Sjt. J.	10040	Sampson, Co. S.M. R. W. K.		8432
Pettit, C.S.M. (A.M.S.M.) T. O.	9002	Savage, Cpl. W.	❀	7291
Phillips, Cpl. P.	9002	Scott, Sjt. C.		8432
Philpot, Ty.Sjt. A. E.	8433	Scragg, R.Q.M.S. J.		8432
Potter, R.Q.M.S. T. F	8432	Seaton, S.Sjt. F. J.		9003
Pratt, Condr. A. J.	8433	Senior, S.Sjt. E. W.		8432
Prescott, S.Sjt. W.	8433	Sernberg, Pte. (actg. Sjt.) C.		8432
Price, Sjt. A. H.	8433	Sharp, actg.S.M. W.		8432
Priest, Gnr. G. M.	❀ 7771	Shaw, Lce.Cpl. B.		8432
Prior, Condr. C. J.	8433	Sheerer, actg.By. Q.M.S. T.		8432
Pritchard, Sjt. W. E.	9002	Shelley, Pte. T.		9002
		Shelton, L.Cpl. J. W.		9002
Quantrill, S.Sjt. D. J.	8433	Shenton, Cpl. A.		10039
Quarrier, Staff S.M. (actg. 1st Cl.		Shepherd, Sub-Condr. S.		6845
Staff S.M.) C. E.	8432	Shore, A.C.S.M. J. G.		9002
		Shrewing, S.Sjt. J.		8432
Rae, Sjt. R. A.	9002	Sidebottom, Pte. J.	§ ❀	9615
Randall, Sjt. (actg. R.Q.M.S.) A. W.	8432	Simpson, Pte. A. R.	❀	7291

* 2/5 W. Yorks. Regt. 27 January, 1916 at Larkhill, when a live Mills bomb was dropped into the trench.

† 20/W. Yorks. For an accident during live grenade throwing practice. This was the second time he had performed such an action.

‡ Group known: M.B.E. (2nd type), 1914 Star & bar trio, 1935 Jubilee and 1937 Coronation, L.S. & G.C. (Geo. V) and M.S.M. (Asst. Surg. 3rd class & 1st class I.S.M.D./I.M.D.).

§ M.S.M. known, 36729 R.A.M.C. (from Halifax). 'For gallantry on the occasion of the mining of a hospital ship '*H S. Oxfordshire*,' East Africa.' See also Ptes. Blockless, Iredale and Jackson who share the same citation. Sidebottom was also M.I.D. *L.G.*

Simpson, S.Sjt. C. A. L.		8433
Sims, Sjt. A. E.		8432
Sinclair, A.C.S.M. C. W.		9002
Slingsby, Co. S.M. T. W.	✿	7291
Smart, actg. R.S.M. A.		8432
Smith, Pte. G.	* ✿	8648
— S.Sjt. J. W.		8433
— By. Q.M.S. S.		8432
— S.S.M. S. H.	✿	7291
— 1st Class Air Mech. V.	† ✿	8648
— Sjt. W.		8432
Smyth, Sadir, Q.M.S. T.		8432
Snellgrove, Sjt. D. R.		9002
Somerfield, S.Sjt. G. J.		8433
Speight, Pte. B.	✿	9002
Spencer, Pte. E. J.	✿	7771
Squibb, actg. A.S.M. H.		8432
Stanton, Q.M.S. (O.R.S.) A. F. C.		8432
Stark, Q.M.S. H. J.	‡	8432
Staton, S.Sjt. W.		8433
Steel, L.C. G.		9002
Steele, Q.M.S. (O.R.S.) W.		8432
Stevens, Sjt. C.		8432
— S.S. (A.S.S.M.) V.		9002
Stickland, Cpl. (actg. M.S.M.) G. J.		8432
Stone, S.M. B. T.		8432
— Sjt. N. P.	§ ✿	10039
Straker, actg. Cpl. H. V.		8432
Strood, Cpl. A. W.		8432

Stuart, S.Sjt. C. E. C. W.		8433
Sufrin, S.Sjt. L.		9002
Suttle, Staff S.M. E. C.		8432
Sutton, Pte. V. S.		7771
Tanner, S.Sjt. (Ty. Sub-Condr.) P.		8433
Taylor, Pte. A. J.	+ ✿	7771
Tebby, Condr. H.		8433
Terry, Sub-Condr. C. E.		6845
Thipthrop, 1st Cl.Asst.Sur. E. E.		8433
Thomas, L.C. (actg. Sjt.) J. W.		9002
Thompson, 1st Cl.Asst.Sur. C.		8433
— R.Q.M.S. H. E.		8432
— C.Q.M.S. T. B.		8432
Tinckell, Co.Sjt.Maj. J.		8432
Tingey, Sub-Condr. J. M.		6845
Titley, Pte. C.		9002
Tobitt, Spr. S. F.	✿	9002
Townsend, S.Sjt. J.		9002
Truscott, Dvr. (Ty.Sjt.) T. F. P.		8432
Tucker, Gnr. A.		8432
Twohig, S.Sjt. P.		8433
Tynan, Sub-Condr. P.		8433
Underhill, Sjt. T. G.		8433
Uttley, Pte. (actg. Sjt.) C. W.		6845
Vaile, F.Sjt. A.		8432

---

7 March 1918 p.2885, for East Africa Force. See also *L.G.* 14 June 1917 (V.C., D.S.O., R.R.C. and two A.R.R.C.s) for gallantry on the occasion of the mining of a Hospital ship with a following note to say that the names of four men of the R.A.M.C. awarded M.S.M.s would appear in a subsequent *Gazette*.

* 2/4 East Yorks. Regt. (T.F.) Single medal in Moss collection. Extract from Regimental Magazine: 'On July 1st (1917), after Church Parade, there was a presentation of Long Service and Good Conduct Medals after which the Governor, General Sir James Willcocks, called forward and congratulated 2/Lieut. F.C.W. Newman. Sgt. A.H. Barry, Cpl. A. Hinchcliffe, Privates Williams and G. Smith (202566) for their bravery in successfully rescuing a Sergeant and two men who had got into difficulties whilst bathing at the Musketry camp, especially complimenting Pte. Smith. His Excellency hoped that a further recognition would come in due course.' Later, same source, the award of the M.S.M. is described as a pleasing sequel. A very unusual gallantry M.S.M. A further ten Valuable Service M.S.M.s were presented in Bermuda and three in Jamaica.

† See Dalzell and Lee *ante*.

‡ M.S.M. known: 36555 40/F.A. R.A.M.C., M.I.D. 5.6.1919 A./C.S.M. North Persian Force. 40/F.A. went from Mesopotamia to Gallipoli, participated in the attempted relief of Kut and entered Baghdad in March 1917.

§ 6/Dorset Regt. France. 21 February, 1916 at Divisional Grenade School.

+ See Gearing *ante*.

Wade, By S.M. W.		8433	Wilder, 1st Class Air Mech. J. F.		9002
Wadsworth, S.Sjt. W.		8433	Wilken, S.Sjt. J. H.		9003
Waldron, Co. S.M. A.		8432	Wilkinson, Sjt. G.		8433
Wall, Sjt. W.	✿	9002	Williams, Pte. A.	† ✿	7771
Wallace, S.Sjt. (L.Sub-Condr.) R.		8433	— Sjt. A. E.	‡ ✿	10040
Walsh, Pte. M.	✿	7291	— By S.M. T. C.		8432
Warg, Pte. F. O.		9003	Williamson, Gnr. C.		8432
Warwick, Condr. T.		8433	Wilson, Gnr. A. L.	§	8432
Waterman, Sjt. R. J.		9003	— Lce.Cpl. T.	+	8432
Waters, Sub-Condr. A.		8433	— Sub-Condr. T.	◊	8433
Wayte, C.S.M. R.	*	9003	— Condr. T. G.	¶	6845
Weatherley, A.Sjt. W. H.	✿	10040	Withington, Co.S.M. H.		8432
Westtote, Cpl. C.		8432	Wood, Condr. J. H.		8433
Wheatley, Sjt. A. H.		8432	Woods, Sjt. A. W.		9003
Whetstone, Sjt. P.		8433	Woodsell, 3rd Cl.Asst.Sur. J. W.	**	8433
Whicker, S.Sjt. A. E.		8433	Wookey, Dvr. F.		8432
White, 1st Cl.Asst.Sur. A. A. W.		8433	Wright, Lce.Cpl. D. C.		8432
— Farr.Q.M.S. C. H.		8432	— Sjt. H. H.		9002
Whitehead, Sadlr.Q.M.S. A.		8432	— S.S.M. J.		8432
— Sub-Condr. W.		8433			
Whitfield, Sjt. R. G.		9003	Yeates, Sjt. (actg. C.S.M.) C.		8432
Whitton, Pte. D.		8432	Young, S.Sjt. R. V.		8433

* Group known: Afghanistan Medal (Charasia, Kabul, Kandahar), Kabul to Kandahar Star (both Pte. 9 Lancers), Queen's South Africa Medal (Cape Colony, Transvaal, Wittebergen, Pte. Worcs.), King's South Africa Medal, 1914/15 Star (Sgt.), British War and Victory Medals (W.O.) and M.S.M. (9/Worcs.). There must be some doubt as to whether this group belonged to one man or two.

† See Gearing *ante*.

‡ 2/7 W. Yorks. 7 February, 1916 at Larkhill firing improvised bombs from a Leach catapult.

§ R.H.A. Group known: 1914/15 trio and M.S.M.

+ 2/Black Watch, a stretcher bearer, died Army of Occupation Germany, 1920. Group known: D.C.M. (Geo. V), Queen's South Africa Medal, 1914 Star trio and M.S.M.

◊ R.A.O.C. also Médaille d'Honneur avec Glaives (en Argent) (Sub-Conductor).

¶ Group known (Seaby 1959, £8): China 1900 (no clasp), 1914/15 Star trio (M.I.D. oakleaf), India General Service Medal (Waziristan 1919-21), Defence Medal, Delhi Durbar 1911, L.S. & G.C. (Geo. V) and M.S.M. Progressively Q.M.S., Conductor, Lieutenant and Captain, Indian Medical Services.

** Group known: Military Cross (*L.G.* 16 August 1917, for tending wounded under heavy fire, 3rd class Asst. Surg. I.M.S.), Naval General Service Medal (Persian Gulf 1909–14, Asst. Surg., R.I.M.S. *Minto*), British War and Victory Medals (erased), L.S. & G.C. (Geo. V, Asst. Surg. I.M.D.), M.S.M. (I.S.M.D.). Born 1883. W.O. 1905, aged 22. 3rd Cl. Asst. Surg. 1910. R.I.M.S. *Minto* 1911. R.I.M.S. *Comet* 1912. 2nd Cl. Asst. Surg. 1917; 1st Cl. Asst. Surg. 1922; Snr. Asst. Surg. 1933, aged 50.

Vol. IV, 1917

Adcock, R.Q.M.Sjt. H.	13202	Bunker, Pte. H.	‡ ✻ 11348
Ambrose, Sjt. J. L.	13202	Burton, Sjt. (A.S.M.) A. W.	13202
Andrews, Cpl. W. C.	✻ 13202	Butler, R.Q.M.Sjt. W. H.	13202
Anderson, Sjt. J.	13202		
Ashbridge, Pte. (A.Sjt.) W. C.	13202	Carroll, Co.S.M. J.	13202
Ashley, Bombr. (now Cpl.) C.	* ✻ 13027	— Pte. (Cpl.) P. (corr.)	13205
Ashton, C.S.M. F. P. W.	13202	Child, S.Sjt. G. H.	13202
— Cpl. H.	13202	Clarke, S.Sjt. (A.S.M.) F.	13202
Atkins, Pte. J. W.	11349	Comer, Gnr. E.	* ✻ 13027
Azeal, Sjt. (A.S.M.) T.	13202	Connors, Sjt. (A.Q.M.S.) W.	13202
		Constable, Bombr. M.	13202
Bailey, S.Q.M.Sjt. T. N.	13202	Convery, Pte. (A.Sjt.) D. J.	13202
Baker, Pte. (Cpl.) E. E.	13202	Cox, Pte. G. R.	11979
— S.Sjt. E. T.	13202	Craddock, Pte. G. C.	13202
Baldwin, R.Q.M.Sjt. B. A.	13202	Critchley, Dvr. G.	* ✻ 13027
Banbury, Sjt. F. H.	13202	Cunningham, Pte. (A.Sjt.) J.	13202
Bannon, S.Sjt. (A.S.M.) J.	13202		
Bate, Cpl. T.	13202	Dale, S.S.M. H.	13202
Bateman, Co. S.M. C.	13202	Darby, Condr. W. A.	§ 10680
Bell, R.S.M. W.	13202	Darke, Sjt. (A.Flt.Sjt.) F. F. W.	13202
Bellringer, 2nd Cpl.(Sjt.) E.	13202	Daughton, Pte. R.	✻ 11348
Bentley, L.C. E. R. T.	13202	Davies, Sjt. J. D.	13202
Bilal Mahabut, Sjt.	✻ 10731	Davis, E.C.Q.M.Sjt. (A.Supt.Clk.) T.	13202
Blaber, Smith S.Sjt. A. E.	13202	Dawson, Pte. C.	11979
Blaygrove, S.M. A. E.	13202	Day, Sjt. J.	13202
Bodiam, S.S.M. W. A.	† 11979	Dedman, Whr. Qrmr.Sjt. A. E.	13202
Bodington, Sjt. (A.S.Q.M.Sjt.) W.	13202	Denyer, S.M. (F. of Wks.) E.	13202
Border, Sjt. H.	13202	Diffey, S.M. J.	13204
Bowyer, Farr. Q.M.Sjt. F.	13202	Dipper, Co. Qrmr. Sjt. C.	13202
Bracken, Pte. B.	✻ 11979	Don, Spr. T.	13202
Bradfield, Sjt. E. A.	13202	Doyle, Pte. M.	+ ✻ 13202
Bradley, Sjt. C. W.	13202	Dugdale, Dvr. (now A.Bombr.) B.	* ✻ 13028
Bream, L.C. G.	11979	Dunn, Cpl. G.	11349
Brittain, By. S.M.	13202	Dungey, Farr. Q.M.Sjt. C.	13203
Brookes, Dvr. (A.Co.S.M.) W. E.	13202		
Bulmer, Sjt. (T.S.S.M.) N.	13202		

---

* See Appendix Y. Also awarded Edward Medal.
† R.A.S.C. M.S.M. and L.S. & G.C. presented by F.M. Lord Plumer in Malta.
‡ 1/4 London R. Served Malta, Alexandria, Gallipoli, Egypt and France. Wounded five times and discharged from wounds. Twice M.I.D.
§ Supply & Transport I.A. Later commissioned.
+ M.S.M. known: 1748 18 F.A. R.A.M.C. for France. He came from Dublin and was later awarded a Military Medal, *L.G.* 18 July 1917, and was K.I.A. 21 March 1918.

Easton, Pte. G. H.	✿ 11348	Harvey, Co.S.M. (T.R.S.M.) H. F.		13203
Edge, Co. S.M. H.	13203	Hawkins, S.Sjt. (A.Q.M.Sjt.) W. S.		13203
Edwards, Sjt. F. P.	13203	Hickson, Sjt. (A.S.Sjt.) E.		13203
— Sjt. H. G.	13203	Hill, S.Sjt. R. H.		11979
— S.S.M. S.	13203	Holden, Co. S.M. (A.R.S.M.) C. G.	§	13203
— R.Q.M.Sjt. W. S.	13203	Holland, Sjt. R. J. H.		13203
Etchells, Pte. J.	✿ 11348	Holmes, Sjt. F. G.		13203
		Homer, Cpl. A.	✿	11348
Fagan, R.Q.M.Sjt. J.	13203	Hood, Pte. G.	✿	13202
Fears, Flt.Sjt. (T.S.M.) L. R.	13203	Horscroft, Sjt. L.		13204
Fenn, 2nd Cpl. (A.Sjt.) E.	13203	Horwood, Sjt. G. E. J.		13203
Ferris, Pte. (A.Sjt.) R.	13203	Hughes, Q.M.Sjt. (F. of Works) W.		13203
Fiddler, S.Sjt. W. H.	13204	Hull, A.Ftr.Cpl. A. R.		13203
Fillmore, S.S.M. R. M.	13203	Hunt, Sjt. L.		13203
Forsythe, S.Q.M.Sjt. (A.S.S.M.) J.	13203	Hurring, Whr. Q.M.Sjt. A. W.		13203
Frankford, Co.S.M. A.	13203			
Franter, Sjt. G. F.	13203	Jackson, S.Sjt. A. E.		13204
French, Pte. (A.S.Q.M.Sjt.) A. H.	11979	— Pte. (A.Sjt.) W. R.		13203
Frost, Sjt. (A.S.S.M.) C. P.	13203	Jaggar, Cpl. A.	✿	13202
		Jennings, Actg. S.M. P. W.		10680
Galbraith, R.Q.M.Sjt. J.	13203	Johnston, Flt.Sjt. H.		13204
Galpin, By. S.M. F. C.	13203	Judge, Co. S.M. (A.R.S.M.) J.		13203
Gardner, Sjt. (A.Sub-Condr.) H. L. F.	11979			
Gibbons, S.Sjt. A. F.	13203	Kemp, Cpl. (A.S.S.M.) A. G.		13203
Gibbs, S.Sjt. (A.S.S.M.) W.	13203	— Farr, Q.M.Sjt. A. S.		13203
Gibson, Co.S.M. (T.R.S.M.) H. F.	13203	Kerswell, Sjt. E. S.		13203
— Pte. (A/L/Cpl.) T. W.	13203	Kidby, 1st Cl.Asst.Surg. W. T.		10680
Gilbert, Pte. (A.S.Sjt.) P. C.	11979	Kite, A.Bombr. W. H.		13203
Gillmore, S.S.M. R. H.	13203			
Goodliffe, S.Q.M.S. (T.S.S.M) R. W.	13203	Large, Sjt. (A.Flt.Sjt.) J. W.		13203
Gorman, R.S.M. F.	13203	Law, By.Q.M.Sjt. F. E.		13203
Green, Sjt. J. W.	13203	Lawson, Sjt. A.	✿	11348
— S.Sjt. W. E.	11979	Leach, Sjt. W. T.		13203
— R.S.M. W. H.	* 13203	Leslie, Sjt. A.		13203
Greengrass, Pte. E. J.	† ✿ 13027	Lewis, R.Q.M.Sjt. F. C. H.		13203
Gregg, Sjt. W.	13203	— Sjt. J. M.		13203
Grist, Sjt. (A.Co.S.M.) W.	13203	Lomas, S.Sjt. E.		13203
Guertin, Pte. W. J. (corr.)	13205	Lovegrove, 2nd Cpl. (A.S.Sjt.) A. E.		13203
		Lusmore, 1st Cl. S.S.M. F. J.		13203
Hall, Sjt. (T.R.S.M.) F. C.	13203			
Hamlin, S.Sjt. (F. of Works) A.	13203	McAdam, Co. S.M. J.		13204
Hammond, W.O. P. P.	‡ 13204	McCardell, S.Sjt. J. R.		13204
Harratly, Sjt. (A.Co.Q.M.Sjt.) J.	13203	McCormick, Sjt. B. E.		13204
Harvey, Cpl. (A.Sjt.) H.	13203	McDonald, Sadd. Cpl. T.		13204

---

    * K.R.R.C. entitled to Queen's South Africa Medal.

    † 24/London R. for Russia. Awarded 1st type B.E.M. *L.G.* 3rd June 1918 for courage in Russia and Rumania in 1916–17. Also awarded Medal of St. George 4th class, *L.G.* 17 October, 1917.

    ‡ Australian Desert Mounted Corps.

    § R.S.M. 8/K.S.L.I. K.I.A. 18 September 1918 on Pip Ridge, Salonika.

McGlasham, Co. Q.M.Sjt. A.	13204
MacKenna, Pte. D.	11979
Magness, Pte. (Cpl.) P.	13203
Major, R.S.M. F. A.	13203
Mangan, C.Q.M.S. W.	13203
Marks, S.Sjt. (A.S.M.) A. W.	13202
Mathery, Pte. R. E.	❀ 13202
Matheson, Pte. (A.Mech.S.M.) F. J.	13203
Maunder, temp. Amt. S.M. E. W.	* 13203
May, Sub-Condr. H. T.	13203
Medlam, Sjt. (A.Flt.Sjt.) H. H.	13203
Menage, S.M. (F. of Works) V. E.	13203
Merritt, 1st Cl. A.M. A. J.	† ❀ 11348
— Co. S.M. (A.R.S.M.) G. W. W.	13203
Mighall, Co. S.M. C. H.	13203
Miles, Sjt. A.	13203
Miller, Sjt. J.	13203
— R.Q.M.Sjt. J.	13203
Milliken, Sjt. W.	13203
Mills, R.Q.M.S. C. H.	13203
Mitchell, Co. Qrmr. Sjt. R. W.	‡ 13203
Morton, Pte. J.	13203
Mulligan, S.Sjt. (A.S.Q.M.Sjt.) T.	13203
Murch, R.Q.M.S. T. A.	13203
Myring, Gnr W. F. (corr.)	13205
Naylor, C.S.M. E. J.	13204
Neill, Dvr. W.	§ ❀ 13028
Neville, L.Sjt. J. R.	13204
Nicholson, Sjt. J. F.	13204
Nicol, Cpl. (A.Sjt.) P. A.	13204
Norris, 2nd Cl. A.M. A. H.	+ ❀ 11979
O'Connor, L.Sjt. (A.S.Sjt.) D. G.	13204
O'Halloran, Bt. S.M. M.	13204
Oldland, Sjt. R. W.	13204
Osborn, Sqdn. S.M. H.	13204
Owen, Co. S.M. W.	13204
Parke, Sjt. W. F.	◊ ❀ 13202
Parrish, Pte. (A.S.S.M.) S.	13204
Parsons, Sjt. (A.S.Sjt.) S. W.	13204
Partridge, Cpl. (A.Col.Sjt.) R.	13204
Pepper, temp.Arm.S.M. W. H.	13204
Perigo, C.S.M. J.	10680
Pettit, temp. Sub-Condr. N.	13204
Pettley, S.M. A. W.	13204
Pitman, L/C (A/Sqdn. S.M.) W. M.	13204
Ponting, Sjt. A.	13204
Powell, Act. Cpl. R.	¶ ❀ 10731
Price, A.Cpl. W.	❀ 11348
Prickett, S.M. H. W.	13204
Prior, temp. Sub-Condr. F. E.	13204
Pugh, C.S.M. S.	13204
Putman, L.C. (A.Sqdn.S.M.) W. H.	13204
Raine, By.Q.M.Sjt. W.	13204
Ranstead, Sjt. C.	❀ 11348
Rawdon, S.S.M. (A.R.S.M.) J. C.	13204
Reader, Cpl. (A.S.Q.M.Sjt.) H. N.	11979
Reed, R.Q.M.S. A.	13204
Rice, L.C. N. (corr.)	13205
Ricketts, Sjt. (A.S.S.M.) H. T.	13204
Ridout, temp. Sub-Condr. H. A. W.	13204
Roberts, Gnr. P.	§ ❀ 13028
Robertson, Flt.Sjt. R. S.	13204
Ross, Co. S.M. D.	13204
— R.S.M. R.	13204

---

* Group known: 1914/15 Star trio (M.I.D. oakleaf), Defence and War Medals, L.S. & G.C. (Geo. V) and M.S.M. Born 1889. Enlisted A.O.C. 1906 and became Arm. S. Sgt. very quickly on the strength of his City & Guilds Certificate in Engineering Fitting. Served in Jamaica for four years. Arm. S.M. in 1915 in Gallipoli, then Salonika. M.I.D. July 1917. L.S. & G.C. as W.O. in 1924 and discharged in 1927. Joined T.A. in 1939 aged 50 as Q.M.S. Discharged from War Service as W.O.I R.E.M.E. 1945, he continued in the T.A.R. until 1954. He missed his Efficiency Medal (Territorial) by just six weeks.

† 71 Sqn. Aust. Flying Corps. Home Forces 5 July 1917. Attempting to save a pilot of a crashed and burning aircraft sustaining severe injuries himself.

‡ K.R.R.C. Entitled to Queen's South Africa Medal and King's South Africa Medal, 3 Bn.

§ See Appendix Y.

+ 47 Balloon Section R.F.C. France.

◊ R.F.C. (Home Forces).

¶ 3/R. Welsh Fus. 8 June 1917 France. For throwing a live grenade out of a trench.

Rowell, Sjt. F.	13204	Talbot, Temp. Sub-Condr. A. N.		13204
Russell, R.Q.M.S. F.	10680	Tarrant, Condr. E.		13204
		Thomson, C.S.M. J.		13204
		Trainor, Pte. (A.L.C.) W.		13204
Salter, Q.M.Sjt. B. B.	13204	Trenam, Sjt. S.		13204
Scarr, Armt.S.Sjt. H. B.	13204	Turkington, Pnr.Sjt. S.		13204
Shenton, Sjt. A.	* 11979			
— (Deletion and Bar awarded)	11980	Varndell, Sjt. H. S. A.		13204
Shepheard, Sjt.(A.S.Sjt.) R. W.	13204			
Short, temp. Armt.S.M. F. P.	13204	Walker, L.C. (A.Cpl.) A.		13204
Shrubsall, Sjt. P. E.	10680	— Sjt. H. J.		13204
Sidders, Fitter Cpl. G. J. M.	13204	— Sjt. J. E.		13204
Sidney, L.C. (A.Sub-Condr.) F. E.	13204	Walsh, By. S.M. H.		13204
Simpson, Flt.Sjt. W.	13204	Wannell, Coy. S.M. W.		11979
— Condr. W. H.	† 13204	Warrington, S.Sjt. H. F.		13204
Sinclair, Sjt. G.	11979	Watson, Condr. P. H.		10680
Smith, Co. S.M. (A.S.S.M.) C. V.	13204	Webb, Mech. S.Sjt. (A.Mech. S.M.)		
— temp. Sub-Condr. H. W.	13204	A. J.		13204
— R.S.M. J.	13204	— Cpl. (A.Sjt.) R. C.		13204
— Co. S.M. R.	13204	West, By.Qrmr.Sjt. E. E.		13204
Springett, Q.M.Sjt. (temp. S.M.) P.	13204	Whiting, S.M. (F. of Works) W. G.		13204
Stenning, Armt. S.Sjt. A. W.	13204	Williams, Sjt. G. E.		11979
Stevens, R.S.M. J. A.	13204	Willis, L.Sjt. A. (corr.)		13205
— Sjt. W. G. T.	13204	Windeatt, Sjt. (A.R.S.M.) C.		13204
Stewart, Co Q.M.Sjt. D.	13204	Worwood, temp. Reg.S.M. G. W.		13204
— Cpl. (A.S.Q.M.Sjt.) W. G.	‡ 13204	Wright, Sjt. E.		11979
Stuart, S.S.M. H.	11979	— Gnr. G. E.	§ ❀	13028
Sturge, By.Qrmr.Sjt. H. J.	13204			
Swinburn, Flt.Sjt. W.	13204	Young, S.Sjt. (A.S.Q.M.Sjt.) W.		13204

* Medal for Gallantry, *L.G.* 26 May, 1917. This Bar for Gallantry at Home whilst serving in the Manchester Regt.
† R.A.O.C. Also D.C.M.
‡ Group in the Moss collection: Military Cross, 1914/15 Star (L./Cpl. A.S.C.), British War and Victory Medals (2/Lieut., M.I.D. oakleaf), M.S.M. M.C. *L.G.* 1.2.19, 2/Lt. H.L.I., formerly A.S.C.; M.I.D. *L.G.* 6.7.17. An unusual combination of an M.C. awarded to an officer after an M.S.M. to an N.C.O. It was awarded for services at Ypres as Intelligence Officer, having gone forward to the enemy trenches many times for information (18th Battn. H.L.I.) (4th Glasgow Regt.).
§ See Appendix Y.

Vol. I, 1918

Abbott, Sjt. C. F.		3255	Banks, A.R.S.M. G. W.	67
— Sjt. H.	*	66	Barber, C.S.M. G. T.	67
— Sjt. P. de M.		76	— Cpl. (A.Sjt.) J. E.	67
Aboukir Ahmed, Mulazim Sena	✿	848	Barfoot, Pte. (A.S.Sjt.) E. H.	67
Acland, Staff Sjt. (A.S.Q.M.S.) J.		66	— Sjt. (A.B.S.M.) F. C.	67
Adams, Sjt. A.		66	Barham, C.S.M. (A.S.M.) G. W.	67
Addy, Sjt. A.J.		76	Barnard, Pte. (A.Sjt.) J.	67
Ahl, Armr. S.Sjt. W. H.		66	Barnes, By.S.M. C.	67
Aiston, Pte. (A.Q.M.Sjt.) J. G. A.		66	— Sjt. P. J.	67
Alexander, S.Sjt. E.		66	Barry, L.C. (A.C.S.M.) D.	67
Allberry, Sjt. H. P.		76	Bartlett, S.Q.M.Sjt. D. H.	67
Allan, Sjt. F.		66	Batten, S.Sjt. J. G.	67
Allen, Cpl. (A.S.Sjt.) J. L.		66	Baugh, Sjt. H. J.	67
— Sjt. (A.C.S.M.) R. F.		76	Baughan, Sjt. (T.S.S.M.) C.	67
Alp, Sjt. C. A.		66	Beach, Pte. (A.L.Sjt.) G. W.	3254
Anderson, Sjt. (T.Sub-Condr.) J.		66	Beale, Cpl. W. R.	67
— Pte. W. E.		66	Beaumont, L.Cpl. (A.Sjt.) R. H.	67
Archer, L.Sjt. W.		66	Beckerleg, Co.Q.M.S. A. J.	67
Armstrong, Sjt. R.		66	Beckett, C.S.M. G. J. (Corr.)	3256
— 2nd Cpl. (A.C.S.M.) W.		66	Behaun, Sjt. H. C.	76
Asher, Cpl. (A.S.Q.M.Sjt.) A.		66	Belford, S.M. D. J. D.	67
Ashton, Sjt. J. H.		66	Bell, L.Cpl. (A.Q.M.S.) D.	67
Ashwin, Cpl. (A.Sjt.) F. R.		66	Bennett, S.S.M. C. W.	67
Ashworth, Sjt. N.		66	— Co.S.M. E. C.	67
Atherton, Sjt. T.		66	— Sjt. F.	67
Atkins, 2nd Cpl. C. P.		76	— Sjt. (A.R.S.M.) F. T. G.	67
Auker, Sjt. W. J.		66	— By.S.M. N. S.	‡ 67
Austin, Sjt. C.		66	— S.M. S.	67
Axson, R.Q.M.Sjt. A.		66	Benson, Co.Q.M.Sjt. F.	67
			Bentley, L.Cpl. R. H.	67
Bailey, R.Q.M.S. F.		66	Benton, Sjt. W. J.	67
— Sub-Condr. G. W. B.		3255	Berbridge, S.Q.M.Sjt. C. E.	67
Bain, S.Q.M.S. W. S.		2974	Bernard, Sjt. W. H.	67
Bale, Pte. A. L.	†	66	Berrie, L.Cpl. V. L.	67
Balfour, Pte. (Sjt.) J.		3255	Berry, Sjt. (A.O.R.Sjt.) J.	67
Ballard, 2nd Cpl. (A.Sjt.) W. A.		66	Bettoney, Pte. J. E.	67
Bamber, Co.S.M. A. W.		67	Bevan, Pte. (A.Sjt.) H. J.	67

* Awarded M.S.M. Annuity 1950 (A.O.144, Grenadier Guards).
† R.A.S.C. Medal presented in Bermuda 25.4.1920 by C.-in-C. Sir James Wilcocks.
‡ Group known: D.C.M. (B.S.M. 252/Sge. Bty. R.G.A.), 1914/15 Star trio (B.S.M./ W.O.II R.G.A./R.A.) Defence and War Medals, 1935 Jubilee, 1937 Coronation, L.S. & G.C. (W.O.1 D.C.M. R.A.) and M.S.M. (253/Sge. Bty. R.G.A.), D.C.M. *L.G.* 3 September, 1918 for rescuing wounded men though wounded himself.

Beveridge, Sjt. G. O. H.	*	67
Biggs, Pte. F. C.		67
Bilsborough, Q.M.Sjt. J.		3255
Birch, Q.M.Sjt. (A.S.S.M.) J. W.		67
Bishop, By.S.M. F.		67
Black, Q.M.Sjt. (A.S.M.) J.		3254
Blackburn, Trp. S.M. (A.R.S.M.) J.		67
— Sjt. W. F.		67
Blackmore, Cpl. F. W.		67
Blackwood, T.R.S.M. (Supt.Clerk) W.		67
Blake, Condr. L. A.		67
Blakemore, Spr. (A.Sjt.) R.		67
Blenkhorn, Pte. (A.Sjt.) E.		67
Blythe, S.Sjt. S. G. W.		3254
Boddy, S.Sjt. R.		67
Bolton, S.Q.M.S, H.		67
Bone, Sqdn. S.M. S. A.		67
Bonner, S.Q.M.S.S. F.		67
Booker, Sjt. G. A.		67
Boorman, 2nd Cpl. W.		3254
Bostock, Sjt. (A.S.S.M.) W.		67
Bougard, S.Sjt.		
(T.Sub-Condr.) W. R.	†	67
Boughey, Sjt. W.		67
Bourton, Sjt. E. S.		67
Bovill, Sjt. (A.Co.S.M.) J.		67
Boyd, S.M. F. of Wks. J.		67
Boyle, R.Q.M.S. J. W.		67
Bradburn, Mech.S.M. J.		67
Brayton, Far. Q.M.S. I.		67
Brett, Sjt. M. J.		67
Brew, L.Cpl. J.		67
Brewer, Co.Q.M.S. R. J.		67
Brewin, Sjt. (A.R.S.M.) S. J.		67
Bridge, Sjt. L. K.		76
Bridges, L.Cpl. (A.S.S.M.) A. C. J.		67
Brookstone, A.Sjt. M. S.		3255
Brown, Sjt. A. H.		3255
— Pte. (A.Cpl.) B. J.		67

Brown, By.S.M. J. A. J.	67
— Sjt. W.	67
— Co.S.M. W. T.	67
Bryant, Dvr. J	1621
— Sjt. W. A.	76
Buckingham, Sjt. A.	67
Buckland, By.S.M. F. J.	67
Buckle, Sjt. H. A.	76
Buckner, Q.M.S. (A.S.M.) A.	67
Buffee Condr. E. W.	67
Bull, R.S.M. T. H.	67
Bullock, Pte. (A.Cpl.) P. A.	67
Bunch, S.S.M. G.	67
Bundock, R.Q.M.Sjt. C.	67
Burdett, R.S.M. D.	67
Burghart, S.Sjt. (A.S.Q.M.S.) C. H. ‡	67
Burnard, Cpl. (A.S.) T. G.	67
Burrows, A.Sub-Condr. R.	3254
Burt, By.S.M. F.	67
Burton, Sjt. R. (R.E.)	67
— Sjt. R. (N. Staffs R.)	67
— Cpl. R.	67
— T.R.S.M. T.	67
Bushnell, Far.Sjt. G. N. R.	68
Butler, Cpl. O. L.	68
Bycroft, Co.S.M. (A:S.Q.M.C.) A.	68
Cager, Cpl. (A.S.) E. W. F.	68
Calcott, Co.S.M. W. E.	68
Cameron, Sjt. D.	77
Camfield, Sjt. A. S.	68
Campbell, L.Cpl. (A.Cpl.) E. W. A.	68
— Co.S.M. J.	68
— Cpl. (A.Sjt.) W. H.	68
Cantrell, S.M. J. B.	68
Carley, Bombr. (A.Sjt.) H.	68
Carman, Co.S.M. (A.Q.M.Sjt.) S. H.	68
Carne, R.Q.M.Sjt. (now 2nd Lt.) P. S.	76
Carpenter, Sjt. W. H. H.	76

---

    * Gerald O'Hagon Beveridge. On the Staff of the Bank of Ireland prior to being called up with his Regiment, the South Irish Horse, on 5 August, 1914, attached to 49 West Riding Div. To France, April, 1915 and was at Festubert, Ypres, Passchendaele, Cambrai, etc. In October, 1916 he transferred to the Military Mounted Police, and was promoted Sergeant Major. His group is known, the 1914/15 Star trio named to South Irish Horse, the M.S.M. to Mil. Mounted Police.

    † R.A.O.C., also B.E.M. (1st type) and Médaille d'Honneur avec Glaives (en Argent). Group known: B.E.M., Queen's South Africa Medal (Cape Colony, South Africa 1902), 1914 Star trio, L.S. & G.C. (Geo. V), M.S.M. and French Decoration as above.

    ‡ Group known: 1914 Star & bar trio, L.S. & G.C. (Geo. V), M.S.M. (R.A.S.C.).

Carroll, Sjt. W.	68	Connolly, Pte. (L.Cpl.) T.	68
Carter, Cpl. G. W.	68	Conradi, W.O. Artfr. F. N.	76
— L. Cpl. (A.Cpl.) H.	68	Cook, Sjt. (A.S.Q.M.S.) A. J. (A.S.C.)	68
Cartwright, Pte. E. L.	68	— Sjt. (A.S.M.) A. J. (R.F.C.)	68
Carver, Sjt. J.	68	Cooke, R.Q.M.Sjt. H.	68
Caswell, Amt. S.Sjt. C. L.	68	— Pte. W. J.	68
Cater, Sjt. W. W.	68	Cookson, Pte. T. B. W.	68
Chadwick, Sjt. A. L.	68	Cooper, Cpl. C. E.	68
Chapman, Pte. (A.Sjt.) W. A.	3254	— Sjt. W. F.	3255
Chare, L.Cpl. (A.Cpl.) A. E.	68	Copperthwaite, W.O., 1st Cl. W. C.	76
Charlesworth, Pte. H.	68	Corless, Sjt. (A.Q.M.Sjt.) T.	68
— Sjt. W. H.	76	Cosher, Spr. T.	68
Cheeseman, Sjt. (now 2nd Lt.) W. C.	76	Coverley, Co.S.M. J. T.	68
Chesters, Pte. (A.Sjt.) P. H.	3254	Cowell, Pte. (L.Cpl.) W.	68
Chick, Gnr. (A.Bombr.) C. E.	68	Cox, Pte. H. W. G.	68
Chirgwin, Flt.Sjt. G. E.	68	— Sjt. J.	2974
Chisnall, Sjt. (T.Sup.Clk.) A. E.	68	— S.Sjt. (T.S.S.M.) J. H.	68
Choate, Sjt. S. S.	77	— Pte. (A.Sjt.) M. G. L.	68
Christie, A.Co.S.M. W.	68	Cracknell, Spr. J.	68
Churchyard, Sjt. (A.By.S.M.) J. T. *	68	Craddock, Sjt. J.	76
Clark, A.R.S.M. F. J.	68	Crisp, Pte. (A.Sjt.) A. J.	68
— Spr. (A.L.Cpl.) J. P.	68	Critchley, Dvr. G. (corr.)	3474
Clarke, Dvr. (A.Sjt.) A. L.	68	Cromarty, Spr. (A.Cpl.) W.	68
— Bombdr. (A.Cpl.) C. E.	68	Croot, S.Sjt. F.ofWks. H. G.	68
— Pte. H.	1621	Crosby, Sjt. (A.S.Sjt.) F.	68
— Sjt. (A.Co.S.M.) J. H.	68	— Sjt. (A.Coy.S.M.) W. G. E.	3255
Clapp, Bomdr. (A.Sjt.) G. S.	68	Croxford, Sjt. F. T.	68
Clements, S.M. F. A.	68	Cruxton, Sjt. (A.S.Sjt.) H. A.	68
Cliff, S.Q.M.Sjt. C. W.	68	Cullen, Supt.Clk. W.	68
Clifford, Cpl. H. L.	68	Cummins, Sjt. (A.S.M.) T.	68
Coates, Co.S.M. A.	68	Cundy, Sjt. (A.S.M.) J. A.	68
— Supt.Clk.Q.M.Sjt. E.	68	Currie, Sjt. (A.S.M. Art. Clerk) W.	68
Cochrane, Pte. (A.Sjt.) W.	68	Curtis, Spr. (A.Sjt.) H. L.	68
Cockaday, Q.M.S. (T.S.M.) J. A.	68		
Colclough, Sjt. F.	68	Dale, R.Q.M.Sjt. F. †	68
Cole, Spr. A. J.	68	Daly, S.Sjt. (A.S.S.M.) S. J.	68
Colebrook, R.Q.M.Sjt. E. S.	77	Daniels, Q.M.S. W. H.	68
Coleman, Gnr. F. E.	68	Darkins, S.Sjt. (A.S.M.) C. H.	68
Collins, Sjt. D.	76	Davey, R.Q.M.Sjt. S.	69
— Pte, (A.Cpl.) H. J.	68	Davies, Q.M.Sjt. D. J.	68
— S.Sjt. (T.Sub-Condr.) J.	68	— S.M. E. B.	76
— Co.S.M. (T.S.S.M.) W.	68	— Sjt. J. C. H.	76
Collison, L.Cpl. (A.Sjt.) H. A.	68	— Cpl. S. C.	68
Connolly, Spr. J. E.	68	Davis, By.S.M. B. J. W.	69

* Group known: D.C.M. (Geo. V, Sgt. D152/Bde.), Queen's South Africa Medal (Cape Colony, Paardeberg, Johannesburg, Dreifontein, Bombr. 83rd Baty.), King's South Africa Medal (Gnr.), 1914 Star (A./Sgt.), British War and Victory Medals (W.O.), and M.S.M. D.C.M. *L.G.* 5 December 1918.

† Group known: 1914 Star (Sgt.), British War and Victory Medals (Captain, R. Lanc. R.), L.S. & G.C. (Geo. V, Q.M.S.) and M.S.M. (Tank Corps).

Davis, Co.S.M. H. H.	69	Eddie, Sjt. F. F.	76
— W.O. J. M.	76	Eley, Cpl. J. O.	69
Dawes, Cp. (A.Sjt.) H. W.	76	Elliott, S.Sjt. A.Q.M.S.) H.	69
Day, 2nd Cpl. (A.Sjt.) E.	69	Ellwood, Pte. F. A.	✿ 3254
— L.Cpl. (T.Sub-Condr.) W. H.	69	Elmy, A.Cpl. W. H.	69
Deakin, R.Q.M.Sjt. M. H.	69	Elsden, Sjt. H. W.	69
Dean, Sjt. W. H.	76	Elsworth, S.S.M. (A.W.O.) R. C.	69
Dennett, Sjt. (A.S.M.) T. R.	69	Embelin, Sjt. B. A.	3255
Denney, Sjt. W. E.	69	Emms, W.O. S. E.	76
Denton, S.Sjt. G. E.	3255	England, Pte. (A.S.Sjt.) W. S.	69
Dawberry, S.M. E. B.	69	Etheridge, Pte (A.Sjt.) E.	69
Dobinson, Sjt. (A.C.Q.M.Sjt.) H. J.	69	Evans, Sjt. C.	76
Dodd, Flt.Sjt. F. W.	69	— Cpl. F. D.	69
Donald, Cpl. C.	69	— By.S.M. H. L.	69
Donnelly, Sjt. P. J.	69	— Pte. (A.Sjt.) L. H.	69
Donohue, C.Q.M.Sjt. H. *	69	— Co.S.M. P. C.	69
Dower, Sjt. W.	69	Ewings, Q.M.Sjt. G. W.	69
Downer, S.Sjt. (A.S.S.M.) C. H.	69	Eyles, Bomdr. G. E.	69
Downs, C.S.M. (A.R.Q.M.Sjt.) C. E.	69		
— Sjt. S.	69	Fairbrother, S.M. P. G.	76
Dowson, Spr. (A.Co.S.M.) C.	69	Farmer, Spr. (A.2nd Cpl.) H.	69
Dray, Sqdn.Q.M. Sjt. H. A. †	69	— S.M. J.	76
Drew, Q.M.Sjt. A. E.	69	Faulkner, Pte. (A.Sjt.) J. W.	69
— Sqn. S.M. (A.R.S.M.) G. W.	69	Fawden, Q.M.Sjt. H. E.	69
— Sjt. H. O. S.	76	Fegan, By.S.M. J.	69
Drummond, S.Sjt. R.	76	Ferguson, Vol. J. S.	3255
Duckworth, Sjt. J.	76	Findlay, Sjt. G.	69
Duggan, Sjt. D. J.	76	Fisher, Sjt. T. C.	3255
— Pte. M.	✿ 2439	Fitzwater, S.S.M. (A.C.S.M.) W. G.	69
Duke, Sjt. (A.S.M.) R. M.	69	Flackfield, Sjt. (T.Co.S.M.) J.	76
Dumjohn, C.Q.M.Sjt. (A.Coy S.M.)		Fletcher, 2nd Cpl. J. D.	76
F. P. W.	3255	— Sjt. T. H.	69
Duncan, Sjt. H.	69	Flood, S.Sjt. (T.S.S.M.) A. W.	69
Dunk, Armt.Q.M.Sjt. H. W.	76	Fogg, S.Q.M.Sjt. (A.Sub-Condr.) H.	69
Dunkinson, Sjt. C.	69	Fontaine, Cpl. L. T.	69
Dunlop. S.Sjt. H. A. S.	69	Foot, L.Cpl. G. B.	69
Durnan, Sjt. (A.Q.M.S.) T. C.	69	Foote, Sjt. W. H.	76
Durnell, Cpl. N.	69	Forbes, S.Sjt. (A.S.M.) J. G. A.	69
		Forrest, L.Cpl. S. V.	77
Eccles, Pte. (A.S.Q.M.) R.	69	Fortescue, Sjt. (T.Co.S.M.)	76

---

    * C.Q.M.S. 13th King's (Liverpool Regiment). Volunteering in September 1914, he was trained at Bournemouth and Aldershot. Proceeding in June 1915, he served at Ypres, Loos, La Bassée, Festubert, Albert, Delville Wood, the Somme, Beaumont-Hamel, Cambrai, Passchendaele, and in the Retreat and Advance of 1918. He was awarded the Meritorious Service Medal for devotion to duty, and in addition, held the 1914-15 Star, and the General Service and Victory Medals. He was demobilised in February 1919. 9 Salter Lane, Eccles.

    † Group known: Queen's South Africa Medal (Cape Colony, Orange Free State, Pte. 8 Hussars), King's South Africa Medal, 1914 Star trio (Sgt. 8 Hussars), L.S. & G.C. (Geo. V S.Q.M.S. M.G.C.), M.S.M. (Geo. V 14 Sqn. Cav. M.G.C.).

Foster, Amt. S.Sjt. (A.S.M.) A. E.	*	69	
— T.S.M. D.		69	
— Pte. E. A.		69	
Fowle, S.S.M. G. A.		69	
Fox, Sjt. F.		69	
Frame, Sjt. W.		69	
Francis, Sjt. G. T.		69	
Franckeiss, Eng.Clk.Sjt. F. J.		69	
Franks, Far.S.Sjt. J.		69	
Fretwell, 2nd Cpl. (T.Sub-Condr.) W.		69	
Fricker, R.Q.M.Sjt. A. E.		69	
Friend, Sjt. W.		69	
Froude, Sjt. (A.By. S.M.) H. G.		69	
Fuller, Sjt. T. A.		69	
Fulton, W.O. G. W.		76	
Gabriel, Dvr. C. N.		1621	
Gage, Cpl. (A.S.S.M.) F.		69	
Gallagher, S.M. T.		69	
Galvin, Sjt. H.		3255	
Gardiner, S.M. J. S.		69	
Gardner, Sjt. J. E.	†	69	
Garret, A.Sjt. J.		69	
Gascoyne, Armt.S.Sjt. (T.Sub-Condr.) R. E.		69	
Gibson, Co.S.M. (T.R.S.M.) H. F. (Deletion)		1621	
— R.Q.M.Sjt. J.		69	
Gillard, Cpl. G.		69	
— S.M. R.		69	
Glover, Sjt. F.		69	
— Sjt. W.		69	
Golds, Spr. (A.Sjt.) A.		69	
Goodall, Cpl. H. H.		76	
Gooderham, Sjt. A. R.		69	
Goodey, S.Sjt. (T.Sub-Condr.) F.		69	
Goodhall, W.O. J. T.		76	
Goodhind, Dvr. S.		69	
Goodman, Co.S.M. J.		69	
Goodwin, R.S.M. G.		69	
— Armr. Q.M.Sjt. W. H.		70	
Gordon, C.S.M. J. B. (corr.)		3256	
— Co.S.M. (A.S.M.) Arty.Clk. S.		70	
Gostling, Sjt. W. A.		70	
Gower, Cpl. (A.Sjt.) W.		70	

Graham, Armt.S.M. (W.O., Cl.1.) S. W.			76
Gray, Sjt. G.			70
Green, Co.S.M. (T.R.S.M.) S.			70
Greenhalgh, L.Cpl. (A.Cpl.) J. H.			70
Gregory, Sjt. A. (Y.&L.R.)			70
— Sjt. (A.Co.S.M.) A. (S. Staffs. R.)			70
Grier, A.Cpl. J.			76
Griffin, Pte. A.			70
— Sjt. G. H.			77
Griffiths, Sjt. (A.S.Sjt.) J. H.			70
Grimshaw, Cpl. (A.Co.S.M.) H.			70
— L.Cpl. W.			70
Guinan, Cpl. (A.Co.S.M.) W.			70
Gunn, C.S.M. J. S.			3255
Guy, Co.S.M. A. H.			77
Gyer, T.Mil.Mech.S.Sjt. E. E.			70
Hadath, Sjt. E.			3255
Haigh, Sjt. W. E.			70
Hall, Amt. S.Sjt. R.			70
Hallam, Sjt. (A.C.Q.M.Sjt.) W. G.			70
Hammond, Sjt. B.			70
— L.Sjt. (A.Sjt.) C. W.	❀		3473
— L.Cpl. W.			70
Hancock, 2nd Cpl. (A.Sjt.) E.			70
Handley, Co.S.M. J. S.			70
Hannah, S.Q.M.Sjt. R.			70
Hannay, A.Sjt. W. C.			3255
Harding, L.Cpl. (A.S.S.M.) J.			70
Hardisty, C.Q.M.Sjt. J.			70
Hardy, Sub-Condr. (A.Condr) L.			70
— Mech.S.Sjt. T. S.			70
Harper, Sjt. H. A.			70
— Sjt. J.			76
— Cpl. (A.C.Q.M.Sjt.) T.			70
Harrington, Co.S.M. D.			70
— S.Sjt. (A.Q.M.Sjt.) E.			70
Harris, R.S.M. G.			70
— S.Sjt. G. A.			76
— Sjt. (A.Co.S.M.) G. S.			70
Harrison, Cpl. F.			70
— Sjt. (A.S.Q.M.S.) W. V.			70
Hartnell, T.S.M. W. G.			70
Harvey, A.S.M. F. A.			70

---

* R.A.O.C. Also M.B.E. and Médaille d'Honneur avec Glaives (en Argent).

† Tank Corps. ('A' Battn.). Also awarded a Military Medal for gallantry near Noyelles on 20 November, 1917. He dealt with enemy field guns firing at his tank at a range of 200 yds. He knocked out one and silenced another, also putting a number of enemy M.G.s out of action.

Harvey, Flt. Sjt. W.		70	Howe, Sjt. G. F.		70
Hastings, Sjt. C. J.		70	Howitt, Co.Q.M.Sjt. C. H.		76
Hayes, 2nd Cpl. S. F.		70	Howson, Far.S.Sjt. J. T.		70
Hayter, Cpl. (A.Sjt.) J.		70	Hughes, T.S.M. F.		70
Head, Q.M.Sjt. (F. of Works) R.		3255	— A.Q.M.Sjt. F.		70
Heal, R.S.M. T.		70	— L.C. (A.2nd Cpl.) J.	❀	3473
Healy, Condr. N. E. W.		70	Hulland, Fitter, G. R.		70
Heaseman, Sjt. H. F.		70	Humpherson, S.Q.M.S. (T.S.S.M.) F.		70
Heath, By.S.M. S. J. G.		70	Humphrey, R.S.M. A. R.		70
— R.Q.M.Sjt. W. H.		70	Hunt, Cpl. C. E.		70
Hellon, Flt.Sjt. W. H.		70	— Sjt. J. J.		71
Hemington, Sjt. J.		70	— Sjt. R. E.		77
Henderson, Spr. (A.Sjt.) A.		3255	— Q.M.S. (A.S.M.) Arty. Clk. T.		71
— Sjt. H. W.		70	Hunter, A.Co.S.M. W.		71
Henley, Sjt. E. J.		70	Hurle, T.S.M. Arty.Clk. E. A.		71
Hester, Sjt. (A.S.M.) H. W.		70	— Sjt. R. E.		71
Hewitt, Sjt. (A.S.Q.M.S.) G. A.		70	Hurst, Sgt. H. O.	❀	2439
Higgs, Sjt. H. W.		70	Hutchings, S.Sjt. (A.S.M.) W.		71
Hilkene, Amt. S.Sjt. A.		70	Hutchison, Pte. (A.Sjt.) A.		71
Hill, S.Sjt. (A.W.O., Cl.1) A. J.		70			
— Sjt. W. H. G.		70	Iliffe, Q.M.Sjt. H. G.		76
Hills, Sjt. F.	*	70	Isaac, Sjt. C.		71
Hineson, By.S.M. E.		76	— S.S.M. C. T.		71
Hinton, Sjt, (A.S.M.) Arty.Clk. A. J.		70	Isaacson, Cpl. (A.Sjt) H. E.		71
Hislop. C.Q.M. Sjt. D. J.		70			
Hoare, Sjt. (T.Sub-Condr.) H. H.		70	Jackson, Co.S.M. G. R.		71
Hockley, Supt.Clk. G. J.		70	— Spr. P. L.	❀	3473
Hockney, Co.S.M. H. H.	❀	3473	James, Cpl. (A.Sjt.) C.		71
Hodge, Sjt. G. A.		70	— S.Sjt. C. F.		71
Holden, Co.S.M. H.		70	— Co.S.M. E.		71
Hole, By.S.M. R. P.		70	— Sjt. (A.Q.M.Sjt.) E. F.		71
Holland, Sjt. W. S.		70	Jamieson, Spr. (A.Cpl.) E.		71
Hollingworth, Sjt,			Jaques, R.S.M. W. E.		71
(A.R.Q.M.Sjt.) A.	†	70	Jarrard, A.C.Q.M.Sjt. A. H.		71
Holloway, Sjt. (A.Q.M.S.) E.		70	Jeffrey, Pte. (A.Sjt.) W.		71
Holmes, T.S.M. S. R,		70	Jeffs, S.Sjt. W. A.		76
Honeywill, L, Cpl. (A.Cpl.) E.		70	Jenkinson, L.Cpl. S.		71
Honnor, Armr.S.M. B. A,		70	Jervis, Pte. (A.S.M.) F. P.		71
Hopkin, Sjt. (A.Q.M.S.) F. M.		70	Johnson, Mech.Q.M.Sjt. G.		71
Hopkins, Sjt. H. C.		76	— Sjt. (A.S.Q.M.S.) G. F. A.		71
Horne, Sqdn. Cpl.Maj. W.		70	— Co.S.M. (A.S.S.M.) T.		71
Horton, R, S.M. A. H.		70	— Pte. (A.Q.M.S.) W.		76
Hossack, Pte. (A.Cpl.) D. T.		70	Johnstone, C.S.M. (T.S.M.) L. G.		71

---

* 24/Manchester (Oldham Pals) *L.G.* 1.1.18. Valuable Service Army in the Field. Details from Regt. Book of Honour: On June 24th 1917, when his company was working east of Bullecourt, during a heavy bombardment, though twice blown up, his courage and determination in keeping his men together carrying on the work in hand, and evacuating the wounded, were most praiseworthy.

† The last serving member of 1st Bn. Duke of Wellington's Regt. who fought at the Somme, died November, 1980, aged 92, in Crosland Moor, Yorks.

Jones, Spr. (A.Sjt.) H. J.	71	Kirby, Q.M.S. (T.Supt.Clk.) F. G.	71
— Col.Sjt. (Q.M.Sjt.) S.	71	— Fitt.Gnr. F. J.	71
— Sjt. T.	77	Kirkhouse, Whr. G.	71
— Sjt. T. F.	3255	Kirkwood, Sjt. G.	71
Jordan, Q.M.Sjt. E.	71	Knowler, Pte. (A.S.Sjt.) W.	71
		Kombo Bin Asmani, Pte. ‡	3255
Keane, Sjt. (A.Co.S.M.) M. W.	71		
— Cpl. T. J.	71	Laing, Sjt. J.	71
Kearns, Sjt. J.	71	Lamb, S.M. C. E.	76
— Cpl. P.	3255	Lambert, Sjt. W. H.	71
Keeley, Co.S.M. F.	71	Lander, S.Sjt. T. §	71
Kellett, Pte. A.	3255	Lang, Sjt. (A.Co.S.M.) F.	71
Kemp, Cpl. (A.S.S.M.) A. G. (corr.)	1407	Langan, Co.S.M. J.	71
— Co.S.M. E.	71	Langrish, Pte. J. G.	77
Kenna, Co.S.M. T.	77	Larbalestier, Pte. C. H.	71
Kennaway, A.S.Sjt. R. J.	71	Laughton, Sjt. E.	71
Kennedy, Cpl. C.	76	Laxton, Spr. R. J.	71
— R.Q.M.Sjt. I.	71	Layton, Gnr. G.	71
— S.Sjt. R. L.	76	Layzell, S.Sjt. K. C. S.	3255
Kerr, Co.S.M. D. R. *	71	Leach, C.Q.M.S. J. V.	71
— S.Sjt. W. H. S.	76	Leaney, S.Sjt. (A.Condr.) F. G. ‡	71
Kidd, Cpl. (A.Col.Sjt.) A. T.	71	Lee, Gnr. (A.Sjt.) T. J.	71
Kidgell, C.Q.M.Sjt. J. E.	3255	Leggett, By.S.M. H.	71
Kimberley, S.M. H.	71	Leicester, S.Sjt. O. H. +	3255
King, Sjt. D.	76	Leigh, Pte. (A.Sjt.) A. B.	71
— Cpl. (A.Sjt.) E. W.	71	— Sjt. W. S.	71
— Q.M.S. (Eng.Clk.) G.	71	Leishman, Co.Q.M.S. J.	71
— Sjt. W.	71	Leonard, Cpl. J. B. ✿	1406

---

* Group was in McInnes collection: 1914/15 Star (68880 C.S.M. R.E.), British War and Victory Medals (Lieut. R.N.R.) and M.S.M. (Inland Water Transport). David Roy Kerr was a Probationary Flight Officer R.N.A.S. in April 1917 and a Lieut. R.N.R. on 10 November 1918. He was 1st Lieut. on the Yacht *'Josephine'* 16 Aug 1918—May 1919.

† East African Intel. Dept.

‡ R.A.O.C., later Conductor. Also D.C.M.

§ See Seigne, Vol. II, 1919. M.S.M. with Intelligence Corps. Also Médaille d'Honneur (en Argent) as R.S.M. 10 R.F., *L.G.* 7.10.19.

+ See notes under Bruce (in II 1918). A second *London Gazette* date found to contain Lotus reverse M.S.M. recipients amongst standard ones is *L.G.* 13.3.18, Valuable Services with the Army in the Field (73 names in all). Included are 9 to I.A. including:— Major O. H. Leicester, whose group of eight medals is on display in the really splendid collection in the R.C.T. Officers' Mess at Aldershot. They are: Queen's South Africa Medal (Cape Colony, Orange Free State, Transvaal), King's South Africa Medal, India General Service Medal (N.W.F. 1908, N.W.F. 1919), 1914/15 Star, British War Medal, Victory Medal (M.I.D.), L.S. & G.C. (Geo. V, F.M. Bust, Swivel Susp.), M.S.M. (Geo. V Kaisar-i-Hind, Eng. S./Sgt. S. & T.C.). The eight I.A. names in this *L.G.* are:— Sgt. C. F. Abbott, C.M.S.C., S.-Cond. G.W.B. Bailey, I.U.L., S./Sgt. G. F. Denton, S. & T.C., 641 Sgt. H. Galrin, Indian Postal Service, Cond. R. Machie, I.M.L., 3501 S./Sgt. J. Rogers, Mil. Wks. Serv. Ind. Bk. Dept., Cond. A. Villiers, I.O.D., Condr. H.R. Selby. I.O.D. (group known, see *infra*).

Leslie, Q.M.S. (A.S.M.) J.		71	MacGregor, Cpl. (A.L.Sjt.) J. G.		76
Lester, Sjt. F.		71	Macindoe, C.Q.M.Sjt. (now Co.S.M.) J.		71
Lethlean, W, O. 1st Cl. L. L.		76	McIntosh, Cpl. (A.Sjt.) E. O.		72
Lewin, Cpl. G.		71	McIver, Sjt. W. E.		72
Lewis, Sjt. S.		3255	MacKay, Sjt. J.		71
Lewsey, Pte. (A.Cpl) H. R.		71	McKenzie, A.Sjt. J. H.		76
Liebert, Cpl. S. F. E		76	Mackey, Co.S.M. J.		71
Lillyman, Sjt. J.		71	Mackie, W.O. G. N.		76
Lincoln, LCpl. W. G.		76	— Condr. R.		3255
Lindsay, Sjt. (A.S.M.) F.		71	McKinnon, Sjt. P.		72
Linney, Sjt. (A, S.Sjt.) H. J.		71	— L.C. W.		3255
Llewelly, Sjt. (A.C.Q.M.S.) T. W.		71	McLaren, Sjt. J. W.		72
Lloyd, T.Sub-Condr. F. C.		71	Macleay, Pte. W. M.		76
Loader, Cpl. (A.Sjt.) T. M.		71	McLernan, Sjt. J.		3255
Locker, Dvr. P. G.		1621	McNaught, Cpl. A.		72
Lockhart, S.Sjt. E. A.		76	— S.Sjt. D.		76
Loney, Mech.S.Sjt. H. G.		71	Maconachie, Pte. (A.Cpl.) J.		71
Loughnane, S.M. T.	*	71	McPherson, Sjt. C.		77
Lovell, S.S.M. G. E.		77	Macqueen, Sjt. W. S.		71
Lowen, Sjt. C. E.		71	McVeigh, By.Q.M.Sjt. W. E.		72
Loweth, 1st Writer (A.Chief Writer)			Magowan, S.Sjt. Artfr. A.		72
A. J.		71	Maile, Spr. J.	✿	3473
Luckett, Sjt. (A.E.C.S.Sjt.) F. C.		3255	Maksudi Manyema, A.Sjt.		3255
Lukes, Pte. (A.L.Cpl.) A. E.		71	Manderson, Sjt. A. J.		72
— Co.S.M. P.		71	Mann, L.Sjt. (A.C.Q.M.Sjt.) J. W.		72
Lyne, Flt.Sjt. C.		71	— Head Condr. O. A.		3255
			Manton, Q.M.S. (A.W.O.) J.		72
McBeath, Cpl. A.		72	Marks, Co.S.M. R. J.		72
McBright, Q.M.Sjt. S.		72	— By.S.M. T. H.		72
McCaig, Pte. G.		3255	Marsh, 2nd Cpl. (A.Cpl.) W.		72
McCarthy, R.S.M. T.		72	Marshall, Cpl. J.		72
MacClafferty, Sjt. E. F.		71	— S.Q.M.Sjt. (T.S.M.) W.		72
McCredie, R.Q.M.Sjt. J. J.		76	Martin, Cpl. (A.Sjt.) C. A.		3255
McCubbin, 2nd Cpl. W. K. J.		72	— Sjt. (T.S.S.M.) J.		72
MacDonald, Vol. Revd. A.	†	3255	— R.Q.M.S. (now Hon.Lt. and		
McDonald, Cpl. R.		76	Qrmr.) R.		72
McDougall, Amt. S.S. G. M.		72	— Pte. T. W.		76
MacFayden, Vol. R.	‡	3255	— Sjt. W. H.		72
McGarry, Sjt. C.		72	— Dvr. W. P.		76
McGeorge, Bomdr. (A.S.M.) H.		72	— Pte. W. T.		72
McGibbon, Co.S.M. (A.S.M. Art. Clk.)			Mason, T.Sub-Condr. H.		72
C. E.		72	Matthews, Sjt. A. W.		3255
McGregor, Sjt. (A.S.S.M.) H. S.		72	— 2nd Cpl. (A.Sjt.) W. S.		72

---

* Group known: 1914 Star trio (W.O.1 M.M.P.), L.S. & G.C. (Geo. V. Sgt.), M.S.M. (both M.M.P.) and French Médaille Militaire. With photograph wearing medals, and French certificate. R.S.M. M.M.P. 5 August, 1914. Retired 14 March 1920. A very rare rank/unit for 1914 Star.

† Padre, Nyasaland Contingent.

‡ Group known: African General Service Medal (Nyasaland 1915), British War and Victory Medals (Lieutenant) and M.S.M. (Nyasaland Vol. R.).

Maxfield, Sjt. J.		72	Nethercott, Cpl. (A.Sjt.) G.	72
May, Sjt. (A.S.S.) W. G.		72	Newberry, Sjt, (T.S.M.) H. P.	72
Mayes, Pte. (A.Cpl.) E.		72	Nixon, By.S.M. O. H.	72
Marwood, S.Sjt. (A.S. M.) H. G.		3255	Norman, R.Q.M.Sjt. J.	72
Meade, T.R.S.M. H. E. G.		72		
Medlock, S.M. G. A.		72	Oates, Sjt. C. F.	72
Mentzel, Sjt. A. E.		72	Oddy, Bnd. Sjt. F. C.	72
Mercer, L.Cpl. J.		77	O'Hara, By.S.M. M.	72
Meredith, Pte. F. S.	❀	3473	O'Hare, L.Cpl. P. J.	72
Miles, Pte. A.		72	Ojerogwe Atwol, Pte.	❀ 848
Millar, Sjt. W. H.		76	Oram, Pte. (A.Sjt.) W. F.	72
Miller, Co.Sjt. C. J.		72	Orchard, S.Sjt. (A, S.M.) C.	72
— S.M. F.		72	— Flt. Sjt. C. R.	72
— Cpl. (A.Sjt.) P. E.		72	Osborne, Sjt.	72
— R.S.M. W. F.		72	Otley, Cpl. (A.S.Q.M.Sjt.) S. S.	72
Mills, S.M. (A.W.O.) L. J.		72	Owen, C.Q.M.S. F.	72
— Cpl. N. G.		76	Oxford, R.S.M. S.	72
— Co.Q.M.Sjt. O. T.		76		
— Co.S.M. W. J.		72	Padget, S.Sjt. A.	72
Milroy, S.Sjt. J.		76	Palmer, Sjt. G. T.	* 72
Mockler, T.Sub-Condr. W. H. F.		72	Paltridge, Mech.S.Sjt. J. W.	72
Molay, R.S.M. W.		72	Parker, Pte. (A.Sjt.) C. V.	72
Mole, Sjt. (A.S.S.M.) T.		72	— Sjt. (A.S.Q.M.S.) J.	72
Mooney, Pte. (A.S.S.) J. A.		72	Parkinson, Dvr. W. (Corr.)	1406
Moore, By.Q.M.S. W. A.		72	Parr, S.Sjt. (A.S.M.) J.	72
Morgan, Sjt. G.		76	Patrick, Sjt. G.	76
Morris, S.Sjt. G. L.		76	Patterson, Cpl. (A.S.S.M.) W. E.	72
— S.S.M. R. J.		72	— S.Sjt. (A.Q.M.S.) W. G.	3255
— Pte. (A.Sjt.) W.		72	Pattison, Sjt. A.	72
— C.Q.M.Sjt. W. R.		72	Payne, Sjt. (A.Q.M.S.) S. A.	72
Morton, T.Sub-Condr. H. R.		72	Peacock, Pte. (A.Sjt.) A. H.	73
Mounce, Pte. L. G.		76	Peake, Amt. Q.M.S. (A.Amt.S.M.)	
Murdoch, R.Q.M.S. R. A.		76	F. E.	† 73
Murphy, Q.M.Sjt. M.		72	Pearce, By.S.M. J.	73
— A.Engr.Clk.Sjt. M. P.		72	Pearson, S.Sjt. A.	73
Murray, Cpl. (A.Sjt.) D. R.		76	— C.Q.M.Sjt. J. H.	73
Murton, Flt.Sjt. C. W.		72	Peasgood, R.S.M. A.	73
			Peck, T.W.O. H. L.	76
Naylor, By.S.M. H. H.		72	Pedder, S.S.M. C. G.	‡ 73
Nelson, Sjt. J. G.		72	Penn, By.S.M. G. J.	73

---

*   Group Known: 1914/15 Star trio, M.S.M. and Special Reserve L.S. Medal (Awarded July 1920, Sgt. R.E., No. 236804).

†   R.A.O.C. Also D.C.M.

‡   Staff Serg. Major, R.A.S.C. An ex-soldier, who had served in the South African war, he was mobilised on the outbreak of hostilities, and proceeded to France in September, 1914. He did great service first with the ambulance, and afterwards on food supply, was promoted to Company Sergt.-Major, and then to Staff Sergt.-Major, was twice mentioned in Despatches, and was awarded the Meritorious Service Medal for his excellent work in the Field. After the Armistice he was sent, in March 1919, to Ireland, where he was still serving in 1920, having completed twenty-three

Penny, Co.S.M. A.	* 73	Quarrie, L.C. J. W.	76
— Pte. (A.Cpl.) H. T.	73
Penwarden, Co.S.M. (A.R.S.M.) J.	73	Rae, By.S.M. (A.R.S.M.) A. G.	† 73
Percivall, R.Q.M.Sjt. T. W.	73	Ramsay, Flt.Sjt. F.	73
Perrin, Sjt. H.	3255	Randall, C.Q.M.Sjt. A. G.	73
Petter, A.Sjt. E. D.	73	Randle, Cpl. (A.Sjt.) J. O.	73
Pettigrew, Sjt. T.	73	Rea, Cpl. T. W.	73
Philbrook, Q.M.Sjt. (A.S.M.) F. A.	73	Read, By.S.M. W.	73
Phillips, Sjt. (A.R.S.M.) E. J.	73	Rees, Sjt. (A.Co.S.M.) T. J.	73
Phillpot, S.Sjt. (T.Sub-Condr.) H. S.	73	— S.S.M. W. R.	73
Pick, Gnr. B.	73	Rekes, Sjt. (T.S.S.M.) H.	73
Pipe, Sjt. O.	73	Render, Dvr. H.	73
Pirie, Cpl. J.	73	Richardson, S.Q.M.Sjt. G.	73
Placey, Co.S.M. H.	73	— Sjt. J.	73
Plank, Pte. A.R.	3255	Richmond, S.M. S.	73
Pollard, Pte. (A.Cpl.) A. H.	73	Rickard, Cpl. (A.Sjt.) T. S.	73
— Sgt. W. H.	❀ 1406	Rider, Sjt. T. W.	73
Pook, C.Q.M.Sjt. F. G.	73	Ridley, Sjt. (A.Co.S.M.) A. E.	73
— Sjt. P. J.	73	— Cpl. (A.Sjt.) S. D.	3255
Poole, W.O. W.	73	Ripley, Cpl. (A.Sjt.) J.	73
Pope, Sjt. E. C.	73	Ritchie, Sjt. H.	77
Pople, Cpl. (A.Sjt.) E. W.	73	Roberts, W.O. F. C.	76
Porter, L.Cpl. (A.S.S.M.) D. G. S.	73	— S.M. F. C. (corr.)	3474
Potter, Q.M.Sjt. T. H.	73	— Sjt. J.H.	73
Pettinger, Sjt. H. H.	73	Robertson, Mech.S.M. W.	73
Powell, L.Cpl. J. H.	76	Robinson, Sjt. (A.Co.S.M.) C.	73
Prance, A.Co.S.M. R.	73	— S.Sjt. G. R.	77
Pratt, L.Cpl. (A.Sjt.) A. L.	73	Robson, L.Cpl. (A.Cpl.) J.	73
— Co.S.M. F. J.	73	— C.S.M. (T.R.S.M.) W.	73
— Sjt. L. A.	73	Rogers, Sjt. H. O.	3255
Prendergast, S.Sjt. E. P.	76	— S.Sjt. J.	3255
Preston, Sjt. (A.S.S.M.) A. N.	73	— 2nd Cpl. L. J.	73
— Sjt. W. H.	73	Roper, Sjt. A.	73
Pringle, S.S.M. J. A.	73	Rose, R.Q.M.S. H.	73
Pringle, Sjt. W.	73	— Sjt. W. R.	73
Prior, S.Sjt. H.	76	Ross, S.Sjt. A. E.	76
Pudney, Pte. (actg.Sjt.) E.	2974	— Vol. H. W.	3255
Punton, P.O. W.	73	Rowan, 1st Cl. S.S.M. T.	73
Pyne, S.Q.M.S. (T.S.S.M.) G. E.	73	Rowles, S.M. A. J.	3255

years' service in the Army. In addition to the Meritorious Service Medal, he held the Queen's South Africa Medal, the 1914 Star, and the General Service and Victory Medals. 38 Halston Street, Hulme, Manchester.

* Group known: M.M. (C.S.M., 173 Tunnelling Coy. R.E.) Queen's South Africa Medal (Cape Colony, Orange Free State, Johannesburg, L./Cpl. R.E.), King's South Africa Medal, 1914/15 Star trio (C.S.M./W.O.II), L.S. & G.C. and M.S.M. (173/Tun. Co. R.E.).

† Group known: Africa General Service Medal (Northern Nigeria 1902, Sgt. 1/Bty. N.N.R.), British War Medal (T./W.O.1 R.A.), L.S. & G.C. (Edw. VII, C.S.M. R.G.A.) and M.S.M. (27/H.A.G. R.G.A.) [Africa General Service Medal in A.O.4/1905 for service at Arghagur Jun–Nov 1902].

Rudderham, A.Sjt. W. E.	3255	Shaw, L.Cpl. A.	74
Rugg, Cpl. M. E.	76	— Cpl. L.	77
Ruhl, Farr.Sjt. H. W.	3255	Shepherd, R.Q.M.Sjt. J.	74
Russell, Cpl. B. H.	73	Shield, Cpl. (T.Sub-Condr.) S.	74
— Sjt. K. S.	76	Shinton, Sjt. S. H.	74
Ryan, S.Sjt. (T.S.S.M.) A. J.	73	Shorney, Pte. (A.Cpl.) F. W.	74
— L.Cpl. (A.Cpl.) T.	73	Sibbalds, S.Sjt. F. V. ‡	74
		Siddle, S.S.M. T. F.	74
Salter, Sjt. (T.Sub-Condr.) J.	73	Silverstone, Mech.S.Sjt. D.	74
Sample, Sjt. A. W. A. L.	73	Silvester, S.Q.M.S. (A.S.S.M.) W.	74
Samuels, C.Q.M.Sjt. (now Co.S.M.) J.	73	Simmons, Pte. (A.S.Sjt.) J. J.	74
Sandroff, Dvr. E.	73	— R.S.M. W. E.	74
Sarbutt, Mech.S.Sjt, D. W.	73	Sinclair, Cpl. A.	76
Sarginson, Sjt. R. H.	73	Slater, Sjt. J.	74
Saunders, Co.S.M. C.	73	Sleigh, Sjt. H.	74
— Sjt. C. S.	73	Smith, Sjt. A.	74
Savill, L.Cpl. (A.2nd Cpl.) W.	73	— Co.S.M. (A.S.S.M.) A.	74
Scarbrow, Q.M.Sjt. C. A.	73	— Sjt. D. R.	76
Schofield, T.M.S.M. H.	73	— Sjt. D. W.	74
Scobie, Cpl. W.	73	— By.Q.M. Sjt. F.	74
Scott, Cpl. (A.Sjt.) A.	73	— Sgt. H. ✸	2439
— S.M. C.	3255	— Pte. (A.Cpl.) H. P.	74
— Cpl. (A.Co.S.M.) J.	73	— Dvr. J.	74
Sedgwick, T.Sub-Condr. J.	73	— S.M. P. G.	3255
Selby, Condr. H. R. *	3255	— S.S.M. Sup.Clk. R.	74
Selden, Sjt. H. W.	74	— Sjt. R. A.	74
Sensier, Sqn. Cpl. Major R.	74	— L.Cpl. T.	77
Sewell, A.Cpl. J. †	74	— Sjt. W.	74
— Sqn. S.M. (T.R.S.M.) W.	74	Smoothey, Co.S.M. J.	74
Sharp, Sjt. C. J.	74	Smyth, Pte. D. ✸	1621
— Award cancelled and D.C.M.		Smyrk, A.S.M. W. J.	74
substituted	2974	Sobey, Far. Q.M.Sjt. J. C. §	74
— Sjt. J.	74	Soilleux, S.Q.M.S. (T.S.S.M.) E. N.	74
— 1st Writer, L. E.	74	Solley, R.S.M. E. E.	76
— Sjt. (A.C.Q.M.S.) R.	74	Sparling, Sjt. R. A.	74
Sharpe, Co.S.M. W. A.	74	Speller, Co.S.M. W. J.	74
Shaver, Gnr. L. A.	76	Spence, Sjt. S. C. ✸	3473

* See Leicester, *ante.* Hon. Lieut. (Asst. Comm.), I.O.D. Commissioned 1.1.19 and killed with Sgt. Mostyn, R.A. in a riot outside Kasur station, on the Ferozepore train 12 April 1919 (Amritsar Riots—see *The Times*). His group is known: Africa General Service Medal (Somaliland 1902–04, Store Sgt. I.O.D.), 1914/15 Star trio (M.I.D. oakleaf), L.S. & G.C. (Sub Cond. I.O.D.) and Lotus Reverse M.S.M. M.I.D. L.G. 1.6.16 and 30.9.18, both East Africa.

† Group known: Tibet (Gyantse, Pte. R. Fus.), 1914/15 Star (Pte.), British War and Victory Medals (Sgt.) and M.S.M. (Chinese Coy., Labour Corps).

‡ Group known in R.C.T. Museum: M.B.E. (1st type, military ribbon), M.M. (Geo. V), B.E.M. (1st type, military ribbon), 1914 Star & bar trio (M.I.D. oakleaf), Defence and War Medals, Jubilee 1935, Coronation 1937, L.S. & G.C. (Geo. V), M.S.M. (A.S.C.) and French Médaille Militaire. Major & Q.M. R.A.S.C. in W.W.II.

§ Awarded M.S.M. Annuity, 1950 (A.O.87), 4 Dragoon Guards.

Spencer, C.S.M. (A.R.S.M.) W. P.		76
Spinks, L, Cpl. A.		74
Spry, Cpl. (A.Sjt.) A. J.		74
Stafford, Sjt. (A.Co.S.M.) W. D.		74
Stagg, T.Sub-Condr. F. G.		74
Standen, Sjt. (A.S.S.M.) H.		74
Stanley, Vol. J. H.		3255
Steed, Bombr. A.S.Sjt.) C.		3255
Steer, Co.S.M. J. H.		76
Stephens, Sjt. (T.S.S.M.) W. A.		74
Stephenson, S.Q.M.S. J.		74
Stevenson, Cpl. J. S.		76
Stobbart, Pte. E. C.		3255
Stoddart, Sjt. (A.C.Q.M.Sjt.) B.		74
Stokes, Cpl. A. J.		74
Stone, Cpl. (A.Sjt.) A.		74
Stott, T.W.O. S. J.		76
Strain, Sjt. A.		74
Strange, Condr. J.	*	74
Strivens, Sjt. A. T.		74
Stroad, Sup.Clk. G. T.		74
Strutt, Q.M.Sjt. (A.S.M.) D. H.		76
Stubbs, Co.Q.M.Sjt. C. R.		76
Sutton, 2nd Cpl. (A.Cpl.) G. D.		74
Sweeting, Flt.Sjt. W. H.	†	74
Sylvester, Sjt. (A.Q.M.Sjt)		74
Tacey, 1st Cl. S.S.M. T. A.		74
Tannahill, Sjt, A.		74
Tansley, Cpl. (A.Sjt.) E. C.		74
Targett, Sup.Clk. H.		74
Taylor, R.S.M. A. H. S.		3255
— Sjt. (A.R.S.M.) C. A.		74
— Condr. F. H.		74
— Sjt. (A.Co.Q.M.Sjt.) F. W. D.		74
— S.Sjt. G. H.		76
— Pte. H. B.	✽	1406
— A.Sjt. H. D.		74
— T.S.M. (A.R.S.M.) H. W.		74
— Sjt. T.		74
— Sjt. W. L.		74
Thake, Sjt. F. W.		74

Thomas, Sjt, T.		74
— L.C. W.	✽	3473
Thomasson, Sjt. W.		74
Thompson, S.M. A.		74
— C.Q.M.Sjt. P.		74
— Cpl. W. F.B.		74
Thomson, L.Cpl. (A.Cpl.) J. McI.		74
Thornhill, A.Sjt. J.		74
Thornly, Sjt. T.		74
Thornton, Sjt. H.		3255
Thurlow, Sjt. H. C. G.		76
Tildesley, Co.S.M. R.		74
Tilt, Bombr. C. W.		74
Tippits, Pte. (A.Cpl.) A. W.		74
Tomkins, Armr. S.Sjt. A.		74
Tomlin, Q.M.Sjt. A. E.		76
Trappett, E.C.Q.M.S. (T.Supt.Clk.) W.		74
Treadaway, 2nd Cl. A.M. (A.Cpl.) F.	‡ ✽	3473
Tribe, S.Q.M.Sjt. V. B.		3255
Tripp, S.Sjt. (A.S.M.) V.		74
Trippas, Sub.Clk.S.M. M.	§	74
Tuke, S.Q.M.Sjt. C. H.		74
Turner, Sjt. (A.S.Sjt.) A. N.		74
— R.Q.M.S. F. G.		76
— A.Sjt. H.		75
— C.Q.M.Sjt. J.		75
— Co.S.M. (A.R.S.M.) J.		75
— Sjt. T. M.		76
— Sjt. W. J.		75
Tustin, Cpl. (A.Sjt.) F.		76
Umney, Cpl. (T.Sub-Condr.) V. V. J.		75
Underwood, Bomdr. (A.Sjt.) R.		75
Unger, Coy.S.M. C. E.		3255
Upton, Sjt. (A.Coy.S.M.) A. F.		3255
Utley, Sjt. (A.S.M.) Arty.Clk.) G.		75
Valentine, Sjt. A.		75
Vaudin, S.M. R. W. V.		3255
Vause, Co.S.M. C. J.		76

---

* R.A.O.C. Also M.B.E.
† Group in Moss collection: 1914/15 Star (Flight Sgt. R.F.C.), British War and Victory Medals (T./S.M. 1 R.A.F.) and M.S.M. Enlisted 27 July 1914. Overseas from 12 December, 1915. Temp. S.M. (Technical) 1 February, 1918. He came from Cirencester.
‡ R.F.C. Home Forces.
§ Group known: M.B.E. (W.O.1 R.B.), Queen's Sudan, Queen's South Africa Medal (Natal), 1914/15 Star trio (M.I.D. oakleaf), Defence and War Medals, L.S. & G.C., M.S.M. and Khedive's Sudan (Khartoum).

Venables, By.S.M. L. W.	·75	Whiston, Sjt. W.		75
Vevers, R.S.M. J.	75	White, R.Q.M.S. A. W. T.		76
Vian, R.S.M. A.	75	— Flt.Sjt. E. E.		75
Villers, Condr. A.	3255	— Q.M.Sjt. H.		75
Vincent, Pte. J.	75	— Sjt. J.		75
		— Pte. (A.Cpl.) W.		75
Waddell, L.Cpl. (A.Sjt.) W. H.	75	— Cpl. W. H. C.		75
Waddingham, Condr. T. E.	3255	Whitehorn, S.St. L. J.		75
Wager, Co.S.M. (T.S.M.) Arty.Clk.		Whitehouse, Sjt. J. W.		75
E. B.	75	Whiteley, Sjt. L.		75
Wainwright, Sjt. (T.S.M.) J.	75	Whitfield, Co.S.M. F. H.		75
Walden, S.Sjt. (T.C.S.M.) H. L.	* 77	— Gnr. G. E.	❁	3473
Walker, C.Q.M.Sjt. F. C.	75	Whitta, By.S.M. J.		76
— Amt. S.Sjt. J.	75	Wignall, Cpl. (Sjt.) W.		75
— Pte. (A.Sjt.) R. W.	75	Wilcox, S.M. Sup.Clk. W.		75
Wallace, Co.S.M. A.	❁ 3475	Wilkinson, Amt. Q.M.Sjt. J.		75
— Cpl. (A.Co.S.M.) E. E.	75	Wilkinson, S.Smith (A.Far.Sjt.) T.		75
Walmsley, Mech.S.Sjt. P.	75	— Sqn. S.M. T. C.		76
Walter, Pte. (A.Cpl.) C. E.	75	Willcockson, Cpl. W. E.		75
Walters, Sjt. J.	3255	Willcox, Sjt. (A.By.S.M.) V. C.		3255
Walthew, S.Q.M.Sjt. J.	75	Williams, S.Q.M.S. F. A.		75
Warburton, S.M. A. J.	75	— L.Cpl. (A.S.M.) G.		75
Ward, Pte. (A.Cpl.) F.	75	Willis, Sjt. (T.S.M.) W. G.		75
— S.Sjt. P. M.	3255	— Pte. (A.L.Cpl.) W. J.		75
— Cpl. W. H.	75	Willson, Amt. S.M. A. H.		75
Warden, Cpl. (A.Sjt.) F. C.	75	— Sjt. W.	† ❁	3473
Wareham, A.C.Q.M.Sjt. S. L.	75	Wilson, Sjt. J. R.		76
Waters, Pte. J.	75	— Sub-Condr. T.		75
Watson, Cpl. (A.Sjt.) A.	75	Wisdom, Q.M.Sjt. W.		75
— Sjt. T.	75	Witts, Pte. A. L.		75
— Condr. T. D.	76	Wonfor, Sjt. W.		75
Webb, Sjt (T.S.M.) H.	75	Wood, Sjt. E. J.		75
— S.S.M. N. E.	3255	— Sjt. R.		3255
Webber, S.Sjt. R.	76	— Amt. S.Sjt. T. W.		75
— Flt.Sjt. T. O.	75	Woodcock, Sjt. J.		75
Webster, C. G.	75	Woodford, 1st Cl.A.M. C. J.	‡ ❁	3473
Webster, Sjt. N. F.	75	Woods, Sjt, A.		75
Weeks, Cpl. A.	75	— Q.M.Sjt. J. A. I.		75
Weiss, S.S.M. B. G.	75	Woollard, W. A. A. F.		76
Welch, Cpl. E. C.	2974	Worsfold, R.S.M. A.		75
— T.Condr. M. C.	76	Wrigglesworth, Pte. G. H.		75
Weldon, 1st Cl. A.M. J. G.	75	Wright, Far.S.Sjt. A. A.		75
Weller, R.S.M. G. H.	·75	— Gnr. J.		75
Wells, Sjt. (A.Q.M.S.) A.	75	— Pte. J.		75
— T.S.S.M. D.	75	— Sjt. J.		75
Welsh, Sjt. H. C.	75	— Sjt. W. L. R.		75
Wheway, Q.M.Sjt. (A.S.M.) T.	75			

---

* N.Z. Army Postal Services later 2/Lieut. N.Z.E.F.
† 105 (Chinese) Lab Coy., Labour Corps (France).
‡ R.F.C. Home Forces.

Vol. II, 1918

Abbott, Sjt. H. J.	7133	Alcock, Pte. J.	7133
Abdale, Sjt. J.	7133	Alden, Pte. (A.Sjt.) F.	7133
Abethell, L.C. (A.Cpl.) C. D.	6507	— Cpl. (A.S.Sjt.) W.	7134
Aby, Farr.Sjt. B. C.	7133	Alder, By.Q.M.Sjt. G.	7134
Ackers, T.Sub-Condr. J. C.	7133	Alderton, Sjt. C. E.	7134
Ackland, Sjt. D. J.	7133	— Cpl. S. H.	7134
Adair, Cpl. K. W.	7133	Alexander, Sjt. (A.Coy.S.M.) A.	7134
Adam, Sjt. (A.S.S.M.) J.	7133	— Sjt. D. M. †	6512
Adams, R.Q.M.Sjt. A. E.	6498	— Sjt. J.	7134
— Pte. (L.C.) D.	7178	— Flt.Sjt. J. C.	6520
— Pte. (A.Cpl.) G. H.	7133	Allan, By.S.M. C. E.	7134
— Cpl. (A.Coy.S.M.) P. H.	7133	— Sjt. J.	7176
— Sjt. R. S.	6498	— Sjt. P. R.	7134
— Coy.Q.M.Sjt. T. G.	7176	Allardice, R.Q.M.Sjt. J. ‡	7134
— L.Sjt. W.	7133	Allcard, Q.M.Sjt. T. W.	7134
Adamson, Cpl. now L.Sjt. A.	7180	Allen, Co.S.M. A.	6507
Adcock, Sjt. F.	7133	— Cpl. A.	7134
Addison, Pte. (A.Sjt.) J. P.	7133	— 1st Cl. Writer, E. F.	7134
Addyman, Pte. (L.C.) A.	7133	— R.S.M. E. R.	7134
Adeney, Sjt. T. W.	7178	— Sjt. (A.Coy.S.M.) E. R.	7134
Adey, Cpl. (A.Sjt.) G. E.	7133	Allen, Spr. F.	7134
Adlam, Coy.S.M. L. W.	7133	— W.O., Cl.1. G. E.	7178
Adsetts, Sjt. L. W.	6498	— R.S.M. G. T.	7134
Agar, Sjt. T.	7133	— Sadd.Sjt. (A.Sadd.S.Sjt.) J.	7134
Aggett, Cpl. F.	7133	Allinson, Dvr. J. G.	7134
— By.Q.M.Sjt. T.	7133	Alliott, Reg.Q.M.Sjt. W.	7134
Ahern, Bombr. J.	7133	Allison, Sjt. H.	7176
Ainscough, Sjt. J. W.	7133	— Cpl. R.	7134
Ainsworth, Pte. (A.C.Q.M.Sjt) B. H.	7133	Allitt, Pte. (L.C.) J. W.	7134
Aird, T.S.M. T. C.	7133	Allsey, Coy.Q-M.Sjt. C. J.	7134
— A.Sjt. W. A.	7133	Allsopp, Sjt. M.	7134
Airlie, Sjt. A. *	6491	Allwork, R.Q.M.Sjt. B. J.	7134
Akers, L.Bombr. D. I.	7133	Ammon, S.Sjt. W. A.	7134
Alabaster, Bombr. (now T.Cpl.) D.J.	7180	Amos, Col.Sjt. J.	7134
Alcock, Cpl. (A.Coy.S.M.) H. C. W. S.	7133	— Sjt. W.	7134

* Group known: Queen's South Africa Medal (Tugela Heights, Relief of Ladysmith, Transvaal, Laing's Nek, South Africa 1901 Pte. Scottish Rifles), 1914/15 Star trio (Sgt. R. Scots. Fus.), Coronation 1911 (Sgt.), M.S.M. (200483 1/4 R.S.F.) and a Fire Brigade Medal (Firemaster 1913). M.I.D. *L.G.* 16.1.18, Allenby's Despatches. A unique Valuable Services award to the Regiment for Egypt.

† M.S.M. known: (98168 R.G.A.) a very rare pre-intervention award for Russia. Only three in this *Gazette* for Russia (although, later, many awards were made for N. Russia, Siberia, S. Russia etc.).

‡ M.S.M. annuity A.O.. 151/1937 (S. Lancs. R.)

Anderson, Coy.S.M. A.	7134	Armstead, Sjt. C.		7134
— S.Sjt. A.	7134	Armstrong, Coy.Q.M.Sjt. B.		7134
— Sjt. D.	7134	— Coy.Q.M.Sjt. H.		7134
— Coy.S.M. E.	* 7134	— F.of W.S.Sjt. J.		7134
— Sjt. (A.Coy.Q.M.Sjt.) E. W.	7134	— Cpl. (A.Sjt.) J.		7134
— Farr.Sjt. F. M.	7134	— Cpl. J. W.		7134
— Trptr. F. R.	7176	— Pte. P.		7134
— Coy.S.M. (Dr.Sjt.) G., *M.M.*	7134	— Coy.Q.M.Sjt. T. G.		7134
— Whr.S.Sjt. J.	7134	Arnall, Sjt. C. A.		7134
— Sjt. J.	7176	Arncil, L.C. R.		7134
— Sjt. J. S.	7134	Arnold, R.S.M., G. R., *D.C.M.*		7134
— T.A.M.T.S.M. R. P.	7134	— Coy.Q.M.Sjt. W. T.		7178
Andrew, Sjt. S.	7134	Artindale, Coy.S.M. A.		7134
Andrews, C.S.M. (A.R.S.M.) E.	6507	Ash, Co.S.M. E. T.		6498
— Cpl. (A.S.M.) F.	7134	— Spr. (A.Cpl.) G. S.		7134
— Pte. F.	7134	Ashbeen, Cpl. (A.Sjt.) A. W.		6520
— Coy.S.M. G.	7176	Ashbolt, Cpl. R. E.		6520
— Sjt. P.	7134	Ashburn, Cpl. A.	✿	7599
— Sjt. P. P.	7178	Ashcroft, Sjt. F.		7134
— Sjt. (A.Q.M.Sjt) W.	7134	Ashdown, Gnr. A. J.		7134
— Coy.Q.M.Sjt. W. H.	7134	Asher, R.S.M. C.		7180
— A.Bombr. (Cpl.) W. W.	7134	Ashford, L.Sjt. G.		7134
Angell, Flt.Sjt. F. T.	6520	— Mech.S.Sjt. W. C.		7134
Angwin, By.S.M. W.	7134	Ashman, Sjt. B. G.		7134
Anniss, Farr.Q.M.Sjt. R. A.	6507	— Pte. S.		7134
Ansell, Bomdr. F. R.	7134	Ashton, Spr. W.		7134
Anstey, 2nd Cpl. (A.Cpl.) E. J.	7134	— Dvr. (A.Cpl.) W. H.		7134
Anthony, 1st Cl. A.Mech.		Ashworth, Spr. H.		7134
(actg.Cpl.) H.	4413	Askham, Coy.Q.M.Sjt. A.		7134
Anwyl, Whr.S.Sjt. W.	7134	Aslatt, Sjt. H. F.		7178
Appleby, S.M. A. N.	7134	Atack, Sjt. O.		7134
Aqutter, Cpl. (A.Mech.S.M.) E.	7134	Atkins, By.S.M. W.	†	7134
Archer, Spr. T.	7134	Atkinson, T.Sub-Condr. A. H.		7134
Armistead, Pte. H.	7134	— Sjt. F.		7134
Armitage, A.Whr.Sjt. J.	7134	— R.Q.M.Sjt. J.		7134

---

* R.S.M., 16th Lancashire Fusiliers. Having previously served with the Colours, he again volunteered in November 1914, and in 1915 was sent to France. He fought with distinction at Albert, the Somme, Beaumont-Hamel, Nieuport and Passchendaele, and in the operations of 1918, and was twice wounded. He was awarded the Military Cross in August 1918 for taking charge of his platoon, and the Meritorious Service Medal for devotion to duty. He also held the 1914–15 Star and the General Service and Victory Medals. 9, Laurel Street, Broughton. Salford. Group was in the H. Y. Usher Collection: M.C. (for Damery, *L.G.* 7 November, 1918), Queen's South Africa Medal (Cape Colony, Lincolnshire Regt.), 1914/15 Star trio (Pte.–W.O.I L. Fus.) and M.S.M. (16/L. Fus.).

† 40517, B.S.M., S.A.A. Section, 29th D.A.C. Flanders, 1917–18, and Cambrai, 1917— For great devotion to duty and to the welfare of his section. On many occasions and in trying circumstances his energy and proved reliability have set a fine example and have ensured thoroughness and efficiency in the work of men under his charge. Flanders, 1918—For general good work. (Belgian Croix de Guerre).

Atkinson, S.Q.M.S. J. G.		6498	Baker, Sjt. W. (Labour Corps)	7135
— Col. Sjt. J. H.		7134	— Sjt. W. (North'd Fus.)	7135
— L.C. (A.Sjt.) J. T.		7134	— Sjt. W. H.	7135
— Coy.Q.M.Sjt. J. W.		7134	— S.Sjt. (A.Q.M.Sjt.) W. T.	7176
— Mech.S.Sjt. M.		7134	Balcombe, Bombr. H. R.	7135
Attaway, Sjt. H. W.		7134	Balderston, R.Q.M.Sjt. W. J.	7135
Attrill, F.of W.S.Sjt. A.		7135	Balding, Sjt. H. A.	6507
Attwood, Sjt. (A.By.S.M.) A. A.		7135	Baldry, Sjt. G.	7135
— Sjt. G. E.		7135	Baldwin, By.Q.M.Sjt. F. A.	7135
Audley, L.C. A.		7135	— Cpl. W. N.	6520
Augood, R.S.M. F.	*	7135	Bale, Coy, S.M. J. G.	7135
Austin, Sjt. A. J.		7135	Ball, Dvr. (L.Bombr.) J.	7135
— By.S.M. H.		7135	— Sjt. O. V.	7135
— Coy.Q.M.Sjt. R. C.		7178	— Sjt. W. H.	7178
Avery, Gnr. H. R.		6507	— S.Q-M. Sjt. W. S.	7178
Axson, Sjt. J.		7135	Ballands, Sjt. L. V.	7135
Axtill, Dvr. S. J.		7178	Balloch, Sjt. Piper. J.	7135
Aylett, T.Sub-Condr. W. F.		7135	Balsom, R.Q-M. Sjt. S. H.	7135
Aylmore, Sjt. A.		7135	Bamber, Sjt. F.	7135
Ayre, Sjt. J. A.		7135	Bamford, Dvr. E. J.	7135
Ayris, A.Sjt. H. J.		7176	Bancroft, L.C. (A.Cpl.) H. W.	7135
Ayrton, A.S.M. A.		7135	Banfield, Pte. F. W.	7176
			Banford, Cpl. F.	7135
Back, Dvr. A.		7135	Banks, Cpl. A.	6498
Bacon, Sjt. H.		7135	— Pte. E. R.	7135
Bailey, Coy.S.M. G.		7135	— Cpl. J. B.	7135
— Sjt. J.		6507	— Sjt. (A.S.S.M.) W. H.	7135
Baillie, Sjt. G. G.		7135	Bannister, L.C. H.	7135
Bain, Pte. (A.Coy.S.M.) H.		7135	Bant, Bombr. S.	7135
Baird, Sjt. E. W.		7135	Barber, Sjt. A. G.	7135
Baistow, L.C. F.		7135	— Gnr. (A.Bombr.) F.	7135
Baker, S.Sjt. C. H.		7178	— Coy.Q.M.Sjt. W. H.	7135
— temp.Sjt.Maj. C. W.	†	6520	Barbour, Sjt. T.	7135
— A.Sjt. E. C.		7135	Barclay, Sjt. A.	7135
— Coy.Q.M.Sjt. E. L.		7135	— Cpl. J. B.	7178
— Sjt. G.		6507	Bardin, F.of W.Q.M.Sjt. J. L.	7135
— Engr. Clk.Q.M.Sjt. (T.Supt.Clk.) J.		7135	Barends, L.Cpl. H. A.	6512
— Pte. (A.Sjt.) J.		7135	Barfoot, Sjt. R. S.	7135
— Cpl. S.		7135	Barham, Dvr. A. I. E.	7135
— Sjt. S. W., *M.M.*		7135	Barker, Cpl. E. ❀	5037
— R.S.M. W.		7178	— Cpl. G. R.	7135

* Group in Moss Collection: 1914/15 Star (S.S.M. 15 Huss.), British War and Victory Medals (2nd Lieut.), Defence Medal, L.S. & G.C. (Geo. V, S.S.M. Rough Rider 15 Huss.), M.S.M. (15 Hussars) Special Constabulary Long Service Medal (Geo. V, Coinage). Enlisted 1896. R.S.M. in 1914. Commissioned April 1918 Royal Fus., att. Tank Corps. Entitled to Regimental Gold Medal for Skill at Arms. Died 1963.

† No. 246 R.F.C. Enlisted 28 March, 1911 into R.E. R.A.F. M.S.M. for services in Egypt. Entitled to 1914/15 Star trio and R.A.F. L.S. & G.C. Awarded M.B.E. in 1934 and commissioned, Flying Officer, later that year. Awarded 1935 Jubilee Medal. Wing Commander 1941. Retired 1946. Died 1975 aged 84.

Barker, Mech.S.Sjt. R.	7135	Barton, Sjt. (A.S.Sjt.) W. S.	6491
— Dvr. W.	7135	Bartram, Pte. J. C.	6498
— Dvr. (A.Sjt.) W. C.	7135	— Col. Sjt. W.	6498
Barmby, S.Sjt. (A.Q.M.Sjt.) E.	7135	Bartrum, Sjt. D. W. L.	7135
Barnard, By.S.M. H,	7135	Bartter, Pte. E.	7135
Barnes, Sjt. (A.Coy.Q.M.Sjt) A.	7135	Baseley, S.Sjt. (A.S.M.) F.	7135
Barnes, Coy.S.M. F. S.	7178	Basket, A.Cpl. W. R.	7135
— Pte. H. E.	7135	Bass, M.F. of W.S.M. A. W. H. D.	7135
— L.C. J. W.	7135	— Coy.Q.M.Sjt. E. J.	7135
Barnett, Spr. B.	7135	Bassett, Coy.Q.M.Sjt.	
— Flt.Sjt. D.	6520	(A.R.Q.M.Sjt.) J.	7135
— Cpl. H. F.	7176	Batchelor, Cpl. A. W.	7135
— Dvr. T.	7135	Batchelor, Coy.S.M. J. *	7135
— Sjt. W.	7135	Bateman, T.Sub-Condr. B. †	7136
Barney, L.C. (A.Sjt.) H.	7135	Bates, Q.M.Sjt. T. N. B.	7136
Barons, Sjt. G. L.	7135	Bath, Sjt. (A.R.S.M.) G.	7136
Barr, Sjt. A.	7176	Batho, C.S.M. C. H.	6498
— Pte. A. B.	6507	Batley, B.S.M. W.	6507
— Cpl. W.	7135	Battersby, Sjt. C. H.	7136
Barrett, Sjt. A.	7135	Battson, Sjt. H.	6498
— Cpl. L. W.	7135	Baty, Pte. (A.Cpl.) C.	7136
Barrie, R.Q.M.Sjt. R.	7135	Baughan, Sjt. W. A.	7136
Barry, Sjt. G.	7135	Baverstock, C.Q.M.Sjt. E.	6507
— Sjt. (A.Coy.S.M.) J.	7135	Bawden, L.C. (A.S.Q.M.Sjt) T. M.	7136
— Cpl. J. T.	6498	Bax, Coy.Q.M.Sjt. W. M.	7136
Bartholomew, S.Sjt. (A.S.S.M.)		Baxter, Cpl. (A.S.Sjt.) C. J.	7136
W. A. B.	7135	— Coy.Q.M.Sjt. G. L.	7136
Bartlett, Gnr. (L.Bombr.) A.	7135	— Sjt. J.	7136
— Coy.Q.M.Sjt. F.	7135	Bayes, Coy.S.M. (Troop S.M.) S. H. ‡	7136
— By.S.M. K. A. W.	6498	Bayley, Sjt. F. J.	7136
Barton, Sjt. A.	6498	— Sjt. R. A.	7136

---

* Group known: British South Africa Co. Medal (for Rhodesia, No. 43 R.E.), Queen's South Africa Medal (Cape Colony, Orange Free State, Transvaal), King's South Africa Medal, L.S. & G.C. (Edw. VII) and M.S.M. (R.E.) (W.W.I medals missing).

† Group was in McInnes collection. Africa General Service Medal (Somaliland 1902–04, 5069 Pte. A.O.C.), 1914 Star (Sgt. A.O.C.), British War and Victory Medals (M.I.D. oakleaf, T./W.O.1 R.A.O.C.), L.S. & G.C. (Geo. V, W.O. R.A.O.C.) and M.S.M. (5–5069 A.O.C.). M.I.D. as S.Q.M.S. (T./Sub Cond.) 10 July 1919. From New Southgate to pension 3 August 1925. Africa General Service Medal rare to A.O.C.: 4 Officers, 2 Conductors, 17 N.C.O.s and 11 Ptes.

‡ Group in Moss collection:— M.B.E. (1st type Military, on first ribbon), 1914/15 Star trio (T./W.O. Class 1 R.E.), L.S. & G.C. (Edw. VII, C.S.M. R.E.), M.S.M., Belgian Order of Léopold, Belgian Croix de Guerre. 26841 Sapper Bayes enlisted into the Royal Engineers in 1892 and was discharged in 1913 with 21 years service and a L.S. & G.C. Recalled to the Colours in 1914 as W.O.1 No. 40648, assigned to 64th Field Coy., part of 9th (Scottish) Division. They embarked for Boulogne in May, 1915 at Folkestone. From there to St. Omer, to Bailleul (18 May), Armentières (26 May) and Festubert (26 June). He participated in the Battle of Loos that September. Action at Poelcappele came next in October and two days later on the 12th they were thrown into the Battle of Passchendaele. He was promoted to

Bayliss, Pte. (A.Cpl.) R. R.	7136	Bell, T.Suptg.Clk. A. J.	7136
— Sjt. Y.	7136	— L.Sjt. E. J.	7136
Baynes, Engr.Clk.Sjt. J. F.	7136	— Sjt. G.	7178
Beach, Pte. (A.S.Sjt.) F.	7136	— Mech.S.Sjt. R. F.	7136
Beadle, Cpl. (T.Sjt.) W. H. D.	7178	— Sjt. W.	7136
Beagley, Pte. G.	7136	Bellamy, S.Q.M.Sjt. G.	7136
Beagley, L.C. J.	7136	Bellgowan, Sjt. G.	7176
Beal, S.Sjt. C. W.	7136	Belson, Cpl. S.	7136
— Dvr. J. F.	7178	Benallick, R.Q.M.Sjt. E. J.	7136
Beale, Supt.Clk. J. H.	7136	Benfield, By.S.M. H. C.	7136
Beamish, Cpl. (A.Sjt.) E.	7136	Benion, L.C. J.	7136
Bean, Coy.S.M. E.	7136	Bennet, Sjt, J. F.	7136
— Sjt. W.	7136	— Sjt. T. P.	7136
Beard, Cpl. (A.Sjt.) W.	7136	Bennett, Sjt. A.	7136
— Sjt. E. A.	4413	Bennett, Pte. A.	7176
Beastall, Coy.S.M. J.	7136	— Col.Sjt. (A./S./M.)	7136
Beaton, Cpl. (C.Q.M.Sjt.) H. S.	6498	— Sjt. A. E.	7136
— Sjt. M.	7136	— Sjt. W.	7136
Beattie, R.Q.M.Sjt. A.	7136	Benson, Sjt. A.	7136
Beaumont, Sjt. G.	7176	— Sjt. D. M.	7178
Beavon, Cpl. W.	7178	— Sjt. (T./S.M.) J. W.	6520
Beck, C.Q.M.Sjt. (T.R.S.M.) A. B.	6507	Bentley, T./Sjt.Maj. J. F.	6520
— A.Sjt. C. F.	7136	— Cpl. W.	7136
— Coy.Q.M.Sjt. J. H.	7136	Berg, A./Sub-Condr. L.	7136
Beckett, R.Q.M.Sjt. N. W.	7136	Berry, Sjt. F.	7136
Bedford, Sjt. (A.S.Q.M.Sjt.) B.	7136	— Coy.Q.M.Sjt. J. T.	7136
Beebee, Gnr. R. R.	7176	— Sjt. (Arty.Clk.) T. A. S.	6498
Beech, Sjt. S.	7136	— Sjt. W. P.	7136
Beechey, Coy.Q.M.Sjt. S. F.	7136	Bessell, Sjt. P. V.	6498
Beedham, Sjt. H.	7136	Best, S./Sjt. (Amt.Q.M.Sjt.) P.	7136
Beedle, 2nd Cpl. (A.Sjt.) W. T. K.	6491	Betts, Pte. (A./Sjt.) G.	7136
Beere, T.Sub-Condr. F. W. H.	7136	Bevan, Spr. (A./2nd Cpl.) T. G.	7136
Beeson, Sjt. H. F., *M.M.*	7136	Bewick, Pte. (A./Sjt.) W. D.	7136
Beevers, Sjt. W.	7136	Bicker, T./Cpl. O. R.	7178
Behar Pte. A.	7136	Bickerton, Dvr. T.	7136
Belben, Sjt. (A.S.Q.M.Sjt.) L. H.	6507	Bickley, Sjt. (A./R.Q.M.Sjt.) W.	7136
Belcher, Cpl. A. A.	7136	Bigg, Supt.Clk. R. W. S.	7136
— R.S.M, B.	7136	Biggs, T./Sjt.Maj. J. F.	6520
— Coy.S.M. C. L.	7136	— Sjt. S. F.	7136
— Sjt. G. S.	7136	Billing, T./S.M. B. *	6520
Bell, L.C. A. E.	7136	— S./S.M. J.	7136

R.S.M. of 14th Division R.E. just as the Germans were planning their Spring offensive on the Somme in 1918. He was tasked with the blowing up of a major ammunition dump located at Montescourt which was directly in the path of the advancing Germans. The final cavalry rearguard crossed the St. Quentin Canal on 23 March and the line stabilised there and Bayes was relieved. He fought at Ypres in September and Courtrai in October before his war ended. He was discharged early in 1919 for the second time.

* R.F.C. No. 232. Enlisted June 1908 into R.E. As Pte. 6 Sqn. earned 1914 Star. R.A.F. M.S.M. for services in France. Died in 1919.

Bilson, Cpl.(A./Sjt.) J.	7136	Blakebrough, Sjt. T.	7137
Bilton, T./S./M. J.	7136	Blanchard, Spr.(A./L./C.) L. M.	7137
Bing, Spr. (A./L./C.) S. H.	7136	Blatch, Coy.S./M. T. B.	7137
Bingham, Cpl.(A./Sjt.) F. M.	7136	Blenkinsop, Coy.Q.M.Sjt. H.	7137
Bingham, Coy.S./M. S.	7136	Bliss, L./Cpl. W. F.	7137
Bingle, Sjt. E.	7136	Blond, Coy.S./M. P. T. M. C.	7137
Binnington, Sjt. T. C.	7136	Blood, Supt.Clk. W. H.	7137
Birch, Coy.S./M. A.	* 7136	Bloom, Sjt. W. G.	7137
— Sjt. F. N.	7136	— Sjt. W. G.	6491
— Sjt. J. T.	7136	Blower, S.Q.M.Sjt. F. D.	7137
Birchall, Gnr.(L./Bombr.) R.	7136	— Cpl. J.	7137
Bird, Sjt. A. H.	7136	Blowman, By.S./M. J.	7137
— Sjt. H. E.	7137	Blows, Q.M.Sjt. G.	7137
— Sjt. J.	7137	Blyth, R.Q.M.Sjt. G.	7137
— L./C. T.	7137	Boags, Sjt. J.	7137
— T./S./S./M. W. A.	7137	Board, Amt.S./Sjt. E. F.	7137
— Pte.(A./Cpl.) W. P.	7137	— L./C. (A./Cpl.) W.	7137
Birkett, Sjt. L. D.	7137	— A./Coy.S./M. W. A.	7137
Birks, Sjt. S.	6498	Boddington, Sjt. F. C.	7137
Birnie, Sjt. J.	7137	Bodinnar, Sjt.(A./Coy.S./M.) J.	7137
Bishop, Sjt. A. T.	7137	Bodle, Sjt. (A./Sub-Condr.) G. F.	6507
— Sjt. D.	7137	Bolam, Mech.S./Sjt. P. F.	7137
— F. C.	7137	Bolan, A./Coy.S./M. R.	7137
Black, Coy.Q.M.Sjt. A.	7137	— Spr. W.	7137
— W.O., Cl.1. G.	7178	Bolton, R.Q.M.S. A. H.	6498
— Pte. (L./C.) G. S.	7137	Bond, Sjt. D. W.	7137
— Pte. (L./C.) J. C.	7178	— Pte. E.	7137
— Cpl. T.	† 7180	Bone, R.Q.M.Sjt. A. S.	7137
— Pte. (A./Sjt.) W.	6498	Bonnard, Cpl. P. H.	6507
Blackburn, Coy.Q.M.Sjt. W.	7137	Bonnett, Flt.Sjt. S. F.	6520
Blackeby, Sjt. W.	7137	Boon, Coy.S./M. H. B.	7137
Blackett, Sjt. R.	7137	Booth, Col.Sjt.(A./S.S./M.) A.	7137
Blackford, Pte. H.	6498	— Sjt. L.	7137
Blackie, Pte.(A./Sjt.) J. J.	7137	— Sjt. R. A.	7137
Blackman, By.S./M. G.	7137	— Gnr. W.	7137
Blain, Coy.S./M./A. J.	7178	Border, Cpl.(A./Sjt.) R. J.	6507
Blair, Q.M.Sjt. T. A.	7178	Borer, Condr., E. G.	7137
— Sjt. W. A.	7178	Borman, C.S.M. F.	6498
Blake, Cpl. (A./Sjt.) E. W.	7137	Borrett, Gnr. H. A.	7137
— Cpl.(A./Coy.Q.M.Sjt.) H. A. W.	7137	Borrows, Sjt.(A./Coy.S./M.) J. E.	7137
— Sjt. W.	7137	Boshier, M.S.Sjt. T. G.	7137

* Born 1878, enlisted Gren. Gds. Group known: Queen's Sudan Medal, Queen's South Africa Medal (Orange Free State, South Africa 1901, South Africa 1902 Cpl), 1914 Star & bar (Sgt.), British War and Victory Medals (W.O.II, M.I.D. oakleaf), M.S.M. (Gren. Gds.), Khedive's Sudan Medal (Khartoum). Served at Mons, Maine, Aisne, Neuve Chapelle, Cambrai with Gren. Gds. Demobilised 1919.

† 12/4137 Sergeant 1/Auckland Regt. D.C.M. *L.G.* 25 June 1918, for the capture of prisoners and M.G.s at Mailly Maillet, 25 March, 1918. Born Opotiki N.Z. 1892. Embarked April 1916, wounded 29 April and 1 October 1918. Re-enlisted July 1942 as 2/Lieut. Home Guard.

Bostock, By.S.M. A.	6507	Bramhall, Sjt.(A./Coy.S./M.) W.		7137
Boswell, Pte.(A./Sjt.) W. G.	7137	Bramley, Coy.S./M. J. *D.C.M.*		7137
Bosworth, Coy.S./M. E.	7137	Brammer, L./C.(A./Sjt.) E.		6491
Botterill, Sjt. H. B.	7137	Bramwell, Cpl.(A./Sjt.) F. S.		7137
Boulden, Cpl. B. R.	7137	Brandie, Pte. (L./C.) J.		7137
Boundy, S./Sjt. H. H.	7180	Brandon, Coy.S./M. H.	*	7137
Bourke, Cpl. A.	7137	— Sjt. J. T.		7137
— Pte.(Cpl.) C. J.	7137	Brannan, Pte. F.	† ❀	4393
Bourne, Dvr.(A./Coy.S./M.) W. J.	7137	Brannon, Pte. T.		7137
Bowater, Sjt. G. H.	6520	Branscombe, Sjt. A. E.		6507
Bowden, S./Sjt. R. J.	7178	Brasington, Sjt. R. E.		7137
Bowers, T./S./M. H. C.	7137	Bray, S./Sjt. B. R.		7180
— R.Q.M.Sjt. H. J.	7178	— Pte.(A./S.Sjt.) B. W.		7138
Bowles, By.S./M. S. C.	7137	— Gnr. F. C.		7138
Bowley, Coy.S./M. P. R.	7178	— Cpl. W.		6498
Bowling, L./C.(A./2nd Cpl.) J.	7137	Brazier, Sjt. A. V.		6498
Bowron, Sjt. A.	7137	Brearley, Bombr. W.		7138
Bowtell, Bomdr. L. D.	7178	Bremner, Cpl. J.		7178
Box, Pte. G. E.	6507	Brennan, Pte. A.	❀	4393
— Sjt. H.	7137	— R./S./M. C.		7138
Boxall, S./S./M. A. E.	7137	— Sjt. T		7138
— S./Sjt. F. G.	7137	Brenand, Sjt. W.		6498
Boyce, Pte.(A./Q.M.Sjt.) C. B.	7137	Brett, Bombr. G. F.		7138
— Coy.Q.M.Sjt. G.	7137	— Sjt. T.		7178
Boyd, Cpl.(A./Sjt.) J.	7137	— Pte. W.		7176
— Sjt. M. C.	7176	Brewer, Sjt. R.		7138
Boyle, Coy.Q.M.Sjt.(T./R.Q.M.Sjt.) J.	7178	Brice, Sjt. J. A.		7176
Boylen, Sjt. P.	7137	— Bombr. W. S.		7138
Boyles, Coy. S./M.(A./R.S./M.) F.	7137	Briden, Sjt. J.		7138
Bratant, S./Sjt. L. L. P.	6492	Bridle, Gnr. A.		7176
Bradfield, A./Coy.S./M. W.	7137	Bridge, Cpl. P. N.		7138
Bradford, Pte. H. J.	6491	Bridges, Pte. W. A.		7138
Bradley, Sjt. A. H.	7137	Briggs, Cpl. C. H.		7178
— Sjt. E. J.	7178	— Sjt. E. C.		7138
— Pte. F. G.	6498	Brindle, L./Bombr. W.		7138
— L./C.(A./Sjt.) J. H.	7137	Brindley, Sjt. C. W.		7178
— Armr.Q.M.Sjt. S. C.	7137	Bristow, Sjt.(T./S./S./M.) J.		7138
Bradshaw, C.Q.M.S. A.	6498	— Sjt. W. E.		7138
Bradwell, Sjt.Maj. W. A.	4413	Britnell, 2nd Cpl.(A./Cpl.) F. W.		7138
Braid, Cpl. F.	7137	Britten, Cpl. E. S.		6498
Brain, A./Cpl. H. J.	7137	Britton, Coy.S./M. H.		7138
Braithwaite, Bombr. W.	7137	Brockbank, Sjt. R. S.		7138

* Group known: D.C.M. (12/Lond R. C.S.M.), *L.G.* 16 January 1919 for Happy Valley, Bray-sur-Somme, 24 August, 1918), 1914/15 Star (Sjt.), British War and Victory Medals (W.O.II), M.S.M. (2/12 Lond. Regt.), Territorial Force Efficiency Medal (Geo. V) and Spec. Const. Long Service (Geo. V, coinage head, Harry Brandon).

† M.S.M. known: 10176 104 Coy. M.G.C. France. Awarded for the unloading of ammunition from a burning railway train shortly after the battle of Arras in 1917. He was wounded in June 1917 and April 1918 and previously served with Yorks. and Lancs. Regt.

Brockett, Sjt. E.	7178	Brown, Coy.S./M. J.	7138
Brocklehurst, Cpl. W	6498	— Pte. J. B.	7138
Brodrick, Bombr.(A./S./M.) P.	7138	— Pte. J. C.	7138
Brogan, L./C. P.	7138	— Sjt. J. D.	6498
Bromham, Sjt. F. E.	7138	— Pte. J. H.	7138
Bromley, Pte.(A./Cpl.) F.	7138	— Sjt.(A./Q.M.Sjt.) J. T.	7138
— Sjt. W. G.	7138	— Q.M.Sjt. L. W.	7138
Brook, Sjt. H.	7138	— By.S./M. M.	7138
Brooker, Cpl. A.	* 6498	— Cpl.(A./Sjt.) P.	7138
Brooks, Pte. A.	7138	— Pte. R.	7138
— Pte.(A./Cpr.) A. J.	6491	— Pte. W.	7138
Brooksbank, Cpl.(L./Sjt.) A.	7178	— Pte.(A./Sjt.) W. D.	7138
Broom, Cpl. R. W.	6520	— Sjt. W. H.	6498
Broomfield, Pte. W. J. S.	7178	Browne, Sjt. W.	7138
Brothwell, Sjt. J. T.	7138	Brownhill, S.Q.M.Sjt. W. R.	7178
Brough, Pte. A.	7138	Browning, R.S./M. F. G.	7138
Broughton, T./Sub.Condr. J. D.	7138	— Sjt. J.	6507
— Cpl.(A./Sjt.) T. W.	7138	Brownlee, By.S./M. W.	7138
Brown, L./C.(A./2nd Cpl.) A. C.	7138	Bruce, Cpl. A. E.	7138
— S./Sjt.(T./S./M.) A. E.	7138	— S./S./M. H. T.	7138
— Pte. A. E.	7138	— Flt. Sjt. R. C.	6520
— Pte.(A./S./Sjt.) A. E.	6507	— Sjt. R. G.	† 6492
— Pte. C. H.	7138	Bryan, Spr. J. E.	7138
— Pte. C. T.	7138	— Cpl. (A./Sjt.) W. H.	7138
— Sjt.(A./Q.M.Sjt.) E. J.	7138	Bryant, 1st A.M. G. E.	6520
— Armr.S./Sjt. F. C.	7138	— Dvr. H.	7138
— Sjt. F. F.	7138	— Sjt. W.	7138
— L./C. F. R.	7138	Bryden, Coy.Q.M.Sjt. W. M.	7138
— Coy.S./M. G. E.	7138	Brydson, Spr. J.	7138
— Coy.Q.M.Sjt. G. S.	7138	Buchan, Pte. J.	. 7138
— Cpl.(A./Sjt.) H.	7138	Buchanan, Pte. H.	7138
— Pte.(A./Sjt.) H. D.	7176	Buckey, Sjt. A.	6498
— Cpl. H. T.	6520	Buckingham, Pte. H.	7138
— Sjt. J.	7138	— Sjt. W. J.	6507

* Group known: D.C.M. (T14/A Bde. R.H.A.) British War and Victory Medals (Sjt. R.A.) and M.S.M. (T Bty. R.H.A. for Italy). (D.C.M. *L.G.* 17 April 1918 and 26 June 1918, also for Italy).

† Apart from the issue of 13 Lotus Reverse M.S.M.s to Senior N.C.O.s in Native Regiments who had European names (probably Anglo-Indians), the Kaiser-i-Hind M.S.M. was also issued in a very limited number of cases to European in the Indian Army. Two gazettings have been traced from the three groups found which contain this variety. The first recipient known is Sgt. R. G. Bruce, 1914/15 Star (No. 985 Sgt. C.M.S.C. I.U.L), 1914/15 Star (Pte./A./Sgt. 985 R. High.), British War and Victory Medals (No. 985 Sgt. R.H.), Indian Type M.S.M. (Engraved Sergt. I.U. List). (*L.G.* 3.6.18, Valuable Services, Egypt). This group is in the McInnes collection. Two other I.A. N.C.O.'s were in this *L.G.* and all three are listed in '*Palestine News*' 13 June 1918 as M.S.M.'s in Egyptian Expeditionary Force and all three are probably I.A. type M.S.M.'s. The other two are S./Sgt. (Sup'y. Sub Condr.) P. E. Hartnoll I.O.D. and S./Sgt. G. Lawrence I.M.L. See also *L.G.* 13 March, 1918 S./Sgt. O. H. Leicester and Conductor H. R. Selby.

Buckland, Sjt. C.	7138	Burnell, Pte. A.	7139
— C.Q.M.Sjt. W.	6507	— Sjt. G. R.	6498
Buckle, Coy.Q.M.Sjt. E. W.	7138	Burnet, C.Q.M.S. H. D.	6498
Buckley, Q.M.Sjt. S.	7138	Burnett, temp. Sjt.Maj. B. C.	6520
Buckmaster, 2nd Cpl.(A./Cpl.)		Burnett, Sjt. W.	7139
W. T. J.	7138	— Cpl. W.	6508
Budd, By.Q.M.Sjt. J.	7138	— Bomdr. W.	7139
Bull, Sjt. F.	7176	Burniston, Sjt. R. A.	7139
— Pte. F.	7138	Burns, Coy.S./M. J.	7139
— S./Sjt. H. J.	7178	— W.O. Cl.1, J. D.	7178
— Sjt. P.	7138	— Pte. J. J.	7176
— Dvr. W. W.	7138	Burnside, A./S./Sjt. W. B.	7176
Bullen, E.C.Cpl.(A./E.C.Sjt.) P. E.	7138	Burr, Sjt.(A/Sqdn.S./M.) A.	7139
Bullock, Sjt. E. (M.G.C.)	7138	Burnell, Sjt. G. E.	6508
— Sjt. E. (Durh.L.I.)	7138	— Sjt. W. A.	7176
— T./Mech.S./M. H. W.	7138	— Pte.A./Sjt. W. F.	7176
Bundy, By.S./M. F. G.	7138	Burrill, Bomdr. J.	7139
Bunn, Sjt. R.	7178	Burrows, Sjt. F.	* 7139
Bunnett, S./Sjt. E. J.	7138	— Q.M.Sjt.(T./S./M.) F. L.	7139
Bunt, Sjt. A.	7138	Burt, Sjt. A.	7139
Bunting, Pte.(A./Sjt.) W. J.	7138	— Coy. S.M.	7139
Bunyan, Sjt. G. F. V.	7138	Burton, Cpl.(A./S.Q.M.Sjt.) E.	7139
Burchall, Cpl. E. A.	7176	— C.Q.M.Sjt.(A./R.Q.M.S.) J.	7139
Burden, Q.M.Sjt. A W.	7138	— Pte. R. H.	7139
— By.S./M. L.	6507	— Spr. R. J.	7180
Burdett, Sjt. J.	7176	Bury, Sjt. F. C.	7178
Burdet, Sjt. S.	7178	Busfield, Sjt. M.	6498
Burford, R.Q.M.S. J. J.	6498	Bush, Coy.S./M. T. A.	7139
Burgess, 2nd Cpl.(A./Cpl.) A. E.	7138	Bushell, Sjt.(A./S./M.) A. W.	7139
— 2nd Cpl.(A./Sjt.) F.	7138	Butcher, Sjt. J.	7139
— Farr.Q.M.Sjt. J.	7138	— Cpl. J.	7139
— Pte. R. J.	7138	— Cpl.(A.C.Q.M.S.) N. A.	❀ 4393
— By.Q.M.Sjt. R. W.	7139	— Sjt. W.	7139
— Coy.Q.M.Sjt.(T./Mech.S./M.) S.	7139	Butler, Coy.Q.M.Sjt. C.	7139
— Coy. S./M. W.	7139	— S./S.M. C.	7139
Burgham, Cpl. W.	7139	— S./Sjt. I. R.	7139
Burke, Sjt. J.	7139	— By.S./M. J. W.	7139
— A./Coy.S./M.Inst. T. W.	7139	— Gnr. M.	7139
— Sjt. V.	7176	— R.S.M. W.	† 6508
— Sjt. W.	7139	Butt, Pte. (L./C.) S. J.	7178
Burkitt, Pte.(L./C.) G.	7178	Butterfield, Cpl. H. D.	7176
Burkmar, Sjt.(A./Bde.Q.M.S.) G.	7139	Butters, C.Q.M.S. W. J.	6508
Burley, Pte. F. H. R.	7139	Butterworth, W.O., Cl. 1 D. C.	7178
Burman, 1st A.M. H.	6520	Button, Cpl.(A./Sjt.) J. J.	7138

* Grenadier Guards. Later Sir Frederick John Burrows, G.C.S.I. (1948), G.C.I.E. (1945), died 1973. Born 1887; married Dora Beatrice (Kaisar-i-Hind Gold Medal). Governor of Bengal 1946–47. D.L. and J.P., Herefordshire.

† 9/S. Lancs. Regt. For Salonika. Group known: Queen's South Africa Medal (Cape Colony, Orange Free State, South Africa 1901, Cpl. 3/S.L.R.), British War and Victory Medals (M.I.D. oakleaf, T./W.O. Cl. 1), M.S.M. and French Medal of Honour.

Buttsworth, S.Q.M.Sjt. C. J.	7178	Cannon, C.S.M. A. W.		6498
Byrne, Sjt. D.	7178	Cant, S.S.M. G. W.		7139
— By.S./M. J. T.	7139	Cantrell, Cpl. A.		7139
— Sub-Comdr. P. A.	7139	Card, Coy.Q.M.Sjt. G.		7139
		— Coy.Q.M.Sjt. R. F.		7139
Cackett, Sjt.(A./Q.M.Sjt.) C., *MM.*	7139	Carden, T./S.M. C. S.	*	6520
Caesar, Sjt. G., *MM.*	7139	Careless, Spr.(A./Sjt.) J. H.		7139
Cahill, Coy.Q.M.Sjt.(A./		Carew, R./S/M. J., *M.C.*	†	7139
Bde.Q.M.Sjt.) W.	7139	Carey, T./S./M.(Arty.Clk.) W. J.		7139
Cairns, Sjt. C. H.	7178	Carlick, Sjt.(A./S.S.M.) C.		7139
— Pte.(A./Cpl.) H.	7139	Carlin, Cpl.(A./L./Sjt.) J.		6508
— Sjt. J.	7139	Carmen, Sjt. J.		6508
Calder, Coy.Q.M.Sjt. J.	7139	Carmichael, Coy.Q.M.Sjt. R. D.		7139
— Sjt. J.	7176	Carnegie, Cpl.(A./S.Q.M.Sjt.) D.		6491
Callander, Pte. C.	7178	Carnell, Cpl. J. H.		7139
Callaway, Sjt. C. R.	7139	Carpenter, Sjt. G.		7139
Callister, Sjt. R. J.	7139	— Cpl. G. W.		6508
Callow, Sjt. F. W., *MM.*	7139	— Farr.S./Sjt. J.		7139
Callum, Sjt. R.	7176	Carr, Gnr. J.		7139
Cameron, Pte.(L./C.) I.	7139	— Sjt.(A./S./S./M.) R. W.		7139
— A./S./Sjt. J. C.	7180	— Sjt. S.		7139
— Sjt. S.	7139	Carrington, temp.Sjt.Maj. H.	‡	5420
Campbell, Farr.Q.M.Sjt. A.	7139	— Pte. J. W.		7139
— R.Q.M.Sjt. A. S.	7139	Carrol, Coy.S./M. M.		7139
— L./C. D.	7139	— Sjt. P. J.		7139
— Sjt. E. I.	7139	Carson, Cpl. J.		7139
— Sjt.(A.By.Q.M.Sjt.) H., *MM.*	7139	Carter, Sjt. A. F.		7139
— Sjt. J.	7176	— R./S./M. A. L. L.		7139
— Sjt J.	7139	— Coy.S./M. H. A.		7139
— Sjt. J. H.	7139	— Coy.Q.M.Sjt. R. J.		7140
— Sjt. N.	7139	Cartledge, Sjt. H. W.		7178
— Pte. S.	7139	Cartwright, Sjt. E.		7140
— Sjt. T.	7139	— Cpl. R. H.		7140
— S./M. W.	7139	— Cpl. T. B.		7140
Campey, Sjt. G. H.	7178	Caselton, T./Sub-Condr. E. J.		7140
Candler, Sjt. J. B.	6508	Casely, Sjt.(A./By.S./M.) J.		7140
Canler, Coy.S./M.(A./R./S./M.)		Casey, Cpl.(L./Sjt.) J.		7140
R., *D.C.M.*	7139	Cass, A./By.S./M. A.	§	7140
Canning, S./M. A.	7139	Cassidy, R.Q.M.Sjt. H. J.		7178

---

* No. 90 R.F.C. Enlisted June 1908 into Grenadier Guards. 1914 Star earned with No. 2 Squadron from 12 August 1914. R.A.F. M.S.M. for services in Italy. R.A.F. L.S. & G.C. in 1926 having reverted to Flight Sergeant.

† Group known: M.C., Queen's South Africa Medal (Cape Colony, Wittebergen, Belfast) King's South Africa Medal (Cpl. R.I.Regt), 1914/15 Star (R.S.M.) British War and Victory Medals (W.O. 1), L.S. & G.C. (Garr. S.M.) M.S.M. (R.I.Regt.). M.C. L.G. 27.7.16

‡ No. 629 R.F.C. Enlisted March, 1914. 1914 Star & bar earned with No. 4 Sqn. in France from 12 August. R.A.F. M.S.M. for services in France.

§ Group known: 1914 Star & bar (Bombr. R.G.A.), British War and Victory Medals (B.Q.M.S. R.A.), 1939/45 Star, Defence and War Medals. L.S. & G.C. (Geo. V,

Casson, Sjt. J.	6498	Chase, Sjt. W.	7176
Castledene, Sjt. H.	7140	Chaston, S./Sjt. C. H.	7140
Catchpole, Flt. Sjt. F. W. C.	6420	— Cpl. H.	7140
Cattell, Cpl.(L./Sjt.) A. F.	6498	Chatfield, T./S./M. C.	7140
Cattley, S./Sjt.(A./S./M.) H. V.	7140	Chattin, Sjt. E.	7140
Cavan, Spr. J. W.	6498	Cheasley, Gnr. E. G.	7140
Cave, Sjt. G.	7140	Chelin, Pte. F.	7140
— Cpl. R. S.	7140	Chennells, L./C. A. J.	7140
Cawthorn, Sjt. W.	7140	Chessell, W.O.,Cl.1, D. L.	7178
Cawthorne, Coy. Q.M.Sjt. E. A.	7140	Chester, R.Q.M.Sjt. C. S.	7140
Challice, Q.M.Sjt. S.	7140	Chetland, By.Q.M.Sjt. A.	7140
Challoner, Amt.S./Sjt.		Chick, C.Q.M.Sjt. J. H.	7140
(A./Amt.S.M.) F. J.	6508	Child, R./Q.M.Sjt. C. H.	7180
— Sjt.(A./Coy.S./M.) W.	7140	Childs, Cpl.(A./S.Sjt.) C.	7140
Chalmers, Sjt. C.	7140	— Sjt. F. J. T.	* 7140
— R.Q.M.Sjt. J.	7140	Chilton, Sjt. C.	6508
Chaloner, Sjt. (A./Coy.Q.M.Sjt.) T.	7140	Chinn, L./C. J. J.	❀ 4393
Chamberlain, Sjt. W.	7140	Chisnell, L./Bomdr. H. G.	7140
Chambers, Sjt. A., *MM*	7140	Chittel, Cpl. J. W.	7140
— By.S./M. L. S.	7140	Chitty, Sjt. L. M.	7176
Champion, Sjt. F. E.	7140	Choat, Cpl. K.	7178
Chance, C.Q.M.S. T. J.	6508	Christie, Condr. A.	7140
Chandler, Sjt. H. A. C.	7140	— Coy.Q.M.Sjt. A.	7140
— Sjt. H. J.	7140	— S./Sjt. K. G.	7176
— Sjt.(A./S.S./M.) W.	7140	— Sjt. P.	7140
Channon, Sjt. O. B.	7178	Christon, Sjt. C. F.	7140
Chaplin, Coy.Q.M.Sjt.(A./R./S./M.) T.	7140	Christopher, Dvr. F.	6498
Chapman, Sjt. A. E.	7140	— Sjt. R.	7140
— A./Cpl. B.	7140	Clare, Coy.S./M. H.	7140
— Sjt. F.	7140	Clark, Pte. (A./Sjt.) A.	7140
— Pte.(A/Cpl.) H. P. A.	7140	— Sjt. A.E.	7140
— Sjt. J.	7178	— Coy.S./M. (A./R.S./M.) E.	7140
— Sjt. (A./Bde.Q.M.Sjt.) L. J.	7140	— Sjt. E. M.	7140
— Coy.S./M. S.	7140	— Gnr. {L./Bombr.) F. J.	❀ 5037
— Sjt. S.	7140	— A./Cpl. G.	7140
— L./C. W.	7140	— Sjt. (A./Coy.S./M.) H. W.	7140
— Sjt. (A./C.S./M.) W.	7140	— Fitt.S./Sjt. J.	7140
— Sjt. W. G.	7176	— Coy.S./M. J. E.	7178
Charles, Sjt. R. E.	7178	— Cpl. J. T.	7140
Charlton, T./R./S./M. A.	7140	— Sjt. R. M.	7140
— Pte. (A./Cpl.) G. B.	7140	— Q.M.Sjt. T. W.	7140
— Q.M.Sjt.L.	7140	— R.Q.M.Sjt. W.	7140
— Fitt.S./Sjt.R.	7140	— L./C. W. H.	❀ 7018
— L./C. (A./Cpl. W. J.	7140	Clarke, Coy.S./M. A.	7140
Chartrand, Cpl.O.	7176	— Spr. (A./Coy.S./M.) C. H.	7140

W.O.II R.A.), M.S.M. (335/Sge. By. R.G.A.), Territorial Efficiency Medal (Geo. VI 1st type 'Territorial,' B.Q.M.S. R.A.), Belgian Croix de Guerre 1939/45.

* Group known: British War and Victory Medals, Territorial Force War Medal (Sgt. R.E.), M.S.M. (7th Anti Aircraft Searchlight Section R.E.) and Territorial Efficiency Medal (Geo. V).

Clarke, R.S.M. C. S.	6498	Cocker, Sjt. J.	7141
— Sjt. F.	7140	Cockerton, Sjt. B. S.	7141
— Dvr. G.	7140	Cocking, Cpl. (A./Coy.Q.M.Sjt.) H.	7141
— C.S.M. H.	6508	Cockle, Sjt. (T.S./M.) H.	7141
— Sjt. (A./Q.M.Sjt.) H.	7140	Cockran, Gnr. R. D.	7180
— Cpl. H. T.	7140	Cocks, Cpl. (A./Sjt.) W. R.	7141
— Cpl. L. J.	7178	Coe, Sjt. W.W.	7141
— C.Q.M.S. M.	6508	Coggin, Sjt. G.	7141
— T./S./M. P. J. C.	6520	Cokeley, Sjt. P.	7141
— Farr.Sjt. R.	6508	Coker, Sjt. T.	7141
— Pte. S. J.	✿ 7018	Cole, Coy.S./M. H.	7141
— Sjt. W.	7140	Cole, Sjt. H. A.	7141
— Cpl. W. G.	6491	— Coy.S./M. I. R.	7141
— Sjt. W. H.	7140	— T./Sub-Condr. J. W.	7141
— Bomdr. W. H.	7140	— Pte. T.C.	7141
Clarkson, Sjt. R. W.	7140	— Spr. (L./C.) V.	7141
Clarvis, Cpl. C.	7140	— Coy.S./M. W. E.	7141
Clayfield, Sjt. A. E.	7140	— Sjt. W. H.	7141
Clayton, Coy.S./M. G. B.	7140	Coleman, A./Coy.S./M. Inst. A.	7141
Clegg, T./S./S./M. H. E.	* 7140	— Pte. A. C., *M.M.*	7141
Clelland, Sjt. W.	7140	— Coy.Q.M.Sjt. C.	7141
Clements. Coy.S./M. H.	7140	— Sjt. (A./S.Sjt.} G.	7141
— Cpl. (A./Sjt.) H. E. P.	7141	— Cpl. G. A.	7178
— Pte. O. J.	✿ 5037	— Sjt. (A./By.S./M.} H. T.	7141
— Sjt. W. H.	6508	— T./S./M. T. G.	7141
— Co.Q.M.Sjt. W. J.	✿ 7018	— Sjt. W. G.	7141
Clerk, W.O.,Cl.1, K. B.	7178	Coles, L./C. (A./Sjt.) P. H.	7141
Clift, Sjt. W.	7141	Collard, Bomdr. W. J.	7141
Clifton, Flt.Sjt. J. E.	6520	Colledge, Sjt. J.	7141
Cline, L./C. H. W.	7176	Collett, Dvr. C.	7141
Clough, Sjt. J. W., *M.M.*	7141	— Sjt. J. W. C.	7141
Clowes, Fitt.S./Sjt. J.	7141	Collier, By.Q.M.Sjt. J.	7141
Clowsley, Lce.Cpl. (A./2nd Cpl.) H.	7141	— T./Amt.S./M. T. F.	7141
Clunie. Sjt. A.	7141	— Sjt. W. C.	7141
Clydesdale, Dvr. J.	7141	Collins, C.Q.M.S. (A./Coy, S./M.) A.	4413
Coates, Sjt. C., *M.M.*	7141	— Sjt. D. (corr.)	4393
— R.Q.M.Sjt. H. E.	7141	— Sjt. E.	7141
— S./M. W.	7141	— Sjt. H.	6520
Coatsworth, Coy.S./M. (A./S./M.)		— Pte. (L./C.) H. A.	7178
A. H.	7141	— Pte. S.	7141
Cobbold, Cpl. (A./Sjt.) A. F.	7141	— Co.S. M. S. A.	6491
Cock, Sjt. (A./S./M.) E.	7141	Collinson, Sjt. J.	7141
Cockburn, Bomdr. (A./Sjt.) G.	7141	Collis, Cpl. A.	7141
— Sjt. H. L.	7178	Colpitts. Sjt. C. F.	7176
— Pte. (L./C.) W.	✿ 4393	Colton, Dvr. J. W.	7141
Cocker, Sjt. F.	† ✿ 4393		

---

* Group known: M.B.E. (1st type, military ribbon, *L.G.* 1919, W.O.I R.A.S.C.), 1914/
15 Star (S.Q.M.S. A.S.C.), British War and Victory Medals (M.I.D. oakleaf, W.O.I
R.A.S.C.) and M.S.M.
† His son, a Lance Cpl. R.E. was K.I.A. 30 June 1942 at Al Alamein.

Colton, L./C. W. C.	* 7141	Cooper, By.S./M. A.	7141
Commander, S./Sjt. C. C.	7141	— Sjt. A.	7141
Comport, C.S.M. E.	6490	— T./S.M. C. H.	6520
Compton, Mech.S./Sjt. H.	7141	— Pte. E.	7141
Condon, Fitt. Q.M.Sjt. T.	7141	— T./S.M. E. H.	6520
Conlan, Dvr. J.	7141	— Sjt. F. G.	7141
Connell, Sjt. D. W.	7178	— Q.M.Sjt. G. P.	6498
— Reg.S./M. F. J.	7141	— Sjt. H.	6508
Connolly, Coy.S./M. R. W.	7141	— Sjt. H. J.	6498
Connor, Coy.S./M. C. J.	7141	— Coy.S./M. J.	7141
— Dvr. J.	7141	— Sjt. J.	6498
Constable, S./Sjt.Maj. A. J.	7141	— Sjt. J.	7176
Constance, Coy.S./M. F.	7141	— Pte. R.	7141
Conway, Cpl. F.	7141	— Sjt. (T./R.S.M.) W.	7141
Cook, R./Q.M.Sjt. A. J.	7178	— Sjt. W. E.	7141
— Cpl. (A./Sjt.) A. S.	7141	— Col./Sjt. (A./By.S./M.) W. G.	7141
— Sjt.E.	6498	Copeland, C.S.M. J.	6491
— Sjt. J. H.	7141	Copper, Sjt. (T./S.M.) E. E.	† 6520
— Sjt. J. W.	7141	Coppin, S./Sjt. C. M.	7178
— By.Q.M.Sjt. (now B.S.M.) P. G.	✠ 7018	Copps, Sjt. H.	6498
Cooke, Gnr. J.	7141	Cops, R.Q.M.Sjt. F. O.	7141
— Sjt. S. G.	7141	Corbett, Sjt. J.	7141
Coombes, Sjt. A. S.	7180	Corbin, Coy.Q.M.Sjt.	
— Sjt. (A./Coy.S./M.) E.	7141	(A./Coy.S./M.) W. J.	7141
Coop, Sjt. H.	7141	Corke, Sjt. G. E.	6498
— L./C. (A./Sjt.) J.	7141	Corkhill, Cpl. N. L.	‡ 7141

* 9 Bn. Tank Corps. Also awarded a Military Medal for an action south of Moreuill on 23 July, 1918. Under heavy shelling and M.G. fire he drove his tank until knocked out by a direct hit. Although wounded, he helped evacuate and bandage other wounded and helped them back.

† R.F.C. No. 188. Born May 1892. Enlisted April 1911 in R.E. Royal Aero Club Aviators Certificate No. 674 as 1A.M. in November, 1913 in a Maurice Farman. Temp. S.M. January 1916. R.A.F. M.S.M. with No. 54 Sqn. R.A.F. L.S. & G.C. April 1929 as S.M.1. Commissioned January, 1931. Awarded 1935 Jubilee Medal. Squadron Leader 1939. Retired 1948. Died 1963.

‡ His medals were sold at Christies in 1989 for £990. A group of miniatures attributed to him are in the McInnes collection: Order of St. Michael and St. George, Companion (C.M.G.), neck Badge, silver-gilt and enamel, Military Medal, G.V.R. (Sjt. 2/6 L'Pool R.), British War and Victory Medals, 1939–45 Star, Africa Star with '8th Army' bar, Defence and War Medals, G.S.M. 1918–62, E. II R., one clasp, Arabian Peninsula (Dr. C.M.G.), Coronation, 1953, Army Meritorious Service Medal, G.V.R. (Cpl. 2/6 L'Pool R.), Egypt, Order of the Nile, Fourth Class breast Badge, silver-gilt and enamel, together with two related O.T.C. shooting medals, silver and bronze, both named and dated, 1923. M.M. *London Gazette* 13.9.18. Miralai (Lieutenant Colonel) Norman Lace Corkill Pasha, C.M.G., M.M., 1898–1966, outstanding in the field of tropical medicine, specialised in nutrition, deficiency diseases and snakes. After his service on the Western Front 1915–19, he graduated M.B., 1925 and joined the Iraq Health Service as professor of Zoology with the Royal College of Medicine, was employed with the Sudan Medical Service, 1930–46. From 1940–44 served with the Sudan Defence Force, as Miralai Corkill Pasha, he organised and led a Sudanese

Corless, Sjt. W. J.	7141	Cox, Cpl. (A./Sjt.) A.	7142
Cormack, Sjt. J. B.	7141	— Sjt. A.	7142
Corney, Coy.Q.M.Sjt. R. O.	7141	— T./Sjt.Maj. A. R.	† 6520
Cornish, Sjt. F. G.	7141	— Sjt. C. F.	7178
Corps, S.S./M. W. F.	7141	— Cpl. E.	7142
Corr, Sjt. M.	7142	— Mech.S./Sjt. F. R.	7142
— By.S./M. M. P.	7142	— Sjt. H.	7142
Corrigan, Q.M.Sjt. L. C.	7142	— Bomdr. (T./Cpl.) P. J.	7178
— Sjt. P.	7142	Crabtree, Sjt. A.	7142
Cosier, M.S.Sjt. E.	6498	— R.Q.M.Sjt. C.	7142
Coskry, Pte. J. G.	7178	— A./S.Sjt. J. H.	7142
Cother, Sjt. A. E.	7178	Craggs, Farr.Sjt. J. M.	7142
Cotton, By.S./M. J. H.	7142	Craig, A./Sjt. J.	7178
Coughlan, Sjt. J. T.	7142	— S.Q.M.Sjt. J. A. V.	7178
Coulson, T./S.S.M. A. A. L.	6508	— Sjt. W.	7142
— actg.Sjt. O. H.	4413	— Supt.Clk. W. J. R.	6512
— Dvr. W.	7142	Craigie, Gnr. S.	7142
Court, Sjt. H.	7176	Crawford, Cpl. H. W.	6520
Courtier, Cpl. C. J.	7142	— Cpl. I. P.	7176
Coutts, Sjt. A.	7142	— Coy.S./M. J.	7142
— Sjt. J., *MM*	7142	Crawley, Fitt.S./Sjt. C.	7142
Couzens, Coy.Q.M.Sjt. W. R.	7142	Credland, Coy.S./M. (R./R.S./M.) F.	7142
Cowell, Sqdn.Q.M.Sjt. N.	* 7142	Creedon, R.S.M. A. P.	6508
Cowen, A./Sjt. T.	7142	Creighton, Flt. Sjt. A.	6520
Cowley, Cpl. (A./Sjt.) J. W.	7142	Cress, Fitt./Onr. T.	7142
— Sjt. P. E.	6498	Crew, 2nd Cpl. (A./Sjt.) E. T.	❀ 4393
Cowling, Cpl. (A./Sjt.) J. T.	7176	Crick, S./Smith(A./F.S./Sjt.) R. G.	7142
Cowperthwaite. Pte. (A./Sjt.) H.	7142	— A./Fitt.Sjt. S.	7142

field ambulance which operated on the lines of communication in the Western Desert campaign—the only armed unit of its type in the Middle East. Appointed Minister of Health, Khartoum, 1944 (Order of the Nile) and Assistant Director Sudan Medical Service 1945. After a brief period as Senior Lecturer in Tropical Medicine at Liverpool, he returned to the Middle East and was appointed Quarantine Expert, Saudi Arabia 1948–50. Health Adviser, Aden Protectorate Health Service for 11 years and was awarded the C.M.G. (1959) for his work there. Nutritional Consultant, World Health Organisation, Tehran, 1962–63. Doctor Corkill's 'recreations' in *'Who's Who'* are given as 'snakes and folk medicine.' There are numerous mentions of him as Regimental Sniper in the 2/6 Liverpool's History. He is also specifically mentioned as leading a number of successful patrols into enemy trenches, for one of which he was awarded the Military Medal.

* Group known: Queen's South Africa Medal (Cape Colony, Orange Free State Transvaal, 29535 Pte. 15th Coy. I.Y.), 1914 Star & bar (27 Sgt., Northumberland Yeo.), British War and Victory Medals (27002 S.Q.M.S. 1/1 Northumberland Huss. Yeo.), M.S.M., Territorial Force Efficiency Medal (Geo. V, 27 Cpl. N.H.Y.). He was the son of Hon. Major Charles Cowell T.D., North'd Huss. Yeo., and he served 39 years in the Regiment. During the Boer War he was captured, then released, with two broken ribs, naked on the Veldt. He walked for three days without boots or clothes until he found British troops.

† R.A.F. M.S.M. No. 2302 R.F.C. enlisting in November 1914. Miniature group known A.F.C., 1914 Star & bar trio and M.S.M. A.F.C. as Captain R.A.F. in *L.G.* 1 January 1919.

Cripps, Bomdr. T. J.	7142		Curd, By.S./M. A. W.	7142
Crisp, Sjt. W. A.	7178		Curling, Pte. (L./C.} C.	7178
Crocker, L./C. (A./Sjt.) F.	7142		Curran, Gnr. J.	7142
Crombue, Sjt. D. I.	7142		Currey, Cpl. T. S.	6498
Crook, Sjt. A. A.	7142		Currie, Pte. J. H.	7176
Crooke, Dvr. F. W.	7142		— S.S./M. W. G.	7176
Crosier, Sjt. J.	7142		Curry, Cpl. J.	7142
Cross, Sjt. (T./S./M.) E. W.	7142		Curtis, L./C. C. J.	7142
— R.Q.M.Sjt. H. R.	7142		— Coy.Q.M.Sjt. S. W.	7142
— Cpl. J. L.	7142		Cussins, Coy.S./M. G., *D.C.M.*	7142
— Sjt. R. J.	7178		Cyra, Sjt. (A./Coy.S./M.) J.	7176
— Bombr. (A./Sjt.) T. H.	7142			
Crossley, Spr. D.	7142		Dagg, Pte. (L./C.) A.	7142
— Coy.Q.M.Sjt. J.	7142		Dalby, A./Farr.Sjt. A.	7142
Croston, Cpl.T.	7142		Dale, S./Sjt. J.	7142
Croucher, L./Bombr. J.	* 7142		— Sjt. J.	6498
Crowe, Sjt. A. E.	7142		— Sjt. S. J.	6498
— Cpl. (A./Sjt.) G.	7142		— Sjt. (A./Coy.Q.M.Sjt.) T. R.	7142
— By.S./M. W. G.	7142		— Cpl. W.	7142
Crowther, Sjt. E.	7142		Dalgleish, Cpl. (A./Sjt.) A.	7142
Crudace, Sjt. A. L.	7178		Dalwood, Pte. (A./Sjt.) C. H.	6498
Crutchley. T./Sub.Condr. A.	7142		Dancer, S./Sjt. (A./S./M.) A. M.	7142
— A./Sjt. H.	7142		Daniel, L./C. (A./Sjt.) S. W.	7142
Crute, Cpl. (A./Sjt.) N. R.	7142		Daniels, Cpl. A. B.	7178
Cryer, Spr. (A./Coy.S./M.) F.	7142		— By.S./M. C. E.	7178
Cuckson, Sjt.C. R. W.	7142		— By.S./M. F. P.	7142
Cudby, C.Q.M.S. C.	6498		— Sjt. T. N.	7142
Cuerdon. Coy.S./M T.	7142		Danks, Pte. (A./Sjt.) H. E.	7142
Cuff, Sjt. J.	7142		Dann, L./C. (A./Col.Sjt.) H.	7142
Cullen, Sjt. H. C.	7142		Darby. Pte. J. R.	7142
Cullen, Sjt. M.	7142		Dare, 2nd Cpl. (A./Cpl.) W. H.	7142
Culliford, L./C. A. J.	7142		Dark, L./C. H. C.	6498
Cullumbine, Cpl. A.	7142		Darley, Sjt. F.,*MM.*	7142
Cumberland, Cpl{L./Sjt.) J. W.	7178		Darters, L./C. W. C.	7143
Cumbleton, Sqn.S./M. H. G.	7176		Davey, Cpl. A. W. T.	6520
Cumming, Bombr. G. A.	7176		— T./R.S.M. H.	† 6498
— Sjt. L. C.	6508		— Bombr. (A./Cpl.) R. J.	7143
— R.Q.M.Sjt. S.	7142		Davidson, Sjt. D. D.	7143
Cummings, Sjt. R. J.	7142		— Coy.Q.M.Sjt. J.	7143

---

* 82918, Lance Bombr., 26th Battery R.F.A. Cambrai, 1917, and Flanders, 1917–18—Has been responsible for the delivery of rations to the battery. Has continually displayed initiative, resource, and great courage throughout this period. In spite of being frequently exposed to shelling and gas, especially during the operations in Flanders, he has never failed to deliver water and rations to the battery. His resourcefulness and invariable stoutheartedness have set a fine example.

† Group of miniatures in Moss collection attributed to this Warrant Officer: D.C.M. (Geo. V, No. 4633 R.Q.M.S. 8/Devons, *L.G.* 16.11.15), Queen's South Africa Medal (no clasp), King's South Africa Medal (two date clasps), 1914/15 trio (M.I.D. oakleaf), L.S. & G.C. (Geo. V), M.S.M. and French Médaille Militaire. M.S.M. for Italy, only 12 to the Regiment for this theatre.

Davidson, Sjt. W.		6508	Deeming, Coy.S./M. R.		7143
Davie, Pte. R.	✿	4393	Delahay, Spr. (A./Cpl.) G. T.		7143
Davies, Cpl. A. D.		7178	Dell, Cpl. (A./L./Sjt.) E.		7143
— Sjt. D.		7143	Delooze, Cpl. J.		7143
— Dvr. D.		6498	Dengate, Pte. (L./C.) A. A.		7178
— Pte. (A./C.Q.M.S.) E. J.		6508	Denham. C.W.M.S. A. C.		6498
— R.Q.M.Sjt. H. A.		7178	— Sjt. G. A. E.		7143
— L./Sjt. J. F.		7143	— Sjt. J. N.		7143
— Gnr. M.		7176	Denley, R.S./M. E.		7143
— Cpl. (A./Sjt.) O. C.		7143	Dennis, Sjt. C. C.		6498
— Gnr. R.		7143	Dennison, Sjt. (A./Coy.S./M.) J.		7143
— Sjt. T. E.		7143	Dent, Gnr. C.		7180
— Gnr. W. A.		7143	— S./Sjt. (A./W.M./Sjt.) E.		7143
— M./S.M. W. G.		7143	— Pte. F.		7143
— Pnr. Sjt. W. J.		7143	— R.Q.M.Sjt. W.		7143
— Pte. (A./Sjt.) W. T.		7143	Derrick, L./C. G.	✿	4393
Davis, Coy.S./M. (A./R./S./M.) A.		7143	D'Esterre, Sjt. C. R.		7143
— R.S.M. A. H., *D.C.M.*	*	7143	Davaney, Coy.S./M. M.		7143
— L./C. C. F.		7176	Devereaux, Sjt. T.		6498
— Pte. (A./Cpl.) G.		7143	Devereux, Sjt. A. E.		7143
— Sjt. H. R.		7178	Devine, Coy.Q.M.Sjt. J.		7143
— A./R.S./M. J.		7143	Devlin, R.S./M. D.		7143
— Sjt. R. E.		7176	Dewar, Sjt. J.		7143
— Pte. W.		7143	— Pte. W.		7180
— By.Q.M.Sjt. W. H.		7143	Dewhurst, Q.M.S.Sjt. A. M.		7143
Daw, By.Q.M.Sjt. A. A.		7143	— Cpl. T.		7143
Dawes, Coy.S./M. A.		7143	Dibley, Sht. H. T.		6498
— C.Q.M.Sjt. F.		6508	Dick, Pte. J. M.		7143
— Pte. (A./Cpl.) F.		7143	Dickenson, Flt. Sjt. R.		6520
Dawson, Cpl. A.		7180	Dickers, By.S./M. W. E.		7143
— Coy.S./M. T., *MM.*		7143	Dickson, R.Q.M.Sjt. H. S. H.		7178
— Coy.S./M. (A./R.S./M.) W.		7143	— Sjt. J.		7143
Day, C.S.M. A.		6508	— Gnr. J.		7143
— Bombr. A. G. W.		6498	— Cpl. (A./S./Sjt.) W. J.		7143
— Cpl. (A./Sjt.) C. T.		7143	Dies, Pte. W. C.		7176
— Cpl. E. H.		7143	Diggle, L./Sjt. W.		7143
— Coy.Q.M.Sjt. F.		7143	Dighton, Cpl. (A./Sjt.) P.		7143
— Sjt. P. H.		7143	Dillon, Gnr. A.		7143
Daykin, Dvr. J.		7143	— Pte. (L./C.) A. E.		7178
De Garis. Sjt. H. E.		7178	Dingley, Sjt. A. E. V.		7143
Deacon, Sjt. I.		7143	Dinsdale, Pte. T. H., *MM.*		7143
Deadman, Sjt. T.		7143	Dion, Pte. J. A.		7176
Dean, Sjt. A.		7143	Dix, C./Q.M.S. A.		6508
— Pte. F.		7143	Dixon, A./S./Sjt. C. L.		7143
— Gnr. T.		7143	— Sjt. J. R.		6498
— Sjt. W.		7143	Dobson, Cpl. (A./Sjt.) E. W.		6508
Deane, Coy.Q.M.Sjt. C.		7143	— Sjt. W.		7143
Debenham, Pte. F. W.		7176	Dodd, Coy.Q.M.Sjt. H.		7143

---

* K.R.R.C. Att. 16 London Regt. Entitled Queen's South Africa Medal and King's South Africa Medal.

Dodd, Sjt. J.	7143	Doyle, Sjt. (A./S./Sjt.) G. A.	7144
Dodds, Coy.Q.M.Sjt. G.	7143	— C.Q.M.Sjt. H.	7144
— Sjt. J. W.	7178	— Pte. (A./Cpl.) M.	7144
Dodge, R./S./M. A. A.	7176	Drake, Pte. B.	7144
Dodgson, Sjt. J.	7143	— By.S.M. (A./R.S.M.) S. R.	6508
Doe, Coy.S./M. A. R.	7176	— Spr. W. F.	7144
Doel, Cpl. G. J. F.	7143	Drane, Pte. A.	7144
Doherty, T./S.M. F. W.	7143	Draper, C.S.M. G.	6508
— Cpl. (A./Coy.S./M.) T. B.	7143	Dray. L./C. (A./Sjt.) A. R.	7144
— Cpl. (A./S./M.) W.	7143	Drew, By.S./M. J. E. †	7144
Doll, A./Sjt. W. A. M.	6512	Drewett, Gnr. A.	6499
Dollins, Cpl. F. J.	7143	Drewitt, Coy.S./M. R. W.	7144
Dolman, Cpl. E. C.	7143	Drinkwater, Pte. A. H.	7144
Dolphin, Pnr. (A./Sjt.) C. E.	7143	Driscoll, Sjt. O. J.	7178
Domone, R.Q.M.Sjt. W.	7143	Driver, Sjt. F.	7144
Domoney, By.S./M. W. A.	7143	Drummond, Q.M.Sjt. C. A.	7178
Donaghy, SJt. F.	7143	— Dvr. W.	7144
Donald, Cpl. E.	7143	Dryburgh, L./C. (A./Cpl.) W. E.	7144
Donaldson, Sjt. G.	7176	Dryden, L./C. (A./Sjt.) P.	7144
— Coy.S./M. J. J.	7143	Drylie, Sjt. A.	7144
Donn, Sjt. F. H.	6508	Duckett, Cpl. R.	7144
— Coy.Q.M.Sjt. R.	7143	Duckworth, B.Q.M.Sjt. E.	7144
Donnachie, Sjt. J.	6499	— Sjt. C.	7144
Donoghue, S./M. P.	7143	— Cpl. D.	7144
Donovan, Coy.Q.M.Sjt. T.	7143	Dudley, Pte. F. A.	7144
Dooel. Cpl. (A./Sjt.) G. B.	7143	— S.S.M. L. A.	6499
Dormer, Sjt. A. A.	6508	— Sjt. J. A.	7144
Doughty, Bombr. R.	7143	— Spr. J. S.	7144
Douglas, S.Q.M.Sjt. A. *	7143	Duff, Sjt. D.	7144
— Pte. J. (A.Cyc.C.)	7144	Duglass, Cpl. J. ✠	7018
— Pte. J. (Dns.)	7144	Dugmore, Mech.S./Sjt. C.	7144
— Pte. J. (R.Scots)	7144	Dumper, Sjt. A. J.	7180
Douthwaite, Sjt. H.	7144	Duncan, Pte. (A./Sjt.) A.	7144
Dow, By.S./M. J.	7144	— Pte. C. B.	7144
— Mech.S./Sjt. J. B.	7178	— Pte. T.	7144
Dowding, Sjt. (A./S./Sjt.) A. E.	7144	Duncanson, Cpl.T./Sjt.) J.	7178
Dower, Pte. A. R.	7176	Dundas, By.S./M. T. H.	7176
Dowler, Cpl. L. J.	7144	Dunford, Coy.S./M. W.	7144
Down, R.Q.M.S. A. J.	6499	Dungey, L./C. (A./Sjt.) G.	7144
Downe, S./Sjt. C. L.	6492	— Cpl. (A./S./Sjt.) R. J.	7144
Downes, Gnr. A.	7144	Dunham, T./R.S./M. R. S.	7144
— Cpl. G. H. W.	7144	Dunkerley, R./S./M. J.	7176
Downie, Sjt. J.	7144	Dunkley, Spr. C.	7176
Downton, Cpl. (A./Sjt.) F.	7176	Dunlop, A./Coy.S./M. W. T.	7144
Dowthwaite, Sjt. J. W.	7176	Dunmore, Gnr. (L./Bombr.) F. C. A.	7144

* As F.Q.M.S. R.A.S.C. Awarded M.S.M. Annuity A.O. 34/1946.

† 3934, D/17th Battery, R.F.A. Flanders, 1917–18, and Cambrai 1917—Has continually displayed coolness, determination and initiative. On several occasions he has had to take action on his judgement when no officer was present and by his resource and devotion to duty has set fine example to the battery.

Dunn, L./C. J. E.	7144	Edwards, Coy.Q.M.Sjt. W.	7144
Dunnage, S.Q.M.Sjt. J. A.	7144	Eele, Gnr. (T./Sjt.) F. W.	7144
Dunnett, Pnr.Sjt. G.	7144	Eeles, Sjt. H. T.	7176
Dunning, Sjt. S. J.	7144	Egenton, Sjt. M. W.	7178
Dunstan, Bombr. G.	7178	Egerton, Coy.S./M. E. H.	7144
Durie, Pte. J. ❀	5037	Eggbeer, A./Sjt. R. J.	7144
Durrant, Sjt. C. G.	7176	Eggleston. Col.Sjt. T. H.	7144
— 2nd Cpl. (A./Sjt.) F.	7144	Eggleton, Cpl. H.	7144
— Cpl. F. W.	7144	Eglingt:on, S./Sjt. R.	7145
— C.Q.M.S. W. A. A.	6508	Eliason, Pte. V.	7178
Dursley, By.S./M. T.	7144	Ellen, Coy.S./M. T. F.	7145
Dutch, Cpl. (A./L./Sjt.) A.	7144	Ellery, Pte. E.	7178
Duthie, Gnr. H.	7144	Ellingham, Sjt. F.	7154
Duthiot. L./C. B. V.	7144	Ellins, Cpl. H.F.A.	7176
Dwyer, Cpl. H. L.	7176	Elliott, Sjt. E.	7145
Dyas, Coy.S./M. G.	7144	— Cpl. G. M. R.	7178
Dyer, Sjt. (A./Drmr.Sjt.) W. J.	7144	— Sjt. H.	7145
Dyke, A./Sjt. A. W.	7176	— S.S./M. J. V., *MM*.	7145
— Mech.S.Sjt. W. C.	7144	— Pte. (A./Coy.S./M.) R.	7145
Dyson, Sjt. (A./Coy.S./M.)	7144	— S./Sjt. T.	7145
		— Sjt T. J.	7145
Eady, L./Sjt. H. W.	7144	— Pte. (L./C.) W.	7145
Eaglestone, Spr. A. E.,*MM*.	7144	Ellis, Dvr. (A./S./Sjt.Whlr.) A.	6499
Eames, Coy.S./M. T. H.	7144	— Q.M.Sjt. A. R.	7145
Earl, S./Sjt. J. E.	7144	— L./Sjt. E.	7145
Easey, Cpl. S.	6499	— Cpl. F.	7145
East, Sjt. (A./Coy.W.M.Sjt.) F. W.	7144	— Mech.S./Sjt. H. W.	6499
Easter, Sqn.S./M. A. E.	7144	— Pte. (A./Sjt.) J.	7145
Easton, Coy.W.M.Sjt.J.	7144	— Q.M.Sjt. (T./S.M.) L. S.	6499
Eastwood, Pte. (A./Cpl.) J. W.	7178	— Pte. (A./Sjt.) W. A.	7145
Eaton, Sjt. H. F.	7180	— Sjt. W. H.	7145
Eccles. Sjt. H.	7144	Ellison, Sjt G.	7145
— Gnr. (A./Sjt.)Arty.Clk. H. L.	7176	— Coy.S./M. J. T.	7145
— T./Sjt.Maj. W.	6520	Elsey, S./Sjt. (A./Q.M.Sjt.)W. J.	7145
Eddowes, Pte. F. E.	7144	Elwell, S./Sjt. (A./S.Q.M.Sjt.) H. A.	7145
Eden, Gnr. (L./Bombr.) G. G.	6499	Embleton, Pte. T.	7145
— Cpl. S. C.	7144	Emerson, Sjt. (A./Q.M.Sjt.) J. T.	7145
Edey. Sjt. J. K.	7144	Emes, Farr.S./Sjt. G. D.	7145
Edgar, Farr.Sjt. W. K.	7144	Emmott, Sjt. W.	7145
Edkins, S.W.M.Sjt. G. G.	7144	England, Gnr. J. H.	7145
Edwards, Sjt. A. O.	7144	English, Sjt. F.	6499
— Sjt. (A./Coy.Q.M.Sjt.) C. C.	7144	— Pte. (L./C.) F.	7145
— Sqn.S./M. C. J.	7144	Enticknapp, Cpl. (A./Sjt.) P. J	7145
— Sjt. D. T.	6508	Eplett, S./Sjt.Artfr. F.	7145
— Cpl. (A./Sjt.) E.	7144	Epps, Gnr. F.	7145
— Pte. F. C.	7144	Eqing, Pte, (A./S./Sjt.) J.	7145
— Cpl. (A./Sjt.) G. H.	7144	Errickcr, Sjt. R. M.	7145
— T./Reg.S./M. J.	7144	Etheridge, Flt.Sjt. C. W.	4413
— Pte. (A./S./M.) J.	7144	Etherington, Sjt. (A./	
— 2nd Cpl. (Engr.Cl.) J. W.	7144	Coy.Q.M.Sjt.} R.	7145
— Coy.S./M. R.	7144	Evans, Coy.Q.M.Sjt. A.	7145
— L./Sjt. S. A.	7144	— Cpl. (A./S.Q.M.Sjt.) A. L.	6499

Evans, Sjt. (A./Q.M.Sjt.) C.	.	7145
— S./Sjt. (A./Q.M.Sjt.) E.		7145
— Sjt. E.	*	6491
— Coy.S.M. G. H.		7145
— Sjt. J.		7145
— Pte. (A./Sjt.) J.		6499
— Coy.Q.M.Sjt. J. C. O.		7145
— Spr. O		7145
— Mech.S./Sjt. R.		7145
— Sjt. T.		4431
— Sjt. T. R.		7145
— L./C. W.		7145
— Sjt. (A./R.Q.M.Sjt.) W. L.		7145
Eve, Sjt. J.		7145
Evennett, Pte. (A./Col.Sjt.) T.		7145
Everitt, L./C. F.		7145
Eves, S./Sjt. (A./S.M.) J. G.	†	6512
Ewart, Cpl. D.	✿	4393
Ewing, Bombr. W.		7145
Eyre, L./C. (A./2nd Cpl.) A. H.		7145
— Bombr. H., *D.C.M.*		7145
Fairbrother, Pte. W. H.		7145
Fairhurst, Coy.Q.M.Sjt. H.		7145
Fairley. A./Q.M.Sjt. J.		7176
Fairs, By.Q.M.S. G.		6508
Fairthorn, C.S.M.(A./R.S.M.) B. W.		6508
Falconer, R.Q.M.Sjt.(A.Sub. Condr.) L. F.		7178
— Coy.Q.M.Sjt. W.		7145
Fale, Sjt. C. J.		6508
Fallaize, Cpl. C. J.		7145
Farmer, Pte. A.		6499
— Sjt. G.		7145
— Coy.Q.M.Sjt. P. J. D.		7145
Farnfield, Sjt. A. W., *D.C.M.*		7145
Farnsworth, S.Q.M.Sjt. F. W.		7145
Farquharson, Coy.Q.M.Sjt. W.		7145
— Spr. W.		7145
Farr, Sjt. W. J.		7145

Farrell, Sjt.(A./Coy.S./M.) J. F.	7145
Fatzeus, Coy.S./M. C.	7178
Faulkner. Sjt. E. L.	7145
— L./Sjt. L.	7145
Fear, Sjt. A. E.	7176
Fearby, Whr.Cpl. H.	6508
Fears, C.S.M. E.	6499
— Sjt. {A./Coy.Q.M.Sjt.) F. H.	7145
Fee, Q.M.Sjt. C. H.	7176
Fehely, Sjt.(A./R.S./M.) E.	7145
Feigherty, E.L.& S.S./Sjt. T.	6491
Felgate, L./C.(A./Sjt.) A. F.	7145
Fellows, S.S.M. J.	6499
Feltham. Sjt. A. C.	7145
Feltus, Cpl. R. C.	7176
Fenn, Cpl.(A.L./Sjt.) E.	7145
Fennell, Cpl. W.	7145
Fenwick, Sjt. J. M.	7145
Ferguson. T./Mech.S./M. F.	7145
— Cpl. F. D. W.	7145
— Sjt. J. A.	7178
— L./C. J. C.	7145
— A./Sjt. J. M.	7178
Ferrell, Pte. G. C.	7176
Fettes, Cpl. G.	7145
Fewster, Coy.S./M.(A./R.S./M.) G.	7145
Fiddaman, Coy.S./M. A.	7145
Field, Pte. A.	7145
— Sjt. R. J.	7145
— Col.Sjt. W. C.	7180
Fielden, Cpl. J.	7145
— Cpl. P.	7145
Fieldhouse. L./C.(A./C.Q.M.S.) A.	6499
Fielding, R.Q.M.Sjt. A. W.	7145
Fifield. Coy.S./M. J. W.	7145
Filer, S./Sjt. L. B.	7145
Fillingham, Mech. S./Sjt. W.	6508
Filyer, Sjt. W.	7176
Finch, Cpl. F.	7145
— Pte.(A./Sjt.) F.	7145

---

* Imperial Camel Corps, for Egypt. Single M.S.M. known, also an Africa General Service Medal (Somaliland 1920) to 334212 Sgt. Evan Evans R.A.F. with M.I.D. oakleaf. A note on his records states he would have been awarded the R.A.F. M.S.M. but for the previous award of the Army M.S.M. An M.I.D. was therefore given.

† Group known: M.B.E. (1st type), 1914 Star & bar trio (Sgt./W.O.1 R.A.M.C.) Defence Medal, Jubilee 1935, Coronation 1937, L.S. & G.C. (Geo. V, W.O.I R.A.M.C.) and M.S.M. (one of five awarded for services on the Mediterranean Lines of Communication). M.B.E. in 1929 as W.O. 1. Served in Malta 1933–37. Temp. Major from 1941 in WW 2. Died 1952 aged 63.

Finch, L./C.(A./2nd Cpl.) P. L.	7145	Foes, Sqdn.Cpl.Maj. W. E.	*	7146
— Coy. S./M.(A./R.S./M.) W.	7145	Fogro, R.Q.M.Sjt. A.		7146
— Sjt. W.	7176	Foley, Bombr. F.		7146
— Flt.Sjt. W. H.	6520	Folkes, F. of W.Q.M.S. W. H.		7146
Findlay, Pte. E. A.	7180	Folwell, 2nd.Cpl. A. T.		7146
— Cpl. W.	7145	Fooks, Sjt. J.		7146
Finlan, Sjt. H.	7145	Foot, Coy.S./M. R. A.		7146
Finlay, Cpl. T. F.	7145	Forbes, C.Q.M.Sjt.(A./C.S.M.) A.		6499
Finlayson, Cpl. D.	7145	— Spr. J. C.		7146
Finucane, R.S./M. F. C.	7145	— Sjt. W.		7146
Firkin, S.Q.M.Sjt. W. G.	7146	Foresey, Cpl. P. G.		7146
Firth, Sjt. C.	7146	Ford, Sjt. A.		6508
— Sjt. F.	7146	— R.Q.M.Sjt. A. J.		7146
— Pte.(A./Sjt.) J. E.	7146	— Flt.Sjt. C. F.		6520
Fisher, Sqdn.Cpl.Maj. B.	7146	— Flt. Sjt. F. G.		6520
— R.Q.M.Sjt. E. E.	7178	— Coy.S./M. G. H.		7146
— Sjt.(A./Coy.Q.M.Sjt.) F. G.	7146	— Sqn.S./M. J.		7146
— Gnr. H. J.	7146	— Pte. W.		7146
— S./Sjt. H. L.	7176	Forder, S./S./M. F. H.		7146
— Q.M.Sjt. J.	7146	Forgan, Pte. J.		7146
— Sjt. J. N.	7146	Forman, Sjt.(A./S./Sjt.) H. A.		7146
— Sjt. R.	7146	Forrest, Coy.Q.M.Sjt. J.		7146
— Bombr.(A./Cpl.) W.	7146	Forster, T./R.Q.M.Sjt. J. A.		7178
Fishlock, Pte. G.	7178	Forsyth, Bombr.(A./Sjt.) J. R.		7146
Fisk, Dvr. J. T.	7176	— W.O. Cl.1, W. F.		7178
Fitzgerald, Cpl. A.	7146	Fortune, Cpl. H.		7178
— Sjt.(A./Q.M.Sjt.) J.	7146	Fossey, Sjt. A. E. V.		7146
Fitzgibbons, Cpl.(A./L./Sjt.) R. J.	7146	Foster, Sjt. A. S.		7178
FitzSimmons, Sjt. G.	7178	— Sjt. G. E.		7146
Flack, L./C. C. F.	7176	— Cpl. H.		7146
Flaherty, Bombr. G. C.	7146	— Sjt.(A./R.S./M.) L. B.		7146
Flanagan, Sjt. J. L.	7146	— Sjt.(A./C.S.M.) W.		6491
Flatley, Sjt. J.	7176	— Pnr. W.		7146
Flaxman, T./S./M. S. A.	7146	Fowden, Cpl.(L./Sjt.) G. L.		7178
Fleckner, C.S.M. A. E.	6508	Fowler, Pte. L. G.		6499
Fleming, Coy.S./M.(now A./S./M.)		Fox, A./Sjt. A. E.		7146
D. W.	7176	— S.Q.M.Sjt. A. O.		7146
— C.Q.M.S. F.	6499	— Amt.(S./M.) C. J.		7146
— Sjt. H.	7146	— Coy.Q.M.Sjt. H. E.		7176
Fletcher, Coy.Q.M..Sjt. J. B.	7146	— Sjt. S. J.		7146
— 2nd Cpl.(A./Sjt.) J. G.	7146	— S./Sjt. T. W.		6508
— L./C. J. T.	7146	Foxall, Pte.(L./C.) J.		7146
— Coy.S./M. W.	7146	Foxley, Pte. J.	❀	5037
Flight, S./S./M. F.	7146	Foyle. C.S.M. L. J.		6508
Flint, Pte. A.	7180	Foz, Dvr. G.		7146
Flynn, By.S./M. T. F. J.	7146	Fraiser, Sjt. W. H.		6499
— Cpl. T.R.H.	7146	France, Fitt.Cpl. G.		7146
Foden, L./C. R.	7146	— Sjt. H. H.		7146

---

* Group known: Queen's South Africa Medal (Relief of Kimberley, Paardeberg, Dreifontein), 1914 Star trio, L.S. & G.C. (Geo. V) and M.S.M. (all Royal Horse Guards).

France, Sjt. M. S., *D.C.M.*	7146	Gadd, Col.Sjt. W. P.	7180
Francombe, Coy.S./M.(A./R.S.M.)		Gainsford, Spr.(A./Cpl.) G. A.	7146
O. C.	7146	Gale, Farr.Sjt. H. C.	7146
Frank, By.S.M. H.	6491	— Sjt. L. H.	7146
Frankland, A./Coy.Q.M.Sjt. H.	7146	Gallagher, Coy.S./M.(A./R.S./M.) J.	7146
Franklin, Bombr. E.	7146	Gallow, Cpl. W. G.	7176
— Spr. G. A.	7176	Galloway, Spr. F. H.	7147
Frankum. Pte. W. J.	7146	— Sjt.(A./Coy.S./M.) J.	7147
Fraser, Sjt. A.	7146	Gamble, Cpl.(L./Sjt.) F. W.	7147
— Sjt. D. S.	7176	Gambles, Pte.(A./L.C.) G. W.	6508
— L./C.(A./Cpl.) J.	7146	Gammon, Pte.(A./Cpl.) A. J.	7147
— R.Q.Sjt. J. B.	7146	Gannon, Sjt.(T./S.S./M.) C.	7147
— R.Q.M.Sjt. J. H.	7146	Gardham, Pnr.Sjt. F.	7147
— Cpl. K. A.	7178	Gardiner, Sjt. A.	7147
— Sjt. M. W.	7176	— Pte. A.	7147
— Pte. (L./C.) W.	7178	— Sjt.(A./S./Sjt.) A. T.	6499
Freeman, R.Q.M.Sjt. G. K.	7178	— Sjt. E. R.	7147
— T.S.M. H. G.	6508	— Coy.Q.M.Sjt. F. W.	7147
— Sjt. J.	7146	— Cpl. W. A.	7176
— Cpl. J.	7146	Gardner, Coy.S./M. F.	7147
— Sjt.(T./S.S./M.) W.	7146	— Coy.S./M.(A./R.S./M.) F. J.	7147
Freemantle, T./Sub.Condr. A. W.	7146	— Pte. W. F.	7147
French, Pte. E.	7146	Gargett, 2nd Cpl. R. S.	7147
— By.S./M. H. J.	7146	Garland, R.S./M. A.	7178
Fretter, Sjt. W. H.	7146	— W.O. Cl. I. J.	7178
Frewin, S./M. H. J. C.	7146	— Coy.Q.M.Sjt. W.	7147
Friend, Sjt. F.	7146	Garner, A./S./Sjt. F. G.	7147
— Sjt. F. J.	7176	— R.Q.M.Sjt. H.	7147
Frimstone, Pte.(L./C.) E.	7146	— Sqdn.S.M. W. B.	6499
Frost, Sjt.(A./R.S.M.) F. C.	7146	Garrett, Pte.(A./Sjt.) J. H.	6491
— S./Q.M.S.(A./S.S.M.) R. R.	* 6512	Garrod, Sjt. G.	7147
— By.Q.M.Sjt. W.	7146	Garwood, Sjt. J. R.	7147
Froud, 1st Cl.S.S.M. W. H.	4413	Gaston, A.R.S./M. T. W.	7178
Fry, Cpl.(A./Sjt.) C. E.	7146	Gatenby, T./Sub.Condr. R.	7147
Fryer, 2nd Cpl. R.	7146	Gates, 2nd Cpl. W. R.	7147
Fuller, By.S./M. A.	7146	Gee, Sjt. J.	7147
— Sjt.(A./Coy.S./M.) C. J.	7146	— L./C.(A./Sjt.) J. H.	7147
— Pte. F. A. O.	7146	— Sjt.(A./Coy.S./M.) W.	7147
Fulton, sjt.(A./Coy.S./M.) J. C.	7146	Gent, Cpl.(L./Sjt.) J.	7147
— Sjt. W.	7176	George, S./Sjt.(A./S.Q.M.Sjt.) A. †	7147
Furness, Bombr. (A./Sjt.) J.	7146	— Amt.S./Sjt. A. A.	7147
Fyfe, Sjt. A.	7146	— Pte. B. W.	7178
Fysh, Sjt. F. W.	7178	— Sjt. P. H.	7178
		— Cpl. W. P.	7178
Gachet, Sjt. W.	7146	Geraghty, Sjt. H.	7147

* A.S.C. for Lines of Communication, Mediterranean.
† Group in R.C.T. Museum: Medal of Order of British Empire, 1914/15 Star trio, General Service Medal (Palestine) Defence and War Medals, Jubilee 1935, Coronation 1937, L.S. & G.C. (Geo. V) M.S.M. and French Médaille Militaire (later Major R.A.S.C.).

Gerald, 2nd Cpl. H. J.	6508	Glennie, Sjt. J.	7147
Gerrard, By.Q.M.Sjt. W.	7147	Glentworth, Sjt. J. P.	7180
Gerrie, S./Sjt.(A./Q.M.Sjt.) W. A.	7147	Glidden, Sjt. J. H.	7176
Gibbon, Cpl.(S./Sjt.) J. C.	7147	Glover, Sjt. F. (E. Kent)	7147
Gibbons, Coy.S./M. H.	7147	— Sjt. F. (Hamps)	7147
— Coy.W.M.Sjt. J. H.	7147	Goacher, Sjt. T. J.	7178
Gibbs, Sjt. C.	7147	Goadby, S.Q.M.Sjt. L. H.	7147
— By.S./M. H. S.	7147	Gobbet, R./S.M. J. *	7147
Gibson, Sjt.(A./Flt.Sjt.) A.	6520	Goddard, Pte.(A./S./Sjt.) H. L.	6499
— Cpl.(L./Sjt.) A. B.	6499	— Pte.(A./S./Sjt.) J. A.	7147
— T./Sub.Condr. C.	7147	Godden, R.Q.M.Sjt. F. P.	7147
— Sjt. D.	6491	— Coy.Q.M.Sjt. G.	7147
— Sjt.(A./Sqdn.S.M.) J.	6491	— Pte. H. C.	7147
— Sjt. J.	7147	Godfrey, R.Q.M.Sjt. C.	7147
— Bombr. J. W.	7147	— Sjt.(S./S./Sjt.) F.	7147
— By.Q.M.Sjt. L.	7178	— By.S./M. G. R.	7147
— Sjt. T.	7147	— A./Sjt. W. B.	7176
Giddings, C.S.M. W. G.	6508	Goffin, Cpl. J.	7178
Gilbert, 1st A.M. A. R.	6520	Goggins, L./C. J.	6499
Giles, Cpl. C.	6499	Gold, Sjt.(A./C.Q.M.Sjt.) C. G. H.	6499
— Sjt. R. J.	7147	Golding, A/C.Q.M.Sjt. R. A.	7147
Gill, L./C. J. W.	7147	— Flt.Sjt. W. J. F.	4413
— L./C. W.	7147	Goldman, Cpl.(S./Sjt.) C.	7147
Gillard, C.Q.M.S. W. K.	6499	Goldsack, Cpl.(A./Sjt.) W. T.	7147
Gillett, Q.M.Sjt.(T./S./M.) W. R.	7147	Goldsmith, Sjt. W.	7147
Gillham, Coy.S.M. W.	7147	Goldsworthy, Sjt. R. G.	7178
Gillies, Sjt. D.	7147	Goll, Pte. H. J.	7147
— Piper, Sjt. J.	7176	Gooch, Spr.(A./2nd Cpl.) H. †	7147
Gillis, By.S./M. D.	7147	— Sjt. S.	7147
Gillman, T./S.M. G.	6520	Good, Cpl. H.	6499
Gilmour, Coy.S./M. D.	7147	Goode, Amt.Q.M.Sjt. E. E.	7147
Gilt, Coy.Q.M.Sjt. H.	7147	Goodman, Sqdn.S./M.(A./R.S.M.)	
Ginger, Gnr. B.	7147	F. A. ‡	7147
Gissing, Flt.Sjt. C. C.	4413	Goodwin, L./C.(T./Sjt.) H. V.	7178
— S./Sjt. H. E.	7178	Goody, R.S./M. A., *D.C.M.*	7147
Gittins, R.Q.M.Sjt. H.	7147	— T./Sub.Condr. B. W.	7147
Glanville, Coy.S./M. T. G.	7147	Gordon, 2nd Cpl. A.	7147
Glassey, S./Sjt. G.	7147	— Sjt.(A./R.S.M.) J.	7147
Glen, Sjt. A.	7176	— S.S.M. J.	7147
Glendinning, Cpl. M.	7178	— R.Q.M.Sjt. J. P.	7176
Glenister, Coy.S./M. F. J.	7147	— Cpl. W. C.	7147
Glenn, Dvr.(A./L./Bombr.) W. H.	6508	Gore, Cpl. E. W.	7179

---

   * 13347 R.S.M. H.Q. 17th Brigade R.F.A. Flanders 1917–18, and Cambrai, 1917—
   For excellent work. He has carried out his duties in a most efficient manner, and by
   his example has set up a very high standard of efficiency.

   † 56818 Sergt. 'B' Battery, R.H.A. Flanders, 1917–18 and Cambrai, 1917—This N.C.O.
   has invariably shown a high sense of duty and devotion to his battery. His continuous
   good work has resulted in a very high standard of efficiency and smartness in his
   sub-section. His work has been beyond all praise.

   ‡ N. Somerset Yeo. Later M.M.

Gore, Pte. H. W.	7176	Gray, Sjt. H.		7148
Goring, Cpl.(A./Sjt.) F. J.	7147	— Dvr.(A./Bombr.) H. R.		7179
Gorman, Sjt.(A./R.S./M.) P.	7147	— C.S.M.(T./R.S.M.) J.		6508
— Cpl. W.	* 6499	— By.S./M. J. E.		7148
Gornall, Cpl.(A./Sjt.) A.	7147	— Sjt. J. N.		7148
Gorton, S.Q.M.Sjt. W.	7147	— S.Q.M.Sjt. J. S.		7148
Gosselin, S./Sjt. J. E.	7176	— R./S.M. W.		7148
Gott, Bombr.(A./Cpl.) R.	7148	Grayson, Cpl.(L./Sjt.) W.		7148
Gough, Sjt.(S./S.Q.M.Sjt.) A. W.	7148	Greasley, Spr. A.		7148
— Coy.Q.M.Sjt. C. C.	7148	Green, Sjt. A.		7148
Gould, Coy.S./M. J. F.	7148	— Sjt. A. J.		7148
Goulding, Cpl.(A./Sjt.) A. D.	7148	— Col.Sjt. F. J.		7148
Gowdy, Pte.(A./Col.Sjt.) J.	7148	— S.Q.M.Sjt. G.		7148
Gowers, Sjt. H. W.	7148	— Sjt. G.		7148
— Sjt. S.	7148	— Cpl.(A./Sjt.) G. B.		7148
Goyen, By.S./M. H. K.	7179	— Coy.S./M. H. G.		7176
Grace, A./S./M. W. C.	7148	— Coy.S./M.(A./R.S./M.) W. H.		7148
Graffham, By.S./M.(A./S./M.) C. H.	7148	Greenbury, Sjt. R. A.		6499
Graham, Sjt. A. F.	7179	Greenfield, Cpl.(Arty. Clerk) G. H.		7148
— R.Q.M.Sjt. D. K.	7176	Greenhead, Fitt.S.Sjt. R.		7148
— Sjt. D. N. H.	7148	Greenhow, Pte. D.		7148
— S.S./M. F. J.	7148	— Coy.S./M. W. G.		7148
— Col.Sjt.(A./W.O.) F. R.	7148	Greenwood, Cpl. A.		7148
— A./Sjt. G.	7148	— Pte. E.		7148
— A./Cpl. J.	7148	— Sjt. E. W.		7148
— Cpl. J. A.	7180	— R.S.M. F. M. C.		6499
— C.S.M. J. W.	6499	— Sjt. T.		6508
— Dvr. R.	7179	Greer, Pte. F.		7176
— Cpl. T. C.	7148	Greetham, Pte. S. J.		7148
— Sjt. W.	7179	Greggains, S.M. C. J. P.		6499
Grandy, Q.M.Sjt.(T./W.O.) C. F.	7148	Gregory, Sjt.(A./Q.M.Sjt.) H.		7148
Granger, Q.M.Sjt.(A3 Clerk) E. W.	7148	— Sjt. H. E.		7148
Granland, Sjt. W. F.	7179	— Gnr. W.		7148
Grant, Coy.S./M. G.	7180	Gregson, Mech.S./Sjt. A.		6491
— R.Q.M.Sjt. G. W.	7179	— L./C. R. E.		7148
— Coy.Q.M.Sjt. J. S.	7176	— Coy.Q.M.Sjt. W. H.		6508
Grattidge, Pte.(A./Cpl.) A. W.	7148	Greenshaw, Sjt. C.		7179
Graves, Sjt. G.	7176	Gresswell, Spr.(A./L./C.) H.		7148
Gray, Cpl. A. A.	7148	Grew, Sjt. F. J.		7148
— Cpl.(L./Sjt.) A. B.	7179	Grey, Cpl. C. H.		7148
— A./Sadd.S./M. A. T.	7148	— Sjt. T. H.		7148
— L./C.(A./Sjt.) C. O.	7148	Gribble, Coy.Q.M.Sjt.(A./		
— Pte.(A./Sjt.) D.	7148	Coy S./M.) C.		7148
— Sjt. G.	7148	Grieve, W.O.Cl.1, T. T.		7179
— S./Sjt. G. F.	7180	Griffin, R./S./M. B.		7148

---

* Hon. Sir William Gorman. R.H.A. W.W.I in France and Italy. M.S.M. for Italy.
Barrister 1921. King's Counsel 1932. M.P. for Royton, Lancs. 1923–24 (Liberal).
Recorder of Wigan 1934–48, Recorder of Liverpool 1948–50. Wing Commander
R.A.F.V.R. 1942–44 (Asst. J.A.G.). High Court Judge (Queen's Bench Division)
from 1950. Knighted 1950.

Griffin, Pte. E.	7148	Haigh, Pte.(A./L./C.) H.		7149
— Sjt. G. A.	7148	Hailwood, R./S./M. F. W.		7149
— By.S./M. P.	7148	Hales, Sjt.(A./C./S./M.) W., *D.C.M.*		7149
Griffith, Sjt. S. V.	7148	— Mech.S./Sjt. W.		7149
Griffiths, Pte. C. W.	7148	Hall, Sjt. A.		7180
— Sjt. H. V.	7179	— Pte.(A./Sjt.) D.		7149
— Sjt. J. N.	7148	— S.Q.M.Sjt. E. H.		6499
Griffs, Sjt. H. E.	7148	— Flt. Sjt. F. S.		4413
Griggs, Coy.S./M. J. W.	7148	— Cpl.(L./Sjt.) G. A.		7149
Grist, Sjt. F.	7176	— Sjt. G. B.		7149
Grocott, Pte. L.	7148	— Sjt.(A./Coy.S./M.) G. E.		7149
Grounds, Sjt. H.	7148	— Sjt. H.		6499
Groundwell, Dvr. H.	7148	— Sjt. J. C.		7149
Grout, L./C. H. S.	7148	— Cpl.(L./Sjt.) J. T.		7149
— Cpl. T. J. G.	6520	— Sjt. P. C. W.		7181
Grove, C.Q.M.S. R. P.	6499	— R.Q.M.Sjt. S.		7149
— Sjt.(A./Mech.S./Sjt.) W. J.	7148	— Sjt. S.		7149
Grover, Sjt. F. R.	6499	— L./C. S. G.		7149
Growcock, Coy.Q.M.Sjt. R. J.	7176	— Amt.S./Sjt. W. C. A.		7149
Grundy, Sjt. W.	7148	Hallas, Coy.Q.M.Sjt.(A./		
Grunnill, Sjt. C.	7148	Bde.Q.M.Sjt.) F.		7176
Guise, Pte. T. C.	7148	Hallatt, S./Smith(A./F.Q.M.Sjt.)		
Gummerson, Sqdn.Q.M.Sjt. E.	7148	L. G.		7149
Gundry, Pte.(A./Sjt.) C. A.	7148	Hallett, L./C. F. J. P.		7180
Gunning, Sjt. J.	7148	— R./S./M. W.		7176
— Cpl. J. H. F. C.	7148	Halsall, R.Q.M.Sjt. J.		7149
Gurney, Sjt. G.	7148	Hambling, Farr.Sjt. R.		7149
Guy, L./C.(A./Sjt.) H.	7148	Hamer, Pte.(A./L./C.) F.		7149
— S./S.M. W. H.	7148	Hamilton, Sjt. B. T.		7149
Guyatt, By.S./M. W.	7148	— Sjt. L.		7149
Gwynn, S./M. C. G.	7148	— R.Q.M.Sjt. W. G.		7149
		Hammond, L./C. A.		7149
Habbitts, Sjt. H. C.	7148	— Coy.Q.M.Sjt. B.		7149
Hack, Coy. Q.M.Sjt. L. A.	6508	— Sjt. H. J.		7149
Hackett, S./Sjt. F.	7148	— Sjt. T. S.		6499
— S./S./M. T. G.	7148	Hampson, Cpl. A.		7176
Haddock, Cpl. W.	7149	Hancock, Sjt. G.		7149
Haddon, R.Q.M.Sjt. J., *M.M.*	7149	Handforth, Cpl. J.	*	7149
— A./Coy.S./M. L. W.	7149	Hankins, Pte. A. E.		7149
Haddow, Sjt. J.	7149	Hanley, R.S./M. J.		7149
Hadley, Sjt. W. H.	7149	— Cpl. J. W.		7149
Hagan, Sjt.(A./S./Sjt.) C.	7149	Hannington, Cpl. G.		6499
Hagger, Sjt. J. C.	7149	Hannon, Pte. J.		7149
Haig, R.Q.M.Sjt. G. L.	7149	Hansell, Pte. A. G.		7176
Haigh, Cpl.(A./Sjt.) C. J. H.	7149	— Sjt. C.		7149
— Dvr. H.	7149	Hanson, Cpl.(L./Sjt.) W.		7149

* 2 Bn. Tank Corps. Also awarded M.M. In Haplincourt Wood, 21 March 1918. He saved at least six tanks from destruction, from close to a S.A.A. dump set alight by a direct hit. Next day his tank was hit four times, once by a gas shell. He led the crew to safety, returned and attempted to recover the Lewis guns.

Harbinson, Sjt. C. J.	7149	Harrison, Sjt. A.		7149
Harby, Sjt. T. W.	7149	— L./C.(A./Cpl.) B.		7149
Harcher, S./Sjt. E. E.	7149	— L./C. C. E.		7149
Harcourt, Pte. C. F.	7149	— Pte.(A./L./C.) G. H.		7149
Hardie, Sjt.(A./C.S.M.) J.	6499	— Coy.S./M. J.		7149
Hardiker, Sjt. R.	7149	— Gnr. J. H.	✽	4393
Hardiman, C.S.M. W.	6508	— Dvr. J. T.		7149
Harding, Bombr.(A./Cpl.) F.	7149	— L./C.L.		7150
— Coy.S./M. J. A.	7149	— R.Q.M.Sjt. S. C.		7150
— T./S./M. T. J.	7149	— Sjt. S. H.		7150
— R.Q.M.Sjt. W. H.	7149	— Sjt. T. W.		7150
Hards, Sjt.(A./Q.M.S.) H. H.	6499	— Sjt.(A./S./Sjt.) W. H.		7150
Hardy, Sjt. A.	7149	— 2nd Cpl. W. H.		7179
— Mech.S./M. J.	7149	Harrop, Sjt. L.		7150
— S./S./M. J.	7149	Hart, Fitt.S./Sjt. A.		7180
Hares, Sjt. J.	7149	— A./S./Sjt. C. D.		6499
Harfield, Pte. S. V.	7149	— Pte.(A./Q.M.S.) D. A.		7150
Hargreaves, R.Q.M.Sjt. L. A.	7149	— A./B.(H.G.) H.		6508
— Sjt. W.	7149	— Sjt. H. W.		7150
— Gnr. W.	7149	— By.S./M. W. W.		6508
Harkness, Sjt. R.	7149	Hartley, S./Sjt. H.		
Harland, Sjt. F. C.	7149	Hartnoll, S./Sjt.(Supply		
Harman, A./Fitt.S./Sjt. A.	7149	Sub.Condr.) P. E.	†	6492
Harmer, Pte.(A./Sjt.) P. S.	7149	Harvey, Coy.Q.M.Sjt. A. R.		7150
Harms, Sjt. L.	7149	— Spr.(A./2nd Cpl.) C. A.		7150
Harn, Cpl. H. P	7149	— Cpl.(A./Sjt.) C. R.		7150
Harnby, R.S./M. J.	7176	— S./Sjt. G. R.		7150
Harper, Coy.Q.M.Sjt. A.	7149	— C.Q.M.S.(A./R.Q.M.S.) H.		6499
— Pte.(A./S./Sjt.) E. J.	7149	— Pte. L.		7150
— Pte. G. E.	✽ 5037	— Pte. L. J.		7180
— L./Sjt. G. S.	7176	— Sjt. T. G.		7150
— Sjt. H. E.	7149	— Sjt. W. R.		7150
Harries, Sjt. D. G.	7149	Hassard, Sadd.Cpl. R. J.		7150
Harris, T./Sub.Condr. A. E.	* 7149	Hastings, Coy.S./M. J.		7150
— Coy.Q.M.Sjt. C.	7149	— S./S. J. W., *D.C.M.*		7150
— Sjt. E. H.	7176	Hatch, By.S./M. F.		7150
— Coy.Q.M.Sjt. E. J.	7149	Hatt, Pte.(A./Sjt.) C.		7150
— Cpl. F.	7149	Hatton, C.Q.M.S. E. S.		6499
— S./S./M. G.	7149	— S./Sjt. H. H.		7179
— Sjt. G.	7149	Hattrick, Pte.(A./L./C.) J. J. H.		7150
— Sjt. J. R.	7176	Hawes, Coy.S.M.(A./R.S.M.) A.		7176
— S./Sjt. S. A.	7149	— Cpl.(A./Sjt.) L. F.		7150
— Sjt.(A./Coy.S./M.) S. R.	7149	— Gnr. R. G.		7150
— Cpl. T.	7149	Hawkesworth, Sjt. J.		6499
— Sjt. W.	7176	Hawkins, Sjt. J.		7150
— Pte. W.	7149	— Pte. J. F.		7150
— Pte. W.	7176	— Cpl. L. C.		7150
— Sjt. W. H.	6499	— R.Q.M.Sjt. R.		7179

---

   * Group known: M.M., 1914/15 Star trio and M.S.M. (all R.A.O.C.).

   † See Bruce *ante.*

Hawkins, Coy.S./M.			Henderson, Pte. C. H.	7176
(A./Dr.Sjt.) W. E.	7150		— Spr.(A./L./C.) E. F.	7150
Hawley, Sjt. A.	7150		— Sjt. H. F.	7150
Haworth, Cpl. F.	7150		Hendry, R.Q.M.Sjt. D. D.	7150
Hawthorne, Sjt. V. H.	7180		— Cpl. D. W.	7150
Hawtin, Cpl.(A./Coy.S.M.) H.	7150		Hennegin, R./S./M. M.	7176
Hayburn, Coy.S./M. J. B.	7150		Henser, S./Sjt.(A./S.M.) W.	6499
Hayes, Dvr. A.	7150		Henshaw, Mech.S./M. C. W.	7150
— Sjt. C.	7150		Henty, Sjt. C. J.	7180
— By.Q.M.Sjt. F.	* 7150		Herbert, S./M. F. G.	7150
— Gnr. H.	7150		— Sjt.(A./Q.M.Sjt.) F. H.	7150
— S.M.L.	6508		— Pte. H.	7150
— R.S.M. P.	6491		Herridge, C.S.M. A. J.	6499
Haynes, L./C. A. J. L.	7176		Heslop, A./S./M. A. W.	7150
— Gnr.(T./Bombr.) F J.	7150		Heveningham, Pte.(A./Sjt.) A.	7150
— Cpl. R. C.	7150		Hevey, R.Q.M.Sjt. W.	7179
— S./M. T. R.	7176		Hewett, R.Q.M.Sjt. E. L.	7150
Hayter, Coy.S./M. J.	7150		Hewitt, Coy.Q.M.Sjt. J.	7150
Hayward, Co.M.(A./R.S.M.) A.	6508		Heycock, Gnr. W. J.	† 7150
— Sjt.(A./Q.M.Sjt.) A. H.	7150		Heyworth, R.Q.M.Sjt. J. L.	7150
— Sjt.(A./Coy.Q.M.Sjt.) W.	7150		Hiam, C.Q.M.S. C. H.	6499
Hazell, Cpl.(L./Sjt.) R.	❀ 7018		Hibberd, Cpl. A. F.	7179
Hazelton, Sjt. G. H.	7150		Hickey, Pte. M.	⌐ 7180
Head, Coy.S./M. G. F.	7150		— Sjt. W.	7150
— Cpl. H. J.	7150		Hickman, Coy.S.M.	
Healas, By.Q.M.Sjt. H.	7150		(T./R.S.M.) A. J.	‡ 6491
Heap, Sjt.(A./Q.M.Sjt.) W.	6499		— L./C. W.	7150
Heard, Sjt. A. E.	7150		Hickson, Cpl.(A./Sjt.) C. E.	7150
Heaslip, L./C.(A./Sjt.) M.	7150		Higgins, By.S.M. A.	6508
Heason, C.Q.M.S.Sjt. H.	7143		— Cpl. B. W.	7179
Heaton, Sjt. R.	7150		— Sjt. E. F.	7150
Heawood, L./C. P.	7150		— Spr. J. P.	7150
Hebblethwaite, R.Q.M.Sjt. E.	7150		— Coy.Q.M.Sjt. T. W.	7179
Hecker, Pte.(A./L./C.) H.	7150		— Sjt. W.	7150
Hedley, Sjt. A.	7150		— Cpl. W.	6499
Heeley, Sjt. E.	7150		Higginson, Sjt. F.	7150
Heffaran, Sjt. T. P.	7150		— Sjt. T. J.	6491
Heggs, Sjt. W.	7150		Higham, Sjt. T.	7150
Heley, By.S./M. C.	7150		Highland, Mech.S./Sjt. W. T.	7150
Helliwell, R./S./M. J.	7150		Hignett, L./C. R.	7150
Helsby, Coy.Q.M.Sjt. R.	7150		Hill, C.S.M. B. R.	6491
Hemingway, Spr. J. C.	7150		— Sjt. E. B.	7150
Hempel, Sjt. F. H.	7150		— S./M.Sjt. E. S.	7176

---

* 614412 B.Q.M.S. 1/1st Warwickshire Battery, R.H.A. (T.F.). Flanders 1917–18, and Cambrai 1917—For exemplary conduct, courage and cheerfulness. His hard and conscientious work has materially contributed to the welfare and efficiency of his battery in which he has served in France since 1914.

† Also French Médaille Militaire. B Bty. 293 Bde. R.F.A. Died 23 November, 1918, aged 23. Buried Etaples. From Port Talbot.

‡ M.S.M. known 32099 1/Garr. Bn., L'Pool Regt. Unique to Regt. for Egypt.

Hill, Sjt. F.	6499	Holland, Coy.S./M. G. A.		7151
— Sjt. J. C.	7150	— Coy.S./M. H. M.		7151
— Sjt. J. W.	7150	Holloway, S.Q.M.Sjt. G. H.		7151
— Cpl. R. A. R.	6520	— Sjt.(A./S./Sjt.) P. G.		7151
Hilland, Farr.Sjt. D. A.	7176	Hollyhead, T./S.M. J. J., *MM.*	‡	6520
Hills, Pte.(A./S./Sjt.) J.	7150	Holman, Tpr. L. E.		6491
— Sjt. W. A.	7151	— Mil.Mech.Mach.Q.M.Sjt. R. S.		6508
Hillyard, By.S./M. H. J.	* 7151	Holyoake, Sjt. G. C.		6508
Hilton, Sjt. A. J.	7151	Holmes, Cpl. E.		7151
— Sjt. H.	7151	— Sjt.(A./S./Sjt.) T. F.	§	7151
— Condr. R. A.	7151	— Sjt. G. F.		7151
Hind, Pte.(A./Sjt.) J. W.	7151	— Coy.Q.M./Sjt. J.		7151
Hindle, Sjt. J. H.	7151	— Sjt. J.		7151
Hines, Cpl. G.	6491	— R.Q.M.Sjt. J. H. T.		7151
Hirst, Sjt. H.	7151	— A./Cpl. M.		7151
Hislop, Sjt. T. H.	7151	Holt, S.M. C. W., *D.C.M.*		6508
Hitchen, S./Sjt. H.	7176	— Dvr. J.		7151
Hitchman, Cpl. A. E.	7151	Homer, Spr.(A./Sjt.) W.		7151
Hoare, R.Q.M.Sjt. R. T.	7151	Hood, Farr.Sjt. A.		7151
Hobbs, Sjt.(A./S./Sjt.) A.	7151	Hooker, 2nd Cpl.(now T./Cpl.) R. E.		7180
Hobday, Pte. W. E.	7179	Hooper, L./C. J. W.		7151
Hoblyn, L./C. S.	7151	Hopcraft, Coy.S./M. H. E.		7151
Hobson, L./C.(A./2nd Cpl.) G. C.	7151	Hopkins, Pte. B.		7151
Hockaday, L./C.(A./Sjt.) F. W.	7151	— Q.M.Sjt. E. A.		7151
Hodder, L./Cpl. W.	7151	— Sjt. E. V.		7179
Hodge, By.S./M. A.	7151	Hopkinson, S./Sjt. W. P.		6491
Hodges, Gnr. G.	7151	Hopper, Amt.S./Sjt. J.		7151
Hodgkin, W.O. Cl.1, R.	7179	Hopton, Cpl.(A./Sjt.) G.		7151
Hodgkins, Pte. G.	7151	Horlock, S./S./M. F. C.		7151
— Cpl. C. H.	7151	Horn, Pte. J.		7151
Hodgson, Sjt. E.	7151	Horne, Farr. Sjt. E. D.		7151
— Sjt. H.	7151	Hornsey, A./R./S./M. F. W.		7151
— P.O. Mech. J. W.	† 6520	Horrell, Pte.(A./Q.M.Sjt.) T. J.		7151
Hodson, Gnr. E.	7151	Horsfield, Cpl.(A./C.M.Sjt.) C. J.		7151
— Coy.Q.M.Sjt. R.	7151	— Coy.Q.M.Sjt. W.		7151
Hoitt, Cpl/.(A./Coy.Q.M.Sjt.) W.	7151	Horton, Gnr. S., *MM.*		7151
Holbrook, Sjt. J.	7151	— Pte. W. H.		7151
Holden, Sjt. T.	6499	Hosie, Mech.S./Sjt. J. D. R.		7151
Holding, Coy.Q.M.Sjt. A. E. W.	7151	Hoskin, Cpl.(A./Q.M.Sjt.) W. T.		7151
Holdsworth, Pte.(A./Cpl.) E. B.	7151	Houghton, S./S./M.		
Holland, Sjt. A.	7151	(T./1st Cl.S./S./M.) A. J.		7151
— By.Q.M.Sjt. D. C.	7151	— Pte. F.		7151
— Sjt.(A./S.S./M.) F. H.	7151	House, Pte. W.		7151

---

* He was the Museum Attendant at the Royal Hospital, Chelsea, from 1960 to 1967. Medals on display: 1914 Star & bar trio, L.S. & G.C. (Geo. V) and M.S.M.

† R.A.F. M.S.M. to F./405 R.N.A.S.

‡ Both M.M. and R.A.F. M.S.M. to 45311 R.A.F.

§ See Seigne, Thomas Frederick, Vol. II 1919. M.S.M. with Intelligence Corps. M.I.D. as R.S.M. 10 R.F. *L.G.* 10 July 1919 and Montenegran Medal for merit in silver as Sgt. R.F./I.C. *L.G.* 9 March 1917.

Houseman, Mech.S./Sjt. H.	7151	Hulme, Cpl. P.	7152
Houston, Sjt. C. N.	7151	Hume, Pte. C. J.	7180
Howard, Cpl. C.	7151	— Pte. T. D.	7176
— Sjt. G. N.	7151	Humphrey, Pte. H.	7152
— Cpl. P. S.	6499	Humphreys, Sjt. J.	7152
— Bombr. T.	7151	— Pte. J. H.	7152
— Sjt. W.	7151	Humphries, By.S./M. H. G.	7152
Howarth, Sjt. W.	7176	— Cpl. H. G.	7152
Howe, Pte.(A./Cpl.) A. E.	7151	Hunt, T./Sub.Condr. A.	7152
— Coy.Q.M.Sjt. E. W. B.	7151	— Bombr. A. H.	7152
— Coy.Q.M.Sjt. R.	7151	— S.M. C. A.	4024
Howell, Sjt. F.	7151	— Col.Sjt.(A./Q.M.Sjt.) C. R.	7152
Howes, 2nd Cpl.(A./Cpl.) J. C. G.	7151	— Cpl. E. G.	7179
— Sjt. W. A.	7151	— Cpl. F.	7152
Howie, Mech.S./Sjt. J.	6491	— Armr.S./M. F. W.	7152
Hoy, Sjt. A. H. M.	6520	— Pte.(T./Cpl.) J. H.	7179
Hoyes, Sadd.Sjt. J.	7179	— Flt.Sjt. J. S. ‡	4413
Huckvale, Pte. J.	7151	— Bombr. R.	7152
Hudson, S./Sjt.(A./S.M.) F. M.	7151	Hunter, Sjt. A.	7152
— Coy.S./M. H.	7151	— Sjt. O. G.	6520
— Cpl. J.	7151	— R.Q.M.Sjt. S.	7152
— Cpl. T.	7151	— Sjt. T.	7152
— Sjt. W. *	7151	— Sjt. W. A.	7152
Huffer, Sjt. H.	7151	Hutridge, Sjt.EA./Coy.S./M.) F. T.	7152
Huggett, Pte. W.	7151	Hurle, Cpl.(A./Sjt.) G. R.	7152
Huggins, Bombr. W.	7151	Hurley, By.Q.M.Sjt. W. G.	7152
Hughes, Pte.(Sjt.) A. D.	7151	Hurrell, S./Sjt. A.	7152
— R.Q.M.Sjt. G.	7152	— T./Sub.Condr. H. R. W.	7152
— Sub.Condr.(A./Condr.) G. F.	7152	Hursey, Coy.S./M. E.	7152
— R.S.M. J.	6491	Hurst, Sjt. H.	7152
— Pte. J.	7152	— Bombr. J. S.	6499
— Pte. R. C.	7152	Hutchings, 2nd Cpl. W. ❀	4024
— Cpl. S.	7152	Hutchinson, Cpl. C.	7152
— Flt.Sjt. S. E.	6520	— Sjt. D.	7176
— Sjt. T.	7152	— Sjt. J. §	7152
— Sjt. W. W.	7152	Hutton, S./M. H.	7152
Hull, Sjt.(A./S./S./M.) J. M.	7152	— S./S./M. J.	7152
— Spr. T. †	7152	— Pte. J.	7152
Hulme, Sjt. J.	7152	Huxford, Sjt.(T./S./S./M.) G. C.	7152

---

* Medal known: 325210 1/1 Cambridge Regt. Only 9 M.S.M.s to the Regt.
† No. 312929 still alive in Marsden, Yorks. in January 1980. He was awarded the M.S.M. serving with 5/A.S. Coy. R.E. for relaying telephone wires under shell fire.
‡ Group of miniatures known D.F.C., 1914/15 Star, British War and Victory Medals and Army M.S.M. It is believed they can be attributed to this man who was 3552 R.F.C., subsequently Lieutenant R.A.F. He was awarded a D.F.C. in *L.G.* 22 December, 1919.
§ Group in National Army Museum: M.B.E. (1st type, military ribbon), 1914 Star & bar, British War and Victory Medals (M.I.D. oakleaf), Defence and War Medals, Jubilee 1935, L.S. & G.C. (Geo. V, awarded 1925), L.S. & G.C., (Geo. VI awarded 1947) and M.S.M. WO 1 1936, Commissioned 1940, later Captain & Q.M. R.A.S.C.

Huxter, Sjt.Maj. T. J.	4413	Jackson, Sjt.(A.R.S./M.) W.	7152
Hyman, Dvr. J.	7179	— Sjt. W.	7152
Hyndman, By.Q.M.Sjt. D.	7152	— 2nd Cpl.(A./Cpl.) W. H.	7152
		Jacob, S.M. S.	6508
Iceton, Cpl. W.	7152	Jacobs, Sjt. F.	7152
Imeson, Pte.(A./L./C.) R.	7152	Jagger, T./Sub.Condr. H. G. F.	6491
Impey, Sjt. A.	7152	Jakeman, Pte. A.	7179
Ing, By.S.M. F. A.	7152	James, T.R.S.M. A. O.	6499
— Pte.(A./Cpl.) H. J.	6499	— S.M. A. T.	4024
Ingall, A./Cpl. E. F.	7152	— Coy.S.M. A. W.	7152
Ingham, Sjt. J. W.	7179	— Pte.(A./Sjt.) C. E.	7152
Ingle, Sjt.(A./C.S.M.) H. C.	6499	— T./S.M. C. W.	6520
Inglis, Gnr. D.	7152	— Sjt. F.	7152
Ingram, Sjt.Arty.Clk.(T.S.M.) R. D. T.	7152	— S.M. H., *M.M.* †	6520
Ings, R.Q.M.Sjt. G.	7152	— Pte.(A./Cpl.) J. H.	7152
Innes, Cpl.(A./Sjt.) J. *	7152	— Cpl. T. E.	7152
Inns, Sjt. H.	7152	— S./Sjt. W.	7152
Ireland, Mech.S./Sjt. A. E.	7152	— R.Q.M.Sjt. W. E.	7179
Ireson, Q.M.Sjt.(A./S./M.) J. R.	7152	— Sjt. W. F.	7176
Ironmonger, Cpl. J. C.	7179	— Coy.Q.M.Sjt. W. S.	7152
Irven, Sjt. C.	7152	Jameson, Sjt. G.	7152
Irvine, Mech.S./M. C. S.	7152	Jamieson, Cpl. J. N.	7152
Irving, R.Q.M.Sjt. W.	7152	— Coy.S./M.(T./R.S.M.) R.	7152
Isaacs, Farr.Sjt. J.	7152	Jamison, Sjt. J.	7152
Ison, Pte.(A./Sjt.) T. E. G.	7152	Jardin, Cpl. A.	7152
Ivanovitch, Cpl. M.	7176	Jarman, T./S.M. A. ‡	6521
Ives, Sjt.(A./Q.M.Sjt.) A. E.	7152	Jasper, Sjt. G.	7152
— Mech.S.M. H. B.	6508	Jeeves, Sjt.(A./S./Sjt.) E. C.	7152
Ivey, Coy.S./M. L.	7152	Jefferies, R.Q.M.Sjt.(A./R.S.M.) L. J.	7152
Ivins, S./M. J. R.	7152	Jeffries, S./M. F. W.	7152
— Sjt. R.	7176	— Pte. H. T.	7180
Ivory, S./Sjt.(A./S.Q.M.Sjt.) C. E.	7152	Jemmett, By.S./M. J. H.	7153
		Jenkins, Sjt. G.	7153
Jackman, Sjt. J.	7152	— Sqdn.S./M. H.	7153
— Pte.(temp.Coy.S.M.) W. F.	4413	— Sjt. H. J.	7153
Jackson, Coy.Q.M.Sjt. E. J.	7152	— Cpl.(L./Sjt.) J. T.	7179
— Spr. F. S. ❀	7018	— Sjt. W. H.	7179
— R.Q.M.Sjt. G. W.	7152	Jenn, Coy.Q.M.Sjt. J.	7153
— Sjt. J. E.	7152	Jenner, S./Sjt. L. W.	7153
— Coy.S./M.(T./Mech.S./M.) V.	7152	Jennings, Coy.Q.M.Sjt. H. M.	7153
— S./Sjt. W.	7181	Jeppeson, Cpl. T. R. G.	7179

---

* 400177 Serjt. John Innes, 400 Field Coy. R.E. K.I.A. at Robecq, 30 April, 1918, aged 30. From Kelvinside, Glasgow.

† No. 320 R.F.C. Enlisted March, 1906 into R.F.A. With 2 Sqn. R.F.C. as Sgt. in France from 12 August, 1914. M.M. L.G. 3 June 1916 as Flight Sergeant, 13 Sqn.,1914 Star trio, R.A.F. M.S.M. for services in France, R.A.F. L.S. & G.C. in 1924 as S.M.1. 4th senior R.A.F. W.O. in 1931.

‡ No. 321 R.F.C. Enlisted November 1906 into R.G.A. With No. 2 Sqn. R.F.C. as Sgt. in France from 12 August, 1914. 1914 Star & bar trio, R.A.F. M.S.M. with No. 5 Sqn. in France.

Jepson, L./C. W. J.	7153	Jones, 2nd Cpl. (A./Sjt.) H.		7153
Jesseman, Sjt. L. W.	7153	— Coy.Q.M.Sjt. H. E.		7153
Jewell, S./Sjt. H.	7153	— Sjt. H. V.		6499
Jewson, L./Sjt. L. T.	7153	— Coy.S./M. J.		7179
Jeynes, Sjt. W.	6499	— R.Q.M.Sjt. J.		7153
Joachin, Coy.Q.M.Sjt. P.	7153	— Cpl.(A./Sjt.) J.		7153
John, Sjt. R.	7153	— Reg.S./M. J. H.		7153
— Pte. W. D.	7179	— Cpl.(A./Sjt.) J. L.		7153
Johnson, S./Sjt. A. E.	7153	— Cpl. M. D.		6521
— Gnr.(A./Sjt.) A. W.	7153	— S.Q.M.Sjt. N. R.		7153
— W.O. Cl.1, B.	7179	— A./Cpl. R.		7153
— Cpl. C. C.	7179	— Sptg.Ck. R. E.		7153
— S.Q.M.Sjt. E. H.	7153	— S./Sjt.(A./Q.M.Sjt.) W.		7153
— Coy. S./M. F. R.	7176	— Whl.S./Sjt. W.		7153
— Sjt. H.	7153	— Q.M.Sjt. W. H.		7153
— Coy.S./M. J. W.	7153	— S.S./M. W. N.		7153
— Sjt. M.	7153	Jopling, Cpl. T. N.		7153
— Cpl. P. F.	7153	Jordan, T./S.S./M. C.		7153
— L./Sjt.(A./Sjt.) S.	7153	— Pte. J. P.		7153
— Sjt. S. W.	7153	— Pte.(A./Sjt.) R. G.		7153
— Q.M.Sjt. W.	7153	Joscelyne, R.Q.M.Sjt. H. B.		7153
— R.Q.M.S. W. L.	6499	Jose, Mech.S./Sjt. J. M.		7153
Johnsson, Pte. R. J.	7179	Joseph, Amt.S./Sjt. F.		6512
Johnston, R.S./M. A. C.	7179	Joules, Spr. W.		7153
— Cpl.(A./S.S./M.) A. G.	7153	Judd, Spr. C. W.		7153
— Cpl.(A./Sjt.) D. C.	7153	— Q.M.Sjt. J.		7153
— C.S.M. J. C.	6508	Jukes, Pte.(A./Sjt.) R.		7153
— Sjt. J. G.	7179	Justham, Sjt.(A./Q.M.Sjt.) J. F. R.		7153
— Sjt. J. W.	7153			
Johnstone, Cpl.(A./Sjt.) A.	7153	Kanard, Pte. H. G.		6508
Joiner, Sjt.(A./R.Q.M.Sjt.) D.	6508	Kane, Sjt. A.		7153
Jolley, Cpl. G. S.	6508	— Pte. R.		7153
Jolly, Coy.S.I.M.(A/R.S.M.) J.	7153	Kay, Sjt. H.		7153
— Coy.S./M. T. B.	7153	— L./Sjt. J.		7153
Jones, L./Sjt. A. (Hrs.)	7153	— Mech.Mach.S./Sjt. J.		7153
— Sjt.(A./Coy.Q.M.Sjt.) A.	7153	Keane, S./Sjt. A.		7153
— Sjt. A. (R.G.A.)	7153	— Cpl. R. S.		7153
— R.Q.M.Sjt. A. H.	6508	Kearns, R.Q.M.Sjt. F. V.		7153
— Sjt.A.(A./Coy.Q.M.Sjt.) C. E.	7153	Keary, Sjt. W. J.		7153
— Coy.S./M. E.	7153	Keefe, By.S./M.(T./R.S./M) A. W.		7153
— Sjt. E. (S. Staff. R.)	7153	— Pte. S. J.	✿	4024
— Sjt. E. W. Rid. R.)	7153	Keeling, Sjt. K. E.		7153
— Pte.(A./L./C.) E. E.	✿ 4393	— Cpl. W. E.		7153
— Coy.S./M. E. R.	7153	Keen, Dvr. E.		7153
— Cpl. F.	6508	— Pte. G.		6499
— Q.M.Sjt. G.	7176	— T./R.S./M. J. S.		7153
— L./C. G.	7153	Keey, S.S./M. C. H.		7153
— Sjt. G. M.	7179	Keightley, Cpl. A. H.		7153
— Sjt. G W.	7153	Keir, Coy.Q.M.Sjt. J. F.		7153
— Sjt. H. (R.W.Fus.)	7153	Kelby, Sjt. A. H.		7153
— Sjt. H. (L'pool R.)	7153	Kelcher, Coy.S./M. J.		7153
— Mech.Mach. S./Sjt. H.	7153	Kellett, Cpl. W. M.		7179

Kelly, Pte.(A./Cpl.) A. B.	7153	Kilcoin, Sub.Condr. C. L.		7181
— Cpl. C.	7179	Kilkenny, L./C. W.		7154
— Sjt. H. C.	7179	Killeen, Pte. J.		6499
— Sjt. J.	7153	Killick, Pte. G. R.		7154
— L./C.(A./Cpl.) J. J.	7154	Killikelly, Sjt. G.	*	7154
Kelsall, R.S./M. J. F.	7179	Killingback, R.Q.M.Sjt. T. H.		7154
Kelso, Pte. J.	7154	Killington, Sjt. J. R.		7154
Kelton, Sjt. K. L.	7179	Kimble, Sjt. J. D.		7154
Kamp, S./Sjt. A. D.	7179	Kinch, 2nd Cpl.(A./Cpl.) A. J.		7154
— Cpl. A. E.	7154	Kinden, C.S.M. D. G.		6508
— Sjt. A. F.	7154	King, Spr. H. E.		4413
— Gnr. C.	7154	— Coy.Q.M.Sjt. J.		7154
— Sjt. G. R.	7176	— Pte. J.		7176
— Sjt. S. W.	7154	— Pte. J. N.		7176
Kenneally, Q.M.Sjt.(A./S.M.) P.	7154	— S.Q.M.Sjt.(now T./Lt.) N. W.		7176
Kennedy, Coy.Q.M.Sjt. W.	7176	— Bombr. P.		7154
Kennelly, By.S./M. J.	7154	— Sjt. P. W.		7154
Kennerley, Cpl. E. W.	7154	— Sjt.(A./S./M.) S. H.		7154
Kenning, S./M. W. E.	7154	— R.Q.M.Sjt. T. H.		7176
Kent, L./C.(A./2nd Cpl.) L.	7154	— Sjt. W.		7154
Kenworthy, C.Q.M.Sjt. A.	6508	Kindgon, Sjt. B.		7180
Kerei, Sjt. H.	7180	Kingscote, S./Sjt. F. G.		7154
Kerr, By.S./M. A.	7154	Kingsford, Coy.Q.M.Sjt.(T./		
— Sjt. F.	7176	R.Q.M.Sjt.) W. J.		7179
— Sjt. J.	6521	Kingsland, L./Bombr. G. C.		7154
— Cpl.(A./Sjt.) R.	6491	Kingwell, Pte.(A./Sjt.) F. S. A.		7154
— Q.M.Sjt. T.	7154	Kinna, S./S.M. J. C.		7154
— Sjt. W. C.	7176	Kinnell, Coy.S./M. J. S.		7176
Kersen, Sjt.(A./S./M.) M.	7176	Kippen, Pte. A. D.		7154
Kersey, Cpl.(A./S./Sjt.) J. B.	7154	Kirby, Flt.Sjt. F. W.		6521
Kerslake, Armt.S./Sjt. W. H.	7154	— A./Sjt. J. T.		7176
Kerton, Sjt. G.	7154	Kirk, Coy.S./M. H.		7154
Kett, Sjt. A.	7154	— Cpl. J.		7154
Kettley, Pte. E.	7154	— L./C.(A./Sjt.) L.		7154
Keyes, Pte. E.	7176	Kirkbride, Cpl.P./O.		
Keys, Pte.(A./Coy.S./M.) D.	7154	(Bn.S./M.) J. L.		7154
Kibble, Sjt. C. E. H.	7154	Kirkin, Coy. S./M. A. G.	†	7154
Kidd, S./Sjt. W. S.	7154	Kirkpatrick, Coy. S./M. S.		7154
Kierran, Gnr. O.	7154	Kirkwood, Sjt.(A./S./M.) N. F.		7154
Kiff, S.Q.M.Sjt. E. H.	7154	Kirsop, Pte. A.		6499

---

* Group sold 1989 for £1400: D.C.M., M.M. (both Sgt. 2/Leinsters), Queen's South Africa Medal (Cape Colony, Tugela Heights, Orange Free State, Relief of Ladysmith, Transvaal, Laing's Nek, Pte. R.A.M.C.), King's South Africa Medal, 1914/15 Star trio (Sgt. Conn. Rangers), Scottish Police 1911 Coronation (P.C.), M.S.M. (6/Conn. R.). M.M. *L.G.* 17 June, 1919, D.C.M. *L.G.* 10 January, 1920 'Near Ghuluwe 29 September, 1918, carried his wounded officer to cover under heavy M.G. fire. Assuming command he worked the platoon around a strongly held enemy position, charged it with the bayonet and killed the whole of the M.G. crews.'

† Group known: 1914 Star trio (Pte./W.O.II A.S.C.), 1939/45 and Atlantic Stars, Defence and War Medals, M.S.M. (A.S.C.); later Commander R.N.

Kirtley, Pte.(A./Cpl.) R. W.	7154	
Kirton, Whr.S./Sjt. J. C. S.	6491	
Kitchen, L./C.(A./S.S./M.) W. G.	7154	
Kitchiner, Cpl. V. C.	7154	
Kite, Sjt.(A./S./Sjt.) C.	7154	
— Cpl. W.	7154	
Kittner, Sjt. B.	7177	
Kleeman, Coy.Q.M.Sjt. W. H.	7179	
Knight, L./C.(A./2nd Cpl.) A.	7154	
— Sjt. G. B.	7154	
— Sjt.(A./S./Sjt.) H. H.	7154	
— R.Q.M.Sjt. J.	7154	
— Sjt.Trptr. J.	* 7154	
Knock, Col.Sjt. A. H.	7154	
Knott, Pte. G.	7154	
— Sjt. J.	7154	
Knox, A./Cpl. A.	7154	
— Q.M.Sjt. A. J.	7181	
— Pte.(L./C.) J. F.	7179	
Kooymans, Cpl. J. W.	7154	
Kyberd, S./M. E.	7154	
Laborde, Pte.(A./Cpl.) H. G.	7154	
Lace, Pte. V.	7154	
Lackford, Cpl. H. F.	6491	
Lacon, Cpl.(A./Sjt.) W.	7154	
Laidlaw, Cpl.(A./Sjt.) G. R.	7154	
Lakeman, Sjt. A.	7180	
Laker, Sjt.(A./R.S./M.) P. J.	7154	
Lally, Spr. J.	7154	
Lamb, Pte. A. P.	7177	
— Sjt.(A./Coy.S./M.) P. (Manch. R.)	7154	
— Col.Sjt.(A./Coy.Q.M.Sjt.) P. (H.L.I.)	7154	
— S.S./M. R. V.	7154	
— Q.M.Sjt. W. J.	7154	
Lambert, R.Q.M.Sjt. R. W.	7154	
— T./R.S.M. W.	6491	
Lamond, Sjt. D.	7154	
Landsborough, Sjt. R.	7177	
Lane, Tpr.(A./S.S./M.) E.	7154	
— R.Q.M.Sjt. J.	7154	
— Farr.Q.M.Sjt. T.	7154	
— Sjt. W. J.	7154	
— Spr.(A./Cpl.) W. M. H.	7154	

Lang, Sjt. W.		7154
— Sjt.(A./Q.M.Sjt.) W. O.		7154
Langford, T./S.S./M. G. H.		7154
Langley, Sjt. T.		7154
— L./C. W. H.		7154
Langridge, Sjt. A.		7154
Langrish, T./Sub.Condr. J. J		6491
Lanham, Bombr. W.		7154
Lankestor, Sjt. D.		7154
Lansley, Sjt. F.		7155
Lappin, Cpl. F.		7179
Large, Sjt. W. W.		7177
Larkins, C.S.M. F. A.		6499
Larmour, Coy.Q.M.Sjt. E. M.		7155
Larner, By.Q.M.Sjt. A. S.		7155
Last, Cpl. C.		7155
Latham, Sjt. C.		6499
— Sjt. W. H.		7155
Laurie, Sjt. J. T.		7177
Law, Sjt. C.		7155
— Pte. W.		7155
— Pte. W. H. F.		7180
Lawley, Cpl. W.		6508
Lawrence, Whl.Cpl.(A./Whl.S./Sjt.) C.		7155
— S./Sjt. G.	†	6492
— C.S.M. J.		6499
— Pte.(A./Sjt.) J.		7155
— Sjt. J. T.		7177
— Cpl.(A./Sjt.) W. J.		7155
Lawson, Sjt. J.		7155
— S./Sjt.(A./Q.M.Sjt.) W.		7155
— 2nd Cpl.(A./Sjt.) W.		7155
Lay, Sjt. D.		7155
Laycock, S./Sjt. J. W.		7155
— Gnr. V. T.		6499
Layton, By.S./M. J.		7155
Lea, Sjt. T.		7155
Leach, Coy.Q.M.Sjt. C. R.		7155
— 2nd Cpl.(A./Sjt.) H.		7155
Leadley, Sjt. F. J.		7155
Lean, S./Sjt.Inst. R. G.		7155
— Pte. T. F.		7177
Leask, Sjt.(A./Coy.S./M.) A.		7155
Leatherbarrow, Suptg.Clk.S.S./M. E. J.	‡	7155

---

* Awarded M.S.M. Annuity 1951.

† See Bruce *ante*.

‡ Group known: O.B.E. (*L.G.* June 1919), 1914/15 Star trio (M.I.D. oakleaf), M.S.M. (1/6 Liverpool Regt.) and Territorial Force Efficiency Medal (Edw. VII). Born 1879 and died 1943.

Le Cheminant, T./Sub.Condr. C.	7155
Le Maitre, Sjt. A. M.	7155
Ledgard, Pte. J. E.	7179
Ledger, Pte.(A./Sjt.) J. A.	7155
Ledingham, S.Q.M.Sjt. A. D.	7177
Lee, Sjt. A.	7155
— Sjt. H.	6499
— L./C. T. H.	7155
— L./C.(A./Sjt.) W. (Nottingham)	7155
— L./C. W. (Alnwick)	7155
— R.S./M. W. T.	* 7155
Leedham, R.Q.M.Sjt. T.	7155
Leeds, Sjt. F. E.	7155
Leeson, Pte.(A./L./C.) W. C.	7177
Legg, Cpl. W.	7155
— Flt.Sjt. W. A.	6521
Leggatt, Sjt. H. O.	7155
Leigh, Pte.(A./S./Sjt.) G.	7155
— Sjt. J. S.	7155
— Coy.Q.M.S.Sjt. W.	7155
Lelliott, Sjt. A. H.	7155
Leman, Bombr. J.	7180
Lemay, L./C. A.	7177
Leonard, Armr.Q.M.Sjt. F.	7155
Leroux, Sjt. H. G.	7179
Lester, Coy.S./M. L. E.	7155
— A./Sjt. R.	7155
— Cpl. R. J.	7155
L'Estrange, Pte.(A./Sjt.) E. G.	6508
Letham, L./C. H.	7155
Letourneau, Pte. A.	7177
Lett, Cpl. R.	7177
Lever, Coy.Q.M.Sjt. B. W.	7155
— Sjt. T. J.	7155
Lewarn, Sub.Condr. H. S.	7155
Lewarne, Cpl.(A./Sjt.) L.	7155
Lewins, Coy.S./M. N. T.	7179
Lewis, Coy.Q.M.Sjt. A. W. J.	7155
— Cpl. C.	7155
— Farr. Sjt. E.	7155
— L./Sjt. J. W.	7155
— Amt. S./Sjt. T.	† 7155
— Pte.(L./C.) T.	7155
Lickorish, Cpl. B.	7155
Lidbury, Pte. J. H.	6499
Liddell, Pte. J.	7155
— Q.M.Sjt.(T./S.M.) T.	6508
Liddiard, Sjt. J. T.	7155

Liggins, Pte.(A./Cpl.) A. G.	7155
Liggitt, Sjt. A.	6508
Lightfoot, M.S./M. G. R.	7155
Lightowlers, Coy.Q.M.Sjt.(A./ R.Q.M.Sjt.) C. G.	7155
Lillie, Gnr. W.	7155
Lilly, T./Sub.Condr.(A./Condr.) A.	7155
Lillywhite, Condr. J.	7155
Lincoln, A./Sjt. J.	7155
Linden, S./S.M. T.	6508
Lindley, S./Sjt.(A./S./M.) J. S.	7155
Lindsay, Coy.S./M. F. J.	7155
— Pte.(A./Cpl.) J. D.	7179
— Sjt.(A./Coy.S./M.) P. J.	7155
— Pte. W.	7155
Linford, Sjt. D.	6508
Lingham, Q.M.Sjt. H. T.	7179
Link, Sjt. C. H.	7177
Littell, B.Q.M.Sjt. L.	6508
Little, R.Q.M.Sjt. H. D.	7155
— Sjt. J.	7155
— A./R.S./M. R.	7155
— Pte. R.	7155
— Pte. W.	7155
Littlejohns, Pte.(T./Cpl.) R. W.	7179
Littler, Pte. T. B.	7155
Littlewood, Sjt. F. A.	7155
Littleworth, Pte.(A./L./C.) T.	7155
Livesay, Bombr. D.	7155
Livesey, Sjt. L.	7155
Livings, L./C. H. R.	7155
Livy, Dvr. D.	7155
Lloyd, Sjt. A. R.	7179
— Coy.S./M.(A./R.Q.M.Sjt.) E. A.	7155
— C.Q.M.Sjt. J.	6508
Loader, Sjt. A.	7155
Loads, Pte. G. B.	7155
Lochrie, Coy.Q.M.Sjt.(A./ R.Q.M.Sjt.) J.	7155
Lock, R./S./M. A. V.	7177
Locke, Cpl. F.	7155
— Sjt.(C.S.M.) H.	6499
Lockerbie, Sjt. J.	7177
Lockton, Pte.(A./Cpl.) J. W.	7155
Lockwood, Cpl. G. W.	7155
Lodge, B.S.M. T.	6508
Loft, T./R.S./M. A. C.	7156
Lofthouse, Sjt. D.	7156

* Awarded M.S.M. Annuity A.O. 76/1947. R.A.
† R.A.O.C. Also Belgian Croix de Guerre and Chevalier Ordre de Léopold II.

Lofts, Pte.(L./Sjt.) G.	7156	McArthur, Cpl.(A./C.S.M.)	
Logan, Sjt. D. M.	7180	G. W. J. H.	6509
— Sjt. W.	7156	— Pte. M.	6492
Logen, Farr./Sjt. J.	7177	Macartney, W.O.Cl.1, C. G.	7179
Lomax, T./S./S./M. R. T.	7156	Macaulay, R.Q.M.Sjt. C. E.	7156
Long, Coy.Q.M.Sjt. F.	7156	McAuley, Coy.Q.M.Sjt. H. J.	7157
— Pte. F. J.	7156	McAuliffe, E.S./Q.M.Sjt. P.	7157
— Sjt. H.	7156	McBain, Cpl.(A./L./Sjt.) D. M.	7157
— 2nd Cpl.(A./Sjt.) H. A.	6499	McBeath, Sjt. D. A.	7177
— Armr.S./Sjt. K.	7156	M'Caffrey, Sjt. J.	7157
Longfield, Sjt. C. D.	7156	McCallum, Sjt. M.	7156
— Q.M.Sjt. H. P.	7156	McCamley, A./Q.M.Sjt. J.	7157
Longley, Bombr. A.	7156	McCarthy, Cpl. C. C.	7157
Lonsdale, Pte. A.	7156	— Sjt.(A./C.S.M.) D.	6509
Looney, By.Q.M.Sjt. R. H.	7156	— Cpl.(T./Sjt.) M.	7179
Lord, C.S.M. E. F.	6508	McClellan, Sjt. C.	7157
— S.Q.M.Sjt. E. R.	7156	McClennand, Pte.A./Cpl. J. J.	7157
Lothian, Sjt. H.	7156	McConkey, Pte. C.	7157
Lousada, Cpl. St.L., *D.C.M.*	* 7179	McConnell, By.S./M.(T./R.S.M.) J.	7157
Lovell, Cpl.(A./Sjt.) E. A.	4413	McConologue, Sjt. J.	7157
Lovelock, Cpl. F. C.	7156	McCord, Col.Sjt. G.	7157
Low, Sjt. G. A.	7156	McCormack, 2nd Cpl.(A./	
Lowdon, L./C. H. A.	7156	Coy.S./M.) F.	7157
Lowe, Coy.Q.M.Sjt. F. W.	7156	McCormick, Dvr. H.	7157
— Spr. L. B.	7156	— L./C. J.	7157
— Sjt. P.	7156	McCready, Sjt. J.	7157
— Sjt. T. E.	7181	McCubbing, By.S./M. A.	7157
— L./C. T. E.	7156	McCulloch, L./C. A. G.	❀ 5037
— Pte. W.	7156	McCurrach, By.S./M. W.	7157
Lowin, Gnr. B.	7156	McCusker, Cpl. J. E.	7157
Lowis, S.S./M. E. J.	7179	McDevitt, Cpl. J.	7177
Loxton, F. of W.Q.M.Sjt. J. W.	7156	McDonagh, Sjt.(A./Coy.S./M.)	
Lucas, R.Q.M.Sjt. F.	7156	J. T., *M.M.*	7157
— S./Smith Cpl. H., *M.M.*	7156	McDonald, Sjt. A.	7177
Lucock, Sjt. W.	6499	— Spr. A. B.	7177
Luffrum, Sjt. A. H.	7156	— Sjt. A. N.	7177
Luke, Cpl.(A./Sjt.) G. A.	7156	MacDonald, Cpl. C.	6508
Lusted, Pte. F. C.	7156	McDonald, Sjt. D. H.	7177
Luxton, Pte.(A./L./C.) R.	7156	— Sjt. E. J.	7180
Lynas, Sjt. I.	7156	Macdonald, L./C.(A./Cpl.) H.	7156
Lynch, Sjt. J.	7156	McDonald, Pte.(L./C.) J. A.	7179
— Sjt. P.	7156	— M.S./M. J. M.	7157
Lyne, Sjt.(A./S.Q.M.Sjt.) H. J.	7156	MacDonald, Sjt. L. A.	6491
Lynn, L./C. W.	7180	McDonald, Coy.S./M. M.	7179
		MacDonald, Pte. W. C.	7177
Mabbett, Pte.(A./L./C.) S. B.	7156	McDonnell, S.S.M. N.	6499
Maber, Sjt. C.	7156	McDougal, R.S./M.	7157
Macalister, R.S./M. A. J.	7156	McDougall, L./C. J.	7157
		— By.Q.M.Sjt. W.	7157

---

* 1724A, 14 Bde. Australian F.A. D. of W. 10 April, 1918. From Victoria, Australia.

McDowell, Farr.S./Sjt. R.	7158	McKenzie, Pte. D.	7180
Mace, Cpl. A. C.	7156	— S./Sjt. J.	7177
McEvoy, S.Q.M.Sjt. W.	7158	— Coy.S./M. J. H.	7180
McEwen, W.O.Cl.1, J. W.	7179	— Sjt. J. R.	7158
— Cpl. R. G.	7177	— Cpl. M. J.	7177
Macey, A./2nd Cpl. C.	7156	— A./B. R.	7158
McFadden, By.S./M. H. D.	7177	MacKenzie, Coy.Q.M.Sjt. W.	7156
McFarland, Sjt. J.	7181	McKeown, R.Q.M.Sjt. D.	7158
Macfarlane, Sjt. R. F.	7156	McKibbin, Sqdn.S.M. V. J.	6492
McFeggans, Col.Sjt.(A./R.S.M.) A.	7181	Mackie, Coy.Q.M.Sjt. J.	7177
McFerran, Sjt. J.	7158	— Sjt. J. R.	7179
McGee, Spr. D.	7158	— Sjt. W. B.	7177
McGernon, S./Sjt. J. G.	7177	McKie, Bombr. W. K.	7158
McGill, Sjt. W.	6499	McKinlay, A./B.(H.C.) J.	7158
McGregor, Gnr. J.	6499	McKinley, R.Q.M.Sjt. T. J.	7179
— A.Supt.Clk.(A./S./M.) J.	7158	McKinnon, Pte. H.	7177
Mcgregor, Fitt.(A./Cpl.) J. G.	7156	MacKintosh, Sjt. D.	7156
McGuckian, Sjt. F.	7158	McKnight, E.Clk.Sjt. W. G. A.	7158
McGuckin, C.S.M. T.	6499	McLachlan, Sjt. I. R.	7179
McHale, Sjt. P.	6499	McLagan, A./S./M. R.	7158
— A./Coy.S./M.Inst. T. J.	7158	McLaughlin, Coy.Q.M.Sjt. A.	7158
McHarg, Sjt. J. C.	6499	— By.S./M. J.	7177
Machin, Sjt. H.	7156	McLean, Fitt. D. L.	7180
McInnes, Pte.(A./Sjt.) C.	7158	— By.S./M. F.	7158
— Gnr. D.	7158	— Sjt. H. H.	7158
McIntosh, Sjt. J.	7158	Maclean, Cpl. R. W. *	7156
Macinosh, L./C. J.	7156	McLean, L./C.(A./Sjt.) W. R.	6499
— L./C. W.	7156	McLeish, Sjt.(A./Col.Sjt.) P. R.	7158
McIntyre, Coy.Q.M.Sjt. A.	7158	McMahon, S./Sjt. B.	7179
MacIntyre, M.S./Sjt. M.	7156	Macmahon, Sjt. J. F.	7156
McIntyre, Spr. R. S.	7177	McManus, Sjt. W.	6509
— Coy.Q.M.Sjt. T.	7179	McMichael, Cpl. J. C.	6521
— Sjt. W.	7177	McMinn, L./Sjt. E.	7158
McIsaac, Coy.Q.M.Sjt. J.	7158	McNair, S./Sjt. J.	7179
McIver, Bombr. E.	7158	McNally, Sjt. A. E.	7158
Mack, Dvr. J.	7156	McNamara, Cpl.(A./Sjt.) E.	6509
McKay, S./M. A.	7158	Mcnamara, Sjt. J.	6499
— Cpl.(A./Sjt.) F. C.	7158	McNamara, Pte. V.	7180
— 2nd Cpl. G. C.	7158	McNamee, Coy.S./M. A.	7158
— Sjt. W.	7158	McNary, Sjt. E., *D.C.M.*	7158
McKearney, Sjt. J.	7158	MacNaughton, Sjt. D. J.	7156
McKechnie, Q.M.Sjt. D., *M.M.*	7158	McNeil, A./R./S./M. R.	7158
McKendrick, C.S.M.(T./R.S.M.) M.	6509	MacPherson, Sjt.(A/Coy.S./M.) A.	7156
McKenzie, Sjt. A.	7158	McPoland, C.Q.M.S. F. J.	6499
Mackenzie, Sjt.(A./C.S.M.) A.	4413	McQueen, 2nd Cpl.(A./Sjt.) F. S.	6500
MacKenzie, Cpl. A. D.	7156	McRae, Pte. T. R.	7177
McKenzie, Coy.S./M.(Dr.Sjt.) D.		McSporran, Cpl. P.	7158
(S. Gds.)	7158	McVey, A./Sjt. A. R.	7177
— Coy.S./M. D. (Mtd.Rif.)	7177	Maddams, A./Sjt. C.	7156

* Sergeant R.E., formerly Glasgow University. Later M.A. and B.Sc.

Maddix, Pte.(L./C.) J.	7156		Marsden, Sjt. A.	7157
Maddock, Spr. R. D.	7156		— Pte. J. B.	7157
Maddox, Sjt. G.	7156		Marsh, Sjt. A. E.	7157
Madigan, Sjt.Drmr. P.	7156		— A./Coy.S./M.Instr. P. R.	7157
Magee, S.M. A. J.	6508		— Cpl.(A./Sjt.) R. G.	6508
— Cpl.(A./Sjt.) J.	7156		— Whr.S./Sjt. T.	7157
Maguire, Sjt. J. F.	7156		— Sjt.(T./S./M.) W. R.	7157
— Coy. S./M. T. M. M.	7156		Marshall, Sjt. A. D.	7157
Maher, Pte. J.	7156		— L./Sjt. A. E.	7157
Mahy, Pte. E. E.	7156		— Coy.S.M.(T./S.M.) F.	6491
Main, A./Cpl. A.	7156		— L.Bombr. G. W.	7157
— By.S./M. L. C.	* 7177		— L./C.(A./Cpl.) H. J.	7151
Mainprice, Sjt. C. M.	7156		— Cpl. N.	7157
Mains, Sjt. J. J.	7156		Marston, Sjt.(A./Q./Sjt.) F. A. J.	7157
Major, L./C. J. W.	7156		Martin, Sjt.(A./S./Sjt.) C.	7177
Makinson, Farr.S./Sjt. G.	7156		— Cpl. E.	7157
Malcolm, Tpr.(T./Sjt.) H.	6492		— Pte.(A./Sjt.) F.	7157
— Cpl. J. M.	7156		— S./Sjt.(A./S./M.) G.	6499
— Cpl. T.	7156		— Pte.(A./L./C.) G.	7157
Mallott, Sjt. C. F.	7156		— P.O. G. M.	7157
Mallows, Sjt. F. W.	7156		— By.Q.M.Sjt. H.	7177
Malone, Sjt. J.	7156		— Cpl. H.	7179
Malpas, Coy.Q.M.Sjt. J.	7156		— Sjt. J. H.	7157
Manley, T./S./S./M. F. C., *M.M.*	7156		— Sjt. J. S.	7157
— R.Q.M.Sjt. G. H.	7156		— Cpl. R.	7157
Mann, Cpl.(A./Sjt.) H.	7156		— S./Sjt.(A./Q.M.Sjt.) S.	7157
— L./C. J. H.	7156		— Pte. T. A.	7157
Manners, Sjt. R.	7156		— Dvr. T. H.	7157
Manning, Cpl.(A./Sjt.) A. E.	7156		— Coy.S./M. W.	7157
— Pte.(A./S./Sjt.) C.	7157		— Pte. W. J.	7157
— T./Sub.Condr. H.	7157		Mascarenhas, A./P./O. S. P.	7157
— R.Q.M.Sjt. J.	7157		Maskrey, Sjt. W. J.	6508
— Cpl.(A./Sjt.) J.	7157		Mason, Sjt. E., *M.M.*	7157
— Spr. W. H.	7157		— Coy.S./M. G.	7179
Mansell, Sjt.(Arty.Clk.) S. R.	7157		— Cpl. H. B.	7157
Manson, L./C. H. M. O.	❀ 4393		— Pte.(A./Sjt.) H. S.	7157
Manton, Sjt. F. G.	7157		— Sjt. J. E.	7179
March, Q.M.Sjt.(A./S./M.) J. E.	7157		— Sjt. J. J.	7157
Mares, Sjt. J.	7157		— Sjt. R. J.	7157
Mark, Sjt. J. G.	7157		— S./Smith(A./Farr.S./Sjt.) S.	6509
Marker, By.S./M. F.	7157		Massey, Bombr. F. C.	7157
Marks, Sjt. C. L.	6521		Masson, Sadd. T.	7157
— Farr.Sjt. W. J.	7157		Masters, A./L./Sjt. W. H.	7157
Marquis, T./Sub.Condr. E.	7157		Mathers, S./Sjt. F. J.	7157
Marr, Cpl. J.	7179		Matheson, Sjt. S.	7157
Marriner, Sjt.(A./S./M.) W.	7157		Mathews, Cpl. E.	7157
Marriott, Sjt. F. H.	6499		— R.Q.M.Sjt. P.	7157

* Group known: M.M. (41426 B.S.M. Can F.A.), 1914/15 Star (Sjt.), British War and Victory Medals (W.O.II), 1911 Coronation (Metro. Police P.C.) and M.S.M. (1/Div. Amm. Col. C.F.A.).

Matthews, L./Cpl. A.	7157	Michailides, L./C. F.	6509
— Flt.Sjt. F. B.	6521	Michin, R.Q.M.Sjt. W.	7158
— Cpl. R.	6491	Micklethwaite, Cpl.(A./Coy S./M.)	
Mauchlen, C./S./M. G.	6509	G. O.	7158
Maudson, Gnr. J. D.	7157	Middlemiss, Sjt. W. A.	7158
Maughan, Cpl. A.	7157	Middleton, Cpl.(A./Sjt.) J.	7158
Maul, Condr. J. H.	6510	— Sjt.(A./Coy.S./M.) L. E.	7158
Mawson, Sjt. J.	7157	— Cpl. R.	7158
Maxted, Sjt.(A./By.S./M.) H. S.	7157	Midgeley, Pte.(A./Cpl.) C.	7158
Maxwell, Cpl.(A./S./Sjt.) M. M. D.	7157	Midgley, Pte.(now Cpl.) E.	7177
May, Flt.Sjt.(T./S.M.) A. R.	* 6521	Miles, R.Q.M.Sjt. E.	7158
— Pte. F. A.	7157	— Cpl.(A./Coy.Q.M.Sjt.) H. M.	7158
— T./S.M. S. H.	6521	— Bombr. T. M.	7158
— By.Q.M.Sjt. W. R.	7179	Millar, Pte. J. H.	7158
Maybank, Sjt. J.	❀ 4393	Millard, Cpl. H.	7158
Mayhew, Pte. G. W.	7157	— Pte. J. W.	7158
Mayman, S./Sjt.(A./Q.M.Sjt.) T. G.	7157	— Gnr. W.	7158
Maynard, Coy.Q.M.Sjt. F. C.	7180	Miller, L./C. A.	7158
Mead, Pte. E.	7158	— 2nd Cpl. H. A.	❀ 7018
Meade, Sjt.(A./Col.Sjt.)		— Sjt. J.	7158
(A./Bombr.Q.M.S.) J. H.	7158	— Pte. J.	7177
Meadows, Sjt. F.	7158	— C.S.M. J. H.	6509
— Dvr. G. S.	❀ 7018	— Coy.S./M. J. W.	7158
Meal, Sjt. W.	7158	— A./L./Cpl. T.	7158
Medhust, L./C.(A./Cpl.) B.	7158	— Coy.Q.M.Sjt. W. (Wellington R.)	7180
Medlam, Sjt. W. J.	7158	— By.S.M.(T./R.S.M.) W.	6500
Medley, Sjt. J. J.	7179	— A.S./Sjt. W. E.	7180
Meiklejohn, L./C. F. A.	7158	Millman, Flt.Sjt. R. H.	6521
Mellor, Cpl.(A./Q.M.Sjt.) A. E.	7158	Mills, Sjt. A.	7158
— Sjt. W.	7158	— Whlr.S./Sjt. A. E.	7158
Melrose, Supt.Clk. G. W.	7181	— Cpl. E.	7177
Melton, C.Q.M.S. W. J. W.	6500	— L./Cpl. J.	7158
Memory, Sjt. E. J.	6492	— By.S./M. J.	7158
Mendel, Pte.(A./Sjt.) G. H.	7158	— Sjt. J. M.	7177
Menelly, Pte. H.	7158	— Coy.Q.M.Sjt. M. E.	7179
Mennel, Cpl. C. T.	7158	— Pte. T.	7179
Menzies, Pte.(A./S./Sjt.) H. E.	7158	— C.S.M. W.	6500
Meredith, Farr.Sjt.(A./Farr.S./Sjt.) A.	7158	Millward, By.Q.M.Sjt. C.	7177
— Sjt. J.	7158	— Cpl. J.	7158
Merewether, Coy.S./M.(A./R.Q.M.)		Milne, Coy.Q.M.Sjt. J. E.	7179
E. F. R.	7158	— Sjt. W.	7177
Metcalf, R.Q.M.Sjt. E. J.	7158	Milner, Sjt. C.	7158
— Sjt. G.	7158	— R.Q.M.Sjt. H.	7158
Metcalfe, T./M.S./M. M.	7158	— By.S./M. T.	7158
Meyers, E.Clk.Q.M.Sjt.(A./Supt.Clk.)		Milnes, C.S.M.(A./R.S.M.) J.	6509
A. S.	7158	Mindham, Sjt. H. J.	7159

---

* R.A.F. M.S.M. in 47 Sqn., Salonika. No. 167 R.F.C. Enlisted into R.G.A. 1906, aged 14. Royal Aero Club Aviator's Certificate No. 863, August 1914. 1914 Star & bar as Sgt., 3 Sqn. M.I.D. Egypt 1.7.16 and 25.9.16. R.A.F. L.S. & G.C. 1924. Still serving as W.O. in 1941.

Minns, Cpl. C.	7159	— 2nd Cpl.(A./Sjt.) C. R.	6500
Minter, Sjt. W. J.	7159	— Sjt. E. B.	7179
Minton, By.Q.M.Sjt. W. R.	7159	— Coy.Q.M.Sjt. F.	7159
Mirams, Coy.S./M. A. J.	7177	— Sjt. G.	6500
Mitchell, Sjt.(A./Q.M.Sjt.) C.	7159	— Pte. H.	7177
— Coy.S./M.(A./R.S.M.) C. G.	7159	— Pte. H. S.	7159
— Pte. D. M.	7159	— Coy.Q.M.Sjt. J.	7159
— By.Q.M./S. F. W.	7159	— Cpl.(A./Sjt.) J. S.	7159
— Cpl.(A./Sjt.) J., *M.M.*	7159	— Pte. W. A.	7159
— S./Sjt. J. S.	7159	Morley, R.S./M. F.	7159
— Cpl. J. W.	7179	— T./M./S./M. H.	7159
— R.S./M. W. A.	7159	— R.Q.M.Sjt. V.	7159
Mitchinson, Coy.S./M. C. J.	7159	— Sjt. W. M.	7159
Moare, S./Sjt.(A./Q.M.Sjt.)		Morrell, Cpl. A. F.	6500
W. H., *M.M.*	7159	— S./Sjt. G.	7159
Moase, Farr.S./Sjt. W. M.	7179	Morris, Coy.S./M. A. D.	7159
Mobbs, W.O.Cl.q, L. J.	7179	— Pte. A. E.	7159
Moffatt, Sjt.(A./Coy.S./M.) R.	7159	— Sjt. B. J.	7180
Mogridge, L./C.(A./2nd Cpl.) S.	7159	— L./C. F.	7159
Moir, A./Whr.Cpl. A.	6509	— (S.) Pte. F. A., *M.M.*	7159
Mollex, Pte. G.	7159	— Sjt. H. A.	6500
Molloy, Q.M.Sjt.(T./S./M.) F.	7159	— Coy.S./M. J. A.	7159
Molyneaux, A./Cpl. C.	7159	— L./C.(A./Sjt.) J. J.	6509
— Pte.(A./Sjt.) T. R.	7159	— Coy.S./M. J. O.	7159
Money, Sjt. J. W.	7159	— Sjt. T. R.	7159
Monk, Sjt. W.	7159	Morrison, S./S./M. E. J.	7159
Montgomery, Coy.S./M. J.	7159	— C.Q.M.S. P.	6509
— Cpl. J. T.	7179	— Coy.S./M. S.	7159
Moody, T./S.S./M. W. E. T.	7159	Morriss, L./C.(A./Sjt.) H.	7159
Moore, By.Q.M.Sjt. A.	7159	Morrow, Pte. S.	7159
— Cpl. E.	7177	Mortimer, Pte. T.	7159
— Sjt. H.	7159	Morton, Sjt. G.	7180
— Sjt. H. E.	7159	— A./B. M. H.	7159
— Sjt.(A./By.S./M.) H. R. C.	7159	— Sjt. R.	7159
— Pte. J.	7159	— Cpl. W. R.	7179
— S.Q.M.Sjt. J. H.	7159	Moseley, R.Q.M.Sjt. E. C. A.	7159
— T./S.S./M. L. V.	6500	Moss, Cpl.(A./Sjt.) A. W.	7159
— Coy.S./M. T.	7159	— Sjt. F.	7159
— Cpl.(A./S./Sjt.) T. H.	7159	— Coy.S./M. J. A.	7159
— Pte.(L./C.) T. McA.	7179	— Coy.S./M. W. C.	7159
— Sjt. W.	7159	Moth, T./Armt.S./M. P.	7159
— Sjt. W. H.	7159	Mott, L./C.(Cpl.) G. H.	7159
Moores, Bombr.(Arty.Clk.) J.	7159	Mould, Coy.Q.M.Sjt. G. W.	7159
— Sjt. R. G.	7159	Moule, Bombr.(A./R.S.M.) T. H.	7159
Moorey, L./C.(A./Sjt.) H. J.	7159	Moulson, S./S./M. L.	7159
Moreton, Spr. A.	7159	Mountsford, Pte. A. H.	7179
— L./C. J. E.	7159	Mouser, S.S.M. G.	6509
Morfitt, Cpl. H.	7159	Mowbray, Sjt. A. J.	7159
Morgan, Sjt. C.	7159	Muir, Cpl. T. *	7180

---

* 7/1121 2/Wellington Regt. N.Z.E.F. D.C.M. as Transport Sgt. *L.G.* 1 Jan 1919. Born Hokitika N.Z. 1895. Embarked August 1915. Died January 1970.

Muirhead, Coy.Q.M.S. W.	6500	Negus, Amt.S./Sjt. R.		7160
Mulkern, Spr.(A./Cpl.) F.	7159	Neill, Coy.S./M. C.		7160
Mullin, Ldg.Sea. T.	7159	Neilson, Cpl. R. M.		7160
Mullineaux, Bombr. H.	7159	Nelson, S./S.M. F.		6509
Mulquiny, Cpl.(T./Sjt.) E.	7179	— Sjt. S.		7160
Mulvaney, Q.M.Sjt. A. J.	7159	Nesbitt, Coy.S./M. A.		7160
Mumford, Pte. E. W.	7159	— Coy.Q.M.Sjt. F.		7160
— Pte.(A./L./C.) J. R.	7159	Ness, Sjt. R.		7160
Muncey, Pte.(A./L./C.) F. W.	7159	Nettleship, Sjt. F.		7160
Mundie, Cpl. R. G.	7159	New, Sjt. T. G.		7160
Mundy, Sjt. S. R.	7160	Newbury, Spr.(A./L./C.) J.		7160
Munn, S.M. A.	* 4024	Newing, Bombr.(A./Sjt.) W.		7160
— Pte.(A./Sjt.) S.	7160	Newman, Sjt. A. H.		7180
Murphy, Cpl.(A./Sjt.) C.	7160	— Bombr. A. S. V.		7160
— Sjt. C. W.	7177	— Sjt. F.		6509
— Sjt. E.	7160	— L./S.(A./Sjt.) H. E. W.		7160
— L./C.(A./Col.Sjt.) E.	6492	— Cpl. L.		7160
— Whr.S./Sjt. F.	7160	— By.S./M. S. H.		7160
— Sjt. J.	7160	Newton, Sjt. A.		7160
— By.S./M. L.	7160	— Col.Sjt.(A./Coy.Q.M.Sjt.) T. B.		7160
— Sjt. M. J.	7160	Newton, Sjt. W. S.		6509
— Cpl. P.	7160	Nicholls, Sjt. G.		7160
— Cpl. R.	6500	Nichols, Cpl.(A./Coy.S./M.) W. G.		7160
Murray, Pte.(L./C.) A. W.	7179	Nicholson, Cpl. G. F.		7160
— S./Sjt. B. R.	7160	— A./Sjt.Instr. J. H.	†	7160
— Pte. T.	7160	Niddrie, Pte. J.		7160
Murrell, Amt. S. M. A. E.	6509	Nightingale, Coy.S./M. G. E.		7160
Murton, Cpl. R.	7160	Nisbett, Cpl. W. M.		7179
Musgrave, M.S./M. A.	7160	Nish, Cpl.(A./Sjt.) E.		6509
Mussabini, T./S./M. M. G.	7160	Nivison, Cpl.(L./Sjt.) S. B.		7160
Mussell, Pte. A. J.	7160	Noak, L./Cpl.(A./Sjt.) H., *D.C.M.*		7160
Musselwhite, L./C. H.	6500	Noble, Cpl. A.		7160
Myers, P./O. H. T.	7160	— Coy.S./M. J.		7160
		Noel, Cpl.(A./Sjt.) W.		7160
Nagle, Pte. C. E.	7160	Nolan, By.S./M. P.		7160
Nairn, Pte. G.	7160	— By.S./M. T. W.		7179
— Cpl.(A./Q.M.Sjt.) M.	7160	Norman, Flt. Sjt. A. S.		6521
Naish, Cpl.(A./S./Sjt.) W.	7160	— Pte.(S./Sjt.) W. D.		7160
Narburgh, C.S.M. E. A.	6509	Norris, S.S./M. G. H.		7160
Nash, Pte.(L./C.) A. H.	7160	Norton, Coy.Q.M.Sjt. H.		7160
Naugher, Pte. W.	6500	— L./C. J. H.		7160
Naylor, Sjt. W.	7160	— Pte.(A./Sjt.) P.		7160
Neal, Sjt.(A./S./Sjt.) J. J.	7177	Nott, Sjt. E. E.		7160
— Sjt. W. J.	7179	Noyle, Sjt. H. W.		7160
Needham, Sjt. E. F.	7160	Nunn, Sjt. A. J.		7160
— 1st A.M. J.	6521	Nurse, Sjt. W., *M.M.*		7160
Neep, Spr. H. D.	7160	Nutt, Coy.Q.M.Sjt. S. St.J.		7160

---

* H.L.I. For Egypt, attached Egyptian Army. L.S. & G.C., A.O. April 1917, Order of the Nile 5th class, *L.G.* 21 September 1923.

† Medal known: No. 672 Army Gym. Staff (only 72 M.S.M.s to A.G.S.).

Nuttall, R.Q.M.Sjt. G.	7160	O'Loughlin, Pte.(L./C.) T. J.	7179
Nuttman, Sjt. G.	6500	Olson, Dvr. C. J.	7177
		Oman, Sjt. J.	7160
Oakes, Pte. J. J.	7177	O'Mara, Supt.Clk. T. N.	7160
— Sjt. J. L.	7160	O'Neil, Sjt. J. T.	7160
Oakley, Sjt. J.	6500	Opie, Sjt.(A./By.S./M.) F. ‡	7160
— Cpl. R.	7160	Orchard, Coy.Q.M.Sjt. A. O.	7181
O'Brien, Coy.S./M. P.	7179	Ord, Q.M.Sjt.(A./S./Sjt.) H.	7161
O'Callaghan, Coy.S./M.		O'Regan, Sjt. J.	7161
(A./R.S.M.) T.	7160	Ormerod, S./Sjt.(A./S.Q.M.Sjt.) J.	7161
O'Connor, Coy.S.M.		Ormesher, Pte.(A./Cpl.) J. E.	7161
(local R.S./M.) A.	6509	Ormisher, Cpl. G.	7161
— R.Q.M.Sjt. J. J.	7160	O'Rourke, A./Sjt. M. ✾	4393
Odell, S./M. A. E.	7160	Ortlieb, Pte.(A./Sjt.) B.	7161
O'Donnell, By.Q.M.Sjt. M. J.	7179	Orton, Coy.S./M. T. E.	7161
O'Donovan, Gnr.(A./L./Bombr.) T.	6509	Orvis, Sjt. H.	7161
Offer, W.O.Cl.1, H. F.	7179	— Cpl. W. J.	7161
Ogden, R.Q.M.Sjt. T.	7160	Osborn, Sjt. C. C.	7161
— Coy.S./M. W. J., *M.C.*	* 7160	— Q.M.Sjt. F. A., *M.M.*	7161
Ogle, S./Q.M.Sjt.(A/Subcondr.) A. A.	7177	Osborne, T./S.M. A. W.	6521
O'Gorman, Sjt. W.	7160	— Coy.S./M.(A./S./M.) G. A.	7161
Ogston, Pte.(L./C.) W.	7160	— Q.M.Sjt.(A./R.S.M.) W. J.	7161
O'Halloran, Sjt.(T./S./M.) M. A.	7160	O'Shea, A./2nd Cpl. W.	7161
O'Hare, Pte. W.	7160	Ostrom, Sjt. H.	7177
Oldcorn, Sjt. T., *D.C.M.*	† 7160	O'Sullivan, L./C.(A./Sjt.) D.	7161
Oldfield, Coy.Q.M.Sjt. H.	7160	O'Toole, Sjt.(T./S.M.) C. J. §	6521
— Bombr.(A./R.S.M.Arty.Clk.) W.	7160	— Cpl. M.	7161
O'Leary, Sjt. J.	7160	Ottley, Sjt. A. T.	7161
Oliver, Sjt. A. M.	7180	Outram, Sjt. H. C.	7161
— Sjt. E.	7160	Over, Sjt. E.	7161
— By.S./M. H. B.	7177	Overall, Sjt. V.	7161
— Sjt.(T./S.S./M.) M. C.	7160	Overhage, R.Q.M.Sjt. A. J.	7177
— Gnr. R.	7179	Owen, Dvr. A.	7161
— By.Q.M.Sjt. T. W.	7160	— Pte. D.	6509
— Sjt. W. T.	7160	— T./Sub.Condr.(A./Condr.) F. R.	7161
Ollerenshaw, L./C. W.	7160	— Pte.(A./Sjt.) H.	7161
Olney, T./S.M. E. S.	6521	— Pte.(A./Q.M.S.) H. B. P.	6509

* 156 Fd. Coy. R.E. M.C. *L.G.* 27 July 1916.

† Group known: D.C.M. (Edw. VII, L./Cpl. R.E.), King's Police Medal (Geo. VI Superintendent, Westmorland & Cumberland Const.), Queen's South Africa Medal (Cape Colony and Transvaal), King's South Africa Medal, 1914/15 trio (Sgt. Mil. Mount. Police), Defence Medal, 1935 Jubilee, 1937 Coronation and M.S.M. (M.M.P.). Born 1879. Enlisted 1898. Retired from Police Force 1945. Died 1969.

‡ 74570 A./B.S.M. 13th Battery R.F.A. Flanders, 1917–18 and Cambrai, 1917.—Has proved himself most capable and has carried out the duties of B.S.M. in a most efficient manner. Under most trying circumstances both in Flanders and at Cambrai he has set a most excellent example of cheerfulness, and the fighting efficiency of the battery has been maintained through his unremitting good work and his tried capacity for handling horses and men in times of great strain and difficulties.

§ No. 942 R.F.C. From Dublin. Enlisted October 1913. Entitled to 1914 Star trio.

Owen, Coy.S./M. J.	7161	Parkes, Cpl. J.	6509
— 1st A.M. S.	7161	— Bombr. J.	7161
— Sjt. W.	7161	Parkhouse, Q.M.Sjt. L.	7161
Owens, Sjt. A. A. A.	7179	Parkin, Fitt. A.	7161
— Sjt. J. P.	7177	— Pte. G. H.	7161
		— Sjt. J.	7161
Pacey, S./Sjt. W. C.	7161	— Spr. J. E.	7161
Pack, Coy.Q.M.Sjt. F. G.	7177	— L./C. W.	7161
— L./C.(A./2nd Cpl.) S. J.	7161	— Sjt. W. T.	7161
Packer, S./M. E. F.	7161	Parkinson, A./Coy.S./M. F.	7161
— Sjt. W. A.	7161	— Cpl. G. H.	7161
Paddock, R.S.M. A. E.	7177	— Gnr. R.	7161
Paddon, Gnr.(L./Bombr.) W. C.	7161	Parks, L./C. H.	7177
Page, Coy.S./M. G. A.	7161	— Supt.Clk. J. T.	7161
Page, T./Sub.Condr. J. F.	* 7161	Parles, Cpl. B.	7161
Pahina, Pte. W.	7180	Parr, Amt.S./Sjt. C.	7161
Paine, Sjt. E. J.	7161	— Spr. W. F. V.	7161
Painter, Pte. F. R.	7161	— Cpl.(A./Sjt.) W.	7161
Palfree, Pte. M. E.	7179	— Q.M.Sjt.(T./S./M.) W. H.	7161
Palgrave, Sjt. C.	7161	Parry, Q.M.Sjt.(T./S./M.) R. R.	7161
Palin, Sjt. J.	7161	Paralor, Sjt. F.	7161
Pallett, Sjt. H. J.	6500	Parsons, Cpl. R.	7161
Palmer, Pte.(L./C.) A.	7179	— S./Sjt. R. W. G.	7180
— Sjt. F. H.	7177	— Pte.(A./Sjt.) S. A.	7177
— Pte. G. F.	7177	— Sjt. T. C.	7180
— Sjt. J.	6500	— Q.M.Sjt.(T./S./M.) T. W.	7161
— Pte. J.	7180	Part, Sjt. A. W.	7161
— Sjt. R. A.	7177	Partington, S./Sjt. E.	7177
— Cpl. W. (R.G.A.)	7161	Partridge, Sjt. R. L.	7179
— Cpl. W. (A. & S. Highrs.)	7161	Pate, R.Q.M.Sjt. F.	7177
Pamplin, Cpl.(A./Sjt.) W. V.	7161	Pateman, Sjt. H.	7161
Panichelli, Pte.(A./Cpl.) F. R.	6509	— Coy. S./M. J.	7161
Pank, Cpl. J.	7161	Paterson, Pte. A.	7161
Panton, Sjt. E. W.	7161	— Cpl. M.	7161
Pape, Sjt.(A/C.S.M.) R.	7161	— Sjt. R.	7161
Parcell, S./Sjt. G. E.	6509	Pathe, T./S.M. J. J.	6521
Paris, Coy.S./M.(T./R.S.M.) J.	7161	Patrick, Sjt. F.	7161
Park, Pte. A.	7161	— Cpl.(L./Sjt.) W. I.	7161
— L./C.(A./Sjt.) E. E.	7161	Patterson, Fitt.S./Sjt. A.	7161
— Pte. R.	7177	Pattison, Sjt. H.	7161
Parke, Coy.S./M. W.	7161	— Sjt. W.	6500
Parker, Sjt.(A./Coy.S./M.) F. J.	7161	Patton, By.S./M. S. J.	7179
— Spr. J. G.	7179	Paul, Coy.Q.M.Sjt. A.	7161
— Cpl. R. H.	7161	— Sjt. H. (R.E.)	7161
— Cpl. S., *MM*	7161	— T./M.S./M. H. (A.S.C.)	7161
— T./Sub.Condr. W.	7161	— T./M.S./M. J.	7161
Parker-Laycock, Sjt. J.	7179	Paulhus, Pte. J.	7177
Parkes, M.S./Sjt. H. T.	7161	Pavey, Sjt. W. J.	7161

---

* Group known: Afghanistan Medal 1878–80 (no bar, Pte. 34th Regt.), 1914/15 Star trio (T./W.O.I A.O.C.) and M.S.M.

Pawson, L./Bombr. W. M.	7161	Penny, Pte. J. W.	7162
Payne, By.S./M. A.	7161	Pennycock, Sjt. J.	7162
— Gnr. A. J.	6509	Pentland, Sjt. W. C.	7179
— Sjt. A. L.	4413	Penwarden, Coy.S./M. F. C.	7162
— Pte.(A./Cpl.) A. V.	7161	Pepper, Sjt. T. L. M.	7162
— Bombr. E. G.	7161	Percy, Coy.Q.M.Sjt. G. W. *	7162
— L./Bombr. H.	7161	Perdue, Sjt.(A./R.S.M.) W. J.	7162
— R.S./M. P.	7018	Perkes, S.S./M. F. G.	7162
— L./C. W. C.	7162	Perkins, Sjt. H. C.	6500
— Pte.(A./Sjt.) W. H.	7162	Perks, Sjt. G.	6500
Peabody, Sjt.(A./S./M.) S. W.	7162	Perris, Sjt. P. D.	7162
Peach, Bombr. C. W.	7162	Perry, Cpl. G.	6500
Peachey, L./Cpl.(A./Sjt.) A.	6492	— Pte. J.	7162
Peacock, Coy.S./M. H. E.	7162	— Sjt. W. S.	7162
— Pte.(A./Cpl.) H. W.	7162	Peterson, Sjt. K. E.	7179
— 1st A.M. R.	6521	Petherham, Pte.(A./Sjt.) R.	7162
— Sjt. T.	7162	Pettingill, Sjt.(A./Q.M.Sjt.) L. E. G.	7162
— Coy.Q.M.Sjt.(A./Q.M.Sjt.) W. R.	7162	Petts, Cpl. E.	7162
Peady, Cpl. T. A.	7179	— Sjt. W.	7179
Peagram, Dvr.(A./Farr.Sjt.) H.	7162	Petty, Sjt. H. A.	6500
Peake, Pte.(A./Cpl.) R. V.	7162	Pexton, Pte.(L./C.) R. H.	7162
Pearce, L./C.(A./Sjt.) F. J.	6509	Peyton, Sjt. S. A.	6500
— Sjt. F. T.	7177	Pheasey, A./Sjt. O.	7162
— Sqdn.S.S./M. W.	7162	Phelan, Sjt. C.	7177
— Sjt. W. E.	7162	Philip, S./Sjt.(A./S.Q.M.S.) A.	
Pearman, Condr. R. J.	7162	(A.S.C.)	6509
Pearson, Sjt. A.	7162	— Sjt. A. (Gord. Highrs.)	7162
— Sjt. F.	7162	Phillips, Coy.S./M. A.	7162
— Sjt. G.	7162	— Sjt. C. E.	7162
— Sjt.(A./Q.M.Sjt.) J. S.	7179	— Cpl. C. H.	4413
Pease, Sjt. G. W.	7177	— Sjt. H. G.	7177
Peattie, Sjt. W.	7162	— Sjt. J.	7162
Pebody, Sjt.(A./Coy.S./M.) C. H.	7162	— Cpl. J.	6521
Peck, M./S./Sjt. E. A. G.	7162	— Sjt. J. D.	7179
Pedlow, Sjt. S. J.	7162	— Sjt. J. G.	7179
Peel, Coy.S.M. F.	7177	— L./C.(A./Sjt.) P. H.	7179
Peers, Cpl. R.	7162	— Sjt. R.	6509
Pegden, Coy.S./M. J.	7162	Philp, L./C.(A./Sjt.) G. C.	7162
Peggie, Sjt. W. D.	7177	Philpott, Sjt. E. W.	7162
Pegler, Coy.Q.M.Sjt. J. A.	7180	— Pte. W.	7177
Pelham, Coy.Q.M.Sjt. F. V.	7162	Philps, Pte. A. C.	7177
Pellatt, Flt.Sjt. L.	6521	Phipps, Pte.(A./Cpl.) D. A.	7162
Pells, Sjt.(A./Coy.Q.M.Sjt.) J.	7162	— Sjt. G. F.	7162
Pemberton, L./C. J.	7162	— Sjt. J. H.	7162
Penman, L./C.(A./2nd Cpl.) G.	7162	— Cpl. R.	7179
Penny, Coy.S.M. F.	7162	Pichard, Coy.S./M. L.	7162
— Coy.S./M. H. S.	7179	Pichering, Sjt. E.	7162

* Group was in McInnes collection: Ashanti Star 1895-6 (Sapper R.E.), 1914/15 Star (47931 Sgt. R.E.), British War and Victory Medals (C.Q.M.S.), L.S. & G.C. (Edw. VII, 22307 Sgt. R.E.) and M.S.M. ('G' C.S.Coy. R.E.).

Pickering, Cpl.(A./Sjt.) T. P.	7162	Poole, C.Q.M.Sjt.(A./C.S.M.) G. E.		6509
Pickersgill, A./R.Q.M.Sjt. F.	7162	— Bombr. H.		7163
Pickess, Gnr. J. B.	7162	— Cpl.(A./S.Q.M.Sjt.) J. L.		7163
Pickup, Dvr. W. T.	7162	— Cpl. L.		6521
Picotte, Cpl. N. E.	7177	— Cpl.(A./Q.M.Sjt.) S.		7163
Piddington, Pte. H. C.	7162	Pooley, Cpl. G. C.		7163
Pieress, Sjt. T.	7162	Popham, Dvr. A. S.		7163
Pilcher, Sqdn.Cpl.Maj. H. E.	7162	Porritt, Dvr. N.		7163
Pinnington, Sjt. L.	7162	Porter, T./S.S./M. C. H.		7163
Piper, Sjt. A. C.	7162	— Dvr. G.		7163
— A./Sjt. A. G.	7162	Postlethwaite, Sjt. F.		7163
— T./S.S./M. G. J.	7162	Potier, Q.M.Sjt.(A./S.S./M.) G.	†	7163
Pitt, Sjt. T.	7162	Potter, Sjt.(A./Coy.S./M.) E. H.		7163
Pittick, Sjt. E.	7162	— Pte. H.		7163
Pitts, Pte. J., V.C.	* 7162	— Cpl. J.		7163
Place, L./Cpl. C.	7162	Potts, Sjt. A. J.		6500
Planner, Pte.(A./Sjt.) H.	7162	— Sjt. A. S.		7163
Plattin, L./Bombr. H. H.	7162	— Sjt. T.		7163
Platts, Sjt. A. S.	6500	Poulter, Cpl. W. J.		7163
Playford, Sjt. J. W.	6492	Pound, Sjt. F. W.		4413
Pleadin, Bombr. J. W.	7162	Powell, Sjt. C. E. F.		7163
Plester, Cpl. W.	7162	Power, Cpl.(A./R.S.M.) J. J.		7163
Pletts, Sph. M.	7162	— Cpl. R. L.		7179
Plomer, C.S.M. M.	6509	Pownall, Sjt. L.		7163
Plowman, Bombr.(A./Cpl.) S.	7162	— Dvr. P.		7163
Pluck, L./C.(A./Sjt.) P. A.	6492	Poyser, Pte.(L./C.) A.		7163
Plum, Cpl. F. G.	7162	— Sjt.(A./S./Sjt.) H. E.		7163
— Sjt. P.	7162	Pracy, By.Q.M.Sjt. G.		7163
Plumb, 2nd Cpl. W. J.	6509	Prater, Sjt. J.		7163
Pointon, Pte.(A./Sjt.) W. H.	6500	Pratley, Sjt.(A./Coy.S./M.) H.		7163
Pollard, Sjt.(A./Q.M.Sjt.) E. A.	7162	— S./Sjt. R. J.		7177
— Sjt. G. H.	7162	Pratt, Sjt. A. J.		7163
— L./C.(A./Coy.Q.M.Sjt.) J. J.	7162	— Gnr. W. E.		7163
— Coy.S./M. R.	7177	Preece, Pte. J.		7163
Pollett, Pte. A. J.	7162	Prentice, S./Sjt. A.		7180
Pomeroy, Sjt. S.	7162	Prescott, Sjt. R. L.		7163
Poole, Spr.(A./Cpl.) E. F.	7162	Prestridge, By.S./M. W.		7163
— Armr.S./Sjt. F.	7162	Pretty, Sjt. S.		6500

---

* Group on display in Ashton under Lyne Museum: Victoria Cross (No. 3429 Pte. Manchester Regt, 6 January, 1900, Caesars Camp, Natal. *L.G.* 26 July 1901: 'On left of the line held a sangar for 15 hours with no food or water, under extensive and heavy fire. The Boers occupied some sangars on the left and rear.' (See also Q.M.S. R. Scott *L.G.* 22 February, 1919). Also Queen's South Africa Medal (Elandlaagte, Defence of Ladysmith, Belfast), King's South Africa Medal, 1914/15 Star trio, Coronation 1937, and M.S.M. He was born in Blackburn in 1877. He stood as a model for the statue of a soldier on the memorial for the Boer War casualties in St. Anne's Square, Manchester. He served in Manchester Regt. in the 2nd W.W. and would probably have been entitled to a Defence or War medal. He died in Blackburn in 1955, having also been awarded a 1953 Coronation Medal.

† K.R.R.C. Also entitled to Rhodesia Medal and Queen's South Africa Medal.

Price, Dvr. A.	7163	Rabett, Sjt. C. G.	7163
— Sjt. G. E.	7163	Race, S./Sjt. H.	7163
— R.Q.M.Sjt. H. F.	7163	Racheil, L./C. A. J.	7163
— Pte.(A./Cpl.) J. B.	7163	Radcliffe, L./C.(A./Cpl.) C. P.	7177
— Sjt. R. G.	7163	— Farr.Q.M.Sjt. J. F.	7163
— Sjt. W. (M.M.P.)	7163	Raddon, R.Q.M.Sjt. W. M.	7163
— Sjt. W. (R.W.Fus.)	7163	Radley, By.S./M. F. E.	7163
Pridham, By.S./M. W.	7163	— Pte. M.	7163
Pring, Coy.S./M. G.	7163	Rae, Cpl. A. I.	7163
Pringle, 2nd Cpl.(A./Sjt.) T.	7163	— S./Sjt. F.	7163
Pritchard, T./Sub.Condr.(A./		— Sjt. H. A.	7163
Condr.) G.	6500	Raine, Pte. J. G.	7163
— Sjt. J. A.	7163	Ralph, Sjt. F. M.	7163
— Sjt. S.	6509	— Pte. V. J.	7163
Procter, L./C. G. S.	7163	— Sad.S./Sjt. W. E.	7163
Pudsey, L./Cpl. D. J.	7163	Ralston, Cpl. E. E.	7179
— Pte.(L./C.) W.	7177	Ramage, R.Q.M.Sjt. A.	7163
Pugh, Cpl. G.	7163	Ramsay, Sjt. R. L.	7177
— S./M. J. E.	7163	Ramsbottom, Coy.S./M. O.	7163
Pullen, Sjt. J. W.	7177	Ramsey, Sjt. A. H.	7179
Pulley, Pte. A.	7163	Randall, Coy.Q.M.Sjt. E. W.	7163
Pulsford, S./Sjt. G. F.	7180	— Pte. F.	7163
Purchase, T./R.S.M. S.	7163	— Sjt. G. H.	6500
Pursehouse, Pte. W. H.	7163	Randell, Armr.Sjt. E. L.	7179
Purser, Q.M.Sjt. A. H.	7163	— SubCondr.(A./Condr.) J.	7163
Purvis, S.Q.M.Sjt. J. H.	7163	Rankin, 1st Cl.A.Mech. J.	4413
Putman, A./Sqdn.Q.M.Cpl. F. G.	7163	Ransom, Gnr. G. W.	7163
Puttick, Spr.(A./Sjt.) A.	7163	— Sjt. E. P.	7163
Puttick-Wynn, S.Q.M.Sjt. A. H.	7179	Raper, Armr.Sjt. H. G.	7179
Puxley, Sjt. S. J.	7163	Rasberry, Sjt. F.	7163
Puxty, Sjt. D. C.	6500	Rashbrook, L./C.(A./Col.Sjt.) W.	7163
— Gnr. T. V.	7163	Ratcliff, Sjt. W. J.	7163
Pye, Cpl. B.	7163	Ratcliffe, Cpl.(A./Sjt.) W. T.	7163
Pyne, S.Sjt. W. V.	4413	Rathbone, Spr. A. W.	7163
Pyper, 2nd Cpl.(A./Cpl.) R.	7163	Rattle, Coy.Q.M.Sjt. E. V.	7179
Pyser, Coy.S./M. R.	7163	Rattray, Sjt. J.	7163
		Raven, Coy.Q.M.Sjt. F.	7163
Quick, C.S.M. H.	6500	Rawles, Sjt. J. E.	7163
Quilter, M.S./Sjt. H. J.	7163	Rawlings, Sjt. G. A.	7164
Quin, Sjt. W. A.	7179	Rawlinson, R.S./M. J.	7164
Quincey, S./Sjt. J. S.	7163	Rawnsley, Coy.S./M. H.	7164
Quinn, A./Cpl. E.	6492	Rawson, Dvr. D.	7164
— R.Q.M.Sjt. J.	7163	Ray, Sjt. R. E.	7164
— Sjt. J. A.	7177	Raymond, Pte. F.	7164
— L./C. W.	7163	Rayner, A./Sjt. C. S.	7164
Quirk, Sjt. J. W.	6509	— S./S./M. H., *M.C.*	* 7164

---

* Group known: M.B.E. (1st type, military ribbon), M.C. (1st class S./Sgt. A.S.C.), Queen's South Africa Medal (Cape Colony, Defence of Ladysmith, Orange Free State, Laing's Nek, Belfast), King's South Africa Medal, 1914 Star trio, L.S. & G.C. (Geo. V), M.S.M. (R.A.S.C.) and French Médaille Militaire. Later Major R.A.S.C. M.C. *L.G.* 18 February 1915, M.B.E. 3 June, 1919.

Rayner, S.M. T., *D.C.M.*	6500	Reynolds, Pte. H.	6500
Reaburn, Cpl.(T./Sjt.) D. A.	7179	— L./C. W.	7177
Read, By.S./M. C.	7179	Rhodes, R.Q.M.Sjt. H.	7164
— C.S.M. E.	* ❀ 7018	Riach, Coy.Q.M.Sjt. J.	7164
— Sjt. F. C.	7164	Rice, Condr. C. M.	6509
— S./Sjt. T.	7164	— By.Q.M.Sjt. E. F.	7164
Reader, L./C.(A./Sjt.) B. H.	7164	— S./Q.M.S. J.	6509
Reading, A./Cpl. C.	7164	Richard, Pte. P.	7177
Reay, Coy.Q.M.Sjt. W. M.	7164	— Pte. W.	7177
Redford, A./Cpl. G. B.	7179	Richards, Sjt. F. C.	7164
Redhead, Sjt. R.	7164	— Sjt. H.	7164
Reed, Pte.(A./Sjt.) A.	7164	— L./C. W. H.	7180
Reeder, A./R.S.M. W. C.	7164	— By.S./M. W. J.	7164
Rees, Gnr.(L./Bombr.) D.	7164	Richardson, Sjt. A. H.	7164
— R.Q.M.Sjt. J. D.	7164	— Pte. D. B.	7179
— Sjt. R. G.	4413	— Coy.Q.M.Sjt. E. L.	7179
Reeve, Pte.(A./Sjt.) H. E.	7164	— Gnr. H.	7164
— M./S./Sjt. W. H.	7164	— Pte. H. R.	7164
Reeves, Coy.Q.M.Sjt. F.	7164	— M.S./Sjt. H. S.	7164
— Cpl.(A./Sjt.) J.	7164	— Sjt.(A./Coy.Q.M.Sjt.) R. (C. Gds.)	7164
Reid, Dvr. A.	7164	— Coy.S./M. R. (North'd Fus.)	7164
— Gnr. A.	7164	— Sjt. W.	7164
— Sjt. P. B.	7177	— L./Cpl. W. H.	7164
— Gnr. W. H.	7164	Riche, Sjt. W. E.	7164
Reidy, Sjt. J.	7179	Riches, Cpl. R. W.	7179
Remnant, L./C. C. A.	7164	Richmond, Fitt.S./Sjt. A.	7164
Rench, Coy.Q.M.Sjt.(T./S.S./M.)		Rickman, Farr.Sjt. H.	7164
W. H.	7164	Riddell, S./Sjt. J. R.	7177
Rennie, Sjt. J.	7180	Riddihough, Coy.Q.M.Sjt. J. J.	7179
— Pte. M.	7164	Riddlesworth, Pte. H.	† ❀ 5037
Renshaw, R.Q.M.Sjt. H.	7164	Ridge, Cpl. E.	7164
Renton, Sjt. S. E.	7164	Ridgewell, Cpl. A. F.	7164
Renwick, Coy.S./M. R. A. M.	7164	Ridgway, Sjt. A.	7177
Reoch, Sjt. J.	7164	Ridings, Coy.Q.M.Sjt. W. P.	7164
Rep, Pte. H. J.	7179	Ridout, S.Q.M.Sjt. H. J.	7164
Reston, Sjt. J.	7177	Ridyard, Coy.S./M. A.	‡ 7164
Reynolds, R.S.M. A., *M.C.*	6500	Rielly, Amt.S./Sjt. J. B.	7164
— R./Q.M.Sjt. B. C.	7164	Rigby, M.S./M. G.	7164
— Cpl.(T.M.S./M.) G. A.	7164	— Coy.S./M. W.	7164

---

* Group known: Queen's South Africa Medal (Cape Colony, Orange Free State, Transvaal, South Africa 1901, Pte. S.L.I.), British War and Victory Medals, M.S.M. (11 Pontoon Park A.S.C.).

† Group known: 1914/15 Star trio (M.I.D. oakleaf), M.S.M. (1st/4th Bn. Cheshire R.), Territorial Force Efficiency Medal (Geo. V), Territorial Efficiency Medal (Geo. V, bar Territorial). M.S.M. for saving life at sea. A Macclesfield man.

‡ Group in Liverpool Regt. Museum: M.M. British War and Victory Medals, M.S.M. The M.M. was for gallantry on 1 September, 1918, at Reincourt. He greatly assisited in forming up the company in no-man's land. After the first attack, and ignoring the heavy hostile shell fire, he gathered up the survivors. The company subsequently captured 160 prisoners and 16 machine guns.

Riggs, S./Smith(A./Farr.S./Sjt.)		Robertson, Sjt. C. C.		7180
A. W.	6509	— R.Q.M.Sjt. C. H.		7165
— Pte.(A./Sjt.) J. F.	7164	— Sjt. D.		7165
— Sjt. L. A.	7164	— S./M. D. C. S.		7165
Riley, Cpl. A.	7164	— Sjt. F. G.		7165
— Cpl. C. J.	7164	— L./C.(A./Sjt.) G.		7165
— Pte. J. T.	7164	— By.S./M. J.		7177
— Cpl.(A./Sjt.) P.	7177	— Sjt. J. (A.S.C.)	*	4413
Rimmer, Sjt. J.	6509	— Sjt. J. (R. Highrs)		7165
— Sjt. R.	7164	— Cpl.(A./R.Q.M.Sjt.) J.		7165
Rintoul, Coy.Q.M.Sjt. A.	7164	— Sjt. J. C.		6521
Rippon, Sjt. T.	7164	— Sjt.(A./S./Sjt.) J. L.		7177
Riste, Farr.S./Sjt. G. F.	6509	— Sjt.(A./Coy.Q.M.Sjt.) P.		7165
Ritchie, 2nd Cpl.(A./Sjt.) R. J.	7164	— Coy.Q.M.Sjt. R.		7165
Ritter, Sjt. R. H.	7179	— R.Q.M.Sjt. W.		7165
Rivers, Sjt.(A./Coy.S./M.)		— Sjt. W. A.		6500
W. E., *M.M.*	7164	— Sjt. W. G. D.		7179
Roach, Cpl. J. J.	7164	— Sjt. W. J.		7165
Robb, Sjt. W. J.	7164	Robins, L./C.(2nd Cpl.) R. J.		7165
Robbins, Sjt. J. E.	7164	Robinson, Pte.(A./Sjt.) A. W.		7165
Robert, Sjt.(A./Coy.S./M.) D., *M.M.*	7177	— L./C. B. B.		7165
Roberts, Cpl. A.	7164	— Cpl. C., *M.M.*		7165
— A./S./M. A. E.	7164	— Sjt. C. E.		7165
— Cpl. E.	7164	— L./C.(A./2nd Cpl.) F. F.		7165
— Spr.(A./Cpl.) F. A.	7164	— Sjt.(A./M.S./Sjt.) G. H.		7165
— R.Q.M.Sjt. G. R.	7164	— Sjt. H. E.		7177
— Pte. J.	7164	— S.Q.M.Sjt. H. E.		7165
— Cpl. J. C.	7164	— Sjt. J.		7165
— Sjt.(A./Coy.Q.M.Sjt.) O. W.	7164	— Coy.S./M.(T./S.S./M.) J.		7165
— Coy.S./M.(A./Dr./Sjt.) P. H.	7164	— T./S.M. J.		6521
— Cpl. R. A.	7164	— Cpl. J. H.		7165
— T.Sub.Condr. R. H.	7164	— Pte. J. W.		7165
— Sjt. R. S.	7177	— Coy.Q.M.Sjt. L. H.		7179
— Sjt. R. W.	7164	— Sjt. R. T.		6509
— Cpl. S. T.	7165	— Sjt. W. M.		7165
— Sjt. T.	7165	— Pte.(A./Sjt.) W. N.		7165
— Cpl.(A./Sjt.) T.	7165	Robson, Fitt. H. G. B.		7165
— Dmr.Sjt. V. C.	7165	— Pte. J.		7165
— Sjt. W. H.	6521	— S.Q.M.Sjt. S.		7165
— Coy.S./M. W. L.	7165	— Pte. W.		7165
— 2nd Cpl.(A./Cpl.) W. R.	7165	Roche, Cpl. P.		6521
Robertson, Sjt. C. (R.F.A.)	7165	— Sjt. W.	†	7165
— R.Q.M.Sjt. C. (R. Scots)	7165	Rochester, Coy.S./M. J. H.		7165

---

* Group known: M.B.E. (2nd type, Military ribbon), British War and Victory Medals (M.I.D., 2/Lt), Defence Medal, 1953 Coronation, and M.S.M. Commissioned *L.G.* 8 July 1918 into A.S.C. w.e.f. 5 May 1918. M.I.D. (Allenby's Despatches) *L.G.* 5 June, 1919. M.B.E. *L.G.* 15 December 1944, Major 3rd Battn. Glasgow Home Guard. The M.S.M. is for the capture of Jerusalem.

† Lancashire Fusiliers. Volunteering in January 1915, he proceeded to France in the following December, and saw much heavy fighting at Loos, Albert, Vimy Ridge,

Rodger, W.O.Cl.1, R. H.	7179	Routledge, Bombr. J.		6509
— Sjt. J. L.	7165	Rowan, Pte. C.		7177
Rodway, Coy.S./M. C. H. S.	7165	Rowden, Sjt.(A./S./Sjt.) P.		7165
— Cpl.(A./Sjt.) H. J.	7165	Rowe, S./Sjt.(A./Q.M.Sjt.) A. V.		7165
Rodwell, Pte. R.	7179	— Gnr. F.		7165
Rote, Sjt. A. V.	7165	— Coy.Q.M.Sjt. H. S.		7165
Rogers, Col.Sjt. A. J. A.	7165	Rowland, Pte. T. W.		7165
— Pte.(A./Sjt.) E.	7165	Rowlands, Spr. H.		7165
— W.O.Cl.1, F.	7179	Rowling, Cpl. T.		7165
— Sjt. G.	6500	Rowntree, Sjt. W.		7165
— L./C.(A./Cpl.) H.	7165	Roxburgh, R.S.M. A.	†	6512
— Coy.Q.M.Sjt. J.	7165	— Sjt. J. T.		7165
— Cpl. J.	7167	Roy, Dvr. L. F.		7177
— Pte. J.	7165	Royall, Pte. H.		7165
— Actg.Flt.Sjt. J. H.	4413	Royden, Sjt. J.		7165
— Sjt. R.	7165	Ruck, Coy.S./M. E. M.		7165
— Sjt. R. J.	7165	Rudd, 2nd Cpl. C.		7165
— Flt.Sjt. S. C.	6521	Rudge, Coy.Q.M.Sjt. F. M.		7166
— Sjt. T.	7165	Ruffells, Sjt. P. H.		7166
— Sjt.(A./Coy.S./M.) W. H.	7165	Rummin, Sjt. T.		7166
— Sjt. W. S.	7165	Rumney, Sjt. B.		7166
Rolph, Bombr. H. J.	6509	Runciman, Spr. J.		7166
Roman, Sjt.(A./Coy.Q.M.Sjt.) C.	7165	Rundle, 1st A.M. J.		6521
Rood, By.S./M. A. J.	7165	Rush, By.S./M.(T./S./M.) W. C.		7166
Rooke, Pte. R.	7165	Rushen, M.S./Sjt. F.		7166
Rooks, Sjt. C.	7165	Rushford, Sjt. I.		7166
Rooney, Pte.(L./C.) A.	7179	Rushton, L./C. G.		7166
Root, Sjt.(A./Q.M.Sjt.) A.	7165	— M.S./Sjt. T.		7166
Rose, Sjt. E. W.	7165	Rushworth, Cpl.(A./Sjt.) A. S.		7166
— L./Bombr. J. F.	7165	Ruskin, Sjt. B. F.		7166
— L./C.(A./2nd Cpl.) P.	7165	Russ, Sjt.(A./Coy.S./M.) A.		7166
— Cpl. W. J.	7165	Russell, Pte. A.		7177
Ross, L./C.(A./Sjt.) A. A.	* 7165	— L./C. C. H.		7177
— Coy.Q.M.Sjt.(A./R.S.M.) G.	7165	— Cpl.(T./R.Q.M.Sjt.) C. L.		7179
— T./F. of W.S./Sjt. J. R.	7165	— Pte.(A./Sjt.) E. E.		6509
Rosser, Sjt. T.	7165	— Coy.Q.M.Sjt.(A./Coy.S./M.) G.		7166
Rothwell, Sjt. F.	6500	— Sjt. H. N.		4413
Roughton, Sjt. H.	7165	— Sjt. J. J.		7166
— R.Q.M.Sjt. J. W.	7165	— Pte.(A./Sjt.) J. J.		7166
Rouke, Pte. J.	❀ 5037	— Pte. J. R.		7166
Rourke, Cpl.(A./Sjt.) R.	7165	— Cpl. W. A.		7166
Rouse, Pte. W. A.	7165	Rutherford, Pte.(A./Sjt.) F.		7166
Routledge, Coy.Q.M.Sjt. F.	7165	— Sjt. J. D.		6509

and Ypres (III). In this last battle he was awarded the Meritorious Service Medal, for devotion to duty in carrying despatches from the dug-outs to head-quarters under heavy shell-fire. Demobilised in August 1919, he held the 1914/15 Star, and the General Service and Victory Medals. 11, Darley Street, Salford.

* Pte. 9/Royal Scots 1914. Clerk to Court Martial Dept., 3 Army H.Q. France 1916. An Edinburgh man. Served in France 1915–1919.

† South African Forces, for Lines of Communication in the Mediterranean.

Rutland, L./C. J.	7166	Savegar, S./Sjt.(A./Q.M.Sjt.) W. C.	7166
Ryae, Coy.S./M.(A./R.S./M.) C. E.	7166	Saville, Pte.(A./Sjt.) T.	7166
Ryan, Dvr. W.	6500	Savins, Sjt. J. L.	7166
Ryder, Sqdn.S./M. A. B. G.	7166	Sawyer, Sjt. D.	7177
— Pte. J.	7166	— R.Q.M.Sjt. H.	7179
Ryman, Flt.Sjt. W. J.	6521	Saxby, Sjt. H.	7166
Rymer, L./C. W.	7166	Sayer, Sjt. T. E.	7166
Rymill, Sjt.(A./Q.M.Sjt.) W. G. P.	7166	Sayers, L./Bombr. F. †	7166
		Saynor, Sjt. E. J.	7166
Saddler, Whlr.Cpl.		Scanlon, Sjt. J.	7166
(A./Whlr.Sjt.) E. J.	6500	Scantlebury, Coy.S./M. E. J.	7166
Sage, Cpl.(A./Sjt.) A. J.	7166	Scard, Sjt. F. J.	7166
Sainsbury, C.S.M. W. H.	6500	Scholes, Cpl.(A./Sjt.) S. H.	6500
St.George, Sjt. G. L.	7180	Scholey, Sjt. F. W. S.	7166
Sales, Gnr. G. H.	7166	Schoon, Sjt. P.	7166
Salmond, Sjt. W. H.	7166	Scorgie, Cpl. C. C.	7179
Salt, Cpl. H.	7166	Scott, Sjt. A. W.	7166
Samms, Sqdn.S./M. G. W. *	7166	— S./Sjt.(A./Sqn.S./M.) C.	7177
Samuels, L./C. W. J.	7166	— A./Sjt. D. H.	7179
Samways, Sjt. W.	7166	— Coy.Q.M.Sjt. D. J.	7179
Sanby, Coy.Q.M.Sjt. W.	7166	— Coy.Q.M.Sjt. F. T.	7166
Sander, By.Q.M.Sjt. L. W.	7166	— Sjt. G.	7166
Sanders, W.O.Cl.1, A. J.	7179	— Sjt. H. ‡	7180
— By.S./M. W. H.	7166	— Sjt. J.	6509
Sanderson, 2nd Cpl. D. S.	7166	— Coy.Q.M.Sjt. J. A.	7179
Sandiford, Sjt. P.	7166	— Pte.(A./Cpl.) J. A.	7166
Santer, Cpl. S. M.	7166	— Sjt. J. W. W.	7166
Sargeant, Sjt. C.	7166	— Sjt. R.	7166
Sargent, R.Q.M.Sjt. E.	7166	— Flt.Sjt. S. J.	7621
Saul, Sjt. F.	7166	— Sjt. T.	7166
Saunders, Sjt.(A./R.S.M.) D.	7166	— Sjt. W. (Linc. R.)	7166
— Pte. H. W.	6500	— Flt.Sjt. W. (Dysart)	6521
— Farr.Sjt. R. A.	7166	— S./Sjt. W. A.	7180
— Sjt.(now T./Lt.) R. C.	7177	Scotter, Spr. W. A.	7166
— Sjt. R. W.	7166	Scragg, Coy.S./M. J.	7166
— Sjt.(A./Coy.S./M.) W. F.	7166	Scrase, Fitt.Cpl. E.	7166
Savage, C.Q.M.Sjt. C.	7166	Screen, L./C. T.	7166
— Sjt.(A./Coy.S./M.) H. W.	7166	Scruton, Q.M.Sjt.(T./S./M.) F. C.	7166

---

* Group known: 1914 Star trio (17th Lancers), L.S. & G.C., M.S.M. (10/Sqn M.G.C.).

† 97552 Gunner 26th Battery, R.F.A. Cambrai, 1917.— Brought to notice for good work as runner near Marcoing on November 30th and December 1st. He carried messages day and night always under heavy shell fire, and was largely responsible for the close touch maintained between the infantry and the artillery. (Divisional Card of Honour No. 1017). Bombr. Flanders, 1917–18 and Cambrai, 1917.— Has acted with the greatest devotion to duty during the operations in Flanders and a Cambrai. His continuous good work as signaller and the fine soldierly spirit he has displayed throughout the most trying circumstances have set a high standard of efficiency and duty to the battery and merit every praise.

‡ Trio known: British War and Victory Medals (Sgt. N.Z.E.F.) and M.S.M. (24. 1813 2/Canterbury Regt.).

Scutt, Sjt. A. W. C.	7166	Shaylor, 2nd A.M. D.	6521
Scarson, Sjt. S. G.	6500	Sheard, Cpl. A. E.	7167
Scatter, Cpl. J. I.	7180	Shearer, Sjt. M.	7167
Secker, S./M. H.	6509	Shearman, E.Coy.Q.M.Sjt. A. R.	7167
Seddon, Sjt. J. E.	7166	Sheed, Cpl.(A./Sjt.) O. J.	7167
— Gnr. J. G.	7166	Sheen, Coy.Q.M.Sjt. J. F.	7167
— L./C.(Pd.A./Cpl.) W. H.	7166	Sheldon, Sjt. J.	6500
Sedgwick, By.S./M. G. R.	7166	Sheldrake, Sjt. H. T.	7167
Sedley, L./C. J. T.	7166	Shellabear, S./Sjt. S. A.	7179
Seldon, L./C. N. A.	7166	Shelton, M.S./M. A. F.	7167
Sellers, Farr.Sjt. A.	7166	Shenton, Sjt. J. S.	7167
Sercombe, S./Sjt. W. F.	6500	Shepherd, Coy.S./M. D. D.	7181
Setterfield, B.S.M. A. A.	6509	— Amt.S./M. R. G.	7167
Seward, Pte. H. W.	7166	Sheppard, Sjt. E. O.	7167
Sewell, Spr.(A./2nd Cpl.) H. J. *	7166	— Sjt. G. G.	7167
— By.Q.M.Sjt. J. L.	7166	Shergold, Sjt. G. R.	7167
Sexton, Sjt.(T./S.S./M.) W. J.	7166	Sherrard, Pte. T.	7167
Shackleton, Cpl.(A./Sjt.) J.	7166	Sherratt, Coy.S./M.(T./S./M.) W. A.	7167
Shakespear, Coy.Q.M.Sjt. B. J.	7179	Sherwin, Pte. W. ❀	4393
Sharman, Sjt.(A./Coy.S./M.) W.	7166	Sherwood, Coy.Q.M.Sjt.(A./	
Sharp, Sjt. C. J. (Corr. D.C.M.		Q.M.Sjt.) T.	7167
substituted)	4024	Shillabeer, Spr. W. H. E.	7167
— Cpl.(T./M.S./M.) G. H.	7166	Shimmin, Sjt. W. H.	7167
— S./Sjt.(A./S./S./M.) P.	7166	Shingler, M.S./Sjt. P.	7167
— T./S.S.M. W.	6509	Shinie, Cpl. J.	7167
— Sjt. W.	7167	Shipley, S./Sjt. G. W.	7167
Sharpe, T./Amt.S./M. F. R.	7167	Shipman, Flt.Sjt. F.	6521
Sharple, Cpl.(A./Sjt.Arty.Clk.) J. W.	7167	Shirley, Farr.Sjt. G. †	7167
Sharpley, Sjt. J. A.	7167	— Sjt. P.	7179
Shaw, Coy.Q.M.Sjt. A.	7167	Shoebottom, Coy.S./M. G.	7167
— Pte. A. E.	7167	Shone, temp.S./M. J. H.	6521
— Sjt.(A./R.S.M.) C.	7167	Short, S.Q.M.Sjt. W. H. A.	7177
— Sjt.(A./Coy.S./M.) D.	7167	Shreeve, Dvr. J. W.	7167
— Cpl. J.	7167	Shrimpton, Sjt.Dmr. A. E.	7167
— Q.M.Sjt.(A./Supt.Clk.) P.	7167	Sibthorp, Pte.(A./Sjt.) S.	7167
— Gnr.(A./Bombr.) R.	7167	Siddons, Cpl.(A./Sjt.) W. T.	7167
— R.Q.M.Sjt. W. G.	7177	Sidgreaves, By.S./M.(A./	
— S./Sjt. W. R.	7167	Reg.S./M.) E.	7167

---

*   Group known in Moss collection: D.C.M. (*L.G.* 26 June 1918, Corp. Henry J Sewell 4th Signal Coy. R.E.), 1914 Star and bar trio, M.S.M., Rumanian Barbatie Si Credinta (Medal for Bravery and Loyalty). From Sheerness. The citation for his D.C.M. reads: 'For conspicuous gallantry and devotion to duty when in charge of forward communications. When all of the wires had been cut by heavy shell fire he succeeded in restoring communications with the help of two linesmen at least eight times while the shelling still continued. He overcame all difficulties by his splendid coolness and determination.

†   614018 Staff Sergt. Farrier 1/1st Warwickshire Battery R.H.A. 1916–18.— This N.C.O. has served with the battery since it came out to France in 1914. His hard work and skill as Farrier and his inspiring example of vigour and resourcefulness have largely contributed to the general efficiency of the battery.

Silcocks, Coy.S./M. A. H.	7167	Slater, Sjt. T.	7167
Silk, Pte. J.	7167	Slee, Pte.(A./Cpl.) H.	7167
Sills, L./C. A. K.	7167	Sleeman, Flt.Sjt. H. L.	4413
Silver, Pte. H. J.	7167	Sleep, Fitt. Gnr.(A.Fitt.S.) C.	7167
Silvester, 2nd Cpl.(A./Sjt.) L. T.	7167	— By.S./M.(T./S./M.) F.	7167
Simcox, Pte. B.	7177	Slight, Gnr. J.	7180
Simkin, Coy.S./M. A. J.	7167	Sloan, Pte. G. S.	7180
Simm, Mech.Mach.S./Sjt. G. C.	7167	— T.Q.M.Sjt. W. J.	7177
Simmonds, Dvr. H.	7180	Sloane, Coy.S./M.(A./R.S.M.) A. L. *	7167
— Gnr. J. G.	7167	— Sjt.(A./Coy.S./M.) C.	7167
Simmons, Sjt. A. E.	6509	Small, Sjt.(A.Coy.S.M.). A.	7167
Simpson, Pte. (A./Cpl.) A.	7177	— Sjt.(A./Coy.S./M.) A. R.	7167
— Pte. H.	7167	— By. Q.M.Sjt. H. E. C.	7167
— B.S.M. J.	6509	Smalley, T./S.M. E. †	6521
— Cpl. J. A.	7167	Smeath, R.Q.M.Sjt. H.	7167
— Sjt. W.	7177	Smiles, L./C.(A./Cpl.) T.	7167
— Cpl. W.	7177	Smith, Coy.S./M. A.	7177
Sims, S./Sjt.(A./Q.M.Sjt.) A. A.	7167	— Sjt. A., *D.C.M.* (Winsford)	6500
— L./C.(A./Sjt.) L. C.	7167	— Sjt. A. (Preston)	6500
Sinclair, Coy.Q.M.Sjt. D.	7167	— Cpl. (A./Sjt.) A.	7167
— Sjt. (A./R.S.M.) G.	6509	— Cpl. A.	7177
— Sjt. J.	7177	— Dvr. A.	7167
— Sjt. J. F.	7167	— C.S.M.(A./R.S.M.) A. A.	6500
— Q.M.Sjt. J. G.	6509	— 2nd A.M. A. E.	6521
Singleton, Sjt. R.	7167	— Pte. A. G.	7180
Siville, Pte. W.	7177	— Pte. A. G.	7167
Skafte, Bombr.(A./Cpl.) W. H.	7167	— Q.M.Sjt.(T./S./M.)	
Skelton, Sjt. H. G.	7167	(Arty.Clk.) A. H.	7167
Skewes, Pte. H.	7177	— Sjt. A. J.	7167
Skidmore, Cpl.(A./Sjt.) S.	7167	— Q.M.Cpl.Maj. A. J.	7167
Skillen, Pte. J.	7177	— R.Q.M.Sjt. A. T.	7167
Skilling, Sjt. H.	7167	— Sjt. C. G.	7167
Skinner, Cpl.(A./Coy.Q.M.Sjt.) G. H.	7167	— Farr.Q.M.Sjt. C. G.	7167
Skull, Gnr. E. T.	7167	— 2nd Cpl. D. W.	7177
Slack, Coy.S./M. W. C.	7167	— Sjt. E.	7168
Slacke, Sjt. J.	7167	— Cpl. E.	7168
Slade, Sjt. G. D. T.	7167	— R.Q.M.Sjt. F.	7168
Slatcher, Coy.Q.M.Sjt. (A./		— Spr.(A./Sjt.) F.	7168
Bde.Q.M.Sjt.) W. J. D.	7167	— R.Q.M.Sjt. F. J.	7168
Slater, Pte. A.	7167	— Sjt. G.	7168

---

* South and North Staffs.: Group known: M.C. (R.S.M.), Queen's South Africa Medal (Cape Colony, Orange Free State, Transvaal, Pte), King's South Africa Medal (Cpl.), 1914/15 Star (Sgt.), British War and Victory Medals (Lieut. & Q.M.), L.S. & G.C., M.S.M., Special Const. Long Service (Chief Inspector) and Russian Cross of St. George 2nd class in gold, *L.G.* 15.2.1917, R.S.M. M.C. *L.G.* 19.8.1916: successfully organising ammunition and tool parties under heavy fire. He and the battalion 1/ 6th N. Staffs. were present on the 1st day of the Somme 1st July 1916. Retired 1925. Living in Wolverhampton 1937.

† No. 467 R.F.C. Enlisted October 1912, from the Merchant Navy. As 1A.M. 2 Sqn. served in France from 12 August 1914. S.M. May 1917. R.A.F. M.S.M. for France.

Smith, Cpl. G.	7168	Snelling, By.Q.M.Sjt. A. E.	7168
— Sjt. G. W. (North'd Fus.)	7168	Snook, Cpl. (L./Sjt.) W. C.	7168
— Sjt. G. W. (R.H.A.)	7168	Snow, Cpl. (A./Sjt.) W. A.	7168
— Sjt. G. W. T.	7168	Snowball, Gnr. J. B.	7168
— Sjt. H.	7168	Soar, Pte. (A./Sjt.) H. W.	7168
— Sjt. H.	7168	Soley, Sjt. F.	7168
— L./Cpl. H.	7168	Sollitt, Sjt. W.	7168
— Pte. (A./Cpl.) H.	7168	Solomon, Pte. W. J. C.	6500
— Farr.Sjt. H. A.	7168	Somers, By.S./M. F.	7168
— Sjt. H. J.	6509	Southern, Cpl. T. H.	7177
— Sjt.(A./Q.M.Sjt.) H. S.	7168	Southworth, S.S./M. J.	7169
— Pte. H. T.	7168	Soutter, Pte. J.	6509
— S.QM.Sjt. J.	7168	Sowden, Cpl. E.	7168
— Coy.S./M.(A./R.S.M.) J.	7168	Spackman, Farr.Sjt. T.	7168
— Sjt. J.	7168	— L./C.(A./Sjt.) W. H.	7168
— Cpl. J.	7168	Spalding, Cpl. E. T. J.	6500
— Spr. J.	7168	— R.S./M. J. W.	7168
— Sjt. J. C.	7180	Spanner, Sjt. H.	7168
— Sjt. J. G.	7168	Sparnon, Coy.Q.M.Sjt. W. H.	7180
— Coy.S./M. J. H.	7168	Spears, Cpl. C.	7177
— Gnr. J. H.	7168	Speed, Pte. F.	6500
— Gnr. N.	7168	Speight, Sjt. A., *M.M.*	6500
— Cpl. N. S.	7168	Speller, R.Q.M.S. N.	6500
— Coy.S./M. R. M.	7168	Spellmann, Q.M.Sjt. M.	7168
— Sjt. S.	7168	Spencer, S./Sjt.(T./S./S./M.) G. W.	7168
— Cpl. S.	7168	— Sjt.(A./Coy.Q.M.Sjt.) J. T.	7168
— C.Q.M.S.(A./Q.M.Sjt.) S. F.	6500	— Coy.Q.M.Sjt. N. B.	7180
— Coy.Q.M.Sjt. S. V.	7168	Spice, Cpl.(A./Sjt.) G. W.	7168
— Cpl. T. (W. Kilbride)	7168	Spicer, Pte. A. T.	7180
— Cpl.(A./Sjt.) T. (E. Perth)	7168	Spillane, T./Amt.S./M. W. T.	7168
— Sjt. T. H.	7168	Spink, Farr.S./Cpl. G. H.	7168
— R.S./M. T. P. V.	7168	Spragg, Q.M.Sjt. G. R.	7168
— Sjt. W.	7168	Spreadborough, Cpl(A./Sjt.) G.	7168
— Pte. W. A.	7180	Spreadbury, Sjt. F.	7168
— A./Cpl. W. A. R.	7168	— T./Sub Condr. H. G. S.	6500
— Coy.S./M. W. L.	7168	Spriggins, W.O.Cl.1, A.	7180
— Sjt. (A./S./Sjt.) W. L.	7168	Springthorpe, Spr.(A./2nd Cpl.) S. C.	7168
— Pte. W. N.	7168	Squire, Sjt.(A./S./M.) P. B.	7168
— Coy.S./M. W. T.	7168	Squires, Sjt. A. J.	6492
— Whlr.S./Sjt. W. T.	7168	Stables, 2nd Cpl.(A./Sjt.) F. H.	7168
— Sjt. W. T.	7180	— Q.M.Sjt. J.	7168
Smithard, Gnr. S.	7168	Stacey, Sjt.(A./Coy.S./M.) S.	7168
Smithies, Coy.Q.M.Sjt. J. R.	7168	— R.S./M. W. T.	7168
Smithson, Cpl. E.	7168	Stafford, Sjt.(A./S./Sjt.) J.	7168
— Q.M.Sjt. M. J.	7168	— R.Q.M.Sjt. T. H.	7168
Smyth, Cpl. D.	7168	Stainton, Cpl.(A./S./Sjt.) L.	7168
— Sjt. R., *M.M.*	6500	Stanbrook, L./C.(A./Sjt.) W. G.	6509
Snailum, M.S./M. R. T.	7168	Standen, Pte. E.	7177
Snaith, S./Sjt. J.	7168	Standing, T./S.S./M. E.	7168
Sneath, Sjt. J.	7168	— Coy.S./M. F. A.	7168
Sneddon, Sjt.(A./Coy.S./M.) R.	7168	Stanford, Cpl. E.	7177
— Coy.S./M. W.	7168	— Spr.(A./Coy.Q.M.Sjt.) J.	7168

Stanton, Sjt. J.	7168	Stevenson, S./Sjt. H. C.		7180
Stapleford, Coy.S./M. J.	7169	— Flt.Sjt. J.		6521
Staples, By.Q.M.Sjt. C. E.	* 7169	Stewart, Cpl. C. W.		7169
Stapleton, T./Sub Condr. A. L.	7169	— Cpl. E. D.		7180
Stapley, Cpl (A./Sjt.) E.	7169	— Cpl. G. H.		7169
Staton, Sjt. H.	7169	— Sjt. J.		7169
Staveley, Dvr. M.	7169	— T./Sub Condr. J. H.		7169
Stead, Cpl. E. J.	7169	— Sjt. J. T.		7169
Stear, Sjt. J.	6509	Stichling, L./C(A./Sjt) R. E.		7169
Stebbing, Sjt. H.	7169	Stidworthy, T./S.M. H. L.		6521
Stedman, A./Coy.S./M.Inst. A.	7169	Stiles, Sjt.(A./M./S./Sjt.) W. H.		7169
— S./M. W. B.	7169	Stinton, S.Sjt. T.		7169
Steel, R.Q.M.Sjt. F. C.	7169	Stirton, Coy.S./M. G. C.		7169
— Pte. (A./Sjt) H.	7169	Stockdale, Cpl.(A./Cpl.S./M.) W.		7169
Steele, S./M. E.	7169	Stocks, Co.Q.M.Sjt. R.		6492
— Coy.S./M. E. A.	7169	Stokell, Coy.S./M. E. R.		7181
— By. S./M. F. C.	7169	Stokes, Gnr.(A./Cpl.) H. H.		7169
— Sjt. H. W.	7169	— Sjt. J. A.		7169
— Farr.Sjt. J.	7169	— 2nd Cpl. W. G.		7169
— Coy.Q.M.Sjt. R. G.	7180	— Sjt. W. P.		7169
— Cpl. W.	6500	Stone, T./Sub Condr. A. E.		6500
— Sqdn.S.M.(A./R.S.M.) W. H.	6492	— S.S./M. T. J.		7169
Steen, Sjt. A.	7177	Stoneman, Sjt. (T./S.S./M.) G.		7169
Steer, Sjt. E. F.	7169	Stow, Sqdn.S./M. G. H.		7169
Stehr, Pte.(A./Sjt.) F. H.	7169	Straiton, Sjt. W. J.		6500
Stein, Pte. A.	7169	Strange, Cpl. E. G.		6521
Stemp, Q.M.S. A. H.	6500	— Gnr. W. E.		7169
Stenner, C.S.M. W. V.	6509	Stangeway, Cpl.(A./Sjt.) J.		7169
Stephen, Sjt. J. F.	7169	Stratford, 2nd Cpl.(A./Cpl.) G.		7169
Stephenson, Cpl. A. W.	7169	Stretch, Coy.Q.M.Sjt. W. J.		7169
— Sjt. C. F.	7169	Street, By.S./M. J. C.		7180
— Coy.S./M. F. L.	7177	— Sjt. S.		7169
— Sjt.(A./Coy.S./M. J. M.	7169	Stribbling, Tpr. W.		7169
— Sjt.(T./S./M.) J. V.	7169	Stride, Sjt. R. M.		7177
— Cpl. W.	6509	Strike, L./Sjt.(A./Q.M.Sjt) A.		7169
Sterling, Cpl. W. A.	7177	Stringer, Dmr. A.		7169
Stevens, 1st A.M. E.	6521	— Sjt. E. J.		7169
— S.Sjt. F. E.	7169	— Pnr.(A./Sjt) J.		7169
— Coy.Q.M.Sjt.	7177	Strivens, Sjt. A. T.		7169
— Sjt. J. A.	7180	Strugnell, Cpl.(A./Sjt.Arty.		
— Pte. R.	7169	Clk.) H. G.		7169
— Sjt. W. G.	7177	Strumey, Sjt. E. J.		7180
— Pnr. W. L. F.	7169	Stuart, F. of W. S./Sjt. A.		7169
Stevenson, Sjt. A.	7169	— Pte. C.		7169
— L./Cpl. E.	❀ 5037	— Q.M.Sjt. C. F.		7169

---

* 41830 Sergt. No. 2 Section 29th D.A.C. Arras and Flanders 1917—For valuable and distinguished service in the field. (M.I.D. 14/12/17). B.Q.M.S. No. 1 Section 29th D.A.C., Flanders 1917–18 and Cambrai, 1917—Has served with distinction. Has proved himself invariable trustworthy and conscientious and has taken the greatest care of and interest in the equipment and welfare of his section.

Stuart, Gnr. H.	7180	Symonds, M.S./Sjt. H. B.	7170
— L./C. L.	7177	Symondson, Cpl.(A./L./Sjt.) J. A.	7170
— S./Sjt.(T.S.S./M.) R.	7169	Symons, Sjt. R. J.	6500
Stubbings, Sjt. H. E.	7169	Synnot, Cpl. G. H.	7180
Stubbley, Sjt. H.	7169	Syzling, R.Q.M.Sjt. C.	7170
Stubbs, Sjt. R. W.	7169		
Sturgess, Cpl.(A./S./Sjt.) J.	7169	Tain, Coy.S./M. P.	7170
— T./Sub Condr. W. H. Y.	7169	Tait, Sjt. R.	7170
Styles, L./C.(A./Sjt) W.	7169	Talbot, Fitt.S./Sjt. A. J.　†	7170
Sullivan, Sjt. (T./S.S./M.) G. M.	7169	— T./Sub Condr. J. M.	7170
— S./S./M. J.	7170	Talboys, Gnr. S.	7170
— S.S./M. T.	7170	Tamblyn, Sjt. S.	7177
Summers, Gnr. H.	7181	Tandy, Coy.S./M. J.	7170
Sumner, Cpl. J.	7169	Tanner, Cpl.(A./Sjt.)	6492
— Q.M.Sjt. N.	7169	Tarbet, Q.M.Sjt.(A./S.S./M.) A.	7170
Surman, S./Sjt. J. R.	7177	Tardrew, Sjt.(A./S./Sjt.) G.	7170
Surrall, Coy.Q.M.Sjt. J. M.	7169	Tarlington, Cpl. A.	6521
Surtees, Cpl. G. F.	6521	Tarr, Pnr. Sjt. D.	7170
— M.S./Sjt. J. E.	7169	Tarrey, R.S./M. E.	7170
Sutherland, Pte. A.　　*	7169	Tatum, Spr. G. A.　　❀	4024
— Spr.(A./Sjt.) W. B.	7177	Taylor, Sjt.(A./S./M.) A.	7170
Sutton, Sjt. D. B.	7169	— Spr. A.	7170
— S.S.M. G. H.	6509	— Sjt. A. E.	7170
— Pte. (A./Sjt.) M.	7169	— Coy.Q.M.Sjt. A. J. R.	7180
Swain, A./Sjt. C. H.	7169	— Pte.(L./C.) B.	7170
Swaits, Coy.S./M. W. C.	7169	— Cpl. D. E.	7170
Swan, L./C.(A./Sjt.) E.	7169	— Coy.Q.M.Sjt. F.	7170
— A.B.P.W.	7169	— Pte. F. J.	7170
Swann, Sjt. R.	7169	— Coy.Q.M.Sjt. G.	7170
Sweet, T./M.S./M. A. G.	7169	— E.C. 2nd Cpl.(A./E.C. S./Sjt.) G. D.	7170
Swettenham, Sjt. G.	7169	— Amt.S./Sjt.(T./Amt.S./M.) G. W.	6509
Swift, Pte.(A./Cpl.) C.	7169	— Pte. G. W.	7170
— Cpl. F.	6521	— By.S./M. H.	7170
— Coy.Q.M.Sjt. J. C.	7177	— Gnr.(L./Bombr.) H.	7170
Swinburn, Sjt. W.	7169	— Cpl.(A./S./Sjt.) H. G.	7170
Swinburne, T./Armt.S./M. J. H.	6492	— Coy.Q.M.Sjt.(A./Coy.S./M.) J.	7170
Swindley, Coy.S.M. C.	7169	— T./R.S./M. J.	7170
Sykes, Amt.S.Sjt.(A./Q.M.Sjt.) A.	7170	— Cpl. J.	7170
— R.S./M. E. N.	7170	— 2nd Cpl.(A./Cpl.) J. W.	7170
Symes, Sjt.(A./Col.Sjt.) H. J.	7170		

*　Group in Moss collection: Queen's Egypt Medal (undated, Gamaizah, 1888 Pte. K.O.S.B.), Indian General Service Medal (Relief of Chitral, 1895 Pte. K.O.S.B.), British War Medal (Cpl. A.S.C.) (Victory Medal missing), M.S.M. (A.S.C.) and Khedive's Star (unnamed and undated). The two Victorian awards are verified in W.O./100/65 and W.O./100/78. The M.S.M. entry shows his home town as Bradford Yorks.

†　51794 Staff Sergt. Artificer A.O.C. (attached 460th Battery R.F.A.). Flanders 1917–18 and Cambrai 1917—This N.C.O. has displayed the greatest devotion to duty. His thorough and conscientious work have contributed very largely to the efficiency of the battery in which he has served since the landing at Gallipoli.

Taylor, Sjt. K. J.	7170	Thomas, L./C.(A./Sjt.) E. H.		7170
— Pte. L.	❀ 5037	— Sjt.(A./Coy.S./M.) G., (A.S.C.)		7170
— Whlr.S.S./Sjt. P. H.	7170	— Sjt.(A../Coy.S./M.) G.		7170
— Sjt. R. A.	7170	— Pte. (A./Sjt.) G. D. W.		7170
— Sjt. R. N.	7180	— Cpl.(A./Sjt.) H.		6492
— Coy.Q.M.Sjt. S.	7170	— Coy.Q.M.Sjt. J.		7170
— Gnr. S. T.	7170	— Cpl. J.		7170
— Sjt. T.	7170	— Cpl. L. (Manch. R.)		7170
— T./S./M. T.	7170	— Cpl. L. (R.E.)		7170
— L./C. T. H.	7170	— Sjt.(A./C.S.M.) O. D.		6492
— Coy.Q.M.Sjt. W.	7170	— Spr.(A./2nd Cpl.) R.		7180
— Sjt. W.	7170	— S./Smith Cpl.(A./Farr. Sjt.) W.		6500
— Sjt. W. B.	7170	— Pte. W. D.		7170
— Q.M.Sjt. W. H.	7170	— Cpl. W. E.		7170
— A./Sjt. W. H.	6500	Thompson, Pte. B.		7181
— Sjt. W. J.	7170	— Sjt. C. F.		7170
Teakle, Sjt. W. H.	7170	— Sjt. C. J.		6521
Teale, Coy.S./M. J. A.	7170	— Sjt. F.		4413
Tedstill, Coy.S./M. G., *M.M.*	7170	— Pte. F. W.		7170
Telfer, Cpl. H.	7170	— Coy.Q.M.Sjt. H. H.		7180
Temperley, L./Sjt. N. G.	7170	— Dvr.(A./L.C.) H. J.		7171
Temperton, Sjt. G. W.	7170	— Sjt. J.		7171
Tench, Coy.S./M.(A./R.S.M.) F. A.	7170	— L./C. J.		7171
Teppett, Cpl. R.	7170	— Q.M.Sjt. J. O.		7180
Terry, Sjt. H.	7170	— Sadd.S./Sjt. J. S.		6500
— Sjt. R.	7170	— By.S./M. P. W.		7171
Thacker, Coy.S./M. A.	7170	— Sjt. R.		7171
— R./S./M. F. W.	7170	— Sjt. R. H.		7171
Thackray, Sjt. W. E.	7170	— Sjt. R. S.		7171
Theaker, By.S./M. G.	7170	— Coy.S./M. S.		7171
Thearle, Sjt. A. J.	7170	Thomson, Coy.Q.M.Sjt. B.		7171
Thew, Coy.S./M.(T./R.S.M.)		— Sjt. J.		7171
W., *D.C.M.*	7170	— Q.M.Sjt. J. A.		7180
Thickett, R./Q.M.Sjt. H.	7170	— Pte.(A./Sjt.) R.		7171
Thirkettle, Sjt. W. J.	7170	— Sjt.(A./Q.M.Sjt.) W.		7171
Thistlethwaite, Dvr. B.	7170	Thorley, C.S.M. F. C.		6509
Thom, Flt.Sjt. G.	6521	Thorn, Sj. G. B. L.		7171
Thomas, Sjt. A.	7170	— Sjt. N.		7177
— T.Q.M.Sjt. A. M.	7170	— S./Sjt. W.		7180
— Cpl. A. W.	7170	Thornbury, Sjt. R. G.		7171
— Gnr.(T./Bombr.) B. G.	7180	Thorne, Sjt. C. C.		7171
— Sjt. C. H.	7170	— R.Q.M.Sjt. C. L.	*	7171
— Spr. E.	7170	— Sjt. W.		7171

---

* Charles Leonard Thorne. Group in Moss collection: O.B.E. (2nd type military), 1914 Star (Colour Sgt. Royal Scots Fusiliers), British War and Victory Medals (W.O.II R.S.F.), Defence and War Medals, Jubilee 1935 and Coronation 1937, L.S. & G.C. (Geo. V, W.O.I 2/R.S.F.) and M.S.M. He was born in 1886 and enlisted into 2/R.S.F. in 1905, serving in the ranks for over 11 years before becoming R.Q.M.S., a rank he held for over three years. Appointed R.S.M. (W.O.1) in 1920, he was commissioned Lieut. and Q.M. in November, 1926. Promoted Captain November

Thornton, S./Sjt. G.	7171	Tooley, Coy.Q.M.Sjt. J.	* 7171
— Sjt. G. W.	6509	Toomey, Sjt.(A./C.Q.M.Sjt.) H. A.	7171
— Coy.S./M. W.	7171	Toon, Cpl. H. E. V.	† 7171
Thorp, Sjt. E. H.	7171	— R.Q.M.Sjt. T.	7171
Thorpe, By.Q.M.Sjt. S. P.	7171	Toop, Sjt. E. A.	7171
Thurlow, Sjt. (A./Coy.Q.M.Sjt.) A.	7171	Topham, Pte. W.	7171
Thurston, Sjt. F. R.	7171	Topping, Pte.(A./L./Sjt.) J.	7171
Tidy, S./S./M. W. T.	7171	Tordoff, Pte. H.	7171
Tilbrook, C.S.M. S. G.	6509	Torr, By.S./M. A.	7171
Tilbury, Mech. S.M. W. H.	6492	Totterdell, Sjt. H. P.	7171
Tiller, Cpl.(A./Sjt.) C. T.	6492	Tough, S./Sjt.(A./Q.M.Sjt.) L. G.	7171
Tilton, Sjt.(A./S./M.) C.	7171	— Cpl. T.	7171
Timbs, Cpl. G. W.	7171	Towhill, Bombr. (A./Cpl.) S.	7171
Timmins, Cpl. G. H.	7171	Towl, Amt.S./Sjt.(A./	
Timson, By.S./M. R.	7171	Amt.S./M.) L. F.	‡ 7171
Tindal, Sjt. A.	7171	Towler, Q.M.Sjt. S. G.	7180
Tindale, Cpl. T. W.	7171	Towner, Coy.S./M. S. C.	7171
Tinkler, A./B. W.	7171	Townley, Sjt.(A./Sqn.S./M.) J.	7171
Tippen, Coy.S./M. L. G.	7171	Townsend, Sjt.(A./Coy.S./M.) E. J.	7171
Tipper, Sjt. E. T.	7171	— Sjt. F.	7171
Tisdall, Dvr. W. G.	7171	Townson, Pte. (A./L./C.) A.	7171
Titley, Cpl.(A./Sjt.) S. E.	7171	Tozer, T./Amt.S./M. H. S.	7171
Titmas, S.B.M.Sjt. W. J.	6492	Tracey, Coy.S.M. J. S.	7177
Titt, Bombr. C. E.	7177	Tranter, By.Q.M.Sjt. H.	6500
Titterington, Sjt. J.	7171	— Coy.S./M.(A./S./M.) J. H.	7171
Tivey, Bombr.(A./Cpl.) G.	7171	Traymor, Coy.Q.M.Sjt. P.	7177
Todd, Sjt.(A./Q.M.Sjt.) R. S.	6500	Treagus, Coy.Q.M.Sjt.(A./	
Tokeley, By.S./M. F. W.	7171	R.S.M.) H. A.	6500
Tom, Pte.(A./Sjt.) G. A.	7171	Treahy, Coy.S./M. J.	7171
Tomkinson, Dvr.(A./Coy.S./M.) A. T.	7171	Trendall, Q.M.Sjt. J.	7171
Tomlinson, Pte. G.	7171	Trenholm, Sjt. W.	7171
— S./Sjt.(A./S.S.M.) W.	6509	Tresidder, Sjt. A. L.	7180
Tompkins, Sadd.Sjt. W. G.	6500	Tressider, Coy.S./M. W. L. A.	7171
Toms, R.S./M. E. R.	7180	Treventhan, Cpl. F. A.	7171
Tonks, L./C. A. B.	7180	Trevitt, R.Q.M.Sjt. P. J.	7171

1934 and given a Brevet of Major in 1938 when he was appointed the Quarter Master of the Staff College at Camberley. He was promoted Lieutenant Colonel in January 1941.

* Group known: 1914/15 Star (Pte. Scots Guards), British War and Victory Medals (C. Sgt.) and M.S.M. (1/S. Gds.).

† 101893 Corpl. 'L' Battery R.H.A. Flanders 1917-18 and Cambrai 1917—For continuous good service. He has been responsible for the battery signals. His conscientious and hard work throughout has been of invaluable service to the battery and has merited all praise. Flanders 1918—During the night operations of June 2nd/3rd near Nieppe Forest he restored telephone communication under heavy fire, including gas, repairing breaks in five places, thus enabling messages to come through from the most advanced infantry up to the time of their gaining their objectives. His assistants being temporarily out of action from gas, he carried on single-handed. (Divisional Card of Honour).

‡ R.A.O.C. Also Belgian Croix de Guerre.

Triggs, 1st A.M. H. W.	6521	Tyrrell, Cpl. R. R.		7172
Tripp, R./S.M. J.	6509			
Trotter, Coy.Q.M.Sjt. H.	7171	Uden, S./Sjt. W.		7172
— Gnr. J.	7171	Ungar, S./Sjt. I. I.		7172
Trufitt, Sjt. J.	6500	Unwin, Cpl.(A./Sjt.) L. P.		7172
Trumpe, Sjt.(A./R.S.M.) R.	7171	Upson, L./Bombr.(A./Cpl.) G. W.		7172
Truss, Sjt. W. G.	7181	Upton, R.Q.M.Sjt. E. A.		7172
— By.Q.M.Sjt. W. H.	7171	Uren, Sjt. A. N.		7180
Tubb, Coy.S./M. J.	7171	Utting, Coy.S./S.M. E.		7172
Tubby, By.Q.M.Sjt. W. J.	7171			
Tuck, L./C.(A./Cpl.) F. C.	6500	Vale, Pte. J.		7172
Tucker, Cpl. A.	7171	Vallance, Cpl.(A./Q.M.Sjt.) W. C.		7172
— Sjt. G. A.	7171	Vanner, Saddler Sjt.(A./Sadd.Sjt.) T.		7172
— L./C.(A./Sub Condr.) P. F.	* 6509	Varley, Pte.(A./Sjt.) W. B.		7172
— Sjt. W. J.	7171	Vassie, Farr.S./Sjt. A. G.		7172
Tuckey, Sjt. C.	7171	Vaughan, Sjt. D.		7180
Tuckwell, Sjt. P. W.	7171	Veitch, Sjt. J.		6500
Tuckwell, C.P.O. W. J.	6521	Venes, Cpl. R.		7172
Tufnel, Sjt. T. G.	7171	Vernon, Dvr. J.		7180
Tugwell, Sjt. C. S.	7171	Veronelli, Cpl.(A./Sjt.) E. E.		7172
— Sjt. (A./Coy.S./M.) H.	7171	Vine, Dvr. H. W.		7172
Tullett, L./C.(A./Sjt.) C. H.	7172	Vingoe, Sjt. A.		7181
Tunstall, Gnr. S.	7172	Vivian, Spr.(A./Cpl.) J. C.		7172
Turcotte, Gnr. E. C.	7177	Voice, Sjt. E. S.		7172
Turnbull, Sjt. R. C.	7180	Vowles, Sjt. W.		7172
Turnell, Sjt.(A./S./S.M.) J.	7172	Voysey, Cpl. C. E.	❀	7018
Turner, Sjt. A. A.	7172			
— Sjt. A. R.	7177	Waddington, Sjt. T.		7172
— Farr.S./Sjt. A. W.	7172	— A./Sjt. W.		7172
— Sjt. E. J.	7180	Wadesen, By.S./M. H. R.		7172
— Sjt. H. J.	7180	Wadsworth, Coy.S./M.(A./R.S.M.)		
— R.Q.M.Sjt. J. C.	7172	E. (W.Rid.R.)		71·72
— Sjt. J. G.	7172	— Coy.By.S./M. E. (R.F.A.)		7172
— Cpl.(A./Sjt.) R.	7172	Waeland, Flt.Sjt. J.	†	6521
— Sjt. S. G.	7172	Wagelein, Sjt. F.		7172
— S./M.Artfr. T. J.	7177	Wagg, Armr.Sjt. C. G. C.		7180
— R.Q.M.Sjt. W.	7180	Wagborne, S./Sjt.(A./Q.M.S.)		
— Sjt. W.	6500	F. W. G.		6500
— By.S./M. W. S.	7172	Waight, Sjt.(A./S./Sjt.)		6492
Turney, Col.Sjt. C.	7172	Waite, Coy.S./M. J.		7172
Turp, L./C. C. W.	7172	— Sjt. J.		7172
Turton, Sjt. A.	7172	Wakefield, Coy.S./M. W. E.		7172
Turvey, Bombr. T.	6500	Wakely, Farr.S./Sjt. G. F.		7172
Tutt, Pte.(A./L./C.) A. E. H.	7172	Wakeman, Pte. (A./Sjt.) E. E.		7172
Twidell, Sjt.(A./S./Sjt.) W. J.	7172	Walden, Pte.(A./Sjt.) C.		7172
Twitichett, Sjt. J.	6500	Waldron, S./Sjt. F.		7172
Tyler, Pte.(A./Cpl.) R. B. W.	7172	Wales, By.S./M. A. J.		7172

* R.A.O.C. Also French Médaille d'Honneur avec Glaives (en Bronze).
† No. 126 R.F.C. Enlisted 28 June 1912. Cpl. 3 Sqn. in France from 13 August, 1914.
    Flight Sgt. 1 September, 1915. R.A.F. M.S.M. in France.

Walker, L./C.(A./Cpl.) A.	7172	Ward, Sjt. W. A.	7173
— Flt.Sjt. F. O.	4413	— S./Sjt.(A./S.Q.M.Sjt.) W. R.	7173
— Sqdn.S./M. G. A.	7172	Warden, Sjt. G. J.	7173
— Sjt. H.	6500	Wardhaugh, Cpl. T. Y.	7180
— Sjt. J.	7172	Ware, Spr.(A./2nd Cpl.) A. P.	7173
— Dvr. J.	7172	Wareham, S./Sjt. A. F. C.	7173
— Coy.Q.M.Sjt. R.	7177	Waring, Pte. H. A.	7173
Wall, Coy.Q.M.Sjt.(A../Coy.S./M.) F.	7172	Warner, T./S./S./M. A. E.	7173
— Sjt. F. J.	7172	Warren, S./Sjt.(A./Coy.	
Wallace, L./Bombr. F. W.	7172	Q.M.Sjt.) F. A.	7173
— Cpl. M. J.	7177	Warwick, R.Q.M.Sjt. F. J.	7173
— A./Sjt. R.	7172	Waspe, Sjt. A.	7173
— Sjt.(A../C.S.M.) W. D.	6492	Wass, F. of Wks.(Q.M.Sjt.) S. H.	7173
— C.S.M. W. H.	6509	Wastman, Sjt. A. E.	7144
Wallbank, E.C.Q.M.Sjt.(T./		Waterhouse, Sjt. W. P.	7173
Supt.Clk.) C.	7172	Waterman, Coy.Q.M.Sjt. C.	7173
Waller, A./Cpl. R. W.	7172	— Sjt. E. T.	6509
Wallis, Cpl.(L./Sjt.) A.	7180	Waters, Sjt. W. G. T.	7173
— Supt.Clk. J.	7172	Waterton, Sjt. H. M.	7173
— Cpl. J. H.	7172	Watkins, S.Q.M.Sjt. A. C.	7180
Wallwork, S./Q.M.Sjt. E. J. S.	7178	— R.Q.M.Sjt. C. W.	7173
Walmsley, S./Sjt.(A./Q.M.Sjt.) P.	7172	— Pte. (A./Sjt.) F. B.	7178
— Bombr. S.	7172	— T./S./M. R. S.	7173
Walsh, L./C.(A./Sjt.) A. B.	7172	— Flt.Sjt. T.	4413
— By.Q.M.Sjt. A. P.	7172	Watling, Cpl. H.	7173
— F. of W. S./M. G. A.	6509	Watson, R.Q.M.Sjt. A.	7173
— E. C. S./Sjt. J.	7172	— Cpl. A.	7173
— Sjt. J. B.	7172	— Coy.Q.M.Sjt. D. L.	7173
— Coy.Q.M.Sjt. P., *M.M.*	7172	— Co.S.M.(T./R.S.M.) G. T.	6492
— 2nd Cpl. (A./Cpl.) T.	7172	— Sjt. H.	7173
— Sjt.(A./Q.M.Sjt.) T. P.	7172	— Dvr. H.	7173
Walters, S./Sjt.(A./S./M.) A. J.	7172	— P./O. J.	7173
— Sjt. E.	7172	— Sjt. J. H.	7173
— Sjt. G.	7172	— Sjt. T.	7173
Walton, Sjt. E. E.	7172	— Sjt. W.	7173
— Coy.Q.M.Sjt. H. G.	7172	— L./C. W.	7181
— Cpl. J.	7172	Watt, Smith Fitt. P. F.	7173
— Sjt.(A./Q.M.Sjt.) W. E.	7172	Watts, Pte. F.	7173
Ward, Sjt. (A./By.S./M.) A.	7172	— Sjt. J.	7173
— 2nd Cpl. A. J.	7172	— S./M. R.	7173
— Sjt. C. G.	6521	Wavell, Pte.(A./Sjt.) J. H.	7173
— S./M. C. H.	7178	Way, Coy.S./K. J. H.	7173
— Pte. D.	7172	— Pte. (A./Cpl.) S.	7173
— B.S.M. E.	6509	Weary, L./C.(A./Sjt.) R. A.	6509
— L./C.(A./Cpl.) E.	7172	Weaver, By.S./M. A.	7173
— Sjt. E. P.	7172	— Cpl. E. J.	7173
— Cpl.(A./Sjt.) G. H.	7172	— Cpl.(now Sjt.) J.	7180
— Cpl. H.	7172	Webb, Cpl.(T./S./S./M.) A. A.	7173
— Sjt. G. E.	7172	— T./Supt.Clk. B.	7173
— By.S./M. J. H.	7173	— Sjt. J.	7178
— A./Cpl. L.	7173	— Coy.S./M. S. L.	7173
— Q.M.Sjt.(A./S.M.) M.	6492	Webber, Cpl.(A./Coy.Q.M.Sjt.) R. W.	7173

Webber, Sjt. S. J.	7173	West, Cpl. C. J. J.		7173
— Cpl. T. C.	7173	— B.S.M. F. J.		6500
— 2nd Cpl.(A./Sjt.) W. J.	7173	— Sjt. G. V.		7178
Webster, Sjt. A.	7173	— R./S./M. S. H.		7178
— M.S./Sjt. E. W. D.	7173	— Sjt. W. J.		7173
— Spr. F. G.	7173	Weston, Cpl. F. H.		7173
— 2nd Cpl. H.	7178	— S./Sjt.(A./S./M.) G.		7173
— Sjt. P.	7173	Westwood, L./C. J. G.		7173
Weedon, Q.M.Sjt.(T./S./M.) W. W.	7173	Wetherell, Sjt. J.		7173
Weight, Sjt.(T./Q.M.Sjt.) F. G.	* 7173	Whalley, L./Bombr. J.		7173
Welburn, S./S./M. A. E.	7173	Whammond, Cpl.(A./Sjt.) D.		7173
Wellington, Sjt.(A./Sjt.S./M.) J. T.	7173	Wharton, Sjt.(A./Coy.		
Wells, Sjt. B. J.	7173	Q.M.Sjt.) G. H.		7173
— Pte.(A./Mech.S./Sjt.) E.	7173	Whatling, Sjt. C. L.		7173
— Cpl.(A./Sjt.) F. G.	7173	Wheadon, Sjt.(A./Coy.S./M.) G.		7173
— Sjt. H.	7173	Wheatley, Cpl. F.		7173
— Pte. J. H.	7173	— Coy.S./M. H. G.		7173
— Pte. J. R. A.	❀ 4393	— Whr.S./Sjt. L.		7173
— Gnr. J. W.	7173	Wheeler, Sjt. A.		7178
— Sjt. W. G.	7173	— C.P.O. 3rd Gr.(E) A. J.	†	6521
Welsh, Sjt. R. S.	6492	— S./Sjt.(T./S./M.) B. V.		7173
Welshman, Cpl. A. D.	7180	Wheelton, Coy.Q.M.Sjt. S.	‡	7173
Welton, Sub Condr. W.	7181	Whelan, Sjt. J. P.		7173
Wensley, Sjt. W.	7173	Wheller, Sjt. W. C.		7173
Werrett, Sjt. W. J.	7173	Whillier, Sjt. E. E.		7173
Wesson, Cpl. A. C.	7173	Whinn, Sjt. J. D. P.		7173

---

* Group in McInnes collection: The Army M.S.M. is one of only 72 to Royal Marines: Africa General Service Medal (Somaliland 1902–04, Pte. R.M. H.M.S. *Mohawk*), 1914/15 Star CH 11722 Sgt. R.M.L.I.), British War and Victory Medals (A./Sgt. Maj), R.N. L.S. & G.C. (Geo. V, Admiral's Bust, Sergeant R.M.L.I.), M.S.M. (1/R. Marines) and Messina Earthquake medal. Born October 1883 in Mitchen, Surrey and enlisted in July 1900 giving a false date of birth of 6 July 1882. He embarked in *Mohawk* in January, 1903 and landed with the Naval Brigade on 21 April, 1904 in Somaliland at Illig and was present at the capture of the town. By 1912 he had had two more sea tours on *Resolution* and *Andromache* and qualified in Musketry seven times. That year he was promoted Sergeant and working in the Q.M.S.'s office. He joined the R.N. Division R.M. Brigade in France in December 1915, two months after earning his L.S. & G.C. He no doubt saw much action in the many battles of Passchendaele, Arras and Welsh Ridge and earned the £34–0–0 war gratuity that went to his widow. For as R.S.M. he was killed in action on 20 September 1918 and is buried in Quant Road British Cemetery, 9¼ miles north-east of Bapaume. He had married when a Corporal in September 1908. They had two sons, Jack (1909–1981) who served in the Merchant Navy and in the Royal Marines from 1923–9, and James (1910–1947) who served in the R.A.F. until his death in Cyprus, where he is buried.

† R.A.F. M.S.M. as F/385 R.N.A.S.

‡ Manchester Regiment, and M.G.C. A Territorial, he was mobilised in August, 1914, and quickly proceeded to Egypt, where he saw heavy fighting in the Suez Canal zone. In 1915 he was sent to the Dardanelles, took part in the landing at Suvla Bay and after the evacuation of the Gallipoli Peninsular, returned to Egypt. Later he

Whitaker, L./C. J. W.	7173
— E.C.Cpl.(A./Sjt.) L.	7173
— Spr.(A./S./Sjt.) T. H.	6492
Whitbread, R.Q.M.S. W.	6509
Whitby, Cpl. J.	7174
Whitcher, L./Cpl.(A./Sjt.) H. S.	7174
White, Sjt. A. J.	7174
— Bombr. B. V.	7174
— S.S.M. D.	6492
— Sjt. E.	7174
— Led.Sea. E.	7174
— S./Sjt. F.	7174
— Pte.(A./Sjt.) F. A.	7174
— Sjt. F. J. (R.F.A.)	7174
— Sjt. F. J. (H.A.C.)	7174
— Sjt. G.	6509
— Sjt.(A./Coy.S./M.) G. N.	7174
— Sjt. G. R.	7174
— Sjt. H. C.	6509
— Pte. J. (Aus.Inf.)	7180
— Pte. J. (Ches. R.)	7174
— Sjt. J. C.	7174
— R.Q.M.Sjt. J. R.	7174
— Dvr. J. W.	7180
— Coy.S./M. P.	7180
— S./S./M. R. W.	7174
— T./S./M. S. J.	7174
— Coy. S./M. W.	7174
— Sjt. W. H.	7180
Whitehead, Sjt. F.	7174
— S./Sjt. H.	7174
— 2nd Cpl.(A./Cpl.) R.	7174
Whitehill, Coy.S./M. G. E.	7180
Whitehouse, Sjt. J.	7174
Whitely, Sjt. T. R.	7178
Whitefield, Sjt. C. S.	7180
Whitham, S./M. J. S.	7174
Whiting, Cpl.(A./Sjt.) H. R.	7174
Whitney, Sjt. A. J.	7180
Whittaker, Cpl. (A./Sjt.) A.	7174
Whittlesey, S./Sjt. F. E.	7174
Whyley, Sjt. G. F.	6500
Whyte, Sjt. J. A. P.	7174

Whyte, Coy.S./M. R. A.	7178
Wibberly, Coy.S./M.(T./S./M.) J. J., *D.C.M.*	7174
Wicks, Pte.(A./Sjt.) G. J.	7174
Widdowson, L./C.(A./2nd Cpl.) W. B.	7174
Widger, Sjt.(T./S./S./M.) B.	7174
Widgery, Cpl. F. S.	7174
Wiencke, Cpl. H. J.	7174
Wigginton, C.S.M. F. G.	6492
— Coy.S./M. J.	7174
Wigham, Gnr. J. R.	7174
Wightman, Sjt. P. R.	7180
Wilce, L./Sjt. A. T.	7174
Wilcox, S./M. G.	7174
— Sjt. J. R.	6500
Wilde, Cpl.(A./Sjt.) H.	7174
Wilding, Cpl. W.	7174
Wilhelm, Cpl. T. C.	7178
Wilkes, Cpl. C.	7174
Wilkie, By.Q.M.Sjt. C.	7174
— A./Sjt. T.	7174
Wilkins, Coy.Q.M.Sjt. H.	7174
Wilkinson, Flt.Sjt. A.	6521
— Sjt. F.	7181
— Sjt.(A./C.S.M.) G. M.	6509
— S./Sjt. H. B.	7180
— Spr. J. R.	7174
Wilks, L./C. R.	7174
— Pte. S. L.	7174
Williams, Cpl. A.	7174
— Condr. A. E.	6492
— Sjt. A. E.	7181
— Sjt.(A./C.S.M.) A. J. (R.E.)	6509
— Sjt. A. J. (Shrop.L.I.)	6509
— L./C. B.	7174
— Sjt.(A./S.Q.M.Sjt.) D. L.	7174
— Sjt.(A./S./Sjt.) E. J.	7174
— Spr. F. J.	7174
— By.Q.M.S. F. M.	6509
— Sjt.(A./Q.M.Sjt.) G.	7174
— S./Sjt. G. A.	7174
— T./Supt.Clk. G. H.	6492
— S.Q.M.S. G. M.	7180

advanced into Palestine, but in March 1917 was transferred to the Western Front, and was in action at the Battles of Ypres (III), Passchendaele and the Somme (II), and in heavy fighting at La Bassée, Nieuport and Dunkirk. He was awarded the Meritorious Service Medal and mentioned in Despatches for conspicuously good work throughout hostilities, and also held the 1914/15 Star, the General Service and Victory Medals and the Territorial Force Efficiency Medal. He was demobilised on his return to England in March 1919. 4, Montague Street, Collyhurst, Manchester.

Williams, Pte.(A./Sjt.) H.	6500	Wilson, Spr. J. E. B.		7174
— S./Sjt.(A./S.Q.M.Sjt.) H. C.	7174	— Sjt. J. L.		7180
— Sjt. H. E.	7174	— Sjt. J. T.	*	7174
— Eng.Clk. Sjt. H. J.	6500	— Cpl.(T./Sub Condr.) J. W.		7174
— Gnr.(L./Bombr.) J.	7174	— S./M. M.		7178
— Dvr. J. A.	7174	— 2nd Cpl. P. J.		7174
— L./C. J. E.	7174	— Coy.Q.M.Sjt. R.		7174
— Sjt. J. L.	7178	— L./C. R. E.		7174
— Q.M.Sjt.(A./S./S./N.) R. C.	7174	— Q.M.Sjt. R. V.		7180
— L./C. R. L.	6500	— S./Sjt. S. P.		7174
— Sjt. S.	7174	— Coy.S./M. T.		7174
— Sjt. S. E.	7180	— R.Q.M.Sjt. T.		7174
— Spr. (A./L./C.) W. J.	7174	— Pte. T.		7180
Williamson, Sjt. G. C.	7174	— Sjt. T. B.		7174
— By.Q.M.Sjt. J.	7174	— Coy.Q.M.Sjt. W. H.		7174
— C.Q.M.Sjt. J. N.	7174	Winch, Coy.S./M. J. R.		7174
— Fitt. Sjt. R.	7180	Wind, Coy.S./M. E.		7174
— Gnr. T.	7174	Windeler, R.S./M. A.		7175
Willis, Sjt. D. G.	7174	Windsor, Sjt. L.		7175
— Sjt.(T./S./M.) J. H.	7174	Winstanley, T./Sub Condr.		
— Sjt. W.	7178	(A./Condr.) J. H.		7175
Willoughby, Sjt. R. T.	7180	Winstone, Sjt. P. C.		6509
— L./C. S. G.	7180	Winter, Flt.Sjt. F. W.		6521
Wills, Cpl.(A./L./Sjt.) N. T.	7174	— Sjt. Dmr. J.		7175
Willson, Sjt. H. B.	7181	— Sjt.(A./Coy.S./M.) T.		7175
Wilshaw, S./M. G. M.	7174	— R.Q.M.Sjt. W. A.		7175
Wilson, Sjt. A. (W. York. R.)	7174	Winzar, Coy.Q.M.Sjt.(A./		
— Sjt. A. (K.R.R.C.)	7174	Coy.S./M.) A. G.		7175
— Sjt.(A./S./M.) A.	7174	Wise, Pte.(A./Sjt.) A. J.		6501
— Coy.S./M. C.	7174	— Coy.S./M.(A./R.S.M.) E.		7175
— M.S./M. D.	7174	— Sjt. G.		7175
— Pte. D.	7174	— Coy.S./M. J. P.		7180
— Cpl. F. E.	4413	Wisken, Sjt. W. R.		7175
— Coy.Q.M.Sjt. F. H.	7180	Wistow, L./Sjt. W. R. J.		7175
— Spr. G.	7174	Witcher, Farr.S./Sjt. E. J.		6509
— Cpl. H.	7174	Withers, Sjt.(T./S.M.) G. H.		6521
— Pte. (A./Sjt.) H. M.	7174	— T./R.S./M. H. O.		7174
— Bombr. J. A.	7180	Witts, C.S.M. F.		6501

* Sergt. 6th King's Own Scottish Borderers. He volunteered in September 1914, and was first engaged as an Instructor of recruits until January, 1915, for which work he was awarded the Meritorious Service Medal. He then proceeded to France and played a prominent part in the Battles of Neuve Chapelle, Hill 60, Ypres (II), Festubert, Albert, the Somme (where he was wounded in action), Arras, Bullecourt, Messines, and Cambrai (where he was gassed in November 1917) and in the Relief and Advance of 1918. After the cessation of hostilities he served on the Rhine with the Army of Occupation until his demobilisation in March 1919. He was awarded the Military Medal for conspicuous bravery in carrying wounded to safety under heavy shell-fire during the Somme Offensive in July 1916, and also held the 1914/15 Star, the General Service and Victory Medals. 41 Derby Street, Ardwick, Manchester.

Wolfenden, Cpl.(A./Sjt.) A.	6510	Worthington, Pnr. F.	7175
Wood, S./Sjt. A. E.	7175	Wray, A./R./S./M. J. J.	7175
— Dvr. B. F.	7175	Wrey, Pte. H. F.	7175
— Pte. C.	7175	Wright, S./M. A. E.	7175
— Arm.S./M. C. A.	7178	— Cpl. C.	7175
— R.Q.M.S. C. W.	6510	— Sjt. F.	7175
— Cpl.(A./Sjt.) E.	7175	— L./C.(A./Sjt.) F. E.	7175
— Pte. E. F.	7175	— Sjt. G. T.	7175
— Pte.(A./Cpl.) F. ✽	5037	— By.S.M. H.	6510
— S./Sjt.(A./S./M.) F. H.	7175	— Sjt. H. A.	7175
— Sjt. G.	7175	— Flt. Sjt. J.	6521
— Dvr. G.	7180	— Sjt. J. R.	7175
— R.Q.M.Sjt. H. (Ches. R.)	7175	— 1st A.M.(A./Cpl.) L.	6521
— By.Q.M.Sjt. H. (R.G.A.)	7175	— Coy.S./M. S. J.	7175
— Sjt. M.	7175	— Cpl. U.	7178
— L./C. P.	7175	— Pnr. Sjt. W. H.	7175
— Fitt.S./Sjt. R. L.	6510	Wyatt, Cpl. C.	7175
— Pte. T. W.	7175	— Coy.S./M. G. W.	7175
— Sjt. W. H. (R.E.)	7175	Wyeth, L./Sjt. C. J.	7175
— Sjt.(A./Q.M.Sjt.) W. H., *M.M.*		Wylie, Sjt. W. T.	7178
(Leins. R.)	7175	Wynn, A./Sjt. F.	7178
Woodburn, Sjt. L.	7175	Wynne, S.S./M. W. H.	7175
Wooderson, Sjt. F.	7175		
Woodfield, C.Q.M.Sjt. J. W.	6501	Yapp, Spt.(A./L./C.) A.	7175
Woodhead, Pte.(A./S./Sjt.) H. C.	7181	Yardley, Coy.S./M. L. P.	7175
Woodhouse, Pte.(A./S./Sjt.) A.	7175	Yates, Sjt. D.	7175
— Sjt. H. A.	7175	— T./M.S.M. L. W.	7175
Woodley, Farr.S./Sjt. R.	7175	— Coy.Q.M.Sjt.(A./R.Q.M.Sjt.) R. H.	7175
— Sjt. W. V.	7175	— Sjt. T. H.	7175
Woodman, Sjt. R.	7175	Yeates, By.S./M. G.	7175
Woodrow, R./S./S./M. W. S.	7175	Yeats, Sjt. J.	7175
Woods, Pte.(L./C.) A. G.	7180	Yielding, F.W.S.Sjt. A.	7175
— Sjt. F. W.	7175	Youle, A./L./C. G. H.	7175
— Cpl. J.	7175	Young, Sjt. A.	7175
— Sjt. W.	7175	— R.Q.M.Sjt. A.	7175
Woodward, Sjt.(A./Q.M.Sjt.) A. E.	7175	— Sjt. A. R.	7175
— S./Sjt.(A./S./M.) F.	7175	— Coy.Q.M.Sjt. B. R.	7180
— Dvr. W. H.	7175	— Sjt. C. A.	7175
Woolcott, Pte. (A./L./C.) J. J.	7175	— Cpl. E. H.	7175
Woolfall, Sjt. R. B., *M.M.*	7175	— L./C. G.	7175
Woolford, Sjt.(A./Coy.S./M.) C.	7175	— A./Ldg.Sea. J.	7175
Woolridge, S./Sjt.(A./Q.M.Sjt.) F.	7175	— By.S./M. J. A.	7178
Worboys, Pte. F. A.	7180	— Farr. Sjt. J. W.	7175
— Sjt. W.	7175	— Sjt. R.	7175
Wordsworth, A./Sjt. T.	6510	— Sub Condr.(A./Condr.) S. L.	7175
Worfolk, Cpl. B.	6501	— Sjt. W. J.	7175
Worgan, Pte. J. R.	7180	Youngman, Sjt. R. (now R./S.M.)	
Workman, Sjt. G., *D.C.M.*	7175	A. H.	7180
Worley, Cpl. (T./S./S./M.) W. H.	7175	Youngs, Sjt. S. B.	7175
Worth, By.S./M. A.	7175		
— S./M. P.	7175	Zipfel, Sjt. A. W.	6501

Vol. III, 1918

Abbott, Sjt. P. de M. (corr.)	10780	Bonsey, Spr. F. H.	10144
Abdullah Abdullahi, Ajt.	10146	Booth, Pte. W. H.	10143
Adlam, C.S.M. L. W. (corr.)	10146	Bowen, Pte. A. J.	§ 10526
Africa, Pte.	10146	Brady, C.S.M. E.	10145
Agutter, Cpl. (A./Mech.S.M.) E.		Brant, Sjt. E.	10145
(corr.)	10146	Brassel, C.S.M. H.	10145
Ahmed Koor, C.S.M.	10146	Bray, Cpl. (A./Sjt.) F.	10144
Ainscow, Pte. E.	10144	— Gnr. F. C. (corr.)	10146
Airey, Sjt. J.	10143	Brink, Dvr.(A./Mech.S.M.) D.	10145
Alderton, Sjt. C. E. (deletion)	10147	Brookes, Sjt. W.	10143
Alexandrides, Cpl. A.	10145	Brown, Spr. F.	10144
Allport, Cpl. (L./Sjt.) N.	❀ 10779	— Farr.S./Sjt. G. E.	10144
Amonoo Aidoo, Q.M.Sjt. S.	10146	— Cpl.(A./Sjt.) T.	10144
Anderson, S./Sjt.(A./S.Q.M.Sjt.) A.		Brownlow, Pte.(A./L./C.) T.	10526
(Corr.)	10146	Burchill, A./Bombr.(A./Cpl.) T.	10145
— Dvr. (A./Sjt.) G.	10145	Burke, S./Sjt. T. J.	10145
— Q.M.Sjt. J.	10145	Burns, Pte. H.	10144
Armarty, Native Cpl. J. W. N.	10146	Buxton, A./Q.M.S. W.	9803
Armstrong, S.M. A. W.	10145		
Ashby, Head Condr. L. F.	10145	Calloway, Pte. W. D.	❀ 10779
Asher, R.Q.M.Sjt. C.	10143	Carmichael, Sjt. J. G.	10145
Aslatt, Sjt. H. F., *MM.* (Corr. of		Carr, Pte. L.	❀ 9256
name)	9257	— Sjt. W.	10143
Atkinson, Pte. (A./L./C.) C.	10525	Cartridge, Sjt. A. G.	10145
		Casterton, C.Q.M.Sjt. R. E.	10143
Baglee, P.O. (R.H.) J. W.	* 7745	Castle, S./Sjt.(T./S.S.M.)	
Bagley, Sjt.(A./R.S.M.) S. E.	† 10144	E. W., *D.C.M.*	10141
Baiden, S./Sjt.(A./S.M.) F. J. R.	‡ 10525	Caton, C.Q.M.Sjt. W.	10143
Barraclough, 2nd Cl.Armr. M. S.	9803	Chadwick, Sjt. A. L. (corr.)	8334
Batchelor, M.D.R. W. H.	10145	Charmbury, Sjt.(A./S.Q.M.Sjt.	
Beckett, C.S.M. R.	10143	C. E. G. A.	10144
Bell, S.M. L. C.	9803	Chatfield, T./R.S.M. W.	10143
Bennett, Pte. A.	§ 10525	Chepbachuka, Barsogat, L./Cpl.	
Bennie, Gnr.(Local Sjt.) A.	+ 10144	(A./Cpl.)	10146
Berry, Sjt. J.	9803	Chetland, By Q.M.Sjt. A. (corr.)	10780
Biddels, L./C. G.	§ 10525	Christy, Condr. A. (corr.)	10780
Bird, Spr. C. W.	◊ 10144	Clarke, C.S.M. J. W., *MM.*	10496

---

* R.A.F. M.S.M. to F/142 R.N.A.S.
† Loyal North Lancs. attach K.A.R., East Africa.
‡ Group Known: 1914/15 trio (M.I.D. oakleaf), L.S. & G.C. (Geo. V), and M.S.M. (R.A.M.C., Devotion to Duty).
§ See Appendix Z.
+ R.G.A. attached Kilwa Battn., E. Africa.
◊ R.E. attached E.A.P.C. E. Africa.

Clayton, Spr. F. J.	* ✿ 10779		Cuthbert, Pte. G. L. M.	10145
Cobb, Sjt. A. A.	10143		— R.Q.M.S. J.	10496
Cole, Sjt. H. A. (corr.)	10146			
Coles, R./Q.M.Sjt. J.	10143		Dagnall, Cpl. F.	‡ 10143
Colley, Sjt. C. H.	† 10526		Darwen, Cpl. I.	10526
Collingwood, Sjt. J. H. A.	10143		Daulman, L./C. H. H.	† 10526
Collins, Sjt.(A./R.Q.M.S.) W. F.	10143		Davies, Cpl.(A./C.S.M.) T.	10143
Commissiong, Sjt.(A./R.Q.M.Sjt.)			Davis, Sjt. G. W.	10144
T. B.	10144		— Pte.(A./Sjt.) W.	10143
Cordwell, Pte.(A./Sjt.) C. H.	10144		Dawkins, Cpl. R. S.	9803
Cotsford, Sjt. R. J.	10144		Dawson, Farr. Sjt. E.	10145
Coulson, Sjt. A. B.	9803		Dempers, Sjt.Instr. T. A.	9803
Cousins, Pte. J.	9803		Dennis, S./S./Cpl. J.	✿ 10779
Cox, Sjt. E. J.	† 10526		Devrill, C.S.M.	10779
Craney, Col.Sjt. J.	9803		Dickinson, O.R.Sjt. J. B.	9803
Crean, L./C. M.	10145		Dixon, Pte. J.	§ 10526
Cresswell, L./C.(T./Sub Condr.) T. E.	10144		Dobson, By S.M. T.	10144
Cresswell, C.S.M. A.	10144		Domoney, B.S.M. W. A. (corr.)	10780
Croft, Gnr. (A./Cpl.) W. P.	10144		Duffy, Sjt. J.	+ 10144

---

* 54th Light Railway Opg. Coy. R.E. (France). Group known: 1914/15 Star and British War Medal (both Notts. & Derbys.), Victory Medal (Sapper R.E.) and M.S.M., also next of kin plaque. K.I.A. 1918.

† See Appendix Z.

‡ Sergt., 2nd Manchester Regiment. He was mobilised in August, 1914, and immediately sent to the Western Front, where he took part in the Retreat from Mons, and was wounded and invalided home. He later returned to France, where he was again wounded and sent home. Afterwards, rejoining his unit, he fought at Hill 60, where he was wounded for the third time and sent home for treatment. On his recovery he returned to France and served in the Retreat and Advance of 1918, in which he was again wounded. He was demobilised in February 1920, and held the Meritorious Service Medal, awarded for devotion to duty, the 1914 Star, and the General Service and Victory Medals. 83A, West Union Street, Salford.

§ See also Appendix Z. Group known: M.M. (2201 Pte. Warwicks. Yeo.), 1914/15 Star (as previous), British War and Victory Medals (Lieutenant), M.S.M. (310104 Pte. Warwicks. Yeo.) and Serbian Medal for Bravery (Obilitch Medal), *L.G.* 15 February, 1917. Also M.I.D. in *L.G.* 1 December, 1916 (Gen. Murrey, C.-in-C. Egypt). On the day of the battle of Romani, August 4th 1916, the Gloucester Squadrons were holding two battalions of the enemy at Hod-Abu-Adi, advancing from Hod-el-Enna, and the Warwicks were ordered to support them. They came into action at Seifanlya, and attacked the Turks who were holding a ridge at Hod-el-Enna (Mount Royston) with three machine guns and a few rifle men. Although inflicting some loss, the advance was checked and at this point Lieut. Stafford and a few men were wounded, but machine guns were brought into action with success, supported by two Troops with rifle fire. At the same time two Troops of 'C' Squadron and one of 'B' galloped round on the right flank, and relieved the pressure on the south side, keeping the situation well in hand until the arrival of the Squadron Leader, Capt. Napier, and eventually the position was taken. Pte. Dixon was 'C' Sqn stretcher bearer and was recommended for his M.M. for attending wounded under heavy fire during the above action. M.S.M. for the 'Wayfarer' incident at sea April 1916.

+ R. Irish F. att. K.A. Rifles.

Dunkerley, Arm.S./Sjt. E.	10144	Grist, S./Sjt. P.		10144
		Grover, A./Cpl. F.		10143
Eales, S./Sjt. C. J.	10145			
Edwards, Armr.S.M. E. F.	9803	Hales, Mech.S./Sjt. W. (deletion)		10780
— Sjt. H.	9803	Hall, Cpl. S.		10143
Eggleston, Sjt. J.	10143	Hallam, Sjt. H.		10143
Elliott, Cpl. W. J.	10145	Hanna, Dvr. H.	✿	9256
Erskine, Armr.S./Sjt. G. A.	10144	Hanrahan, S./Sjt.(A./S.M.) J.		10526
		Hardy, 1st Cl.A.M. J. I.	✿	9256
Farndon, Pte. F.	* 10526	Hargreaves, Sjt. F. W.		10143
Fergusson, Sjt. J. A. (corr. of name)		Harman, Mech.S./Sjt. E. V.		10145
	9257,10146	Harrington, Pte. J. R.		9803
Ferjella, Abdulla, Sjt.	10146	Hart, L./C. J. N.		10496
Ford, Spr.(A./L./C.) W.	✿ 10779	Harburn, Co.S.M. J. B. (corr.)		10780
Forkin, C.S.M. W.	10143	— deletion		10780
Fourie, M.D.R. H. J.	10146	Haydon, Pte. C.		10143
Fox, Sjt. T.	10143	Herbert, R./Q.M.Sjt. H.		10143
Fraser, 2nd Gr. Clerk G. M.	10146	Higgins, S./Sjt. A. E.		10145
Freeman, Cpl. W.	10145	Hinds, Pte. A. H.	✿	9256
Fyfe, Sjt. K. B.	9803	Hinsley, Cpl. R. J.	‡	10144
Fynn, S./S.M. H. C. K.	10145	Hogan, S.M. J. F.		10526
		Holland, Sjt.(A./S.S.M.) F. H. (corr)		10780
Gabre, Michael Tigre, Sjt.		Holohan, C.S.M.(A./R.S.M.) T.	§ ✿	10779
(A./R.S.M.)	10146	Horne, Cpl. M. J.	◊	7745
Gardiner, C.Q.M.S. F. W. (corr.)	10780	Hough, Sjt. B., *M.M.*	*	10526
Garside, Pte.(A./Cpl.) P.	10143	Howard, Spr.(A./Cpl.) J.		10144
Gauld, Pte. (A./L./C.) A.	✿ 10779	— 1st A.M. W. H.	¶	7745
Geddes, Gnr. J. D.	† ✿ 10779	Howe, Spr. W.		10144
Giddens, Bombr.(A./Cpl.) J.	10144	Hunt, C.S.M.(A./S.S.M.) L. H.	✿	9256
Gore, Spr. H.	✿ 10779	Husband, Sjt. W. J. M.		9803
Gosden, Sjt. F. J.	10145	Hymer, Sjt. W. T.		10143
Goss, M.D.R. J. A.	10145			
Goulding, Spr.(L./C.) J., *D.C.M.*	✿ 10779	Iceton, Cpl. W. (corr.)		10146
Grant, C.Q.M.Sjt. G. H.	10145	Iddeson, Pnr. J. S.		10145
Greenbury, Cpl.(A./Sjt.) R. O. (corr.)	10780	Ingham, Sjt. J. W. (corr. of name)		
Greenhow, Pte. D. (corr.)	10780		9257, 10146	
Greenwood, C.S.M. C.	10145	Ireland, Spr. (A./Sjt.) A. B.		10144
Gregory, Sjt. H. E. (corr.)	10780	Ives, Sjt.(A./C.Q.M.S.) A. E. (corr.)		10780

---

* See Appendix Z.

† The only Gallantry M.S.M. to Tank Corps. Group in McInnes collection: British War and Victory Medals (109543) and M.S.M. (11 Bn. T.C. for France) a gallantry award *not* listed in *Tank Corps Book of Honours and Awards.*

‡ It is not known if this is the R.A.F. M.S.M. or the Army type, but the awards were announced by the War Office and probably relate to actions performed prior to the formation of the R.A.F. on 1 April, 1918. Hardy was 57 Sqn. R.A.F.

§ R.E. for East Africa, attached Kilwa Sig. Coy.

+ Pair known: L.S. & G.C. (Geo. V, 5097 C.Q.M.S., Leinsters) and M.S.M. (3/Leinsters attached West India Regt.) he came from Cork. The medal was earned in France.

◊ No. 9546 Aust. Flying Corps. See Spike *infra.*

¶ No. 92534 Aust. Flying Corps. See Spike *infra.*

Jackson, Sjt. O.	9803	Lawson, Cpl. J. W.	† 10145
Jarvis, Sjt. T. K.	10143	Le Roux, Sjt. P. L.	9803
Jeffery, S./Sjt.(T./Sub Condr.) W.	10144	Lea, S./Sjt. J.	10145
Jenkins, Sjt. W. J.	9803	— L./C. W. A.	10143
Johns, Sjt. J. W.	10145	Leaver, C.Q.M.S. B. W. (corr.)	10780
Johnson, S.M. G. A.	9803	Lees, Sjt. R.	10143
Johnstone, S.M. T. W.	10145	Lemon, Bombr. J. (corr.)	10146
Jonas, L./Sjt. S.	10143	Lester, Cpl. R. J. (corr.)	10146
Jones, S.M. H. E.	9803	Leuty, Q.M.Sjt.(F. of W.) M. H.	10145
— C.S.M. J., *MM.*	10143	Lewis, Sjt. G.	‡ ❀ 10143
— Farr.Q.M.S. J. W.	* 10526	— T./Sub Condr. R. W.	8334
— Sjt. W. G.	10144	Leyshon, Pte. W.	10526
Jordan, 2nd Cpl.(A./Sub Condr.)		Liles, Spr. N.	❀ 10779
E. W. G.	❀ 10779	Lillington, Sjt. H. W.	10145
Juma, R.S.M.	10779	Lindsey, Sjt.(A./C.S.M.) P. J. (corr.)	10146
		Lister, Sjt. E.	10143
Kalifa Dambeli, Interpreter	10146	— Pte.(A./Cpl.) J. T.	10144
Keadle, Sjt. W. H.	❀ 10143	Loader, Sjt. A. J. (corr.)	10146
Kenny, Condr. J. L.	10145	Loker, C.Q.M.S. F.	10144
Kentish, By S.M. (now 2nd Lt.) E. G.	9256	Lomas, C.Q.M.S. J. T.	10144
Kiernan, Gnr. O.	10146	Lovejoy, Cpl. J.	10145
— Deletion of second ann.	10147, 10780	Lowis, S.S.M. E. J. (corr. of name)	9257
Kilby, Sjt. G. E.	10143	Lowle, Sjt. J. P.	10145
King, Cpl. W. S.	10145		
Kirtland, C.S.M. C. T.	10144	Mabbett, Pte. S. B. (corr.)	10780
Kleynhans, Cpl. N. W.	10145	McCormack, Sjt. E. H.	§ 10526
Knox, S.M. J. H. J.	10145	McDougal, R.S.M. A. (corr.)	10146
Kriehn, Pte. A.	❀ 9256	McEvoy, Sjt. W.	9803
		McFadden, Cpl. J.	10145
Langford, Sjt. J.	10143	McGuckian, Sjt. J. (corr.)	10146

---

* See Appendix Z.
† Group in Moss collection: O.B.E. (2nd type, Military ribbon), 1914/15 Star trio (Gunner/Cpl. R.M.A., with M.I.D. oakleaf), Defence and War Medals, Royal Naval L.S. & G.C. (Geo. V, 1st type, St. Cl. R.M.), Army M.S.M. (Geo. V, Corp. R.M.A.). John Lawson enlisted into the R.M.A. in 1911. He went to sea firstly in H.M.S. *King George V* and H.M.S. *Hercules*, then transferred to H.M.S. *Queen Mary* in 1913, in which he saw service at the Battle of Heligoland Bight in 1914. He spent the remainder of the Great War ashore with the East Africa Expeditionary Force, being both mentioned in despatches and awarded the Army M.S.M. one of only two such awards to 'Royals' for East Africa during W.W.I; indeed in total only 15 Army M.S.M.s were awarded to R.M.A. He was awarded his L.S. & G.C. in 1926 as a Staff Clerk R.M. and eight years later was commissioned Lieutenant & Q.M. and three years later promoted to Captain. He was latterly Paymaster of the R.N. School of Music and then 'Q' Staff Officer at R.M.O., where he remained until his retirement in 1948, having been promoted to Lieutenant Colonel (Q.M.) in 1943 and awarded his O.B.E. in *L.G.* of 1 January 1948. He died on 25 August 1970.
‡ See also Rodrigues *infra*, both Railway Corps E.A. Forces.
§ Group known: Queen's Sudan Medal (11420 Pte., R.A.M.C.), 1914/15 Star trio (M.I.D. oakleaf, 35076 Sgt., R.A.M.C.), L.S. & G.C. (Edw. VII), M.S.M. (R.A.M.C., Devotion to Duty) and Khedive's Sudan Medal (Khartoum).

McGuiness, Sjt. T.	10144	O'Brien, Spr. C.	❀ 10779
McGuire, Cpl.(A./Sjt.) J.	10526	Odlum, C.Q.M.S. G. M.	10146
Mackay, Sjt. Instr. D. C.	9803	O'Neill, S./Sjt. C. E. E.	10145
Madi, R.S..	10779	Ord, S./Sjt.(A./S.Q.M.S.) H. (corr.)	10146
Malcolm, Pte. H.	10144	O'Shea, Flt.Sjt. E. J.	§ ❀ 10143
Malzer, Pte. J.	❀ 9256	Ottewill, Pte.(A./Mech.	
Martin, Sjt. F.	10496	S./Sjt.) A. H.	10145
Masters, Pte.(A./Cpl.) S.	10145	Owen, Gnr. A./B.S.M.) B. A. D.	10145
Mattock, Sjt.(A./S.M.) F. H.	10145	— Pte.(A./Sjt.) H. (corr.)	10146
Mayers, Sjt. A. H.	9803		
Maylia, L./C. J.	❀ 10143	Palmer, Pte. G. A.	10144
Meade, Sjt. J. M. (corr.)	10780	Parkin, Fitt. A. (corr.)	10146
Meintjes, Pte.(A./Q.M.S.) E. A.	10145	Parkins, Cpl. (A./Sjt.) A. E.	10145
Meredith, Sjt. J.(second entry of		Parsons, C.Q.M.Sjt. S.	10144
award cancelled)	10147	Paterson, Cpl.(A./Sjt.) W.	10145
Merry, L./C.(A./Cpl.) T.	❀ 8334	Paton, Col.Sjt. L.	9803
Miles, C.S.M. J.	10144	Patrick, Spr.(A./CPl.) W.	10145
Mill, Pte. A.	* ❀ 9256	Paulo, Native Pnr.	10146
Mohamed Ibahim, Pte.	10146	Peach, Pte. W.	10144
Moore, A./Bombr. H. H.	10145	Pears, 2nd Cpl.(A./Sjt.) T. H.	10145
— S./Sjt.(A./S.Q.M.S.)		Pearson, Sjt. J. E.	‡ 10526
W. H., *M.M.* (corr.)	10780	Pemberton, Q.M.S. J.	10144
Morris, C.S.M.(A./R.Q.M.S.) G. H.	10144	Pepper, Sjt. T. L. M. (corr.)	10146
— S./Sjt. R. N.	10145	Pesa, Native Pnr.	10146
Morrison, Pte. G. A.	† ❀ 9256	Phillips, Sjt. J.	10145
Motingwoi, Arap Bongoi, L./Cpl.	10146	Phipps, Sjt. H. G.	10145
Murphy, L./C.(A./Clr.Sjt.) E. (corr.)	9257	Pickering, Cpl. G.	10145
Murtrie, Sub Condr. M.	10145	— Cpl.(A./Sjt.) T. P. (corr.)	10146
Muskett, S./Sjt. J. H.	9803	Pickman, S./Sjt. A. J.	10144
Mycock, C.Q.M.S. J. W.	10144	Pollard, By.S.M. A.	10496
		Poole, Cpl.(A./S.Q.M.S) J. L. (corr.)	10146
Nesbit, C.S.M. A. (corr.)	10146	— C.S.M. R. R.	10145
Newman, S./Smith Cpl. J.‡	10526	Pope, Sjt. J.	10144
Nichols, Cpl.(A./C.S.M.)		Powditch, C.S.M. C.	10144
W. G. (corr.)	10146	Pratt, 2nd Cpl.(A./Cpl.) H. B.	10145
Nicholson, Pte.(A./Cpl.) A. T.	10145	Prince, Sjt.(T./Sub Condr.) P. A.	10145
Noble, R.Q.M.S. W.	10144	Pritchard, Sjt. E.	+ 9803
Nolan, S.M. P.	9803	Purchase, Q.M.S. C. G.	9803
Norman, S./Sjt. F. W.	9803	Pyne, Pte.(A./Cpl.) A. V. (corr.)	10146
North, Pte. (A./Sjt.) D.	10144		
Nyundu Bin Kassaga, Sjt.	10145	Radford, Sjt. F. S.	10144

---

* It is not known if this is the R.A.F. M.S.M. or the Army type, but the awards were announced by the War Office and probably relate to actions performed prior to the formation of the R.A.F. on 1 April 1918. Mill was R.A.M.C. att. 57 Sqn. R.A.F.

† 1st Anzac Bn. Imp. Camel Corps, for Egypt.

‡ See Appendix Z.

§ It is not known if this is the R.A.F. M.S.M. or the Army type, but the awards were announced by the War Office and probably relate to actions performed prior to the formation of the R.A.F. O'Shea was 2 Aeroplane Supply Depot R.A.F.

+ M.S.M. known: For German South West Africa 1914/15 (Railway Regt.).

Rattray, R.S.M. A.	10146	Smith, Q.M.S. D. F.	9803
Read, Cpl. T.	10144	— Linesman F.	9803
Reily, Sjt. R. R.	10145	— C.Q.M.S. F.	10496
Rheeders, Pte. J. A.	9803	— Pte.(T./Cpl.) G.	† ✱ 9256
Richardson, Sjt. A. E.	10145	— S./Sjt. Maj. S. J.	10146
— Pte. D. B. (corr. of name)	9257	— Whr. S./Sjt. W. T. (corr.)	10780
— Sjt. L.	10145	Spencer, Pte. J. J. H.	‡ 10526
— Pte. T.	10144	Spick, Sjt. W.	10144
— S.M. W.	9803	Spike, 1st A.M. E. L.	§ 7745
— Cpl. W.	10145	Stanway, C.Q.M.Sjt. H.	10144
Roberts, Sub Condr. H. V. H.	10145	Staples, Pte. G.	10144
Robertson, C.Q.M.S. R. (corr.)	10780	Stenmark, Sjt. O.	10146
Robinson, Cpl.(A./Sjt.) G.	10145	Stephens, S./Sjt. H.	10145
— Sjt. G. H. (corr.)	10780	Stirton, C.S.M. (deletion)	+ 10147
Robson, Spr.(A./Cpl.) A.	✱ 10779	Stokes, S.M. H. S.	9803
Rodrigues, T./Sjt. A. C.	* ✱ 8334	Stow, Sqdn S.M. G. H. (corr.)	10146
Roscoe, Pte.(A,.cpl.) J.	10144	Strivens, Sjt. A. T. (deletion)	10147
Ross, Sjt. T.	10145	Stubbs, Sjt. H.	10146
Rowan, Sjt. J.	10144	Sturges, Cpl.(A./S./Sjt.) J. (corr. of	
Rowley, Cpl.(A./Sjt.) S. G.	10144	name)	9257
Rowling, Cpl.(A./Sjt.) T. (corr.)	10146	Sulley, Sjt. E.	10496
Royle, Sjt. (A.S.S.M.) W. J.	10145	Sullivan, Sjt. P.	10496
Rummings, Sjt. T.(corr.)	10146	Sunderland, L./C. T. C.	10144
Rutter, Pnr. F.	10146	Sutherland, Sjt. J.	10145
Ryan, C.S.M.(A./R.S.M.) C. E. (corr.)	10146	Swain, Sjt. A. E.	7745
		Swanepoel, C.S.M. D. A.	10146
Sabe, Bukeit, R.S.M.	10146		
Sancto, L./C. H. E.	✱ 9256	Tait, Cpl. J.	10144
Sanderson, Sjt. J.	10145	Tawera, C.S.M.	10779
Scott, Pte.(A./L./C.) J. W.	✱ 10779	Thirkell, Tpr. H. S.	✱ 8334
Seabrooke, Bombr. J.	✱ 10779	Thomas, C.S.M. J. G. (corr.)	10146
Seale, Pte. H. S.	10145	Thorpe, Cpl. A.	10144
Shaffi Ahmed, Native Offr.	10146	Tillet, C.S.M. H.	10146
Sheard, Cpl. A. E. (corr.)	9257, 10146	Tisdall, Dvr. W. G. (corr.)	10146
Sheridan, S.M. H. P.	9803	Tolson, A./R.S.M. F.	10145
Sibu, C.S.M.	10779	Trenfield, Cpl. E. G.	‡ 10526
Skea, Cpl. L. A. P.	10145	Trezona, Sjt. W. F.	10145
Slinger, Cpl. J. W.	10144	Tumbo, Native Pnr.	10146
Smallwood, 2nd Cpl. J.	10145	Turner, Sjt. F.	10144
Smethurst, Cpl. F.	10144		

---

* See also Lewis *ante*. These two awards were also gazetted on page 7599 of 27 June 1918 but no entry for these is found in *L.G.* Index, nor has a cancellation been found for either. They were both Railway Corps, East African Forces.

† Austr. Provost Corps att'd. H.Q. Anzac Mounted Div., for Egypt.

‡ See Appendix Z.

§ No. 812 Australian Flying Corps. See Horne and Howard *ante*. R.A.F. M.S.M.s for meritorious service and devotion to duty on the occasion of an outbreak of fire at a Government Establishment at Stanford, Lincolnshire.

+ M.S.M. awarded 17 June, 1918, 200226 C.S.M. 2/Tank Corps. D.C.M. substituted 21 October 1918.

Underwood, Sjt. H.	10144	Wilkens, S.M. J.	9803
		Wilkes, L./C. J. A.	* 10526
Van Rensburg, Pte. J.	10145	Wilkey, R.Q.M.Sjt. G. C.	10144
Veino, Pte. L.	10526	Wilkinson, Sjt. J. H.	10144
Viant, S./Sjt. (T./Sub Condr.) A.	10145	— Cpl. J. S.	10144
Vickers, Cpl.(A./Sjt.) J.	10144	Williams, Sjt. T.	10145
Vincent, Cpl.(A./S.Q.M.Sjt.)	10145	Wilson, C.S.M. D.	10145
		— Pte.(A./Sjt.) H. M. (corr.)	10780
Walker, S./Sjt. S.	9803	— Spr. J.	10145
Ward, R.Q.M.Sjt. R. F.	10144	— C.S.M. J. H.	10144
Warder, Amt.S./Sjt.(T./Amt.S.M.)		Withiel, Mech.S./Sjt. S.	† 10145
J. W.	10145	Woest, Sjt. P. J.	9803
Warner, Pte. T.	* 10526	Woodward, Pte. A.	* 10526
Watt, Mech.Elect.(Q.M.Sjt.) A.	10145	Wrench, Sjt. J. C.	9803
Watts, Sjt. M. H.	10145		
Way, Pte. T. J.	10145	Young, Pte. H. M.	* 10526
Webster, Cpl. J.	10144		
Wellington, A./S.S.M. J. T. (corr.)	10146	Zeiler, Sjt.Instr. F. F.	9803
Whitbread, Gnr.(A./Sjt.) B. P.	10145		
White, 2nd Cl.Asst.Surg. E. D.	10145	*Meritorious Service Medal—Bar:*	
— C.SM. F.	10144		
Whitehead, Pte. P. N.	9803	Elliott, R.Q.M. Sjt. J.	‡ 10143

---

  * See Appendix Z.

  † Group known: Cape of Good Hope General Service Medal (Transkei), British War and Victory Medals (S.S.M. S.A.S.C.), War Medal, M.S.M. (M.T. S.A.S.C., for E. Africa).

  ‡ Group in McInnes collection. This is one of only seven bars to M.S.M.s. The other six are for gallantry, this is the only one for valuable service. His award for gallantry was gazetted on Page 7599 of *L.G.* 27 June, 1918 although this reference is absent from the *L.G.* Indexes (see also Rodrigues and Lewis, *ante*). Details from Regimental History of Northumberland Hussars Yeomanry: 'On the morning of 19th March 1918 at La Neuville-en-Beine, a limbered G.S. waggon with two horses broke away from the driver and went full gallop through the crowded streets of the village. This W.O. though nearly 60 years of age, seeing that a terrible accident was about to happen, flung himself at the rein of the near leader as the limber dashed by, and, by good fortune, caught it. He held on, allowing himself to be dragged, thereby bringing his full weight onto the bit, with the result that the horses were brought up. That anyone should attempt to stop a runaway pair of horses in this manner (and succeed) shows remarkable bravery and resource. This gallant act diverted a very serious accident at the risk of great personal injury to the above W.O.' W.O. Elliott served the whole time the regiment was in France (6.10.14—June 1919)—a record which does this fine old soldier infinite credit. His group consists of: 1914 Star & Bar (23, R.Q.M.S. Northld Hrs.), British War and Victory Medals (M.I.D.) (23, W.O.II Northld Hrs.), M.S.M. & Bar (H/270001 R.Q.M. Sjt. 1/1st North'd Hrs. Yeo.) and Territorial Force Efficiency Medal (Edw. VII—erased). He hailed from Rothbury and was a well known soldier at all the Camps of the N.H. Yeo. in the 1890's and 1900's.

Vol. IV, 1918

Allan, Spr. W.	12103	Cooper, Pte.(A./Sjt.) W.	12103
Allen, 1st Cl. Writer E. F. (corr.)	11842	Corcoran, L./C. J.	12103
— Spr. G.	❀ 11841	Crabtree, Q.M.Sjt. J. H. (corr.)	11842
Ambler, Pte. G.	12103	Craig, Cpl. J. P.	12103
Andrews, S.M. F. G.	14906	Crean, C.Q.M.Sjt. J. P.	12104
Appleton, Cpl.(A./S./Sjt.) G. A.	12103		
Axtens, Pte. C. R.	12103	Davenport, Pte. S.	12104
		Davey, R.Q.M.Sjt. E. R.	12104
Bagley, C.S.M. H. T., *D.C.M.*	12103	Davis, Sjt. J.	12104
Ball, C.S.M. H.	12105	— L./Sjt. J. F. (corr. of name)	11842
Barker, Sjt. F. C.	12105	Day, Sjt. A. F.	12104
Barnard, Sjt. H. J.	12103	de Monte, 4th Cl. Asst. Surg. A. N.	12105
Bath, L./C.(A./Cpl.) H. A.	12103	Dixie, Sub Condr. W. J.	12105
Bennett, Smith/Sjt. A.	❀ 12423	Drummond, Pte.(A./L./C.) W.	12104
— Cpl. (local Sjt.) J. R., *M.M.*	12103	Duggan, Pte. M. (corr.)	14671
Bentley, Spr. A.	12103	Dunkerley, By Q.M.Sjt. J. H.	12104
Berry, Sjt. C.	12105		
— 2nd Cl.A.M. F. R. (deletion)	14671	Edwards, Pte.(A./S.M.) J. (corr.)	11842
Betteridge, 1st A.M. L.	* ❀ 14328	Evans, Sjt. E.	❀ 12423
Bishop, C.Q.M.Sjt. C. U.	12103	Evans, Pte. W. E. (deletion and	
Blake, L./C. J., *M.M.*	12103	Bar to M.M. substituted)	14671
Bourne, Pte.(T./Sjt.) W. C.	12103		
Bruce, Sub Condr. H.	12103	Favers, Q.M.Sjt.(A./S.S.M.) T.	12104
Bull, Pte. F. (corr.)	12842	Ferris, Sjt. C. E.	12104
Burkimsher, R.S.M. W.	14906	Fischbacher, Pte. C.	12104
Bushby, Pte. W. N.	12103	Flannery, Pte. J. M.	12104
Butterfield, S.M. T. W.	14906	Flynn, By S.M. T. F. J. (corr.)	14671
		Foster, L./C.(local Sjt.) J. A.	12104
Candy, Cpl. R. H. F.	12103		
Cann, Sjt. R. J.	12103	Gaffney, Pte. M. (deletion)	14671
Carpenter, Sjt. B. C.	❀ 12423	Gale, Pte. G.	12104
Carrol, Pte. J.	12103	Garner, Spr. W. T.	❀ 11841
Carter, Gnr.(A./S.M.) J.	12103	Gell, Pte. S. W.	12104
Channell, L./C.(A./Sjt.) S.	12103	Graham, Col.Sjt.(A./W.O) F. O.	
Charlton, S./Sjt. E. H.	14906	(corr.)	11842
Clifford, actg. Cpl. G.	14329	Green, Sqdn.Q.M.Sjt. F. W.	12104
Cocker, Sjt. F. (corr.)	11842	— L./C. W.	12104
Connor, C.S.M. J.	12103	Greenwood, Sjt. W.	12104

---

* Gallantry; R.A.F. M.S.M. 'On 26/27 July, 1918, a fire broke out in this airman's petrol lorry, in France. He drove 200 yds. away from a farm, averting a dangerous fire and a possible loss of life to both troops and civilians.'

Grimes, L./C. G. C. — * 12104
Grundy, S./Sjt. H. L. E. — 12105
Guise, Pte.(local Sjt.) T. C. — 12104

Hall, Sjt. A. (corr.) — 11842
— Pte.(A./Sjt.) F. W. — 12104
— C.S.M. G. A. — ✿ 11841
Harding, Pte. A. W. — 12104
Harper, C.Q.M.Sjt. A. (corr.) — 11842
— S./Sjt. C. — 12105
Harris, Pte. (A./Cpl.) A. E. — 12104
Harvey, Sjt. D. S. — 12104
Haswell, Hd. Comdr. J. C. — 14906
Hathaway, Pte. G. — ✿ 12423
Hawkins, S.M. R. — 10146
Hiley, S./Sjt. J. — 12105
Hodder, Pte. C. F. — 12104
Holmes, Sub Condr. G. H. — † 12105
Hopwood, Pte. F. — 12104
Howe, Pte.(A./Cpl.) A. E. (corr.) — 11842
Hughes, Sjt.(A./S./Sjt.) A. E. — 12104
Hunt, Pte. S. (corr.) — 12424
— S.M. W. H. G. — 12104
Hunter, Pte. (A./Cpl.) J. G. — 12104

Jemison, Pte. R. — ✿ 11841
Johnson, Pte. (A./Sjt.) A. — 12104
— Pte.(A./L./Sjt.) O. — 12104
Jones, L./C. A. — 12104
— Pte. D. — 12104
— Sub Condr. H. — 12105
— Sjt.(A./S./Sjt.) J. H. — 12104

Keating, R.Q.M.Sjt. J. — 12104

Latter, S./Sjt. H. — 12104
Legge, Pte. T. H. — 12104
Lindsay, S./Sjt.(A./Condr.) R. W. — 12105
Love, S./Sjt. R. — 12105
Lyness, C.S.M. A. — 12104

McCrae, L./C. A. — 12104
MacDonald, Pte.(A./C.Q.M.Sjt.) G. A. — 12104
Mace, Farr.Q.M.Sjt. C. — 12104
Macfarlane, S.M. D. K. — 14906
MacGregor, Pte. J. — ✿ 11841
McRae, Cpl. A. — 12104
Martin, A.B. (H.G.) G. M. (corr.) — 11842
— C.S.M. W. T. — 12104
Mash, A./R.S.M. W. J. — ‡ ✿ 11841
Melhuish, Pte.(A./Sjt.) H. C. — 12104
Mennie, Pte.(A./Sjt.) S. R. — 12105
Miles, Pte.(A./Cpl.) W. J. — 12104
Milner, Pte. E. — ✿ 11841
Mitchell, Pte. J. — 12104
Moncrieff, Pte. R. — ✿ 11841
Moorman, S./Sjt.(Sub Condr. P.T.) W. B. — 12105
Morfitt, Cpl. H. (corr.) — 13402
Moroney, Sjt. T. — 12104
Morris, S.M.Instr. R. G. — 14906
Moul, 4th Cl.Asst.Surg. S. W. A. — 12105
Mullins, R.S.M. M. F. — 14906
Munckton, S./Sjt.(A./S.S.M.) A. — 12104

Noble, Gnr. H. — ✿ 11841

Ogden, R.Q.M.Sjt. T. (corr.) — 14671
Ongley, Cpl.(A./Col.Sjt.) A. — 12104
O'Regan, Sjt. D. — 12104

Pearse, L./C.(2nd Cpl.) W. — 12105
Perry, C.Q.M.Sjt. E. R. — 12104
— Sjt. W. H. — 12104
Pickard, R.S.M. W. — 12104
Pizzey, Local Cpl. A. F. — 12104
Plummer, By S.M. A. J. — 12104
Pollen, Gnr. A. — 12104
Poole, S./Sjt.(Sub Condr.) E. E. T. — 12105
Price, Sjt.(A./S./Sjt.) H. G. — 12104
Probyn, R.Q.M.Sjt. P. D. — 12104

---

* Group known: M.B.E. (Mil., 1st type), British War Medal, Victory Medal and Territorial Forces War Medal, M.S.M. and Territorial Efficiency Medal (Geo. V, with bar). R.Q.M.Sgt. 4th (Terr.) Bn. The Devonshire Regt.

† M.S.M. known: Military Works Service, I.A. George Henry Holmes, born 1879. Twice M.I.D. in W.W.I (12 March 1918 and 21 February 1919), Major (Commissariat) 1933. Retired 1934.

‡ Group known: D.C.M. (A./R.S.M. 16 R.B.), 1914 Star & bar (Cpl. 3/R.B.), British War and Victory Medals (W.O.1, M.I.D. Oakleaf), M.S.M. (16 R.B., for Gallantry), D.C.M. *L.G.* 21 October 1918 (disregard of personal suffering under heavy shelling).

Puga, Farr.Sjt. J.	12104	Taylor, Pte. J.	§ ❀ 11841
Redman, Sjt.(A./C.S.M.) W. J.	12104	Wadham, L./C.(A./Sjt.) S. C.	12104
Reeder, Pte.(2nd Cl.) C. A.	* ❀ 14328	Wakelen, Armr.S./Sjt. A. G.	12104
Rees-Jones, T./Sjt. H.	12105	Ward, Sjt.(A./R.S.M.) S. N. B.	12104
Rhodes, Sjt. E. J.	12105	Waters, Sjt. G. T.	12104
Robertson, Cpl. J. M.	12104	Watts, Sjt.(A./C.Q.M.Sjt.) T.	12104
Robinson, C.S.M.(A./S.M.) A.	12104	Weight, Sjt.(A./Q.M.Sjt.) F. G.	
Rogers, S./Sjt. C. F.	† 12105	(corr.)	11842
Rudd, Pte. J.	12104	Westbrook, S.M. E. C.	14906
Rushforth, Sjt. I. (corr. of name)	11842	Wheele, Pte. W. H.	12104
		Wilkinson, Sjt. J.	12105
Sabine, Pte. H. E.	12104	Williams, Sjt. A.	❀ 11841
Saunders, Sjt. A.	12104	— Gnr. J. (corr.)	14671
Scant, Pte. J. E.	12104	Williamson, Sjt. F. J.	❀ 12423
Seaman, Pte. 1st Cl. S. A.	‡ ❀ 14328	Wilson, Sjt. A. E.	12104
Smith, Gnr. F. H. D.	12104	— Cpl. W.	❀ 11841
— S./Smith P.	12104	Winchester, Sjt. L.	12104
— S./Sjt. W.	12104	Wood, R.S.M. H.	14906
Stewart, Pte. C. (deletion)	14671	Woodrow, Pte. A. H.	12104
Stiff, Sjt. P. F.	12105	Woodward, L./C. H. T.	❀ 11841
Stoneman, L./Sjt. W.	12104	Wynne, S.S.M. W. H. (corr.)	13402
Talbot, Sjt. W. E.	12104		
Tarr, R.Q.M.Sjt. S.	12104	Young, 2nd Cpl. A.	12104

---

* R.A.F. M.S.M. award for gallantry and devotion to duty in action. See R.A.F. Communiqué No. 3, 21st/27th October, 1918.

† Group in Moss collection: 1914 Star trio (Staff Sgt. S. & T. Corps), India General Service Medal 1908 (Waziristan 1919–21, Mahsud 1919-20, Afghanistan N.W.F. 1919, Staff Sgt. 64th Mule Corps), India General Service Medal 1936 (N.W.F. 1936–37, Major R.I.A.S.C.), Jubilee 1935, Coronation 1937, L.S. & G.C. (Geo. V, Sub-Conductor I.A.S.C.), M.S.M. (Geo. V, Staff Sgt. Supply and Transport Corps, [for Mesopotamia]).

‡ R.A.F. M.S.M. award for gallantry and devotion to duty in action. See R.A.F. Communiqué No. 3, 21st/27th October, 1918.

§ For Gallantry in Gibraltar. 1st Garr. Bn. Cheshire Regt.

Vol. I, 1919

Abbott, Sjt. G. W.	1487	Adams, Spr.(A./Sjt.) W. S.	982
— Sjt.(A./R.S.M.) H. C., *D.C.M.*	972	— Q.M.Sjt.(T./Mily. F. of W.)	
— S.M. H. C.	* 2701	W. T.	977
— Ch.Mech. J. B.	99	Adamson, S.M. J.	2696
— Sjt. J. T.	992	— Air Mech. 1st Cl. J. W.	99
— Mech.S./Sjt. O. T.	1004	Addlesee, Coy.S.M. J. R.	987
— S./Sjt. P. de M. (corr.)	2146	Agar, Pte.(L./C.) G.	1015
Abdul Gadr Bilal, L./C.	✿ 1256	Aiano, Air Mech. 1st Cl. C. J.	99
Abdul Ranman Mohammed El		— Sjt. R.	2696
Amrusi, Bashshawish	† 62	Ainley, 2nd Cpl. F. W.	1020
Abernethy, Ftr.S./Sjt. S.	975	Ainslie, Pte.(A./S./Sjt.) R.	1010
Accleton, Pte.(A./Sub Condr.) H.	1014	Ainsworth, Cpl.(A./Sjt.) F. G.	980
Acheson, Q.M.S. A.	2697	Airey, Coy.Q.M.Sjt. W.	991
Ackroyd, Bombr. H.	974	Aitchison, Pte.(A./L./C.) G.	988
Acton, Mech.S./Sjt. W. H.	1004	Aitken, Cpl. A.	1023
Adam, T./R.S.M. J.	970	— Sjt.(T./S./Sjt.) G. K. R.	1020
Adams, Sjt. A.	988	— Gnr. H.	68
— Sjt. C.	972	— S./S.M. J.	2698
— Sjt.Clk. D. C.	99	— Sjt. J.	984
— Ch.Mech. E. A.	99	— Coy.Q.M.Sjt. T.	975
— Dvr.(A./Cpl.) E. C.	982	Ajusa, Sjt.	1946
— Cpl. E. D.	973	Akast, C.S.M. A. C. S.	2692
— Sjt. F.	977	Aker, Sjt. J.	988
— Sjt.Maj. F. A.	99	Albiston, S./Sjt. C.	1023
— Q.M.S.(O.R.S.) F. I.	989	Alcock, Coy.S.M. H.	995
— B.S.M. F. J.	970	Aldcroft, Arm.Sjt. W.	1016
— Sjt. F. S.	2701	Alderson, Sjt. S.	1006
— Sjt. G.	2689	Alderton, Spr. C.	982
— Bdr.(A./Sjt.)(A.C.) G. W.	977	Aldous, S.M. C.	§ 2694
— A./Mas.Clk. H. C.	‡ 99	Aldred, Coy.Q.M.Sjt. G.	997
— Fitt.Sjt. H. W. C.	2997	Alexander, Sjt. G. M.	984
— C.S.M. J.	2696	— Sjt.(A./C.Q.M.S.) H. T.	978
— Eng.Clk.(S./Sjt.) J. W.	1488	— Q.M.S. J.	+ 2697
— Spr. W.	982	— Sjt. J.	990

* Group known: Queen's South Africa Medal (Tugela Heights, Orange Free State, Relief of Ladysmith, Transvaal, South Africa 1901, Cpl. Devon Regt.), L.S. & G.C. (Geo. V) and M.S.M. (Mil. Prov. Staff Corps).

† Coy. S M 1st Bn. Egyptian Army.

‡ Group known: British War and Victory Medals (M.I.D. oakleaf), India General Service Medal (Waziristan 1919–21), R.A.F. M.S.M. and R.A.F. L.S. & G.C. Later Wing Commander during W.W.II. Enlisted early in 1915, No. 3337.

§ Awarded M.S.M. Annuity A.O.144/1950 (Norfolk Regt.).

+ Awarded M.S.M. *and* Annuity A.O. 231/1925 as C.S.M. R.G.A. Immediate M.S.M. as Q.M.S. Labour Corps. Group known containing both M.S.M.s.

Alexander, Pte. O. E. R.		68	Amos, S.M. C., *D.C.M.*	‡	2695
— Coy.S.M. T.		998	Ampleford, Sjt. C.		972
Allaker, Pte.(A./Sjt.) S. A.	*	1015	Amy, Pte.(A./C.Q.M.S.) F.		1010
Allam, Sjt. J. A., *M.M.*	†	978	Anderson, Pte. F. S.		1001
Allan, Pte. D. N.		969	— By.S.M. H.		975
— S./Sjt. H.		1016	— Sjt. J. H.		62
— Sjt.(A./Coy.Q.M.Sjt.) W.		996	— Q.M.S. R.		1945
— Pte. W.		70	— 2nd Cpl. R. W.		1016
Allanson, By.S.M. J. D.		975	— C.Q.M.S. W.		1489
Allar, S./S.M. H.		1003	— Sjt. W.		1002
Allaway, Pte.(Q.M.Sjt.) W. J.		994	— Pte.(A./Sjt.) W.		2700
Alldridge, Sjt. S. H.		972	Andow, Sjt. J. R.		1005
Allemand, Ch.Mas.Mech. E. A.		99	Andrews, Sjt.(A./C.S.M.) A. F.		978
Allen, C.Q.M.Sjt. A.		69	— Mech.S./Sjt. A. H.		2692
— Cpl. C. H.		1020	— Sjt. C. J.		978
— P.O. Teleg. D.		2360	— Pte.(A./Cpl.) E.		1010
— Sjt. G. N.		997	— S./S.M. E. O.		1020
— Cpl. J.		980	— P.O. Teleg. F. J.		2360
— Spr.(A./Sjt.) J. A.		2998	— Sjt. H.		972
— T./Sub Condr. R. S.		1013	— Actg. C.P.O. J. E.		3591
— Pte. (L./C.) W.		990	— By.S.M. R. A. R.		970
— C.S.M.(A./R.S.M.) W. J.		2691	— Sjt. W.		975
Allender, Q.M.S. L. E.		1020	— Cpl. W.		976
Allford, C.S.M.(A./S.M.) J.		2693	Angel, C.Q.M.Sjt. W. V. S.		1004
Allgood, Gnr. A.		969	Annett, Pte. E. E.		2998
Allison, S.Q.M.Sjt. F.		1004	Annette, Cpl.Clk. W. J.		99
Allman, Q.M.S. J. G.		2694	Annetts, Sig. S. F.		2361
Allom, Pte.(A./S./Sjt.) S.		1490	Ansell, Q.M.Sjt. F. C.		989
Allsopp, Sjt. C.		990	— Q.M.S. J.		1489
Almond, Gnr.(A./Sjt.) E.		977	— Sjt. J. G.		975
Alp, C.Q.M.Sjt. C. A.		987	Anslow, C.S.M. P.		995
Alsop, Cpl.(A./Sjt.) J. H.		1012	Applesby, E.R.A.1st.Cl. T.		2360
— Sjt. W.		991	— Sjt. W. J.		984
Altman, Sjt.(A./C.Q.M.S.) W. E.		992	Appleton, S.M. B.	§	2691
Ambridge, Pte.(L./C.) S. R.		993	— Sjt. Mech. W. S.		99
Amery, Bombr. A.		974	Apps, Sjt. C. G. B.		991
Ambrose, Pte.(A./Sjt.) R. M.		1015	Arblaster, Sjt. E.		3000

---

   * Group was in McInnes collection: China 1900 (no clasp, 308 Dvr. 5/Section, Vickers Maxims), 1914 Star and bar (618 L./Cpl. M.M.P.), British War and Victory Medals (M.I.D. oakleaf, Pte. A./Sgt. M.M.P.) and M.S.M. (618 M.M.P.). His China Medal was issued on 19 June 1902, rolls signed in Athlone and Shanhaikwan. 131 China medals were issued to 'Vickers Maxims.' In 1914 the strength of the Military Mounted Police was 514 all ranks, increased by 253 by mobilisation. Apart from a small staff retained in U.K., all earned the 1914 Star with the B.E.F. M.I.D. 4 January, 1917 (Gen. Haig, services at G.H.Q.).

   † M.M. and M.S.M., both R.E., known.

   ‡ Group known (M.S.M. missing): D.C.M. (Edw. VII, R. Sussex R.), India General Service Medal (Hazara 1888), Queen's South Africa Medal (five clasps), L.S. & G.C. (Edw. VII).

   § R.G.A. in Gibraltar.

Arbon, Sjt. R. 997
Archibald, Cpl. A. 3841
— Pte. G. F. 1001
Arlette, Sjt.Mech. T. B. 99
Armes, Cpl. A. 987
Armitage, Sjt. J. W. 2695
— 2nd Cpl.(A./Cpl.) R. 1488
— Q.M.Sjt. S. 1488
Armour, T./S.M. R., *M.C.* 986
Armstrong, T./S.M. A. 2693
— Sjt.(A./C.Q.M.S.) J. 989
— Cpl.(A./Sjt.) J. J. 973
— Sjt. T. 995
Arnott, 2nd Cpl.(A./Cpl.) J. 982
Arscott, Dvr.(A./Sjt.) G. D. 2699
Arthur, Cpl. A. R. 1000
Arundel, S.M. W. F. 2700
Ascroft, Sjt. C. W. 1945
Ash, Pte.(A./C.S.M.) A. 2696
Ashbrook, S./Sjt. E. L. 61
Ashby, S./Sjt. W. S. 1006
Ashcroft, E.,C.Cpl.(A./Sjt.) T. P. 980
Ashdown, S.M. G. 990
— Pte.(A./Sjt.) W. T. 1015
Ashfield, Condr. E. 2701
Ashford, C.S.M. G. W. 2692
— Q.M.Sjt. M. 994
Ashley, L./C.(A./S.M.) A. 1490
— Sjt. W. H. 993
Ashman, S.M. F. W. 2694
— T./S.M. G. R. 2688
Ashmore, S.M. F. 1945
Ashton, Pte.(A./Sjt.) A. 1490
— Sjt. F. G. 1016
Ashton, Sjt. F. N. 1006
— Pte. W. 1001
Askenbeck, Sjt. A. 2702
Asker, A./Sjt. W. J. 99
Askins, Pte. A. 988
Aspden,Q.M.Sjt. J. 993
Asprey, Pte. (L./C.) F. 1001
Athey, Pte. A. R. 1013
Atkin, S.Q.M.Sjt. T. 1004
Atkins, S.M. A. 2689
— Cpl.(A./Sjt.) F. W. 1008
Atkinson, Sjt. A. 986
— Sjt. C. 68
— C.Q.M.Sjt. E. 989
— Sjt. J. 978
— C.S.M. R. C. 2999
— Pte.(L./C.) W. E. 986
Attewell, Sjt. H. C. 993
Attle, Pte. A. F. 1010
Attwood, Gnr. W. J. 974
Augustsen, Dvr. A. 1016
Ault, Sjt. F. H. W. 1006
Austen, Sjt. W. 978
Austin, C.S.M. F. 2693
— Clr.Sjt. F. H. 1488
— S./Sjt. F. W. 2703
— 2nd Cpl.(A./Cpl.) J. 68
— Pte. J. ❀ 1256
— S.M. W. 2695
— Pte.(A./Cpl.) W. 992
Auty, Sjt. J. 993
Avent, Cpl.(A./Sjt.) A. G. 2694
Avery, B.S.M.(A./S.M.) J. 1487
— Pte. P. 2998
Ayers, Sjt. M. T. W. 986
Ayling, Pte.(A./S./Sjt.) C. 2699
— Sjt. J. A. 1016
— Sjt. Clerk S. B. 2050
Ayres, C.S.M. A. W. 1004
Aytha, Cpl.(A./C.S.M. Instr.) I. 2701

Baber, S.M. A. 2691
— Ftr.S./Sjt. J. 971
— C.S.M. W. J. 2698
Bacon, Bombr. R. 68
— 2nd Cpl. W. McP. 982
Badenoch, Pte.(L./C.) A. 1001
Badger, Sjt. W. E. 994
Baggott, Sjt. W. H. 970
Bagnall, Spr. A. J. 60
Bagshaw, T./S.S.M. R. 1003
Bailey, Q.M.S. G. H. 2702
— C.S.M.Sjt. H. 978
— Q.M.Sjt. H. E. 986
— S./Sjt.(A./Q.M.Sjt.) J. E. 1490
— C.S.M. P. W. 997
— Ldg.Sea. T. W. 3863
— Sjt. W. 978
— S./S.M. W. A. 2701
— Mech.S./Sjt. W. J. 1004
Bailey, S./Sjt. W. J. F. 62
Bailie, Sjt. J. 1020
Bain, Cpl. H. R. 1020
Bainbridge, Spr. H. 982
Baird, S./Sjt. H. A. 1020
— C.S.M. W. 1016
— Sjt. W. A. 1006
Baker, Sjt. A. D. 1016
— S./Sjt. A. E. 1006
— Pte. A. E. 1010

Baker, Sjt. C. J.	997	Bamforth, Cpl. B.		995
— S.Q.M.S. D.	2689	Banbury, C.S.M. H. H.		998
— P.O. 1st Cl. G. F.	3861	Bancroft, Condr. G. F.		2700
— S./Sjt. H.	* 1490	Banfield, Cpl.(L./Sjt.) G.		2999
— Pte.(A./L./C.) J.	1013	Banham, Bdr. C. R., *M.M.*		970
— S.M. S. H.	1016	— Pte.(A./Sjt.) R.		1015
— Dvr. T. A.	974	Banks, Pte. (A./Sjt.) B. V.		2695
— Sjt. W.	68	— Cpl. C.		970
— 2nd Cpl.(T./Sub Condr.) W. E.	1014	— By.Q.M.S. H.		971
— Farr. S./Sjt. W. J.	† 971	— C.S.M. J. E.		998
Balch, C.Q.M.S. F.	2692	— Sjt. T.		992
Baldrey, C.Q.M.S. H. M.	978	— C.Q.M.Sjt. W.		989
— Condr. J.	2999	Banner, C.Q.M.Sjt. G.		988
— Sjt. (A./C.Q.M.S.) W.	987	— C.S.M. J. F.		998
Baldwin, Farr.S./Sjt. J.	975	— Pte. L. E.		1016
— Cpl. J. E.	980	Bannerman, Engmn. G.		3861
Bale, Sjt. J.	1488	— Sjt.(A./Q.M.S.) J.		2697
— Cpl. R. E.	2690	— Pte. J.		996
Balkwill, S.M. J.	2695	Bannister, Sjt. H. J.		69
Ball, C.S.M. A.	977	— C.S.M. P. F.		998
— Pnr. G. E.	60	Banwell, C.Q.M.Sjt. H. G.		60
— W.O. Cl.1, Spdt. Clerk G. E.	3572	— Cpl. L. G.		1003
— Sjt. S. R.	2694	Barber, Q.M.Sjt.(T./S.M.) C.		61
— Sjt. Art.Clk.(A./Q.M.Sjt.) T. W.	975	— Cpl.Obs. E. A.		99
— S./Sjt. W. J.	2702	— Cpl.Major W.	‡ 2689	
Ballantine, Cpl. J.	1008	— S.M. W. J.		70
— Sjt. R.	978	Barbery, Cpl. H. L.		980
Ballard, C.S.M. G. H.	1489	Barclay, Q.M.Sjt. J. H.		996
Balls, Pte. W. R. J.	60	— Pte. R.		1020
Bamber, C.S.M. H.	2694	Barcroft, Q.M.Sjt. H.		993
Bamberger, Sjt. A. E.	999	Bardell, Sjt.(A./R.Q.M.Sjt.) S.		992
Bambridge, C.S.M		Barden, S./S.M. F. H.		1003
(A./S.M.) C., *D.C.M.*	995	Bardner, Sjt. J.		984
Bamfield, C.Q.M.Sjt. W. H.	978	Barfoot, Pte. E. Y.		2694

---

* Lieut. & Q.M. Hugh Baker (No. 75102). M.B.E. M.S.M. 141 Field Amb. R.A.M.C. killed 1 June 1940 at Dunkirk aged 53.

† 18757, 92nd Battery R.F.A. Flanders 1918—Has served in the battery for over three years. Thoroughly hard-working, efficient and painstaking, he has carried out his work in a most efficient manner. By his zealous efforts, personal example and keen supervision, he has imbued those under him with energy and enthusiasm. He has constantly taken up ammunition to the gun line and has never failed to complete his duty. (French Croix de Guerre 19/6/19).

‡ A pair of medals to Regimental Corporal Major Walter Barber, Royal Horse Guards, are known: L.S. & G.C. (Geo. V, Regt. Cpl. Major) and M.S.M. (No. 733 Corpl. Major R.H.G.), one of only nine immediate M.S.M.s awarded to R.H.G. (plus 11 to Guards M.G. Regt. (R.H.G.) (3rd Battn.)). Born 1877. he enlisted in November, 1898, previously a stableman from Pontefract, Yorks., and was appointed Rough Rider in November, 1901 and L./Cpl. R.R. two weeks later. Cpl. R.R. in September, 1903 and Corporal of Horse R.R. in January, 1906, he qualified at the School of Musketry. Hyde. in July 1908 and gained a 1st class Certificate of Education in

Barker, Pte.(A./C.S.M.) A.	70	Barrett, Sjt. F.		972
— Sjt. C. (Gren. Gds.)	984	— L./C. W.		1020
— Sjt. C. (Aus. Inf.)	1020	Barritt, Pte.(A./Sjt.) B. A.		2699
— Farr.S./Sjt. G.	1004	Barritte, Ch.Mech. R.		99
— E.R.A., 2nd Cl., R.	3591	Barron, Sjt. F. P.		1012
— Sjt. R. A.	2092	Barrow, Cpl. F. F.		1008
Barkray, R.S.M. J.	2690	— Pte. P.		2998
Barlow, Cpl. A.	973	Bartholomew, Cpl. F. G.		1020
— Pte. F.	1490	Bartleet, S./Sjt.(A./Q.M.S.) J. J.		2700
Barnard, S.M. J. B.	99	Bartlett, Cpl.(A./Sjt.) C. J.		61
— Dvr. L.	974	— Sjt. J. G.		3840
— Cpl. (A./C.S.M.) P. G.	980	— S./Sjt. J. V.		1020
Barnes, B.Q.M.S. F. J.	2690	Barton, Pte.(A./Sjt.) E.		1015
— Mech.S./Sjt. G. F.	978	— Pte.(A./S.Q.M.S.) J. F.		1489
— Pte.(A./Sjt.Instr.) G. J.	1016	— Gnr. S. W.		1016
— B.SM. G. R.	60	Bartram, Sjt. E.		978
— Cpl.(A./S./Sjt.) J.	1014	Barwick, S.M. J., *M.C.*	*	2693
— Pte. (A./Sjt.) J. A.	1001	Basford, Pte.(A./Mech.S./Sjt.) C. E.		2699
— Pte. J. A.	1010	Basham, Pte. W. A.		993
— Sjt. M.	1006	Basnett, Sjt. A. H.		1020
Barnett, Ch.Mech. E. B.	99	Bastie, Gnr. F. W.		974
— Sjt. F.	985	Batchelor, Sjt. A. G.		972
— C.Q.M.S. M. C.	2693	— Gnr. H. A.		974
— Pte.(A./L./C.) R. C. S.	1010	Bate, Cpl. F. J.		998
— Pte. W. T.	996	Bateman, Sjt. T. A.		1006
Barnicoat, Spr.(L./Cpl.) F.	982	Bates, Pte. G. F. H.		970
Barr, Spr.(A./Sjt.) H.	2998	— Sjt. H. J.		975
— Sjt. Mech. J.	99	— 3rd Cl.Mst.Gnr. J. G., *D.C.M.*	†	2691
— T./S.M. R. W.	977	— By.Q.M.S. T. J.		975
Barrett, Sjt.(A./Q.M.Sjt.) W., *M.M.*	1016	Batey, Sjt. R.		68
Barrell, C.S.M. G.	985	Batsford, Sjt. G. R.		1490
— S./S.M. L.	1016	Battell, Sjt.Mech. E.		99
Barret, Cpl.(A./Sjt.) A. C. H.	976	Battersby, Cpl.(A./Sjt.) W. T.		1012
Barrett, Cpl. C. C. C.	992			

April 1910 and had less than twelve years service when he was appointed Sqdn. Cpl. Major Rough Rider in September, 1910. He re-engaged to complete 21 years that month and became Regimental Corporal Major on 10 September, 1914 a rank he held through the war until in May 1920; having extended his service the previous year beyond 21 years he was appointed W.O.1 Permanent Staff Instructor Gloucester Yeomanry until his final discharge in April 1922 with 24 years and 167 days service, all in the U.K. His pension was 5/4d. per day for life. His Army number was 304007. He had been mentioned in despatches 27.3.1919 (see war Office Communiqué). It would be interesting to know how he wore the oakleaf, having neither British War Medal nor Victory Medal.

* Group known: M.C. (*L.G.* 18 February, 1915, S. Maj. 1/Scots Gds.), Queen's South Africa Medal (two clasps, Pte. Scots Gds.), 1914 Star & bar (S.M. S.G.), British War and Victory Medals (W.O.1), L.S. & G.C. (A.O. 130 April 1919) and M.S.M.

† Group known: D.C.M. (Edw. VII), Queen's South Africa Medal (Natal, Orange Free State, Transvaal), King's South Africa Medal, L.S. & G.C. (Edw. VII) and M.S.M.

Battle, Amt.S./Sjt.(T./ Amt.S.M.) F. J.	1014
Batts, T./S.M. E.	2701
Battson, Sqdn. S.M. F.	60
Batty, By.S.M. W. E. F.	970
Baugh, Col.Sjt. A.	2360
Baulch, T./S.M. W.	2698
Baverstock, S.M. A. T.	1015
Bax, Cpl. R. J.	1008
Baxter, Q.M.Sjt. A. R.	61
— Sjt. H.	997
— C.Q.M.S. J. P.	1020
— Pte. S. J.	1016
Bayley, Sjt. F. J.	1006
Baylis, Sjt. C. H.	2690
Baynes, R.Q.M.S. J. H.	1020
Bazeley, Sjt. H. A.	1006
Bazley, Spr.(A./Sjt.) T. H.	982
Beach, B.Q.M.S. W. W.	2690
Beale, Sjt. C. M.	1020
Beall, Pte.(A./Cpl.) F.	61
Beames, Sjt. A. E.	1020
Beamish, Spr.(A./Sjt.) G. H.	982
Bean, Pte.(L./C.) A.	1016
— C.S.M. F. W., *MM.*	998
Bear, C.S.M. H. C., *D.C.M.*	994
Beard, By.S.M. J. G.	970
Beard, Pte. L. D.	1016
— Q.M.Sjt. P. S.	1011
— C.S.M. R., *MM.*	984
Bearne, Spr.(A./2nd Cpl.) L. W.	60
Beasley, Sjt. C.	999
— Mech.S./Sjt. J. W.	1004
— Sjt. S. C	2694
Beatham, Cpl. T.	980
Beatson, Sjt. G.	68
Beattie, S./S.M. R.	1003
— C.S.M.(A./S.M.) W. J.	2692
Beaumont, Sjt. E.	995
— T./S./S.M. J.	1003
Beaver, Q.M.S. R.	2691
Beavers, 2nd Hnd. A. T.	3861
Beavon, S.Q.M.Sjt. A.	1004
Beckett, C.S.M. F. F.	977
— Pte. H. H.	1010
— Cpl. P.	991
Beckham, T./S.M. J. J.	2690
Beckley, Sjt.(A./Sub Condr.) A. A.	* 1945
— Pte.(A./Sjt.) T.	982

Beckwith, E.R.A. 2nd Cl. J. J.	2360
Bedford, 2nd Cpl. C.	982
— Spr.(A./2nd Cpl.) H. E.	2692
Bee, S./Sjt.(A./Q.M.S.) W. W.	1490
Beech, Spr.(L./C.) P.	982
Beedle, Sjt. S.	2698
Begg, F. of W. S./Sjt. J. M.	978
Behan, Sjt. J. J.	1016
Beisly, Sjt.(A./Q.M.S.) R. J.	61
Belcham, Condr. A. F.	2701
Belcher, Q.M.Sjt. W. P.	993
Bell, S./Sjt. A.	1005
— Sjt.(A./C.Q.M.S.) E.	2698
— C.S.M. F.	2694
— Sjt. G.	972
— Sjt. G. T.	1016
— Cpl.(A./Sjt.) H.	994
— Pte. H.	995
— Sjt. J.	989
— C.Q.M.S. M. C.	70
— Ch.Mas.Mech. M. J.	99
— Pte.(A./Cpl.) W.	70
Bellamy, C.S.M. J. H.	987
Bellinger, Sjt. J. C.	1017
Bellingham, Sjt. C. W.	1020
Belsham, Pte. (L./Cpl.) A. E.	982
Belton, Pte. W. H.	1017
Bence, S./Sjt. H.	2699
Benfield, Sjt. H. H.	1488
Benham, Sjt.(A./C.S.M.)	1012
Bennett, Sjt.(A./S.S.M.) A. E.	2699
— S./Q.M.S.(T./S.S.M.) C. G., *MM.*	2699
— Farr.Sjt. G.	1006
— Pte.(A./S./Sjt.) G.	2700
— W.O. H. J.	2702
— Sjt. H. T.	1945
— By.S.M.(A./R.S.M.) J. J.	971
— Ldg. Sea. R. C.	3861
— Sjt. S. G.	68
— C.Q.M.Sjt. T.	997
— Gnr. T.	977
— C.Q.M.S. T. J.	1020
Bennetts, Sjt. H.	1020
Benning, Q.M.Sjt. W. J.	69
Bennington, C.S.M. S.	2998
Benson, C.S.M.(A./Q.M.S.) J. A.	986
— C.Q.M.Sjt. J. E.	978
— C.S.M. P. J.	977
Benstead, Sjt. H. G.	993

* R.A.O.C. Also Ordre de Léopold (Chevalier).

Bent, S./Sjt.(A./S.Q.M.Sjt.) E.	1006	Binnie, Cpl. J.	1008
Bentham, Cpl.(A./Sjt.) J.	1012	— Col.Sjt. J. S.	2693
Bentley, Pte. A. T. G.	1003	— Pte.(L./C.) T. G.	998
— Sjt.(A./S./Sjt.) D.M.S.	1012	Binning, T./Supt.Clk. A. J.	977
Beresford, T./S./S.M. J.	1003	Binnington, Sjt. W.	1488
— C.S.M. R. H.	2698	Binstead, Sjt. J. A. S.	99
Berkeley, Sjt. A. E. V.	972	Birch, Spr.(A./2nd Cpl.) A.	982
Bernard, C.S.M. W.	986	— Spr. A.	982
Berris, C.S.M.(A./S./S.M.) R.	1004	— Q.M.S.(A./S.M.) G. V.	1488
Berrisford, Sjt. A.	994	— 3rd Writer J. L.	2660
Berry, S./Sjt. A.	1024	Bird, Sjt. F.	1006
— Pte.(A./Sjt.) A. W.	1015	— Dvr. T.	1010
— Sjt. J.	991	— F. of W. Q.M.S. T. F.	2692
— Gnr. R. O.	1256	Birse, Q.M.Sjt. A. L.	986
— Sjt. R. S.	1012	Birtle, Sjt. J.	985
— Q.M.Sjt. W.	991	Bishton, Sjt. D. G.	1020
— Sjt. W.	989	Bissell, S./S.M. F. F.	2698
— Cpl. W.	60	Bissett, Ch.Mech. W.	99
Bertram, S.M. R.	2695	Black, Sjt.(A./C.S.M.) W.	978
— Sjt. W. T.	995	— Sjt. W., *M.M.*	1006
Bessell, Q.M.Sjt. S. J.	987	Blackburn, Sjt. F.	1020
Best, Q.M.Sjt. J. W. E.	986	— Cpl.(A./Sjt.) S. N.	980
— Sjt. R. G.	975	— Pte.(A./Cpl.) T. B.	1015
Beston, S./Sjt. (A./S.S.M.) W. J.	2699	Blackery, Sjt. D.	990
Betts, Sjt. F. S.	1488	Blackett, Art.Cpl. J. S.	981
— C.Q.M.Sjt. G.	989	Blackler, Sjt. J.	987
Bevan, Pte. H.	993	Blackman, Sjt.(T./S.S.M.) C. E.	2699
— R.Q.M.S. H. H.	1020	— Sjt. G. T.	997
— C.E.R.A. T. F.	2360	Blackmore, Sjt. C.	988
Bevan-Brown, Cpl.(A./Sjt.) R. E.	1012	— Cpl. J. A.	981
Beveridge, C.Q.M.Sjt.(A./Q.M.Sjt.) A.	996	— C.Q.M.Sjt.(T./M.S.M.) J. R.	1004
— Pte. 2 P.M.	99	— F. f W. S.M. J. W.	977
Bickford, Sjt. E. H.	1002	— C.S.M.(A./S.M.) W. H.	2997
Bickle, Pte.(L./C.) (A./Sjt.) F. J.	2999	Blackwell, Sjt. C.	69
Bidder, Pte. T.	1003	— Pte.(A./Bdr.) M. C.	1024
Biddle, S.M. E. L.	985	Blade, Q.M.Sjt. R. J.	986
Biffen, C.Q.M.Sjt. A. G.	988	Bladon, Pte. L./C. A.	1016
Bigg, Pte.(A./Cpl.) A. G. A.	1010	Blaikley, Pte.(A./Sjt.) E.	1003
Biggs, Sjt. A.	999	Blair, Sjt. A. T.	1017
— Sjt. (A./S./S.M.) F.	1006	Blake, Spr.(L./Cpl.) H.	982
— S.M. W. G.	1488	— C.Q.M.S.(A./Q.M.S.) H. T.	* 2691
Bigley, F. of W. (S./Sjt.) J.	2692	— S.M. J.	2696
Bille, Vet.Sjt. A. M. I.	1017	Blakeley, C.Q.M.Sjt. A. F.	1004
Billingham, Sjt.(A./S.M.) C. J.	2700	— Ftr./Cpl. F.	973
Billinghurst, Pte.(A./L./C.) A. J.	1010	Blank, Sjt. W. C.	978
Bills, T./S.M. T.	2695	Blease, B.Q.M.S. J. F.	2691
Binks, Sjt. H.	1006	— 2nd Cpl.(A./Cpl.) W.	2999
— C.Q.M.S. J.	2999	Blenkey, By.S.M.(A./R.S.M.) M.	971

* Awarded M.S.M. and Annuity, A.O. 103, June, 1945 as B.Q.M.S. R.A. Both are extant, with his W.W.I medals and L.S. & G.C.

Blood, Sjt.(A./Sub Condr.) F. R.	1946	Boulter, Gnr. F. E.	974
Bloodworth, S./Sjt. A. J.	2702	— Sjt. H. E.	2697
Bloom, C.S.M. G. G.	998	Boulton, Ftr. W.	974
Bloomer, Pte.(A./Sjt.) H.	61	Bourke, Sjt. E. E.	1020
Bloomfield, Pte. W.	1010	— Cpl.(T./R.S.M.) E. T.	1020
Blount, T./S./S.M. B.	1003	— C.Q.M.S.(A./Q.M.S.) L. M.	2696
Bloustein, C.Q.M.S. H. M.	1020	Bourne, Sjt. W. J.	972
Blowers, By.S.M. G. S.	971	Bowden, Pte.(A./Sjt.) C. G.	1013
Blunden, Sjt. (O.R.) F.	970	— Spr. W. D.	982
— Bmdr. R.	977	Bowditch, By.S.M. F. H.	1020
Blunt, T./S.M. O. J.	2691	Bowdler, Pte. C.	1010
Blyth, Sjt. J., *M.M.*	989	Bowen, Cpl.(L./Cpl.) A. E.	1000
— T./S.S.M. P. R.	1003	— Cpl. D. W.	70
Blythe, Pte.(A./Cpl.) P. F.	1016	Blower, Sjt. A. F.	986
Boaler, Pte.(A./W.O.Cl.II) J.	2696	Bowes, Cpl.(A./Mc.Sjt.) N. S.	981
Bodger, Pte. E. J.	987	Bowgett, C.S.M.(A./S.M) R.	2696
Boggie, By.Q.M.Sjt. K. D. H.	971	Bowler, Sjt.(A./C.Q.M.Sjt.) A.	978
Bolam, Pte.(L./C.) J. S.	69	— Cpl. A. F.	994
Bolland, Q.M.Sjt. H.	988	— S.Q.M.Sjt. G. H.	1004
Bolshaw, Col. H.	994	Bowles, Sjt.(A./Q.M.S.) W.	2693
Bolton, S./S.M. A. H.W.	1003	Bowley, Pte.(L./C.) R. L.	1016
Bonacina, Sjt. L.	1024	Bowra, Sjt. H. S. C.	972
Bond, Sjt. E. J.	1002	Bowyer, Condr. C.W.	2700
— Dvr. (L./C.) J.	11020	— B.Q.M.Sjt. R.	975
Bone, S./Sjt. W.	1012	Box, Cpl.(A./Sjt.) E. J.	1015
Bonfield, By.S.M. J. E.	971	— C.S.M. W. R.	1020
Boniface, Sjt. A. S.	901	Boxshall, T./S.M. C. E.	2695
— S.M. J.	2695	Boyce, Sjt. D. R.	1024
— T./Arm.S.M. J. H.	1013	— C.Q.M.Sjt. F. J.	69
Bonney, Sjt. R. C.	987	— Pte. H. W. J.	986
Bonser, Gnr. F.	974	— Bdr. S. C.	973
Booker, Pte.(A./Sjt.) F.	1016	Boyd, C.Q.M.Sjt. J. G.	999
Bool, Sjt.Clk. R. W.	99	— C.Q.M.S. V.	1020
Boorman, Cpl. G. F.	981	Boyden, S./S.M. J. W.	2698
Boosey, Sjt. E. A.	1017	Boyle, Pte.(A./Sjt.) A. F.	1017
Boost, Sjt. T. W., *M.M.*	972	Bracken, Sjt. G.	989
Booth, Sjt. F.	997	Bracksieck, Cpl.(A./Sjt.) W. F.	981
— Sjt. H. D.	978	Bradbury, Ch.Mas.Mech. E. A.	99
— C.S.M. M. G.	977	— Cpl. E. S.	1020
Bootle, Pte.(A./Q.M.Sjt.) W. A.	990	— Sjt. R. H.	1017
Borstel, Sjt. R.	1020	Bradfield, Spr. C.	982
Bosanquet, C.Q.M.S. B.	2695	Bradford, Pte. A. H. * ❀	1256
Bosley, S./Sjt. W. F.	1490	— Cpl.(L./Sjt.) W.	1017
Bostock, Cpl. W.	68	Bradley, Sjt. H.	979
Botham, S./Sjt. H. G.	1017	— Dvr. J.	982
Bothwell, S.M. H.	2703	— By.S.M.(A./R.S.M.) L.	971
Botterill, Sjt. J.	1006	— Pte. L.	986
Bottomley, C.S.M. E. T., *M.M.*	998	— C.S.M. P. H.	2696
Boughtflower, Condr. J.	2999	— Dvr. W.	974

* M.M., British War Medal, and M.S.M. known (R.A.O.C.).

Brady, C.S.M. E.	1946	Briggs, C.S.M. F.	997
Braga, W.O. J.	2702	— Cpl. F. B.	1008
Brain, S.M. T.	2691	— C.S.M. G.	992
Bramble, C.Q.M.Sjt. J.	999	— Pte.(L./Sjt.) J.	1015
— Ch.Mech. W.	99	Bright, Cpl. R.	1008
Bramhall, Sjt. J.	979	— Pte. R. R.	1013
Bramley, Pte. H.	1013	Brignall, Sjt. J. T.	975
Brand, Sjt. J.	1017	Brind, Sup.Clk. F. W.	2695
— Sjt. L. R.	1020	Brindle, Sjt. S.	1006
Brander, Cpl. D.	1017	Brindley, S.M. E. E.	2694
Brandon, Cpl. M. L.	993	— Col.Sjt. T.	992
Brannan, Sjt. T.	1489	Brinnard, Cpl. G. M.	1488
Branson, C.Q.M.Sjt. C. E.	900	Brisbin, Pte. P. R.	1017
Bray, Sjt. F.	979	Brisco, Cpl.(A./Sadd.S./Sjt.) J. T.	1006
— Sjt. J.	979	Bristow, Sjt. W.	1489
Braybrooke, 2nd Cpl.(A./C.S.M.)		Brittain, Pte. A.	1010
W. L.	982	— Pte.(A./S.Q.M.S.) E. G. H.	2699
Brayne, Cpl. R. W.	1008	Brittlebank, Cpl. F. S. J.	986
Brazier, P.O. P. J.	* 3863	Britton, Cpl.(A./Sjt.) L. C.	1000
Breaden, Sjt. T. A. H.	1020	Broadhurst, Sjt. V.	† ❀ 1256
Breeze, C.P.O. G.	3591	Broadley, Pte.(A./Sjt.) G.	1015
Breheny, Cpl. T. C.	1020	Brockman, Pte. G. A.	60
Breingan, C.Q.M.Sjt. A.	996	Broderick, C.S.M. (T./S.M) A.C.) M.	975
Brennan, Q.M.Sjt.(T./S.M.) J. A.	1011	— Cpl. W.	975
Brennan, Cpl. M.	981	Brodie, S./Sjt.(A./S.Q.M.S.) D.	61
— Spr. W.	68	— C.Q.M.Sjt. J.	997
Brennen, Sub Condr.(A./Condr.)		— Sjt. J.	1020
W. A.	1013	Bromley, Mec./Mach.S./Sjt.	
Brentnall, Q.M.S. G.	2697	(A./Q.M.S.) W.	978
Brett, Pte. A. E.	984	Brook, Pte.(L./C.) F. E.	2696
Bretton, S.M. H.	1489	— Cpl. H.	1012
Brewer, Sjt. B. W. J.	979	Brooke, Pte.(A./Sjt.) H.	2700
— Pte. G. C.	1010	Brooker, Pte.(A./Cpl.) W. J. A.	2699
— Sjt. R.	997	Brookes, Pte. E.	1945
Brewster, Sjt. J. L.	970	Brookfield, Sjt. J.	989
Bricknell, Q.M.S. E.	2694	Brookman, B.S.M. F.	1487
Bridges, Sjt.(A./S.Q.M.Sjt.) A. M.	1006	Brooks, Clr.Sjt.(A./W.Cl.1) C.	3572
— Sjt. J. T.	68	— Cpl.(A./Q.M.Sjt.) F. H.	985
Bridle, Gnr. A. J.	977	— Cpl.(L./Sjt.) J.	61
— Sjt. S. H.	1006	— Pte. W. J.	997
Brien, Sjt. Dmr. A. J.	986	Broomfield, Mech.Sjt. A. T.	978
Briggs, Sqdn.Q.M.S.(A./S./S.M.) A.	2699	Brothers, Sjt. I.	979
— C.Q.M.Sjt. E.	999	Brotherton, C.Q.M.Sjt. W.	983

---

* R.N. M.S.M. as F18403 R.N.A.S.

† R.E. Volunteering in June 1915, he was sent to France later in the same year, and took part in numerous engagements including those at Vermelles, Albert, the Somme, Ypres, Cambrai, Lens, Bapaume, and Le Câteau. He was awarded the Meritorious Service Medal for extricating his men from a poison gas area, and also held the 1914–15 Star, and the General Service and Victory Medals. He was demobilised in February 1919. 61, Kemp Street, Ancoats, Manchester.

Broughton, Cpl. R. H.	973	Brownlee, C.S.M. R.		1020
Brown, Sjt. A.	992	Bruce, CQ.M.Sjt. G. S.		984
— Spr. A.	982	— Sjt. J.		3840
— Cpl.(A./S.M.) (A.C.) A. E.	976	— Cpl. J.		1000
— S./S.M. A. G.	1017	— Pte. (A./Sjt.) R. T.		1010
— C.Q.M.Sjt. A. J.	991	Bruckner, Sjt. C. A.		1020
— Cpl. A. R. T.	1020	Bruerton, Sjt. H.		988
— Sjt. C. J.	986	Brunsden, C.Q.M.S. C.		1023
— Pte.(A./C.S.M.) E. M.	2697	Brunt, Sjt. A. E.		988
— Sjt. E. W.	1017	Bryant, Cpl.(L./Sjt.) C. W.		992
— Pte.(A./Cpl.) F.	80	— Sjt. E.		1006
— Pte. F.	2361	— Gnr. F. T. F.		970
— Sjt. F. A.	984	— C.Q.M.Sjt.(A./Q.M.Sjt.) J. G. D.		1017
— Sjt. G	1017	Bryce, Spr. A. D.		982
— Pte.(A./Sjt.) G.	1015	— Pte.(A./S.M.) J.		62
— Sub Condr.(A./Condr.) G. J. F.	3000	— Dkhnd. J.		2360
— Sjt. H.	979	— C.P.O. Teleg. T.		3861
— Sjt. H. C.	1020	Bryden, Spr. (A./Sjt.) C.		982
— Sjt. Mech. H. V.	99	— Cpl. W. H.		1008
— Pte.(L./C.) H. W.	1003	Bryenton, Sjt. W. H.		1020
— Cpl. (A.C.) J.	976	Bryne, C.Q.M.Sjt. T. S.		978
— Cpl. J.	973	Bubb, C.S.M. (T./R.S.M.) C. P.		2702
— S./Sjt. J. E.	998	Buchan, Sjt. L. S.		1006
— S./S.M. J. H.	61	Buchanan, Sjt. S. R.		984
— Q.M.Sjt. J. K.	997	Buck, Farr.Sjt. A		1017
— Spr. (L./Cpl.) J. L.	982	— Clr.Sjt.(C.Q.M.S.) F. E. J.		70
— Farr. S./Sjt. J. T.	978	— Sjt. J. N.		997
— Sjt. J. W.	1020	— Sjt. T.		991
— Sjt. L. W.	1002	— Pte.(A./Sjt.) T. A.		1016
— Sjt.(A./Q.M.S.) N.	1490	— Sjt. W. J.		999
— C.Q.M.S. R.	69	Buckenham, By.S.M. A. H., *MM.*		971
— Sjt. R.	2691	Buckett, S.Q.M.Sjt.(T./Sub Condr.)		
— Sqdn.Q.M.Sjt. T. H.	997	E. S.	*	1014
— Q.M.Sjt. W.	996	Buckland, 1st Writer E. C.		2361
— Cpl.(A./S./Sjt.) W.	1014	Buckle, Cpl.(A./S./Sjt.) C.		2692
— Gnr. W. D.	1017	Buckley, Pte. F.		1010
Browne, Pte.(L./C.) L. O.	1016	— Sjt. H. G.		979
Browning, S./Sjt.(T./S.S.M.) A. C. S.	61	— Pte.(A./Sjt.) P.		1015
— C.Q.M.S. J.	2689	— C.S.M. S.		998
— Cpl. R.	69	Budd, Q.M.Sjt. W. G.		985

---

* Group known: Queen's South Africa Medal (Cape Colony, Pte. A.O.C.), King's South Africa Medal (Cpl. A.O.C.), 1914 Star & bar (S/Sgt. A.O.C.), British War and Victory Medals (T.W.O.1 A.O.C.), L.S. & G.C. (Geo. V, S/Sgt. A.O.C.). and M.S.M. With photographs and news cuttings giving full details of his career, together with a certificate from the Army Ordnance Corps for 'Specially Meritorious Services in times of the greatest pressure at the Advance Ordnance Depot at Le Mans 1914,' signed by D.O.S. Brit. Army in France, 13 December, 1917. Served 49 years, first as a 10 year old at the Duke of York's Military School, then aged 14 he joined the Ordnance Store Corps. After 25 years in R.A.O.C. and its predecessors, left in 1919 as a Lieutenant. In charge of recruiting at Thornton Heath from 1920 for 20 years.

Budgen, Sjt. E. J.	979	Burrill, Sjt. W.		972
Buffham, Sjt. J. W.	997	Burrows, Sjt. A. N.		1006
Bugg, Sjt. W. J.	1488	Burton, Cpl.Mech. A. H.		99
Bule, Sjt. N.	996	— S.M. A. W.	*	2701
Bull, M.A.A C. T.	2360	— S.M. C. A.		2700
Bulled, Pte.(A./Sjt.) H. A.	1016	— S.Q.M.Sjt. D. H. Q., *MM.*		1005
Bullen, Pte.(A./Sjt.) F. H.	1015	— Sjt. E. G.		975
Bulley, Sjt. T.	2999	— Cpl. F. J.		1008
Bullock, C.Q.M.Sjt.(A./M.S.M.) A.	1004	— 2nd Cpl. J.		1024
— Sjt. F. H. T.	988	— Farr.Sjt. W. H.		972
— C.S.M. G.	2692	Burville, A./Ch.Mech.		
— Farr.Q.M.Sjt. W. J.	971	W. S., *D.S.M.*	†	99
Bulmer, Q.M.S. E. H.	69	Busby, Pte.(A./Sjt.) J. P. V.		1015
Bulpitt, Pte.(A./Q.M.S.) L. G.	61	Buschell, Cpl. E. H.		2695
Bunker, Cpl.(A./Q.M.S.)	1490	Bush, Cpl.(T./Sub Condr.) A. G.		1014
Bunn, Mech.S./Sjt. V. W.	1005	— Clr.Sjt. J.		3572
Bunnett, Pte. C. H. B.	1010	Bushby, Pte.(A./Cpl.) J.		1010
Burbage, Sjt. W. P.	986	— W.O. W.		2702
Burch, Farr.Sjt. A.	979	Bushell, Sjt. W. K.		2696
Burden, Sjt. A.	972	Bushnell, Sjt. G. E. J.		71
— Sjt. A. N.	1017	Butcher, 2nd Cpl.(A./Sjt.)		
— Sjt. C. A.	994	C. J., *MM.*		982
— Pte.(A./Sjt.) W. R.	1017	— T./S.M. J. R.	‡	2690
Burdick, S.M. C.	2689	Butler, Ftr.S./Sjt. A. V.		975
Burge, Pte.(L./C.) F. G.	992	— Spr. C.		982
— Spr. R.	❀ 1256	— Sjt.(A./S.M.) H.		62
Burgin, T./Sub Condr. A.	1013	— Sjt. H.		68
Burke, Sjt. F. E.	1945	— Sjt. L. W.		972
Burke, Q.M.Sjt. T.	998	— 2nd Cpl.(A./Sjt.) P. F., *MM.*		982
Burkett, Sjt.(A.C.) G. P. W.	2691	— Pnr.Sjt. T.		984
Burkitt, Sjt.(A./Q.M.S.) J. E.	2693	Butlin, R.Q.M.S. H.		1024
Burnard, Sjt. W. E.	60	Butt, Sjt.(A./S.Q.M.S.) A. G. L.		2699
Burne, Cpl. R. W.	1000	Butterfield, Ftr. G. F.		970
Burnet-Smith, Pte. E. J.	2997	Butters, Sjt. A		1020
Burnett, Q.M.S. E. E.	2696	— T./S.M. W.		2697
— C.S.M. (A./S.M.) G.	984	Butterworth, Farr.S./Sjt. J.		971
Burney, Sjt. T.	996	Button, Sjt. J.		979
Burns, Cpl.(A./C.Q.M.S.) J. H.	61	— L./C.(A./Sjt.) L. J.		982
— C.S.M.(A./S.M.) J. J.	2696	Buxton, Pte.(A./Sjt.) A. D.		2699
Burnside, Farr.Q.M.Sjt. J.	971	Bylers, Sjt. P.		1017
Burr, Farr.Sjt. J.	979	Byrne, Pte. A. M.		1003
Burrell, T./Sub Condr. H. E.	1013	— By.S.M.(A./R.S.M.) C.		971
— Sadl.S./Sjt. P.	1017	— Sjt. E.		972
Burridge, Cpl(A./S.Q.M.S.) F. A.	61	— Pte.(A./Sjt.) H. C.		991

* For Bermuda (R.A.M.C.).
† R.A.F. M.S.M., formerly No. 2117 R.N.A.S.
‡ The only M.S.M. to Bucks. Yeomanry. Group known: Queen's South Africa Medal (Talana, Defence of Ladysmith, Orange Free State, Laing's Nek, Belfast), King's South Africa Medal (both 3929 Sgt. 18 Huss.), L.S. & G.C. (Edw. VII, S.S.M. 18 Huss.) and M.S.M. (11205390), plus two temperance medals.

Byrne, Sjt. J.	1020	Cameron, C.S.M. J.	990
— Pte.(L./C.) T. J.	1001	— W.O. Cl.1, J. B.	1020
		— Cpl.(A./Sjt.) J. T.	1017
Cabell, Pte. H.	2998	— Spr. J. W.	982
Cadd, Sjt. M. M.	68	— Pte. W. J.	1001
Cade, Cpl.(A./Q.M.S.) L. H.	2700	Cammish, Pte. R.	1001
Cadger, Sjt. I.	1017	Camp, P.O. 1st Cl., J J.	2360
Cadman, S.M. H.	2694	Campbell, Sjt. A. C.	2702
— Ch.Mech.(E) H.	* 99	— C.Q.M.Sjt. D.	992
Caffell, Gnr. R.	2997	— Sjt. D.	1488
Caffrey, S.M. A. W.	2691	— Dvr. J.	1020
Caffyn, Sjt. L. J.	997	— Pte. 1 J. D.	99
— C.Q.M.S. S. C.	2998	— Spr.(A./Sjt.) P.	982
Cagby, S./S.M. W. G.	† 2698	— Wh.S./Sjt. R	1020
Cairns, Sjt. J.	985	— Q.M.Sjt. R. A.	§ 70
— Sjt. R.	999	— Cpl. W.	69
— Cpl.(A./Sjt.) S	1012	— Cpl.(A./Sjt.) W. D.	1012
— Sjt. T.	984	Campion, C.S.M. W. F.	992
Caldcleugh, Cpl. C.	1000	Campkin, C.Q.M.Sjt. H.	978
Calder, C.Q.M.Sjt. G.	988	Candy, By.S.M. G.	1017
— Sjt.(A./S.Q.M.S.) J. M.	2702	Cannon, Cpl.(A./Sjt.) W.	2695
— Pte.(A./S./Sjt.) W. H.	2702	— Pte. W. C.	69
Caldwell, Farr.Q.M.Sjt. J.	971	Canvin, Ftr.S./Sjt. H. A.	975
— S.M. J. H.	2697	Cape, C.S.M.(A./1st Cl.W.O.) J. G.	1945
Callander, Cpl. C.(corr)	1257	Capelen, C.S.M. M., *D.C.M.*	69
Calligan, Cpl.(A./S.Q.M.S.) W.	2699	Capon, Gnr. W.C.H. S.	974
Callow, Sjt. G.	999	Capper, Pte.(A./L./Sjt.) F.	1013
Callowhill, C.Q.M.Sjt. A. T. A.	999	Careless, Pte. C. H.	1001
Calver, S.Q.M.Sjt. J. H.	1489	Cargill, Pte.(L./C.) W. J.	998
Calvert, Ftr.(A./Ftr.S./Sjt.) F. J.	68	Carlile, Q.M.S. J. D	2700
— Spr.(L./C.) H.	982	Carlyle, C.S.M. R.	984
— Gnr. T.	974	Carmichael, 2nd Hnd. H.	3861
Cameron, Pte.(A./S./Sjt.) A.	1013	Carnegie, Sjt. H. R.	1002
— Pte.(A./Cpl.) A.	1001	Carnon, Q.M.Sjt. F. W.	1002
— C.Q.M.Sjt. C.	1017	Carolan, Sjt.(T./Sub Condr.) W.	1014
— S./S.M. D.	2698	Carpenter, C.S.M.(A./R.S.M.) C. O.	2702
— Sjt. E.	975	— B.S.M. W. A.	2691
— Sjt.(T./Sub Condr.) H. R.	‡ 1014	— Bmdr. W. N. H.	974

* R.A.F. M.S.M. formerly No. 4479 R.N.A.S. Commissioned in R.A.F. 1937, shown as awarded A.F.M. also.
† A.S.C. for Ceylon.
‡ R.A.O.C. served 47 years. Later Lieut. Colonel. Group known: O.B.E., British War and Victory Medals, Defence Medal, Jubilee 1935, Coronation 1937, L.S. & G.C. and M.S.M.
§ Group was in McInnes collection: 1914/15 Star (17037 Cpl. Manchester Regt.), British War and Victory Medals (W.O.II Manchester R.), M.S.M. (20/Manchesters, 5th Manchester Pals). To France 9 November, 1915. 118 men of the Regiment killed on the first day of the Somme, 1 June, 1916. 20th Battn. were part of XV Corps, 7 Div. The 20/Man. were transferred to the Italian theatre on 23 November, 1917. This M.S.M. is for service in Italy.

Carr, Sjt. J., *MM.*	985	Castle, P.O.(A./C.P.O.) J. H.		2689
— Sjt. J. T.	2702	— S./Sjt. S. J.		1023
— Pte.(T./Cpl.) R. T.	1021	Caswell, Sjt. C. C.		988
— Sjt. T. L.	979	Cater, Sjt. F. H.		990
— Sjt. W. C.	993	Cato, Dvr. J.		982
Carrick, 2nd Cpl. W.	982	Catterall, S.M. R.		993
Carrig, Sjt. T.	1023	Caulton, 2nd Cpl.(A./Sjt.) P.		982
Carrigan, C.S.M. (A./S.M.) J.	990	Cave, Spr.(A./2nd Cpl.) H. W.		983
Carroll, S./Sjt.(A./S.M.) H. J.	1012	— Sjt. J.		2999
— Cpl.(A./Sjt.) L. M.	1945	Cavey, Sjt. E. P.		1017
Carruthers, Sjt. A.	1006	Cawsey, Sjt. G.		1021
Carson, Sjt. J.	1017	Cawthorne, Sjt. J.		992
Carstairs, S.M. W.	1489	Chadd, C.S.M. E.		1004
Carter, C.S.M. A. J.	1004	Chadwick, C.Q.M.Sjt. A. R.		994
— Sjt. E. G.	994	— Sjt.(A./C.Q.M.S.) E.		2698
— S./S.M. G. J.	2701	— R.Q.M.Sjt. H.		970
— Farr.S./Sjt. G. J.	1005	— T./Sub Condr. S. V.		1490
— C.S.M. J.	1004	Chalk, E.		975
— Pte.(L./C.) J.	1017	Chalmers, Sjt. A.		1017
— Ldg.Sto.W. J.	2361	— Sjt. J. E.	‡	99
Carthy, Sjt. M., *D.C.M.*	* 1945	Chamberlain, Sjt.(A./S./Sjt.) C.		2700
Cartwright, Sjt.(A./Q.M.Sjt.) G	984	— Spr.(L./C.) J.	❀	1256
— C.Q.M.S. M. M. H.	1021	— R.S.M. J. C.		975
Carver, Sjt. E. A. E. K.	1021	Chambers, C.S.M. R. J.		998
Case, Cpl.(T./S.S.M.) W. A.	2699	Champion, S./Sjt.(A./Q.M.S.) A. G.		1012
Casey, S.M. J.	† 3841	— Cpl. E. J. W.		71
— B.S.M. W.	1487	Champney, Sjt. A.		975
Cash, Spr. A. W.	1021	Chandler, Condr. F.		2701
Cashman, Sub Condr.(A./		— Cpl.(A./S.Q.M.S.) H. A. V.		1014
Condr.) E. J.	61	— Sjt. W. J.		1006
Cassells, Cpl. H.	990	Chant, Pte. S. C.		70
Cassidy, By.S.M. C.	975	Chaplin, Sjt. C.		990
— Cpl.(A./C.S.M.) H.	1016	— C.S.M. H. G.		977
Castell, Sjt. A. J.	1017	Chapman, Sjt. A., *MM.*		997

* R. Irish Rif. attach. Gold Coast Regt. for East Africa.
† Pair known in Moss collection: British War Medal (Serial number 1, W.O.1 Rifle Brigade) and M.S.M. (200001 18 Garr. Battn. R.B.) shown as valuable service in the War in the *London Gazette,* but 18th Garrison Battn. R.B. served from 1916–1919 in Burma, so it is likely the award is for this theatre. In 1915 the Rifle Brigade who had no Territorials Battalion had seven former National Reserve (Garrison) Battalions attached, being the 18th to 24th. The 18th (London) Battn. came into being on 11 November 1915, formed from various Territorial units around the Capital. R.S.M. Casey, the senior W.O. was No. 1. They sailed for India in *'Miltiades'* and *'Ballarat'* on 26 November, 1,000 all ranks and then were sent to Rangoon on 2 January 1916, were they served out the war. They had a detachment guarding convicts on Andaman Islands, provided escorts to Basra (and these only qualified for both British War and Victory Medals) and some were employed on mine-sweepers offshore from Bombay. In November 1919 they sailed for home in the *'Herefordshire'* and were immediately dispersed.
‡ R.A.F. M.S.M. for Egypt, No. 280 Australian Flying Corps.

Chapman, C.Q.M.Sjt. C. B.	1005	Christian, S./Sjt.(A./		
— C.Q.M.S. C. H.	2699	Sub Condr.) R. E.		2701
— Sjt. J.	999	Christie, S./Sjt. (A./S.M.) J.		1012
— Pte.(A./Sjt.) J. E.	80	— C.S.M. J. A.		70
— F. of W.S.M. W.	977	— Pte. R. M.		1017
Chappell, T./S.M. J. F.	977	— Pte.(A./Cpl.) W. H.		998
Chapple, B.S.M. W. J.	2690	Christison, Sjt. D.		3840
Charbonneau, Sjt. M.	1017	Chubb, Sjt.(T./S./S.M.) T.		1006
Chard, C.S.M.(A./S.M.) T.	987	Church, Sjt.(T./S./S.M.) C.		1006
Charles, Sjt. F.	995	Churchill, Sjt.(A./S./Sjt.) H. D.		2700
Charlesworth, Sjt. J. R.	2700	Chuter, Cpl.(A./Q.M.S.) L.		2998
Charlton, Sjt. W. R.	99	Ciark, T./S.S.M. J.		2698
Charman, Sjt. F.	986	Clamp, Sjt. H.		1487
— Pte. F. W.	1013	Clancy, Q.M.Sjt.(A./Supt.Clk.) P. J.		996
Charnock, Ftr.Sjt. A. E., *M.M.*	970	Clapton, Sjt. R. J.		1017
Charter, Cpl. C. W.	1945	Clark, S./S.M. A. C.	‡	2701
Chatto, Sjt. R. H. S.	1021	— Pte. C. E.		1010
Cheater, Sjt.(A./S./Sjt.) H. C.	* 2700	— Pte. E.		1010
Chedd, Ch.Mech. R. J.	99	— Pte. E. S.		994
Cheesman, Cpl.(A./Sjt.) E.	1012	— Sjt. F. A.		2699
Cheesmore, Dvr. T.	68	— Sjt. G.		994
Cheeswright, Pte.(A./L./Sjt.) F. V.	996	— Dvr. G.		1010
Cheney, C.Q.M.S.(A./C.S.M.) A.	988	— Cpl.(A./Sjt.) G. S.		1008
Chenier, Sjt. A.	1017	— Bmdr. H.		977
Cherry, Pte. H. D. E.	1001	— T./Sub Condr. H. W.		1013
— Sjt. H. J.	1006	— Q.M.Sjt. J.		991
— Sjt. J. T.	997	— T./Sjt. J. W.		3000
Cheshire, C.S.M. B.	1004	— Sjt. P. J.		984
— Sjt. R.	972	— Sjt. R.		979
Chester, Sjt. F.	979	— S.Q.M.Sjt.(T./Sub Condr.) S. C.		1014
— 2nd Cl. Mt.Gnr. J. A.	2691	— Q.M.S. T. G.		1023
Cheverton, Farr.Q.M.S. W.	2690	— Pte.(A./Cpl.) W. A. N.		997
Chicken, CQ.M.Sjt. R. H.	985	— B.S.M. W. H.		2691
Child, C.Q.M.Sjt. F.J.	999	Clarke, Sjt. Clerk A.		2050
Childs, Dvr. T. K.	974	— Ship's Cpl.1st Cl. A.		2360
Chinnery, C.S.M. W. G.	998	— Pte.(L./C.) A.		995
Chisholm, T./Sub Condr. W. A.	1013	— Spr.(A./2nd Cpl.) A. B.		2998
Chittenden, Cpl. A.	990	— Pte.(A./S./Sjt.) A. C. H.		1014
Chivers, Sjt. H.	1021	— Cpl. A. E.		1017
Chiverton, Sjt. R. J.	1006	— C.S.M. C.		1017
Choules, Sjt. C. T.	997	— Sjt. F. H.		1017
Christensen, By.S.M. H. F.	1021	— Q.M.Sjt. G.		987
Christer, T./S.M. A. E.	† 2693	— Sjt. H.		976

---

* R.A.M.C., for Gibraltar.

† M.S.M. Annuity awarded A.O.92 September, 1948. Royal Fusiliers.

‡ Group known: M.B.E. (1st type, military, *L.G.* 3 June 1930, W.O.1 R.A.P.C.), Queen's South Africa Medal (Cape Colony, 816 Sgt. A.P.C.), L.S. & G.C. (Geo. V, A./S.S.Mjr.) and M.S.M. Alfred Charles Clark was born 3 May, 1876, in the ranks 20 years 361 days, W.O.1 one year 265 days. S.S.M. 7 January 1917.

Clarke, Pte.(A./Cpl.) H. S.	2998	Clowes, Sjt. R.		991
— Sjt. J. H.	1006	Clubb, Q.M.Sjt. J.		996
— S./Sjt. L. H.	1012	— Sjt. J. A., *M.M.*		1006
— Sjt. L. J.	972	Clunne, Q.M.S. G J.		1021
— Pte.(L./C.) N. W. B.	995	Clutterbuck, S.M. E.		2690
— Spr. (A./L./C.) P.	983	Clymo, Q.M.Sjt. E. H.		1002
— Q.M.Sjt.(T./S.M.) R.	61	Coates, Sjt. B. C.		979
— R.Q.M.S.,W.O.Cl.2, R. D.	1017	— Cpl. E. G.		991
— Pte.(L./C.) T.	992	— Cpl. H. B.		1003
— Sjt. W. H.	996	— S./Sjt. H. G.		3000
Clarkson, Cpl.(A./Sjt.) J.	1012	— Sjt.(A./C.S.M.) W.		1490
— Sjt. V. J.	2699	Coatesworth, Pte.(A./L./C.) J. F.		1010
Claxton, Cpl. E.	99	Cobb, S./S.M. J. R., *D.C.M.*	*	2689
— Sjt. J.	972	— Sjt.(A./S.Q.M.Sjt.) W. H.		1006
Clay, C.S.M. J. W. W.	998	Cochrane, Pte.(L./C.) C. T.		1017
Clayden, Cpl. W. J.	1012	Cockayne, Pte.(A./C.Q.M.S.) W.		1010
Clayton, 2nd Cpl. C. J.	962	Cockburn, Sjt. A.		979
— Sjt. J. R.	1489	— Cpl.(A./Sjt.) D. W.		61
— S.Q.M.S.(A./S.S.M.) R., *D.C.M.*	1489	Cocker, Sjt.(A./C.S.M.) E. A.		979
— Pte.(A./Cpl.) S. H.	1001	— Pte. E. J.	†	994
Claytor, C.Q.M.S. G.	69	Cockerton, Pte. (L./C.) H. R.		1001
Clear, Pte.(A./L./C.) D.	1016	Cockings, By.S.M. E. G.		975
Cleary, Sjt. G. E. K.	1006	Cockram, Sjt. W. W., *M.M.*		987
— 2nd Cpl.(A./Cpl.) T.	60	Cocks, Schmaster P. H.	‡	2701
Cleere, Ch.Mas.Mech. E. E.	99	Coffen, Sjt. H. H.		1021
Clegg, Cpl. C.	1008	Coggles, B.S.M. A. W.		60
— Q.M.S. J.	2698	Cogliolo, Sjt. R.		992
— S./Sjt. J. S.	1006	Coker, Sjt. W. A.		1017
Clem, Q.M.S. F.	985	Coldwell, T./S.M.(A.C.) A.		975
Clemens, Gnr. F. B.	977	Cole, S.M. A. B.		2692
Clemenson, Pte. W. E.	1010	— Sjt. C. A.		1002
Clements, C.S.M.(T./S.M.) A.	2694	— S./S.M. E.		2698
Clench, Pte. C. H.	986	— S./Sjt.(A./S.Q.M.S.) F.		61
Cleverley, Gnr.(A./Ftr.S./S.Sjt.) A. J.	977	— Sto.P.O. J. C.	§	3861
Clifford, Spr.(A./2nd Cpl.) C.	2692	— 2nd Cpl. W. J.		982
Clinch, Pte.(A./Cpl.) H.	998	Coleman, Cpl. G. J.		975
Clisby, Sjt. T. H.	2699	— CS.M. H.		1488
Clive, Sjt. J.	976	— W.O. H. F.		2702
Clough, Cpl.(A./C.S.M.Instr.) B.	2701	— Sjt. S. H.		1002
— Pte.(A./C.S.M.) T.	71	— C.S.M. W., *M.M.*		69
— Pte.(A./Cpl.) W. H.	935	— Pte.(A./Sjt.) W. F.		1015

---

*   Group known: D.C.M. (Edw. VII, 4010 Sgt. 7 D G, *L.G.* 15 November 1901 and 31 October, 1902, for Driekloor 20 May 1901), Queen's South Africa Medal (Cape Colony, Orange Free State, Johannesberg, Diamond Hill, Belfast, Sgt.), King's South Africa Medal (Sgt. Maj.), L.S. & G.C. (Geo. V, S.S.M.) and M.S.M. (also 7 Dragoon Guards).

†   1/K.R.R.C. Entitled to Queen's South Africa Medal.

‡   For Bermuda (Corps of Army Schoolmasters).

§   Group known: 1914/15 Star trio, R.V.M. (silver), R.N. L.S. & G.C. (Edw. VII, H.M.Y. *Victoria & Albert*) and R.N. M.S.M. (*Lupin*, Mediterranean 1918).

Coles, S./S.M. A.	2701	Comoy, Pte.(A./C.S.M.) A. H.		986
— C.S.M.(T./S./S.M.) J.	2699	Condon, Sjt. J.		997
— C.Q.M.S. P. H.	994	Conibear, Col.Sjt.(A./S.M.) J. H.	*	2695
— Spr.(A./Sjt.) S.	2692	Conlon, S./Sjt. T.		2702
— C.Q.M.S. W.	999	Connell, Pte.(A./Sjt.) M.		1015
— Mech.S./S. W. E.	1005	Connor, Pte. M. W.		2998
Coley, Pte.(A./Sjt.) W. T.	2696	Connors, S./Sjt. W.		1017
Collard, C.S.M. C. T. A.	1946	Conor, S./S.M. C. W.		2701
Colledge, Sjt. A.	1006	Conran-Smith, Pte. L. N.		1017
— Cpl.Mech.(Eng.) A. M.	99	Conway, Pte.(A./Sjt.) A.		1013
Collett, Cpl. E.	2998	— Pte.(L/C.) E. W.		1016
— C.F.R.A. 1st Cl. F.	3691	Cooch, R.S.M. A. G.		1017
Colley, Sjt. H.	1003	Coogan, Cpl. C. D. R.		1000
— C.Q.M.S. W. J.	1002	Cook, Engmn. A.		3863
Collier, Ch.Sto. J. M.	3860	— Sjt. A. C.		1006
— Cpl. R.	1008	— C.S.M. A. S.		70
— Pte(A./Cbl.) V. E.	1001	— Sjt.(A./C.S.M.) A. T.		2699
Collinge, Q.M.S. W. R.	990	— Cpl. C.		994
Collings, Sjt. S.	2999	— Sjt. E. H.		1017
— S.M. T. M.	997	— Sjt. F.		2999
Collingwood, CE.R.A. 2nd Cl. R. E.	3591	— Pte.(A./Sjt.) G.		1015
Collins, W.O. A. B.	2702	— Cpl.(A./Sjt.) H.		1012
— Mech.S./Sjt. E. J.	1005	— Pte.(L./C.) H.		1016
— L./Sjt.(A./Sjt.) F. C.	2689	— Dvr. H. P.		1021
— Cpl. H.	973	— Eng.Clk.Cpl. J.	†	981
— Pte.(A./Cpl.) H. G.	1001	— Sjt. J. T.		1006
— Sjt.(A./C.Q.M.S.) J.	979	— T/S.M. P. F.		2700
— Pte.(L./C.) M. S.	1017	— S./S.M. S.		1017
Collinson, Sjt. H. J.	1006	— Eng.Clk. 2nd Cpl.(A./E.C.Sjt.) S. G.		981
Colloney, Sjt. T.	1489	Cooke, Sjt. H. A., *M.M.*		1021
Colpitts, Pte.(A./Cpl.) J.	1010	— Q.M.S. H. M.		989
Colquhoun, Sjt.(K.O.S.B.)	990	— Sjt. W.		69
Coltham, C.S.M.(A./S.M.) W. E.	2997	Coomber, Dvr.(A./Cpl.) G. J.		1010
Coltman, Sjt.(A./C.) J	976	— S./S.M. J.		2698
Colver, C.S.M.(A./S.M.) G. W.	2696	Coombes, Spr. F.		68
Colville, S./S.M. D.	2698	— Armt.Q.M.Sjt.(T./Arm.S.M.) P. H.		1014
Colvin, W.O. Cl. 2, R. A.	2697	— Supt.Clk. W. J.		2690
Comaskey, Armr.S./Sjt. D. W.	2999	Cooper, Sjt. A.		979
Combe, Cpl. J. T.	1008	— C.S.M. A. A.		1004
Comerford, C.S.M. P.	998	— Sdlr.S./Sjt. A. C.		971
Commins, By.S.M. A. J.	975	— Farr.Q.M.S. A. E.		2997
Commons, Sjt. T. F.	1023	— S./Sjt. A. E.		2702

---

* For Bermuda (K.O.S.B.).

† Group known: 1914/15 trio, 1939/45 and Burma Stars, Defence and War Medals, and M.S.M. Recommended 22 September 1918 'For continuous good work and devotion to duty from February to September 1918. This N.C.O. has always shown great initiative and tact, and his work has been of the utmost value. He served at Arras from March to April 1918 and on the Somme in August and September, 1918. (R.E.)

Cooper, Mech. E. A. G.	1945	Cousins, Gnr. A.	974
— Sjt. Mech. F. R. J.	* 99	— C.Q.M.S.(A./S.S.M.) A. E.	2699
— W./S./Sjt. H., *D.C.M.*	971	Coussins, Q.M.Sjt. H. W.	2691
— Pte. H.	1010	Coutts, Farr.S./Sjt. J.	1017
— S./Sjt.Maj. H. J.	61	Cowan, C.Q.M.Sjt. G. C.	978
— Sjt. K. A.	62	Coward, Spr.(A./C.Q.M.S.) G.	2692
— Pte.(A./S./Sjt.) R. D.	1945	— Pte. H. B.	990
— S./Sjt. R. W.	1021	Cowderoy, Pte.(A./L./C.) F.	1001
— Q.M.Sjt. S.	1011	Cowe, Sjt. D. W.	1489
— Clr.Sjt. W. C.	2695	Cowgill, Cpl. F.	973
— C.S.M. W G. M.	1017	Cowie, Cpl.Mech. W.	99
— Pte.(A./Sjt.) W. M.	1490	— Pte.(A./Sjt.) W. H.	62
Copland, Cpl.(A./Sjt.) A. M.	973	Cowley, Cpl. C. A.	1000
Copleston, Sjt. S.	1006	Cowper, Sjt. C. E.	62
Copping, Pte.(L./C.) C	1010	Cox, S.M. A.	2690
— C.S.M. G. A.	1004	— Mech.S./Sjt. B.	1005
— C.S.M.(A./R.S.M.) H.	61	— Pte.(A./Sjt.) F.	1016
Coppinger, Cpl.(A./C.Q.M.S.) C.	988	— Pte. G. H.	70
Copplestone, Ch.Mas.Mech. A. J.	99	— Pte. G. W.	1010
Corbett, C.S.M. E. A.	989	— Pte.(A./Sjt.) H.	3840
— C.Q.M.S. H. G.	1021	— Bmdr. H. D.	977
Cordery, CQ.M.Sjt. C. H.	999	— F. of W. Q.M.S. H. T.	† 2692
Cordwell, Cpl.(A./Sq.S.M.) C.	1008	— Sjt.(A./C.S.M.) J.	2701
Core, C.Q.M.S.(A./C.S.M.) T. M.	2697	— Q.M.Sjt. J. E.	989
Corke, W.O. Cl. 1, Supt.Clk. W.	3572	— Pte. J. W.	1001
Corkindale, Dvr. J.	974	— C.Q.M.Sjt. S. W. J.	987
Cormican, Cpl.(A./Sjt.) J.	1008	— S./Sjt.(A./S.M.) W.	62
Corner, Sjt.(A./By.S.M.) W.	972	— C.Q.M.Sjt. W. C.	1002
Cornish, Sjt. A. H.	1021	— Cpl. W. H.	981
Corps, Spr.(A./C.S.M.) T.	2998	— Sjt. W. T.	972
— C.S.M. W.	2692	Coxon, Pte.(A./Cpl.) J.	‡ 1016
Costar, S./Sjt. J. H.	62	Coyle, R.Q.M.S. H.	1017
Cote, Cpl. F A.	1017	Crabbe, Sjt. J.	1017
Cottam, Pte. S.	1001	Cracknell, 1st Cl.Mt.Gnr. J. J.	2691
Cotterell, Farr. Cpl. A. S.	973	— Col.Sjt. L. T.	2694
Cotton, Sjt.(A./S./Sjt.) F. E.	2700	Craddock, C.S.M. C. C.	977
— T./S.M. T., *D.C.M.*	975	Craft, Sjt. J.	99
Cottrell, By.S.M. C. D.	1021	Crafter, Mech.S./Sjt. A. A.	1005
Couldrey, Sjt. G.	1003	Cragg, Q.M.Sjt. H. B.	1011
Coulter, C.Q.M.S.(A./Q.M.S.) H. E.	1017	Craig, Pte.(A./L./C.) A.	1016
Counsell, Sjt. J. C	1945	— Cpl. A. C.	70
Courtenay, Pte.(A./Sjt.) J.	2701	— S./S.M. G.	2698
Cousal, 2nd Cpl.(A./Cpl.) C.	982	Crampton, S./Sjt. J.	2999
Cousins, S.Q.M.S. A.	1489	Crane, 2nd Cpl.(A./Sjt.) G. A.	982
— Cpl. A.	3840	Cranston, Cpl. W.	1008

* No. 651 R.F.C. Enlisted June 1906 into 3/Coldstream Guards. As 1A.M. earned 1914 Star with the Aircraft Park in France. R.A.F. M.S.M. for France. Entitled to India General Service Medal (Waziristan 1925) and R.A.F. L.S. & G.C.
† R.E. For China.
‡ See award of bar 20 October, 1919.

Craske, Pte. L.	2695	Cross, S.M. H.	3841
Craven, Ch.-Elect.Art.		— Sjt. H.	1017
2nd Cl., C. F	* 3863	Crossley, Sjt. W	990
— Pte.(L./C.) G. H.	1021	Crouch, L./Bombr. A. A.	68
— Dvr.(A./C.) W.	1010	— C.Q.M.Sjt. C. A.	997
Crawford, S./Sjt.(A./Condr.) J.	1014	— 2nd Cl.Mstr. Gnr. E. A.	2691
— C.S.M. J.	1021	— Sjt. Mech. J. H.	99
— Cpl. S.	1021	Croucher, Pte.(A./Sjt.) A. T. W.	1001
Crawley, Cpl. A. G.	1488	Croughton, Sqdn.Q.M.S. G. J.	2701
— By.S.M. A. H.	975	Crow, Sjt.(A./S./Sjt.) W. R.	2701
— C.Q.M.S.(A./S.M.) H. E.	† 2696	Crowhurst, Cpl. F. C.	998
Creamer, C.Q.M.Sjt. H. J.	991	— Pte.(A./S./Sjt.) G. H.	§ 1490
Creek, Flt.Clk. J.	99	Crowther, C.S.M. W. A.	998
Cremins, Col.Sjt. O.R.S. G. W.	‡ 996	Croxford, C.Q.M.Sjt. E. A. B.	1002
Creswick, C.S.M. F.	1017	Cruchley, R.S.M. A. C., *M.M.*	1017
Crewys, T./S.M. E.	2693	Cruddace, Ch.Mech. A.	99
Crichton, S./Sjt. T.	1021	Cruft, Cpl. J. G.	976
Crickmore, Sjt. R.	972	Cuickshank, Sjt.(A./S./Sjt.) C. S.	1002
Cripps, Spr.(A./Sjt.) T.	60	— C.Q.M.S. P.	1024
Crisford, Sjt. G. T.	1017	Crump, Sjt. W.	979
Crisp, Sjt.Dmr. F. W., *M.M.*	69	Cruttenden, Q.M.Sjt. J.	1002
— Cpl.(L./Sjt.) G. E.	1008	Cuckson, Q.M.Sjt. T. M.	998
— By.S.M. S. W.	971	Cue, Cpl. W.	1021
Critchard, Cpl. J.	981	Cuenod, Gr.(A./S./Sjt.) A. B.	1017
Critchett, Pte. H. D.	1017	Cugley, C.Q.M.S. J. F.	1021
Critchley, C.S.M. G. F.	70	Culley, Pte.(A./Cpl.) B. A.	1010
Croasdell, Pte.(A./Q.M.Sjt.) W. H.	71	— Spr.(L./C A./Cpl.) G. T.	983
Crocker, Farr.Sjt. J. W.	1017	Culshaw, C.S.M. F. G.	993
Croft, C.S.M. F.	2702	Cumming, Q.M.Sjt. T., *D.C.M.*	996
— Sjt.(A./Mech.S./Sjt.) R. A.	2699	— Sjt. W. S.	996
Crofts, 2nd Cpl.(A./S./Sjt.) W. A. J.	1014	Cummings, Mech.S.M. J. A.	2698
Crombie, Sdr.S./Sjt. J.	971	Cuneo, Q.M.Sjt. G. M.	62
Crompton, Ftr.Gnr. S.	977	Cunliffe, S.S.M. F	1003
Cronk, C.S.M. G.	2694	Cunningham, Spr. F. J.	983
— C.Q.M.S.(A./Q.M.S.) S., *M.M.*	2696	— C.E.R.A. 2nd Cl. H.	3861
Crook, Cpl.(A./W.O. Cl.2,		— Pte. J.	1021
S.Q.M.Sjt.) R.	3572	— B.Q.M.Sjt. R.	60
— Sjt. T. W.	1023	— C.S.M. W.	1488
— Mech.S./Sjt. W.	1005	Cunnington, Cpl. J.	973
Crooks, Sjt. J.	990	Cupit, S.M. V. G.	992

* Group known: 1914/15 Star trio, R.N. L.S. & G.C. (Geo. V), R.N. M.S.M. (H.M.S. *Gibraltar*, Northern Patrol 1918) and Messina Earthquake Medal.

† Group in Loyal North Lancashire Regt. Museum: 1914/15 Star trio, Defence and War Medals, Jubilee 1935, Coronation 1937, L.S. & G.C. (Geo. V) and M.S.M. Later Major, L. North Lancs. Regt.

‡ Group known: Queen's South Africa Medal (Cape Colony, Transvaal, Wittebergen, Pte. Leinsters), 1914 Star and bar (Sgt.), British War and Victory Medals (C./Sgt.), L.S. & G.C. (Geo. V, C./Sgt. Leinsters) and M.S.M. (Leinsters—only 23 to the Regiment).

§ M.S.M. known: T./2348 M.P.S.C. Unique to the Corps for Salonika.

Curell, Sjt.(A./S.S.M.) C. P.	2699	Darling, Sjt. A.		993
Curley, Sjt.(W. D. W.	1006	— T./S.S.M. H.		61
Currier, Ft.S./Sjt. H.	1487	— Sjt. (T./M./S.M.) J. F.		70
— Sjt. J. A.	1017	Darmon, Sig.Sjt. R. J		987
Curry, S.M. G. D.	2700	Darrell, Sjt.(A./C.S.M.Instr.) R.		2701
Curties, L./C. F. A.	1021	— 2nd Cpl.(A./Sjt.) W. T.		982
Curtis, Cpl. A. W	3840	Dartnall, Cpl.(A./Sjt.) H. T.		1012
— Dkhnd. F. O.	2360	Daville, Sjt A. E.		999
— S./S.M. G. W.	* 2698	Dashwood, Cpl.Mech. J. E.		99
— C.Q.M.Sjt. P. L.	984	— Farr.S./Sjt. J. H.		970
— Sjt. S. B.	998	Dath, Pte. O. D.		1017
— Sdlr.S./Sjt. S. E.	1017	Davall, Pte. A. A.		1010
Curwen, Bmdr.(A.C.) S.	977	Davenport, Q.M.Sjt. J. H.		60
— C.Q.M.S. W. G.	1021	Davey, C.Q.M.S. (A./		
Cusick, Ldg.Sea. J. A. T.	2361	Mech.S.M.) A A.		1489
Cusworth, Pte.(L./Cpl.) C. T.	985	— Sjt. Mech. E. H.		99
— Pte. J. S.	1010	— C.S.M. F. H.		1004
Cutler, Pte.(A./S./Sjt.) H.	2699	— Ch.Mech. R. J. J.		99
— Pte.(A./Sjt.) J.	1015	— T./S.M. S. J.		2690
Cuttle, Pte.(A./Sjt.) G. S.	1017	— S.M. T.		1490
		— Sjt. W. G.		1021
Daffern, Sjt. A.	1006	David, Sjt. I. M.		1012
Dailey, Sjt.Clk. G. W.	99	Davidson, S./S.M. C		1003
Dakin, Sjt. F. E.	1021	— C.S.M. C. W		1017
— Corr of name	4136	— Cpl. J. T. A.		981
— Sjt. G.	996	— W.O. R.		2702
Dale, Sjt. G.	979	Davies, Sigr. Cpl. A.		973
— Sjt. J.	1945	— Sjt. A. C.		997
Dales, Mech.S./Sjt. G.	1489	— Pte. A. L.		1010
Daley, Sjt. J.	999	— Ch.Mas.Mech. D.		99
— Cpl. J. O	1017	— Sjt. E. (R.W. Fus. T.F.)		989
— By.S.M. P. T	971	— Sjt. E. (O.B.L.I.)		2998
Dallaston, Cpl. W. R.	3840	— S.M.Instr. E. J.		60
Dallimore, Sjt. J. E.	976	— Engmn. F.		3861
Dalling, Sjt.(A./S./Sjt.) W. E.	2999	— Cpl. (A./Sjt.) F. W.		981
Daly, Sjt. E. J.	1021	— C.S.M. G. H.		1489
— S.M. J.	2697	— Farr.S./Sjt. H. G.		1005
Danby, Q.M.Sjt. S. H.	69	— Cpl. H. M.		1023
Dando, Sjt.(A./C.Q.M.S.) F. J.	60	— T/S.M. J.		990
Dangar, Col.Sjt.(O.R.Sjt.) H. C.	984	— Pte. J. O.		70
Daniels, Sjt. J. L.	986	— Cpl. J. W.		1488
— Pte. (A./Sjt.) S W.	71	— Q.M.Sjt. L. T.		1002
— Cpl.(A.S./Sjt.) W. J.	1008	— C.Q.M.Sjt. M. H.		1002
Darby, C.S.M. A.	995	— Sjt. (A./C.Q.M.Sjt.) P. M.		60
Dare, T./S.M. P.	997	— S.M. T.	†	1011
Dargan, S./SM. W. L., *D.C.M.*	1003	— Pte. T.		1001
Darleson, Sjt. A. R.	979	— Cpl.(A./Sjt.) T. M.		981

* A.S.C. For Malta. Medal presented by F.M. Lord Plumer, Governor of Malta, 6 April 1920.
† Later awarded Military Cross (S.M. R.W.Fus., *L.G.* 14.1.16).

Dickens, Pte. J. D.	1010	Doe, S.M. C. W.		2690
Dickenson, Ch.Mech. G.	* 99	— Pte. J. W. R.		1001
Dickinson, Mech.S./Sjt. A.	1005	— Q.M.Sjt. P., *M.M.*		987
— Pte. A.	1013	— S./Sjt. W. R.		80
— Cpl. R.	988	Doery, Dvr. E. B.		1021
Dickson, Sjt. E. L.	979	Doggett, F. of W. S.M. F. H.		2692
— Pte.(L./C.) J. G.	996	Doherty, Sjt. A.		1006
— Cpl. P. M.	973	— C.Q.M.S. J. E.		1021
Dillon, Farr. Cpl. G.	1021	Dolahenty, Cpl. J. V.		1021
— Corr.	4136	Dolan, Sjt. J. T.		1946
— Cpl. M. V.	1021	— Pte.(A./Cpl.) M.		989
Dines, C.S.M. (T./S.M.) A. H.	70	Dolley, Pte.(T./Sub Condr.) L. W.		1014
Dingle, Sjt. C.	1017	Doman, Pte. H. J.		2998
Dinmore, Pnr. J.	983	Dominy, Sjt. J. H.		1017
Dinning, Ord.Sea. J.	3592	Donagan, S.Q.M.S. B. B.		1021
Disbrey, Sjt. W. T.	1012	Donald, Q.M.S. A. W. S.		2699
Divall, B.S.M.(A./S.M.) W. H.	2997	— Sjt. (T./R.S.M.) J., *M.M.*		979
Dix, Mech.S./Sjt. C. N.	1489	— Sjt. T. A.		972
— Sjt. G. F. A.	60	Donaldson, Sjt. W.		68
— Cpl. G. L.	1017	Donnelly, Sjt. J.		996
Dixon, S.M. H., R.A.M.C.	61	— S.M. T.		1011
— S.M. H. (Y.L.I.)	2696	— C.S.M. W. A.		1004
— Sjt. H.	1489	Donnison, S./Sjt. H.		1017
— S.M. R. H.	2692	Donoghue, Dvr.(A./C.S.M.) S.	†	61
— C.P.O. W.	3861	Doody, C.Q.M.S. C. L.		2699
— Sjt. W. D.	979	Dooley, Sjt. H. H.		996
Dobinson, Sjt. C. R.	986	— Sjt. J. M.		1021
Dobson, C.S.M. C. (M.G.C.)	1489	— Sjt. W.		999
— C.S.M. C. (R.D.C.)	2698	— Sjt. W. J. B.		1488
— Sjt. C.	976	Dore, Sjt. F.	‡	994
— Sjt. C. E.	2702	Dorman, Sjt. J.		984
— Amt.S./Sjt. H.	2999	Dorning, Mech.Cpl. A. E. C.		1945
— By.Q.M.Sjt. H. T.	1017	Dorrington, Q.M.Sjt. F. C.		994
— Sjt. L. S.	1017	Double, C.Q.M.Sjt. W.		992
— Cpl. W. F.	1012	Douglas, Cpl. A., *D.C.M.*		976
Dockerill, Sjt. H.	987	— Pte.(A./S./Sjt.) H. H.		2702
Dodd, Pte.(A./C.Q.M.S.) E. V.	2698	— Sjt. P.		70
Dodds, Sjt. A. E.	1021	Douglass, Sjt. Dmr. A.		984
— S./Sjt. G. C. C.	1017	— S.M. W. J.		2695
— T./Cub Condr. W. P.	1490	Dovey, Sjt.(A./C.Q.M.Sjt.) R. A.		994
Dodge, By.S.M. A. A.	975	Dow, C.Q.M.Sjt. F. W.		986
Dodson, C.S.M. W. J.	1004	Dowdall, Pte.(A./Cpl.) W. E.		1014
Dodsworth, Sjt.(A./S./Sjt.) A. W.	1489	Dowell, Farr.Sjt. W. L.		1017

* R.A.F. M.S.M. No. 4769 R.F.C. Died in service 6 July 1946 as Flight Sergeant R.A.F. His son was K.I.A. as Sgt. 605 Sqn. R.A.F. on 1 July 1944.
† Group formerly in McInnes collection: 1914/15 Star (1283 Pte. Manchester Regt.), British War and Victory Medals (1283 W.O.II Manchester R.), M.S.M. (T./422642 2nd Donkey Transport Coy. R.A.S.C.), Territorial Force Efficiency Medal (Geo. V, T422642 C.S.Mjr. R.A.S.C.). From Ashton under Lyne.
‡ 2/K.R.R.C. Entitled to Queen's South Africa Medal and King's South Africa Medal.

Down, C.Q.M.S.(A./3rd Cl. Master Gnr) J. W.	* 🌸	1256
Downes, Sjt. R.		986
Downham, Sjt.Mech. H.		99
Downie, C.S.M. J.		2691
— T./S.M. J.		984
Downs, Sjt.Clk. G		2050
Dowse, Sjt. E., *MM*.		985
Dowsett, S./S.M. A. W.		2701
Dowson, C.S.M.(A./R.S.M.) H.		1017
Doxey, C.P.O. F.		3591
Doyle, Cpl. H.		68
Drake, Sjt.(A./Q.M.S.) A.		2692
— W.O. Cl. 1, J. L.		1021
— Sjt. R., *MM*.		991
— Sjt.(T./S.S.M.) T. W.		2699
Drakeford, Farr.Sjt. C. C		972
Dransfield, Pte.(A./Cpl.) L.		995
Draper, S.M. C.		2696
— Sub Condr. F. H.		2701
Drayton, Cpl. W. R.		3840
Dresser, T./S.M. W.		998
Drew, Sjt. J. H.		1017
Drinnan, Cpl. A. W.		1017
Driscoll, C.P.O. P		2360
Driver, Gnr.(L./Bmdr) F.		974
— T./S./S.M. G.		1489
— Sjt. T. W.		1489
— L./Cpl.(T./Sub Condr.) T. W.		71
Drummond, Pte.(A./ Q.M.Sjt.) A. G.		995
Dubberley, Cpl. H. A.		99
Dubbin, Cpl.(L./Sjt.) J.		2695
Duckworth, S./Sjt. E. E.		969
Dudding, S./S.Cpl. Carr. Smith J.		981
Dudeney, Sjt.(A./C.S.M.) E.		1016
Dudney, Mech.S.M. A. H.		1003
Duffus, Pte. W.		1001
Duggan, Sjt.(A./S.M.) J. G.		990
Duke, Cpl.(A./S.M.)(A./C.) F.		1488
— Q.M.S. H.		1017
— Cpl.(A./Q.M.Sjt.) H.		1012
— S.M. J.		989
Dulborough, Pte.(L./C) E. J.		1016
Dumbleton, Sjt. C. H.		1002

Duncan, Sjt. H.		1490
— Sjt. J.		2697
— 1st Cl.Mst.Gnr. J. L.		2691
Duncanson, Sjt. J.		992
Dunford, Clr.Sjt.(A./ Q.M.S.) H. H.		2695
Dungate, Pte. C. J. A.		994
Dunk, Ch.Mech. J. W.	†	99
— C.S.M. W.		999
Dunkason, S.M. S.		2696
Dunkley, Sjt. F.		993
Dunley, Sjt. J. L.		996
Dunlop, S.M. W. D.		986
Dunmall, C.S.M.(T./S./S.M.) R.		61
Dunn, Cpl.A., *MM*.		986
— Sjt. E.		2701
— C.E.R.A. 1st Cl. E.		3860
— Sjt. G. W. H.		985
— A.M.1 h.		99
— Q.M.Sjt. L. A. H., *MM*.		992
Dunachie, Sjt. W. C.		972
Dunnett, S./Sjt. D.		1017
Dunstan, Sjt.(T./B.Q.M.S.) E.		2702
Dunster, F./Sjt. A. E.		99
Durling, Sjt. A. W.		1489
Durrant, S./Sjt.(A./S.Q.M.Sjt.) H.		1006
— S.M.Supt.Clk. J. W.		2690
Durston, Pte.(L./C.) H. L.		1016
Dutson, C.S.M. F. E.		1004
Dutton, Clr.Sjt.(A./W.O.Cl.1 S./S.M.) A.		3572
— Sjt.Clk. F. W.		99
Dwyer, Sjt. C.		989
— S./Sjt. E. W.		2702
Dyer, C.Q.M.Sjt. A. H.		69
— Bomdr.(A.C.) A. M.		977
— Ch.Sto. G.		2360
— Pte.(A./S.M.) G. H.		1010
— Sjt. J.		1017
— Cpl. J.		990
— C.Q.M.S. R.		2998
Dyett, Q.M.Sjt. W. J.		999
Dymock, Pte. W. A.		1017
Dymond, Cpl.(A./Sjt.) J. G.		987
Dyson, Spr. A.		983

---

* R.G.A. Gallantry in Aden.

† Group known: M.B.E., 1914/15 Star (2144 R.N.A.S.), British War and Victory Medals (202144 F./Sgt. R.A.F.), 39/45 Star Defence and War Medals (Wing Commander), 1935 Jubilee, 1937 Coronation, R.A.F. M.S.M. and R.A.F. L.S. & G.C. (Geo. V, S.M.1) and Bar.

Eadie, C.S.M. J. R.	1017	Edwards, Cpl.(A./Sjt.) W. H.	981
Eadon, Sjt. F. B.	2696	— Cpl. W. H.	1021
Eagle, Sjt. H. B.	1021	Eggett, Gnr. L.	970
— C.S.M. W. T.	2698	Eggleton, B.Q.M.S. J.	2691
Eaglesim, Sjt. A.	996	Egley, S./Sjt.(T./S.Q.M.S.) B.	2702
Earith, Sjt. W. S.	976	Elborough, Pte.(A./Cpl.) J. H.	1010
Earley, Pte.(L./C.) J. A.	70	Elcombe, S.M. W. G.	71
Earll, C.S.M. J.	977	Eldridge, E.R.A. 2nd Cl. W. G. P.	2360
Earnshaw, Q.M.Sjt. J.	989	Eley, Pte. C. E.	993
Easton, Pte.(A./L./C.) A.	1014	Elgar, Dvr. J. R.	974
— R.Q.M.S. W.O. Cl.2, J. D.	1017	Elkington, Cpl.(A./L./Sjt.) H.	1012
Eastwood, Ch.Elect.Art. 2nd Cl. C. B.	3863	Ell, Sjt.(A./C.S.M.) A. W.	1006
Eather, Cpl. V. W.	1023	Elliott, S./S.M. A.	2698
Eaton, Pte. W. H.	1017	— Pte.(A./Sjt.) A. E.	1015
Eatough, Pte. R.	1001	— Pte. F. N.	1003
Ebbrell, C.Q.M.Sjt. J. J.	978	— C.E.R.A. 2nd Cl. G.	2360
Eccles, T./S.M. J.	1488	— Pte.(A./Cpl.) G. A.	991
Eddison, Col.Sjt.(O.R.S.) H.	988	— S./S.M. G. E.	61
Eden, R.Q.M.S. E. G. D.	1023	— Cpl. H.	1017
Edgar, Sjt. T.	994	— Sjt. J. W.	1006
Edmonds, Sjt. F. P. O.	979	— F./Clk. S. C.	99
— Bombr.(A.C.) J. R.	3840	— C.P.O. V.	969
Edmunds, Ch.Mech. E. T.	99	— Sjt. W. J. W.	999
Edwards, Cpl. A.	1008	Ellis, C.S.M. A.	984
— Pte.(L./C.) A.	1017	— Sjt. E.	1487
— Sjt. E.	1006	— Clr.Sjt. G.	2697
— Pte.(L./C.) E.	1001	— C.Q.M.Sjt. H.	997
— C.S.M.(W.O.2nd Cl.) E. E.	2359	— Pte.(L./C.) H.	1001
— Sjt. F. H.	991	— Pte. H.	1001
— Pte.(A./S./Sjt.) G. F.	1015	— B.S.M. S. T.	1487
— Farr.S./Sjt. H.	1005	— Sjt.(A./Q.M.Sjt.) W. †	970
— 1st Cl.Mstr.Gnr. J.	2691	— Gnr. W.	1021
— Dvr.(A./Farr.Sjt.) J.	983	Ellison, C.S.M. R.	994
— W.S./Sjt. J. A.	70	Elphec, Sjt. W. J.	997
— Ftr.Sjt.(A./Ftr.S./Sjt.) R. *	972	Elson, C.S.M. W., *D.C.M.*	985
— Pte.(A./S./Sjt.) R. A.	1010	Elstone, C.S.M.(T./S.M.) E. J.	992
— Cpl. R. B.	1017	Elsworth, Sjt. C.	1006
— Q.M.Sjt.(A./S.M.) R. W.	1490	— Cpl.(A./Sjt.) W.	68
— Cpl.(A./Sjt.) T.	3841	Elwell, Pte. G. W.	71
— P.O. 1st Cl. T. C.	3863	Emberson, B.Q.M.Sjt. P. W.	975
— Ldg.Sig. W. A.	2360	Embleton, S./S.M. A. J.	70

---

* 201132 A./Fitter Staff Sergt., H.Q. 17th Brigade R.F.A. 1916–18 This N.C.O. has been with the H.Q. 17th Brigade R.F.A. since the latter landed in France, and has carried out his duties throughout in a manner which deserves the highest praise. Absolutely fearless and ready to endure any hardship, he has been able by his work and endurance to keep the guns of the brigade in first class order, often under most distressing conditions.

† Awarded M.S.M. Annuity A.O. 92 September, 1948, as Orderly Room Sgt. (Q.M.S.), King's Shropshire L.I.

Emeney, T./R.S.M. W.		971
Emerson, R.S.M. A. L.	*	1023
Emery, Spr.(A./Cpl.) H.		983
— Sjt. M.		985
Emmanuel, S./Sjt. E.		1489
Emmett, Pte.(A./Sjt.) H.		970
Emslie, E.R.A. 3rd Cl. W. N.		2361
Endacott, Pte.(A./Sjt.) F. W.		2699
England, Sjt. A.		1012
— Sjt. J. E.		1021
— Sjt. P. A.	† ✤	1256
— Q.M.Sjt. R. P. H.		992
English, Sjt. S. C.		972
Entwistle, Cpl. T.		1000
— Sjt.(T./S.M.) T. S.		68
Epworth, Sjt. F. W. F.		1012
Erskine, C.Q.M.Sjt. R. C.		1005
Erswell, Condr H. W		62
Ervine, Q.M.Sjt. A. G., *M.M.*		996
Esmonde, S./S.M. J.		2698
Ess, Sjt. F. J.		979
Essam, C.S.M. W.		1002
— C.Q.M.S. W.		988
Estermann, Sjt. H.		1945
Etchells, Sjt. W.		999
Etheridge, Sjt. A. E.		3000
— Pte.(A./L./C.) C.		1010
Eton, Spr.(A./S.M.) A. L.		2692
Evans, W.O. Cl. 2 (S.Q.M.) A. C.		3572
— Cpl.(A./W.C. Cl. 2 S.Q.M.Sjt.) E		3572
— Pte.(A./Sjt.) E.		1015
— Sqdn.Q.M.S. E. T.		2699
— S./Sjt. F. J.		70
— S.M. G. R.		1023
— Cpl. H.		981
— Cpl. H. S.		1008
— Sjt. J.		991
— Cpl. J. A.		1000
— Q.M.Sjt. J. E.		990
— Pte. J. H.		1001
— S./Sjt. J. T.		1018
— Pte.(A./L./C.) J. W. (R.A.S.C.)		71
— Pte.(A./L./C.) J. W. (Mil.Police C.)		1016
— L/C.(A./C.S.M.) M. H.		2701
— Ch.Mech. P. W.		2050
— Sjt. R.		1002
— Sjt. R. K.		1018

Evans, By.S.M. R. N.	971
— Q.M.Sjt. T.	992
— Sjt. T. J.	990
— Ch.Mech. T. W.	99
— Sjt. T. W.	999
— Sjt. W. D.	1024
— Eng.Clk. (2nd Cpl.) W. D.	982
Eveleigh, Sjt. W.	999
Everett, Sjt.(A./S./S.M.) P.	1945
Everitt, Pte.(A/C.Q.M.I.) W. A.	1490
Eversden, Pte. A. J.	1010
Everson, A./Sjt.W.O.Cl.II(	
C.Q.M.S.) C. W.	3572
Everton, Q.M.Sjt. E.	991
Eves, Cpl.(A./Sjt.) J. A.	981
Evis, Pte. E. A.	1003
Ewart, R.Q.M.S. H.	1021
— Corr.	4136
Ewing, C.Q.M.Sjt. D. A.	989
Exton, Sjt. H. J.	1018
Eyles, Supt.Clerk (W.O.Cl.I) J. S.	3572
Fabian, Pte. A. W.	2699
Fage, Cpl.(A./Sjt.) F. J.	981
Fagg, Sjt.(A./W.O. Cl.I) C. G.	3572
Fail, C.Q.M.Sjt. H.	69
Fairbairn, Pte. F.	1023
— Sjt. G. A.	1018
Fairweather, Dvr. F.	1010
Faithorn, S.M. E.	2694
Falconer, Cpl. G.	996
— Q.M.Sjt. J. G.	1489
Fallowfield, Cpl.(A./Condr.) B.	1014
Fallows, C.S.M. H.	999
— Pte. P.	989
Fannon, Sub Condr. J. T.	62
Fairclough, Sjt. F	989
Farley, Cpl. J.	993
Farmer, Pte.(A./Sjt.) A.	1016
— By.S.M. A. W.	975
— Sjt. C. A.	1006
— Pte. E.	2998
Farnden, Cpl. H. A.	993
Farnham, Supt.Clk. S.	2692
Farquharson, S.M. W. T.	986
Farr, S./Sjt.(A./S.S.M.) P. L.	2699

---

* Otago Regt. N.Z.E.F. later as W.O.1 N.Z.P.S. awarded New Zealand M.S.M., 28 October, 1944.
† British West Indies Regt.

Farrant, S.Q.M.Sjt.(T./		Fensome, Sjt. S.		988
Sub Condr.) F. H.	1013	Fenton, Sjt. H.		994
Farrell, C.Q.M.Sjt. J. A.	970	Ferguson, Cpl. A. J.		1009
— C.S.M. W.	991	— S./Sjt. C. H.		1021
Farrer, Farr.Sjt. R. J.	1021	— Ldg.Sea. J.		2360
Farrow, Q.M.Sjt. J. S.	994	— Sjt. L.		979
Farthing, Farr.Sjt. S. S. G.	972	— S./Sjt. R. A.		2702
Faulconbridge, B.S.M. H.	2690	Fernandez, Mr. J. F.	†	2361
Faulding, Sjt. W.	972	Fernie, S.Q.M.S.(A./S.S.M.) P. W.	‡	2701
Faulkner, Q.M.Sjt. G.	1489	Ferris, Clr.Sjt. G.		2694
— Sjt. S. J.	1018	— Pte. G.		1018
Fawcett, Pte.(L./C.) W. E.	993	— Pte.(A./R.Q.M.S.) H.		2702
Ferne, Sjt. C.	976	Fewings, Pte.(L./C.) R.		1016
Featherstone, C.Q.M.Sjt. A. E.	990	Fiddler, Sjt. J.		2699
— Pte.(A./S.M.) J.	2700	Fiddy, Q.M.S. A.	§	2696
— Sjt. W. A.	979	Fido, Sjt.(A./C.S.M.) F.		1015
Featonby, Sjt.(A./Q.M.Sjt.) D.	999	Fiehn, Sjt. H.		1002
Feaver, Far.Q.M.Sjt. G.	2690	Field, Sjt. C W.		990
Feehally, S./Sjt.(A/S.S.M.) J.	* 2701	— Spr. H.		983
Feeny, S.M. C. J.	977	— Sjt. L. G.		1006
Fellows, Sjt. D.	1012	— Spr.(A./C.S.M.) W.		2692
Fender, Sjt. G. E.	972	— Cpl. W. G.		1009
Fenneberg, Sjt. J. H.	987	Fielder, 2nd Cpl.(A./Sjt.) W. H.		982
Fenner, Pte.(L./C.) W. T.	986	Fields, Pte. G.	+	990

* Group known: C.B.E. (2nd type, Colonel and Paymaster) Queen's South Africa Medal (Natal, Belfast), King's South Africa Medal, Jubilee 1935, Coronation 1937, L.S. & G.C. (Geo. V) and M.S.M. (No. 1210 A.P.C.).

† R.N. M.S.M. for service in Nyasaland Volunteer Reserve.

‡ For Jamaica (A.P.C. No. 795).

§ 2/Northants. R. Group known: M.B.E. (2nd type), Queen's South Africa Medal (Transvaal, Orange Free State, Cape Colony), King's South Africa Medal, 1914 Star and bar trio, Jubilee 1935, L.S. & G.C. (Geo. V), M.S.M. and Territorial Force Efficiency Medal (Geo. V).

+ Medals on display in K.O.S.B. Regimental Museum: India General Service Medal (1895) (Relief of Chitral), Queen's South Africa Medal (Cape Colony, Paardeberg, Johannesburg), King's South Africa Medal (1/K.O.S.B.) 1914/15 Star trio and M.S.M. (2/K.O.S.B.), the first three being erased examples. 2/K.O.S.B. fought on the western front throughout 1914–18 except for four months on the Italian Piave front in late 1917. The recommendation for the M.S.M., dated 23 September, 1918, and made by Lt. Col. Furbar Commanding 2nd Battn. K.O.S.B. reads:— 'This man is over 50 years of age and has rendered extraordinary fine work for a considerable period. Especially during active operations he has performed a very valuable and courageous service in charge of ration and ammunition carrying parties, cheerfulness and utter disregard of personal safety have at all times greatly inspired the men with him, and his courage and devotion to duty have been most exemplary and beyond all praise' He was demobilised on 17 February 1919. Born *circa* 1867, he lived most of his civilian life in Doncaster. He had enlisted under age and told how Queen Victoria had once inspected the Battalion and commented that he was too young to be posted to India. He had been discharged prior to W.W.I and re-called for the duration. The M.S.M. was presented on a parade at Pontefract. He died in 1940.

Fields, Pte.(A./Sjt.) W. T.	1015	Floyd, C.S.M. F.	69
Fiford, A.M.1(A./Cpl.Mech.) S. E.	99	Fluck, Sjt. F. J.	70
Fillingham, W.O Cl.I		Foggo, Sjt.(A./S./Sjt.) T. D.	1006
(Supt.Clerk.) J. J.	* 3572	Foley, Sjt.(T./S./S.M.) J.	1006
Fillmore, Gnr.(A./By.		— C.S.M. S.	998
Q.M.Sjt.) T. C.	974	— Pte. S. H.	1001
Finbown, C.Q.M.Sjt. A. E., *MM.*	1002	Foote, Pte.(A./2nd Cpl.) J. C.	1018
Finch, Pte.(A./S./Sjt.) W.	1014	Forbes, C.Q.M.Sjt. R. S. J.	999
Findlay, Pte. W.	1945	Ford, Spr.(A./Sjt.) B. B	983
Finlayson, Cpl. J. A. V.	995	— L./Sjt. B. F., *MM.*	1021
Finlinson, Pte.(A./Cpl.) J.	1016	— C.S.M. G. H.	1004
Finnie, C.Q.M.Sjt. W.	996	— Sjt. H., *MM.*	998
Fish, Q.M.Sjt. G. W.	985	— C.S.M. J.	2695
— Cpl. R.	2999	— Cpl. J.	1488
Fisher, C.S.M. G. F.	1021	— Bombdr. R. O.	1021
— Armr.S./Sjt.(T./		— Sjt.(A./S.M.) W. E.	2701
Armr.S.M.) G. W.	1490	Fordham, Cpl. F. C.	1000
— Cpl.(A./S.M.) (A.C.) H.	976	Fordyce, Spr.(A./S.M.) R.	2692
— Pte. H.	985	Forrest, Cpl.(A./Sjt.) J.	1012
— C.S.M.(A./S.M.) J.	984	Forrester, Cpl. J. F., *MM.*	996
— Cpl.(A./S.M.) W. H.	2701	Forsdyke, Q.M.Sjt. F.	1002
Fishwick, S./Q.M.Sjt.(A./		Forster, Sjt. A. P.	1006
Condr.) O.	1013	— Cpl. L. H.	2998
Fisk, C.S.M.(A./S.M.) A.	2696	— Sqdn.Q.M.S. T.	2701
— Bmdr. E. J.	974	— Pte.(A./Cpl.) W. A.	1010
— Ftr.S./Sjt. T.	975	Forsyth, Pte.(L./C.) G.	1001
Fitton, Sjt.Mech. E. C.	99	Forth, Pte. E.	984
Fitzgerald, C.Q.M.Sjt. P.	1005	Foss, Q.M.Sjt. S. E.	1011
— Pte. W.	2999	Foster, Sjt. A.	993
Fitzheny, Cpl. E.	981	— Pte.(A./Sjt.) A.	2694
Fitzpatrick, S.M. P.	2697	— Sjt. C. F.	1018
Flack, Ftr.CPl. A. J.	973	— Sjt. F. C.	1021
Flanagan, Q.M.S. J.	2700	— S./Sjt. F. W.	1023
Flannaghan, Sjt. A.	988	— Sjt. G. C.	985
Flattley, R.Q.M.S. T.	1021	— C.S.M. (I. of M.) P.	2694
Fleming, B.S.M. E. W.	2690	— C.S.M. R.	999
— C.S.M. J.	990	— By.S.M.(A./R.S.M.) W.	971
Fletcher, Cpl.(A./Sjt.) A. W.	1009	— S./S.M. W. A.	2702
— C.Q.M.S. J. K.	1021	Fotheringham, Pte.(L./C.) J. G.	992
— Sjt. N. J.	1021	Foulds, Pte. J. J.	990
Flett, Ft.Sjt. F.	1021	Foulstone, Pte. (A./Cpl.) J.	995
Flewker, Gnr. F.	977	Fowler, Sjt. F.	69
Flockhart, Ldg. Trmr. J. N.	3861	— Cpl.(A./Sjt.) F.	1012
Flood, Sjt. E. J.	1018	— Q.M.Sjt. G.	1011
— By.S.M. E. J.	975	— Sjt. W. S.	1006
— Cpl.(A./C.S.M.) T. F.	1009	Fowles, C.S.M.(A./S.M.) S., *D.C.M.*	2697
Flower, Pte.(A./Sjt.) W.	1015	Fox, Sjt. A. H.	986
Floyd, Pte.(A./Cpl.) E.	983	— Sjt. C. W.	999

* Awarded M.S.M. Annuity A.O. 10/1933. Queen's Royal West Surreys. M.S.M. for services at a Records Office.

Foxcroft, C.S.M. F. H.	2697	Freemantle, Q.M.Sjt. E.		986
Foxley, C.Q.M.S.(A/C.S.M.) T., *M.M.*	978	Freestone, By.Q.M.Sjt. H.		971
— Pte. T.	1010	French, C.P.O. A. E.		2360
Foyle, Pte.(A./Sjt.) R. B.	2998	— C.Q.M.S. F.		2695
Frampton, C.S.M. A. J.	2701	— P.O. 2nd Cl. G. S.		3861
France, Dvr. C.	983	— Sjt. W. C.		2590
Francis, Pte. A. M.	1018	Fricker, Sjt. A. P.		1021
— Spr. C. J.	983	— Spr.(A./L./C.) H.		983
— S./Sjt. C. R.	1018	Friday, Pte. I. F. W.		99
— C.E.R.A. 2nd Cl. G.	2360	Friend, Pte. A. F.		2998
— Pte. G. H.	69	— Pte.(A./Cpl.) A. J.		1013
— S.S.M. H. G.	1003	— Pte. E. A.		2998
— Pte.(A./Sjt.) J.	2998	— Sjt. W. H.		999
— Pte.(L./C.)(A./S./Sjt.) J. E.	1010	Frier, Armt.S.M. J.		2700
— S./Sjt. J. W.	1006	Fripp, Ldg.Sto. C.		3861
— Pte.(A./Sjt.) P. E.	71	Froggatt, Pte.(A./Q.M.S.) R.		2694
— T./S.M. T.	1011	Frost, C.Q.M.Sjt. A. A.		1002
— Cpl.(A./Sjt.) T.	981	— Pte.(A./C.,A./Sjt.) B. A.		1010
— C.Q.M.Sjt. W.	989	— Cpl. Mech. C. H.		99
Franckeiss, Clr.Sjt.(C.Q.M.S.) E.	70	Froud, R.S.M. H. R.		975
Frankham, Cpl.(A./Sjt.) H. H.	1490	— By.S.M. W. F.		971
Frankland, Ch.Engmn. F.	3861	Froude, Sjt.(A./C.Q.M.S.) G. H.		1006
— Cpl. H. R.	969	Frudd, Sjt. (A./S.M.) E.		99
— S.Q.M.Sjt. L.	1005	Fry, Sjt. I.		992
Franklin, S./Sjt. A.	1012	— Sjt. J.		1021
— Ch.Arm. W.	2361	— C.S.M. W. J.		2692
Franks, S./Sjt.(A./S.M.) F.	1945	Fryer, S.Q.M.S. M. F.		2689
— Gnr. H. C.	974	Fulford, Pte. W. J.		987
— S./Sjt. S. R. B.	1012	Fuller, Cpl.(A./Sjt.) F.		981
Fraser, Sjt. H. D.	1018	— Pte. L.		998
— Sjt. J.	1021	Fulton, Q.M.S. G. S.		2695
— A./Mas.Mech. P.	99	Funnell, Sjt. A. H.		1018
— S./Sjt. T. H.	1018	Furguson, F. of W. S.M. H. A.		2692
— Sjt. T. S.	1018	Furlong, Sjt. J. V.		1021
Frazer, Bmdr.(A.C.) J. A.	977	Furness, C.S.M. G. H.		999
Fredjohn, Pte.(A./Sjt.) M.	* 80	Furniss, Cpl. C. A.		987
Freeborough, Cpl.(A./S./Sjt.) L.	61			
Freeburn, Q.M.S. V. C.	1021	Gadd, Spr.(A./Sjt.) C. A.		983
Freeman, Q.M.S. F.	† 2694	— Sjt. H.		999
— Sjt. H. W.	1021	— Mas.Mech. J. J.		99
— T./Sub Condr. N. A.	1013	Gaffney, Spr.(A./S.M.) P.		2692
— Cpl. R.	70	Galbraith, Q.M.Sjt. J. W.		996
— Pte.(A./Cpl.) W. G.	993	Gale, Sjt.(A./C.S.M.)		1006
Freemantle, Pte.(A/S.M.) A. H. O.	2702	— Q.M.S. E.		2693

---

* M.S.M. known: 557385 9th Bn. Labour Corps. One of the very early awards for the N. Russian theatre the original force being despatched in mid-1918. Also entitled to Russian Medal of Zeal with the St. Anne Ribbon.

† Group known in the R.G.J. Museum. Queen's Egypt (Tel el Kebir, Suakin 1884, El Teb Tamaai), British War and Victory Medals (C.Sgt.), L.S. & G.C. (Victoria) M.S.M. and Khedive's Star.

Galea, Sjt. W. S.	1018	Garrett, Pte.(A./L./C.) B.		1013
Gales, S.M.(Q.M.S.(A./S.M.) A.	2691	— Sjt. H.		990
Gall, Pnr. D.	983	— S./Sjt.(A./Q.M.S.) S. O.		1012
— T./S.M. G.	982	Garrioch, Pte.(A./Cpl.) B. W.		1010
Gallagher, R.Q.M.S. H. H.	1021	Garrod, Sjt. G.		991
— Bombr.(A./Sjt.) J. H.	2691	Garside, S./S.M. C., *M.C.*	*	80
— C.P.O. W. J.	969	— Sjt.(A./C.S.M.) E.		1000
Gallehawk, Sjt. B. C.	999	— Sjt. H.		998
Galley, Sjt. G.	989	Gartside, Sjt. J.		994
— Pte. H. W.	2999	Garvie, Ftr. W.		974
— Sjt. J.	972	Gascoyne, Amt.S./Sjt.		
Gallia, Cpl. M.	1488	R. E. (corr.)	†	1257
Gallop, Sqdn.S.M. W. E.	60	Gasper, Sjt. J.		1018
Galloway, Sjt.(A./C.S.M.) E. H.	997	Gasser, S./S.M. H.		1003
— Ch.Sto. J.	2361	— L./C.(A./C.S.M.) J. G.		2697
— C.Q.M.Sjt. R., *M.M.*	990	Gaw, Sjt. W.		989
Gamble, Farr.Sjt. H.	1018	Gay, F. of W. S.M. J.		2692
— Cpl. J. T.	995	Gayes, C.S.M. W. E.		977
Gamblin, Ch.Mech. E.	99	Gayler, Sjt.(A./C.S.M.) T. H.		1488
Gammon, Sjt. R.	1006	Gear, Sjt. H. E.		976
Gandy, L./C. J. W., *M.M.*	1021	Geddes, Cpl. G. A.		996
Gann, Pte. H. A.	986	— S.M. W.		2697
Ganson, Sjt. W.	1018	Gee, Sjt. F. W.		1021
Garden, Pte.(A./M.S.M.) W.	2999	Geissler, Pte. C. R.		1018
Gardiner, E. C. 2nc Cpl.(A./Sjt.) G.	982	Gelder, S./S.M. E C.	‡	2698
— Spr.(A./S.M.) H. R.	2692	Gellatly, Sjt. S. H.		998
Gardner, S.M. A.	2691	Gennery, Sjt. S. P.		976
— T./S.M. H.	2698	Gent, S.S.M. F. C.		68
— C.S.M. (A./S.M.) H. W.	2698	— Pte.(A./Sjt.) J. R.		1015
— Q.M.S. H. W.	990	Gentle, W.O., Cl. 2, F. B.		1021
— C.Q.M.Sjt. J.	984	Gentry, 3rd Writer, G. G.		3862
— Cpl. R. H.	1009	George, C.S.M. (A.C.) H.	§	2691
— C.P.O. 3rd Cl. R. P.	3863	— Sjt. L. K.		972
Gardon, Sjt.(A./By/S.M.) E.	972	— By.S.M. R. L.		971
Garland, Sjt. E. D.	1006	— Pte. (A./Sjt.) W. H.		987
— By.Q.M.Sjt. H.	971	German, Pte. R. A.		1001
— Pte.(A./S.Q.M.S.) J. W.	2694	Gerrard, S./S.M. R.		2698
Garner, Sjt. A. H.	979	Giannina, Sjt. (A./S.M.) P.		2701
Garnett, Q.M.S. A	2693	Gibb, Spr. J. R.		983
Garraway, Sjt. E.	2998			

---

* Group sold 1990 for £858: M.B.E. (for Archangel, February 1920), M.C. (for Egypt, June 1916), Queen's South Africa Medal (Cape Colony, Orange Free State, South Africa 1902, Pte. A.S.C.), 1914/15 Star trio (M.I.D. for N. Russia), L.S. & G.C. (Geo. V, 1st class S.S.M., M.C.) and M.S.M. (for Russia). Retired Captain 1936 with 35 years service. Born April 1883 and enlisted into A.S.C. in 1901. Served in Sinai January 1915 to May 1916 and in Archangel between June 1918 and September 1919.

† R.A.O.C. Also D.C.M.

‡ A.S.C. For Gibraltar.

§ R.G.A. For Malta.

Gibbon, C.S.M.(A./			Gillespie, Sjt. S. C.		1018
S./S.M.) P. H. T.		1004	Gillette, Sjt. E. T.		986
Gibbons, Bmdr. (A./Sjt.) A. T.		977	Gilling, Sub-Comdr. H. T.		2701
— C.Q.M.Sjt. V.		1005	Gillingham, Sjt. (A./C.S.M.) A. A.		1006
— W.O,Cl. II. (S.Q.M.S.) W.	*	3572	Gillman, C.S.M. A.		999
Gibbs, C.S.M. G.		1488	Gillmor, Sjt. P.		1018
— C.S.M. M. H.		2695	Gilman, Sjt.Maj. G.		99
Gibson, P.O. D. H. J.		3863	Ginger, Sjt. W.		1944
— Pte.(A./W.M.S.) F.		2697	Ginn, T./S.M. J. G. B.		977
— Pte.(L./C.) F.		985	Girard, C.Q.M.S. S.		978
— Sjt. G. E.		979	Girling, Cpl. F. J.		1009
— Sjt. G. H.		1006	Gissing, Cpl. (A./Sjt.) C. S.		2702
— 1st A.M. H. J.	†	99	Gittens, Sjt. M.		1000
— By.Q.M.Sjt. J.		971	Gjertsen, Pte.(A./L./C.) T. A.		1010
— Gnr. O.		974	Gladdle, Sjt. J. M.		1006
— C.Q.M.Sjt. R.		997	Gladwell, By.S.M.(A./R.S.M.) W.		971
— C.Q.M.S. R. E.		1021	Glanville, C.S.M. W. G.		1945
— Sjt. W.	‡	979	Glascodine, By.Q.M.Sjt. W. H.		971
— Flt.Sjt. W.		99	Glass, S.M. R.		2697
Gifford, Sjt. E C.		972	Glasspool, C.S.M.(A./S.M.) H.		2695
— Sdlr. Q.M.S. J. I.		1004	Gleeson, Sjt. A. G.		1021
Gilbert, C.Q.M.Sjt. A.		990	— Q.M.Sjt. A. J.		998
— Sjt. C. F.		979	Glennon, C.Q.M.Sjt. W.		990
— C.S.M. J. W.		1004	Glenville, W.O., Cl.II, Q.M.Sjt.		
— B.Q.M.S. T. W.		2690	(A./W.O., Cl.I., Spdt. Clerk)		
Gilchrist, Sjt. A. J. S.		1021	J. C.		3572
— C.Q.M.Sjt. G.		990	Gliddon, Sjt. F. J.		991
— C.S.M. (A./S.M.) W.		2697	— Ch.Mec. T. L.	+	99
Gilder, Clr.Sjt. A.		2694	Gloag, R.S.M. D. C.		1018
Giles, By.S.M. E. H.		975	Gloster, S./Sjt. A. A.		61
— E.C. Cpl. (A./E.C.Sjt.) F.		981	Glover, Pte.(A./Sjt.) A. W.		1015
Gill, C.Q.M.Sjt. A. E.		993	— Pte. C. H.		1010
Gill-Houghton, S.Q.M.Sjt. F. G.	§	1945	— S./Sjt. P. W.		1012
Gillard, Pte.(A./Sjt.) J. S.		1013	— Mech./S.M. S.		1003

* Pair known: L.S. & G.C. (Edw. VII, Clr. Sgt. Rl. Munster Fus.) and M.S.M. (Depot R. Mun. F.) for services in Record Offices.

† No. 12392 R.F.C. Pair in Moss collection British War Medal and R.A.F. M.S.M. Born in Northumberland. Enlisted in 1915 aged 18. Posted to France 1916 with 13 Sqn. A mechanic servicing the Squadrons R.E.8 reconnaissance aircraft, he was frequently pressed into service as air gunner observer. In 1919, upon discharge, he emigrated to U.S.A. where he disappeared without trace the next year.

‡ 'A' Battn, Tank Corps. Group known: Queen's South Africa Medal (Cape Colony Orange Free State, South Africa 1901, 14987 Pte. R.A.M.C.), 1914 Star & bar (C.M.T. 3455 Pte. A.S.C.), British War and Victory Medals (R.T.S. 3455 A.W.O.2 A.S.C.) and M.S.M. (75001 Hy. Brch., M.G.C.) 'for excellent work with the workshop party at Beaucourt, Ancre, 1916.'

§ Awarded M.S.M. Annuity A.O.87/1950. R.A.P.C. M.S.M. for East Africa.

+ R.A.F. M.S.M. No. 210 R.F.C. Enlisted July 1912. With 3 Sqn. earned 1914 Star & bar as Cpl. in France from 13 August 1914. Awarded French Médaille Militaire for gallantry 21–30 August 1914 (see *L.G.* 9 November 1914).

Goad, Mech./S.Sjt. R V.	978	Gore, C.Q.M.Sjt. E. J. S.	995
Goalen, C.S.M. G. H.	977	— Gnr. F.	974
Goatley, Pte. G. H.	1013	— Cpl. J. R.	1000
Gobie, Spr.(A./C.Q.M.S.) T.	2692	Goreham, Cpl. E. J.	70
Goddard, A.M. 1 J. H.	2050	Gorle, Pte. J. W.	1001
— Spr. W. R.	983	Gornell, C.S.M.(A./Q.M.Sjt.)	
Godden, C.S.M. (A./S.M.) H.	2696	J., *D.C.M.*	984
Godfey, C.Q.M.Sjt. A. C. G.	992	Gorse, Q.M.Sjt. R.	988
— Sjt.(T./S./Sjt.) J. D.	1023	Gosky, Ch.Mech. C. E.	99
— Pte. 2 L. A.	2050	Goss, CS.M. H. T.	999
— Pte. (A./C.S.M.) R.	2698	Gotts, Sjt. J. W.	1488
— Dvr. (L./C.) W.	983	Gough, Dvr. D.	974
Godwin, Sjt. W. H.	1488	— Sjt. H. G. P.	2699
Golden, Pnr. T.	1001	— Sjt.(A./S.S.M.) T. H.	3841
Golder, Pte.(A./C.S.M. Instr.) A. W.	2701	— Dvr.(A./L./C) W. G.	983
— Cpl. (A./Sjt.) F. J.	1014	— Q.M.S. W. S.	2999
Golding, C.S.M. H. L.	1023	Gould, Pte.(A./Cpl.) A.	996
— C.Q.M.Sjt. R. A. (corr.)	1257	Goulding, C.S.M. H.	977
Goldsmith, Clk. 1 A. A.	99	Gow, S.M. A.	3840
— C.S.M. W. E.	1004	Gower, C.S.M. W. A.	977
Goldthorpe, C.S.M. E.	994	Graber, F. of W. Q.M.Sjt. F. A.	60
— Sjt. F. W.	1488	— Q.M.Sjt.(T./E.S.S.M.) W. F.	977
Good, Sjt. (A./C.S.M.) P.	1488	Grace, Cpl. J. E.	973
Goddall C.QM.S. (A./S.M.) F.	2999	— Sjt. S.	2697
Goodchild, Cpl. E. E.	70	Grady, Pte.(A./Cpl.) C.	995
— Sjt. P. M.	2690	Graham, Q.M.Sjt. E. J.	997
Goode, Pte. T. E.	1010	— Q.M.Sjt. H.	977
Goodenough, S./Sjt.(A./S.M.) F.	2700	— C.S.M.(A./S.M.) J.	2697
Gooderham, B.S.M. O. M.	2997	— Sjt. N. H.	987
Goodey, S.Q.M.Sjt.(T./S.S.M.) A. A.	70	— C.Q.M.Sjt.(O.R.S.) T. H.	996
Goodhand, C.S.M. D. W.	977	— C.Q.M.Sjt. W. A.	997
Goodhew, Cpl. W. A.	70	— Sjt. W. M.	979
Gooding, T./S.M.(A.C.) G. B.	975	Grahame, S./Sjt.(A./Q.M.Sjt.) F. D.	1012
— Sjt. R.	2361	Grainger, Sjt. H.	979
Goodman, Spr. E.	983	Graley, Sjt. P.	70
— Sjt.(O.R.S.) G. W. H.	2998	Granger, Cpl.(A./Sjt.) A. H.	1009
Goodrich, C.P.O. P. B.	969	Grant, S./Sjt. D.	1018
Goodspeed, Pte. R.	970	— Pte.(L./C.) E. H.	1001
Goodwill, Sjt.(A.C.)(A./S.M.) F.	1488	— Sjt. I. M.	1006
Goodwin, Cpl. A.	985	— Pte. J. A.	1018
— S.M. G.	2700	— C.Q.M.S. P.	1021
— Sjt. R. B.	1006	— Fitt.Cpl. T.	1018
Goodyear, C.S.M. G.	2695	Grantham, B.S.M. R.	68
Goom, Pte.(A./Sjt.) W.	2700	Grassby, Arm.S.M.G	1018
Gordge, Q.M.S. J. H.	1024	Gravestock, Sjt. J. W. G.	1018
Gordon, S.M. A. G. M.	2690	Gray, S.M. A., *M.C.*	984
— Ch.Mech. F. E.	99	— Sjt.(A./S.M.) A.	2695
— R.S.M. H.	1018	— Sjt. A.	1489
— C.Q.M.S. J.	2698	— Sjt. E. A.	1000

* M.C. L.G. 27.7.16, 3/Coldstream Guards.

Gray, Sub Condr.(A./Condr.) E. E.	1013	Greenslade, Sjt. W. S.	2701
— Cpl. F. T. G.	1009	Greenwood, Pte. J. H.	2703
— Sjt. G.	1018	— S.Q.M.Sjt.(A./S.S.M.) L.	1005
— R.Q.M.S.(W.O.Cl. 2) J.	1018	— Cpl. L. M.	1009
— Bmdr. J. A.	974	— Sjt. M. R.	972
— Pte.(A./Cpl.) J. B.	1016	— Q.M.Sjt.(T./S.M.) S. C.	1011
Gray, Sjt.(A./S.Q.M.S) William	1006	Gregory, C.E.R.A. 2nd Cl. H. S.	3591
— Sjt. W.	60	— Cpl. W. J.	973
— Sjt. W. H.	989	Gregson, Sjt. A.	992
Graydon, S./Sjt. W.	1018	Greig, Pte. A. W. *	1010
Grayling, Sjt. G.	972	— O.M.S.(A./C.S.M.) G. A.	1018
Greatorex, F. of W. S./Sjt. A.	978	— Cpl.(A./C.Q.M.S.) J.	2697
Greaves, Pte. E.	994	Gresham, C.Q.M.S.(A./C.S.M.) H. H.	2697
— Sjt. R.	996	Gresty, Pte.(A./S./Sjt.) J.	2700
Green, Col.Sjt.(A./C.Q.M.Sjt.) A.	986	Grey, Sjt.(A./S.M.) R. E.	987
— Ldg. Sea. A.	2361	Gribbon, Pte. G.	1001
— C.S.M.(A./S.M.) C.	2696	Grierson, Cpl. W.	996
— Sjt. C. (Notts. & D.R.T.F.)	993	Griffe, Pte.(L/Cpl.) M.	986
— Sjt. C. (R.W. of Surr. R.)	985	Griffin, By.S.M. F.	971
— Pte.(A./Sjt.) C P.	989	— S./Sjt. G. E.	1021
— Farr.Sjt. E.	972	— Pte.(A./Cpl.) J.	989
— Sjt. E. J.	1490	— By.S.M. P. L.	1018
— R.S.M. F. J.	1003	Griffith, Cpl.(A./R.Q.M.S.) T. E.	973
— S./Sjt.(T./S./S.M.) G.	1006	Griffith-Williams S./Sjt.(A./Q.M.S.)	
— Pte.(A./Sjt.) G.	1015	H. M.	1012
— Cpl.(L./Sjt.) G. R.	1003	Griffiths, By.S.M. A.	975
— S./Sjt.(T./S./S.M.) G. W.	1006	— Sjt. D. W.	991
— Sjt. H. J.	2692	— Sjt.(A./S./Sjt.) F Y.	2699
— Pte.(L./C.,A./C.S.M.) I. E.	1010	— Cpl.(T./S./S.M.) G. A.	1009
— Q.M.Sjt.(A./S.M.) J. E.	1011	— Pte.(A./Cpl.) H. J.	1013
— Sjt. J. F.	1023	— A.M. J.	99
— Pte.(A./Cpl.) J. S.	1010	— Q.M.S.(T./S.M.) J. D.	2700
— L./C.(A./Sup. Clk.) O. C.	2694	— L./C.(A./Sjt.) P.	2698
— Sjt. O. E.	992	— B.S.M.(A./S.M.)(A.C.) R. J.	2691
— Pte.(A./Sjt.) R. W.	1015	— Pte.(L./C.) S.	989
— Sjt. V.	1006	— Sjt. T. G.	69
— Sjt. W. B.	1002	— Cpl.(A./Sjt.) W.	998
— Cpl. W. C.	973	— Cpl. W. J.	1009
Greenall, Q.M.S. W.	2693	Grigsby, W.O. H. J.	2702
Greenford, Condr. C.	2999	Grimshaw, Mech.S./Sjt. J. H.	1005
Greenhill, M.S./Sjt. F. J.	998	— Sjt. T.	993
— Dvr. W.	974	Grindells, C.Q.M.Sjt. A. H.	988
Greensides, Sjt. W.	998	Grindey, 1st Writer W. A.	2863
Greenslade, Sjt. W.	1002	Grindrod, Sjt. J.	70

* M2/082643 Pte. 29th M.T. Coy. A.S.C. (attached H.Q. 29th Divl. Artillery). Flanders 1918—For continued exemplary service as driver of the R.A. car. Has shown a high degree of skill and nerve, and persistent devotion to duty. In the most trying circumstances he has never failed in coolness and courage, whilst the care he has bestowed on his car is proved by the fact of the immunity from trouble after more than three years continuous work at the front. (Belgian Croix de Guerre 4/9/19).

Groenewald, Sjt. P. H.	1946
Grogan, Sjt. A. T.	1021
Groom, Cpl. A. G.	1003
Groome, C.S.M.(A./S.M.) W. C.	2695
Grover, Sjt.(A./S.M.) F. M.	2692
Groves, Mech.S./Sjt. A. L.	978
Groves, Sjt. H. J. H.	1012
Grundy, T./S.M. W.	1488
Gubbins, Pte.(A./Sjt.) J. L	1018
Gubby, Sjt. W. J.	2840
Guinea, A./Ch.Mas.Mech. G. R.	99
Guiver, T./R.S.M. C.	975
Gullidge, S./S.M. G. F. C.	1003
Gundry, C.Q.M.S. F. H.	2998
— Sjt.(A./C.Q.M.S.) T. G.	1000
Gunn, Sjt. J.	996
Gunthorpe, Ftr.Cpl. A. C. G.	973
Gurney, Q.M.Sjt. R.	988
Guthrie, Sjt.(A/S./Sjt.) A.	1012
— Ch.Mas.Mech. S. J.	99
— C.S.M. W.	1021
Gutteridge, Sjt. F. E.	976
Guy, Sjt. A.	972
— Gnr. (A./Sjt.) E. A.	2703
— C.S.M. T.	999
Guyver, Cpl. G. F.	1945
Gwilliam, Sjt.(A./Q.M.S.) J.	2997
Gyton, Spr. F. G.	983
Hackett, S./S.M. C. S.	1003
Hackling, Spr.(A./Sjt.) H. W.	983
Hadden, Cpl. W. R.	1018
Haddock, Pte. F. G.	994
Hadley, Cpl.(A./Sjt.) H. W.	987
Haggarty, Cpl. C.	973
Haggerston, Sjt. W.	69
Haggertay, C.S.M. H. J.	2692
Haig, Sjt.(A./C.) T.,	976
Haigh, Pte. F.	1010
Haines, Spr. V.	983
— Sjt. W. A.	979
Haith, C.Q.M.Sjt. R.	997
Hale, Ftr. S./Sjt. T.	975
Halfacre, Sjt. A.	991
Haliday, C.S.M.(A./S.M.) T. G.	2695
Hall, Sjt. A. (Som.L.I.)	988
— Sjt. A. (N.Z.Engrs.)(corr.)	1257
— Dvr. A. E.	1010
— Sjt. A. W.	70

Hall, By.S.M. B. A.	971
— Sjt. C.	991
— Pte. C.	990
— C.Q.M.Sjt. C. H., *M.M.*	992
— Amr.S./Sjt. D.	1013
— Sdr.Cpl.(A./Sdr.Sjt.) F. C.	973
— C.Q.M.Sjt. F. S.	1002
— Dvr.(L./Bmdr.) F. S.	974
— S./Sjt. F. W.	1006
— Cpl. H.	1009
— Pte. J. R.	985
— C.S.M.(T./Mech.S.M.) L.	1004
— Q.M.Sjt. N.	993
— Ldg. Sea. T. W.	2361
— 2nd Cpl.(A./Sjt.) W. J.	68
— S./S.M. W. N.	61
— C.S.M. W. S.	2699
Halle, Sjt. C. E.	1021
Halley, Cpl.(L./Sjt.) T. C.	990
Hallion, Pte. P.	1015
Halliwell, Bmdr. T. E.	974
Hallows, Sjt. T. E. P.	979
Halls, C.Q.M.Sjt. F. L.	990
Hallworth, Cpl. J. H.	70
Hamblin, Cpl. I. C.	1488
Hambridge, Sjt.(A./S.M.) W. J.	976
Hamer, Sjt. T. A.	1012
Hamilton, L./C.(A./Cpl.) J.	3840
Hammond, Pte.(A./Sjt.) A. P.	2698
— Sjt. G. W.	1021
— Farr.Sjt. T.	972
— B.S.M. W.	2690
Hanchard, 2/Cpl.(A./S./Sjt.) S. A.	1945
Hancock, T./S.M.(A.C.) C. H.	2690
— C.Q.M.Sjt. C. W.	1002
— Sjt. G. P.	972
— Farr.Sjt. R. J.	1023
Hand, Cpl. J.	❀ 1256
Hands, C.Q.M.Sjt. H. T.	986
— Cpl. S.	1013
Handy, S./S.M. F.	1003
Hankin, Sjt. F. R. W.	1945
Hanna, C.S.M. J.	990
— Sjt. J. M.	1006
Hannibal, S.M. W. H.	977
Hansell, Q.M.S. A. J.	2694
Hansen, A./Ch.Mas.Mec. H. P.	* 99
Harcourt, Sjt. V.	1021
Hardie, C.Q.M.Sjt. A. J. F.	1005

* R.A.F. M.S.M. No. Aus/458, 68 Sqn. Australian Flying Corps in Egypt.

Hardie, C.S.M. J.	2697	Harris, Sjt.(A./S.M.) A. E.	1015
— S./Sjt.(A./Sub Condr.) R. D.	3000	— Sjt. C.	2695
— Pte.(A./L./Sjt.) W.	62	— C.S.M. C. H.	1488
Hardiman, Sjt. G. H.	69	— Sjt. C. W.	2698
Harding, Sjt. (T./Sub Condr.) A. S.	* 2701	— Pte.(A./Q.M.S.) E.	2698
— Cpl. E. S.	1023	— Sjt. E. A.	987
— Pte.(A./Sjt.) G. C.	992	— Ch.Mec. F.	99
— C.E.R.A. 1st Cl. J. E. A.	3860	— Pte. F. D.	987
— Gnr. J. B.	974	— Pte. F. T.	1001
— Sjt.(A./S.S.M.) P. A.	979	— Sjt. G. O.	1007
— S./S.M. P. C.	2701	— C.S.M. G. S.	999
— Ch.Mas.Mec. R.	99	— Sjt. J. M.	991
Hardstone, S./Sjt. A. E.	1006	— Spr.(A./C.) W. A.	983
Hardy, C.Q.M.Sjt. A.	1005	— Sjt. W. G.	1021
— C.P.O. J.	3591	— Cpl. W. M.	1000
Hare, S./Sjt. P.	68	Harrison, S./S.M. A. J.	2701
Harfield, Cpl.(A./Sjt.) A. G.	981	— Q.M.S. C	2690
Hargraves, Farr.Sjt. J.	1018	— Clr.Sjt.(O.R.S.) E.	991
Harkness, F./Sjt. J.	99	— Sjt. F. N.	1013
— By.Q.M.S. T.	971	— Sjt. F. R.	979
Harland, Sjt. S.	2697	— Cpl. G.	981
Harling, By.S.M. W. J.	† 971	— Cpl.(A./L./Sjt.) H.	986
Harlow, Sjt. H. J.	994	— Bombr. H.	+ ※ 1256
Harman, Sjt. C. J.	‡ 99	— Sjt. H. P.	71
Harmsworth, C.Q.M.Sjt. H. J.	69	— Sjt. J.	991
— T./Sub Condr. R.	1013	— Sjt. (T./S.M.) J. W.	979
Harnwell, Spr.(L./C.) S. A.	983	— Sjt. P.	2999
Harper, Sjt. C.	1946	— C.P.O. R.	969
— Cpl.(A./Sjt.) D. T.	§ 99	— Pte. R.	61
— Pte.(A./S./Sjt.) E. S.	2700	— Mech.Q.M. T.	977
— Q.M.S.I.(A./R.S.M.) H. H.	1002	— Farr.Sjt. T.	979
— Sjt. W. E.	1006	— A.M. W.	99
Harrington, Sjt. W. J.	979	— Sub Condr. W	3000
Harris, S./S.M. A. A.	1015	Harrold, Dvr. A.	974
		Harrop, Teleg. E.	3863

* For China (R.A.O.C.).
† 940003, B.S.M. 460th Battery R.F.A. Flanders 1918—For continuous good service and executive ability as Sergeant-Major of his battery. His personal keenness and example have maintained a high standard of general efficiency in the battery. Flanders 1918—This W.O. displayed the most praiseworthy courage on two separate occasions when his battery wagon lines near Becelaere were shelled. On the night 4th/5th October when a dug-out was hit he extricated four men under fire, bandaged the wounded and got them safely away. On the night 7th/8th October the lines were again heavily shelled and he spent two hours attending to wounded men and horses. Furthermore, three ammunition wagons caught fire, realising the danger of an explosion, he immediately organised a party and put the fire out. (D.C.M. (immediate) 12/3/19).
‡ R.A.F. M.S.M. No. Aus/222, 68 Sqn. Australian Flying Corps in Egypt.
§ R.A.F. M.S.M. No. Aus/120, 68 Sqn. Australian Flying Corps in Egypt.
+ R.G.A. for Gallantry in Aden.

Harrow, S./S.M. J. E.	* 2698	
Hart, S./Sjt. G. W.	1011	
Hart, Pte.(A./Condr.) J. A.	1014	
— Pte.(A./L./C.) P.	1010	
— By.Q.M.Sjt. V. L.	971	
— Cpl. W.	995	
Hartford-Liddiard, Cpl. (A./ C.Q.M.S.) F.	2692	
Hartgrove, S.M.(A.C.) T. A., *M.C.*	† 973	
Hartigan, S./Sjt. F. P.	1021	
Hartley, Cpl. A.	1009	
— Clr.Sjt.(O.R.Sjt.) J. A.	1488	
Hartnett, B.S.M.(A./S.M.) H. J.	1487	
Hartwell, Ch.Mec. H. W.	99	
— S.Q.M.S.(A./Sub Condr.) W.	1018	
Harvey, T./S.M. A. E.	1002	
— Sjt. A. J.	2696	
— S./S.M. A. W.	2698	
— S./Sjt. A. W.	1013	
— Sjt. A. W., *M.M.*	979	
— By.S.M. F.	973	
— Sjt. H.	2998	
— S.Q.M.S.(T./S.M.) P.	1006	
— Sjt. (A./C.S.M.) R.	1018	
— Sjt. Clk. T.	99	
— 2nd Cpl. T.	1944	
— Sjt. T. H.	988	
— Cpl.(A./Sjt.) T. R.	1013	
— Sjt. W.	1944	
Harvie, Sjt. E. P.	993	
Harwood, Clr.Sjt. F.	2694	
— Cpl.(A./Sjt.) H.	1009	
— Sjt. T. W.	2699	
Hasham, E.R.A. 2nd Cl. C.	2360	
— Sjt. H. F.	972	
Hastie, Cpl.(A./S.Q.M.S.) J.	1009	
— W.O. R. L.	62	
— By.S.M. W. M.	971	
Hastings, S./Sjt. C. T.	1007	
— Pte.(A./Cpl.) H. H.	1001	
— Pte.(L./C.) M.	990	
Hatch, Pte.(L./Cpl.) H. G.	986	
Hateley, Cpl. F.	973	
— S.M. T. S.	2698	
Hattersley, Pte.(A./Cpl.) A.	995	
Hatton, S./S.M. A. E.	61	
— Sqdn.S.M. T. M.	2699	
Haunant, Ch.Sto. H.	3591	
Haunch, Cpl. H. H.	1000	
Haward, Spr. C. L.	983	
Hawes, S.Q.M.Sjt. R.	61	
Hawken, S./Sjt.(A./S.M.) C. A.	2700	
Hawker, Pte. H.	1012	
Hawkes, Pte. F. C.	❀ 1256	
— Pte.(A./Sjt.) W. G. W.	1013	
Hawking, Pte. F.	987	
Hawkins, Pte.(A./S./Sjt.) C. H.	1014	
— C.S.M. H.	2691	
— Sjt. P. N.	976	
— Dr. W.	1010	
— Cpl. W. C.	1488	
Hawksworth, Q.M.S.(T./S.M.) J. H.	1011	
Hay, Q.M.Sjt. A.	1011	
— Sjt. A. J.	2702	
— Cpl. R.	981	
Hayes, Sjt. A. C. R.	991	
— S.M.Instr. J.	2701	
— S.M. N.	993	
— C.S.M. P., *D.C.M.*	999	
— Spr.(A./C.Q.M.S.) R.	2692	
— W.O.Cl.1 (Supt. Clerk) S. H.	3572	
— Sjt. W. G., *M.M.*	976	
Hayler, Cpl.(A./Sjt.) E. G. A.	985	
Hayman, P.O. R. E.	3862	
— Pte.(L./Cpl.) W. G.	985	
Haynes, C.S.M. J. W.	977	
— Pte. J. W.	2361	
— 1st Cl. Mst.Gnr. W.	‡ 2691	
Haysom, Sjt. F.	990	
Hayward, Q.M.S. A.	2696	
— Sjt.(A./C.Q.M.S.) A. J.	2699	
— Sjt. C. F.	1000	
— Sjt.(A./Supt.Clk.) E.	2692	
— Sjt. R.	2692	

---

* A.S.C. for China.

† Group known: M.C. (*L.G.* 14 January 1916, Sgt. Maj. Artillery Clerk), 1914 Star (Q.M.S.), British War and Victory Medals (W.O.II R.A.), L.S. & G.C. (Geo. V, Q.M.S.), M.S.M. (R.G.A.). Thomas Anthony Hartgrove, 21 years 10 days in the ranks, S.M. 11, February 1915. Born 1 September, 1879.

‡ Group known: British War Medal (80744 W.O.1 R.A.), L.S. & G.C. (Edw. VII, 80744 3rd class Master Gunner R.G.A.) and M.S.M. for West Africa—the only one to this theatre for R.G.A., one other to R. Hamps. Fowkes 3 June 1919.

Haywood, S./S.M.(T./S./S.M.) R. E.		1010
— Sub Condr. W. G.		2701
Hazell, Bndmst. A.		2695
— C.S.M. H. R.		2691
Hazlehurst, C.S.M. J.		61
Head, Cpl. E.		2690
— T./Sub Condr. J. N.		1013
Headon, Sjt. H. W.		1000
Heal, C.S.M. A. L. J.		69
Heald, 2nd Cpl. C. W.		982
Healey, C.S.M. A. J.		1488
Hearne, S./Sjt. W. J.		1018
Heath, C.Q.M.Sjt. W. T.		993
Heathcote, Sjt.(A./C.Q.M.Sjt.) W.		991
Heather, Cpl. N., *M.M.*		1013
Heathfield, Sjt. Mec. R. C.		99
Hedges, L./C.(A./Q.M.S.) G. H.		2693
Hedingham, Q.M.Sjt. G.		993
Hefford, Sjt. A.		987
Heggie, Q.M.S. A. V.	*	2700
Heilig, S./S.M. B. A. E.		1003
Helliwell, C.S.M. I. H.		997
Hellwig, C.S.M. H. E.		999
Helmsley, Sjt.Mec. W.		99
Hemelryk, Sjt.(A./S./Sjt.) G. E.		1007
Hemingway, Cpl.(A./Sjt.) E.		994
Hemming, Cpl.(A./Sjt.) R.		973
— A.M.I. J. W.		99
Hemsley, Sjt.(A./Q.M.S.) R.		2701
Henaghan, L./C.(A./Sjt.) G. J		2692
Henderson, C.S.M. A.		977
— Pte.(A./Q.M.S.) A.		1018
— S.M. G. H.		2693
— Dvr. H., *M.M.*		974
— C.Q.M.Sjt. J.		984
— S.M. J.		991
— Sjt.(A./C.S.M.) J.		1021
— Pte.(L./C.) J. H.		68
— Cpl.(A./Sjt.) J. M.		2692
— Sjt. R. H.		979
— S./Sjt. R. T.		2699
— Q.M.Sjt. S. L.		995

Henderson, Sjt. W. J.		1946
Hendrie, C.Q.M.Sjt. F. N.		995
Hendry, 2nd Cpl.(A./ C.Q.M.S.) H. R.		982
Henly, Sjt. H. L.		2702
Hennessey, Sjt. J. M.	†	1946
Henrici, Whlr.S./Sjt. R. H.	‡	1005
Henry, Pte. A. L.	§ ✱	1256
— Sjt. J.		987
— Pte.(A./Sjt.) M.		1010
— Q.M.S. W. T.		1018
Henson, 2nd Cpl. H. A.		1021
— F. of W. S./Sjt. H. T., *M.M.*		978
Henthorne, Pte.(A./Cpl.) W.		2998
Hepburn, Pte. J. W.		1003
— Sjt.(A./C.S.M.) M.		979
Hepworth, Sjt. J. W.		1007
Herapath, Sjt.(A./C.S.M.) L. M.		2691
Herbert, 2nd Cpl. J.		982
— Q.M.Sjt. S. C.		1003
Herridge, C.Q.M.Sjt. W. C.		985
Heslin, By.S.M. J.		971
Heslop, Sjt.(A./C.Q.M.S.) A.		2691
— S.M. T.		997
Hesson, Sjt. B., *D.C.M.*		979
Hetheringtom, Pte. W.		1021
Heun, C.S.M. F.		1004
Hewett, Sjt. A. J.		986
— C.Q.M.S.(T./S.M.) F.		1005
— Cpl.(A./Sjt.) T. W. F.		2690
Hewitson, Sjt.(A./S./Sjt.) R.		2999
Hewitt, Spr. A.		983
— By.S.M. E. J., *M.M.*		971
— Mech.S./Sjt. F.		1005
— Sjt. R.		979
— Pnr.(A./Sjt.) R. G.		2692
— Mech.Q.M.S. W. R.		2692
Hews, Pte.(A./Sjt.) R. G. W.		2700
Hibbert, Sjt. P. M.		995
— C.S.M. T.		1488
Hick, C.Q.M.S.(A./Q.M.S.) G.		2694
Hickling, Sjt. R.		1007

---

* R.A.M.C. for Malta.

† Group known in a Zimbabwe Museum: 1914/15 Star trio, W.W.II Southern Rhodesian Service Medal, Permanent Forces Beyond the Sea L.S. & G.C., M.S.M. (1710 B.S.A.P.) and Special Const. L.S. Medal. (British South Africa Police were awarded 13 M.S.M.s in W.W.I).

‡ Group known: Queen's South Africa Medal (Natal, South Africa 1901), British War and Victory Medals and M.S.M.

§ For Gallantry, B.W.I. Regt.

Hickling, 1st A.M. W. O.	99	Hill, Cpl. R. G. W.	1021
Hickman, Sq.Q.M.S. A.	2997	— Cpl.(L./Sjt.) R. J.	1009
— Pte. H.	1001	— Sjt. S.	70
— S.M. S. J.	2695	— Q.M.Sjt. T. C.	1011
Hicks, Dvr. A.	2359	— Sjt.(A./S.Sjt.) T. D.	61
— S./Sjt. R A.	1007	— S.M. W. ‡	1018
— C.E.R.A. 2nd Cl.(now Act.Art.		Hilliar, 2nd Cpl.(A./Sjt.) T. E.	1488
Eng.) W. H.	2360	Hillier, Sjt. G. W.	1012
Hickson, Sjt. B.	1007	— Pte.(A./Col.Sjt.) H. V.	995
Higgin, Cpl. J. W.	1000	Hilliger, Pte.(A./Sjt.) W. W. §	986
Higginbotham, C.S.M. H.	999	Hillman, T./S.M. E. E.	993
Higgs, C.S.M. B.	1004	— Sjt. H. C.	1000
Highfield, Sjt. J.	979	Hills, 2nd Cpl. F. B.	982
Higson, Sjt. B. C.	998	— S./S.M. J.	2698
— A./Cpl. J. R.	99	— Sjt. W. E.	1487
— Pte.(L./C.) W. F.	995	Hillworth, Cpl. H. L.	1009
Hildich, Sjt. W.	987	Hinam, C.Q.M.S.(T./R.S.M.)	
Hill, Col.Sjt. A.	2360	W. T. C.	1021
— C.Q.M.S.(T./S./S.M.) A. E.	1005	Hinchcliffe, Sjt. J. +	1007
— Tech.Q.M.Sjt. A. W. *	998	Hind, Q.M.Sjt. G.	994
— Pte. A. W.	1010	Hinde, Col.Sjt.(A.S.M.) B.	2694
— Sjt. C. H.	61	Hindle, Sjt. A.	972
— Sjt. E.	1000	— S./Sjt. J.	61
— C.Q.M.S. F. †	2699	— C.Q.M.Sjt. J. A.	990
— F./Clk. F. A.	99	Hindmarsh, S.M. J. A. ◊	2697
— Sjt.(A./Q.M.S.) F. C.	1007	Hinds, Bombr.(A./C.S.M.Instr.) C.	1016
— Cpl. F. H.	1009	— Sjt. S.	985
— Sjt.(A./S.Q.M.S.) F. P. C.	2699	Hines, Cpl.(A./Sjt.) W. R.	1488
— Sjt. G. W.	1021	Hinton, Sjt. F. G.	993
— Pte.(A./Cpl.) H.	988	Hinxman, Sjt. F. H.	972
— S.M. H. J.	2689	Hipkin, C.S.M. W.	987
— Condr. H. M.	2701	Hird, Pte. J.	1001
— Cpl.(A./Sjt.) J.	1945	Hire, Supdt.Clk. E. A. ¶	970
— Pte. J. S.	970	Hirst, Cpl. A.	995
— Sjt. J. T. J.	2702	— Pte. J.	985
— Mech.S.M. O. W	1003	— Gar.Q.M.S. T. H.	2702
— Sjt. R.	1018	Hiscock, Pte. H.	1001

---

* 14 Bn. Tank Corps. Group known: Queen's South Africa Medal (Cape Colony, Orange Free State, Transvaal, South Africa 1901, 4871 L./Cpl. R.Berks.), 1914/15 Star trio (439 Sgt. M.M.G.S./R.A.) and M.S.M. (205223).

† Group known in R.C.T. Museum: M.C., 1914 Star trio, R.V.M. (Bronze, Edw. VII), L.S. & G.C. (Geo. V) and M.S.M.

‡ Canadian Army Medical Corps.

^ Medal known with documentation. He received the M.S.M. for services as an interpreter. Subsequently served in Russia during the intervention period. He was later a member of the Intelligence Police. M.S.M. named to G/95760 Royal Fusiliers. (See Seigne Vol. II 1919).

+ Later awarded M.M.

◊ Awarded M.S.M. Annuity A.O.103/1945, R.S.M. Argyll & Sutherland Highlanders).

¶ Awarded M.S.M. Annuity 1946.

Hitch, Q.M.Sjt. F. H. D.	993	Holland, Condr. F. W.	2700
Hitchcock, S./Sjt. P. W.	998	— C.S.M.(A./S.M.) W.	2694
Hitchings, Farr.Q.M.S. H.	3000	— C.S.M. W. F.	999
— Sjt. W. L.	990	Holliday, By.S.M. H.	975
Hitchman, Spr.(A./Sjt.) C. G.	60	— Arm.S./Sjt. J. J.	1013
Hoad, 2nd Cpl. W. G.	982	— Q.M.Sjt. S. A.	986
Hoare, Pte.(L./C.) J.	992	Holliman, Q.M.Sjt. T.	68
Hobbs, Q.M.Sjt. A. C.	1489	Hollingsworth, By.Q.M.Sjt.(A./	
— Pte.(A./Sjt.) C. E.	1490	By.S.M.) E. T.	971
— Cpl. L. P.	992	— Sjt. J. E.	995
— Cpl.(A./Sjt.) S. C.	981	Hollins, Cpl.(A./Sjt.) A.	981
Hobling, T./Sub Condr. L. C.	2700	Holloway, Cpl.(A./C.Q.M.S.) A. W. F.	1009
Hobson, R.Q.M.S. B. C.	1021	— S.M. T.	2693
Hodder, Cpl.(A./Sjt.) F. W.	1009	Hollyer, T./S./S.M. J. R. S.	2698
Hodge, S.Q.M.Sjt. B.	970	Holman, Mech.S./Sjt.(T./M.S.M.) F.	61
Hodges, Farr.Sjt. F.	979	Holman, Ldg. Sig. H. R.	3862
— Sjt. S. H.	1002	Holmes, T./Sub Condr A.	1013
Hodgkinson, Sjt. H.	983	— C.E.R.A. 2nd Cl. E.	3860
— S./Sjt.(A./S.S.M.) P.	2699	— Sjt.(A./G.Q.M.S.) E. F.	2699
Hodgson, C.S.M. A.	2692	— A./Cpl. F. G.	981
— Ch.Mec. G.	99	— Sjt. J.	1023
— Sjt. T.	1021	— Cpl. J.	1013
— Pte.(L./C.) T.	989	Holroyd, Sjt.(A./S./Sjt.)(A./C.) J.	976
Hodson, Pte.(A./Cpl.) A.	1001	Holt, Sjt. O.	979
— Spr. J.	983	— Pte. S.	1001
— Ftr.S.Sjt. J. W.	975	— Pte.(L./C.) T.	988
Hogan, S./S.M. C. L. A.	1003	Homer, Bmdr. G.	974
— W.O. Cl. 1. R. J	1021	Honeychurch, C.E.R.A. 2nd Cl. J. F.	3860
— S.Q.M.S. W. G.	1021	Honeysett, Sjt. C.	976
Hogden, C.Q.M.Sjt. P. H.	991	Honner, L./C(A./Sjt.) W. R. E.	2693
Hogberg, Ch.Mec. F. J	99	Hood, Mech.Q.M.S. G. N.	2692
Hogbin, Pte.(A./S.Q.M.S.) E. R.	2700	Hook, C.Q.M.Sjt. G.	999
Hogg, By.S.M. A. E.	971	Hooker, Sjt.(A./C.S.M.Instr.) J. F.	1016
— Sjt. J.	979	Hooper, Pte.(A./Q.M.S.) C.	2696
— Spr. S. F. N.	983	— Sjt.(A./S./Sjt.) F. J.	1000
— Sjt. W. A.	1018	— B.Q.M.Sjt. H. S.	975
Hoggart, C.Q.M.S. M.	2999	— G./S.M. H. W. S.	2693
Holberry, Q.M.Sjt. J.	987	— Gnr. J.	974
Holdaway, Condr. F.	* 2701	— Cpl.(A./Sjt.) W. H.	2692
Holden, S./S.M. W. F.	1003	Hope, S.M. J.	2697
Holderness, Sqdn. S.M. T.	2699	Hopkins, By.Q.M.S. C. W.	1018
Holdershaw, S./Sjt.(A./S.Q.M.S.)		— Cpl. H. V.	1001
W. C. T.	1007	— Q.M.Sjt. J. W.	988
Holdstock, Sjt. A. E.	1000	— S./Sjt.(A./Q.M.Sjt.) W.	1012
Hole, Sjt.(A./C.Q.M.Sjt.) F. J.	1002	— Cpl. W. G.	70
Holehouse, Sjt. F.	994	Hopkinson, Pte.(A./Sjt.) A. H.	1016
Holgate, Cpl.(A./Sjt.) L.	1021	— S./Sjt. J. J.	2700

* Group known: Tibet (Gyantse, Sgt. S. & T. Corps), India General Service Medal (N.W.F. 1908, Afghanistan N.W.F. 1919, M.I.D. oakleaf), 1914/15 Star trio, L.S. & G.C. (Geo. V), M.S.M. and Volunteer Long Service in India (Geo. V, Tpr. 5 Punj. L.H.).

Hopley, Sjt. M.	976	Howard, C.Q.M.Sjt. J.	994
Hopper, Sjt. W.	70	— Sjt.(A./C.S.M.) J.	2698
— Cpl.(A./Q.M.Sjt.)		Howarth, Col.Sjt. S. J.	993
Engr.Clerk W. H.	68	Howatson, 1st Cl.	
Horn, S.M. (A.C.) T.	975	Asst. Surg. G. A. S.	3000
Hornbuckle, Sjt. J. F.	1021	Howe, Res. Ward Master A. G. D. §	2361
Horne, Sjt. C. L.	1023	— Sjt.(A./C.Q.M.S.) W. R.	2691
— Sjt.(A./C.S.M.) H. G.	979	Howell, Cpl. A.	986
Horner, Sjt. L. C.	1021	— Q.M.S. H. G.	2693
Hornsby, Pte.(A./Sjt.) J. T.	1010	— Sjt. R.	976
Horridge, Sjt.(A./S.M.) J. D.	2703	— C.E.R.A. 1st Cl. W. J.	2360
Horrocks, Pte.(A./L./Sjt.) A.	986	Howie, Sjt. A.	989
Horsley, Sjt. E. J.	69	— Pte. (A./Sjt.) J.	990
Horsman, Spr.(A./L./C.) A.	983	— Q.M.Sjt. R.	984
— Q.M.Sjt. H.	991	Howitt, C.P.O. R. R.	3862
Horton, Spr. G. E.	1488	Howlett, S.M. F.	2696
— Sjt. J.	1946	Howson, Pte. P.	1010
Hoskins. C.S.M. C. J.	987	Hoxley, Cpl.(A./Sjt.) W.	981
— Sjt. F. H.	1007	Hoy, Bmdr. A. J.	977
— Sto.P.O. S. H.	2361	Hubbard, Cpl.(A./Sjt.) L. L.	981
Hostler, Sjt.(A./C.S.M.) A. W.	979	— Sjt. T. M.	988
Hotchkiss, Cpl. A.	994	— Bmdr. W.	974
Hotine, Clr.Sjt. H.	2697	Hubert, Sjt.(A./S./Sjt.) C. R.	1945
Hough, Cpl. F.	993	— Sub Condr. J.	2701
Hough, W.O. Cl.II, S.Q.M.S.(A./		Hudson, T./S.S.M. A. R. G.	2698
W.O.C Cl. I) J.	3572	— Mech.S.M. H.	1003
Houghton, Cpl.(A./Sjt.) W. P.	2691	— Sjt. H. C.	992
Houlding, Pte.(A./Sjt.) E.	1015	— Sjt. (A./C.S.M.) H. W.	1000
Hounsell, Q.M.S.(T./S.M.) R. C. E.	2692	Hugg, Sjt. J. J.	1018
Hourigan, Spr. T.	983	Huggett, Sjt.(A./S.M.) A. W.	1015
Housden, S./Sjt. V. G.	1023	Hughes, T./S.M. A.	2694
House, S.M. A. G. *	2697	— T./S.M. A. J.	977
— Sjt. R.	2701	— Sjt. A. W.	979
Houston, A.B. G. †	3862	— Sjt.(A./S.M.) D.	979
— S./S.M. W. J. ‡	2698	— Cpl. E. J.	2698
Howard, Sjt.(A./C.S.M) C. J.	1000	— C.Q.M.S. F. V.	1021
— Mas.Mec. H. S.	99	— Sto. H.	2359

---

* Enlisted 1891 1/H.L.I., Crete 1898, Boer War, S.M. 1/H.L.I. 1908. L.S. & G.C. A.O.72/1912. D.C.M. *L.G.* 3 June 1915. M.S.M. in 4/H.L.I.

† Pair known: R.N. L.S. & G.C. (H.M.S. *Gentian*, No. 23922 R.F.R. Ch/B9379), and R.N. M.S.M. (also H.M.S. *Gentian*). This ship was lost in the Gulf of Finland on 16 July 1919 in action against the Bolsheviks, a Flower class fleet sweeping sloop of Arabian type.

‡ A.S.C. For Gibraltar.

§ Group known: St. John's Serving Brother, 1914 Star (M10237 Jun. Res. Asst. Dunkirk), British War and Victory Medals (Reserve Wardmaster R.N.), Coronation 1911 (St. John Reverse—Sgt.), R.N. M.S.M. (Res. Ward Mr. attd. R.A.F. Dunkirk 1918), R.N.A.S.B.R. L.S. Medal (449 Res. Wd. Mstr. R.N.A.S.B.R.) and St. John's Service Medal (462 Amb. Offr. No. 3 Dist. Wigston M.R. Div. St.J.A.B. 1918, with three extra clasps). Only 13 names on the R.N.A.S.B.R. Roll for Dunkirk, 1914.

Inglis, By.S.M. F.	971	Jacques, Sjt. R.		1487
— Sjt.(A./C.S.M.) J. M. M.	69	Jaffrey, Ftr.Cpl. W.		1488
— Col.Sjt.(A./S.M.) W.	2695	Jago, Sjt. P. P.		1018
Ingram, Pte.(A./Sjt.) E. D.	1014	James, S. M. A.		2691
Inskip, C.S.M. D. W.	1022	— Pte.(A./Cpl.) A.		1014
Ireland, Cpl.(A./Q.M.Sjt.) A. P.	1013	— Sjt. A. E.		988
— Gnr. T. H.	974	— Cpl.(A./C.Sjt.) B.		1001
Irvin, Sjt. T. G.	976	— Q.M.Sjt.(A./S.M.) C. E.		1011
Irving, Ch.Mec. H.	99	— Spr.(A./Cpl.) C. H.		983
— Sjt. H. V. C.	1022	— P.O. Teleg. E. J.		2361
— Pte. N. W.	61	— Mas.Clk. F.	†	99
Irwin, Spr. S.	983	— T./R.S.M. G. H. J.		970
— O.R.Sjt. T. A. F.	* 1946	— Sjt.(A./By.Q.M.Sjt.) J.		976
Isaacs, A./C.Q.M.S. D. J.	1022	— Dvr. J.		974
Isherwood, C.Q.M.Sjt. E.	1006	— Cpl. M.		1009
Isles, Gnr. H. E.	1018	— Sjt. R. L.		989
Isley, Cpl.(A./Sjt.) C. H.	986	— Spr. V. H.		1022
Islip, R.S.M. J.	2680	— Spr.(A./Sjt.) W. T.		983
Issit, Pte. H. W.	1001	James-Peck, Sjt. J.		980
Isted, Pte.(A./Cpl.) F.	69	Jamieson, S./Sjt. T. C.		1024
Ives, Pte. W.	983	Jamison, T./S.M. W.		996
Izzard, Engmn. A.	3862	Jaques, S./S.M. F.		2698
		Jardine, Sjt. J., *M.M.*		976
Jack, Q.M.S. R.	2693	— 2nd Cpl.(A./Cpl.) P.		982
Jackson, Cpl. A.	981	Jarlett, Sjt. C.		1007
— By.Q.M.Sjt. A. E.	972	Jarrett, Pte. F. W.		984
— Cpl. E. L.	1022	— Sjt. H. E.		1007
— Spr. E. W.	983	Jarvie, Pte.(A./Sjt.) W. Y.		2999
— Sjt. F. R.	1490	Jarvis, Ch.Mas.Mec. C.	‡	100
— Q.M.Sjt. W.	989	— Pte. D. J.		1018
— Sjt. W.	1007	— Sjt. P. R.		989
— Farr.Sjt. W. J.	970	Jasper, W.O. Cl. I		
Jacobs, By.S.M. A. E.	971	(Spdt. Clerk) H.	§	3572
Jacobs, Vict. C.P.O. C. J.	2360	Jeans, C.S.M. F. C.		2998
— Sjt. D. A.	978	Jefferies, Sjt. G. C.		1945
— R.Q.M.S. (W.O.Cl. 2) S. J.	1018	Jeffrey, Cpl.(A./C.Q.M.Sjt.) B. H.		981
— Sjt. W. T. G.	1000	— S.M. W. E.		977

---

* M.S.M. known. For East Africa: 11747 K.A.R.

† No. 152 R.F.C. Born 1888. Enlisted January 1908 into 1/Coldstream Guards. Central Flying School June 1912. Royal Aero Club Aviators' Certificate No. 864 28 July 1914. 1914 Star & bar as Sergeant 4 Sqn. in France from 9 September. 1914. M.I.D. *L.G.* 30 November, 1915, French Médaille Militaire *L.G.* 24 February 1916. 6th senior R.A.F. W.O. in 1931. Group known: M.B.E., 1914 Star & bar trio, Defence and War Medals, R.A.F. M.S.M., R.A.F. L.S. & G.C. (Geo. V, S.M.1) and Médaille Militaire.

‡ R.A.F. M.S.M. No. 159 R.F.C. Born 1882. Enlisted July 1912. Royal Aero Club Aviators' Certificate No. 524, June 1913 as Sergeant, Earned 1914/15 Star trio as a Warrant Officer. R.A.F. L.S. & G.C. in 1930. Served in W.W.II.

§ Pair known: L.S. & G.C. (Edw. VII, 56003 C.S.M. R.G.A.) and M.S.M. (for services in Record Officers (Home)). Attached Depot E.Kent Regt. at Canterbury.

Jeffreys, Sjt.(A./S./Sjt.) D.	1018	Johnson, Q.M.Sjt. W. R. G.	69
Jeffries, Pte. H.	998	Johnston, Cpl.(A./Sjt.) E.	1009
— Cpl. P. J.	981	— S./S.M. J.	1003
Jeffs, Sjt. E. C.	1023	— Sjt. J.	1000
— Sjt. F. G.	979	— L./Cpl.(A./2nd Cpl.) J. M.	983
— F./Clk. R. H.	100	— Clr.Sjt.(A./S.M.) W	2696
Jenkins, C.S.M. A.	978	Johnstone, Sjt. J. C.	2840
— Sjt. C.	989	— S./Sjt. J. W.	1018
— Sjt. E.	1022	Joliffe, T./S.M. B. J.	2698
— Cpl. H.	989	Jolly, L./C.(A./S./Sjt.) T. W. ❀	1256
— S.M. H. A.	2695	Jones, Cpl.(A./Sjt.) A.	1018
— Pte.(L./C.) L.	992	— 2/Cpl. (A./Sub Condr.) A.	1945
— Sjt.Clk. W. A.	100	— A.M.1 A. A.	100
— Sjt. W. F.	2697	— A.B. A. C.	3591
Jenkinson, Sjt. J. E.	68	— Cpl. A. P.	70
Jenner, Sjt.(A./C.S.M.) G.	993	— C.Q.M.S. A. W.	1018
— Ch.Mec. G. W.	100	— Sjt.(T./S./S.M.) A. Y. D.	1007
Jennings, T./C.M. J. E. *	2689	— Sjt.(A./C.Q.M.S.) D.	1000
Jensen, Pte. J.	1018	— S./SM. D. A.	2698
Jenson, Sjt. N., *MM.*	979	— C.S.M.(T./Mech.S.M) D. L.	1004
Jenvey, Sjt. F.	988	— Sjt.Mec. E.	100
Jepson, C.Q.M.Sjt. E. J.	985	— Sjt. E.	1900
Jeram, Cpl. F.	1001	— S./Sjt.(T./S./S.M.) F. E.	1007
Jessop, Cpl. R. T.	1022	— 2nd Cpl.(A./Sjt.) F. G.	982
Jiggins, Col.Sjt.(O.R.S.) S. E.	995	— Sjt.Mec. F. J.	100
Jinks, By.Q.M.Sjt. A. E.	972	— Condr. F. L.	1013
Jobson, Sjt. H. C.	1022	— Sjt. G. E.	1018
Johns, Cpl.(A./Sjt.) T. L.	1018	— Q.M.Sjt. H.	989
Johnson, C.S.M. A.	999	— Gnr. H.	974
— Cpl. A.	1018	— W.O. Cl.1, S./S.M. H. A.	3572
— Cpl.(L./Sjt.) A. C.	2693	— C.Q.M.Sjt. H. S.	999
— Gnr.(A./By.Q.M.Sjt.) A. S.	970	— Q.M.S. J.	2701
— Cpl. C. P.	100	— Sjt. J. †	2696
— S.M. D.	2694	— Spr.(A./L./C.) J.	2693
— Sjt. E.	979	— Pte. J.	1014
— C.Q.M.Sjt. F. J.	987	— Q.M.Sjt. J. E.	994
— Sjt. F. P.	1022	— Sqdn. S.M. J. H.	970
— Pte. (L./C.) H.	993	— T./Sub Condr. J. H.	2700
— Expl.Q.M.S. J.	2690	— Q.M.Sjt. J. L.	992
— Cpl.(A./Sjt.) J. F.	2840	— Pte.(A./S.Q.M.S.) J. L.	2700
— Sjt. O.	970	— 2nd Cpl.(A./Sjt.) J. S.	982
— S./Sjt. O. W.	1003	— S./S.M. M. G.	1003
— Gnr. S.	3840	— Cpl. M. H. A.	1003
— Sjt. W. D.	979	— S.M. P. P.	1011
— F. of W. S.M. W. F.	2692	— R.S.M. R., *M.C.* ‡	970

---

* Group known: Queen's South Africa Medal (Relief of Kimberley, Paardeberg, Dreifontein, Diamond Hill, Wittebergen, Cpl. of Horse 2/Life Guards), L.S. & G.C. (Edw. VII) and M.S.M. (Temp./Cpl. Major).

† K.S.L.I. For Singapore

‡ R.F.A. M.C. *L.G.* 19 August 1916.

Jones, Cpl. R.	1001	Keane, F. of W. Q.M.Sjt. N.		978
— S.Q.M.Sjt. R. A.	1005	— T./S.M. S.		997
— R.S.M.(A./S.M.) T.	2690	Kearney, Spr. (A./Cpl.) T. W.		983
— C.S.M. T.	1489	Kearns, Sjt. J. C.		979
— C.S.M.(A./S.M.) T. E.	2701	Keating, F. of W Q.M. F. J. J.		978
— Sjt. T. E.	69	— B.S.M. H. C.		1487
— Pte. T. G.	1945	Keats, Pte. R.		1010
— Dvr. T. M.	68	Keattch, Cpl A.		993
— Condr. T. P.	2999	Keay, Cpl.Clk. G. E.		100
— Sjt. W.	3840	Keech, Sjt. E.		1018
— Pte. W.	988	Keeley, Pte.(L./C.A./Sjt.) C.		1010
— C.S.M. W. C.	61	Keeman, Sjt. W.		1000
— C.Q.M.Sjt. W. J.	1005	Keen, C.S.M.Instr. A. J.		2690
Sjt. W. T.	989	Keenan, Sjt. C.		1023
Jordan, C.S.M. T. E.	992	— Sjt. J., *M.M.*		972
Joseph, Ch.Clk. A.	1946	— C.S.M.(T./R.S.M.)(A.C.) W.		975
Jowsey, Spr. J. A.	1018	Keeping, S./S.M. A. E.		1003
Joy, Pte. C.	1018	Keeves, C.Q.M.S. E. W.		1022
— Pte.(L./C.) J. C. M.	2696	Keighly, Sjt.(A./Q.M.S.) W.		1012
Joyce, Sjt. H. T.	976	Keith, Sjt. J.		996
— Sjt. J.	1007	— Ch.Elect.Art. 2nd Cl. R. J. L.		2360
— Pte. J.	1001	Kelleher, Cpl. J.		989
— S./Sjt.(T./Sub Condr.) J. H.	71	Keller, Sjt. H. E.	*	2690
— Sto.P.O. R.	3591	Kellett, Sjt. F.		989
Joyner, Cpl.(A./Q.M.Sjt.) E.	991	— Sjt.(A./C.)(A./S.M.) T. W.		1488
Jubb, Farr.Sjt. H.	1487	Kelly, Q.M.Sjt. D.		984
Jubber, Whlr.S./Sjt. C	1005	— Cpl. D. J.		976
Juden, Cpl. J.	1001	— Sjt. E. L.		1022
Judge, T./S./S.M. A. E.	2698	— A.M. 2 J.		100
Jupp, Gnr. F.	2997	— Cpl. J. W.		987
		— Sjt. L. S.		1022
Kable, Cpl. R. R.	1022	— S. and C.S.Cpl. M.		2997
Kachepa, L./C.	1946	— Sjt. T.		998
Kafwiro, Sjt.	1946	— Trpr.(A./Cpl. of H.) T.	†	984
Kavanagh, Farr.Q.M.Sjt. M.	971	Kember, Pte.(A./Sjt.) J.		2701
— S./S.M. P.	1489	Kemp, Cpl.(A./C.S.M.) C. H.		2692
Kay, Sjt. A. W.	984	— Sjt. F.		995
— Cpl.(A./Sjt.) F.	1013	— Mas.Mec. J.	‡	100
Kean, Sjt. A.	1022	Kemplay, Cpl.(A./Q.M.Sjt.) E. L.		1489

---

* Group known: Queen's South Africa Medal (Cape Colony, Paardeberg, Dreifontein, Transvaal, Wittebergen, Driver A.S.C.), King's South Africa Medal, Defence Medal, M.S.M. (Wilts. Yeo.), Spec. Const. L. S. (Sgt. Horace E. Keller). Served with 2/1st R. Wilts. Yeo. in England and Ireland in W.W.I, thus no British War Medal or Victory Medal.

† This is the only M.S.M. to a man of Machine Gun Guards (Life Guards). There are however two others to Guards Machine Gun Regt. (Life Guards): S.C.M. W. Butson and Q.M.C.M. C. M. Dawes, both in *L.G.* 3 June 1919.

‡ Group Mounted as worn in Moss collection: Order of St. John Officers badge in silver, R.A.F. M.S.M., British War and Victory Medals, Defence and War Medals, 1911 Coronation (St. John's Ambulance Brigade), 1935 Jubilee and St. John's Long

Kempshall, Sjt. G. A.	994	Kerrison, Q.M.Sjt.E. P., *D.C.M.*	*	988
Kempster, Sjt.(T./S.S.M.) G.	2699	Kerry, Ch.Mec. A. L.		100
Kench, S.M. W. E.	2700	— Pte.(L./C.) J. M.		1001
Kendall, Sjt. F.	1018	Kerswell, Q.M.Sjt. G. S.		985
— Sjt. F. H.	1022	Kerton, Pte.(A./Sjt.) A.		1013
— Sjt. H., *M.M.*	994	Ketterer, Q.M.Sjt. J.		1003
Kendell, S./Sjt.(A./Sub Condr.) J. W.	2997	Kettley, Cpl. J. W.		1001
Kennedy, Q.M.Sjt.(A./S.M.) H.	1011	Key, Sjt. W.		991
— Sjt. J.	1018	Kidby, Pte.(A./Sjt.) A.		71
— Farr.S./Sjt. P.	972	Kidd, C.Q.M.S. C. W.		2697
Kennell-Webb, Pte. W.	1018	— Q.M.Sjt. J.		996
Kenneth, S.M. G. D.	3841	Kidman, Cpl.(A./Sjt.) S. J.		1013
Kenny, Sjt. O. P.	1022	Kielly, Bombdr. R.		1018
— Q.M.Sjt. T.	997	Kilby, Sjt. G. E.		1256
Kent, Pte.(A./Cpl.) E. G.	1003	Kilgar, Engmn. P.		3862
— S./Sjt. L. C.	62	Kilimanjaro, Pnr.		1946
— S.Q.M.Sjt. L. J.	61	Kilkenny, S.M. W.		100
— Pte. M.	1001	Killick, S./Sjt. C. C.		1018
— S./Sjt. R.	1018	Kimm, 2nd Cl. Schoolmaster		
— Condr. W.	2702	G. W. P.	†	2701
Kenyon, Pte. N.	1013	Kinch, Cpl. W.		1018
Kenzie, Amt.S./Sjt.(T./Amt.S.M.)		King, S.M.(W.O.Cl.1) A. J.		1018
B. C.	61	— Q.M.Sjt. E.		994
Keppel, C.S.M. G.	2698	— S.M. E. O.	‡	2695
Kernohan, Sjt.(A./C.S.M.) W.	68	— Sjt.(A./S.M.) E. W.		1490
Kerr, Cpl.(A./L./Sjt.) J. B.	1018	— BS.M. F. E.		2690
— L./C.(A./C.Q.M.S.) R. D.	3840	— Pte. G.		989
— S.Q.M.Sjt. S.	989	— Pte. G. A.		71
— Farr.S./Sjt. T.	970	— Sjt. J.		1022
— Cpl. W.	1009	— Sjt. M. E.		979

Service Medal with 6 extra clasps (S.Sgt. W. W.'Stow Div. 1923). No. 8101 R.F.C. Enlisted in 1915. Probationary 2nd Lieut. R.A.F. 1 April 1918. Left the services and qualified M.B. Ch.B. Manchester 1927. In 1930 was Flight Lieutenant R.A.F., Gen. Hosp. Hinhidi, Iraq. Serving Brother St. John's 23 November 1928 and Officer (St.J.A.B.) 22 May, 1936. June 1939 promoted to Sqn. Leader and June 1941 to Wing Commander. Group Captain in 1946. Still noted in St. John's Medal Directory in 1962.

* Group sold Christie's, 1990, for £2750: D.C.M., George Medal, 1914/15 trio and M.S.M., with R.S.P.C.A. silver medal dated September, 1940. The George Medal was awarded for gallantry during the London Blitz in February 1941, when he was serving in the Police (*L.G.* 15 November 1940), when he rescued a woman in very dangerous circumstances in a bombed building. The D.C.M. was awarded in *L.G.* 1 January 1917, 7/Bedfordshire Regt.

† For Malta (Corps of Army Schoolmasters).

‡ Group known: Queen's South Africa Medal (Cape Colony, Orange Free State, Transvaal, South Africa 1901, 190 Pte. 2/Hants.), Defence Medal, Imperial Service Medal (Geo. V, Ernest Otto King), M.S.M. (380802 17/Hamps. R.) and Territorial Force Efficiency Medal (Geo. V, 284 C./Sgt. 5./Hants.). Later Captain R.A.O.C. (T.A.) and was Inspector of Telegraph Messengers at Southampton. Joined the Volunteers in 1898, W.O.II, 1915 and W.O.1 in 1917. Lieut. R.A.O.C. 1922.

King, Q.M.Sjt. S.	904	Kynaston, Cpl. H.	987
— E.C.Sjt. T.	979		
— S.M. W.	994	Lacy, T./Mech.S.M. T.	61
— 2nd Cpl.(A./Sjt.) W.	982	Ladd, Pte.(A./W.O. Cl. 2, S.Q.M.S.)	
— Gnr.(A./Bdr.) W. A.	977	J. W.	3572
— Sjt.(A./S.S.M.) W. J.	60	— Sjt. W. A.	979
— Sjt.(A./R.Q.M.S.) W. L.	1018	Laing, Sjt. A. R.	68
Kingan, Sjt.(A./C.S.M.) R.	3841	— Pte. (A./Sjt.) C.	1018
Kinggett, Sjt.Mech. J.	2050	— Sjt. D. J.	1002
Kings, Cpl. A. T.	1009	Laird, Sjt. D.	990
— S./Sjt. E. M.	2702	— Sjt. J., *MM.*	979
Kingston, Sjt. A. C. W.	1022	— Sjt.(A./C.S.M.) W. A.	990
Kingstone, Sig./Cpl D.	973	Laithwaite, Ch.Mas.Mec J.	100
Kinloch, Sjt.(T./S./S.M.) P.	1007	Lake, S./S.M. J. W. V.	2698
Kinnaird, Cpl. C.	981	— Q.M.S. T. E.	2695
Kinnell, Ftr.Cpl.(A./Ftr.Sjt.) A.	973	Lakelin, Cpl. H.	998
Kinnersley, Cpl. N.	1009	Lamb, Farr.S./Sjt. F.	1005
Kinross, 2nd Cpl.(A./S./Sjt.) J.	1014	— Cpl.(A.C.) F. W.	976
Kirby, Sjt. C. B.	1018	— Cpl. W. R.	985
— Armr.S./Sjt. C. E.	1013	Lambert, Sjt. A.	992
— Cpl.Mec. E. G.	100	— Pte.(A./L./C.) E.	1010
— C.S.M. F. E.	2999	— S./Sjt. W. H.	1007
— Q.M.S.(T./S.M.) T.	2700	Lambie, Q.M.Sjt. A.	989
Kirby, Sjt. W. J.	976	— Pte. (A./Cpl.) J.	995
Kirfield, Sjt. J. W.	1022	Lambkin, C.S.M. J. S.	1024
Kirk, L./Bombr. A. W.	1488	Lampard, Spr. H. E	983
— S.M. J.	2697	Lancaster, C.Q.M.S. H., *MM.*	1022
Kirkby, Pte. G.	62	— S./S.M. H. H.	1003
Kirkdale, Sjt.(A./C.S.M) W.	1007	Lane, S./Sjt. (A./S.M.) A.	2700
Kirkham,. Spr. T.	1488	— S.M. W. J.	1011
Kirkland, Cpl.(A./Sjt.) H. A.	988	Lang, Bombdr. C. H.	1022
Kitching, Sjt. M.	1007	— Sjt. D. G.	1022
Kitson, W.O.Cl.1, E.	1022	— Sjt. S. J., *D.C.M.*	1022
— Q.M.S.(A./S.M) P.	2695	— S./Sjt. V. L.	1018
Kivell, C.Q.M.S. C. L.	1024	Lang, C.Q.M.S. W. A.	2691
Knapton, Yeo.Sigs. A. A.	2360	Langdon, B.Q.M.Sjt. F. K.	68
Knee, Q.M.S.(A./S.M) W. J.	2999	Langeson, Sjt.(A./By.S.M.) C. N.	1018
Knight, Sjt. C. E.	994	Langham, S.M. H.	2694
— Pte.(A./C.Q.M.S.) C. J.	2698	Langley, S./Sjt.(A./Condr.) F. C.	1014
— Sjt. H. L.	991	Langlois, Pte. W.	1013
— Q.M.S. T. F.	2696	Langtry, Clr.Sjt. H.	2696
— E.R.A. 2nd Cl. W. H.	3860	Lanning, Sjt. J.	998
Knill, Cpl. A.	1001	Lansdell, B.Q.M.S. L. H.	2690
Knoll, C.Q.M.Sjt. J. P.	1002	Lansley, C.Q.M.Sjt. G. W.	999
Knott, Sjt.(A./S.Q.M.S.) J.	2690	Lantsberry, Cpl. G. E. A.	1001
Knowles, Pte. J.	1001	Lapworth, C.Q.M.S. O.	69
Knox, Cpl. (A./Sjt.) F.	995	Larcher, Pte.(T./	
— Sjt.(A./By.S.M.) W. J.	1022	Sub Condr.) S. H.	* 1014
Kohler, C.S.M.(W.O. Cl. 2) E. F.	1022	Large, Gnr. H. W.	2997

* R.A.O.C. Also Médaille d'Honneur avec Glaives (en Argent).

Lark, Sjt. W. J.	1024	— C.Q.M.S. J.	1022
Larkin, Q.M.S. C. A.	2691	Leather, Pte.(A./Cpl.) R. L.	1010
Larsen, Sjt. H. J.	992	Leathley, Dkhnd. L., *D.S.M.*	2361
Lashbrook, Ch.Mec. P.	100	Leavey, Sadd.S./Sjt. C. J.	1005
Last, Sjt.(A./Sqdn.S.M.) A.	2701	Ledger, T./S.M. F. W.	975
Latimer, Q.M.Sjt. J.	995	Lee, Cpl. C.	990
Lavender, Pte.(A./Sjt.) H.	62	— By.S.M. C. H.	971
— Cpl. T.	1001	— Pte.(A./Sjt.) E. J.	1016
Laver, W.O. Cl.1 (S./S.M.) G. H.	3572	— S./Sjt. G. H.	1007
Laverack, Col.Sjt		— Sjt. J.	1022
(O.R.S.) T. V., *MM.*	991	— Sjt. J. H.	993
Lavin, Clr.Sjt. T.	2695	— S./Sjt. J. W.	1007
Law, Pnr.(L./Cpl.) A. H. V.	983	Leehan, B.S.M. E.	2691
— Sjt. D. P.	* 1000	Leeming, W.O. W.	2702
— Cpl. L. F.	1009	Lees, Pte. F. W.	995
Lawler, Sto. T.	2361	— Cpl. J.	60
Lawrence, C.Q.M.S. A.	1018	— Q.M.Sjt. J. M.	1012
— Gnr.(L./Bmdr.)(A.C.) C	977	Legg, S.M. L. C.	2690
— S.M. C. H.	100	Leggett, Pte.(A./S.Q.M.S.) H.	2700
— Sjt. G. L.	991	— Sjt. S. H.	68
— Sjt. J. C.	1022	Leggott, Sjt. G. H.	68
— B.Q.M.Sjt. J. W.	972	Lehane, C.S.M.(A./S.M.) P.	2997
— Sjt. M. E., *D.C.M.*	1018	Leibermann, Sjt. R.	1000
Laws, Pte.(A./S./Sjt.) G.	1013	Leigh, Ch.Mec. J. N.	100
Lawson, Sjt. B. F.	2361	— Sjt. S. H.	1022
— Cpl. F.	2997	Leigh-Hunt, C.Q.M.Sjt. H.	986
— Pte. G. T.	1010	Leighfield, C.S.M. W. C.	994
— Mech.S./Sjt. H.	2999	Leitch, Pte.(A./L./C.) P.	1001
— Pte. L. W.	1001	— C.Q.M.Sjt. S. A.	995
— Cpl. W.	984	Lemon, C.Q.M.Sjt. H.	1005
— Mech.S./Sjt. W. W.	60	— S.M. J., *D.C.M.*	994
Lawton, Dvr A.	71	Leng, S./S.M. J. R.	1003
— Pte.(A./Sub Condr.) J. A.	1014	— Sjt. R. A.	993
Laycock, Pte.(A./Sjt.) J. R. T.	988	Lennon, S.M. J.	1945
Layfield, Pte.(A./Sjt.) W.	1003	Leonard, Cpl.(A./R.S.M.) E. J.	976
Le Brun, C.P.O. Teleg. C. J.	2360	— Pte.(A./Sjt.) L.	70
Le Lacheur, Sjt.(A./Q.M.S.) P.	1490	— 1st Cl. Mst.Gnr. W.	† 2691
Le Roy, Sjt. B.	1000	— Cpl.(A./C.S.M.) W.	1009
Leach, Ch.Mas.Mec. G.	100	Leppard, Sjt. C. T.	979
— S./Sjt. W. E.	2702	Leppington, S./Sjt.(A./Q.M.S.) W C.	1012
— S./Sjt.(T./Sub Condr.) W. J.	1014	Leroy, Condr. D.	80
Leach, S.M. W. T.	1011	Leslie, Sjt. H. J.	984
Leahy, Farr.S./Sjt. P.	1005	Lesseman, By.S.M. G. W.	971
Leak, Pte. R.	985	Lester, Eng.Clk.(A./Sjt.) A. J.	1488
Leaney, B.Q.M.S. W. J.	2690	— Cpl. F.	981
Leary, Sjt. C.	976	— Cpl.(A./Sjt.) P. A.	100

---

* Group was in McInnes collection: Natal Medal (clasp 1906, Tpr. Zululand M.R.),
  British War and Victory Medals (38926 Sgt. Northants. R.), Defence Medal, M.S.M.
  (86061 144/LC), Special Constabulary L.S. (Geo. V, 1st type, Inspector).

† R.G.A. For Gibraltar.

Lester, Arm.Sjt. P. J.	1024	Little, By.S.M. W. H., *M.M.*	971
Lethbridge, C.P.O. 3rd Cl. G.	3863	Littlewood, Q.M.S. C. H. J.	2693
Letson, C.Q.M.S. H.	996	— Farr.Sjt. F.	2997
Letts, Sub Condr. F. C.	2702	— Pte.(A./Sjt.) H.	1013
Letty, Pte.(A./Sjt.) D.	1016	— Sjt. J.	100
Levings, Sub Condr. F. G.	62	Livingstone, Sjt. H.	1007
Lewinden, Pte. C.	1010	— S./Sjt. H. W.	1018
Lewis, S./Sjt.(A./Sub Condr.) C.	3000	— C.S.M. J.	2691
— Sjt. C. G.	1022	Llewellyn, Sjt. T.	1488
— Supt.Clk. E. A.	2692	Lloyd, Sjt. A. S.	987
— Bombdr.(A./Cpl.) E. E.	1022	— Sjt. C.	1000
— R.Q.M.S. E. H.	1022	— Dvr. D.	1010
— Pte.(A./Sjt.) F. C. V.	1016	— Pte. E. E.	980
— Sjt. G. H.	1007	— Sjt. F. J., *M.M.*	1002
— Spr. G. H. C.	2998	— Pte. H. C.	1010
— Q.M.S. H. J.	2696	— C.Q.M.Sjt. L.	989
— T./Sub Condr.(A./Condr.) J. H.	1013	— Sjt. P. T.	972
— Sjt. J. S.	1488	— H.Condr. T.	1945
— Q.M.Sjt. T.	985	— Cpl.(A./Sjt.) W.	2695
Lewsey, C.S.M. M. W.	989	— Pte.(L./C.) W. H.	69
Leyland, By.S.M. T.	975	— Q.M.S. W. J.	1018
Liddel, Sjt. J.	2698	Lock, Sub Condr. J.	2702
Liddell, Sjt. W. T.	979	Locker, Cpl. A.	984
Lidstone, F. of W. Q.M.S. A. R.	2692	Lockhead, Pnr.(A./Sjt.) J.	1946
Lightfoot, C.Q.M.Sjt. A.	978	Lockley, C.S.M.(A./R.S.M.) J.	991
— S./Sjt. R.	2703	Lockwood, C.E.R.A. 2nd Cl. G. F.	2360
Lincoln, Pte.(A./Mech.S.S.) J. C.	2700	— S.M. J. W.	1011
Lindsay, S.M. H., *M.M.*	988	— Mech.S./Sjt. T.	1489
— Pte.(A./Sjt.) J.	1003	— Spr.(A./2nd Cpl.) W. S.	981
— Sjt. W. P.	987	Lockyer, Sjt. S.	985
Lindsley, Q.M.Sjt. J.	1489	Lodge, R.Q.M.S. E. G.	1022
Lincham, Pte.(A./Sjt.) M.	1015	— 2nd Cpl. P. F.	68
Lines, Cpl. H. A.	1009	— Ch.Mec. W. *	100
Ling, Sjt. A.	1940	Loeber, Cpl.(A./Sjt.)(A.C.) C. W.	975
Linnell, Cpl. E.	1000	Loftus, Sjt. T. D.	984
Linthwaite, Pte.(A./S.Q.M.Sjt.) J. W.	62	Lomax, Pte.(L./C.) T. V.	989
Linton, B.S.M. A.	1487	Long, 2nd Cpl.(A./Cpl.) A.	982
Lipman, W.O. L. B.	2702	— Sjt. A. A.	1018
Lipscombe, C.S.M.(T./Mech.S.M.) G.	1004	— S.Q.M.S. B S.	61
Lister, Mech.S./Sjt. J.	1003	— Arm.S./Sjt. G.	1013
— Sjt. J. J.	1007	— W.O. Cl. 1, G. H., *M.M.*	1022
Little, Sjt. O. H.	1000	— A.B. L. J. †	2361
— Pte. W. A.	1001	— Pte.(A./Mech.S./Sjt.) H. W.	2697

---

* R.A.F. M.S.M. No. 948. 1914 Star only known. Enlisted November 1913. To France with 2 Sqn. (2A.M.) 12 August, 1914. Promoted Flight Sergt. (Photographer). L.S. & G.C. (S.M.2) 1931. Awarded 1935 Jubilee Medal. Commissioned August 1937. Wing Commander 1942. Still serving 1946.

† Single R.N. M.S.M. known impressed *'Cassandra'* Baltic Sea 5 Dec 1918. A light cruiser sunk by a mine. Of the complement of 344, 11 were killed by the explosion, the balance being transferred to accompanying destroyers (see also Appendix T).

Longbottom, Pte.(A./Sjt.) E.	1015	Lucas, C.S.M. C.	999
Longden, Sjt. J.	993	— Pte. E.	71
Longhurst, Sjt. C.	979	— S.M. J. C. §	977
— Pnr. C. R.	983	Luck, C.S.M. C. A. V.	984
Longland, Dvr. J.	974	— Q.M.S. W.	997
Longpre, Sjt. C.	1013	Lucke, Sjt.(A./S./Sjt.) R. M.	1007
Longstaff, Sub Condr. H.	2700	Luckie, Sjt. G. E.	979
Loomes, P.O. F.	3860	Ludgate, Sjt. J. T.	1944
Loosemore, Sjt. J. W. ✿	1256	Luff, Sjt. R. J.	1007
Lord, Gnr. F.	68	Luffman, Ch.Sjt.(A./S.M.) W.	2701
— Sjt. J.	1022	Lukehurst, Sjt.(A./C.S.M.) C.	979
Lorne, Sjt. G. W. *	972	Lumsden, C.S.M. J. S.	992
Louth, C.S.M. W. G. E.	994	Lund, Sjt. J. W.	988
Love, Sjt. H.	1018	Lunn, Cpl. R.	996
Lovelace, Sjt. Mec. F.	100	— C.S.M. W.	2698
Lovell, C.S.M. A. V.	997	Lunt, Pte.(A./Sjt.) E.	986
— Sjt. Mec. P. J.	100	Luntley, S./Sjt. J.	1945
Lovelock, R.S.M. H. W. †	1002	Lyall, T./S.M. W. H.	2701
Loveridge, Cpl. A.	987	Lyles, Sjt. (O.R.S.) M. J.	1000
Lovett, Q.M.S. J.	997	Lynch, S./Sjt. J. +	3000
Lovick, Pte.(A./S./Sjt.) W.	1015	— C.S.M. J.	2691
Low, Sjt. F. C.	998	— Sjt. J.	972
— Sjt. G.	995	— Sjt. T. G.	993
Lowe, Pte.(A./L./C.) E. L.	1011	Lyon, Sjt. J.	1000
— C.S.M.(T./R.S.M.) E. M. ‡	978	Lyons, T./S.M. P. C	60
— Sjt. F. V.	2698	— Cpl. W. M.	1022
— Sjt. H., *M.M.*	979		
— Sjt. J. H.	1007	Mabbutt, Gnr.(L./Bombr.) A. J.	974
— A.M. 1, L. H.	100	MacAdam, Cpl. C.	996
— Pte.(T./Sub Condr.) S. G.	1014	McAinsh, Cpl.(A./Sjt.) W. ✿	1256
— Spr. W. F.	1945	McArdle, Cpl. T.	981
Lower, Sjt. A.	3840	McArthur, Sjt. Mech. J.	100
Lowes, Q.M.S. W.	995	— Pte.(A./Cpl.) W.	1013
— Q.M.S. W. R.	991	McAteer, S.M. H. ◊	995

* 62917 Sergt. and B.S.M. No. 2 Section 29th D.A.C. 1914–15—For continuous hard work and devotion to duty. He landed with the 29th Division at Gallipoli on April 25th, 1915, and remained with the Division till it reached the Rhine in December, 1918. (Mention 21/5/18).

† P.W.O. Civil Service Rifles. K.I.A. 28 September 1918, aged 38. From Chelsea. Clerk at the Bank of England.

‡ Group sold by Glendining, 1969 for £10: B.S.A. Coy. Medal (Rhodesia 1896, Bugler 43 Coy. R.E.), L.S. & G.C. (Geo. V, Sgt. R.E.) and M.S.M. (W.W.I medals missing).

§ Unusual group, known: 1914/15 Star trio (W.O.II R.A.), R.N. L.S. & G.C. (Victoria, Stoker 'Victoria & Albert'), Army L.S. & G.C. (F. of W. Q.M.S. R.A.) and M.S.M.

+ Group sold by Baldwin, 1960, for £7.10.0, now in R.C.T. collection: India General Service Medal (Abor 1911–12), L.S. & G.C. (Geo. V) and M.S.M. (both Supply & Transport). M.S.M. for Mesopotamia, W.W.I medals not present.

◊ 7/H.L.I. Served in 1/H.L.I. in Boer War. Queen's South Africa Medal (Cape Colony, Wittebergen, South Africa 1901, South Africa 1902), Territorial Force Efficiency Medal (Edw. VII) and M.S.M. known.

McBretney, C.Q.M.S. A. C.		988	— Sjt.(A./C.S.M.) J.	1018
McCabe, Cpl. C.		1009	Macdonald, Clr.Sjt.(A./C.Q.M.S.)	
— Clk. 1, E.		100	J. M., *D.C.M.*	986
McCafferty, Gnr. J.	❀	1256	McDonald, Spr. P.	983
McCaffery, L./C.(A./S.M.) P.		2701	Macdonald, T./S.M. R.	‡ 2694
McCall, S./S./Cpl. J.		973	MacDonald, L./C.(A./Sjt.) W.	1490
McCann, Pte. T.		995	— Ldg.Sea. W.	3862
McCardle, Cpl. O.		985	McDonald, Pte.(A./L./C.) W.	1011
McCarthy, C.P.O. 3rd Cl., E. H.		3863	McDonnell, C.S.M. J.	999
— By.S.M.(A./R.S.M.) F.		975	McDonough, C.Q.M.S. S. B.	1022
— Sjt.(A./C.S.M.) J.		2692	McDougall, S./Sjt. A. D. H.	1024
— Sjt. P.		2999	— Cpl.(A./Sjt.) A. M.	1001
— Q.M.S. T. D.		984	— Sjt.(A./W.O.Cl. 2) D. C.	1019
— Sub Condr. W. T.		2702	MacDougall, S./Sjt. T. F.	1012
McCartney, A./Q.M.S. A.		2691	McDowell Dowell, pl.(A./Sqdn.	
McCleery, Ch.E.R.A.			Q.M.S.) A. N.	2701
W. J., *D.S.M.*	*	2359	McEvoy, Q.M.Sjt. J. R.	1488
McClellan, S./Sjt. W. M.		1019	McEwan, Sjt. F. W.	3000
McCluskey, Dvr. J.		974	McFadden, Ldg.Sto. D.	2359
McCollum, R.Q.M.S. C. S.		1019	— Cpl. J.	984
McComb, Cpl. R.		1001	— Q.M.Sjt. R.	997
McConnell, C.S.M. D. M.		1488	McFarland, Pte. A. H.	1022
McConvill, Sjt. A.		69	McFarlane, Dkhnd. A.	3862
McConville, C.Q.M.S. T.		996	— C.Q.M.Sjt. C.	996
McCoshen, Pte.(A./Sjt.) D.		2702	McGillivray, Pte. H.	1019
McCoy, Pte. L.		69	MacGillivray, Sjt. J.	970
— Sjt. T.		1000	McGrath, Sjt. D.	68
MacCreadie, Farr.S./Sjt. W.		970	— Spr. J.	983
McCready, Sjt. D.		1946	— S./Sjt. T.	1022
McCrossan, Cpl.(L./Sjt.) J.		990	McGreevy, Cpl.(L./Sjt.) H. J.	1019
McCulley, Sjt. J.		984	MacGregor, C.Q.M.Sjt. A.	978
McCurdy, Sjt. R.		1012	McGregor, F. of W. Q.M.S. J. G.	§ 2692
McDerment, C.S.M.(A./S.M.) W.		2702	MacGregor, Cpl. R.	1001
McDermot, Sjt. T.		2998	McGregor, F. of W. S.M. R.C.	2692
McDonagh, Pte.(L./C.) P. J.		987	McGuigan, Cpl. A. C.	996
MacDonald, Sjt. A.		1018	McGuiness, Pte.(A./Sjt.) W. E.	1015
— Q.M.Sjt. D.		1012	McGuire, C.S.M. J. H.	1004
McDonald, Sjt. D.		996	McIlveny, Pte.(A./Sjt.) H. E.	1015
MacDonald, Pte. D.		970	McIlvride, Pte. A. B.	1019
McDonald, C.S.M. D. F.		997	McInnerney, Cpl. W.	3841
— Sjt. D. R.		1488	McInroy, C.Q.M.S. C. B.	1022
— Sjt.(O.R.S.) E.	†	984	McIntosh, Q.M.S. A.	2697
— Clr.Sjt. E.		2697	— S./S.M.(A./S.M.) J.	2690
MacDonald, Pte. H.		970	McIntosh, Cpl.(L./Sjt.) J.	984
MacDonald, C.S.M. J., *D.C.M.*		2694	— Cpl. J. M.	1019

---

* R.N.R. and R.N. M.S.M.
† Trio known: British War Medal, Regular Army, L.S. & G.C. (Geo. V) and M.S.M. (2/Scots Gds).
‡ For Bermuda (East Yorks.).
§ Trio known: China 1900 (no clasp, Balloon Coy. R.E.), L.S. & G.C. (Geo. V), M.S.M.

McIntosh, Pte.(A./Sjt.) J. M.	1015	McLachlan, Sjt. J.		1022
McIntyre, S.M. A. B.	2692	McLagan, Pte.(L./C.) W. E. G.		1019
— Sjt. H.	995	McLaren, C.S.M. A.		1002
— C.S.M. H. L.	978	— Q.M.Sjt. A. L. V.		990
— Cpl. J., *M.M.*	992	— S./Sjt. P. C.		2702
— Cpl.(A./Sjt.) R. L.	970	McLaughlin, Sjt. A., *D.C.M.*		2697
McIver, Far.S./Sjt. C.	970	— Gnr. T.		974
McKail, 2nd Cpl.(A./C.Q.M.) T.	982	MacLaurin, C.Q.M.Sjt. A.		996
Mackay, C.S.M. J.	1946	McLean, P.O. A.		2360
— Q.M.S. J.	1018	— Sjt. F. E.		997
McKay, By.S.M. J. C.	971	— Sjt. G. D.		1019
— S.M. M.	2703	MacLean, S./S.M.(Q.M.S.) J. S.		2697
— Sjt.(A./C.S.M.) R. R.	2999	McLear, Pte. P.		1002
— Pte. S. F.	1019	McLelland, C.P.O. D.		969
— Pte.(L./C.) T.	997	McLeod, S.M. G. A. N.		1019
Mackay, Sjt. W.	1489	— Q.M.S. J.		2694
MacKay, Cpl.(A./Sjt.) W.	1001	— Sjt. J.		973
McKechnie, Sjt.(T./Mech.S.M.) H.	1007	— Pte.(A./L./C.) N.		1490
McKee, Cpl. J.	1019	McLindon, T./S.S.M. B.		1945
McKellar, Sjt. H.	1489	McMahon, S.M. J. H.		1945
McKenna, Supt.Clk. J. O. F.	2693	McManus, Pte.(A./Sjt.) C.		1016
Mackenzie, Clr.Sjt. G. A. P.	2697	MacMillan, S.M. D. M.		2697
McKenzie, Pte.(L./C.) J.	1016	McMullen, Sjt. H. H.		1488
MacKenzie, Sjt. J. M.	1015	MacNab, Q.M.Sjt. A.		992
Mackenzie, By.S.M. L.	971	McNally, Sjt. W. H.		1019
— Condr. T.	2702	McNaughton, Sjt. J.		976
McKeown, Pte.(A./L./C.) J.	1016	McNeil, Pte.(L.C.,		
McKerihan, W.O.1st Cl. C. R.	1022	T./M.S.M.) A. E.		1011
McKerrow, Sjt. T.	989	— Sjt. W. J.		979
McKett, C.S.M.(A./		MacNiven, C.Q.M.Sjt. J.		992
S.M.Instr.) J. E.	2701	McPherson, Ch.Mas.Mec. J.		100
McKevitt, Pte.(A./Sjt.) B.	2697	MacPherson, Sjt. W.		1022
Mackey, Q.M.S. A.	2689	MacQueen, Ch.Mas.Mec. H.	*	100
— C.Q.M.Sjt. F.	994	McQueen, Cpl. J.		984
McKie, Cpl. C. M.	1019	— By.Q.M.Sjt. J. W., *M.M.*		972
Mackie, C.Q.M.S. M.	1022	McSloy, Sjt. J.		998
— By.S.M. W.	975	McStocker, By.S.M. C.		971
McKilligan, Clr.Sjt. W. J.	2697	McTurk, Pte. J.		1019
McKinley, F. of W. Q.M.Sjt. M.	60	McVey, W.O. Cl. 1 (S.M.) J.		3572
— Cpl.(A./Sjt.) W., *M.M.*	976	McVicker, Cpl. H. E.		985
MacKinnon, Sjt. D.	2697	McWade, Pte. W. A.		2700
Mackinnon, Sjt. Clk. D.	100	McWean, Q.M.Sjt. T.		986
McKinnon, C.S.M.(now		McWilliam, Sjt. C. C.		2692
2nd Lt.) E. G.	1022	McWilliams, Pte. D.		996
— P.O. R. A.	969	Madden, Armt.S./Sjt.(A./Armt.		
McKnight, Pte.(A./Cpl.) G. A.	983	Q.M.Sjt.) F. C.		1013
Mackrill, 2nd Cpl. H. A.	982	Maddock, Q.M.S. E.		1018
Mackway, Sjt.(A./C.S.M.) B.	1000	Maggs, Sjt. O. J.		992

* R.A.F. M.S.M. No. 744 R.F.C. Enlisted June 1913. No. 3 Sqn. in France from 13 August, 1914. S.M. August 1917.

Maguire, Clr.Sjt. J. J.	* 2694	Mantell, S.M. A. V.		2695
Maher, Sjt. D. K.	1022	Manton, Pte.(L./C.) H. J.		68
— Q.M.S. J.	2998	Maples, L./Cpl.(A./Sjt.) J.		71
— Sjt. J. J.	1022	March, R.Q.M.S. N. N.		1022
Mahon, Cpl. D.	1009	Marchant, L./C.(A./Cpl.) J.		1946
Mahoney, Sjt. C., *M.M.*	986	Marcon, C.Q.M.Sjt. J.		995
— By.S.M. J.	975	Marfleet, Sjt.Clk. R. J.		100
— Sjt. O. W.	1002	Margarson, Cpl.(A./Sjt.) J. A.		1009
— C.Q.M.Sjt. W. B.	978	Margetts, Sjt. P. W.		998
Maiden, Q.M.Sjt. E. J.	1490	Marker, Sjt. G.		1007
Maidman, Spr.(A./C.S.M.) P. W.	2693	Markey, 1st Cl.Schmaster G.		2701
Maidment, Sjt. C. E.	1007	Markham, Q.M.Sjt. H. W.		997
Main, Sjt.(A./S.Q.M.S.) B.	1007	— M./S.Sjt. S. H.		70
Major, Pte.(L./C.)(A./		Marks, Sjt. G.		976
Sub Condr.) J.	1945	— Cpl. W.		981
Making, Sjt. L.	990	Marley, C.S.M.(A./S.M.) A. J.		2696
Malcolm, Pte.(A./Cpl.) H.	989	Marlor, Sjt.(A./C.S.M.) S.		989
Male, Pte.(L./C.) H. H.	2998	Marlow, Pte.(A./Sjt.) J. F.		1019
Mallen, 2/Cpl. (A./		Marney, Sjt. W.		997
S.Q.M.Sjt.) G. K.	1945	Marr, Sjt. J. W.		1007
Mallett, Saddlr.S./Sjt. R.	1005	Marriott, Far Q.M.Sjt. E. E.		970
Malley, C.Q.M.Sjt. H.	991	Marrison, Sjt.(A./C.S.M.) F.		1007
Malone, 2nd Cpl.(A./Sjt.) P. J.	982	Marsden, C.S.M. Instr.		
Maloney, Sjt.(T./R.S.M.) M.	1014	(A./S.M.) J.	†	6262
Malpress, C.P.O. W.	969	— C.Q.M.Sjt. J. R.		1488
Maltby, Pte(A./L./C.) D.	71	— Cpl. J. W.		993
Malthouse, C.S.M. E J.	1018	Marsh, S.Q.M.Sjt. A.		998
Mancer, Pte. E.	1011	— S.M. A. V.		2690
Manders, Ch.Mech. R. F.	100	— Sjt.(T./Sub Condr.) C.		61
Manley, Q.M.S. G. H.	2693	— Pte.(T./Sub Condr.) E. W.		1014
— W.O. Cl. 1, Supt.Clk. W. J.	3572	— Q.M.Sjt. H. W.		985
Mann, Sjt. A. E.	992	— Ch.Mas.Mec. S. G.		100
— Spr.(A./Cpl.) J.	983	— C.S.M. W. (Ches. R., T.F.)		989
— Whlr. Cpl. J. L.	973	— C.S.M. W. (Bedf. R.)		2694
— By.Q.M.Sjt. R.	972	Marshall, Sjt. C. S.		1007
Manning, S.Q.M.S. H. J.	2702	— Cpl. G. G.		994
— Cpl. W. J.	1022	— Q.M.S. J.		2694
Mansell, W.O. Cl. 1, G. H.	1022	— Cpl.(L./Sjt.) J.		996
— Sjt.(A./C.S.M.) T., *D.C.M.*	979	— S.M. J. A.		2691
Mansfield, C.Q.M.Sjt. J. S.	1002	— Sjt. T.		1019
Manson, Sjt. A. C.	1019	— S.M. W.		2689

---

   * Later R.Q.M.S. 10th Manchester Regiment. He volunteered in September 1914, and completing his training in the following year was drafted in France. There he played a distinguished part in the Battles of Loos, St. Eloi, Vimy Ridge, the Somme, Beaumont-Hamel, Arras and Ypres. He was awarded the Meritorious Service Medal for conspicuous services under fire. Owing to an accident he was invalided home, and on his recovery retained at various stations for important duties. Demobilised in March 1920, he held also the 1914/15 Star, the General Service and Victory Medals. 64, Collyhurst Street, Collyhurst, Manchester.

   † Army Gym. Staff.

Marshall, Pte.(A./L./C.) W. H.	1011	Matthews, Gnr.(L./Bmdr.) C. E.	974
Marsland, S./S.M.(T./		— Sadd.Q.M.S. G. E.	2997
S./S.M.) M. H.	1003	— By.S.M. G. J.	971
Marson, Sjt.(T./R.S.M.) C. H.	1014	— Sjt. J.	989
Mart, C.P.O. A. G.	3591	— Dvr. J.	974
Martin, C.Q.M.Sjt. A.	992	— Sjt. J. B.	1000
— Sjt. A.	985	— Sea. R.	3860
— Sjt. A. R.	998	— Cpl.(L./Sjt.) W. E.	2999
— Sqdn.S.M. B. G.	970	Mattingly, Sjt. E. G.	979
— Pte.(A./C.S.M.) C. J.	986	Mattock, B.S.M. H. J.	2690
— Ch.Mas.Mec. D., *M.M.*	* 100	Mattocks, Clr.Sjt. J.	993
— Sjt. D. D.	1007	Maudsley, Sjt. F.	1019
— Cpl.(A./S./Sjt.) F. V.	1014	Maule, Q.M.S. E. A. F.	2693
— Sjt.(A./S./Sjt.) G. W.	1007	Maw, P.O. J. L.	2361
— Sjt. L.	1007	Mawhiney, S./Sjt. J. B.	1022
— E.R.A. 2nd Cl. O. G.	2360	Mawhinney, Sjt. W.	1024
— Sjt. T.	995	Maxey, By.S.M. A. E.	971
— T./R.S.M. T. B.	970	Maxfield, C.Q.M.Sjt. G. P.	989
— 1st Cl.Mst.Gnr. T. L.	2691	Maxwell, A./W.O. Cl. 1, S./S.M.	
— Dvr. V. J. L.	1022	A. L. H.	3572
— Pnr.(A./2nd Cpl.) W.	2998	— T./S.M. W.	991
— T./Sub Condr. W. H.	1013	May, Sjt. G.	1007
Martyn, Sjt. W.	1019	— 1st Cl.Mst.Gnr. G. T.	† 2691
Maskell, A.B. J	3591	— Farr.Q.M.Sjt. J.	68
Mason, Spr.(A./Sjt.) C.	2693	Mayell, Armt.Q.M.Sjt.(A./	
— Cpl. F.	981	Armt. S.M.) A.	1945
— Sjt. F. W.	995	Mayhew, Sjt.(A./C.S.M.) A. F.	1000
— Mech.S.M. P. J.	2699	Maynard, C.S.M. W. H.	984
— Cpl.(A./Sjt.) P. J.	981	— Pte.(A./Sjt.) W. H.	1015
— Cpl. W.	70	Mayor, C.Q.M.Sjt. C.	993
— Sjt. Clk. W. E.	100	Meachem, C.Q.M.S. A. G.	1019
Massey, Sjt. J.	70	Mead, Pte.(L./C.) F.	988
— C.Q.M.Sjt. J. E.	997	Meade, Mech.S.M. J.	‡ 2692
Masters, Cpl. C.	1009	Meadows, Clr.Sjt.(A./S.M.) F.	2694
— Sjt. R. H., *D.C.M.*	1003	— Sjt. I. A.	1000
Matheson, Farr.S./Sjt. D.	970	Meads, Sjt. A. F. C.	1007
Mathews, Sub Condr. F.	62	Meakin, C.Q.M.Sjt.(T./S./S.M.) F.	1005
— Cpl.(A./Sjt.) J.	976	— Sjt. G.	2701
Mathieson, Sjt. R. A.	1022	Mear, Farr.S./Sjt. W. J.	2690
Mathison, S.M. A.	2696	Mears, C.Q.M.S. J. W.	1019
Matley, Pte.(A./Q.M.S.) W.	60	— Pte.(L./C.)(A./Cpl.) R. E.	1945
Mattey, Sjt. B.	1000	Meates, Q.M.S. C. F.	1022
— Cpl.(A./Sjt.) L.	922	Mee, Sjt. J.	994
Matthews, Sjt. A. G.	976	— Cpl. W. H.	981

---

* No. 252 R.F.C. Enlisted February 1904. Cpl. with 3 Sqn. in France 13 August 1913.
F./Sgt. (Temp. S.M. (T)) October 1915. An Observer with No. 7 Sqn. R.F.C. in
April 1916. Military Medal *L.G.* 11 October, 1916. M.I.D. *L.G.* 7 December, 1917.
R.A.F. M.S.M. Died 24 February 1919 M.I.D. *L.G.* 3 June 1919 and 11 July 1919.

† R.G.A. For China.

‡ R.E. For Gibraltar.

Meech, Sjt. G. O.	1003	Millar, Ch.Shipwt. R. J.		3860
Meehan, C.S.M. E. R.	1489	— C.Q.M.S. W. P.		978
Meek, Pte.(A./L./C.) M.	1011	Miller, Pte.(L./C.) A.		981
Meeks, S./Sjt. F.	1007	— Whlr.S./Sjt. D.		1006
Meeson, 2nd Cpl.(T./Sub Condr.)		— Spdt.Clk. D.		60
G. F.	1014	— Dvr.(A./Cpl.) D.		1011
Melbourne, Ch.Sto. J. A.	3860	— Cpl.Mec. D. D.		100
Melton, W.O.Cl.II(Spdt.Clerk) R.	3272	— Sjt. E.		980
Melvin, Sjt. J. G.	1000	— C.Q.M.S. E. C., *M.M.*		1019
Menard, Sjt. P. G.	1019	— C.S.M.(A./S.M.) F.		2696
Mendham, Q.M.Sjt. C.	1019	— S./Sjt. F. H.	*	2701
Mendoza, F./Clk. W.	100	— S.M. G., *D.C.M.*		1489
Menzies, S./Sjt. D. C.	1022	— Sjt. J. F.		1000
Mercer, Sjt. C W.	1000	— Sjt. J. H.		987
Merchant, Cpl. H. W.	1488	— Mech.S./Sjt. T. J.		1005
Merck, Sjt. T. H.	1012	Milles, Sjt. T.		980
Meredith, Sjt.(A./		Millett, Sjt. A.		976
C.Q.M.S. Instr.) E.	2701	— Pte. L.		984
— Cpl. R. D.	1946	Millichamp, Cpl. T.		3860
Merralls, Farr.Q.M.Sjt. J. C.	970	Milligan, Sjt. J., *M.M.*		69
Merrett, Cpl. T. D.	981	Milliken, Sjt. E., *D.C.M.*		1022
Merrick, S.M. J. J.	2693	Millner, C.Q.M.S. G. H.		978
Merrilees, Sjt. Clk. A.	100	Mills, Sjt. A. H.		1000
Merritt, Sjt. C.	998	— C.Q.M.S. A. W.		2695
Merry, C.S.M.(A./S.M.) A.	985	— Dvr. J.		974
— By.S.M. A. T.	1022	— By.Q.M.Sjt. S. H.		972
Merryday, Pte. M.	1019	— Q.M.S. W. G.		2696
Mertens, Spr. W.	983	— Ch.Sto. W. G.		2360
Metcalf, Dvr. C.	974	Millward, B.Q.M.S. F. E.		2997
Metcalfe, Pte. A. L.	1002	Milne, C.Q.M.S. A. E.		1019
— Sjt. F. H.	998	Milne, S./Sjt.(A./Q.M.S.) A. J.		2999
Mews, Cpl. S. A.	981	Milner, B.S.M. A. B.		2690
Micklethwaite, Sjt. F.	991	— Farr.Cpl.(A./Farr.S./Sjt.) M. F.		61
Middleditch, Q.M.S. F. J.	2996	— Cpl. S.		1001
Middlehurst, Sjt. J.	979	— Cpl. W. J.		973
Middlemas, Pte.(A/Cpl.) G. W.	61	Milnes, Q.M.Sjt. J.		984
Middlemess, Sjt. F. S.	1022	Milton, CS.M.(A./S.M.) A.		2697
Middleton, S./Sjt. G. D.	1012	— Cpl. F.		1009
Midgley, Sjt.Mec. H. B.	100	— Sjt. S. G.		69
— Sjt. H. J.	979	— S./Sjt.(A./M.S.M.) W. J.		2999
Milburn, R.Q.M.S. W.	1022	Minal, Sjt.(A./C.Q.M.S.) W.		1488
Miles, Spr.(A./Sjt.) H. E.	983	Minns, Spr.(A./S.M.) W.		2693
— C.S.M. J.	993	Mint, C.S.M. J. D.		999
— C.S.M.(A./S.M.) J. R.	997	Mitchell, Farr.S./Sjt. A.		972
Mill, Sjt. R. E.	992	— Cpl. A.		995
Millar, Sjt. B.	1019	— Dmr. A.		1024
— S./S.M. G. H.	1004	— Cpl.(T./Sjt.) A. G.		1022
— Q.M.Sjt. J. M.	994	— R.S.M. C.		2702
— Col.Sjt. (O.R.S.) J. W.	988	— Sjt.(A./C.S.M.) F. H. S.		1000

* For Gibraltar (R.A.O.C.).

Mitchell, Dvr.(A./Sjt.) F. J.		983	Monks, S./S.M. W.	1004
— S.M. G.		2694	Monksfield, Cpl. F. C.	988
— W.O. Cl.1,Spdt.Clerk H.		3572	Monteith, Sjt. W., *M.M.*	980
— Sjt.(A./C.Q.M.S.) H. G.		986	Montgomery, Sjt. K. H.	1019
— C.Q.M.S.(A./C.S.M.) J.		2698	Moody, Q.M.S. C. T.	2998
— 2nd Cpl. J. A.		982	— Pte.(A./Sjt.) F. H.	2700
— Pte. W.		1011	— Sjt. J. F.	981
— Cpl. W. A.		981	— Sjt. R.	70
— Sjt. W. H.		1945	Mooney, Sjt. C. J.	1022
Mizen, Ftr. E. H. J.		974	Moorcroft, Ftr.Q.M.Sjt. T. G.	971
Moat, Spr.(A./Cpl.) J.		2693	Moore, S.M. A. H.	1019
Mobbs, Pte.(L./C.) P.		1016	— Sjt. C. C.	1003
Moffat, Pte.(A./Sjt.) D. J.		1014	— Mech.S./Sjt. E. J.	1005
— Cpl.Mec. R.		100	— Sjt.(T./S.S.M.) G.	1007
Moger, Q.M.S. A. E. G.		2696	— S./S.M. H.	‡ 2689
Mogford, Pte.(A./C.S.M.) R. W.		986	— Cpl. J.	1009
Mogg, 2nd Cpl.(A./C.Q.M.Sjt.)			— Yeo.Sig. T.	2360
A. G., *M.M.*		982	— Farr.Sjt. T. W.	976
Mohomed, Bilal, Pte.	✿	1256	— Sjt.(A./Col.Sjt.) W. A.	996
Moignard, Sjt. E. J.	*	1007	— S.M. W. E.	§ 100
Moir, Sjt. H. L.		1019	— Sjt. W. J.	1489
Mol, Sjt. R.		70	Moran, Cpl. P.	984
Mole, Sdlr.Sjt. J. T.		970	Mordecai, Sjt. M. J.	1490
Moles, Cpl.(A./Sjt.) W. T.		2703	Morden, Cpl. G. A.	1019
Mollekin, Pte. (A./Sjt.) H.		1015	Morey, Cpl. W. G.	1022
Moncur, Sjt. D. G.		1022	Morgan, By.S.M. A. H.	975
— G.S.M. J., *M.C.*	†	2693	— C.Q.M.Sjt. B.	992
— A.M. 1st Cl. M.		100	— Sjt. C. G.	1019
Monk, Pte. W. H.		986	— Sub Condr. E.	3000
Monkhouse, S./Sjt. R.		1012	— Cpl. H.	1022
— Armt.S./Sjt.(A./Armt.Q.M.Sjt.) T.		1490	— Sjt. H. V.	1019

* R.A.S.C. G.H.Q. Didier, Paris.
† Group known: M.C., Queen's South Africa Medal, (Cape Colony, Transvaal, Wittebergen, Sgt. Scots Guards), King's South Africa Medal (Col. Sgt.), 1914 Star & bar (S.M.), British War and Victory Medals (M.I.D. Oakleaf), R.V.M. (Silver, Edw. VII), 1911 Coronation, L.S. & G.C. (Edw. VII, S.M.) and M.S.M. M.C. *L.G.* 18 February 1915 (Coldstream Gds.).
‡ Group known: Queen's South Africa Medal (Cape Colony, Orange Free State, Transvaal, South Africa 1901, South Africa 1902, Pte. 4677 7th Dragoon Gds.), British War Medal (W.O.II 4677 7 D.G.), General Service Medal (Iraq, D20451 W.O.1 7 D. Gds.), Defence Medal, L.S. & G.C. (Geo. V, D.20451 S.S.M. Rough Rider 7/D.G), Royal Victorian Medal (Geo. V, R.S.M. 7 D.G.) and M.S.M. (7 D. Gds).
§ No. 5 R.F.C. 1914/15 Star known, and miniatures in McInnes collection. Enlisted December 1889. 2 Cpl. 1/Balloon Section R.E. in South Africa. Queen's South Africa Medal (4 clasps). Edw. VII, L.S. & G.C. 1907. S.M. R.F.C. August 1912. Service Overseas in W.W.I from December, 1915. M.I.D. *L.G.* 4 January, 1917 and 1 January 1919, also French Médaille d'Honneur en vermail, August, 1918, R.A.F. M.S.M. and Roumanian Barbatie Si Credinta with 9 Sqn—*L.G.* 15 July, 1919. Senior W.O.I April 1918 on the R.A.F.'s formation.

Morgan, S.M. J.	2695	Moss, Spr.(A./2nd Cpl.) S V.	1488
— Whlr.S./Sjt. M.	1024	— C.S.M. W. H.	987
— C.Q.M.S. T. E.	2693	Mott, Sjt. S. A.	1007
— E.C. Q.M.S. W.	2692	Mouel, Farr.S./Sjt. P., *M.M.*	972
— Sjt. W. E.	1019	Moulding, Sjt. F.	973
Morhen, S./Sjt.(A./S.M.) J.	1016	Moulds, Pte.(L./C.) E.	1011
Morisette, 2nd Cpl. S.	1019	Moult, Cpl. F. H.	976
Morison, S./Sjt. H. B.	1024	Mound, S./S.M. F. D.	2999
— C.Q.M.Sjt. J. L.	995	Mountford, Pte.(L./C.) J. T.	1016
Morrall, S.M. H.	2694	Mousley, Armr.S./Sjt. W. J.	2701
Morris, S./S.M. B. G.	1004	Mowatt, Sjt. H. M.	1019
— Sjt. C. G.	980	Mowbray, Sjt.Clk. F.	100
— S./Sjt.(A./C.S.M.) D. H.	1019	Mowe, Sjt. W.	980
— 1st Cl.Schmaster .	2701	Moxon, Sjt.(A./C.Q.M.S.) W.	2694
— Sjt. F.	2690	Moyser, Q.M.Sjt. W.	987
— Pte.(A./S.M.) G. E.	2700	Muckersie, Cpl.Mec. D.	100
— Ch.Shipwt. G. H.	2360	Mudd, Sjt. R. H.	1000
— Sjt. G. H.	1022	Mueller, Cpl. R. R.	1022
— Cpl. H. B	1022	Mugleton, Pte.(A./Sjt.) W. J.	1490
— Ch.Mech. H. S.	2050	Muir, S.Q.M.Sjt. A.	1005
— Pte. J.	1019	— Spr.(A./C.S.M.) A.	2998
— Pte.(L.C.) R.	1024	— Pte.(A./L./C.) F. W.	1945
— C.S.M. T. H.	!))$	— E.C.S./Sjt. J.	978
— Pte.(A./Sjt.) W.	1019	Mulchinock, Sjt.Clk. H. L. N.	100
— Sjt. W. F.	60	— Spr.(A./2nd Cpl.) W.	983
Morrison, Pte.(A./Sjt.) F.	1013	Mulholland, S.M. W.	2694
— C.Q.M.S.(A./C.S.M.) H.	988	Muli, C.S.M.	1946
— Cpl. H.	991	Mullarkey, Q.M.S. J.	2694
— By.S.M.(A./R.S.M.) J.	971	Muller, Pte. H. M.	1024
— Cpl. J. A.	1022	Mulligan, Spr.(A./S.M.) J.	2693
— Cpl. J. P.	1009	Mullinger, C.S.M. F.	997
Morse, C.S.M. H.	60	— Sjt. S.	998
Morsman, Spr.(A./Sjt.) F.	983	Mulliss, Cpl. F. R.	994
Mortimer, Sjt.(A./R.S.M.)		Mulrooney, C.S.M. F.	994
H. E., *M.M.*	1019	Mumby, Sjt. E. E.	986
Mortimore, Sjt. P. J.	1003	Muncey, Sjt. E. W.	997
Mortlock, C.S.M. C.	2695	Munday, Sjt. A. E.	3840
Morton, CPl. E. D.	981	— C.Q.M.S. G. E.	1489
— S./S.M. R. J.	2699	Mundell, Gnr. W.	1019
— A.M. 3rd Cl. W.	100	Munnery, Farr.Sjt. W. J.	1005
Moseilhi, Osram, Shawish *	62	Munns, Gnr. J. T.	974
Moseley, Sjt. W.	973	Munro, Sjt. J. S	992
Mosely, Sjt.(A./C.S.M.) P. C.	980	— Ldg.Deckhand W.	2361
Moss, Dvr.(L./Cpl.) C.	983	Munslow, Cpl.(A./Sjt.) J.	1009
— Pte. F. A.	71	Muntzer, S.M.Inst. A.	977
— S./Sjt.(T./S.M.) H. L.	1012	Murdoch, Sjt. J.	68
— Gnr.(A./Ftr.S./Sjt.) J. E.	977	Murdoch, C.Q.M.S. J. D.	1022
— Q.M.Sjt. S.	987	Murie, Sjt. W.	984

---

* Sjt., Medical Corps Egyptian Army.

Murison, Pte.(A./Sjt.) G.	* 1946	Nash, C.S.M. J.	997
Murphy, S./S.M.(T./S./S.M.) A.	1004	— Sjt. W.	1019
— Ch.Mech. A. C.	100	— Sjt. W. T.	1489
— By.S.M. C. A.	975	Naughton, Condr. T. H.	2702
— C.S.M. J., *MM.*	70	Naylor, Sjt. J. W.	1007
— S.M. J.	2694	Neal, Pte. A. E.	970
— Sjt. J.	2699	Neale, C.S.M. C. L. H.	994
— Pte.(L.C.) J.	70	— Pte.(A./Sjt.) J. A.	1011
— Sjt. J. N.	1022	— C.S.M. R. C.	978
Murray, C.S.M. A. H. G.	1022	Neary, Sjt. L.	990
— Q.M.Sjt. C.	989	Needham, Sjt. T. G.	1003
— Sjt. D.	1019	— S.S.M. W. G.	70
— C.S.M. G.	2702	Neighbour, C.Q.M.Sjt. S. J.	986
— Sjt. G.	2700	Nelson, Cpl. G. O., *D.C.M.*	981
— S./Sjt. H. R.	1022	— C.Q.M.S. J.	2695
— Ftr.S./Sjt. J.	975	— Pte. J.	993
— 2nd Cpl. J.	982	— Farr.S./Sjt. L.	1022
— A.M. 1 J. B.	2050	— S./Sjt. W. J. R.	1946
— Mr. J. L.	† 2361	Neri, Farr.Sjt. A.	1022
— S./S.M. R	1945	Nesbit, C.Q.M.Sjt. J. T.	997
Murry, Mech.S.M. J. W.	2692	Nessling, By.S.M. J.	971
Musamunanga, Sjt.	1946	Nettleton, Sjt. F	991
Muskett, C.S.M. J. C.	1019	Neville, By.S.M. P.	975
Muzzell, Sjt.(A./Sqdn.S.M.) F. W. B.	970	Nevitt, Q.M.S.(A./3rd Cl.Mst.Gnr.) T.	2691
Myatt, W.O. Cl. II (A./W.O. Cl.I) F.	2697	New, Ch.Mas.Mec. J.	100
Myers, By.S.M. J.	975	— By.S.M. J. F.	975
— Mech. S./Sjt. S. W.	1005	Newbury, Pte.(A./L.C.) H.	994
— Pte.(A./Sjt.) W. T.	1014	Newcombe, Ch.Sto. S.	3591
		Newman, R.Q.M.S.(E.R. Condr.) C. S.	1022
Nadin, Pte.(L./C.)(A./Sjt.) G.	2999	— Pte.(A./Cpl.) F.	990
Nairn, Sjt. J. R.	980	— Q.M.Sjt. F. A.	1002
Napier, Sjt. J.	‡ 984	— Sjt. N.	2702
Naphine, Cpl. G. H.	1009	— Sjt. R. H.	973
Narborough, Pte. R. B.	1024	— Pte.(A./Sjt.) T. H.	1015
Nash, Pte. B.	2702	— C.Q.M.Sjt. W.	978
— Spr. F. J.	983	— Pte.(L./Cpl.) W.	1013
— R.S.M. F. T.	1004	Newnham, Sjt.(A./M.S./S.) C.	1007
— Sjt. H.	987	Newns, Res.Ward Master J. E.	2361

* Group was in the McInnes collection. The M.S.M. is the only one awarded to the Rhodesian Regt: Queen's South Africa Medal (Cape Colony, Orange Free State, Transvaal, South Africa 1901, South Africa 1902, 2986 3rd class Tpr. S.A.C.), 1914/15 Star (1310 Pte. 2/Rhodesian Regt.), British War and Victory Medals (129 Sjt. E. Afr. Road C.), South African Service Medal 1939–45 and M.S.M. (1310 Pte. A./Sgt. 2/Rhod. R.). M.S.M. for services in East Africa. He served two years in the South African Constabulary in the Boer War. Enlisted into Rhodesian Regt. August 1915 aged 34, a Presbyterian, a stonemason from Bloemfontein. He went to German East Africa in October 1915 until August 1918, when he was transferred to the E. A. Road Corps.

† R.N. M.S.M. serving with the Nyasaland Volunteer Reserve.

‡ As Major, Pioneer Corps (No. 159416). K.I.A. aged 50 28 April, 1945 Buried Celle War Cemetery.

Newton, Pte. A.	992	Nolan, T./S.M. R.		995
— Dkhnd, J. H.	3860	— C.S.M. W.		990
— Farr.S./Sjt. M.	1487	Noone, Sjt. P.		989
— Pte.(A./Col.Sjt.) M.	988	Norbury, Sjt. G.		989
— S./Sjt. R. A.	62	Norgate, Ldg.Sig. G. C. A.		3591
— Ch.Mec. S. H.	100	Norman, Sjt. C.		1024
— Sjt. S. W.	69	— C.P.O. N.		3862
Niblett, Sjt. R. W.	1000	— S./S.M. R. W.	*	2699
Nichol, Sjt. P., *M.M.*	1019	Norris, Cpl. A. F.		1009
Nicholas, Cpl.(A/Condr.) F. U.	1014	— Pte. G.		1945
Nicholds, Pte.(L./C.) W.	1002	— Sjt.(A./C.Q.M.S.) H.		1489
Nicholls, Ch.Sto. S. R.	2361	— S./Sjt.(A./S.S.M.) P. A.		2701
— C.S.M.(A./S.M) W.	1489	— Pte.(A./L./Sjt.) P. R.		2698
— B.S.M. W. J.	1487	— Cpl. R. B.		992
Nichols, S.M. B. J.	985	North, Pte. C. H.		1002
— Sjt. C. W.	980	— F. of W. S.M H.N.		977
— Pte.(A./Cpl.) F.	996	— Sjt. W. G., *M.M.*		988
Nicholson, Sjt. H. H.	1000	Northey, C.E.R.A. 2nd Cl. H. J.		2360
— C.Q.M.Sjt. J.	995	Norton, Sjt. E.		986
— C.S.M. J.	999	— Ch.Mas.Mec. F.	†	100
— Ftr.Cpl. S. M.	973	— Q.M.Sjt. J.		991
— Sjt. W.	1012	Norwood, Sjt. D.		1019
Nickels, Pte.(A./Sjt.) W.	2696	Notting, Cpl.(A./Sjt.) A.		981
Nicklin, Sjt. E. L.	987	Nottingham, Cpl. H.		1003
Nicks, C.S.M. M. T.	987	Nowell, Sjt. C.		1007
Nickson, Pte.(L./C.) F.	70	— Pte. J. A.		1019
Nicod, Ch.Mec.(A./Mas.Mec.) A. A.	100	Noyce, Sjt. G.		969
Nicol, Cpl. O. R.	973	Nunn, Pte.(A./Sjt.) F. E.		1013
Nicoll, R.Q.M.S. J. W. A.	1022	Nuttall, Pte.(L./C.) H.		70
Nield, Sjt. W. T.	1000	— C.Q.M.S. J. R.		1489
Nightingale, Sjt. G.	69	— Sjt.(A./Q.M.Sjt.) J. W.		1000
— Pte.(L./Cpl.) T.	996	Nutting, Sjt. E. H.		1019
Nimms,Sjt. A.	1007	Nye, T./S.M. A., *D.C.M.*	‡	2695
Nisbet, Sjt.(Signr.) D.	1003			
— T./S.M.(A.C.) S. G. C.	975	Oakes, Pte. A. R.		60
Nixon, C.S.M. A. W. J.	1019	Oates, Pte. F.		2998
— Sjt. C. H.	998	— R.Q.M.S. F. A.		1022
— Sjt. J. E.	984	Oatway, C.Q.M.Sjt.(A./S.M.) H. R.		978
Noakes, Pte.(A./S.M.) W. J.	1011	O'Connell, Sjt. A. F.		2692
Nolan, Sjt. J.	1000	O'Connor, Sjt. J.		1024
— Pte.(L./C.)(T./S./S.M.) J.	1011	— Cpl.(A./C.S.M.) J.		1009

---

* Group known: Queen's South Africa Medal, 1914 Star trio L.S. & G.C. (Geo. V) and M.S.M. F.M. Lord Plumer, Governor of Malta, presented S./S.M. Norman R.A.S.C. with both his L.S. & G.C. and his M.S.M. on the Island on 6 April, 1920.

† Group known: 1914/15 Star trio (Lincolnshire Yeomanry, M.I.D. oakleaf), R.A.F. M.S.M. (No. 403594) and Territorial Efficiency Medal (Geo. V, Linc. Yco.).

‡ Group known: D.C.M. (Victoria, 3238 C./Sgt., *L.G.* 27 Sept 1901), Queen's South Africa Medal (Cape Colony, Johannesburg, Diamond Hill, Wittcbcrgcn); slightly wounded 23 July 1900 Reif's Nek. L.S. & G.C. (Edw. VII) and M.S.M. (4/R. Sussex Regt.), also Annuity in Army Order 76 June 1947 as S. Major.

O'Connor, S.Q.M.Sjt.(T./S./S.M.) M. E.	1005
— Dvr.(A./2nd Cpl.) T.	983
O'Dowd, Cpl. B. C.	2999
— S./S.M. T. E.	2702
Ogbourn, Ch.Mec. E. A.	100
Ogden, Pte.(A./Sjt.) C.	986
— Sjt. F. J.	1007
— Cpl.(A./Q.M.S.) P. E.	989
O'Keefe, By.S.M.(T./R.S.M.) P.	971
Oliphant, Q.M.Sjt. L.	995
Oliver, Q.M.Sjt.(O.R.S.) C.	993
— Amt.S./Sjt.(A./Amt.S.M.) E. J.	61
— Farr.Sjt. G. J.	980
— Pte.(A./S.Q.M.S.) H. J.	2700
— C.S.M. J.	2691
— Sjt. J.	2694
— C.Q.M.S. J. G.	1019
— Cpl. R. F.	976
Olley, E.R.Cpl. E. W.	1022
— Sjt. W.	987
O'Neil, Sjt.(A./C.S.M.) D.	2696
O'Neill, Q.M.Sjt. A.	991
— Sjt. J.	980
Onley, Cpl.(A./Sjt.)(A.C.) E.	976
O'Rawe, Pte. J.	996
O'Reilly, Gnr.(L./Bombr.) B.	970
— L./Cpl.(A./C.S.M.) J.	986
Orgles, Sjt. G. R.	980
Orme, Sjt.Dmr. A. C.	990
— S.Q.M.Sjt. W.	1005
Ormerod, Sjt. J.	989
Ormond, Cpl.(A./S./Sjt.) E. F.	1015
Ormrod, Gnr. S.	977
Orr, Cpl. J.	992
— CPO 3rd Cl. J. McC.	3863
Orrick, C.Q.M.Sjt. W. C.	978
Osborn, Sjt. G. C.	998
— Pte.(A./Sjt.) S.	983
Osborne, Cpl. G.	988
— By.S.M. L. M.	971
— S.M. T. A.	2693
O'Shea, Sjt.(A./S.Q.M.S.) M.	1007
Osmond, Cpl. G.	973
— Cpl.(A./Sjt.) J.	973
— S./Sjt. R. R.	1945
Ostick, Sjt.Mec. J. L.	100
Ostler, Ch.Mec. C.	100
Otterson, Q.M.S.(A./S.M.) W.	1490
Otway, Gnr. J.	974

Owen, Cpl.(A./Sjt.) A. W.	981
— Sjt. C. J.	1019
— C.S.M.(A./S.M) C. T.	2695
— S./Sjt.(T./S.S.M.) J. H.	2699
— Pte. S. H.	1019
— C.Q.M.Sjt. T. W.	989
— Ch.Yeo.Sig. W.	3862
Owens, Sjt.(A./S.M.) W.	1945
Oxlade, S./S.M.(T./S./S.M.) G.	1004
Oxley, Sjt. A.	998
— C.S.M.D.D.	1019
— Cpl. H. E.	973
Oxton, C.Q.M.Sjt. J.	989
Pacey, Sjt. A. L.	1022
— Cpl. W.	973
Packer, By.S.M. E.	975
— B.S.M. F. J.	68
— T./S.S.M. G.	70
— Cpl.(L./Sjt.) G.	987
— C.Q.M.S. W. H.	* 2691
Paddon, S.Q.M.Sjt.(O.R.S.) F. C.	970
Padley, Cpl. J. M.	969
Page, Sjt. A.	3000
— Supt.Clk. E. H.	988
— C.S.M. E. R. W.	2692
— S./S.M. F.	1004
— 2nd Cpl. F. L.	1022
— Sjt. G. E.	2702
— C.S.M.(T./S./S.M.) R. H. H.	1004
Pagett, Sjt. F. E.	985
Paice, C.Q.M.Sjt. R. G.	1005
Pailthorpe, S./Sjt. H. N.	3000
Pain, Ftr.Cpl. S. D.	973
Paine, Pte. H.	993
— T./S.M. W. T.	1946
Painter, A./W.O. Cl. 2(S.Q.M.Sjt.) F. J.	3572
— Pte.(A./Cpl.) R. H.	70
Palfrey, 2nd Cpl.(A./Cpl.) W.	982
Palk, Pte.(A./S./Sjt.) E. C.	2700
Pallant, Pte. F. M.	1013
Palmer, C.Q.M.Sjt. A.	978
— Pte.(A./Cpl.) L. W.	2998
Papenius, S./Sjt.(A./S.M.) W. C.	1945
Papps, Sjt. Shkr. T. W.	984
Pardoe, Q.M.Sjt. C. W.	997
Parish, Pte.(L./C.) W	991
Park, S./Sjt. J.	1007

* For Bermuda (R.G.A.).

Park, Cpl. J.	981	Passmore, S./Sjt. W. P.		1022
— Spr. N. J.	983	Patefield, Sjt. J.		1000
Parker, Sjt.(A./C.S.M.) A.	2997	Pater, Pte.(A./L./C.) S. P.		1005
— Pte.(A./S./Sjt.) A.	1015	Paterson, Dvr.(A./Sjt.) H.		1011
— Pte. A. W.	1011	— Mech.S.M. H. G. C.		1004
— Sjt. F.	980	— Pte.(A./L./C.) P. E.		2700
— Cpl. F. R.	69	Patience, Sea. W.		3860
— Sjt.(A./S./Sjt.) G.	1007	Paton, 2nd Cpl.(A/C.S.M.) C. B.		982
— Q.M.Sjt.(T./S.M.) H.	1012	Patrick, C.Q.M.Sjt. W. C. C.		1005
— Sjt. H.	985	Patrickson, F. of W., Q.M.S. J. W.		2692
— Sjt. J.	989	— Q.M.Sjt. T. H.		1489
— Cpl. J. H.	1001	Patten, S./Sjt.(T./Supt.Clk.) A.		980
— Mech.S.M. P. B.	1004	Patterson, Pte. C. L.		1945
— Sjt. R. J.	68	— S.M. S.		2694
— Sjt. S.	980	— T./S.M.(A.C.) S. W.		2690
— Cpl.(A./Sjt.) W.	1009	— Cpl. W.		2692
— Cpl. W. H.	981	Pattinson, C.Q.M.Sjt. A.		984
Parkes, T./S.M. G. S.	992	Pattison, Col.Sjt.(A./Q.M.S.) A.		988
Parkhouse, Pte.(A./Cpl.) F. G.	61	— Gnr.(L./Bdr.) G. W.		977
Parkhurst, F./Sjt. W E.	100	— C.Q.M.S. J.		2999
Parkin, Bombr. R.	974	Patton, Col.Sjt. W. J.		2694
Parks, Sjt.(A./C.Q.M.Sjt.) W. G.	980	Paul, Sub Condr. A.		62
Parlett, T./S.M.(A.C.) H. S.	68	Paulson, Sjt. R. A.		1022
Parmenter, Cpl.(A./Sjt.) F.	976	Pautard, C.S.M. H.		2697
Parnaby, Cpl. R. H.	973	Pavitt, Pte. W. G.		986
Parnell, Sjt. A. E.	69	— E.C.Sjt. W. J.		980
— Sjt. D. A.	2690	Pawson, Cpl.(A./Sjt.) F.		1013
Parratt, Sqdn.Q.M.S.(A./S.S.M.)		Paxton, Cpl. C. W.		1019
C. H.	2701	— Payne, C.S.M. C. E.		2698
Parrott, Sjt. H.	1007	— Sqdn.S.M. H. T.		2699
Parry, Sjt. F.	2699	— B.S.M.(A./S.M.) W. F. H.		1487
— Pte.(A./Sjt.) I. O.	1016	Paytrees, By.Q.M.Sjt. A. H.		972
— S./Sjt. W.	1007	Peach, Gnr.(L./Bdr.) B. A.	*	979
— Q.M.Sjt. W. H.	985	Peachey, Pte.(L./C.)(A./Sjt.) A. E.		1945
Parsons, Sjt. A. A.	1007	— By.Q.M.Sjt. H. O.		972
— Mech.S./Sjt.(A./Mech.S.M.) G. O.	2999	Peacock, P.O. A. E. V. G.		3860
— A.B. H.	2361	Peake, S./S.M. L.		2699
— Cpl.(A./S.M.)(A.C.) H. H.	976	Pearce, Whr.Cpl.(A./Whr. S./Sjt.) E.		1009
— T./S.M. H. J.	2695	— Sjt G. P.		1007
— Sjt. J.	2999	— Spr. H. D.		988
— Sto. T.	2361	— S.M. M. H.		1019
— Ch.Mec. W. H.	100	Pearson, C.S.M. F. J. H.		985
Partridge, Pte.(L./C.) A. C.	1005	— C.S.M. S. N.		978
— A.M. 1. H. W.	100	— C.Q.M.Sjt. T. H.		978
Pasley, Pte. W. A.	996	— Sjt.(A./C.Q.M.Sjt.) W.		980
Pasquill, Pte.(A./L./C.) A.	1013	— Sjt. W.		996

---

* 59544 Lance Bombr. 'L' Battery R.H.A. Flanders, 1918—This N.C.O. has shown very exceptional courage and coolness while acting in charge of the Brigade medical station. He has often been left in sole charge and has never failed under the heaviest fire in his skilful attention to the wounded of R.H.A., R.G.A., and Infantry units.

Pease, Sjt.(A./C.S.M.) D. C. M. B.	980	Peterson, S./S.M. P.	1489
Peat, Sjt. G.	1000	Pettitt, Cpl.(A./Sjt.) J.	1009
— Q.M.Sjt.(O.R.S.) W.	992	Petts, Ch.Mec. S. J	100
Peck, Pte.(A./Sub Condr.) C. D.	1480	Peverett, Sjt. E. J	68
Peckham, P.O. C. H.	969	Pheasey, C.S.M.(A./R.S.M.) E.	978
Peddar, Spr.(A./2nd Cpl.) A.	985	Phelon, Sjt.(A./S./Sjt.) S. G.	1014
Peddie, S./Sjt. A. W.	1007	Phillips, C.Q.M.Sjt. A.	1002
Pedley, T./Sub Condr. F.	1013	— Sjt. A. R.	1488
— C.Q.M.Sjt. J.	991	— Pte.(A./Sjt.) E.	2700
Peebles, C.Q.M.Sjt. D.	1005	— Sjt.(A./C.Q.M.Sjt.) F. A.	992
Peet, Sjt. T.	987	— Sjt. G.	1488
Pegg, Cpl.(A.C.) W. E.	976	— Pte.(A./Sjt.) G.	991
Peirce, Sjt. H. E.	985	— S./Sjt. G. N.	1489
— E.C. 2nd Cpl.(A./E.C.Sjt.) W. A.	982	— Cpl.(A./Sjt.) G. P. P.	2699
Peiser, Pte. A. J.	1946	— By.Q.M.Sjt. H.	972
Pelling, C.Q.M.Sjt.(A/S.M.) W. J.	978	— Pte.(T./Cpl.) H. C.	1022
Pemberton, C.Q.M.Sjt. S. A.	978	— Sjt. J.	1022
Pembroke, Sjt. F. E.	1007	— Cpl. L. C.	100
Pendreich, Cpl.(A/S.Q.M.S.) J.	1009	— Cpl. L. D.	2703
Pendrey, Spr.(A./Sjt.) W.	983	— Dvr. R. J. ❋	1256
Penfold, Cpl. E.	985	— Sjt.(A./S./Sjt.) S. J.	1490
Penn, Sjt. F.	994	— Pte.(A./Cpl.) W. A.	1019
Pennell, C.S.M. G. *	989	— C.Q.M.Sjt. W. H.	978
Pennells, C.Q.M.Sjt. S. G.	985	Phillpotts, Pte.(L./C.) O. E. C.	998
Penwarden, Sjt. S. H.	1003	Phipps, Cpl.Mec. H.	100
Penwill, Pte. C. L.	2998	— Sjt. L. J.	2695
— S./S.M. W. A.	2699	Phythian, Q.M.Sjt. H.	989
Pepper, Sjt. B. W.	973	Pickman, S./Sjt. A. J.(deletion of	
Perdue, Cpl.(A./S.M.)(A.C.) R. H.	976	second announcement)	1257
Perfect, Sjt. F.	1007	Pickstock, Farr.Sjt. S.	980
Perkins, C.Q.M.Sjt. A. F.	991	Pickup, Pte.(A./Sjt.) J. G.	1015
— Mech.S./Sjt. A. J.	1005	Pidduck, Sjt. W. J.	998
— Pte.(A./S./Sjt.) H.	1015	Pidgeon, C.S.M. S. S.	2692
— Sjt. P.E.	2999	Pidgley, Dvr. W. J.	2997
Perrin, S.M. C. H.	100	Pierce, Sjt.(A./S.M.) A. J.	3841
— T./Sub Condr.(A./Condr.) E. J.	1013	Pigg, Sjt. W. J.	1007
— Spr.(A./2nd Cpl.) G. J.	983	Piggott, Dvr. J. J.	1011
Perrins, Mech.S./Sjt. C. J.	2999	Pike, Q.M.Sjt. C.	993
Perry, Cpl.(A./Sjt.)(A.C.) A.	976	— Sjt. F. C.	1019
— Spr.(A./Cpl.) B. H.	983	— S./Sjt. P. R.	980
— Pte. E. W.	1013	— Pte.(L./C.) W. E	998
— Pte. T. F.	1024	Pikes, Sjt. E. J.	1002
Petch, Pte.(A./L./C.) J.	1016	Pilch, C.S.M. C. J.	2692
— Ch.Mec. R. W.	100	Pilcher, Sjt.(A/By.Q.M.Sjt.) W. J.	969
— Sjt. W.	986	Pillar, M./S./Sjt. A. G.	70
Peters, C.Q.M.Sjt. P. C.	1002	Pinches, Sig. O.	974
— S./Sjt.(A./Condr.) S. G.	62	Pinchin, S.S.M. J.	1004

* Group known: 1914 Star (Sgt. 2/Welsh R.), British War and Victory Medals (W.O.II Welsh R.), M.S.M. (69 Coy. Lab. Corps) and Special Reserve L.S. & G.C. (Geo. V, Sjt. 3/Welsh R.).

Pink, S./S.M. G. W.	1004
— Pte.(A./Sjt.) J.	3840
Pinkerton, Art.Cpl. J. D.	981
Pinnock, Cpl.(A./C.S.M.) F. J.	2698
Piper, S./Sjt.(Local Sub Condr.) J.	3000
Pirie, Sjt. W. T.	1003
Pitchforth, Sjt. H.	1007
Pitman, C.Q.M.Sjt. C. E.	69
Pitt, Sjt. B.	980
— C.Q.M.S. C. C.	1022
Pittkin, B.Q.M.S. R. E.	2690
Pittock, E.C.Sj.(A./E.C.Q.M.S.) S.	980
Pitts, S./Sjt. A. H.	2702
Place, Sjt. A.	2691
Plaice, B.S.M. S. J.	2999
Plampin, Sjt. W. H.	990
Plant,Sjt.(A./C.S.M.Instr.) C. W. *	1016
— C.Q.M.S. J. W.	1488
Platford, C.Q.M.Sjt. J. J.	991
Platt, Sjt. A. E.	980
Player, Pte.(L./C.) A. L.	1002
Playfair, Sjt. J. L., *M.M.*	1019
Pleydell, W.O. A. D.	2702
Plint, M./S./Sjt. A. F.	70
Plum, Sjt. E.	988
Pocock, S.M. E.	2692
Pogson, Pte.(A./S./Sjt.) A.	2700
— Sjt. E., *D.C.M.*	991
Pollard, Sjt. A.	1012
Polli, Sjt. P.	1007
Pollock, C.S.M. J.	70
Pomeroy, Sjt.(A/C.Q.M.Sjt.) F. R.	1000
— Sjt. H. E.	1007
— S./Sjt. L. E.	998
Ponsford, Spr.(L./Cpl.) W. G.	983
Ponting, Sjt.(A./Sub Condr.) S. F.	1490
Poole, S./Sjt. F. A. L.	2702
— C.E.R.A. 1st Cl. W.	3863
— Pte.(A./Sjt.) W. R.	1014
Pooley, Sjt. H.	980
Pope, C.S.M.(A./S.M.) G.	2693
— Dvr. H. A.	2700
— Bmdr. W. A.	977
— 3rd Cl. Asst. Surg. W V.	2702
Pordage, Pte.(L./C.) F. C.	1016
Portch, T./S./S.M. A. J.	2699
Porteus, A./S.M. J.	2703
— Pte.(A./Sjt.) J.	1016

Porter, Sjt.(A./C.S.M.) A.	980
— Sjt. E. A.	987
— Sjt. R. A. J.	2693
— Q.M.Sjt. S.	991
— Sjt. W. L. F.	1024
Potter, By.S.M. A. E.	971
— Cpl.(A./Sjt.) C.	981
— Sjt. E. T.	986
— (A./C.Q.M.Sjt.) Sjt. R.	980
— S.M. W.	2690
Potts, Bmdr.(A./Sjt.)(A.C.) C.	977
Poulter, Sjt.(T/S./S.M.) R.	1007
Pouncy, By.S.M. W. H.	971
Powell, Sjt. W.	976
Power, Cpl. (A./Sjt.) J.	1009
— Sjt. M. J.	1946
— Q.M.S. S. A.	1024
Powers, Q.M.S. E. J.	2696
Powls, Sjt. (A./C.S.M.) F.	988
Poynter, B.S.M. H. R.	2691
Pragnell, Sjt. F. T.	993
Pratt, Pte.(A./S./Sjt.) A. D.	2700
— C.S.M. E. A.	2702
— Pte.(A./S.M.) E. J.	71
— Sjt. J.	2693
Preece, Sjt. D.	992
— Spr.(A./Sjt.) W. H.	2693
Preedy, C.S.M. C. A.	999
Preston, Sjt. J.	1007
— Q.M.S.(A./S.M.) S. D.	2700
Price, Q.M.Sjt. A.	992
— C.Q.M.Sjt. E.	986
— S.M. G., *D.C.M.*	2693
— Cpl. H. J.	1019
— S./S.M. R.	1015
— C.S.M. R. R.	1004
— Sjt. S. R.	1003
— S./Sjt. M.(O.R.Sjt.) V.	970
— F. of W. Q.M.S. W. G.	2692
— C.S.M. W. H.	1488
Priddle, Sjt. T.	1002
Priestland, Cpl.(A./Sjt.) J. W.	2696
Prime, Sjt.(A./Q.M.S.) B.	1012
Prince, Sjt. A.	2998
— Pte.(A./Cpl.) A. W.	1003
— Sjt. C. W.	1000
— A.M.3 S.	100
Pringle, Sjt. E.	2698

* Group known: British War and Victory Medals (M.I.D. oakleaf, A./W.O.II D.C.L.I.), L.S. & G.C. (Geo. V, Sgt. D.C.L.I.) and M.S.M. (Army Gym. Staff).

Pringle, C.S.M. G.	996	Quinn, C.Q.M.S. H.	999
— C.Q.M.S. J.	1019	— R.Q.M.S. J. T.	2702
Prior, Pte.(A./Sjt.) F.	2999	— Sjt.(A./Sub Condr.) M.	1945
— Sjt. J.	1000	— E.Clk.Q.M.S.(T./Spdt.E.Clk.) T. J.	60
Pritchard, Sjt. F.	1007	Quintrell, Sjt. S. B.	1024
— Sjt.(A./S./Sjt.) F. P.	2701	Quirk, Sjt. W. J.	1024
— Farr.Sjt. G.	980		
— Ftr.S./Sjt. H.	975	Raby, Q.M.Sjt. W.	991
— Sjt.(A./C.Q.M.S.) J.	61	Rackham, By.S.M. A. G.	1022
— Cpl. S.	990	Rackshaw, Pte. R.	3840
Procter, Armr.S.M. E.	2700	Radbourne, S./S.M. A. P.	2699
— Cpl.(A./Sjt.) W.	974	Radcliffe, Cpl.Clk. D. D.	100
Proctor, Sjt. E.	980	Rae, Sjt.(O.R.S.) D. M.	1019
— Sqdn.Q.M.S.(A./Q.M.S.) F. J.	3840	— Q.M.Sjt. W.	1488
— Dvr. J. T.	974	Raeburn, Sjt.Clk. J. A.	100
Prosser, S.M. G. T.	2696	Rafter, Sjt. M. E.	62
— C.S.M.(A./S.M.) T. J.	984	Raftrey, C.S.M. P.	988
Pruce, C.Q.M.S. I.	978	Rainbert, Cpl.Mec. E. F.	100
Pryke, Sjt. J. F.	976	Rainbow, Condr. W. H. *	1946
Puddy, Sjt. L.	970	Rainey, Sjt. S.	970
Pudsey, Cpl. D. A.	988	Rali Kiwanuka, A./S./Sjt.	1946
Pugh, Sjt. C. T.	980	Ralph, Sjt.(A./C.) H.	976
— C.S.M. M.	2695	Ramm, C.S.M.(T./R.S.M.) W.	1022
Pughe, Cpl. R. L.	981	Ramsay, Pte.(A./Cpl.) A.	983
Pulfer, F./Clk. G. H.	100	— Sjt. R. G.	1022
Pullen, Cpl.(A./C.Q.M.S.) C. S.	1003	Rance, Sjt. S. T.	1000
— T./S.M. G. W.	70	Randall, Pte.(L./C.) A.	987
— Pte. H. G.	993	— Pte.(L.C.)(A./Cpl.) A. H.	1003
— Sjt.Sjt. J.	998	— Sjt. G. H.	985
— Sjt. W. J.	1488	— C.S.M. R. J. J.	999
Pumford, Pte. W. H.	1002	— Mech.S./Sjt.(T./M.S.M.) S. G.	1005
Punter, Q.M.Sjt. C. E.	985	— Sjt.(A./S.M.) S. W.	987
— S.S.M. P.	2699	Randles, Sjt. J. H.	989
Purdie, S./S.M. C. L., *M.M.*	1024	Rands, Q.M.S. H. J.	2695
Purdy, R.Q.M.Sjt. A.	970	Ranford, S./Sjt. J. W.	1012
Pussey, Sub Condr. A. S.	1946	Ransome, Cpl.(A./S./Sjt.) S. R.	2700
Pye, Sjt. C. A.	2702	Rasberry, Pte. T.	994
— Pte.(A./Sjt.) E. C.	1015	Ratcliffe, Sjt. J. A.	1007
— Sub Condr. J.	2702	Rathbone, Sjt. G.	1945
Pyett, C.Q.M.Sjt. A.	991	Raven, C.S.M.(A./S.M.) G. E.	2695
Pyle, Sjt. W. D.	1022	Rawcliffe, Dkhnd. H.	2360
Pynor, C.Q.M.S. S. E.	1022	Rawding, C.S.M. J. F.	992
		Rawlins, Exp.S.M. B	2690
Quick, S.S.M. G.	1489	Rawlinson, T./Sub Condr. E.	1014
— Pte. W. H.	1011	— Cpl.(A./C.Q.M.S.) J. F.	1009
Quigley, Pte. J. G.	1019	Rawnsley, Cpl. A. J.	1022
— Q.M.S. J. H.	1019	Rawson, By.Q.M.S.(A./By.S.M.)	
Quinn, Sjt. D.	990	W., *M.M.*	972

---

* Trio known: British War and Victory Medals (Driver Mesopot. Railway) and M.S.M. (East African Railway).

Raymond, C.P.O. F.	*	2360	Reid, Cpl. G.		1019
Rayner, Sjt.(A./Q.M.S.) G. W.		969	— Pte.(A./S./Sjt.) G.		2700
Rayson, Sjt. W. J.		976	— Pte. M.		1019
Read, Sjt. F.		988	— Sjt. R. B.		1019
— Cpl. J. S. M.		1946	— Spr. W.		983
— Spr. R. H.		983	Reidy, Sjt. E.		1022
— Q.M.S. W.		2690	Reilly, Q.M.S. J.		2697
— Engmn. W.	†	3862	— Col.Sjt. J.		2694
Reader, S.M. L. N.		100	— T./Sub Condr. J.		2701
Reading, Sjt. (A./S./S.M.) W.		1015	Reinman, Pte. H. E.		2693
Reddin, E.R.,W.O. Cl. 1, H. K.		1022	Rennie, Gnr.(L./Bdr.) E. J.		977
Redford, Cpl. A.		2696	— C.S.M.(T./M.S.M.) J. C. M.		1004
Redhead, Sjt. J. W.		1022	— C.Q.M.S. J. G.		995
Redman, Sjt. G. B.		980	Renouf, Sjt. G. B.		1007
— R. of W. Q.M.S. H. J.		978	Renshaw, B.Q.M.S. W. H.		2690
Redmond, Cpl.(A./Sjt.) J.		981	Revelle, Pte. O.		984
Redpate, Ch.Mec. J.		100	Revill, F. of W. S.M. F C.		2692
— Dvr. W.		983	Reynolds, Armt.S./Sjt.(T./		
Reed, Pte C. E. R.		2998	Armt.S.M.) A. B.		1014
— B.Q.M.S. F. C.		2997	— F. of W. Q.M.S. A. W.		2692
— C.S.M. P.		997	— C.Q.M.S. E.		989
— Cpl. S.		974	— Q.M.S. H.		2696
— Pte.(A./Sjt.) W. (A.V.C.)		1016	— Sjt. J. H.		976
— Pte.(A./Sjt.) W. (Mil. Police)		1016	Rhaney, Ch.Mech. T. A.		2050
— Cpl.Clk. W. H.		100	Rhatigan, S./Sjt.(T./Supt.Clk.) T.		980
Rees, S.M. F. T.		2691	Rhind, C.S.M.(T./S.M.)		
— T./Sub Condr. T. J.		1014	G. McR., *M.C.*	‡	990
Reeve, Sjt. A. G.		60	Rhoades, Ch.Mas.Mec.		
— Sjt. J. W.		973	W. E., *A M.*	§	100
Reeves, Sjt. A.		997	Rhodes, Pte. V.		1002
— Sjt. E. C.		980	Rial, C.Q.M.S. H.		985
— Sjt. J. H.		1024	Rice, R.Q.M.S. E. H.		1022
— C.S.M. S. T.		999	— Pte.(T./Sjt.) P. J.		1024
Reid, E.C.Cpl.(A./E.C.Sjt.) A.		981	— Sub Condr. T.	+	2702
— Sjt. G.		1003	— Q.M.S. W.		2692

---

* R.N. M.S.M. Awarded D.S.M. *L.G.* 22 April, 1919.

† R.N.R. R.N. M.S.M. known, impressed *'Kidwelly Castle'* Minesweeping 1918, and a B.E.M. (*L.G.* 20 January 1942), a gallantry award for a firefight between an armed trawler and a Focke Wolfe Condor aircraft.

‡ 7/Scot. Rifles. M.C. *L.G.* 11 April 1918.

§ An R.A.F. M.S.M. No. 1744 R.F.C. Enlisted November 1914. Awarded the Albert Medal. in *L.G.* 1 January, 1918 'At an airfield in France on 14 October 1916 a bomb exploded in the mouth of a dugout forming a bomb store. Sgt. Rhoades and 2/ Lieut. F.R. Smith entered the smoke filled dugout and rescued a severely injured man who had been thrown down into the store by the bomb.

+ Thomas Rice. Group in Moss collection: M.B.E. (Sub Cond. I.O.D., *L.G.* 22 February 1919 for valuable services in India), Queen's South Africa Medal (Talana, Orange Free State, Transvaal, Pte. R.Irish Fusiliers), King's South Africa Medal (Cpl. R.I. Fus.), British War Medal (Sub Conductor Indian Ordnance Dept.), War Medal 1939/45, Indian War Service Medal, L.S. & G.C. (Geo. V, Staff Sgt. Ordnance

Richard, Q.M.S. G. T.	2702	Rigby, Q.M.S. P. C.		993
Richards, Cpl. A. N.	2997	— Sjt. R.		69
— Cpl.(A./Sjt.) F. W.	1009	Riley, Sjt. H. W.		985
— S./Sjt. G. A.	2702	— E.Clk.(2nd Cpl.) J		982
— Mech.Q.M.S. J.	2692	— Pte.(A./C.S.M.) J. E.		1016
— Cpl. J. A.	1009	— C.Q.M.S. W. H.		1024
— C.S.M. T.	984	Rillstone, Pte.(L./C.)(A./Cpl.) S. H.		1011
— Cpl.(A./Sjt.) W.	981	Rimmer, Sjt. R.		980
— Pte. W.	1002	Rimmington, B.S.M. F. W.		2691
— Cpl.(A./Sub Condr.) W. H.	1945	Rinder, By.Q.M.S. J. A.		972
— Bombr. W. R.	1022	Riordan, M.O.Cl. 1, S.		1022
Richardson, F./Clk. A. E.	100	Ripley, By.Q.M.S. D. B.		1019
— Sjt. E.	973	— A.M. 1, R.		100
— Pte.(A./S./Sjt.) E. F.	1011	Ripton, 2nd Cpl.(A./Sjt.) W.		1014
— Pte.(A./Sjt.) F.	1013	Risiott, Carpenter's Mt. A.		2360
— S.M. F. E. M.	2695	Ritchie, Engmn. R.		3862
— Sjt. H.	2698	— Gnr. W. T.		2703
— Pte. H.	1019	Ritson, F./Sjt. A.		100
— Col.Sjt.(A./S.M.) H. E.	2694	Ritter, Gnr. F. G.		1022
— Dvr. J.	1011	Rivett, Sjt. A.		1007
— Cpl.(A./Sjt.) P. C.	976	— F. of W. Q.M.S. C.		2692
— S./Sjt.(A./Condr.) S. E.	1014	Rix, Sjt. W.		1015
— Whlr.Cpl. W. B.	974	Rixon, Sjt. E.		980
— Cpl. W. C.	1022	Roach, Sjt.(A./S./Sjt.) J.		2699
Riches, Pte.(L./C.) A.	1002	Robb, S./Sjt. C. C.	†	2703
Richmond, Q.M.S. F.	984	— Ftr.S./Sjt. W. M.	‡	68
— Sjt. J. (E.York R.)	988	Roberson, Cpl.(A./W.O. Cl. 1) E. C.		3572
— Sjt. J. (R.A.S.C.)	1007	Roberts, Dvr. C. A.		1019
Rick, Dvr. R.	1011	— S./Sjt. D. S.		1490
Ricketts, Sjt. R. A.	1024	— Condr. E.		2701
Rickman, C.P.O. H.	* 3591	— Cpl.Clk. E. C.		100
Rickwood, Sjt. W.	985	— S./S.M. F.		1004
Riddell, C.S.M. F.	2698	— Pte.(A./Sjt.) F.		1014
— Pte.(A./Sjt.) R.	2698	— Q.M.S.(A./S.M.)(A.C.) G.		2691
Riddles, C.S.M. H.	1004	— Sjt.(A./S.Q.M.S.) H.		1007
Ridge, C.P.O. W. P.	3591	— C.Q.M.S. H.		999
Riding, Sjt. G.	1007	— Cpl.(A./Sjt.) H. A.		1015
Ridley, Dvr. N.	❀ 1256	— Cpl.(A./Sjt.) J.		1009
— C.Q.M.S. T.	991	— Dvr.(A./Cpl.) J.		60
— Sjt. W.	1007	— Sjt. J. T.		1019

Dept.), M.S.M. (I.O.D.). Born September 1877, he enlisted as 5431 into 1st Battn. R. I. Fus. *circa* 1895 and transferred to 2nd Battn. during the Boer War. After some 20 years service in the Indian Ordnance Dept. he was commissioned Lieut. & Asst. Commry. in August, 1925, Captain and Deputy Commry. August 1928 and Major and Commry. August, 1931. He re-engaged in 1939 in India aged 62.

* Group in Moss Collection. See Appendix S.

† New Zealander. Otago Regt. Later 2/Lt.

‡ Group known: British War and Victory Medals (Sgt.), M.S.M. (R.G.A.) and Al Valore Militaire (Silver), the last in 317 Siege Baty. R.G.A. 27 October 1918 at Maserada and the Piave for 'recovering a cannon in violent aerial bombardment.'

Roberts, Sjt. L.	68	Robinson, C.Q.M.S. S.	1489
— Pte. L. S.	1011	— Pte.(A./S./Sjt.) S.	1945
— Sjt. R.	983	— C.S.M. W.	999
— Pte. S.	985	— S./Sjt. W. E.	998
— Spr.(L./Cpl.) T. H.	983	— T./S.M. W. G.	* 2690
— S./Sjt.(A.Q.M.S.) W.	998	— Q.M.S. (A.C.) W. H.	2691
— Dvr. W.	974	— Ftr.Sjt. W. J.	973
Robertshaw, Sjt. W. G.	1007	Robson, Clk. 1, E. C.	100
Robertson, Pte. A.	1022	— L./C.(A./Cpl.) E. E.	2693
— T./S.S.M. A. R.	2697	— F. of W. Q.M.S. F. A.	60
— C.Q.M.S.(A./C.S.M.) C. F.	999	— Q.M.S. H. L.	992
— Pte. D.	1019	— E.R.A. 3rd Cl. J. H.	2360
— W.O. Cl. 2 S.Q.M.S.(A./W.O.Cl.1		— Spr.(A./C.Q.M.S.) T. J.	2693
S./S.M.) E.	3572	Roche, Eng.Clk. Q.M.S. M.	2692
— Cpl. H. B.	996	Rockingham, S.M. J. H.	† 2699
— Q.M.S. J.	994	Rodger, Sjt.(A./C.Q.M.S.) J.	1019
— Cpl.(A./Q.M.S.) R. J.	1013	Rodgers, C.Q.M.S. (T./R.Q.M.S.)	
— C.S.M. R. W.	2702	H. H. S.	1022
— Mech.S./Sjt.(A./Mech.S.M.) T.	1945	Rodrequez, Sjt. J. H.	1022
— Q.M.S.(T./S.M.) W.	61	— Corr. of name	4136
— Bandmaster W.	2694	Roe, Sjt. C. K.	987
Robey, Gnr.(A./Bombr.) C. A.	3000	— Spr. J.	983
Robins, Cpl. A.	1009	— By.S.M. T. S., *D.C.M.*	971
Robinson, Ftr.S./Sjt. A.	975	Rogers, Pte. F.	1013
— Pte. A., (M.G.C.)	70	— Sjt. F. J. M.	980
— Pte. A (R.A.M.C.)	1945	— Sjt. G.	993
— Ch.Mec. A. A.	100	— Pte. H. E.	2999
— Pte.(A./Cpl.) A. A. L.	991	— B.S.M. H. J.	1487
— S./Sjt.(A./Q.M.S.) A. R.	1012	— W.O. Cl. 2, S.Q.M.S. (A./S.S.M.)	
— Sjt.(A./3rd Cl.Mstr.Gnr.) C. H.	2691	W.O.Cl.1) J. G.	3572
— 2nd Cpl.(A./Sjt.) D. A.	1944	— Cpl. R.	1003
— Pte.(A./S./Sjt.) E.	1015	— Pte.(A./Q.M.S.) S.	988
— L./C.(A./Sjt.) F.	1490	— S./Sjt. T. W.	2999
— Sjt. F. (R.E.)	980	Rolph, C.Q.M.S. N.	1019
— Sjt. F. (Mil. Pol. Corps)	1015	Rolt, Sjt. A. T.	991
— Pte. (L./C.) G.	993	Rook, Mech.S.M. B. F.	2699
— Sjt. H. T.	985	Rooney, Pte.(A./Sjt.) S. C.	1011
— C.Q.M.S. J. C.	1022	Roper, Sjt.(A./S./Sjt.) A.	973
— S./Sjt.(A./S.S.M.) J. R.	3840	— Sjt.(A./Condr.) L. J.	1014
— Sjt. J. W.	1487	Rosair, 2nd Cl.AsstSurg. H. B.	3000
— By.S.M. R. A., *D.C.M.*	975	Roscoe, S.M. F.	2694
— S./S.M. R. W.	61	Rose, Sjt. C. A.	973

* Group known: M.B.E. (2nd type, civil ribbon, *L.G.* 1.1.1953, Chairman Cav. Old Comrades Assoc.), Queen's South Africa Medal (Defence of Ladysmith, Orange Free State, Transvaal), King's South Africa Medal (both Cpl. 5 D.G.), Defence Medal, L.S. & G.C. (Geo. V, Sqn. S.M. 5 D.G.) and M.S.M. (4/Reserve Regt. of Cav.).

† Trio known: British War Medal (W.O.1 A.S.C.), L.S. & G.C. (17th Lancers Sqn. Sgt. Maj.) and M.S.M. (S.M. R.A.S.C.). Awarded M.S.M. annuity 1946. L.S. & G.C. 1912. He came from Leeds.

Rose, Sjt. Mec. D. M.	100	Roy, S.M. T.	2697
— By.S.M.(A./R.S.M.) F. J.	971	Royle, Mech. J. B.	1945
— Sjt. J.	1007	Ruff, Sjt. R. J.	2695
— S./Sjt. S.	998	Rule, Q.M.S.(O.R.S.) W. C.	2998
— Armt.S./Sjt. W. B.	* 1014	Ruler, Sjt. A. G.	980
Rosenbaum, Sjt. M.	1019	Rumball, Mech.S.M. G.	1004
Rosenberg, T./S.M. W. F. H.	2698	Rumble, P.O. 1st Cl. S.	3862
Roskell, Cpl. R. N.	981	Rumbold, Cpl.(A./Sjt.) G. T.	2691
Ross, Cpl. A.	1945	Rumfitt, Pte.(A./C.Q.M.S.) C.	1011
— S.M. A. R.	1019	Runacres, By.S.M. C. S.	975
— Pte.(A./Sjt.) E.	2701	Rundle, A./E.R.A. 4th Cl. A. C.	2361
— Cpl. G., *MM.*	996	Ruse, S.M. F. H.	1011
— Pte. G. A.	1945	Rushmer, C.Q.M.S. S. R.	1019
— S./Sjt.(A./Q.M.S.) H. W.	1008	Rushton, Ldg. Cook's Mt. C.	2361
— C.S.M. J.	991	Russell, Cpl. A.	981
— C.Sjt. J.	1002	— Sjt. A. G.E.	69
— Pte.(A./C.Q.M.S.) J.	2698	— Pte.(A./S.Q.M.S.) A. J.	2700
— Sjt. R.	995	— S./Sjt. E. J. M.	1008
Rothwell, Q.M.S.(A./S.M.) G.	1012	— S./S.M. E. W.	61
Roud, Pte. W. J.	988	— Cpl.(A./S./Sjt.) H.	61
Rough, C.Q.M.S. P. C.	1005	— Whr.A./Sjt. H. J.	969
Roughsedge, Pte.(A./Sjt.) R. L.	1014	— C.S.M.(A./S.S.M.) J.	2699
Round, Sjt. W. J., *MM.*	984	— Sjt.(A./C.Sjt.) J. J.	969
Rounsley, Cpl.(A./S./Sjt.) W.	1009	— Sjt. R. W. G.	1008
Rourke, By.S.M.(A./		— C.Q.M.S. W.	978
R.Q.M.S.) E. H.	975	— Farr.S./Sjt. W. J.	972
— Sjt.(T./S.M.) T.	71	— Sjt. W. J. (R. Ir. R.)	988
Routledge, Clr.Sjt.(A./C.Q.M.S.) F.	999	— Sjt. W. J.	2999
Rowberry, Q.M.S. A.	2694	Rusted, Sjt. R.	1000
Rowden, S.M. F.	100	Rutherford, Sjt.(A./R.S.M.) A.	61
Rowe, S./Sjt. B.	1489	— S./Sjt. G. B.	998
— A./Cpl. H.	100	— Pte. J.	1002
— Cpl.(A./Sjt.) W. N.	† 1009	Rutter, Q.M.S. G.	71
Rowland, Eng. F.C.	2360	Ruxton, By.S.M. A. W.	971
— Sjt. G.	2692	Ryan, C.S.M. J.	995
— Pte. M. J.	1002	— S.M. J.	2700
— W.O. Cl.2, S.Q.M.S. (A./		— C.S.M. J. J.	2697
W.O. Cl.1) W.	3572	— Cpl. R. A.	1009
Rowlands, Sjt. H.	997	Ryder, S.M. E.	2701
— By.Q.M.S. T. C.	972	Rymills, B.S.M. F. G.	2691
Rowley, W.O. Cl.2,(A./S.M.) E.	2697	Ryno, Cpl. A.	1488
— S./Sjt. L. E.	1024	— S, Cpl. (S.W. Bord., Hemel	
Rowsell, T./S.M. J. H.	985	Hempstead)	990
Rowson, Pte.(A./Sjt.) S.	2700		
Roxburgh, C.S.M.(W.O.,		Sackley, Sjt.(A./C.S.M.) T.	1008
Cl.2) R. T.	1019	Sadikik, S. M.	‡ 1946

---

* R.A.O.C. Also M.M.
† Forfeited but restored 1925.
‡ King's African Rifles. Group known: 1914/15 Star (565 Sgt. 1/K.A.R.), British War and Victory Medals (R.S.M.), African General Service Medal (Geo. V, Nyasaland 1915, Sgt. Depot. Coy.), Jubilee 1935, Coronation 1937 and M.S.M.

Sadler, Sjt. J. A.	976	Savage, Cpl.(A./Sjt.) A. R.	61
Sagar, By.S.M. J. E.	975	— S./Sjt. T.	1945
Sage, S.M. J.	2700	— Sjt.(A./Q.M.S.) W.	987
Sainsbury, Sjt. A. L.	998	Savill, Sjt. J. G.	993
St. Leger, Spr. F.	983	Sawer, C.S.M. F.	2692
Salisbury, C.Q.M.S. J. E.	993	Sawkins, S./S.M. J	1489
— Bombr. J. H.	2997	— Sjt. W. H.	973
Salmon, C.S.M. J.	987	Sawwood, Cpl. H.	1001
— T./S.M. W. H.	970	Sawyer, Sjt. E. W.	1945
Salter, Cpl.(L./Sjt.) C.	* 69	— C.S.M. F. C.	1004
— Cpl.(A./C.S.M.) J. L.	981	Saxton, Sjt. W.	973
— Pte. W. M.	1019	Sayer, Col.Sjt. A.	2703
Sambrook, C.Q.M.S. G. A.	2695	Sayers, C.S.M. J.	999
Sammons, Pte. W. A.	† 1024	Scadding, W.O.Cl.1, T. W.	3572
Sample, Pte. A.	1019	Scaife, C.S.M. M. M. S.	992
— Sjt. P. W. R.	1008	— Sjt.Mech. T. W.	100
Samuels, Sjt. M	1003	Scarborough, Cpl.(L./Sjt.) J. W.	991
Sander, Sjt. A. J.	980	Scarff, Pte. G. E.	1002
Sanders, Sub Condr. A.	2702	Scarlett, Cpl. E. H.	981
— S./Sjt. A.	2701	Scatchard, Pte.(L./C.) W.	1011
— Q.M.S. F.	‡ 987	Schmidt, W.O. F. A.	1023
— Pte.(L./C.) J. C.	1019	Schofield, Cpl.(A./Sjt.) C.	1009
Sanderson, Gnr.(L./Bombr.)(A.C.)		— Spr. (A./Sjt.) C. E.	983
G. H.	977	— Ch.Mas.Mech. F.	100
Sandman, Gnr.(L./Bombr.) J. J.	974	— Mech.A./Sjt. J. H.	1005
Sandys, By.S.M. W. G.	975	— S./Sjt. P.	·61
Sansome, Cpl. R.	69	Scholes, Cpl. J.	995
Sare, C.S.M. T. H.	1002	Schronen, Sjt. C. F.	1946
Sargeant, Pte. F. H.	1014	Schulmovitch, Pte.(L./C.) S.	1002
Sargent, Farr.Sjt. R. A.	973	Schwarz, Sjt. S.	§ 1008
Saunders, C.S.M. A.	999	Scobie, Sjt. J. C.	1019
— Cpl. A.	974	Scoffin, Q.M.S. H.	2691
— Pte.(A./Sqdn.S.M.) F.	62	Scollay, S.M. E. F., *MM.*	993
— S.Q.M.S. F. A.	62	Scorah, Clr.Sjt. H.	2697
— Gnr. G. E.	1019	— Sjt. L.	980
— Ftr.Cpl.(A./Ftr.Sjt.) J.	974	Scott, Pte. A.	2361
— C.S.M. P. G.	997	— Q.M.S. A. W.	2692
— Farr.S./Sjt. W.	972	— Sjt. C. A.	1000
— Sadlr.Sjt. W.	1022	— Q.M.S. C. E.	994
— Sjt.(A./Q.M.S.)(W.O. 2nd Cl.)		— C.Q.M.S. F. T.	995
W. J.	2361	— Deletion	4136

* Group in Moss collection: M.M. (9/S. Staffs. Regt.), 1914/15 Star trio (Pte.—Cpl.), and M.S.M. (15765 on all five, this for Italy). M.M. *L.G.* 16 August 1917: 'This Lance Corporal has shown great courage and resolution in charge of transport. On 6 June his convoy came under heavy shell fire and several animals were hit. Some drivers took cover. He rallied them and galloped the convoy safely through.'
† Wellington Regt., N.Z.E.F. Served also in W.W.II and entitled to B.E.M., War Medal, N.Z. War Service Medal and N.Z. Territorial L.S. Medal.
‡ Pair known: Imperial Yeo. L.S. & G.C. (Edw. VII, Royal North Devon Yeo.) and M.S.M. (16 Devon R.).
§ R.A.S.C., Prisoner of War Section. No. S4–187367. From Ekaterinaslav, S. Russia.

— T./S./S.M. F. W.	1004	Seabrook, Ch.Mech. A.		100
— Sjt. G.	61	Seaford, S.M. G.		2695
— Cpl.(A./Sjt.) G. A.	981	Seago, Q.M.S. G.		987
— Sjt. G. H.	973	Seagrave, Q.M.S. F.		991
— S.M. H.	997	Seal, C.Q.M.S. E.		1019
— Cpl.(A./Sjt.) H.	1023	Sealy, Cpl. S.		981
— Sjt. J. H.	1000	Seaman, Sjt. J. H.		992
— Pte.(A./Sjt.) J. J.	1015	Seamons, Pte. G.		1013
— Gnr. M.	68	Searle, Sjt. F. S.		1003
— Q.M.S. R., V.C.	* 2696	— Pte.(A./Sjt.) K. W.		1011
— Sjt.(A./Q.M.S.) R.	989	— Motor Mech. W. A.	§	3860
— Pte.(A./Sjt.) R. J. W.	986	Seccombe, Mr. A. E.	+	2361
— S.M. T. J.	2690	Seckerson, Q.M.S. A. E.		2693
— C.Q.M.S. W.	1019	Seckington, Sjt. C.		984
— Spr.(L./C.) W.	983	Seears, Cpl. H. E.		1001
— Cpl. W. F.	981	Seed, Cpl. R.		974
— Sjt. W. J.	2699	— R.Q.M.S. W. E.		970
— Q.M.S. W. M. K.	984	Seely, Cpl.(L./Sjt.) R. E.		1013
Scott-Badcock, S.M. W. H.	† 1011	Sefton, C.Q.M.S. W. H.		978
Scranney, By.S.M. T. W.	971	Selbie, Sjt.(T./S./Sjt.) D. W.		1024
Scrouston, Cpl. H.	70	Self, Sjt. S.		2698
Scudds, C.S.M. C.	‡ 60	Sellens, 2nd Cpl.(A./Cpl.) A. J.		982
Scullion, Sjt. P.	1008	Sellers, Sjt. G. A.		976
Scuse, Sdlr.Cpl. E. J.	970	Senior, Q.M.S. A. F.		2700

---

* Group on display in Ashton under Lyne Museum (see also Pte. Pitts, V.C., M.S.M. 17 June 1918). He was wounded at Caesars Camp at Ladysmith on 6 January 1900, with Pitts. Both share a similar citation:— Victoria Cross, Queen's South Africa Medal (Elandslaagte, Defence of Ladysmith, Belfast), King's South Africa Medal (Cpl), War Medal 1939/45, Coronation 1937, Coronation 1953, L.S. & G.C. (Geo. V) M.S.M. (all medals named to Manchester Regt.). No. 4535, he was born in 1874 in Haslingdon and was R.S.M. of the 3rd Battn. at Cleethorpes 1914/18. He died in Downpatrick, Co. Down in 1961.

† Sqn. Ldr. R.A.F.V.R. (No. 75559), died 16 March 1941, Alexandria, Egypt.

‡ C.S.M. 103rd Coy. R.G.A., Verdala, Malta, for service in Egypt.

§ Group known: British War and Victory Medals and R.N. M.S.M. (impressed H.M.M.B. *Salmon*, North Sea 5 July 1916). Approx 52°15′ N. by 1°54′ E. at about 2300 hrs to midnight during 6/7 July HM motor boat *Salmon*, on patrol duty off Lowestoft heard buzzing sounds on hydroplane at intervals. When about 1.30 a.m. the buzzing re-commenced, it seemed to be much nearer and rapidly approaching—the sound being like that of a dynamo running, until, within a few minutes, it seemed to be right under the boat. Engines were immediately put full speed ahead and depth charge was dropped. This exploded about 100 yards astern of 'Salmon' and almost immediately a much more violent explosion followed, throwing up a column of water 50 ft high. A large number of air bubbles came to the surface, and a strong smell of acetylene gas were noticed. No further sounds were heard on hydrophone. At 10.40 a.m. S.S. 'Lady Ann' passed a circle of oil, 50 ft. in diameter near this position.

+ Trio known: China 1900, R.N. L.S. & G.C. (Edw. VII) and R.N. M.S.M. Served as a pensioned Chief Writer in Hong Kong from 1912–16.

Seppings, Mech.S.M. E.	2692	Sheerman, Sjt.(A./W.O. Cl.2	
Serjent, Cpl. F. J.	974	S.Q.M.S.) G. F.	3572
Sess, Cpl. W.	1014	Shefford, Sjt. R.	997
Severs, T./S./S.M. G.	1004	Sheldon, Spr.(A./C.Q.M.S.) R. J.	983
— Sjt. J., *MM.*	980	Shelley, Cpl. R.	994
Sewell, 2nd Cpl.(A./Cpl.) C.	2997	Shelton, By.S. M.	970
Seymour, Pte. E. J.	1019	— S.M. H. B.	1011
— Sjt.(T./S./S.M.) G. A.	1008	— S./Sjt.(A./S.Q.M.S.) P.	1019
— Sjt. J. J.	1019	Shepherd, T./Sub Condr.	
Shadbolt, Cpl. A. G.	1001	(A./Condr.) A.	1014
Shadrack, Sjt. A.	1008	— Sjt. A. L.	1019
Shakeshaft, Sjt.(A./S.Q.M.S.) E.	2699	— Cpl. A. N.	1023
Shannon, Spr.(A./Sjt.) J. A.	983	— C.S.M. D. H.	987
Sharman, 2nd Cpl.(A./S./Sjt.) B. J.	1014	— Armt.S.M. G. R. *	1014
— Cpl.(A./Sjt.) J.	1009	— S./S.M. P. W.	61
Sharp, Sjt. B.	988	Shepherdson, Farr.S./Sjt. E. F.	1023
— Q.M.S.(T./S.M.) E.	1012	Shepley, S./Sjt.(A./S.M.) F.	1012
— Pte. E.	1011	Sheppard, By.S.M. F.	971
— C.Q.M.S. F.	1488	— Pte.(A./Sjt.) F. G.	1019
— Cpl.(A./R.S.M.) H.	981	— Q.M.S. R. H.	2692
— Pte.(A./Cpl.) H.	1015	— Ch.Mec. W. J.	100
— Pte.(A./C.S.M.Instr.) J. H.	1016	Shepperd, Ldg.Teleg. H. E. W.	3591
— Q.M.S. O. G.	1023	Sheridan, C.S.M.(A./S.M.) T. J.	2695
Sharpe, 2nd Cpl.(A./Sjt.) A.	2997	Sherriff, Sjt.(A./S./Sjt.) G.	1008
Sharples, Pte. J. A.	1023	Sherring, Q.M.S. G.	2701
Sharrott, Q.M.S.(A./S.M.) G. H.	2693	— By.S.M. H. F.	971
Shaw, Sjt. A. E.	1008	Sherwood, T./S.M. S. C.	997
— Pte.(A./Sjt.) C.	1015	Shevlin, Sub Condr. W.	2702
— Sjt. C. A.	1019	Shewan, S./Sjt. G.	1008
— Cpl.(A./Sjt.)(A.C.) H.	976	Shields, C.S.M. J. †	994
— S./Sjt. H. C.	1019	Shilling, C.S.M. C.	2693
— C.Q.M.S. J.	1005	Shillitto, S.M A. W.	989
— C.Q.M.S. P. T.	994	Shipcott, Cpl. H. J.	1001
— Cpl. V. R. W.	1023	Shipp, Dkhnd. J. W.	3862
— T./S.M. T.	3840	Shipperbottom, A./Sjt. F.	100
— Sjt. W. H.	2999	Shipton, Sjt. A.	980
Shawyer, C.S.M. C.	1004	Shipway, Sjt. G. F.	980
Shearlock, 2nd Cpl. L. W.	982	Shires, Spr.(A./C.S.M.) H.	2998
Shearman, C.Q.M.S. F.	60	Sholl, Cpl.(A./Sjt.)(A.C.) R. F.	976
— C.Q.M.S. H. N.	1005	Shore, Sjt. J.	989
Sheehy, C.Q.M.S. J.	999	Shorland, Sjt.(A./S.M.) W. L.	2700

---

* R.A.O.C. Also M.M.

† C.S.M. 7th Manchester Regt. Volunteering in August 1914, he sailed to Gallipoli in the following August, and served in the landing at Cape-Helles, and Suvla Bay. After a short period in Egypt, where he was in action at Katia and Romani, he proceeded to France, and there fought at the Battles of Arras, Ypres, Nieuport, and the Somme. He was awarded the Meritorious Service Medal for gallantry in the Field in 1918. He also held the 1914/15 Star, and the General Service and Victory Medals, and was demobilised in March 1919. 31, Sedan Street, Pendleton, Salford.

Short, Cpl. F. L.	1001	Sissons, Pte. W. G.	1002
— Cpl.Mec.(A./Sjt.Mec.) G.	100	Sistrom, 2nd Cpl. R.	982
Shorten, Sjt. W.	987	Skelly, Sjt. J.	998
Shotter, Sjt. A. J.	1488	Skingsley, C.Sjt.(O.R.Sjt.) A. M.	1002
— Mech.S./Sjt. E. C.	1005	Skinn, Cpl.(A./C.S.M.) F. T. E.	981
Shrive, T./S.M. J.	60	Skinner, Mech.S./Sjt. F.	1005
Shrives, Supt.Clk. J. A.	988	— Sjt. L.	1019
Shufflebotham, W.O. Cl.2, S.Q.M.S.		Skipp, Farr.Q.M.S. H. A.	1004
(A./W.O. Cl.1,S./S.M) C.	3572	Skipper, C.Q.M.S. A.	1002
Shuttle, Sjt.(A./Q.M.S.) A. R.	1016	Slade, Cpl.(A./Sjt.) F.	981
Shuttleworth, Cpl. F.	1009	Slater, Sjt. E. P.	995
Sibbald, Sjt.(A./S.Q.M.S.) A. O.	1008	— Sjt. J.	68
Siddall, S./Sjt.(A./S.Q.M.S.) G. E.	1008	— S.M. T.	1019
Siddins, Condr. N. M.	1023	Slatford, S.Q.M.S. H.	2690
Siddle, Sjt. W. H.	980	Slatter, Pte.(A./R.S.M.) H.	2702
Siddons, C.S.M. W.	987	Slattery, B.S.M. D.	2691
Sidney, Pte.(L./C.) C. L.	1016	— Pte.(A./L./Cpl.) F.	62
Silver, Sjt. S. H.	986	— Sjt. H.	1946
Silvey, C.S.M. R.	996	Sleath, Q.M.S. C. G.	69
Sim, S.Q.M.S. R. J.	2690	Sleight, Sjt.(T./C.S.M.) G. H. B.	62
Simes, S.M. P. T.	1011	Slim, Sjt. T.	70
Simister, Pte.(A./Sjt.) N. M.	1019	Slinn, Sjt. E.	1000
Simmonds, Sjt. D.	1000	Sloan, Gnr.(L./Bdr.) F. W.	977
— Cpl. T. A.	974	— Q.M.S. R.	2694
Simmons, Clr.Sjt.(A./C.S.M.) A. E.	2696	Smales, Cpl.(L./C.) J. R.	988
— Cpl.(A./Sjt.) A. H.	2999	Smart, Sjt.(A./Q.M.S.) F. T.	984
— Pte. C. H.	1011	— Cpl. J.	1009
— Sjt.Mec. E. G.	100	Smeaton, C.Q.M.S. G.	2691
Simms, Armr.S./Sjt. F.	1014	Smellie, C.Q.M.S. J.	3840
— Sjt.(A./Q.M.S.) G.	2690	Smith, C.Q.M.S. A.	999
Simon, Pte.(A./S.Q.M.S.) R.	986	— S.M. A. (Y.L.I.)	2695
Simper, Pte. F.	1011	— S.M. A. (R.W.Fus.)	2695
Simpson, By.S.M. C. W.	971	— Sjt.(A./S.Q.M.S.) A.	1008
— Cpl. D.	996	— Sjt. A. (Gren. Gds.)	984
— Supt.Clk.(Q.M.S.) E.	989	— Sjt. A. (R.W.Kent R.)	993
— Q.M.S. E.	1002	— Cpl.(A./Sjt.)(A.C.) A.	976
— Sjt. J.	976	— Spr.(A./L./Cpl.) A.	983
— Pte.(L./C.) J.	1002	— Sjt. A. E. (R.Fus.)	986
— Sqdn.S.M. J. P.	970	— Sjt. A. E. (Essex R.)	992
— Gnr. (L./Bdr.) L. G. S.	977	— Farr.S./Sjt. A. G.	972
— Ch.Mec. R.	100	— Sjt. A. J.	1020
— Sjt. S. L.	1023	— Pte.(A./Sjt.) B. G.	1011
— S.M. T.	1011	— Sjt. C. A.	1020
— S./Sjt. W.	61	— F. of W. S./Sjt. C. E., *M.M.*	978
Sims, Bmdr. R. W.	977	— Farr.S./Sjt. C. J.	978
— C.Q.M.S. T.	985	— Pte. C. S.	1011
Sinclair, Cpl. D. H.	1001	— Sjt.(A./S.Q.M.S.) C. V.	2702
— Cpl. J.	987	— Sjt. C. W.	987
— C.S.M.(A./R.S.M.) R.	68	— Sjt. D. L.	980
— Singleton, Pte.(A./Sjt.) T.	1015	— Ch.Mec. D. M.	100
— Bmdr.(A./Sjt.)(A.C.) W.	977	— S./Sjt. E.	1489
Sissons, Pte.(A./Cpl.) B.	2700	— Sjt. E.	1489

Smith, S./Sjt. E. A.	1008	Smith, Pte.(A./Cpl.) S. B.	1011
— Cpl. E. T. F.	2050	— S.M. T.	2693
— T./S.M. F.	2690	— Sjt.(A./C.S.M.) T.	2692
— Sjt. F.	987	— P.O. T. F.	969
— Pte. F.	1020	— Q.M.S. T. G.	989
— Ch.Mec. F. B.	100	— Col.Sjt.(A./Q.M.S.) W.	997
— Cpl. F. J.	1001	— Cpl. W.	1001
— Armt.S./Sjt. F. P.	1014	— Pte.(A./Sjt.) W.	1016
— C.S.M. F. W. C.	997	— Pte. W.	2999
— C.Q.M.S. G.	993	— Cpl. W. A.	986
— Cpl. G. C.	994	— Supt.Clk. W. D.	2697
— C.P.O. G. H.	2361	— Sjt.Mec. W. E.	100
— Q.M.S.(T./S.M.) G. R.	1012	— Pte.(A./Cpl.) W. G.	1016
— Gnr.(L./Bdr.) G. W.	977	— Sjt. W. H.	995
— Q.M.S. G. W. M.	2696	— Farr.Sjt. W. H. J.	973
— C.Q.M.S. H.	986	— Condr. W. M.	2702
— Q.M.S. H.	989	Smithers, Sjt. F. W.	973
— T./S.M. H.	997	— Pte.(T./Cpl.) H.	1024
— Sjt. H.	1023	Smitten, Pte.(L./C.)(A./Cpl.) A.	1011
— T./Sub Condr.(A./Condr.) H. A.	1014	Smurthwaite, W.O. Cl.1, R.S.M.	
— Sjt. H. D.	1008	W. J.	3572
— E.C.Cpl.(A./E.C.S./Sjt.) H. G.	981	Smyth, Ch.Mas.Mec. P.	100
— Sjt. H. H.	2698	— Sub Condr. R.	2702
— Sjt. H. J.	985	Snarey, C.Q.M.S. F. A.	70
— Cpl. H. P.	1009	Snashall, C. of H. (A./Sqdn.C.M.)	
— Cpl.Mec. H. W.	100	A. R.	2689
— S./Sjt. J.	1024	Sneddon, Q.M.S. W.	2696
— C.S.M. J.	999	Sneesby, Sjt. F.	1012
— Sjt. J.	1008	Snell, Sjt.(A./Condr.) H. J.	2702
— S.M. J. A.	2697	Snelling, Sjt. L. A.	1000
— Cpl.(A./S.Q.M.S.) J. D.	2699	Snider, Pte. A.	1023
— C.Q.M.S. J. H.	993	Snook, Sjt. H.	1020
— Condr. J. N.	2702	Snow, C.S.M.(A./R.S.M.) F., *D.C.M.*	994
— S.Q.M.S. J. T. H.	70	— Cpl.(A./C.S.M.) W.	991
— C.Q.M.S. J. W.	993	Snowdon, S.M. G., *M.M.*	2692
— A./C.S.M.(W.O. 2nd Cl.) L.	2361	Soame, Exp.S./Sjt.(A./Exp.Q.M.S.) J.	2690
— 3rd Cl.Mstr.Gnr. N. L. O.	2691	Somerford, Sjt. S.	1023
— S./S.M. P.	1004	Somers, L./C. J.	1023
— Sjt. P. C., *M.M.*	973	Soper, Sjt. F. J., *M.M.*	987
— Col.Sjt.(A./C.S.M.) P. J.	986	— C.Q.M.S. G. J.	2691
— Sjt. P. S.	993	Sorrel, Sjt.(A./C.S.M.) A. W.	988
— Col.Sjt. P. W.	2693	Souch, Pte.(L./C.) H. G.	988
— By.Q.M.S. R.	972	South, Sjt. A. E.	1489
— C.S.M. S.	986	Southern, Dvr.(L./Bmdr.) M.	974
— Sjt. S.	995	Southgate, C.Q.M.S. T. H.	987
— Cpl. S.	1013	— Ch.Mas.Mec. W. J. *	100

* R.F.C. No. 753. Enlisted March 1905 into R.G.A. As 1A.M. to France from 12 August 1914 with No. 2 Sqn. S.M. March, 1916. Serving with No. 52 Sqn. in France when awarded R.A.F. M.S.M. Earned India General Service Medal (Mahsud 1919–20).

Sparkes, Sjt. A. J.	998	Stamp, Pte.(A./S./Sjt.) E. C.	61
Sparks, C.S.M.Instr. R. J.	1014	Standen, Sjt.(A./C.Q.M.S.) D. J.	1000
Sparrow, B.Q.M.Sjt. F.	975	Stanfield, Pte. S.	993
— Pte.(A./Sjt.) L. A.	1015	Stanford, Cpl. (T./Farr.Sjt.) D.	981
— Sjt. S. F.	985	Staniforth, C.Q.M.S. T. T.	978
Spayne, Sjt. J.	990	Stanley, Cpl. A. R.	1489
Spedding, C.S.M. T.	70	— Q.M.S. J. R. W.	988
Speed, Cpl. A. E.	981	— Sjt. W.	1008
Speedie, Dvr. A.	✿ 1256	Stannard, Sjt. A. E.	993
Speight, Dvr. J. E.	1020	Stansfield, Cpl.Mech. J.	100
Speller, Sjt. A. S.	990	Staple, EClk.(A./Sjt.) A. G.	981
— Pte.(A./L./C.) T.	1016	— Condr J. W. E.	1014
Spencer, C.S.M. H. F.	1004	Stapleford, By.S.M. F. E.	975
— S.Q.M.S. J.	68	Stapleton, Pte.(A./Sjt.) R. N.	1015
— Cpl.(A./C.Q.M.S.) J.	1009	Stares, Pte.(L./C.) J. F.	1016
— Sjt. P. J.	978	Starr, Pte.(A./Sjt.) A.	71
— Pte.(A./Sqd.Q.M.S.) R.	1019	Startin, C.Q.M.S. E. C.	1002
Sperring, Cpl. A. H.	1009	Staton, Gnr. A.	974
Spice, Sjt. G.	973	Statters, Sjt. A. W.	980
Spicer, C.S.M. A. E.	2693	Stead, C.S.M. A. C.	978
— Pte.(A./S./Sjt.) W. C.	2701	Stead, Pte.(A./C.Q.M.S.) A. E.	2698
Spiers, Dvr.(L./C.) F.	1023	Steane, G.N. P.	2702
— Pte.(L./C.) W. J.	1002	Steddy, Cpl. H. G.	976
Spillane, Sjt. J. H.	1946	Stedman, Pte.(A./C.S.M.) H. J.	1016
Spiller, Sjt. H.	990	Steel, Cpl. A. B.	974
Spinner, Cpl. J. J.	981	— Cpl.(A./Sjt.) W. E.	981
Spires, C.S.M. C. H., *M.M.*	997	Steele, Mech.S./Sjt. C. H.	1005
— Sub Condr. J.	2702	— By.Q.M.S. F. A.	972
Spitty, Pte.(T./Cpl.) C. P.	1023	— Sjt. J.	1024
Spokes, Cpl. J. L.	68	Steer, C.Q.M.S. A. H.	1005
Spooner, Spr.(A./L./C.) A. G.	2993	— Sjt.(A./Q.M.S.) H.	1012
Spraggs, Sjt. E. O.	1024	— Sjt. W.	987
Spring, R. H.	1008	Stehr, C.S.M. W. C.	1489
Sprunt, Bombr. W.	2690	Stendell, C.Q.M.S. R. H.	988
Spry, F./Sjt. C. H.	100	Stenton, C.S.M. S.	2697
Spurlock, Sjt. H.	980	Stephen, By.S.M. F.	971
Squibb, Sjt. G. E.	1008	— Sjt. W.	973
Squire, Cpl. G. H.	1013	Stephens, Ch.Mech. C. D.	100
Squires, P.O. F. J.	3860	— Sjt. E.	995
Stacey, S./Sjt. E.	70	— Pte.(A./Sjt.) F.	1016
— S.M. H. G.	2700	— Offrs.Std. 1st Cl. H.	3591
— S./S.M. S. G.	2701	— Gnr. N.	1023
Stachan, Sjt. C.	996	— Q.M.S. W. H.	985
Staffiere, Cpl.Mech. J.	100	Stephenson, Spr. H.	983
Stafford, Condr. F. S.	2700	— Q.M.S. P.	2694
Stagg, C.S.M.(A./S.M.) R. F.	2689	Stevens, S./S.M. A. H.	2701
Stait, C.S.M. A. C.	997	— R.S.M. C. J.	970
— Clr.Sjt.(A./Q.M.S.) W. E. R.	2695	— S./Sjt. E. J.	3000

Stevens, Sjt.(A./C.S.M.) F.	1008	Stone, Sjt. G. W.		991
— C.S.M. G. W.	* 2692	— Farr.S./Sjt. H.		1005
— S.M. H.	2697	— Cpl.(A./Q.M.S.) J. R.		1020
— S.M. H. T.	2697	— Pte.(A./S.M.) R. F.		1945
— Q.M.S. J.	69	— Sjt.(A./Sjt.) W. F.		1008
— Farr.Sjt. L. E.	980	Stonex, Sjt. H.		995
— Col.Sjt. S.	998	Stott, By.S.M. C.		971
— Sjt. W. G.	68	— C.S.M. J.		2694
— S./Sjt.(A./Q.M.S.) W. H.	1012	— C.S.M. W.		991
— Q.M.S.(A./S.M.) W. H.	2702	Stowe, Pte. O. H.		1013
Stevenson, Q.M.S. J.	995	— Sjt. W.		1000
— Cpl.(A./C.S.M.) N.	996	Strachan, Sjt. J.		70
— Sjt.Clk. R. C.	100	Strafford, Cpl. J. H.		1001
— Cpl. W.	992	Straker, Sjt.(A./C.Q.M.S.) S. E.		1003
Stewart, C.S.M. C. A.	999	Strange, Sjt. F. C.		976
— S./Sjt. C. B.	1024	Strangward, S./Sjt. A. W.		1008
— Clr.Sjt.(A./W.O. Cl.1) C. E.	3572	Stratford, 2nd Cpl. D. R.		1023
— Sjt. G.	1490	— Pte.(A./Sjt.) L. S.		69
— S./Sjt. G. C.	1023	Stratton, Sjt. T.		980
— Sjt. J.	992	Straw, Pte.(A./L./Sjt.) J. W.		1490
— Sjt. P.	998	Street, S./S.M. F. W.		1945
— Pte.(A./L./C.) P.	1013	Streeter, Sjt. E. T., *M.M.*		985
— Sjt. R. R.	980	Strickland, Spr. A.		983
— Sjt. S. H.	2702	— Cpl.(A./C.S.M.I.) J.		1490
— Gnr. W.	977	Strike, Sjt. T. J.		1008
— Sjt. W. R.	1020	Stringer, Q.M.S.(T./S.M.) F.		988
— Q.M.S. W. S.	1020	Stritter, By.S.M. R. W.		970
Stezaker, Q.M.S. W.	990	Strode, Sjt. J.		1003
Stiles, S./Sjt.(T./S.M.) G. L.	2700	Strong, Pte.(A./L./Cpl.) H.		1011
Still, Mech.S.M. F. W.	2999	— Sjt. P. G. L.	†	1003
Stirton, S.M. S. A.	1024	Strudwick, C.Q.M.S.(A./R.Q.M.Sjt.)		
Stock, S.M. G.	2694	E. E.		993
— Sjt. G. A.	980	Stuart, C.S.M. C. R.		1488
Stockton, L./C.(A./C.S.M.) W. C.	2693	— Sjt. G. G.		980
Stockwell, Sjt. F.	973	— Sjt. R. C.		1023
— Pte. S.	1002	Stunnell, Sjt. W. G.		1012
Stoddart, S.Q.M.S. T. A.	2702	Strugess, T./Mech.S.M. H.		1004
Stokes, Spr. A.	1020	Sturrock, Mech.S./Sjt. J. T.		2999
— Cpl.(L./Sjt.) A. W.	987	Styles, Sjt. A. E.		1020
— Sjt. H.	973	Suar Effendi Karar Yusbashi		1946
Bmdr. R. E. M.	977	Such, Sjt. H. V. G.		986
Stone, Ch.Mas.Mech. A. E.	100	Suddaby, Q.M.S. A. E. B.		978
— By.S.M. A. J.	971	Sudworth, S./S.M.(A./S.M.)		
— Sjt. E. G.	69	P., *D.C.M.*		2690
— F. of W. Q.M.S. G. O.	978	Suffill, Sjt. S. G.		988

* Group known: Queen's Egypt (The Nile 1884–5, 18145 Sapper R.E.), 1914/15 trio (47933 W.O.II R.E.), L.S. & G.C. (Victoria, Sgt. R.E.), M.S.M. and Khedive's Star.
† Family group known: M.B.E. (awarded 1960), 14/15 trio (15 Lond. Regt.) and M.S.M. His father's pair South Africa Medal (1879) and L.S. & G.C. (Victoria), and his sister's Imperial Service Medal.

Sugden, C.S.M.(A./S.M.) A.	988		Sword, S./Sjt. E. H.	1023
— Pte.(A./Sjt.) E. N.	2694		Sydenham, Sjt. T.	1008
Sugg, Sjt.(A./C.S.M.) E.	2997		Sykes, Q.M.S.(O.R.S.) G.	991
Sullivan, Cpl. E. G.	1009		— Sjt. J. E.	1009
— Farr.Sjt. J.	973		— A.M. 2, T. B.	100
— Sjt. W.	996		— Q.M.Sjt. W.	994
Summerbell, Sjt. F.	994		Symes, Sjt. E. H.	970
Summerfield, C.Q.M.S. J.	994		— Spr. F. G.	984
Summers, Sjt. A.	1000		Symington, Pte. C. P.	985
Summersccales, Cpl. A.	2690		— Sjt. J. W.	980
Summersell, 1st Cl. S./S.M. A.	2699			
Sumner, Farr.Sjt. G. H.	* 973		Talbot, C.Q.M.S. H. S.	978
— Mech.S.M. P. V.	2699		— Pte.(A./S./Sjt.) J. C.	61
— C.S.M. W.	986		Tanner, S.M. A. E.	2695
Sumners, Q.M.S.(T./S.M.) C.	1012		— C.Q.M.S. W. A.	3840
Surridge, Pte. J. H.	1002		Tarling, Sjt. J.	973
Sustins, C.Q.M.S. E. E.	999		Tarratt, Sjt. G. A. W.	1006
Sutcliffe, Gnr. A.	977		Tate, S./Sjt. T.	3840
— Mech.S./Sjt. J. H.	1005		Tatum, B.Q.M.S.(A./B.S.M.) C. H.	60
Sutherland, C./Sjt.(T./S.M.) A.	2697		Tay, Sjt. C.	970
— Sjt. G.	1000		Taylor, Ch.Mas.Mec. A.	† 100
— S.Q.M.S. J.	1005		— Sjt.Mec. A. A.	100
— C.S.M. K.	999		— T./S.M. A. F.	997
— Sqdn. Q.M.S. W.	2701		— Cpl.(A./Sjt.) A. R.	1015
— Sjt. W.	1000		— Sjt. E.	2695
Sutton, Sjt. J. A.	1000		— Cpl.(A./Sjt.) E. E.	2690
— Cpl. Dvr. O.	2360		— Sjt. E. H.	1000
— Sjt. S. J.	980		— Cpl. E. O.	1020
Swain, F. of W. S./Sjt. H.	978		— C.Q.M.S. F.	978
— C.Q.M.S. H. M.	2691		— Pte.(A./Sjt.) F. J. S.	1015
— By.Q.M.Sjt. J.	972		— By.Q.M.S. G. E.	972
— Cpl. W.	990		— Sjt.(A./C.S.M.) G. F.	980
Swallow, Q.M.S.(A./S.M.) J	2695		— Pte. G. K.	1945
Swanston, Spr.(A./Q.M.S.) J. A.	983		— Garr.Q.M.S. G. W.	2693
Swanton, Cpl. R. W.	1020		— Cpl.(A./Sjt.) H. B.	3840
Swarbrick, Cpl. J.	974		— Bombr.(A./Sjt.) H. E.	68
Sweetman, Cpl. E. J.	974		— C.Q.M.S. J. C.	985
Swift, Pte. (A./Cpl.) J. A.	1016		— T./Sjt. J. N.	3000
Swinhoe, Farr.Sjt. A. E.	973		— S./Sjt. J. R. K.	2702
Swinnerton, Cpl. (A./Sjt.) S.	981		— Cpl. J. T. N.	70
Swire, A.M. 2, H. W.	100		— Cpl.(A./Sjt.) L.	1013
Swithenbank, Cpl. C.	1001		— Sjt. P. F.	980
Swithinbank, Sjt. H.	1000		— Sjt. P. H.	980

* 46308 Farrier Sergt. 26th Battery R.F.A. Flanders 1918—A first-class workman and full of perseverance, this N.C.O. has carried out his duties in a highly efficient manner. He has almost invariably come up in charge of wagons at night and in spite of frequent shelling has never failed to deliver his ammunition. He has served in the 17th Brigade R.F.A., throughout the Gallipoli campaign and since then in France.

† R.A.F. M.S.M. in France with 69 Australian Sqn. as No. Aus/740.

Taylor, Sjt.Clk. P. N.	100	Thomas, Sjt. F.	995
— S.M. R.	2701	— Sjt. F. V.	1023
— Pte.(A./Cpl.) R. D.	1002	— Sjt. H. B.	1009
— S./Sjt. S. G.	1023	— Sjt. H. J., *MM.* ‡	984
— Cpl.(A./Sjt.) T.	1013	— Arm.S./Sjt. H. W. H.	1014
— Pte. T. E.	1011	— Q.M.S. J. F.	1002
— Sjt. Piper W.	996	— Cpl. P.	1023
— Pte. W.	69	— Pte.(A./C.Q.M.S.) W. I.	992
— Sjt.(A./C.S.M.) W. C.	1008	Thomerson, Col.Sjt.(A./C.S.M.) H. A.	986
— By.S.M. W. E.	971	Thompsett, S./Sjt. W. A.	2999
— C.Q.M.S. W. F.(O.B.L.I., T.F.)	992	Thompson, Pte. A. E.	996
— C.Q.M.S. D. F. (N.Z.E.)	1024	— Cpl.(A./Q.M.S.) A. W.	2693
— Cpl. W. H.	981	— Sjt. C.	987
— Bmdr. W. H.	974	— Sjt. E. B.	1020
— S.Q.M.S. W. P.	1005	— Cpl. G. S.	981
Teague, S.M. A.	1489	— S./Sjt. H.	2699
Te Au, Pte. G. D. *	1024	— T./S.M. J. E.	2694
Tee, S./Sjt. C. R.	1945	— C.Q.M.S. J. H.	997
Tegete, Col.Sjt.	1946	— Sjt. R.	1020
Telfer, Sjt. T.	1000	— Q.M.S. R. H.	990
— Cpl. W.	70	— Sjt.(A./Q.M.S.) S.	1000
Telford, Q.M.S. R.	1020	— S./Sjt. S. F. J.	1008
Tellick, C.P.O. P. G.	3591	— Ch.Mech. T.	100
Tempay, C.Q.M.S. R. F.	995	— Q.M.S. T. (Notts and D. R.)	992
Temperton, Sjt. G. W.	976	— Q.M.S. T. (Leins. R.)	2697
Temple, Sjt. H.	2692	— Cpl. T.	1013
— Q.M.S. W. V.	986	Thomson, Sjt. D.	996
Templeton, C.S.M. W. J.	2691	— Spr. J. C.	2998
Terrell, Cpl. W. J.	981	— Sjt. L. E.	1023
Terrill, Cpl.(A./S./Sjt.) C. E.	1009	— Pte. L. E.	985
Terry, Cpl. A. J.	1946	— C.S.M. W.	1004
— Cpl. F.	1009	Thorn, Pte.(A./Cpl.) F.	1002
— Condr. W.	2702	Thorne, Pte. G. C.	1003
— Cpl.(A./Sjt.) W. E.	1020	— C.S.M. J. E.	68
— S.M. W. H.	2700	Thornhill, Sjt. W. E.	1012
Teversham, Sjt. F.	1008	Thornley, Sjt.(A./C.Q.M.S.) G.	980
Thacker, S./Sjt. C. I.	1012	Thornton, L./Bombr. (A.C.) A. G.	3840
Thackray, Act. E.R.A. 5th Cl. J.	2361	— Cpl.(A./L./Sjt.) C. J.	61
— Cpl. W.	998	— Sjt. R. S.	1008
Thatcher, Cpl.(A./Q.M.S.) H. E. H.	1013	Thorp, C.Q.M.S. G.	978
— Mech.Cpl. H. O.	1945	Thorpe, P.O. A. J. J.	3861
Theobald, Sjt. H. D.	980	— C.Q.M.S. G.	978
Thexton, Cpl.(L./Sjt.,		— Cpl. P.	1009
A./C.Q.M.S.) J. †	1009	— T./S.M. W.	2690
Thirkill, Cpl. R.	1009	— Cpl.(L.Sjt.) W. G.	1020
Thom, Whlr.S./Sjt. D.	1005	Thow, Pte.(L./C.) W.	996
Thomas, Spr.(A./C.S.M.) C. H.	2693	Throp, C.S.M. H. J.	997

* No. 16/525A, Maori (Pioneer) Battn. N.Z.E.F.
† Also entitled to M.B.E. and 1953 Coronation.
‡ Awarded M.S.M. Annuity A.O. 34/1946. Grenadier Guards.

Thursby, Cpl. N.		1001	Toye, Q.M.S.(T./S.M.) W. S.	1012
Thurston, Bomdr. D.		1023	Tozer, Sjt. G.	1020
Thwaites, Sjt.(TG./Mech.S.M.) T. S.		1008	Trafford, Sjt. H. E.	1020
Tilley, Sto.P.O. E.		3591	— Sjt. W. G.	985
— By.Q.M.S. F. J.		972	Traquair, A.M. 3, J.	100
— Sjt. J.	*	2696	Traviss, Col.Sjt R. H.	986
— S./S.M. W. W.		2699	Tremlett, Spr.(A./Sjt.) F. A.	984
Tilston, F. of W. A./Sjt. T. H.		978	Trenear, Cpl.(A./Sjt.) A. B.	1009
Timbers, Arm.S./Sjt. M. C.		1014	Trethewey, W.O. Cl. 1, H.	1023
Timmins, F. of W. Q.M.S. E. J.		978	Trevanion, By.S.M. D. E.	1023
— Sjt. W.		994	Trewavis, Sjt. H. J.	1023
Timmons, Greaser P.		2361	Trewhella, Sub Condr. M.	2702
Timms, Sjt. B. O. W.		1023	Tribe, Spr.(A./Cpl.) T. G.	3840
— Spr.(A./Sjt.) L. E.		1945	Trickey, C.Q.M.S. J. P.	3840
Timperley, Q.M.S. W.		989	Trigwell, Ftr.S./Sjt. C.	975
Tindale, Q.M.S. J. H.		2693	— Cpl.(A./C.S.M.) C. H.	1015
Tingey, Cpl. T. A.		981	Trinder, Sjt. A. E.	993
Tingle, Sjt. J. C.		1008	Triplett, Cpl. F. A.	1023
Tinkham, Q.M.S. A.	†	2692	Trivett, S.M. G.	2694
Tinlin, C.S.M. T.		70	Trotman, Cpl.(A./Sjt.) J.	1001
Tinsley, Pte. W.		990	— Pte. W.	1002
Tite, Sjt. W. J.		985	Trotter, Pte.(A./Cpl.) A. V.	1020
Titt, C.S.M. E.		999	Trowbidge, S./S.M.(A./S.M.) A. T.	2690
Toal, Clr.Sjt. P. J.		2697	— Pte.(A./Sjt.) J. A.	1015
Tobin, Ch.Mas.Mec. E. J.		100	Trueman, Cpl. F. W.	1009
— 3rd Cl.Asst.Surg. P. W.		1946	Tucker, Sjt. E.	1008
Tocher, Farr.Sjt. C.		1020	— C.Q.M.S. H.	995
Todd, B.S.M. A. P.		2690	— Q.M.S. H. F.	997
— S./Sjt. E. W.		1020	— Teleg. J.	2360
Tomkins, Sjt. W.		991	— Sjt. J. A.	980
Tomlin, C.Q.M.S. W. R.		987	— Sjt. P. W.	980
Tomlinson, Sjt. A.		2690	Tuckwell, B.S.M. T.	2691
— Sjt. H.		973	Tuff, Sjt. R. H.	1023
Tompkins, Farr.Sjt. W. H.		970	Tuffield, Sjt. H. R.	973
Toms, S./Sjt. J. M. S.		2702	Tulford, Sjt. T. H.	1000
Tonkin, W.O. Cl. 1, F. H.		1023	Tullie, C.Q.M.S.(A./C.S.M.) R. J.	2999
Toobey, Sjt. R. I.		1008	Tully, Sjt. A.	62
Toon, Ftr.S./Sjt. A.		975	Tunnicliffe, Pte. C. J.	987
Toone, Dvr. D.		1011	Tunny, Spr.(A./2nd Cpl.) J. W.	984
Topp, Sjt.Clk. A.		100	Turbett, C.Q.M.S. D.	995
Topping, Pte.(T./S./S.M.) C. J.		1011	Turcotte, Sjt. L.	1020
Totty, Cpl.(A./Sjt.) J.		1487	Turmaine, C.Q.M.S. F. W.	985
Tough, C.Q.M.S. J. W.		996	Turnbull, Tnr.(A./Sjt.) E. R.	1945
Touhy, Sjt. J.		1024	— Sjt. P.	988
Townend, Q.M.S. E. W.		993	Turner, C.Q.M.S. A.	989
Towns, Sjt.(A./C.Q.M.S.) K. W.		990	— Sjt. A.	998
Townsend, Sjt. J. B.		1023	— T./R.S.M. A. E.	998

* K.S.L.I. For Singapore.
† Group known: India General Service Medal (Punjab Frontier 1897–8), China 1900 (Relief of Pekin), L.S. & G.C. (Edw. VII) and M.S.M. (R.E.).

Turner, Pte.(A./Sjt.) A. R.	1020	Umpleby, C.Q.M.S. G. A.	1020
— Sjt. C.	68	Underwood, Sjt. F.	1008
— W.O. Cl. 1, C. W.	1023	— Sjt. J.	976
— Sjt.(A./C.S.M.) E. J.	2997	Unsworth, Sjt. W.	989
— Pte. E. S.	1011	Uren, Sjt. W. J.	1000
— Sjt.(A./C.S.M.) F. R.	987	Usher, Sjt.(A./S./Sjt.) H. A.	1945
— Sjt. G.	1945	Usherwood, T./Sub Condr. J.	1014
— S.M. H.	985		
— Sto.P.O. H. W. J.	2360	Vacher, S./S.M. R. C.	2699
— C.Q.M.S.(A./Q.M.S.) J., *M.M.*	996	Vance, Sjt. C. N.	995
— Sjt. J.	1023	Varcoe, Pte.(L./C.) R.	995
— Pte. J.	2998	Varley, R.Q.M.S. A. A.	1023
— Sjt. M. A.	2997	Varney, Sjt.(A./S./Sjt.) A. W.	2699
— Farr.Cpl. T.	1020	Vaughan, Q.M.S. A.	2695
— Cpl. T. H.	982	— Pte. M. E.	68
— S.M. W.	2696	Vause, Pte. G.	1489
— Sjt. W.	976	Veale, Pte. 1, F. T.	100
— Spr.(A./Sjt.) W. A. J.	2693	Venables, S./S.M. J.	2701
— Ch.Mas.Mec. W. G.	* 100	Venner, Sjt. H. C.	973
Turp, Farr.Sjt. B.	970	Vere, Sjt. S. H.	980
Turpin, Pte. J. R.	1023	Verity, Cpl.(A./Sjt.)(A.C.) G. F.	975
Turrall, Cpl.(A./Sjt.) F.	1001	Verlaque, Pnr. D.	1946
Turrell, Sjt. T.	976	Vernon, Sjt.(A./C.Q.M.S.) H. J.	988
Tweedale, Cpl. E.	994	— C.S.M. H. S.	997
Twine, Cpl. S.	69	— Sjt. R. G.	2690
Twiss, Pte.(A./S./Sjt.) M. R.	1020	Verrall, Cpl. H. R.	995
Twohig, C.P.O. D.	2360	Vezina, Pte. J. E.	1020
Twomey, Mech.S./Sjt. J.	1005	Vialls, Q.M.S. O. J.	2690
Twyford, Pte. 1, J. S.	100	Vicars, Sjt. B. G.	969
Tyldesley, Col.Sjt. A. J.	994	Vickers, S.M. C.	† 2694
Tyler, 2nd Cpl.(A./Cpl.) H.	982	Vickerstaff, Bmdr. C.	974
— 2nd Cpl. J. W.	982	Vickery, S.M. T.	‡ 2694
Tyler-Jones, Cpl.(A./W.O. Cl. 1,		Victory, C.S.M. H. J.	3840
S./S.M.) A.	3572	Vigar, Pte.(A./Sjt.) A. G.	1015
Tynan, C.S.M.(A./S.M.) F.	996	Vigour, Sjt. R. W.	975
Tyrrell, Cpl.(L./Sjt.) C. B.	1003	Vince, S.M. A. H.	2690
Tysoe, C.Q.M.S. A. H.	1023	— Col.Sjt.(C.Q.M.S.) A. P.	985
Tyson, Cpl. W. H.	991	— Sjt. H.	1020
Tytherleigh, Spr. G. A.	1945	Vincent, S.M. H.	2690
Tytler, Sub Condr. S.	2702	— Pte. R.	990
		Vine, S.Q.M.S. C. J.	1005
Udall, S./Sjt.(T./S./S.M.) A. H.	1008	Viner, S./Sjt. E.	1014
Udell, Sjt.Clk. F. J.	100	Vines, S./Sjt.(A./S.Q.M.S.) E. G.	1014

---

* No. 128 R.F.C. Enlisted April 1907 into R.F.A. Later No. 3 Sqn. R.F.C., earning 1914/15 Star trio. M.I.D. 4 January 1917 and 13 May, 1917 as Flight Sgt. and 30 May 1918 as S.M. in Italy. R.A.F. M.S.M. also for Italy.

† M.S.M. annuity awarded in Army Order 10 of 1933 only 14 years after his M.S.M., indicating he was a long-serving W.O. when W.W.I started, perhaps with Victorian Medals.

‡ Awarded M.S.M. Annuity A.O.18/1946. Somerset L.I.

Viney, C.Q.M.S. W. C.	999	Walker, B.Q.M.S. G. F.	68
Vinton, Sto.P.O. T. H.	2360	— Farr.S./Sjt. H.	975
Vivian, C.E.R.A. 1st Cl. W.	2360	— Cpl.(L./Sjt.) H.	69
Voase, S.M. F.	2696	— Sjt. H. V.	994
Voce, Mech.S./Sjt. R.	1005	— Cpl.(A./Q.M.S.) J.	3840
Voller, Gnr. G.	977	— S.M. J. H.	2703
Volum, L./C. J. G. H.	1023	— Sjt. L.	1000
Von Ehren, Q.M.S. H.	2691	— Sjt. R. (Sco.Rif.)	990
Vowles, E.C.S./Sjt.(A./E.C.Q.M.S.)		— Sjt. R. (Lab. C.)	1000
G. A.	978	— Cpl.(A./Sjt.) S. F. H. M.	1015
Voyce, Sjt. C.	3840	— Sjt. W.	1020
Vyse, Cpl. A. H.	2998	— Spr.(A./Mec.S./Sjt.) W. E.	2693
— S./Sjt.(A./Q.M.S.) W. L.	2700	Wall, R.Q.M.S. A. G.	1023
		— C.S.M. C. A.	1004
Wadham, C.Q.M.S.A. H.	1005	Wallace, Ch.Mec. J. A.	100
Wadley, Pte. W.	990	Wallbutton, Dvr.(A./Sjt.) W.	1011
Wagger, C.S.M. W.	2999	Waller, Cpl.(L./Sjt.) W. L.	2698
Waghorn, Sjt. W.	2691	Walley, Pte.(A./Sjt.) W. H.	1015
Wagstaff, Cpl.(A./Sjt.) A.	3841	Wallington, Pte.(A./Cpl.) G.	71
Wahrmund, Gnr.(A./Sjt.) F.	1944	Wallis, S./Sjt. (T./S.S.M.) C.	2699
Waine, Q.M.S. H.	70	Walser, Cpl.(A./Sjt.) C. J.	1488
Waining, E.R.A. 3rd Cl. A.	2361	Walsh, C.Q.M.S. A. A.	999
Wainwright, Sjt. G. A.	1946	— S./Sjt.(A./S.S.M.) J.	2701
Wakefield, C.Q.M.S.(A./		— Pte. J.	995
S.M.) H. G.	2696	— Cpl.(L./Sjt.) M. A.	68
Wakeford, S.M. D.	2696	Walter, S./Sjt.(A./S.M.) R.	1012
Wakelin, Pte.(A./C.Sjrt.) S. J.	1003	Walters, W.O. L. T. W.	2702
Wakeman, Sjt. E. J.	970	Walton, S./S.M. F. H.	2699
Walden, Sjt. D. E.	1489	Walton, Cpl. F. W.	974
— Supt.Clk. H. S.	2692	— Pte. H.	985
— Sjt. O. A.	1003	— Cpl. W. G.	1023
Walder, Cpl. F. H.	974	— E.C.Cpl.(A./E.C.Sjt.) W. J.	982
Waldrin, Pte. A. G.	❀ 1256	Warburton, Q.M.S. A.	† 2696
Waldron, C.Q.M.S. R. G.	990	— Sjt.(A./C.S.M.) A.	980
Wale, Sjt.(A./S.M.) L.	2694	Ward, Cpl.(A./Sjt.) A. E.	982
Wafford, Sjt. F. J., *MM.*	3840	— C.Q.M.S. A. J.	999
Walker, S.M. A.	2694	— Sjt. C. C.	986
— Sjt. A.	984	— Sjt. E.	998
— Ch.Mec. E.	100	— Sjt. F.	980
— Q.M.S. E.	990	— Cpl. G. A.	1009
— Sjt. E.	994	— S.M. H. J.	2701
— Pte.(A/Col.Sjt.) G.	988	— Sjt.(A./S.Q.M.S.) H. S.	1008
— S.M. G.	* 988	— Cpl. J. G.	974
— Pte. G.	1011	— Cpl. R.	1001
— S.M. G. A.	2700	— L./C.(A./Cpl.) T. E.	2693

* Group known: Queen's South Africa Medal (Cape Colony, Transvaal, Orange Free State South Africa 1901, N. Staffs.), British War and Victory Medals (M.I.D. oakleaf), L.S. & G.C. (Geo. V), M.S.M. (13/York Regt.), Russian Cross of St. George and Belgian Croix de Guerre.

† 5/K.R.R.C. Also entitled to Queen's South Africa Medal, 4 Bn.

Ward, Pte. T. W.	2702	Watt, Pte. J.	1020
— Spr. W. R.	1945	— C.S.M. W.	2695
Wargent, C.P.O. W. H.	3591	Watton, Pte. I. C.	2998
Warne, S./Sjt. C. H.	1012	Watts, Sjt.(T./Sub Condr.) A. W.	1014
— Sjt. H. V.	1020	— Sjt.(A./S.S.M.) F.	1015
Warrack, S./S.M. W.	1004	— Cpl.(A./S./Sjt.) G. T.	1014
Warren, C.S.M. A.	999	— Cpl. L. W.	989
— Pte. A. E.	1023	— Cpl. W. F.	1009
— Arm.Q.M.S.(T./Arm.S.M.) C. A.	1014	Waugh, Cpl.(A./Q.M.S.) E. A.	2698
— Cpl.(A./Sjt.) C. H. N.	1001	— Tpr. R.	970
— C.E.R.A. M. P.	2361	Way, S.M. J. H.	2693
— Q.M.S. W. H.	2693	Wears, Sjt. R.	995
Warrington, Pte. A. V.	1002	Weatherell, Pte.(L./C.) C.	998
Warwick, Q.M.S. S.	994	Weatherill, Q.M.S. S.	988
Watchman, Sjt. R.	1024	Weatherley, Sjt. R. A., S.O	2999
Waters, Cpl. H. J.	* 100	Weaver, C.S.M. J.	978
— Sjt. R. J.	1945	— B.S.M. W. E.	‡ 2691
Waterson, Army Sch. W. E.	2999	Weavers, F./Sjt. F.	101
Watford, By.S.M. P. C.	971	— C.S.M. T.	1489
Watkins, Sjt.Mec. C. E.	100	Webb, Mech.S.M. A.	1004
— Sqdn.S.M. R.	970	— Sjt. A.	992
Watson, Cpl.(A./Sjt.) A. J.	1023	— Sjt.(A./C.Q.M.S.) A. E.	986
— S.Q.M.S. C.	1005	— Pte. A. G.	1011
— Q.M.S. C.	2697	— Q.M.S. A. W.	1002
— S.M. C. B.	1020	— S./S.M. C.	61
— Sjt.(A./Q.M.S.) G.	991	— Pte. D. J.	1002
— C.Q.M.S. G.	990	— S.M. E.	§ 3840
— Pte. H. M.	1013	— Sjt. E. F.	2702
— Cpl. J. H.	974	— C.Q.M.S. H.	991
— L./C.(A./Sjt.) J. H.	2698	— Pte.(A./Sjt.) H.	1015
— Pte.(A./S.Q.M.S.) J. W.	2700	— C.S.M. J.	1488
— Sjt. R.	992	— Sjt. M. E.	1008
— C.S.M. S. J.	978	— Cpl.(A./Sjt.) W. D.	1001
— S./Sjt. W., *M.M.*	† 998	Webber, Cpl. A. E.	986
— Sjt. W.	992	— C.Q.M.S. G. H.	992
— Pte.(A./L./C.) W. A.	986	— Cpl. S. A.	982
— Pte.(A./Cpl.) W. H.	1011	Websdale, Pte.(A./Sjt.) H. S.	1013

* No. 14975 R.F.C. R.A.F. M.S.M. earned in France following the recovery of some engines from aircraft which had crashed beyond the front line trenches. He was later better known by his stage name of Jack Warner, who played Sgt. Dixon of Dock Green. His group was the only one seen by the compiler, as worn, containing an R.A.F. M.S.M. The full group was O.B.E., British War Medal, Victory Medal and R.A.F. M.S.M.

† Group in Tank Corps Museum: M.M., British War and Victory Medals and M.S.M. M.M. as Sgt., 'C' Battn. Tank Corps at Feuchy Chapel, 13 April, 1917. During a heavy gas shell bombardment he helped repair tanks. On two occasions he worked 48 hours continuously under difficult circumstances.

‡ R.A. M.S.M. annuity awarded in A.O. 73/1949.

§ Group known: Queen's Sudan (L./Cpl. R. Warwicks.), L.S. & G.C. (Edw. VII, Sgt.) M.S.M. (Labour Corps) and Khedive's Sudan (Atbara and Khartoum, as Cpl).

Webster, Pte.(L./C.) G. E.	1016	Weston, A.M. 1 A. C.	101
— Sjt. H. R. F.	980	— Q.M.S. F.	2695
— Cpl. J.	1009	— Sjt. P. H.	994
— Q.M.S. W. A.	2998	— Sub Condr. W. *	2702
Weddell, C.S.M. H. L.	1945	— T./S.M.(A.C.) W. H.	975
Wedgwood, Sjt. J. K.	1023	Westwood, Cpl. E.	69
Weeks, Sub Condr. A. H.	2702	— Sjt.(A./S.Q.M.S.) H.	1008
— Ch.Mech. A. L.	101	Wetherell, Q.M.S. J.	995
Weidenhofer, Dvr.(A./Bomdr.) F. W.	1023	Wetton, Pte.(A./Cpl.) W.	1011
Weight, Sjt. S.	1023	Weymouth, Cpl. F. G.	101
Weir, C.Q.M.S. A. J.	1024	Whale, S./Sjt.(A./S.M.) J.	62
— S./Sjt. D.	1008	Whammond, Bmdr. J. R.	977
— Pte.(A./Sjt.) F. P.	1020	Wheal, Sjt. G.	976
— S.M. G.	996	Wheatcroft, Pte.(A./Sjt.) W.	2700
Welch, T./S.M. G. A.	2690	Wheaver, Cpl. A. B.	977
— Sjt. J.	980	Wheeler, Q.M.S. C. F.	1012
Weldon, Q.M.S.(T./S.M.) T. McD.	1012	— Condr. E.	2701
Welfare, S./Sjt. C.	1008	— B.Q.M.S. G. J.	2690
— Pte. F.	1011	— Pte.(A./W.O. Cl. 1 Spdt.Clk.)	
Welford, Mech.S./Sjt. A.	1005	H. T.	3572
Wellfare, F. of W. S./Sjt. J.	978	— Pnr.Sjt. J., *M.M.*	988
Wellings, Cpl.(A./Ftr.Sjt.) J.	974	— Cpl. (A./Sjt.) W. H.	1013
— Farr.Sjt. T.	973	Wheelhouse, Pte. E.	1020
Wellington, S./Sjt. E. L.	1023	Whelan, Cpl.(A./S.Q. ..) J. W. †	1009
Wells, Sjt. C.	998	— Cpl. (A./Sjt.) T.	3000
— Spr. H. C.	984	— Sjt. T. M.	1023
— Pte.(A./L./C.) H. H.	1011	Whibley, Q.M.S. R. J.	2695
— C.S.M. J. E.	999	Whife, Sjt. B.	2691
Welsby, By.Q.M.S. E.	972	Whillans, C.Q.M.S. J.	999
Welsh, Sjt. A. E.	1003	Whitbread, T./S.M. E.	970
— Cpl. F. D.	1020	Whitcombe, Q.M.S. H.	2691
— Sjt. H.	980	White, Sjt. A. F.	995
— Farr.Q.M.S. H. J.	970	— C.S.M. A. H.	69
West, C.Q.M.S. E. G.	3840	— Sjt. A. J.	973
— M.S.S./A.Mech./S.M. F. J.	1005	— R.S.M. C. E.	1024
— Sjt. G.	998	— Sjt. C. H.	973
— Spr. L. G.	984	— Q.M.S. C. J.	994
— Condr. R.	2701	— Pte.(L./C.) D.	1016
Westall, Cpl. W. W.	998	— Cpl. D. J.	987
Westbrook, Sjt. J.	1023	— Sjt. E. B.	973
Westcott, C.S.M. F.	997	— Pte. E. G.	1945
— Cpl.Mech. G. H.	101	— Gnr.(A./Sjt.) E. T.	977
Westhorpe, Q.M.S. P.	997	— 3rd A.M. F. J.	101
Westley, F./Clk. E. J.	101	— Sjt. G.	995

* Group known: British War Medal (Lieutenant). L.S. & G.C. (Geo. V, Sub-Condr. Indian Misc. List, engraved in script) and M.S.M. (I.M.L.) 'For services with the Indian Army in the War.' Indian type suspension on British War Medal.

† Group known: M.B.E. (1st type, military ribbon, 1st class S.S.M., R.A.S.C.), 1914 Star (Pte), British War and Victory Medals (M.I.D. oakleaf, W.O.II), L.S. & G.C. (Geo. V, W.O.II) and M.S.M. Retired from R.A.S.C. 16 May, 1937.

White, A./Sjt.Maj. G. G. R.	101	Wilde, Cpl.(A./Sjt.) W. B.	80
— Sjt. H. G., *M.M.*	✿ 1256	Wilderspin, C.S.M. F. C.	999
— C.S.M. H. J.	68	Wildman, Sjt. V. G.	1023
— Cpl. J. A. (R.F.A.)	974	Wile, Sjt. M.	973
— Cpl. J. A. (Ontario R.)	1020	Wiles, Sjt. G.	998
— Sjt. R.	1008	— By.S.M.(A./R.S.M.) S. T.	971
— Bomdr.Sig. T. A.	1024	Wilkes, Cpl.(A./C.Q.M.S.) J.	1009
— Sjt. W.	1008	Wilkie, Sjt. T. B.	3840
— M.E. Q.M.S. W. E.	60	Wilkins, C.S.M.(A./S.M.) F., *M.M.*	986
— Cpl. W. T.	* ✿ 1256	— By.Q.M.S. W.	972
Whitehead, Q.M.S. T.	989	Wilkinson, Sjt. A.	980
Whitehurst, Pte. W.	2698	— Cpl. A.	994
Whiteley, Pte. W.	989	— Pte.(L./C.)A. W.	987
Whitelock, L./C.(A./Sjt.) H	2693	— S.M. C. A.	1011
Whitemore, Pte. R.	1011	— Farr.S./Sjt. F.	972
Whitfield, B.S.M. R.	1487	— Sjt.(A./C.Q.M.S.) G. H.	2695
Whitlam, Sjt.(A./Q.M.S.) S.	985	— W.O. H. H. G.	2702
Whitmore, Cpl.(A./S./Sjt.)		— Sjt. H. O.	2999
(A.C.) P.	977	— Sjt. J.	994
Whitney, Pte.(A./Sjt.) G. S.	987	— Arm.S./Sjt. R. J.	1014
— S.M. J. J.	2696	— Mech.S.M. S.	1004
Whitrow, C.Q.M.S. H. G.	1023	— Pte.(A./C.S.M.) W. P.	1016
Whittaker, Pte.(A./C.S.M.) F. N.	2998	Wilks, Sjt. J.	3840
— C.Q.M.S. R.	994	Will, C.S.M. W. J. J.	1004
— Bomdr. W. L.	977	William, 2nd Cpl.(A./Sjt.) J. H.	982
Whittingham, Ch.Mas.Mech. J.	101	Williams, Sjt. A.	998
Whittington, Rfmn. C. E.	2703	— Supt.Clk. A.	2692
Whittle, Sjt. A. W.	1000	— S./Sjt.(A./Mech.S./Sjt.) A. A. A.	1945
— T./Sub Condr. F.	1014	— T./Sub Condr. A. W.	1014
Whittlesey, Yeo.Sigs. E.	2361	— Arm.Q.M.S.(A./Arm.S.M.) C. A.	1014
Whitty, E.R./S.S.M.		— C.Q.M.S. C. J.	1020
W.O.2, H. F.	1023	— Sjt. D. S.	1008
Whitworth, S./Sjt.(T./S.M.) R.	2700	— Ch.Mec. F.	101
Whyte, C.Q.M.S.(A./Q.M.S.) A. K.	1020	— By.S.M. F.	1020
Wickstead, T./S.S.M. G. H.	2699	— Sjt.(A./C.S.M.) F.	1000
— Sjt.(A./S./Sjt.) S. C.	1008	— Sjt. F. (R.E.)	980
Wiesener, Sjt. W. G.	1023	— Sjt. F. (R.A.S.C.)	1008
Wigglesworth, Sjt. A.	1008	— Pte.(A./L./C.) F	990
Wight, Sjt.(A./S./Sjt.) J.	2700	— C.Q.M.S. F. C.	69
Wigmore, T./Sub Condr. F. G.	1014	— Sjt.(A./C.S.M.) F. C.	980
— Sjt. G. F.	980	— 2nd Cpl.(A./Cpl.) F. C.	1488
Wilbow, C.S.M. A. J.	1023	— Sjt. F. M.	69
Wilbraham, Cpl. J.	1009	— Cpl. F. W.	1009
Wilcock, T./S.M. J. F.	989	— F. of W. Q.M.S. G. C.	2692
Wilcocks, Cpl.(A./Sjt.) S.	982	— R.Q.M.S. G. H.	1023
Wild, C.S.M. F.	1004	— Sjt. II.	1000
— Bmdr.Sig. H.	977	— Mech.S./Sjt. H. E.	978
— 2nd Cpl. J. G.	1945	— T./S./S.M. H. S.	1004
Wilde, Pte.(L./Cpl.) G. S.	1014	— T./S.M. I. W.	2695

* R.G.A. For Gallantry in Aden.

Williams, Sjt.(A./C.S.M.) J., *M.M.*	990
— Spr. J.	984
— S./S.M. J. D.	1004
— C.S.M.(A./S.M.) R.	2695
— Sjt. R. D.	1020
— Ch.Mec. R. R.	101
— Sjt. S.	995
— Sjt.(A./S./Sjt.) W. G.	1008
— Q.M.S. W. H.	2998
Willis, S.M. H. E.	2698
— S.Q.M.S.(A./R.S.M.) W.	978
Willison, Q.M.S. W. H.	1023
Willmot, Cpl.(A./S./S.) A. L.	1015
Wills, Sjt. A.	3840
— S./Sjt. E. C.	1024
Willson, Pte.(A./Sjt.) A. J.	992
Wilmer, Pte. V. A. G.	2997
Wilmore, S./Sjt. H.	1012
Wilson, 2nd Cl.Mstr.Gnr. A.	2691
— Bdr. A. C.	1023
— Sjt. A. E.	1008
— 2nd Cpl.(A./Cpl.) A. J.	982
— W.O. Cl. 1, A. M.	1023
— Clr.Sjt. A. P.	2694
— S./Sjt. B. S.	969
— Q.M.S.(A./S.M.) C.	2700
— Pte. C. J., *M.M.*	1020
— Cpl. C. L.	1945
— Cpl. G.	1009
— Sjt. G. F.	996
— Sjt. G. T.	980
— C.Q.M.S. J.	2692
— Clr.Sjt.(A./C.S.M.) J.	2693
— Q.M.S. J. A.	995
— Sjt. J. G.	68
— Sjt. J. L.	70
— Pte.(A./Cpl.) L.	991
— Pte. P.	1002
— Sjt. P. J.	1023
— Q.M.S. R.	990
— Sjt. R. J.	1945
— T./S.M. S. F.	2698
— By.S.M. T., *M.M.*	1020
— Cpl. (A./Q.M.S.) T.	995
— Cpl.(A./C.S.M.) T.	1009
— Cpl. T. A.	1488
— C.Q.M.S. T. F.	984
Wilton, Ch.Mec. G. T.	101
Wiltshire, Clr.Sjt.(A./S.M.) T.	2696
Winchcombe, A.M. 1, W. H.	101
Windass, Pte. W.	988
Windeat, Sjt.(A./Garr.S.M.) C. L.	61

Windebank, Sjt.(A./S./Sjt.) P.	1945
— Cpl. W. J.	1010
Wingate, Sjt.(A./S./S.M.) R.	1015
Wingfield, Sjt. F.	1020
— Q.M.S. H. J.	992
Winning, Sjt. J. P.	1020
Winstanley, Pte.(L./C.) J. J.	1011
Winter, Sjt. F.	984
— Dvr. J. H.	68
Winterburn, Sjt. F.	2702
Winters, Q.M.S. M. R.	1020
Winward, Armt.S.M. H. H.	2701
Wise, A./Cpl. F. J.	101
— S.Q.M.S. H.	1005
— Sjt. J.	2691
Wishart, Sjt. J.	976
Wiskar, S.M. H. W.	2701
Witcombe, Sjt. E.	69
Withers, C.Q.M.S. J. A.	60
— S.M. T.	2695
Witney, S.M. A. W.	1024
Wolfe, S./Sjt.(A./Q.M.S.) I.	1012
Wolstencroft, C.S.M.	1004
— Spr.(A./L./C.) J. A.	3840
Wolsenholme, C.Q.M.S. J. J.	997
Wombwell, Sjt.Dmr. R.	984
Womphrey, Q.M.S.(A./S.M.) I. T.	2692
Wones, Sjt.(A./S.Q.M.S.) B. B.	2702
Wood, Pnr. A.	3840
— Cpl. A. J. R.	1010
— Sjt. A. M.	1008
— Sjt.Clk. A. R.	101
— Sjt. C.	986
— Cpl.(A./Sjt.) C. V.	1020
— Mech.S./Sjt. F.	1488
— Sjt. F. D.	1012
— Col.Sjt.(C.Q.M.S.) H. V.	985
— Cpl.Mec. J. T.	101
— Cpl.(A./Sjt.) J. W.	2695
— Pte.(A./Sjt.) J. W.	1011
— Sjt.(A./Q.M.S.) K.	988
— Sjt. T. H.	995
— S.M. T. V.	2696
— Cpl. W. C.	1010
Woodall, Pte. C.	994
Woodard, T./Sub Condr. A. E. L.	1014
Woodcock, Sjt.Clk. T.	101
Wooderson, By.S.M. F. J.	975
Woodhall, Pte.(A./S.M.) A.	62
Woodhouse, Q.M.S. W. P.	1020
Woodin, Q.M.S.(O.R.Sjt.) E.	970
Woodland, Sjt. G. A.	68

* A.S.C. M.C. *L.G.* 23 June 1915.
† No. 370 R.F.C. Group known: 1914 Star (Sgt.), British War and Victory Medals (S.M.1 R.A.F.), Defence and War Medals (M.I.D. oakleaf) and R.A.F. M.S.M. Enlisted December, 1912. As 1A.M. with 3 Sqn. in France from 13 August, 1914. S.M. from March 1916. (M.I.D. *L.G.* 1 January, 1945 as W.O. R.A.F.).
‡ R.E. Malta.
§ Group known: D.C.M. (352026 B.S.M. R.G.A.), British War and Victory Medals, Territorial Force War Medal, M.S.M. and Territorial Force Efficiency Medal (138 C.Q.M.S. Hants. R.G.A.).
+ R.A.O.C. Also Russian Silver Medal with the Riband of St. Stanislas.

Young, Cpl.(A./Col.Sjt.) S.	995	Young, Ch.Sto. W. A.	3861
— Pte.(A./Sjt.) S. W.	1003	Younger, Q.M.S. J.	1020
— C.Q.M.S. W.	999		
— Sjt. W. (H.L.I)	* 995		
— Sjt. W. (C. Ontario R.)	1020	Zeederberg, Supt.Clk. H.	1024

* Pipe Major 2/H.L.I. 1909–1920.

Vol. II, 1919

Abbott, Sjt. C.		7014	Adams, S./Sjt.(T./S.Q.M.S.) R.	6945
— Pte. G. J.		6893	— Sjt.(T./Mech.S./Sjt.) R. A.	6901
— S./Sjt.(A./Q.M.S.) J. J.		6946	— Pte.(A./Cpl.) S.	7019
— Sjt. O. H.		6873	— C.Q.M.S. T.	6912
— A.B. P.		4734	— Dkhnd. W.	8202
— C.Q.M.S. P. J.		6885	— Cpl. W. C.	6912
— Sjt. R. W. H.		6873	— B.S.M. W. G.	6869
— Cpl. W.		6868	— Pte.(A./R.S.M.) W. T.	6957
— Sjt. W. J.		7020	Adamson, Pte.(A./C.S.M.) A. A.	6905
Abdul, Gardi Rizik, Sjt.		6971	— Pte.(A./Cpl.) J. E.	6882
Abdulla Zena Mulazim Tani		6971	Addison, C.Q.M.S. G.	6872
Abel, Pte.(A./S.Q.M.S.) H.		7020	Ager, Cpl.(L./Sjt.) W. G.	6955
Abell, C.Q.M.S. W. H.		6900	Aiken, S./Sjt. A. D.	6912
Abraham, Cpl. R. S.		6903	Ainsworth, Dvr. G. F.	6869
Abrahams, Sjt. J. J. A.		6916	— Cpl. S. H.	6903
Abrahart, Sjt. F. G.		6901	Airey, Ch.Mech. J. W.	7036
Abram, Pte. J.		6896	Aisbatt, Cpl. A.	6876
Acheson, C.S.M. G.	*	6886	Aisthorpe, 2nd Hnd. Horace	4732
— Master Gnr. 1st Cl., W. H.		7011	Aitchison, Pte.(L./C.) A.	6905
Acker, R.S.M. W. R.		6912	Aitken, C.Q.M.S. G. G.	6872
Ackert, Spr. H. A.		6912	— Pte.(A./S.Q.M.S.) J. M.	7020
Ackhurst, Sjt. Instr. A. H.		6912	Albrechsten, S.S.M. O. W.	6970
Adam, C.S.M. J. W. D.		6970	Albutt, R.S.M. R. J.	‡ 7014
Adams, Cpl. of Horse A. E.	†	6881	Alchin, Pte., (L./C.) C.	6885
— Ch. Writer, E. J.		7907	Alcock, F./Sjt. A. G.	§ 7036
— C.Q.M.S. E. S.		7013	Aldhouse, T./S.M. B. L., *D.C.M.*	6907
— Sjt. F.		6912	Aldridge, Pte.(A./S.Q.M.S.) A.	7019
— S./Sjt. G. J.		6901	— C.Q.M.S. C. W.	6880
— Sjt. H.		6874	— Sjt. T.	6912
— C.Q.M.S. J.		7013	— Farr.Sjt. W. G.	6874
— Cpl. (A./C.S.M.) J.		6896	Alexander, Supt.Clk. G.	+ 7011
— Sjt. J. H.		6887	— Bombr. H.	6868

---

* R.G.A. in Gibraltar.
† Group known: 1914 Star & bar (Tpr. R.H.G.), British War and Victory Medals (Cpl. of H.), L.S. & G.C. (Geo. V, W.O.II) and M.S.M. Joined the Coldstream Guards in 1908, transferred to 4 Dragoon Guards in 1909 and Royal Horse Guards in 1912. His M.S.M. is named to Guards Machine Gun Regt.
‡ R. Welsh Fus. in Gibraltar.
§ No. 558 R.F.C.; R.A.F. M.S.M. for France. Enlisted March 1902, was Sapper (Balloonist and Engine Driver) at the Balloon School R.E. on the formation of R.F.C. Discharged before W.W.I and recalled to serve with the Aircraft Park from 16 August 1914 as 1A.M. Flight Sergt. March, 1918.
+ Group known: British War Medal (R.E.), L.S. & G.C. (Geo. V) and M.S.M. (for services in Gibraltar).

Alexander, Mech.S.M. P.	*	6898
— Pte.(L./C.) T. L.		6943
Alford, C.Q.M.S. H. F.		6882
— F./Sjt. R. E.	†	7036
— S.M. T. H.		7036
Allan, Pte. C. W.		6908
— Sjt.(A./C.Q.M.S.) D.		6933
— Sjt. G.		6882
— R.S.M. J. S.		6916
— Pte.(A./Cpl.) J. S.		6905
Allard, Sjt. G. E.		7011
Allcock, Gnr.(L./Bombr.) F.		6869
— Pte.(A./Sjt.) G. R.		7019
Allder, C.Q.M.S.(A./C.S.M.) W. H.		7018
Allen, Sjt. A. G.		6890
— Sjt. A. J. H.		6916
— Cpl. F. G.		6896
— Cpl.(A./C.Q.M.S.) H.		6876
— Cpl. H. F.		6954
— Cpl.(A./Sjt.) J. R.		6934
— Whlr.S./Sjt. J. T.		6900
— T./S.M. S.		6871
— R.Q.M.S. S. G.		6916
— Pte. W. S.		6945
Allison, Pte.(A./Q.M.S.) A. E.		6933
Allitt, Supt.Clk. H.		6880
Almon, Sjt. J. M.		6912
Alpe, Cpl.(A./C.S.M.) E. F. R.	‡	6882
Alton, Hd.Condr. H.		6970
Alvis, Cpl.(A./Sjt.) W. G.		6903
Ambrose, C.Q.M.S. B. E.		6900
Amor, C.S.M. A. H.		6882
Amos, Ldg.Sea. C. W.		6447
— S.S.M. F.		6898
— C.Q.M.S. W. J.		6886
Anderson, B.S.M. A.		6916
— Pte.(C.S.M.) A.		7022
— Cpl.(T./Q.M.S.) A. K.		6916
— Cpl. A. M.		6896
— Farr.Sjt. C.		6867
— Cpl.(S./Sjt.) C. W.		6934
— Sjt. D.McM.		6894
— L.A.C. G.		7036
— A./Sjt. H.		7021
— Cpl. H.		6892
— S./Sjt. J. (Manitoba R.)		6912

Anderson, S./Sjt. J. (R.A.M.C.)	6907
— C.S.M. J. (Lab. C.)	6895
— Pte.(L./C.) J.	6883
— Sjt. J. D.	6953
— R.S.M. J. F.	6916
— Cpl. M.	6892
— F./Sjt. O.	7036
— B.Q.M.S. P.	6954
— S./S.M. R. G.	7023
— F. of W. S./Sjt. R. W.	7012
— C.S.M.(A./Q.M.S.) T.	7012
— Sjt. T.	6874
Anderton, T./S.S.M. A. A.	6808
Andrew, Sjt. J. H.	6874
— R.Q.M.S. W. J.	7017
Andrews, Pte. F.	6887
— Sjt.(T./C.S.M.) H. C.	6874
— T./Sub Condr. J.	6909
— Sqdn.Q.M.S. J. I. G.	6866
— Pte.(L./C.) M.	6898
— Sjt. R., *MM*.	6991
— Cpl.(A./Sjt.) R. L.	6876
— Whlr.S./Sjt. W.	7018
Angear, Sjt. J. I.	6874
Angier, R.S.M. C.	7010
Angus, Cpl. F.	6896
Anlezark, T./R.S.M. W.	6890
Annand, Sjt. W. J.	6918
Ansell, Sjt. J. G. (R.G.A.) (corr.)	7703
— Pte.(L./C.) J. G. (Mil. Mounted Police)	6911
Anstee, Fitt.S./Sjt. A. J.	6870
Anstey, Sjt. G. T.	6885
Anthony, Armr.Q.M.S. J.	6934
— Sjt. M.	6874
— B.Q.M.S. W. E.	6867
Antrobus, C.Q.M.S.(A./C.S.M., W.O. II) H.	7010
Aplin, Sjt. W. E.	6874
Appleby, Cpl.(Sjt.) R. R. C.	6916
Applegate, Q.M.S.Instr. H. S.	7012
Appleton, Pte.(L./C.) T. E.	6905
Appleyard, Cpl. F. H.	6896
Apps, Ch.Shipwt.2nd Cl., H. E.	7907
Archer, Sjt. A. A.	6884
— R.S.M. W.	6890

---

* R.G.A. in Gibraltar.

† R.A.F. M.S.M. for service in the Mediterranean. Formerly F1214 R.N.A.S.

‡ See Seigne *infra*. M.S.M. 10/R. Fus. and French Médaille d'Honneur avec Glaives en Argent 14 July 1919.

Archer, Q.M.S. W. H.	* 6894	Asplin, Cpl.(A./Sjt.) A. J.	6957
Archibald, A./S.Q.M.S. A. J.	† 7021	Astill, S.M. R.	6871
Ariss, R.S.M. W.	6866	Aston, R.Q.M.S. A.	7013
Armitage, Bombr.(T./S./Sjt.) C. L.	7023	— Ch. Mech. E. C	7036
— Pte.(A./Cpl.) W.	6911	Atherton, Sjt.(A./C.S.M.) A.	6885
Armstrong, T./Armt.S.M. A. L.	‡ 6909	— Sjt. W.	6888
— C.Q.M.S. H. G.	6916	Atkin, S./Sjt. J.	6953
— C.S.M. J.	6899	— Cpl.(A./Sjt.) J.	6908
— C.S.M. J. E.	7013	— Sjt. S. H.	6916
— Pte. W.	6886	Atkins, Pte. C.	6910
— Gnr.(L./Bombr.) W. J.	7011	— Sjt. F	6908
Arnold, C.S.M. A. J.	6888	— Cpl. G. T.	6903
— Farr.Q.M.S. G. E.	6865	— Pte.(A./C.S.M.) M. L.	6945
— Dvr. J.	6869	— C.Q.M.S.(A./C.S.M.) S. H.	6892
Arnott, Sjt. G.	7010	— M.A.A. Squire A.	7907
Arnup, Sig.(L./Bombr.) C. J.	6871	Atkinson, Cpl. A. F.	6887
Arrowsmith, P.O. F. G.	8068	— Sjt. E.	6893
Arscott, T./Sub Condr. F.	6909	— Cpl. E. M.	6903
Arthur, S./Sjt.(A./S.Q.M.S.) A.	7018	— Cpl. G.	6884
— Sjt.(A./C.S.M.) A.	7019	— Sjt. G. R.	6887
— S.S.M. D. W.	6898	— Sjt. Instr. H.	6912
— L./C. C. J. McC.	7022	— Army Schmaster J.	§ 7021
Ash, S./Sjt. H. T.	6971	Attenborough, C.Q.M.S. B. E.	6884
— Pte.(A./Sjt.) S.	7019	Attey, Sjt. E.	6891
Asha Mukasa Efendi		Attrill, Sadd.(T./Sadd	
Mulazim Awaal	6971	S./Sjt.) M. S.	6905
Ashby, Sjt. F. J.	6870	Auger, Sjt. F. W. B.	6911
Ashcroft, Cpl.(A./Sjt.) W. H.	6883	August, Pte. F.	6956
Ashford, Sjt. E.	6874	Auld, Spr. J.	6879
— Sjt. G. F.	6956	Austin, Sjt.	6971
— Sjt. J.	6901	— C.Q.M.S. A. W.	6891
Ashley, A.C. 1, B.	7036	— Cpl. F.	6916
— Cpl. R.	6908	— Pte. F. C.	6905
Ashton, Pte.(A./Cpl.) C.	6905	— Pte.(A/S./Sjt.) F. W.	7020
— Pte. E.	6908	— Q.M.S. G. A.	6907
— Pte.(A./C.Q.M.S.) H.	6885	— Sjt. I. T.	6934
— R.S.M. J.	6912	— Supt.Clk. W. T.	7011
— Actg. C.E.R.A. 2nd Cl. J. A.	8203	Auty, Cpl.(A./Sjt.) A.	6908
— S.M. J. F. J.	6865	Avenell, Ldg.Sea. C. E.	4735
— C.S.M. J. W.	7015	Averell, Farr.S./Sjt. T. H.	6867
Ashwell, Cpl. F.	6903	Aylott, Spr.(A./2nd Cpl.) W. G.	7012
Ashworth, C.Q.M.S. W.	6873	Aylward, Cpl.(A./Sjt.) W. R.	6912
Askwith, Cpl. E. A.	6912	Ayres, C.Q.M.S. T.	6885
Aspin, C.S.M. S.	6945	— Pte.(A./C.Q.M.S.) W. C.	6888
Aspinal, Q.M.S. J.	6871	Ayton, Spr. W.	6916

* Group known : 1914 Star trio (Pte./W.O. A.S.C.) and M.S.M. (Tank Corps).
† Single known: Canadian Postal Corps. 5 awarded to the unit. This is the only one for home service in Canada.
‡ Awarded M.S.M. Annuity A.O. 92/1948 as Arm. Q.M.S. R.A.O.C.
§ C. of A.S. in Malta.

Baard, Sjt. H. W.	6970	Bain, C.S.M. J.		6872
Babb, C.P.O. Teleg. H.	7907	— Pte.(A./S.Q.M.S.) J.		7022
Babbage, Pte.(A./Sjt.) A. L.	6934	— Sjt. W. D.		6886
Babington, S.Q.M.S. J. H.	7023	Bainbridge, Sjt. G. S.		6970
— Sjt. P. A.	6912	Baines, Cpl. W. E.		7036
Bach, T./S.S.M. H. C.	6898	— Spr. W. E.		6879
Bachrach, Pte. S. E.	6934	Bains, Sjt. W. J.		7036
Backer, 2nd Hnd. J.	4733	Baird, C.S.M. J. S.		6912
Backhouse, Q.M.S. R. V.	6912	— Sjt. T.		6934
— Sjt. W. E.	6874	Baker, C.S.M.Instr. A.		6912
Bacon, Q.M.S. A.	6882	— Pte.(A./R.S.M.) A.		6883
Badcock, S./Sjt.(A./S.S.M.) R. E.	7018	— Pte. A. A.		6883
Baddeley, Pte.(A./Cpl.) R. F.	6883	— Pte.(A./L./Sjt.) A. E.		6908
Badenoch, Sjt. A.	6912	— Sjt. A. W.		6898
Badger, Cpl.(A./S./Sjt.) A. G.	7019	— Sjt. B.	✿	7701
— Spr.(L./C.) E. A.	6879	— Pte.(A./Sjt.) B. G.		6909
Badman, Sjt. E. B.	6894	— Sjt.(A./C.S.M.) E.		6957
Bagge, S./Sjt.(A./Sub Condr.) A. A.	6934	— Pte.(A./S.M.) H.		7022
Baggott, Sjt. A. T. J.	6901	— Pte. H. C.		6898
Baggs, Sjt. A. E.	6912	— Pte. (A./Sjt.) H. T.		6893
Bagshaw, R.Q.M.S. R. I., *M.M.*	6912	— R.Q.M.S. J.		7011
Baguley, C.Q.M.S. K.	6900	— Cpl.(A./Sjt.) J. A.		6868
Baigent, C.S.M. E. C.	7011	— T./S.M. J. J.		6907
Baigrie, Sjt.(A./C.S.M.) J.	7018	— Q.M.S.(A./S.M.) R. L.		6871
Baikie, Farr.S./Sjt. J. W.	6873	— Pte.(A./S./Sjt.) S. A.		6905
Bailey, Sjt. A. (W. India R.)	6064	— Cpl. T.		6954
— Sjt. A. (R.A.S.C.)	6901	— Pte. W.		6880
— Sjt. A. B.	6874	— Pte.(L./C.) W. G.		6890
— C.S.M. A. E.	6899	— L./C. W. H.		6916
— Pte.(L./C. C. F.	6885	— Pte.(A./S./Sjt.) W. S.		6905
— C.Q.M.S. C. H.	6891	Bakewell, Amt.Q.M.S. W.		7020
— Sjt.(A.C.) C. T. J.	6870	Balcke, Cpl. C. E.		6916
— Sjt. E.	6890	Baldock, Dvr.(L./C.) H.		6945
— C.Q.M.S. F. H.	6872	— Sjt. R. E.		6894
— Sjt.(A./B.S.M.) J. C.	6912	Baldwin, Farr.Q.M.S. B.		6943
— C.Q.M.S. J. R.	6891	— Sqdn.S.M. C. A.		6865
— Cpl. S.	✿ 6064	— Sjt. E.	*	6866
— R.Q.M.S. W.	7017	— Cpl. F. C.		6876
Bain, Sjt.(A./Sqdn.S.M.) D. S.	6865	— Sjt. J. A.		6874
— C.Q.M.S. H.	6970	— Pte.(A./Sjt.) R. A. J.		6957

* Sgt. Ernest Baldwin, Northumberland Yeo. Valuable service France & Flanders. Details from Regt. History: This N.C.O. has shown great devotion to duty throughout the whole campaign. I cannot speak too highly in praise of this N.C.O.'s ability, determination and sense of duty, both in times of danger and also of rest. Nothing could be more noticeable than the hold he has over men in times of danger and difficulty. These superb qualities have been brought out on numerous occasions during this war, and nowhere more noticeably than during the severe trials during November 4th to 6th last in the fighting at Forêt de Mormal. His group is known: 1914 Star & bar trio (602 Northumberland Hussars), M.S.M. and Territorial Efficiency Medal.

Baldwin, R.S.M. W. J.	7016	Banks, C.Q.M.S. G. A.	6900
Bales, Cpl. F.	6903	— A.B. G. A.	6865
Ball, C.S.M. A. (corr.)	6065	— R.Q.M.S. W.	6891
— S.M. A. E.	7011	— T./S.M. W. C.	6957
— Sjt. A. F.	7023	Bann, Sjt. W.	6874
— Ch.Mech. G.A .	7036	Bansemer, S./Sjt.	6970
— C.S.M. H.	6891	Baragwanath, Sjt. T. V. †	6971
— C.Q.M.S. H.	6887	Barber, Sjt. F. G.	7011
— Sjt. H.	6889	— Sjt. W. G.	6901
— Sjt. S. *	7014	Barclay, Pte.(L./C.) A. F.	6881
— Cpl.(A./Sjt.) W. W.	6934	— C.Q.M.S. J.	6881
Ballantyne, Sjt. R.	6916	Barcroft, F./Sjt. J. W. ‡	7036
Ballard, Cpl. C. T.	6954	Bardo, R.Q.M.S. A. A.	6886
— Q.M.S. F. R.	6871	Barker, B.S.M. A.	6912
Balligall, Sjt. G.	6888	— F. of W. Q.M.S. A. R.	7012
Ballinger, Pte. W.	6890	— S.Q.M.S.(A./S.S.M.) E. A.	7021
Balloch, C.Q.M.S.(A./S.M.) R. H.	6872	— C.S.M. E. T.	6955
Balls, Pte.(A./Cpl.) E. C.	6884	— Sjt. F.	6865
Balmer, Pte. R. R.	6865	— C.Q.M.S.(A./C.S.M.) J. W.	7017
Bamber, C.Q.M.S. F.	6872	— S.Q.M.S. R.	6899
Bambrick, L./C. R. B.	6912	— Sjt.(A./C.S.M.) R. A.	7012
Bamford, S.Q.M.S. R.	7018	— Cpl. R. W. J.	6957
Bampton, Cpl.(T./Mech.S./Sjt.) C. C.	6903	— S./Sjt. W.	6901
— S.S.M. F. S.	6898	— Sjt. W. de G.	6908
Bamsey, Sjt. A. J.	6870	Barlow, Cpl. C. A.	6868
Bancroft, Cpl. J.	6908	— Sjt.Clk. J.	7036
Bandy, Farr.Q.M.S. J.	6865	— C.S.M. J. E.	6956
Bangay, S.Q.M.S. C. S.	6899	— R.S.M. W. A. §	6881
Banister, C.S.M.(R.S.M.) W. O.	6884	— C.Q.M.S. W. G.	6872
Banks, C.S.M.Instr. A.	6912	Barnard, C.Q.M.S. C. H. F.	7014
— Cpl. A.	6974	— Cpl. H. A. B.	6903
— Pte.(A./Cpl.) A. E.	6911	Barnes, Cpl.(A./Sjt.) E.	6876

---

* Group known: Queen's South Africa Medal (Natal, Transvaal, Orange Free State, Pte. R.W.F.), M.S.M. (R.W.F.), Territorial Force Efficiency Medal (Edw. VII, R.W.F.) & bar. Plus a diary kept by Pte. Ball in the Boer War.

† Hunt's Scouts, German S.W.A.

‡ R.A.F. M.S.M. 217 Sqn. Dunkirk.

§ Group in Moss collection: Queen's South Africa Medal (Orange Free State, Transvaal, South Africa 1901, South Africa 1902, 4182 Sergt. R.I. Highrs.), 1914/15 Star (3/6587 C.Q.M.S. R. Highrs.), British War and Victory Medals (W.O.1), L.S. & G.C. (Geo. V, C.Q.M.Sjt. R. Highrs.) and M.S.M. (61931 R.S.M. 8/R. Scots). Born in 1870 he enlisted about 1891 and served with 1st Battn. in Boer War. Discharged from 3rd Battn. to a pension in 1911. Employed in the Customs & Excise at Perth. Recalled September 1914 and posted to 8/R.H. as C.Q.M.S. 'D' Coy. C.S.M. in March 1916 and R.S.M. later. L.S. & G.C. in April 1916, wounded in July of that year and left 8 R.H. Finally served as R.S.M. 8 R. Scots until demobilised 22 May 1919. Again employed by Customs & Excise in Perth until he retired in June 1935. Awarded an M.S.M. annuity in A.O. 118/1946 and died at Westminster Hospital in August 1949. He was buried in a Regimental Grave in Perth with four other Black Watch Association Veterans.

Barnes, T./S.M. E. G. W.	6907	Basey, R.Q.M.S. W.	6888
— T./S.M. E. J.	6907	Basford, Sjt.(B.S.M.) W.	6866
— Sjt.(A./C.S.M.) G. R. E.	6874	Bass, Spr.(A./S.M.) G. W.	7012
— C.S.M. H.	6955	Bassett, T./S.S.M. A. C.	6898
— Q.M.S. J.	6890	— C.Q.M.S. J. S.	6872
— Ch.Mech. J. H.	* 7036	— Sjt. L.	6901
— Sjt. J. W.	6901	Bassindale, Sjt. I. R.	6874
— T./Armt.S.M. L. J.	6909	Bastabal, F./Sjt. J. C.	7036
— Sjt. R. W.	6874	Baston, Condr J. P.	6912
— Sjt. S	6885	Batchelor, Cpl.(A./Sjt.) T.	6957
Barnett, S./Sjt. M. M.	6916	— Ch.Mec. W. O.	7036
— C.S.M. W.	6916	Batcock, Cpl.(T/S./Sjt.) F.	6908
Barnicoat, M.F. of W. S./Sjt. H.	6873	Bate, 2nd Cpl. J.	6878
Barnikel, Cpl.(A./Sjt.) T. H.	7017	Bates, C.Q.M.S.(A./R.S.M.) A. G.	6872
Barnshaw, Cpl. J. G.	6903	— Pte.(A./S.M.) J. V.	6970
Baron, E.Clk.(A./Sjt.) F. J.	6932	— T./R.S.M. R.	7015
— Pte.(A./Sjt.) R. W.	6910	— L./C.(T./C.S.M.) R. W.	6916
Barr, Pte. B.	6888	Bathe, B.Q.M.S. S. J.	6867
— Sadd.Sjt. H. J.	6934	Batho, C.Q.M.S. J. A.	6872
— Spr.(T./Cpl.) J.	6879	Battam, Sjt. T.	6874
Barrett, S./Sjt. C. W.	6901	Battersby, Sjt.(A./R.S.M.) G. W.	‡ 6976
— Cpl. G.	6955	Batty, Sjt. G. J.	6916
— Sjt.(A./S./S.M.) J.	6946	Baudains, B.S.M. P. M.	§ 6912
— C.S.M. R.	7011	Baxendall, Spr.(A./C.S.M.) E. R.	7012
— C.Q.M.S.(A./Garr.S.M.) W.	7021	Baxter, Sjt.(A./R.S.M.) J.	6892
Barrie, S./Sjt. J.	6970	— Sjt. J.	6912
— Pte. J. C.	6912	— S./Sjt.(A./Q.M.S.) J. W.	6907
— Q.M.S.(A./R.Q.M.S.) L.	6891	Bayldon, Pte. C. E.	6887
— Cpl.(T./Sjt.) S. W.	6916	Baylis, T./S.S.M. A. J.	6898
Barritt, T./S.M.(A.C.) J. N.	6869	Bayliss, Sjt.Clk. B. R.	7036
Barron, Pte.(T./S./Sjt.) J. H. M.	6905	Bayne, C.Q.M.S. W.	6919
Barrow, Sjt. A.	7019	Bazley, S./Sjt. F. W.	6954
— C.Q.M.S. F. W.	6893	Beaby, 1st Writer L. G.	7511
— Sjt. J. F.	6954	Beadle, Spr.(A./Sjt.) A. F.	6974
Barry, Sjt. F.	6975	Beadsmore, Pte.(A./Cpl.) E.	6905
— Sjt. G. P.	✿ 7701	Beagarie, Q.M.S. W. H.	7013
Bartholomew, Sjt.(A./C.Q.M.S.) F.	7011	Beale, T./Sub Condr. C. M.	6909
Bartlett, Sjt.(A./S.Q.M.S.) J.	7020	Beales, Sjt. A. W.	6955
— Dkhnd. W. C.	5113	Beames, Sjt. F.	6933
Bartley, Cpl. F.	6903	Beamish, Cpl. T.	6868
Barton, Sjt.(A./Q.M.S.) B. J.	7012	Beaney, Pte. J.	6865
— S.S.M. F. C.	† 7021	Beard, Ldg.Sto. H.	7907
— Ldg.Sto. F. W.	8068	— Sjt. J.	6955
— Pte. J. H.	6905	— C.S.M. S.	6912

* R.A.F. M.S.M. for Egypt to Aus/266 Australian Flying Corps.
† For Bermuda (A.P.C.) Group known: Queen's South Africa Medal (Cape Colony, Orange Free State), King's South Africa Medal (both Sgt.), British War Medal, L.S. & G.C. (Edw. VII, S.Q.M.S.) and M.S.M.
‡ R.G.A. Aden.
§ No. 732. Artillery of the Island of Jersey.

Beasley, Pte. H.	6889	Bell, Sjt. H. W. W.	6912
— Sjt. J. C.	6911	— Pte. (T./Sjt.) J.	6905
Beatey, Sjt. W. E. H.	7014	— Farr.Sjt. P.	6874
Beatson, Mech.S./Sjt. F. H. P.	6933	— Farr.S./Sjt. R.	6867
Beattie, Ch.Yeo.Sigs. J. W.	8068	— Pte. R.	6905
— T./Supt.Clk. W. G. L.	6956	— C.Q.M.S. W.	6882
Beaumont, Pte. A. D.	6905	— 2ndCpl. (T./Sjt.) W.	6878
— Q.M.S. A. E.	6907	Bellamy, Sjt. F.	6912
— Cpl. W. J.	7036	— C.Q.M.S. (A./C.S.M.) J. A.	7018
Beavan, Pte. (L./C.) W.	6885	Bellsham, C.Q.M.S. H. E. †	6881
Beavis, Cpl. E.	6970	Belt, Cpl. (T./Sjt.) H. A.	6903
— Sjt. (A./Q.M.S.) W.	6908	Benbow, C.Q.M.S. J. T.	6956
Beazer, Cpl. F. C.	6876	Benham, Sjt. (A./C.S.M.)	
Beck, T/S.S.M. A.	6898	G. W. (corr.)	6065
— C.Q.M.S. A. W.	6872	Benn, Sjt. J. L.	7021
— Pte. J.	6944	Bennett, Pte. (L./C.) A.	6911
— F./Sjt. J. W.	6916	— Pte. (A./Sjt.) A. P.	6911
Beckey, Gnr. W. T.	6871	— Pte. (A./Sjt.) F. H.	6905
Beckwith, A.C.1, W. J.	7036	— 2ndCpl. H.	6878
Bedding, T./S.S.M. W. A., *MM.*	7018	— Supt.Clk. H. W.	6882
Bedford, Dvr. (L./C.) A. N.	6906	— Pte. J. E.	6896
— Bombr. (A./Sjt.) A. T.	7011	— Spr. (2ndCpl.) J. H. W.	6879
— Sjt. D.	6884	— Sjt. Mech. J. M. ‡	7036
— T./S.S.M. W. T.	6933	— C.Q.M.S. R.	6886
Bee, C.Q.M.S. G.	6889	— S./Sjt. (A./S.M.) R. H.	6934
Beech, Cpl. A. H. A.	6868	— Cpl. R. N.	6868
— B.S.M. M.	6866	— C.S.M. (A./S.S.M.) T.	6899
Beechey, C.S.M. T. W.	6955	— Q.M.S. (O.R.Sjt.) T. H.	7014
Beeching, R.Q.M.S. A. W.	6890	— C.Q.M.S. W	6943
Beeney, Pte. (A./Sjt.) E.	6912	— Pte. W.	6944
Belcher, S.M. C. H.	6886	— Cpl. W. G.	6870
— Sjt. C. T.	6898	— Sjt. W. T.	6887
— 2ndCpl. G. E.	6878	Benson, C.Q.M.S. G. E.	6955
— Farr.Sjt. S. J.	6867	Bentley, Sjt. G.	6883
Bell, Sjt. A. H.	6944	— Sjt. H.	6974
— C.S.M. C. F.	6932	— Sjt. P.	6933
— Sjt. (A./R.Q.M.S.) C. G.	6912	Benwell, Dvr. W. J.	6957
— C.Q.M.S. E. R.	6885	Benz, Spr. (L./C.) F. C.	7012
— Pte. (A./Cpl.) E. T.	6891	Berchdolt, E.R./Cpl. G. A.	6916
— C.S.M. G. * ❀	7702	Beresford, Sjt. C.	6895
— Gnr. (A./Sjt.) G. W.	7011	Berridge, Sjt. H. L.	6885
— Pte. (A./Sjt.) H.	6905	Berry, Sjt. A.	6945

* Later awarded M.M. 32nd Bn. M.G. Corps.

† Group known: 1914 Star & bar (6315 Pte. Coldstream Guards), British War and Victory Medals (W.O.II Cold. Gds.) and M.S.M. (417 Coy. Q.M. Sgt. 4/Gds. M.G. Regt.).

‡ R.A.F. M.S.M. for Egypt to Aus/275 Australian Flying Corps. Later A.F.M., *L.G.* 26 December, 1919 then a bar to A.F.M. for his participation in the air-race to Australia in a Vickers Vimy. Also entitled to India General Service Medal (Afghanistan N.W.F. 1919).

Berry, Sjt. (A./S./Sjt.) D.		6908	Bingham, T./S.M. (A.C.) A. E.		6869
— Sjt. J.		6893	— Pte. (L./C.) C.		6945
— Pte. O.	✿	6064	— Cpl. (A./S.Q.M.S.) R. L.		6866
— Spr. (L./C.) T. M.		6879	Binner, S.Q.M.S. A. L.		6899
— C.Q.M.S. W.		6872	Binns, Gnr. A. O.		6869
Berryman, W.O.Cl.1, A. R.		6934	— Cpl. J. A.		6894
Best, Cpl. (A./Q.M.S.) C. A.		7018	Bintcliffe, Sjt. G.		6892
— Sjt. (A./C.Q.M.S.) E.		7011	Birch, Pte. (A./Cpl.) A.		6910
— Pte. F. V.		6892	— Cpl. H.		6912
— C.Q.M.S. J. A.		7016	— Sjt. R.		6889
— Pte. (A./Sjt.) J. C.		6886	— Sjt. R.C.		6882
Beswarick, Cpl. (A./Q.M.S.) A.		6933	— Pte. (L./C.) S. S.		6911
Beswick, Pte. J.		6894	Birchenough, Sjt. C. A.		6888
Bethel, S./S.M. J. G.		7023	Bird, Pte. (A./Cpl.) A. F. R.		6905
Betts, Pte. A. E.		7018	— AC.1, C. H.		7036
— Ch.Mec. W.	*	7036	— 2ndCpl. (A./Sjt.) E. W.		6878
Bevan, Sjt. E.		6874	— A./S.Q.M.S. F. H.		7022
— Sjt. G. W. J.		6901	— Mas.Mec. L. M.		7036
— Sjt. H. J.		6889	— Sjt. W.		6884
Beven, A./W.O.2ndCl. T.		4197	— F./Sjt. W. J.		7036
Beveridge, Sjt. H. J. C.		6892	Birkbeck, Sjt. D. M.		6894
Bickell, Sjt. R. J. G.		6908	Birkin, Cpl. J.		6868
Bickford, C.Q.M.S. A.		6944	Birkinshaw, Cpl. Mec. F. T.		7036
Bickham, Sjt. A. W.		6874	— Sjt. T. W.		6874
Bicknell, F/Clk. J.		7036	Birnie, Sjt. J.		6894
Biddle, Sjt. H. W.		6882	Birt, Sjt. J.W.		6888
Bieler, Pte. A. C.		6912	— Cpl. Clk. S. E.	†	7036
Biggerstaff, SubCondr.			Birtles, A./O.R.Sjt. A.		7022
(A./Condr.) T. J.		6912	Birtwell, C.Q.M.S.		
Biggs, Sjt. W. T.	✿	7702	(A./R.Q.M.S.) E.		6887
Bill, Sjt. F.McD.		6912	Bisgrove, E.R./S./Sjt. R. C.		7022
Billet, Sjt. F. B.		6912	Bishop, C.P.O. A. C., *D.S.M.*		4734
Billing, Sjt. G., *M.M.*		6884	— Pte. A. H.		6883
— 2ndHand S.		6448	— Cpl. A. S.		6916
Billings, O.R.Sjt. R.		7016	— Sjt. (A./C.S.M.) F. C.		6932
— Sjt. W.		6908	— Sjt. R. C.		6954
Billington, Spr. E.C.(L./C.) F.		6879	— S./Sjt. W. A.		6901
Bin Haji Juma, R.S.M.		6971	— L.A.C.(A./Cpl.) W. A.		7036
Bines, R.S.M. J.		6869	— Sjt. W. F.	‡	7011
Binfield, Cpl. F.		6896	— Sjt. (A./C.Q.M.S.) W. H.		6874
Bingham, Sjt. A.		6891	Bishopp, R.Q.M.S. H. H. S.		6976

---

* No. 6116 R.F.C. Group known: British War and Victory Medals (Flt. Sgt.), Defence and War Medals, R.A.F. M.S.M. (for Egypt) and R.A.F. L.S. & G.C. (EIIR 1st type). He must have left the R.A.F. between the wars, rejoined in W.W.II and stayed in until at least 1953.

† Group known: B.E.M. (Geo. V, Flt Sgt. *L.G.* 11 May 1937), British War and Victory Medals (M.I.D. oakleaf Cpl. R.A.F.), 1939/45 Star, Defence and War Medals (Flight Lieut. R.A.F.), R.A.F. M.S.M. (I Force, France), R.A.F. L.S. & G.C. (Geo. V, Sgt.) and King Faisal of Iraq General Service Medal.

‡ Hamps. R. Aden.

Bissell, Sjt. G.	* 6935	Blatchford, Sjt. R. A.	6943
Bissett, S./Sjt. G.	6910	— R.S.M. W. H.	6866
Bittlestone, S./Sjt. R.	7018	— Sto.P.O. W. J. L.	8068
Black, C.S.M. A.	6912	Blease, Mech. S./Sjt. E.	6900
— Sht. A. H.	6912	— T./S.S.M. G. H.	7018
— Pte. D.	6932	Blencowe, Pte. (A./Sjt.) W. T.	7020
— Cpl. G. E.	6912	Blewitt, Cpl. J.	6903
— Sjt. (A./C.Q.M.S.) S.	6874	Blezard, Sjt. (A./S./Sjt.) W. A.	6908
— T./Supt.Clk. T. L.	7011	Blood, Sjt. (A./SubCondr.) F. R.	
— Pte. (A./Cpl.) W.	6911	(corr.)	7703
Blackaby, Cpl. A.	6898	Bloomfield, C.Q.M.S. P. H.	6891
Blackall, Farr.Sjt. W. R.	6918	— R.S.M. W.	6866
Blackburn, Mech. S.M. H.	7018	Blowers, C.Q.M.S. B. H.	6884
— Pte. (A./Cpl.) J. W.	6911	Bloxham, C.S.M. B. N.	6881
Blackett, B.Q.M.S. R.	6867	— Bloy, C.S.M. (A/R.S.M.) G.	6890
Blackie, Cpl. J. S.	6881	Blunson, R.Q.M.S. G.	6888
Blackledge, Dvr. R.	6912	Blydenstein, Sjt. (A./S./Sjt.) E. H.	7022
Blackman, Sjt. A. J.	6898	Blyth, C.Q.M.S. D. M.	6888
— C.Q.M.S. H. E.	6954	— A.B. J.	6865
— Ch.Mech. V. H.	7036	— T./S.M. W.	6871
Blackmore, Cpl. A. W.	6970	Blythe, Sjt. F. E.	6889
Blackstock, Spr. (L./C.) J.	6879	Boakes, T./Mech. S.M. W. T.	6898
Blackwell, E.R.Sjt. F. M.	6934	Boaler, Sjt. F. A.	6867
Blair, Sjt. (A./C.Q.M.S.) J.	6895	Boardman, C.Q.M.S. G. M.	6888
— 2ndCpl. J.	6878	Bode, Q.M.S. (T./S.M.) J.	6946
— Mech. S./Sjt. J. W.	6933	Boden, Sjt. A.	6901
— Cpl. W. B.	6943	Bodger, S./Sjt. E.	6907
Blake, C.Q.M.S. A. C.	6900	Bolam, C.S.M. B.	6891
— C.S.M. E. J.	† 7018	— Sjt. J.	6894
— Sjt. F.	6932	Boley, Sjt. A. G. V.	6954
— Pte. (A./Sjt.) H.	7018	Bolger, C.P.O. P. J.	8202
— F.ofW.Q.M.S. H. J.	6871	Bolt, C.S.M. F.	6954
— Mech. S./Sjt. R. R.	6900	Bolton, Cpl. E.	6944
Blakeley, Pte. A.	‡ 6881	— C.S.M. (A./R.S.M.) E. L.	6944
— Sjt. T.	6908	— Pte. (A./Cpl.) G.	6905
Blakey, C.Q.M.S. G. C.	6897	— A./C.S.M. G. S.	7022
— A./Sjt. H.A.	7022	— Pte. J.	6934
Blanchard, Bombr. W. L.	6870	— C.Q.M.S. (A./R.Q.M.S.) J. H.	6897
Bland, Cpl. A. W.	6903	Bond, Sjt. A. W.	6888

---

* R.E. Arabia; see also Owen *infra*.

† 2nd Bn. West India Regt. (from Sierra Leone).

‡ King's Own (Royal Lancaster Regt.). Mobilised at the outbreak of war in August 1914, he was shortly afterwards drafted to France and took part in the Battles of the Marne, the Aisne, La Bassée, Ypres, Neuve Chapelle, Hill 60, Loos, Vimy Ridge, the Somme and Arras. He suffered from gas poisoning at the third Battle of Ypres, and was sent home, but on his recovery returned to his unit and was in action until the cessation of hostilities. He was awarded the Meritorious Service Medal for devotion to duty in the Field, and also held the 1914 Star, and the General Service and Victory Medals. He was discharged in February 1919. 6, Hyde View, Grey Street, West Gorton, Manchester.

Bond, Cpl. (A./L./Sjt.) F.	6908		Bowden, S./Sjt. E.	6957
— Pte. F. J. G.	7019		— C.S.M. N.	6882
— C.P.O. G.	7511		— C.Q.M.S. (A./C.S.M.) R.	7015
— Sjt. G. F.	6912		Bowen, Sjt. C. A.	6916
— F./Sjt. H. F.	7036		— Sjt. J. W.	6901
— Sjt. I. T.	6870		— Pte. W.	6955
— C.Q.M.S. J. E.	6872		Bower, Cpl. A. V.	6870
— C.Q.M.S. J. H.	6916		— F.ofW.Q.M.S. C. W.	7012
— Cpl. W.	6876		— Sjt. (A./C.Q.M.S.) L. G.	7017
Bonell, Pte. V. C.	6912		Bowerman, Dvr. W. F.	6866
Bonfield, C.Q.M.S. R.	6889		Bowers, Dvr. R.	6869
Boniface, T./Armt.S.M. J. H.	6909		— Sjt. R. B.	6892
Bonner, Pte. F. D.	6905		— Sjt. W.	6911
Bonny, Sjt. C.	6901		Bowes, Sjt. G. E.	6874
Boodson, Sjt. D.	* 6935		Bowie, Pte. (A./Sjt.) J.	6910
Boorer, Cpl. A. J.	6876		— Cpl. (L./Sjt.) W.	6893
Boorman, Pte. F.	6896		Bowker, Farr.Sjt. E. G.	6874
Boote, Sjt. C. H.	6901		Bowler, Cpl. L.	7036
Booth, Cpl. A. L.	6903		Bowley, Sjt. H. C.	7036
— S.Q.M.S. C.	6899		Bowmaker, C.S.M. E. V.	6872
— Pte. F. A.	6905		Bowman, Cpl. (A./Sjt.) E.	6932
Booton, Cpl. W. A.	6908		— Pte. (L./C.) F. V.	6905
Booza, Pte. N. J.	6919		— 2ndCpl. J. R.	6878
Boraston, Sjt. C.	6898		Bown, C.S.M. (R.A.S.C.)	6945
Bore, S./Sjt. W. E. M.	6907		Bownass, Pte. R.	6905
Boreham, C.Q.M.S. H. E.	6889		Bowyer, C.Q.M.S. G., *MM.*	6894
Borkett, R.Q.M.S. E. G.	6933		— A.M.1, H.	7036
Borthwick, Sjt. J. H.	6895		Box, Sjt. E. V.	6944
Bose, Sjt. (A./R.Q.M.S.) J.	6998		Boxall, Sjt. (T./S./Sjt.) A.	6908
Bosley, Sjt. H. L. W.	6912		— Master Gnr. 3rd Cl. G.	‡ 7011
Boswell, Pte. E. G.	6880		Boyce, R.Q.M.S. J. W.	6887
Bothwell, C.Q.M.S. N. D.	6892		Boyd, C.P.O. 3rdCl. E. A.	6448
Bott, Pte. (A./S.M.) C. C. F.	6905		— Pte. W. W.	6912
— Sjt. N., *MM.*	6944		Boyes, Sjt. (A./S.Q.M.S.) G. W.	6957
Bottomley, Pte. (A./Sjt.) G.	6909		Bracegirdle, R.Q.M.S. F. W.	7015
— Sjt. R. O.	6933		Bracewell, Pte. (A./Sjt.)	6896
Boucher, Cpl. (A./Sjt.) E. B	7036		Brackenbury, Gnr. J. G. F.	6866
Boughey, B.S.M. A. V	6866		Bradbury, C.S.M. F. W.	6974
Boulger, Sjt. (A./S./Sjt.) A.	7022		Bradford, Pte. (A./Sjt.) D.	6893
Boultbee, C.Q.M.S. B. H.	6912		Bradish, Pte. (T./Cpl.) J. H.	6905
Boulton, C.Q.M.S. D. H.	6900		Bradley, Cpl. A.	6890
— Sjt. G. T.	6901		— Pte. (A./L./C.) C.	6911
Bourne, Sjt. A. E.	6870		— Cpl. H. W.	6903
— Engr.Clk. Q.M.S. C. G.	† 7012		— Pte. W.	6888
— Ch.Elect.Art.H. J.	7511		Bradsell, Sjt. W.	6885
Bovey, L.A.C.(A./Cpl.) P. A.	7036		Bradshaw, Cpl. (A./Sjt.) A.	6954
Bowden, S.Q.M.S. A. H.	6899		— Sjt. Mech. F.	7036

* R.A.S.C. Arabia; see also Owen *infra*.
† R.E. Gibraltar.
‡ R.G.A. Gibraltar.

Bradshaw, Sjt. J. A.	6908	Bridgment, Cpl. (L./Sjt.) P. W.	6889
— Pte. (L./C.) J. C.	6891	Briggs, Pte. (A./Sjt.) A. F.	6905
— E.R./C.S.M. R. L.	6916	— S.M. E.	6907
— Sjt. W.	6874	— Cpl. E.	6903
Brady, Sjt. G.	6874	— Cpl. (A./Sjt.) F.	6876
— W.O.Cl.1, P. L.	7022	Bright, Pte. B. W.	6887
Bragg, Pte. J	6896	Brighton, Cpl. G. F.	6891
— Cpl. (A./C.S.M.) J. B.	6876	Brignall, Sjt. G. L.	6934
— Sjt. R. W.	6943	Brimelow, Spr. (L./C.) F. G.	6879
Braiden, Dvr. R.	6943	Brind, Spr. (L./C.) F. H.	6879
Braidwood, Pte. D. C.	7019	Brindle, Sjt. (T./Q.M.S.) L.	6908
Brailey, Farr.Sjt. W.	6867	Brindley, Cpl. Clk. F.	7036
Braim, E.C.Cpl. (A./E.Sjt.) L.	6876	— S./Sjt. H.	6911
Brain, O.R.Sjt. A. E.	7017	Bristow, Pte. A. B.	6905
Braines, Bombr. A.	6868	— Sjt. (A./C.S.M.) G. J.	6943
Brainwood, T./R.S.M. H. C.	6916	— Sjt. P.	6901
Braithwaite, C.S.M. H.	6893	Brittan, C.S.M. S.	6955
Braitling, Bombr. (T./Cpl.) W. W.	6916	Britton, R.S.M. E. P., *D.C.M.*	6880
Bramner, C.S.M. E.	6944	— Pte. R. W. M.	6905
Bramwell, R.Q.M.S. T. R. A.	6891	— Cpl. (A./Q.M.S.) W. T.	6882
Brand, Sjt. E. H.	6954	Broad, Pte. W. W.	6905
Brannan, Cpl. H.	6876	Broadbelt, C.Q.M.S. C. W.	6872
Brasier, Farr.S./Sjt. H. J.	6867	Broadbent, R.Q.M.S. C.	7017
Brassey, Cpl. J.	7011	— Sjt. (A./R.S.M.) H. H.	7012
Bratt, Sjt. R.	6901	Broadhurst, Cpl. J.	6868
Bray, R.S.M. F. I.	6916	Broadsmith, Sjt. R. J.	6891
— Ch.Elect.Art.2ndCl. H. W.	4197	Brockett, S.M. H. C.	6971
— Bombr. Sig. J. L.	6871	Brocklehurst, Cpl. F.	6943
Braybrook, Sjt. P. W.	6954	Brocklesby, S./Sjt. W.	7020
Brayshaw, Gnr. E. H.	6869	Brodrick, Cpl. (A./Sjt.) C. J.	6912
Brazier, Sjt. H. L.	6874	Broocke, Sjt. A. O. A.	6908
Breach, Ch.Sto. E.	8068	Brook, Mech. S./Sjt. H.	6873
Brearey, Cpl. W.	6896	Brookbanks, Sjt. G. R.	6955
Breed, T./SubCondr. A. F.	6909	Brooke, Sjt. C. M.	6911
Breen, S./Sjt. (A./S.S.M.) P.	7021	— S.S.M. P. R.	6866
Brefitt, C.Q.M.S. E.	6890	Brooker, Sjt. A. A. T.	6901
Brennan, Pte. (A./Sjt.) G.	7021	Brookes, 2ndCpl. (A./Cpl.) C.	6878
— Gnr. M	6954	— C.S.M. G.	6886
— Detect.Sjt. R. P.	7022	— C.S.M. (A./S.M.) W.	6893
— T./SubCondr. (A./Condr.) V. T.	6909	Brooks, Mech. S./Sjt. A. D.	6900
Brett, Sjt. B. J.	6885	— Clr.Sjt. (A./W.O.Cl.1S./S.M.)	
— Cpl. (A./S.M.) F. V.	6882	C. (corr.)	:6065
— Sjt. W. T.	6916	— Pte. (A./Sjt.) C. A.	6905
Brew, C.Q.M.S. R. E.	6916	— Sjt. E.	6957
Brewer, 2ndCpl. (A./Cpl.) B.	6878	— Sjt. F.	6944
— Sjt. (T./Supt.Clk.) W. H. R.	6943	— MasterGnr. 3rdCl.G.	7011
Brewster, Q.M.S. (O.R.S.) W. A.	6894	— Cpl. (T./C.Q.M.S.) G. S.	6876
Brideaux, Q.M.S. W. P.	7012	— Pte. (A./Sjt.) J.	6883
Brider, Cpl. A.	6876	— Sjt. J. E.	6901
Bridgeman, Cpl. (A./Sjt.) A.	7017	— C.P.O. 3rdCl., P. H.	6504
Bridger, C.S.M. Instr.J. H.	6912	— Sjt. W. A.	6933

Brooks, T./S.S.M. W. J.	* 7018	Brown, Sjt. J. W.	6884
Brookshaw, R.S.M. W. H.	6890	— C.S.M. I.(A./Q.M.S. I.) J. W.	7013
Broomer, Cpl. (L./Sjt.) F.	6880	— Sjt. J. W.	6944
Broomham, Sjt. J. O.	6882	— R.S.M. L.	6916
Brooshooft, Sjt. B. E	6891	— Cpl. (A./C.Q.M.S.) L. R.	7011
Brophy, Pte. E.	6865	— T./S.S.M. L. S.	6898
Brotton, Sjt. F.	6895	— Q.M.S. M. C.	7021
Brough, Sjt. C	6901	— R.Q.M.S. M. W.	6888
— S.Q.M.S. H.	6953	— S.M. R.	6871
Broughton, Pte. E.	6945	— Cpl. (A./S./Sjt.) R. H.	6934
— Pte. J.	6896	— E.R.A.4thCl.R. L.	8068
Brown, Cpl. A.	6911	— Pte. (L./C.) R. T.	6905
— Spr. (A./Cpl.) A.	6879	— Pte. (T./S.Q.M.S.) S. W.	6905
— Pte. (A./Cpl.) A.	6934	— A.B. T.	6865
— Pte. (L./C.) A.	6905	— S.M. T. M., *D.C.M.*	6912
— R.Q.M.S. A. B.	6912	— B.Q.M.S. W.	6869
— S./Sjt. A. E.	6901	— B.S.M. W.	6916
— Pte. (L./C.) A. E.	7015	— Ch.Writer W. C.	6865
— Sjt. C. D.	6916	— C.S.M. W. E.	7012
— Pte. (A./Cpl.) C R.	6909	— Pte. W. E.	6918
— Sjt. D. K.	6910	— C.S.M. W. M.	6899
— C.S.M. (A./R.S.M.) E.	6890	— Sjt. W. T.	6912
— Pte. (L./C.) E. H.	6883	Brownbridge, Cpl. T. J.	6882
— C.S.M. F.	7011	Browne, S./Sjt. (A./S.M.) E. B.	7020
— C.Q.M.S. F. C.	7018	— S.Q.M.S. V. E.	6956
— Mech. S./Sjt. F. W.	6957	Brownhill, T./Armt.S.M. R. F.	6909
— C.Q.M.S. G.	6944	Browning, Pte. C. J.	7015
— Cpl. G.	6903	— Pte. (L./C.) G. H. W.	6909
— Pte. (L./C.) G.	6882	— Sjt. H.	6932
— Sjt. (A./S./Sjt.) H.	7020	— Pte. T. E.	6887
— Bombr. (Cpl.) H.	6866	Brownlow, T./R.S.M. C. F.	7016
— Pte. (A./S./Sjt.) H.	6910	Bruce, Pte. (L/C.) A.	6956
— Cpl. H.A.	6912	— Sjt. J.	6908
— Dkhnd, H. T.	4732	Bruder, Cpl. C. E. P.	6876
— C.Q.M.S. J.	6872	Brunsdon, Pte. (L./C.) S. G.	6886
— S./Sjt. J.	6971	Brunt, Sjt. J. G.	6946
— Sjt. J.(R.A.S.C.)	6901	Brunton, Pte. (A./Cpl.) W. G.	6934
— Sjt. J.(R.A.M.C.)	6910	Bryan, Col.Sjt. C.	6448
— Sjt. J.(R.M.L.I.)	7907	— Sjt. (A./C.S.M.) J.	6874
— Sjt. J.(S.A.Inf.)	7023	— Sjt. (A./S./Sjt.) R. A.	7019
— A.M. T. J.	7036	Bryant, Armr.S./Sjt. (A./	
— Pte. J.(ManR.)	6891	Armt.Q.M.S.) A. E.	† 6910
— Pte. J.(North'dFus)	6944	— Ch.Writer A. J.	7511
— S./Sjt. J. A.	6918	— T./SubCondr. (A./Condr.) G.	6909
— Cpl. J. E.	7019	Brydon, Pte. (L./C.) M. T.	6896
— F./Sjt. J. H.	7036	Bryson, F./Sjt. J.	7036
— Pte. (A./S.Q.M.S.) J. P.	6912	Buchan, T./S.M. A.	6871
— Sjt. J. R.	6895	Buchanan, Pte. (A./Cpl.) D.	6886

* R.A.S.C. Also D.C.M. Served in W.W.2 as Major, M.B.E. (awarded 1927).
† R.A.O.C.; also Croix de Guerre.

Buchanan, Pte. (A./S./Sjt.) D. D.	6909	Burgess, Cpl. W.		6890
Buck, C.Q.M.S. A.	6872	— Ch.Sto.W. J.		6504
— Pte. (L./C.) J.	6911	Burke, Ch.Arm.A. E.		8069
— R.Q.M.S. W. M.	6889	— B.Q.M.S. J., *D.C.M.*		6869
— C.S.M. W. T.	6883	— C.Q.M.S. J., *M.M.*		6893
Buckle, Sjt. P. S. W.	6865	— L./Sjt. L.		6916
Buckley, Sjt. T.	7019	— C.Q.M.S. T.		7015
Budd, Sjt. (A./R.S.M.) D. J. B.	7017	Burley, Pte. C. W.		6905
Budden, Cpl. W.	6890	Burlington, Pte. (L./C.) F. W.		6945
Buddery, Pte. E. P. G.	6946	Burn, Ch.Writer G. H.		7511
Buffey, Cpl. (L./Sjt.) J. H.	6944	— T./S.M. J. R.		6871
Bufton, Cpl. (A./Sjt.) S. A.	6876	Burne, Sjt. R.		6874
Bulbeck, C.S.M. E. H.	6872	Burnham, P.O. 1st Cl. T.		8202
Bull, Pte. C.	6905	Burnhill, Sjt. T. W.		6908
Bullen, Sjt. (T./C.S.M.) H. J.	6874	Burns, Cpl. C. G.		6916
— Pte. (L./C.) J.	6905	— C.S.M. E.		6954
— Cpl. (A./C.Q.M.S.) J. A.	7019	— 2nd Cpl.(A./Cpl.) J.		6878
— Whlr.Cpl. (A./Sjt.) W.	6868	— Sjt. J. S.		6912
— Sjt. W. A.	6874	— S.S.M. W.		7016
Bulling, Sjt. A.	7017	— C.Q.M.S. W. S.		6916
Bullman, Pte. C.	6905	Burrows, Spr. C. T.	†	6879
Bullock, A./Sjt. A. P.	7022	— Cpl.(T./Sqdn.S.M.) J.		6934
— Spr. (L./C.) L.	6879	— Sjt. R.		7013
Bulow, Sjt. N.	6943	— B.S.M.(A./R.S.M.)		
Bungay, R.S.M. F.	6869	W. *D.C.M., M.M.*		6866
Bunker, C.S.M. F. G.	6956	— S.B.S. W. J.		8069
Burbury, Arm.S./Sjt. W. H.	6957	— S.B.S. W. J.		8069
Burch, Sjt. D. W.	6874	Burry, Sjt. J. J.		7010
— C.S.M. H.	6880	Bursell, Sjt. S.		7023
Burchell, Gnr. C.	* 6979	Burt, T./S.M. W. G.		7011
Burchett, F./Sjt. C. C.	7036	Burton, Sjt. (A./Q.M.S.) A. H.		7012
Burden, Cpl. Sig.F. E.	6870	— Pte. G.		6905
Burdett, Sjt. C.	6874	— Cpl.(A./Sjt.) R.		7020
— Sjt. W. A.	6932	Busch, Sjt. J. H.		6916
Burford, Sjt. W.	6889	Bush, Sjt. G.		6889
Burgess, Pte. (A./Cpl.) A.	6970	— Sjt. S. W. A.		6943
— Cpl. (A./Sjt.) C.	6876	— Q.M.S.(A./S.M.) W.		6907
— Cpl. C.	6868	Bushell, C.P.O. G. E		5112
— Sjt. F.	6892	Butcher, S.S.M. F. C.	‡	6899
— Sjt. F. W.	7013	— C.S.M. G. J. H.		6893
— Ch.Engmn.H. R.	4732	— C.S.M. W. H.		6893
— Cpl. J. S.	6898	Butler, C.Q.M.S. A. M.		6865
— E.R./Cpl. L. G.	6916	— Sjt. C.		7023
— Farr.S./Sjt. T.	6953	— T./S.M. J.		6889
— Cpl. (A./Sjt.) T. C.	6880	— Sjt. J. A.		6895
		— Sjt. M. H.		6954

---

* R.G.A. Aden.
† Awarded M.S.M. Annuity Sept. 1948.
‡ Group known: 1914/15 Star (S.S.M. A.S.C.), British War and Victory Medals (W.O.1 R.A.S.C.), M.S.M. (R.A.S.C.), Volunteer Long Service Medal (Edw. VII, Sjt. 1/VB R. Sussex R.) and Territorial Force Efficiency Medal (Geo. V, S.S.M. A.S.C.).

Butler, Pte.(L./C.) R. D.	6911	Callaway, C.Q.M.S. F.	6892
— A.C. 1, Richard H.	7036	Callender, Sto. P.	7907
— Sjt. W. H.	6889	Calver, Pte. G.	6905
Butlin, S.Q.M.S. G. H.	6942	Calvert, R.S.M. H.	7016
Butson, Sqdn.Cpl.Maj. W.	6881	— Pte. T. W.	6896
Butt, Sjt. E. A.	6901	Calway, Farr.Q.M.S. P. I.	7022
— Pte. G.	6890	Camble, C.S.M. G.	6893
— Pte.(L./C.) P.	7017	Cameron, Spr. A.	6879
Butterfield, Sjt.(A./C.S.M.) F.	6895	— Cpl.(A./Sjt.) C.	6882
— B.Q.M.S. L.	6867	— 1st Cl. S.S.M. D. (corr.)	6065
Butterwick, Cpl.(A./Sjt.) A. H.	6903	— Sjt. F. C.	6892
— S./Sjt. J. H.	6910	— Sjt. J. (R. Dub. Fus.)	6893
Buttling, S./Sjt. W. J.	6912	— Sjt.(A./C.Q.M.S.) J. R.	6891
Buzza, B.Q.M.S. A. E.	6869	Camfield, S.M. J. F.	7036
Buzzard, B.S.M. M. A.	6866	Camm, F./Sjt. W.	7036
Bwanali, Sjt.	6971	Campbell, Sjt. A. (Can. Mtd. Rif.)	6912
Byers, Spr. J. H.	6912	— C.Q.M.S. A. L.	6892
— Cpl. S.	6886	— C.Q.M.S. C	6889
Byrne, Cpl. A	6876	— Pte. H.	6883
— Pte. J. T.	* 6934	— C.S.M. J.	6899
Byron, Sjt. E.	6912	— Cpl. J.	6891
Bysouth, Pte. G. H.	6905	— Pte.(A./Cpl.) L. O.	6912
— Sjt. Mech. G. J.	7036	— Pte.(L./C.) R.	6894
Byworth, Sjt. J. C.	6874	— Sjt. T. S.	6901
		— Sjt. W.	6943
Caddick, Cpl. J. J.	6888	Campion, Cpl.(A./C.Q.M.S.) J. J.	7018
Caffarey, Sjt. J. G.	6884	Canham, Sjt. A. R.	7023
Cahill, Sjt.(A./C.Q.M.S.) J., *M.M.*	6893	Cann, Pte.(A./Mech.S./Sjt.) P. W.	7019
Cain, Cpl. J. W.	6876	Cannon, Pte.(T./Sjt.) T.	6934
Caird, Pte. S.	8202	Canty, Cpl. J.	6913
— L./Sjt. V. R.	6916	Capon, Ch.Sto. A. B. P.	4734
Cairns, Sjt. A.	6893	— C.S.M.(A./R.S.M.) F., *D.C.M.*	6885
— Sjt. J. (deleted)	6066	— Spr.(A./Cpl.) R G.	6879
Cakebread, Spr. A. W.	6879	Capper, S.M. J. L.	7013
— T./S.S.M. E. J.	6899	Carey, Sjt. T.	6874
Calder, Sjt. D	6912	— Pte. T.	6956
— Pte. R.	6912	Carlile, Pte.(A./Cpl.) P.	6871
Calderbank, Sjt. H.	6889	— S./Sjt.(A./S.S.M.) W.	6911
Calderwood, Cpl. R.	6876	Carlyle, Sjt. J.	6870
Calkin, Sjt. H. G.	6894	Carnarton, C.Q.M.S. H.	6913
Call, Sjt. J. E.	6912	Carpenter, Dvr. C.	6954
Callaghan, S./Sjt. J. F.	6910	— C.S.M. H.	6872
Callam, Cpl. F. O.	6903	— S.Q.M.S. W.	7020

* Initially L./Corpl., Lancashire Fus. He volunteered in May 1915, and proceeding to Egypt in the following March, played a prominent part in the defence of the Suez Canal and was in action in Katia and Romani. Later he was transferred to the Royal Army Medical Corps, and did excellent work as a nursing orderly in the hospital at Alexandria, where he was awarded the Meritorious Service Medal for devotion to duty. He also held the General Service and Victory Medals, and was demobilised in August, 1919. 8, Commission Street, Salford.

Carr, Q.M.S. D.		6912	Catchpole, Pte. W. D.		6909
— V.Q.M.S. G. S.		6913	Catherall, Spr. C. H.	✿	7701
— Q.M.S. J. B.		6865	Catley, Sjt.Instr. H. W.		6912
— E.C.2nd Cl. Cpl.(A./Q.M.S.)			Cattell, C.S.M. C. J.		6885
J. E. R.		6878	Catterall, C.Q.M.S. C. R.		6895
— Sjt.(A./C.S.M.) M.		7019	Cattermole, Sjt. F. A.		6866
— Sjt. W. T.		6916	Cave, Pte. J.		6896
Carrick, Dvr.(T./Bombr.) W.		6918	— P.O. J. S.		4735
Carrington, F./Sjt. F. J.		7036	Cavell, Sig. C.P.		4734
— P.O. J. B. J.		4734	Caven, R.S.M. J.		6894
Carrodus, Pte.(L./C.) J.		6887	Cavin, Sjt. G. A.		6913
Carroll, Cpl. F. S.		6896	Chadderton, Gnr.(A./L./Bombr.)		
— Pte. P. P.		6896	H. H.		6871
— Sjt.(A./R.S.M.) W.		6886	Chadwick, Sjt. Mech. A. E.	‡	7036
Carruthers, Sjt. W. J.		6970	— C.P.O. E. J.		7907
Carter, Pte. C. W. D.		6884	— C.S.M. G.		7013
— Sjt. D.		6880	Chalk, C.Q.M.S. T. P. N.		6884
— Pte. F.		6913	Chalmers, Sjt. T. G.		6901
— Pte. F. G.		6905	Chaluka, Clerk E.		6971
— Whlr.Sjt.(T./Whlr.S./Sjt.) G.		6945	Chamberlain, Pte.(A./Cpl.) A. C.		6896
— T./S.S.M. G. J., *M.C.*	*	7018	Chambers, Cpl.(L./Sjt.) F.		6889
— Q.M.S. H.		6894	— Spr. F. H.		6879
— C.S.M. J.		6884	— C.Q.M.S. G. F.		6990
— Cpl. J.	✿	6064	— Teleg. R. O.		5111
— C.Q.M.S. L. F.		6913	Chamoto, Pte.(L./Cpl.)		6970
— B.Q.M.S. S		6867	Champkins, Pte.(A./		
— T./S.M. T. E.		6907	L./Cpl.) E. M. W.		7017
— Cpl. W.		6876	Chance, 2nd Cpl.(A./Sjt.) R.		6878
Cartmell, Pte.(A./Sjt.) E.		6934	Chandler, Sjt. F. C.		6888
— Pte.(A./Cpl.) T.		6905	— C.Q.M.S. J.		6881
Cartwright, C.S.M.(A./			Chapelhow, C.Q.M.S. J.		6954
R.S.M.) A. H.	†	7014	Chapham, Pte. D.		6945
— C.S.M. H.		6890	Chapin, Cpl. C. H.		6913
— C.S.M.(A./R.S.M.) T. H.		7016	Chaplin, Sjt. H. H.		6881
— S./Sjt. W. F.		6910	Chapman, B.S.M. A.		6943
Carvell, Q.M.S.(A./S.M.) C. F.		6956	— Cpl.(T./Sjt.) E. S.		6916
Carver, Bombr.(A./Sjt.A.C.) A. A.		6871	— Sjt. G. L.		6913
— Cpl.(L./Sjt.) F. W.		7019	— Pte.(A./Sjt.) H.		7019
Casey, C.Q.M.S. P.		6872	— S.M. J. F.		6971
— R.Q.M.S. W.		6916	— T./S.S.M. W.		7018
Castle, Ch.Mech. L. G.		7036	— Dvr. W.		6954
Castleton, Cpl. G. H.		6903	— Spr.(A./2nd Cpl.) W. W.	✿	7701
Caswell, C.S.M. J. H.		6872	Chappell, Cpl. J. R.		6888
— Cpl. T.		6903	Chard, Farr.Sjt. F.		6900

---

* A.S.C. M.C. *L.G.* 18 February, 1915.
† Group known in S. Lancs. Regt. Museum: Queen's South Africa Medal (Tugela Heights, Orange Free State, Relief of Ladysmith, Transvaal, Laing's Nek, Pnr. Sgt. S. Lancs), King's South Africa Medal, British War Medal (Cheshire R.), L.S. & G.C. (Geo. V, Ches. Regt.) and M.S.M. (1/Garr Btn. Ches. R.) for Gibraltar.
‡ R.A.F. M.S.M. for Egypt to Aus/281, Australian Flying Corps.

Charge, Pte. C. W. T.		6905	Christian, S./Sjt.(A./Sub Condr.) R. R.	
Charlcroft, Cpl.Mech. J.	*	7036	(corr.)	7703
Charles, Sjt. R.		6867	Christie, T./Arm.S.M. A.	6934
Charlesworth, Cpl. A. H.		6884	— Pte. A. F. G.	6881
— S.M. H.		6907	— Sjt. D.	6901
Charman, C.Q.M.S. J.		6886	— C.Q.M.S. D.McK.	6881
Charmbury, Sjt.(A./S./Sjt.) T.		7019	— Pte.(A./Sjt.) W. A.	6911
Charnock, Sadd.S./Sjt. G. E.		6867	Christmas, Cpl.(A./Sjt.) I. G.	6894
Charters, Pte.(A./S.Q.M.S.) F. V.		7019	Christopher, C.Q.M.S. A.	6913
Chase, C.Q.M.S. L. J.		6913	Church, Sjt. A. E.	6908
Chatburn, Sjt. H. B.		6908	— Pte. A. E.	6905
Chatwin, Armr.S./Sjt. T. J.		9691	— R.Q.M.S. E. O.	6867
Chautter, Sjt.(T./S.S.M.) W. R. A.		6945	— Sto. P.O. G. P.	8069
Cheal, Sjt. G.		6874	— Sjt. W. H.	6910
Cheale, F. of W. Q.M.S. J. W.		7012	Churchill, S.S.M. R.	6899
Cheeseman, Spr.(T./Sjt.) A. E.		6879	Churchin, C.S.M. F. H.	7012
Chennell, Sqdn.Cpl.Maj. F. C.		6881	Clack, C.S.M. R. W.	6899
Chester, F./Sjt. J. J.		4512	Clactworthy, C.S.M. W. M.	6899
Chesterman, S./Sjt.(A./Q.M.S.) J. C.		7020	Clague, T./Sub Condr. W. A.	6957
Chettleburgh, Sjt.(A./S./Sjt.) W. G.		7020	Clampin, Pte. H. G.	6905
Chetwyn, 2nd Cpl.(T./Sjt.) G.		6878	Clapcott, Cpl. E.	6903
Chevell, Sjt. R L.		6979	Clapp, Sjt. B. C.	6881
Chewter, Flt.Clk. W.		7036	Clapton, Cpl.(T./Sjt.) F.	6908
Chick, R.S.M. C. C.		6889	Claridge, Cpl. B.	6898
— Cpl. W. F.		6908	Clark, Sjt. D.McIntyre	6892
Chida, Sjt.(A./C.S.M.)		6971	— Sjt. E A.	6901
Chidgey, Farr.S./Sjt. H. A.		6900	— Cpl. E. T.	7036
Child, Sjt.(A./Q.M.S.) H. G.		6889	— Cpl. G	6876
— Pte.(S./Sjt.) J.		6957	— Sjt. G. S.	6901
— Pte.(A./L./Cpl.) W.		7018	— A./S.M. H.	7021
Childs, Sjt. F. M.		6913	— Spr.(T./Sjt.) H.	6879
— Sjt. G.		6885	— Cpl.Clk. H.	7036
— Sqdn.Cpl.Maj.(Instr. of Fencing)			— Sjt. J.	6865
J. W.		7010	— Sjt. J. J.	6916
Chipps, Dvr.(L./Bombr.) C.		6869	— C.Q.M.S. R.	6881
Chisholm, Spr.(A./Cpl.) G.	❀	7701	— Ship's Cpl. 1st Cl. R. E.	5111
— S.Q.M.S.(A./S.S.M.) W.		7021	— Gnr.(A./Bombr.) T	6871
— Cpl. W.		6896	— S.S.M. W.	7021
Chislett, Sjt. G. C.		6943	— Sjt. W.	6867
Chiswell, 2nd Cpl.(A./Cpl.) J. A.		6878	— Cpl. W.	6895
— C.S.M. S. L.		7017	— Dvr. W.	6869
Chitendeni, C.S.M.		6971	— Pte.(A./Sjt.) W J.	6905
Choake, M.A.A.(A./Ch.M.A.A.) C. H.		7511	Clarke, Cpl. B.	6876
Chown, Cpl.(A./Sjt.) A. J.		6903	— T./S.M. B. G.	7020
Christian, Gnr.(A./Sjt.) D. F.		6913	— Sjt. E.	7022
— Sjt.(A./C.S.M.) F. A.		6874	— T./S.S.M. E. A.	6956
— Sjt. H. A.		6908	— Sjt. E. H.	7015
			— C.Q.M.S.(A./C.S.M.) F.	6881

* No. 1695 R.F.C. Enlisted September, 1914 and Motor Cyclist by trade. R.A.F. M.S.M. (I Force, France).

Clarke, Sjt.(A./C.S.M.) F. A.	6912	Clissold, C.Q.M.S. P. L.	6900
— C.Q.M.S. F. H.	6895	Clively, Cpl. G.	6903
— R.S.M. G.	* 7016	Close, Sjt. F.	6887
— Pte. H. J.	6905	Clough, Sjt.(A./R.S.M.) J.	‡ 7014
— S.Q.M.S.(A./R.Q.M.S.) J.	7010	— Pte. M. J.	6905
— C.Q.M.S. J.	7014	Clover, C.Q.M.S. H. W.	6897
— C.S.M. J.	6899	Clutterbuck, C.Q.M.S. C. J.	6889
— Gnr.(A./Cpl.) J.	6871	— Sjt. W. R.	6887
— Cpl. J.	6913	Coast, Sjt. H.	6901
— Spr.(T./Cpl.) J. A.	6943	Coates, Sjt. H., *M.M.*	6944
— Whlr.Sjt. J. E.	6945	— Sjt. W. C.	6911
— Sjt. J. J.	6908	Cobb, Pte.(A./S.S.M.) G W.	6905
— S./Sjt. O. J.	6910	Cobden, L.A.C. C.	7036
— Pte.(A./Cpl.) P. W.	6909	Cobley, Cpl. R. H.	6898
— C.Q.M.S. S.	6900	Cochrane, C.S.M. J.	6881
— Pte. S.	❀ 6064	— Farr.Sjt. J. G.	6913
— Pte. T.	6890	— Sjt. R.	6901
— Cpl. T. J.	6903	Cock, 3rd Writer, H. A.	4732
— B.Q.M.S. T. R. G.	6953	Cockburn, Sjt. T.	6895
Clarkson, Cpl.(A./Q.M.S.) A. L.	6957	Cockell, 2nd Cpl.(A./Sjt.) R. A.	6878
— Sjt. G. H.	6891	Cocking, C.S.M. T.	6882
— Sjt. R.	6882	Cocks, S./Sjt. B. P.	7022
Clavering, Cpl. H.	6891	— Whlr.S./Sjt. F. T.	6900
Clayton, S./Sjt. A.	6910	Cocksedge, T./Mech.S.M. F. M.	6956
— Spr.(A./Mech.S./Sjt.) A. E.	7012	Coe, Sjt. Drm. F. T.	6885
— Q.M.S. G. L.	7016	— Sjt. W.	6901
— C.S.M. J.	† 6899	— Dvr. W.	6869
— T./R.S.M. N. R.	6893	Coffey, R.Q.M.S. T. B.	6916
— Sjt.(A./S./Sjt.) P. E.	6908	Coggins, Sjt. J. E.	6889
— Pte.(T./Sjt.) W.	6911	Coira, Cpl. P. F.	6918
Cleaveley, C.S.M. A.	6899	Coke, Pte. R.	6905
Cleavin, Sadd.Q.M.S. W. T.	6867	Colbourne, S./Sjt. O. H.	7018
Clegg, Pte. J.	6905	Colclough, Pte.(L./C.) H.	6905
Clements, Sjt. A.	6895	Coldwell, Pte.(A./Cpl.) B. A.	6892
— C.P.O. G.	5112	— Pte. D.	6887
— Gnr.(A./Sjt.) H. W.	7011	Cole, BS.M. E. G.	6913
— R.S.M. J.	6869	— C.Q.M.S. F. H.	6897
— Sjt.(A./S.M.,A.C.) S. W.	6870	— Cpl.(A./Sjt.) F. J.	6903
Clemmit, Pte. W.	6910	— S./Sjt. H. J. R.	6916
Clews, C.S.M. J. C.	6919	— Sjt. P. M.	6945
Cliffe, Pte. F.	❀ 6064	— Sjt. T. H.	6955
Clifford, Sjt. H. E.	6867	— C.S.M.Instr. W.	6912
— Sjt.(A./C.S.M.) T.	7016	— C.S.M. W. C.	6954
Clift, Sjt. A. A.	7021	— B.Q.M.S. W. H.	6869
Clippingdale, Sjt. L. A.	7011	Cole-Edwards, Sjt. J. N.	6970

* 6/K.R.R.C.; entitled to Queen's South Africa Medal.
† Group known: Queen's Sudan (21st Lancers), 1914 Star & bar, British War and Victory Medals (W.O. R.A.S.C.), L.S. & G.C. (Geo. V), M.S.M. (A.S.C.) and Khedive's Sudan (Khartoum, 21st Lancers). 'A' Sqn. at Omdurman.
‡ West Yorks. R. For Malta.

Colelough, 2nd Cpl. G. F.	6878	Comaish, Cpl. W. A.	6970
Coleman, Ch. Yeo. Sigs. J. A.	7907	Compton, C.S.M. B. G.	6872
— S./Sjt. V. A.	6910	Comrie, 2nd Cpl. W. A.	6918
Coles, Dvr. A. E.	6906	Condon, Sjt.(A./F./Sjt.) C. H.	7036
— Cpl. F.	6911	Condron, Condr A.	6934
Coleshill, Cpl. F. H.	6903	Conley, L./C. H. M., *MM.*	6913
Coley, Sjt. J. T.	6944	Connolly, Sjt. A. H.	6970
Colgan, C.S.M. J.	6882	— Pte. H. V.	6883
Collcott, C.Q.M.S. G.	6872	— T./Sub Condr. W.	6909
Collens, R.Q.M.S. G. P.	6916	Connor, Sjt. J.	6901
Collett, Pte.(A./Sjt.) H. F.	6905	— S./Sjt. L.	6913
— Shipwt. 2nd Cl. H. J.	5112	— C.Q.M.S. W.	6895
— Sjt. R. C.	6901	Conolly, Gnr.(A./Sjt.) J.	6913
Colley, Pte. J. N.	6934	— Farr.S./Sjt. J.	6867
Collie, Pte.(A./Col.Sjt.)D.	6880	— C.Q.M.S. W. F.	6872
Collier, Cpl. E.	6868	Constable, T./S.M. C.	7020
— S./Sjt. J. G.	6957	— C.S.M.(A./R.S.M.) G.	7014
Collington, Pte.(A./Cpl.) P. L.	6896	— Sjt.(T./C.S.M.) J.	6874
Collinge, Sjt. C. E.	* 6908	— Sjt.(A./C.S.M.)(R.A.S.C.)	6901
— Sjt. F.	6874	Constant, S.S.M. A. S.	6899
— Pte.(A./S.M.) J. W.	7022	Cook, S./Sjt.(A./S.Q.M.S.) D. M.	6901
Collings, Cpl. E	6896	— Sjt. E. H. (corr.)	7703
Collins, C.Q.M.S.(A./		— B.S.M. E. W.	6869
R.Q.M.S.) A. E.	6955	— Pte. F. H.	6905
— S./S.M. A. G.	6916	— Sjt. H.	6901
— Sjt. A. J.	6886	— A./S.S.M. J.	7022
— Pte. C. E.	6896	— S./Sjt. S.	6901
— C.Q.M.S. E.	6872	— Sjt. T. A.	6932
— Q.M.S. G. H. A.	6913	— C.S.M.(A./R.S.M.) W.	7012
— Sjt. G. W.	6901	— Sjt. W.	6945
— Master Mech.(W.O. Cl.II) H. E.	7022	Cooke, Sjt.(A./S.M.) J., *D.C.M.*	6911
— B.S.M. J.	7011	— T./Sjt. W. H.	6934
— Cpl. J. T.	7010	Cookson, Sjt. W. G.	6867
— Sjt. L.	6874	Coombes, C.Q.M.S. H. H.	6872
— Pte.(L./C.) M.	6883	— S.M. R. B.	6907
— Pte.(L./C.) M. S. (corr.)	7703	Coombs, R.S.M. W. F.	7016
— Pte. N. W. G.	6905	— T./S.S.M. W. F.	6899
— Flt. Sjt. T.	7036	Coop, R.S.M. A.	6933
Collinson, S./Sjt. E. H.	6907	Cooper, R.S.M. A.	6913
— Sjt. G. E.	6933	— B.S.M. A.	7011
— Pte. H.	6905	— Sjt. A.	6874
Collison, T./Mech.S.M. C. S.	6956	— Sjt. B. S.	6874
Collister, Sjt. T. H.	6913	— Sjt. C. F.	6890
Colluney, Sjt.(corr.)	6065	— Q.M.S. C. G.	6907
Colman, S./Sjt. T. W.	6957	— Cpl.(A./Sjt.) C. H., *M.M.*	6876
Colquhoun, C.Q.M.S.		— Cpl.(A./Sjt.) E.	6903
(A./R.S.M.) F.	6884	— Cpl. E. E.	6898
Colwell, Farr.Sjt. F.	6874	— Cpl.(A./S./Sjt.) E. H.	7019

* Group known: Queen's South Africa Medal (no bar, Ord. St.J.A.B.) Bronze St.J.A.B South Africa Medal (Edw. VII, Hebdon Bridge Corps) and M.S.M. (R.A.M.C.).

Cooper, Q.M.S. E. L.	6871	Cornford, Sjt. G. P.	6913
— C.Q.M.S. F.	6891	Cornish, S./Sjt. A. B.	6913
— Bombr. F. G.	6871	— Sjt. F. S.	7036
— S.Q.M.S.(A./S.S.M.) F. W.	7021	— Sjt. J.	6893
— Sjt. H.	6895	Cornthwaite, A./Sjt. J.	6913
— C.S.M. H. B.	6887	Cornwell, C.S.M. W. G.	6895
— C.Q.M.S. H. H.	6872	Corps, Cpl. A. G.	6870
— Cpl. H. J.	6911	Corry, P.O. Teleg. A. G.	8069
— 1st Cl. S./S.M. H. J. (corr.)	7703	Corsbie, T./S.S.M. P. H. D.	6933
— R.Q.M.S.(A./R.S.M.) J.	6955	Cory, R.Q.M.S. C.	6897
— A./Cpl. J. A.	7036	— Sjt. H. A.	6870
— Q.M.S. M.	6919	— T./S.S.M. P.	6933
— Pte. R.	7017	Costello, Sjt. F.	6970
— C.S.M. W. G. M. (corr.)	7703	Costigan, Sub Condr.(A./Condr.)	
Cope, Dr. E.	6907	F. R., *M.C.*	* 6909
— Sjt. H.	6882	Costin, Cpl.(A./C.S.M.) E. G.	6877
Copestake, C.S.M. W. E.	6895	Cottam, S.Q.M.S. J.	6899
Copland, T./S.M. J.	6932	— Cpl. J. F.	6908
Copp, S.B.S. G. F.	4735	Cotter, Sjt. J.	6874
Coppard, F.Q.M.S. H. A.	6976	Cotton, Cpl. A	6877
Coppin, S./Sjt. C. H.	7019	Cottrell, Sjt. I. R., *M.M.*	6874
Copping, T./S.S.M. H. A.	6956	— C.P.O. J. C.	7907
— T./S.S.M. L. C.	6899	Couchman, R.Q.M.S.(A./	
Copplestone, Ch.Shipwt. W. H.	7511	R.S.M.) C. A.	6884
Copson, C.S.M. J. W.	6886	— F./Sjt. F.	7036
Corbet, Pte. D.	6893	Coughlan, Sjt. C.	6913
Corbett, Cpl. G.	6911	Couling, Sjt. J. J.	6944
— Pte.(T./S./Sjt.) J.	6905	Coull, Pte.(A./L./C.) W.	6892
— Cpl. R. R.	6913	Coultas, A.C. 1, J. W.	7036
Corbishely, Spr.(A./Sjt.) G. H.	6879	Coulter, Pte.(A./Sjt.) J. H.	7021
Corby, Sjt. F. J	6908	— Cpl. R. H.	6916
Corcoran, Ldg.Sto. T.	7512	Coultham, Pte.(L./C.) H.	6883
Cordwell, C.Q.M.S.(A./		Coulthurst, A.M. 3 S.	7036
R.S.M.) H. H.	6886	Coupe, Sjt. G.	6874
Core, Pte.(A./Q.M.S.) F.	6895	Couper, Fitt.S./Sjt. A.	6867
Corfield, Pte.(A./Sjt.) F.	6880	Court, Farr.Q.M.S. A.	6865
Cork, S.S.M. W. T.	7021	— Pte.(L./C.) C. S.	6911
Corke, S./Sjt. E.	6901	— S./Sjt. H. T.	6912
— Sjt. E. R.	6898	— Cpl. S. C.	6903
— A.B. H. C.	4735	— B.S.M.(A./R.S.M.) T. H., *D.C.M.*	6953
Corker, C.S.M. W.	6955	Courtney, S.S.M. H. M.	† 7021
Corkhill, Sjt. F.	6901	Cousins, Pte.(A./Cpl.) M. H.	6883
Corlett, S./Sjt.(A./S.Q.M.S.) P.	7019	Couttie, Sjt. A. C.	6881
Cormack, C.S.M. W.	6886	Coverdale, 2nd Cpl. A.	6878
Cornaby, Sjt. G. C.	7014	Covey, Sjt.(T./S./Sjt.) H.	6901
Cornell, Cpl.(A./C.Q.M.S.) C.	6876	Cowan, Sjt.(A./S./Sjt.) G. A.	6901
Cornelous, C.S.M.(A./R.S.M.) E.	7017	— Cpl.(A./Sjt.) H. G.	6883
Corney, T./Sub Condr. H.	6909	— Cpl.(T./Mech.S./Sjt.) W. R.	6877

* M.C. *L.G.* 1 January 1917, Sub Cond. A.O.C.
† A.P.C. For Ceylon.

Cowburn, C.Q.M.S. R.	6889	Craine, Sjt. A. G.		6916
Cowden, Cpl. C.	7036	Crampin, Sjt. A., *MM.*		6895
Cowdray, Sjt.(A./Mech.S.M.) F.	6901	Cran, C.S.M. J. G.		7018
Cowe, Ldg.Dkhnd. T. S.	4733	Crane, C.S.M. E. R.		6916
Cowey, B.S.M. T. G	6866	Crankshaw, Sjt. E.		6901
Cowley, A.M.T.S./Sjt. H. R.	6913	Cranston, Sjt.(A./C.S.M.) J.		6886
— T./Sub Condr. W. T.	6909	Crauford, Dvr. J. L. W.		6916
Cowling, Sjt. E	6955	Craven, Sjt.(A./R.S.M.) F.		6933
— R.Q.M.S. T.	6893	— Pte.(L./C.) H. (corr.)		7703
— Q.M.S. W.	7015	Crawford, E.C.Sjt.(A./Q.M.S.)		
Cowper, 3rd Cl.AsstSurg. G. J.	7021	C. W. McD.		6874
Cox, Ch.Mech. A.	7036	— Cpl. J.		6892
— Mech.S./Sjt. B. (corr.)	6065	— B.Q.M.S. J. W.		6869
— Cpl.(A./Sjt.) C.	6908	— S.M. S. C.	*	7036
— C.S.M.(A./R.S.M.) E. C.	6897	— S./Sjt. W.		6901
— Sjt.(A./R.S.M.) E. H.	6956	— Cpl.(R. E.)		6877
— Cpl. H.	6882	Crawley, Gnr. J. J.		6869
— Pte.(A./Sjt.) J. F.	6909	Crees, C.S.M. J.		6884
— Sjt. J. H.	6889	Creese, Pnr.Sjt. A. J.		6891
— Mech.S.M. J. W.	6899	Creighton, Cpl.(A./Sjt.) F. O.		6932
— R.Q.M.S. P. W.	6887	— T./S.S.M. T. P.		7018
— Sjt. R. H.	6874	Cremin, Pte.(A./S./Sjt.) D.		7020
— Sjt. S.	6870	Cressell, S./S.M. G.		6976
— C.S.M.(A./R.S.M.) S. A.	6891	Cresswell, Sjt. R.		6901
— Gnr.(A./L./Bombr.) W. C.	6871	Creswell, C.Q.M.S. A. W.		6895
— C.Q.M.S. W. E.	6889	Crewdson, Engmn. W.		4732
Coxon, S./Sjt. J.	6913	Crichton, C.Q.M.S. D. F.		6888
— R.Q.M.S. W.	6891	Crick, Sjt. A. J.		6889
Coy, S.Q.M.S.(A./S.S.M.) E.	7021	Cripps, Cpl. F.		6903
— A./S.M. J. W.	7021	Cripwell, S./Sjt. S. T.		6910
Coyle, C.E.R.A. 1st Cl. G. D.	8069	Crisp, Cpl. E.		6910
Coyne, C.S.M. T.	6880	— Cpl. G.		6877
Cozens, T./R.S.M. G. H., *D.C.M.*	6969	— Cpl.(A./S.M., A.C.) V. H.		6870
Crabbe, Pte.(L./C.) J., *MM.*	6891	Crispin, Ch.Mech. A. E., *D.S.M.*	†	7036
Crabtree, B.Q.M.S. H.	6867	Critch, Sea. W. G.	‡	8203
Cradden, C.S.M. J.	7014	Croad, L.A.C. V.		7036
Craddock, Cpl. W.	6903	Crocker, S.S.M. A. G. B.		7023
Cragg, S./Sjt.(A./S.M.) E.	6907	— Pte.(A./Sjt.) W. J.		7017
— Pte. E.	6919	Crockett, S./Sjt.(A./S.S.M.) F. C.		6901
Craig, Pte.(L./C.) A.	6909	— C.S.M. G.		6872
— S./Sjt. A. C.	7019	— C.Q.M.S. G. L.		7018
— R.S.M. W.	7023	Crofton, Gnr. A.		6871
— Cpl. W.	6913	Cronk, Sjt. F. J.		6895
— Pte. W. A.	6865	Cropper, Pte. H.		6903

---

* No. 713 R.F.C. Enlisted May 1913 as S. C. Hogg. Discharged 1914 under KR 392 (IX) 'Unfitted for the duties of the Corps, ' but re-enlisted during W.W.I after April 1918 and awarded this R.A.F. M.S.M.

† Pair known (F2519 C.P.O. Mech. R.N.A.S. 1917) and R.A.F. M.S.M. (3056 R.A.F.) for service in Mesopotamia.

‡ R.N.R. (Newfoundland).

Cropper, Pte.(A./Cpl.) J. E	6909	Currall, Pte.(L./C.)	6911
Cross, R.Q.M.S. H.	6894	Curran, Sjt. C. S.	7012
— R.Q.M.S. J.	7016	— Sjt. Mech. H. A.	7036
— S.B.A. R.	5112	— Cpl.(A./S.M.) T.	6957
— E.R.A. 1st Cl. R. C.	8069	Currell, S./Sjt. A.	6907
Crosse, Q.M.S. R. H.	7020	Currey, S./Sjt.(T./S.M.) J.	6912
Crossingham, Sjt. H. W.	6898	Curtis, Mech.S.M. C. G.	6899
Crossley, S.M. A.	6907	— Cpl. G. G.	6877
— T./S.M. B. E.	6907	— Sjt. G. H.	6933
Crosswell, Cpl.(A./Sjt.) S.	6877	— Cpl.(A./S.Q.M.S.) R. G.	7019
Crotty, C.S.M. R.	6955	— C.S.M. R. H.	6913
Croucher, Sjt.(A./R.S.M.) R.	6943	Curwin, C.Q.M.S. W. G. (corr.)	7703
Crow, Sjt. A. C.	6889	Cutler, Cpl. Mec. H. W.	7036
— Pte.(A./Sjt.) C. E.	6883	Cutter, C.Q.M.S. T.	6881
Crowhurst, Sjt.(A./B.S.M.) E., *M.M.*	6876		
— Cpl.(A./Sjt.) P. O.	6945	Dace, Sjt. G.	6874
Crowley, R.S.M. W. F.	6945	Daffern, Sjt. A.	6901
Crowther, Pte.(L./C.) E.	6958	Dagg, Sjt. W.	6894
— Sjt. G.	6882	Daglish, C.Q.M.S. A.	6886
— A./S.M. M.	7021	Dainty, Pte. E.	6905
— S./Smith, W.	6911	— Cpl.(A./C.S.M.) F. E.	6877
Cruickshank, S.C.M. A.	6895	Dalby, Pte.(A./Cpl.) J.	6909
— C.S.M.Instr. J.	6912	Dale, Cpl.(A./Sjt.) A. W.	6908
Crutchley, Sjt. W. G.	6957	— C.Q.M.S. W. I.	6889
Crute, Cpl. W.	6903	Dales, Sjt. R. L.	6913
Cryan, Sjt. J. H.	6870	Dalgleish, R.S.M. J.	7011
Cudd, Pte. A. S. J.	6905	— 2nd Cpl. J.	6878
Cuddon, T./S.S.M. E. M.	7018	Dalindyebo, Sjt. D.	6919
Cudmore, Cpl.(A./Sjt.) G. A. H.	6943	Dall, B.S.M. A.	6866
Cullen, T./Sub Condr. R. K.	6909	Dalton, Pte. E. A. G.	6913
— Cpl.(A./Sjt.) W.	7012	— Sjt. W. J.	6913
Culley, C.Q.M.S. W.	6885	Dalwood, Sjt. H. B.	6870
Cullum, T./Sub Condr. W. G.	6909	Dambuza, Native Chapln.	* 6919
Culpan, C.Q.M.S. J.	6894	Dams, Pte.(A./S./Sjt.) H.	7020
Culver, Sjt.(A./F./Sjt.) A. W.	7036	Danby, Cpl. R.	6891
Culverhouse, Cpl.(A./Sjt.) J.	6877	Dandridge, C.S.M.(T./	
Culverwell, Sjt.Mech.J. A. H.	7036	S.S.M.) A. W.	6945
Culwick, C.Q.M.S. W. C.	6886	Daniel, Cpl. H. G.	6903
Cumming, Pte.(L./C.) J. H.	6909	— S.Q.M.S. J. L.	6933
— A./Sjt. W. G.	6913	Daniels, Supt.Clk. G. A.	6871
Cummings, Gnr. A.	6943	— Sjt. P. S.	7019
— Sjt. J. H.	6913	Dann, Exptl.S./Sjt.(A./Exptl.	
Cummins, Pte. D.	6893	Q.M.S.) E.	7011
Cundick, Cpl.(A./Sjt.) T. F.	6884	— C.Q.M.S. F.	6881
Cunniffe, Pte.(L./C.) B.	6911	Dannatt, Sjt. W. E. J.	6953
Cunningham, Dvr. A. C.	6916	Darby, Spr. E. A.	6879
— Sjt.(A./Q.M.S.) H.	6908	— Cpl. F. S.	6877
Cureton, Mech.Q.M.S. C. E.	7012	Darcy, B.S.M. C.	6869
Curman, Dkhnd, H.	5112	— Ch.Mec. G	7036

* South African Labour Corps.

Dardell, E.R.A. 2nd Cl. J.	7907	Davies, Gnr. W. A.	6871
Dare, S./Sjt.(A./S.M.) J. R.	6907	Davis, B.S.M. A.	7011
Dargin, Sjt. R. A.	6916	— Cpl. A.	6904
Dargue, Spr. D. H.	6879	— Pte. A. E. J.	6896
Dark, C.Q.M.S.(A./R.S.M.) F.	6882	— Cpl. A. H.	6916
Darley, Cpl. F.	6911	— Sjt. C. J.	6874
— Cpl.(A./S./Sjt.) W. F. I.	7020	— C.S.M.(A./R.S.M.) C. R.	7014
Dart, Sjt. J. C.	6874	— Dvr.(A./C.S.M.) F.	6957
Dascombe, B.S.M. W. C.	6866	— Sjt. F. T.	6874
Davenport, Sjt. E.	6885	— Pte. G. W. F.	7019
— Sjt. J. W.	6898	— Pte.(A./L./C.) H. E.	7019
Davey, Sjt. A. G.	6932	— Sjt. I.	6957
— Farr.Q.M.S. C. S.	6932	— S./Sjt. J. L.	7021
— Sjt. D.	6945	— C.Q.M.S. S.	6884
— F./Sjt. E. A.	7036	— Sjt.(A./C.S.M.) S.	6901
— Sjt. E. F.	6891	— C.S.M. T.	7018
— C.S.M. G.	6893	— R.Q.M.S. W. E.	6944
— Sjt. T. A.	6885	— S./Sjt. W. J.	6873
— Spr.(L./C.) W. A.	6879	Davison, S./Sjt. J.	6901
David, C.S.M.	6971	— T./Sub Condr. J. E.	6909
Davidson, C.E.R.A. A. B.	4197	Daviss, Cpl. V. C. M.	6865
— Sjt. A. E.	6945	Davos, S.S.M. C. W.	7018
— Condr. A. W. E.	* 7021	Dawes, Cpl.(A.C.)(A./Sjt.) C. E.	6870
— Sjt. G.	6957	— Q.M.Cpl.Maj. C. M.	6881
— Pte.(T./Sjt.) H.	6909	— B.Q.M.S. S. A.	7010
— C.S.M. J.	6885	Dawson, Pte.(A./Sjt.) F. S.	6913
— Spr.(L./C.) R.	6879	— F./Sjt. H.	7036
— C.Q.M.S. S.	7013	— Cpl. J.	6868
— Sjt. W.	6865	— C.S.M. W.	6890
— Sjt. W.	6955	— Cpl.(T./C.Q.M.S.) W.	6877
Davies, Cpl. A. E.	6913	Davy, S./Sjt. S. I.	7021
— B.Q.M.S. C. J. S.	6916	Day, P.O. A. L.	4734
— Pte. D. J.	6905	— Pte.(A./Sjt.) A. V.	6934
— B.S.M. D. L.	6866	— Pte.(A./Sjt.) C.	6909
— Cpl. E.	6892	— S./Sjt. F.	6913
— Sjt. F.	6874	— Sjt. F. N.	6916
— Sjt.(A./S./Sjt.) F. T.	7019	— Pte. G. C.	6916
— Sjt. H.	6955	— Pte.(A./R.S.M.) H. A.	7015
— S./Sjt. H. E.	6894	— Dvr. J.	6954
— Pte. H. J.	6905	— Trmr. J.	5112
— T./R.S.M. J.	6869	— S./Sjt. J. G.	6894
— Spr. J.	6879	— Sub Condr. P. W.	7021
— Sjt. J. E.	6888	Daykin, Master Gnr. 2nd Cl. R. S.	7011
— Sjt.(A./C.Q.M.S.) J. P.	7012	De Carteret, Supt.Clk. H.	7011
— Pte.(A./Sjt.) R.	6911	De Roux, Sjt. A. A.	6910
— Dvr. R. W.	6907	Deacon, R.S.M. G. L. W.	6916
— 2nd Cpl. S. M.	6878	Deadman, Pte.(A./Col.Sjt.) E. A.	6883
— C.S.M. S. W.	7016	— F./Sjt. H.	7036
— Cpl. T. C.	6903	Deady, Sjt. G. W.	6913

* I.A. For Hong Kong.

Deakin, Sjt. G.	6945	Devine, S.S.M. G.	6899
Deal, Cpl.(A./C.Q.M.S.) H. A.	6894	Devonald, F./Sjt. J.	7036
Dealtry, T./Sub Condr. W.	6909	Devonshire, 2nd Cpl.(A./Q.M.S.)	
Dean, A./C.Q.M.S. D. G. H.	7022	E. G. C.	6878
— Pte. F. E.	6905	Dew, Cpl.(A./Sjt.) R.	7018
— C.Q.M.S. H.	6872	Dewar, Sjt. H. C.	6916
— Sjt. H. W.	6874	Dewdney, Pte.(A./Sjt.) J.	6910
— Pte.(L./C.) W. G.	6919	Dewey, Pte.(A./Sjt.) A.	6883
Deane, C.Q.M.S. B. W.	6900	Dewhirst, C.Q.M.S. E	6891
— Sjt. Drmr. H.	6887	Dewhurst, Pte.(A./Sjt.) R.	6865
Deans, Pte. W. F.	6909	Dewsbury, Cpl. F. R.	6896
Dear, Farr.Sjt. A. S.	6953	Diamond, Pte.(A./Sjt.) W. G.	6911
Dearden, Pte.(A./Cpl.) N.	6905	Dick, S./Sjt. J. U.	6913
Dearling, Pte.(A./L./Sjt.) R. L.	6934	Dicken, C.Q.M.S. P.	6891
Dearlove, Sjt. J.	6976	Dickens, Sjt. C. W.	6874
Deary, C.Q.M.S. F. H.	6894	— Sqdn.Q.M.S. T. E.	6865
Death, Sjt. F. E.	6874	Dickenson, Mech.S./Sjt. A.	6900
— Fitt.S./Sjt. J.	7011	— A.C. 2, C. J.	7036
— T./S.S.M. R. A.	* 7018	— Sjt. J.	7016
Deaville, B.Q.M.S. R.	6867	Dickie, C.Q.M.S. J., *M.M.*	6913
Deboise, 2nd Cpl. A. S.	6878	Dickinson, Cpl. E. D.	6885
Degnan, Sjt. L.	6895	— E.R.A. 1st Cl. F. J. F.	8202
Delahunt, C.Q.M.S. S. D.	6886	— R.Q.M.S. W. T.	6916
Delworth, Cpl. D.	6904	Dicks, B.S.M. F.	6943
Demay, Sjt. R., *M.M.*	6874	Dickson, S./Sjt. W. C.	6907
Denholm, 2nd Cpl.(A./Sjt.) D.	6878	Diggle, Pte.(A./Q.M.S.) E.	6865
Dennett, Cpl. T.	6887	Dilley, Ch.Mech. F. E.	7037
Dennis, A.C. 1, A. E.	7036	Dimond, Bombr. R.	6975
— Pte. C. H.	7014	Dingle, Sjt. C. (corr.)	7703
— Gnr.(L./Bombr.) E.	6871	Dingwall, Gnr. J.	6869
— Sjt. W.	7021	Dinning, Cpl. H.	6916
Dennison, Cpl.(A./C.Q.M.S.) W. E.	6896	Dinsdale, Pte. C. F.	6890
— Q.M.S. W. J.	6907	Dira Effendi, Yuzbashi Juma	6971
Denniss, Sqdn.Q.M.S. A. J.	6865	Disher, Cpl. S. H.	6916
— Pte.(A./Sjt.) H. W.	6905	Diver, T./Sub Condr.(A./Condr.) C.	6909
Denny, Pte.(A./Sjt.) A. W. J.	7020	Dixon, C.Q.M.S. A.	6955
— Pte. B. A.	6883	— Pte. H.	6909
— Pte.(A./Cpl.) B. W.	6884	— Q.M.S. H. C.	6907
Densham, P.O. W. C.	6504	— C.S.M. J. H.	6956
Dent, Fitt.S./Sjt. C. H.	6870	— C.Q.M.S. R.	6891
Deny, S./Sjt. J. D.	6933	Dobby, Sjt. A.	6881
Derbyshire, Sjt. W.	6890	Dobinson, Bandmaster H. S.	7016
Derrett, R.Q.M.S. H. T.	6884	Dobson, T./Armt.S.M. P.	6909
Dersley, Pte. J.	† 6957	Dockerill, Sjt. J.	6882
Desmoulins, Pte.(A./S./Sjt.) W.	7019	Docwra, C.S.M. D. W.	6899
Dessez, Pte. C. V.	❈ 6064	Dodd, Cpl.(A./L./Sjt.) A. F.	6896
Desveau, Cpl. J. W.	6913	— S./Sjt.(A./Q.M.S.) L. R.	7020

* Medal presented in Bermuda by C.-in-C., Sir James Wilcocks, 25.4.1920, together
  with his M.M. and L.S. & G.C. (R.A.S.C.).
† R.A.O.C. Also Médaille d'Honneur avec Glaives (en Bronze).

Dodd, C.Q.M.S.(A./R.Q.M.S.) W.	6885	Douglas, Spr.(L./C.) S. F.	6879
Dodds, Pte.(A./R.Q.M.S.) D. G. H.	7022	— A./S.Q.M.S. W.	7022
— C.Q.M.S.(A./R.S.M.) G.	7013	— Sjt. W.	6901
— Sjt. R.	6943	Douglass, 1st Cl.Army	
— Cpl.(A./Sjt.) R. A. M.	7010	Schoolmaster J. D. T.	7021
Dodson, B.Q.M.S. H., *M.M.*	6870	Dove, T./Mech.S.M. W. B.	6899
Doe, Sjt. F. V.	6867	Dow, Sjt.(A./S./Sjt.) A. A.	6908
Doherty, Sqdn.S.M. R. W.	6934	— Master Gnr. 2nd Cl. H. J.	7011
Doig, Sjt. C. L.	6913	Dowd, R.Q.M.S. L.	6892
Dolamore, Pte.(L./C.) W. T.	6883	Dowdling, Pte. A. H. W.	6865
Dolan, Cpl. J. J.	6913	Dowker, Mech.S./Sjt. W. H.	6900
Dolby, Whr. E. A.	6869	Dowler, Sjt. E. D.	6916
Dolding, F./Sjt. R.	7037	Dowling, Pte. F.	6880
Dolman, Cpl. M. E.	6889	— B.Q.M.S. J. F.	6916
Donagh, C.S.M. C.	7014	Down, S./Sjt. C. R.	6873
Donald, Shipwt. 1st Cl. T.	8069	— S.Q.M.S.(A./S.S.M.) H. P.	7021
Donaldson, Sto.P.O. D.	5111	— S./Sjt. W. G.	6910
— Sjt. E.	6896	— Cpl.(A./L./Sjt.) W. J.	6934
— Pte.(A./Condr.) E. R.	6946	Downes, Dvr. M. M. B.	6976
— Cpl.(A./Sjt.) J. B.	7037	— B.S.M. W. P.	6953
— R.S.M. J. W. A., *D.C.M.* *	7022	Downie, S.M. C. E.	7037
Doncaster, T./Sub Condr. C. W.	6909	Downing, Pte.(A./Cpl.) T. H.	6909
Done, Sjt.(A./C.Q.M.S.) H.	6883	Downs, Cpl(A./Sjt.) E. A.	7037
Donelly, Sjt. E. J.	6913	— T./S.M. E. J.	7020
Donji Ashagar, Cpl.	6971	Dowse, C.Q.M.S. A.	6872
Donkin, Sjt. A.	6874	— Pte. J. J.	6934
Donnelly, S./Sjt.(A./S.M.) A., *M.M.*	6907	Dowsett, R.S.M. E.	7014
Donovan, Sjt. P.	7013	Doxey, Sjt.(A./C.Q.M.S.) J. W.	6874
Dool, Pte. W. J.	6892	Doyle, B.S.M.(T./R.S.M.) P. J.	6916
Dorian, Pte.(L./C.) C. J. C.	6909	— B.S.M. S. G.	7011
Dorling, Cpl. A. T.	6898	Drake, Sjt.(T./S.S.M.) F. W. (corr.	
— T./S.S.M. F. W., *M.M.*	7018	of initials)	6065
Dorrington, W.O. Cl.1, F. R.	7022	— Sjt. J.	6874
Dorrity, Cpl.(A./C.Q.M.S.) J. H. †	6956	Draper, C.Q.M.S.(A./C.S.M.) H. J.	6872
Dorse, R.Q.M.S. L.	7022	Drawley, Sjt. E. J.	6898
Double, Sjt. A. J.	6885	Dreer, Cpl.(A./R.S.M.) W. J.	6945
Douglas, C.Q.M.S. J.	6881	Drew, Cpl.(L./Sjt.) A.	6881
— Sjt. L.	6887	— Pte.(A./Sjt.) D.	7021
— Pte.(A./Sjt.) R.	7022	— Mech.S./Sjt. F.	6900

---

* Group known: D.C.M. (Geo. V, C–40330 S.M. 1/BDE Canadian Art., *L.G.* 5 August, 1915), China Medal 1900 (no clasp, 80085 Sgt., Vickers Maxim Bty.), 1914/15 Star (B.S.M.), British War and Victory Medals (W.O.1 C.F.A.), L.S. & G.C. (Edw. VII, 80085 B.S.M. R.H.A.) and M.S.M. (Can. F.A.).

† James Henry Dorrity. Enlisted into the Royal Irish Fusiliers in August, 1914 and took part in the landing at Suvla Bay in August, 1915, and was wounded at Chocolate Hill. Promoted Sergeant, he served in the Struma Valley operations in 1916, and on the Doiran front in 1917; he lost part of a hand on Grand Coronne. Subsequently sent to G.H.Q. in Constantinople, he acted as an escort to the King's Messenger with the rank of C.S.M. His M.S.M. was for his service in the Balkans. Before the war he was an employee of the Bank of Ireland.

Dring, Pte.(A./C.Q.M.S.) A	7018	Dungar, Pte.(A./Sjt.) F. H.		6898
— Sjt. J.	6913	Dunham, C.S.M. C. E.		6872
Driscoll, Sjt.(A./C.S.M.) B.	6881	— R.Q.M.S. J. W.		7014
— C.S.M.Instr. J.	6912	Dunlevey, Trp.(A./Cpl. of Horse) H.		6881
— M.A.A. M.	5111	Dunlop, Sjt.(Clr.Sjt.) A.		6892
Driver, Cpl. J.	6943	Dunn, Ldg.Sto. C.		8069
Drummond, S.S.M. D.	6899	— Elect.Art.2nd Cl. F. E. A.		7907
Drury, Gnr. J. R.	6871	— Pte. H.		6892
— Pte.(A./Sjt.) W.	6911	— Cpl. P. W.		6957
Dryden, Cpl. A. S.	6913	— Sjt. R. G.		6916
DuCharme, Spr. D.	6970	— Sjt. S. H.		6874
Ducker, Whlr.Cpl. D. F.	6904	Dunne, Sjt. J.		6916
Duckworth, Cpl. F. W.	6868	Dunstan, Cpl. G. W.		6932
— Cpl. G.	* 6877	Durham, C.Q.M.S. L.		7014
Dudley, Pte. A. G.	6896	Durling, Sjt. A. W. (corr.)		6065
— Pte.(L./C.) H. J.	6958	Durnell, C.Q.M.S. W.		6884
— Ldg.Teleg. R. L.	4734	Durnford, Sjt. F. C.		7017
— Armr.S./Sjt. T. H.	6910	Durrant, Sto.P.O. A.		7512
Duff, Sjt. J.	6955	— Sjt. D. E.		6910
Duffey, S.M. L. A.	6970	Durston, C.Q.M.S.(A./S.M.) I. W.		6872
Duffill, Fitt.S./Sjt. G. E.	6870	Dutch, Pte.(A./Cpl.) R. J.		6955
Duffin, C.Q.M.S. D. I.	6970	Duthie, C.Q.M.S.(A./C.S.M.) A. R.	†	6872
Duffy, C.Q.M.S. H. J.	6916	Duxbury, Sjt. J.		6894
— C.S.M. J.	6895	Dyer, Sjt. E. A.		7037
— R.S.M. P.	6871	— Cpl. R. H.		6877
Dugdale, Pte. A.	6885	— Pte.(A./Cpl.) S. A.		6909
Duggan, Sjt. T. L.	6901	— Sjt.(A./C.S.M.) W.		6874
Duhig, Sjt.(T./C.Q.M.S.) T. B.	6943	Dyke, E.C.S./Sjt.(A./Supt.Clk.) E. S.		6873
Duke, Armr.S./Sjt. A. V.	6916	Dyson, R.Q.M.S. H.		7023
Dukes, Mech.S.M. A. E.	7011			
Dullage, Pte.(A./C.Q.M.S.) W.	6898	Eade, C.Q.M.S. A. M.	‡	6865
Dunbar, Cpl.(A./Sqdn.S.M.I.) F. D.	7010	Eades, S./Sjt. W. J.		7021
Duncan, Sjt. G.	6890	Eagers, Ch.Mec. A. C.		7037
— Pte.(A./Sjt.) G.	7019	Eakin, Cpl. E. H. R.		6890
— S./Sjt. G. M.	6913	Ealey, Sjt.(A./C.S.M.) A. H.	§	6874
— Cpl. J.	6892	Eallett, S./Sjt. R. B.		6907
— Pte. J.	6905	Earl, R.Q.M.S.(A./R.S.M.) G. A.		6933
— Cpl.(T./Sjt.) V. S.	6916	Earle, Ch.Mas.Mec. W. W.		7037
Dundas, B.S.M. G. W.	6869	Earnshaw, Pte. W.		6905

---

* Group known: 1914/15 Star trio (81639 2/Cpl/A-Sgt. R.E.), Defence Medal, M.S.M. (202 Field Coy. R.E.). Born 1895, enlisted in Manchester, died 1966. M.S.M. for saving company records under fire. Commissioned into Home Guard in Middlesex, rose to Captain. Led a Y.M.C.A. group mission to Sweden in 1951.

† Group known: British War and Victory Medals, War and Defence Medals, M.S.M. (R.E.) and Militia Long Service Medal (and two bars, Geo. V). Temp. Capt. R.E. 1941.

‡ R.N. M.S.M. issued 4 July 1919, withdrawn, Army M.S.M. issued 3 June 1919 (R.M.).

§ Group known: Africa General Service Medal (Somaliland 1902–04, R.E. – Signals), 1914 Star & bar trio, L.S. & G.C. (Geo. V) and M.S.M. (R.E.).

Earrey, Pnr.Sjt. G. A.	6889	Elgar, Pte.(A./Cpl.) L. K.	7021
Earwaker, Sjt. R.	6901	Elks, Cpl.(A./Sjt.) A.	6904
Easdown, S./Sjt. W. F.	6957	— Sjt. C.	6867
Eason, Pte.(L./C.) W. C.	6898	Ell, Sjt.(A./C.S.M.) A. W. (corr.)	7703
East, Cpl.(A./Sjt.) H. J.	6877	Ellams, Fitt.S./Sjt. G	6870
Eastwood, Q.M.S. C. H.	6913	Elles, Sjt.(A./C.Q.M.S.) J. P.	7012
Eaton, Cpl. A.	6887	Elliott, 2nd Cpl. C. D.	6913
— Gnr. E.	6954	— Cpl. E.	6894
— L.A.C. H. C.	7037	— Cpl.(A./Sjt.) E. G.	6877
Eayers, Cpl. F.	6877	— C.S.M. G.	6916
Eccles, C.S.M. D.	6865	— Sjt.Clk. J.	7037
— S./Sjt. H.	6957	— C.S.M. J. W.	6872
— C.Q.M.S. W.	6886	— Pte. R. S.	6905
Eddy, Sjt. J.	6902	Ellis, 2nd Cpl.(A./C.S.M.) F.	7012
Ede, Sjt.(A./Mech.S.M.) W.	* 6902	— Sjt.(A./S./Sjt.) F. J.	6934
Ede-Clendinnen, Condr. E. F.	6916	— S.M. H.	6913
Eden, Sjt. E. S.	6884	— Pte. J.	6905
Edgar, T./S.S.M. D., *D.C.M.*	6956	— Sjt. J. B. W.	6874
— Sjt. J.	6916	— Cpl. J. E.	6896
— Sjt. M. R.	6910	— Pte.(L./C.) J. T.	6905
Edgeller, Sjt. G. F.	6874	— Dvr. P. C.	❀ 6063
Edgeworth, Q.M.S. E. J.	† 7015	— E.R.A. 2nd Class P. S.	‡ 4734
Edgington, Sjt. W. J.	6908	— Pte. R. J.	6886
Edie, C.S.M. J. B. (corr.)	7703	— Pte.(A./S.Q.M.S.) W.	7022
Edmonds, Cpl.(A./Sjt.) G.	7021	— Q.M.S. W. J.	6907
— Sto.P.O. W. J.	7907	Ellison, Cpl.(A./Sjt.) H.	6908
Edwards, B.S.M. F.	6866	— Pte. W.	6905
— Pte. F.	6905	Ellor, Spr.(A./Sjt.) W. N.	6879
— A./Clr.Sjt. F. J.	7022	Ellott, Cpl. A. H.	6904
— Sjt. G.	6953	Ellsey, C.S.M. H. W.	6897
— Pte.(A./Sjt.) H. P.	6905	Ellwood, Cpl. G. W.	6877
— Sjt. H. T. C.	6919	Elmer, C.S.M. S.	6899
— Pte. L. E.	6883	Elmslie, Sjt. A. M.	7016
— Cpl. L. J.	6877	Elphick, C.S.M. P. C.	6872
— B.Q.M.S. R. W.	6867	Elton, Cpl.(A./Sjt.) J. J.	6913
— C.S.M. S.	6883	— Gnr.(L./Bombr.) W.	6869
— Sjt. S.	6957	Emanuel, A./Yeo.Sigs. A. B.	6448
Elboy, C.S.M. J.	7021	Emerson, R.S.M. W.	7015
Eley, Sjt. F. W.	6874	— Sjt. W.	6902
Elford, S./Sjt. C. R.	7021	Emerton, Cpl.(A.C.A./Sjt.) A. J.	6932
Elgar, P.O. A. E.	4735	Emery, S.M. A. C.	7037

---

* Group known in R.C.T. Museum: 1914 Star & bar trio, General Service Medal (Iraq W.O.1), 1939/45 and Africa Stars, War Medal, Indian War Service Medal, Jubilee 1935, Coronation 1937, L.S. & G.C. (Geo. V) and M.S.M. (Later Major & Q.M. R.A.S.C.).

† Awarded M.S.M. Annuity A.O. 118 July, 1946 (Northamptonshire Regt.)..

‡ Group known: 1914/15 Star (E.R.A.3 R.N.), British War and Victory Medals (E.R.A.2) and R.N. M.S.M. (Destroyer Convoys and Escorts July—November 1918), in boxes to widow. Lost overboard 19 February, 1919, his body recovered and buried at sea.

Emery, Pte. R. G.	6898	Eves, Spr.(A./C.Q.M.S.) T.	7012
Emmanuel, S./Sjt. E. (corr.)	6065	Ewald, C.S.M. F. C.	6872
Emmott, Sjt. H. G.	6902	Ewart, T./S.M. J.	6871
Enefer, C.Q.M.S. P.	7018	Ewens, Sjt. G.	6865
England, L.A.C.H. H.	7037	Ewing, Pte. J.	6905
— Pte.(A./Sjt.) W.	6957	Ewings, 2nd Cpl.(A./E.C.Sjt.) H.	6878
English, S./C.S. C. E.	6934	Ewins, Sjt.(A./C.Q.M.S.) F. J.	7012
Ennis, C.S.M. H. G.	6893	Exley, Spr. F.	6879
Ennor, T./S.M. C.	6907	Eyden, Cpl. C. F.	7037
Enticknap, Sjt. J.	6916	— R.S.M. S. J.	7013
Errington, Sjt. F.	6870	Eyles, Sjt. F.	6953
Estell, Cpl.(A./R.Q.M.S.) A	6933	Eyre, Pte. J.	6883
Etchells, Sjt. H.	6882		
Etches, S.Q.M.S. R.	6934	Facer, S.Q.M.S. T. H.	7010
Etherington, Mech.Elect.Q.M.S.		Fagg, S./Sjt. C. H.	7012
W. G.	* 7012	Faint, T./S.S.M. H., *D.C.M.*	6956
Eustace, Cpl. S. W.	6919	Fair, Shipwt. 1st Cl. W. H. G.	8069
Eustis, B.Q.M.S. G. H.	6916	Fairchild, 2nd Cpl. F. W.	6878
Evans, Sjt. A.	6944	Fairey, B.S.M. G. E.	6866
— Sjt.(A./C.Q.M.S.) A. W.	6954	— Sqdn.Q.M.S. J. D.	6866
— B.Q.M.S. B. A.	6867	Fairweather, Arm.S./Sjt. A.	6974
— S./Sjt. C. R.	6913	— Pte.(A./C.S.M.) R.	7017
— Cpl.(A./Sjt.) D. L.	6877	Faithful, Sjt. A. J.	6954
— C.S.M. F. H.	6872	Falconer, C.Q.M.S. D.	6974
— C.S.M. F. W.	6957	— Pte. D.	6892
— B.Q.M.S. G.	6867	Fama, S.S.M. L. C.	7023
— S.S.Cpl. G.	6868	Fanning, 2nd Cpl.(A./Sjt.) D.	6910
— Dvr. G. E.	6907	Fanthum, Sjt. R.	6902
— Sjt. H.	6867	Farah Dooleh, Sjt.	6971
— Cpl.(A./Q.M.S.) J.	6908	Fargher, Sjt. J. M.	6902
— Pte. J. P.	6883	Farish, Sjt.(A./C.S.M.) J.	6874
— Ch.Writer L. L.	4197	Farleigh, Cpl W. H. A.	6932
— Sjt. R. E. (H.A.C.)	6874	Farler, Pte. A.	6913
— Sjt. R. E. (N. and D.R.)	6889	Farley, Pte.(A./Sjt.) A. E.	6911
— C.Q.M.S. T.	6933	— Sjt. H.	6887
— C.S.M.(A./R.S.M.) T.	7014	Farmer, Armr.S./Sjt. A. W.	6910
— Sjt. T. E.	7019	— Sjt. H.	6910
— Engmn. W.	8202	Farmery, Sjt. A. H.	6911
— Cpl. W. J.	6896	Farnish, Pte.(A./L./Sjt.) J.	6896
Eveleigh, Ch.Mec. C. E.	7037	Faro, S./Sjt.Eng.Clk J. L. L.	6873
— T./S.S.M. L. G.	6956	Farquharson, S./Sjt. W. E.	6901
Evens, Sjt. N.	6874	Farr. Sjt. T.	6945
Everitt, Sjt. H.	7019	Farran, S./Sjt. R. S.	6901
— Pte. W.	6934	Farrell, Supt.Clk. A. J.	7011
— Pte.(A./C.S.M.Instr.)		— R.Q.M.S. F.	6890
W. A. (corr.)	6065	Farrer, L.A.C. B. F.	7037
Everson, Cpl. A	6886	Farrin, Pte. L.	6891
— Sjt.(A./W.O. CL. 2)(S.Q.M.S.)		Farrow, Mech.Electn.Q.M.S. A.	7012
C. W. (corr.)	6065	— S.M. S.	7037

---

* R.E. For Malta.

Farthing, Sjt. A.	6902	Findlay, Cpl. R. L.	6943
Fathers, Ch.Writer E. G.	7907	Fineberg, Sjt. A.	6970
Faulkner, C.S.M. P.	6881	Finer, Cpl. J.	6945
Fawcett, Pte.(A./Cpl.) A.	6905	Finlay, Ch.Ship's Cook F.	7907
Fayers, Sjt.(A./R.S.M.)A. E.	6913	— C.S.M. R. G.	6872
Fazey, C.Q.M.S. J. W.	6891	Finlayson, Sjt. R. H.	6913
Feast, F./Sjt. R. W., *D.C.M.*	* 7037	Finley, Cpl.(A./Whlr.S./Sjt.) A.	6904
Feaver, Sjt.(T./S.Q.M.S.) W. J.	6902	Finmore, Q.M.S. J.	6871
Feeney, Sjt. J.	6898	Finnemore, Sjt. A.	6882
Fellows, Cpl. B.	6904	— Cpl.(A./Sjt.) W. F.	6904
— Sjt. J.	6867	Finnie, C.S.M. D.	6913
Felton, F./Sjt.(T./S.M.) R. W.	7037	Firth, S.Q.M.S. G. E.	7018
— Pte. S.	6885	— Sjt. H. K.	6887
Fenn, Q.M.S.Instr. W.	7012	— Sjt. J. E.	6902
Fennell, C.S.M. F	6899	— Pte.(A./C.Q.M.S.) R.	6887
— R.Q.M.S. S.	6887	— Cpl.(A./Sjt.) R. E.	6868
Fenton, S.S.M. A. T.	7023	— Sjt.(A./R.Q.M.S.) W.	6884
— W.O. Cl. 1, J. P.	7022	Fischer, R.Q.M.S. F. J. G.	6913
Fenwick, T./Sub Condr. R. J.	6909	Fisher, Pte.(L./C.) A.	6911
Ferglisson, Sjt. A. P.	6902	— F./Sjt. A. J.	7037
Ferguson, C.Q.M.S. A.	6919	— Cpl. D. G.	6904
— B.Q.M.S. E. B.	6932	— Sjt. E. D.	6874
— Sjt.(A./S.M.) H.	7012	— C.S.M. F.	6889
— Cpl.(A./Sjt.) J.	6933	— T./S.M. F. H.	6871
— Sjt. J. R.	6874	— Pte. H. (corr.)	6065
— Q.M.S.(A.C.) W.	7011	— Spr.(A./2nd Cpl.) J.	6879
Ferneyhough, Cpl. C.	6868	— Pte. J. A.	6883
Fernihough, Pte.(L./C.) J. J.	6958	— Spr. M.	6919
Ferrer, Cpl. A.	6893	— Sjt. R. E.	6916
Fidler, Cpl.(A./S.M.) H.	6870	— Sjt. S.	6870
Fido, Pte. W.	6957	Fitch, Condr. C. M.	6970
Fiegehen, C.Q.M.S. A. L., *M.M.*	6945	— Q.M.S. G.	6913
Field, Sjt. P., *M.M.*	6887	Fitt, C.Q.M.S. G.	6890
— Mech.S./Sjt. W.	6873	— F. of W. Q.M.S. P. W.	7012
Fieldwick, Cpl. A. G.	6893	Fitter, Sjt. E.	6888
Fife, Pte. W.	6905	Fitton, C.S.M. B.	6956
— Sjt. W. B.	6955	— Sjt. R.	6865
Figures, Armt.S./Sjt. W. S.	6910	Fitzbucke, Sjt. E. G.	6913
Fides, Cpl.(A./Sjt.A.C.) C. H.	6870	Fitzgerald, Sjt. G.	6895
— Cpl.(A./C.S.M.) T.	6904	— P.O. H. A. F.	7512
Filtness, R.S.M. C.	7017	— Sjt.(A./Sqdn.S.M.) J.	6911
Fincham, Cpl.(A./Sjt.) E. F.	6957	— C.Q.M.S.(A./R.S.M.) J.	7018
Finchcombe, C.Q.M.S. E. E.	6872	Fizelle, C.Q.M.S. J. W.	6872
Findlay, Pte.(L./C.) F.	6893	Flack, Sjt. G. F.	6910
— Pte.(A./Cpl.) P. L.	6886	Flanders, Farr.Sjt. E. D.	6874

---

* Group known: D.C.M. (Victoria, *L.G.* 2 August 1900, Cpl. 5 Dragoon Gds.), Queen's South Africa Medal (Natal, Transvaal, Orange Free State), King's South Africa Medal (both Cpl. 7 D.G.), British War and Victory Medals (Flt Sgt. R.A.F.), Coronation 1911 (Metropolitan Police Reverse) and R.A.F. M.S.M. (9092—I Force, France).

Flannagan, Cpl.Sig. M.	6868	Ford, Sjt. E. M.	6954
Flannery, C.S.M. J.	6889	— T./S.S.M. G.	6899
Flavin, Pte.(A./R.Q.M.S.) E. J.	6913	— Sjt. G. E.	6933
Fleet, Sjt. E. H.	7014	— B.S.M. J. T.	6869
— Cpl.(A./Sjt.) W. R.	7012	— E.R.Cpl.(T./S.Q.M.S.) P. O.	6916
Fleming, Sjt. J.	6892	— T./S.M. W. H.	7020
— A./R.S.M. J.	7022	— Sjt. W. J.	6913
— Cpl. J.	6904	Fordham, Sjt. D.	7017
— Cpl.(A./Sjt.) R.	6913	Foreman, F./Sjt. R. L. M.	7037
Fletcher, Pte.(L./C.) A. B.	6905	Forrest, Sjt. J. A.	6883
— O.R.Sjt. F. W.	7014	Forrester, C.S.M. A. P.	6872
— C.S.M. J.	6885	— Gnr. J. ✿	6064
— Sjt. J. W.	6885	Forshaw, T./S.M. W	6871
— C.S.M. N. J.	6954	Forster, R.S.M. B. G. C., *D.C.M.*	6913
— C.Q.M.S. S. A.	6872	— Q.M.S.(A./S.M.) E. J.	7020
— B.S.M.(A./R.S.M.) T. B.	6866	— Farr.Q.M.S. G. A. *	6866
— Sjt.(A./S./Sjt.) W.	6934	— Pte.(L./C.) J.	6905
Flete, E.C. 2nd Cpl.(A./Sjt.) R. J.	6878	Forsyth, Sjt. J.	6868
Flight, Condr E.	7021	— Sjt. J. R.	7023
Flint, Sjt. L. E.	6911	Forsythe, Sjt. J.	6913
Florance, Pte. E. G.	6905	Fortune, Ch.Mec. J.	7037
Flowerday, Cpl.(L./Sjt.) W.	6883	Fosbury, Sjt. J.	7021
Flowers, C.S.M. A.	6882	Fosdick, Spr. S. J.	6916
Floyd, Sjt. H.	6874	Fosh, Pte.(T./Cpl.) J. A.	6909
Fluck, A./Sub Condr. T. A.	6913	Foss, Sjt. A. E.	6902
Flux, T./Supt.Clk. T. W., *D.C.M.*	6871	Foster, Sqdn.Q.M.S.(A./C.S.M.) A.	7018
Flynn, Sjt.(A./C.S.M.) J.	6902	— Sjt. G. (Aust. F.A.)	6916
— Sjt. J. P.	6881	— Sjt. G. (R.A.F.)	7037
— Sjt.(A./M.S.M.) M. J.	6902	— Sjt. G. C.	6874
Foard, Pte.(A./Sjt.) A. H.	6909	— Sjt. H. J.	6902
Foghill, Sqdn.S.M.(A./		— Cpl. J.	6888
R.S.M.) S. W.	7010	— Pte.(A./S.Q.M.S.) J. A.	7017
Foley, Sjt. J.	6883	— Dvr. J. W.	6869
Folland, Engr.Clk.S./Sjt. V. M.	7012	— Sjt. W.	6870
Follett, C.S.M. S. H.	7013	Foulkes, S./Sjt. T. F.	6934
Fooks, Whr.Cpl. E. H.	6868	Fowkes, C.Q.M.S. J. E. †	7015
Foott, Sjt. J. O.	6889	Fowler, Sjt. H.	6913
Ford, Pte. A.	6888	— R.S.M. R. S.	6913
— C.S.M. C.	6893	— Pnr.(A./Cpl.) R.W.	6880
— S.Q.M.S. C. W.	7022	Fowles, T./S.M. F.	6907

---

* George Alex Forster, Farrier Q.M. Northumberland Huss. Valuable Service France & Flanders. Details from Regt. History: This old regular N.C.O. has done most meritorious service throughout the campaign. Having 31 years service, practically unbroken, he has rarely been away from duty during the war. Many times has been obliged to work under great difficulties and danger, and in a special instance out of many similar ones, was the devotion to duty showed during a period of heavy shelling on October 24th in the vicinity of Le Câteau when the Regt. was working on the XIII Corps Front.

† Hampshire Regt. For West Africa.

Fowles, F./Sjt. G. C.	* 7037	Free, Dvr. K.	6907
Fox, Sjt. A. E.	6933	Freman, Sjt.(A./C.Q.M.S.) A.	6943
— Warrt. Offr. E. A.	† 7037	— T./S.M. C.	6871
— Pte. G. F.	6893	— Pte.(A./Mech.S.M.) F. C.	7019
— Pnr.(L./C.) H. G.	6880	— Sjt. J. H.	6902
— Condr. J.	7021	— Pte.(A./Cpl.) W. C.	6896
— C.Q.M.S. O.	6889	Freeth, Ldg.Sea Fritz Henry	7907
— Pte. W.	6880	French, B.S.M. A.	6866
— Amr.S./Sjt. W. H.	6913	— C.Q.M.S. F. (corr.)	7703
Foy, 2nd Cl.Asst.Surg. F. H.	7021	— A.B. W. T.	7907
— Sjt. H.	6885	Freshwater, F./Sjt. A. G.	7037
— Sjt.(A./C.S.M.) J.	7016	Frewin, B.Q.M.S. C. H.	6867
Fraley, T./S.S.M. E. T.	7018	— Sjt. O.	6944
Frampton, Sjt. E. C. W.	6902	Fricker, C.S.M. A. W.	6916
France, 2nd Cpl. W. G.	6878	— Cpl. W. L.	6890
Francis, Sjt. A. E.	6902	Friday, L.A.C.(A./Cpl.) G. R.	7037
— S./Sjt.(A./S.M.) C.	7022	Friend, Pte.(A./L./C.) D. W.	6889
— Sjt.(A./C.S.M.) G. H., *M.M.*	7012	Frith, Pte.(A./Sjt.) E.	6905
— Sjt. H.	6874	Froome, Sqdn.S.M.(A./	
— R.S.M. J.	6886	R.Q.M.S.) G.	7010
— Sjt. R. H.	6874	Frost, Pte. F.	6884
— Cpl.(A./Sjt.) W.	6884	— Pte.(A./Sjt.) H. M.	6898
Frankham, S./Sjt. W. J.	6902	— Cpl.Sigr. L. W.	6870
Franklin, A./Cpl. A.	6913	Fry, Sjt. A.	.6913
— T./Sub Condr. C.	7020	— Sub Condr. F. N.	7021
— Pte. C. C. W.	6905	— Farr.Sjt. H.	6867
— Pte.(Cpl.) E.	6888	— C.S.M. R.	. 7016
— 2nd Cpl.(A./Cpl.) L.	6878	— Sjt. W.	6888
— Farr.S./Sjt. W. A.	6954	Fryar, Sjt. L.	6894
Frankling, Sjt. F. W.	‡ 6866	Fryer, S./Sjt.(A./S.S.M.) P. R.	7021
Franks, Sjt. S.	6885	Fulcher, T./S.S.M. C. H.	6899
Fraser, Cpl. A.	6898	— C.S.M.(I.M.) J. J.	7014
— Sqdn. Sjt. C.	6919	Fuller, Pte. J. W.	6911
— Sjt. D.	6908	Fullerton, Sjt. G. J.	6874
— Pte.(A./Sjt.) L.	6883	Fume, Cpl.	6970
— A.M. 1 W. McK.	7037	Funnell, Sjt. F.	6902
Frazer, C.S.M. A. E.	6891	— R.Q.M.S. F. C.	7015
— Cpl.(A./Sjt.) J. K.	7020	— Sjt. F. H.	6916
Frears, C.Q.M.S. J. H.	6887	Furlong, Cpl. E. J.	6913
Freck, T./Sub Condr. P.	6909	— Sjt. H. L.	6908

---

* Group known: Queen's South Africa Medal (Relief of Kimberley, Paadeberg), King's South Africa Medal (both R.A.M.C.), 1914/15 Star trio and R.A.F. M.S.M. (134900, for France).

† R.A.F. M.S.M. for France, to Australia Flying Corps.

‡ 614048 Sergt. 1/1st Warwickshire Battery, R.H.A. (T.F.). Flanders 1918—From 16th September till the cessation of hostilities this N.C.O. acted as B.S.M. He showed persistent gallantry and devotion to duty. His fine example in the most trying circumstances was a constant encouragement to the men, and his ability and leadership contributed greatly to the way in which the battery adapted itself to the conditions of moving warfare.

Furlong, Cpl. R. J.	6868	Garrett, Sjt. A. J.	6870
Furlonger, Farr.Sjt. C. J.	6957	Garrod, R.Q.M.S. T.	6891
— L./C. F. T.	6913	Garside, Shipwt. 1st Cl. L.	4734
Furneaux, Sjt. S. R., *M.M.*	6874	Garston, Spr. J. A.	6879
Furnell, R.S.M. H. C.	6956	Garton, Sjt.(A./C.Q.M.S.) E. E.	6874
Furness, C.Q.M.S. F.	6892	Gascoine, Sjt. A. H.	6932
Furrell, Cpl.(A./Sjt.) C. L.	6913	Gascoyne, B.Q.M.S. F. C.	7011
		Gasmier, C.Q.M.S. H. M.	6916
Gabre Gorgio, Pte.	6971	Gates, 2nd Cpl.(A./Sjt.) A. S.	6878
Galbraith, R.Q.M.S. W.	6888	— Pte. H.	6933
Gale, Q.M.S. E.	7013	— Sjt. W. H.	6902
— 2nd Cpl.(T./Sjt.) F. S.	6878	Gatrell, Cpl. G.	6888
— Sjt.(A./C.Q.M.S.) J. W.	6895	Gaukroger, Pte.(L./C.) L.	6897
— C.Q.M.S. M.	7016	Gaunt, L./C.(T./Cpl.) A. D.	6916
Gall, Cpl. J.	6904	Gaunt, Pte.(L./C.) W. H.	6905
Gallacher, A./P.O. J.	6865	Gausden, T./S.S.M. H.	7018
Gallaugher, Sjt. W.	6886	Gayfer, Sjt. S.	6874
Gallehawk, Sjt. H. R.	6887	Gaynon, P.O.Teleg. F.	4734
Galliford, Sjt. F. J.	7010	Gaynor, Pte. J. P.	6916
Gallimore, Pte. G., *M.M.*	6891	Gearing, Pte. A.	6888
Galway, C.E.R.A. 2nd Cl. F.	4197	Gearon, Mech.S./Sjt. C. F.	6873
Gambell, Sjt. A. A.	6902	Geary, Sjt.(A./C.S.M.) G. F. J.	7015
Gammon, Sjt. J. H.	6913	— Pte.(A./S.C.M.) J.	6905
Gange, R.S.M. E. W.	7014	Geddes, Pte.(A./Cpl.) F.	6970
Gardener, T./S.M. H.	6871	Gedge, Pte.(A./Sjt.) W.	6913
— C.S.M.(A./R.S.M.) W.	7702	Gee, Pte.(A./Cpl.) E. S.	6905
Gardiner, Ch.Writer A. C.	7512	— C.S.M R.	6895
— C.Q.M.S.(A./R.S.M.) A. R.	6880	Geeson, Pte.(L/C.) H. L.	6970
— Sjt. C. S.	6892	Geilern, S./Sjt. B. H.	6933
— T./R.S.M. J.	6886	Geldeard, Pte.(A./Cpl.) W. E.	6886
— Cpl. S. W.	6890	Gell, C.S.M.Instr. A. F.	6912
Gardner, Ch.Mec. G.	7037	Gemmel, T./S.S.M. A.	6933
— Sjt. G. J.	6902	Gentles, Sjt. J. A.	7023
— Sjt. W. H.	6910	George, Sjt.	6971
Garlick, Pte. H.	6909	— C.Q.M.S. E. S.	6872
Garner, T./Sub Condr. O. P. H.	6909	— Sjt. G. C.	6933
Garnett, Sjt. H.	6891	— Pte. H. W.	6913
— C.S.M. J. H.	* 6872	German, Sjt. G. W.	6910
— Sjt. P. V.	7019	— Sjt. R.	6913
Garraway, S./Sjt. H. L.	6913	Germon, C.S.M. C.	6971
Garrett, Sjt. A. G.	6888	Gerrand, Cpl.(T./Sjt.) P. A.	6919

---

* C.S.M. R.E. He volunteered in August, 1914, and early in the following year was drafted to the Dardanelles, where he saw much heavy fighting at Cape Helles, Suvla Bay, Chunuk Bair, and at the Evacuation of the Gallipoli Peninsula. He was then transferred to France, and played a prominent part in the Battles of the Somme (II), Amiens, Bapaume, and Havrincourt, where he was gassed in action in September 1918. He was awarded the Meritorious Service Medal for continuously good work throughout hostilities, also held the 1914–15 Star, and the General Service and Victory Medals, and was demobilised in January 1919. 63, Russell Street, Moss Side, Manchester.

Gerrard, C.S.M. G.	6885	Gill, E.R.Cpl. V. A.	6916
— C.Q.M.S. R.	6894	— Pte.(T./Sjt.) W. I.	6958
Giardelli, Cpl. V. A. E.	6904	— Spr.(A./2nd Cpl.) W. T.	6879
Gibb, C.Q.M.S. J.	6872	Gillard, Spr. H. J.	6879
Gibbons, C.Q.M.S. M. H.	6916	Gilleghan, Cpl. A	6877
— Cpl.(L./Sjt.) W. J.	6886	Gillespie, Pte.(L./C.) H. H.	6919
Gibbs, E.C. and D. 2nd Cpl		— Pte. J.	6883
(A./Sjt.) B. P.	6878	— Ch.Yeo.Sigs. J. B.	4734
— Cpl. G. T.	6896	— Sjt. T.	6902
— Sjt. J. W.	6957	Gillett, B.Q.M.S. F. E.	6913
Gibson, Sjt.	6971	— Pte.(T./Cpl.) W. E.	6916
— F./Sjt. C.	7037	Gillies, Sjt. C. M.	6913
— Cpl.(A./C.) C. R.	6870	Gillis, Sjt. A. L.	6913
— 2nd Cpl. J. (R.E.)	6878	Gills, Actg.C.E.R.A. 2nd Cl. N. C.	7907
— 2nd Cpl. J. (C.E.F.)	6913	Gilmoor, Sjt.(A./Q.M.S.) J. H. B.	6874
— Pte.(A./Sjt.) N.	6911	Gilmour, Bandmaster A.	7023
— S./Sjt. W.	6974	Girling, C.Q.M.S. W.	6889
— Sjt.(A./S.S.M.) W.	7019	Giza, Sjt.	6970
— Sjt. W. C.	6870	Gladdy, S.Q.M.S. F.	6899
— Ldg.Dkhnd. W. G.	4733	Gladman, Sjt. J. A.	6910
Giddins, Cpl. G. H. L.	6910	Glanton, P.O. C.	7907
Giffney, Sjt. J.	7023	Glass, B.Q.M.S. E. W.	6867
Gilbert, Cpl. A. E.	6894	— Pte. W.	6905
— Farr.Sjt. G.	6970	Glaze, Pte.(L./C.) B. C.	6882
— Cpl.(A./Sjt.) G.	6877	Gledhill, S./Sjt. J. F.	6970
— Sjt. H. T.	6916	Glen, 2nd Cpl.(A./Sjt.) J.	6878
— C.S.M.(A./R.S.M.) J.	6933	Glencorss, Sjt. C. M. G.	7023
— Sjt. J. B.	6889	Glithro, Sjt. J. J.	6874
— R.Q.M.S.(A./C.S.M.) S. H.	6895	Glover, Sjt. H. S.	7015
— Cpl. W.	6889	Goatly, C.Q.M.S. W. A.	6932
— Dvr. W.	6907	Goddard, Sjt. A.	6868
Giles, R.Q.M.S. A.	* 7013	— S./Sjt. E.	6907
— Cpl. C. H.	6913	— Cpl. W. H.	6944
— Gnr.(L./Bombr.) G.	6869	Godding, Pte. H.	6957
— S./Sjt.(A./S.M.) H. J. H.	6907	Godfrey, Sjt. A. G.	6874
— Pte.(L./C.) H. T.	6898	— Cpl.(A./S./Sjt.) C. V.	6910
— Sadd.Q.M.S. L. H.	6865	— Sjt. H.	6955
— Gnr.(A./Farr.Sjt.) P. P.	† 6976	— C.Q.M.S. J. S.	6900
— E.R.A. 1st Cl. T. W.	8069	— Sjt. P. C.	6885
Gilford, Pte.(A./S.S.M.) W. H.	7019	Godman, T./Supt.Clk. S. J.	6871
Gilks, Farr.S./Sjt. W. J.	6957	Godsmark, Sjt. A. E.	6874
Gill, S./Sjt. F.	7021	Godwin, Sjt.(A./C.Q.M.S.) E. J.	7017
— F./Sjt. J. H.	7037	— B.S.M. E. J.	6866
— Dvr. L. H.	6907	— 2nd Cpl.(T./Sjt.) P. A.	6878
— R.S.M. S.	7010	— Sjt. R. J.	6946

---

* Group known: D.C.M. (15443 S.S.M. 18 Bn. I.Y.) (*L.G.* 27.9.01 A.O./15/02), Afghanistan Medal (no clasp, Queen's Hussars), Queen's South Africa Medal, L.S. & G.C. (Victoria), M.S.M., Volunteer Long Service Medal (Edw. VII) and Territorial Efficiency Medal (Geo. V).

† R.F.A. For Aden.

Godwin, Cpl. R. S.	6910	Gostling, Sjt. H. V.	6910
Goff, S./Sjt. S. G.	6910	Gough, Sjt. A. E.	6884
Goldrick, Sjt. D. E.	6916	— Sjt. H. T.	6882
Goldsmith, F./Sjt. J.	7037	Gould, Sjt.(A./R.S.M.) A.	7014
Goldsworthy, Pte. W. T.	7015	— Pte.(A./S.Q.M.S.) A.	6866
Goldthorpe, Cpl. W.	6904	— Sjt. L. McL.	6913
Gollan, Spr. T. H. B. ✿	7702	— Sjt. W. J.	6917
Golland, C.S.M.Instr. A.	6912	Gourlay, C.Q.M.S. J., McK.	6886
Gomani, Sjt.	6971	Gover, Mech.Electn.Q.M.S. J. O. E.	7012
Gomer, Mech.S./Sjt.(A/Q.M.S.) P. W.	6873	Gow, Gnr. J.	6871
Gonsalves, C.Q.M.S. M. A.	6919	Gowan, Cpl. E. G.	6868
Gooch, Cpl. E. A.	6904	Gower, Sjt.(A./C.S.M.) E.	6885
Good, Cpl. W A.	6877	— B.S.M. H. J.	7011
Goodall, S./Sjt.(A./Q.M.S.) G.	6907	Gowers, Sjt.(A./R.S.M.) G. L.	6886
Goodchild, Sjt. G. R.	6944	Grace, L./C. E. C.	6917
Goode, Sjt. C.	6955	Gracey, Dvr.(A./Sjt.) R.	6970
— Sqdn.S.M. S.	7018	Grady, Pte. P.	6905
— Sjt. W A.	6894	Graham, Pte. A	6970
Gooderson, Ch.Sto. F. L.	7512	— Sjt. A. H.	6890
Goodey, S.S.M. W.	7018	— Sjt. G. M.	6913
Goodfellow, R.Q.M.S. G. W.	7010	— Sjt. H.	7013
Gooding, S./Sjt.(A./S.M.) C.	6934	— S./Sjt. J.	6907
— Sjt.(A./C.Q.M.S.) F.	6943	— Cpl.(A./Sjt.) J.	6882
— Sjt. W. H.	6898	— Cpl. J. H.	6908
Goodlad, Dkhnd. R.	4732	— C.S.M. L. W.	6917
Goodland, Pte.(A./Sjt.) P. H. E.	6880	— Pte. M.	7907
Goodman, Q.M.S. A. G.	7016	— Sjt. P. J.	6919
— Whlr.S./Sjt. A. H.	6900	— Cpl. T.	6904
Goddricke, C.Q.M.S. S. E.	6943	— R.Q.M.S. T. R.	6913
Goodridge, Mech.S./Sjt. H. R.	6900	— Spr.(A./Sjt.) W.	7012
Goodson, Cpl.(A./C.Q.M.S.) G. A.	6890	— Pte. W. M.	6897
Goodwin, T./W.O. Cl. 1, C. A.	7022	Grainger, C.S.M. A. G.	7012
— C.Q.M.S. J. L.	6891	— Pte. W. H. ✿	7702
— Sjt. J. T.	6908	Grandy, S./Sjt. D.	6907
— Sjt. R. I.	6870	Grange, R.S.M. C. H.	7017
— B.S.M. W. E.	6953	Grant, Pte. C. S.	6913
— Pte. W. I.	6889	— Pte.(A./Cpl.) D. J.	7017
Goold, Sjt. W. D.	6913	— Ch.Mec. J.	7037
Gordon, Pte. D.	6956	— Q.M.S. S. J.	7014
— Pte.(L./C.) D. R.	6892	— Pte.(A./Cpl.) T. M.	6909
— T./W.O. Cl. 1, H. B. G.	7022	Grapps, Cpl.(A./Sjt.) H.	6888
— C.Q.M.S. J.	6894	Grave, Sjt. J.	6933
— Pte.(T./Cpl.) J. F.	6917	Graveley, R.Q.M.S. W. K.	6913
— Sjt. J. F.	6895	Gravener, Sjt. J.	6870
— T./S./Sjt.(A./Sub Condr.) W.	6958	Graves, R.S.M. H.	6956
Gore, T./S.S.M. A. R.	7018	— Cpl.(L./Sjt.) S.	6890
Goring, S.Q.M.S. L. T.	6899	— Sjt. T. H.	6895
Gorst, S./Sjt. F. A.	6917	Gray, B.S.M. A.	6866
Gosley, Pte. H. F.	7019	— S./Sjt. A. N.	7019
Gosling, Sjt. A. W.	6870	— T./S.M. A. S., *MM.*	6871
Gosney, Pte. R. T.	6897	— C.Q.M.S. G.	7023
Gostling, C.S.M.(A./R.S.M.) F.	7013	— Sjt. D. R.	6913

Gray, Sjt. G. (corr.)	7703	Greenwood, Pte.(L./C.) H.	6884
— Cpl. H.	6877	— Pte. L. E.	6913
— Sjt. J.	6953	— Sjt. T.	6880
— Spr. J.	6879	— Q.M.S. W. E.	7014
— C.Q.M.S. R.	6873	Greet, Ch.Writer, W. C.	7512
— Bombr. W. H.	6868	Gregory, E.C. 2nd Cpl.(A./Sjt.) F. W.	6878
— Sjt. W. J.	6956	— Cpl. H.	6896
Greaves, Cpl. B.	6904	— Pte.(A./S./Sjt.) P.	7020
Greedy, Pte.(A./Cpl.) W. H.	6887	— Cpl. R.	6883
Greef, Sjt. J. P.	6970	— L.A.C. R. W.	7037
Green, Cpl.(A./Sjt.) A.	6894	— F./Sjt. S.	7037
— T./Mech.S.M. A. A.	6945	— Cpl.(L./Sjt.) T. H.	6957
— C.S.M. A. E.	6872	Greig, C.S.M.(T./R.S.M.) J.	6892
— Sjt. A. H.	6910	— Sjt. J.	6895
— Pte.(L./C.) A. J.	6911	— Sjt. J. C.	7023
— Q.M.S. B. A.	6907	— C.Q.M.S. R.	6888
— S.Q.M.S. C.	7023	Grey, Pte. S. H.	6888
— T./S.S.M. C. E.	7018	Grier, Pte. J.	6897
— Cpl.(A./Sjt.) D. M.	6908	Griffin, Pte. C. R.	6893
— Sjt. F.	6887	— Dvr.(L./C.) R. H.	6880
— C.P.O. H.	8069	Griffith, Cpl.(A./Sjt.) A.	7037
— Sjt. J. A.	6868	— 2nd Cpl.(A./Sjt.) O. H.	7012
— C.Q.M.S. J. F.	7018	Griffiths, Sjt. A. T. (R. Berks R.)	6889
— Engmn. J. L.	4197	— Sjt. A. T. (R.A.S.C.)	6902
— Sjt. J. W.	6854	— Sjt. C. W.	6945
— Sjt.(A./C.S.M.) L. E.	* 6874	— Mech.S./Sjt. F. F.	6900
— Cpl. T. H.	6904	— Pte. H.	6905
— Sjt. T. W.	6892	— S.Q.M.S. J.	6899
— C.Q.M.S. W. E.	6885	— Sjt.(A/S./Sjt.) R. W.	7019
— Sjt. W. P.	6911	— Pte.(L./C.) T. J.	6911
Greene, T./Mech.S.M. J.	6933	— Q.M.S. W. A.	6907
Greenhorn, C.Q.M.S. A.	6913	— Sjt.(A./C.Q.M.S.) W. C. H.	6887
Greenstock, B.S.M. A.	7010	— Er./W.O. Cl. 1, W. E.	6917
Greenwood, Sjt. A.	6902	Grigg, Sjt. M. H.	6919
— Spr. A	6954	Grigge, Pte. J. J. C.	6946
— Sjt. F. E.	6874	Griggs, C.Q.M.S. W.	7017
— Pte. H.	6894	Grills, Ch.Writer T.	6865

* Group known in Moss collection: D.C.M. (Geo. V, Serjt. 47 Div. Signal Coy. R.E. T.F.) 1914/15 Star (Serjeant), British War and Victory Medals (A./C.Q.M.S.), M.S.M. and Territorial Efficiency Medal (Geo. V, Serjeant, London Div. R.E.). A Territorial soldier, Green and 2/Lond. Div. Sig. Coy. arrived in France on 9 March, 1915 and moved into the Ypres sector taking part in the Battle of Aubers on 9 May, 1915 and again seeing action of Festubert from 15 to 25 May. Shortly afterwards, his D.C.M. was gazetted on 3 June 1915 'For consistent gallantry and good work when maintaining telegraphic communications, notably during a period of heavy bombardment.' His Territorial Efficiency Medal for 12 years service (war service counting double) was awarded during this period. The company saw active service up until November 1918, with Green rising through C.Q.M.S. to C.S.M. being at various times at Loos, Messines, Cambrai, Bapaume, Amiens, Albert and the Pursuit to Mons.

Grimes, C.Q.M.S. J. A.	6887	Gunn, Dvr. W. W.		6869
Grimsdell, Cpl. F. W.	6887	Gunnell, C.S.M.(A./C.Q.M.S.) F.		6886
— Farr.Sjt. J.	6867	— C.S.M. F. C.		6888
Grimsditch, R.Q.M.S. E.	6895	Gunning, 2nd Cpl. E.		6878
Grimwood, S.S.M. A. C., *D.C.M.*	6899	Gunther, Sjt. W. H.		6890
— Sjt. H.	6894	Guppy, Sjt. C. W.	§	6976
Grindrod, R.Q.M.S. E., *M.M.*	6881	Gurney, T./S.S.M. E		6899
Grisdale, Sjt. W. J.	6883	— Sjt. L. W.		6870
Grisley, Sjt. W. C.	6902	Gurr, C.Q.M.S.(A./R.S.M.) G. F.	+	7021
Grognet, Sjt. S. S.	* 6945	Gutteridge, Pte.(A./Cpl.) T. F.		6909
Groom, Farr.Sjt. W. A.	6942	Guy, Sjt. D. S.		6913
Groome, Sjt C. E.	6874	— Pte.(A./L./Sjt.) F.		7010
Gronow, Pte.(A./Cpl.) W E.	6897	— Pte.(A./C.S.M.) L.		7021
Grose, Sjt. S. N. W.	6917	Guyton, 2nd Hnd. R. E.		4732
Grove, Sjt.(A./C.S.M.) T.	6894	Gwatkin, C.Q.M.S. F W. S.		6873
Grover, Sjt. G. J.	7013	Gwynne, Sjt. W.		6890
— C.S.M. J.	7017			
Groves, C.S.M.(A./R.S.M.) E.	† 7017	Hack, R.Q.M.S. M. S.		6893
— Pte.(A./Sjt.) P. H.	6893	Hackett, T./R.S.M. E. C.		6893
Grundy, Master Gnr. 3rd Cl. T. G. B.	7011	— Pte. F. E.		6885
Guckin, Bombr. T.	6868	— Pte.(L./C.) G. W.		6911
Gude, C.S.M.(A./R.S.M.) G. G.	7017	— Sjt. H.		6944
Guering, T./R.S.M.)	7017	Hackman, S./Sjt. G. T.		6910
Guest, C.S.M.(A./R.S.M.)		Hackwill, Sjt.(A./C.Q.M.S.) G. W.		7017
J. J., *D.C.M.*	7013	Haddleton, Spr. W.		6879
— C.Q.M.S.(A./S.M.) T. H. H.	6873	Hadley, Q.M.S. F. W.		6882
Guinn, Pte. R.	6892	— Sjt.(A./C.S.M.) G.		6955
Guled Kahin, Sjt.	6971	— Sdlr.S./Sjt. H. J.		6870
Gummer, 1st Cl. Army		Haedaker, C.Q.M.S. R.		6884
Schoolmaster H. S.	‡ 7021	Hagerud, Spr. G.		6913
Gumsley, T./S.M. G. W.	6932	Haggar, Sjt. J. T.		6889

* Severin Stephen Grognet, from Anglo-French family. Four brothers served in W.W.I. Group in McInnes collection: 1914/15 Star trio (M.I.D. oakleaf, Sgt. Manchester Regt.) Defence and War Medals and M.S.M. (24th Manchesters). An Oldham man who served in the 'Oldham Pals,' a painter & decorator previously. Served in France & Flanders and Italy. Demobilised 22 March 1919. In W.W.II he served in the U.K. in R.A.S.C. M.I.D. twice, *L.G.* 30 May 1918 and 3 June 1918, for Italy. M.S.M. citation: 'As Transport Sgt. he displayed great courage in the front line, keeping his company supplied with all necessary material, rations and equipment. He was an inspiration to all.' Died in 1970.

† Awarded M.S.M. Annuity A.O.92/1948. Royal Scots Fusiliers. Also awarded M.M.

‡ C. of A.S. For Gibraltar.

§ Group known: M.S.M. for Aden: 1914/15 Star (Sergt. 3/Gde., I.U. List), British War and Victory Medals (5662117 S./Sgt. I.U.L., M.I.D. oakleaf *L.G.* 7.4.19 for Aden, 8554 Pte. (A./Sgt.) 2nd Bn. Somerset L.I. att'd. C.M.S.C. and *L.G.* 23.7.20 Sgt. C.M.S.C. I.A. Aden Field Force), India General Service Medal (Afghanistan N.W.F. 1919, 5662117 Sgt. C.M.S.C., M.I.D. *L.G.* 3.8.20 Afghanistan Command and Staff), L.S. & G.C. (Geo. V, fixed susp., S./Sgt. I.C.C.) and M.S.M. (C. of M.S.C., I.A.). Promoted to Conductor, Indian Army Corps of Clerks, 16 Feb 1932.

+ Pair known: L.S. & G.C. (Edw. VII, C./Sgt. R. Irish Regt.) and M.S.M. (M.P.S.C.).

Haggarty, Sjt. H.	6886	Halling, Cpl.(A./Q.M.S.) H. W.	6870
Hagger, Sjt. C. C.	6894	Hallows, Pte.(L./C.) H.	6955
— Sjt. S. H.	6874	Halls, Sjt. W. J.	6943
Haigh, Sjt. L. G.	6913	Halpin, Sjt. G.	6880
— R.Q.M.S. W.	6883	Halsall, C.S.M. T.	7012
Hailey, C.Q.M.S. J. G.	6873	Halsey, Pte. E. L.	6905
Hainsworth, Pte.(A./L./C.) E. V.	6884	Halton, Spr. W. S.	6954
— Air Mech. 1st Cl. F.	6504	Hamban Doma, R.S.M.	6970
Haldane, Pte. H. B.	6889	Hambleton, Sjt. T.	6943
Hale, Cpl.(A./Sjt.) T. J.	6904	Hamblin, Sjt.(A./C.Q.M.S.) W. T.	7019
Hales, Sjt. A.	6956	Hamblyn, Pte.(A./Cpl.) A. M.	7011
— Sjt. J.	6888	Hamilton, Sjt. J.	6913
Haley, Sjt.(T./C.S.M.) U. A. J.	6917	— Sjt. J. G.	6892
Halford, Ch.Arm. C. J.	5112	— Sjt. K. W.	6913
— C.S.M. W. G.	6899	— Sjt. W.	6913
— Pte. W. H.	6890	— Pte. W.	6891
Haliburton, C.Q.M.S. R. L.	6913	— Sjt. W. F.	6913
Halksworth, Sjt. J. F. M.	6902	Hamister, L./Sjt. G. H.	6917
Hall, C.S.M. A.	7014	Hamlin, F./Sjt. H.	7037
— Pte. A. C.	6905	Hamlyn, Sjt. W. H.	6875
— Pte.(A./Sjt.) A. P.	6911	Hammond, S./Sjt.(A./Q.M.S.) F. J.	6907
— Pte.(A./S./Sjt.) E. C.	7020	— Sjt. F. R.	6902
— T./Sub Condr. E. H.	6909	— S./Sjt. G.	6901
— P.O. E. W.	8069	— Sjt. G. W.	6889
— S.B.S. F. T.	4735	— B.Q.M.S. H.	6867
— Sjt. G.	6881	— Sjt. H.	6970
— Bombr.(A./C.) H. F.	7011	— 2nd Writer H. E.	5112
— Gnr.(A./Cpl.) H. J.	6943	— Sjt. T.	7023
— Pte. H. W.	6891	— R.S.M. W. J.	7010
— S./Sjt. J. (R.A.S.C.)	6901	Hamnette, Cpl. R. J.	6877
— S./Sjt. J. (R.A.M.C.)	7020	Hampshire, Pte. W.	6897
— Spr.(L./C.) J.	6879	Hampson. R.Q.M.S. A. W.	6883
— Spr.(L./C.) J. S.	6879	— Sjt. W.	6902
— Pte. J. W.	6903	Hampton, S.M. J. F.	6907
— Sjt. R.	6870	— R.S.M. W. E.	7011
— E.R.A. 2nd Cl. R. F. E.	7512	Hanbury, Sjt.(A./S.M.) A. E.	7012
— F. of W Q.M.S. S. H.	6871	Hancock, C.Q.M.S. C. E.	6873
— C.P.O. T.	4198	— Sjt. F. C.	7037
— Spr.(A./S.M.) T. W.	7012	— S.M. L. H., *M.C.*	* 6899
— Spr.(L./C.) V.	6879	— Q.M.S. R.	7012
— R.Q.M.S. W.	6891	Handford, Cpl. W. T.	6904
— Pte.(L./C.) W. A.	6944	Handley, Cpl. R. W.	6904
— Cpl. W. F.	6868	Hands, T./R.S.M. W.	6866
— C.Q.M.S.(A./S.M.) W. G.	6873	Handy, Spr. A.	6954
— Farr.Sjt. W. G.	6953	— S.Q.M.S. F. (corr.)	7703
— 2nd Cpl.(T./C.S.M.) W. J.	6878	Haney, Sjt. D.	6954
Halliday, C.Q.M.S. C. E.	6873	Hanlon, C.Q.M.S. P. J.	6887
— R.Q.M.S. I.	7014	— Sjt. W	6885
— C.Q.M.S. J. D.	6900		

* A.S.C. M.C. *L.G.* 18 February, 1915.

Hann, Cpl. of Horse C. L.	* 6881	Harris, Pte. E. C.	6890
— C.S.M. G. P.	6865	— C.S.M. F.	7018
Hannaford, Cpl. S. R.	6877	— C.Q.M.S. F. E.	6881
Hannant, Ch.Sto. Henry (corr. of		— Cpl.(A./Sjt.) F. J.	6970
surname)	6450	— Sjt.(A./M.E.S./Sjt.) H. E.	7012
— C.S.M. W.	6957	— Pte. J.	6944
Hanrahan, M.A.A. P. J.	7907	— R.Q.M.S. J. M.	6894
Hanworth, C.Q.M.S. F., *D.C.M.*	6885	— Dvr. J. W.	6869
Harbridge, R.Q.M.S. G. H.	7015	— R.S.M. R. E.	6914
Harbot, S.M. A. E.	7037	— T./S.M. T., *D.C.M.*	6871
Harbron, R.Q.M.S. E.	6956	— Mech.S./Sjt. W.	6933
Hard, Er./S.Q.M.S. A. G.	6917	— W.O. Cl. 1, W. A.	7022
— C.S.M. J. F.	6872	— C.S.M. W. J.	6872
— S.S.M. T.	7021	— Sjt. W. T.	6887
Hardie, Er./S./Sjt. A. E.	6917	Harrison, C.P.O. C.	7907
Hardiman, Sjt. A.	6913	— Sjt. C. A.	6896
Harding, Cpl.(A./Sjt.) A.	6943	— Cpl. F.	7037
— R.Q.M.S. C. G.	7016	— Sjt. F. P.	6908
— Ch.Writer E.	7512	— Sjt. F. T.	6902
— F. of W. S./Sjt. J.	6873	— Mech.S./Sjt. H. G.	6900
— Sjt. J. J.	6944	— R.Q.M.S. J.	7014
Hardingham, R.S.M. J. P.	7016	— Sjt. J.	6908
Hardwick, C.S.M. H.	6889	— Sjt. J. H.	6914
— Sjt. R. W.	6913	— Sjt. R.	6902
Hardy, L.A.C. M. E.	7037	— C.S.M. T. W.	6899
Hare, Sjt.(A./C.S.M.) G.	6882	— Sjt. W.	6914
— Sjt. G. A.	6875	— R.Q.M.S. W. E.	7014
Harford, Sjt. C. W.	7010	— Pte. W. J.	6934
Hargreaves, Condr. F. W.	7021	Harsant, S./S.M. A. R.	6956
— Pte.(A./Cpl.) J.	6888	Harsley, Sjt. F.	6894
Harkess, Pte.(L./Cpl) G. R.	6909	Hart, T./R.S.M. A. H. C.	6886
Harman, C.S.M. E.	6899	— Sjt. C.	6919
— S./Sjt. F. W.	6933	— Pte.(L./C.) C. A.	6957
— Sjt. S. L.	6913	— Sjt. E. W.	6917
Harmer, Sjt. J.	6875	— Spr. H.	6879
Harmon, C.Q.M.S. S.	6886	— S./Sjt.(A./S.M.) J. A.	6907
Harned, Pte. E. J.	6913	— T./Supt.Clk. S. A.	6871
Harnett, Pte. W. J.	6943	— Q.M.S. T. D.	7015
Harper, Engmn. A. G. B.	6447	— R.Q.M.S. W. B.	6897
— C.Q.M.S. J. H.	6873	— C.Q.M.S. W. F. C.	6886
— Sjt. T. W.	6944	Harte, Cpl.(A/C.Q.M.S.) P.	6932
Harratt, Spr. C. E.	6917	Hartenstein, L./C. E.	6917
Harrington, Pte.(L./C.) T.	6909	Hartley, Sjt. F.(R.A.S.C.)	6902
— Pte. W. F.	6893	— Sjt. F. (Aust. F.A.)	6917
Harris, Ch.Writer A. C.	6865	Harverson, Pte.(A./C.Q.M.S.) W. W.	7018
— Sjt. E. A.	6885	Harvey, S./S.M. A.	6887

* Group was in McInnes collection: 1914/15 Star (erased), British War Medal (Cpl. of Horse R.H.G.), Victory Medal (erased), L.S. & G.C. (fixed suspension, W.O.II R.H.G.) and M.S.M. (Guards Machine Gun Regt.). Served in 3 (R.H.G.) Bn. G.M.G.R., No. 5566, was 1526 in R.H.G., later 304154. From East Peckham.

Harvey, C.Q.M.S.(T./R.Q.M.S.) A. P.	6917	Hayes, Sjt. F.		6875
— Sjt. A. J.	6910	— Pte. F. W.		6897
— Sjt. A. W.	6902	— E.C. & D. Spr.(A./Sjt.) H. A.		6879
— Sjt. G. A.	6875	— C.Q.M.S. H. W.		6873
— Sjt. J.	6888	— Sjt.(A./C.Q.M.S.) J.		6875
— Spr.(A./Sjt.) J.	6879	— Pte. W. C.		6906
— Sjt. R.	6889	— C.Q.M.S. W. H.		6873
— Sjt. T.	6889	Hayes-Jones, Pte. F.		6906
— Q.M.S. W.	7012	Hayman, C.Q.M.S. C. F.		7018
Harwood, Sjt. A. H.	6875	Hayne, Q.M.S. W. B. J.		6871
— T./S.S.M. A. H.	6899	Haynes, C.Q.M.S. A. H.		6895
— Pte.(A./Cpl.) W.	6911	— C.S.M.(R.Q.M.S.) F. W.		6891
Haskens, Sjt. W. E.	6970	— Pte.(A./Sjt.) H. V.		7019
Haskins, Sjt. T. H.	6944	— Cpl(A./S.S.M.) T. H.		7019
Hassard, Cpl. A. B.	6896	— Cpl. W. J.		6904
— Cpl.(A./S.M.) H. W.	6970	Hayter, Pte. F. W.		6906
Hastings, Sjt. F.	6902	— C.S.M. H. J.		6899
— C.Q.M.S. H. W.	6873	Hayward, Pte. J.		6914
Hastwell, Sjt. J. R.	6881	— Sjt. P. G.		6889
Hatch, Pte. F. G.	6906	— Cpl.(A./Sjt.) P. H.		6955
Hatcher, Dvr. A. G.	6869	— B.S.M. W. H.		6943
Hatherley, Pte. A. A.	6917	Hazel, Sjt. H. W.		6868
Hatton, Cpl. G. B.	6904	Hazley, Sjt. J. H.		6886
Havard, C.S.M. G.	6914	Head, Dvr. E. E.		6907
Havelock, Cpl. E. C.	6877	— Pte. T. C.		6909
Haw, Sjt. Drmr. R. J.	6889	— C.Q.M.S. W. A.		6919
Haward, Sjt.(A./C.Q.M.S) L. E.	7017	Heald, T./Sub Condr. H.		6909
Hawes, S./Sjt. G. H.	6919	Heale, C.Q.M.S. F. J.		6898
— Cpl. W. de C.	6914	Healey, Pte.(L/C.) J. W.		6906
Hawker, Pte.(A./Cpl.) E. G.	6911	— Sjt. P.		6891
Hawkeswood, Cpl.(A./Sjt.) D. H.	6890	Healy, Sjt. J.		7012
Hawkings, Sjt. E.	6957	Heaney, Q.M.S. J.		7016
Hawkins, Sjt. A. C.	6875	Heap, Cpl.(A./Sjt.) B.		6914
— Mech.S./Sjt. A. V.	6900	— C.S.M.(A./R.S.M.) J.		7013
— T./S.S.M. F.	7018	— Q.M.S. L.		6907
— B.S.M. F. N.	6869	Heard, R.Q.M.S. F. W.		6884
— Spr. G.	6879	Hearn, Q.M.S.(A./S.M.) C. G.		7020
— Sjt. I.	7013	— Pnr. T.		6954
— Sjt. S. W.	6875	Heasman, Pte. S. P.		6914
Hawkless, L./C. E.	6917	Heath, 2nd Cpl. A.McL.		6919
Hawley, Pte. T. M.	6892	— C.S.M. W. J.	*	7011
Hay, Q.M.S. C.	6914	Heatley, Sjt. W.		6875
— Sjt. G.	6914	Heaton, Gnr.(L./Bombr.) N. H.		7011
— C.E.R.A. 1st Cl. J.	8203	Heaven, Sjt.(A./C.S.M.) F.		6945
— Sjt. J.	6886	Hedge, B.S.M. W. J.		6866
Haydock, S.Q.M.S. J.	6899			

---

* Trio known: British War Medal, L.S. & G.C. (Geo. V) and M.S.M. (for Hong Kong), all R.G.A.

Hedges, R.S.M. F., *M.C.*, *D.C.M.*	* 6894	Herbert, C.Q.M.S.(A./S.M.) J.	6865
— Cpl.(T./S./Sjt.) L. F. G.	6904	— B.Q.M.S. P. M.	6917
— R.Q.M.S. W. C.	6888	— Sjt.(A./C.Q.M.S.) R. E.	7016
Hedingham, Q.M.S. G. C. (corr.)	7703	Herdson, S./Sjt. C. H.	6919
Hedley, Bombr. E. W.	6868	— (correction)	7023
— Cpl. W.	7037	Herman, A./Cpl. J. M.	6914
— Q.M.S. W. H.	6064	Hern, Slt.Sjt. F.	7037
Heesom, Cpl.(A./Sjt.) F.	6970	Herridge, Pte.(A./S.Q.M.S.) F. R.	7019
Hefford, Sjt. A.	6883	Herrington, Cpl. E.	6911
Hegarty, C.Q.M.S. W. S.	6900	Hesp, 2nd Cpl. G.	6878
Heley, Sjt. F. C. F.	6932	Hession, Sjt. E. J.	6932
Hellen, Pte.(A./Cpl.) S.	6909	Hetherington, Sjt.(A./R.Q.M.S.) T.	6865
Helman, Mech.S./Sjt. A. W.	6875	Hewins, Cpl. F. G.	6898
Hemley, S./Sjt.(T./C.S.M.) A. L.	6917	Hewitt, Pte.(A./Cpl.) A. E.	6897
Hemlin, Pte.(A./R.S.M.) A. D.	7017	— Sjt. H. E.	6908
Hemming, Sjt. R.	6955	— B.S.M. R. J.	6869
Hemmings, R.Q.M.S. E., *M.M.*	6944	— Spr. W. S.	6879
Hemsley, Sjt. C. P.	6870	Heyes, S./Sjt. P.	6907
— Ldg.Sig. P.	4734	Heys, Sjt. J. R.	6902
Henderson, E.C.Sjt. C. F. W.	6875	Heythuysen, Pe. C. T. V.	6890
— Pte. J.	6882	Heywood, Sjt. C.	6890
— Sjt.(A./C.Q.M.S.) J. E.	6883	— Spr.(L./C.) R.	6879
— Flt.Sjt. J. R.	† 7037	Hexham, C.E.R.A. 2nd Cl. W. J.	4198
— C.S.M. K.	6892	Hexter, C.P.O. W.	4734
— C.S.M.(A./R.S.M.) T. M.	7013	Hibberd, Sjt. A. B.	6908
— Spr.(T./Sjt.) W.	6879	Hibbert, C.Q.M.S. J. H.	6894
— Sjt.(A./S./Sjt.) W. J.	6894	Hickey, Sjt. F.	7019
Hendley, Sjt. A.	6875	— R.S.M. J. R.	6917
Hendrie, Cpl. J. H.	6868	Hickling, Mech.S./Sjt. E.	6900
Hendry, Cpl. D. R.	6970	— C.Q.M.S. F. H.	6887
— Sjt. W. J.	6898	Hickman, R.Q.M.S. C.	7023
Henigan, Sjt. G.	6870	— Sjt. W. J.	6898
Hennery, C.S.M.(A./R.S.M.) A. J.	6891	Hicks, R.Q.M.S. C. J.	6933
Henri, B.Q.M.S. T. C.	6867	— Sjt. J. G.	6943
Henry, R.Q.M.S. T. B.	6914	— Sjt. P. A.	6890
Henshall, Sjt. F. B.	6876	— Sjt.Clk. S. V.	7037
Henson, Sjt. F. V.	6875	Hickson, Cpl.(T./S.Q.M.S.) H. W.	6974
— Sjt. H.	7014	Higgins, Sjt. Maj. 1 H. R.	7037
Hepton, Cpl. W. H.	6904	— C.Q.M.S. P.	6882
Hepworth, C.S.M. N.	6881	— Sjt.(A./C.Q.M.S.) W.	7012
Herbert, Sjt. B. W.	6910	— Pte. W.	6906
— Mech.S./Sjt. C. W.	6900	— Pte.(A./Sjt.) W. J.	6882
— Pte. E. J.	6919	Higgs, Sjt. F.	6890
— Sjt. G. B.	6875	Higham, Pte. T. L.	6888

* 16 Bn. Tank Corps. Enlisted into R.B. (No. 29 1st Bn.) D.C.M. *L.G.* 18.2.15, C.Q.M.S. 1/R.B. and M.C. *L.G.* 27.7.16, C.S.M. 1/R.B. Also M.B.E. *L.G.* 3.7.26, W.O.1 (R.S.M.) 2/RTC. Group known: M.B.E., M.C., D.C.M., 1914 Star trio (M.I.D. oakleaf), L.S. & G.C. and M.S.M. (305299). Also Royal Humane Society Medal.

† Group known: British War and Victory Medals and R.A.F. M.S.M. (5582 Flt Sgt. on all three). He was Cpl-rigger to Albert Ball, V.C., in 60 Sqn.

Highman, Sjt. A. J., *M.M.*		6892
Hildreth, T./S.S.M. E.		6899
Hiley, Sjt. F. H.		6955
Hill, Sjt. A. E.		6902
— Pte. A. E.		6890
— Sjt. B.		6914
— Pte.(A./S.Q.M.S.) C.		7019
— Pte.(A./Sjt.) E G.		6914
— Sjt.(A./C.S.M.) F.		6970
— Ch.S.B.S. F. C.		7907
— Pte.(A./Sjt.) F. R.		6914
— Amt.S./Sjt. H.		7020
— Pte.(A./Sjt.) H.		6970
— C.Q.M.S. H. G.		6894
— Flt.Sjt. J. T.		7037
— Pte. L. V.		6944
— Master Gnr. 3rd Cl. P.	*	7011
— Sadd.S./Sjt. R.		6932
— Sjt. R. H.		7013
— Cpl. R. W.		6868
— Actg.Ch.Yeo.Sigs. T.		4198
— R.Q.M.S. T. H.		6953
— Flt.Sjt. T. M.		7037
— S.Q.M.S. W.		6956
Hillier, 2nd Cpl.(A./Cpl.) W.		6954
Hills, Pte.(L./C.) A. P.		6906
— Sjt. C. A.		6865
— C.Q.M.S. E. J.		6889
— Pte.(L./Cpl.) J.		6909
— Cpl. T. R.		6934
— Ch.Yeo.Sigs. W. A.		7512
Hilton, S./Sjt. A.		6957
— C.Q.M.S. H.		6883
— Sjt. J. H.		6889
Hinchcliffe, Sjt. I.		6902
Hind, Pte. A.		6891
Hinde, C.Q.M.S. A. F.		6932
Hindle, Sjt. A. W.		6902
Hindley, Pte.(A./Cpl.) J. W.		6946
Hindmarsh, Bandmaster C.		7015
— C.Q.M.S. J.		7018
— Sjt. T. W.		7013
Hinson, Pte. W. F.	❀	6064
Hinton, B.S.M. H.		6866
Hipwell, A.M. 1, Joseph		7037
— Sjt. W. S.		6890
Hipwood, C*M.M.* H.		7037
Hird, Pte. B. T.		6897
Hirons, Ldg.Sig. J.		4734
Hirons, Sjt. L. T.		7037
— Farr.S./Sjt. W.		6867
Hirst, Pte.(A./Sjt.) A. L.		7022
— C.S.M. B. C.		6914
Hiskett, T./S.M. W. R.		6871
Hitchcock, Gnr. A. V.		6871
— Sjt. C.		6933
Hitchcox, Hd.Condr. S. W.		6970
Hitchens, T./Armt.S.M. S. H.		6909
Hitchins, L./C.(T./Cpl.) H. H.		6917
Hoar, S./Sjt.(A./R.S.M.) A. J.		7019
— Vict.C.P.O. A. W.		7512
— Sjt. B.		7037
— Pte.(A./L./Sjt.) B. H.		6933
— Sjt. H. A.		6885
Hobbs, Cpl. G. G.		6914
— Sjt. J.		6882
— Mech.S./Sjt. J. R.		6900
— Sjt. P.		6974
Hobson, Cpl. A.		6868
— C.S.M.Instr. A.		6912
— 2nd Cpl. T.		6878
Hodder, Pte.(A./Sjt.) E. W.		6914
Hodge, Sjt. H. T.		6875
— Yeo.Sigs. W. J. H.		4734
Hodges, Sjt. C. M.		6914
— R.Q.M.S. H.		6888
Hodgkinson, Q.M.S. W. J.		6907
Holdgson, Pte.(A./Cpl.) A. E.		6906
— Cpl. C. E.		6877
— Pte.(L./C.) E. S.		6897
— Sjt. G.		6902
— Sjt. J.		6887
— Gnr. S.		6869
— Pte.(A./Sjt.) W.		6906
— Pte. W. O.		6906
Hodkinson, Sjt. J.		6908
Hodson, B.S.M. F.		6866
— Sjt. G. H., *M.M.*		6944
Hogan, S./Sjt. E. E. M.		6933
— Sjt. L. C. V.		6887
— Sjt. P.		6880
Hogben, Pte.(A./S./Sjt.) A. G. W.		6958
— C.S.M. R. J.		6933
Hogg, Cpl. A.		6877
— Pte.(L./C.) D.		6886
— Cpl.(T./C.S.M.) G. H. A.		6877
— Dvr.(L./Bombr.) J.		6932
— Sjt. J. B.		6875

* R.G.A. For Malta.

Hoggarth, Dvr. M. E.	6914	Holywell, Spr. R.	✿ 7702
Holcombe, Farr.Q.M.S. A. F.	6866	Honan, Sjt. J.	6917
Hold, A./Condr. H.	6909	Honey, Sjt. F., *M.M.*	6894
Holden, Sjt.(A./C.Q.M.S.) A.	6895	Honeysett, Sjt.(A./R.S.M.) J. S. †	6882
— F./C. G. R.	6917	Honor, Sjt. H. J.	7011
— Cpl.(A./Sjt.) H.	6908	Hood, A./Cpl.Clk. A. W.	7037
Holder, C.Q.M.S.(A./CS.M.) C. R.	6888	— R.Q.M.S. J.	6888
— Pte.(A./Cpl.) J.	6957	Hook, Pte. G. N.	6917
Holding, Spr. B. S.	6879	Hooke, C.Q.M.S.(A./R.Q.M.S.) W. S.	6893
Holland, C.Q.M.S. F.	6889	Hool, T./Sub Condr. P. W.	7020
— Pte. H. A.	6883	Hooper, Cpl.(T./S.Q.M.S.) J.	7019
— Sjt. J. A. E.	6893	— C.S.M. W. J.	6872
Hollands, C.Q.M.S. E. T.	6885	— Armt.S./Sjt. W. O.	6910
Hollaway, 2nd Cpl.(A./Sjt.) B.	6878	Hooson, Sjt. W. E.	6908
Hollinghurst, Farr.S./Sjt. J.	6900	Hooten, Pte.(A./Sjt.) G. H.	6911
Hollingsworth, F./Sjt. R. *	7037	Hope, Sjt.(A./S.M.) A.	7020
Hollins, Cpl.(A./C.S.M.) F.	6904	— Gnr. J. G. R.	6869
— Farr.S./Sjt. G.	6900	Hopkins, Sjt.(A./C.S.M.) A. C.	6875
Hollis, Sjt.(A./C.S.M.) S. R.	7010	— T./S.S.M. C. W., *D.C.M.*	6899
— C.Q.M.S. W.	6873	— T./S.M. F.	6907
— Engmn. W. J.	4732	— Spr. G.	6879
Holloway, C.P.O. A. J.	4734	— R.Q.M.S. N. L.	6917
— Gnr. C.	6871	— Sjt. O.	6908
— Sjt.(T./C.S.M.) H. C.	6902	— C.Q.M.S. S. J.	6943
— Pte. L.	6906	Hopper, Sjt. H.	6910
Holm, Sjt. T.	6875	Hordern, Pte.(A./Cpl.) A. J.	6883
Holme, Sjt.(A./C.S.M.) G. H.	7013	Hornby, Cpl. F. N.	7037
— R.Q.M.S. W. F.	7015	— Sjt. L.	6875
Holmes, Cpl.(A./Sjt.) A.	6888	Horne, Pte.(A./C.Q.M.S.) P.	7017
— Sjt. A. J.	6917	— B.S.M. P. E.	6917
— F. of W.(T./S.M.) A. S.	6871	— Pte.(A./C.Q.M.S.) T. H.	6933
— Sjt. B.	7021	Horner, C.S.M. A. S.	6917
— Sjt. G. S.	6887	— Farr.S.Cpl. I.	7010
— C.Q.M.S.(A./R.Q.M.S.) H.	6894	— Sjt.(A./Mech.S.M) J. H., *M.M.*	6902
— C.S.M. H.	6899	Hornsby, S./Smith T.	6869
— S./Sjt. H.	6901	— Cpl.(A./S.M.) W. J.	6870
— Sjt. H.	6894	Horrocks, Sjt. W.	6891
— S.S.M. J. H.	7021	Horsbourgh, Flt.Sjt. D. J.	7037
— Pte. J. H.	6906	Horsey, Sjt. G. H.	6917
Holness, Pte.(A./Sjt.) A.	6911	Horsfall, Cpl. T.	6877
Holt, Sjt. A.	6881	Horsley, Sjt. W.	7011
— Sjt. J. D.	7037	Horsman, Pte.(A./2nd Cpl.) J.	6910
Holten, Mech.Q.M.S. A. E.	7012	Horton, B.Q.M.S.(A./R.Q.M.S.) F.	7010
Holyoake, L. A. C. H.	7037	— Sjt. H.	6886

---

 * No. 823 R.F.C. Enlisted August 1913. Entitled to 1914 Star & bar trio, Defence and War Medals, 1935 Jubilee, 1937 Coronation, R.A.F. M.S.M. and R.A.F. L.S. & G.C. (1931). W.O. 1935. Commissioned 1939 and rose to Wing Commander in W.W.II. Post-war was Parade Marshal for Battle of Britain Cathedral Services in Lincoln. Councillor in the town in the early 1950's. Alive in 1975.

 † See Seigne *infra*. 10/R. Fus., M.I.D. *L.G.* 20 December 1918.

Hoskin, Flt.Sjt. E.	7037	Hudson, Sjt. A. B.	6919
Hoskins, Dvr. A. G.	6954	— Dkhnd, F. A.	4732
Hostler, Dvr.(T./Cpl.) A. E.	6880	— A.M. K. L.	* 7037
Hotchkiss, Pte. H.	6914	— Cpl. S.	6884
Hough, C.Q.M.S. J. W.	6873	— S.S.M. T.	7023
— Cpl. T.	6904	— Sjt. W.	6910
Houghton, Sjt. E.	6875	— C.S.M. W. A.	6899
— Pte. G.	6906	Huggett, Pte.(A./Sjt.) J.	6911
— T./S.M.(A.C.) H. C.	6869	Hughes, C.S.M. A.	7012
— Cpl. T. E.	6904	— Pte.(A./Sjt.) A.	6911
— Sjt. W. H.	6932	— Sjt. A. H.	6882
Houldsworth, 2nd Cpl. J.	6878	— B.Q.M.S.(A./B.S.M.) E. F. B.	6867
Houlston, Cpl. C. V.	6904	— Sjt.(A./C.S.M.) G.	7013
Hourigan, Cpl. D. P.	6917	— Sjt. G. (R.A.S.C.)	6902
— Pte. J.	6917	— Sjt. G. (R.G.A.)	7011
House, Dvr.(A./Sjt.) A. E.	6914	— Cpl. (A./Sjt.) H. A.	6896
Housego, Sjt. F. W.	6875	— C.S.M. H. J.	6917
Houstin, S./Sjt. A. T.	6901	— Sjt. J.	6953
Howard, Pte.(L./C.) A.	6955	— L./C. J. B.	6917
— Dvr. G. E.	6914	— Pte. J. C.	6886
— C.Q.M.S. H.	6873	— Sjt.(A./C.Q.M.S.) J. W.	7015
— Pte. H.	6909	— Sjt. J. W.	6881
— C.S.M. J. H., *M.M.*	7014	— Sjt.(A./R.S.M.) L. E.	6882
— Cpl.(A./Sjt.) J. N.	7011	— Sjt.(A./C.S.M.) L. F.	6945
— C.S.M. W.	6872	— Sjt. P. J.	6917
— Sjt. W. F.	6902	— Sjt. R. S.	6885
— C.S.M.(A./R.S.M.) W. L.	6889	— Sjt.(A./C.S.M.) T.	6902
Howarth, W.O. Cl. 1, J. F. L.	7022	— Whlr.Cpl. W. K.	6904
Howden, B.S.M.(A./R.S.M.) A.	6866	— Sjt. W. McK.	6868
Howdle, Sjt. B. W.	6884	Hull, B.Q.M.S. J.	6867
Howe, Sjt.Instr. A. H.	6912	— Cpl.(A./S./Sjt.) W., *M.M.*	6904
— Sjt. C. F.	7017	Humfrey, Cpl. H. F.	7037
— S.M.(A.C.) C. J.	7011	Humphrey, Sjt. E. F.	6945
Howell, Sjt.(T./S.S.M.) A. V.	6945	— Sjt. R.	6870
— Sjt. E. C.	6902	— Sjt.(A./C.Q.M.S.) W. M.	6882
— Cpl.(A./Sjt.) E. J. W.	7011	Humphreys, Sjt. A. C.	6895
— S.Q.M.S. W. F. H.	7021	— Sjt.(A./S./Sjt.) E. F.	7019
Howles, Sjt.(A./C.Q.M.S.) J. W.	7017	— Sjt. J.	7019
Howlett, R.Q.M.S. A. G.	6914	— Sjt. L. C.	6886
— Cpl.(A./Sjt.) E. H.	6884	— C.Q.M.S. P. J.	6873
Howling, S.Q.M.S. A.	7020	Humphries, Cpl. A	6904
Howorth, Pte. W.	6934	— Arty.Cpl. R. C.	6877
Hoy, R.S.M. W.	6971	Hunt, Sjt. C. F.	6875
Hoyle, C.S.M. J.	6887	— Pte.(A./Cpl.) C. W.	6906
Hubbard, S.M. H.	6871	— Sjt. E. E.	6868
— Sjt.Mec. I. M. S.	7037	— Pte.(L./C.) F.	6897
— Sjt. T., *D.C.M.*	6884	— Gnr.(A./L./Bombr.) F. G.	6869
Hucker, Cpl.(A./Sjt.) H. A.	6896	— Cpl.(T./C.S.M.) H.	6904
Hudson, Sjt. A.	6910	— P.O. H. C.	8202

* R.A.F. M.S.M. for Mesopotamia as Aus/12 Australian Flying Corps.

Hunt, T./R.S.M. H. P.	7010	Hymes, B.Q.M.S. H.		6917
— F. of W. Q.M.S. H. V.	6871	Hynd, T./Sub Condr. L. H.		6909
— Whlr.Q.M.S. J.	6899	Hynes, Sqdn.Q.M.Cpl. J. P.		6881
— S./Sjt. J. B.	6919	— S./Sjt.(A./S.M.) T.		6907
— Bombr.(A./Cpl.) J. H.	6871	Hyslop, C.S.M. W.		6917
— Pte.(L./C.) J. W.	6911			
— Cpl. W. J. B.	6896	I'Anson, Pte.(L./C.) E. J. (corr.)		7703
Hunter, Pte. A.	6909	Ibbotson, Sjt. N.		6868
— S./Sjt. B.	6933	Iddison, T./Sub Condr. H.		6909
— Sjt. F.	6875	Ilsley, C.S.M. E. C.		7015
— R.Q.M.S. G.	7015	Ingall, Sjt. J. T.		6933
— C.Q.M.S. R. S.	6957	Ingamells, T./S.M. W. H.		6907
Huntley, Cpl. R. G.	6882	Ingham, Sjt. G. E.		6875
Hurd, Cpl. E. J.	6904	Inglesby, Pte.(A./Sjt.) S. G.	‡	6971
Hurford, T./R.S.M. E. E.	6868	Ingoe, Sjt. R. H.		7512
Hurley, Pte. J.	680	Ingram, 2nd Cpl. A.		6943
Hurlock, Pte.(A./L./C.) G. C.	6897	— Sjt.(A./C.Q.M.S.) A. G.		6889
Hurndall, Cpl.Mec. W. F.	7037	— Sjt. A. W. McA.		6914
Hurrell, Sjt. W. J.	6875	— Pte.(A./Sjt.) C.		7019
Hursthouse, Sjt.(A./C.S.M.) J.	* 7016	— Cpl. N. C.		6904
Hussey, C.S.M. W. Le W.	6914	Ingrouille, R.Q.M.S. T. J.		6914
Hutchins, S.S.M. H. F.	6914	Inns, R.Q.M.S. H.		6945
— E.C.Sjt.(A./E.C.Q.M.S.) J. A.	6875	Insole, C.S.M. G. H. B.		6914
— Sjt. J. G.	6889	Ionn, Sjt. C. F.		6894
Hutchinson, Spr.(A./2nd Cpl.) F.	6943	Ireland, Sjt.(T./C.S.M.) H.		6875
— Pte.(A./Sjt.) H. E.	6971	— Sjt. J. W.		6887
— Gnr.(L./Bombr.) L. R.	6871	— Pte.(L./C.) W.		6906
— Pte.(A./Sjt.) S.	6934	Iremonger, 2nd Cpl. F. H.		6878
— Supt.Clerk T. (corr. of surname)	7703	Irvine, Cpl.(A./Sjt.) A.		6896
Hutchison, 2nd Cpl.(A./Cpl.) S. A.	6878	— Sjt. J.		6881
Hutt, F. of W. S./Sjt. A. G.	6873	Irving, Pte. D.		6888
— Pte. F. G.	6898	— S./Sjt.(T./Mech.S./Sjt.) J.		6901
— C.S.M. W. R.	7012	Isaac, Flt.Sjt. S. F.		7037
Huxley, T./S.S.M. A. C.	6899	Isaacs, T./Sub Condr. G.		6934
Huxtable, Pte.(A./C.Q.M.S.) L.	7018	Isbell, Pte. R.		6911
Hyde, Cpl.(A./Sjt.) J. T.	† 6870	Isden, B.S.M.(A./R.S.M.) J.		6869
— Sjt. R.	6881	Ison, Sjt. E. E.		6955
— Spr.(A./Cpl.) W.	6932	Isted, Sjt. A. C.		6917
Hyland, Cpl. R. C.	6898	Ivatts, Flt.Sjt. W.		7037

---

  * Later C.S.M. 8th Manchester Regiment. Mobilised with the Territorials in August 1914, he was drafted to Egypt in September, and served as a Sergeant there until early in 1915. He was then transferred to the Dardanelles, and played a prominent part in the Landing at Cape Helles, and in the first and second Battles of Krithia; he was badly wounded in action in May 1915, and invalided home. On his recovery was promoted to Company Sergeant-Major, and rendered valuable services as an Instructor until his discharge in March 1919. Awarded the Meritorious Service Medal and the General Service and Victory Medals. 76, Gibson Street, Ardwick, Manchester.

  † Awarded M.S.M. Annuity 1945.

  ‡ Hunt's Scouts, German S.W. Africa.

Ivens, Pte.(A./Sqdn.S.M.)	
A., *D.C.M.*	6911
Iverson, Cpl.(A./Sjt.) H. A.	6882
Ives, C.Q.M.S. F.	6873
Jack, Cpl.(A./Sjt.) A. D.	6888
— Sjt. F.	6902
— S./Sjt.(T./Q.M.S.) J.	6907
Jackman, Cpl. C. G.	6877
Jackson, S./Sjt. A.	6971
— Spr.(A./Sjt.) A.	6879
— Sjt.Mec. A. D.	7037
— Flt.Sjt. A. E. C.	7037
— Pte. (A./Sjt.) B., *M.M.*	6906
— Sjt. B. H.	6890
— Pte.(A./Sjt.) C. H.	6884
— Dvr. E. ✿	6063
— Pte.(A./Sjt.) F.	6914
— Farr.Sjt. F. A.	6867
— Sqdn.Q.M.S.(A./S.S.M.) G. W.	6894
— Sjt. Harry	7037
— Sjt. H.	7016
— A./Sjt. H.	7022
— Sjt. H. W.	7016
— Pte. J.	6906
— 2nd Cpl. J. T.	6878
— Sjt. L.	6957
— R.Q.M.S. R. *	7014
— Sjt. R.	6886
— R.S.M. T., *D.C.M.*	6945
— Sjt. W. J.	6902
— Whlr.Cpl. W.	6914
— Cpl. W.	6877
— Dvr.(T./Sjt.) W.	6907
— Sjt. W. F.	6887
Jacobs, Sjt. C. V. M.	6875
— S.S.M. H. W.	7021
Jacques, Sjt. H.	6895
Jaggard, A./C.S.M. G.	7022
James, Sjt. A. E.	7015
— Farr.Sjt. A. J. T.	6971
— Cpl. A. T.	6888
— Cpl. C. W.	6888
— S./Sjt. E.	6957
— Pte. E. S.	6891

James, Ch.Shipwt. 2nd Cl. F.	8069
— Sjt. G. E.	6887
— Cpl. G. P.	6934
— C.S.M. J.	6956
— S./Smith Sjt. W. A.	6901
— T./S.S.M. W. J.	6890
— C.Q.M.S.(O.R.Sjt.) W. T.	7010
— Ch.Mech. W. T.	7037
Jameson, Sjt. E.	6914
Jamieson, Mech.S./Sjt. R. B.	6900
Janes, S.S.M. H. C.	7023
Jansen, W.O. Cl. 1, R. F.	7022
Jaques, 2nd Hnd. A. W.	4732
Jaram, Sjt. H.	6868
Jardine, Sjt. R.	6894
Jarvie, Cpl.(T./C.S.M.) L. R.	7022
Jarvis, Cpl. A.	6934
— Sjt. E. P.	6953
— Pte.(A./S./Sjt.) J.	6906
— Sjt. J. T.	6953
— C.Q.M.S. T. E.	6954
Jauncey, Sjt. J.	6908
Jay, Sjt. H. H.	6902
— Sjt.(T./S.Q.M.S.) W. F.	6902
Jeffcott, Spr.(T./Sjt.) H. W. T.	6879
Jefferies, Cpl. A. G.	6904
— Spr.(T./Sjt.) R.	6879
— Sjt. W. H.	6914
Jeffers, S./Sjt.(T./	
Mech.S./Sjt.) G. A.	6901
Jeffery, Sjt. W. H.	6943
Jefferys, L.A.C. F.	7037
— C.S.M. H. A.	6872
Jeffrey, Sjt. W. H.	6902
Jeffreys, Sjt. R.	6910
Jeffries, Sjt. F. E.	6893
— Pte. R. W.	6897
Jeffs, C.S.M.(A./R.S.M.) G. R.	7013
Jelly, F.W./Q.M.S. H. F.	6932
Jenkin, R.Q.M.S. W. E.	6917
Jenkins, S./Sjt. A.	6907
— C.Q.M.S. A. R.	6881
— C.Q.M.S.(A./C.S.M.) B. H.	6888
— Cpl. F. J.	6917
— Pte. G. D.	6914

* Medal known: 3/Cheshire R. (from Douglas, Isle of Man). Part of the I.O.M. Volunteer Battn., the only such one existing after the formation of the Territorial Army in 1908. A company was formed in I.O.M. in 1915 and posted to 16/King's (Liverpool) Regt. Later trans. to 3/Cheshires to become 1st (Manx) Service Coy. The Regt. history shows Jackson as M.I.D.

Jenkins, Flt.Sjt. W.	7037	Johnson, Pte. H.	6884
Jenkinson, Sjt. D.	6902	— S./Sjt. H. W.	6901
— Sjt. G. H.	6902	— Cpl. of Horse J. †	6881
— Pte. H.	6884	— Pte. J.	6906
Jenner, Cpl. A.	7037	— Pte.(A./C.Q.M.S.) J. H.	7019
Jennings, S./Sjt. F.	6914	— Sjt.(A./R.Q.M.S.) L.	7015
Jennison, R.Q.M.S. G.	6892	— S./Sjt. R. G.	7022
Jenson, Pte.(A./Cpl.) R.	6906	— Sjt. T.	6875
Jenvey, Sjt. F. J.	7033	— Sjt. W.	6870
Jephcott, Pte.(L./C.) F. V.	6946	— Sjt. W. A.	6902
Jepson, Sjt.(A./C.S.M.) J.	6884	— 2nd Hnd. W. H.	4732
— Sjt.(A.C.) J. C.	6943	Johnston, T./Sub Condr.	
Jermey, C.Q.M.S. E. W.	7017	(A./Condr.) A. S.	6909
Jervis, Spr.(L./C.) J.	6879	— Sjt.(A./S.M.) J. ‡	7020
Jesseman, Pte.(A./Sjt.) W. A.	7019	— Cpl. J.	6954
Jessiman, C.S.M. J	6895	— Sjt. T.	6902
Jestico, 2nd Cpl.(A./Cpl.) G. J.	6878	— 2nd Cpl.(A./Cpl.) W. M.	6932
Jewell, S.S./Cpl. F. *	6868	Johnstone, 2nd Cpl. A.	6878
Jewitt, Spr. F. ✿	7702	— C.S.M.(A./R.S.M.) S.	6893
— Cpl. R. S.	6904	Joiner, Sjt. F. J.	6890
Jobling, P.O.(A./C.P.O.) H.	7010	Jolliffe, C.Q.M.S. B.	6944
Jobson, Pte.(L./C.) H.	6911	Jolly, Cpl. P. W.	6881
Joel, T./S.M. D., *D.C.M.*	6871	Jones, Sjt. A.	6944
Johns, Pte. T. H.	6956	— Spr.(L./C.) A.	6879
— Ch.Mec. W.	7037	— Pte.(T./Sjt.) A.	6910
Johnson, Farr.S./Sjt. A.	6953	— C.S.M. A. R.	7014
— Pte. A.	6906	— Sjt. B. (R.F.A.)	6868
— Pte.(A./L./C.) A. H.	6911	— Sjt. B. (N. Zealand Force)	6919
— Pte. A. W.	6881	— Pte.(A./C.S.M.) B. C.	6898
— Sjt. B. W.	6945	— Cpl. B. G.	6877
— 2nd Cpl. D.	6932	— S./Sjt. B. J.	6907
— Sjt. E.	6875	— Sjt. C.	6875
— Dvr. E.	6943	— Spr.(A./Cpl.) C.	7012
— Ch. Writer E. A.	8069	— Sjt. C. C. §	6944
— S./Sjt. F.	6914	— Pte.(A./Sjt.) C. F. B. S.	6883
— T./Sub Condr. F.	6909	— Sjt. C. L.	6954
— Cpl. F. P. (corr.)	7703	— Sjt. D.	6917

* 32501 Corpl. S./Smith 26th Battery R.F.A. Flanders 1918—During the operations of September and October he was almost nightly employed in bringing up ammunition and, in spite of frequent shelling and gassing, never failed to carry out his duties. He came with the battery to France in 1916. A thoroughly efficient and conscientious workman, he has imbued those under him with the same spirit.

† Group known: 1914 Star & bar (Cpl. R.H.G.), British War and Victory Medals (Cpl. of Horse), L.S. & G.C. (Geo. V) and M.S.M. (3/Guards Machine Gun Regt.) He served in France from August 1914 to May 1915 and was evacuated with the effects of shell shock. He returned to France with the Gds. M.G. Regt. and served there until February 1919.

‡ R.A.M.C. Malta.

§ See Seigne *infra*. This is the only M.S.M. for Italy to 10/R. Fus. M.I.D. as A./L.Cpl. 20 December, 1918.

Jones, Cpl. D.	6877		Jones, C.Q.M.S. R. H.		6955
— R.Q.M.S. D. D., *M.C.*	* 7013		— C.S.M. S.		6884
— Cpl. D. E.	6904		— Pte. S.		7020
— Cpl. D. I. P.	6904		— Spr. S. A.		6879
— C.S.M. D. T.	6888		— Sjt. T.		6870
— Pte. E.	6955		— C.Q.M.S. T. A.		6890
— Sjt. E. H.	6918		— Sjt. T. C.		6957
— Sjt. E. I.	6914		— B.Q.M.S. T. E.		6914
— A./Cpl. F.	6914		— C.Q.M.S. T G.		6944
— Pte. F.	6946		— Cpl.(A./Q.M.S.) T. H.		6887
— Sjt. G. A.	6914		— Pte.(A./Sjt.) T. W.		6906
— Pte.(A./Sjt.) G. F.	6911		— S.M.I. William	‡	7037
— C.Q.M.S. G. H.	6895		— A.M. 1, W. J.		7037
— P.O. G. H.	5112		— C.Q.M.S. W. L.		6893
— Sjt. H.	7037		— Cpl.(A./Q.M.S.) W. T.		6908
— R.S.M. H. A.	7013		— Sjt. W. W.		6895
— Sjt. H. E.	6875		Jordan, T./B.S.M. A.		7016
— Cpl. H. J.	6904		— Spr.(L./C.) J. G.		6879
— Sjt. H. M.	6975		Jordon, T./S.S.M. R. G.		7018
— Farr.Sjt. H. M.	6943		Joshua, C.S.M. J.		6888
— M.A.A. H. P.	8202		Joubert, Condr. G.		6970
— Sjt.(T./C.S.M.) H. W. T.	6919		Jowers, Sjt. A. C. W.		6898
— R.S.M. I.	7015		Jowett, T./S.S.M. J. T.		6899
— Sjt. J. (R.F.A.)	6868		Joy, Cpl. F. G.		6910
— Sjt. J. (Mon. R.)	6897		Joyce, Sjt. J. C.		6868
— A.M. 2 James	7037		— T./Sub Condr. S. G.		6934
— C.S.M.Instr. J. B.	7021		Joyner, Pnr. E. F.		6880
— S./Sjt. J. I.	7019		Joynt, Pte.(A./2nd Cpl.) W. D.		6914
— Sjt.(T./C.S.M.) J. R.	6875		Judd, Sjt.(A./S./Sjt.) A. O.		6946
— Cpl. J. R.	6888		Judge, Sjt.(T./C.S.M.) E. W.		6875
— Pte.(L./C.) J. W.	6945		Judkins, Sjt. F.		6943
— Cpl. L.	6877		Jukes, Ch.Sto. W.		8069
— L./C. L. C.	6917		Julian, C.Q.M.S. C.		6881
— Pte. L. G.	6911				
— Sjt. M.	6945		Kagugwe Erita, Sjt.		6971
— Flt.Sjt. P.	7037		Kamkwamba, Cpl.		6970
— R.Q.M.S. R., *D.C.M.*	† 6893		Kane, Dvr. E.		6907
— Sjt. R. B.	7021		Katepoli, C.S.M.	§	6971

---

* M.C. 1 January, 1917 R.Q.M.S. Coldstream Guards.

† Group known: D.C.M. (Geo. V, 2/R. Mun. Fus., *L.G.* 13 February 1917), 1914 Star trio (M.I.D. oakleaf) and M.S.M. (R. Muns. F.).

‡ Group known: Queen's South Africa Medal, 1914 Star trio (M.I.D. oakleaf), R.A.F. M.S.M., R.A.F. L.S. & G.C. and Karageorge with Swords. Enlisted Balloon Company R.E. in November 1900 and served in Boer War. Later in the Air Battalion and was Sgt. 3 Sqn. in France from 13 August, 1914. S.M. June 1916. R.A.F. L.S. & G.C. November 1918 (one of the first six such awards). His R.A.F. number was 30.

§ Group known: Ashanti 1900 (Pte. 2/Central African Regt.), Africa General Service Medal (Somaliland 1902–04, Jidballi, East Africa 1913–14 Cpl. 2/K.A.R.), 1914/15 Star trio (Cpl/C.S.M. K.A.R.), K.A.R. L.S. & G.C. (Geo. V) and M.S.M. (No. 113 2/ K.A.R.). M.S.M. for East Africa.

Kavanagh, Sjt. G. B.	6914	Kemp, Pte.(A./C.Q.M.S.) W.		7019
— Sjt.(C.S.M.) J.	6917	— Cpl. W. A.		6904
— Cpl. W.	6877	Kempster, Sjt.(T./1st Cl.S.S.M.) G.		
Kay, Sjt. A. J.	6875	(corr.)		6065
— Pte.(A./Sjt.) J.	7019	— T./S.S.M. G.		6976
Keane, Sjt.(A./B.Q.M.S.) J. J.	6868	Kendal, Sjt. F. W.		6898
— Sjt. L. L.	6870	Kendall, Pte.(L./C.) H.		7019
Keaney, T./S.M. M.	6871	Kenefick, Cpl. J.		6908
Kearney, Spr.(A./Sjt.) T. W. (corr.)	7703	Kennedy, Farr.S./Sjt. G.		6866
Kearns, B.S.M. E. E.	6917	— Sjt. J. (Lon. Fus.)		6885
Kearvell, 2nd Cpl. J. H.	6878	— Sjt. J. (R.A.S.C.)		6902
Keating, L./Sjt. O.	6917	— Gnr.(Cpl.) J. S.		7022
— C.S.M. T.	6893	— Cpl. P.		6877
Keats, S./S.M. L.	6914	— Pte. R. K.		6897
Keddie, Cpl. G. C.	6881	— T/S.S.M. T. M.		6899
Keeble, T./S.M. J. D.	7020	Kennett, Mech.S./Sjt. S. E.		6894
Keedy, Dkhnd. G. R. A.	4732	Kenny, R.S.M. J.	*	7016
Keefe, Sjt. R. F. J.	6943	— S./Sjt. J. H.		6917
Keel, Pte.(L./C.) G. H.	6897	— S./Sjt. P.		6919
Keeler, Sjt. W.	7012	Kent, Cpl.(A./Sjt.) A. J.		6877
Keeling, Pte.(A./Sjt.) G. H.	6909	— Sig.Sjt. J.		6870
Keen, 2nd Cpl. A. A.	6878	— Bombr. S. D.		7011
— B.Q.M.S. S.	6867	— Sto.P.O. W. G.		7907
— Pte.(A./S./Sjt.) W. A.	7020	Kentisbeer, Sjt. R. J.		6944
Keenan, Sjt. W.	6902	Kentish, Cpl. F.		6904
Keene, Cpl.(A./Sjt.) S.	6908	Kenwright, Pte.(A./Sjt.) F. H.		6886
Keep, R.S.M. W.	6866	Kenyon, Sjt. H.		6884
Keighly, T./Sub Condr. A. C.	6909	— Sjt. J.		7038
Keiller, Sjt. J.	6888	— Pte.(A./Sjt.) J.		6911
Keith, Dvr. A. W.	6917	Keogh, Cpl. W.		6896
Kelleher, Sjt. N.	6954	Kerr, T./S.M. D. M.		6907
Kelleway, 2nd S.B.S. H. W.	7512	— Sjt. G.		6908
Kellond, Pte.(L./C.) H. J.	6883	— Sjt. H.		6970
Kellow, Pte.(A./Sjt.) W.	6906	— Pte.(A./C.Q.M.S.) R. D.		6892
Kelly, Sjt. A. H.	6875	Kerridge, C.Q.M.S. C. R.		6884
— T./Sub Condr. A. H.	6909	Kerry, Sjt. D.		6880
— C.Q.M.S. C. D.	6892	— Sjt. F.		6956
— Sjt. D.	6956	— Sjt. F. A.		6969
— Gnr. D. J.	6871	Kershaw, Cpl. C.		6877
— S./Sjt. E.	7020	— Sjt. H.		6933
— Cpl.(A./Sjt.) J.	6904	— Cpl. W.		6868
— Pte.(T./Cpl.) J. F.	6906	— Pte.(A./Sjt.) W.		7020
— C.E.R.A. 1st Cl. J. H.	7512	Kershler, Cpl.(T./R.Q.M.S.) J. W.		6917
— Cpl.(A./Sjt.) T.	6891	Kerswill, Cpl. S. H.		6904
Kelsall, Sjt. R. W.	6902	Kett, Sjt. H. J.		6914
Kelsey, Cpl. G.	7038	Ketteridge, C.S.M.(A./R.S.M.) H.		6891
Kemp, Sjt. C. E.	7010	Kew, Sjt. R.		6910

---

* Group known: British War Medal (R.S.M. R Irish Rifles), L.S. & G.C. (Col. Sgt. R.I.Rif., Victoria), M.S.M. (R. Irish Rifles, for valuable services in India). As Colour Sergeant late R. Irish Rifles he was awarded an annuity in A.O. 127 of 1932.

Khairalla Kenyon, C.Q.M.S.	6971	Kingsley, Pte. J. E. W.	6898
Khan, Pte. C.	6917	Kingston, Sjt. R.	6914
Kidd, Pte. W. A.	6906	— Pte.(A./Sqdn.S.M.) W.	6906
Kieran, Sjt. E.	6902	Kington, 2nd Writer L. G.	7512
— Sjt.(A./C.S.M.) F. A.	6892	Kinkead, Sjt. A. F.	6891
Kierton, Sjt. A. A.	6868	Kinnaird, Sjt. J.	6881
Kilby, Sjt. G. E. (deletion of		Kinrade, Cpl. S. K.	6904
duplicate)	7703	Kinsella, T./Sub Condr. A. F.	6909
Kildea, T./S.M. R.	6907	Kinsman, Sjt.(A./C.S.M.) H. J.	7015
Kildgour, 2nd Cpl. A.	6878	Kirby, T./Sub Condr. A. F.	6909
Killey, Pte. G. W.	6914	— Sjt.(A./C.Q.M.S.) L. E. H.	6895
Killick, Sjt.(A./B.S.M.) F.	6868	— Pte.(A./Cpl.) T.	6890
— Pte.(A./Sjt.) G. St. J.	6914	Kirch, Pte.(A./S.Q.M.S.) E.	6932
Kilmartin, Pte. J.	6897	Kirk, Sjt. H.	6884
Kilner, Pte.(L./C.) W.	6887	— C.Q.M.S. J.	6873
Kilpatrick, S./Sjt. E. J.	6917	— S./Sjt.(A./S.S.M.) W. T.	6957
Kilvington, Dvr. H.	6869	Kirkaldy, Cpl. A.	6877
Kimp, Actg.Ch.Yeo.Sigs. W. J.	8202	Kirkham, Cpl. A.	6908
Kimpton, Pte.(A./L./C.) E. C.	6897	— S./Sjt. G.	6873
Kincaid, Pte.(A./L./Sjt.) H. E.	6909	Kirkman, Pte.(A./C.S.M.) A. H.	6883
King, L./Sjt. A. F.	6917	Kirkwood, R.Q.M.S. T. J.	6914
— Ch. Writer C. S.	7512	Kirton, Pte. H.	6906
— Pte.(A./Cpl.) E.	6906	Kitchen, S.M. A. E., *M.M.*	6907
— R.Q.M.S.(A./B.S.M.) E. F.	6870	Kiza Yowana, Pte.	6971
— Pte. E. H.	6897	Kneeland, Pte.(A./Sjt.) C. R.	6914
— R.Q.M.S. F.	6889	Knight, Sjt. A.	6892
— C.S.M. F.	6959	— S./Sjt. B. R.	6914
— Flt.Sjt. F.	7038	— C.Q.M.S. E. H.	6932
— Cpl. F. U.	7019	— Cpl.(A./Sjt.) F. G.	6908
— Pe.(A./Sjt.) G.	6911	— Pte.(A./L./C.) G. W.	6911
— Cpl. G.	6868	— C.Q.M.S. J. H.	6944
— S.S.M. G. H.	6899	— C.S.M. M. T., *M.M.*	6944
— Pte. G. U. H.	6906	— Sjt. W.	6910
— T./S.S.M. H. D.	7018	Knights, Sjt. F. H.	6884
— Clr.Sjt. J.	7907	— Sjt. W. J.	6902
— Armr.S./Sjt. J. H.	6910	Kniveton, Pte.(A./Sjt.) G.	6911
— Cpl. J. H.	6917	Knott, A./S.M. J.	7021
— Cpl. J. R. ❀	7702	Knowles, Pte. G.	6897
— Cpl.(A./Sjt.) J. T.	6904	— C.Q.M.S. W.	6873
— Pte.(A./Sjt.) L. W.	6866	Knox, R.Q.M.S. J. E.	7015
— C.S.M. O. M., *D.C.M.*	6888	— Dvr. J. S. J.	6919
— Pte.(A./Sjt.) R. F.	7015	Kohler, S.M. A.	6970
— Q.M.S. W.	6934	Kora, Sjt. S. A.	6919
— R.Q.M.S. W. F. W.	6894	Kurton, Pte.(L./C.) C.	6944
— S./Sjt.(A./S.M.) W. H.	6910	Kyle, T./S.M.(A./C.) G. G.	6869
— Cpl.(L./Sjt.) W. H.	6865		
— C.Q.M.S. W. W.	6898	La Haye, Sjt.(A./C.Q.M.S.) J.	6894
Kingham, Cpl. C.	6877	Labbett, Sjt. E.	6884
Kinghorn, Sjt. A.	6914	Laccohee, Ldg.Sea. H.	4734
Kingsbury, Sjt. T.	7038	Lacey, C.S.M.(A./S.M.) G. W. *	6976

    * R.G.A. For Aden.

Lachance, Cpl. J. E.	6914	Lanford, Pte. S.	6865
Lahiff, Sjt. R.	6890	Lang, Sjt. A. E.	6902
Laidlaw, Sjt. W. F.	6914	— R.S.M. S. F.	6893
Laing, Ldg.Sto. J. McK.	6504	Langford, B.S.M. J.	6869
Laird, Sjt.(A./C.Q.M.S.) T.	6892	Langley, Pte.(S./Sjt.) A. J.	7022
Lake, Sto. 1st Cl. C.	7512	Langton, Mech.Sjt. R. †	6894
— Sjt. D.	6894	Lansdowne, F./Clk. W.	7038
— Pte.(A./Cpl.) H. B.	6898	Lansley, Pte. W. G.	6906
— Ch.Mec. J. J.	7038	Lapsley, Sjt. F. G.	6917
Lakeman, Sjt. C. C.	6943	— Cpl.(A./Sjt.) S. R.	6886
Laker, C. F.	7011	— Cpl. W. B.	6877
Lamb, Dvr.(A./Cpl.) C. A.	6907	Larder, Pte.(A./L./C.) J. W.	6893
— Sjt. H.	6885	Lark, Cpl. C.	6957
— Sjt. J.	6890	Larson, Sjt. A.	6875
— Q.M.S. W.	6871	Last, Pte.(L./C.) J. W.	6889
Lambert, Ch.Mec. A. J. *	7038	— Cpl. P. A.	6914
— Pte.(A./Q.M.S.) C.	7020	Latham, 2nd Cpl. C.	6878
— C.Q.M.S. E.	6873	— Sjt.(C.S.M.) G. L.	6956
— A.B. G.	8202	— Gnr.(L./Bombr.) W.	6871
— S.S.M. G. E.	7021	Lathom, Spr.(L./C.) J. E.	6879
— S./Sjt. H. C.	6911	Latter, C.Q.M.S. H. E. ‡	7013
— S.Q.M.S. J.	7023	Lavender, Cpl.(C.Q.M.S.) J.	6897
Lambie, Pte. A.	6885	Laventhal, S./S.M. S.	6971
Lambourne, Cpl.(T./Sjt.) T.	6904	Lavill, Dvr. G.	6869
— S.Q.M.S. W. J.	6865	Lavington, Sjt. G.	6910
Laming, Sjt. G. E.	6880	Law, Sjt. J. H.	6914
Lamond, Sjt. H. G.	6955	— Sjt. W. H., *M.M.*	6875
Land, C.S.M. W.	6883	Lawday, Spr.(A./C.S.M.) F. W.	7012
Lane, Pte.(L./C.) A.	6911	Lawes, Whlr.Cpl.(T./Whlr.S./Sjt.)	
— C.Q.M.S. A. E.	6889	F. C.	6904
— Cpl. C. H.	7038	Lawford, Clr.Sjt. G. A.	6504
— Sjt. E.	7023	— Sjt. P. T.	6868
— Sjt.(A./C.Q.M.S.) M.	6944	Lawley, T./Armt.S.M. L. W.	6909
— Sjt.(A./Sqdn.Q.M.S.) M. T.	6875	Lawlor, Sjt. T. J.	7023
— Pte. T. G.	6976	Lawrance, R.S.M. W. G., *M.C.* §	6893

* Group known: 1914/15 Star trio (1062 Pte./F./Sgt. West Kent Yeo. and R.A.F.) and R.A.F. M.S.M. (403695) for Egypt.
† Tank Corps. He volunteered in November, 1914, and proceeding to France in 1916, served with distinction at the Battles of the Somme, Messines, Ypres, Cambrai, Havincourt, and Valenciennes, and in heavy fighting at Neuve Chapelle, Richebourg, St. Vaast, Canal de L'Escat, Masnières and Achiet-le-Grand. He was wounded at Ypres in August 1917, and on two occasions his tank was struck by shells and put out of action. He was awarded he Meritorious Service Medal and mentioned in Despatches for conspicuous bravery in the Field, and was demobilised in February 1919. He also held the General Service and Victory Medals. 15, Elias Street, Manchester.
‡ Grenadier Guards, for Singapore.
§ Group known: M.C. (R.S.M. 1/R.B. *L.G.* 1 January 1917), Queen's South Africa Medal, King's South Africa Medal, 1914 Star & bar trio, L.S. & G.C., M.S.M. (Geo. V) and M.S.M. (Geo. VI F.D.), this last issued under the terms of A.O.98/1953..

Lawrance, Pte.(T./Sjt.) W. W.	6911	Ledgard, Sjt. J.	6894
Lawrence, Sjt. A. E.	6910	Lee, S.Q.M.S. C. B.	6933
— Sjt. F. J.	6875	— Flt.Sjt. C. E.	7038
— Gnr.(A./Bombr.) F. J.	6869	— Cpl.(A./L./Sjt.) F.	6957
— Spr.(A./C.S.M.) F. J. S.	7012	— Ch.Writer H.	7512
— Cpl. J. S.	6904	— C.P.O. J.	7907
— Sjt. R. R.	6911	— Dvr. J.	6869
— C.Q.M.S. T. G.	6888	— Sjt.(A./C.S.M.) S.	6891
Lawrenson, Sjt. I. L.	6881	— Sjt. S.	7016
— Sjt. J.	6902	— F.W./S.M. S. C.	6932
Lawrie, Cpl. T.	6932	— Q.M.S. T.	7020
Laws, Bombr. G.	6871	— Sjt. W. H.	6882
Lawson, Sjt.(A./C.S.M.) D.	6902	— Spr. W. H.	6879
— Sjt. H.	6891	— S./Sjt. W. J.	6907
Lax, Sjt. C.	6891	— F./Sjt. W. S.	7038
Laycock, Pte.(A./L./C.) S.	6914	Leech, Cpl.(A./Sjt.) T.	6868
Layfield, Sjt. H.	6875	Leeds, Sjt. A. A.	7013
Layton, A./Cpl. H. L.	7038	Leeke, Bombr. O.	6868
Lazzeri, Cpl.(A./Sjt.) E. J.	6904	Lees, Cpl. E. L. D.	6919
Le Deau, Cpl. D.	6914	— Sjt.Drm. E. M.	6886
Le Guelence, Cpl.(T./Sjt.) C. P.	6877	— C.Q.M.S. J.	6957
Le Leu, Sjt. H.	6914	Leese, Sjt. H.	6868
Le Lieve, Farr.Sjt. C.	6953	— Q.M.S. J.	6871
Le Page, Sjt. G.	6868	— Sjt. J.	6870
LeSauteur, C.P.O. W. P.	8069	— S.S.M. R. W.	6899
Leach, R.S.M. F.	6932	Leggatt, Mech.S./Sjt. F. H.	6945
— Sjt. F. E.	6934	Legge, Cpl. C.	6904
— Sjt. H. P.	6875	Leigh, Spr.(T./Sjt.) T. H.	6879
— S./Sjt. J. E.	6934	Leishmann, Sjt. W.	6902
Leadbeater, R.Q.M.S. H.	6956	Leitch, Pte. G.	6886
Leadbetter, Cpl. C.	6932	— C.S.M. H.	6932
— Pte. E. G.	6906	— Dvr. W. M.	6919
Leaf, Sjt. T.	6875	Lemon, Sjt.(A./C.Q.M.S.) R.	6895
Leahy, T./R.S.M. J.	6866	Lenahan, S.Q.M.S. T.	7018
— Sjt. J. J.	6970	Lenny, Cpl. T. F.	6890
Leake, Sjt. G.	6891	Leppard, Cpl. A.	6896
Leaning, Dvr. R.	6907	Lerotholi, 1st Cl. Induna M.	6919
Leaper, S./Sjt. W. A.	6914	Lesnewitz, Pte. A	6914
Lear, Sjt. T.	6955	Lethaby, Pte. J.	6894
Leary, 2nd Cpl. J. C.	6878	Levey, C.S.M. O. S. H.	6897
Leatherband, Pte.(A./C.S.M.) C. E.	6882	Levy, Sjt.(A./Flt.Sjt.) E.	7053
Leatherbarrow, 2nd Lt.(A./S.Q.M.S.)		Lewarn, F. of W. Q.M.S. J. H.	6872
J. K.	6970	Lewin, Sjt. B.	6857
Leathers, Pte.(T./Sjt.) P. N.	6906	— Vict.C.P.O. F. J.	8202
Leavers, B.S.M. A.	6866	Lewington, C.S.M. C.	6856
Leavy, Cpl. M. J.	6877	Lewis, Cpl.(A./Sjt.) A.	7012
Leckenby, Cpl. J.	6877	— Pte. A.	6906
Lecluse, Sjt.(A./C.S.M.) E. A.	6875	— S./Sjt. E.	* 6970

* Group known: Queen's South Africa Medal (Cape Colony, Orange Free State, Transvaal, Kitchener's Fighting Scouts), 1914/15 Star trio with bilingual Victory

Lewis, S.M. F.	7038	Little, Sjt. J.	6875
— Cpl. F. J.	6914	— Spr. J. E.	6879
— C.S.M. G. A. J.	6917	Littler, C.S.M. A.	6899
— C.P.O. G. F. M.	5112	Littley, C.S.M. H.	6899
— Sjt. H.	6875	Litton, Cpl.(A./Sjt.) E. G.	6975
— L./Sjt. H. G.	6917	Livesey, Pte.(L./C.) F.	6886
— C.S.M. J.	7014	— Sjt. R.	6955
— Cpl.(A./Sjt.) J.	6911	Livingstone, Sjt. W.	6914
— S./Sjt. J. J.	6901	Llewellyn, Sjt. J. S.	6883
— Sjt.Mec. J. N. E.	7038	Lloyd, C.P.O. A.	7512
— Cpl. O.	6904	— Ch.Motor Mech. A. F.	4733
— Flt.Sjt. Ralph	7038	— 2nd Cpl.(A./Sjt.) A. H.	7012
— Sjt. R. W. T.	6898	— C.Q.M.S. E.	6900
— Ch.Shipwt. 2nd Cl. W. B.	7512	— Dvr. E. P.	6917
— 2nd Cpl. W. H.	6954	— C.S.M. F. G.	6899
Ley, Cpl. A. P.	6957	— E.C.Sjt.(A./E.C. Q.M.S.) G.	6875
— Sjt. F.	6954	— C.S.M. J.	7011
Leyshorn, C.Q.M.S.(A./S.M.) W. J.	6873	— Sjt. P. F.	6908
Liddiard, Sjt. W G.	6954	— Sjt. R. H.	6902
Liddle, S.Q.M.S. J. A.	7018	— C.S.M. T.	6899
Liebermann, C.Q.M.S. W. J.	6944	— Hd. Condr. T.	6970
Lifford, C.Q.M.S. W.	6900	— Farr. Sjt. W.	6875
Likeman, B.S.M. W. E.	6943	— T./Sub Condr. W. J. * ✱	6064
Lillburn, Pte. L.	6906	Loasby, Cpl. A. H.	6908
Lilley, Sjt.(A./Sqdn.S.M.) J.	7019	Lobley, B.Q.M.S. W. J. J.	6867
Lillicrapp, C.S.M.(A./R.S.M.)		Lochead, Pte. J.	6957
A. B., *MM.*	6872	Lock, Pte.(A./C.S.M.) M.	7011
Lillie, Sjt. A.	6914	Locke, Cpl. A. V.	6904
Lilly, S.M.Instr. J.	6971	— Sjt. C. H.	6884
Lind, Cpl.(T./Sjt.) A.	7022	— S./Sjt.(A./Q.M.S.) C. H. J.	7020
Linder, L./C. H.	6914	Lockhart, Pte. J.	6892
Lindley, Pte. J.	6905	Lodder, C.S.M.(Instr.Gnr.) G. R. †	7011
— Armr. T. N.	6865	Loder, S./Sjt. H. J.	7020
Lindo, T./W.O. Cl. 1, A. E. McN.	7022	Loe, Farr.Sjt. and C.S. T. O.	6875
Lindsay, Sqdn.S.M. W.	6865	Lofthouse, Pte.(A./Cpl.) F.	6906
Lindsell, Dvr. W.	7011	Logan, Sjt. N.	6893
Line, S.S.M. O. F.	7021	— Farr.S.M. R.	6865
Lingley, Whlr.S./Sjt. T. T.	6945	— Mech.S./Sjt. S. H.	6873
Linklater, C.Q.M.S. L. J.	6917	Loggie, R.Q.M.S. A. B.	6917
Linnet, S./Sjt. N.	6907	Logie, S./Sjt. J.	6901
Linsdell, T./S.S.M. H. T.	6899	Lomas, T./S.M. E. D.	6871
Linthwaite, R.Q.M.S. W. J.	7014	Lomax, B.Q.M.S. J. G.	6867
Lipscombe, Pte. E. F.	6880	— R.S.M. R. H.	7023
Lister, R.S.M. C.	6943	London, Sjt. W. S.	6917
Little, Sqdn.Q.M.S.(A./S.S.M.) A. J.	6894	Long, Farr.S./Sjt. A. E.	6867

Medal (2/South Africa Rifles), M.S.M. (South Africa Special Service Corps) for East Africa.

* R.A.O.C. Gallantry 16 August 1918 at Boulogne, a fire in an ammunition repair factory.

† R.G.A. For Singapore.

Long, B.Q.M.S. E. C.	6867	Low, C.Q.M.S.(A./C.S.M.) R. W.	7018
— Sjt. F. C.	6870	Lowden, Mech.S./Sjt. C. W.	6900
— T./Sub Condr. L. R.	7020	Lowe, Cpl.(A./Sjt.) G.	6944
— B.S.M. S. E.	6866	Lowery, Pte. A. E.	6914
— Ldg.Sea. W.	* 4734	— Cpl. J. B.	6945
Longbottom, S./Sjt. W.	6958	Lowman, Sjt. F. H.	6875
Longhurst, Cpl. E.	6868	— Q.M.Cpl.Maj. W. H.	7010
— T./Sub Condr. W. L.	6909	Lowrie, S./Sjt. A.	6901
Longmore, Sjt. S.	6892	Lowry, C.Q.M.S. A. J.	6890
Longstaff, Sjt. J. R.	7038	Loxton, Sjt. J. R.	6944
Longstaffe, Pte. J.	6892	Loy, Sjt. P.	6894
Longstone, Cpl.(A./Sjt.) R.	6904	Lucas, Pte. F. J. E.	6897
Lonnon, Ch. Writer G. F.	7512	— Pte. F. P.	6911
Looker, Sjt. A. E.	6970	— Pte.(L./C.) G. T.	6934
Loombe, S.Q.M.S. R. M.	6899	— C.S.M. W.	6957
Loosemore, Sjt. F. J.	6902	— Cpl. W. F.	6904
Lord, Farr.S./Sjt. J.	6900	Luck, Cpl. C. E.	7011
— Pte.(A./Cpl.) J. E.	6865	Luckett, Sjt.(A./C.Q.M.S.) P. J.	6895
— Sqdn.Cpl.Maj.(A./		Luckin, C.S.M. E. C.	6892
R.Q.M.C. Mjr.) W. C.	† 7010	Luckman, Sjt. J.	6944
Lorimer, Cpl. E. L. D.	6882	— C.Q.M.S. T.	6884
Lorraine, R.S.M. T.	7014	Ludbrook, Q.M.S.(O.R.Sjt.) H. C. F.	7013
Loten, C.Q.M.S. A. O.	‡ 6932	Ludgate, Sjt. A. J.	6902
Lott, C.S.M. G.	6897	Luke, B.Q.M.S. J.	7010
Louden, Farr.Q.M.S. H.	6914	Lukes, Pte. J. T.	6898
Loughman, R.Q.M.S. E.	6895	Lumb, Pte. A. L.	6906
Louis, Sjt. L. R.	6943	— Bombr.(A.C.) G. E.	7011
Lovatt, Pte. P. C.	6906	Lumness, Mech. S. B.	6900
Love, C.Q.M.S. A. F.	6917	Lumsden, Condr. G. S.	7020
— Sjt.(A./C.Q.M.S.) C. J.	6895	— Sjt. W.	6914
— Spr. D. R.	6879	Lund, Pte. E.	6914
— Sjt. F. H.	6884	Lunn, Q.M.S.(A./S.M.) H. C. A.	6907
— Cpl. F. H.	6904	— Pte.(A./Sjt.) L. C.	6887
Loveland, C.S.M.Instr. W. J.	6912	— Spr. W. C.	6879
Lovell, Dvr. C. J.	6869	Lunt, C.Q.M.S. J. W.	7702
Lovelocks, Cpl. A. S.	6870	Lupton, L./Bombr. R. J.	§ 6976
Lover, Mech.S./Sjt. F. E.	6894	Luscombe, Vict.C.P.O. R. E. C.	7512
Loveridge, T./S.S.M. A. E.	6956	Lusty, Sjt. C.	6908
Lovett, Pte. C. A.	6911	Luxon, Sjt. A. J.	6910
— Sjt. E. J.	6902	Luxton, Actg.C.P.O. H. W.	7512
— Cpl. O.	6885	Lyall, C.S.M. J. W., *MM*.	6885
Low, Pte.(A./Sjt.) F. W.	6944	Lynas, Cpl. J.	6877

---

* Group known: Naval General Service Medal (Persian Gulf 1909–14 *'Perseus'*), 1914/
15 Star trio, R.N. L.S. & G.C. (Geo. V, *'Victory'*) and R.N. M.S.M. (P39 Patrol
1918).

† Group known: Queen's South Africa Medal (Relief of Kimberley, Paardeberg,
Dreifontein, Johannesburg, Diamond Hill, Wittebergen), King's South Africa Medal
(both Cpl. R.H.G.), L.S. & G.C. (Geo. V, S.C.M.) and M.S.M. (R.H.G.).

‡ Imperial Camel Corps for Egypt.

‡ R.G.A. For Aden.

Lynch, Sjt. D.	6954	McCartley, Bombr.Sig.(A./Cpl.) J.	6871
— C.S.M. T.	* 6882	McCarty, S./Sjt.(A./C.S.M.) W.	6914
Lynd, Sjt. A. E.	6875	McCasker, L./Cpl. N. L.	6917
Lynn, Sjt. R. J.	6914	McCeady, Pte. C. T.	6897
Lyon, S.M. G. F.	6934	McClay, Sjt. H.	6883
— Spr.(L./Cpl.) J.	6879	McCleary, P.O. W. L.	4734
— C.Q.M.S. S.	7014	McCleery, Sjt. E.	7018
Lyons, Pte.(A./Cpl.) G.	6906	McClellan, Sjt. G. B.	6914
— S.Q.M.S. G. T.	6917	McClure, Sjt. R. D.	6902
— S.Q.M.S.(A./S.S.M.) H. C.	7021	McComb, C.S.M. R. J.	6872
— Cpl. M.	6877	McCombry, Sjt. G. J.	6902
— Condr. P.	6971	McConnell, R.Q.M.S. T. A.	6956
Lyrett, Sjt. F. C.	6886	— Gnr. W.	6914
Lyster, Cpl. F. O.	6943	McCormack, Pte. E.	6892
Lyth, Sjt. A.	† 7019	— Sjt. J	7012
		McCormick, C.S.M. E.	6899
Mabbett, Sjt. C. J.	6943	— Farr.Sjt. J. W.	6914
— Cpl. W. J.	6888	McCormick, S.M. N.	7038
Maberley, Cpl.(T./Sjt.) C. P.	6917	McCoubrey, Cpl.(T./C.Q.M.S.) T. J.	6877
Mabey, A.B. J. T.	5111	McCoy, Sjt. J. (M.G.C.)	6894
Macallan, Pte. J.	6914	— Sjt. J. (R.F.A.)	6954
M'Ardle, Pte. B.	6892	McCreadie, M.F. of W.S./Sjt. H.	6873
McArthur, Pte.(A./Sjt.) W.	7022	McCreedy, Ch. Writer H. J.	8069
McAteer, Sjt. J. J.	7018	McCullough, Cpl.(A./Sjt.) S. ❀	6064
Macauley, Sjt. R.	6919	McCutcheon, Flt.Sjt. D.	7038
McBain, Q.M.S. J.	6885	McDermid, Sub Condr. R. J.	6917
McBeath, Sjt. R. L. R.	6914	McDonald, Ch.Yeo.Sigs. A. J.	7907
McBride, L./Cpl. J. O.	6917	— Sjt.(A./S.M.A.C.) D.	6870
McBryde, Cpl. D. H.	6892	Macdonald, Dkhnd. D.	4732
McBurnie, C.Q.M.S. R.	6954	MacDonald, S./Sjt. F.	6901
McCaigh, Pte. A.	6885	McDonald, Pte.(L./C.) G. M.	6917
McCairn, C.Q.M.S. J. S.	6892	Macdonald, Sjt.(A./S./Sjt.) H.	6914
McCallum, C.Q.M.S. A. S.	6873	McDonald, Pte.(L./Cpl.) H. B.	6911
— R.S.M. J.	7016	— C.Q.M.S. J.	6888
— Sjt. J. A.	6919	MacDonald, Pte. J.	6906
McCann, Farr.S.M. T.	7010	McDonald, Sadd.S./Sjt. J. D.	6945
McCarthy, Cpl. B. S.	6917	— Ldg. Dkhnd. M.	6447
— T./W.O. Cl. 1, C. J.	7022	— Dkhnd. M.	5113
— R.S.M. D.	7010	— Sjt. P.	6902
— C.Q.M.S. J.	6888	— C.Q.M.S. R.	6884
— C.Q.M.S. T.	6917	— Sjt. R. S. ❀	6064
— Sjt.(A.R.S.M.) T. R.	7015	MacDonald, Mas.Clk. T.	7038

* Group known: India General Service Medal (Punjab Frontier 1897–98, 5644 Pte. 2/ R. Irish Regt.), Queen's South Africa Medal (Transvaal, South Africa 1902, Cpl), 1914/15 Star (3408 Sjt. R.I.Regt.), British War and Victory Medals (W.O.II), Delhi Durbar 1911, and M.S.M. (102692 43/R.Fus.). Born Oola, Co. Limerick, enlisted 23 November, 1895. Discharged 19 January, 1914. Re-enlisted 23 March, 1915. To Labour Corps 29 September 1917 and to 43/Royal Fusiliers 27 August, 1918. Only 21 men of the R. Irish Regt. earned the 1911 Delhi Durbar Medal.

† R.A.S.C. For Hong Kong.

MacDonald, Cpl.(L./Sjt.) V. H.	6880	McKay, Cpl.(A./Sjt.) J.		6919
McDonough, C.Q.M.S. W.	6895	Mackay, Cpl.Mec. J.		7038
MacDougall, Pte. J. A.	6892	MacKay, Sjt. N.		6902
McDowell, R.S.M. A. H.	6919	McKay, S./Sjt. P.		6910
McDowell-Dowell, Cpl.(A./		McKee, C.Q.M.S. H.		6892
S.Q.M.S.) A. M. (corr.)	6065	McKenna, Spr. B.	✸	7702
Mace, Ch.Mec. W. C.	7038	— Cpl. J.		6877
McEwan, Sjt. D.	6875	— Pte. P.		6883
McFadyen, Q.M.S.(T./S.M.) W. H.	6912	McKenzie, S./Sjt. A.		6971
McFarlane, Pte. E.	6944	MacKenzie, T./S.S.M. C. M.		6899
— Pte.(L./Cpl.) J.	6945	McKenzie, Pte.(L./Cpl.) D. D. A.		6898
MacFarlane, 2nd Cpl. J.	6970	— E.R.A. 1st Cl. J.		8069
Macfarlane, S.M. I. R.	7038	— Cpl. J.		6904
McFarlane, Cpl. R.	6893	— Sjt. J. L.		6914
McGaffin, Sjt. J. A.	6917	Mackenzie, Sjt.Mech. W. H.		7038
McGaffney, T./Sub Condr.) J.	6909	McKeown, Sjt. R. O.		6914
McGarrity, Pte. J.	6886	McKie, Cpl. J.		6877
McGarry, Pte. T.	6892	Mackie, Pte. R.		6865
McGeagh, C.Q.M.S. A. H.	6913	— 2nd Cpl.(A./Sjt.) W.		6878
McGeorge, Ch.Shipwt. J. W.	8069	— Sjt. Piper W. C. K.		6886
McGhie, Ch. Writer J. F.	6504	McKinlay, Sjt. J.		6868
— Sjt. W. W.	6886	McKinnon, Cpl. J. P.		6914
McGovern, Pte. J. J.	6919	MacKintosh, R.Q.M.S. A.		6892
McGrail, C.S.M. J.	6900	Macklem, Sjt. N.		6914
McGrath, Pte. C. J.	6919	McKnoulty, Dvr. P.		6917
— Pte. E.	6933	McLachlan, Ch. Writer W. S.		8202
McGready, S.M. S.	7021	McLaren, C.Q.M.S.(A./S.M.) D.		6873
McGregor, B.Q.M.S. A. P.	6870	— Sjt. L.		6881
MacGregor, Sjt. D. J. E.	6902	— W.O. Cl. 1, P. C.		7023
— Pte.(A./Cpl.) J. H.	6897	— Sjt. R.		6917
McGregor, Pte. L. E.	6913	McLaughlin, Pte. D.		6914
MacGregor, Sjt. R.	6875	— Cpl. J.		6919
McGrotty, B.S.M. G.	7011	McLean, Pte. A.		6934
McGuinness, Pte. E.	* ✸ 6064	— Spr. H.		6879
McHaffie, Gnr.(L./Bombr.) J.	6943	— P.O. J.		4734
MacHardy, Sjt. W.	6888	MacLean, Mech.S./Sjt. L.		6900
Machin, T./Sub Condr.(A./Condr.)		McLean, Sjt. W.		6875
E. A.	6957	MacLeay, Mech.S./Sjt. J.		6873
— Gnr. F.	✸ 6063	McLellan, C.Q.M.S. R.		6873
McIlraith, Sjt. T.	6885	McLennan, E.R./Sjt. R. R.		6917
McIlroy, Sjt.(A./R.S.M.) W.	6885	MacLeod, 2nd Hnd. A.		5448
McIlwraith, Sjt. J. A.	6875	McLeod, P.O. D.		8202
McIvor, S./S.M. E. J.	6919	— Pte.(A./Cpl.) H.		6911
— Sjt. T.	6954	— R.Q.M.S. J.		6892
Mackay, C.S.M. D.	6900	McLoughlin, Pte.(L./Cpl.) H.		6892
McKay, S.S.M. G.	6899	Maclure, L.A.C. J. W.		7038
MacKay, Whlr.S./Sjt. J.	6900	McMahon, Sjt. E.		6917

---

    * 5/Connaught Rangers attached H.Q. 30th Div.

McMahon, Ch. Armr. W.	*	6865	McStay, Sjt. J. H.		6894
McManus, Pte.(T./Sjt.) C.		6911	McSwiney, Condr. D.		6909
McManus, B.Q.M.S. J.		6867	— Sjt. T.		7038
McMenamin, S.M.Instr. J., *D.C.M.*	†	7011	MacTaggart, Cpl. A.		6904
McMillan, Spr.(C.S.M.) A. B.		7022	Madden, S./Sjt. M.		6901
— Sjt. R.		6932	Maddick, Actg.Ch.Yeo.Sigs. H. T.	‡	5112
— Cpl.(A./Sjt.) W.		6914	Maddin, Pte.(L./Cpl.) G.		6946
McMollen, Pte. J.		6886	Maffey, Sjt. F. L.		7010
McMullen, W.O.Cl 1, A. J.		6934	Mafuri, R.S.M.		6971
McMully, Spr. W. J.		6879	Magee, Sjt. H. T.		6882
McMurray, Pte.(A./Cpl.) D.		6888	Magombo, C.S.M.	§	6971
MacMurray, Pte. V. F.		6914	Magowan, Master Gnr. 2nd Cl. A.		7011
McMurtrie, Cpl. G. B.		6908	Maguire, Sjt. J. H.		6889
McNally, Sjt. F. J.		6917	Maher, B.Q.M.S. S. R.		6867
— Cpl.(A./Sjt.) G. S.		6877	Mahomed, Bin Baghid, R.S.M.		6971
MacNamara, Cpl. D.		6877	Mahoney, Cpl.(T./Sjt.) J.		6911
McNamara, S./Sjt.(A./S.M.) W. J.		6907	Mahony, Sjt. A. P.		6917
McNeil, S./Sjt. C.		6873	Mahood, Pte. G.	✿	7702
— T./R.S.M. S. E.		6970	Maidment, Cpl.(A./Sjt.) A. C.		6877
McNeillie, S./Sjt. W.		6970	— Pte. P.		6943
McNicoll, C.S.M. J. G.		6881	Maile, T./S.M. A. E.		6899
McNiven, A./R.Q.M.S. C. H.		6914	Main, Sea. D.		7907
MacOwan, Cpl. W.		6914	— Sjt. J. G.		6932
McPhail, Sjt. R. C.		6914	Maine, S.S.M. C. H.		7018
MacPhee, C.S.M. J.		6956	Major, Sjt. A. W.		6902
Macpherson, C.Q.M.S. A.		6914	— Pte.(A./L./C.) G. W.		6893
— Pte. M.		6906	— S.S.M. P. E.		7018
McPherson, Sjt.(A./R.S.M.) V. D. H.		7016	Makamba, Sjt. H.		6919
Macpherson, C.Q.M.S.		7016	Makeham, Sjt. F. C.		6875
McPhie, R.S.M. M.		7017	Mallett, C.S.M.(A./R.S.M.) J.		6885
MacRae, C.S.M. J.		6914	Malley, Pte. M.		7018
Macready, Sjt. G. J.		7014	Mallon, Sjt.(A./C.S.M.) J.		6895

---

* Pair known in Moss collection: Royal Naval L.S. & G.C. (Edw. VII, Chief Armourer H.M.S. *Jupiter*) and Army M.S.M. William McMahon would of course also be entitled to W.W.I medals. Only some 47 Army M.S.M.s were awarded to Naval recipients during the War, mostly to ratings and P.O.s of R.N.V.R. Only six were issued to R.N. This is therefore a very rare medal especially taking into account the following issues to R.N./R.M. combined:— M.M.s 570; 23 bars; one 2nd bar. D.C.M.s 72; 2 bars; one 2nd bar. M.C.s 137; 8 bars; one second bar.

† D.C.M. as Sergeant, Coldstream Guards, in South Africa, see *L.G.* 27 September, 1901. This M.S.M. was for Valuable Services at the Army School of Signalling. In Army Order 141 of 1949 he was awarded an annuity for the M.S.M.

‡ Group known: Queen's South Africa Medal (Tugela Heights, Orange Free State, Relief of Ladysmith, Johannesburg, L.S. H.M.S. *Tartar*), 1914/15 Star trio (C.Y.S.), R.N. L.S. & G.C. (Geo. V, *Roxburgh*) and R.N. M.S.M. (*Roxburgh*, July–Nov. 1918), with Marine Society Reward of Merit 15 May, 1902, six R.N. Temperance Society medals, South African War Veterans' Badge and silver medallion 1913 H.M.S. *New Zealand*.

§ Pair known: Africa General Service Medal (Somaliland 1902–04, Nyasaland 1915, Pte. 2/K.A.R.) and M.S.M. (3/1 K.A.R.).

Malone, Sjt. T.	7017	Marlow, Sjt. W. H.	6910
Maltby, C.Q.M.S. J. D.	6900	Marples, C.Q.M.S. W. Y.	6873
Malthouse, Sqdn.Q.M.S. G.	6957	Marpole, Whlr.S./Sjt. W. H.	6900
Mammen, Pte.(A./Sjt.) S. V.	6897	Marr, T./Cpl. E. T.	6919
Mandy, Pte. A.	6892	— Pte. H.	6906
Manger, R.Q.M.S. H. E.	6889	Marrett, Pte.(A./Q.M.S.) E. A. R.	6893
Manifold, Sjt. W.	6875	Marriner, Cpl.(A./Sjt.) A. E.	6877
Manion, C.Q.M.S. J.	* 7016	Marriott, Cpl. J. H.	6868
Manley, S.Q.M.S. J. L.	7010	— Sjt. R. A.	6914
Mann, Sjt. H. W.	7017	Marsden, C.Q.M.S. J. R. (corr.)	6065
— Sjt. P. A.	6917	— Pte. W.	6897
— C.S.M.Instr. R. S.	6912	Marsh, S./Sjt. G. M.	6917
Manners, C.P.O. J. J. C.	7512	Marshall, Ch.Engmn. Amos (*alias*	
Mannin, Sjt. F.	6902	Ernest)	8069
Manning, Pte. A.	6906	— T./R.S.M. C. H.	7018
— Q.M.S. H. S.	7020	— Sjt. C. L. S.	6917
— Sjt. W. H.	6914	— Farr.Q.M.S. F.	7010
Mansfield, Sjt. T. H.	6910	— Pte. F. A.	6882
Mant, Engmn. J. B.	4198	— Cpl.(A./Sjt.) F. H.	6908
— P.O. J. H. C.	7512	— S.Q.M.S. G.	6945
Mantell, Mech.S./Sjt. H.	6900	— Mech.S./Sjt. G. W.	6900
Mantle, Sjt. S.	6870	— C.S.M. J.	6917
Manvell, Armr.S./Sjt. W.	6910	— S.M. John	7038
Mapple, Mech.S./Sjt. E. H.	6900	— Cpl. R.	6908
March, Clk. 1 (A./Cpl.Clk.) A.	7038	— Pte. R. C. R.	6888
Marchant, Sqdn.S.M. A. D.	7010	— C.Q.M.S. W. B.	7017
— Pte. C. A. W.	6914	— Sjt. W. G.	6914
— Pte.(A./L./C.) C. W.	7021	— Gnr.(L./Bombr.) W. H.	6871
— A.B. H. W.	7512	Martin, Fitt.S./Sjt. A. A.	6870
— Ch.Sto. R.	7907	— Cpl. A. D.	6914
Marchington, L./C. H.	❀ 6064	— Sjt. A. E.	6911
Marcus, Pte.(T./Sjt.)	6909	— Sjt. A. F.	6954
Marcuse, Pte.(A./C.S.M.) M.	6883	— Sjt. B. F.	6902
Marden, C.P.O. E. E.	4734	— S.M. C. E.	† 7038
— Ch.Shipwt. 2nd Cl. J. W.	6447	— Farr.Sjt. D.	6943
— Pte.(A./Q.M.S.) W. A.	6883	— Sjt. D. D.	6902
Margerison, A./Cpl. W.	7038	— Mech.Q.M.S. F.	6872
Marhoff, Pte.(A./Sjt.) A.	6911	— S.Q.M.S. G.	6970
Mark, C.Q.M.S. G.	6865	— Sjt. G. A.	6902
Markham, T./Mech.S.M. F.	6899	— Sjt. J.	6895
Markland, C.Q.M.S. H. R.	6889	— Cpl. J.	7019
Marlow, C.Q.M.S. J.	6885	— T./Sub Condr. J.	6909

---

* Group in Manchester Regt. Museum: D.C.M. (Geo. V), Africa General Service Medal (West Africa 1909–10), 1914/15 Star trio (M.I.D. oakleaf), L.S. & G.C. (Geo. V) and M.S.M.

* R.A.F. M.S.M. No. 175 R.F.C. Enlisted May, 1908, into R.E. Was with the Balloon School on formation of Air Battalion of R.E. 1A.M., R.F.C. H.Q. in France from 12 August, 1914. S.M. November, 1916. R.A.F. M.S.M. with 74 Sqn. in France. Order of Chevalier of Léopold II of Belgium and Belgian Croix de Guerre in *L.G.* 15 July 1919. R.A.F. L.S. & G.C. May 1926. Still serving in 1931.

Martin, Bombr. J.		6866	Matthews, E.C.Sjt. W. G.		6873
— Sjt. J. B.		6902	Mattison, Pte.(A./Sjt.) J.		6894
— Sjt. J. W.		6891	— Cpl.(A./Sjt.) W. E.		6877
— Sjt.(A./C.S.M.) S.		6875	Maude, Sjt. I. C.		6868
— B.S.M. W., *M.M.*		6943	Mauler, T./S.S.M. G.		6899
— Sjt. W. H.		6875	Maver, B.Q.M.S. R.		6867
— R.Q.M.S. W. K.		6881	Mawhinney, Sjt.(A./C.S.M.) F.		6886
Martinsen, Pte.(A./Sjt.) C.		7017	Maxwell, Flt.Sjt. A.		7038
Martinson, Pte.(L./C.) E.		6909	— Sjt. J.		6894
Marwood, Ldg.Sig. G. E.		4734	— S.M. W. R.		7038
Maslin, Sjt. A.		6868	May, Sjt. E. T.	*	7018
— Ldg.Sea. G. A.		7512	— E.R./Cpl. F. W.		6917
Mason, B.Q.M.S. A. E.		6953	— Sjt. J.		6881
— Farr.Q.M.S. C.		6910	— S.M. L. A.		7038
— Pte. C.		6955	— Flt. Sjt. N. H.		7038
— Sjt. C. S.		7038	— Mech.S.M. W. G.		6871
— R.Q.M.S. E. G.		6884	Maydon, Sjt.(A./S./Sjt.) F.		6908
— R.Q.M.S. F.		6865	Mayfield, R.S.M. U. S.		7017
— Sjt.(A./C.S.M.) G. F.		6881	Mayl, T./Mech.S.M. P. W.		6899
— T./R.S.M. J.		6892	Maynard, C.Q.M.S. E. B.		6887
— C.S.M. J.		7013	Mayne, S./Sjt. O. H.		6919
— Sjt. T.		7038	Mead, Sjt.(A./Q.M.S.Instr.) G. O.		7017
— C.S.M. W. E.		6890	Meadows, Pte.(A./Sjt.) A. E.		6909
Masse, Sjt. G.		6914	— Cpl. R. H.		7012
Massey, C.S.M. W.		6885	— C.S.M. S. G.		6932
Masson, T./Supt.Clk. W. C.		6871	Meads, Pte.(A./C.S.M.) A. L.	†	6883
Masters, Cpl. W. H.		6945	— Pte. H. H.		6944
Masterton, Sjt.(A./C.S.M.) C.		6895	Meagher, Sjt. E.		6908
— Sjt.(A./C.S.M.) H. G.		7019	Meaney, E.C. and D.S./Sjt. C. R.		6873
Mateyo, C.S.M.		6971	Mearns, Sjt.(A./Q.M.S.) P., *M.M.*		6892
Mather, Cpl. H.		6877	Medland, S./Sjt.(A./S.M.) J.		6907
Mathers, L./C. W.		6917	Medley, Sjt. E.		6945
Matheson, Sjt. D.		6954	Mee, Pte.(A./S./Sjt.) E. J.		6910
— R.Q.M.S. J.		6893	— S./Sjt. H.		6910
— A./R.S.M. K.		7022	Meek, Sjt. C. F.		6954
Matongwe, Pte.(L./C.)		6870	Meggison, B.S.M. J.		6869
Matthew, C.S.M.Instr. H. C.		7021	Meiklejohn, C.S.M. W.		6900
Matthews, Cpl. G. H.	✱	6064	Meister, Pte. M. L.		6914
— C.Q.M.S. J. P., *M.M.*		6873	Melhuish, R.Q.M.S. J. J.		7010
— Sjt. R. H. E.		6870	— Cpl. W. G.		6877
— C.Q.M.S.(A./C.S.M.) W. E., *M.M.*		6888	Mellor, Armr.S./Sjt. J.	‡	6910

---

* Group known: Queen's Egypt (Tel el Kebir, Drummer Gren. Gds.), Imperial Service Medal (Geo. V, Coinage Head), M.S.M. (Royal Defence Corps), Volunteer Long Service (Edw. VII, Sgt. Bugler 24 M'Sex. V.R.C.) and Khedive's Star 1882.

† See Seigne *infra*. 10/R. Fus. also M.I.D. 10 July, 1919, and French Médaille d'Honneur avec Glaives en Argent as Sgt. 10 R.F. 17 March, 1920.

‡ Group known: 1914/15 Star trio (M.I.D. oakleaf 24 Dec 1917 as Armr. Sergt. Maj.), L.S. & G.C. (Geo. V, 7578663 S. Sgt. R.A.O.C.) and M.S.M. (A1170 R.A.O.C.). He was the subject of an article in *Medal News* in July 1986 as being one of a party chosen to represent the R.A.O.C. in the Victory March in Paris on 14 July 1919. In 1914 he was part of a detachment in Sierra Leone.

Mellor, 2nd Cpl. J.	6878	Miles, 2nd Cpl.(A./Sjt.) W. H.	6932
Melton, Pte.(A./Cpl.) G. G.	6932	Millar, R.S.M. D.	7017
Melville, Sjt. A. D.	6914	— Sjt. J. Y.	* 6910
— Pte. J. C.	6897	— C.Q.M.S. R.	† 7016
— Spr. R.	❀ 7702	— S./Sjt. T. H.	6934
— S./Sjt. W.	6917	— Sjt. W.	6976
Menkens, Sjt. W. E.	6875	— Cpl. W.	6877
Mennie, Sjt. W.	6895	Miller, F. of W. S./Sjt. A., *M.M.*	7012
Menzies, C.Q.M.S. F.	6885	— Sjt.(A.C.) A. C.	6870
— Sjt. G. H.	6919	— E.C. 2nd Cpl. A. D.	6878
Mercer, Fitt.S./Sjt. R.	6943	— Sjt. A. E.	6891
Meredith, Flt.Sjt. A. J.	7038	— Sjt. A. R. R. A.	‡ 7016
— Cpl. T. M.	6957	— Pte.(L./C.) C.	6906
Merret, S.M.Instr. E. W.	6971	— Cpl.(A./C.Q.M.S.) D.	6896
Merrick, Cpl.(A./Sjt.A.C.) A. E.	6870	— Ch.Writer E. G.	8069
— Sjt. E.	6954	— Q.M.S. E. J.	6872
— Sjt. J. L.	6898	— Cpl. G. R.	6944
Merrill, L./C. J. A.	6917	— S./S.M. G. T.	7023
Merrix, Sjt. H. A.	6868	— S./Sjt. G. W.	7019
Merry, Pte.(L./C.) R.	6881	— R.Q.M.S. H.	6917
Mervyn, Pte. F.	6897	— Flt.Sjt. H.	§ 7038
Metcalf, Sjt.(A./S.Q.M.S.) P. B.	7019	— Cpl. H.	7038
— Cpl.(A./R.Q.M.S.) T.	6956	— Pte. H.	6897
Metcalfe, Sjt. J.	6875	— T./S.M. H. G.	7020
Metson, A.C. 1, A.	7038	— C.Q.M.S. I. P.	6917
Mew, S./Sjt. W. H.	6910	— Cpl.(A./Sjt.) J. R.A.	6877
Mickie, Pte.(A./Sjt.) C. A.	6909	— C.S.M.(T./R.S.M.) R.	❀ 6063
Middleton, Pte.(A./Cpl.) D.	6909	— Ldg.Sea. R. P.	4733
— Sjt. E.	6902	— Spr. S. L.	6879
— S.Q.M.S. J.	6933	— Sjt. W. (Lab. C.)	6895
— T./Sub Condr. R.	6909	— Sjt. W. (R.A.S.C.)	6902
Milburn, Pte.(A./Cpl.) E.	6882	— C.Q.M.S. W. K.	6886
Miles, T./S.S.M. G. P.	6899	Millest, S./S.M. H. C.	6899
— C.P.O. J. F.	4732	Millican, C.S.M.Instr. F.	6912
— Pte. V.	6838	Milligan, Sjt. T.	6893

* S.E/12872 Sergt. A.V.C. attached 460th Battery R.F.A. Flanders 1918—By his devotion to duty and self-sacrificing love of horses this N.C.O. has won for himself a great reputation in the battery to which he is attached. During the final operations in Belgium wagon lines were frequently heavily shelled. Sergeant Millar was invariably in the lines, soothing the horses, caring for the wounded, and inspiring confidence, He has been invaluable in keeping the battery mobile and efficient. (Belgian Croix de Guerre 4/9/19).

† 52/H.L.I. Awarded Territorial Force Efficiency Medal (Geo. V) 6/Gordons. Pair known 243811 on M.S.M., 10029 Sgt. on Territorial Force Efficiency Medal.

‡ R.E. For Aden.

§ Group in Moss collection: 1914/15 Star (1A.M. R.F.C. No. 1513) British War and Victory Medals (F/Sgt. R.A.F.), India General Service Medal (Afghanistan N.W.F. 1919), R.A.F. M.S.M. (one of only four R.A.F. M.S.M.s for India) and Serbian Obilitch Medal (*L.G.* 15 February, 1917. One of only two to R.F.C. or R.A.F.). He enlisted on 13 August 1914 a fitter/turner by trade.

Mills, Spr.(A./Sjt.) F.		7013	Mitchell, Pte.(A./Sjt.) H. R.	6886
— C.Q.M.S. G.		6889	— R.Q.M.S. J.	6917
— C.S.M. J.		6872	— Q.M.S.(O.R.Sjt.) J.	7016
— Sjt. J. E.		6917	— Sjt. J.	6914
— Sjt. L.	*	6886	— Cpl.(A./Sjt.) N. H.	6908
— Dvr. P. A.		6945	— Sjt. S.	6911
— Pte. P. J.		6893	— Pte. T. F.	6897
— Sjt. S. H.	†	6865	— Armr.S./Sjt. W. J.	6910
— Sjt.(A./C.Q.M.S.) W.		7013	— E.R.S./Sjt. W. S.	6917
— Sjt. W. H.		6908	Mittell, Cpl.(A./Sjt.) W. S.	6870
— Pte. W. R. C.		6956	Mobbs, C.S.M. A. J.	7015
Millson, Pte. R. J.		6906	Mock, Dvr.(L./C.) W.	6880
Millward, Sjt. (A./Sjt.) J.		6898	Mockett, P.O. 1st Cl. W. S.	4734
Milne, Cpl.(A./Sjt.) J.		6906	Moddy, C.S.M. H.	6881
— Pte.(L./C.) J.	‡ ❀	7702	Moffit, Bombr. P.	6871
Milner, Sjt. C. U.		7023	Moir, Sjt. W.	6875
— Sjt. E.		6890	Monachan, Pte. J.	6956
— C.S.M. R. W.		6914	Moncur, Sjt. J.	6908
Milnes, R.Q.M.S. J.		6880	Monery, Flt.Sjt. G.	7038
— Pte.(A./C.Q.M.S.) N.		7013	Money, Sjt. F. E.	6976
Milson, Sjt. W.		6902	Monico, Mech.Sjt. C. J.	6933
Milton, Sjt.(T./S./Sjt.) A. R.		7022	Monk, Pte. A. C.	6895
Minney, Cpl. G.		6904	— Sjt. F.	6875
Minnis, Pte. G.		6914	— Sjt. H. N.	6914
Minns, Fitt.Cpl.(A./Fitt.Sjt.) F. W.		6954	Monks, C.S.M. J.	6893
Mirfield, Whr.Sjt. F.		6867	Montclare, Pte.(A./C.S.M.) T. R.	6883
Missen, L./Sjt. A. J.		6917	Moody, Sqdn.S.M.(I.M.) G. C.	7010
Mitchell, Pte.(A./Cpl.) A.		6906	Moon, C.P.O. F.	7512
— Pte.(A./Cpl.) A. M.		6970	— Sjt. J.	6945
— T./S.M. E.		6907	Moore, Farr.Sjt. A.	6867
— C.Q.M.S. E. E.		6873	— Sjt. B.	6945
— S.Q.M.S. E. R.		6917	— Pte. G.	7014
— Sjt. G C.		6880	— Sjt. G. W.	6914
— Pte. H. J.		6888	— Sjt. I.	6881

* Group known in Moss collection: 1914/15 Star (Private K.O.S.B.), British War and Victory Medals (Sergeant K.O.S.B.), Defence Medal and M.S.M. A Bacup, Lancashire, man he enlisted in September 1914 into 7/K.O.S.B. soon to be merged with 8 (Service) Battn. As Company Accountant he went to France 9 July 1915 with 46 Inf. Brigade H.Q. He was demobilised 31 March 1919. A citation has been traced for his M.S.M. 'For continuous good work and devotion to duty from 25 February to 31 December 1918. This N.C.O. has shown conspicuous ability and untiring perseverence in the execution of his duties, especially during the operations South of Soissons in July, and during the enemy retreat in October, 1918. Orders had to be issued at very short notice under adverse circumstances. Whatever the conditions he did the best possible, never sparing himself. His work as Chief Confidential Clerk has been of the greatest value to Brigade H.Q.' He was a Captain in the Home Guard in W.W.II.

† Group known: Queen's South Africa Medal (Orange Free State, Transvaal, South Africa 1902 Pte. 3/Huss.) L.S. & G.C. (Geo. V) and M.S.M. (3/Huss.).

‡ M.F.P. att'd. Marseilles Base L. of C. Area.

Moore, T./S.S.M. J.	6899	Morley, Cpl.(A./Sjt.) G. A.		6886
— Sjt. J.	6902	Morman, T./S.M. W. P. S.		6934
— Ord.Sea. J.	6447	Morrell, S./Sjt.(A./S.M.) C.		6934
— L./C.(T./Cpl.) J. L.	6917	— Pte.(T./Sjt.) F. G.		6910
— S.M. J. R.	7038	Morris, Sjt. A.		6886
— Engmn. J. W.	6447	— Sjt. F.		6875
— R.S.M. L. A.	6955	— Dvr. F. W.		6914
— S.M. I. L. R.	7038	— S.M. G. R., *M.M.*		6907
— C.S.M.(A./R.S.M.) R.	7015	— S./Sjt. G. W.		6901
— Sjt. S. F.	6910	— Pte.(A./Sjt.) H. V.		7020
Moorely, R.Q.M.S. W. A.	6895	— Cpl. O. C.		6886
Moores, Cpl. J.	7017	— C.S.M. R.		6957
Moran, Cpl. A.	6908	— Sjt. R.		6868
— Pte. J.	6885	— E.C.Cpl.(A./Q.M.S.) R. J.		6877
— Sjt.(A./C.Q.M.S.) W.	7013	— Mas.Mec. .		7038
Morck, C.S.M. A. C. T.	6900	— R.Q.M.S. W.		6891
Moreby, Cpl. R. A.	6889	— Sjt. W. H.		6944
Morel, B.S.M. G. E.	6869	Morrisey, Sjt. J. A.		6914
Morey, Sjt. P.	7023	Morrison, Cpl. A. L.		6904
— Cpl.(T./Sjt.) T. G.	6911	— Sjt. D.		6892
Morfitt, T./S.M. J. R.	6934	— C.S.M. J.		6891
Morgan, Sjt.Clk. A. E. G.	7038	— Pte. J. B.		6934
— S./Sjt. E.	6901	— Sjt. R.		6868
— Pte. F. H.	6906	— Sjt. W. C.		6875
— Sjt. F. W.	6914	— Pte. W. V.		6892
— Cpl. G. T.	6904	Morriss, 2nd Cpl.(A./Cpl.) F. H.		6943
— S./Sjt.(A./S.Q.M.S.) J.	7020	Morrissey, C.S.M. J.		6900
— 2nd Cpl.(A./Sjt.) J. C.	6946	Morter, P.O. G. J.		5111
— Sjt. J. E.	6932	Mortimer, Sjt. C. E.		6902
— Cpl. L.	7038	— S.M. E. J.		7011
— Sjt. M. L.	6875	Morton, Sjt. D.		7022
— S./Sjt. M. T.	6934	— Sjt. G.		6943
— Sjt. R.	6895	— F./Sjt. J. A.		7038
— Farr.Q.M.S. T.	* 7010	— Actg.W.O. 2nd Cl. T.		4198
— S./Sjt. T.	6957	— Sjt. T. J.		6888
— Pte.(A./Cpl.)T.	6909	Mosdell, C.Q.M.S. J. V. B.		6873
— Sjt. W.	6885	Moser, Cpl.(A./Sjt.) C. W. L., *M.M.*		7011
Moriarty, Cpl.(T./S./Sjt.) D.	6904	Moss, Sjt. A. E.		6875
Morison, Cpl. G. E.	6877	— Q.M.S. A. T.	†	6872

---

* R.A. Awarded M.S.M. annuity A.O. 10/1933.

† Group in the Moss collection: British War and Victory Medals (W.O.II R.E. M.I.D. oakleaf), Defence Medal, M.S.M. and French Médaille Militaire. A Derbyshire man, Moss joined the R.E. was given the number 175087 and at some stage in 1916 posted to 258 Tunnelling Coy. R.E. in France. 258 was the last Tunnelling Company formed; from May 1917 they operated with the 1st A.N.Z.A.C. Corps at Bullecourt, in 1918 they served with XIX Corps at St. Quentin, Rosières and Avre and in the summer they were part of the British Third Army at Albert, Bapaume and Epéhy. Sometime prior to the end of the war Moss was given a new number, WR256657, a war reserve number, indicating he was no longer fit for front line duties. His Médaille Militaire was gazetted four days after his M.S.M., on 7 June 1919.

Moss, Pte. J., *MM.*	6889	Murch, Q.M.S.(A./S.M.) F. W.	7020
— Sjt. J. G.	6893	Murchison, Sjt.(A./B.Q.M.S.) A.	6954
— T./S.S.M. W. F.	* 6899	Murcy, Sjt. R. P.	6944
— Sjt. W. N.	6875	Murgatroyd, L.A.C. T. W.	7038
Mostyn, Cpl. R.	6904	Murnagham, R.S.M. G. A. G.	6890
Mottershead, Flt.Sjt. A.	7038	Murphie, Sjt. J.	6894
Mottram, Sjt. S. A.	6895	Murphy, C.S.M.(A./R.S.M.) F.	6885
Moule, Sjt. G.	6890	— E.C.Cpl.(A./E.C.Sjt.) J.	6877
— Pte.(A./Sjt.) G. H.	6914	— Pte.(T./C.S.M.) J.	6906
Moulton, Cpl. S. L.	6896	— Sjt.(T./R.S.M.) M. J.	6917
Moundrill, C.Q.M.S. F.	6944	— P.O. P.	8203
Mounsey, C.Q.M.S. W.	6887	— Pte. W.	6917
Mountain, Cpl. J. F.	7019	Murray, Sea. A.	4733
Mountney, Cpl.(T./Sjt.) S.	6954	— Condr. A. A.	6970
Movat, Sjt. J.	6881	— Sjt. D.	6875
Moy, C.S.M. W. O.	6943	— R.S.M. E.	7014
Moyes, R.Q.M.S. J.	6886	— Cpl.(T./Sjt.) J.	6877
Moyle, T./W.O. Cl.1, T. A.	7022	— Cpl. J.	6877
Mugford, B.S.M.(A./R.S.M.)F.	6953	— E.R.A. 1st Cl. S.	7512
Muir, C.Q.M.S. A.	6894	— Sjt. V.	6875
— Pte.(A./L./C.) F. W. (corr.)	7703	— S./Sjt. W. J.	7022
— R.Q.M.S. J.	6881	Murrell, Pte.(A./Cpl.) C.	7021
— Pte. J.	6891	— C.S.M.(I.M.) G. A.	‡ 7021
— T./R.S.M. P.	7010	— T./R.S.M. H. E.	7015
Mulcahy, C.S.M. J.	7017	Musgrove, Spr. H.	6879
Mulhall, S./Sjt. J.	6934	Musker, C.Q.M.S. K.	6883
Mullane, Pte.(A./Sjt.) E. J.	7015	Mustart, S./Sjt. A. S.	6907
— C.S.M. M.	7011	Muston, Pte. W	6917
Muller, Sjt.(A./S./Sjt.) S.	7019	Mutch, Sjt. T. W. L.	6914
Mullett, Cpl. R.	6904	Mutimer, S./Sjt. J.	7021
Mulley, Sjt. G.	6870	Mutter, Ch.Writer W. J.	8069
Mullins, C.Q.M.S. H.	6882	Myers, T./S.M. B.	6871
— Pte.(A./Cpl.) J.	7014	— R.Q.M.S. G.	6933
Mulvenny, Sjt. P.	6955	— S.S.M. O. B.	6899
Mummery, Cpl. J.	6945	Myerscough, Pte.(L./C.) L.	6883
Muncaster, C.S.M. J.	6891		
— Cpl. J.	6868	Naggomero, R.S.M.	6971
Munday, Armr.S./Sjt. A. T.	6910	Nagle, Sjt. M.	7016
Munn, Pte.(A./C.Q.M.S.) H.	6955	Nairn, Sjt. J.	6910
Munns, C.Q.M.S. C.	6954	Naisby, Sjt. H. B.	6881
— C.Q.M.S.(A./C.S.M.) W. J.	7018	Napper, R.S.M. C. F.	6970
Munro, S./Sjt. J.	6976	Nash, B.Q.M.S. A. J., *MM.*	6867
— Pte.(A./L./Sjt.) J.McG.	† 7015	— Sjt. F.	6875
Munsey, Bombr. W. C.	6868	— Sjt. J.	6914
Munton, Sjt.(A./S.Q.M.S.) J. C.	6957	— Sjt. J. J.	6885

* His L.S. & G.C. (Geo. V, W.O.II) and M.S.M. (R.A.S.C.) are in the Moss collection without his W.W.I medals. S.M. Moss's father was awarded an annuity M.S.M. together with a pair of medals for Egypt in 1882.
† Indian Army, for Aden.
‡ M.S.M. known. School of Musketry No. B/331. Only 12 M.S.M.s to the unit.

Nash, Sjt. W	6888	Newman, C.S.M. C., *D.C.M.*		6893
— Cpl.(A./Sjt.) W.	6877	— S./Sjt. C T.		7021
Natzler, T./Sub Condr. G.	6909	— S.S.M. J.		6899
Nawa Bin Nyame, C.S.M.	6971	— Sjt. J. W.		6954
Naylor, Sjt. Mec. C.	7038	— Pte. L.		6897
— T./Sub Condr. H. B	6909	— Sjt.(A./C.S.M.) W. H. E.		7016
Neal, T./Sub Condr. D W.	6909	Newport, Sjt. J.		6910
— C.S.M.Instr. G. H.	6912	Newth, Cpl.(A./Sjt.) F.		6887
— Sjt. J. W.	6875	Newton, E.R./W.O. Cl. 1, A. E.		7022
Neale, Pte.(A./Cpl.) A. H. G.	6882	— Sjt. G. L.		6915
— Sjt. H.	6914	— Sqdn.S.M. H. W.		7022
Neatham, Sjt.(A./R.Q.M.S.) F. H. W.	7010	— C.S.M.(A./R.S.M.) W. G.		6887
Nehemiah, Headman	6970	Niblett, Sjt.(A./S.S.M.) F. B.		6504
Neighbour, S./Sjt. J. W.	6910	Nicholl, C.S.M. H.		6915
Neill, R.S.M. A.	6866	Nicholls, Sjt. A.		6902
— Sjt. J. G. C.	6888	— Cpl. A. H.		6943
Neish, S./Sjt. W. G.	6914	— Farr.Sjt. B.		6915
Nelson, L.A.C. C. B. R.	7038	— Pte.(L./C.) E.		6942
— Sjt. J.	6895	— Sjt. J. E.		6875
— C.Q.M.S. J. E.	6945	— R.Q.M.S. W.		6884
— C.Q.M.S. T. L.	6956	— Sea. W. C.		4733
Nevard, S./Sjt. J.	6957	Nichols, Condr. L.		6915
Neve, T./S.M. C.	6866	Nicholson, Pte. B.		6915
— Sjt. F. N.	6865	— Pte.(A./Sjt.) C. W.		7019
— Sto.P.O. W. G.	4735	— Cpl. D.		6904
Nevin, Sea. J. P.	4733	— Sjt.(O.R.Sjt.) F.		7015
Nevitt, Pte. S.	6906	— S.M. H. F. C.		7038
New, Pte.(A./Sjt.) A.	6911	— S./Sjt. H. K.		6919
— Mech. S./Sjt. A. E.	6900	— C.Q.M.S. H. P.		6894
Newall, F./Sjt. W.	7038	— R.Q.M.S. H. S.		6881
Newberry, Sjt.(A./Sub Condr.) A. D.	6914	— Sjt. N.		6902
Newblatt, Sjt. S. N.	6890	— Farr.Sjt. T.		6867
Newbon, Sjt.(A./S.S.M.) E. A.	6902	— Gnr. T.		7011
Newbury, Spr.(T./Farr.Sjt.) A.	6879	Nickells, R.Q.M.S.(A./R.S.M.) J.		7015
Newby, Sjt. G. A., *M.M.*	6884	Nickless, Sjt. H.		6945
Newcomb, F./Clk. J.	7038	Nield, S./Sjt. H. B.	*	7702
Newcombe, Cpl. F.	6894	Nightingale, Cpl. D.		6877
Newham, Sjt. W. L.	6885	Nisbet, C.S.M. W. J.		6872
Newholm, S.M. I. H.	7038	Niven, Dvr. A.		6943
Newicutt, Pte. T.	6906	— Pte. W.		6886
Newman, S.Q.M.S.(A./S.S.M.) A.	7021	Nixon, Sjt.(A./S.M.) A.		7014

* M.S.M. only known with copy of a letter General H.Q. North Russian Expeditionary Force, 17th Nov. 1918: The 'Meritorious Service Medal' in recognition of your meritorious service. The following is the official account of your service, for which the award has been made: 'Owing to the shortage of Officers, this N.C.O. was left in charge from the first landing until the beginning of Oct., of all Signals organisation at Bakharitza. This included installing and controlling the Signal Office, fitting up and running wireless and instrument repair shops, handling, unpacking, classifying, storing and issuing about 80 tons of wireless stores of a highly varied nature, testing equipment and putting into commission all wireless stations, keeping of

Nixon, C.S.M.Instr. E.	6912	Oakes, C.S.M. H.	6890
Nkwale, C.S.M. N. N.	6971	— Pte. W. H.	5113
Noad, Sjt. A.	6875	O'Brien, C.S.M. J.	6933
Noakes, Pte.(A./Sjt.) A. E.	6883	— T./S.M. J.	6869
— Cpl.(L./Sjt.) A. H.	6944	— Sjt.(A./C.Q.M.S.) J.	7015
Noble, C.Q.M.S. T. A.	6891	— Sjt. J.	6875
Noblet, B.Q.M.S. W. J.	6867	— S.S.M. J. W.	7023
Nock, 2nd Cpl.(A./Sjt.) A. J.	6878	— C.S.M.O.	7016
Nolan, C.Q.M.S. J.	6943	— Spr.(A./2nd Cpl.) P.	7013
Noon, Pte. H.	6866	— R.Q.M.S. W.	6883
— S./Sjt. P. H.	7019	Ockelford, Sjt.(A./C.S.M.) C. W.	7012
— Sjt.(O.R.C.) W.	6880	O'Connor, B.S.M. J. T.	6917
Noonan, Sjt.(A./C.Q.M.S.) J. A. C.	6893	— Pte. V. P.	6893
Noor Sileit, Pte.(L./C.)	6971	Oexle, C.S.M. W. H.	7017
Norkett, Condr. H. W.	7021	Ogg, T./Sub Condr. R. K.	6909
Norman, Pte.(A./C.S.M.) A. H.	6955	Ogilvie, Dvr. G. L.	6917
— Sjt. J.	6902	O'Gorman, Dvr. G.	6917
Normington, Sjt. A. L.	6945	Ohlsen, Cpl. E.	6943
Norrie, S.S.M. E. R.	7023	O'Keeffe, Sjt. J.	6885
North, Cpl. F.	6934	Oldacre, B.S.M. H.	6866
— Sjt.(A./C.Q.M.S.) F. E.	* 7018	Oldfield, Sjt. H. S.	6895
— Spr.(L./C.) H. G.	6879	O'Leary, Sjt.(T./C.S.M.) E. E.	6943
— Cpl. J.	6890	— Spr.(L./C.) M. R.	6879
— Pte.(L./C.) M.	6887	Olive, Sjt. F.	6889
— Gnr.(L./Bombr.) R.	6871	— Sjt. F. L.	6969
— Ldg.Sea. T. H.	5112	Oliveira, Pte.(A./Sjt.) J. D.	6894
Norton, Pte. F. W.	6906	Oliver, Sjt. C. N.	6943
— Sjt.(A./C.Q.M.S.) R. C.	6875	— Sjt.Clk. D. C.	7038
Noyce, Sjt. L. A.	6890	— Sjt. F. W.	6915
Noye, Sjt. J.	4512	— T./S.S.M. G.	6899
Nunn, Cpl. E. A.	6883	— T./Sub Condr. H.	6909
— C.Q.M.S. G. S.	6882	— C.Q.M.S. H. G.	6882
— Cpl.(A./Sjt.) J. E.	6911	— C.Q.M.S. J.	6882
Nurse, Sjt. H. G.	6887	— Sjt. W. J.	6887
Nutt, Sjt.(A./R.S.M.) J.	7014	Ollett, S./Sjt.(A./S.Q.M.S.) C.	6970
Nuttall, Sjt. H.	6933	Olley, Cpl.(A./Sjt.) H. C.	6956
— Bombr. H.	6943	Ollis, F./Sjt. C.	7038
		O'Looney, Cpl. J. P.	6868
Oake, Cpl.(A./C.S.M.) G.	7012	Omolo Bin Ogudu, Sjt.	6971
Oakes, Sjt. A.	6891	O'Neill, Sub Condr. G. P.	7021
— Pte. G. W.	6906	— S.S./Cpl. J.	6911

wireless parties. He showed the greatest energy and resource, and performed all these duties most efficiently. It is hard to realise how this N.C.O. got through his daily work in the 24 hours.' I heartily congratulate you upon the honour which has been conferred upon you. Ironside, Brig. General, Commanding-in-Chief, North Russia Expeditionary Force. A Scarce award with a citation for Russia.

* Group was in McInnes collection: Queen's South Africa Medal (Orange Free State, Transvaal, South Africa 1901, South Africa 1902, 3070 Sergt. 20 Hussars), L.S. & G.C. (22328 Sgt. R.D.C.), M.S.M. to 60 Coy. Royal Defence Corps. (Only 54 M.S.M.s to R.D.C. The L.S. & G.C. is probably even more scarce.)

O'Neill, Sjt. J. H.	6917		Owens, Cpl.(A./Sjt.) E. S.	6896
— R.Q.M.S. W.	7014		— Sjt. O.	6885
Onyett, C.S.M. A. S.	6933			
Opie, Sjt. N.	6917		Pack, Sjt. A. J.	6969
Oram, Pte.(A./C.Q.M.S.) R. B.	7017		Packer, Sjt. F. H.	6976
Organ, Ch. Writer W. S.	7907		— Pte.(A./Sjt.) H. G.	6909
Ormonde, Gnr. E.	6871		Paddock, Sjt. J. L.	6918
O'Rourke, L./C. T. E.	6917		Paddon, Sjt. W. H.	6910
Orphan, Sjt.(A./S.Q.M.S.) T. J.	7019		Padfield, Sjt. G.	6884
Orr, Pte. A.	6915		Padgett, Gnr. T.	6869
Orton, Sjt. C.	6875		Paffrey, C.Q.M.S. H. E.	6888
Osborn, Sjt. A. C.	7038		Page, T./R.S.M. A.	6856
— 2nd Cpl. A. F.	6878		— Sjt. A. G.	7038
Osborne, Sjt. E. R.	6870		— T./Sub Condr. C. F.	6909
— S.Q.M.S. M. M. E.	6942		— Cpl. H.	6870
— S.S.M. S.	6899		— Cpl. P.	6890
— Sjt. W.	6887		— Cpl. R.	6974
Osbourne, R.S.M. E. G.	7010		— S./Sjt. R. G.	6915
O'Shea, Cpl. J.	6956		— SSjt. W.	6955
Osman, T./R.S.M. E. W.	7015		— Sqdn.Q.M.S. W. A.	6865
Osmond, Cpl. G. W.	6904		Paice, B.S.M. W. J.	7010
Ostick, 2nd Cpl. G.	6878		Pain, T./S.S.M. G.	6956
Ostler, Sjt. W. E.	6908		— C.Q.M.S. R. G.	6918
Oswick, Cpl.(L./Sjt.) F.	6887		Painter, W.O. Cl.2, S.Q.M.S.(A./	
Otis, Cpl. J. T.	6915		W.O. Cl. 1) F. J. (corr.)	6065
Ottley, Ch.Mec. O.	7038		Palfrey, Pte. J.	6906
Ousley, Sjt. F. W.	6881		Palham, Pte. H. A.	6906
— Sjt. R. W.	6902		Palimoni Lugiana, Pte.(L./C.)	6971
Outterside, Pte. E.	6882		Pallin, Sjt. T. G.	6934
Ovenden, Mech.Elect.			Palmer, Cpl. A.	6883
Q.M.S. E. W.	* 7012		— Sjt.(T./C.S.M.) A. C.	6875
Over, Pte.(L./C.) A. R.	6898		— Pte.(A./S.Q.M.S.) A. R.	7022
Overall, Pte.(T./Sub Condr.) W. A.	6946		— Sjt. A. S.	6898
Overton, Pte. S. H.	6906		— Pte. C.	6865
— Sjt. T.	6868		— T./S.M. C. F.	7020
Owen, C.Q.M.S. A. A.	† 6890		— Cpl.(A./Sjt.) C. W. F.	6896
— Pte.(A./Sjt.) A. E.	6945		— Sjt. E.	7013
— S./Sjt.(A./R.S.M.) C. V.	7017		— Sqdn.Cpl.Maj. E.	7010
— Sjt. D.	6888		— R.S.M. E. H.	6895
— C.S.M. E.	6882		— Sadd.Sjt. G. A.	6868
— Mech.S./Sjt. H.	‡ 6935		— Q.M.S. J. G.	6934
— S./Sjt. J.	6933		— Spr. W. H.	6879
— Q.M.S. J. H.	7021		Pankhurst, S./S.M.(A./1st Cl.	
— Sjt. S.	7013		S.S.M.) F.	7702
— C.Q.M.S. W. E. C.	6885		Pankhurt, Sjt. E. J.	6875
— S./Sjt. W. H.	6934		Papworth, Cpl. C.	6885

* R.E. For Hong Kong.
† 2/K.R.R.C. Entitled to Queen's South Africa Medal.
‡ For Arabia. Group known: 1914/15 Star (Staff Sgt. R.E.), British War and Victory Medals and M.S.M. Only three awards for Arabia. See Bissell and Boodson *ante*.

Papworth, C.S.M. J. M.	6893	Partridge, Sjt. H. H.		6890
Parbott, Sjt. J. T.	6889	— Sjt. W. A.		6956
Parfitt, S.S.M. A. F.	7023	Pascoe, L./C. A. J.		6918
Pargeter, Pte. S.	6897	— C.S.M. T. T.		6872
Parish, Sjt. C. G.	6893	Passell, Gnr.(L./Bombr.) A. C. P. W.		6871
Park, Pte. W. G.	6906	Pate, C.S.M. J.		6872
Parker, Sjt. A.	7019	— Pte.(A./C.Q.M.S.) R.		6906
— Cpl.(A./Sjt.) A. G.	6877	— C.Q.M.S. T. J.		6885
— Sjt. H. J.	6908	Pater, Cpl.(A./Sjt.) F. D.		6891
— P.O. J. E.	7512	Paterson, Sjt. A.		6892
— Sjt. J. R.	6918	— Sjt. E. H.		6883
— C.Q.M.S.(A./R.Q.M.S.) W. G.	6956	— Sjt. J.		6868
— S./Sjt.(A./Q.M.S.) W. O.	6907	— Pte.(A./C.S.M.) W.		6970
Parkes, Sjt.(A./Bd.Mr.) A.	6895	Paton, Cpl.(A./C.S.M.) C. B. (corr.)		7703
— Sjt. E.	6894	— Cpl.(A./Sjt.) J.		6915
— A.M. 2dn Cl. F. H.	7038	Patrick, Sjt. F. G.		6898
— Sjt.(A./C.S.M.) W. G.	6875	— T./Sub Condr. H. F.		6909
Parkin, Sjt. C.	6891	— Sjt. J.		6902
Parkinson, Sjt.(A./S.Q.M.S.) C. H.	7022	Pattenden, Pte.(A./Sjt.) H. A.		7019
— C.Q.M.S. C. R.	6900	Patterson, F./Sjt. F. H.		7038
— S./Sjt. G.	6907	— C.Q.M.S. I.		6919
— S.S.M. W.	6899	— C.Q.M.S. J.		6886
Parnham, Sjt. C.	6902	Pattinson, Sjt. J.		6954
Parr, C.S.M.Instr. R. S.	6912	Pattison, S./Sjt. R. S.		6915
— Pte.(A./R.Q.M.S.) T.	6955	Patton, Sjt. S.		6918
Parrett, Dvr.(A./Sjt.) G. R.	7019	Paul, C.Q.M.S. H. E.		6873
Parrott, Pte.(A./L./C.) W. R.	6911	— R.S.M. R.		6953
Parry, S./Sjt. A. G.	6945	Pavy, Cpl. C. F.		6918
— Sjt. A. O.	6875	Paxman, Cpl. H. L.		6877
— A./Cpl. C.	7038	Payne, Pte. A.		6884
— Clk. 1st Cl. D.	7038	— Gnr. E.		6954
— Sjt. G.	6902	— S.M. G. W.		6946
— Sjt. H.	6868	— Sjt. J.	†	6883
— Ldg.Sea. H.	4735	— Sjt. R. C., *D.C.M.*		6875
— Pte.(A./Cpl.) J. L.	6909	Paynter, Ch.Sto. W.		5112
Parsons, Sjt. C. R.	6898	Peach, C.Q.M.S.(A./S.M.) J. W.		6873
— Sjt. F. C.	6893	Peachey, B.Q.M.S. H. O. (deletion)		7703
— Dvr.(A./Sjt.) G. E. H.	6907	Peacock, Pte. S. A.		6906
— Cpl. G. M.	6904	— Cpl. T. L.		6877
— Sjt. J. A.	6875	Peak, C.Q.M.S. F.		6893
— C.Q.M.S. M. M.	6918	— Sjt. H. T.		6875
— Sjt. R. C.	6933	Peake, Sjt. J. N.		6875
— Mech.S./Sjt. W.	6970	— R.Q.M.S. P.		7014
— T./Amt.S.M. W. J.	* 7020	— C.Q.M.S. S.		6857
— Sjt. W. R. W.	7015	Pealing, S./S.M. W.	‡	7021
Parton, Pte.(A./S.S.M.) E.	7019	Pearce, Sjt. A. C.		6908
— S.M. F. S.	7020	— Pte. A. T.		6954

* R.A.O.C. M.S.M. for Malta.
† As Staff Q.M.S., R.A.S.C. awarded M.S.M. annuity in A.O. 87/1950.
‡ A.P.C. For Malta.

Pearce, Sjt. (A./S.S.M.) C.		7019	Penny, Sjt. D. G.		6915
— Sjt. E. G.		6895	— Cpl. F. C.		6908
— A.C. 2, F. R.		7038	— Engmn. J. H.		6447
— C.S.M. H.		6954	Pentland, Pte.(A./Cpl.) F. W.		6957
— Sjt. H.		6946	— B.Q.M.S. M.		6867
— Cpl. J.		6908	Penwarden, Sjt. J.		6915
— S./Sjt.(A./S.M.) W. G.		6946	Penwill, 1st Cl. S.S.M. W. A. (corr.)		6065
— S.M. W. H.		7038	Peplow, R.Q.M.S. J. J.		7014
— Detect.Sjt. W. H.		7022	Percival, Pte. W		6934
Pearson, Cpl. C.		6975	Percy, C.Q.M.S. S.	†	7015
— C.Q.M.S. C. H.		6891	Perdrian, Dvr. J. A.		6918
— C.S.M. H.	*	6867	Perfect, Pte. J. A.		6906
— Sjt. H.		6956	Perfitt, Sjt.(A./Flt.Sjt.) J. A.		7038
— R.S.M. P. J.		6886	Perigo, Mech.S./Sjt. H.		6900
Peasgood, C.S.M. A.		7017	Perkins, Pte. G. H.		6906
Peat, C.Q.M.S. H.		7012	— B.Q.M.S. R. J.		6866
Peck, Farr.S./Sjt. A. H.		6867	Perks, S./Sjt. C.		6908
— Pte.(A./Sjt.) G.		6911	Perrett, Ch.Shipwt 2nd Cl. W		7512
— Sjt. P. D.		6902	Perry, T./S.M. F. G.		6909
Peckham, Sjt.(A./R.Q.M.S.) S.		6892	— Bombr.(A./B.Q.M.S.) G. P.		6976
Peddy, 2nd Cpl. G. H.		6878	— C.Q.M.S. H.		6888
Peebles, Cpl. J.		6904	— Pte. J. F.		6915
Peel, T./Armt.S.M. J. P.		6909	— C.Q.M.S. P.		6898
Pegg, A.C. 1 (A./Cpl.) A. W.		7038	— Sjt. R. J.		6918
Pelham, Cpl.(A./Sjt.) G.		6954	— C.P.O.Teleg. T. L.		7907
Pellett, Sjt. G.		6908	— Ch.Mec. W.		7038
Pelley, S./Sjt. (A./S.M.) A. H.		6907	Pery, Pte. H.		6956
Penberthy, C.S.M. P. R.		6872	Peters, Pte. A. L.		6906
Pendleton, Pte. A.		6888	— C.Q.M.S. G.		6880
Penfold, S.M. H. A.		7038	— L.A.C. W.		7038
— Cpl.(L./Sjt.) R. F.		6882	Pether, C.S.M. H.		6915
— Sjt. W. H.		6893	Petitt, Spr. C. W.		6879
Penn, Cpl.(A./L./Sjt.) C. W.		6945	Petrie, Sjt. C. W.		6875
— C.Q.M.S. F.		6889	— Cpl. J. A.		6956
— C.Q.M.S. J.		6891	— S.Q.M.S. N. J. C.		6899
— Farr.S./Sjt. J. A.		6900	Pett, Spr. H.		6879
— R.S.M. J. T.		6918	— Sjt. H. F.		6898
Penney, Cpl.(A./Sjt.) G. C.		7017	Pettitt, Sjt. C.		6894
Pennington, Cpl W.		6883	Pettyfer, Sjt.(A./C.Q.M.S.) C. J.		6932

* Group was in McInnes collection: O.B.E. (1st type, military ribbon T./Cpt.), India General Service Medal (Burma 1885/87, 1036 Pte. 2/Liverpool R.), British War Medal, Territorial Force War Medal and Victory Medal (all 4, W.O.II, R.A.), Coronation 1911 (B.S.M. 3/Welsh R.F.A.), M.S.M. (735002 C.S.M. R.F.A.), Volunteer L.S. & G.C. (Edw. VII, 1676 Sgt. 1/Cheshire RGAV) and Territorial Force Efficiency Medal (Geo. V, 735002 W.O.II R.F.A.). He first enlisted in Warrington in January 1885 being born in Essex in 1866. He was discharged in 1896 having served in India and Burma from 1886 to 1892.

† Group known: 1914/15 Star trio (M.I.D. oakleaf C./Sgt. D.C.L.I.), Africa General Service Medal (Nigeria 1918, Duke of Cornwall's L.I.), L.S. & G.C. (Geo. V) and M.S.M.

Peverley, S./Sjt. R. S.	7021	Pimm, Sjt. H. C.	6915
Philip, Sjt. A.	6894	— Spr. J. H. ✤	7702
Philippart, Cpl. A. E.	6904	Pinchen, B.S.M. R. H. H.	6866
Philipson, Sjt. A. S.	7038	Pinder, Pte.(A./Sjt.) E.	6909
Phillips, Sjt. B. S. V.	6875	Pinhay, C.P.O. G. H.	8202
— T./S.M. C.	6880	Pinnigar, Sjt. W. G.	6890
— Cpl. H.	6957	Pint, C.Q.M.S.(A./C.S.M.) P. M.	6956
— Sjt. H. J.	6910	Pipe, Spr.(L./C.) F. H.	6932
— S./Sjt. H. J. C.	6918	Piper, C.Q.M.S. J. F.	6884
— Cpl.(A./Sjt.) H. R.	6954	Pitkin, Q.M.S. C.	7020
— Sjt. L.	6891	Pitman, Cpl.(L./Sjt.) A. F. A.	6880
— C.Q.M.S. M. T.	6955	Pitt, Spr.(T./Sjt.) F. T.	6880
— Pte. W. A.	6906	— Q.M.S. G.	6956
— Dkhnd. W. H.	4733	Pittendreigh, Pte.(L./C.) T.	6945
— T./Sqdn.S.M. W. H. A.	6934	Pitts, S./Sjt. S. T.	7021
— S./Sjt. W. J.	6915	Plaice, S.M. W.	7038
Philpott, Sjt. W. H.	6902	Plane, B.S.M. G.	6866
Philps, Farr.Sjt. T. A. H.	6870	Plant, Pte. E.	6865
Pibworth, C.S.M. S.	6889	Plaskett, Ch.Elect.Art. A. J.	8079
Picken, B.S.M. T. W.	6866	Platt, Sjt. C. F.	6889
Pickerill, C.Q.M.S.(A./S.M.) G. W.	6873	Pleace, Sjt. G	7014
Pickering, Pte.(A./S./Sjt.) A. P.	7019	Plum, Cpl. E. G.	6932
— Supt.Clk. J. A.	6871	Plumb, Sjt. H. F.	6903
Pickersgill, Sjt. W.	6884	Plumley, Sjt.(O.R.Sjt.) H.	7014
Pickett, Sjt. J.	6945	Plummer, Pte.(A./L./C.) J. H.	6911
Pickford, C.S.M.Instr.(A./		Poad, Q.M.S. F. H. L.	6907
S.M.Instr.) G.	7021	Pocock, C.Q.M.S. A. G.	6873
— Sjt. J.	6885	— C.S.M. H.	6889
Pickston, Pte.(A./Sjt.) J.	6976	Pointing, Master Gnr. 1st Cl. A.	7011
Pickup, Cpl. T.	6868	Pollard, C.Q.M.S. W.	6890
Pickwell, Cpl. E.	6884	— C.Q.M.S. W. H.	6889
Pidduck, Pte. W. T.	6915	Polley, Sjt. A.	6910
Pierce, Sjt. J. J.	6888	Pollock, B.Q.M.S.(A./B.S.M.) D.	6867
— Cpl.Mec. R. W.	7038	— Ch. Blacksmith G.	8069
Piercey, Sjt. M.	6918	— B.S.M. J. P.	6866
Piggott, Sjt. W.	6902	Ponter, Sjt. W.	6933
Pigott, Q.M.S.(A./R.Q.M.S.) T. W. *	6932	Pool, Cpl. W. J.	6882
Pike, A./C.S.M. W. H.	6915	Poole, Pte. A.	6884
Pikesley, Sjt. C.	6888	— Pte.(A./C.Q.M.S.) H.	6882
Pilgrim, Ldg.Sig. A.	7908	— Eng.Clk.S./Sjt. N.	7012
Pilkie, C.Q.M.S. A. E.	6915	— T./S.S.M. S.	6889
Pilkington, Cpl. G.	6954	— Sjt. W. H.	6883
— W.O. Cl. 1, I. H.	6934	Pooley, C.S.M. E. R.	6971
— Spr.(A./Sjt.) J. W.	6879	— S./Sjt. H. E.	7012
— Sjt. T. E.	6910	Poore, Sjt. A. J.	6875
Pilling, Pte.(A/Cpl.) J. H.	7020	Pope, Cpl.(A./Sjt.) C. S.	6915

---

* Group known in Edinburgh Castle: Queen's Egypt (Gemaizah 1888), India General
Service Medal (Relief of Chitral, Punjab Frontier), both K.O.S.B., 1914/15 Star
trio, L.S. & G.C. (Victoria). M.S.M. (for Egypt Lothian & Border Horse), Territorial
Efficiency Medal (Geo. V, L. & B.H.) and Khedive's Star (undated).

Pope, Farr.Sjt. G.	6903	Preston, S.M. E.	6907
— Pte.(A./S.S.M.Sjt.) G. F.	7019	— Cpl. H.	6904
— R.S.M. H. H.	6871	— C.S.M.Instr. W. H.	7016
— Cpl. J. H.	6882	Prestt, S./Sjt. L.	6908
— F. of W. Q.M.S. W.	7012	Price, Pte.(A./Sjt.) A.	6883
Pople, C.S.M. W. A.	6872	— Cpl. H.	6943
Porteous, W.O. Cl.1, J.	7023	— Pte.(A./C.Q.M.S.) H. E.	7016
Porter, Pte. A.	7020	— C.Q.M.S. H. G.	6918
— S./Sjt. D. F.	6935	— Pte. S. W.	6888
— Ch.Sto. F. C.	7512	Pridmore, Cpl. T.	6889
— Sjt.(A.C.) H. J.	6870	Priestley, Pte.(L./C.) C. H.	6883
— Mech.S./Sjt. R. W.	6900	Priestly, Pte. L.	6909
— C.S.M. T.	6933	Priestner, Bombr.(A./Cpl.) W.	6868
Postill, Ch.Mec. H.	7038	Prime, Sjt. G. G.	6890
Pothecary, Pte. J.	6956	Primrose, Mech.S./Sjt. A.	6900
Potter, Sjt. A.	6875	Prince, Cpl.(A./Sjt.) H. J.	6877
— R.Q.M.S. J.	6933	— Q.M.S. H. W.	6907
— R.S.M. J.	7014	— Sjt. J. D.	6894
— Pte.(A./Cpl.) J. C.	6897	Pringle, Sjt. S. S.	6903
— Pte. W. D.	6906	Prior, Cpl. A.	6897
Potts, T./S.M. W.	6907	— E.C. and S. 2nd Cpl. A. A. W.	6878
Poulter, Cpl.(T./C.S.M.) A., *MM.*	6877	— T./R.S.M. A. H.	6970
— Condr. J.	7021	— Pte.(A./Cpl.) A. J.	6906
— R.Q.M.S. W. H.	6933	— Sjt. F.	6875
Poulton, A./Sjt. P. C.	6915	— Pte.(A./Cpl.) F.	6909
Pover, Cpl. E.	6915	— Sjt. O. C.	6918
Pow, Spr.(A./Sjt.) T.	✼ 7702	Pritchard, R.Q.M.S. F. A.	6889
Powell, Ch.Engmn. A. D. C.	4733	— Sea. J. R.	5112
— C.Q.M.S. C. R.	6900	— C.S.M. T.	7017
— Sjt. F.	6903	— Bombr.(A./Sjt.) T. F.	6869
— Sjt.Mec. G. C.	7038	— Sjt. W.	6890
— Sjt.(A./Sjt.Dmr.) H.	6884	— Cpl.(A./Sjt.) W. C.	6898
— S./Sjt. H. E. W.	7023	Pronger, Sjt. E.	6890
— C.S.M. J. C., *MM.*	7013	Proud, R.Q.M.S. J. C.	6891
— Sjt. J. E.	6888	Prout, 2nd Cpl. G.	6878
— S./Sjt. T. C. H.	6918	Prudames, C.Q.M.S.(A./R.Q.M.S.)	
— Pte.(L./C.) W. F. D.	6898	S. M.	6884
Power, Pte.(A./S.S.M.) G. A. V.	7019	Prudhorn, Sjt. T.	6915
Pratley, Pte. T.	✼ 6064	Pryor, C.Q.M.S. D.	6882
Pratt, Cpl.(A./Sjt.) A. J.	6893	— 2nd Cpl. R. W. N.	6878
— R.S.M. E. R.	* 6866	Pugh, Sjt. J.	6945
— Spr.(L./Sjt.) J. W.	6880	Pulfrey, F./Sjt. A.	7039
Preece, Sjt. E.	6875	Pullen, Cpl.(A./C.Q.M.S.) C. S.	6898
— F./Sjt. G. H.	7038	— Sjt. L. T.	6875
— Gnr.(A./Sjt.) W. A.	7011	Punch, Sjt.(B.Q.M.S.) F. S.	6918
Prentice, Cpl. J. R.	6877	Purcell, Sjt. H. A.	7016
Presswell, W.O. Cl. 1, R. J.	7022	— B.S.M.(A./R.S.M.) W. H.	6866
Preston, S./Sjt. A.	6908	Purdue, P.O. J. E	6448
— L.A.C. C.	7038	Purse, Gnr.(L./Bombr.)(A.C.) G. S.	6871

* Awarded M.S.M. Annuity A.O.144, 1950. Royal Artillery.

Pursey, Sjt. J. F.	6910		Ramson, T./S.S.M. T. H.	6899
Purslow, F./Sjt. W. C.	7039		Rance, Cpl. A. W.	6877
Purves, T./S.M. J.	6907		— Pte. F. W.	6955
Purvis, S.S.Cpl. and C.S. G. S.	6954		Rand, Cpl. W.	6915
Putley, Sjt. H.	6933		— Sjt. W. E.	6956
Putname, Sjt. W. J. B.	6875		Randall, Cpl.(L./Sjt.) A.	6884
Pyall, 2nd Cpl.(A./E.C.Sjt.) H. C.	6943		— Sjt. G.	6889
Pye, B.Q.M.S. S. J.	* 6867		— Cpl. G. H.	6904
Pyle, C.Q.M.S. L. E.	6887		— L./C. L. E.	6918
Pyne, Sjt. H. W.	6865		— Pte.(A./Q.M.S.) L. J.	6933
Pyrke, Actg.C.P.O. G. A.	4735		— Mech.S.M. W.	6899
Pywell, R.Q.M.S. A.	7015		Randle, C.E.R.A. 1st Cl. G. R.	4734
			Rands, C.Q.M.S. T.	6873
Quar, Pte. C.	6893		Rangeley, T./S.M. E. J.	6871
Quayle, Cpl. W. S.	6885		Rangi Alijabu Alongi, Sjt.	6971
Quelch, Q.M.S. W. H.	6907		Rankine, Sjt. J.	6895
Quick, Pte. T.	6897		— Sjt.(A./C.S.M.) W. J.	6932
Quigley, Cndr.(Sub Engr.) J.	6934		Rann, C.Q.M.S. J. C.	6890
Quin, Cpl. S. J.	6898		Ransom, Sjt.(A./C.S.M.) A. T. E.	6903
Quinlisk, Cpl. J.	6891		— S.M.I. J. W.	7039
Quinn, Pte. M.	6897		Rapley, Sjt. C. T.	6887
— 2nd Cpl.(A./Sjt.) W. J.	6878		— Sjt.(A./C.Q.M.S.) H.	6970
			Raspin, Pte. J.	6915
Rabson, 2nd Cpl. R.	6878		Rasten, W.O.Cl. 1, F. H.	7022
Race, Mech.S./Sjt. J. B.	6900		Ratcliff, Pte. M.	6906
Rackham, Pte. H. S.	6871		Ratcliffe, Sqdn.Cpl.Maj. (Rough	
Radbourne, Cpl. G. T.	❀ 7702		Rider) J.	7010
Radcliffe, Cpl. P.	6877		Rattray, Pte. J. McH.	6919
Radford, Pte.(A./Q.M.S.) H.	6888		Rautenback, S./Sjt. J. W.	6970
— C.S.M. W.	6900		Raven, Pte.(A./Sjt.) C. E.	6911
Radigan, Pte.(A./Sjt.) F.	6915		Ravenhall, Pte. W.	6906
Radmore, Ldg.Sea. W. J.	4734		Raverty, P.O. T. A.	4734
Rae, C.S.M. G. J.	† 6892		Rawcliffe, Cpl. V.	6945
— Cpl. J. H.	6915		Rawley, Dvr. F.	6869
Raeburn, B.S.M. J. G.	6866		Rawlins, Q.M.S. E. H. P.	6907
Railton, C.Q.M.S. T.	6873		Rawson, Cpl. H. M.	6890
Raine, Gnr. F. C.	6871		Ray, Pte. F. E.	6897
Ralph, Sjt. A. H.	6903		— Pte.(A./Sjt.) R. E.	7014
Ramsay, A./Sub Condr. J. B.	6915		— C.S.M. W.	7017
— Cpl.(A./Sjt.) W.	6974		Rayfield, A./R.S.M. E.	7022
Ramsden, R.Q.M.S. A. V.	6885		Rayment, 2nd Cpl.(T./S./Sjt.) A. C.	6918
— Cpl. D. C. G.	6970		— Pte. J.	6934
— Pte. H.	6865		Raymond, Mech.S./Sjt. W. F.	6970
Ramsey, Cpl.(A./Sjt.) J. M.	6904		Raymont, S./Sjt. E. R. W.	6910
— Mech.S./Sjt. W. W.	6900		Rayner, Dvr. S. J.	6945

* Group known: Queen's South Africa Medal (four bars, 962 Pte. C.I.V. Essex Vol. Art), British War and Victory Medals and M.S.M. (all B.Q.M.S. R.F.A.) and Territorial Force Efficiency Medal (Edw. VII, No. 2 B.Q.M.S. 2/E.A.B. R.F.A.) (East Anglian Brigade).

† 2/H.L.I. L.S. & G.C. A.O./Oct/1917.

Rayner, F./Clk. W. R.	7039	Reid, Pte.(L./C.) E. J.	6906
Raynor, Pte. E. N.	6880	— Sjt. F. H.	6865
Read, Supt. Clk. A. J. F.	6932	— Cpl. F. T.	6915
— C.S.M. F.	6872	— R.Q.M.S. H.	6915
— Pte.(L./C.) J.	6944	— Cpl. J.	6877
— A.B. W. J.	4734	— Cpl.(A./Sjt.) R.	6934
Reading, Cpl. F.	6894	— Cpl. R. (corr.)	7703
Reardon, Sjt. T. L.	6876	— Sjt.(A./C.S.M.) T.	6886
Reason, L.A.O.(A./Sjt.) A. E.	7039	— Cpl. W. L.	6915
— F./Sjt. W. G.	7039	— Sjt. W. T.	6915
Reay, Cpl. E. C. G.	6877	Reilly, T./S.M. A. R.	7020
Reddall, Pte.(A./Sjt.) J. P.	7019	— Sub Condr J. H. J.	* 7021
— F./Sjt. W.	7039	Reily, Pte. E.	6883
Reddaway, Gnr. R. H. M.	6871	Relf, Sjt. H.	6943
Reddin, T./Supt.Clk. J.	6871	Relph, B.S.M. H. C.	6953
Redding, Sjt. Mech. J.	7039	Remmett, Pte.(L./C.) C. W.	6866
Refearn, T./Sub Condr. T.	6909	Remnant, Sjt. G.	6886
Redford, Dvr.(A./C.S.M.) W.	6907	Renaud, Cpl. J. G.	6915
Redhead, Sjt. G.	6887	Rendall, Pte.(A./L./C.) F.	6911
Redman, Q.M.S. H.	7010	— Sjt. H. J.	6868
Reece, Spr.(A./Sjt.) H. G.	6880	Rendle, Sjt.(A./C.S.M.) C. H. R.	6898
— Sjt. J.	6876	Rennie, Sjt. D.	6892
— Pte. T.	❀ 6064	Reuben, Sjt. D. B.	6932
Reed, Ch.Mec. J. R.	7039	Reynolds, Cpl.(A./Sjt.) C. C.	6908
— Pte.(A./Sjt.) W.	7020	— Pte.(A./Mech.S./Sjt.) E.	7020
— S.Q.M.S. W. A.	6865	— Pte. G.	6883
Reeds, T./Armt.S.M. H. D.	6909	— Pte. J.	6906
Reeman, Sjt.(A./C.S.M.) C. P.	6954	— R.Q.M.S. S. A. C. G.	6893
Reepe, Clr.Sjt. C. H.	5111	— Bombr.(P. A./Cpl.) W.	6869
Rees, Pte.(L./C.) A. J.	6898	— Pte.(L./Cpl.) W., *M.M.*	6884
— Pte. E. L.	6888	Rhind, Sjt. Mec. D.	7039
— Cpl. P. C.	6868	— C.S.M. F.	7023
— Condr. R.	7021	Rhodes, Sjt. A. T.	6876
Reeve, Sjt. J. W. (corr.)	7703	— S./Sjt. A. W.	7021
— S.S.M. W.	7018	— Sjt.(A./C.S.M.) C. H.	6890
— 2nd Cpl.(A./Sjt.) W.	6878	— Sjt.(A./S./Sjt.) S. G.	7020
Reeves, Cpl.(T./Sjt.) C. W.	6954	Rhys, S./Sjt. H.	6901
— Sjt.(A./C.Q.M.S.) F. G.	6891	Rice, S.M.II E.	7039
— T./Sub Condr. F. J.	6910	— C.S.M. J.	6872
— Cpl. F. J.	6904	Rich, Condr. H. W. W.	7021
— Sjt. J.	6915	Richards, R.Q.M.S. D. W. L.	6893
— Sjt. T., *M.M.*	6890	— Dvr. E.	6907
— Clr.Sjt. W. T.	7908	— C.S.M. G. D.	6918
Rega, Cpl. of Horse E.	6881	— Sjt. G. H.	6908
Regan, E.R./W.O. Cl. 1, C. C. A.	7022	— Pte. L. V.	6897
Reid, C.S.M. C. R. W.	7017	— Sjt. T.	6903

* Group known: India General Service Medal (Edw. VII, N.W.F. 1908 Sgt. I.U.L.), L.S. & G.C. (Geo. V, S./Sgt. I.M.L.) and M.S.M. (I.M.L. James Henry Joseph Reilly). Born 1878. Sub Condr. 1915. Condr. 1922. On the Staff, Peshawar, 1916–1922.

Richards, Flt.Sjt. W.	7039	Riley, Sjt. D. R.	6908
— L.A.C.(A./Cpl.) W. G.	7039	— R.S.M. J.	7015
— L.A.C. W. M.	7039	Rimmer, Sjt.(A./Q.M.S.) J.	6876
Richardson, Cpl. A.	6894	Riordan, Sjt. S. W. R.	6970
— Pte.(L./C.) D.	6906	Rise, A.B. F. † ❀	7701
— C.Q.M.S. E.	6873	Rishworth, T./R.S.M. T.	7010
— Sjt. E.	6903	Ritchie, Sjt. J.	6915
— Sjt. F. C.	6903	— Pte. W.	6883
— Sjt. G. A. (Lond. R.)	6898	Rivers, Sjt. J. C.	6915
— Sjt. G. A. (R.E.)	6954	Rivett, B.S.M. F.	6869
— Spr. G. A. E.	6880	Robb, Pte.(A./L./C.) W.	6892
— Arm.S./Sjt. H.	6971	Robbins, Cpl.(A./Sjt.) E. W.	6904
— 1st Cl.Asst. Surg. H. A.	7021	Roberson, Whr.S./Sjt. G.	6957
— Pte.(A./Cpl.) J. C.	6915	Robert, C.Q.M.S. J.	6933
— Pte. J. H.	6909	Roberts, T./S.S.M. A.	6899
— C.Q.M.S. O. E.	6885	— Sjt. A.	6910
— Spr. W. ❀	7702	— Cpl. A.	6957
— Whr.Cpl. W. H.	6868	— Sjt. C. J.	7039
Richens, Sjt. D.	6895	— Sjt.(A./Sqdn.S.M.) D. T.	6865
Richford, Sjt. C. G.	6903	— Cpl. Ernest	7039
Richings, Sjt.(A./B.S.M.) F. E.	6954	— Dvr.(A./Sjt.) E. G.	6907
Richmond, Sig.Sjt. A.	6870	— R.Q.M.S. G.	6897
— C.Q.M.S.(A./R.Q.M.S.) F.	6884	— Cpl. G. W. T.	6904
— S./S.M. W. V.	6956	— Spr.(A./R.Q.M.S.) H. C.	7013
Rickard, Sjt.(A./C.S.M) S. G., *D.C.M.*	6876	— Sjt. H. J.	6064
Rickards, Sjt. A. H.	6911	— C.Q.M.S. J.	6888
— F./Sjt. W. H.	7039	— Cpl. J.	6904
Ricketts, T./Sub Condr. C. W.	6910	— R.Q.M.S. J. H.	6893
Ridding, C.S.M.(A./Q.M.S.) H.	6893	— R.Q.M.S. J. H. (G.M.G.C.)	7013
Riddington, Sjt. C. A.	6885	— Pte. J. H.	6890
Riddle, Sjt. N.	6908	— Sjt. J. T. (corr.)	7703
Riden, Sjt. C. R. F.	6876	— Farr.Cpl. J. V.	6904
Rider, Spr. H.	6915	— Sjt. L. B.	6887
Ridgeway, Sjt. C.	6910	— C.Q.M.S. N. G.	6898
Ridgwell, Cpl. F. L.	6904	— Cpl.(A./Sjt.) R.	6877
Riding, Pte.(A./Sjt.) A. E. H. *	7020	— Sjt. R. A. J.	6918
— F./Sjt. J. P.	7039	— Pte.(A./Cpl.) S.	6909
— Sjt. T.	6888	— S.M. Thomas	7039
Ridley, Sjt. A.	7022	— Sjt. T. C.	6890
— S.M. G.	6954	— Cpl. W.	6955
— Ch.Elect. Art. J.	8069	— Bosn. W.	8202
Rigby, Cpl. A. E.	6944	— C.Q.M.S. W. A. (R.E.)	6873
— Pte. H. ❀	7702	— C.Q.M.S. W. A. (Midd. R.)	6890
Rigden, C.S.M. J. H.	6945	— Sjt. W. E.	6911
Riggs, Pte.(T./Sjt.) P.	6910	— Sjt. W. G. C.	6910
Riley, R.Q.M.S. A., *M.C.*	6944	— R.S.M. W. R.	6915

---

* Group known: British War Medal (16809 A Sgt. R.A.M.C.) L.S. & G.C. (Geo. V, 16809 Pte. (A Cpl) R.A.M.C.) and M.S.M. (for Services in Singapore). Only seven M.S.M.s for this theatre.

† RNVR, (Army Gallantry M.S.M.). Drake Bn. R.N. Div.

Robertson, S.S.M. A.		7018	Rodgers, Pte. J. A.		6919
— 2nd Cpl.(A./Sjt.) A.		6879	Rodway, R.Q.M.S. W. J.		7014
— Pte.(A./Sjt.) A.		6956	Rodwell, Gnr.(A./Cpl.) T.		6915
— Pte. A.		6906	Rogan, Spr. J.	❀	6064
— Spr. A. G.	❀	7702	Rogers, Sjt.(A./S./Sjt.) A.		6910
— Mech.S./Sjt. A. M.		6900	— B.Q.M.S. C. T.		6932
— Sjt. A. N.		6918	— Cpl. F. C.		6897
— Sjt. H.		6876	— Cpl.Mec. G. D.	§	7039
— Spr.(T./Cpl.) H.		6880	— R.Q.M.S. G. E.		7010
— Ch.Mech. S. R.	*	7039	— R.S.M. J.		6885
— Condr. W. D.		7021	— F./Clk. M. J. H.	+	7039
Robicheau, Sjt. L. P.		6915	— 1st Writer L. S.		7512
Robins, S.M. F.		7039	— C.S.M.(A./R.S.M.) T.		6887
— Sjt. R.		6876	— C.Q.M.S. W. E.		6890
— Pte. W. J. J.		6871	— C.S.M. W. E.		6895
Robinson, C.E.R.A. A. W.		7512	— S./Sjt. W. J.		6919
— Sjt. E.		7039	— 2nd Cpl. W. J.		6879
— T./R.S.M. E. C.	†	6869	Rolfe, P.O. B.		6865
— Sjt. E. D.		6876	— C.Q.M.S. T. W.		6900
— Cpl.(A./Sjt.) E. H.		6877	Rollings, A.M. 1, R. L.	◊	7039
— B.S.M. F.		6869	— Pte.(A./L./C.) W. J.		6894
— Cpl. G. A.		6911	Rollitt, C.S.M. J. W.		6900
— Sjt. H.		6876	Rolls, Pte.(L./C.) S. C.		6934
— Sjt. J.		6893	Rood, Cpl. J. A.		6918
— Cpl.(L./Sjt.) L. H.		6891	Root, F./Sjt. F. C.		7039
— S./Sjt. R. M.		6970	— Cpl. H.		6877
— Pte.(T./Sjt.) R. M.		6909	— Pte. H. G.		6909
— C.Q.M.S. T. W.		6895	Roper, Pte.(A./L./C.) D.		6912
— R.Q.M.S. W.		6975	— S./Sjt. F. J. F.		6873
Robison, A./Sjt. R. A.		7022	— Sjt. G.		6876
Robson, Sjt. A. H.		6903	Rosamond, T./S.M.(A.C.) J. B.		6869
— S./Sjt. E.		7021	Rosbrook, Sjt. W. H.		6870
— Sjt. E. A.		6881	Rose, Gnr. B. G.		6871
— Mech.Elect.Q.M.S. E. P.	‡	7012	— F./Sjt. C. A. E.		7039
— Cpl.(A./Sjt.) J.		6877	— Sjt.(A./Sqdn.S.M.) F. W. F.		6911
— C.Q.M.S. M. W.		6932	— T./Sub Condr. H.		6910
— Sjt. W. H.		6898	— Pte. H. C.		6884
Roche, Cpl. G.		6877	— Cpl. J. F.		6904
Rodgers, S./Sjt. G. F.		6908	— Cpl. P. G. G.		6911
— Sjt.(A./R.Q.M.S.) G. V.		7013		

---

* R.A.F. M.S.M. for Egypt to Aus/105 Australian Flying Corps. See also M.S.M. (Army) *L.G.* 17 December, 1917 and cancellation *L.G.* 17 June 1924.
† Group known: 1914/15 Star trio, Coronation 1911 (S.S. Major R.G.A.), M.S.M. (4/ London Howitzer Batt. R.G.A.), Territorial Force Efficiency Medal (Edw. VII) and Rumanian Barbatie si Credinta.
‡ R.E. For Singapore.
§ R.A.F. M.S.M. for Egypt to Aus/236, Australian Flying Corps.
+ R.A.F. M.S.M. for Egypt to Aus/124, Australian Flying Corps.
◊ Group known: British War and Victory Medals (8162 R.N.A.S.), Jubilee 1935 and R.A.F. M.S.M. (208162 R.A.F. H.M.S. *Celandine*, Mediterranean).

Rose, C.Q.M.S.(A./C.S.M.) W. F.	* 7018	Royle, Pte. G.	6915
Roseby, A./C.S.M. H.	7022	Ruck, Spr.(L./C.) A. J.	6880
Rosewell, R.S.M. T. H.	6918	Rudd, Sjt. J.	6957
Rosindale, Sjt. F.	6910	— Sjt. R.	† 7011
Roskey, Pte.(A./Sjt.) J. H.	7020	Rudderham, Shipwt. 1st Cl. P. L.	8069
Ross, Sjt.(A./C.S.M.) A.	6882	Rudolph, S.M. F. W.	7039
— B.Q.M.S. A. S.	6870	Ruff, Sjt. W.	6868
— Sjt. D.	6956	Rukin, Sjt. M.	6903
— S./Sjt.(T./Q.M.S.) F. C.	6912	Rule, C.Q.M.S. H.	6892
— Pte.(A./Sjt.) G. T.	6906	Rumbold, Ch.Sto. F.	7908
— Sjt. H. A.	6876	— Sjt.(A./C.Q.M.S.) J. A. V.	6871
— Eng.Clk.S./Sjt. H. L.	7012	Rumsby, Cpl. T.	7039
— Sjt. J.	6876	Rumsey, Sjt. P. C.	7039
Rotherham, C.S.M. J.	6955	Runcie, Sjt. W.	6892
Rothwell, Sjt. E.	6876	Ruse, Sjt. G. O.	6870
— Cpl.(A./Sjt.) W.	6883	Rush, Cpl. D. W. A.	6918
Roughon, C.S.M.Instr. S.	6912	Rushbrook, Sjt. H. G.	6903
Round, Fitt.S./Sjt. H.	6943	Rushby, Spr.(A./C.S.M.) T.	7013
Rouse, Q.M.S. C. A.	7017	Rushworth, Pte. J.	6886
— Sjt.(A./S./Sjt.) G.	7019	Russell, Sqdn.S.M. B. F.	7022
— Sjt. G.	6886	— Farr.S./Sjt. C.	6900
Routledge, R.Q.M.S. J.	6884	— T./S.S.M. C. A.	6956
Routley, R.Q.M.S. P. F.	6888	— C.Q.M.S. E. E. R.	7023
Rovery, R.S.M. C.	6893	— F./Sjt. F.	7039
Rowan, Spr.(A./2nd Cpl.) J.	6880	— C.Q.M.S. G. F. A.	6900
— Sjt. W. E.	6885	— Sjt. H.	6903
Rowberry, Sjt.(A./C.Q.M.S.) J. F.	6895	— Pte. P.	6885
Rowbotham, Sjt. W. J.	6915	— C.S.M. R.	7016
Rowbottom, Whlr.S./Sjt. F.	6900	— C.S.M.(A./R.S.M.) W. R. J.	6872
Rowden, C.S.M. A. G.	7017	Rutherford, C.S.M. D. C.	6872
Rowe, T./S.S.M. F., *MM.*	6899	— Farr.Q.M.S. J.	6865
— Sjt. F.	6884	Rutter, Sjt. F.	6888
— C.Q.M.S. F. G.	6882	Ryan, T./W.O. Cl. 1, J. A.	6918
— S./Sjt. J. E.	6915	— Sjt. J. A.	6894
— W.O.Cl. 1, R.	6934	— 2nd Writer P.	6865
— Sjt. R. S.	6876	— Sjt. T. W.	6889
— Sjt. W. C.	6918	— C.S.M.(A./R.S.M.) V. A. S.	‡ 7018
Rowland, Sjt.(A./C.S.M.) W. A.	6955	Ryde, Pte.(A./Cpl.) H.	6889
— Sjt. W. F.	6970	Ryland, Dvr. G.	6869
Rowlands, C.S.M.(A./R.S.M.) F. R.	6889		
— Sjt. H. J.	6934	Sabari, Cpl.	6970
Rowles, Mech.S./Sjt. W. A.	6901	Sabuni, Sjt.	6970
Rowley, Sjt. A. J.	6891	Sadler, Mech.S./Sjt. F. E.	6901
— Sjt. E. A.	6887	Sage, B.S.M. A. W.	6866
— C.Q.M.S. J. R.	6873	Sageman, Pte.(A./L./C.) W. E.	7017
Rowsell, Pte. H. R.	6918	Sainsbury, Cpl. H. V.	6955
Royals, Sqdn.Q.M.Cpl. J.	6881	Saint, Gnr.(L./Bombr.) H. S. R.	6871

* For Bermuda (R.A.S.C.).
† Awarded M.S.M. Annuity 1949 (A.O. 14). R.A.
‡ 1st Bn. West Indian Regt. (from Jamaica).

St. Pierre, A./C.Q.M.S. A. T.	7022	Saxelby, S.Q.M.S. W. H.	6899
Sale, Cpl.(L./Sjt.) G.	6955	Saxon, Sjt. N.	6891
Salim Effendi Mustapha, Mulazim		Saxton, Pte. A. T.	6883
Tani	6971	Saxton, Sjt. Y., *M.M.*	6885
Salkeld, Gnr. J. C.	6869	Sayer, Sjt.Instr. C.	6912
Salmon, Sjt. Harry R.	7039	— Pte. H. W.	7013
— F./Sjt. Howard R.	7039	Sayers, Sjt. E. (R.F.A.)	6868
Salmons, S.M. I. J.	7039	— Sjt. E. (R.A.M.C.)	6910
Salsbury, Sjt. T. F.	6945	Scamell, Spr.(A.E.C.Sjt.) J. G.	6880
Salt, C.S.M. L.	6881	Scanlan, Cpl. T.	6908
Salter, Army Schoolmaster G. H.	* 7021	Sceats, C.Q.M.S. D. B.	6898
— Pte.(A./Sjt.) G. H.	6909	Schalk, Sjt. J. J.	6886
Sampson, Sjt. C.	6870	Schirn, Sig.Sjt. A. G.	6870
— Sjt.(A./S./Sjt.) F. W. H.	6957	Schlarb, Spr.(A./Sjt.) C. H.	6954
Samson, Sjt.(A./C.S.M.) A. J.	6898	Schmidt, Cpl. W. H.	6904
Samsoni, S./Sjt.	6971	Schoeman, Cpl. P. R.	6970
Sanders, Sjt. W. I.	7011	Schofield, 2nd Cpl.(T./Sjt.) T.	6954
Sanderson, Cpl.(A./Sjt.) J .H.	6904	Scholfield, Sjt. W. H.	6910
— Sjt. M. C.	6954	Schoneveldt, S.M.Instr. S. C.	6971
— Spr. N. S. (corr.)	6065	Schoombie, Pte. D. J.	6970
— T./S.S.M. R. E.	6970	Scimgour, E.R.A. 3rd Cl. W	7512
— S.Q.M.S.(A./R.Q.M.S.) W. J.	† 6953	Sclater, S./Sjt. J. R.	6919
Sandow, C.Q.M.S. H. R.	6918	Scobell, Dvr. J.	6970
Sands, R.Q.M.S. A.	7014	Scott, R.Q.M.S. A., *M.M.*	6893
Sandys, Sjt. E. J., *M.M.*	6876	— F./Sjt. A.	7039
Sangster, S./Sjt. A.	6957	— Ldg.Sig. C.	5112
Sanigar, Sjt. H. F.	6868	— S./Sjt. D.	7012
Sansam, Sjt.(A./C.S.M.) W.	6954	— Cpl. E. L.	6918
Sargent, R.S.M. A.	6884	— T./S.M. G.	6871
Satterthwaite, Sjt. W. A.	6894	— Dvr. G.	6907
Saunders, T./Sub Condr. F. J.	6910	— Sjt. G. G.	6876
— S./Sjt.(A./S.M.) G. H.	6908	— E.C.S./Sjt.(A./Q.M.S.) H. J.	6873
— Cpl.(L./Sjt.) H. B.	6933	— T./Sub Condr. H. R.	6910
— Pte.(A./Sjt.) M. M. R.	7702	— Gnr.(L./Bombr.) H. S.	6871
— Sjt.(A./C.Q.M.S.) P.	6892	— C.S.M. J. (R.E.)	6872
— R.Q.M.S. T.	6897	— C.S.M. J. (R. Highrs.)	6955
— Dvr. W.	6907	— Sjt. J. (R.E.)	6876
Savage, T./S.M. A. D.	6907	— Sjt. J. (R. Sc.)	6954
— Pte.(L./C.) E.	6894	— Sjt. J. (Mil. Foot Pol.)	6911
— S.M. G. H.	7039	— Sjt. J. F.	6893
Saville, S./Sjt. H.	7021	— Sjt. J. M.	6903
— S.M. S. D.	6957	— Sjt. (A./C.S.M.) J. W.	6956
Sawasawa, Pte.(L./C.)	6971	— Sjt. J. W.	6881
Sawyer, Pte.(A./Sjt.) F. C.	6911	— E.C. S./Sjt.(A./E.C.Q.M.S.)	
— C.Q.M.S. H.	6944	J. W. T.	6873
— Pte.(L./C.) W. J.	6906		

---

* For Malta.

† Group known: 1914/15 Star trio, M.S.M. (120029 Lothian & Border Horse), Territorial Efficiency Medal and Greek Military Cross (*L.G.* 21 July 1919), a unique combination to any Yeomanry unit.

Scott, Sjt. R. B.	* 6953	Seymour, Sjt. C. M.	6957
— Spr. T. C.	6970	Shackleford, Pte.(A./Cpl.) G. V.	6906
— Sjt. W. (R.G.A.)	6954	Shadwick, S./Sjt. T. P.	6901
— Sjt. W. (S.A.S.C., M.T.)	6970	Shanahan, C.S.M. D.	6885
— Sjt. W. C.	6882	Shannon, C.S.M.(T./R.S.M.) H. E.	6945
— C.S.M. W. W.	7017	— R.Q.M.S. J.	7013
Scoulding, Spr.(A./C.S.M.) J. T.	7013	Shaper, T./R.S.M. H.	7017
Scully, Cpl. C. F.	6915	Shardlow, Bandmaster B. J.	7023
Seaborne, T./S.S.M. R.	6899	Sharkey, Sjt. L.	6890
Seabrook, L./C. W. W.	6918	Sharman, Cpl.(A./Sjt.) A. E.	6889
Seal, S.S.M. T. E.	6970	— 2nd Hnd. W. S.	4733
Sealey, T./R.S.M. W.	7013	Sharp, Sjt. A.	§ 6865
Searle, T./S.S.M. W. A.	6970	— Pte. A.	6934
Sears, Sjt.(A./R.Q.M.S.) F. J.	6887	— Sjt. A. E.	6918
Seaton, L./C. R.	6918	— Cpl. A. E.	6880
Seay, Condr. C. A.	6919	— C.Q.M.S.(A./S.M.) F.	6873
Secrett, Pte.(L/C.) T.	† 6865	— Sjt. J.	6918
Seddon, Pte.(A./L./C.) W.	6911	— Pte. W. J.	6915
Sedgwick, S./Sjt. J.	6915	Sharpe, S./Sjt. M. A.	6957
Seed, T./M.S.M. R.	7018	— T./S./Sjt. W. H.	6934
Seeley, Sjt. J.	6885	Sharples, Sjt. J.	6889
Seigne, Pte. L. J. L.	‡ 6883	— Dvr. S.	6907
Selkirk, C.Q.M.S. F. C.	6933	Sarrock, Sjt.(A./F./Sjt.) R. G.	7039
Sellar, L.A.C. C.	7039	Shatwell, Sjt. F.	6895
Sellek, Sjt. S. F.	6876	Shaw, Sjt. A. G.	6903
Selves, C.S.M.(A./R.S.M.) W.	7014	— F./Clk. D.	7039
Semple, R.Q.M.S. J. A.	6886	— Sjt.(A./C.S.M.) G.	6974
Senior, Cpl. C. H.	6904	— Bombr. H.	6869
— Sqdn.S.M. G.	7010	— Sjt. J.	6892
— Sjt. H.	6894	— C.S.M.(A./R.S.M.) J. B.	7022
Sergent, Cpl. W. J.	6904	— Gnr. J. C.	6869
Serson, Sjt. P.	6915	— Cpl.Clk. P. R.	7039
Seton, Sjt.(T./C.S.M.) J. F.	6876	— Cpl.(L./Sjt.) S.	6955
Seymour, Spr. A.	6880	— Sjt. W. (R. Sc. Fus.)	6885

---

* Group known: 1914/15 Star trio (1696 Pte–Sgt. Lothian & Border Horse) and M.S.M. (120331 L. & B.H.). From Kelso. A and D Sqn. were in the Balkans and subsequently served with the Army of the Black Sea.

† Was Field Marshal Haig's batman from 29 November 1900 to 31 October, 1925. Born 1875 enlisted as No. 5186 into 11 Hussars. Died 1942. Group known: Queen's South Africa Medal, King's South Africa Medal, 1914 Star trio, Delhi Durbar 1911, L.S. & G.C. (Edw. VII), M.S.M., Médaille Militaire (1914), French Médaille d'Honneur, Medal of King Albert of the Belgians. M.S.M. named to 11 Hussars.

‡ See article in *Medal News* April, 1990. Group known: British War and Victory Medals (Pte. R.W. Kent R.) and M.S.M. (10/R. Fus.). The M.S.M. is for service as an Intelligence Policeman a unit which served as 10/R. Fus. Born in London of French parents, his linguistic abilities were used by the Intelligence Corps. There would appear to be 36 M.S.M.s to I.C. or 10 R.F.

§ Group known in Moss collection: 1914/15 Star trio (Private R.M.L.I.) and M.S.M. Of the 72 Army M.S.M.s issued to the Royal Marines only some 30 are to men of R.M.L.I.

Shaw, Sjt. W. (R.A.S.C.)	6903	Shotbolt, Sjt. R.	6898
— Cpl. W.	6904	Shrubshall, Ch.Mec. F.	7039
— Ch.Mec. W.	7039	Shrubsole, Cpl.(A./Sjt.) F.	6877
— Spr.(A./Sjt.) W. A.	7013	Shuttle, C.S.M.Instr. A. R.	6912
— S./Sjt. W. H.	6901	Shuttleworth, Pte.(L./C.) E.	6909
— Cpl. W. J.	6904	— W.O. Cl. 1, L. B.	7022
Sheable, B.S.M. F.	7010	Sibson, Sjt. J. B.	6915
Sheard, Sjt. O. F.	6919	Side, Sjt. F.	6876
Shearing, Sjt.(A./Q.M.S.) H.	7021	Siggs, Sjt. G. G.	6945
Shears, Cpl. H. S.	7039	Sills, L.A.C. L.	7039
Sheffield, Q.M.S. E.	6872	— C.Q.M.S.(A./C.S.M.) W. H.	6976
Sheldon, S./Sjt. F.	6901	Silversides, B.Q.M.S. J.	6867
— Cpl. W.	6911	— Pte. R. W.	6897
Shelley, B.S.M. D. F.	6866	Sim, S./Sjt. J. G.	6910
— Farr.Sjt. G. S.	6876	Simcock, Cpl.(A./S./Sjt.) F. B.	6904
Shenton, Sjt. A.	6903	Simmonds, C.Q.M.S. H.	7017
Shepherd, Sjt. A. J.	6918	— T./S.M. J.	6871
— C.S.M.(A./R.S.M.) D. H.	6884	— Farr.Sjt. J.	6957
— Cpl. P. C.	7039	Simmons, Sjt.(A./Q.M.S.) C. G.	6882
— Cpl. W. E.	6904	— Sjt. G. C.	6915
— E.C. and D. 2nd Cpl.(A./Sjt.)		— S./Sjt. H. S.	6910
W. G.	6879	Simnett, T./S.M. P.	6871
Sheppard, R.S.M. A.	6871	Simons, Spr.(T./Sjt.) A. F.	6945
— Spr.(A./2nd Cpl.) H. S.	6880	— Cpl. F. G.	6904
— C.E.R.A. 2nd Cl. W. H.	8202	— 2nd Cpl. G. E.	6879
Sherman, Sjt. T.	6915	— Spr. T. ❀	7702
Sherwin, P.O. J. F.	4198	— 2nd Cpl.W.	6879
Sherwood, Pte.(A./Sjt.) A. C.	6915	Simpson, Cpl. A.	6892
— Sjt. A. W.	6918	— R.Q.M.S. C.	6865
— Cpl.(L./Sjt.) R.	6894	— Sjt. C.	6903
Shield, Ch.Shipwt. F.	7908	— Gnr. E.	6866
Shields, C.Q.M.S. G. W.	6893	— S./Sjt. J.	6934
— C.S.M. J.	6954	— Sjt. J. H.	6883
Shiell, Cpl. L. G.	6870	— Bombr. J. R.	6869
Shillabeer, C.P.O. W. J.	5112	— Cpl. R.	6877
Shillito, Bombr. J. C.	6869	— Sjt. R. G.	6886
Shimmans, Sjt. R.	6885	— Dvr. W. E.	6907
Shine, Sjt.(A./S.Q.M.S.) J.	7022	Sims, Sjt.(A./S./Sjt.) F. T.	6876
Shipley, Cpl.(A./Fitt.Sjt.) G.	6870	— Pte. H.	6880
Shoebridge, Cpl.(A./Sjt.) E. G.	6896	Simson, P.O. V. C.	7908
Shoetensack, Pte. W. G.	6893	Sinar, Pte. J.	6944
Shone, C.Q.M.S. P.	6885	Sinclair, S./Sjt. A. D.	6919
Short, B.S.M. C. F.	6918	— Mech.S./Sjt. H. J.	6970
— C.Q.M.S.(A./Mstr.Gnr. 3rd Cl.)		— S.S.M. H. W.	7023
F. J.	7011	— Sjt. S.	6892
— Pte.(A./Cpl.) F.	6909	Siney, Sjt.(T./S./Sjt.) J. J.	6912
— C.S.M. (I.M.) H.	7015	Singer, Cpl. R.	6877
— S.S.M. J.	6953	Singleton, Whr.S./Sjt. R.	6867
— S.M. 2 R. T.	7039	— S.Q.M.S. R. H.	6933
— R.Q.M.S. S.	6945	— E.R.Sqdn.S.M. W.	6918
— Pte.(L./C.) S.	6880	Sinnock, T./Sub Condr. H.	6910
Shorter, C.S.M. H. G.	6894		

Sirrett, Actg. Warrt. Offr. 2nd Cl. J.	*	4196	Slocombe, C.Q.M.S. A. W.	6898
Sisman, C.S.M. Instr. A. L.		6912	— Whlr.Sjt. R.	6933
Skae, Cpl. J.	✿	6064	Sloman, Sjt.(A./C.S.M.) S. J.	7017
Skedgwell, Dvr. W. T.		6907	Slora, Sjt.(A./C.S.M.) J.	7012
Skidmore, Spr. H. J. M.		6880	Sloss, Cpl.(A./F./Sjt.) J. McK. †	7039
Skillicorn, Dvr. J. N.		6869	Slough, S.M. P. E.	6915
Skilling, Cpl. A. W.		6904	Smailes, S./Smith R.	6880
Skinner, Sjt. A.		6885	Smale, R.Q.M.S. E. H.	6881
— Spr.(L./C.) B.		6880	Small, Sjt.(A./C.S.M.) J.	7016
— Sjt. F.		6915	— Pte. W. G.	6906
— C.Q.M.S. F. G.		6915	— Pte. W. J.	6915
— Sjt. T. R.		6870	Smart, R.S.M. A., *M.C.* ‡	6886
— Cpl. W. A.		6904	— Cpl. G. J.	6918
— Sjt. W. J.		6903	— Sjt. H. C. B.	6876
Slack, Sjt. S.		6884	— R.S.M. H. W.	6893
Slade, Dvr. H. R.		6918	— Sjt. J. P.	6915
Slater, S./Sjt. A. A.		6919	— Sjt. R.	6876
— R.Q.M.S. B.		6945	— Engmn. R. W.	4733
— T./S.M. E. D.		6892	Smedley, Cpl. W. H.	7014
— Pte. E. W.		6883	Smee, Cpl. J. F.	6868
— C.Q.M.S. F. A.		6943	Smellie, A.Yeo.Sigs. R. G. P.	4198
— C.Q.M.S.(A./R.S.M.) J.		7013	Smith, Q.M.S.Instr. A.	7021
— Pte. R.		6906	— C.S.M. A.	6895
Sleep, Sjt. H. C.		6876	— Farr.S./Sjt. A.	6867
— 2nd Cpl. J. W.		6915	— S.M. A.	7039
Sleet, 2nd Hnd. R.		6447	— Cpl. A.	6894
Sleigh, R.Q.M.S. A.		6882	— Pte. A. (R.Sc.)	6881
Slender, C.Q.M.S. A.		6954	— Pte. A. (M.G.C.)	6956
			— Sjt. A. E., *M.M.*	6887

---

* Corrected to Sirett 22 January 1920, see *infra*. Group in McInnes collection: British War Medal (R.M.A. 5109 Act Q.M.S.), R.N. L.S. & G.C. (Edw. VII, R.M.A.), R.N. M.S.M. (A./W.O.II Cl 'Recruiting Newcastle') and R.M. M.S.M. (Geo. VI, 1st type, on blue ribbon, Clr. Sgt. 20.9.45). He was the only man to be entitled to both types of M.S.M.—the Royal Naval 1919–28 and the Royal Marine 1848–1951. See Snape, Vol. III 1919. Born 5 November, 1875 in London, he enlisted in January 1894, by trade an engine cleaner; shortly after his marriage in 1899 he was promoted Sergeant and was awarded his L.S. & G.C. in February, 1909, when he had for the past 3½ years been an Instructor of Gunnery. Appointed Recruiting Sgt. in York in 1912 he transferred to the Royal Fleet reserve in January, 1915 but continued to serve as Q.M.S., Recruiting, in Newcastle upon Tyne. He was awarded a £10 gratuity in 1916 and was demobilised in December 1918. In 1923 he rejoined the R.F.R. finally retiring on pension in June 1925. Sirett saw plenty of sea service from enlistment to 1910 in *Inflexible, Benbow, Dreadnought, Irresistible, King Edward VII,* and *Africa.* His R.M. M.S.M. and annuity were approved on 30 August 1946 and he died on 25 March, 1956 aged 81.

† See Vol. IV 1920.

‡ Group known: M.C. (R.S.M., Royal Highlanders), Queen's South Africa Medal (Paardeberg, Dreifontein, Cape Colony, Wittebergen), King's South Africa Medal (both Cpl. Black Watch), 1914 Star (C.S.M.), British War and Victory Medals (W.O.1) and M.S.M.

Smith, C.Q.M.S. A. H.	6918	Smith, W.O. Cl. 1, H. C.	6918
— S./Sjt. A. H.	7021	— Sjt. H. C.	6910
— E.Clk.Sjt. A. H.	6932	— Sjt. H. H.	6876
— Cpl.(L./Sjt.) A. H.	6890	— Sjt. H. L.	6890
— S./Sjt. A. L. (R.A.M.C.)	6908	— Sub Condr. H. W.	7021
— A./S./Sjt. A. L. (Can. A.O.C.)	6915	— C.S.M.(A./R.S.M.) J., *D.C.M.*	6892
— Sjt. A. McD.	6891	— S./Sjt. J.	6915
— Gnr. A. T.	6871	— Sjt. J. (R.A.O.C.)	6910
— Sjt. A. W.	6884	— Sjt. J. (Lab.Corps.)	6945
— A./Sjt. A. W.	7039	— Cpl.(A./Sjt.) J.	6904
— C.P.O. C.	8069	— Cpl. J.	6904
— 2nd Cpl. C.	6879	— Engmn. J.	4733
— Spr.(A./Cpl.) C.	6880	— Pte. J.	6886
— E.C. Cpl.(A./Sjt.) C. B.	6877	— C.S.M. J. A.	6954
— Q.M.S.(A./S.M.) C. E.	7020	— Sjt. J. H.	6910
— Cpl. C. McL.	6877	— Cpl.(T./C.S.M.) J. J.	6918
— C.Q.M.S. C. S.	6954	— Pte.(A./Cpl.) J. S.	6909
— R.Q.M.S. D.	6918	— Farr.Sjt. J. T.	6954
— C.Q.M.S. E.	7015	— Sjt. J. T.	6910
— S.Q.M.S. E.	* 7021	— Cpl. J. V.	6877
— Sjt. E. R.	6890	— Sjt. L. E.	6903
— B.Q.M.S. F.	6867	— Dvr. L. G.	6869
— T./S.M. F.	6871	— Sjt. L. M.	6918
— Sjt. F., *MM.*(R.E.)	6876	— Sjt. M. M.	6889
— Sjt. F. (R.F.A., D.A.C.)	6868	— Sjt.(T./S./Sjt.) M. M. V.	6908
— Sjt. F. (W. Rid. R.)	6887	— S./Sjt. N.	6901
— Sjt. F. (N. and D.R.)	6889	— Cpl. O. F.	6877
— Sjt. F. (R.F.A., T.M.B.)	6868	— C.S.M. P.	6955
— Pte.(L./C.) F.	6889	— S./Sjt. P.	6915
— Pte. F. A.	6946	— C.Q.M.S. R.	6888
— Signlr.Sjt. F. C. V.	7010	— C.S.M. R.	6956
— Pte.(L./C.) F. E.	6906	— Pte. R.	6946
— Sjt. F. J.	6898	— C.Q.M.S. R. C.	6873
— Cpl. F. S.	6877	— Sjt. S.	6887
— C.S.M. G.	7015	— Cpl. S.	6918
— Sjt. G.	6876	— S./Sjt.(A./S.S.M.) S. A.	6911
— Sjt.Drm. G. D.	6880	— Pte.(A./Sjt.) S. R. B.	6909
— Mech.S./Sjt. G. E.	6901	— Sjt.(A./C.S.M.) T.	7012
— Sjt. G. F.	6884	— Sjt.(A./S.M.) T.	6870
— Spr.(L./C.) G. F.	6880	— Sjt. T.	6870
— Cpl. G. H.	6877	— Sjt. T. A.	6910
— T./Sub Condr. G. W. M.	† 7020	— S./Sjt. T. B.	6915
— Sjt. H. (Suff. R.)	6884	— Pte. T. L. C.	6970
— Sjt. H. (Can.A.S.C.)	6915	— Cpl.(O.R.Clk.) T. P.	6865
— Sjt. H. (W. Rid. R.)	6944	— Cpl.(A./Sjt.) T. S.	6868
— Sjt. H. (R.E.)	6954	— Cpl.(A./Sjt.) T. W.	6908
— Pte. H. A.	6906	— B.S.M. W.	7011

* Group known: British War Medal (W.O.II A.P.C.), L.S. & G.C. (Geo. V, S./Sgt. A.P.C.), M.S.M. (No. 978 A.P.C. for services in Gibralfar).
† R.A.O.C. For Ceylon.

Smith, Dvr. W.	6869	Sowden, C.S.M. W.	6944
— Pte.(A./S./Sjt.) W.	7020	Sowerby, Spr.(L./C.) G. A.	6880
— C.Q.M.S. W. A.	6891	Sowray, T./R.S.M. F. J., *D.C.M.*	6871
— C.Q.M.S. W. G.	6873	Spalding, Pte. F. ❀	7702
— Cpl. W. G. ❀	6064	Sparey, Cpl.Mec. T. A.	7039
— Pte. W. G.	6898	Sparkes, S.Q.M.S. W. H.	7018
— Sjt.(A./C.S.M.) W. H.	6911	Sparkman, Spr. R.	6918
— Sjt. W. H.	6888	Sparks, Cpl. R. W.	6904
— Cpl. W. H.	6878	Sparrow, S./Sjt. A. K.	6915
— R.Q.M.S. W. M.	6955	— Cpl. G. A.	6904
Smithyman, R.S.M. F. M.	6970	Spearing, C.Q.M.S. J. J.	6873
Smurthwaite, S./Sjt.(A./S.Q.M.S.) A.	6957	Speck, Cpl. H.	7039
Smyth, Ch.Mas.Mec. P. *	7039	Speight, Sjt. F.	6943
Smythe, Ch. Writer F. J.	7512	Speller, R.S.M. F., *M.C.* ‡	7013
— O.R./Q.M.S. J.	7013	Spence, Sjt. A. R.	6910
Snape, Sjt.(A./Q.M.S.) W.	6865	— Spr.(A./C.Q.M.S.) R.	7013
Snare, A.B. R. M.	7908	Spencer, Pte.(A./Sjt.) E.	6933
Snelgar, T./S.S.M. H. J.	6899	— Pte.(A./Mech.Q.M.S.) G. A.	7020
Snook, Sjt. Mech. H.	7039	— Cpl. H.	6878
— Sjt. J.	6910	— Pte.(L./C.) H. B.	6865
Snow, C.Q.M.S. H. C.	6898	— C.S.M. H. N.	6933
— Pte. W. H.	6974	— Cpl. J.	6932
Snowball, Sjt. F. V.	6910	Spice, Cpl. W. L.	6894
Snowden, Pte. J. D.	6906	Spicer, C.S.M. D. W.	6893
Soars, Engmn. T. C.	4733	— 2nd Cpl.(A./Cpl.) R. W.	6879
Soden, Spr.(L./C.) J. A.	6880	Spiers, Armr.S.M. W. H.	7020
— T./S.S.M. T.	6899	Spilsbury, Sjt. R. G.	6903
Solman, Sjt. F. H. C.	7017	Spink, Sjt. A.	6903
Soloman, Cpl.(A./Sjt.) A. F.	7013	Spinney, Sjt. E.	6887
Somerton, Sjt. R. C.	6884	Spokes, C.Q.M.S. L. J.	6890
Somerville, Dvr.(A./Sjt.) J.	6957	Spooner, S./Sjt. H.	6894
Sommers, Sjt.(A./C.S.M.) L.	6932	— F. of W. S.M. W. C. §	7012
Somper, L.A.C. H.	7039	Spriggs, E.C. Cpl.(A./Q.M.S.) A. C.	6878
Soper, Sjt.(A./S.M.) F. H.	6956	Springbett, Act.C.P.O. C. T.	4735
Sorrell, S.Q.M.S. A.	6872	Square, R.S.M. H. S.	6915
— Teleg. F. †	5111	Squire, Sqdn.Cpl.Maj. (Rough Rider)	
— Cpl. G. A. V.	6943	F. H.	7010
South, Dvr. A.	6957	— Cpl. P.	6896
— Sjt. W. H.	6915	— Squires, T./Sub Condr. H.	6910
Southam, R.S.M. F. R.	7010	— Pte. M.	6883
Southwell, Sjt. J. W.	7012	Stacey, Pte. A. J.	6886

* No. 3187 R.F.C. R.A.F. M.S.M. (I Force, France), duplicated 1 January 1919 and one cancelled *L.G.* 17 June, 1924.
† Group known: 1914/15 Star trio Z216 RNVR), Defence Medal, R.N. M.S.M. (*Fratscati*, Adriatic, July–November 1918). Part of the anti-submarine division (Mobile Barrage Force). Participated in repelling the raid by Austrian Destroyers 23 April, 1918 as wireless operator on a trawler.
‡ Military Cross *L.G.* 4 June 1917 as C.S.M. Machine Gun Guards. The M.S.M. is to 4/ Guards M.G. Regt.
§ For Jamaica (R.E.).

Stacey, S./Sjt. F.	7019	Steele, R.Q.M.S. A.	7015
Stacey, S.M. H. J.	7020	— C.Q.M.S. A. S.	6891
— Pte. W. R.	6897	— Sjt. F.	6882
Stack, Cpl.(A./Sjt.) M.	6915	— Dvr.(T./Sjt.) F. W.	6976
Stackhouse, C.S.M. Instr. P. C.	6912	— C.S.M. W.	6945
Stafford, Pte.(A./Sjt.) L. V.	6943	Steggles, Pte.(A./Sjt.) A. W.	6915
Stagg, Sjt. E. F.	6954	Stentiford, Sjt. P. J.	6884
Stairs, Sjt. C.	6868	Stephens, Sjt. C. B.	6890
Stamp, Pte. T. H. *	6971	— Sub Condr. G. R. T.	7021
Standen, Pte.(A./Sjt.) H. A. B.	7013	— Sjt. S. C.	6918
Standerwick, Sjt. H. J.	6908	— Ch.Sto. T. H.	7512
Standing, Sjt. C.	6934	Stephenson, Sjt. A. L.	6891
Stanford, Cpl. N. J.	6918	— C.Q.M.S. D.	7023
Stanley, Clr.Sjt. A. E.	6919	— R.Q.M.S. F.	6944
— Sjt. D.	6894	— Cpl. F. M.	6868
— S./Sjt. H.	6915	— Pte.(A./Sjt.) L.	6885
— Sjt. H. F.	6903	— B.Q.M.S. W. R.	6867
— S./Sjt. J. E.	6901	Steptoe, Sjt. F. J.	6944
— T./R.S.M. S.	7020	Sternslow, S.S.M. A. J.	6970
Stannage, C.S.M. R. G.	6900	Stevens, 2nd Cpl.(A./S./Sjt.) A. J.	6957
Stannard, Cpl.(L./Sjt.) H.	6882	— Spr. B. C.	6880
Stanton, Sjt. E.	6876	— Q.M.S. E. H.	7020
— Mech.S./Sjt. H. F.	6901	— Vict. C.P.O. F. H.	4735
Stanway, C.Q.M.S. H. J.	6873	— Pte.(A./L./C.) F. J.	6911
Stapleton, Pte.(A./Cpl.) J.	6906	— A./Sub Condr. F. S.	6915
Stapley, Ch.Shipwt. F. C.	8069	— Dvr. R.	6919
Starbuck, Cpl. L. A.	6878	— Ldg. Sig. T. G. †	7908
Starck, Pte. P. W.	6970	— Pte.(T./Q.M.S.) W. J.	6912
Stares, Ch.Yeo.Sigs. E. J.	5111	Stevenson, Sjt.(A./C.S.M.) A.	7015
Stark, Sjt. T. F.	6892	— Pte.(A./Sub Condr.) A. H.	6976
Starkey, Sjt. E.	6895	— Sjt. D. S.	6918
— Cpl. G.	6904	— W.O. Cl. 1, E. T.	6934
Statham, Pte. A.	6906	— C.S.M. J. K.	6895
Statia, S.Q.M.S. C. V.	6915	— Cpl.(A./S.Q.M.S.) P. P. L.	7017
Stead, Engmn. H.	6447	— R.S.M. W.	7013
Steadman, S.M. W. R.	6907	— Pte.(A./Sjt.) W.	6915
Stearns, Pte. E.	6919	— Sjt. W. C.	7012
Stebbings, Spr. J. E.	6880	Steveson, Pte.(A./Cpl.) J. J.	6897
Steed, Sjt. B. L.	6865	Steward, Pte. F. E.	6918
— Ch.Sto. R.	7908	Stewardson, Spr.(L./C.) W. G.	6880
— 1st Writer S. J.	7512	Stewart, B.S.M. A.	6866
— Pte.(A./Sjt.) W.	6934	— Sjt. A.	6876
Steedman, Sjt.(A./Q.M.S.) A.	7015	— Sjt. A. A. B.	6895
Steel, B.Q.M.S. W. J.	7010	— Cpl.(A./L./Sjt.) A. D.	6892

* Hunt's Scouts, for German S.W. Africa.
† Group in Moss collection: 1914/15 Star trio (M.I.D. oakleaf, Leading Seaman R.N.), R.N. L.S. & G.C. (Yeoman of Signals, H.M.S. *Dragon*), R.N. M.S.M. (H.M.S. *Garry*) and Roumanian Barbatie Si Credinta (*L.G.* 17 March 1919). H.M.S. *Garry* destroyed submarine UB10 19 July 1918. M.I.D. *L.G.* 17 January, 1919. Also Marine Society Reward of Merit issued 3 August, 1915.

Stewart, Cpl.(A./Sjt.) E. M.	6932	Stowe, T./S.S.M. C. W.	6899
— S./Sjt. H. F.	6918	Stoyle, S.Q.M.S.(A/S.S.M.) E.	7021
— R.Q.M.S. J.	6955	Stoyles, Sjt. T.	6957
— S./Sjt.(A./Q.M.S.) J.	7022	Strachan, Cpl.(A./Sjt.) H. E.	6908
— Sjt. J.	6915	— Sea. P.	6448
— W.O. Cl. 1, L. W.	6934	Stradling, C.S.M. J. E.	6895
— Dkhnd. R.	4733	Strain, C.Q.M.S. C. G.	6890
— Pte. T.	6894	Straiton, Sjt.(A./Sub Condr.) W. L.	6957
— R.S.M. W. F.	6866	Strange, C.S.M. F. G.	7012
— Flt. Sjt. W. H.	7039	Stratford, T./R.S.M. G. F. F.	6955
— Sjt. W. Y.	6903	Street, C.S.M. G. C.	6881
Stilges, Vict.C.P.O. W. H. (&		Stringer, R.Q.M.S. H.	6887
correction)	7908, 8203	— Sjt. H.	6903
Stinson, Sjt. F.	6915	Stroud, B.Q.M.S. S. J.	6867
Stinton, R.Q.M.S. H. L.	6882	Struthers, Sjt. G. A.	6876
Stirk, T./S.M. H. R.	6866	Strutt, Sjt. W. H.	6891
Stirrup, Pte. E.	6906	Stuart, Pte. A.	6892
Stitt, Sjt. A. W.	6955	— R.Q.M.S. C.	* 7016
Stock, S./S.M. L.	6899	— Sjt. H.	6898
Stockbridge, Spr.(A./Cpl.) W. J.	6880	— Sjt. J. W.	7018
Stockman, Sjt. J. C.	6887	Stubbs, Sjt. G. T.	6903
Stockton, Sjt. W. C.	6895	Stuchbury, B.S.M. C.	6866
Stockwell, C.Q.M.S. C.	6933	Stuckberry, Sjt.(A./C.Q.M.S.) J. N.	6896
Stokes, C.S.M. A. E.	6890	Stupple, T./Sub Condr. E. H.	6910
— C.S.M.(A./R.Q.M.S.) J.	7016	Sturges, Pte. W. I.	6898
— C.Q.M.S. W.	6915	Sturgess, Sadd.Sjt.(A./Sadd.S./Sjt.)	
Stone, Ch. Writer A. W.	7908	A. C.	6903
— Cpl.(S./Smith) F.	6866	Sturt, Sjt. P.	6891
— S.M. F. S.	7039	Styles, Sjt. W.	7018
— S.Q.M.S. G. W.	6933	Suckling, Sjt. C.	6868
— P.O. 1st Cl. J.	8202	— C.Q.M.S. T. N.	6918
— C.S.M. J. H.	6918	Suddard, Pte.W. T.	6915
— C.S.M. M. C.	6892	Suddes, Pte. J.	6897
— Sjt. P.	6903	Sudell, Sqdn.S.M. W.	† 7010
— T./W.O. Cl. 1, P. M.	7022	Sullivan, Ldg.Sto. J.	7908
— T./Sub Condr. R.	7020	— Pte.(L./C.) J. E.	6911
— Sjt. W.	6884	— S./Sjt. L. J.	6970
— 2nd Cpl. W. E.	6879	— F./Clk. W. E.	7039
— Sjt. W. H.	6911	Summerfield, Cpl.(A./S.M.) C.	6956
Stoot, Sjt.(T./C.S.M.) R.	6876	— Sjt. V. A.	6893
Storey, C.Q.M.S. I. J.	6883	Summers, Cpl.(A./Sjt.) C. C.	6908
— Pte.(A./Cpl.) N. C.	7020	Summersgill,Q.M.S. H.	6907
— C.Q.M.S. W.	7016	Summersides, C.Q.M.S. T.	7016
Stout, Sjt. J.	6896	Sumner, Pte. R.	6906
Stovell, Cpl. F.	6915	Surridge, Cpl.Mec. D. G.	7039
Stovold, S./Sjt.(A./S.M.)W. T.	6946	Sutcliffe, Ch.Mec. D. G.	7039

---

* H.L.I. L.S. & G.C. 1911.

† Pair known: M.S.M. and Territorial Force Efficiency Medal (Geo. V). All W.W.I
  service with Duke of Lancaster's Own Yeomanry was in Ireland. Originally
  recommended for Medal of the Order of British Empire.

Sutherland, Sjt. D.	6892	Tainsh, C.Q.M.S. T. T.		6887
— S.Q.M.S. W. (corr.)	7703	Talbot, R.Q.M.S. A.		7014
Suthers, C.S.M. R.	7016	— C.S.M. C. H.		6872
Suttell, Cpl.(L./Sjt.) F. W.	6882	— F./Clk. W. O.		7039
Sutton, E.S.T./S.M. A.	6932	Tallis, R.S.M. T. E.		7013
— Cpl.(A./Sjt.) C. J. B.	6878	Tame, Sjt. J.		6903
— Pnr. E. R.	6880	— Ch.Mec. W. O.		7039
— Ch. Writer F. J.	7512	Tandy, Cpl.(A./R.Q.M.S.) E. E.		6882
— Sqdn.Q.M.S.(A./S.S.M.) H., *MM.*	6894	Tann, R.S.M. G.		7017
— Dvr. H.	6907	Tannahill, Cpl. J.		7039
— Farr.Cpl.(A./Farr.Sjt.) H. E.	6904	Tanner, Pte.(L./C.) P.		6906
— Dvr.(A./Cpl.) P.	6907	— Sjt.(A./C.S.M.) S.		6876
— Cpl.(L./Sjt.) P. J.	6898	Tansley, Sjt. F. A.		6943
— Cpl.(A./Sjt.) T.	6878	Tappenden, C.Q.M.S. H.		6895
— Sjt. T. R.	6896	Tapper, F./Sjt. C. E.		7039
Swain, Sjt. H. R.	6890	— C.Q.M.S. J.		6889
— Cpl. W.	7039	Tappere, Sjt. A. F.		6903
Swan, C.S.M. C.	7016	Tarbath, Cpl. H. W.		6918
— Sjt. R.	6876	Tarling, Sig. F. C.		4734
Swann, Cpl. W. J.	6944	Tarlton, Cpl. H.		6868
Swanson, T./R.S.M. D.	6934	Tarry, Cpl. J. A.		6868
Swarbrick, Dvr.(A./Cpl.) F.	6907	Tart, R.Q.M.S. J. R.		6884
Swartz, Pte.(A./C.Q.M.S.) E. E.	6915	Tasker, C.Q.M.S.(R.S.M.) E.		6887
Swayne, Cpl. A. P.	6896	— Spr. F. A.	❀	6064
Sweeney, Sjt.(A./C.S.M.) M.	6896	Tassell, Sjt. J. D.		7039
Sweet, Cpl.(A./C.S.M.) D. J.	6904	Tatler, Sjt. J. W.		6903
— Mech.S./Sjt. S. W.	6901	Tawton, B.S.M.(A./R.S.M.) W.		6966
— Pte.(A./S./Smith Cpl.) W.	6957	Taylor, R.S.M. A., *D.C.M.*		6893
Sweeting, B.S.M. G.	6918	— Pte.(A./L./C.) A.		6894
Swift, Sqdn.S.M.(A./R.S.M.) A.	7010	— Sjt. A. E.		6886
— 2nd Cpl. A.	6879	— Pte.(A./R.Q.M.S.) A. E.		7016
— Cpl.(A./Sjt.) A. M.	6904	— C.Q.M.S. A. G.		6873
— Pte. E. G.	6898	— Cpl.(A./Mech.S./Sjt.) A. G.		6904
— Sjt. H.	6884	— Pte. A. G.	❀	6064
Swinnerton, Sjt. Instr. R.	6912	— Sjt. C. (R.E.)		6876
Swinson, Cpl. F. L.	6904	— Sjt. C. (R. Berks. R.)		6889
Syer, Pte.(L./C.) A.	6889	— Sjt. C. (M.G.C.)		6894
Sykes, Cpl. H.	7011	— Cpl. C. H.		6904
— Pte. H.	6946	— 2nd Cpl. C. H.		6878
— C.Q.M.S. L. T.	6887	— S./Sjt. C. St.J.		6915
— B.Q.M.S. R. W. G.	6943	— 2nd Cpl. E.		6943
Symonds, Cpl of Horse R.	6881	— Sjt. E. F.		6908
— Cpl. W. J.	6878	— Sjt.(A./C.S.M.) F.		6882
Symons, Bombr. A. H.	6871	— Pte.(A./L./C.) F. A.		6911
— Pte.(A./Sjt.) E. W.	6906	— S./Sjt. F. W.		7021
— S.Q.M.S.(A./S.S.M.) J. H.	6911	— C.Q.M.S. G.	*	6882
— C.Q.M.S. K. W. F.	7015	— Cpl. G.		6888

---

* Group known in Moss collection: Two Queen's South Africa Medal medals one
(Relief of Ladysmith, Cape Colony, Corporal K.R.R.C.) the other with the bars
Cape Colony, South Africa 1902, British War and Victory medals (Colour Serjeant,

Taylor, Sjt. G. A.	6908	Templeton, C.S.M. D.		6872
— C.Q.M.S. G. S.	6892	— C.Q.M.S. W.		6892
— B.S.M. G. W.	6896	Tennant, Pte. F. J.		6897
— Sjt. G. W.	6876	Terras, Spr.(A./Cpl.) A. D.		6880
— Cpl. G. W.	6881	Terrey, Sjt. E. S.		7022
— S.M. H. (corr.)	7703	Terry, Sjt. F. J.		7039
— S./Sjt. H.	6908	— Sub Condr. T.		7021
— Cpl. H.	6889	— Pte.(L./C.) W.		6896
— Pte. H.	6883	Tester, T./R.S.M. J.		7018
— Sjt. J.	6908	Tetley, Pte. F. J.		6897
— C.S.M. J. A.	6895	Tewkesbury, Cpl. of Horse C.		6881
— Sjt. J. A.	6893	Thacker, Farr.S./Sjt. F.		7019
— Cpl. J. E.	6908	— Sjt. H. J.		6903
— Pte.(A./Sjt.) J. H.	7020	Thain, C.Q.M.S. A. E.		6898
— Bombr.(A./Cpl.) J. R.	6871	Thatcher, Pte. A. J.		6897
— Spr.(L./C.) L.	6880	Thaw, S.M. W.		7039
— Cpl.(A./Sjt.) M.	6904	Theed, R.S.M. W. R.		7015
— Spr.(L./C.) R. C.	6880	Theobald, Sjt. W. A.		7039
— S./Sjt. R. E.	6945	Theodore, Spr. G.	✱	6064
— Pte. R. J.	6894	Thewlis, T./W.O. Cl. 1, O. A.		7022
— F./Sjt. R. P.	7039	Thirtle, Sjt. H. G.		6896
— Cpl. S. (R.E.)	6878	Thody, Sjt. B. E.		6898
— Cpl. S. (R.A.S.C.)	6904	Thom, C.S.M. F.		6872
— Pte.(A./Sjt.) T.	6883	Thomas, Mech. A. C.		6448
— Pte.(A./Sjt.) V.	6891	— Cpl. C.		6904
— R.S.M. W.	* 7016	— S./Sjt. C. G.		7010
— Sjt. W. (Lab. C.)	6896	— Sjt. E. (R.G.A.)		6932
— Sjt. W. (R.D.C.)	7018	— Sjt. E. (Mil. Foot Police)		6957
— C.Q.M.S. W. H.	6881	— Cpl. E.		6896
Teale, Cpl. F. W.	7019	— Pte. E. T.		7015
Teather, Sub Condr. R. T.	7021	— E.C. 2nd Cpl.(A./Q.M.S.) G. B.		6879
Tedham, C.S.M. W. G. H.	6900	— Pte. G. J.		6897
Tedray, C.P.O. A.	5111	— Sjt. H.		6918
Telfer, C.Q.M.S. R.	6915	— Sjt.(A./T.S.M.) J.		6876
Tellett, C.Q.M.S. F.	6885	— F./Sjt. J. B.		7039
Temperton, Sjt. G. W. (deletion of		— Ch. Writer J. E.		7512
duplicate)	7703	— Pte.(A./Sjt.) J. W.		6883

Hampshire Regt.) and M.S.M. (C.Q.M.S. Garrison Battn. Hamps. R.). Both Q.S.A.s
are verified, the first with 3rd Battn. with whom he was wounded at Spion Kop and
evacuated to U.K. on 2 February 1900 and the second with 4th Battn. on his
return on 3 May, 1902. He was a cricket bat maker, serving in the 1st Vol. Bn.
Warwickshire Regt. when he enlisted aged 19 yrs. 9 months into 3/K.R.R.C. on 29
July 1892. On 23 December 1897 he was transferred to the Army Reserve with his
consent prior to the expiry of his paid Army service in the rank of Lance Sgt. to his
home in Sparkbrook, Birmingham. He was recalled on 9 October, 1899 and promoted
Sergeant the same day. He was finally discharged time expired on 11 April 1904.
Twelve years later aged 44 he went to France in April 1916 with the Garrison
Battn. of the Hampshire Regt.

* 3.K.R.R.C. Also entitled to Queen's South Africa Medal and King's South Africa
Medal.

Thomas, Sjt. P.	6896		Thorne, C.S.M. R. K.	6895
— E.C. Cpl.(A./Q.M.S.) R.	6878		Thornett, Pte. R.	6888
— Cpl. R. W.	6919		Thornley, Sjt. S.	6910
— S./Sjt. S. R.	6901		— Pte. T.	6906
— Ch.Yeo.Sigs. W.	* 7512		Thornton, Sjt. A.	6945
— Sjt. W. D.	6932		— Sjt. E.	6896
— Pte. W. H.	6906		— Cpl.(A./Sjt.) J.	6904
— Eng.Clk.Q.M.S. W. R	7012		— Supt. Clk. J. J.	6943
Thompsen, Cpl. H. E. N.	6878		Thorpe, F. of W. S./Sjt. B. W.	6873
Thompson, R.Q.M.S. A. E. (Ess. Reg.,			— Cpl.(A./Sjt.) S. W.	6896
7th Bn.)	6933		— Cpl. W. (M.G.C.)	6894
— S./Sjt. A. E. (New Zealand Force)	6919		— Cpl. W. (R.G.A.)	6943
— Sjt. A. E. (Ess Reg., 5th Bn.)	6933		— Sjt. W. E.	6903
— Sjt.(A./C.S.M.) A. H.	6896		Thould, Sjt. F.	6915
— Sjt. C.	6896		Thrasher, C.S.M. H. S.	6895
— 2nd Cpl.(A./Cpl.) C. J.	6879		Thrift, R.Q.M.S. W., *D.C.M.*	6882
— Pte.(A./Cpl.) C. S.	6884		Thrower, P.O. 1st Cl. F.	6448
— T./Sub Condr. E.	6910		— C.S.M. G.	6884
— Trmr. E.	5111		Thurlow, Pte. D.	6906
— Pte.(L./C.) E.	6892		— Sjt.(A./S./Sjt.) E. E.	6971
— Pte.(A./Cpl.) F. A.	7020		— Sjt. R.	7023
— Pte.(A./Sjt.j) F. J.	7016		Thurman, Sjt. H.	6918
— Sjt.(A./R.Q.M.S.) G.	6896		Thwaites, L.A.C. F. W. B.	7039
— Sjt.(A./C.Q.M.S.) G.	6896		Ticehurst, Cpl. A. T.	6905
— Sjt. G.	6903		Tickner, A.C. 1, S. A.	7039
— Cpl. G.	6904		Tiddy, Cpl.(A.C.) T. E.	7011
— F. of W. S.M. G. C.	† 7012		Tidman, T./S.M. J. A.	6871
— Gnr.(L./Bombr.) H.	6871		Tidy, Pte. J.	6943
— Pte. H. J.	6897		Tierney, Pte. J.	✿ 6064
— Cpl. H. L.	6896		— S./Sjt. W.	6915
— T./S.S.M. J.	6945		Tilbrook, Sjt. H. A.	6903
— Sjt. J. R.	6876		Tilby, Sjt.(A./S.M.) R. J.	7020
— Sjt. J. T.	6896		Tilley, Condr. F. L.	7021
— Sjt. R. G.	6918		— Cpl. H. J.	6870
— Spr.(L./C.) T.	6880		Timms, R.S.M. A.	6915
— C.Q.M.S. T. A.	6873		— T./Sub Condr. R. H.	6910
— Q.M.S. W.	7013		Timson, Sqdn.S.M.(A./R.S.M.) E.	7010
— E.R.A. 3rd Cl. W. J.	7908		Tincknell, C.S.M. F. W.	6915
— Pte.(A./Cpl.) W. L. N.	7020		Tingey, C.Q.M.S. C. A.	6873
Thomson, T./S.M. C.	6871		Tingley, Sjt. Mec. C.	7039
— Dvr. H.	6880		Tinley, Sjt. W.	6903
— S./Sjt. J.	6908		Tippings, Pte.(L./C.) W.	6906
— Cpl.(A./Sjt.) J.	6892		Tipple, Sjt. W.	6876
— 2nd Cpl.(A./Cpl.) J.	6954		Titchener, Dvr. G. L.	6907
Thorne, Sjt.(R.S.M.) M. M. T.	6955		Titcombe, P.O. 1st Cl. C.	4735

---

 * Group known: East & West Africa Medal (Witu 1890, Leading Seaman, H.M.S.
  Turquoise), British War Medal, R.N. L.S. & G.C. (Victoria, Yeo. of Sigs., *'Terror'*)
  and R.N. M.S.M. (H.M.S. *Victory*).
 † For Bermuda, (R.E.). Group known: British War Medal (W.O.1), L.S. & G.C. (Geo.
  V) and M.S.M.

Titheridge, Sjt. W. C.	6903	Trebilcock, Sto.P.O. W.	8069
Titley, Pte.(A./Sjt.) M. M. J.	7014	Trehane, Sjt. H. B.	7020
Titmons, Yeo.Sigs. A. S.	7908	Trehearn, Q.M.S. W. J.	7016
Toben, S./Sjt. H.	6901	Tremaine, C.Q.M.S. T. H.	6944
Todd, Pte. D. P.	6906	Tribe, Sjt. H.	6903
— Cpl.(A./Sjt.) F. D.	6905	— Sjt. W. H.	6903
— R.Q.M.S. H. A.	6881	Trimmer, R.Q.M.S. H. W.	6919
Todhunter, Sjt. J. W.	6943	— Cpl. W.	6911
Toft, Sjt. C. W., *MM.*	6911	Trissler, Pte. J.	6915
Toghill, Sjt. F.	6882	Trodd, Cpl. R. R.	6915
Toler, Cpl. C. W.	6911	Troke, Sjt.(T./Q.M.S.) G. A.	6912
Tolhurst, Farr.S./Sjt. H.	6953	Trollope, Gnr.(A./Sjt.) W. T.	* 7011
Tollfree, Sjt.Clk. T. H.	4512	Trotman, F./Clk. A. C. W.	7039
Tombs, Gnr. C. F.	6943	Trott, Sjt. E.	6915
— C.Q.M.S. W. H.	6918	— B.S.M. J., *MM.*	6869
Tomison, Sjt. W. H.	7039	— Cpl. W.	6905
Tomkinson, Q.M.S. F. W.	6907	— C.Q.M.S. M. M. J.	6880
Tomlinson, Sjt. P. W.	6868	Trotter, Cpl.(A./Sjt.) A. W.	7039
Tompkin, C.S.M. H. M.	6893	— C.S.M.(A./S.M.) G.	7013
Tompson, Sjt. A. A.	6886	Trow, Pte.(L./C.) J. E.	6906
Toms, Cpl.(L./Sjt.) F. E.	6969	Truckle, L.A.C. N.	7040
— Spr.(A./Cpl.) W. J.	6880	Trueman, C.Q.M.S. G. V.	6881
Tonkin, C.Q.M.S. W. L.	6932	Trumble, Pte.(A./Sjt.) A.	7018
Tookey, Farr.S./Sjt. W. O.	6867	Trupp, Sjt. A. J.	6876
Tooth, Sjt.(A./C.S.M.I.) C. J.	6944	Truss, Cpl.(A./Sjt.) T. E.	6910
Topp, T./S.S.M. E. C.	6899	Trubbenshauer, T./W.O. Cl.II, E. C.	7022
Topper, Cpl. W. H.	6878	Tucker, Sjt.(T./C.S.M.) A.	6876
Toweland, Cpl. J., *MM.*	6932	— Sjt. A.	6881
Tough, C.Q.M.S. S.	6918	— Pte. E. H.	6887
Towers, Sjt. A. C.	6942	— Mech.S./Sjt. G. F.	6976
Towill, Cpl.(A./Sjt.) G. H.	6896	Tuckwood, S.S.M. C. H.	7018
Towle, Pte. E. W.	6906	Tudge, C.Q.M.S.G. H.	6889
Townley, Sjt. H. W.	6908	Tuffen, Pte. A.	6945
Townsend, Pte.(A./C.S.M.) V. R.	6970	Tuffin, Sjt. N.	6970
— Cpl.(A./S./Sjt.) W. A.	6905	Turkington, Pte.(A./S./Sjt.) R.	6906
Townsend, Q.M.S. C.	6915	Turnbull, C.S.M. G.	6900
Townson, Sjt. W.	6892	— E.R.A. 3rd Cl. T.	7908
Towsend, Sjt. J. F.	6866	Turner, C.S.M. A.	6932
Tozer, Cpl. A. L.	6868	— Sjt. A.	6903
— Sjt. A. S.	6943	— Mech.S./Sjt. A. W.	6873
— W.O. Cl. 1, H. J.	7022	— Sjt. E.	6876
Tracey, F./Sjt. W. A.	7039	— Cpl. E. W.	6905
Train, Cpl. W.	6895	— Cpl.(A./Sjt.) F.	6908
Trainor, Pte.(T./Sjt.) A.	6906	— C.Q.M.S. F. H. D.	6882
Travers, B.S.M. R. H.	6866	— C.S.M.Instr. F. W.	6912
Traylor, Sjt. W. M.	6955	— S./Sjt. G. A.	6970
Treasure, Sqdn.Q.M.S.(O.R.Sjt.) R. E.	7010	— Sjt. G. W., *MM.*	6883
— Farr.Sjt.(A./Farr.Q.M.S.) W. R.	6865	— Farr. Sjt. H.	6867

* Group known: British War Medal (R.A.) and Victory Medal, General Service Medal (Iraq, M.I.D. 1921) and M.S.M. (R.F.A. for services in India).

Turner, Sjt. H.	6887	Usherwood, Cpl.(A./Sjt.) N. H.		7012
— Spr.(A./2nd Cpl.) H.	6880	Ussher, Q.M.S. J. H.		6919
— Sjt. J.	6887			
— Pte. J.	6974	Vallis, Q.M.S. H. G.	‡	7014
— Sjt. N. V.	6910	Valter, Cpl. C. L.		6868
— Q.M.S. (I.G.) R.	7011	Vance, Farr.Q.M.S. H.		6867
— Spr. S. J.	6880	Vann, Sjt. T. E.		6903
— C.S.M. T.	6900	Vanner, S.Q.M.S. J.		6899
— Mas.Mec. W.	7040	Vanstan, R.Q.M.S. F. J.		6918
— Pte.(A./Sjt.) W.	6887	Varey, R.Q.M.S. N.		6884
Turnley, R.Q.M.S. A. P.	6918	Varley, Cpl.(A./L./Sjt.) J. H.		6887
Tutt, Sjt.(A./C.S.M.) G.	7015	— S./Sjt. W. T.		6901
Tuttiett, Sjt. J. T.	6956	Veale, C.P.O. R.		8069
Twaite, Sjt. H	6915	Veater, Ch. Writer E. J.		6865
Twizell, Sjt. F.	6882	Veevers, C.S.M. F.		6885
Twycross, C.S.M. L. E.	6872	Veitch, B.S.M. C. A.		6869
Twynham, S./Sjt. P. E.	6971	Venables, Cpl. T.		7040
Tyers, Whlr.S./Sjt. J. T.	6900	Veness, Sjt.Mec. W. E.		7040
Tyler, C.E.R.A. 1st Cl. E. S.	4198	Venner, R.Q.M.S. A. B.		6884
— P.O. Teleg. F.	* 7512	Venton, Pte.(A./Sjt.) E. W.		6912
— Pte.(A./S.Q.M.S.) G.	7020	Ventress, Sjt. S. T.		6868
— Sqdn.Q.M.S. H.	6894	Verity, Supt.Clk.(Draughtsman) B. C.		6932
— R.Q.M.S. H.	6956	Verney, Pte. T.		6889
— Pte.(A./L./C.) J.	6911	Vernon, Pte. J.		6897
— Sjt. J. E.	6896	Vessey, 2nd Cpl. W.		6879
Tyrell, Pte.(A./Sjt.) F.	7020	Vial, Sjt. J. C.		6954
Tyrrell, R.S.M. A. J., *M.C.*	† 7014	Vick, C.E.R.A. 2nd Cl. W. H.		8069
— Sjt.(A./R.S.M.) F. G.	7010	Vickers, Pte.(A./Sjt.) J. C.		6892
		Vincent, Sjt. A.		6944
Umney, Pte. C.	6888	— sjt. G. A.		6915
Underhay, Q.M.S. H. R.	6448	— sjt.(A./Q.M.S.) W. J.		6876
Underhill, 2nd Hnd. (now Skpr.)		Vine, Sjt. P.		6911
G. W.	6447	Viner, Pte.(A./Sjt.) R. F.		7015
Underwood, Sjt. A.	6903	Vining, Pte. W. R.		6906
— Spr. J. C.	✤ 7702	Vinson, Sjt. T. S.		6943
Unsworth, Pte.(A./Sjt.) J.	6934	Vokes, C.S.M.(A./R.Q.M.S.) S.		7011
— Q.M.S. S.	6907	Volk, Mas.Clk. G	§	7040
Upfold, R.Q.M.S. H.	6918	Voller, Cpl. W. A.		7040
Upton, Offrs.Std. 1st Cl. W. H.	7908	Volze, Sjt. J. H.		6915
Uren, Sjt.(T./C.S.M.) F.	6918			
Urquhart, Cpl. J.	6955	Waddams, Sjt.(A./C.Q.M.S.) P. G.		7015
Usherwood, Sjt. A. E.	7013	Waddell, A./Condr. F. J.		7022

* Group known in Moss Collection: 1914/15 Star trio, Africa General Service Medal (Somaliland 1920 H.M.S. *Clio*) and R.N. M.S.M. (H.M.S. *Rival*).

† 8/Devons. R. M.C. *L.G.* 27 July, 1916.

‡ R.Scots Fus. For Sierra Leone.

§ Group in Moss Collection: South African War Services Medal 1939–45, 1914/15 Star (Chief Petty Officer 3rd class R.N.A.S.), British War and Victory Medals (S.M.2 R.A.F.) and R.A.F. M.S.M. (I Force, France, No. 203427). Came from Durban, South Africa.

Waddell, Sjt.(A./S./Sjt.) W. H.	7019	Walker, Sjt. J. L.	6898
Waddington, C.Q.M.S. G.	6919	— Ch.Mec. J. N.	7040
— Gnr.(A./Sjt.) G. E.	7011	— Cpl.(A./Sjt.) J. R.	6908
— Sjt. R. A.	6903	— Sjt. J. W.	6908
Wademan, C.S.M.(A./R.S.M.) F.	* 6970	— Pte. (A./Sjt.) J. W.	6897
Wadham, C.Q.M.S. A. H.	6900	— R.S.M. L.	6866
Wadmore, S./Sjt.(A./Q.M.S.) E. A.	6908	— Bombr. L.	6869
Waggitt, C.Q.M.S. J. C.	6915	— Cpl.(A./L./Sjt.) M.	6885
Waghorn, Pte. E.	6897	— C.Q.M.S. P. E.	6887
— A.B. J.	4734	— Sjt.(A./C.S.M.) T. E.	6891
Wagstaff, Cpl. J. W.	6878	— T./S.M. W.	6871
Wain, Pte. C. H.	6909	— Sjt. W. A.	6894
Wainscott, C.E.R.A. 1st Cl. G. H.	8069	— S.M. W. H.	6970
Wainwright, Cpl.(A./Sjt.) A.	6905	Walkinshaw, Pte. E.	6883
— Pte. A.	6897	Walkley, S./Sjt. T.	6957
Waite, Cpl. H. J. A.	6868	Wall, Sjt. H. H.	6886
Wakefield, B.Q.M.S. F. W. G.	6867	— C.Q.M.S. W. T.	6900
— Sjt. J. A. V.	6908	Wallace, B.Q.M.S. T.	6867
Wakeford, R.S.M. D.	7016	Waller, Shlr.Sjt.(A./Whlr.S./Sjt.)	
Wakeham, C.S.M. J. H.	6865	G. R.	6903
Wakelin, Sjt. D.	6876	— Whlr.S./Sjt. J. H.	6900
Wakely, S.Q.M.S. G. W.	7021	— Cpl.(A./Sjt.) S. G.	6910
Wakelyn, S./Sjt. A., *M.M.*	6915	Walliker, Q.M.S. L. G.	7014
Wakem, Sadd.S./Sjt. A. W.	6900	Wallis, Sjt. C. B.	6903
Walbey, Sjt. H.	6896	— S./Sjt. F. F.	6901
Walcroft, Sjt. W.	6893	Wallisbuhl, C.Q.M.S. E. G.	6918
Waldock, Sjt. J.	6945	Walliter, Sjt. W. W.	6882
Walford, Pte.(A./L./C.) J. T.	6911	Wallwork, Cpl. A.	6905
Walker, Cpl.(A./Sjt.) A.	6892	Wallworth, Cpl. A. R.	6878
— Pte. A.	6886	Walmsley, Sjt. Instr. E.	6912
— Sjt. A. C.	6876	— C.Q.M.S. G. W.	6894
— Cpl. A. C.	6894	— C.Q.M.S.(A./R.Q.M.S.) J.	6891
— Clk. 1 A. T.	7040	— Pte.(L./C.) J.	6887
— Pte. B. G.	6918	Walsh, Sjt. A.	6896
— Sjt.(A./B.S.M.) C.	6954	— C.Q.M.S. A. A.	6895
— Sjt.(A./S.M.)C. T.	7011	— L./C. E. J.	6918
— Pte.(L./C.) E.	6890	— Cpl. H. A.	6896
— Pte.(A./Cpl.) E.	6909	— T./R.S.M. J.	7016
— Cpl. F.	6911	— Sjt. J. (Ir. Gds.)	6880
— 2nd Cpl.(A./Cpl.) F. M.	6879	— Sjt. J. (Mil. Mounted Police)	6911
— Cpl.(A./S./Sjt.) F. O.	6910	— Pte.(A./Sjt.) J., *M.M.*	6911
— Sjt. G. A.	6889	— Pte. W. ❀	7702
— Pte. G. C.	6889	Walter, L.A.C. A.	7040
— Sjt. G. W.	6868	— C.S.M. F.	6900
— Sub Condr. H.	7021	— R.S.M. T. W.	7012
— C.Q.M.S. H. D.	6918	Walters, Sjt. A.	6915
— Spr. (L./Cpl.) J.	6880	— R.Q.M.S. R.	6881
— T./S.M. J. C.	7020	— Pte. T.	6897
— Sjt. J. H.	6894	— Spr. W. G.	6880

* For East Africa, K.R.R.C. Also entitled to Queen's South Africa Medal 2/K.R.R.C.

Walthen, Pte.(A./Sjt.) W.	6909	Wasley, Sjt. G.	6876
Walton, Dvr. E. W.	6869	Water, C.Q.M.S. W.	7016
— T./1st Cl. S.S.M. F. H.	7020	Waterfield, Pte.(L./C.) T.	6906
— Pte.(A./Cpl.) G.	6909	Waterhouse, Sjt. A. W.	6894
— Sjt. H. H.	6915	Waters, Pte. A. W.	6865
Want, T./Sub Condr.) B.	6910	— C.S.M. W. G. T.	6890
Warby, C.S.M. J. W.	6872	— Cpl.(T./C.Q.M.S.) W. H.	6905
Warcham, T./Sub Condr. C.	6910	Waterson, Fitt.Sjt. C. R.	6918
Ward, Sjt. A. J.	6933	Watkins, B.Q.M.S. E. S.	6918
— Q.M.S. A. S.	6907	— Gnr. F.	6869
— T/S.S.M. B.	6970	— Gnr. T.	6869
— Pte.(A./C.S.M.) C. G.	7020	— Sjt. (A./R.Q.M.S.) W. H.	6933
— C.Q.M.S. C. H.	6945	Watmough, Ch.Mec. J.	7040
— C.S.M.(T./R.S.M.) E.	6884	Watson, A.M.T./S.M. A.	6915
— Sjt. F.	6956	— T./Sub Condr. A.	6910
— Sjt. F. C.	6932	— Sjt. B.	6891
— Pte. 1, G. A.	7040	— S.M. C. B. (corr.)	7703
— Mech.S./Sjt. J. G.	6901	— Gnr.(A./Sjt.) C. C.	6871
— Sjt.(A./Sqdn.S.M.) P. J.	6911	— R.Q.M.S. D.	6933
— R.S.M. T.	6871	— Farr.Sjt. D.	6915
— Farr.S./Sjt. T.	6953	— Sjt.(A./C.Q.M.S.) G.	6876
— Bombr.(L./Cpl.) W.	6869	— Sjt.(A./C.Q.M.S.) J.	6919
— Sjt. W. T.	6956	— Pte.(A./Cpl.) J.	6865
— Pte.(L./C.) W. W.	6897	— Mech.S./Sjt. P.	6901
Wardall, Sjt.(A./C.S.M.) F. H.	6956	— Pte.(A./Cpl.) S. A.	6897
Wards, Cpl.(A./Sjt.) W. B.	6891	— Sto. 1st Cl. W.	7512
Ware, Sjt.(A./C.S.M.) J.	6896	— Cpl.(A./Sjt.) W. H.	6954
— Pte. J.	6906	— Sjt.(A./S./Sjt.) W. R.	7020
Warham, R.Q.M.S. J. C.	6893	Watt, Condr. H. J.	6918
Waring, C.S.M. F.	6900	— Spr. W.	6880
— C.Q.M.S. T.	6892	Watts, S./Sjt. A. E.	6910
— S.M. W. E. S.	7020	— Cpl. G.	6890
Warley, Sjt. J. H.	7040	— Sjt. G. E.	6876
Warlow, Supt.Clk. S.	7011	— Sjt. G. F.	6903
Warman, Sjt. A. J.	7012	— L.A.C. J. W.	7040
— B.Q.M.S. A. S., *MM.*	6867	— Pte.(T./C.S.M.) R. H. W.	6906
Warner, Pte.(A./Sjt.) A. C.	6883	— Mech.S./Sjt. T. H.	6901
— C.Q.M.S. J. L.	6976	— C.Q.M.S. W.	7015
— Sjt. P. W.	6876	Waudby, Pte.(L./C.) C.	6884
— Cooper. W. T.	7908	Waugh, Sjt.(A./R.Q.M.S.) C. H.	7017
Warren, Cpl.(A./Sjt.) C. S.	6905	Wavell, Dvr. W. W.	6869
— Cpl. E. C.	6896	Way, Dvr. E.	6907
— Sjt. F. C.	6957	Wayman, Sjt.(A./C.Q.M.S.) W. S.	6887
— B.S.M. G. A.	6918	Weakick, Sea. T.	5112
— Yeo.Sig. G. W.	4734	Wealthy, B.S.M. J.	7010
— Sjt. H. W.	6915	Wear, Cpl. S.	6891
— E.R.A. 3rd Cl. L.	7908	Wearing, Cpl. T.	6868
— Sqdn.S.M. R.	6956	Weatherill, Sjt. J. A.	6894
Warrender, Pte. J.	6906	Weaver, F. of W. S./Sjt. W.	7012
Wasama, Abib, Cpl.	6971	Weavis, Sjt.(A./S./Sjt.) E.	6957
Wash, F./Sjt. C. E.	7040	Webb, S./Sjt. A.	6910
Washford, Sjt. H. J.	6915	— Cpl.(A./Sjt.) A.	6905

Webb, Cpl. C.	6878	West, C.S.M.(A./R.Q.M.S.) E.		7011
— Cpl. D. R.	6908	— C.Q.M.S. F. C.		6873
— B.S.M. F.	6918	— Sjt.(A./C.Q.M.S.) F. E.		7015
— Sjt. H. R.	7021	— Sjt. G. F.		6876
— Q.M.S. H. S.	7016	— C.S.M. H. W.		6888
— Cpl. J. E.	6905	— Sjt.(A/C.S.M.) T. E.		7015
— C.Q.M.S. J. H.	* 7013	— C.S.M. W.		7013
— Cpl. J. P.	6896	— Sjt. W. A.		6915
— Sjt. L. R., *M.M.*	6876	— Sjt. W. C.		7013
— Sjt. S. F.	6918	Westbrook, C.S.M. A.		7013
— C.Q.M.S. W. C. L.	6898	— C.Q.M.S. G.		7015
— Spr. W. E.	6880	— Pte.(A./Sjt.) H.		6889
Webber, F. of W. Q.M.S. G. H.	7012	Westfield, S.S.M. E. N.		7018
— Elect.Art. 3rd Cl. H. T.	7908	Westhorpe, P.O. 1st Cl. J. J.		5112
— Sjt. R. R.	6911	Weston, Gnr. C. E.		6932
Webster, Sjt. C. B.	6876	— S.S.M. R. G.		7018
— Sjt. D. F.	6876	— Cpl.(A./S./Sjt.) S.		6905
— Pte.(L./C.) F.	6886	— Pte.(A./L./Sjt.) W. J.		7013
— Pte.(L./C.) H. O.	6883	Westwell, Pte.(A./Sjt.) A. W.		7014
— Pte. P. H.	6906	Wetherill, Sjt. A. E.		6876
— Bomb. R.	6943	Wetherwilt, L./Sjt. G.		6915
— 2nd Hnd. R. B.	6447	Wetton, Cpl. C		6944
Weddell, S./Sjt. A. C.	7023	Weymouth, Pte.(A./Sjt.) J. E.		6887
Wedgbury, Sjt. A.	6908	Whale, Sjt.(A./Q.M.S.) C. A.		7012
Wedgewood, Sjt.(A./Q.M.S.) W.	6890	— Sjt.(A./S.S.M.) E. W. T.		7019
Weedon, Sjt. A. H.	6868	Whaley, Farr.Q.M.S. F. C.		7018
Weeks, Q.M.S.(I.G.)) H. E.	7011	Whall, Sjt. J. R.		6896
— C.Q.M.S. J. W.	7023	— Pte. W. E.		6891
Weir, Pte.(A./S./Sjt.) L.	7020	Wharton, S./S.M. E. H.		6956
Welch, Sjt. E. V.	6918	— Pte.(A./Cpl.) H. J. C.		6890
— Ch.Yeo.Sigs. G. H.	7908	Wheatley, Sjt. J.		6903
— Sjt. J. F.	6896	— Sjt. J. W. H.		6945
— F. of W. S./Sjt.(A./Q.M.S.) T.	6873	Whebell, C.S.M.(A./Drill Sjt.) C. J.		6881
Welfare, C.Q.M.S.(A./S.M.) A. H.	6873	Wheelans, Pte.(A./L./Sjt.) A. G.		6892
Welford, Sjt. A. J.	6945	Wheeldon, S./Sjt. A.		7020
— C.Q.M.S. T. W.	6915	Wheeler, Condr. F. (corr.)		7703
— Sjt. L. W.	6975	— Pte. F. S.		6897
Wellan, Sjt.(A./C.S.M.) A.	7018	— C.Q.M.S. G. C.		6873
Wellings, Sjt. L. C.	6918	— Pte. H. T.		6906
Wellman, Clr.Sjt. E.	7023	— T./Sub Condr. J. E.		6910
Wells, Cpl. A. B.	7040	Whelan, Sjt.(T./S.Q.M.S.) M.		6903
— R.Q.M.S. G. F.	7015	Whelen, S./Sjt. W. M.		6873
— T./Mech.S.M. W. R.	6899	Whenham, S.M. F. C.	†	7040
— Cpl.(T./Sjt.) W. T.	6954	Whiddon, S./Sjt. H.		7019
Welsby, Cpl. N.	6915	Whimpey, Pte.(A./Sjt.) C. F. R.		6906
Welsh, Sig. R.	6869	Whiston, C.S.M. S.		7017

* East Kents, for Singapore.
† No. 349 R.F.C. Enlisted September 1912. Entitled to 1914 Star and bar trio, Defence and War Medals, 1935 Jubilee, R.A.F. M.S.M. and R.A.F. L.S. & G.C. Cpl. in 1914. S.M. in 1917 Commissioned in 1935. Sqn. Ldr. in W.W.II; retired 1946.

Whitaker, Spr. A. H.	6880	Whitley, Pte. S. O.		6976
Whitall, Pte. E. H.	6906	Whitlock, S./Sjt. A. L.		6915
Whitby, C.Q.M.S.(A./R.S.M.) H. J.	7018	Whittaker, Sjt. J. E.		7017
White, C.Q.M.S. A.	6915	— Pte.(A./S.M.) R. A.		7022
— Sjt. A.	6918	Whittam, Sjt. J. E.		6876
— Dvr. A.	6915	— Sjt.(A./C.Q.M.S.) M.		6876
— Farr.Sjt. C.	6915	Whittle, Dkhnd. L. J.		5111
— S.Q.M.S.(A./S.S.M.) C. G.	7021	— S./Sjt. T.		6901
— Spr. E.	6880	— S./Sjt. W. J.		6901
— R.Q.M.S. E. L.	6915	Whittlestone, Cpl. J.		6896
— Cpl.(A./Sjt.) E. T.	6944	Whittmore, T./S.S.M. P. C.		6899
— Cpl. F.	6896	Whitton, S./Sjt. H. T.		6971
— F./Sjt. F. C.	7040	— C.S.M. J.		6881
— Pte.(A./S.Q.M.S.) F. C.	7020	Whitwell, S./Sjt.(A./C.S.M.) F. E.		6918
— Pte.(A./Sjt.) F. H.	6911	— Sjt.(T./S.Q.M.S.) M. L. M.		7019
— Pte.(A./Sjt.) G. F.	6886	Whitworth, Pte.(A./Sjt.) A.		6886
— Sjt. H.	6955	— Sjt. E.		6944
— Q.M.S. J.	6907	— R.Q.M.S. H.		6945
— Cpl. J.	6957	— T./W.O. Cl. 1, W.		7022
— Q.M.S. J. H.	6919	Whorlow, Pte. G.		6897
— Ch.Sto. J. J.	8069	Whyatt, Cpl. E. B.		6878
— Cpl. (A./Sjt.) P. A.	7040	— Sjt. J. W.		6896
— Pte.(A./Sjt.) T. E.	7017	Whybrow, R.Q.M.S. A.		6885
— R.Q.M.S. T. G.	7016	— B.S.M. D. W.		6869
— Sjt. T. J.	6915	Wickham, C.Q.M.S. E.		6895
— C.Q.M.S. W.	6900	Wickins, C.Q.M.S. J. N.		6918
— Sjt. W.	6868	Wicks, CS.M.(A./R.S.M.) R. L.		6889
— Sjt.(A./C.S.M.) W. R.	6903	— B.Q.M.S. W.		6935
— C.S.M. W. S.	6882	Wickson, Pte. W. J.		6946
White-Fraser, Sjt.(A./C.S.M.) G.	6915	Wiffen, Sjt. H. G.		6934
Whitefoot, Sjt. T. W.	6915	Wigg, Mech.S./Sjt. H.		6901
Whitehead, S.M. C.	7040	Wiggall, Cpl.(L./Sjt.) P. E.		6886
— T./R.S.M. F. W.	6954	Wiggans, S./Sjt. R.		6933
— C.Q.M.S. G.	6891	Wiggett, Sjt. F. J.		6896
— Sjt. R.	6945	Wiggins, Pte. J. J.		6897
Whitehouse, Sjt.(T./Sqdn.S.M.) E.	6903	— Cpl. R.		6878
Whitelaw, C.S.M.Instr. J.	7016	Wigglesworth, F./Sjt. A.		7040
Whiteley, Cpl. H. C.	6878	Wightman, Cpl. W. F.		6943
— R.S.M. W.	* 7014	Wilby, Dvr.(L./C.) S. J.		6880
Whitefield, Cpl. E. E.	6870	Wilcocks, C.Q.M.S. A.		6957
— Pte. R.	6906	Wilcox, Sjt. H. B.		6876
Whitham, C.Q.M.S. W.	6889	Wild, Pte.(A./L./C.) F.		6897
Whiting, C.S.M. J.	6976	— C.Q.M.S. H.		6889
— S.M. J.	† 7020	— Spr. H.		6880
Whitley, S.M. A.	7040	— Ldg. Sig. W. F.	‡	4735
— Spr. J. W.	6880	Wildblood, Sjt.(A./C.Q.M.S.) F. H.		6886

---

* I.A. For Aden.

† R.E. For Aden.

‡ R.N. M.S.M. for local Defence Flotillas. Died 8 January 1947 when Master at Arms, H.M.S. *Excellent*, aged 52. Buried at Portsmouth.

Wilden, Sjt. D.	6896	Williams, Cpl. G. K.		6915
Wildish, Dkhnd. C.	4733	— Sjt.(A./C.Q.M.S.) H.		6876
Wildman, B.S.M. J. C.	6866	— C.S.M. H. H.		7017
Wiles, R.Q.M.S. A. E.	6893	— Pte.(A./Cpl.) H. J.		6897
— C.Q.M.S. C. J.	6889	— Sjt. H. R.		6919
— Ldg. Sto. G. E.	8069	— Sjt.(A./C.S.M.) J.		7014
Wilkes, Pte. (A./Sjt.) J.	6897	— Bombr.(A./Sjt.) J. E.		6871
Wilkins, T./Armt.S.M. H. A.	6910	— Spr. J. H.		6918
Wilkinson, Gnr. A. S.	6869	— Cpl.(A./Sjt.) J. R.		6933
— Spr. E. W.	✿ 7702	— L./C. M.		6918
— S./Sjt. F.	6901	— Pte.(L./C.) O. W.		6883
— Sjt. F. B.	6903	— Pte.(L./C.) P.		6883
— C.Q.M.S. G.	6873	— Pte. R.		6915
— Cpl. H.	6888	— Sjt. R. J.		6886
— Sjt. J. A.	6903	— C.Q.M.S.(A./R.Q.M.S.) S.		6898
— Ch. Mec. R.	7040	— C.P.O. T.		7908
— Cpl. R.	6896	— L.A.C. T.		7040
Wilks, 2nd Cpl. M.	6879	— Spr.(L./C.) T.		6880
— Sqdn.S.M. (R.R.) W.	7010	— Dvr.(T./Cpl.) T.		6907
Will, T./W.O. Cl. 1, W. C.	7022	— Pte.(A./L./C.) T.		6911
Willcock, Cpl. C. H.	6878	— Cpl.(A./C.Q.M.S.) T. E.		7015
Willcocks, C.Q.M.S. H. C.	6873	— S./Sjt. T. F.		6901
Willgross, Cpl.(A./Sjt.) J. W.	6898	— Spr.(L./C.) T. L.		6880
William, Pte.(A./L./C.)		— E.R.A. 2nd Cl. T. W.		4734
W., *D.C.M., M.M.*	* 6912	— Sjt. V. T. M.		6888
Williams, Sjt. Mec. A.	7040	— S.Q.M.S. W.		6918
— Sjt. A.	6903	— R.S.M. W.		7016
— C.S.M.(A./R.S.M.) A. C.	6888	— Sjt. W. C.		6903
— S./Sjt. A. E.	6910	Williamson, Sjt. C. F.		6957
— Sjt. A. E.	6903	— Pte. D.		6934
— Pte.(L./C.) A. E.	6906	— C.S.M.(A./S.S.M.) H.		6915
— S./Sjt.(T./Q.M.S.) A. G.	6934	— Sjt. H.		6885
— Sjt. A. L.	6876	— T./Sqdn.Q.M.S. K. McF.		6935
— Sjt. C.	7040	— Sjt. W.		6903
— Cpl. C.	6886	Willis, Pte. A.		6911
— C.S.M. D.	6895	— T./R.S.M. A. S., *M.M.*		6907
— Pnr.(A./Cpl.) D.	6880	— C.Q.M.S. E. H.		6881
— C.Q.M.S. E.	6944	— Farr.Cpl.(T./Farr.S./Sjt.) H. J.		6905
— Gnr. E. T.	6954	— Sjt.(A./C.S.M.) J.		6896
— Pte.(A./Cpl.) F.	6955	— Cpl.(L./Sjt.) K. L.		6887
— Sjt. F. G.	7017	— Sjt.(A./C.S.M.) L.		6896
— Sjt. G.	6911	— Sqdn.Q.M.Cpl. W. E.		7010
— T./Armt.S.M. G.	6910	Willison, L./C. G. H.		6915
— Pte. G. A.	6906	Willshire, Pte.(A./L./C.) G. J.	†	6911
— Cpl. G. E.	6896	Wilmhurst, Sjt. C. A. J.		6903

---

  * Group known: D.C.M. (14356 Pte. 2/G. Gds.), M.M. (L./Cpl. 2/G.Gds.), 1914/15 Star trio (Pte. & Cpl. Gren. Gds.) and M.S.M. (P14444 M.F.P.). Also Liverpool City Police Long Service Medal (Const. 45711), presented 8 June 1932.

  † Group known: 1914/15 Star trio (L./Cpl. M.M.P.), Metropolitan Police 1911 Coronation Medal (P.C.) and M.S.M. (M.M.P.).

Wilmore, Sjt. A. E.		6892	Windrum, R.S.M. J.		6971
Wilmot, Sjt. M. M. W.		6918	Windsor, Sjt. C. C.		6868
Wilmott, C.Q.M.S. P. F.		6873	— Sjt. E. G.		6890
— Cpl.(A./Sjt.) W. P.		7018	Wingrave, S./Sjt. H. C.		6901
Wilshaw, B.Q.M.S. E. E.		6870	Winkle, Sjt. A. E.		7019
Wilsher, Pte.(A./L./C.) G. W.		6912	Winkley, Sjt.(A./S.S.M.) W. E.		6866
Wilshere, Sjt. D.		6887	Winkworth, Pte.(T./Cpl.) J. N.		6918
Wilson, R.S.M. A.		6865	Winn, R.S.M. H.		7015
— T./S.M.(A.C.) A. A.	*	7011	Winning, C.Q.M.S. T. A.		6891
— S.Q.M.S.(A./Supt.Clk.) C.		7015	Winslet, C.P.O. H.		7908
— S./Sjt. C. C.		6901	Winstanley, C.Q.M.S. J. H.		6873
— Sjt. C. E.	✿	6064	Winston, Sjt. T. C.		6896
— Sjt. C. J.		6885	Winter, Sjt. H. B.		6918
— Pte. C. R.		6897	Winterbottom, T./Sub Condr. E.		6957
— S./Sjt. E.		7021	Winterburn, Sqdn.Cpl.Maj. J. W.		6881
— Pte. E. H.		6909	Winton, S.M. E.		6907
— B.S.M. F.		6869	— Q.M.S. (I. G.) J. E.		7011
— Sjt. F. G.		6908	Wishey, Cpl.(A./Sjt.) B.		6905
— Sjt. G. (R.E.)		6876	Wisdon, Pte. T. V.		6916
— Sjt. G. (Midd. R.)		6890	Wiseman, Dvr. W.		6919
— T./S.M. (A.C.) G. B.		6869	Wishart, S./C.S.M. J.		7022
— Sjt.(T./S.M.A.C.) G. B.		6870	Witcombe, S.B.S. E. H.		8202
— Sjt. G. H.		6882	Witherington, R.S.M. W. O.		6865
— Q.M.S. H. de L.	†	6956	Withers, Sjt. F. C.		6887
— F. of W. S./Sjt.(A./Q.M.S.) H. G.		6873	— Cpl. W. G. A.		6896
— C.Q.M.S. H. J.		6889	Withey, R.Q.M.S. J. H.		6955
— C.S.M.(A./R.S.M.) J.		6884	Withington, Cpl. B.		6878
— C.S.M. J.		6895	Witt, Sjt. W. W. J.		6876
— S./Sjt. J.		6945	Wixted, Cpl. T. A.		6957
— Farr.S./Sjt. J.		6870	Wolfenden, Q.M.S. T.		6881
— Sjt. J. (R.A.S.C.)		6903	Wolff, Sjt. H.		6918
— Sjt. J. (R.A.V.C.)		6946	Wood, C.Q.M.S. A.		6893
— Pte. J.		6956	— Cpl. A. E. G.		6896
— T./Sub Condr. J. A.		6934	— T./Mech.S.M. A. H.		6899
— Sjt. L. J.		6903	— Cpl. A. W.		6878
— Sjt. Mec. T.		7040	— S.S.M. C.		6916
— Mech. S.M. T. R.		6871	— Engmn. C. E.		4733
— R.Q.M.S. T. T.		6885	— C.Q.M.S. C. L.		6873
— Sjt. Instr. W.		6912	— Pte.(A./L./C.) C. W.	✿	6911
— Sjt. W. M.		7040	— Sjt.(A./R.Q.M.S.) E.		6882
Wilton, Mech.S./Sjt. A.		6901	— Pte.(L./C.) E.		6906
— Sjt. G.		6910	— Cpl.(A./L./Sjt.) F. A.		6885
Windram, L./Sjt. T.		6918			

---

* R.G.A. For Hong Kong.

† Group known: Queen's South Africa Medal (Cape Colony, Tugela Heights, Relief of Ladysmith, Transvaal, Cpl. K.R.R.C.), King's South Africa Medal (O.R.Clk. K.R.R.C.), 1914/15 Star (C/Sjt.), British War and Victory Medals (M.I.D. oakleaf W.O.1), Delhi Durbar 1911 (Sgt.), L.S. & G.C. (Geo. V, C./Sgt.) and M.S.M. (No. 404 throughout. 3/K.R.R.C.) for Salonika. Henry De Lacy Wilson M.I.D. Salonika *L.G.* 28 January 1919.

Wood, M.Elect.S.M. F. T.	* 7012	Woolen, Pte. W.		6882
— Sjt. F. V.	6890	Woolley, Pte. J.		6887
— Sjt. F. W.	6903	Woolrich, Cpl. J. J.		6916
— B.S.M. G. E.	6866	Woolston, Spr.(A./Sjt.) A. V.		7013
— Ch. Writer G. H.	8202	Woolvine, Cpl. G. H.		6955
— B.Q.M.S. H.	6867	Wooster, R.Q.M.S. A. E.		6894
— C.S.M. J.	7018	Wootten, Mech.T./S.M. C. G.		6871
— Pte.(A./L./C.) J.	6897	Worby, Sjt. T.		6911
— Sjt. J. W.	6884	Wordingham, Sjt. T. H.		6882
— Sjt.(A./S./Sjt.) J. W. M.	6974	Worlidge, Pte. A. V.		6910
— Pte.(A./Sjt.) L. W.	6897	Worrall, Sjt. F.		6891
— Sjt. P.	6903	Worsfold, Cpl. Mec. R.		7040
— Cpl. T.	6910	Worth, Gnr. W. H.		6916
— C.S.M. W.	6895	Worthy, C.S.M. G. W.		6872
— S.M. W.	4512	Would, B.S.M.(A./R.S.M.) H. C.		6867
— Pte.(A./R.S.M.) W. J.	6883	Wray, Cpl. C. A.		6888
— C.Q.M.S.(A./R.Q.M.S.) W. J. A.	6885	— Sjt.(A./C.S.M.) T., *D.C.M.*		7016
— S./Sjt. W. P.	6908	Wreford, T./R.S.M. T. J.		7012
Woodburn, C.Q.M.S. L.	6887	Wren, C.Q.M.S. A. E.		6873
Woodcock, Sjt. J.	6945	— Sjt. E.		7011
— Pte.(A./Sjt.) J. R.	6934	Wrigglesworth, Sjt. L. M.		6884
— Bombr.(A./Sjt.) (A.C.) S. W.	6871	Wright, C.S.M. A. P. P.		6893
Wooderson, Sjt. F.	6891	— Sjt. C.		6889
Woodfield, Pte.(A./Q.M.S.) W. T.	6898	— R.S.M. D. G. H.		6916
Woodford, Pte.(A./Cpl.) F.	6884	— C.S.M. E. G.		6900
— Sjt. J. H.	7017	— Sjt. E. I.		6908
— S./Sjt.(T./Q.M.S.) T.	6912	— S.M. E. L.		6899
Woodhouse, S.M. E. C.	6934	— Cpl.(A./Sjt.) F.		6884
Woodisse, O.R. Sjt. T.	6970	— F./Sjt. F. E.	† 7040	
Woodley, Gnr. G.	6954	— Sub Condr. F. L. H.		6912
— Offrs. Ch. Stwd. W. W.	4198	— B.S.M. F. R.		6867
Woodrow, Sjt. K.	6876	— C.Q.M.S. G.		6895
— Pte.(A./L./Sjt.) W. J.	6889	— Armt.S./Sjt. G. E.		6916
Woodruff, Cpl. R. T.	6916	— Q.M.S. G. W.		6907
Woods, B.Q.M.S. E. J.	6867	— C.S.M.(A./R.S.M.) H.		6955
— C.Q.M.S. G.	6887	— T./Sub Condr. H.		6910
— Pte. J.	6897	— Pte.(L./C.) H.		6883
Woodward, Sjt. C.	6944	— C.S.M. H. J.		6872
— S./Smith(A./Cpl.) F. J.	6905	— R.Q.M.S. J., *D.C.M.*		6866
— Pte. G. E.	6897	— Sjt. J.		6876
— R.Q.M.S. H.	6895	— Pte.(A./C.Q.M.S.) J.		7020
Woodyard, Sjt. J.	6918	— C.Q.M.S.(A./C.S.M.) J. H.		7018
Wookey, Spr. A. T.	6880	— B.S.M. J. W.		6867
Woolgar, Pte.(A./Cpl.) H.	6906	— Spr.(A./Cpl.) J. W.		6880
Woollcombe-Boyce, Pte.(A./Sjt.)		— Spr. M. O.		6880
K. W.	6912	— Cpl. R. H.		6898

* R.E. Singapore.
† No. 19925 R.F.C. Formerly Balloon Section R.E. later Sqn. Ldr. (Eng. Off.). Group known: O.B.E., 1914/15 Star trio, Defence and War Medals (M.I.D. oakleaf), 1935 Jubilee, 1937 Coronation, R.A.F. M.S.M. and R.A.F. L.S. & G.C.

Wright, Cpl.(A./Sjt.) R. M.	6905	Yorke, C.S.M. A. R.		6945
— Farr.S./Sjt. S.	6867	Youd, Sjt. A. E.		6876
— Ch. Writer S. A.	6504	Youde, A.M. 3 (A./Cpl.) W.		7040
— Cpl.(A./Sjt. A.C.) S. C.	6870	Young, 2nd Cpl.(A./Cpl.) B.		6879
— Sjt. S. P.	6876	— C.Q.M.S. F.		6894
— Sjt. T.	6911	— R.Q.M.S. G.		6918
— Sjt. W.	6896	— Sjt.(A./R.Q.M.S.) H. B.		6896
— Sqdn.Cpl.Maj.(Instr.) W. H.	* 7010	— A.B. H. L. W.		4735
Wrigley, Sjt. L.	6894	— Sjt. J.		6916
Wyatt, Sjt. A. E.	6916	— Condr. S.		7020
— Sjt. J. N.	6934	— A.B. S. E.		4735
— Cpl.(A./Sjt.) W.	6868	— Fitt.S./Sjt. T.		6870
Wylde, B.S.M. F.	6869	— Sjt. T.		6876
Wyness, Sjt. I. K. F.	6918	— Sjt. W.		6903
Wythe, Sjt. W.	7018	— Mas.Mec. W.		7040
		— Pte.(A./Cpl.) W.		7014
Yarnell, R.Q.M.S. J. E.	6885	— A./C.Q.M.S. W. C.		7022
Yates, Dvr. F.	6869	— Sjt.(A./Q.M.S.) W. T.		6908
— C.S.M. G.	6895	Younger, C.Q.M.S. S. W.		6918
— Sjt. H.	6903	Youngs, R.S.M. G.		6969
— Pte. H.	6898	Yuile, B.Q.M.S. J., *M.M.*		6867
— Fitt.S./Sjt. J.	6870			
— Pte.(A./Cpl.) J. W.	6885	Zanelli, P.O. J. R. A.		7908
— Sjt. S.	6893	Zell, S.M. I. A.		7040
— Sjt. T. H.	6868			
— Cpl. W.	6868			
— C.Q.M.S. W. A.	6873			
Yelling, Cpl.Mec. J. T.	7040	*Meritorious Service Medal, Bar:*		
Yendole, Sjt.(A./C.S.M.) G. H.	6884			
Yeo, C.P.O. W. H.	7512	Carmody, Cpl. T. J.	† ❀	7701

*　Awarded M.S.M. Annuity 1947. (Army Order 18). A pair of medals are known: L.S. & G.C. (Edw. VII, S.C.M., Inst. of Fencing, Life Guards) and M.S.M.
†　530 3 Sqn. (Australian Flying Corps) for gallant conduct rescuing a pilot from a burning aircraft. Medal, also for gallantry *L.G.* 21 August, 1917.

Vol. III, 1919

Abbott, Sto. R. H.	8385	Balsom, Pte. A. W.	8386
Adams, Sjt. G. (corr.)	8360	Banks, Sjt.(A./C.S.M.) H.	11774
— C.P.O. W.	8943	Bannigan, R.S.M. J. F. M.	* 11997
Ahern, Ch. Writer P.	9111	Barber, E.R.A. 3rd Cl. C.	9835
Ainsworth, Sjt. W.	11773	Barden, Pte. E. J.	11775
Aldis, Farr.Q.M.S. R. G.	11774	Barker, Pte.(A./C.Q.M.S.) H. C. P.	11775
Allison, 2nd Writer C.	8385	Barkley, Mech.S./Sjt. H. G.	11778
— Sqdn.S.M. C. E.	11777	Barnes, Sjt. W. H.	11774
— Supt.Clk.(W.O.I.) S. A.	11579	Barnett, C.E.R.A. 1st Cl. F. J.	9111
Allsop, Pte. J.	11773	Barnicott, Pte.(A./Sjt.) J. D.	11775
Alp, C.Q.M.S. C. A. (deletion, award		Barrett, Pte. J. A.	11777
having been gazetted		Bartlett, Ch. Shipwt. F. R.	9111
previously)	8361	Barwick, Staff Clk.(W.O.II) (actg.	
Amey, S.B. S. H.	9111	Supt. Clk. W.O.I) G. W.	† 11579
Anderson, Cpl. F. McK.	11778	Bates, Cpl.(T./Sub Condr.) G. P.	11779
— Mech. J. P.	9111	— Pte.(A./S.M.) J. V. (corr.)	10589
Ansell, C.P.O. R. J.	9111	Bawden, T./Sub Condr. C. A.	10320
Anthony, L. A. T.	11780	Baxendale, 2nd Writer W.	8385
Antoney, R.Q.M.S. G.	11776	Baxter, Sjt. B.	11579
Arkell, C. B.	11780	Bayley, C.P.O. S. W.	9833
Armitage, Cpl. H. V.	11778	Beale, Army Sch. Mstr. D. E.	11779
Arnold, Sjt.(A./R.Q.M.S.) G. W.	11776	Beard, Sjt.(A./C.Q.M.S.) F. C.	11774
Askew, Cpl.(A./Sjt.) G. A.	11774	Bebbington, 2nd Cpl. W.	11775
Asquith, S./S.M. H.	10319	Bedford, Sjt. D. (corr.)	10589
Atherton, Sjt.(A./C.S.M.) A. (corr.)	10589	Bell, Sjt. J. T.	11778
Atkins, Cpl. C. J.	9111	Belshaw, C.P.O. J.	8939
— P.O. Teleg. H. T.	9111	Benbow, 2nd Cpl. W. P.	11775
		Bendall, Ch.Arm. E. E.	9111
Badger, Sjt. B. R.	❀ 8359	Benham, Sjt.(A./Q.M.S.) G. W.	
Bagg, Spr.(A./Cpl.) W.	10319	(corr.)	9395
Bailey, Sjt. J.	11776	Bennett, Sjt.(A./S./S.M.)	
Baker, Cpl. C. F.	11778	A. E. (corr.)	8360
— Sjt. F. A.	11779	— Pte.(A./Sjt.) H. M.	11778
— Pte. H.	11776	— Ch. Writer W. R.	11579
Ball, Sjt. H. (corr.)	10589	Betterton, Cpl. J.	11776
Balls, C.P.O. W. U.	9111	Bibb, Sjt.(A./R.S.M.) E.	‡ 11774
Balsom, Gnr. (A./Sjt.) A.	11774	Bicknell, A./Bombr. F. (corr.)	10589

---

* 2128 2nd Brigade Australian Field Artillery. See also Pte. W. Bristow. *L.G.* 30th
  January 1920. Devotion to duty as a P.O.W, during an epidemic. See also Wood
  and Worsfield *infra*.

† Group known: Naval General Service Medal (Persian Gulf 1909–14 Pte. '*Hyacinth*'),
  1914 Star trio, R.N. M.S.M. (R.M. & London).

‡ Medal known (No. 1941 R.E.). Three times M.I.D. 12th March 1918, 27th August
  1918 and 5th June 1919.

Biggs, Bombr. H.	❀ 10587	Broomfield, Mech.S./Sjt.	
— Pte. J. A.	11773	A. T. (corr.)	8360
— Sjt. W.	11779	Brough, B.S.M. W., *M.M.*	11774
— Sjt. W. T. (corr.)	10589	Brown, Cpl.(A./C.) J. (corr.)	8360
Bilk, Ch. Offrs. Std. F. C.	9111	— Pte. L.	11776
Bingham, Bombr. H.	11774	— Ch. Writer W. C.	8385
Birch, Bombr.(A./Sjt.) F.	11774	— (Haunton) P.O. 1st Cl. W. J.	8385
Bishop, Ch. Writer A. H. C. E.	9111	— Staff Clk.(W.O.II)(actg.Supt.	
— 3rd Writer J. C.	8385	Clk. W.O.I) W. McK.	† 11579
Bissell, S./S.M. F. F. (corr.)	8360	— Cpl. W. R.	❀ 8359
Black, C.Q.M.S. J. M.	11774	Browning, C.S.M. W. F.	11778
Blackburn, Cpl. A. J.	11775	Bryant, Pte. G.	11775
— C.S.M. C.	10319	— C.P.O. H.	9111
Blackman, Sjt. W. E. C.	* 11579	Buck, Pte.(A./Sjt.) H. M.	10319
Blagrove, S.M. A. E. (corr.)	8360	Buckell, C.P.O. H.	11579
Blake, P.O. 1st Cl. E.	11579	Buckenham, B.S.M. A. H. (corr.)	10589
Blakeman, C.E.R.A. G. W.	8943	Buckle, Sjt. P. S. W.	‡ 8385
Blount, C.S.M. A.	11778	Buckley, P.O. 1st Cl. R. E.	8943
Blythe, Sjt.(A./S.M.) R. L.	11778	Bullard, Gnr. D.	8943
— C.S.M.(W.O.II) S. G.	9111	Bulley, Ch. Writer F. W.	§ 9111
Boardman, C.S.M. J.	11776	Bumstead, Mech.S./Sjt. W. E.	11778
Boatswain, Spr.(A./R.S.M.) A. G.	11775	Burcher, Sjt.(A./S./Sjt.) G. H.	11778
Bodley, Dvr. W. H.	10320	Burden, Ch. Sto. C. H.	9111
Bolan, C.S.M. R. (corr.)	8360	Burdett, 2nd Writer, W. H.	8385
— R.S.M. W.	11774	Burgess, Cpl.(A./Sjt.) H.	11774
Bond, Pte. F. J. G. (corr.)	10589	— Ord. Sea. H. G.	11579
— Mech.S./Sjt. T. E.	11778	Burnley, Clr. Sjt. H.	9111
Bottomley, Sjt. R. O. (corr.)	10589	Burrows, Sjt. S.	11776
Boucher, Pte. (A./Sjt.) J.	11779	Burt, Supt.Clk.(W.O.I) G.	11579
Boulton, Sjt. F. M. E.	11579	Bury, Clr.Sjt. W. R.	11579
Bourke, Cpl.(A./Sjt.) J. T.	11779	Bushell, Ch.Shipwt. 2nd Cl. J. W.	9111
Bowden, Pte. R.	11775	Butler, S.S.Cpl. E.	11773
Bowen, Pte. C. H.	11775	Buxton, Gnr.(A./Sjt.) H. S.	11774
Bowles, R.Q.M.S. H. A.	11777		
Brewster, Mech.S.M. H. J.	10319	Cairns, Sjt. D.	11777
Bridge, Pte. C. K.	11775	Calcott, Calcott, Sub Condr. T.	11779
Bridger, P.O. W.	8943	Calder, Pte.(A./S./Sjt.) W. H.	
Briggs, Cpl.(A./Sjt.) H. P.	11579	(corr.)	10589
Bristow, C.S.M.(A./R.S.M.) G. E.	11776	Callender, Pte.(A./Cpl.) W. G.	
Broadbridge, Sjt. W.	9111	(corr.)	10589
Broadhurst, Sjt. W. F.	❀ 8359	Cann, Pte.(A./Mech.S./Sjt.) P. W.	
Brockman, A.B. J. W.	11579	(corr.)	10589
Brooker, C.S.M. E.	11777	Cantrell, Ch. Arm. W. G.	9833

---

* Group known: British War Medal, Victory Medal, Defence Medal, Royal Victorian Medal, R.N. L.S. & G.C. and R.N. M.S.M.

† Killed 12 August, 1940 aged 60—Lieut. & Q.M. R.M.

‡ R.M.L.C. R.N. M.S.M. but withdrawn. See Army M.S.M. *L.G.* 3 June 1919.

§ Group known: China 1900 (*Pique*) 1914/15 Star trio, R.N. L.S.& GC (*Medea*) and R.N. M.S.M. (*Resolution*).

Carleton, Clr.Sjt.(A./S.M.,	
W.O. I) W.	8943
Carter, Sjt. W.	11774
Carthew, Pte.(A./L.C.) R.	11778
Cash, Sjt.(A./C.S.M.) G. H.	11777
Cattle, Gnr. S. J.	8943
Cearns, 1st Cl. Assist. Surgn. W.	11779
Chadwick, R.Q.M.S. H. (corr.)	9395
Chalmers, Shipwt. 2nd Cl. J. M.	8943
Chapman, C.Q.M.S. J.	11774
Chase, C.S.M. J. W.	11776
Cheason, B.S.M. S.	11774
Child, Clr.Sjt.(A./Q.M.S. W.O. II)	
J. J.	8385
Childs, Spr. (A./Sjt.) F. W.	11775
Chowns, Sjt.(A./R.S.M.) D.	10319
Church, Pte.(A./Sjt.) H. J. B.	11776
Clark, Sjt.(A./C.S.M.) G. E.	11776
— Yeo Sigs. H. J.	9111
— T./S./S.M. J. (corr.)	10589
— Sjt.(A./Q.M.S. W.O.II) J.	8385
— C.S.M. R.	11778
Cochrane, Sjt. J. H.	11778
Colan, Sjt. O. J.	11579
Colbourne, S./Sjt.(A./Sub Condr.)	
W. G.	11779
Coleman, Sjt.(A./S./Sjt.) A. L.	11778
— Sub Condr. J. W.	11779
Collis, S./Sjt. (A./Sub Condr.) G. F.	11779
Conning, C.E.R.A. W. T.	8943
Connolly, Sjt. S.	11774
Constable, Pte.(A./Sjt.) D. W.	11775
Convers, Condr. A. W.	10319
Cook, C.S.M. (W.O. II) F.	11579
Cooper, Sjt. C. G.	11774
— Clr.Sjt. G. J.	9111
— Farr.Sjt. J. W.	11774
— 4th Cl. Assist. Surgn. L. B.	11779
— Pte.(L./C.) R.	11779
— Pte. S.	11775
Copestake, A.B. W. J.	11579
Copplestone, Ch. Sto. J. A.	11579
Cornwell, Cpl. H. G.	11775
Cosford, Pte. G.	✽ 10587
Cosgrove, C.P.O. J.	9111
Cottom, Sjt. J. H.	11774
Cough, Pte.(A./Sjt.) S. A.	11777
Coulton, 2nd Cpl.(A./Sjt.) G. C.	11779
Court, Sjt. A. S.	11778
Coward, Q.M.S.Instr.	
(W.O. II) C. F.	11579
Coweson, A.B. D.	10199

Cowthard, Ch. Ship's Cook T. P.	9111
Cowton, C.P.O. Mech.	
2nd Gde. A. E.	9111
Cox, C.S.M. H. V.	11777
— Sjt.(A./Staff Clk.	
W.O. II) V. L.	11579
Crampton, Q.M.S. D.	11778
Craven, P.O. 1st Cl. J. W.	11579
— Sjt. T. S.	11773
Crawley, Sjt. F.	11579
Creech, C.S.M. E.	11777
Cresswell, Condr. H. B.	11778
Crewe, Pte. A.	11779
Crofts, S.B.S. C. E.	11579
Crompton, Ch. Yeo. Sigs. E.	9111
Crook, Pte.(A./Cpl.) E.	11777
Crutchloe, Pte.(A./R.S.M.) J. C.	11775
Cull, Pte.(A./Sjt.) E. A.	11776
Cullen, C.P.O. W. G.	9111
Cumper, Q.M.S.(A./R.S.M.)	
J. B., *D.C.M.*	10320
Cunningham, Cpl.(A./	
Sub Condr.) A.	11779
Curley, S./Sjt.(A./Sub Condr.) J.	11779
Curtis, Spr.(A./S./Sjt.) A. C.	11775
— C.S.M. S.	11776
Curwen, C.Q.M.S. W. G. (corr.)	10590
Cushion, Cpl.(A./Sjt.) C. A.	11774
Cutting, A. B.	11780
Drade, Sjt. W. H.	11775
Dalrymple, Sjt.(A./C.S.M.) J.	11774
Dalton, Sub Condr. J.	11778
Dampier, Spr.(A./Sjt.) T. A.	11775
Daniell, Cpl.(A./S.M.)	
(W.O. I) A. H.	11579
Daniels, P.O. 1st Cl. H.	11579
Darlow, Staff Clk.(W.O. II)(actg.	
Supt. Clk. W.O. I) H.	11579
— Sjt.(A./Supt. Clk. W.O.I) W. J.	11579
Davidson, Sub Condr. W. L. L.	11779
Davies, Cpl.(A./Sjt.) C.	11778
Davis, Sjt. A.	11778
— Ch. Writer H. E.	9111
— C.Q.M.S. S. (corr.)	10589
Davison, T./Xub Condr. W.	11778
Dawkins, Sjt. J.	11779
— Greaser W.	9833
Day, Farr.Sjt. A.	11774
— Sjt.(A./S.Q.M.S.) S. G.	10320
de Carle, Cpl. P. J. I.	11579
Deag, B.Q.M.S. W. F., *D.C.M.*	11774

Dealler, Spr.(A./Sjt.) W. T.	11775
Deamer, Pte. R. A. J.	❀ 10587
Dear, Sjt. L. A.	* 11778
Deaville, Sjt. J.	11777
Delahaye, Sjt. F. T.	❀ 8359
Danny, S./Sjt. J. D. (corr.)	10589
Devoy, Pte. J.	11778
Dew, B.Q.M.S. A. G.	11774
Dex, A./L.S. C. V.	8737
Dickens, Gnr.(L./Bombr.) F.	❀ 8359
Dicks, Farr.S./Sjt. S. J.	11774
Dickson, S.M. R. H. (corr.)	8360
Didsbury, Q.M.S. W. A.	11774
Disley, Cpl. W.	11777
Dixon, C.Q.M.S. J. H.	11777
Dobiear, C.P.O. A.	8737
Dobson, R.S.M. G. H.	11776
Docwra, Pte.(A./Cpl.) S.	11778
Dodd, Clr.Sjt.(A./C.S.M. II) C.	11579
Donovan, Sjt. W. J.	11779
Donovan, Ch. Writer E. C.	11579
Douglas, Pte.(A./S./Sjt.) H. H. (corr.)	10589
Dowling, Sjt. J. P.	11774
Downer, Pte.(A./Sjt.) E. J.	❀ 10587
Dowson, Sjt.(A./R.S.M.) T.	11774
Doyle, Pte.(L./C.) T.	11776
Drayton, Cpl. W. R. (corr.)	8361
Drinkwater, R.S.M. L.	11777
Driscoll, Sjt. W. E.	11579
Drury, Sjt.(A./S.S.M.) E. J.	11773
Drysdale, Pte. J.	11778
Duckworth, Cpl.(A./Sjt.) J.	11774
Duff, Pte.(A./L./C.) W.	11777
Dunford, P. O. F.	9111
Dungey, L./C.(A./Sjt.) G. (corr.)	8360
Durie, Sjt. J.	11779
Dyce, Pte.(L./C.) E.	11777
Eade, Clr.Sjt.(A./S.M., W.O. I) A. M.	† 8385
Earnshaw, Sjt. H. H.	11774
Eastaway, Sjt. H. J.	11579
Eaton, 2nd Writer G. E. W.	9111

Eccles, S.M. W.O. I. D. E.	8385
Edwards, Pte.(A./Cpl.) E.	11779
Elliott, M.A.A. A. W. G.	9111
Ellis, Q.M.S.Instr.(W.O. II) C.	11579
Enstice, Cpl. E. J.	11776
Evans, Staff Clk.(W.O. II) E.	11579
— Ch. Writer G. F.	9111
— Pte.(A./L./C.) T.	11778
Eyden, R.S.M. J. (corr.)	10589
Farnsworth, C.Q.M.S. W.	11777
Farrell, Cpl.(A./S./Sjt.) J.	11778
Fazakerley, Sjt. O.	11776
Ferris, Pte.(A./R.Q.M.S.) H. (corr.)	10589
Field, C.Q.M.S. W.	11774
Fieldhouse, Sjt. W.	10319
Fielding, Sjt. J.	11776
Findlay, S./Sjt.(A./S.M.) W. B.	10319
Finley, Sjt. W.	11778
Fisher, 1st Writer H. J.	8943
— Ch. Boatman, W. H.	8943
— Armr.S./Sjt. W. J.	❀ 8359
Flanagan, S.M.(W.O. I) W. J.	11579
Flawn, S.M.(W.O. I) F. J.	‡ 11579
Florence, R.Q.M.S. E.	11777
Foden, T./Sub Condr. W. M.	11779
Ford, Sjt. C. E.	11779
Forsyth, Sjt. W.	11774
Fosbury, Pte.(A./Sjt.) L. F.	11776
Foster, Pte. D. S.	11778
— C.E.R.A. 2nd Cl. P. E.	11579
Fox, C.S.M. H.	11776
— Pte.(A./L./C.) J.	11779
Frampton, W.O. Cl. II, A. J. (corr.)	9395
France, Sjt.(A./S.M.) R. A.	11778
Fraser, Sjt. J.	11774
Freckleton, 2nd S.B.S. L. G.	8737
Freeman, Pte.(A./Sjt.) A. J.	11775
— Staff Cl.(W.O. II) F. A.	11579
— Pte. H.	11773
Fremantle, C.S.M.(A./S.M.) A. H. O. (corr.)	10589
Fry, Cpl.(A./Sjt.) F. J.	11776

* Trio known: British War and Victory Medals and M.S.M. (R.A.S.C.). Recipient states that the M.S.M. was awarded for driving a blazing lorry full of H.E. shells away from an ammunition dump in Mesopotamia.
† See Vol. II 1919.
‡ Group in R.M. Museum: British War and Victory Medals, Defence and War Medals, R.N. L.S. & G.C. (Geo. V, Admiral's Bust) and R.N. M.S.M. Later Captain R.M.

Gales, Smith Q.M.S.(A./Fitt. S.M.)		Gooderham, 2nd Hnd. E. R.	9112
A. (corr.)	10589	Goodwin, Sjt. P. C.	✿ 8359
Gallichan, Pte. A. J.	11777	Gopp, Pte.(A./Sjt.) J. I.	10319
Gandy, S./Sjt. D. (corr.)	10589	Gouge, Lce. Sjt. W. A.	11580
Garbe, Supt. Clk. (W.O. I) F. J.	11580	Gozney, C.E.R.A. 1st Cl. G. W.	9111
Garbutt, Pte. (L./C.) E.	11777	Grant, Sjt.(A./C.S.M.) G. A.	10319
Gardener, P.O. 1st Cl. H. W.	8943	Graves, Pte.(A./Sjt.) F. R.	11775
Gardner, Sqdn.S.M. S. J.	11773	Green, Supt. Clk.(W.O. I) E. C.	11580
— Q.M.S.(W.O. II) T. C.	11580	— Q.M.S.Instr.(W.O. II) F. H.	11580
Garner, Pte.(A./S./Sjt.) J. H.	11775	— Pte.(A./Sjt.) H. A.	11777
Gasser, L./C.(A./C.S.M.) J. G.		— Sjt. H. C.	10319
(corr.)	8360	Greenhalgh, C.S.M.(W.O.2) J.	‡ 9833
Gates, Gnr. H. W.	8943	Grice, Q.M.S.(A./S.M.) C.	11778
Gedge, Ch. Sto. F.	8943	Griffiths, Spr.(A./R.S.M.) L. W.	11775
Gerken, E.R.A. 3rd Cl. F. A.	9833	— S./Sjt. W. G.	11778
Gethin, Dvr. R. D.	11778	Grigg, Ch. Yeo. Sigs. J.	11580
Gibb, Sjt. D.	11778	Grills, Ch. Writer T.	8385
Gibson, Sub Condr. A.	11779	Grimley, T./Sjt. F. R.	11779
Gidley, Pte.(A./Sjt.) F. J.	11775	Gristwood, Pte.(A./R.Q.M.S.) R.	11773
Giles, A./C.E.R.A. 2nd Cl.		Gritt, Cpl.(A./Sjt.) F.	10319
Norman Charles (corr.)	9112	Groome, Spr.(T./Sjt.) L. J.	11775
Gillespie, C.S.M. W. J.	11777	Groves, Bombr. A. E.	11774
Gillman, S.M.G. (award of 1st Jan.		Gunning, S./Sjt. E.	11779
1919, cancelled, having been			
previously gazetted)	8990	Hadley, Amt.S./Sjt. A. A.	§ 10319
Gissing, Cpl.(A./Sjt.) G. S. (corr.)	* 10589	Hague, Sjt. H.	11779
Glenister, Pte. A. J.	11777	Haig, Sjt. C.	11776
Glinn, 2nd Writer G. E.	9833	Haines, C.E.R.A. 1st Cl. H. E.	9111
Glynn, 1st Writer A. E.	11580	Hainsworth, Pte.(A./L./C.) E. V.	
Godsell, Clr. Sjt. E. F.	† 8943	(corr.)	10589
Godwin, Sjt. H. J.	11777	Hale, P.O. W.	+ 9111
Gonsalves, A. D.	11780	Hall, Cpl.(A./Sjt.) F. J.	10319
— G. F.	11780	— Sjt. W. J.	¶ 11580

* Group known: 1914/15 Star trio (30453 C.A.S.C.) and M.S.M.

† Group in Moss collection: British War Medal (R.M.A./2364) R.N. L.S. & G.C. (Victoria) and R.N. M.S.M. (*'Cyclops,'* Services during the war). Only 35 to R.M.A. 1919–1928.

‡ Group known: 1914/15 Star trio (Col. Sgt. R.M.A.) R.N. L.S. & G.C. (Geo. V), R.N. M.S.M. (Services in Corfu). and two safe driving awards.

§ M.S.M. known: (T./1566 R.A.O.C.). A citation for this award is given in the Official History of the R.A.O.C. For North Russia (Archangel Command). The D.A.D.O.S. Dvina Force, Major Croydon, with much ingenuity designed an emergency sight for guns badly wanted for use against the enemy's long range artillery They were at length brought up to Bereznik by sleigh and Arm.S./S Hadley A.O.C. constructed a sight from parts of other sights. On the first trial a direct hit was obtained on a target. To carry out the work he had only a bench in a hut and a very meagre supply of tools.

+ Group known: China 1900, R.N. L.S. & G.C. (Edw. VII) and R.N. M.S.M. (Services in Canada).

¶ R.N. M.S.M. Killed 24 October 1944 aged 58.

Halls, Cpl.(A./Sjt.) C. G.	11773	Haycock, Sjt.(A./C.Q.M.S.) A.	11776
Hallum, Pte.(A./Sjt.) D. C.	11779	Hayes, Cpl. T.	11777
Halstead, Sjt. R. E.	11773	Hayward, Cpl. A.	✸ 8359
Hamer, Sjt. F. W.	11778	Hayward, Sjt.(A./C.Q.M.S.) A. J.	
Hammersley, Arm.S./Sjt.(A./		(corr.)	9395
Amt.S.M.) A. G.	11779	Hazle, 2nd Cl. Assist. Surgn. W.	11779
Hammond, C.S.M. J.	11774	Heap, C.S.M.(A./W.O. Cl. 1) J.	
Hanchard, B.S.M. E.	11774	(corr.)	10589
Hanford, B.S.M. H. C.	11774	Hearne, Arm.S./Sjt. A. T.	11779
Hanlon, Clr.Sjt. T. E.	11580	— Ch. Sto. J. M.	9111
Hann, S.M. W.O. 1, G. P.	* 8385	Hedges, Pte.(L./C.) J.	11777
Hardaker, C.Q.M.S. R. (corr.)	10589	Hemens, Pte.(A./C.Q.M.S.) W. G.	11775
Hardie, P.O. 1st Cl. R. J.	8737	Henderson, Cpl.(A./Sjt.) J.	11580
Harding, Sjt. F. W.	11775	Henneberry, Sjt.(A./C.S.M.) R.	11774
Harradon, C.P.O. J.	8385	Henwood, Pte. C. H.	11778
Harrigan, Pte.(A./Cpl.) W.	11777	Herbert, Clr.Sjt.(A./S.M.	
Harris, Ch. Writer A. C.	8385	W.O. 1) J.	‡ 8385
— C.E.R.A. 2nd Cl. A. G.	9111	Heskins, C.S.M. W.	11777
— Ch. Yeo. Sigs. G. F.	8385	Heywood, Sjt. C.	10319
— Sjt. R. W.	11778	Hickie, Sjt. D.	11778
Harrison, Mech.S./Sjt. J.	11778	Higgins, Pte.(A./L./C.) J. D.	11779
Harrow, 1st Cl. S./S.M. J. E. (corr.)	10589	Higgs, Pte. E. M.	11775
Hart, Cpl.(A./C.S.M.) H.	10319	Hill, C.P.O. A. E.	11580
Hartland, Pte.(A./R.S.M.) H.	11776	— P.O. W.	§ 9111
Hartley, Sjt.(A./R.S.M.) R. H.	11776	Hillard, C.Q.M.S. E. F.	11776
Hartwell, C.S.M. A. G.	† 11777	Hilton, C.Q.M.S.(A./Mech.S./Sjt.) G.	11778
Harvey, Pte.(A./Sjt.) E. C.	11779	Hinder, 4th Cl. Assist. Surgn.	
— Pte.(A./Sjt.) G.	11776	B. A. P.	11779
— Sjt. G. W.	11775	Hinton, Q.M.S.Instr.W.O. 2 (A./	
Harwood, Ch. Sto. G.	9833	S.M. W.O. 1) H. W.	11580
Haswell, Gnr.(A./R.S.M.) R. H.	11774	Hobbs, Clr.Sjt. E. F.	+ 9833
Hatherall, Act. C.P.O. J.	11580	Hobdey, Cpl.(A./C.Q.M.S.) H. A.	11777
Hatton, Sqdn.D.S.M. P. M. (corr.)	8360	Hobgen, Gnr.(L./Bombr.) G.	11774
Hawes, Sjt. M.	11580	Hocking, C.P.O. J. H.	8385
Hawkesworth, Pte.(A./Sjt.) M.	11775	Hoddinott, Sjt.(A./R.S.M.) C. T. W.	11776
Hawkins, R.S.M. A. G.	11775	Hodgins, Sjt.(A./Q.M.S.) W. H.	11777
Haworth, C.Q.M.S. F., *D.C.M.* (corr.)	10589	Hodgkinson, C.Q.M.S. W.	11776

---

* R.M.L.I. R.N. M.S.M. withdrawn, Army M.S.M. issued 3 June 1919.

† Group known 1914/15 Star (P.O.M. R.N.A.S.), British War and Victory Medals (C.S.M. M.G.C.), M.S.M. (M.G.C.) and Russian Silver Medal for Zeal. He flew with R.N.A.S. in early 1915 then served as an instructor with the Armoured Car detachment (R.N.A.S.). He was transferred to M.G.C. and saw service in the Balkans then in Mesopotamia.

‡ R.M.L.I. R.N. M.S.M. withdrawn, Army M.S.M. issued 3 June 1919.

§ Group known: Africa General Service Medal (Somaliland 1902–04, AB *'Porpoise'*), 1914/15 Star trio, R.N. L.S. & G.C. (Geo. V, P.O. *'Research'*) and R.N. M.S.M. (*'Royal Sovereign'*).

+ Group known: 1914/15 Star trio, R.N. L.S. & G.C. (Geo. V), R.N. M.S.M. (Services in Corfu), and French Médaille Militaire. French medal awarded for services as Legation Guard, Corfu, Greek Isles.

Hogben, Sjt. S. R.	11774	Isaacs, Sjt.(A./S./Sjt.) C.	10320
Holden, Pte.(A./R.Q.M.S.) F.	11775	Isherwood, Pte.(A./L./C.) C.	11778
Holland, Staff Clk. W.O. 2 (A./		Islip, Pte.(A./Sjt.) S. H.	11778
Supt.Clk. W.O. 1) R. B.	11580		
Hollings, C.S.M. J. G.	11777	Jack, C.Q.M.S. J. A.	10319
Holyoake, M.C. Cpl. R. H.	11774	Jacklett, Cpl. J. W.	11778
Holmer, W. W.	11780	Jackson, Sjt. L. M.	11776
Honey, 3rd Writer G. V.	8385	— Mech.S./Sjt. W. C.	11778
Hood, C.P.O. W. D.	9111	Jacobs, A./C.P.O. F. H.	9111
Hook, Cpl.(A./Sjt.) J.	11580	Jameson, Sub Condr. A. N.	11779
Hopkins, T./S.M. F. (corr.)	10589	Janes, C.E.R.A. 2nd Cl. W. J.	9111
Horridge, Sjt.(A./S.M.) J. D. (corr.)	10589	Jenkins, C.P.O. A. J.	9111
Horswill, P.O. 1st Cl. W. R.	8943	— Ch. Shipwt. 1st Cl. H.	9111
Hotchkiss, Mech.S./Sjt. T. E.	11778	— Pte. J.	11776
Hough, B.Q.M.S. W.	11774	Jennings, C.P.O. A. A.	9111
Houghton, C.S.M.(A./R.S.M.) W.	11776	— C.P.O. D. S.	10199
Howard, S./Sjt. J.	11778	— Ch. Writer S. E.	11580
— C.P.O. T. H.	8738	Jervis, C.S.M. C. F.	11778
Howarth, Ldg. Sea. R.	11580	John, Pte.(A./Sjt.) R.	11776
Howe, Pte. L.	11778	Johns, C.P.O. H. J.	9834
Howlett, Sjt.(A./S.M. A.C.) F.	11774	— Pte. J.	11580
Hudson, T./S.S.M. A. R. G. (corr.)	9395	Johnson, Pte.(A./Sjt.) A.	11775
— Sjt.(A./C.Q.M.S.) F.	11774	— S./Sjt. A. R.	11778
— S.M. J.	* 11775	Johnston, C.P.O. J.	9111
Hughes, Sjt.(A./C.S.M.) (W.O. 2)		— S./Sjt. W.	10319
J. J., *D.S.M.*	11580	— C.S.M. W. H., *D.C.M.*	✻ 8359
Hulme, Greaser J.	8385	Johnstone, Vict. C.P.O. W. A.	11580
Humby, Ch. Ship's Cook W.	9111	Jones, Sjt. A. M.	✻ 8359
Humphries, Clr.Sjt.(A./Staff Clk.		— Pte. E.	11776
W.O. 2) G.	11580	— Mech. E. B.	9111
Hunt, Pte.(A./Sjt.) J. H. C. F. C.		— E. W.	11780
(corr.)	10589	— C.S.M. J. P.	11777
Hussey, Cpl.(A./Sjt.) A.	11779	— Pte. R. J.	11777
— Pte.(A./R.S.M.) W. N.	11777	— C.P.O. T.	8385
Hyde, Gnr. T., *M.M.* (corr.)	8360	— 2nd Writer T. J.	† 8385
Hynd, P.O. Teleg. H. D.	9111	— P.O. 1st Cl. V. H.	11580
		— Ch. Writer W. F.	‡ 11580
Ifian, Pte. O.	11779	Joscelyne, Pte.(L./C.) E. L.	11775
Illman, 3rd Writer S. E.	8385	Joyce, S./S.M. A. H.	10320
Irwin, Pte. J. J.	11779	Jupp, P.O. Teleg. F.	§ 9834

---

* R.A.F. M.S.M. No. 1169 R.F.C. Enlisted 23 March 1914. earned 1914 Star. T./S.M. December 1917.

† R.N. M.S.M. to R.N. Transport Service. Group known: O.B.E.(1942), 1914/15 Star trio, Defence Medal, Coronation 1953 and R.N. M.S.M. (Alexandria, Egypt).

‡ Family group sold 1990 for £1,265. Father: Baltic 1854, Arctic 1876 and R.N. L.S. & G.C. (Victoria), Son: 1914/15 Star trio, R.N. L.S. & G.C. (Geo. V) and R.N. M.S.M. (Pembroke) and Grandson: British War Medal, Victory Medal, Defence Medal and R.N. L.S. & G.C. (Geo. VI).

§ Group known: 1914/15 Star trio, 1939/45 and Africa Stars, Defence and War Medals, R.N. M.S.M. (*'Barham'*) reputedly for erecting jury aerials at the Battle of Jutland. Lieut. (Tel.) in North Africa in 1941.

Kavanagh, Farr.Q.M.S. M. (corr.)	10589	Leaman, C.E.R.A. 1st Cl. W.	9111
Kay, Sjt. J.	11777	Leary, S./S.M. W.	10320
— Pte. W.	11776	Ledlie, T./Sjt. F. B.	11779
Keefe, Lce. Cpl. G. A., *D.S.M.*	11580	Lee, Clr.Sjt. G.	11580
Keen, S./Sjt.(A./S.S.M.) A.	* 11778	— Clr. Sjt. W.	9834
Keep, Sjt.(A./R.Q.M.S.) A. F.	11777	Legg, T./R.S.M. R.	11776
Keeton, Sjt.(A./Mech.S./Sjt.) W. H.	11778	Leigh, Sjt. T.	11777
Kelly, Ch. Sto. E. C.	9111	Leserve, S./Sjt. G. F.	11778
— Sjt. J.	11776	Lewis, Sjt. B. (corr.)	10589
Kelsey, Supt.Clk.(W.O. 1) T. C.	11580	— Sjt. W. J.	11774
Kemp, C.S.M. L. G. L., *D.C.M.*	11777	Leyland, Pte. T.	11776
Kendell, Sjt. F. G.	11778	Lindsay, Sjt.(A./Mech.S.S.M.) H. V.	11778
— S./Sjt. J. W. (corr.)	9395	Littlejohn, Cpl. W.	11778
Kennett, S.M. G. D. (corr.)	10589	Littleton, Ch. Sto. J.	8385
Kenny, Sjt.(A./Q.M.S.) T.	11776	Lloyd, R.Q.M.S. H. C.	11776
Kenten, Ch. Mech. 2nd Cl. C.	9111	— Cpl.(A./Sjt.) W. (corr.)	10589
Keogh, Sjt. E.	11778	Lodge, Bandmaster 1st Cl. H.	9111
Kimber, Ch. Writer A. T.	11580	Loft, Cpl.(A./Sjt.) W. H.	11777
King, Sjt. E.	11774	Lofthouse, Pte. J. A. E.	10319
Kings, S./Sjt. E. M. (corr.)	10589	Long, Spr.(A./C.S.M.) L. W.	11775
Kingsley, Cpl. C. H. (corr.)	10589	Love, B.S.M. F. E.	11777
Kirby, Ch. Writer W. W.	11580	Lovejoy, C. E.	11780
Kirkham Pte. J.	11778	Lowndes, C.P.O. Mech. 3rd Cl. A. B.	11580
Kitchen, Army Sch. Mstr. L. A.	11779	Lunt, C.S.M.(A./R.S.M.) A.	11776
Kitson, S./Sjt.(S./Sub Condr.) W. J.	11779	Luxmore, Cpl. B. M.	11778
Knight, Cpl. (A./C.Q.M.S.) A. E.	11774		
Knuckey, Spr. D. D. R.	11779	McCaig, Pte. A. (corr.)	10589
Koller, Sjt. C. F., *M.M.*	11778	McCoshen, Pte.(A./Sjt.) D., C.F.C. (corr.)	‡ 10589
Laird, Sjt. D. (corr.)	10589	McCullough, 2nd Writer R.	8386
Lambert, Sjt. F. E.	11774	McDerment, C.S.M.(A./S.M.) W. (corr.)	10589
— C.P.O. G. H.	11580	McDermott, Pte. J.	11775
Lamerton, C.P.O. W.	† 11580	McDonald, Sjt.(A./C.S.M.) F. H. E.	11779
Lane, Sjt. A.	11775	— J.C.C. D.	11779
Langdown, Dkhnd. R. C. T.	11580	— Sjt. J. H., *M.M.*	11776
Large, Pte. D. W.	❀ 8359	McEvely, Ch. Yeo. Sigs. J. T.	9111
Law, B.S.M. J. C.	11774	Macey, C.S.M.(R.Q.M.S.) F.	11775
— A./C.P.O. W. H. J.	9111	McGee, Cpl. A.	11777
Lawrence, Sjt. J.	11776	McGrath, 1st Cl.Assist. Surgn. P. J.	11779
— Ch. Sto. W.	9111	McInnes, Sjt. J. (corr.)	10589
Lawrie, 4th Cl. Assist. Surgn. L. J.	11779	McIntosh, P.O. H.	9111
Layen, Pte.(A./S.M.) L. E.	11778	McIntyre, Pte.(A./Sjt.) J. S.	11776
Lazarus, Pte.(A./S./Sjt.) J.	10319		

* Group known: British War Medal (T.W.O. Cl.1 A.S.C.), Territorial Force War Medal (Sgt. A.S.C.), M.S.M. (for Mesopotamia) and Territorial Efficiency Medal (Geo. V, C Q.M. Sjt. R.A.S.C.).
† Group known: China 1900, 1914/15 Star trio, R.N. L.S. & G.C. (Geo. V) and R.N. M.S.M. (R.N.V.R. S.A.). Formerly Chief Staff Inst. (London Div.) R.N.V.R. then Staff Inst. (Cape Town Div.) R.N.V.R. Served in German S.W.A. in W.W.I.
‡ Canadian Forestry Corps.

McIntyre, Ldg. Sea. V. A. E.	9111	Milton, C.P.O. D. P.		9111
McLaren, Sjt. L. (corr.)	10589	— Ch. Writer H. B.	†	8943
McManus, Pte. C. (deletion, award		— Clr.Sjt.(A./C.S.M., W.O. II) J.		11580
duplicated)	10590	Mitchell, C.S.M.(W.O. II)(A./S.M.,		
McMillan, Cpl.(A./L./Sjt.) J., *M.M.*	11777	W.O. I) A. E.		11580
Main, Sjt. H. J.	11777	— C.E.R.A. 2nd Cl. C. W.		9111
Major, Sjt. H. W.	11779	— C.Q.M.S. R. M.		11777
Malcolm, Mech.S./Sjt. J. A.	11778	— Ch. Shipwt. W. P.		9834
Male, Sjt. A. J.	11777	Mole, Sjt. A. H.		11777
Malekin, Ch. Writer J. McD.	11580	Montgomery, Cpl. A. F.		11778
Malins, Sjt. F.	11773	Moody, Staff Clk.(W.O. II) G.		11580
Manning, Sjt.(A./R.S.M.) P. V.	11774	— Ch. Ship's Cook W. J.		9111
Margetson, Ch. Yeo. Sigs. H. B.	8738	Moore, Pte.(A./Cpl.) E. W.		11775
Martin, Dvr.(A./R.S.M.) A. B.	* 11774	— Sjt. G. E.		11779
— Dvr.(A./Cpl.) A. H.	11774	— Ch. Mech. R.		9834
— Sjt. H.	11580	Morant, S.M. H. O.		11778
— Sjt. W. A. T.	11580	Morss, Pte. W.		11776
Masters, Q.M.S.(W.O. II) F. M.	11580	Morton, Pte.(A./Cpl.) J. F.		11777
Mathieson, Pte. R. A. J.	11776	Moss, Pte.(A./Cpl.) E.		10319
— Pte.(L./C.) W.	11775	Mothersole, S./Sjt. L. V.		11778
Maton, S.M.(W.O. I) C. E.	11580	Moxon, Farr.S./Sjt. E.		11774
Matthew, C.S.M.Inst. H. C. (corr.)	10589	Muckelt, Sjt.(A./S.M.) J. W.		11776
Meade, Spr.(A./C.S.M.)L. A.	11775	Mugford, M.A.A. T.		9834
Meatyard, Sjt. W. H., *M.M.*	11580	Munday, Ch. Yeo. Sigs. R. H. J.		9111
Meek, C.P.O.Mech. 2nd Cl. D. S. M.	11580	— C.Q.M.S. T. W.		11777
Meredith, Sjt.(A./C.S.M.Inst.) E.		Munro, Sjt.(A./Staff Clk., W.O. II)		
(corr.)	8361	J. M.		11580
Merritt, Pte.(A./Cpl.) E.	8386	Munting, C.Q.M.S. A.		11775
Michell, P.O. 2nd Cl. E.	10199	Musselwhite, Sjt.(A./R.S.M.) W. T.		11774
Mileman, Pte.(A./Sjt.) T. W.	10319			
Miles, C.S.M. J. (deletion, award		Narracott, Pte. F. K.		11580
having been gazetted		Nash, Sjt. F. G.		10319
previously)	8361	Naylor, 2nd Writer H. L.		8386
Millar, Sjt. G. H.	11779	Neal, A./Condr. J. S.		11779
Miller, Pte.(L./C.) A. (deletion,		Newport, Cpl. H. H.		11776
award having been gazetted		Newton, Sjt. E. J.		11777
previously)	8361	Nicholas, Ch. Arm. C. H.		8738
— T./Sjt. H.	11779	Noe, Pte.(A./Sjt.) F.		10320
— Mech.S./Sjt. T. J. (corr.)	8360	Nolan, Pte.(A./Cpl.) T.		11580
Millett, Arm. J. W.	8738	Norbury, Pte.(A./Cpl.) R. T.		11775
Milne, C.S.M. J. R.	11778	Norton, Sjt. F.		11776

---

* R.F.A. He joined in March 1916, and seven months later proceeded to Mesopotamia.
During his service overseas he played a prominent part in severe fighting at Kut,
Sanna-i-Yat, and on the Tigris front, and participated in the capture of Baghdad.
He was awarded the Meritorious Service Medal for consistently good work in the
Field, and was also mentioned in Despatches. He held the General Service and
Victory Medals, and was demobilised in June, 1920. 73, Church Street, Pendleton.

† Group in Moss collection: Queen's South Africa Medal (no clasp, H.M.S. *Monarch*),
British War Medal, R.N. L.S. & G.C. (Victoria, H.M.S. *Wildfire*) and R.N. M.S.M.
(Naval Base, Lowestoft).

Norton, Ch. Elect. Art. H. W.	8943	Peasnell, Lce. Sjt. F. A.	11580
Nowlan, 2nd Cpl. A. J.	11779	Peat, Ldg. Sea, J. E., *D.S.M.*	8943
Noy, Pte.(A./Sjt.) E.	11779	Pegrum, Pte. F. W.	11775
		Pelham, Sjt. W. T.	11776
O'Brien, Ldg. Sea. T.	11580	Perkins, Vict.C.P.O. R. L. W.	8943
O'Dowd, Cpl. J.	9834	— S./Sjt.(A./S.S.M.) J. F.	11778
Ong, C.P.O. T., *D.S.M.*	11580	— Deputy Supt. M. St. P.	11780
Ordish, C.S.M.(W.O. II)(actg. Supt.		Perrett, P.O. 1st Cl. W. H.	9111
Clk. W.O. I) A. W.	11580	Perrin, Sjt. A. E.	11779
O'Regan, C.P.O. T.	9834	Pettengill, P.O. 1st Cl. W.	11580
Orme, C.Q.M.S. A.	11776	Pharo, Sjt. F.	11774
O'Rourke, Q.M.S.(A./S.M.) P. J.	11778	Phillips, Supt. Clk. (W.O. I) F. W.	11580
Osborne, Supt. Clk.(W.O. I) H. J.	11580	Piatt, Sjt. J. F.	11774
Osgood, Sjt. C. J.	11774	Pickering, Deputy Supt. H.	11780
O'Shaughnessey, Sjt. J.	11774	Pigott, Gnr. F.	11774
Owen, S.S.M. R. A.	10319	Pink, C.P.O. A.	11580
— Supt.Clk.(W.O. I) W.	* 11580	Pinkney, Ch. Yeo. Sigs. P. R.	9111
		Plant, Sjt. J.	† 11775
Packer, C.S.M. F.	11779	Podmore, Sjt. F. W.	11776
Page, Sjt.(A./R.Q.M.S.) W. E.	11775	Ponsford, Sjt. J.	11580
— C.P.O. W. H.	8386	Porter, Spr.(L./C.) C.	10319
Paine, Sjt. H. W.	11776	Potter, Sjt. C. R.	11580
Pallett, Pte.(A./Sjt.) W. F.	11777	Power, Pte.(A./S.S.M.) G. A. (corr.)	10589
Palmer, Farr.S./Sjt.(A./Farr.Q.M.S.)		Prescott, Pte.(A./C.Q.M.S.) J. H.	11777
A. V.	11780	Preston, Cpl.(L./Sjt.) J. W.	11580
— Pte. G.	✹ 8359	— 3rd Writer N. E. L.	8386
Pankhurst, S./Sjt.(A./S.S.M.) R. A.	11778	Priestly, Pte. L. (corr.)	10589
Parfitt, Supt.Clk.(W.O. I) C. F.	11580	Pritchard, Sjt. E.	11774
Parker, R.S.M. F. L.	11777	Protheroe, Sjt.(A./C.S.M.) G. A. J.	11778
— Ch. Sto. G.	9111	Prynn, Ch. Arm. R.	8938
Parkin, Pte. H.	11778	Purvis, A.B. R. W.	9111
Parkinson, R.Q.M.S. W.	11775	Putnam, Cpl.(A./Sjt.) A. W. F.	11580
Parr, C.S.M. J. W.	10319	Pye, Art. Ch. Writer E. P.	8738
Parsons, Sjt. A.	11777	Pyke, Spr. F. W.	✹ 8359
— Sjt. A. O. L.	10319	Pyne, Sjt. W.	11779
Parton, Pte.(A./S.S.M.) E. (corr.)	10589		
Pascoe, C.P.O. T.	9111	Qua, Sjt. J.	10319
Patten, Pte. W. R.	11776	Quartley, Ch. Sto. A. L.	‡ 9111
Pearce, Pte.(A./Sjt.) E.	11776	Quinlan, Sjt.(A./C.Q.M.S.) J. T.	11777
— Pte.(A./C.Q.M.S.) R. A.	11776		
— Supt. Clk. (W.O. I) W.	11580	Radford, Cpl. C. E.	11774
Pearm, P.O. H.	8386	Randall, Pte. A. V.	11777

---

* Group known: China 1900, 1914 Star & bar trio, R.N. L.S. & G.C. and R.N. M.S.M. Pensioned 1906, R.M. M.S.M. annuity but seemingly no medal 10 March 1943; died 17 December 1943.

† M.S.M. and Victory Medal known: (3184 9/R. Warwicks) Formed part of the North Persian Force. Viscount Slim served with this Battalion.

‡ Group known: British War and Victory Medals, Antarctic Medal (Edw. VII, bar 1902–04, *Discovery*), R.N. L.S. & G.C. (Geo. V, *Naiad*) and R.N. M.S.M. (*Sovereign*). He was an American citizen who took part in Scott's first voyage.

Randall, Pte. W. H.	11775	Rose, Sjt. J. A.	11774
Randell, Mech.S./Sjt.(T./		Routledge, Sjt. M. E.	11779
Mech.S.M.) S. G. (corr.)	8360	Rudge, B.Q.M.S. W.	10319
Ranner, P.O. 1st Cl. E. W.	11580	Rumsey, Ch. Writer S. A.	11580
Rebello, Deputy Supt. C.	11780	Russell, E.R.A. 3rd Cl. J.	9111
Record, P.O. 1st Cl. C. H. P.	11580	— Cpl.(A./Sjt.) R. H.	10320
Redfern, Cpl. G.	11777	Rutter, Cpl. T., *D.C.M.*	11773
Redwood, Arm. S. C.	9111	Ryan, 2nd Writer P.	8386
Reed, Pte. H. T.	11776	Ryott, Mech.S./Sjt. L. A.	11778
Reid, Cpl. G. (corr.)	10590		
— Spr.(A./Sjt.) G.	11775	Sainsbury, M.A.A. W. G.	9111
Rendell, Sjt.(A./C.Q.M.S.) G. H.	11775	Salt, C.E.R.A. 1st Cl. R. T.	9834
Reynolds, C.P.O. J.	11580	Salter, C.S.M.(W.O. II) C. G.	11580
Rhead, Sjt. T. A.	11777	Sampson, Ch. Sto. R.	9111
Richards, Pte.(A./S.S.M.) F. P.	11778	Sancto, Spr.(A./Sjt.) A.	11775
— C.Q.M.S.(T./C.S.M.) P. T.	11774	Sanders, S./Sjt.(A./S.M.)	
Richardson, Sjt. J. E. L. * ❀	8359	G. H. (corr.)	10589
— Pte.(A./Sjt.) J. J.	11776	Sanderson, Supt.Clk.(W.O. I) A. G.	11580
— Spr. W. (corr.)	10589	Santry, Sjt. T.	10319
Richman, Sjt.(A./R.S.M.) R. E.	11775	Sargison, C.P.O. E. J.	11580
Rist, Sjt. W. P.	11580	Sawyer, S./Sjt. G. G.	11779
Robbins, Ch. Shipwt. 1st Cl. A. H.	9111	Scotland, Spr. J.	11775
— Sjt. C. W.	11779	Scott, C.P.O. Teleg. G.	9112
Roberts, P.O. 1st Cl. F. W.	8386	Selwyn, Sjt. P. J.	11777
— Sjt. W.	11776	Sewerin, R.Q.M.S. H. W. R.	11775
Robertson, E.R.A. 3rd Cl. A. J.	8934	Shaddick, Pte.(T./S.S.M.) C. H.	11778
— C.S.M.(A./R.S.M.) R. W. (corr.)	10589	Shepherd, Sjt.(A./C.Q.M.S.) E.	11774
Robinson, Staff Clk.(W.O. II)(A./		— C.Q.M.S. F.	11777
Supt.Clk. W.O. I) A. J. D.	11580	— Armt.S.M. G. R. (deletion, award	
— Deputy Supt. W. E.	11780	having been gazetted	
Rogers, Flt.Clk. J. H.		previously)	8361
(announcement of 3rd June		— C.Q.M.S. J.	11777
1919 cancelled, reward		Sheppard, S./Sjt.(A./Condr.) J.	11779
having been previously		Sherring, Ch. Sto. C. G.	9834
gazetted)	8990	Shinn, Pte. J. ❀	8359
— Sjt. J. H.	11773	Shipway, C.Q.M.S. H. J.	11777
— C.Q.M.S. R.	11776	Sillitoe, Clr. Sjt. T.	11580
— Pte.(A./L./C.) R. G.	11778	Silverberg, Pte.(A./S./Sjt.) E. A.	11779
Rolfe, S./S.M. C. T.	11778	Sinclair, C.Q.M.S. J. B.	11779
Ronketti, C.Q.M.S. P. A.	11775	Skilling, A.B. B.	8386
Rook, Mech.S.M. V. F. (corr.)	10589	Skinner, Sjt. A.	10319
Roscoe, S./Sjt. F. S.	11778	Sleep, Ch. Writer W. H.	9834

---

* Motor M.G. Service for Gallantry in Mesopotamia. 'On 12 August, 1918 a general advance was made on Derbend but the cars still travelled by rail. The Bolsheviks retired from Derbend after desultory fighting, and the town was occupied on 15 August, 1918 at 9.20 a.m. The train on which the armoured cars were travelling was smashed in a collision south of Derbend and the armoured car personnel were responsible for the rescue of many men under conditions calling for gallantry and endurance. These two N.C.O.s received the M.S.M. for their gallant behaviour on this occasion (see J. J. Smith *infra*).

Sloan, Pte.(L./C.) R.	11776	Stevens, Q.M.S.(A./S.M.) W. H. (corr.)		10589
Sly, Pte. E. W.	11776	— Sjt.(T./S.S.M.) W. L.		10319
Smallwood, Sjt. H. G.	❀ 10587	Stevenson, Cpl.(A./Sjt.) J.		11779
— S./Sjt. S.	11778	Stocks, C.Q.M.S. A.		11774
Smart, Ch. Writer J. F.	8386	Stokes, 2nd Writer G. E.		8386
Smith, Pte.(A./S.M. W.O. I) A. G.	11580	Stoodley, Sjt. A. E.		11775
— Sjt.(A./S.Q.M.S.) C. V. (corr.)	10589	Stott, Sjt. H.		9834
— Pte.(A./Sjt.) F.	11580	Stowar, A./C.E.R.A. 2nd Cl. P.		9112
— B.S.M.(A./R.S.M.) J.	11774	Strevens, C.S.M.(W.O. II) J. P.		11580
— Sjt. J. J.	* ❀ 8359	Stroyan, S./Sjt. P.		11779
— Supt. Clk.(W.O. I) J. W.	11580	Stuart, Sjt. J.		11774
— E.R.A. 2nd Cl. J. W.	9112	Sutherland, C.Q.M.S. J. B.		11779
— Cpl.(A./Sjt.) R. C.	11777	Sutton, Sjt. F.		11774
— Pte. W.	11778	Sutton, C.E.R.A. 1st Cl. W. G.		9112
Smitten, L./C.(A./Cpl.) A. E. (corr.)	8360	Swanson, Spr.(A./Cpl.) J. A. McI.		10319
— Pte.(A./L./C.) F.	11776	Symonds, Spr.(A./Sjt.) G. J.		11775
Snape, Q.M.S.(W.O. II) W.	† 8386			
Snell, Sjt.(A./Condr.) H. J. (corr.)	10589	Tabor, Cpl. A. E.		11775
Snelling, S./Sjt.(A./Sub Condr.) G.	11779	Tallack, Shipwt. C. F.		8386
Snook, Ch. Writer W.	11580	Tattersall, Condr. O.		11779
Sobey, Sjt. A. E.	11778	Taylor, C.S.M. A.		11777
Soole, Cpl. W. G.	10319	— Pte.(T./S./Sjt.) A.		10319
Spanswick, A.B. A. E.	8943	— Pte.(A./S./Sjt.) G.		11779
Speed, Supt.Clk.(W.O. I) E. W.	11580	— Ch. Yeo. Sigs. G. A.		9112
Spencer, Sjt. H.	11774	— Sjt. W. E.		11778
Spraggon, Pte.(A./S.M.) C. R.	11778	Tee, Ch. Writer A. T.		11581
Spruce, Elect. Art. 1st Cl. S. W.	9112	Terry, Sjt. B. N.		11775
Stafford, Sjt. F. E.	11775	Thatcher, S.M.(W.O. I)		
Staite, C.S.M.(A./R.S.M.) H.	11776	C. J., *D.S.C.*	§	11581
Stalham, Pte. J. S.	8386	Thoburn, Pte.(A./Cpl.) W.		11776
Stamp, Spr.(L./C.) E.	11775	Thomas, Q.M.S. B.		10320
Stanton, Pte. J. W.	11775	— Dvr. D. R.	❀	10587
Stapley, S./Sjt.(A./S.S.M.) W. Y.	11778	— Pte.(T./Sjt.) G.		11777
Steane, S.M. P. (corr.)	10589	Thorn, S. & C. Smith W. J.		11775
Stedman, Ch. Sto. J. A.	9834	Thornton, Sjt. W. J.		11581
Steed, Sjt. B. L.	‡ ❀ 10587	Thorpe, Pte.(A./Sjt.) A. E.		11777
Stembridge, C.S.M. F.	11776	Tiddy, Cpl.(A.C.) F. E. (corr.)		10589
Stephens, Pte. H. V.	❀ 8359	Till, Cpl. H. D.		11775
— Offrs. Std. 1st Cl. P. J.	9112	Tilly, S./S.M. W. W. (corr.)		8361
— Ch. Sto. W.	8386	Tinckler, Spr. H. T.	❀	8359
Stephenson, 3rd Writer A. R.	8386	Tomlin, Sjt. G.		11776
Stevens, Clr.Sjt. T. E.	8943	Toms, S./Sjt. J. M. S. (corr.)		10589

---

* Motor Machine Gun Service. Gallantry in Mesopotamia. (see also J. E. L. Richardson above).

† R.N. M.S.M. R.N. Transport Service. Later withdrawn as Army M.S.M. already issued *L.G.* 3 June 1919. 9 May 1945 issued with Royal Marine M.S.M. and Annuity. A unique pair. See Sirrett, Vol. II 1919.

‡ R.M.L.I., an Army Gallantry M.S.M. Attached R.M. Labour Corps.

§ R.N. M.S.M. The D.S.C. was earned at Zeebrugge on 23 April, 1918 with R.M.L.I., one of only two D.S.C.s earned during W.W.I by Sergt. Majors of the Royal Marines.

Tongue, Sjt. R. E.	11778	Ward, C.S.M.(A./R.Q.M.S.) W.	11776
Tooth, P.O. 1st Cl. O.	11581	Wardell, Sub Condr. C.	11779
Townsend, Staff Clk.(W.O. II) W.	11581	Wark, Cpl. A.	❀ 8359
Toy, Sjt.(A./C.S.M.) J. J.	11774	Warren, Dvr.(A./Cpl.) B. A.	11774
Traill, Sjt. A. S.	8386	Warring, Ch. Sto. W.	11581
Tregunna, B.Q.M.S. W.	11774	Waterfield, Sjt. J.	11774
Troke, Pte.(A./Sjt.) G. D. F.	11776	Waters, Pte. H. J.	❀ 8359
Trout, Ch. S.B.S. E. J.	11581	Watkins, Supt. Clk.(W.O. I) H. M.	11581
Truss, Sjt.(A./R.S.M.) H. J.	11774	Watling, Q.M.S.(W.O. 2) W.	11581
Tuck, Sjt. F.	9112	Watts, C.P.O. A. G.	8738
Tucker, Sjt. A.	11775	— S.M.(W.O. 1) J.	11581
— Sjt. E. (corr.)	8360	— Sjt. J.	11773
Tuckerman, Mech.Sjt.(A./S./Sjt.)		— Sjt.(A./C.S.M.) R. E.	11774
R. H.	11774	— Cpl.(A./Sjt.) W. A., *D.C.M.,*	
Turnbull, Clr.Sjt. J.	11581	*M.M.*	† 11581
Turner, Pte. A. P.	11777	Weaver, Sjt. C. W.	11777
— C.S.M.(T./R.S.M.) H. A.	11777	Webber, Supt. Clk.(W.O. 1) W. E.	11581
Tyrer, Sjt.(A./S./S.M.) W.	11778	Webster, Cpl. J. (deletion, award	
		having been gazetted	
Ulyatt, Sjt. J. N. (corr.)	10589	previously)	8361
		Weightman, Sjt. R.	10319
Veale, C.P.O. Mech. 3rd Gde. A. H.	9112	Weir, Mech.S./Sjt. C. F.	11778
Veater, Ch. Writer E. J.	8386	Welch, C.S.M.(W.O. 2) J. R.	8943
Verion, Pte.(A./Sjt.) R. J.	10319	Wells, Cpl. J. P.	11776
Vernem, A. W.	11780	Werry, Q.M.S.(W.O. 2) J.	11581
Verrall, Cpl. A. H.	10319	West, Mech.S./Sjt.(A./Mech.S.M.)	
Voller, Ch. Sto. F. J.	9112	F. J. (corr.)	8360
		— P.O. J.	9112
Wade, Sub Condr.(S.P.T.		— Cpl.(L./Sjt.) T.	11777
Condr.) J.	11779	Westerman, Pte.(A./Sjt.) R. A.	11773
Wagstaff, Pte. F. H.	* ❀ 10587	Westmore, P.O. 1st Cl. W. F. F.	11581
Wakeham, Ch. Writer E. W.	9112	Whattaker, Sjt.(A./C.S.M.) J. W.	11774
Walker, Mech. J. H.	9112	White, Sjt. A.	11777
— T./R.S.M. W.	11775	— T./Sub Condr. E. F.	11779
— Spr. W.	11775	— C.E.R.A. 2nd Cl. C. F.	9112
— Pte. W. J.	11779	Whitlock, P.O. T. F. I.	9834
Waller, Sjt. A.	11776	Whittaker, Sjt. J. E. (corr.)	10589
Wallineer, Dkhnd. H. M.	11581	Whurr, C.E.R.A. 2nd Cl. E. J.	11581
Wallis, P.O. A. E.	8943	Wickman, 2nd Cpl.(A./C.Q.M.S.) F.	11775
Walmsley, R.Q.M.S. G. F.	11773	Wickstead, T./S.S.M. G. H. (corr.)	8361
— Pte. T.	11778	Wild, Sjt.(A./C.S.M. W.O. 2) E. G.	11581
Walter, Pte. J.	11778	Wilde, Sjt. O. M.	11774
Ward, Cpl.(C.Q.M.S.) A. E.	10319	Wilkie, Sjt. T. B. (deletion, award	
— C.Q.M.S. B. J.	11773	duplicated)	10590
— Spr.(A./Sjt.) J.	11775	Williams, Pte.(A./Sjt.) A. T.	11779
— Pte. T. W. (corr.)	8361	— Sjt.(A./C.S.M. W.O. 2) E. G.	11581
— — Corr.	10589	— T./Sjt. G. E.	11779

* 7th Hussars, for Gallantry in Mesopotamia.
† R.N. M.S.M. Ply.9874, R.M.L.I. His D.C.M. and R.N. M.S.M. only are in the R.M. Museum, Eastney.

Williams, Yeo. Sigs. J. W.	9834	Wood, S./Sjt. E.		11779
— Pte.(A./Sjt.) T. E.	11775	— Clr.Sjt. E. J.		11581
— Sjt. V.	11779	— Mech.S./Sjt.(A./S.M.) J. T.		11774
Williamson, Sjt. G.	11773	— Pte. R.	*	11997
Willoughby, Pte. A. R.	11776	Woodcock, C.S.M. W.		11777
Wills, Q.M.S.Instr.(W.O. 2)(A./S.M.		Woodley, Pnr. C. H.		11775
W.O. 2) G. E.	11581	Woods, Pte.(A./Sjt.) C. V.		10319
— P.O. 1st Cl. H. C.	11581	Woolridge, Farr.S./Sjt. Z.	❀	10587
Wilson, Q.M.S.Instr.(W.O. 2)(A./S.M.		Worsfold, Gnr. E. A.		11774
W.O. 1) B. I.	11581	— Pte. F. J.	†	11997
— Pte.(A./Sjt.) J. G.	11775			
— Cpl.(A./C.S.M.) T. (corr.)	8360			
Winsborough, Vict. C.P.O. R. G.	9112	Yaxley, S.B.S. B. R.		8738
Witcher, R.Q.M.S. A. E.	11774	Young, Clr. Sjt. A.		11581
Witchers, Cpl. C. H.	11581	— S./Sjt.(A./Sub Condr.) H.		11779
Wolstenholme, Pte.(A./Cpl.) A. L.	11776	— Sjt. J. A.		11774
Wood, Pte. C. W.	❀ 10587	— Sjt. W.		11774

* 1466 2nd Bn. Australian M.G. Corps—see Bannigan *ante*.
† 6/SR/6987, 1st Bn. Middlesex Regiment—see Bannigan *ante*.

Vol. IV, 1919

Abbot, C.S.M. M. 15464
Abraham, Bombr. (A./ Sjt. A.C.) J. A. 12762
Adams, R.Q.M.S. G. 12764
Addison, Sqdn. S. M. J. 12755
Adkins, Cpl. W. W. 12527
Aiken, Sjt. J. 12757
Airlie, Pte. E. ❀ 12875
Aitken, Cpl. (A./Sjt.) G. 12757
— actg. Ldg. Sea. J. 15430
Albery, Sjt. A. G. 12765
Albrow, Pte. (A./Cpl.) E. J. 12758
Alcock, L.A.C. J. E. 15840
— S.M. S. J. 12754
Aldridge, Col. Sjt. H. N. 15460
Alexander Cpl. (A./Sjt.) H. J. 12765
— W.O. Cl. 1, J. A. 15464
Allison, Sjt. T. W. 12762
Allitt, C.Q.M.S. H. (corr.) 15725
Allsopp, Pte. C. E. 12758
Allum, Sjt. E. H. 12757
Almond, Spr. (A./2nd Cpl.) F. 12754
Alsop. Pte. A. 12758
Ambler, Gnr. (A./L./Bombr.) C. 12753
— C.P.O. G. * 13744
Amos, Spr. H. 15447
Anderson, Pte. (A./Cpl.) F. A. 12758
— Sjt. R. McM. (corr.) 14275
Anthony, Sjt.(A./S./Sjt.) J. C. 15464
Appelby, Cpl. (T./Sjt.) R. R. C. (corr. of surname and rank) 14275
Apple, 2nd Cl. Mast. Gnr. E. W. 15460
Appleyard, Cpl. (A.C.) G. H. 15439
Archibald, Cpl. J. 12764
Armston, Q.M.S. W. 15462
Arnold, Sjt. T. G. 15439
Asbrey, S./Sjt. C. 12761
Ashenhurst, T./S.M. J. T. 15460
Ashforth, Pte.(A./L./C.) G. 12758
Ashton, O.R.Sjt. A. 15439
— A.M. 2, R. C. 15840
Ashwell, Sjt. H. C. † 12527, 15840
— Pte. (A./S.M.) S. M. 15464
Ashworth, Pte. W. 15463
Askins, Cpl. J. 12757
Aspley, C.Q.M.S.(A./Q.M.S.) W. T. 15447
Astley, Farr.S./Sjt. W. 12762
Atkinson, Pte.(A./Cpl.) J. P. 15463
Axson, Pte.(A./S.M.) C. W. 15462
Aylett, Sjt. P. 12757
Ayling, Sjt. R. W. 12757

Babbs, Sjt.(A./S./Sjt.) B. H. 12757
Back, Pte.(A./Q.M.S.) A. E. 15461
Backhouse, Q.M.S. R. V. (corr.) 12878
Bacon, Sjt.(A./Q.M.S.) D. 12755
Baggott, Cpl. F. T. 12757
Bailey, Pte.(L./C.) A. V. 12758
— Sjt. E. 15462
Bailey, Pte.(L./C.) E. M. 15463
Bailie, Pte. J. 15440
Bain, Sjt. A. A. 12757
— Sto. P.O. W. 15431
Baker, Pte.(A./C.Q.M.S.) F. A. 12765
— Actg. Sjt. G. W. 15430
— Pte.(T./Sjt.) H. 12763
Bakewell, Sjt.(A./S./Sjt.) G. J. ❀ 12875
Baldrey, B.Q.M.S. A. 15447
Baldwin, Sjt.(A./Q.M.S.) A. C. 15461
— R.S.M. J. C. 12764
— Sjt. T. 12761
Bale, Q.M.S. C. B. 15461
Ball, Sjt. H. 15444
Ballinger, Cpl. A. 12757
— Cpl.(A./Sjt.) H. G. 15463
Bamber, Pte.(A./S.Q.M.S.) M. S. 15464

* R.N.V.R. (S. Africa) No. 6. Entitled to Queen's South Africa Medal (Defence of Ladysmith, Natal Naval Volunteers), 1914/15 Star trio, Coronation 1911 and R.N. M.S.M. Also R.H.S. Bronze Medal. He was on *'Pegasus'* when she was sunk by *'Königsberg.'* Then served in German East Africa. He manned naval guns ashore in two wars.

† R.A.F. M.S.M. One cancelled in *L.G.* 17 June 1924.

Bambridge, Sjt. H.	12754	Beeson, Sjt. J. W.	12760
Bancroft, Pte. H. V.	12758	Belcher, C.Q.M.S. C. H.	15462
Banham, R.Q.M.S. F.	12756	— Pte. G.	12758
Barber, Sjt. J.	12755	Bell, Supt. Clk. W. K.	15443
— Cpl.(A./Sjt.) R.	12763	Bendry, B.S.M. G.	15447
Barden, Sjt.(A./C.S.M.) W. J.	12756	Benham, Pte. W. J.	15440
Barker, Sjt. C. E.	15840	Benn, Spr.(L./C.) A.	12754
— Q.M.S. H. C. P. (corr.)	15726	Bennett, C.Q.M.S. A.	12756
— Whlr. T. A.	12753	— Pte. H.	12755
Barkwitch, Pte. F.	12758	— Farr.Cpl.Maj. H. J.	15439
Barlow, 2nd Cpl.(A./C.S.M.) H.	12764	Benson, A./S.M.(W.O. I) J.	15430
— C.S.M. J.	15461	Berry, Mech.S./Sjt. H.	12760
— Pte. W.	12758	— Pte.(A./S./Sjt.) W.	12760
Barnes, Supt. Clk. F. C.	15460	— Sjt. W. K.	15464
— Q.M.S. G.	15464	Berryman, Pte.(A./C.S.M.) F. L.	12758
— Cpl.(T./S./Sjt.) G. A.	12760	Bertram, T./Sjt. J.	12761
— Sjt. R. W. (corr.)	15725	Best, C.Q.M.S. H. C.	12134
Barnett, Pte.(A./S.M.) H. A.	15464	Bevan, S./Sjt. P. S.	12760
— Sjt.(A./S.S.) W. L.	12762	Biggar, Pte. T.	12758
Barratt, Sjt. L. M.	12574	Bigham, T./R.S.M. J.	12764
Barrett, B.Q.M.S. C.	15439	Bilby, Sjt. H.	12757
— Sjt. E. H.	12757	Billingham, Pte.(A./Cpl.) R. E.	15448
Bartle, Sjt. A. W.	15460	Billington, Sjt. C.	12757
Bartlett, Pte.(A./S./Sjt.) A. J.	15464	Bills, Pte.(A./Sjt.) W. H.	12761
Barton, Sjt. J. S.	15461	Binfield, Cpl. F. (corr.)	12878
Bass, C.S.M. S. J.	12756	Binns, Spr. J. G.	12754
Batchford, S./Sjt.(A./		Birkett, Sjt.(A./C.S.M.) W.	12760
S.Q.M.S.) E. F.	* 12135	Bisgrove, E.R./S./Sjt. R. C. (corr.)	14275
Bater, Pte. G. R.	12760	Bishop, Sjt. H.	12757
Bates, R.Q.M.S. J.	12756	Black, Sjt. A. H. (corr.)	12878
Baxendale, Pte. J. E. K.	12758	Blackburn, Pte.(A./Cpl.) G. P.	15462
Baxter, C.S.M. J.	15460	— S./Q.M. J.	12760
— S./Sjt.(A./Q.M.S.) J. W., *M.M.*		— Cpl.(T./Mech.S./Sjt.) R. T.	12760
(corr.)	15725	Blackett, Q.M.S. M. H.	15443
Bayliss, M.F. of Wks. , W. G.	15460	Blackwell, Pte. H. R.	15464
Baynton, Gnr. C.	❀ 12875	Blaik, Pte.(A./S.Q.M.S.) J.	12764
Bazley, S./Sjt. A. W.	15464	Blake, Sjt. A. J.	12761
Beacham, C.P.O. Mech. 2nd Gr. A.	12779	Blakeman, C.Q.M.S.(A./C.S.M.) T. H.	12756
Beak, Sjt.(A./R.Q.M.S.) W. F. J.	12753	Blakemore, Cpl.(A./Sjt.) E. A.	12764
Beale, Sjt. C. A.	12760	Bland, Pte.(A./S.Q.M.S.) C. T.	15464
— Sjt. F.	12763	— Pte. G. U.	12134
Beaufoy, Cpl.(A./S.Q.M.S.) S. J.	15460	Blay, Pte. J.	12758
Bechley, Pte. E.	12755	Bloomfield, S.Q.M.S.(A./R.S.M.)	
Beck, Sjt. J.	12760	A. G.	12764
Bedford, Pte. W. H.	12758	Boaler, Pte.(L./C.) H. J.	12759
Bee, Sjt. H.	12757	Boast, Spr.(L./C.) C. E.	12754
Beesley, Pte. N.	12758	Bolton, Pte.(L./C.) A.	15462

---

* Group known: King's Police & Fire Services Medal (for Meritorious Service), British War and Victory Medals, Defence Medal, 1935 Jubilee, M.S.M. (for Murmansk) and two Fire Brigade Long Service Medals.

Bolton, Pte.(A./Sjt.) A. H.	12758	Brookbanks, S./Sjt.(A./Supt.Clk.)	
— Cpl. H.	12757	W. E.	12754
Bone, Sjt. G.	15460	Brookbrank, Pte.(A./Sjt.) A. E.	15460
Boniface, T./Armt.S.M. J. H.		Brooke, Cpl. H. A.	† 12763
(deletion)	12879	— E.R.A. 3rd Cl. P. A.	15431
Booth, Sjt.(A./S.M.) F.	15464	— Pte. R.	12758
Borrell, T./S./Sjt. A. D.	12761	Brooks, Sjt.(R./S./Sjt.) A. G.	12754
Boston, Cpl. T.	12754	— 2nd Hnd. B. E.	13748
Boucher, Pte.(A./S.M.) J. S.	15464	Brown, R.S.M. A. E.	12754
Boultbee, C.Q.M.S. R. H. (corr.)	12878	— Sjt. C.	12762
Boulton, Sjt.(A./B.Q.M.S.) B. H.	12762	— Pte.(A./Sub Condr.) C. J. A.	15440
Bourne, Pte.(A./Sjt.) J. J.	12758	— Cpl.(A./S.Q.M.S.) D.	15448
Bowater, C.S.M.(A./R.S.M.) E.	12755	— T./S.S.M. G.	12134
Bowden, C.S.M.(A.Q.M.S.) E. C. R.	15461	— C.S.M.(A./R.S.M.) H.	12755
— S./Sjt.(A./Q.M.S.) F. C.	15440	— Ch. S.B.S. H. J.	12779
— Pte.(A./Cpl.) J. P.	12758	— Cpl. H. J.	12754
— Pte.(A./Sjt.) L.	15440	— C.Q.M.S. J.	15460
Bowen, Sjt. C. A. (corr.)	12879	— 2nd Cpl.(A./Cpl.) J.	12763
— Sjt. J. W. (corr.)	12878	— C.S.M. J. C.	12755
Bowles, Cpl. F. S.	12627	— S.M. 2, J. T.	15841
Bowman, Cpl. A.	12758	— Sjt. J. W.	15443
Bown, C.S.M. E. C. (corr.)	15725	— S.S.M. R. E.	15464
Bowsley, S.M. H.	12764	— Pte.(A./Sjt.) S. D.	12755
Bowyer, Sjt. E.	12757	Browne, 1st Cl.S.S.M. E. B.	15463
— Sjt. W.	12757	Bruin, C.Q.M.S. A. F.	12755
Boyd, S./Smith(A./		Brusey, Skpr. H.	‡ 12781
Farr.S./Sjt.) F. W.	15463	Bryan, C.S.M. E. E.	12134
Brace, S./Sjt. A. G.	12762	Bryant, Sjt.(A./C.S.M.) C.	12757
Bradfield, S.M. W. B.	12762	— Cpl.(A./S.M.) J.	15464
Bradish, Sjt. W. P. C.	15462	— Condr. T.	12765
Bradshaw, Cpl.(A./Sjt.) O.	12785	Buchanan, C.Q.M.S. J.	15462
Bramall, Spr.(A./L./C.) T.	12762	Buck, C.S.M. C. J.	12764
Bramwell, Sjt. J. H.	15462	Buckenham, B.S.M. A. H., *M.M.*	
Brannan, Sjt. B.	12757	(corr. of amendment)	14275
Bray, Pte. H. W.	12758	Buckland, Cpl.(A./S.S.M.) W. A.	15443
Brazil, S.Q.M.S. G. P.	15464	Buckle, Pte.(A./S.M.) H.	15464
Brenchley, B.S.M. E. G.	15460	— Sjt. S. W. (deletion)	13749
Bridge, Ldg. Mech. C.	15841	Buckley, C.S.M. J. P.	12756
— C.S.M. R.	12756	Bull, Sjt.(A./C.Q.M.S.) A. E.	12765
Briggs, Cpl.(A./S./Sjt.) W. H.	15463	Bullock, Cpl. T. J.	12760
Brighting, S.S.M. H. L.	15465	Bunn, Sjt.(A./C.Q.M.S.) A.	12757
Brindley, S.M. E.	15461	Burbery, Pte.(A./Sjt.) A. T.	15440
Brine, Ch. Writer G. E.	* 12779	Burch, Pte.(A./Sjt.) A.	15464
Brisland, Pnr. J.	12754	Burgess, S.B.S. C. J.	12779
Britton, Cpl.(A./S.Q.M.S.) H.	15462	Burke, Pte. W. E.	12760
Broadway, Dvr. W. R.	12755	Burley, Pte. C. W. (corr.)	12878
Bromehead, Q.M.S. E. C.	15465	Burness, Pte.(A./S./Sjt.) C. S.	15464

* Group known: 1914/15 Star trio and R.N. M.S.M. (Admiralty Office, Paris 1919).
† R.G.A., Turkana.
‡ New Zealand Naval Auxiliary Service. Minesweeping July—December 1918.

Burnett, Supt. Clk. V. W.	12764	Carnie, T./S.M. A. B.	15460
Burnham, Cpl. E. J.	12760	Carpenter, Sjt. A. R.	12760
Burton, Spr. J.	12134	Carr, Pte.(A./Sjt.) C. W.	12760
Burnwood, Pte.(A./Sub Condr.) L. F.	15443	— Sjt. H. C.	12763
Bush, Cpl.(T./C.Q.M.S.) F. J.	15462	Carrington, Q.M.S.(A./S.M.) H.	15463
Butler, Pte.(A./Sjt.) N. G.	15440	Carroll, Pte. J. F.	14670
— Sjt.(A./C.S.M.) W.	15460	Carss, Pte.(A./S./Sjt.) T. T.	15463
Bywater, Cpl. H.	12758	Carter, Farr.Q.M.S. A.	12760
		— Sjt. A. N.	15464
Cadman, Spr.(A./C.Q.M.S.) E.	* 15447	— Sjt. F. P.	15460
Caffrey, C.Q.M.S.(O.R.Sjt.) W.	† 15461	Cartledge, S./Sjt. T. A.	12762
Cairns, Pte.(T./S./Sjt.) D. J.	12760	Cartwright, Sjt. J. W.	12756
— R.Q.M.S. J.	12756	Castle, Pte. H.	12758
— Pte.(A./Sjt.) S. G.	12765	Caswell, T./S.M. J. C. W.	12762
Calderwood, Sjt. J.	15841	Catley, R.Q.M.S. P. C.	12755
Call, Sjt. J. E. (corr.)	12878	Catling, Pte. G.	15461
Callaghan, Gnr.(A./Sjt.) R. D.	15460	Catt, S./Sjt. C. F.	12760
Callander, Sjt. G. A.	15443	Catto, S./Sjt. H.	12763
Calvert, Pte.(A./S.Q.M.S.) E. C.	15464	Caunce, Sjt.(A./S./Sjt.) H.	15464
Calvo, Cpl.(A./C.S.M.) L. E.	12134	Cave, Pte. G. A.	12758
Cambridge, Sjt. E. A.	15841	Chadwick, Pte. H.	12758
Cameron, Pte.(A./S.M.) W.	‡ 15464	Chambers, Q.M.S. R. W.	15461
Camp, T./Q.M.S. H.	15461	Channer, Sjt. S. T.	12751
Campbell, Pte.(A./Sjt.) W. J.	15464	Chantler, Sjt. T./S.S.M. W. R. A.	
Campe, Pte.(A./Cpl.) H.	12758	(corr. of surname)	12878
Candelin, Sjt. G. H.	15463	Chapman, Pte.(A./Sjt.) F. G.	15463
Cank, Cpl.(A./Sjt.) W.	15447	— C.S.M. R. F.	15464
Cann, Pte.(A./Sjt.) J. S.	15461	— Sjt. T.	15460
— P.O. Mech. S. G.	12779	Charnock, Sjt.(A./Sub Condr.) N. H.	12763
Canning, C.S.M. W.	12763	Chase, Spr. M.	15439
Card, T./Sjt. R.	12761	Chate, T./S./Sjt. E. C.	12761
Carkner, A./S.M. R. C.	15464	Chatfield, Pte.(A./S.Q.M.S.) A. W. P.	15463
Carman, Sjt.(A./S.M.) E. A.	12760	Chetcuti, Sjt.(A./C.S.M.) E.	§ 12763
Carnell, Cpl. A. J.	❀ 12875	Chirgwin, Spr.(A./C.Q.M.S.) R. W.	12754
— T./Sjt. C. J.	12761	Chitty, Q.M.S. W. H.	15460

---

* Single M.S.M. known in Moss collection: M.S.M. (WR 199094 Spr. (A./C.Q.M.S.) R.E.). For valuable services rendered with the British Army of the Black Sea. He served with the Inland Water Transport (R.E.) in Mesopotamia, a service consisting of approx. 465 officers and 1,400 O.R.s. They operated vessels, marine engineering, dockyards, shipbuilding, native craft, pilotage, coal and barge depots, etc., etc., from Baghdad, through Persia and along both the Tigris and Upper and Lower Euphrates. Their main task was transporting men and material from Basra to Baghdad.

† Group known: 1914/15 Star trio (Sgt./C.Sgt. Suffolk R.), Indian General Service Medal (Malabar 1921–22, W.O.II Suff. R.), L.S. & G.C. (Geo. V, fixed susp., W.O.II Suff. R.) and M.S.M.

‡ Group known: D.C.M. & bar (C.S.M. 2/Gordon High.), 1914 Star trio (M.I.D. oakleaf, L./Cpl—W.O.II), 1939/45 Star, War Medal, L.S. & G.C. (Geo. V, W.O.II), M.S.M. (Gord. High.) and Médaille Militaire.

§ Royal Malta Militia Regt. For Balkans.

Christian, S./Sjt.(A./Sub Condr.) R. F.	
(corr. of amendment)	14275
Christopher, Sjt.(A./S.M.) J.	12763
Clactworthy, C.S.M. W. M. (corr.)	15726
Clapham, Pte. D. (corr. of surname)	14275
Clappen, T./Sjt.(A./S./Sjt.) H. G.	12761
Clark, Cpl.(A./Sjt.) D. W.	12764
— Sjt. G. S. (deletion of duplicate	
award)	14276
— Sjt.(A./Q.M.S. W.O.II) J.	
(deletion)	* 13749
— Sjt. W. P.	12764
Clarke, Pte. C. R.	15461
— C.Q.M.S. S. (corr.)	12878
— C.P.O. Mech. 3rd Gr. T.	12779
— S./Sjt. W. G.	12761
Claydon, Pte. J. H.	12758
Clee, Pte. A. H.	❀ 12875
Clement, Cpl.(A./S./Sjt.) H. E.	15443
Clinch, 2nd Cpl.(T./Sjt.) T. V.	12754
Clubb, Sjt. N. H.	15430
Cluett, C.S.M. A.	12756
Coates, Armr.S./Sjt. A. E.	12761
— Pte.(A./S.Q.M.S.) C. W.	15463
— Sjt.(A./C.S.M.) T. W.	12757
— Sjt. W. H.	12762
— Pte. W. M.	15440
Cochrane, Ldg. Mech. D.	12779
Cockburn, C.S.M. W.	12756
Coggins, S.M. A. J.	12761
Coghlan, S.S.M. E. E.	15464
Cohen, Cpl. B.	12758
Colata, Pte.(A./Sjt.) J.	15444
Colby, Exptl./S.M. H. J.	12764
Cole, S./Sjt. H. J. R. (corr.)	12879
— Cpl.(A./Sjt.) W.	12758
— Cpl. W.	15460
— Sjt. W. E. (corr.)	14275
Coleman, T./S.M. R. F.	12754
— Cpl. T. J.	† 12762
— Supt. Clk. W. J.	12764
Coles, S.Q.M.S. A. J.	15465
— Pte.(L./C.) J. A.	15440
Collett, Sjt. R. C. (corr.)	14275
Collett, Pte.(A./S./Sjt.) T.	12760
Collie, Sjt. R.	15440
Collyer, C.Q.M.S.(A./R.Q.M.S.) H.	12762
Colman, S.M. S. H.	15461
Comber, Cpl.(T./Sjt.) F. H.	12760
Connolly, S.S.M. J. J.	15465
— T./S.S.M. J. M.	15463
Connor, Sjt. J. (corr._)	15725
Constable, Sjt.(A./C.S.M.) G. (corr.)	15725
Coo, By.S.M. G. V.	12756
Cook, Spr.(A./Sjt.) C. A.	15447
— Skpr. F. H.	‡ 12781
— Sub Condr. H. C.	15449
— Sjt. R.	12757
— C.Q.M.S.(A./Q.M.S.) W.	15462
Cooke, Spr. A.	12754
— C.S.M.(A./S.M.) H.	15443
— Sqdn.S.M. R. A.	15460
Cookson, Gnr. R.	12754
Coombes, T./S.S.M. W. F. (corr. of	
surname)	14275
Copp, Sjt. T.	12754
Copping, T./S.M. E.	§ 15461
Corfield, Cpl.(A./Sjt.) A. A.	15447
Corlett, S./Sjt.(A./S.Q.M.S.) P.	14275
Cornish, 2nd Cpl. F. G.   ❀ 12875, 14273
Corrin, C.P.O.Mech. 3rd G. A. T.	12779
Cosgrove, Pte. A.	12758
— C.S.M. R.	12134
Costello, T./S.M.(A.C.) F.	15460
— Pte. M.	12762
Coulson, C.Q.M.S. F. C.	15460
— Cpl. H.	15841
Coupland, Sjt.(A./C.Q.M.S.) T.	15439
— S./Sjt.(A./S.M.) W. J.	15448
Coutts, Pte.(A/Q.M.S.) W.	15447
Cowan, A./S./Sjt. G. A. (corr.)	14275
Cowdrey, Sjt.(A./Mech.S.M.) F.	
(corr. of surname)	14275
Cowern, C.S.M. J.	15447
Cowie, Pte.(A./S./Sjt.) G.	15464
Cox, Pte.(A./Sjt.) B. J.	12754
— A./Cpl. H. J.	15841
— Sjt. J. T.	12757

* R.M.L.I. See Army M.S.M. 3 June, 1919.
† R.A.S.C. for Italy. Awarded Bar to M.S.M. *L.G.* 11 July 1924.
‡ New Zealand Naval Auxiliary Service. Minesweeping July—December 1918.
§ Group known: 1914 Star & bar (L./Cpl. S. W. Bord.), British War and Victory
   Medals (Sjt. S. W. Bord.) and M.S.M. (1 Garr. Bn. S.W.B.) for Gibraltar.

Craig, Sjt.(A./S.Q.M.S.) A. J.	* 12764	Dale, W.O. Cl. 1, C. S.	15464
Craik, Pte.(A./Sjt.) W.	14273	Dallas, Pte.(A./Sjt.) S.	15440
Crawford, Sjt. A.	15440	Daniels, Sjt. A.	12757
— Cpl. D. (corr.)	15725	— Gnr. D. J.	15448
— Spr.(A./L./C.) R.	15439	Darcy, C.S.M. P.	12755
Croce, S.M.(A.C.) G. N.	15460	Darvil, Cpl.(A./Sjt.) W. E.	12758
Crocker, S./Sjt.(A./Sub Conder) A. E.	15449	Davenport, S.M.	
— Sjt. C. H.	15460	V. H. S., *M.C.*, *D.C.M.*	‡ 15461
Croke, T./S.M. T.	15461	David, Flt. Sjt. W. T.	15841
Crook, Dvr. C.	12753	Davidson, Sjt. C.	15465
Crooks, Cpl. T.	12758	Davies, Pte. J.	§ 12763
Crosbee, Sjt. W. A.	15443	— Sjt. L. J.	12762
Crosby, Cpl.(L./Sjt.) C. G.	15461	— Pte. R. T.	12758
Cross, Sjt.(A./Q.M.S.) G.	15460	— Sjt. W.	15461
— T./S.M. G.	15460	— Pte.(A./L./C.) W.	12755
Crouch, Sjt. W. A.	12760	— Sjt.(A./Q.M.S.) W. A.	12762, 15448
Crowther, Pte.(L./C.) E. (corr.)	12878	Davis, C.S.M. A. V.	12756
— Gnr. G. A.	12134	— T./S./Sjt. J. P.	12761
Crute, Cpl. W. (corr.)	14275	— Pte. R.	12758
Cuddy, Q.M.S. J. P.	12764	— Pte.(A./Sjt.) S. J.	12764
Culliman, S.M. P.	† 15462	Dawe, Pte.(A./Cpl.) E.	12759
Cunningham, Pte.(L./C.) J. S.	12755	Dawson, Spr.(A./Cpl.) H. H.	+ 12762
Curchod, Pte.(A./Q.M.S.) H. J.	15461	Day, 2nd Cpl.(A./Sjt.) A. F.	15439
Curran, Cpl.(A./S.M.) T. (corr.)	12878	De la Haye, A./S.Q.M.S. W. P.	15464
Curtis, W.O. Cl. 1, A. R.	15443	Deamer, S.Q.M.S. E.	12765
Curtis, S./Sjt. J.	15439	Dean, S.S.M. G.	◊ 15465
Cushing, S./S.M.(A./R.S.M.) F. W.	12765	Dearnely, Cpl.(A./Sjt.) F.	12760
Cussens, Q.M.S.(A./C.S.M.) J. T.	12134	Dedman, Sjt. G. H.	12760
Cutteridge, Sjt. B. J.	12757	Denton, Sjt. A. H.	12760
Cutting, Dvr. E.	15443	Denyer, Sjt.(A./S.Q.M.S.) G.	12760
		Dewe, T./S.S.M. J.	12134
Daffern, Sjt. A. (deletion of duplicate		Deykes, Sjt. A.	12759
award)	14276	Dibben, Sjt. L., *M.M.*	12754
Dainty, Pte. E. (corr.)	14275	Dick, C.Q.M.S. P. (corr.)	15725

---

* Trio known: Queen's Egypt (El Teb—Tamaai, Cpl. 10 Hussars), M.S.M. and Khedive's Star. (M.S.M. for service in U.K.).

† D.C.M. (4366 R.S.M. R. Munster Fus.) (A.O./193/1919), 1914 Star trio and M.S.M. Was a P.O.W. 4½ years being captured at Etreux in August 1914. It is difficult to see how his M.S.M., gazetted for Valuable Services in the War (*i.e.* usually U.K. or home country), could be for anything other than as a P.O.W., as is his D.C.M. Yet it is not gazetted under A.O./193/1919.

‡ Border Regt. M.C. *L.G.* 23 June 1915. D.C.M. *L.G.* 1 May 1915. Bar to D.C.M. *L.G.* 5 August 1915.

§ W. Riding Regt. Turkestan.

+ Group known: 1914/15 Star trio (Cpl. R.E.), Defence Medal, Imperial Service Medal (Geo. VI—Major), M.S.M. (R.E. for Italy) and Cadet Forces Medal (Major).

◊ New Zealand Permanent Staff. Group known: Queen's South Africa Medal (Johannesburg. Orange Free State. Cape Colony, 2/N. Zealanders), King's South Africa Medal (two date clasps, Superintendent, Provincial Transport Constabulary), M.S.M. and New Zealand Long & Efficient Service Medal.

Dickenson, Mec.S./Sjt. A. (deletion)	12879	Dudley, Pte.(L./C.) H. J. (corr.)	12878
Dickinson, Cpl. W.	12760	— Dvr. W. T.	12760
Digsby, Pte.(A./Cpl.) E. G.	12759	Duffey, S.M. L. A. (corr.)	15726
Dilley, Sjt. J.	12760	Duncalf, Cpl. W.	12758
Dimery, S.Q.M.S. S.	15464	Duncan, Pte. A.	12759
Dinning, Pte.(L./C.) J. W.	12760	— Cpl.(A./Sjt.) J.	12755
Dishington, Cpl. E.	12758	— Sjt. P. R.	12761
Dix, C.S.M. S. C. H.	12756	— Pte. W.	12760
Dobbin, Cpl. C., *M.M.*	12758	— Pte.(A./Sjt.) W. G.	12134
Docherty, Garr.S.M. T.	* 12764	Dunford, Farr.Sjt. E.	12134
Dockerill, C.Q.M.S.(O.R.Sjt.) U.	15461	Dunlop, Pte.(A./C.Q.M.S.) R. G.	12765
Dodd, C.S.M. H. M.	12762	Dunn, Sjt. W. R.	15440
Dodwell, Sjt. H.	15460	Dunsford, Cpl.(A./Sjt.) A.	12758
Dolan, Sjt.(A./C.S.M.) D. M.	12757	Dunthorne, Pte. W. J.	15448
Donaghy, Cpl.(L./Sjt.) J.	12758	Dyer, Pte. E. C.	15447
Donald, Mech.S./Sjt. F. B.	12760	Dyne, Q.M.S. W.	12756
Donaldson, R.S.M. J. W. A., *D.C.M.*		Dyson, Pte. E. J.	15461
(corr.)	12878	— S.Q.M.S. H.	15463
— S.S.M. W. H.	† 15465		
Dornan, S./S.M. T. D.	12759	Eade, Clr.Sjt.(A./S.M.W.O. 1) A. M.	
Douglas, T./W.O. Cl. 1, A. J.	15464	(deletion)	13749
— Pte. J.	15463	Eades, Sjt. S. H., *D.C.M.*	12754
Douthwaite, Pte.(A./Sjt.) G.	12754	Eales, Sjt.(A./C.Q.M.S.) W. H.	15460
Dove, Ch. Writer S. D.	15430	Eames, Pte.(A./Cpl.) T. G.	12135
Dowding, Pte.(T./Sjt.) A. W.	12760	Earl, S./S.M. I. M. H. E.	12764
Dowling, Pte. T. G. H.	12760	— Spr.(A./Sjt.) S. H. L.	12754
Dowson, Engmn. H.	12782	Eato, Sjt.(A./C.S.M.) H.	15439
Doyle, Sjt. J.	15460	Eaton, T./S.M.(A./C.) C. H.	15448
Drane, Pte.(A./Cpl.) F. D. S.	12135	— Cpl. C. W.	12760
— Q.M.S. C. K.	15448	Ebbs, Cpl.(A./S.M., A.C.) J. H.	12762
Drinkald, Pte. J. O.	12763	Ebsworth, C.Q.M.S. T.	12756
Duckworth, A.C.1,(A./Cpl.) D.	‡ 15841	Eccles, S.M. W.O. 1, D. E. (deletion)	13749
— Gnr.(A./Sjt.) J. I.	§ 12763	Ede, Sjt. A. H.	12764

---

* Group known: Queen's South Africa Medal (Transvaal, South Africa 1902, 4915 Sgt. Scottish Rifles), British War Medal (4915 W.O.1 Sco. Rif.), L.S. & G.C. (Geo. V, Q.M.S. Garrison Staff) and M.S.M. (Sco. Rif.). Born in Glasgow, he was originally in 2nd Bn. M.S.M. for service in Malta. Only perhaps 17 M.S.M.s were actually for services in Malta, although references have been traced of another six presented on Malta to men who may have been awarded the medal for another theatre. In addition two M.S.M.s were earned by Maltese recipients in the Balkans—Chetcuti and Spiteri *L.G.* 16 October 1919 and one in South Russia—Cassar 29 July 1921.

† New Zealand Perm. Staff Group known: Queen's South Africa Medal (Cape Colony, Orange Free State, Transvaal, South Africa 1901 and South Africa 1902), Perm Forces beyond the Seas Long Service Medal, M.S.M., New Zealand M.S.M. (Cpl. 2 March, 1931) and N.Z. Long & Efficient Service Medal.

‡ Group in Moss collection, formerly in McInnes collection: British War and Victory Medals (277178 R.A.F.), 1939/45, Burma, and France & Germany Stars (with Pacific and Atlantic bars), War Medal, R.A.F. M.S.M. (for North Russia), Russian Medal for Zeal with St. Anne Ribbon, and King Feisal of Iraq General Service Medal.

§ R.G.A. For Turkestan.

Edgar, R.Q.M.S. A. D.	12764	Fandam, T./S.M. H.	15463
Edginton, Sjt.(A./S./Sjt.) G.	12757	Farenden, C.S.M. J. E.	15461
Edwards, Ldg.Sig. A. E.	13748	Farnell, Sjt. R.	12134
— Pte.(A./Sjt.) D. K.	15463	Farrimond, Pte. E.	12750
— Pte.(A./Sub Condr.) E. J.	15440	Faulkner, C.S.M.(A./R.S.M.) W.	12755
— Cpl.(A./S.Q.M.S.) F.	12760	Fawcett, C.Q.M.S. C.	15461
— B.S.M. F. (corr.)	15725	Fensom, Cpl.(A./Sjt.) G. E. M.	12134
— Sjt.(A./C.S.M.) G.	15460	Fenton, Q.M.S. J.	15461
— T./S.M. J. H. M.	15443	Ferguson, Pte. A.	15461
— Pte.(A./S.Q.M.S.) L. M.	15464	— Sjt. A. R. (corr. of surname)	14275
— Pte.(A./Sjt.) R.	12759	— Sjt. J.	12762
— Sjt. S. (corr.)	15725	— Pte.(A./Sjt.) J.	12761
— Sjt. W. B. W.	✤ 14273	Fernce, C.S.M. H.	12764
Egginton, Sjt. J. B.	12757	Ferneyhough, C.Q.M.S. A. E.	12756
Eggleton, Sqdn.Cpl.Maj. (I.F.)		Fernihough, Pte.(L./C.) J. J. (corr.)	12878
(A./Q.M.S.I.) F.	15460	Ferry, Pte. W.	12759
Einchcombe, C.Q.M.S. E. E. (corr.		Fetch, Q.M.S. J.	12756
of surname)	15725	Fiddes, Cpl.(A./Sjt.)	
Ekins, Pte. W. G.	✤ 12875	A. F., *D.C.M., M.M.*	* 14670
Elder, C.S.M.(A./S.M.) J. D.	15447	Filkin, Pte.(A./S.Q.M.S.) P.	15464
Eldridge, L.A.C. E.	15841	Filsell, Sjt. F. J.	12762
Elliott, C.S.M. G. (corr.)	12879	Fingzies, R.Q.M.S. R.	12765
— Pte.(A./L./C.) T. W.	12759	Firth, S./Sjt. C.	12762
— Pte. W. F.	12765	— Pte. J. R.	12759
Ellis, Sjt.(A./R.S.M.) F. S.	12757	Fisher, Farr.Sjt. W. G.	12134
— Cpl.(L./Sjt.) P.	12758	— Armt.S./Sjt. W. J. (corr.)	14275
— C.Q.M.S. W.	12756	Fitzgerald, Cpl. A.	12758
— W.O. Cl. 1, (Supt.Clk.) W. H.	15462	FitzGerald, Ch. S.B.S. R. C.	12779
Ellison, C.S.M. F.	12754	Fitzpatrick, Q.M.S.(A./S.M.) F. H.	15462
Ellwood, Sadd.S./Sjt. W.	12760	Flanders, Farr.Sjt. E. R. (corr.)	12878
Elmes, C.S.M. G.	12134	Fleming, Pte. A.	15440
Elmslie, Sjt. A. M. (corr.)	14275	— Sen.R.A. A. E.	12779
Eltringham, 1st Writer J. G. E.	15430	— Cpl.(A./C.S.M.) P.	15447
Elvish, Sjt. D.	15462	— C.Q.M.S. P. J.	12756
Emett, Pte. (A./Cpl.) T.	12759	— S.M. R.	15462
Emmott, C.Q.M.S. W.	15461	Fletcher, Pte.(A./Cpl.) A.	12755
England, Sjt.(T./C.Q.M.S.) A.	15462	— Cpl. J.	12754
English, S./Smith C. E. (corr.)	15726	— C.S.M. R.	12756
Ennis, Pte.(A./S./Sjt.) W.	15463	Flood, T./S.M. H. A.	15443
Erasmus, Pte. H.	12759	Flotman, Sjt. P. J.	12761
Eriksen, Sjt. E.	15464	Foard, Spr.(L./C.) P. G. ✤ 12875,	14273
Essam, S.M. E. J.	15460	Forbes, Cpl.(A./Q.M.S.) J. E.	15460
Evans, Pte. R.	12759	Ford, Armr.S./Sjt. H. D.	12761
		— Sjt. J. W. (corr.)	12878
Fairclough, By.S.M. C.	12762	Forrest, Sjt. A.	12757

---

* Essex Regt. 'For exceptional devotion.' The names of five men, gazetted here for
'exceptional devotion in the performance of military duties' also appeared in A.O.442
of 1919. Pte. J. F. Carroll, 11/Lond R., Sgt. A. F. Fiddes, D.C.M. M.M., 6/Essex R.,
L./Cpl. R. C. Jones, 1/Leinster R., Sgt. R. G. Lawton, R.A.V.C. and Sgt. G. N.
Reynolds, 6/Essex R.

Foster, Pte. A. J.	12759	Gamlen, S./Sjt. T. H.		12761
— Q.M.S. W. J.	15462	Gander, Dvr.(T./C.S.M.) E. G.		12760
— Pte. W. J.	12763	Gane, Pte.(A./Sjt.) A. C.		15440
Fotherby, Sjt. H., *M.M.*	12755	Garcia, Pte.(L./C.) C. F.		12760
Foulds, Cpl. F.	12758	Gardner, T./S./Sjt. J. L.		15443
Fowles, Sjt. G. R.	12753	— Sjt.(A./C.S.M.) W.		12754
Fox, Pte.(A./S.M.) P. C.	15464	Garmston, Sjt. W. H.		12757
— Spr.(A./Sjt.) W.	12754	Garner, C.P.O.Mech. 3rd. Gr. P.		12779
— Pte.(L./C.) W. P.	12762	— Sjt. R.		12760
Francis, Sjt. A.	15464	Gash, S.M. F.		15462
— S./Sjt. H.	12760	Gaskin, Farr.S./Sjt. C. F. J.		12760
— Ch.S.B.S. R.	15431	Gasser, L/C.(A./C.S.M.) J. G. (corr.)		12878
Frank, S.S.M. H. L. S.	† 15465	Gatland, T./S./Sjt. G. A.		12761
Franklin, Spr.(A./Cpl.) C. L., *D.C.M.*	12754	Gayler, C.S.M. T. H. (corr.)		15725
— Sjt. F. W. (corr. of surname)	14275	Geary, Sjt.(A./S.M.) H. C. G.		12762
— Pte.(A./Cpl.) J. W.	15439	— C.Q.M.S. T.		15461
Fraser, S./Sjt. A. D.	15443	Gellatly, Pte.(A./S.M.) H. J. C.		15464
— C.Q.M.S. J.	12756	Genn, Mech.S./Sjt. C.		12134
Freear, T./Sub Condr. H.	12761	George, A./C.S.M.(W.O. II) W.		15430
Freeland, Skpr. J.	12781	Gerhardi, Pte.(A./Sjt.) T. E.		12134
Freeman, C.S.M. W. H. J.	12760	Gibbins, Sjt.(A./S./Sjt.) A. L.	‡ 15463	
Freestone, C.S.M. A. H.	15460	Gibbons, Cpl.(A./Sjt.) A.		12760
Freudemacher, S.Q.M.S. E. L.	12760	Gibsen, Sjt. A.		15461
Frost, Cpl.(A./Sjt.) A. J. F.	12758	Giddings, Cpl.(A./Sjt.) F. M.		15463
— T./S.M. J. F.	15460	Gildea, C.P.O. G.		15459
Fulker, C.Q.M.S.(A./R.S.M.) H.	12765	Giles, Cpl.(A./Sjt.) F. H.		12760
Fullard, Sjt. W.	12134	Gill, Sjt. E. J.		12757
Fullbrook, T./S.S.M. J.	† 15463	— Cpl. I.		12758
Funnell, Cpl. W. G.	15841	Gillespie, S.M. W.		15462
Furry, C.Q.M.S.(A./Q.M.S.) B. D.	15464	— C.S.M. W. J. (corr.)		15725
Furseman, Cpl. C.	12758	Glanville, S.S.M. W. L.	§ 15465	
Furze, Cpl.(A./Sjt.) F. J.	12760	Gledhill, C.S.M. W.		12760
Fyffe, C.S.M. J.	12756	Glendinning, Gnr. F. W.		15444
		Glover, Sjt. F. J.		12761
Gadd, C.Q.M.S.(A./C.S.M.) W. G.	12755	— Bandmr. K. S. (corr.)		14275
Gallichan, Sjt. W. H. K.	12760	— Sjt.(A./C.S.M.) W. E.		12760
Gamble, C.S.M. G. (corr of surname)	14279	— Ch.S.B.S. W. J. H.		12779

---

* N.Z.P.S. Later awarded New Zealand M.S.M. as No. 326 W.O.1, N.Z.P.S., 15 November, 1929.

† Group was in McInnes collection: Queen's South Africa Medal (Belmont, Modder River, Orange Free State, Transvaal, 12189 Corpl. A.S.C.), King's South Africa Medal (Sergt. A.S.C.), British War Medal (S–12189 W.O.1 R.A.S.C.) and M.S.M. (S–12189 R.A.S.C.) (for services in the Union of South Africa). Only 25 for this theatre, of which 14 were to South African Forces. Born 14 December, 1876; in the ranks 19 yrs. 194 days; appointed S.S.M. (S. & T.) 15 December, 1914; retired 4 June, 1917.

‡ R.A.S.C. For Malta. Presented 6 April 1920 by F.M. Lord Plumer, Governor of Malta.

§ No. 6/235, Canterbury Rifles, N.Z.E.F. Later as No. 421 W.O.1 N.Z.P.S. awarded N.Z. M.S.M. on 15 November 1929.

Glynn, Pte.(A./C.S.M.) P.	12760	Green, Sub Condr. A. T.	† 15463
Godber, Sjt. A. F.	12760	— Pte.(A./C.S.M.) B. J.	12761
Goddard, Dvr. A. W.	12760	— Sjt. F. (corr.)	14275
— Sjt. G. R.	15460	Greenham, Spr.(A./2nd Cpl.) H.	12754
— C.S.M. T. S.	12755	Greenland, Spr.(T./Sjt.) J.	12754
Godden, Sjt.(A./S./Sjt.) J. R.	✿ 12875	Greenwood, A./C. 1, C. H.	12527
Godman, T./Supt.Clk. S. J.	12754	Gregory, Sjt. A. C.	15449
Godwin, S./S.M. A.	15444	— Q.M.S. A. W.	15444
— S.Q.M.S.(A./S.S.M.) E. R.	15463	— 2nd S.B.S. J. J.	12779
Goldstone, Cpl. S.	12758	— C.Q.M.S. J. R.	12756
Godlthorp, S./Sjt. H.	12761	— T./S./S.M. T.	12759
Gonsalves, C.Q.M.S. M. A. (corr.)	12379	Gregson, Sjt.(A./Q.M.S.) A.	15443
Gooch, S./Sjt. L. D.	15463	Grenham, Cpl. F.	12760
Goodwin, Sjt. F. W.	12756	Grey, Cpl. T. M.	12760
— C.S.M. J. T.	15462	Griffen, S.S.M. H. F.	15465
Gordon, Sjt.(A./S.M.) F. N.	15464	Griffiths, T./Sub Condr. C. H.	12765
— Pte.(T./Cpl.) J. F. (corr.)	12879	— Pte.(A./S.M.) G. C.	15464
— Cpl. R.	15461	— Pte. W. J.	12759
Goree, Pte.(L./C.) G. E.	12754	Griggs, C.S.M. E. H.	‡ 12134
Gorsuch, C.Q.M.S. C.	12756	Groat, Spr.(L./C.) G.	12754
Gothard, A./C.Q.M.S. S.	15462	Groombridge, C.S.M. H. A.	12760
Gould, Sjt.(A./Sub Condr.) W. H.	✿ 15724	Grose, Sjt. S. N. W. (corr.)	12879
Goulden, S./Sjt. H. H.	15464	Grossman, T./S.M. J.	12765
Goulding, Mech.S.M. H. P.	15460	Guerin, T./R.S.M. J. (corr. of	
Gourd, Vict.C.P.O. G. T. A.	* 15431	surname)	15725
Gourdie, Sjt.(A./S.M.) A.	15447	Guiver, C.S.M. C.	12754
Gourlay, Farr.Sjt. W.	12761	Gully, Sjt. J. H.	15443
Govan, Cpl. P.	12758	Gunning, Pte. J.	12755
Gowland, S./S.M. R. H.	15464	Guscott, Q.M.S. R. T.	15462
Graham, Q.M.S.(A.C.) A. M.	15460	Gutteridge, Dvr. J. K.	12760
— Bdr.(A./Sjt.) G.	12764	Guyatt, Pte.(A./Sjt.) W.	12760
— Dvr. J.	12760	Guypson, Sub Condr. J. C.	12763
Granger, Sjt.(A./C.Q.M.S.) H.	12754	Gyton, C.P.O.Mech. 3rd Gr. G. H.	12779
Grant, Cpl.(A./Sjt.) C.	12758		
— S./Sjt. H.	12760	Hacker, Sjt.(A./C.S.M.) A. J.	12757
Gratwick, Pte.(A./Mech.S.M.) P. J.	12765	Hackett, Pte.(A./Sjt.) A.	15463
Gray, Sjt. A.	15464	Haddon, Eng.Clk.Sjt. F. W.	12760
— C.S.M. E.	12756	Hadgraft, S./Sjt.(A./S.Q.M.S.) F.	12765
— Sjt.(A./S.M.) R. E. (corr. of		Haigh, Cpl. A. E.	12758
surname)	14274	Hale, S.M. F. G.	15461
— Sjt.(A./C.S.M.) W.	12757	Hall, Sjt. A. J.	12761
— S./Sjt. W. S.	12135	— C.S.M. T.	15462

---

  * Group known: Africa General Service Medal (Somaliland 1908–10, *'Philomel'*), 1914/ 15 Star trio, R.N. L.S. & G.C. (Ships Std., *'Albemarle'*) and R.N. M.S.M. (*'Glory'*) (Murmansk).

  † R.A.O.C. South Africa.

  ‡ Group known: Queen's South Africa Medal (Laing's Nek, Belfast, Pte. 381 A.P.O.C.), King's South Africa Medal (Cpl.), British War and Victory Medals (Major), M.S.M. (570005 R.E.) and Order of St. Stanislas (4th class in gold and enamel). M.S.M. for Murmansk. Temp. Lt. Col. in Ireland 1922–23.

Hall, Sjt.(A./R.S.M.) W.	12764	Hartland, Sjt.(A./Q.M.S.) W. T.	15460
Hallett, C.Q.M.S.(A./Mech.S.M.)		Hartlebury, Cpl. E.	15461
W. J.	12760	Hartley, A./Rmr.S./Sjt. C. H.	12761
Halls, C.Q.M.S. F.	12756	— Mech.S./Sjt. R. K.	12760
Hallsworth, S./Sjt. W. H.	* 12763	— Pte.(A./Q.M.S.) W.	15464
Halman, S./Sjt. E.	15440	Harvey, Pte.A./Sjt. J.	15439
Hamilton, C.S.M. T. C.	12756	— Sjt. P. C.	12757
Hammerton, Sjt. R. W.	15439	Harwood, C.Q.M.S. F. H.	15461
Hammond, Sjt. R. S.	12757	— Sqdn.Q.M.S.(O.R.Sjt.) P.	15460
— Sjt. T. J.	12754	Hathaway, Condr. M. L.	15465
— C.S.M. W.	12756	Hatt, S.S.M. A. R.	15465
Hampshire, Pte.(A./Sjt.) H.	12759	Hatton, Pte.(A./L./C.) R.	12761
Handley, Cpl.(A./S./Sjt.) J. W.	15463	Haughton, Pte.(A./Cpl.) W. R.	15447
Hanks, C.S.M. A. C.	12756	Hawke, Sjt. E. J.	15447
Hanley, Pte. H. A.	❁ 12875	Hawker, C.P.O. G.	15430
Hanlon, Sjt.(A./B.Q.M.S.) J.	12762	Hawkins, Pte.(A./S.Q.M.S.) H. F.	15463
Hann, T./R.S.M. G. C.	12761	— Cpl.(A./Sjt.) W. C.	15447
— S.M. W.O. 1, G. P.	13749	Haworth, Pte. A.	12761
Hannah, C.S.M.(A./R.S.M.) W. G.	12755	Haycock, C.S.M. A. E.	12756
Hansell, Pte. E. H.	12754	Hayes, Pte. E.	15448
Harding, S./Sjt.(A./S.M.) F. H.	15463	Haynes, T./Amt.S.M. F. H.	15448
— T./S.M. J. H.	15447	Head, C.Q.M.S. G. H.	12762
— Pte. J. T.	† ❁ 12875	Heap, Sjt. T.	12765
Hardy, S.Q.M.S. E.	12760	Heath, P.O.Mech. R. A.	12779
— T./Sub Condr.(A./Condr.) G.	12761	— Cpl. T. W. E.	12527
Hargreaves, Pte.(A./Sjt.) E.	15444	Heaton, Cpl.(A./S.Q.M.S.) W. F.	15448
Harley, Sjt. H. E.	15443	Hedinburgh, Whr.S./Sjt. W. A.	15463
— S.Q.M.S. W. H.	15462	Hedley, Sjt. D. A.	15464
Harper, Sjt.(A./S.M.) G. F. C.	15443	Hefford, Sjt. A. (deletion)	15726
Harris, T./Mech.S.M. C.	12760	Hegan, C.Q.M.S.(O.R.Sjt.) W. H.	15461
— S.M. C. V. N.	15464	Hellinger, Sjt. A.	15841
— Cpl.(A./S./Sjt.) G. H. B.	15443	Hemming, Cpl.(A./S.M.) A. L.	12754
— Cpl. G. L.	15841	Hemmings, Pte.(A./L./C.) C. W.	12759
Harrison, Pte.(A./Sjt.) J. W.	12761	Henderson, Cpl.(A./S./Sjt.) A. O.	12760
— R.S.M. S. J.	15465	— Sjt.(A./C.Q.M.S.) J., *M.M.*	12757
— Pte. W.	12759	— Farr.S./Sjt. J.	12763
Harrop, 2nd Cpl. D. W.	12134	— Spr.(A./Sjt.) J. S.	15460
Hart, Cpl.(A./S./Sjt.) H. T.	12761	Henniker, Supt.Clk. G.	12764
— C.S.M.Instr. J.	15439		

* Group was in McInnes collection: Queen's South Africa Medal (Cape Colony, Transvaal, Wittebergen), King's South Africa Medal (both Sergt. 77 Batt. R.F.A.), 1914/15 Star (unnamed), British War and Victory Medals (Conductor, M.W.S.), General Service Medal (South Persia, Condr. M.W.S., M.I.D. oakleaf), Delhi Durbar 1911, L.S. & G.C. (Geo. V, engraved Staff Sgt. I.A.) and M.S.M. (Mily. Works Serv. I.A.). He was born on 31 December, 1876 and served from 1894, initially in R.A. His Regimental Number in M.W.S. was No. 1. M.I.D. for S. Persia *L.G.* p.7759 in 1920. The M.S.M. was for service in S. Persia from 12 October, 1918 to 22 June, 1919. He was commissioned 1 January 1928, rose to the rank of Major *w.e.f.* 30 December, 1930 and retired at Bombay 31 December, 1931.

† 13 Hussars, for Gallantry in Mesopotamia.

Herbert, Clr.Sjt.(A./S.M. W.O. I) J.	
(deletion)	13749
Herdman, Spr.(A./Sjt.) J.	12754
Herdson, S./Sjt. C. H. (deletion)	12879
Herrod, T./Sjt. J. H.	12761
Heslup, F. of W. Q.M.S. W.	15460
Hetrick, Pte.(A./S./Sjt.) R.	15464
Hewdey, Pte.(T./Sjt.) F.	12761
Hewett, Sjt.(A./C.S.M.) T. E.	15460
Hewitt, B.S.M. T.	12134
Hicks, S.B.S. C. W.	12779
Higgin, S./Sjt.(A.C.) M. H.	12764
Higginbottom, C.Q.M.S.	
(O.R.Sjt.) C.	15461
Higgins, C.S.M. E. B.	* 15465
High, Pte.(L./C.) A. L.	15440
Highcock, T./Sub Condr.) F.	12761
Higman, C.S.M. W. W.	12764
Hill, Col.Sjt.(A./C.Q.M.S.) C.	15462
— B.Q.M.S.(A./S.M.) C. E.	15447
— Cpl.(A./S./Sjt.) G.	15463
— C.E.R.A. 2nd Cl. G. H.	15431
— Sjt.(A./S.Q.M.S.) R.	12134
— Pte. W.	12759
Hillary, Cpl. A. J.	12758
Hilliard, C.S.M.(A./S.M.) C. E.	15462
Hilton, Q.M.S. F. H.	12762
Hincks, B.Q.M.S.) G. W.	15460
Hindmarsh, Q.M.S. H. J.	15464
Hiney, C.S.M. R. T.	12764
Hipkiss, C.S.M. D. J.	12765
Hipperson, C.S.M. C. F.	12764
Hird, Pte.(A./Sjt.) J. F.	15448
Hirst, S./Sjt. T. C.	12760
Hitchman, Sjt. W.	12757
Hoare, S./Sjt. A.	† 15440
Hobbs, W.O. Cl. 1, E. W.	15464
— Sjt. S. A.	12757
Hobday, Pte.(A./Sjt.) J. P.	15462
Hocking, P.O. R. G.	13747

Hoddle, S.B.S. H. G.	12779
Hodge, S./Sjt. H. S.	12765
Hodges, Pte.(A./S.Q.M.S.) H. T.	15464
Hodgkinson, Pte. J.	12759
— Sjt.(A./C.S.M.) S.	12134
Hogarth, Pte.(L./C.) J. E.	12759
— Sjt. J. M.	12757
Holden, Mech. S.M. H.	12759
— C.S.M.(A./R.S.M.) N.	12764
Holder, Sjt. E.	12756
Hole, Pte. E. W.	12761
Hollamby, C.Q.M.S. E. T.	12754
Holland, Bombr. W.	12762
Holliman, Pte.(A./S.Q.M.S.) H.	12765
Holloway, S./Sjt. R.	12761
Holmes, Pte.(A./Cpl.) A. G.	12761
Holt, W.O.Cl. 1, Supt. Clk. A.	15461
— C.Q.M.S. L.	12756
Honey, Cpl. A. W.	12753
Honeyball, Q.M.S. J. F.	‡ 15461
Hood, Pte.(A./Sjt.) J.	12765
Hooker, E.R.A. 3rd Cl. H. E.	12782
Hope, C.Q.M.S. A.	15461
— 1st Writer G. W.	15430
Hopkins, Pte.(A./Sjt.) F. J.	12761
Hopson, Pte. F. R.	§ 15463
Horchover, S./Sjt. D. M.	12765
Horner, Sjt.(A./Mech.S.M.) A. H.	
(corr.)	12878
Horsfield, Armt.S./Sjt. E.	12763
Horton, Cpl.(A./Sjt.) H.	12760
Houghton, Sjt.(A./C.Q.M.S.) J. H.	12767
Howard, Pte.(A./S.M.) E. H.	15464
— Pte.(A./Cpl.) G. R.	12761
— Q.M.S. W.	15463
Howarth, T./S./S.M. H.	12759
Howell, Sjt. W.	12757
Howie, T./Sub Condr. C. C. C. McK.	12763
Howse, Dvr.(A./Sjt.) A. E. (corr.)	12878
Hubbard, Pte.(A./) G. E.	15464

---

* For Jamaica (R.G.A.).

† M.S.M. and Victory Medal known, R.A.O.C. No. 07926. This is the last M.S.M. gazetting for France & Flanders. This award probably relates to post-hostilities work in relation to the numerous ammunition dumps. His Victory Medal shows Sgt. A.O.C., his M.S.M. S./Sgt. R.A.O.C.

‡ Group known: Queen's Mediterranean Medal, L.S. & G.C. (Edw. VII, Q.M.S. North. Fus.) and M.S.M.

§ Group known: British War and Victory Medals, Defence Medal, Coronation 1937 and Coronation 1953, M.S.M., Special Constabulary L.S. (Geo. VI, 1st type, clasps 1943 and 1949) and Medal of St. George (Silver).

Huddleston, Spr. A. M.	12763	Ison, Cpl.(A./S.Q.M.S.) J. W.	12134
Hudson, Sjt. E. E.	12753	Iudkevitch, Sjt. R. M. N.	† 12134
— S.M. 1, J.	12527		
— P.O. W.	15430	Jack, Sjt. J.	12757
Hughes, Pte. C. S.	15439	Jackson, By.Q.M.S.(A./R.S.M.) E.	12762
— Pte. D. T.	12759	— S.Q.M.S. E.	15463
— P.P. Teleg. J.	13747	— Pte.(A./Sjt.) F.	12761
— Farr.S./Sjt.(A./S.S.M.) T.	12760	— Sjt. L. (corr.)	12878
— Sjt.(A./S.Q.M.S.) W. A.	15460	Jacobs, Sjt.(A.C.) H. H.	12762
Hulse, C.P.O.Mech. 3rd Gr. H.	12779	— Q.M.S.(A./S.M.) W. R.	15460
Humphreys, Sjt. J. E.	12761	James, C.S.M. J. C.	12756
— Sjt. R. J.	12755	— Pte. V. G.	✤ 15724
— T./S.M. S.	15447	Jarrett, S./Sjt. F.	15464
Humphries, C.Q.M.S. G. S.	12756	Jarvis, Sjt. J. H.	15460
— Cpl.(T./S.Q.M.S.) W. J.	12760	Jayne, Sjt. W. H.	15460
Hunneybell, C.S.M. G.	12756	Jenkins, C.S.M. W.	15439
Hunt, Cpl. A. J. B.	12134	Jennings, 2nd Cpl.(A./Sjt.) R. W.	15447
— Sjt.(A./S.M.) G. H.	12762	Jobbins, Pte. J.	12759
— P.O. J. E.	15430	Johnson, Pte.(A./Sjt.) A.	12759
— S.M. W. H.	15461	— Cpl. O. J.	12758
Hurcombe, Spr.(L./C.) E.	12754	Johnston, S./Sjt. A. D.	15464
Hurd, Bandmr. J. L. T.	15461	— R.S.M. E. A.	15465
Hurndall, C.S.M. J. J.	12756	— Pte.(A./Sjt.) J.	12755
Hurtell, S.Q.M.S. A.	15463	— C.Q.M.S.(A./C.S.M.) J. M. M.	12755
Hurst, Dvr. W. M.	✤ 12875	— Sadd.Cpl.(A./Sadd.Sjt.) R.	12753
Hutchins, S./S.M. H. H.	15463	Jones, T./S./Sjt. A.	12762
Hutchinson, C.S.M. G. H.	12756	— T./S./S.M. A. E.	15443
Hyland, Sjt.(A./C.S.M.) G.	12767	— Armr.S./Sjt. A. E.	15463
Hynes, B.Q.M.S. H. (corr. of		— Act.Arms.Mate A. W.	‡ 13747
surname)	14273	— C.Q.M.S.(A./R.Q.M.S.) D.	12756
		— Cpl. D. W.	15439
Ibbs, Mech.S./Sjt. F. S.	15447	— R.Q.M.S. E.	12755
Igglesden, S./Sjt. H.	12760	— S./Sjt.(A./S.Q.M.S.) E. S.	✤ 12875
Iles, Sjt. F. W.	12760	— Pte.(A./Sjt.) F.	12759
Ingle, Sjt. D.	12757	— C.Q.M.S. F. J. R.	15449
Ingleton, Q.M.S. E. W.	12762	— Pte. G. N.	§ ✤ 12875
Ingram, Armr.S./Sjt. F.	15463	— Yeo. Sigs. H.	13748
Ings, Q.M.S.(O.R.Sjt.) G. F.	* 15461	— C.Q.M.S. J.	12756
Inkson, Pte.(A./Sjt.) P. N.	15463	— Cpl. J.	12758
Innes, B.S.M. G.	15443	— Pte.(A./C.Q.M.S.) J. E.	15463
Instone, Pte.(A./Spl.) P. R. T.	12761	— Cpl. J. P.	12758
Ireland. Sjt. F. C.	15461	— Pte.(A./S.M.) J. T.	15464
Irving, S./S.M. G. E.	15463	— Pte.(A./Cpl.) L. G.	12759
— C.S.M.(A./S.M.) W.	15447	— Cpl. O.	12758

* C./Sgt. George Frederick Ings, aged 54, from Tunbridge Wells, No. 6278071, The Buffs, and H.Q. 37 Infantry Brigade; killed 7 March, 1939. (Palestine? N.W.F.?).
† Interpreter R.E. Archangel.
‡ R.N. M.S.M. Group in Family. Served 1914–19 then in Cardiff Police to 1951. Born 1896. Died 1978.
§ N. Somerset Yeo. attd. 6 Dragoons.

Jones, Cpl.(A./S.M.) O. E. L.	15448	Kent, T./Sub Condr.(A./	
— Pte. R.	12759	Condr.) H. V.	12763
— Pte.(A./L./C.) R. C.	14670	— Sjt. R. H.	12757
— T./S./Sjt. S. J.	12762	Kenyon, T./S.S.M. A. R.	15440
— Sjt. S. J.	12762	Kerby, Pte.(A./Mech.S.M.) A. P.	12765
— C.S.M. T. (E. Lancs. R.)	12762	Kerr, S.M.1 J.	§ 12527
— C.S.M. T. (R.W.Fus.)	15447	— S./S.M. R. A.	+ 15443
— Pte. W. E.	12759	— Pte.(A./C.Q.M.S.) R. D. (deletion)	15726
Joy, Pte.(A./Cpl.) J. C. M. (corr.)	15725	Kerswill, Cpl. S. H. (corr.)	14275
Joyce, C.S.M. F. J.	12764	Kidson, Pte. J. G.	12759
— Sjt. G. E.	15440	Kilpatrick, S./Sjt. E. J. (corr.)	12879
— Sjt. W. H.	15464	King, Sjt. A.	12757
Jury, C.Q.M.S. T. S.	15447	— Cpl.(A./S./Sjt.) L. W.	15448
		— Sjt. R.	15464
Kaine, Sjt. J. T.	* 15463	Kingston, T./R.S.M. F. J.	12753
Kampff, Sjt. W.	15448	Kirby, Sjt. T.	12761
Kane, Pte.(L./C.) A. A.	12759	Kirkpatrick, Q.M.S. A.	15461
Karle, Pte. F.	12759	Kitson, S.Q.M.S. H.	15464
Kavanagh, Sjt.(C.S.M.) J. (corr.)	12879	Knight, Sjt. A. E.	12757
Kay, A./C. 2 (A./Cpl.) C. A.	† 15841	— Flt.Sjt. A. S.	15841
— T./C.S.M. F. T.	15462	— Sjt. E.	12757
Kearns, Ch. Motor Mech. J. J.	‡ 13748	— Sjt.(A./C.Q.M.S.) H.	15461
Keeble, B.S.M. G.	15465	Knowles, By.Q.M.S. W.	12753
Keefe, Pte. E.	12759		
Kell, Spr.(A./Cpl.) J. F.	15443	Labond, Pte.(A./Cpl.) L.	15462
Kellaway, S.B.S. J. R.	13744	Labourer, No. 15333 (59th Chinese	
Kellett, Cpl. F.	15447	Lab. Co.)	14273
— Pte.(A./Cpl.) T.	12755	Lake, C.Q.M.S. H.	12756
Kelleway, Sjt. F.	15460	— Sjt. R. E.	12763
Kelly, Sjt. E. A.	12755	Lala, Cpl.(A./Sjt.) G. W.	15444
— Cpl.(A./S./Sjt.) E. K.	15448	Lamb, Pte. E.	15449
Kember, Sjt.(A./Condr.) E. H.	15443	— Res Wardmaster S. H.	12779
Kemp, Pte.(A./S./Sjt.) C. S.	15464	Lambert, Cpl.(A./Sjt.) T.	12758
Kempster, Sjt. L. U. C.	15443	Lammiman, Cpl.(A./Sjt.) G.	15439
Kennedy, S./Sjt. E. A.	15464	Lancake, Cpl.(A./Sjt.) D.	❀ 12875
— T./Supt.Clk. H.	15439	Lancaster, Cpl. O.	12758
Kennett, Sjt. A.	12757	Lane, Cpl. G.	12758
Kenny, S./Sjt. J. H. (corr.)	12879	Lang, T./Sub Condr. T. H.	15443

---

* A.P.C. Malta.

† Group known: British War Medal (Boy Mech. R.N.A.S.), Victory Medal (A./Cpl. R.A.F.), R.A.F. M.S.M. (for N. Russia), Special Const. L.S. (Geo. VI) and Russian Medal for Zeal.

‡ Group known: British War and Victory Medals R.N. M.S.M. (Motorboat 557, Zeebrugge Force).

§ R.A.F. M.S.M. No. 215 R.F.C. Enlisted 11 August 1910; entitled to 1914 Star trio and R.A.F. L.S. & G.C. Retired 1934.

+ Medal known: 3/125A N.Z. Medical Corps. 44 awards in this Gazette for Egypt and Palestine, 31 of these non–U.K. personnel. Kerr was M.I.D. 21 January, 1919 (Allenby). The 'A' suffix indicates originally with another branch of the N.Z. service.

Lange, Act.P.O. G.	* 13749	Levick, Sjt. S. R.	15460
Langham, Cpl. C. H.	12758	Lewin, Sjt. B. (corr. of amendment)	14275
Langley, Sjt. R. C.	12757	Lewis, Cpl.(A.C.) A. G.	15460
Langlois Hamon, Sjt. P. F.	12763	— C.Q.M.S. C.	12756
Langtry, C.Q.M.S. H.	15462	— S./Sjt. D. L.	15465
Larnder, Cpl.(A./L./Sjt.) J. H.	12755	— T./S.M. H. V.	12762
Last, Pte.(A./S./Sjt.) C. J.	15464	— Cpl.(A./S.Q.M.S.) S.	15463
Latilla, Sjt. W. H.	15463	Lidstone, Sjt. L. G.	15463
Laughton, C.S.M. W.	12756	Lill, C.Q.M.S. F. A., *M.M.*	15439
Lavender, Sjt. H. E.	12757	Linder, L./C. R. G. (corr.)	12878
Laverack, C.S.M.(A./R.S.M.) A.	12754	Lines, Pte.(A./L./C.) H. C.	12759
Lawrence, Q.M.S. W.	15462	Lingley, Whlr.Sjt. T. T. (corr.)	14275
— C.S.M. W. G.	12756	Linington, S./S.M. J. J.	12134
Lawson, Pte. A.	12759	Lipscombe, C.S.M. F.	15462
— Spr.(A./Sjt.) F.	15447	Lister, Cpl. J.	12527
— T./Q.M.S. R. J.	15443	— Sjt. J. T.	14273
Lawton, Cpl.(A./Sjt.) R. G.	14670	Littler, C.Q.M.S. R.	12756
Laxton, Cpl.(L./Sjt.) T.	12758	Littlewood, Pte.(A./Sjt.) C.	15461
Laycock, Pte.(A./L./C.) S. (corr.)	12878	Llewellyn, Pte. A. L.	12759
Lea, Pte.(A./C.Q.M.S.) F.	12759	Lloyd, C.Q.M.S.(A./C.S.M.) A. W.	15439
Leach, Sig.Sjt.(A./B.Q.M.S.) C. H.	12754	Lockwood, Sjt. F.	12757
— R.S.M. F. (deletion, M.B.E.		Logan, Pte.(L./C.) S. J.	12754
substituted)	14276	Logie, S./S.M. R. V.	15465
— Cpl.(A./S./Sjt.) G. W.	15463	Long, C.Q.M.S. D.	12754
Leadbeater, Sjt. F.	12757	Longworth, By.Q.M.S. P.	12755
Leadbeter, Sjt. J. H.	12754	Loosley, Sjt.(A./C.S.M.) A. J.	15448
Leaman, Sjt. G. H.	12763	Lord, Q.M.S.(O.R.Sjt.) S.	15461
Leech, Pte. V. O.	12759	Lott, Pte.(A./L./C.) H. L. G.	12759
Leeder, Cpl. S. E. H.	15443	Love, A./S.M. H. E.	15464
Leeming, Pte.(A./L./C.) J.	12759	Lovett, Sjt. C. A. (corr.)	15725
Lees, 2nd Writer E. A.	13748	Lucas, Pte.(A./Q.M.S.) A. E.	15464
— Pte. E. J.	12759	Lundon, S.Q.M.S. D. H.	15464
— S.M. J.	† 15440	Lunn, T./S.M. J.	15447
Legg, Spr.(A./C.S.M.) N. E.	15460	Lunness, Mech.S./Sjt. S. R. (corr.	
Leggatt, Pte.(A./S.Q.M.S.) E. E.	12134	of surname)	14275
Leggett, Mech.S./Sjt. F. H. (corr.		Lyons, S.Q.M.S. G. T. (corr.)	12879
of surname)	12878		
Leicester, Pte. T.	12756	Maber, C.Q.M.S. A. T. S.	12762
Leigh, S./S.M. F. J.	15463	McArthur, Sjt. A.	12763
Leighton, Sjt.(A./S./Sjt.) J. M.	15464	— Pte. N. (corr.)	15725
Leinster, T./Sjt. J.	12761	McBain, Cpl. A.	12763
Leonard, Sjt.(A./C.Q.M.S.) A.	15461	McBryde, Cpl. D. H. (corr.)	15725
Leslie, C.S.M. W. J.	15443	McCabe, S.Q.M.S. A. E.	15463

---

* R.N. M.S.M. R.N.V.R. An escaped P.O.W. from Yozgod, Turkey, August 1918. See also Newton *infra*.

† Group known: Queen's South Africa Medal (Cape Colony, South Africa 1902, 5392 Sgt. 3/Gren. Gds.), British War and Victory Medals (1352 W.O.1, M.P.S.C.), L.S. & G.C. (S/Sgt. M.P.S.C.), M.S.M. (M.P.S.C.) and Territorial Efficiency Medal (2205056 W.O.II R.E.). Born 1877. In the ranks 19 years 329 days. Warrant Officer 1915. Retired Regular Army 1920.

McCaffery, C.S.M.(A./R.S.M.) J. A.	12134	Macoubrey, Pte.(A./S./Sjt.) D.	12135
McCallum, Cpl. J.	12758	MacPherson, C.Q.M.S. T. (corr.)	15725
McCoubrey, Sjt. G. J. (corr. of		McQuade, Cpl.(A./C.S.M.) A. E.	15463
surname)	14275	MacRae, C.Q.M.S. J.	15462
McCreedy, 2nd Hnd. J.	12752	Maiden, Spr. W. S.	* 12763
McDermott, Pte.(A./Sjt.) P. D.	12764	Main, Cpl.(A./S./Sjt.) L. J.	12763
McDonald, Cpl.(L./Sjt.)(G. Gds.)		Major, Sjt.(A./Sub Condr.) H. W.	15448
(corr. of surname)	15725	Malcolmson, Q.M.S.(O.R.Sjt.) B.	15460
— Sjt.(A./C.S.M.) F. H. E. (corr.)	15726	Maloney, Sjt. P. J.	12757
McDonnell, C.Q.M.S. C. F.	15465	Mann, A./Sjt. C. F.	15841
McEwan, Cpl. W.	12761	— T./Q.M.S. T.	15461
McGeachan, Spr.(A./Sjt.) J. M.	15460	Manners, S./S.M. A. E.	15464
McGregor, Pte.(L./C.) A. C.	12759	Manning, S.Q.M.S. F. V.	15464
MacGregor, S./Sjt. J.	15464	Mansfield, Gnr.(A./Fitt.Sjt.) W.	12753
McInerney, C.S.M.(A./S.M.) T.	15464	Mantle, F. of Wks. Q.M.S. A. W.	15460
McIntosh, Pte.(A./Sjt.) J. S.	12761	Marks, C.P.O. H. A.	15459
MacIntyre, Sjt. D.	12756	Marler, Pte. A./Sjt. B. K.	12759
McIntyre, C.Q.M.S.(A./C.S.M.)		Marr, Pte.(A./Cpl.) H. W.	15462
D. F., *D.C.M.*	12763	Marten, Q.M.S. Instr. F. S.	15463
Mackay, S.M.(A./Supt.Clk.)	12755	Martin, Sjt. D. D. (deletion)	12879
McKay, Pte.(A./Cpl.) A.	12135	— Cpl. G. W.	15439
Mackay, Sjt.(A./S./Sjt.) J.	12761	— Sjt.(A./C.S.M.) H.	12134
McKellar, Pte. J.	15440	— Sjt. J. H.	15439
Mackenzie, S./Sjt. A. M.	15463	Massey, C.Q.M.S.(O.R.Sjt.) W. H.	15462
— Gnr. J.	15447	Massie, Engmn. E.	12782
McKenzie, Pte. R.	12759	Masters, Q.M.S. S. W.	15462
McKinney, Sjt. J.	12757	Mathews, Sjt.(A./S.M.) A. D.	15464
McKinnon, Sjt.(A./C.Q.M.S.) J.	12757	Matthews, By.Q.M.S. W. J.	12762
Mackintosh, Pte.(L./C.) D. W.	12759	May, Sjt. G. W.	12763
McKirdy, Sjt. C.	12757	Maynard, Sen.R.A. H. E.	12779
McLachlan, S./Sjt. B. G.	15464	Meech, Pte. R. J.	12759
M'Lachlan, Sjt.(A./Q.M.S.) L. B.	12765	Meehan, Pte.(A./Sjt.) B. C.	† 12763
MacLaren, Sjt.(A./C.S.M.) A	12757	Meenan, Pte. F.	12759
McLaren, Pte.(A./Sjt.) C. R.	15464	Meeres, Cpl. T. W.	12758
MacLaughlan, Pte.(corr. of surname)	12878	Meers, S.Q.M.S. D. H.	15464
McLean, Pte. J. G.	12759	Meeson, R.S.M. R. C.	12764
— Sjt. W. G.	15464	Melsom, Cpl. G. W.	12755
McLellan, Ch. Sto. S.	13748	Melton, Pte.(A./Sjt.) H.	12759
McMullan, Sjt.(A./S.Q.M.S.) F.	12134	Menzies, Cpl.(A./S.M.) W.	15464
Macnamara, S.Q.M.S.(A./S.S.M.)		Miatt, T./S.S.M. A. J.	15463
M. W.	15448	— M.A.A. W.	15430
McNaughton, Sjt. T.	15448	Michael, Pte.(A./Cpl.) G. G.	15440

---

* Group known: Queen's South Africa Medal (Cape Colony, Tugela Heights, Relief of Ladysmith, Transvaal, Laing's Nek), King's South Africa Medal (both 26537 Sapr. R.E.), 1914/15 Star (97802 Cpl. R.E.), British War and Victory Medals (97802 Spr. R.E.) and M.S.M. (143rd A.T. Coy. R.E.), for services with the British Military Mission to Turkestan (Army of the Black Sea). By the end of 1918, two anti–Bolshevik governments had been established, one in Turkestan. Only 12 M.S.M.s for this theatre.

† 7 Hussars—Turkestan.

Middlemas, Pte.(A./L./C.) A. E.	12759	Morrison, Flt. Sjt. J. F.	12527
Mildenhall, S.M. W. G.	15448	Morrissey, C.S.M. J. (corr.)	12878
Miles, S.M. C.	15462	Mortimer, Mech.S.M. J.	15460
Mill, Sjt.(A./C.S.M) R.	12757	Mortley, Q.M.S. W. G.	15462
Millard, L.A.C. A. L.	15841	Morton, Sjt. F.	12756
Miller, C.Q.M.S. G.	15464	Mouland, F. of W. Q.M.S. W. T.	15460
Milne, T./R.S.M. G.	12764	Moulgang, Cpl.(A./Sjt.) F. D.	15841
— Cpl. W.	12760	Mountague, Sjt. J. G.	12760
Milnes, R.Q.M.S. J. (deletion)	12879	Mountstephen, Pte.(A./S.M.) W. A.	15464
Milton, R.S.M. G. W.	12755	Muir, Sjt. P.	15463
Mingay, Pte.(A./S.M.) A. H.	15464	— Sjt. S. H.	15841
Mitchell, Ch. Wirter D. C.	15430	Mullen, Sjt. J. A.	15464
— S./Sjt. H.	12760	Mullins, By.S.M. J.	† 12753
— C.S.M. J. H., *D.C.M.*	12754	Munro, Gnr.(A./Fitt.S./Sjt.) A.	12754
— E.R.S./Sjt. W. S. (corr.)	12879	— Sjt. H. M.	15440
Mock, Pte.(A./Sjt.) H. J.	15463	Murcutt, Pte. T. (corr. of surname)	12878
Mockford, Pte.(A./Sjt.) G.	15448	Murphy, T./S.S.M. C.	15463
Moliver, C.P.O.Mech.3rd Gr. H.	12779	— C.S.M. J. E.	15464
Money, Sjt. F. E. (corr.)	15725	Murray, 2nd Writer H. G.	15430
Monk, Gnr. J.	12762	— W.O. Cl. 1, J. S.	15464
Monro, C.S.M. J.	12756	Murrell, T./R.S.M. H. E. (corr.)	14275
Moore, F. of W. Q.M.S. A. H.	12134	Myers, C.Q.M.S. J.	12756
— Cpl. C.	12758		
— Cpl.(A./Sjt.) G.	* 12760	Napier, Sjt. D. A.	15440
— Cpl. J. T.	❀ 14273	Napper, R.S.M. C. F. (corr.)	15726
— Sjt.(A./C.Q.M.S.) R. B.	12757	Naylor, Gnr.(A./Sjt.) W.	‡ 12763
— Sjt. R. W.	12757	Neilson, Cpl. T.	12758
— Sqdn.Cpl.Mjr. W.	15459	Nelson, Spr. P. M.	12754
— Sjt.(A./C.Q.M.S.) W. F.	15443	Nesham, Sjt.(A./C.Q.M.S.) T.	12762
Moran, Spr.(L./C.) T. F. J.	12754	New, Cpl. C.	15841
Moreton, Pte. H.	12761	Newcombe, Sjt. F. W.	12755
Morgan, Dvr. D. L.	15447	Newman, Yeo.Sigs. C. A.	13744
— Sjt.(A./S.M.) P.	15447	Newton, P.O. F. C.	§ 13749
— Cpl. T.	12758	— Sjt.(A./S.M.) P. A.	15448
— Sjt. W., *M.M.*	12757	Nice, Sjt. J. V.	12756
— Cpl.(T./S.Q.M.S.) W. A.	12760	Nichol, S./S.M.(A./R.S.M.) V.	15462
— Sjt. W. D.	15463	Nicholls, Pte.(L./C.) F. V.	12759
Morley, Sjt. A.	12762	Nichols, Q.M.S. I.M.(A./R.S.M.)W.	12764
Morris, Farr.S./Sjt. H. J.	12754	Nicholson, Pte. A.	12759
— Cpl.(A./Sjt.) T. M.	15447	— T./Mech.S.M. A. M.	12760
— Pte.(A./Sjt.) W. J.	❀ 12875	— Pte. B. (corr.)	12878
Morrish, Sjt.(A./S./Sjt.) T. J.	15443	Nicol, Pte. J.	12761
Morrison, Sjt. F. (corr.)	12878	Nicoll, C.S.M. H. (corr. of surname)	12878

---

* Group known in the Moss collection: 1914 Star trio (Pte./Cpl. A.S.C./R.A.S.C.), two
Military General Service Medals (one impressed Sqn.Q.M.S. R.A.S.C., the other
W.O.II R.A.S.C., both with the clasp Palestine), Coronation 1937, L.S. & G.C.
(Geo. V, bar Regular Army, W.O.II) and M.S.M.

† Artillery Training Depot, German S.W. Africa.

‡ R.G.A. Turkana.

§ R.N. M.S.M., see Lange *ante*. Escaped P.O.W. from Yozgod, Turkey.

Nixon, Pte.(A./Sjt.) L.	15447	Packham, Cpl.(A./Sjt.) T.	† 12762
Noble, Pte. J.	12759	— T./Sjt. W. B.	12761
— Pte.(A./Sjt.) R.	12135	Page, Dvr. G.	15448
Nolan, S.M. D.	15464	— Cpl. S. J.	12764
— S./Sjt. E. W. P.	15464	Pain, C.Q.M.S. R. G. (corr.)	14275
— C.S.M. F. J.	12756	Painting, C.S.M.(A./Q.M.S.) C.	12764
— R.S.M. P. E.	12754	Palmer, T./Sub Condr. A.	12761
— Pte.(A./Cpl.) Timothy (corr.)	12784	— Sadd.Sjt. G. A. (deletion)	15726
Noon, S./Sjt. P. H. (corr.)	15725	— S.Q.M.S. H. J.	12765
Noott, Sjt. S. A.	12762	— Sjt. J.	12762
Norman, Sjt. E. H. F.	15447	— S./Sjt. P. W.	15444
Northgraces, Cpl. D.	12758	— Q.M.S. W.	‡ 15463
Northover, Sjt.(T./C.S.M.) A. H.	12754	— Sjt. W. T.	15461
Nugent, Sjt. W.	15463	Papworth, Cpl. G.	12527
Nuttall, C.S.M. H.	15464	Park, Pte.(A./Sjt.) J.	12755
— Pte.(A./Sjt.) H. L.	12759	Parker, Pte. A. E.	12759
		— Pte.(A./L./C.) E.	12759
O'Brien, S./S.M. E. F.	15464	— Spr.(A./S./Sjt.) E. B.	§ 15447
— Sjt. E. G.	12760	— Spr.(A./2nd Cpl.) J.	12754
— S.M. J. G.	15465	— C.Q.M.S.(A./Q.M.S.) L.	12755
— Bmdr. T.	12754	Parkes, Sjt.(A./C.S.M.) W. G.	
— Sjt.(A./C.S.M.) T. J.	12764	(deletion of duplicate award)	14276
O'Connor, Pte. H. C.	12763	Parkinston, Q.M.S. W. H.	15465
O'Gorman, Q.M.S. R.	15460	Parsons, Sjt. C., *D.C.M.*	12757
O'Leary, Ch.S.B.S. T. J.	12779	— P.O. Mech. S.	12779
Oliver, Pte.(L./C.) M. F.	12759	Partridge, S.Q.M.S. E.	15449
Olver, Cpl. R. F. (corr. of surname)	14275	— Gnr. H. D.	+ 12763
— S.B.S. W. G.	12779	Parvin, M.F. of W. Q.M.S. W.	15460
O'Reilly, Pte.(A./Sjt.) M.	15463	Pascoe, C.S.M. W.	15430
Ormiston, Pte.(A./Cpl.) R.	12755	— Pte.(A./Sjt.) W.	15463
Orton, S./Sjt. M.	12763	Passingham, Whlr.Cpl. A. J.	12762
Osborne, Pte. H.	15439	Patey, Cpl. W. H.	12758
— T./S./Sjt. L.	12761	Patrick, Sjt. A.	12755
— S./Sjt. M. T.	15464	Pattenden, C.Q.M.S. W. E.	12756
O'Sullivan, S.S.M. G. W.	* 15465	Payne, Ch.S.B.S. W. H.	12779
Ovenden, Sjt. A. A.	15448	— Sjt. W. J.	12527
Owen, C.S.M. A.	15462	Pays, Flt.Sjt. J. E.	12527
Owen, M.F. of Wks. Q.M.S. R. J.	15460	Peacock, R.Q.M.S. C. W.	12764
— Cpl.(A./Sjt.) Instr. R. J.	15461	Peadon, S./Sjt. S. A.	15464
		Pearse, C.S.M. P. R.	12754

* No. 6/1158 N.Z.P.S. Later as W.O.1 N.Z.P.S. awarded New Zealand M.S.M. 9 April, 1929.
† Group known: 1914/15 Star (1084 L./Cpl. R.E.), British War and Victory Medals (Sjt. R.E.), M.S.M. (538019 R.E.), (for services in the Balkans), Greek War Cross, 1914–18 3rd class, Territorial Force Efficiency Medal (Geo. V, Sjt. R.E.).
‡ M.P.S.C. for Malta.
§ Group known: British War and Victory Medals (195210 Spr. R.E.) and M.S.M. (for services with the Army of the Black Sea). Plus several Shooting Medals for the late 1920's including the Bell Medal.
+ R.G.A. for Turkestan.

Peart, 2nd Writer R.	15430	Posse, Pte.(A./S.M.) W. H. C.	15464
Peckitt, Pte.(T./S./Sjt.) S.	12761	Potter, T./S./S.M. S. C.	12759
Pellett, Sjt. F.	15448	Pow, C.Q.M.S. C. J.	12756
Pelling, Sjt. S.	12134	Powell, Pte.(A./S./Sjt.) A. L.	12135
Penhalluriac, W.O. Cl. 1, F. J. R.	15464	— Sjt.(A./C.S.M.) E. O.	15447
Pepin, Sjt. W. F. G.	12757	— Pte.(A./Sjt.) H.	12761
Pepper, Sub Condr. A. J.	12763	— 2nd Cpl.(T./C.S.M.) S.	12754
Percy, S./S.M. T. O.	15463	— Pte. T.	12759
Perkins, S.Q.M.S. A.	15463	Powley, C.Q.M.S. H.	12754
— Cpl. J. W. H.	15443	Poynor, Sjt.(A./R.Q.M.S.) W H.	15439
Perkis, 2nd Cpl.(A./Sjt.) J. R.	12765	Pragnell, Pte.(A./Sjt.) W. H.	15460
Perry, Sjt. F.	12761	Prater, Garr. S.M. G.	15462
— Pte. J. F. (corr.)	12879	Pratt, C.Q.M.S. A. E.	12755
— Sjt. J. H.	12757	Preece, C.Q.M.S.(A./C.S.M.) W. C.	12763
Peters, Armr.S./Sjt. H. J.	12134	Prentice, Pte. T.	15449
Pettit, S.M. A.	15463	Press, Sjt. T. R.	15461
Pettitt, S.M.(W.O. I) D. J.	15430	Preston, Pte.(A./Sjt.) H. J.	12761
Petty, Sjt. A. G.	15447	— W.O. Cl. 1, Supt. Clk. W. H.	15462
Phelps, Pte.(A./R.S.M.) H.	12764	Price, Pte.(A./Sjt.) F.	12761
— Pte.(T./S./Sjt.) H. H.	12761	— Sjt. H.	15440
Phillips, Q.M.S. G. W.	15461	— Pte.(A./L./C.) J. C.	15462
— Sjt. J.	12757	— Sjt. P.	12757
— R.Q.M.S. J. E.	12756	— S./Smith(A./Farr.Sjt.) W.	15463
Philliskirk, Pte.(A./Cpl.) T. G.	* ❀ 15724	— C.S.M. W.	15465
Pickering, L.A.C. A. J.	12527	— S.M. W. E.	12762
Pickston, Pte.(A./Sjt.) J. (corr.)	12878	Priestley, Cpl. J.	12758
Pierce, Pte.(A./Cpl.) C. E.	12759	Prime, Q.M.S. H.	15460
Piggott, C.Q.M.S. E.	12756	Proom, C.S.M. C.	12756
Pike, Pte.(A./Sjt.) P. J.	12764	Prudhoe, Cpl. F.	12758
Pile, Sjt. A. T.	12761	Prudhom, Sjt. T. (corr. of surname)	12879
Pilgrim, C.S.M. F.	12765	Pryer, S.M. C., *M.C.*, *M.M.*	† 15461
— Sjt. F. C.	12757	Pullen, Cpl.(A./C.Q.M.S.) C. S.	
Pimm, Pte.(A./Cpl.) J.	12763	(deletion)	15726
Pinhorne, C.Q.M.S. W.	12756	— A./C. I. R. J.	15841
Pit, C.S.M.(A./S.M.) C.	15443	Purcell, Q.M.S. P.	15462
Pitts, S./Sjt. J. S.	12761	Pursey, Sjt. H. J.	15447
Plowman, Pte.(A./S.S.M.) R. L.	12761	Purvis, Farr./Sjt. W.	12762
Pointer, T./Sjt. A. F.	12761		
Pollard, Pte. A. T.	15440	Quantrell, Sjt. W. H. W.	15841
Pollitt, Sjt.(A./C.Q.M.S.) H.	12757	Quick, T./Sjt. J.	12761
Poole, Cpl.(A./C.Q.M.S.) H. A.	12134		
— Sjt. J.	12527	Radband, Cpl.(A./W.O. Cl.1) G.	15463
Pope, Pte.(A./S.Q.M.S.) G. F. (corr.)	15726	Radd, S./Sjt. E.	15463
Porteous, Q.M.S. E. G.	15461	Radnell, Mech.S./Sjt.(T./Mech.S.M.)	
— W.O. Cl. 1, J. (deletion)	12879	S. G. (corr. of amendment)	12879
Porter, Cpl.(A./R.S.M.) B.	15439	Rae, Pte.(A./Cpl.) T. H.	15444
— C.S.M. R.	12755	Raeside, Sjt. J.	12760
— Act. P.O. R.	15430	Rafter, Cpl. M. E. (corr.)	12878

---

*   37 (Chinese) Coy., Labour Corps.
†   Norfolk Regt. M.C. *L.G.* 20 October, 1916.

Railton, R.Q.M.S. .D.	12756	Reid, Sjt. E.	12762
Ramsey, S./Sub Condr. J. B. (corr. of surname)	12879	— C.Q.M.S. F. C.	12755
Ranson, T./S./S.M. T. H. (corr. of surname)	14275	— Cpl. T.	15444
		— Sjt. W. G.	12757
Rapson, Skpr. W.	* 12781	Relf, Pte.(T./C.S.M.) A. E.	12761
Raw, By.S.M. P. E.	† 12764	Rennie, Q.M.S. T.	15447
Ray, R.S.M. R. K.	12764	Rewhorn, T./Sub Condr. T.	15448
Read, Sjt. B.	15462	Reynolds, Pte.(T./Sjt.) G. N.	14670
Reade, C.S.M. C.	15439	— T./S./Sjt. H.	12761
Reardon, Sjt. T. L. (corr.)	15726	— Cpl.(L./Sjt.) J.	12758
Reay, S./Sjt. G. E.	15448	Richards, Sjt.(A./S./Sjt.) A.	✿ 12875
— Pte.(A./Sjt.) J. M.	12765	— C.Q.M.S. F.	12759
Redfern, C.P.O. W. G.	12781	— Cpl. M.	15461
Reed, Cpl. A. H.	15724	— Sjt.(A./C.S.M.) N. C.	15439
— Sjt. J.	‡ 12756	Richardson, Sjt.(A./C.S.M.) A.	15463
Rees, C.S.M. D.	12756	— Cpl. F. W.	12758
— Cpl. P. C. (corr.)	14275	— Cpl.(A./Sjt.) R.	12764
Reeve, 2nd Cpl. W. E.	15439	— S.M. W. (corr. of amendment)	14275
Reeves, T./Sub Condr. G. L.	12761	Richings, Cpl. F. W.	12134
Reid, Sub Condr. D.	15443	Ricketts, Q.M.S. H. G.	§ 15462
		Riley, O.P.I. T. B.	12738

* New Zealand Naval Auxiliary Service, Minesweeping June—December, 1918.

† Group in McInnes collection: British War Medal (5237 W.O.II R.A.), Defence and War Medals, M.S.M. (337549 R.G.A.), Territorial Force Efficiency Medal (Geo. V. 337549 S.Mjr. Durham R.G.A.) (awarded in May 1917) and Special Constabulary Medal (Geo. V, Coinage Head, Percy E Raw). W.O. 329 confirms the award of the British War Medal only, for services in U.K. during the German Bombardment of the Town of Hartlepools on Wednesday 16 December, 1914. The other five medals were also earned for service in the United Kingdom—a very unusual group. On the 15th December, S.M. Raw is noted as detailing the guard to mount the various posts and as B.S.M. would have been very active during the bombardment by three German Capital ships—*Seydlitz, Blücher* and *Möltke*. All three ships were damaged by British fire, their casualties were 80 killed and about 200 wounded. Seven British seamen and eight soldiers were killed and a further 13 seamen and 11 soldiers were wounded. Approximately 120 civilians were killed and perhaps 300 were wounded. Lt. Col. Robson was made a Companion of the D.S.O. and Sgt. T Douthwaite was awarded a D.C.M. The first two M.M.s awarded on 4 April 1916 went to the two gun captains, Sgt. Mallin and Bombr. Hope. Undoubtably, Raw's service would have helped earn this M.S.M.

‡ Group known: 1914/15 Star trio (Warwicks. Yeo.) and M.S.M. (100th M.G.C.). 100th M.G.C. formed in August 1918 from the Warwicks. and South Notts. Yeomanry. They went into action early in September in France. The Regimental History includes details of an action at Beaurevoir:— 'During the night Sergt. J. Reed, who had been gassed and was left behind in a pill-box as not fit to march, made good use of the time by helping some American machine gunners, who were without an officer, to locate themselves and come into action. The gallant Sergeant, in spite of his unwillingness to succumb, had to be ordered to hospital next morning.' He had served in Gallipoli, Egypt and Palestine before France.

§ R.A.S.C., M.S.M. and L.S. & G.C. presented by F.M. Lord Plumer, Governor of Malta, on the Island on 6 April, 1920.

Riley, Pte.(A./L./Sjt) W.	12765	Rudolff, Gnr.(A./Sjt.) G.	12134
Roadnight, Cpl.(A./Sjt.) A. W.	15448	Russell, T./S.M. F.	12764
Roberts, Sjt.(A./S./Sjt.) D. C.	15440	— Pte.(A./Sjt.) N. H.	15463
— Sjt. E.	12755	Rutland, Supt. Clk. F. E.	12755
— Spr. J. T.	* ※ 14273		
— Sjt. T.	12757	Sackville, Cpl.(A./Q.M.S.) G. H.	15463
— Pte. W.	12759	Sales, R.Q.M.S. W. J.	12756
Robertshaw, Pte.(A./Sjt.) H. F.	15461	Salisbury, C.Q.M.S.(O.R.Sjt.) W. E.	15461
Robey, Gnr.(A./Bombr.) C. A. (corr.)	15725	Salmon, C.Q.M.S. H.	12756
Robinson, Cpl. A.	12758	— S./Sjt. H. C. D.	15465
— Pte.(A./C.Q.M.S.) B. D.	12759	Salsedo, Pte. J. J.	12755
— Pte. G. A.	12759	Salt, Sjt.(A./S.Q.M.S.) C. T.	12755
— Sjt.(T./C.Q.M.S.) H.	12762	Samsome, Pte.(A./Cpl.) G.	12759
— Sjt. R. F.	15447	Sanders, F. of W. Q.M.S. H. T.	15460
— Cpl. S.	12762	Satherly, T./R.S.M. C. W.	12754
Robson, Pte.(A./C.S.M. I.M.) J. G.	15461	Saunders, Pte.(A./C.S.M.) J. J.	15462
— Sjt. W.	12757	Sayer, Armr.S./Sjt. J. A.	15448
Roddis, Pte.(A./Sjt.) A. G.	12761	Scaife, Sjt. J.	12757
Rodnight, Sjt. W. C.	12764	Scattergood, P.O. G.	13747
Roebuck, Cpl. A.	12758	Schacht, Pte. W. F.	12759
Rogers, Pte.(T./Sjt.) E. E.	12761	Schofield, Farr.Sjt. H.	15447
— C.S.M. S. J.	12756	Schuchard, C.	15443
— C.S.M. W.	12755	Scobie, Sjt. H. E.	12757
Rolfe, Sjt.(A./S.S.M.) F. H.	15443	Scott, R.S.M. A. H.	12756
Rolt, P.O. Mech. H. L.	12779	— T./Supt.Clk. C. J. A.	12754
Roney, B.S.M. H. N.	15447	— T./Armt.S.M. E. O.	12761
Rood, Cpl. J. A. (corr.)	12879	— C.S.M. J. (deletion)	12879
Rose, S./Sjt. D. E. L.	15465	— Sjt.(A./C.S.M.) J.	12757
— Sjt. J.	12756	— Sjt. L. A.	15431
— By.S.M. J. W.	12754	— Cpl. L. T.	12758
— T./Sjt. L.	12761	— Pte. R.	12765
— Cpl. W. A.	12758	— Sjt. W.	12757
Ross, Pte.(A./S.M.) H. G.	15464	Seall, Cpl. W. A.	12134
— Pte.(L./C.) J.	15448	Searle, Sjt.(A./C.Q.M.S.) G.	12764
— Q.M.S.(A./S.M.) W.	14273	Seddon, Pte.(A./L./C.) H.	12759
Rossall, Sjt. J.	15440	Sedgwick, Cpl.(A./Sjt.) C. W. H. B.	12765
Rossine, Sjt. A.	12756	Sellens, Eng.Clk.Spr.(A./Sjt.) P.	15439
Roughley, Sjt.(A./S./Sjt.) J.	15463	Sellers, T./S.M.(I.G.) G.	15460
Rountree, S./S.M. E. G.	15465	— Cpl. J.	12758
Rouse, B.Q.M.S. H.	15447	Seton, S.B.A. C. C. C.	15431
Routledge, Col.Sjt.(A./C.Q.M.S.) F.		Sevier, Sjt. T. J., *M.M.*	12134
(deletion)	15726	Seward, Cpl. S. F.	12754
Rowe, S./Sjt. J. E. (corr.)	12819	Sewell, Pte.(A./Sjt.) E.	† 12765
Rowett, Sjt. R. H.	12757	Seyfang, Cpl.(A./S.Q.M.S.) R. A.	15463
Rowland, Pte.(A./Sjt.) J.	15447	Seymour, Spr. A. (corr. of surname)	15726
Rowley, Spr.(L./C.) C. H. R.	12134	— Sjt. W.	15460
Roy, S./Sjt.(A./Q.M.S.) E. G.	15464	Shaftoe, Shipwt. 3rd Cl. H. L.	15431

---

* R.E. For Gallantry with the Army of the Black Sea.

† Group known: Tibet Medal 1903–4 (clasp Gyantse), 1914/15 Star trio and M.S.M. (all Royal Fusiliers). Group sold by Baldwin 1939, £3–17–6.

Shail, S./S.Maj. G.	12763	Slater, P.O. Mech. D. D.		12779
Shales, Q.M.S. E. J.	12754	Slaughter, Cpl.(A./R.Q.M.S.) H.		12764
Shanks, Pte.(A./Sjt.) W.	12763	Sleath, Sjt. J. H.		12757
Sharp, S./Sjt. F.	12762	Small, Spr. T. H.		12754
Shaw, Q.M.S.(A./S.M.) A. B.	15440	Smallwood, Sjt. A.		15460
— Sjt. G.	12763	Smeaton, C.S.M. J.		12756
Shears, Pte.(A./S.Q.M.S.) H. P.	15464	Smeed, sjt.(A./C.S.M.) J. W.		15463
Sheed, Sjt. F.	15463	Smith, Gnr. A. E.		15447
Sheldon, Pte. C.	✤ 12875	— Spr.(A./Sjt.) A. W.		12754
— M.A.A. F.	15430	— T./Sub Condr. E. C.		15440
Shepherd, C.S.M.(A./R.S.M.) D. H.		— Cpl. E. W.		15460
(deletion)	12879	— O.R.Sjt. H.		15461
— Sjt. F. H.	15462	— P.O.(C.) H. C.		12779
— Cpl.(A./Sjt.) G. F.	12756	— S./Sjt.(A./S.S.M.) J.		15464
Sheppard, Cpl.(A./Sjt.) A. E.	15439	— T./R.S.M. J.		12764
Sherrard, S./Sjt. T. J.	15465	— Cpl. J.		12762
Sherwood, Pte.(A./Sjt.) S. V.	12759	— Cpl.(A./C.S.M.) J. A.		12134
Shields, P.O. E. R.	13747	— A./R.S.M. J. B.		15462
— Sjt.(A./C.S.M.) S. R.	15443	— Sjt. J. D.		12757
Shinn, S.Q.M.S.(A./S.S.M.) A. J.	15448	— Q.M.S. J. E.		15461
Shipton, Pte.(A./L./Sjt.) W. J.	15463	— C.S.M. J. W.		12756
Short, Cpl.(A./S.Q.M.S.) C. E.	15440	— Pte. J. W. B.		12759
Shroff, Cpl.(A./Sjt.A,C) V.	12763	— S./Sjt. L. A.		15448
Shuttle, C.S.M.Instr. A. R. (deletion)	15726	— Pte. R. E.		15448
Siddle, Cpl. T.	12758	— Cpl. R. H.		12758
Sidey, Pte. J.	12765	— T./Sjt. W.		12761
Sidmouth, T./S./Sjt. G. J.	15463	— C.Q.M.S. W. A.		12756
Simmons, Q.M.S. F. H.	12762	— C.E.R.A. W. C. R.		13748
Simpson, Sjt. J.	13439	— Ch. Writer W. F.		15430
— Sjt.(A./C.S.M.) W.	12757	— Pte.(A./C.Q.M.S.) W. F. J.		15439
— Whlr.S./Sjt. W. E.	12760	— W.O. Cl. 1, Supt. Clk. W. H.		15461
Sinclair, Pte. J.	12759	— Dvr.(A./C.Q.M.S.) W. R.		15463
— Sjt. W.	12764	Smitten, Pte.(A./Cpl.) A. E. (corr. of		
Singleton,Cpl.(A./Sjt.) J. F.	12762	amendment)		12879
Sinott, T./S./Sjt. M.	12761	Smyth, Sjt. W. H.		15439
Sisley, Sub Condr. J. L.	15443	Snape, Q.M.S. W.O. II, W. (deletion)		13749
Sivorn, Pte.(L./C.) E.	12763	Snell, Whrl.(T./Whlr.S./Sjt.) H. W.		12760
— C.Q.M.S. T. E.	12756	Snellgrove, Pte. L.		12780
Skene, B.S.M.(A./S.M.) J. L.	15447	Snowball, Cpl. H.		12758
Skilbeck, C.S.M. A.	12755	Snowden, Sjt. G. R.		12756
Skingsley, P.O. G.	13747	Soden, T./S.M. T. (corr.)		12878
Skinner, Pte.(A./Cpl.) F.	15462	Southern, Pte.(A./Sjt.) A. J.		12765
— Sjt.(A./B.Q.M.S.) R.	15465	— Pte. J. H.	* ✤	12875
— B.S.M. W., *M.M.*	15443	Spargo, Sjt. C. A. G.		12764
— Sub Condr. W.	12763	Sparks, Cpl.(A./Sjt.) W.		15439
Skipper, Cpl. C. W.	12758	Speak, Sen.R.A. W. E.		12779
Slade, Pte.(A./S.M.) W.	15464	Spinney, Sjt. F. (corr. of surname)		12878
Slann, Cpl. W. W.	12758	Spiteri, C.Q.M.S.(A./R.S.M.) C.	†	12763

* 39 P.O.W. Coy. Labour Corps.
† Royal Malta Militia Regt, for the Balkans.

Spragg, S./S.M. A. W.	15465	Taylor, Pte.(A./Sjt.) W.	15461
Squibb, Clr.Sjt. A. G.	15431	— Sjt. W. F.	12762
Squire, Pte. G.	12759	Tealby, T./S./Sjt. H. A.	12761
Squires, Pte.(A./C.Q.M.S.) D. P.		— Pte.(A./Sjt.) W. J.	15464
(corr. of surname)	14275	Tennant, Pte. S. E. (corr.)	12878
Standring, Sjt. C. (corr. of surname)	14275	Theobald, Pte.(A./Sjt.) F.	12135
Stares, Ch.Yeo.Sigs. Ernest John		Theobalds, Cpl.(A./S.M) E. Y.	15464
(corr.)	15433	Thewlis, E.R./W.O. Cl. 1 O. A.	
Stark, Sjt.(A./C.S.M.) J. D.	15447	(corr.)	14275
— Pte.(A./L./C.) J. H.	15440	Thomas, Sjt. E. (corr.)	12878
Stearn, Sjt.(A./C.S.M.) E. W.	15443	— Dvr.(A./Sjt.) E.	* 12135
Steed, Sjt. B. L. (deletion)	15726	— Spr.(L./C.) E. J.	12763
Steeley, Cpl.(A./S./Sjt.) A.	15463	— Sjt. I. C.	12754
Steer, Sjt. G.	15460	— Supt. Clk. J. H.	15463
Stephenson, C.I.(A./S.S.M.) J. A.	15463	— W.O. Cl. II, Supt.Clk.(A./	
— Cpl. P.	12763	W.O. Cl. I) W.	15461
Stevens, C.Q.M.S. B. B.	12757	Thompson, 2nd Cpl.(A./Cpl.) C. J.	
Stewart, Sjt. A. (R. Scots)	12134	(deletion and D.C.M.	
— Sjt. A. (Aust. F.)	15464	substituted)	14276
— Cpl.(A./S./Sjt.) C.	12765	— Spr.(L./C.) H.	12754
— Sjt. D.	15449	— C.S.M.(I.M.) R.	15462
— S./Sjt. J. P.	15464	— Pte. W. T.	12765
— Sjt.(A./S.M.) T.	15464	Thomson, Sjt. G. H.	15464
Stickland, Sjt.(A./S.M.) W. W.	12755	Thorman, Cpl. L. P.	12761
Stobart, C.P.O. A. E.	15430	Thorn, Cpl.(T./Sjt.) F.	12760
Storey, 1st Cl.Mastr.Gnr. W. H.	15460	Thwaites, S.M. A. P.	15464
Stratford, C.Q.M.S. A. J.	12754	Tickle, Sjt. W.	15841
Street, Pte. C.	12761	Tickner, P.O. H.	13747
— Sjt. F. E.	15463	Tierney, Pte. J.	12759
Stribbling, C.S.M.(A./S.M.) C. F.	15462	Tilley, Sjt. F.	15841
Strickland, Bombr. G. J.	12134	Tippins, Pte.(L./C.) W. (corr. of	
Stroud, By.S.M. W. H.	12753	surname)	14275
Sturdy, Sjt. W.	12755	Titcombe, P.O. F. G.	15431
Sussex, Pte.(A./Sjt.) W.	15447	Tod, Q.M.S. G.	15464
Sutton, Sjt. R. T.	12763	Todd, Armr.S./Sjt.(A./	
Swindley, Pte.(A./Q.M.S.) R. E.	15464	Armr.Q.M.S.) D.	12761
Syrett, Sjt. F. C. (corr. of surname)	14275	Tomey, C.S.M. H.	❀ 12875
		Tomsett, Ch. Shipwt. 2nd Cl. C. L.	15431
Tait, Pte. J.	15443	Tonkin, Pte.(A./S.Q.M.S.) R. W.	12765
Tappere, Sjt. A. F. (corr.)	14275	Toogood, Flt.Sjt. G. H.	12527
Taylor, Fitt.S./Sjt. A.	12754	Tosdevine, Sjt. A. S. V.	15447
— Sjt.(A.C.) A. H.	15460	Towers, Sjt.(A./By.Q.M.S.) E. C.	12753
— S./S.M. C.	12134	Townley, C.S.M. E. O.	12764
— Bombr. E. E.	15460		

---

* R.A.S.C. Volunteering in October 1914, he was retained on important duties at home stations until 1917, when he was drafted to Russia. He then saw much severe fighting, and was awarded the Meritorious Service Medal for conspicuous bravery in carrying rations to the forward areas under heavy shell-fire. He was demobilised in August, 1919, and also held the General Service and Victory Medals. 31, Windsor Street, Rochdale Road, Manchester.

Townsend, Sjt. J. F. (corr. of surname)	14275	Wale, Gnr.(L./Bombr.) A. E.	12754
Toye, C.S.M. D. A. W.	15465	Walker, Cpl.(A./S.S.M.) D. J.	15460
Tracy, C.P.O. Mech. 3rd Gr. A. W. H.	12779	— 2nd Cpl. J.	15440
		Walker, A.O.H. 2, J. H.	12527
Trimnell, C.Q.M.S. A. F.	15444	Walkley, S./Sjt. T. (corr.)	14275
Trott, C.Q.M.S. W. J. (corr.)	15726	Wall, Pte.(A./L./C.) A. J.	* 12763
Trotter, Pte.(A./Sjt.) W. M.	15449	— C.S.M. J. J.	15461
Trow, Pte.(L./C.) J. E. (corr.)	12726	Wallace, B.Q.M.S. T. (corr. of name)	15726
Trussler, Pte. J. J. (corr. of surname)	12879	Walsh, C.Q.M.S. A. A. (deletion)	15726
		Walters, Pte.(A./Cpl.) A.	12759
Tudor, C.S.M. L. A.	12755	— Dvr. E. J.	15444
Turnbull, S.B.S. E. J.	12779	Waltisbuhl, C.Q.M.S. E. G. (corr. of surname)	14275
Turner, Sjt. W. J.	12762	Walton, S.S.M. F. H. (deletion of award ann. 23 Feb. 1919)	14276
Underwood, C.P.O. 3rd Gr. C.	12779	Wang Yu Bhan	† ✿ 14273
Unsworth, Cpl.(A./Sjt.) W. W.	12135	Ward, Pte. A. E.	12763
Uren, S.Q.M.S. R. N.	15465	— C.S.M.(A./R.S.M.) C. H. G.	12764
		Wareham, Pte. H.	15447
Van Hoof, C.Q.M.S. A. C.	15465	Waring, Spr.(A./L./C.) F. D.	15447
Vassie, Pte.(A./Sjt.) D.	15462	Warr, T./S.M. E.	‡ 15460
Venart, Supt. Clk. J. H.	15460	Warren, C.S.M. J. Y.	15465
Veneear, Sqdn.S.M. J. E.	15439	Wathen, Pte.(A./Sjt.) W. (corr. of surname)	15726
Venn, Sjt.(A./Q.M.S.) E.	12754		
Virgo, Pte.(A./Cpl.) S. R.	12759	Watkiss, Supt. Clk. (W.O. I) H. M. (corr. of surname)	12784
Vogan, Cpl.(A./Sjt.) J.	12134		
		Watson, 1st Writer G. S.	15430
Waddington, Sjt. R. A. (corr.)	12878	— Sjt. J. E.	15439
Wade, Cpl.(A./Sjt.) J.	12134	Webb, C.P.O. A. E.	12782
Wadham, C.Q.M.S. A. H. (deletion of duplicate award)	14276	— S.S.M. F. W.	15465
		— Spr. G. H.	✿ 15724
Wakeford, Sjt. C. D.	12754	— C.S.M. W.	12762
Wakeham, S./Sjt. F.	12754	Webber, S.B.S. V. A. W.	§ 15431
Wakeling, Pte.(A./S.M.) A. A.	15464		

---

* R.A.S.C. for Turkestan.

† Labourer 59 (Chinese) Coy., Labour Corps, France.

‡ Group known: Queen's South Africa Medal (Defence of Ladysmith, Orange Free State, Laing's Nek, Belfast, 3830 Cpl. A. WEBB 19 Hussars), King's South Africa Medal (South Africa 1901, South Africa 1902 3830 A. WEBB Sgt. 19H.), L.S. & G.C. (Edw. VII, 3830 Sq.S.M. I. of M. E. WARR 19 Hussars) and M.S.M. (W. Som. Yeo.). L.S. & G.C. 1911. They would appear to be to one man.

§ Group known: 1914/15 Star trio (S.B.S. R.N.), R.N. M.S.M. (Mercantile Marine Reserve, Hospital Barge 245, Dvina River) and R.N.A.S.B.R. L.S. & G.C. (Geo. V, awarded August 1922). Born September 1886. Joined Chichester Div., S.J.A.B. February 1906. In 1909 as a Naval Reservist joined R.N.A.S.B.R. Mobilised 1 August 1914 on H.M.S. *Theseus*. In December 1914 to Armed Merchant Cruiser *'Oropesa,'* re-named *'Champagne'* and loaned to French Navy. Discharged from her in March 1916, Served on board H.M.S. *Albion* July 1916 to November 1918. Transferred to Hospital Ship *'Kalyan'* for service in North Russia. Presented with the M.S.M. by the King, 14 August 1920. Citation in ADM 137/1704 '... devising

Webster, Pte.(A./Sjt.) J. W.	* 15449	Wilkins, Pte.(A./Sub Condr.) A. J.	15448
Weekes, Pte. H.	† 12763	Wilkinson, Sjt. A. E.	15463
Weeks, Pte. T. C.	15447	Williams, C.Q.M.S. G.	15461
Welham, Pte.(A./Sjt.) J. L.	15462	— Sjt.(A./C.S.M.) H. P.	15443
Weller, B.S.M. H. J.	14273	— S./Sjt.(A./Sub Condr) W. S.	15449
West, C.Q.M.S. H.	12755	Willson, L./C. H. C. (corr.)	12879
— C.S.M.Instr.(A./S.M. Instr.) J.	15460	Wills, 1st Writer D.	15430
Westbrook, C.S.M.(A./Q.M.S.) H.	12764	Wilmington, R.S.M. C.	12764
Westlake, Pte. W. J.	15440	Wilmott, C.Q.M.S. F. P. (corr.)	15726
Wetherill, L./Sjt. G. (corr. of		Wilson, Sjt.(A./C.S.M.) A.	15439
surname)	12879	— Sjt.(T./S.M.)(A.C.) G. B. (deletion)	12879
Wheatley, S.M. J. W.	15462	Wilson, Sjt. L. J. (corr.)	15726
Wheeler, Cpl. C.	12754	— R.S.M. T. H.	+ 12764
— C.Q.M.S. G. C. (corr.)	15726	— Cpl.(A./C.S.M.) W. H.	15447
Whelton, Cpl.(A./S.S.M.) T.	15448	Wiltshire, C.S.M.(A./Q.M.S.) A. E.	15460
Whimpey, Pte.(A./Sjt.) C. F. R.		Winch, C.S.M. H. J.	12755
(corr.)	15726	Winchester, Sjt. C. H.	15841
Whitall, Pte. F. H. (corr.)	14275	Withington, P.O. W.	◊ 15431
White, W.O. Cl. 1, A. J. H.	15464	Witney, Q.M.S. L. H.	12753
— S.Q.M.S. W. J.	15465	Wood, R.S.M. E. C.	15465
Whitehead, Pte. A.	✿ 14273	— Sjt. H.	12763
Whitfield, Pte.(A./S.M.) F.	15464	— S.M. H. F.	15460
Whiting, Cpl. A. G.	12754	— C.S.M. J. P.	15447
Whitlock, Pte.(A./S./Sjt.) G. H.	12765	Woodburn, C.Q.M.S. L. (deletion)	15726
Whitmore, Sjt.(A./S.M.) R.	15464	Woods, Sjt. J.	15462
Wicks, B.Q.M.S. W. (corr.)	15726	Wookey, Spr.(L./C.) A. T. (corr.)	15726
Wickson, Gnr. J.	‡ 12763	Woolley, Sjt. A. H. T.	15464
Wiebkin, Expl.Q.M.S.(A./Mstr Gnr.)		Woolnough, Pte.(A./C.Q.M.S.) S. R.	12755
F. A.	15460	Worley, Sjt.(A./C.S.M. I.M.) B. W.	12764
Wiffen, Pte.(A./C.Q.M.S.) W. G.	§ 15462	Worster, Pte.(L./C.) C. W.	12763
Wigley, Sjt. F. J.	12762	Worthington, C.Q.M.S.(A./	
Wilcox, Pte.(L./C.) F. O.	15440	R.S.M.) F.	15462
Wild, Cpl. H.	15440	Wright, Pte.(A./S./Sjt.) D. C.	15464

and carrying out improvements to the method employed in slinging cots for serious cases. His work was excellent regardless of personal danger in charge of stretcher parties recovering wounded from on board H.M.S. *Glowworm* after the recent explosion ...' *'Glowworm'* was a river gunboat with a crew of about 50, wrecked by the explosion of Army Barge NT 326 *Edinburgh* in the early hours of 26 August 1919. Some 26 men from the *'Glowworm'* were either killed, missing or died of wounds, and some 15 were injured. (See *Medal News*, March 1992.

* Pair known: British War Medal (G 25084 A–Sgt. R. West Kents, M.I.D. oakleaf) and M.S.M. (2/R. West Kent R.). From Hammersmith; twice M.I.D., both under Sea Transport Indian Army headings, 27 August 1918 and 21 February 1919.

† Worcs., for Turkestan.

‡ R.F.A., for Turkestan.

§ 25/Bn. Training Reserve. Single M.S.M. known. Only 5 to the unit, the other four being for gallantry.

+ Awarded M.S.M. Annuity A.O. 141/1949. (Royal Highlanders).

◊ 'One of the casualties on the *'Glowworm,'* (see Webber, *ante*). Wounded in both arms, he greatly assisted in anchoring the ship and rallying the survivors.'

Wright, S.M. E. L. (corr.)	14275	Young, Ch. M. Mech. J.	‡ 15841
— Gnr. S. G.	12753	— Sjt. L. A.	15461
Wroe, Pte.(A./W.O. Cl. I Supt. Clk.)		— Pte. R.	15443
W. G.	* 15462		
Yaxley, T./Sjt. W. J.	† ✿ 15724	*Meritorious Service Medal, Bar:*	
Young, R.Q.M.S. A. J.	12755		
— Condr. F. W.	12762	Coxon, Cpl. J., M.S.M.	§ ✿ 12875

———◇◇◇———

---

* Depot/K.R.R.C. Entitled to Queen's South Africa Medal.
† 60 (Chinese) Coy., Labour Corps.
‡ R.A.F. M.S.M. (North Russia). No. 461 R.F.C., enlisted 26 November, 1912. Also entitled to 1914 Star trio. In Syren Force in 1919.
§ Group known: 1914/15 Star and British War Medal (GS 9851 Pte. 5 D.G.), Victory Medal (erased) and M.S.M. & Bar (P 10969 Mily. Mounted Police). Medal 18 January 1919 'For valuable services in France & Flanders.' The bar, for gallantry, is also for France & Flanders. 7 bars only were awarded.

Abram, Pte.(A./L./Sjt.) F.		946	Bates, Pte.(A./Cpl.) J.		161
Aitken, Cpl.(T./Sjt.) A.		2740	Batt, Pte.(L./C.) W.	+	1226
Allenby, Pte. E.		1227	Beale, Sjt. J. R.		160
Alleway, Pte.(A./S.Q.M.S.) H. J.	*	946	Beasley, C.S.M. E.		945
Allford, S.M. T. R.		162	Beck, S./Sjt. C. F. (corr.)		1785
Andrews, Sjt. C.		684	Bell, Pte. W.		946
— S.H. M.		1227	— Pte. W. J.		1226
— Pte. T.	†	1226	Bennett, P.O. W. R.		2863
Annells, C.S.M. T.		946	Benson, 2nd Cpl. E. A.		2740
Anthony, Pte.(A./Sjt.) H. M.	‡ ✿	3517	Bentley, Cpl.(A./Sjt.) L.		162
Ashton, Pte.(T./Cpl.) J.		946	Bishop, Pte.(L./C.) J. W.		1226
Aston, Sjt. J. M.		163	— Gnr. S.		1226
Austin, Pte. H.		1226	Blay, Sjt. J. S. (corr.)		1786
Awford, Cpl. A. V.		163	Bleakman, Ldg. Sea. E. H.		2863
			Boardman, Cpl. W.	+	1226
Babister, Sjt. W. J.		1225	— Sjt.(A./R.S.M.) W. C.		163
Baddams, Cpl. W.		162	Boodrie, Asst.Surg.(4th Cl.) E. R. B.		1803
Baker, Sjt. F. G.	§	684	Book, Pte. T. E.		1226
Balcombe, Dvr. E.		161	Boon, C.Q.M.S. W., *M.M.*		1227
Bance, C.Q.M.S. G. E., *M.M.*		163	Borley, T./Sub Condr. G. W.	◊	946
Bangs, S./Sjt. F.		1803	Boyce, Sjt. A. H.		1226
Barber, Pte.(A./Sjt.) A. H.		163	Boydell, Sjt. H. N.		162
Barham, C.P.O. F. C.		2863	Boves, Sjt. W.	¶	684
Barling, Shipwt. 1st Cl. F. W.		2863	Bozie, Pte.(A./Cpl.) A. G.		163
Barrett, Bombr. F.		162	Bracher, C.Q.M.S. J. H.		945
Bartram, S./S.M. J.		161	Bradley, C.S.M. P.		162
Bateman, Pte. W.		1226	Bramley, Pte. J.		1226

* R.A.O.C. For Siberia.
† Group sold by Baldwin, 1965, for £7: 1914 Star trio (1/R. Lancs. Regt.), Defence and War Medals, M.S.M. (A.O. 193/1919 P.O.W.), Territorial Efficiency Medal (Geo. VI, R. Sigs.). Thomas Andrews, from Willesden, London, No. 10733, enlisted on 12 September, 1912 and was discharged on 11 October, 1919 as a result of wounds. To France 23 August 1914 and reported missing on 26th at Le Câteau. The Bn. had over 400 casualties on that day.
‡ R.A.S.C. For Gallantry in Ireland. Also in A.O.114.1920. He came from the Isle of Wight.
§ Group known: British War and Victory Medals (M.I.D. oakleaf, S./Sgt. I.U.L.), General Service Medal (South Persia), 1939/45 and Burma Stars, War Medal, Indian War Service Medal, Delhi Durbar 1911, Jubilee 1935, Coronation 1937, L.S. & G.C. (Geo. V, Sgt. I.C.C.), M.S.M. (C. of M.S.C.). M.S.M. for South Persia.
+ See Bristow *infra.*
◊ R.A.O.C. For Siberia.
¶ Yorks. Regt. Bushire.

Brashaw, Cpl.(A./Sjt.) F. J.	* 1226	Burgess, Pte. H. G.	§	1227
Brassey, Sjt. W.	945	Burt, Yeo. Sigs. J. S. K.		948
Brazear, Pte. W.	1227	Burton, Ch. Motor Mech. J.		949
Brees, Vict.C.P.O. A. A.	2861	Butler, Pte.(A./Sjt.) R. G.		162
Brickel, Ch. Yeo. Sigs. A. P.	2863	Byng, Pte. N. C.	+	1227
Briggs, Bombr. H. O.	160			
Bristow, Pte. W.	† 1226	Canning, Sjt. C. F.		946
Brooks, T./Sub Condr. G. H.	‡ 946	Carter, C.S.M. A. V.	◊	945
Broomfield, Offrs. Ch. Std. C.	2863	— Sjt. E. F.	¶	2740
Brown, Sjt. A. G.	946	— Sjt. W. (corr.)		1785
— Pte. J.	2861	Cash, Yeo. Sigs. G. R.		2863
— Pte. S.	163	— Pte. J. R.		1227
Browne, Cpl. J. J.	946	Cave, Sto. P.O. O. H.		2863
Buck, C.Q.M.S. G. H. B.	163	Chaffe, Pte. A. H.		2864
Budden, Pte.(A./Sjt.) S.	162	Challis, C.S.M. F. W.		163
Bumstead, R.S.N. R.	1227	Chaney, S.M. (now Capt.) J. S.		1223
Bunting, Act. Sto. P.O. H. J.	2863	Charter, Pte. E.		1226
— Pte.(A./S.S.M.) J.	162	Chatfield, Pte. R.		1226
Burchell, Cpl. E. H. (corr.)	1785	Checketts, Pte. H. J. F.		1226
Burden, Sjt.(A./C.Q.M.S.) C. T.	946	Chold, Col. Sjt. R. H.		946

---

* See Bristow *infra*.

† *Bristow*. 11155 4/R. Fus., was one of 10 M.S.M. recipients who received the medal for devotion to duty when prisoners of war during epidemics of cholera and typhus at Wittebergen and Gardelegen in Spring and Summer 1915. Bristow also received a D.C.M. in *L.G.* 15 December 1916 where he is shown as R.A.M.C. formerly Royal Fusiliers. It is thought he was repatriated early in 1916. His group is known: D.C.M. (Pte. R.A.M.C.), 1914 Star & bar (Pte. 4/R. Fus.), British War and Victory Medals (A./Sjt. R.A.M.C.) and M.S.M. (4/R.F.). The names of the other nine are detailed in *O.M.R.S. Journal* Autumn 1981 by Major J D Sainsbury T.D. They are:— 12927 L./Cpl. Batt, 4th Bn. R.F., 14523 Cpl. W. Boardman, 4th Bn. R.F., 9219 Sgt. F. J. Brashaw, 1st Bn. Cheshire R., 1882 Pte. A. Dolton, 4th Bn. R.F., 10561 Pte. W. J. Gooderham, 2nd Bn. W. Riding R., 9111 Pte. F. G. Goulder, 1st Bn. R. Scots Fus., 10366 Pte. S. Kellett, 2nd Bn. W. Riding R., 7226 Pte. W. M. Manser, 1st Bn. Scots Gds., 9052 L./Cpl. G. R. Niell, 2nd Bn. W. Riding R., 9939 Pte. J. T. V. Roberts, W. Riding R. All caught the diseases and all received M.S.M.s in this gazette.

‡ R.A.O.C. For Siberia.

§ Medal known: M2/082579 R.A.M.C. From Kew. (A.O./193/1919 P.O.W.).

+ Noel Coy Byng. Group in Moss collection: 1914 Star trio (Pte. 550364 16/London Regt., from Catford), 1939/45 and Africa Stars, Defence and War Medals and M.S.M. (this for devotion to duty and valuable service whilst a prisoner of war under the terms of A.O. 193/1919). In W.W.II he was 2/Lieut. Intelligence Corps 13 July 1940, Lieutenant 15 January 1941 and Temp. Captain 9 January 1942.

◊ Group known: Queen's South Africa Medal (Cape Colony, Rhodesia, Transvaal, South Africa 1901, 50th Coy., 17th I.Y.), British War and Victory Medals (W.O.II Hamps. R.) and M.S.M. (for Siberia).

¶ Group known: 1914 Star trio. (Pte./Sgt. R.A.M.C.) and M.S.M. (R.A.M.C.). Plus miniatures of these four and Russian Orders of St. Anne & St. Vladimir, Serbian Medal for Zeal and Greek Military Cross.

Chirgwin, E.R.A. 2nd Cl. J. P.		2863	Delara, R.S.M. G., *D.C.M.*	1226
Clancy, C.S.M. P., *M.M.*	*	161	Dennett, Cpl. T. (corr.)	1785
Clarke, Q.M.S. A. S.		163	Dixon, Sjt. A.	945
Clay, Pte. E. S.	†	684	Dolphin, Pte.(L./C.) J.	1226
Clee, Pte. J. T.		1226	Dolton, Pte. A.	§ 1226
Clinton, Pte. J. W.		2739	Doughty, Pnr. H.	+ 2740
Cloke, pte.(A./Sjt.) E. W.		946	Dow, Sjt. J. R.	163
Cole, S.Q.M.S.(A./S.S.M.) F.		946	Duff, Sjt. W. K.	162
Coleman, Blacksmith 1st Cl.			Dungate, Sjt. E. J.	160
W. J. C.		2863	Dunk, Sto. P.O. C. F.	2863
Conaron, C.Q.M.S. R.		161	Dunn, Pte. J.	1226
Constable, Pte. G., *M.M.*		1227	— Sjt. W. G.	2740
Cook, Pte. A. W. N.		684	Dwyer, Sjt. W. E.	684
— Sjt. M.		946		
— B.S.M. W.		1226	Easby, Sjt. R.	945
Cooper, Pte.(A./S.S.M.) A. E.		946	Edgar, C.Q.M.S. M.	945
— Gnr. E.		1226	Edwards, T./S.M. R. W. (corr.)	1785
Corbett, S.M. J. F. C. (corr.)		1785	Eed Ahmed Abdel El Wahad,	
Cornish, 2nd Cpl. F. G. (deletion of			Shawish	2262
duplicate award)		1786	Eggleston, Sjt. S., *M.M.*	161
Costa, Pte.(A./Sjt.) J.		160	Eggleton, C.Q.M.S. A. H.	945
Courtman, Pte. J.		1226	— Pte.(L./C.) H.	946
Crampton, R.Q.M.S. H. W.		945	Elliott, P.O. Teleg. F. E.	2863
Crane, S.B.S. S.		2863	Elphick, Pte.(L./C.) A. H.	◊ 684
Creedon, C.S.M. M. P.		945	— R.S.M. R. J.	1223
Cripwell, Q.M.S.(M.F.W.) T.		945	Emmes, S.Q.M.S. J. S.	161
Cryer, Ftr.Cpl.(A./Ftr.Sjt.) H. P.		163	Evans, Sjt. W.	163
Cubitt, Pte. E. A.	‡	946		
Cullimore, Sjt. H.		946	Fairclough, Sjt. F. (corr. of surname)	1785
			Faulkner, Pte. C.	1227
Davidson, Sjt. W. J. J.		160	Feast, P.O. A. G.	¶ 2863
Davies, Spr. D. E.		160	Felstead, Pte. H. E., *M.M.*	1227
— C.Q.M.S.(A./R.Q.M.S.) H., *M.M.*		160	Field, T./Sub Condr. J. F.	946
Davis, Pte. H. V.		1226	Foard, Spr.(L./C.) P. G. (deletion of	
Dawson, Sjt.(A./B.S.M.)		160	duplicate award)	1786
De Ramer, R.S.M. F.		164	Foden, T./Sub Condr. W. M. (corr.)	1785
Dean, Sig. C. T.		948		

---

* Group known: M.M. (for Russia), 1914–15 Star trio (C.S.M. 1/London Regt.), Defence Medal amd M.S.M. (for Murmansk). M.M. and M.S.M. 29/London Regt.

† Rifle Brigade. Bushire.

‡ R.A.O.C. For Siberia.

§ See Bristow *ante*.

+ Pair known: M.S.M. (49828 R.E.) for services with the British Military Mission in South Russia, and Russian Medal of Zeal with St. Stanislas Ribbon (49828 Spr Hubert Doughty). This must have been one of the last uses of the rank of Pioneer in the *London Gazette*, as it was abolished in A.O.441 of December, 1919.

◊ Rifle Brigade, for South Persia (Bushire).

¶ As C.P.O. P/JX 152640, killed 8 February, 1942, H.M.S. *Volunteer*, aged 51. R.N. M.S.M. for services in the Baltic.

Forbes, Pte.(A./Sjt.) W.	* 1802	Good, C.E.R.A. G. H.	2863
Ford, C.E.R.A. 2nd Cl.,		Goodchild, Pte. H. A. J.	946
W. W., *D.S.M.*	2863	Gooderham, Pte. W. J.	+ 1226
Francis, S.M. P. C.	946	Goodman, Cpl. W. T.	1226
— R.Q.M.S. W. A.	1226	Gordon, T./R.S.M. J.	946
Fraser, Cpl. A.	160	Goude, Pte. H. F.	1227
Freemantle, Spr.(A./Sjt.) J. B. W.	2740	Gough, Pte.(A./Sjt.) S. A. (corr.)	1785
French, C.S.M.(A./R.S.M.) G. A.	945	Goulder, Pte. F. G.	+ 1226
— Pte. W. H.	1226	Gray, Ldg. Teleg. R. G. R.	2863
Friend, Pte. G. J.	† 2864	— Cpl. T. M. (corr. of surname)	1786
Froggatt, T./C.Q.M.S. H.	1227	Grey, Fitt. Cpl. G. J.	◊ ✿ 683
Fudge, Snr. Writer L.	2861	Griffin, 2nd Cpl.(A./Sub Condr.)	
		H. R.	2740
Gadsby, Pte.(A./Sjt.) T. J.	‡ 684	Griffiths, Pte. A. T.	946
Gale, Q.M.S. E. (deletion of		Grubb, Sjt. T. J.	¶ ✿ 944
duplicate award)	1785	Gulliver, Sto. P.O. E. G.	2863
Galletley, S./Sjt. M. G.	161		
Gardener, Pte. G. E.	1226	Haile, Pte. A.	2861
Gardner, Pte. F.	163	Hall, S./Sjt. P.	** 163
Garlick, C.E.R.A. 2nd Cl. A.	2863	Halsall, Sjt. J., *D.C.M.*	†† 163
Garratt, Pte. W.	1226	Hamilton, C.S.M. G. A.	‡‡ 946
Gennings, Sjt. A. T.	2740	— R.S.M. H.	1227
George, C.S.M. R.	945	— Pte. H.	684
Gerrard, Pte. G. C.	1226	Hammersley, Amt.S./Sjt.(A./	
Gibb, C.S.M. A.	1227	Amt.S.M.) A. G. (corr.)	1785
Gibbs, 1st Cl. S./S.M. R. W.	2740	— Sjt. H. W.	163
Gilchrist, Cpl.(A./Q.M.S.) A.	946	Hanckel, L./C. F. C.	1227
Giller, Pte. L. J.	946	Harnett, S.Q.M.S. W.	1225
Goddard, Cpl. F. W.	946	Harris, Ldg. Sea. A. E.	§§ 948
Godley, Sjt.(A./T./		— Ldg. Sea. G. A.	2863
Mech.S./Sjt.) F. J.	§ 1378	Harrison, Pte. F. A.	1226

---

* O.R. Sgt. 1/H.L.I. in Kurdistan. Died 30 September, 1919, 4½ months before this Gazette.

† See Volume II 1920.

‡ 7 Hussars. S. Persia.

§ Tank Corps, for services in Finland, to be dated 11 November, 1919.

+ See Bristow *ante.*

◊ R.F.A. Gallantry in Baluchistan.

¶ H.L.I. For gallantry at Archangel. M.M. previously awarded on 13 August, 1918, deleted 22 January 1920.

** R.A.O.C. Also 2nd class Silver Medal of St. Anne.

†† Group was in McInnes collection: D.C.M. (22427 Pte. M.G.C.) 1914/15 Star trio (2853 Pte./Sgt. Liverpool Regt.) and M.S.M. (345002 R.E.). D.C.M. *L.G.* 14 December 1916, 165 Coy. M.G. Corps, for France & Flanders, carrying ammunition to an isolated post under shell and M.G. fire even though wounded. The M.S.M. is for service with the Archangel Force in North Russia.

‡‡ H.L.I. S. Persia.

§§ Single R.N. M.S.M. was in McInnes collection impressed *'Bibiabat'* Caspian 8 August, 1919. Two ex-Tsarist ships were converted to seaplane carriers for service against the Bolsheviks, *'Orlionok'* and *'Bibiabat.'* In August they attacked Ashurada in

Harvey, S.Q.M.S. H. J.		946
Hashagen, Pte.(A./Sjt.) S. W.		946
Hawkins, S.M.I. B. H. R.		164
Heaney, Pte. J.		1226
Heatley, Sjt. R.		1226
Herrerd, T./Sjt. J. H. (corr. of surname)		1786
Heyward, M.C. S./Sjt. H. G. R.		2740
Hickey, Sjt. J.	*	1378
Hillier, Sjt. A.	†	1802
Hodgson, Pte. (A./Sjt.) S. J.		2740
Hodson, Pte. F. J.		161
Hollings, C.S.M. J. C. (corr.)		1785
Hopewell, Pte. (T./Sjt.) S. A.		1223
Hopkins, Pte.(A./Sjt.) F. J. (corr.)		1786
Hopper, Sjt. G. T.		945
Horsfield, B.S.M. A.		944
Hough, B.Q.M.S. W. (corr.)		1785
Howard, Sjt. F. J., *M.M.*		163
Howell, Sjt.(A./C.S.M.) J. A.		945
— Sjt.(A./C.S.M.) R. H.		945
Howes, Ch. Sto. J.		2863
Hubbard, C.S.M.I.(A./S.M.) E.		164
Hudson, Sto. P.O. A.		2863
Hughes, Pte. J.		1227
Hunt, Col.Sjt.(A./C.Q.M.S.) F.		946
Hutchison, Ldg. Teleg. J. B.	‡	2863
Irwin, C.S.M. J.		945
Isherwood, L./C. M.		1226
Ivens, Spr. T. E.	§	164
Jackson, C.Q.M.S. E. E.		161
James, P.O. G. W.		2863
— Yeo. Sigs. J. R.		2863
— Pte.(A./Sjt.) W. E.		684
Jayne, Snr. Writer W. N.		2861
Jeffrey, Sjt. H. J.		1226
Jessiman, Sjt. W.		1227

Jewell, Sto. P.O. S.		2863
Jones, Shipwt. 4th Cl. E. H.		2863
— Sjt.(A./C.S.M.) H.		163
— Pte.(A./Sjt.) J.		161
— Dvr. W. H.		161
Jordan, Pte.(T./S.Q.M.S.) H.		946
Joyce, Pte. P.		163
Jupe, C.Q.M.S. P. F.		946
Kean, Dvr.(A./Sjt.) F.		2470
Keating, S./Sjt. C.	+	162
Keeble, Sjt.(A./C.S.M.) H.		163
Kellet, Pte. S.	◊	1226
Kempster, T./S.S.M. G. (deletion of duplicate award)		1786
Kennard, Act. Ch. Arm. W. T.		2863
King, Sjt. W. (corr.)		1785
Kitson, S./Sjt.(A./Sub Condr.) W. J. (corr.)		1786
Laird, Sjt. W. W.		160
Lamb, Condr. A.		163
— Ldg. Teleg. G. J.		2863
Langford, Cpl. W. S.		2740
Langley, Armr.S./Sjt. A.		163
Laycock, Pte.(L./C.) S. (corr.)		1786
Lee, C.S.M. G. F.		160
Lewington, S.M. G.		161
Lewis, C.S.M. J.		160
Lilley, S.M.Instr. J. (corr. of surname)		1785
Lindsay, S.Q.M.S.(A./S.S.M.) F.		2740
Lingley, Whr.S./Sjt. T. T. (corr.)		1786
Little, Sjt. C. J.	¶	2740
Lloyd, Hd. Condr. T. (deletion of duplicate award)		1786
Logan, Sjt.(A./S./Sjt.) T.		162
Long, Cpl.(T./Sjt.) A.		163
Longinotto, Mech.S.M. B. A.		162

North Persia, and captured 200 prisoners and several barques loaded with arms and ammunition. See also A.B. A. Wade *infra.*

* R.A.S.C. For Finland.

† M.G.C. Kurdistan.

‡ See Appendix T. Group in Moss collection: 1914/15 Star trio and R.N. M.S.M.

§ See Tovey *infra.* For Japan. (R.E.).

+ R.A.M.C. From Dublin. M.S.M. for Archangel. Later Surgeon Captain, C.B.E. (1945), R.N.

◊ See Bristow *ante.*

¶ Tank Corps, for South Russia. Group known: British War and Victory Medals (A./ S/Sgt. M.G.C.), M.S.M. (201625 T C), Russian Medal of Zeal on St. Stanislas Ribbon.

McAfee, Pte. W. D.		2740	Mellor, Pte. T. J.	163
McAlister, Pte. A.		1227	Melvin, Pte. W.	1226
McCormick, Pte. J.	*	1784	Merrett, S.M.Instr. E. W. (corr. of	
McCready, Pte. C. T. (corr. of			surname)	1785
surname)		1785	Messam, Pte.(L./C.) G.	1227
McDavid, Pte. H. G.		1226	Metcalfe, C.S.M. F. S., *D.C.M.*	162
MacFarlane, Sjt.(A./S./Sjt.) A.		161	Miller, Pte. J.	1226
Macintyre, Pte.(T./Cpl.) D.		1227	Milman, S./Sjt.(A./S.Q.M.S.) A.	2740
McIntyre, Pte. L.		1227	Milner, Pte. J.	946
Mackay, S.M.(A./Supt.Clk.) W. G.			Milsom, Ch. Sto. J.	2863
(corr.)		1786	Minkshlin, Pte. A.	163
McKenzie, Pte. J. M.		1227	Mitten, Cpl. H. M.	1227
Mackereth, Amt.S./Sjt.(A./			Molloy, Pte. R.	1226
Amt.S.M.) W.		163	Monaghan, Sjt. B., *M.M.*	163
Macklin, Ch. Writer F. C.		2863	Moon, Pte. N. N.	◊ 1802
McLachlan, Pte.(A./S./Sjt.) H. E.		945	Moorby, Q.M.S. H. P.	946
McLaren, Pte. A.		1227	Morgan, S./Sjt. A.	163
MacLaughlan, Pte. D. (corr.)		1786	Morrison, O.R./Q.M.S.(A./	
McLean, Cpl.(A./Sjt.) J.	†	1803	R.S.M.) W.	¶ 684
McLeod, Pte. N.		1227	Moss, 2nd Hnd. A. J.	949
McMullen, Pte. F.		946	Moulds, Pte. G. R.	** 684
McNaughton, Sjt. J. (corr.)		1785	Murray, Sjt.(A./C.S.M.) J.	160
Mannerings, T./Sjt.(A./C.Q.M.S.)				
T. F. J.		163	Netherway, Pte. M. J.	2861
Manning, Sjt. E. A.		162	Newby, T./Sub Condr. W.	946
Manser, Pte. W. M.	‡	1226	Newstead, Cpl.(A./Sjt.) T. W.	2740
Mappley, Sjt. P.		1227	Nicholson, 2nd Cpl. A. V.	160
Margetts, Farr.Sjt.(A./Farr.S.M.)			Niell, Pte.(L./C.) G. R.	‡ 1226
J. E.	§	946	Nixon, Pte. F.	1226
Marsh, Cpl.(A./Sjt.) A. E. G.		162	Nock, Pte. L.	162
Martin, Pte.(L./C.) C. J.		163		
Mather, Pte. R.		1226	Oakes, Pte. A.	163
Mathieson, T./sjt.(A./C.S.M.)			Obourne, Sjt.(A./Q.M.S.) S. H.	2740
G. W., *D.C.M.*		945	Occomore, Sjt. T. R.	945
Matthews, Sjt. W. G.		946	Oday, Cpl.(A./Sjt.) G. H.	2861
Maxwell, Sjt. D. H.	+	163	Ogden, S./Sjt. J.	162
May, Cpl. G. F.		160	O'Laughlin, Dvr.(A./Sjt.) M.	1802
Meagher, Spr.(A./Sjt.) N. J.		2740	Olding, P.O. Teleg. P. J., *D.S.M.*	†† 2863
Meldrum, Sjt. T.		2740	Owens, Sjt. F.	2740

---

   * Scot. Rif. For exceptional devotion in the performance of military duty.
   † R.A.S.C. For South & Central Kurdistan.
   ‡ See Bristow *ante*.
   § Royal North West Mounted Police, for Siberia, the only M.S.M. to this service.
   + A unique M.S.M. to Officers' Training Corps. For North Russia (Archangel Command).
     He is shown as I of C. (? Instructor of Cookery, ?Inspector of Communications).
   ◊ Devons. For South & Central Kurdistan.
   ¶ S. Lancs. Regt. For Bushire.
  ** R.A.M.C. For Bushire.
  †† R.N. M.S.M. for the Baltic, D.S.M. for Jutland 1 June 1916.

Packer, Sjt. F. H. (corr.)		1785	Rae, C.E.R.A. 1st Cl. J. M.	2863
Page, T./R.S.M. A. (corr.)		1785	Randles, C.Q.M.S. A.	945
Palmer, Cpl. A. H.		162	Rawlings, Pte. A. J.	1227
Papillon, Pte. J. B.	* ❀	1784	Read, C.S.M.(T./R.S.M.) W. A.	1226
Parkin, Col.Sjt.(O.R.S.) H.		946	Reeve, A.B. A. F.	948
Parkinson, Pte. F. T.		1226	Reeves, C.P.O. T.	2863
Parr, Act.C.E.R.A. 2nd Cl. H.		2863	Reich, Pte.(A./C.S.M.) T. O. ◊	1802
Parry, Pte. W. O.	†	684	Reid, Pte. W.	1227
Parsons, Pte.(A./Sjt.) D.		946	Reynolds, Spr.(A./C.Q.M.S.) F. G.	2740
— Ldg. Sig. E. M.		2863	Richardson, Sjt. H. C.	2740
— Pte. F. A. J.	‡	2864	Riddell, Gnr.(A./Sjt.) J. O.	945
Paterson, Pte. W.		1227	Roberts, Pte.(A./Sjt.) A. ¶	1802
Peacock, Sjt. E. T.		1226	— Spr.(T./2nd Cpl.) C. S.	163
Pearce, Pte. H. H.	§	1802	— Dvr. G. E.	1226
Pears, Pte. G.		1226	— Pte. J. T. V. **	1226
Peck, 2nd Cpl. W. N.		160	— Sjt. W. J.	946
Peet, Pte.(L./C.) D. W.		1227	Robertson, Cpl.(A./Sjt.) J.	1227
Perkins, Pte. B. F. J.		1227	Robinson, Sjt. J.	946
Perrin, Pte.(A./L./C.) F. W.		945	— Bosn. W. C.	2861
Phelps, Pte. H. C.		1227	Rodnight, Gnr.(A./Bombr.) W. C.	
Pikles, Pte. A.		1227	(corr.)	1786
Pink, A.B.(Sigmn.) K. J.		2861	Ronald, Cpl.(A./Sjt.) A. ††	1802
Plenderleith, S./Sjt. R.		945	Rose, Pte. W.	1227
Pointon, Pte. W. S.		1226	Russell, Pte.(A./Cpl.) P. ‡‡	1802
Pole, Sjt.(A./C.S.M.) W. H.		163		
Poole, C.P.O. H.		2863	Salmon, Pte.(A./Sjt.) T. F.	161
Potter, C.Q.M.S. E. R. W.		945	Saul-Brown, Sjt. G. M.	163
Poulter, Cpl.(A./Sjt.) R. M.		160	Sayers, Pte. C. F. W.	1227
Powell, Cpl. T. D.		163	Scannell, Elect.Art.(3rd Cl.) W. B.	2863
Preston, Cpl. L.		162	Schonfeldt, S.M.Instr. S. G. (corr.	
Price, Sjt.(A./C.S.M.) W. R.		160	of surname)	1785
Priggen, Pte.(A./Sjt.) F. H.		163	Scott, Pte. R.	1227
Prigmore, Pte. P. J.	+	1378	Shambrock, Pte. T. A. E.	1226
Pritchard, Cpl. E.		161	Sharpe, Sjt.(A./C.Q.M.S.) A.	163
Prosser, Bombr. T.		1225	— Sjt.(A./C.Q.M.S.) W. J., *D.C.M.*	163
Punton, Pte. E.		1226	Shelton, Cpl.(A./S./Sjt.) C. S.	946
Purser, Cpl. H. M.		1227		

---

*   Canadian War Graves Dept.
†   Norfolk Regt, for Bushire, South Persia.
‡   See also Friend, Vol. II 1920. Group known: British War and Victory Medals (R.M.L.I.) and R.N. M.S.M. (H.M.S. Grafton, Novorossich, 14 October 1914).
§   7 Hussars. For South & Central Kurdistan.
+   200213. Tank Corps. For Finland.
◊   R. West Surrey Regt. For South & Central Kurdistan.
¶   Group known: British War Medal, India General Service Medal (Afghanistan N.W.F. 1919) both to A. Sgt. N. Staffs., and M.S.M. (2/N. Staffs. R.) for operations in Southern & Central Kurdistan.
**   See Bristow *ante*.
††   Yorks. Regt. For South & Central Kurdistan.
‡‡   North Staffs. For South & Central Kurdistan.

Shepherd, C.S.M. G.	* 1803	Stuart, Sjt. A. H.	160
— Pte. J.	1226	— Condr. C. E. C. W.	◊ 1803
— Pte. M. F.	946	Sylvester, Yeo. Sigs. C. W.	2863
Sheppard, S./S.M. W. C.	163		
Sherry, Pte.(A./Sjt.) J. W.	† 1802	Tatham, C.Q.M.S. G. E.	946
Shvets, Pte. B.	163	Taylor, Sjt.(A./R.Q.M.S.) A. E.	
Sidwell, Pte. F. E.	1227	(corr.)	1785
Simmonds, Sig. D. L.	948	— Pte. J.	1226
— Ch. Ship's Cook H. E.	2863	Tennant, Pte. A.	2739
Sirett, Act. W.O.(2nd Cl.) John		Ternent, Motormn.(2nd Cl.) T.	2861
(corr. of surname)	‡ 950	Terry, Cpl.(A./Sjt.) H.	2740
Skelwes, Pte.(A./Cpl.) C.	§ 1378	Tew, Pte. E. J.	1227
Smith, Cpl. A. E.	946	Thompson, C.Q.M.S. B. (corr. of	
— P.O. A. J.	2863	surname)	1785
— S.M.I. E. H.	164	Thorn, B.S.M. H. J.	160
— Sjt. H. R.	162	Thurston, 2nd Hnd. E. J.	949
— Pte. J. W.	2864	Tobitt, Pte. E. J.	945
— Sjt. P.	2740	Tongue, Sjt. R. E. (corr.)	1785
— Pte.(A./Sjt.) R.	162	Toon, Cpl. F.	1225
— P.O. Teleg. W.	948	Tovey, Sjt. G.	¶ 164
Sol Ibrahim Abdulla Kidr	2262	Townsend, M.C./Cpl. G.	** 684
Soppitt, Pte. W. C. B.	161	Travis, Pte.(A./Cpl.) A.	2740
Spence, Cpl. A.	+ 1226	Tribe, C.S.M. E.	945
Stamp, Sjt. A. W.	2740	Triggs, Pte.(A./Sub Condr.) R. G.	945
Stephens, Cpl. J. E.	163	Turner, Pte. H. J. J.	1226
Stepney, Pte.(L./C.) D. G.	2861		
Stevens, B.Q.M.S.(A./R.S.M.) E. A.	160	Vincent, C.S.M. A., *D.C.M.*	163
Stevenson, Pte. E. N.	2861	Voaden, Sto. P.O. B. W.	2863
— R.Q.M.S. N.	160		
Steward, A. B. J.	2863	Wade, A.B. A.	†† 948
Stiff, Pte. A. J.	1226	Wain, S./Sjt. A.	161
Still, Pte. A. J.	2864	Walker, C.Q.M.S. P. E. (corr.)	1785
Stocks, C.Q.M.S.(A./R.S.M.) A.		Wallace, Spr.(T./2nd Cpl.) B. D.	2740
(corr.)	1785	Walsh, Pte. J.	1226
Stone, C.S.M. W. J.	160	— Sjt.(A./R.S.M.) R.	946
Streeter, Sjt. W. F.	160	Walters, C.S.M. F. I.	164

---

* I.A. For South & Central Kurdistan.
† Hamps. Regt. For South & Central Kurdistan.
‡ See Vol. II 1919 *ante*.
§ R.A.S.C. For Finland
+ Group known: Queen's South Africa Medal (Cape Colony, Orange Free State, South Africa 1902, Cpl. Scots Gds.), 1914 Star & bar trio (Cpl. Scots Gds.) and M.S.M. (A.O. 193 of 1919 as P.O.W.). M.I.D. *L.G.* 30 January, 1920.
◊ I.A. For South & Central Kurdistan.
¶ Group known: British War and Victory Medals, 1939/45 and Africa Stars, War Medal and M.S.M. (Royal Engineers), for services in Japan in sole charge of loading operations of heavy locomotives attached to the British Military Mission (Siberian Command). See also Ivens *ante*.
** For Bushire with South Persia Rifles.
†† Single R.N. M.S.M. known, *'Orlionok,'* Caspian 8 August, 1919. See Harris *ante*.

Want, R.S.M. A.	1226	Williamson, Pte. F. J.	‡	2861
Wareham, 1st Writer E. E.	2863	Willox, Pte.(A./Sjt.) J. D.		161
Warnock, Sjt. W. P.	162	Wills, Spr. G. F.		160
Watson, Pte. D.	161	Wilson, Spr.(A./Sjt.) J. G. (corr.)		1786
Watt, Pte.(L./C.) R.	160	Windrum, T./S.M.Instr. J. A. (corr.)		1785
Watts, S./Sjt. J. E.	163	Withers, Pte.(A./L./C.) T.		161
Weaver, Pte. H. L.	2864	Wolland, Pte. J. H.	§	684
Welsby, Sjt. H.	162	Woods, 2nd Cpl. A. J.		162
White, S.M.I. F.	164	Woodsford, Sjt. A. W.		1225
Whitehead, Ldg. Teleg. E. T.	* 2739	Woolstenholmes, Pte. W.		2864
Whitlock, Farr.S./Sjt. W. H.	163	Wootten, C.Q.M.S. H. J.	+	162
Whyte, Armr. Crew (1st Cl.) J. B. D.	2861	Wray, Sjt. F. A.		945
Wilkinson, Sjt. A.	163	Wrigglesworth, P.O. T.		2863
Williams, Sjt. A. T. (corr.)	1785			
— 2nd Cpl. C. F.	946	Yaseen Said Mohammed		
— Pte.(A./S.Q.M.S.) C. J.	161	Husein Rash, Shawish		2262
— Cpl.(A./Sjt.) F.	946	Young, S./Sjt.(A./Sub Condr.) H.		
— R.S.M. F. W.	† 684	(corr.)		1786
— L./C. T.	1226	— Pte.(A./Sjt.) L. G.	◊	946

———◆◆◆———

* This would appear to be an Army M.S.M. issued for service with the Army of the Black Sea, the last such to R.M. and R.N. recipients, but see the one to Boatswain Chapple, Mercantile Reserve, *infra*.

† R.E. For Bushire (S. Persia).

‡ Group known: 1914/15 Star trio (Ply/15043 R.M.L.I.) and R.M. M.S.M. ('Kama River' Siberia 1919).

§ R.A.M.C. For Bushire (S. Persia).

+ See Wotton, Vol. IV 1920.

◊ Pair known: British War Medal (S/391138 A./Sgt. R.A.S.C.) and M.S.M. also R.A.S.C., for services in Siberia.

Vol. II, 1920

Aird, Pte. P.	6437	Chapple, Bosn. W.	†	4694
Anderson, 2nd Cl. Asst. Surg. C. L.	5912	Clarke, Sub Condr. H. A.		5477
Andrews, Cpl. G. I.	4021	Coles, Pte.(L./C.) J. A. (corr.)		4017
— Sjt. H.	5476	Cook, Clk. 3, R. W.		4021
Armitage, Flt. St. P.	4021	Cranwell, A.C. 2. J. A.		4021
Ashenhurst, T./S.M. J. T. (corr.)	4017	Crosbee, Sjt. W. A. (corr.)		4017
Ashton, Sjt. J. M. (corr. of surname)	4017			
Aston, Pte. A. E.	6437	Deane, Sjt. W. J.		5477
		Dickerson, Sjt. E. A.	‡	5448
Barnes, Pte.(L./C.) F.	5476	Dinsdale, Pte. T. H. (corr.)		4017
Beard, S./Sjt. E. J.	5476	Douglas, Sjt. W. A.		4016
Beaver, L.A.C. M. S.	4021	Duffy, S.M. L. A. (corr.)		4018
Bell, Dvr. A., *MM*.	5448	Duncan, Pte. R. J.		5912
— Cpl. J.	5476	Dunning, Pte. H. D.		5476
Belshaw, Cpl. F.	5476	Durham, S./Sjt.(A./Condr.) C.	§	5477
Beresford, Pte.(A./Sjt.) J.	* 5476	Durrant, Pte. D. C.		6437
Blount, A./C. 2 R.	4021			
Boak, A./C. 1 S.	4021	Ellings, Pte. (L./C.) A.		5476
Bozie, Cpl. A. G. (corr.)	4017	Emms, S.Q.M.S. J. S. (corr.)		4017
Bradfield, Sjt. F. M.	4016	Evans, Pte. D. E.		5912
Browne, 3rd Cl. Asst. Surg. W. A.	5912	Ewing, Condr. J.		5477
Bruce, Pte.(A./Sjt.) C. H.	5912			
Bryant, Cpl.(A./S.M.) J. (corr.)	4017	Fallen, L.A.C. F.		4021
Bucke, C.Q.M.S. G. H. B. (corr.)	4017	Favell, P.O. Henry Allen (corr. of		
Burden, Sjt. A. E.	5477	surname)		5100
		Filby, Pte.(A./Sjt.) A. G.		5476
Cann, Pte.(A./Sjt.) J. S. (corr.)	4017	Fish, Pte.(A./Sjt.) H. L.		5911
Carruthers, T./Sub Condr. A.	5912	Fogg, C.S.M. E. G.		5476
Carter, Sjt. J. G.	5476	Ford, Cpl.(A./Sjt.) H. G.		5911
— L.A.C. S. H.	4021	Friend, Ord. Sea. George James		
Chao Wan Te, Coolie	✿ 4016	(corr. of rank)	+	5100

* See bar 18 February 1921. This medal was awarded on North West Frontier with K.R.R.C.
† Mercantile Marine Reserve, for N. Russia.
‡ South Persia Rifles.
§ Group known: Queen's South Africa Medal (Cape Colony, Orange Free State Transvaal, 78 Batty. R.F.A.), 1914 Star & bar (S./Sgt. S. & T.), British War and Victory Medals (M.I.D. oakleaf), India General Service Medal (Afghanistan N.W.F. 1919, A./Sub Cond.), Defence and War Medals, Jubilee 1935, Coronation 1937, L.S. & G.C. (Geo. V, S./Sgt.), M.S.M. (for N.W.F. India). Recalled in 1940 and was a P.O.W. camp guard on Salisbury Plain.
+ Group known in Moss Collection: British War and Victory Medals (Boy 1st class R.N.), War Medal 1939/45, R.N. M.S.M. (H.M.S. Grafton, Novorossick, 14 October, 1919) originally p.2864/1920. See also Parsons, *ante*. Vast quantities of allied (French,

Funnell, Pte.(A./Cpl.) A. E.		* 5448	Holmes, Sjt. A. G.		5476
			Hoskins, S.M.I. J.		4021
Geldart, Sjt. Mech. E. F.		4021	Howard, F./Sjt. G. E.	§	4021
George, Gnr.(A./Mech.S./Sjt.) L. H.	†	5476	— T./Cpl. N.		5448
Gibson, S./Sjt. P. J.		5477	Humphrey, A.M.I. T.		4021
Glendinning, Gnr. F. W. (corr.)		4017	Hunt, Pte.(A./L./C.) T. J.		5477
Gordon, Sqdn.S.M. G.		5911			
— Sjt. J. A.		5448	Jaynes, A.M. 2, A. L.		4021
Green, A.C. 1, G.		4021	Jessiman, C.S.M. J. (corr.)		4017
Greenhow, Pte. G. O. R.		6437	Jones, Sjt. W. G.		5476
Greenwood, Q.M.S. H. A. B.		5912	Joyce, Sjt. J. C. (corr.)		4017
Griffiths, Pte. A. L.		5448			
— Pte.(A./Sjt.) R. C.		5476	Kelly, Sjt. P.	+	5448
			King, Sjt. E. (Lrs.)	◊	5448
Hall, T./S./Sjt. P. (corr.)		4017	— Sjt. E. (R.A.S.C.) (corr.)		4017
Hardy, A.C. 2, W.		4021	— Sjt. H.		5912
Hare, Pte.(A./Sjt.) F. J.		5476	Knight, Sub Condr. W. R.		5477
Hargreaves, Cpl. R.		5476			
Harris, Cpl.(A./C.S.M.) A.		5476	Landau, Cpl. C.		5912
— Sjt. E. A. (deletion of duplicate)		4018	Langtry, C.Q.M.S. H. (deletion of		
Hart, Pte. F. E.		5476	duplicate award)		4018
Harwood, Col.Sjt.(O.R.Sjt.) E. H.			Lawrence, Q.M.S. W. (corr.)		4017
(corr.)		4017	Leahy, S./Sjt. E. B.		5477
Hawkes, Sjt.(A./W.O. Cl.II)			Leppard, Cpl. A. (corr.)		4017
W. G. W. (corr.)		4017	Levesseur, Pte. B.		4016
Heason, Cpl. W. F. (corr.)		4017	Levett, Cpl.(L./Sjt.) J. W.	¶	5448
Hewitt, Pte. A. W.		5912	Lewis, Sjt. W. F.		4021
Hickman, Pte.(A./S./Sjt.) H. C.	‡	5476	Lister, Sjt. J. T. (corr.)		4017
Hodges, Pte.(A./S.Q.M.S.) H. T.			Liu Dien Chen, 1st Class Ganger	✤	4016
(corr.)		4017	Locke, Cpl. J. R.	**	5448
Holliday,Cpl. W.		4021	Long, Cpl.(T./Sjt.) A. (corr.)		4017
Hollins, C.S.M. F. (corr.)		4017	Loosley, Sjt.(A./C.S.M.) A. J. (corr.)		4017

British and White Russian) stores were held here. Many batteries of 18-pdr. field guns and 4.5-in. howitzers were landed for use by Denikin's front line troops, but it was a nightmare running up to the final evacuation in March 1919, Typhus, freezing weather and starvation, together with Red Army bullets, killed hundreds every day.

* See notes under Pte. (A./Sgt.) Smith W., *infra*.

† Group known in Moss collection: British War Medal (Gunner R.F.A.), India General Service Medal (Afghanistan N.W.F. 1919, Staff Sgt. R.A.) and M.S.M. (for N.W. Frontier of India). With miniatures.

‡ Pair known: India General Service Medal (Afghanistan N.W.F. 1919) and M.S.M. (275361 1 (Garr.) Bn. Som. L.I.), M.I.D. *L.G.* 3.8.20 under Commander & Staff, the only M.I.D. to 1/Garr. Bn. S.L.I.). The S.L.I. provided the Garrison at Amritsar, Punjab, at the time of the Massacres in April 1919. M.S.M. for N.W.F. of India.

§ R.A.F. M.S.M. N.W. Frontier of India, with 52nd Wing.

+ S. Lancs. R. S. Persia.

◊ 21st Lancers. S. Persia.

¶ R. Sussex Regt. att. S. Persia Rifles.

** York Regt. att. S. Persia Rifles.

McCartney, L.A.C. J.	4021	Morgan, Sjt.(A./C.S.M.) J.	5476
McCulloch, 2nd Lt. Writer Robert		Murray, Sjt. R. J., *M.M.*	‡ 5448
(corr. of surname)	6340		
McDiarmid, W./T.Op. 1st Cl.		Nalty, Sjt. H. V.	4016
Ronald Fraser (corr. of		Napper, R.S.M. C. F. (corr.)	4018
surname)	5100	Newman, Pte. A. E.	5912
MacDonald, Sjt. F. M.	4021	Norris, Sjt. E.	4021
McDonald, Cpl.(L./Sjt.) V. H. (corr.)	4018	Nunn, Flt.Sjt. F. W.	§ 4021
— Sjt. W. H.	5477		
McGill, S./Sjt. W. J.	5477	O'Brien, Sjt. A.	6437
McKay, Sjt. G.	5912	Old, A./C. 1, E.	4021
Mackenzie, S.Q.M.S. A. M. (corr.)	4017		
Malkin, Cpl. E.	4021	Page, Sjt. A. H.	6437
Manger, Pte. C. E.	5448	Pain, Sub Condr. H. B.	+ 5477
Mann, S./Sjt. F. C.	5912	Pamphilon, A.M.2 N.	4021
Markwick, Pte.(A./Sjt.) E. G.	5476	Peden, Sjt. A. C.	4016
Mason, Pte.(A./Sjt.) J. W.	5912	Petts, Sjt. G.	◊ 5448
Masters, Sjt. S. R.	5911	Philpott, Sjt. B.	5476
Menzies, Cpl.(A./S.M.) W. (corr.)	4017	Pickering, T./Sub Condr. W. K.	¶ 5912
Middleditch, Pte. B.	5476	Pilsbury, L.A.C. W.	4021
Mill, F./Sjt. M. F. G., *D.F.M.*	* 4021	Prentice, Pte.(A./R.S.M.) T. (corr.)	4017
Mitchell, F./Sjt. L.	† 4021		
Money, Sjt. F. E. (corr.)	4018	Randall, Sub Condr. P. B.	** 5477

---

* R.A.F. M.S.M. for South Russia. D.F.M. *L.G.* 1 January 1919. Wing Commander in 1942.

† Group known: 1914/15 Star (2A.M. R.F.C.), British War and Victory Medals (S.M.2 R.A.F.), General Service Medal (Kurdistan), 1939/45 Star Defence and War Medals (M.I.D. oakleaf), Jubilee 1935, R.A.F. M.S.M. (for S. Russia), R.A.F. L.S. & G.C., Medal of St. Stanislas and King Feisal's Active Service Medal. Enlisted Dec 1914. Commissioned 1936. Wing Commander 1942. Died 1954.

‡ Tank Corps, for services with the British Military Mission in South Russia. Awarded M.M. for gallantry near Marcoing and Noyelles 20/21 November, 1917, when a Private in 'A' Bn. Tank Corps. He drove his tank four times into action and helped inflict heavy casualties on the enemy.

§ R.A.F. M.S.M. (South Russia). No. 504 R.A.F., enlisted 10 December 1912. 1914 Star from August. Court Martialled December 1914 and given two years hard labour for quitting post. Later earned Russian Medal for Zeal.

+ Group sold in 1955 for £12.10.0. Queen's South Africa Medal (Belmont, Moddar River, Paardeberg, Johannesberg, Diamond Hill, Belfast, South Africa 1901, Bomb. R.F.A.), Tibet Medal 1903–04 (Sgt., Supply & Transport), 1914 Star trio (M.I.D. oakleaf), India General Service Medal 1908 (Afghanistan N.W.F. 1919, Mahsud 1919–1920, Waziristan 1919–21), L.S.& G.C. (Geo. V) and M.S.M. (for N.W.F. of India).

◊ R. Sussex Regt. attached South Persian Rifles.

¶ Group known: British War and Victory Medals (M.I.D. oakleaf T./W.O.1 A.O.C.), India General Service Medal (Afghanistan N.W.F. 1919, Sub Cond.) and M.S.M. for N.W. Frontier (Baluchistan). (Baluchistan is in Central Asia).

** Group known: Queen's South Africa Medal (Transvaal, Orange Free State, Cape Colony, Drummer 2/S.W.B.), King's South Africa Medal, 1914 Star (S/Sgt. I.O.D.), British War and Victory Medals (Sub Cond. I.A.O.C.), India General Service Medal

Reeman, C.S.M. C. P. (corr.)	4017	Stainton, Pte. P.		5476
Robinson, Spr. A. G. (corr. of		Stewart, C.S.M. T.		6438
surname)	4017	Stock, Cpl.(A./Sjt.) R.		5912
Rountree, S./S.M. E. G. (corr. of		Stote, Sjt.(A./C.S.M.) A.	‡	5476
surname)	4017	Sumbler, Spr.(A./Sjt.) W. J.		5476
Ruskin, L.A.C. D.	4021	Swift, Pte. H.		6437
		Swingler, Sjt.(A./S.M.) J. F.	§	5911
Salter, C.Q.M.S. F. A. (corr. of				
surname)	4017	Taylor, Sjt. A.	+	5448
Sargent, Asst. Surg. H. L.	* 4656	— Sjt. (A.C.) A. H. (corr.)		4017
Saunders, Pte.(A./Sjt.) R., *M.M.*		— Cpl. C. H. (corr.)		4017
(corr.)	4017	Thompson, A.C. 1, G. D.		4021
Sheed, Pte.(A./C.Q.M.S.) F. (deletion		— R.S.M. T. E.		5476
of first announcement)	4018			
Shepperd, S./S.M. W. C. (corr. of		Unjohn, Pte.(A./Sjt.) F.	◊	5912
surname)	4017			
Shvets, Pte. V. (corr.)	4017	Virgo, Sjt. G. A.		5477
Slade, Sjt. G. D. T. (corr.)	4017			
Smith, Cpl. C. E.	4021	Walker, Sjt. P.		5912
— B.S.M. D'A.	6437	Walklett, Pte. G. H.		6437
— Sjt. F. J.	4021	Wallis, Sjt. W. J.	**	5448
— Pte.(A./Sjt.) W.	† 5448	Wang Chen Ching, Labourer	❀	4016
Spurgeon, Pte.(A./Sjt.) F. J. A.	5476	Wang Yu Bhan, Coolie (corr.)		4017

(Afghanistan N.W.F. 1919, Waziristan 1919–21, Waziristan 1921–24), L.S. & G.C. (Engraved to European in Indain Army, S./Sgt. I.O.D.) and M.S.M. (I.O.D.) for services on N.W. Frontier of India). He was aged 14 on enlistment.

* East African Medical Corps for Northern Turkana.

† His medals are still in the family. The citation for the M.S.M. is given in official sources as follows: 'For devotion to duty in the Field from the 1st to 6th January 1920. Cpl. Smith accompanied Lieutenant Peploe, R.N., in an icebreaker from Taganoy to Yeisk and Mariupol; at the latter place on 5th January while breaking out and rescuing two ships abondoned by their crews came under close hostile artillery fire. The example set by him under very trying circumstances had a great effect on the Russian crew and it was undoubtably due to the fine example set by Cpl. Smith and the others with him that the ships were rescued and the whole conveyed safely back to Yeisk with stores, troops and refugees. (See also L12448 Pte. (A./Cpl.) A. E. Funnell, 3/Royal Sussex Regt.). On 16 July 1921 the War Office advised ES/50928 Lance Corporal (Acting Sergeant) William Smith R.A.S.C. (Harrogate) that His Majesty the King had granted permission to accept and to wear the Russian Silver Medal for Zeal on the ribbon of St. Stanislas (0137/5/1243). A full report and a resultant letter are in Appendix X.

‡ Group known: British War Medal, Territorial Force War Medal, Indian General Service Medal (Afghanistan N.W.F. 1919, M.I.D. oakleaf), Defence Medal, M.S.M. and Territorial Force Efficiency Medal (7/Hamps. Regt.).

§ Group known: British War Medal (Sgt. R.A.), India General Service Medal (A./W.O.1 R.A., Afghanistan N.W.F. 1919, Waziristan 1919–21), L.S. & G.C. (Geo. V, Cpl. R.F.A.) and M.S.M. (for Baluchistan).

+ R.G.A. attach South Persia Rifles.

◊ S. Lancashire Regt. for Baluchistan.

** 7 Hussars, att. South Persia Rifles.

Wardell, C.S.M. F. H. (corr.)	4017	Wiseman, Sjt. T. L.		4021
Warlow, 1st Cl. Mast. Gnr. A. J.	4016	Witcher, Cpl.(A./Sjt.) W.		4021
Whelton, Cpl. T. (corr.)	4017	Woodcroft, Sub Condr. J.	‡	5477
Whitworth, Cpl. H.	4021	Woolley, Pte. A. J.		5477
— T./S.M. R. (corr.)	4017	Worthington, Cpl. E.		6437
Wilkinson, Pte. C.	* 6437	Wren, Pte. A. W.		5476
Williams, Pte. D. B.	6438	Wright, Sjt.(A./Mech.S./Sjt.) F. C.	§	5477
— Sjt. T.	† 5448	— R.Q.M.S. F. J.	+	5912
Willmott, C.Q.M.S. F. P. (corr.)	4018			
— B.Q.M.S. G. H.	5476	Yorke, Sjt. H. B.	◊	6437

---

* Group was in McInnes Collection: British War and Victory Medals and M.S.M. (W. Yorks. Devotion when a P.O.W.).

† S.L.I. attached S. Persia Rifles.

‡ Group know: Queen's Sudan Medal, 1914/15 Star trio, India General Service Medal (Afghanistan N.W.F. 1919), L.S. & G.C. (Victoria), Delhi Durbar 1911, M.S.M. (N.W.F. of India) and Khedive's Sudan (Khartoum).

§ Group known: British War and Victory Medals (M2/113581 A S./Sgt. A.S.C.), India General Service Medal (Afhganistan N.W.F. 1919, M.I.D. oakleaf *L.G.* 3.8.20, 630 (M.T.) Coy. R.A.S.C.), Defence Medal and M.S.M. for N.W. Frontier.

+ R W Kents, for Baluchistan.

◊ M.S.M. known: No. 2 Madras S. & M. Motor Cycle Section, for Devotion to duty as a P.O.W.

Aggett, Cpl. F. W. G.	* 7424	Boucher, Pte.(A./S.M.) J. S. (corr.)		7444
Aggus, A./Sjt. T. G. A.	7424	Bowtle, Pte. W. D.		8968
Aitkenhead, A.C.2 J.	† 7424	Bramble, Sjt. C. W.		8966
Aldridge, Pte. W.	8968	Brammer, C.S.M.(I.G.) H. J.		8966
Allan, Pte. E. H.	8967	Braund, A.C. 1 E. W.	+	7424
Allen, Cpl. W. J.	8967	Brazil, S.Q.M.S. G. P. (corr.)		7444
Andrews, Cpl. F. G.	8966	Brindley, R.S.M. E. E. (deletion of		
Axworthy, Q.M.S. A. E.	8966	duplicate award)		7445
		Bristowe, Sjt.(A./R.Q.M.S.) C. H.		8967
Baker, Cpl.(A./Sjt.) H. W. V.	7443	Brookbank, Pte.(A./Sjt.) A. E.		
Bamber, Pte.(A./S.Q.M.S.) M. S.		(corr. of surname)		7444
(corr.)	7444	Brooks, Pte. J. W. H.		8967
Barber, Sjt.(A./C.Q.M.S.) H.	8966	— Sjt. T.		8967
Barden, Pte. E. T. (corr.)	7444	Brown, Col.Sjt.(O.R.S.) G. H. H.		8967
Barfoot, C.S.M. W. H. J.	8967	Bryan, Sjt. J. D.		8967
Barker, T./R.S.M. E.	8966	Bryant, Pte.(A./Sjt.) H. W.		8967
— Sjt.(A./C.S.M.) R. A. (deletion of		Buckle, Pte.(A./S.M.) H. (corr.)		7444
duplicate award)	7445	Bulcock, R.Q.M.S. T. A.		8967
Barnard, B.S.M. G.	8966	Bulman, Cpl. F. F. F.		7424
Bartlett, Pte.(A./S.S.M.) A. J. (corr.)	7444	Burden, Sjt.(A./C.Q.M.S.) C. J. (corr.)		7445
Beeden, Condr. A. W.	‡ 9511	Burnett, Sjt. J.		8968
Berry, Col.Sjt.(O.R.S.) A. C.	8967			
Biggs, T./S.S.M. F. (corr.)	7444	Cameron, Pte.(A./S.M.) W. (corr.)		7444
Binfield, Pte. H. E.	9511	Candy, Sjt. E. C. N.		8967
Blackmore, Pte. D. H.	8966	Carkner, A./S.M. R. C. (corr.)		7444
Blackwood, L.A.C. W. C.	7424	Carrol, T./R.S.M. A. V.		8966
Bloss, Pte. A. W.	8968	Carter, Band Sjt.(A./Bandmr.) F. W.		8968
Bluff, Col.Sjt.(O.R.S.) J. F.	8968	Cartwright, Cpl.(A./Sjt.) H.		7443
Booth, Sjt. A. D., *A.F.M.*	§ 7424	Caunce, Sjt.(A./S./Sjt.) H. (corr.)		7444
— Pte. B.	8967	Chaplin, Pte.(A./S./Sjt.) W. J.		8966

---

   * R.A.F. M.S.M. for South Russia. Group known: M.B.E., 1914/15 Star trio, 1939/45 and Africa Stars, Defence and War Medals, Jubilee 1935, R.A.F. M.S.M., R.A.F. L.S. & G.C. and St. Stanislaus Medal.

   † Group known: British War and Victory Medals (3A.M. R.A.F.), R.A.F. M.S.M. and Russian Medal for Zeal.

   ‡ Group known: British War and Victory Medals (Cond. I.A.), India General Service Medal (Waziristan 1919–21, Major I.A.O.C.), L.S. & G.C. (Edw. VII, Sub-Conductor O.D.), M.S.M. and Volunteer Long Service Medal (Geo. V, Gunner, 1st Corripore Bde., Mobile Art., I.D.F.). M.S.M. for N.W.F. India.

   § R.A.F. M.S.M. for Somaliland. A.F.M. in *L.G.* 12 July, 1920.

   + Group known: British War and Victory Medals, India General Service Medal (Waziristan 1925, Sgt. R.A.F.), R.A.F. M.S.M. for S. Russia, R.A.F. L.S. & G.C. (F./Sgt.) and St. Stanislaus Medal.

Chapman, Sjt. E. C.	8966	Drake, Pte.(A./S./Sjt.) R.		8967
Cheffins, Flt.Sjt. W. H.	* 7424			
Childs, T./R.S.M. H.	8968	Elcombe, Pte. H. W.		8968
Chipperfield, T./Sjt. W.	8966	Ellis, Pte.(A./Sjt.) E. A. S.		8968
Chiverton, T./Bombr. E.	8966	— L.A.C. J.		7424
Clay, A.C. 2 L. C.	7424	Escott, C.Q.M.S.(A./R.Q.M.S.) F. H.		8967
Clements, Sjt. G. J.	8966	Ewington, Pte.(A./Sjt.) D.		8968
Clift, Pte.(A./Sjt.) W. B.	8966			
Coates, T./Sjt. B. M.	8967	Field, T./Sub Condr. J. F. (corr.)		7445
Coe, Cpl. C. R.	7424	Finch, S.M. 1, S. P., *D.S.M.*	§	7424
Collier, B.S.M. W. J.	8966	Fisher, Sjt.(A./R.S.M.) W.		8965
Collins, Gnr. W. S.	8968	Fortescue, R.Q.M.S. T. H.		8966
Conway, W.O. Cl. 1, J. F.	8968	Fowler, Cpl. A. G.		9511
Cooper, Pte.(A./S.S.M.) A. E. (corr.)	7445	— Pte.(A./Sjt.) W. S.		8967
— Pte. C.	8966	Fox, Pte.(A./S.M.) P. C. (corr.)		7444
— A.C. 1 L. V.	7424	Franklin, T./R.S.M. W.		8966
— Pte.(A./Sjt.) S. T.	8967	Fraser, S./Sjt. A. D. (corr.)		7444
Coward, Sjt. H. H.	7424	Fry, R.S.M. W.		8966
Cowie, Pte.(A./S./Sjt.) G. (corr.)	7444			
Cox, Pte.(A./Sjt.) B. J.	8968	Gaiger, R.S.M. F. S.		8967
Cozens, Sjt. W. G.	8968	Gardner, Col.Sjt. A.		8967
Craske, Pte. W. R.	8968	Gawn, B.S.M. H. J.		8966
Crook, Flt.Sjt. A. J.	7424	Gibbs, Pte.(A./Sjt.) A. E.		8967
Curtis, R.S.M. A.	8967	Goacher, Cpl. H. G.		7424
		Graham, Cpl.(A./Sjt.) J. (corr.)		7444
Dales, Sjt. Sig. H. R.	8966	Grant, A.C. 1 J.		7424
Davies, Sjt.(A./S.M.) J. H.	8967	Gray, L.A.C. J. R.		7424
— A.M. 3 Ll. S.	7424	Green, Bombr. A. E.		8966
Davis, C.S.M. S. G.	8966	Greenwood, B.S.M. D.		8966
— Sjt. J.	8965	Gregge, Pte. J. J. C.(corr. of		
Davison, Ch. Writer J. O. A.	† 9055	surname)		7444
Dawson, Sjt.(A./B.S.M.) D. (corr.)	7445	Griffiths, Pte.(A./S.M.) G. C. (corr.)		7444
De La Haye, A./S.Q.M.S. W. P.				
(corr.)	7444	Hailstone, Pte.(A./Sjt.) J. E.		8967
Delaney, C.Q.M.S. W.	‡ 8966	Hall, Sjt. W.		8968
Devey, Sjt. H. S.	8966	Hammond, B.S.M. L.		8965
Dopson, R.S.M. A. C.	8968	Hansford, Cpl. T. S.		8967
Downes, T./S.M. E. J. (corr. of		Harfield, T./R.S.M. G.		8967
surname)	7444	Harris, Sjt. W. J.		8968
Downey, Sjt.(A./C.Q.M.S.) A. P.	8967	Hatchard, C.S.M. F. W.		8966

---

* Group known: 1914 Star trio (Lincoln R.), Africa General Service Medal (Somaliland 1920), R.A.F. M.S.M. (for Somaliland) and R.A.F. L.S. & G.C.

† Group known: Africa General Service Medal (Somaliland 1908–10, *Fox*), 1914/15 Star trio, R.N. L.S. & G.C. (*Julius*), R.N. M.S.M. (South Russia, March—June 1920) and Russia Medal for Zeal.

‡ Group known: Queen's South Africa Medal (South Africa 1902, 17709 Bombr. 63 Coy. R.G.A.), 1914 Star trio (B.Q.M.S. R.A.), L.S. & G.C. (Geo. V, C.Q.M. Sgt. R.G.A.) and M.S.M. (R.G.A.). M.S.M. for services in India.

§ R.A.F. M.S.M. for South Russia. Formerly No. 556 R.N.A.S.

Hawkins, T./R.S.M. A., *D.C.M.*	8966	Last, Pte.(A./S./Sjt.) C. J. (corr.)		7444
— Cpl.(A./Sjt.) W. C. (deletion of		Laughlin, Pte. A. G.		8968
duplicate award)	7445	Lawley, Pte.(A./L./Sjt.) W. F.		8967
Head, Pte.(A./Sjt.) G. H. R.	8967	Lawson, Pte. A.		8967
Hearne, Pte.(A./Sjt.) H. W.	8966	Le-Petit, B.S.M. S. T.		8966
Henry, Armr.Q.M.S. G.	8968	Leach, S./Sjt. F. E. (corr.)		7444
Hilder, R.Q.M.S. W. H.	8966	Licence, Sjt. P.		8966
Hirst, R.Q.M.S. H.	8966	Lock, Dvr. L. F.		8966
Hobbs, T./Sjt. E. E.	8965	Lockyer, L.A.C. E. E.		7424
— Sjt. G. B.	8966	Longhurst, Pte.(A./L./Sjt.) H. P.		8966
Holdstock, Pte. R. J.	8968	Love, A./S.M. H. E. (corr.)		7444
Howard, Armr.S./Sjt. F.	8968	Lowe, R.S.M. W. H.	*	8968
Howlett, Pte.(A./Sjt.) L. M.	8967			
Hubbard, Pte.(A./Q.M.S.) G. E.		McAllister, C.S.M. J.		8968
(corr.)	7444	McCann, S./Sjt. J.	† ❀	9511
Huck, R.Q.M.S. W. S.	8967	McCulloch, Spr. A.	‡ ❀	7443
		Macken, Cpl.(A./Sjt.) A. G.		8967
Iggulden, Pte. H. A.	8968	McMinn, R.Q.M.S. D.		8967
		Maddocks, T./Sjt. W. E.		7424
		Major, Cpl.(A./S./Sjt.) H. A.		8966
Jones, Dvr.Whlr. H. (corr.)	7445	Marsh, Pte.(A./Cpl.) H.		8967
— Pte.(A./S.M.) J. T. (corr.)	7444	— Pte. R. E.		8968
Joseph, Deputy Supt. S. P.	9511	Maulkin, Pte.(A./Sjt.) A. G.		8966
Joyce, Pte. P. (corr. of Regt.)	7445	Maunder, Pte. A. C.		8966
		Maynard, Pte. C. C.		8967
Kearley, Gnr.(A./W.O. Cl. II) C. J.	9511	Melton, W.O. Cl. II, R. (corr.)		7444
Kelloway, Pte.(A./Sjt.) J.	8968	Milledge, Sjt. J. W.		8967
Kemp, Pte.(A./S./Sjt.) C. S. (corr.)	7444	Moggridge, Gnr.(A./R.S.M.) G. H.		8966
Kerslake, Pte.(L./C.) B. H.	8967	Molden, Sjt.(A./S./Sjt.) C. J.		8968
Killeen, Pte. J. A.	8966	Moores, S.M. J. R., *M.M.*		8968
King, A.C. 1 R.	7424	Morrall, S./Sjt.(A./S.M.) C. (corr. of		
Knight, C.S.M.(A./R.S.M.) W. H.	8968	surname)		7444
Knowles, A.C. 2 J.	7424	Moseley, Pte.(A./Q.M.S.) R. B.		8966
		Mountstephen, Pte.(A./S.M.) W. A.		
Lakeman, Pte. H. S. B.	8967	(corr.)		7444
Lambert, Sjt. E.	8967	Murdoch, W.O. Cl. 1 H. J.		8968

---

* Group in D.L.I. Museum: O.B.E. (1st type, Military, 1914–15 Star trio (W.O.I), India General Service Medal (Afghanistan N.W.F. 1919, Lt. & Q.M.), 1939–45 and Africa Stars, Defence and War Medals (M.I.D. oakleaf, Lieut.-Colonel), Jubilee 1935, Coronation 1937 and M.S.M. (for India).

† S./Sgt. R.A. att. S. & T. Corps (Woolwich). For Gallantry in Mesopotamia. For gallant conduct and devotion to duty on 20th December 1919. He not only saved more than one man from drowning, but after hours in the icy water, arranged for shelter and food for men and animals who were unable to cross to their lines.

‡ Sapper, 8/Bn. Canadian Railway Troops. Gallantry in France. At Poperingue on 12th August 1918, this man with two others assisted in detaching burning wagons from a train containing cylinders of poison gas and removing them to a place of safety. Despite the escaping gas the fire was ultimately extinguished thereby averting a serious accident.

Murphy Q.M.S. T. G.	* 8967	Reeve, Cpl.(A./Q.M.S.) J. A. A.	8966
Murray, Pte.(A./Sjt.) C. C.	8965	Richards, Pte. J. W.	8968
Mynheer, Sjt. A. V.	8968	Roberts, Pte. E. R.	8967
		Robins, Pte. G. A.	8966
Newcombe, Sjt. H. W.	8966	Roblett, Q.M.S. J. J.	8966
Norman, Pte.(A./Sjt.) H. M.	8966	Robson, Sjt.(A./C.S.M.) J.	8966
Nuttall, Cpl.(A./Sjt.) H. L. (corr.)	7444	Ross, Pte.(A./S.M.) H. G. (corr.)	7444
		Rowbotham, A./C. 1 A.	† 7424
O'Brien, R.Q.M.S. T. H.	8966		
Odell, Cpl.(A./Sjt.) R.	8967	Sadler, A.C. 2 H.	7424
Ongley, C.S.M.(I.G.) A.	8966	Schuchard, S./Sjt. C. (corr.)	7445
		Schulze, B.S.M. G. W.	8966
Painter, Sjt. W. J.	9511	Scott, Pte. A. J.	8967
Palmer, Sjt. J., *MM.*	8967	— Sjt. W.	8966
Parton, T./S.M. F. S. (corr.)	7444	Sharp, Flt.Sjt. W.	7424
Pattinson, L.A.C. (A./Cpl.) T. A.	7424	Shaw, S./Sjt.(A./Q.M.S.) F. W.	8968
Paul, Pte.(A./S.M.) G. F.	8967	— Sjt. J.	8966
Payne, C.S.M. A. G. E.	8966	Sheffield, Q.M.S. E. (corr.)	7444
Peacock, Cpl. A. H.	7424	Shephard, Flt.Sjt. A. A.	7424
Penicud, Flt.Sjt. L.	7424	Shepherd, Sjt. J. B.	8966
Penn, Gnr.(A./Sjt.) T. C.	8966	Sheppard, Cpl. H. D.	8966
Phillips, Pte.(A./Sjt.) J. W.	8967	Short, L.A.C. M. H. W.	7424
Pitchford, Pte.(L./C.) V.	8965	Simpson, T./S.M. L. T.	8967
Plank, L.A.C.(A./Cpl.) W. J.	7424	— Sjt. P. A.	7424
Pollard, C.S.M.(A./R.S.M.) W.	8968	Singleton, Pte.(A./Sjt.) J. S.	8967
Poote, S.M. E.	9511	Slade, Pte.(A./S.M.) W. (corr.)	7445
Pound, Cpl. S. W. H.	7424	Smith, Cpl. C. G.	8966
Price, Pte. D. E.	8968	— Flight Sjt. E. G.	7424
— Pte.(A./Sjt.) E.	8966	Southcott, Cpl. G. E.	7424
Priestley, B.Q.M.S. W. C.	8966	Stanley, Sjt. F.	7424
Purdie, W.O. Cl. 1, J.	8968	— Pte. G. R. D.	8966
		Statham, Q.M.S. A.	8966
Raison, C.Q.M.S.(A./C.S.M.) J. H.	8966	Steed, Cpl. L. W.	8968
Randall, Pte.(A./S./Sjt.) R. J.	8968	Steer, R.S.M. J. S.	‡ 8967
Randell, Pte. R. H.	8968	Stevens, Sjt. W. G.	8966
Rawlings, T./Sjt. H. L.	8968	Stewart, Sjt.(A./S.M.) T. (corr.)	7445

---

* Group was in McInnes collection: British War Medal (5308 W.O.II York R.), Indian General Service Medal (Afghanistan N.W.F. 1919, R.Q.M.S.), L.S. & G.C. (C.Sjt. Yorks. R.) and M.S.M. (1st Yorks.). In India throughout W.W.I, to Afghanistan in 1919, Egypt in 1920 and Palestine later that year.

† Group in K.S.L.I. Museum: British War and Victory Medals, R.A.F. M.S.M. (for S. Russia), R.A.F. L.S. & G.C. and Russian Medal for Zeal. Wing Commander in W.W.II; retired in 1947.

‡ Group known: M.B.E., 1914/15 Star trio, India General Service Medal (Afghanistan N.W.F. 1919), General Service Medal (Palestine, Captain), 1939/45, Africa and Italy Stars, Defence and War Medals (Lt. Colonel), Delhi Durbar 1911, L.S. & G.C. (Geo. V) and M.S.M. (services in India).

Stone, Pte.(A./Sjt.) E. G.	8966	Waudby, Dvr.(A./Bombr.) C. G.		8966
Stuart, Condr. C. E. C. W. (deletion		Webster, L.A.C.(A./Cpl.) F. O.		7424
of duplicate award)	7445	West, S./Sjt. H. C.		9511
— Cpl. F. M.	* 7424	West-Skin, Pte. J.		8966
Summers, C.S.M. J. B.	8968	Wexted, Cpl. T. A. (corr. of surname)		7444
Swarbrick, Spr.(A./Sjt.) J. R.	7443	Whinnett, Sjt.(A./C.S.M.) A.		8967
Swindley, Pte.(A./Q.M.S.) R. E.		Whitburn, Pte.(A./Sjt.) A. K.		8968
(corr.)	7445	White, Cpl. E. C.		7424
		— Pte. F. H.		8968
Taylor, Pte. C.	8968	— B.S.M. R.		8966
— Pte.(A./Sjt.) R. E.	8968	Williams, Sjt. A.		8966
— W.O. Cl. II, R. H.	8967	— 2nd Cpl. C. E. (corr.)		7445
— B.Q.M.S. T.	8966	— Cpl.(A./Sjt.) F. N. (corr.)		7445
Telford, Cpl. J.	7424	Wilson, Pte.(L./C.) G.		8967
Thackaray, Sjt. W.	8965	— Pte.(A./Sjt.) T. W.		8967
Thornback, Sjt.(A./S.M.) F. W.	8967	— Pte.(A./Sjt.) W.		8966
Thwaites, S.M. A. P. (corr.)	7445	Wolff, Pte. E.		8968
Tindall, Pte.(A./Sjt.) C. C. P.	8968	Wood, C.S.M. F. G. S.		8966
Tobitt, Pte. J. E. (corr.)	7445	— Pte.(A./Sjt.) R.		8967
Tritton, Mech.S.M. A. D.	8966	Worthington, Sjt. J. (corr.)		7444
Turton, L.A.C. J.	7424	Wren, A.C. 1 J. T.		7424
		Wright, Pte.(A./S./Sjt.) D. C. (corr.)		7445
Walker, L.A.C. J. W.	† 7424	Wynton, S./Sjt. H. A.		9511
Wallace, T./W.O. Cl. II (O.R.S.)		Wyper, Pte.(A./Sjt.) J. M.	‡ ❀	7443
R. P.	8967			
Waller, Sjt. J. W. (corr. of surname)	7444	Yen Teng Feng, 1st Cl. Ganger	§ ❀	7443
Wallis, Pte. W. H.	8967			
Ward, Sjt.(A./Sqdn.S.M.) J. H.	8965			
Warwick, Pte.(A./Sjt.) P.	8968	*Meritorious Service Medal, institution*		
Waterman, C.Q.M.S. F.	8966	*of a bar to, to be awarded to*		
Watson, C.S.M. J.	8968	*Indian Troops*		8413
Watt, Pte.(A./Sjt.) W. S.	8967			

---

* Group known: British War and Victory Medals, R.A.F. M.S.M. (S.Russia) and Medal for Zeal. Enlisted January, 1916. A rigger aero. S.Russia from 24 May, 1919, 47 Sqn. (Crimean Group). Evacuated 31 March 1920.

† Group known: British War and Victory Medals, R.A.F. M.S.M. (S.Russia) and next of kin bronze plaque.

‡ Pte./A./Sgt. I/H.L.I. (Eccles), for Gallantry in India. On 21st March 1918, during bombing practice at Bangalore, one of the officers was almost about to throw a bomb when he dropped it behind him. Sgt. Wyper, with great presence of mind, seized the bomb and threw it clear.

§ 130th Chinese Labour Corps. Gallantry in France. On 23rd May 1919, at Bailleul during an explosion he worked continuously for four hours removing tarpaulins from unexploded stocks of ammunition and drenching them with water. (Probably paired with a bronze British War Medal).

Vol. IV, 1920

Royal Warrant establishing revised rules and ordinances	11310	Bryant, T./Sjt. A. M.	10389
		Burbidge, Sqdn.S.M. A. E.	10167
Alexander, W.O. Cl.1 J. A. (corr. of description)	10392	Byrne, C.Q.M.S. T. S. (corr. of description)	10391
Allen, Clr.Sjt. J.	11002	Callow, Pte.(L./C.) J. H.	10168
Anthony, L. A. T. (corr. of description)	10391	Carey, Pte. E.	10389
Arnold, Sjt. T. G. (corr.)	10392	Chapin, Cpl. C. H. (corr. of description)	10391
Ashton, Sjt.(A./W.O. Cl. 1) F.	10168	Chappell, Bo's'n W. (corr. of description)	10392
Baker, C.Q.M.S.(A./C.S.M.) E. (corr.)	12037	Charters, Cpl. J.	10388
— Pte.(A./R.Q.M.S.) W. G.	10389	Clark, Clr.Sjt.(A./S.M.) C. W.	10168
Baldock, Sjt. R. E. (corr. of description)	10391	— S./Sjt.(A./S.Q.M.S.) W. J. (corr. of description)	10391
Baldry, B.Q.M.S. A. (corr. of surname)	12037	Clarke, Pte. W.	10388
Barber, Pte.(A./Sjt.) E.	10389	Coles, S.Q.M.S. A. J. (corr. of description)	10392
Barker, Garr.S.M. J. W.	10167	Condliffe, Sadd.S./Sjt. M. J. G.	12037
— C.Q.M.S. R.	10389	Cook, B.S.M. M. F.	10389
Bazley, S./Sjt. A. W. (corr. of description)	10392	Cooke, Pte. A. W. N. (corr. of description)	10392
Bedwell, Sjt. J. W. (corr. of description)	10391	Coope, Clr.Sjt.(A./S.M.) B.	10168
Beeson, Sjt. J. W. (corr.)	12037	Cribb, Armr.S./Sjt. W.	10389
Bellairs, Ch.S.B.S. C. A.	12600	Cutting, A. B. (corr. of description)	10391
Bellringer, Sjt. E. (corr. of description)	10391	Daine, Sjt.(A./S.Q.M.S.) P.	10389
Birch, Cpl. H. (corr. of description)	10391	Dale, W.O. Cl.1 C. S. (corr. of description)	10392
Bishop, Sjt. J., *D.C.M.*, *M.M.*	10389	Davidson, 1st Cl. S.S.M. C. (corr. of description)	10391
Blacker, S./Sjt. J. F.	10168	Davies, Cpl. A. E. (corr. of description)	10391
Blyth, Sjt.(A./S.M.) R. L. (corr. of surname)	10391	— Q.M.S. W. A. (deletion of duplicate award)	10392
Bosworth, P.O. P. W.	11002	Davis, Pte.(A./C.S.M.) W. (deletion of duplicate award)	12038
Bradford, C.S.M. H.	10168		
Breakspear, B.S.M.(A./W.O. Cl. 1) J. T.	10388	Day, Sjt. F. S. J.	10168
Briant, Pte.(A./Sjt.) G. F.	10389	— Cpl. F. W.	10389
Briggs, T./S.S.M. A. (corr. of description)	10391	Dimmick, Dvr.(A./Sjt.) H. G.	* 10388
Brookes, Sjt. C. C.	10389	Donnithorne, Pte.(A./Cpl.) F.	10389

---

* Group known: British War Medal, Territorial Force War Medal (Driver R.A.), India General Service Medal (Waziristan 1919–21) and M.S.M. (217 Bde R.F.A.). From Bridport. M.S.M. for Waziristan. M.I.D. *L.G.* 10.6.21, corrected 29.6.23 (No. 3 Wireless Sqn. R.A.).

Douglas, T./W.O. Cl.1 A. J. (corr. of description)	10392	Griggs, Clr.Sjt.(O.R.S.) W. (corr. of description)	10391
Douglass, S.Q.M.S. A. (corr. of surname)	10391	Hackett, Clr.Sjt.(A./S.M.) J. G. I.	10168
— 1st Cl. Army Schoolmstr. J. D. T. (corr. of date)	10168	Hall, Pte.(A./Cpl.) A. H.	10389
Down, S./Sjt. J. H.	10168	Hamilton, A./Sjt. J. W. M.	10168
Dunning, Sjt.(A./C.Q.M.S.) H. D. (corr.)	12037	— Sjt. W. (corr. of description)	10391
Durno, Sjt. A. T.	10168	Hanham, Sjt. A. V.	10168
Dwyer, Sjt. W. E. (deletion of duplicate award)	12038	— Corr.	12037
		Hargreaves, Pte. J. C.	10389
Eastham, Sjt. T.	10167	Harris, Ch. S.B.S. G. S.	12600
Eddy, Sjt. J. (corr.)	12037	Henshall, S./Sjt.(I.) E.	10168
Elliott, Spr. C. G. M.	10389	Higginson, Sjt.(A./C.Q.M.S.) A.	10389
Etchells, Pte. J. (corr. of description)	10391	Hill, Sqdn.S.M.(A./S.M.) F.	10167
Everson, Sjt.(A./W.O. Cl.2) C. W. (corr. of description)	10391	Hillyard, Pte.(A./Cpl.) F. S.	10389
Evres, T./W.O. Cl. 2 R.	10389	Hilton, T./Mech.S.M. G. (corr. of description)	10391
		Hobbs, W.O. Cl. 1, E. W. (corr. of description)	10392
Flynn, W.O. Cl. 2 F. C.	10389	Hodson, W.O. Cl. 2, J. P. M.	10389
Forster, Cpl. J. (corr.)	12037	Hogg, Sjt. T., *M.M.*	10165
Fowles, Sjt. W. H.	10168	Hoggan, Sjt.(A./S.M.) G.	10168
Francis, S.M. P. (corr. of description)	10392	Holloway, Sto.P.O. A. J.	9693
Fraser, C.E.R.A. 1st Cl. A.	9693	Holt, Pte. R.	10168
		Homer, W. W. (corr. of description)	10391
Giller, Cpl.(A./R.Q.M.S.) L. J. (corr.)	12037	Hooker, Armt.S./Sjt.(A./Armt.S.M.) A.	10389
Givens, Pte. J.	10389	Hopley, R.Q.M.S. W. F. L.	10168
Glover, C.S.M. W. E. (corr.)	12037	Howard, Sjt. H.	10389
Gollings, Sqdn.S.M. E. A.	10167	Hylton, Sjt. V. F. (corr.)	12037
Gonsalves, A. D. (corr. of description)	10391		
Gonsalves, G. F. (corr. of description)	10391	Imber, Pte.(A./Sjt.) H. E.	10389
Goodall, Q.M.S.(A./S.M.) G. (corr. of description)	10391	Ison, Cpl.(A./S.Q.M.S.) W. J. (corr.)	12037
Gordon, Sjt.(A./S.M.) F. N. (corr. of description)	10392	Jackson, T./S.S.M. F. W.	* 10389
Gould, Sjt. L. McL. (corr. of description)	10391	James, Pte.(A./Cpl.) J. H. (corr. of description)	10391
Greene, Sjt. H. O.	10168	Jenkins, Pte. J. H.	10389
Griffin, S./S.M. H. F. (corr. of description)	10392	Johnson, C.S.M.(I.) A.	10167
		— R.S.M. E. A. (corr. of surname)	10392
		Johnston, C.S.M.(A./R.S.M.) S. (corr. of description)	10391

---

* Group known: O.B.E. (2nd type, military ribbon, *L.G.* 30 November, 1940, Major, Officer in charge of Barracks, Cairo), 1914/15 Star (A.Q.M.S. A.S.C.), British War and Victory Medals (T.W.O.1 R.A.S.C.), General Service Medal (Geo. VI, Palestine, Q.M. & Lieut. R.A.S.C.), 1939/45 and Africa Stars, Defence and War Medals, Jubilee 1935, Coronation 1937, L.S. & G.C. (Geo. V, S./Sgt. R.A.S.C.), M.S.M. (R.A.S.C.), 5th class Order of St. Anne, Russian Medal for Zeal. Born 1885, in the ranks 18 yrs., W.O.II 6 yrs., W.O.I 3 yrs., Lieut. & Q.M. 10 yrs. Major 1940. Died 1954. M.S.M. for South Russia.

Johnstone, Garr.S.M. J.	10168
Jones, S./Smith E. W.	10389
— C.S.M. F. J. R. (corr.)	12037
Joyce, Sjt. W. H. (corr. of description)	10392
Keble, R.S.M. G. (corr. of description)	10392
Kennedy, S./Sjt. E. A. (corr. of description)	10392
Kilbee, Pte. W.	10389
Kilford, Spr. A. E.	10389
Killick, Armt.S./Sjt. A. J.	10389
Kincaid, Cpl.(L./Sjt.) H. E. (corr. of description)	10391
Kirkpatrick, Cpl.(A./W.O. Cl.1) J. C.	10388
Kitney, Sjt. W. F.	10389
Latham, T./W.O. Cl.1, H. R.	10389
Leighton, Sjt.(A./S./Sjt.) J. M. (corr. of description)	10392
Lettington, C.S.M.(A./S.M.) C. D.	10167
Lewis, S./Sjt. D. L. (corr. of description)	10392
Lister, Sjt. J. T. (deletion of duplicate award)	10392
Loftus, Sjt.(A./R.S.M.) R. E.	10168
Long, S./Sjt. J. T. H.	10168
Lovejoy, C. E. (corr. of description)	10391
Lyles, Sjt.(O.R.S.) M. J.	10391
McCarthy, Bombr.Sig.(A./Cpl.) J. (corr. of description)	10391
McConachie, Pte.(A./Cpl.) W. A.	10389
McCully, Sub Condr. A. J.	10168
McDonald, Sjt. W. H. B.	10168
McKeag, Pte.(A./S./S.M.) W.	10389
McLean, Sjt. W. G. (corr. of description)	10392
Major, Sjt.(A./S.C.) H. W. (deletion of duplicate award)	12038
March, Dvr. W. H.	10389
Martin, C.P.O. Cook A. L.	11002
Masterson, Sjt.(A./C.S.M.) H. G. (corr. of description)	10391
Matthews, T./R.S.M. W. W.	10168
Maybury, A./Sjt. A.	10168
Meadows, A./Sjt. J.	10168
Messenger, T./S./Sjt. T. H.	10389
Mingay, Pte.(A./S.M.) W. H. C. (corr. of description)	10392
Moggridge, Gnr.(L./Bombr.) G. H. (corr.)	12037
Mole, Clr.Sjt.(A./R.S.M.) (I.) E. J.	10168
Molyneux, Spr.(A./Sjt.) J.	10389
Moody, Pte.(A./Sjt.) S. H. (corr.)	12037
Moore, Cpl. J. (corr. of description)	10391
Morrison, Armr.S./Sjt. G. A.	10389
Murphy, C.S.M. J. E. (corr. of description)	10392
Murray, W.O. Cl. 1, J. S. (corr. of description)	10392
Neale, Sjt. J. A. (corr. of description)	10391
Newbould, Pte.(A./S.S.M.) W.	10389
Nichol, Cpl.(A./Sjt.) W.	10389
North, Sjt. R.	10168
O'Connell, Sjt.(A./C.S.M.) A. F. (corr. of description)	10391
Osborne, A./Sjt. E. G.	10168
— S./Sjt. M. T. (corr. of description)	10392
Pallister, P.O. Teleg. H. J.	11002
Palmer, Pte.(A./Sjt.) W. J.	10168
Parker, S./Sjt.(I.) F.	10167
Patterson, S./Sjt. K. A.	* 10168
Peadon, S./Sjt. S. A. (corr. of description)	10392
Penhalluriack, W.O. Cl. 1, F. J. R. (corr. of description)	10392
Peyton, Spr. H. J.	10389
Phillips, Sjt.(A./S.M.) W.	10168
Pickstock, Farr.Sjt. S. (corr.)	12037
Plowman, T./S.S.M. R. L. (corr. of description)	10391
Porter, Sjt.(A./R.S.M.) B. (corr. of description)	10392
Posse, Pte.(A./S.M.) W. H. C. (corr. of description)	10392
Pritchard, Sub Condr. E. J.	10168
Randall, Mech.S./Sjt.(T./Mech.S.M.) S. G. (corr. of amendment)	10392
Rawlings, S./Sjt.(I.) C.	10168

---

* Pair known: British War Medal (Argyll & Suth. High) and M.S.M. (Army Clothing Dept., for services in India).

Rebello, Dep. Supt. C. G. (corr. of description)	10391
Rendell, Cpl.(A./Sjt.) C. E.	10389
Richardson, Spr. G.	10389
Roberts, Clr.Sjt.(A./R.S.M.) C. T.	10168
— Pte. J.	10389
Rogerson, B.S.M. J.	10389
Rollins, Sub Condr. C.	10168
Rowe, Sjt.(A./S./Sjt.) H.	10389
— Sjt. W. R., *M.M.*	* 10389
Russell, Cpl.(A./C.S.M.) R. H. (corr.)	12037
Salter, C.S.M. W. M. (corr.)	12037
Saunders, C.Q.M.S. A. (corr. of description)	10391
Sharp, S./Sjt.(A./S.S.M.) S. F. (corr.)	12037
Shepherd, Q.M.S. F. H.	10168
Shore, Pte. A. H.	10389
Sloss, Flight Sjt. J. McK.	† 10167
Smith, Pte.(A./Cpl.) N.	10389
— S./Sjt.(I.) R.	10168
Soper, Sjt.(A./S.M.) F. H. (corr. of description)	10391
Squire, Cpl. G. H. (corr. of description)	10391
Stevenson, A./Sjt. C.	10165
Stewart, Sjt. A. (corr. of description)	10392
— Bombr. D.	‡ 10389
— C.S.M. W. J., *D.C.M.*	§ 10389
Stowe, Pte.(A./Sjt.) S. A.	10389
Swanston, C.Q.M.S. J. A. (corr. of description)	10391

Tarnke, Pte.(A./Sjt.) F. K.	+ 10389
Taylor, S./Sjt. W. E.	10168
Trusler, Pte.(A./Cpl.) W. D.	10389
Tyrell, Pte.(A./S.Q.M.S.) F. (corr.)	12037
Uren, S.Q.M.S. R. N. (corr. of description)	10392
Vernem, A. W. (corr. of description)	10391
Wade, Q.M.S. J. W.	10168
Wakeling, Pte.(A./S.M.) A. A. (corr. of description)	10392
Walding, Sjt.(A./S.M.) B.	10168
Wallace, L./Bombr.) V. W. (corr. of description)	10391
Warren, C.E.R.A. 2nd Cl. F. W.	11002
Welch, Pte. J. (corr. of surname)	10392
Wharton, Clr.Sjt. J. A.	◊ 10168
White, S.Q.M.S. W. J. (corr. of description)	10392
Williams, S./Sjt. A.	10168
— T./S.Q.M.S. T. J. (corr.)	12037
Wilson, Sub Condr. G.	10168
— Sjt. G. H.	10165
— Sjt. J. W.	10389
Wolland, Pte. J. H. (corr. of description)	10392
Wood, Cpl.(L./Sjt.) P. (corr. of description)	10391
Woolff, Pte. E. (corr. of surname)	12037
Woollett, Cpl.(A./Sjt.) S.	10389
Worden, S./Sjt.(I.) H.	10168

* Group in Regimental Museum: M.M., British War and Victory Medals, India General Service Medal (Waziristan 1921), Defence Medal, Jubilee 1935, L.S. & G.C. (Geo. V), M.S.M. (for South Russia), and M.S.M. (Geo. VI Fid. Def.) (Royal Signals).

† No. Aust. 11, Aust. Flying Corps. For Valuable Services as a P.O.W. A.O. 193, 1919, cancelled *L.G.* 15 March, 1921 as originally issued *L.G.* 3 June, 1919.

‡ Group in Moss collection: 1914/15 Star trio (Bombr. R.F.A./R.A.), M.S.M. (for South Russia) and Russian Medal for Zeal with the Ribbon of St. Anne. He was one of the group of British Military Mission personnel who evacuated from Novorossik in November, 1919, having served with Denikin in early 1919 and Ekaterinden in 1920.

§ 6 Dragoons, N.W. Frontier Afghanistan.

+ For South Russia serving in Royal Fusiliers attached to Intelligence Corps.

◊ Group known: Queen's South Africa Medal (Cape Colony, Orange Free State, Transvaal), King's South Africa Medal (both Cpl. Cheshire R.), British War Medal (C. Sgt. Yorks. Regt.), L.S. & G.C. (Geo. V, C. S. Inst. E.C. Vol. Rifles) and M.S.M. (1/York Regt.), for India.

Wotton, Clr.Sjt.(O.R.S.) H. J.		Wyles, Sjt.(A./C.S.M.) H.	10388
(corr. of description)	* 10392	Yacomen, S./Sjt.(I.) J. W.	10168

---

* See also Wooton, p.162 Vol. 1/1920. Trio known: British War and Victory Medals
(R. Hants.) and M.S.M. (for Archangel).

Vol. I, 1921

* 5718378, 2/Dorsets (Nottingham). Joint citation with Gollop, *infra*.
† Military Police Corps; also in A.O.20 January 1921, to be dated 31 October, 1920.
‡ R.E.; also in A.O. 20 January 1921, to be dated 20 September 1920.
§ Sotheby's, July 1991. M.S.M. *L.G.* 18.2.21, Valuable Services Waziristan. A most interesting group of 14 awards to Conductor V. D'Auvergne, Supply & Transport Corps, comprising: Military Cross, Geo. V. (reverse engraved Lieut., S. & T. Corps), Distinguished Conduct Medal, Victoria (Staff Sergt., Comst. Transpt. Dept., renamed), Egypt, 1882, undated, 2 clasps, The Nile 1884–85, Abu Klea [copy] (Corpl., 16th Lancers, renamed), India General Service Medal, 1854, 5 clasps, Burma 1885–7 [copy], Sikkim 1888, Chin Lushai 1889–90, Samana 1891, Hazara 1891 Sergt., I.T. Corps, renamed), India General Service Medal, 1895, 3 clasps, Relief of Chitral 1895, Punjab Frontier 1897–98, Tirah 1897–98 [copy] (Sergt., C.T. Dept.), Third China War, 1900, no clasp (Staff Sergt., Comst. Transpt. Dept., renamed), Tibet, 1903, 1 clasp, Gyantse 1904 [copy] (Sub. Condr., S. & T. Corps), British War and Victory medals (Lieut., Political Service, both named), India General Service Medal, 1908, 1 clasp, Afghanistan N.W.F. 1919 (Condr., S. & T. Cps.), Coronation, 1937, Army L.S. & G.C., Victoria (Condr., S. & T. Corps., S. & T.C., renamed), Khedive's Star, 1884–6, mounted for display, the Egypt medal pitted but otherwise very fine and better. Conductor V. D'Auvergne, who was never awarded the M.C. or D.C.M., or indeed several of the above described campaign awards, possessed a depth of imagination which one can only stop to admire. Furthermore, he had the necessary flair and composure to promote his bluff in the most respected circles. A born raconteur, never short of 'thrilling tales' for his admiring audience, and blessed with a classic Indian Army Officer appearance, he was able to carry through the act until his death in Calcutta in 1940. Had he lived a little longer, he might have proved an excellent technical advisor to David Niven for his portrayal of 'the Major' in *Separate Tables*. The fact that he did see limited service in India and Tibet, and receive the M.S.M. does little to compensate for the extraordinary scale of his Flashman-like approach to collecting (and renaming) undeserved awards. At least George Macdonald Fraser's revived character always ends up in the thick of it, even if subsequent adulation and awards turn out to be misplaced. No such argument seems to exist in the case of Conductor D'Auvergne, whose junior rôle in the Supply and Transport Corps must have been a far cry from the more elaborate tales of 'derring-do' which he conjured up during his travels. Such was his success in acting out the role of a twice decorated Officer (with a combination of awards which would secure a place in the *Guinness Book of Records*), that he felt safe

Ewing, Pte.(A./Cpl.) J. P.		1363	Keane, Pte. J. H.	1363
			Kell, Pte. S.	1363
Feather, Sjt. J.	*	1363	Kyle, Sjt. G. W.	1362
Gallagher, 2nd Cpl.(A./Sjt.) W.	† ❀	2172	Lingwood, S./Sjt. R. W.	+ 1363
Godman, T./Supt.Clk. S. J.			Lyons, T./Sjt. T. F.	2172
(Notification of award in				
L.G. 16 Oct. 1919 deleted,			Mathieson, Pte. W.	1363
duplicate award)		1364		
Gollop, Pte. F. W. G.	‡ ❀	2172	O'Flaherty, T./S.Q.M.S. J.	1363
Granger, Cpl. A. E.		1363		
			Parkinson, Pte.(A./C.Q.M.S.) S. G.	1363
Heaton, Cpl. W. F. (corr.)		1364	Payne, Pte. V.	1363
Heaver, Pte.(A./Sjt.) W. A.		1363	Ponder, Sjt. F. A.	1363
Hepburn, Sub Condr. T.		1363		
Holroyd-Doveton, Sjt. M.		1362	Randall, W.O. Cl. 1, S. G. (corr.)	1364
Hoole, Pte.(A./Sjt.) T. C.		1363	Riddex, Pte.(A./Cpl.) A. C.	◊ 368
Howick, Pte.(A./Sjt.) A.		1363		
Hutchison, S./Sjt.(A./Supt.Clk.) J. G.			Saville, Pte.(L./C.) B. C.	1362
(corr.)		2173	Scott, Mech.S.M. A. R.	¶ 558
			Sloss, Flight Sjt. J. McK. (corr.)	2173
Jewell, Pte.(A./L./Sjt.) W. J.	§ ❀	2172	Spooner, Sjt. R. A. H., *M.M.*	1363

---

enough to publish some short stories. Thus appeared a wonderful tome, entitled *Zindari*, which included a portrait photograph of 'Captain D'Auvergne, M.C., D.C.M.' wearing the above medals (!), and a set of stories guaranteed to stir the coldest of hearts. Entertainment of the first degree can be found on every page, and it has to be said that if just a tenth of these tales bore direct resemblance to D'Auvergne's actual conduct, he would be more than worthy of the highest approbation.

* Group known: 1914/15 Star trio (Sgt., W. Yorks. R.), India General Service Medal (Waziristan 1919–21, Mahsud 1919–20, Waziristan 1921–24) and M.S.M. (1/D.W.R. attached 23/Div. Sig. Co.).

† 016237, R.A.O.C. (Stockton-on-Tees). See Jewell, *infra*; joint citation.

‡ 5719524, 2/Dorsets (Upper Parkstone). *L.G.* 15.3.21. For gallantry and devotion to duty during a fire at the Arsenal at St. Thomas' Mount (India) on the night of 18/19 June 1920. These soldiers were the first to undertake the removal of the bombs from the immediate vicinity of the flames, which they continued to do until ordered to rejoin the guard. The work was of a highly dangerous nature, involving risks of explosion. See Biddlecombe, *ante*.

§ 027967, R.A.O.C. (Carnbrea) *L.G.* 15.3.21. Gallantry and Devotion to Duty during a fire in an ammunition store shed at Basra (Mesopotamia) on 3.7.19. These N.C.O.'s, by a total disregard of personal danger, materially assisted in averting what might have proved a serious disaster by dismantling stacks and boxes of phosphorus and incendiary shells some of which were actually burning. In spite of the fumes and risk of burning and explosions, they continued the work of removal until the bay of the store was cleared. See Gallagher, *ante*.

+ Group known: 1914 Star & bar trio (M.I.D. oakleaf, Sgt.), India General Service Medal (Waziristan 1919–21, S. & T. Corps), 1935 Jubilee, L.S. & G.C. (Geo. V) and M.S.M. (2/E. Yorks. Regt.).

◊ 2/R.S.F.; also in A.O. 20 January 1921; to be dated 16 August 1920.

¶ R.A.S.C. For Siberia; also in A.O. 20 January 1921.

Stanynought, Sjt. F. B.	1362	
Thomson, Pte. G.	1363	
Thornback, C.Q.M.S.(A./S.M.) F. W. (corr.)	2173	
Turner, Sjt. S. J. (corr.)	2173	
Tyrrell, Pte.(A./S.Q.M.S.) F. (corr.)	1364	
Walker, Spr. G. W. (corr.)	1364	

Walsh, A./Sjt. H. T.			1363
Warwick, A./Sjt. D. J.		✿	2172
Williams, C.Q.M.S. J. (corr.)			2173

Meritorious Service Medal, Bar:

Beresford, Sjt. J.		* ✿	1362

* 3/K.R.R.C. *L.G.* 18.2.21. Bar to M.S.M. for Gallantry in Waziristan. For gallantry and devotion to duty on 11th March 1920, whilst serving with Waziristan Force when in a heavy snow storm he remained on duty transmitting important messages when the remainder of the staff had collapsed from the effect of oil fumes, thereby keeping open the only possible means of communicating at considerable risk to his health. (His M.S.M. was in *L.G.* 14.5.20 for N.W.F. India).

Vol. II, 1921

——⟩∞⟨——

---

* R.A.F. M.S.M. No. 313 R.F.C.; enlisted 28 April 1906 into R.F.A. 1914 Star & bar awarded, and R.A.F. L.S. & G.C. 1924.
† R.A.F. M.S.M. for Waziristan. Pair known: India General Service Medal (Mahsud 1919–21, Waziristan 1919–21) and R.A.F. M.S.M. Served 1915–21. Aero Rigger. M.I.D. 20 Sqn. 1 August, 1920.

Vol. III, 1921

Adlan, Cpl.(A./Sjt.) E. W.	7196	Jones, Pte. T. E.	§ ❀	6010
Anthony, Spr.(A./L./Sjt.) H. A. R.	7195	Josephs, Dpty.Supt. S. P. G. (corr. of name)		6011
Black, Sjt.(A./C.Q.M.S.) G. H., *D.C.M., M.M.*	* 7196	Kelleway, S.B.S. James Rixon (corr. of surname)		7137
Bowtle, Pte.(A./Sjt.) W. D. (corr. of rank)	6011	Massey, S./Sjt.(Supy. Sub Condr.) B.		7196
Boxall, Cpl.(A./W.O. Cl. II) H.	7195	Miller, W.O. Cl.1, D., *D.C.M.*	+	7196
Brown, Cpl.(A./Sjt.) D. J. O.	† 7196			
Cassar, Pte. P.	‡ 6010	Parish, Lt.Sto. William John		5560
Cooper, Gnr. E. (deletion of duplicate award)	6011	Pearce, Sdlr.Cpl. A. T. (corr. of rank)		6011
Dawson, Pte.(A./Sjt.) J. E. H.	7196	Playford, Sadd.Sjt. J. L.		7195
D'Souza, Telegraphist P.	6010	Pont, S./Sjt.(A./Sub Condr.) J. W.		7196
Donohue, Sjt. J. A., *M.M.*	7196	Richards, Pte.(A./Sjt.) J. W. (corr. of rank)		6011
Fleet, 2nd Cpl.(A./Sjt.) R. J. (corr. of surname)	6011	Sexton, S./Sjt.(A./ Sub Condr.) W. E.		7196
Gaywood, T./Sjt. W. H.	7196	Sole, S./Sjt. F. G.		7195
Graham, W.O. Cl.2(A./S.M., A.C.) A. M. (corr. of rank)	6011	Spiller, Condr. W.		7196
		Stonehouse, L./Cpl.(A./Sjt.) J.	◊ ❀	7641
Jackson, Sjt.(A./Sub Condr.) W. G.	7196	Sturgeon, Sjt. L. A. W.		7195

* M.G.C. See also A.O. 397/1921. To be dated 7 February, 1921, as are all twenty in this *L.G.*

† Group known: 1914 Star & bar (Pte. A.S.C.), British War and Victory Medals (Cpl. A.S.C. M.I.D. oakleaf), General Service Medal (Iraq, NW Persia) and M.S.M. (R.A.S.C., Mesopotamia). M.I.D. 9 September 1921, attached H.Q. Staff. M.S.M. for Iraq.

‡ Maltese Employment Company. For South Russia.

§ M/15536 R.A.S.C. (Oswestry). *L.G.* 29.7.21 for Gallantry in Egypt. At Kantara 28th June 1920 during a train wreck on the Palestine Military Railway, this soldier though badly injured himself—one arm being practically useless—behaved in a most courageous manner, dragging injured from the burning wreck. Being exhausted, he fell insensible on the sand, but on recovery continued to help carry the injured to a place of safety.

+ For Mesopotamia to Royal Ulster Rifles.

◊ 1852996, R.E. (Folkstone). *L.G.* 28.9.21. Gallantry in the performance of military duties in Mesopotamia. For gallant conduct and devotion to duty on the occasion of a fire amongst motor lorries, at Mosul on 28th June 1920. Arriving late on the

Taynton, Pte.(A./Sjt.) J. H.	7196	Wakeford, R.S.M. D. (delete		
Than Maung, Mate (A./Havildar)		duplicate award)		6011
(delete duplicate award)	6012	Walker, Sjt.(A./Mech.S./Sjt.) R.		7196
		Williams, Sjt.(A./W.O. Cl.1) A. V.	*	7196

scene this N.C.O. immediately became conspicuous for his disregard of danger and for his leading of the sappers. He immediately started to look around for new points from which the fire could be attacked. On several occasions he endeavoured to get into the back of one of the lorries and remove tins of petrol and other inflamable material which had not up until this time caught fire, but in each one he was driven back by the excessive heat. By his action and example he was responsible for getting the fire in this lorry under control.

* Group known: 1914 Star & bar (S25019 Cpl. A.S.C.), British War and Victory Medals (M.I.D. oakleaf, Sgt. A.S.C.), General Service Medal (Iraq, S1228 A./W.O.1 R.A.S.C.), L.S. & G.C. (S1248 W.O.II R.A.S.C.) and M.S.M. (R.A.S.C., for Iraq).

Attrill, S.M.I. W. C.	8496	Hitchcock, L.A.C.(A./Cpl.) H. C.	8496
		Honeybone, Flt.Sjt. J. W. +	8496
Bebington, Flt.Sjt. F.	8496		
Briggs, Cpl. S. J. *	8496	Morrison, W.O.Cl.1, E. J. (corr.)	9611
Bunting, Flt.Sjt. C. F. R. †	8496		
		Oakley, Flt.Sjt. C. ◊	8496
Cocks, C.P.O. A. ‡ ✿	9150		
Cooling, L.A.C.(A./Cpl.) G. F.	8496	Petch, A.C.1, H.	8496
Croft, Flt.Sjt. G. C.	8496		
		Ramplin, S.M.1, C. ¶	8496
Dobson, Flt.Sjt. A. E.	8496	Smith, S./Sjt. (I.) (T./Tpt.S.M.) M.	
		(corr.)	9611
Hart, L.A.C.(A./Cpl.) Frank H.	8496	Sparkes, Sjt. S. W.	8496
Hepple, Sjt. G. W. (Notification of			
award in *Gazette* 26 Oct. 1921		Tuckey, Flt.Sjt. J. H.	8496
cancelled, award being in			
Gazette 10 Nov. 1916) §	9785	Wilson, Flt.Sjt. B. W.	8496

---

* Group known: 1914/15 Star trio (Cpl/W.O.II R.E.), General Service Medal (Iraq, Cpl. R.A.F.), Defence and War Medals, Jubilee 1935, R.A.F. M.S.M. (for Mesopotamia), R.A.F. L.S. & G.C. (W.O.) and Territorial Force Efficiency Medal (Sgt. 2/E. Anglian Field Coy. R.E.).

† No. 864 R.F.C. Joined September 1913. 1914 Star earned from 16 August, 1914. R.A.F. M.S.M. for Mesopotamia. M.I.D. *L.G.* 10 October 1927 for Iraq (30 Sqn). Entitled to General Service Medal for Iraq and NW Persia.

‡ R.N. M.S.M. in recognition of courage and promptitude displayed by him when a saluting gun misfired on H.M.S. *Hawkins* on 19 August 1921.

§ Group known: B.E.M. (Geo. V, 2nd type, F./Sgt. R.A.F., June 1927), 1914 Star & bar trio (M.I.D. oakleaf), General Service Medal (Iraq, M.I.D. Oakleaf), India General Service Medal (N.W.F. 1935), Jubilee 1935, Army M.S.M. (Sgt. R.F.C.) and R.A.F. L.S. & G.C. No. 780, enlisted June 1913. In France from 16 August 1914. M.I.D. Cpl. *L.G.* 15 June 1916 and Sgt. *L.G.* 10 October 1922. Served in W.W.II. Discharged 1944.

+ R.A.F. M.S.M. for Mesopotamia. No. 1215 R.F.C., enlisted 11 February 1911 into R.E. Also entitled to General Service Medal (Iraq) and 1914 Star trio.

◊ Group known: General Service Medal (Iraq), India General Service Medal (Mohmand 1933 N.W.F. 1935), India General Service Medal (N.W.F. 1936–37), Jubilee 1935, Coronation 1937, R.A.F. M.S.M. and R.A.F. L.S & G.C. Served in W.W.I in U.K. (No. 3929) and also entitled to medals for W.W.II.

¶ R.A.F. M.S.M. No. 145 R.F.C. Enlisted 1906 into Rifle Brigade; also entitled to 1914 Star trio, General Service Medal (Iraq) and R.A.F. L.S. & G.C.; retired 1931.

Vol. I, 1922

Adams, Pte.(W.O. Cl. 1) W. T. (corr.
of rank)   2585

Ankers, L./Cpl. H. D.   * 2583

Carter, Pte. H.   † 2583

Childs, Sjt. A. W.   2583

Hartnett, Condr. G. W.   2583

Hatch, By.S.M. F. (deletion of
notification in Gaz. 17th
June 1918, duplicate award)   2586

Hills, Gnr. J.   2583

Jones, C.S.M. T. (deletion of
notification in Gaz. 12th
Dec. 1919, duplicate award)   2586

Leadbeater, Pte. R.   ‡ 2583

McLeod, S./Sjt. W. G. M. (corr. of
name)   2585

Maxwell, Pte.(A./Sjt.) D. H. (corr.
of rank)   2585

Millard, S.Q.M.Sjt.(A./1st Cl.
S./S.M.) C. J. (corr. of rank)   2585

Pankhurst, Pte. G.   2583

Pettit, Dvr. E. R.   2583

Sanford, Sjt. F.   2583

Snellgrove, Pte.(A./Sjt.) Louis (corr.)   963

Stocks, Gnr. W. K.   2583

Thomas, W.O. Cl.II, P. (corr. of
rank)   2585

Vigar, Pte.(A./Sjt.) V. G. (corr. of
name)   2585

Wilson, Sjt. G. H.   2583

---

* R.A.S.C. Devotion to Duty as a P.O.W. in Eastern Anatolia.
† M.G.C. Devotion to Duty as a P.O.W. in Eastern Anatolia.
‡ M.G.C. Devotion to Duty when a P.O.W. in Eastern Anatolia.

Vol. II, 1922

Bennett, Sjt. F. S.	* 3616	Stonehouse, Sjt. C.	+ 3616
Dalton, Pte. J. J.	† 3616	Thorogrood, Pte. A. J.	◊ 3616
Lilley, Sjt.(A./S./Sjt.) A.	‡ 3616	Wagstaff, Sjt. J. P.	¶ 3616
Moyse, Cpl. A.	§ 3616		

---

* 7 Hussars, for North Persia, (Indian Unattached List). Single M.S.M. known.
† K.R.R.C. For North Persia (4th Bn.).
‡ I.A. For North Persia (Corps of Military Staff Clerks).
§ 82 Coy. R.G.A. For North Persia.
+ 2/W. Yorks. Regt. For North Persia. Formerly Duke of Wellington's Regt.
◊ 2/Beds. & Herts. For North Persia.
¶ 7th Hussars. For North Persia, att. 18 Hussars.

Vol. III, 1922

Cooke, Pte.(A./Sjt.) W. H. (corr. of
    rank and regt.)   6903
Copland, T./S.M. J. (deletion of
    duplicate award in Gaz.
    3rd June 1919)   6903

Dobbs, T./Lt. C. G. (medal forfeited) 5961

Kent, Pte. L. J. (medal forfeited)   6158

Le Marinel, A.B. Sidney   * ❀ 5358

McDonald, Sjt. W. H. B. (deletion
    of duplicate award in Gaz.
    20th Oct. 1920)   6903

Maloney, Pte. P. J. (medal forfeited) 5961

Oldfield, Pte. H. (medal forfeited by
    sentence of Field G.C.M.)   6158

Rowe, Pte. W. N. (medal forfeited) † 5961

Vigar, Sjt. V. G. (corr. of name)   6903
— Amendment in Gaz. 29th
    March 1922 cancelled   6903

---

* A Jerseyman. Group known: 1914/15 Star trio and R.N. M.S.M., impressed number,
  rank, and name only. He deserted on 27 November 1922 and his medals were
  forfeited. He later re-qualified and medals were re-issued 'In recognition of his
  presence of mind and plucky action in dealing with a bomb in Shanghai, China.'
† Restored in 1925.

Vol. IV, 1922

Blight, Sjt. Samuel Wyatt	7134	Luscombe, Flight Sgt.		
Brooker, Sjt. Albert Victor	7134	William Phillip		7134
Dathan, Sjt. T. W.	* 9119	Mountfield, S.M. Cornelius Francis		7134
Figg, Sjt. Arthur	† 7134	Oland, Flight Sjt. Henry Alfred		
Forbes, late temp. Qrmr. and Lt.		Charles	‡	7134
James George Annand				
(award forfeited in		Taverner, Cpl. George Edwin		7134
consequence of conviction		Tucker, S.S.Inst. W. H. E.	§	9119
by Civil Power)	7049			
Garrod, L.A.C. (A./Cpl.) Frederick	7134			
Hawkes, Sjt. J.	8956	*Medal, List showing order in*		
		which worn		7871

———❖———

* 2/Gordon Highlanders. For South Persia.
† Enlisted December 1915. M.S.M. for Iraq 1920–21. Entitled to India General Service Medal (N.W.F. 1935). Later W.O. R.A.F. (No. 19797). Killed 26 May, 1941.
‡ Group known: British War and Victory Medals, W.W.II War Medal, R.A.F. M.S.M., for Iraq 1920–21, R.A.F. L.S. & G.C. and Russian Medal of St. George.
§ 16/5 Lancers. For South Persia.

Vol. I, 1923

Vol. II, 1923

Bannister, Pte. V. A.	4134	Long, Pte.(A./Sjt.) A. H.	4134
Barnes, Pte.(A./W.O.I) J. W.	3673	Lyon, Cpl. G.	3673
Bowler, Ftr.Sjt. E. G.	3673		
Bryon, Sig.(Cpl.) F. A. W.	4134	Moore, Condr. P.	3673
		Morgan, Sjt. M. J. C.	4134
Collins, Cpl. F.	4134	Murphy, 2nd Cl.	
Cooper, Spr.(L./C.) V.	4134	Asst. Surg. S. B. W.	† 3673
Cornwell, Sjt. A.	3673		
Cummings, Sig. J. T.	3673	Pawson, Bombr.(A./Sjt.) A. J.	3673
		Phaure, 3rd Cl. Asst. Surg. A. E.	3673
Denning, C.S.M. H., *M.M.*	4134		
Dunne, Sjt. J., *M.M.*	4134	Shields, Sjt. P. E.	3673
		Smith, Sub Condr. F. W. F.	4134
Francis, Pte.(L./C.) L. W. Le'B.	3673	Sullivan, W.O. I. G.	3673
Harding, S./Sjt.(A./Condr.) E. S.	4134	Todd, Sjt. A.	3673
Hawkes, Sjt. J. (forfeited)	3674		
Hollis, S./Sjt. L.	3673	Wilson, L./C. J., *M.M.*	‡ 4134
Lewis, Sjt.(A./Sub Condr.) E. J.	3673	Young, Pte.(A./Sjt.) P. C.	3673
Lilley, Pte.(A./Mech.S.M.) G.	* 4134		

* Group known: British War and Victory Medals (M.I.D. oakleaf), India General Service Medal (four clasps, Afghan N.W.F. 1919, Waziristan 1919–21, Mahsud 1919–20, Waziristan 1921–24) and M.S.M. (R.A.S.C. 4/Indian Brigade). The M.S.M. is for service in Waziristan. April to Dec 1921. George Lilley was born in 1889 in Wisbech and enlisted in March 1916. He served in Mesopotamia from July 1917 to March 1919 and was M.I.D. in *L.G.* 12 January 1920. He served in India from March 1919 to March 1924. Private, acting Sergeant Major is not often seen. He died aged 90 in September 1979.

† Group in Moss collection: British War and Victory Medals (3rd class Asst. Surgeon, Indian Medical Dept.), India General Service Medal (clasps Afghanistan N.W.F. 1919, Waziristan 1919–21, Asst. Surgeon I.M.D.), L.S. & G.C. (Geo. V, 1st class Asst. Surgeon I.M.D.) and M.S.M. (this last to be dated 23rd October, 1921). Born in October, 1886, Stanley Beresford William Murphy become a 4th class Asst. Surgeon in March, 1907 and served at Naini Tal, Allahabad and Lucknow. He became 3rd class Asst. Surgeon March 1912 and served in this rank throughout the War with the Indian 8th Division. As a 2nd Class Asst. Surgeon he served in Afghanistan and Waziristan and was then posted in succession to the British Military Hospitals at Ranikhet, Agra, Simla and Calcutta. His final promotion to 1st class came in March 1924, five years before his discharge in 1929.

‡ Group in McInnes collection: Military Medal (23110 A./Sgt. 3/Div. Sig. Coy. R.E., *L.G.* 24 January 1919), Queen's South Africa Medal (Tugula Heights, Relief of Ladysmith, Laing's Nek, Transvaal, South Africa 1901, 2/Scottish Rif.), 1914 Star & bar (Sapper R.E.), British War and Victory Medals, India General Service Medal

(Waziristan 1919–20, Mahsud 1919–20, Waziristan 1921–24, T./Sgt.), L.S. & G.C. (Geo. V, 23110 A./Sgt., M.M., R.E.), M.S.M. (1850359 L./Cpl. A./Sgt., M.M., R.E.). The M.S.M. is for service in Waziristan, to be dated 24 May 1922. John Wilson was born in 1880 in Upavon, Wiltshire, and was in all probability in the débâcle at Spion Kop. He was with 3 Div. Signalling Coy. at Mons, with the Second Corps. He was involved in many battles in W.W.I. 3/Div. Sig.Coy. were in the midst of much action, including the retreat from Mons, Le Cateau, Marne, Aisne, Ypres 1914 Nonne Boschen, Hooge 1915, Somme 1916, Bazentin, Delville Wood, Ancre, Scarpe 1917 Menin Road, Polygon Wood, Cambrai, St. Quentin, Bapaume Albert 1918, Canal du Nord, Selle and Sambre.. But Waziristan and Mahsud were not easy campaigns. The terrain, the climate and the tribesmen ensured that the 94 M.S.M.s awarded were well earned. He was discharged in 1926.

Vol. III, 1923

Moody Spr. J. F.   6275

Vol. IV, 1923

Bilton, S.B.A. William   * 8327   Richards, Acting S.B.P.O.
Alfred Gilbert   * 8327

Eyles, L.S.B.A., Charles Victory   * 8327

[Vol. 1, 1924—No entries]

---

* 'For Gallant Services in September last, at the destruction by earthquake and fire
of the R.N. Sick Quarters, Yokohama, Japan. All three were R.N.A.S.B.R. men.

Vol. II, 1924

---

* R.A.F. M.S.M. for Kurdistan in 1923. No. 755 R.F.C. Boy Entrant June 1913 aged 15. S.M.1 1933. Commissioned 1940. Group known: General Service Medal (Kurdistan), R.A.F. M.S.M., R.A.F. L.S. & G.C.

† Group known: 1914/15 Star trio (Gnr—Bombr. R.G.A.—R.A.), India General Service Medal (Afghanistan N.W.F. 1919, Waziristan 1919–21, Waziristan 1921–24) and M.S.M. (11 Pack Battery R.G.A.).

‡ Group in Regimental Museum: British War and Victory Medals (Sapper R.E.), India General Service Medal (Waziristan 1921–24, with M.I.D. oakleaf), General Service Medal (Palestine), Defence and War Medals (Major, Royal Signals), 1937 Coronation, L.S. & G.C. (Geo. V, Regular Army) and M.S.M.

§ See Vol. II 1919.

+ No. 23 R.F.C. Enlisted Febraury 1903 into the Air Bn. R.E. S.Maj. 1914. M.I.D. *L.G.* 22 June 1915. Entitled to 1914 Star & bar trio, General Service Medal (Kurdistan), R.A.F. M.S.M. (for Kurdistan, Nos. 6, 30 and 63 Sqn. R.A.F., March–June 1923) (M.I.D. *L.G.* 6 November 1924) and R.A.F. L.S. & G.C.

◊ See Appendix W.

Jones, Sgln. G. A.   * ✸ 5321   *Meritorious Service Medal, Bar:*

Coleman, Pte.(A./Sgt.) T. J.   † ✸ 5320

———◇◇◇———

* 2309293, Royal Corps of Signals (Walthamstow). *L.G.* 11.7.24. For Gallantry in Thrace. On 28th November 1922, when patrolling a telegraph line in Thrace he showed marked gallantry and devotion to duty in beating off single handed two armed brigands.

† R.A.S.C. Awarded M.S.M. 16 October 1919 (Italy), *L.G.* 11.7.24. Bar to M.S.M. for Gallantry. This N.C.O. was directly in charge of the British Fire Brigade in Constantinople and in this capacity has been present at about 200 fires during the period of 22 months. The Gallantry and Devotion to Duty displayed by this N.C.O. have resulted in the prevention of great material stock being destroyed and in the saving of many lives. Regardless of danger he has invariably placed himself in the position from which he could best direct the work of the Brigade and has on several occasions only escaped death by the closest margin. His group, 1914/15 Star trio and M.S.M. and bar, is known.

Vol. IV, 1924

Garnett, Guardsman A. (forfeited)   8423

Vol. I, 1925

Desmond, Corp.(A./Rly.Trans.S.M.) Francis   * 1769

Doman, Sjt. Harry, *D.C.M.*   † 1769

Greenhalgh, Corp.(A./C.S.M.) Arthur   ‡ 1769

Lambert, Sigmn.(A./L./Sjt.) Noel Victor   1769

Lane, Pte.(A./Sjt.) Wilfred   1769

Lewin, Sjt.(A./C.S.M.) William James   1769

Saunders, Warr.Off. C.S.M. Joseph, *D.C.M.*   § 1769

Smith, Pioneer Sjt. Jesse   1769

———❖———

[Vol II, 1925—No entries]
[Vol III, 1925—No entries]

* 1/Royal Inniskilling Fusiliers.

† D.C.M. *L.G.* 10 January 1920 as 1402 Cpl. 4/R.B., att. 3 Div. Signalling Coy. in Mesopotamia. M.S.M. as 1/R.B. & I.U.L.

‡ Group known in Moss collection: General Service Medal (Iraq, Kurdistan, A./Sgt. R.E.), India General Service Medal (Waziristan 1919–21, Waziristan 1921–23, Burma 1930–32, C.S.M. R.E.), 1939/45 and Burma Stars, Defence and War Medals, Coronation 1937, L.S. & G.C. (Geo. V, bar Regular Army, W.O.1), M.S.M. (for Waziristan) and India Independence Medal 1947. Only those five M.S.M.s awarded in 1926, 1927 and 1928 were issued later than these eight issued for Waziristan. 314075, later 1854281, Arthur Greenhalgh was born in Sheffield, South Yorkshire. He enlisted into the R.E. in 1919 as a Sapper and was assigned to the Inland Water Transport Section, Later that same year he was posted to India, an acting Sergeant attached to the Sappers & Miners. In 1925, sporting three medal ribbons (General Service Medal, India General Service Medal, and M.S.M.), he re-engaged to complete 12 years service and after service in Burma in 1930 he signed on to complete 21 years. In 1934 he was promoted to W.O.II and in the same year to W.O.I. His L.S. & G.C. came that year, suggesting he had three years previous service before 1919, which might also explain his early and rapid promotions. It is not known if he earned medals during W.W.I. In W.W.II he served in the Indian Engineers and was still serving in 1947 when he was awarded his last medal.

§ D.C.M. *L.G.* 11 March 1916 as 9219 C.S.M. 2/Welch R.

Vol. IV, 1925

[Vol II, 1925—No entries]
[Vol III, 1925—No entries]

Rowe, Pte. W. M. (restoration)   **6349**

[Vol I, 1926—No entries]

Vol. II, 1926

Edwards, Sgt.(Local C.S.M.)   *   3455

————◇◇◇————

---

   * Group known: D.C.M. (8102 Sgt. 2/Norfolk Regt.) (for gallantry and distinguished services rendered in connection with the *defence* of Kut-al-Amara), *L.G.* 23.10.19, British War Medal (8102 2/Norfolk R.), India General Service Medal (Waziristan 1919–21, 5763209 Sgt. 2/Norf. R.), General Service Medal (Kurdistan, 5763209 Norf. R.), L.S. & G.C. (Geo. V, fixed susp., 5763209 Sgt., D.C.M., Norfolk R.) and M.S.M. (attached Iraq Levies).

Vol. I, 1927

[Vol III, 1926—No entries]
[Vol IV, 1926—No entries]

Dickinson, Lce. Corp. E. J.   * ❀ 1046

———✕✕✕———

---

* 7812380, (Fulham). *L.G.* 15.2.27. Gallantry in the performance of military duties in Waziristan. On the afternoon of 4th June 1926, at Damdil Post, N. Waziristan, L.Cpl. Dickinson (Royal Corps of Signals), noticed that the S.A. Ammo. Magazine was on fire. Without hesitation he ran into the magazine and helped to remove several boxes of explosives to a safe distance. L.Cpl. Dickinson was in no way concerned with the charge of the magazine, but instantly gave his assistance at a time of great danger. By his gallant conduct he helped very materially to prevent a serious explosion and consequential loss of life.

Vol. II, 1927

Matheson, Staff Serjeant Murray
    Boulten   * ❀ 3447

Turner, Sub-Conductor George
    Edmund   † ❀ 3447

[Vol III, 1927—No entries]
[Vol IV, 1927—No entries]
[Vol I, 1928—No entries]

---

* 1022628, I.A.O.C. *L.G.* 27.5.27. S./Sgt. Matheson's citation is a repeat of Sub Cond. Turner's, *infra*, except that the second last sentence reads in addition: 'and assisted in pouring water over the burning boxes of explosives.' These two M.S.M.s are effectively the last two awarded under the immediate award rules. The one on *L.G.* p.2675 dated 13.4.28 to A./B.S.M. A. H. Frame, M.M., Canadian Artillery, was in respect of Valuable Services in N. Russia and was to be dated from 6th June 1919.

† Group known: M.B.E. (1st type, military ribbon), British War and Victory Medals, General Service Medal (Iraq), India General Service Medal (Waziristan 1921–24), L.S. & G.C. (Geo. V, running script as issued to Indian Army) and M.S.M. There is a citation in the *London Gazette*. 'On 6 April 1926 a fire broke out in a truck of explosives at Ferozepore Arsenal near the Magazine. Sub-Conductor Turner knew that the truck contained explosives, but in spite of this he entered the truck and assisted to unload it. By his gallant conduct he helped to extinguish the fire and materially prevented a serious explosion and consequent loss of life.' Turner was born 27 August 1881. His M.B.E. is verified in the Indian Army List of January, 1928. It is interesting to speculate that if this incident had occured in 1928, then an Empire Gallantry Medal would have been the new and natural alternative. If this *had* occured, Turner, had he lived long enough, would have exchanged his E.G.M. for a George Cross. He retired in 1931. All Turner's medals are named to the Indian Army Ordanance Corps.

Vol. II, 1928

[Vol III, 1927—No entries]
[Vol IV, 1927—No entries]
[Vol I, 1928—No entries]

Frame, Actg. Battery Sgt. Major
    A. H., *M.M.*　　　　　 * 2675

---

* See Matheson, Vol. II, 1927

Appendices

London Gazette Headings

YEAR 1916

18th October   pages 10041–5

War Office 18th October, 1916. His Majesty the KING has been graciously pleased to award the Meritorious Service Medal to the undermentioned Warrant Officers, Non-commissioned Officers and Men, in recognition of valuable services rendered during the present war:—   (403 names)

11th November   pages 10933–5

His Majesty the KING has been graciously pleased to award the Meritorious Service Medal to the undermentioned Warrant Officers, Non-commissioned Officers and Men, in recognition of valuable services rendered with the Armies in the Field during the present war:—   (202 names)

YEAR 1917

1st January   pages 52–5

Awarded the Meritorious Service Medal:—   (390 names)

24th January   page 927

Awarded Meritorious Service Medal:—   (1 name)

1st February   page 1146

Awarded Meritorious Service Medal in recognition of valuable services in East Africa:—   (18 names)

13th February   pages 1574–5

His Majesty the KING has been graciously pleased to award the Meritorious Service Medal to the undermentioned Warrant Officers, Non-commissioned Officers and Men, in recognition of valuable services rendered with the Armies in the Field during the present war:—   (107 names)

15th February   page 1596

War Office 15th Feb., 1917:—His Majesty the KING has been graciously pleased to approve of the undermentioned rewards for Distinguished Service in the Field, with effect from 1st January, 1917, inclusive, except where otherwise stated:—   (2 names)

1917 (Contd.)

12th March   pages 2487–8

His Majesty the KING has been graciously pleased to award the Meritorious Service Medal to the undermentioned Warrant Officers, Non-commissioned Officers and Men, in recognition of valuable services rendered with the Armies in the Field during the present war:—   (89 names)

page 2488

His Majesty the KING has been graciously pleased to approve of the award of the Meritorious Service Medal to the following Warrant Officers, Non-commissioned Officers and Men in recognition of valuable services rendered with the Armies in the Field during the present war:—   (21 awarded)

17th April   page 3700

His Majesty the KING has been graciously pleased to award the Meritorious Service Medal to the undermentioned Non-commissioned Officers and Men for gallantry in the performance of military duty:—   (14 names)

(Also Meritorious Service Medal Correction. 'With reference to the awards of Meritorious Service Medals published in Gazette of 12th Ultimo, the undermentioned names should have appeared under the heading "for gallantry in the performance of military duty," not for "services rendered with the Armies in the Field during the present war." Officers in charge of Records will, accordingly, make the necessary corrections in their records.')

26th April   page 3949

His Majesty the KING has been graciously pleased to award the Meritorious Service Medal to the undermentioned Non-commissioned Officers, for gallantry in the performance of military duty:—

(2 names)

pages 3949–50

His Majesty the KING has been graciously pleased to award the Meritorious Service Medal to the undermentioned Warrant Officers, Non-commissioned Officers and Men in recognition of valuable services rendered with the Armies in the Field during the present war:—   (105 names)

11th May   page 4602

His Majesty the KING has been graciously pleased to award the Meritorious Service Medal to the undermentioned Non-commissioned Officers and Men for gallantry in the performance of military duty:—   (5 names)

26th May   page 5197

His Majesty the KING has been graciously pleased to award the Meritorious Service Medal to the undermentioned Non-commissioned Officers and Men for gallantry in the performance of military duty:—   (7 names)

1917 (Contd.)

26th May *(Contd.)*   pages 5197–8

His Majesty the KING has been graciously pleased to award the Meritorious Service Medal to the undermentioned Warrant Officers, Non-commissioned Officers and Men, in recognition of valuable services rendered with the Armies in the Field during the present war:—   (39 names)

4th June   pages 5491–3

Awarded The Meritorious Service Medal for valuable services rendered with the Armies in the Field:—   (293 names)

18th June   page 6027

His Majesty the KING has been graciously pleased to award the Meritorious Service Medal to the undermentioned Non-commissioned Officers and Men for gallantry in the performance of military duty:—   (9 names)

                                                                         pages 6027–8

His Majesty the KING has been graciously pleased to award the Meritorious Service Medal to the undermentioned Warrant Officers, Non-commissioned Officers and Men in recognition of valuable services rendered with the Armies in the Field during the present war:—   (90 names)

9th July   page 6845

His Majesty the KING has been graciously pleased to award the Meritorious Service Medal to the undermentioned Non-commissioned Officers and Men for gallantry in the performance of military duty:—   (3 names)

                                                                         page 6845

His Majesty the KING has been graciously pleased to award the Meritorious Service Medal to the undermentioned Warrant Officers, Non-commissioned Officers and Men, in recognition of valuable services rendered with the Armies in the Field during the present war:—   (22 names)

18th July   page 7291

His Majesty the KING has been graciously pleased to award the Meritorious Service Medal to the undermentioned Warrant Officers, Non-commissioned Officers and Men for gallantry in the performance of military duty:—

                                                                         (8 names)

28th July   page 7771

His Majesty the KING has been graciously pleased to award the Meritorious Service Medal to the undermentioned Non-commissioned Officers and Men for gallantry in the performance of Military duty:—   (10 names)

1917 (Contd.)

28th July *(Contd.)*   page 7771

> His Majesty the KING has been graciously pleased to award the Meritorious Service Medal to the undermentioned Warrant Officers, Non-commissioned Officers and Men, in recognition of valuable services rendered with the Armies in the Field during the present war:—   (10 names)

16th August   pages 8431–3

> His Majesty the KING has been graciously pleased to award the Meritorious Service Medal to the undermentioned Warrant Officers, Non-commissioned Officers and Men, in recognition of valuable services rendered with the Armies in the Field during the present war:—   (286 names)

21st August   page 8648

> His Majesty the KING has been graciously pleased to award the Meritorious Service Medal to the undermentioned Non-commissioned Officers and Men for gallantry in the performance of military duty:—   (10 names)

29th August   pages 9002–3

> Awarded the Meritorious Service Medal, for valuable services rendered with the Armies in the Field, in Mesopotamia:—   (89 names)

                                                                     page 9002

> His Majesty the KING has been graciously pleased to award the Meritorious Service Medal to the undermentioned Non-commissioned Officers and Men for gallantry in the performance of military duty:—   (9 Names)

> His Majesty the KING has been graciously pleased to award the Meritorious Service Medal to the undermentioned Warrant Officers, Non-commissioned Officers and Men in recognition of valuable services rendered with the Armies in the Field during the present war:—   (9 names)

17th September   page 9615

> His Majesty the KING has been graciously pleased to award the Meritorious Service Medal to the undermentioned Warrant Officers, Non-commissioned Officers and Men for gallantry in the performance of military duty:—
>
>   (12 names)

28th September   pages 10039–40

> His Majesty the KING has been graciously pleased to award the Meritorious Service Medal to the undermentioned Non-commissioned Officers and Men for gallantry in the performance of Military duty:—   (9 names)

1917 (Contd.)

28th September *(Contd.)*   page 10040

    His Majesty the KING has been graciously pleased to award the Meritorious Service medal to the undermentioned Warrant Officer, Non-commissioned Officer and Men in recognition of valuable services rendered with the Armies in the Field during the present war:—   (4 names)

17th October   page 10680

    Awarded the Meritorious Service Medal for valuable services rendered with the Armies in the Field:—   (7 names)

18th October   page 10731

    His Majesty the KING has been graciously pleased to award the Meritorious Service Medal to the undermentioned Non-commissioned Officers for gallantry in the performance of military duty:—   (2 names)

2nd November   page 11348

    His Majesty the KING has been graciously pleased to award the Meritorious Service Medal to the undermentioned Non-commissioned Officers and Men for gallantry in the performance of military duty:—   (9 names)

19th November   page 11979

    His Majesty the KING has been graciously pleased to approve of the award of the Meritorious Service Medal to the undermentioned, for gallantry in the performance of military duty:—   (2 names)

    His Majesty the KING has been graciously pleased to award the Meritorious Service Medal to the undermentioned Warrant Officers, Non-commissioned Officers and Men, in recognition of valuable services rendered with the Armies in the Field during the present war:—   (16 names)

12th December   page 13027

    His Majesty the KING has been graciously pleased to award the Meritorious Service Medal to the undermentioned Non-commissioned Officers and Men for gallantry in the performance of military duty:—   (8 names)

17th December   pages 13202–4

    His Majesty the KING has been graciously pleased to approve of the award of the Meritorious Service Medal to the undermentioned Warrant Officers, Non-commissioned Officers and Men, in recognition of valuable services rendered with the Armies in the Field during the present war:—   (200 names)

YEAR 1918

1st January pages 66–77

His Majesty the KING has been graciously pleased to approve of the award of the Meritorious Service Medal to the undermentioned Warrant Officers, Non-commissioned Officers and Men, in recognition of valuable services rendered with the Armies in the Field during the present war:—   (905 names)

14th January page 848

His Majesty the KING has been graciously pleased to approve of the award of the Meritorious Service Medal to the undermentioned Non-commissioned Officers and Men for gallantry in the performance of military duty:—   (2 names)

His Majesty the KING has been graciously pleased to approve of the award of the Meritorious Service Medal to the undermentioned Non-commissioned Officers and Men, in recognition of valuable services rendered in the performance of military duty:—   (3 names)

28th January page 1406

His Majesty the KING has been graciously pleased to approve of the award of the Meritorious Service Medal to the undermentioned Non-commissioned Officers and Men for gallantry in the performance of military duty:—   (3 names)

His Majesty the KING has been graciously pleased to approve of the award of the Meritorious Service Medal to the undermentioned Non-commissioned Officers in recognition of valuable services rendered with the Armies in the Field during the present war:—   (2 names)

4th February page 1621

His Majesty the KING has been graciously pleased to approve of the award of the Meritorious Service Medal to the undermentioned Man in recognition of gallantry in the performance of military duty:—   (1 name)

page 1621

His Majesty the KING has been graciously pleased to approve of the award of the Meritorious Service Medal to the undermentioned men in recognition of valuable services rendered with the Armies in the Field during the present war:—   (4 names, including 3 South Africans)

23rd February page 2439

His Majesty the KING has been graciously pleased to approve of the award of the Meritorious Service Medal to the undermentioned Non-commissioned Officer and Men for gallantry in the performance of military duty:—   (3 names)

His Majesty the KING has been graciously pleased to approve of the award of the Meritorious Service Medal to the undermentioned Non-commissioned Officer in recognition of valuable services rendered with the Armies in the Field during the present war:—   (1 name)

1918 (Contd.)

8th March   page 2974

    Awarded Meritorious Service Medal:—   (4 names)

13th March   page 3254

    His Majesty the KING has been graciously pleased to approve of the award of the Meritorious Service Medal to the undermentioned Man, for gallantry in the performance of military duty:—   (1 name)

                                                              pages 3254–5

    His Majesty the KING has been graciously pleased to award the Meritorious Service Medal to the undermentioned Warrant Officers, Non-commissioned Officers and Men, in recognition of valuable services rendered with the Armies in the Field during the present war:—   (73 names)

19th March   page 3473

    His Majesty the KING has been graciously pleased to approve of the award of the Meritorious Service Medal to the undermentioned Warrant Officers, Non-commissioned Officers and Men for gallantry in the performance of military duty:—   (13 names)

2nd April   page 4024

    His Majesty the KING has been graciously pleased to award the Meritorious Service Medal to the undermentioned Non-commissioned officer and Men for gallantry in the performance of military duty:—   (3 names)

    His Majesty the KING has been graciously pleased to award the Meritorious Service Medal to the undermentioned Warrant Officers in recognition of valuable services rendered with the Armies in the Field during the present war:—   (3 names)

10th April   page 4393

    His Majesty the KING has been graciously pleased to approve of the award of the Meritorious Service Medal to the undermentioned Non-commissioned Officers and Men for gallantry in the performance of Military duty:—   (17 names)

11th April   page 4413

    Awarded Meritorious Service Medal for distinguished services in the field in connection with Military Operations culminating in the capture of Jerusalem:—   (31 names)

13th April   page 4500

    Awarded Meritorious Service Medal for valuable services in North Russia:—   (1 name)

1918 (Contd.)

25th April   page 5037

His Majesty the KING has been graciously pleased to approve of the award of the Meritorious Service Medal to the undermentioned Non-commissioned Officers and Men for gallantry in the performance of military duties:—   (12 names)

3rd June   pages 6491–2

His Majesty the KING has been graciously pleased on the occasion of His Majesty's Birthday, to approve of the award of the Meritorious Service Medal to the undermentioned Warrant Officers, Non-commissioned Officers and Men, in recognition of valuable services rendered with the Forces in Egypt:—

(71 names)

pages 6498–501

His Majesty the KING has been graciously pleased on the occasion of His Majesty's Birthday, to approve of the award of the Meritorious Service Medal to the undermentioned Warrant Officers, Non-commissioned Officers and Men, in recognition of valuable services rendered with the Forces in Italy:—

(237 names)

pages 6507–10

His Majesty the KING has been graciously pleased, on the occasion of His Majesty's Birthday, to approve of the undermentioned rewards for valuable services in connection with Military Operations with the British Forces in Salonika:—   (195 names)

page 6512

His Majesty the KING has been graciously pleased, on the occasion of His Majesty's Birthday, to approve of the award of the Meritorious Service Medal to the undermentioned Non-commissioned Officers in recognition of valuable services rendered in Russia:—   (3 names)

page 6512

His Majesty the KING has been graciously pleased, on the occasion of His Majesty's Birthday, to approve of the award of the Meritorious Service Medal to the undermentioned Warrant Officers and Non-commissioned Officers in recognition of valuable services rendered with the British Forces on the Mediterranean Lines of Communications:—   (5 names)

12th June   page 7018

His Majesty the KING has been graciously pleased to approve of the award of the Meritorious Service Medal to the undermentioned Warrant Officers, Non-commissioned Officers and Men for gallantry in the performance of military duty:—   (10 names)

1918 (Contd.)

12th June *(Contd.)*

His Majesty the KING has been graciously pleased to approve of the award of the Meritorious Service Medal to the undermentioned Warrant Officer in recognition of valuable services rendered with the Armies in the Field during the present war:— (1 name)

17th June pages 7133–81

His Majesty the KING has been graciously pleased to approve of the award of the Meritorious Service Medal to the undermentioned Warrant Officers, Non-commissioned Officers and Men, in recognition of valuable services rendered with the Forces in France during the present war:— (4251 names)

27th June page 7599

His Majesty the KING has been graciously pleased to approve of the award of the Meritorious Service Medal to the undermentioned Warrant Officer and Non-commissioned Officer:— (2 names)

16th July page 8334

His Majesty the KING has been graciously pleased to approve of the award of the Meritorious Service Medal to the undermentioned Warrant Officer, Non-commissioned Officer and Men for gallantry in performance of military duty:— (4 names)

6th August page 9256

His Majesty the KING has been graciously pleased to approve of the award of the Meritorious Service Medal to the undermentioned Warrant Officers, Non-commissioned Officers and Men for gallantry in the performance of military duty:— (11 names)

His Majesty the KING has been graciously pleased to approve of the award of the Meritorious Service Medal to the undermentioned Warrant Officer in recognition of valuable services rendered with the Armies in the Field during the present war:— (1 name)

22nd August page 9803

His Majesty the KING has been graciously pleased to approve of the award of the Meritorious Service Medal to the undermentioned Warrant Officers, Non-commissioned Officers and Men, for valuable services in the Field, and in connection with the campaign in German South-West Africa 1914-15:— (41 names)

29th August page 10143

His Majesty the KING has been graciously pleased to approve of the award of the Meritorious Service Medal to the undermentioned for gallantry in the performance of military duties:— (3 names)

1918 (Contd.)

29th August   pages 10143–4

His Majesty the KING has been graciously pleased to approve of the award of the Meritorious Service Medal to the undermentioned in recognition of valuable services rendered with the Armies in the Field during the present war:—

(77 names)

pages 10144–6

His Majesty the KING has been graciously pleased to approve of the award of the Meritorious Service Medal to the undermentioned Warrant Officers, Non-commissioned Officers and Men, in recognition of valuable services rendered with the Force in East Africa during the present war:—   (146 names)

4th September   page 10496

His Majesty the KING has been graciously pleased to approve of the award of the Meritorious Service Medal to the undermentioned for valuable services in France & Flanders:—   (8 names)

6th September   pages 10525–6

His Majesty the KING has been pleased to approve of the following awards for devotion to duty on the occasion of the destruction or damage by enemy action of Hospital Ships, Transports and Storeships. Dated 3rd June, 1918:—

(28 names)

13th September   page 10779

His Majesty the KING has been graciously pleased to approve of the award of the Meritorious Service Medal to the undermentioned Warrant Officer, Non-commissioned Officers and Men for gallantry in the performance of military duty:—   (16 names)

His Majesty the KING has been graciously pleased to approve of the award of the Meritorious Service Medal to the undermentioned Native Warrant Officers in recognition of valuable services rendered With the Forces in East Africa during the present war:—   (5 names)

7th October   page 11841

His Majesty the KING has been graciously pleased to approve of the award of the Meritorious Service Medal to the undermentioned Warrant Officers, Non-commissioned Officers and Men for gallantry in the performance of military duty:—   (13 names)

15th October   pages 12103–5

His Majesty the KING has been graciously pleased to approve of the award of the Meritorious Service Medal to the undermentioned Warrant Officers, Non-commissioned Officers and Men, in recognition of valuable services rendered with the Forces in Mesopotamia during the present war:—   (120 names)

1918 (Contd.)

21st October   page 12423

> His Majesty the KING has been graciously pleased to approve of the award of the Meritorious Service Medal to the undermentioned Non-commissioned Officers and Men for gallantry in the performance of military duty:—   (5 names)

19th December   page 14906

> His Majesty the KING has been graciously pleased to approve of the award of the Meritorious Service Medal to the undermentioned Warrant Officers and Non-commissioned Officers for valuable services rendered within the Union of South Africa in connection with the campaigns in German South-West Africa and German East Africa:—   (13 names)

YEAR 1919

1st January   pages 60–62

> His Majesty the KING has been graciously pleased to approve of the award of the Meritorious Service Medal to the following Warrant Officers, Non-commissioned Officers and Men, in recognition of valuable services rendered with the Forces in Egypt:—   (150 names)

                                                                                pages 68–71

> His Majesty the KING has been graciously pleased to approve of the award of the Meritorious Service Medal to the undermentioned Warrant Officers, Non-commissioned Officers and Men, in recognition of valuable services with the British Forces in Italy:—   (221 names)

                                                                                page 80

> His Majesty the KING has been graciously pleased to approve of the award of the Meritorious Service Medal to the following Warrant Officers, Non-commissioned Officers and Men, in recognition of valuable services rendered with the Forces in Northern Russia:—   (7 names)

18th January   pages 969–1024

> His Majesty the KING has been graciously pleased to approve of the award of the Meritorious Service Medal to the following Warrant Officers, Non-commissioned Officers and Men, in recognition of valuable services rendered with the Armies in France & Flanders:—   (4407 names)

24th January   page 1256

> His Majesty the KING has been graciously pleased to approve of the award of the Meritorious Service Medal to the undermentioned Non-commissioned Officers and Men for gallantry in the performance of military duty:—   (19 names)

> His Majesty the KING has been graciously pleased to approve of the award of the Meritorious Service Medal to the undermentioned for gallantry in the performance of military duties in Aden:—   (3 names)

1919 (Contd.)

24th January *(Contd.)*   page 1256

His Majesty the KING has been graciously pleased to approve of the award of the Meritorious Service Medal to the undermentioned for gallantry in the performance of military duties in East Africa:—   (2 names)

His Majesty has been graciously pleased to approve of the award of the Meritorious Service Medal to the undermentioned Non-commissioned Officer, in recognition of valuable services rendered with the Armies in the Field during the present war:—   (1 name)

31st January   pages 1487–90

His Majesty the KING has been graciously pleased to approve of the award of the Meritorious Service Medal to the following Warrant Officers, Non-commissioned Officers and Men, in recognition of valuable services rendered with the British Forces in Salonika:—   (197 names)

7th February   pages 1944–6

His Majesty the KING has been graciously pleased to approve of the award of the Meritorious Service Medal to the undermentioned Warrant Officers, Non-commissioned Officers and Men, in recognition of valuable services rendered in connection with Military Operations with the Forces in East Africa:—

                                  (129 names)

22nd February   pages 2689–703

His Majesty the KING has been graciously pleased to approve of the award of the Meritorious Service Medal to the undermentioned Warrant Officers, Non-commissioned Officers and Men, in recognition of valuable services rendered in connection with the war:—
(1007 names including 32 for India, 8 Gibraltar, 1 West Africa, 4 Bermuda, 1 Ceylon, 5 China, 6 Malta and 1 Singapore)

3rd March   pages 2997–3000

His Majesty the KING has been graciously pleased to approve of the award of the Meritorious Service Medal to the undermentioned Warrant Officers, Non-commissioned Officers and Men, in recognition of valuable services rendered with the British Force in Mesopotamia:—   (171 names)

15th March   page 3572

His Majesty the KING has been graciously pleased to approve of the award of the Meritorious Service Medal to the undermentioned Warrant Officers, Non-commissioned Officers and Man, in recognition of valuable services rendered in connection with the war in record offices:—   (39 names)

1919 (Contd.)

22nd March

page 3840

His Majesty the KING had been graciously pleased to approve of the award of the Meritorious Service Medal to the following Warrant Officers, Non-commissioned Officers and Men, in recognition of valuable services rendered with Armies in France & Flanders:— (40 names)

His Majesty the KING has been graciously pleased to approve of the award of the Meritorious Service Medal to the following in recognition of valuable services rendered with Armies in India:— (1 name)

His Majesty the KING has been graciously pleased to approve of the award of the Meritorious Service Medal to the following Warrant Officers, Non-commissioned Officers and Men, in recognition of valuable services rendered with the British Forces in Salonika:— (4 names)

page 3841

His Majesty the KING has been graciously pleased to approve of the award of the Meritorious Service Medal to the undermentioned Warrant Officers and Non-commissioned Officers in recognition of valuable services rendered in connection with the war:— (10 names)

3rd June

pages 6865–6919

His Majesty the KING has been graciously pleased to approve of the award of the Meritorious Service Medal to the following Warrant Officers, Non-commissioned Officers and Men, in recognition of valuable services rendered with the Armies in France & Flanders:— (5116 names)

pages 6932–5

His Majesty the KING has been graciously pleased to approve of the award of the Meritorious Service Medal to the following Warrant Officers, Non-commissioned Officers and Men, in recognition of valuable services rendered with the Forces in Egypt:— (235 names)

page 6935

His Majesty the KING has been graciously pleased to approve of the award of the Meritorious Service Medal to the following Non-commissioned Officers, in recognition of valuable services rendered with the Forces in Arabia:— (3 names)

pages 6942–6

The KING has been graciously pleased, on the occasion of His Majesty's Birthday, to approve of the award of the Meritorious Service Medal to the undermentioned Warrant Officers, Non-commissioned Officers and Men, in recognition of valuable services rendered with the British Forces in Italy:— (265 names)

1919 (Contd.)

3rd June *(Contd.)*   pages 6953–8

The KING has been graciously pleased to approve of the award of the Meritorious Service Medal to the following Warrant Officers, Non-commissioned Officers and Men, in recognition of valuable services rendered with the British Forces in the Balkans:—   (356 names)

                                                                                        page 6971

The KING has been graciously pleased to approve of the award of the Meritorious Service Medal to the following Warrant Officers, Non-commissioned Officers and Men, in recognition of valuable services rendered with the British Forces in the Union of South Africa:—   (13 names)

His Majesty the KING has been graciously pleased to approve of the award of the Meritorious Service Medal to the undermentioned Non-commissioned Officers and Men, for valuable services rendered in the Field in connection with the campaign in German South-West Africa:—   (3 names)

                                                                                        pages 6969–71

His Majesty the KING has been graciously pleased to approve of the award of the Meritorious Service Medal to the undermentioned Warrant Officers and Men, in recognition of valuable services rendered in connection with Military Operations with the Forces in East Africa:—   (146 names)

                                                                                        page 6974

The KING has been graciously pleased, on the occasion of His Majesty's Birthday, to approve of the award of the Meritorious Service Medal for valuable service rendered in connection with Military Operations in North Russia (Archangel Command):—   (17 names)

                                                                                        pages 6975–6

The KING has been graciously pleased, on the occasion of His Majesty's Birthday, to approve of the award of the Meritorious Service Medal for valuable services rendered in connection with Military Operations in North Russia (Murmansk Command):—   (12 names)

                                                                                        pages 6976

His Majesty the KING has been graciously pleased to approve of the award of the Meritorious Service Medal to the following Warrant Officers, Non-commissioned Officers and Men, in recognition of valuable services rendered with the Forces in the Aden Peninsula:—   (17 names)

1919 (Contd.)

3rd June *(Contd.)*   pages 7010–23

    His Majesty the KING has been graciously pleased to approve of the award of the Meritorious Service Medal to the undermentioned Warrant Officers, Non-commissioned Officers and Men, in recognition of valuable services rendered in connection with the war:—

(1063 names including 43 for India, 7 Gibraltar, 6 Hong Kong, 8 Malta, 6 Singapore, 3 Ceylon, 1 Jamaica, 1 Sierra Leone, 1 West Africa and 3 Bermuda)

17th June   page 7702

    His Majesty the KING has been graciously pleased to approve of the award of the Meritorious Service Medal to the undermentioned Warrant Officer, Non-commissioned Officers and Man, in recognition of valuable services rendered with the Forces in Northern Russia (Archangel):—   (5 names)

                                          page 7701

    His Majesty the KING has been graciously pleased to approve of the award of the Meritorious Service Medal to the undermentioned Warrant Officer, Non-commissioned Officers and Men, for gallantry in the performance of military duty:—   (28 names including 3 for Mesopotamia)

3rd July   page 8359

    His Majesty the KING has been graciously pleased to approve of the award of the Meritorious Service Medal to the undermentioned Warrant Officers, Non-commissioned Officers and Men for gallantry in the performance of military duty:—

(20 names including 1 for Egypt, 3 for Mesopotamia and 2 for Salonika)

27th July   page 9500

    His Majesty the KING has been graciously pleased to approve of the award of the Meritorious Service Medal to the undermentioned for valuable service:—

(4 names)

13th August   pages 10319–20

    His Majesty the KING has been graciously pleased to approve of the award of the Meritorious Service Medal to the following Warrant Officers, Non-commissioned Officers and Men, in recognition of valuable services rendered with the British Force in North Russia (Murmansk Command):—   (11 names)

20th August   page 10587

    His Majesty the KING has been graciously pleased to approve of the award of the Meritorious Service Medal to the following Non-commissioned Officers and Men for gallantry in the performance of military duty:—

(10 names including 3 for Mesopotamia)

1919 (Contd.)

22nd September   pages 11773–80

His Majesty the KING has been graciously pleased to approve of the award of the Meritorious Service Medal to the following Warrant Officers, Non-commissioned Officers and Men, in recognition of valuable services rendered with the British Forces in Mesopotamia:—   (509 names)

29th September   page 11997

His Majesty the KING has been graciously pleased to approve of the award of the Meritorious Service Medal to the following Warrant Officer and Men for devotion to duty during an epidemic in a Prisoners of War Camp, Germany:—   (3 names)

3rd October   pages 12134–5

His Majesty the KING has been graciously pleased to approve of the award of the Meritorious Service Medal to the following Warrant Officers, Non-commissioned Officers and Men, in recognition of valuable services rendered with the British Force in North Russia—Archangel Command:—   (34 names)

                                                     page 12135

His Majesty the KING has been graciously pleased to approve of the award o: the Meritorious Service Medal to the following Warrant Officers, Non-commissioned Officers and Men, in recognition of valuable services rendered with the British Force in North Russia—Murmansk Command:—   (24 names)

His Majesty the KING has been graciously pleased to approve of the award of the Military Medal to the undermentioned Man for bravery in the Field with the British Force in North Russia—Murmansk Command:—   (1 name)

16th October   pages 12753–61

His Majesty the KING has been graciously pleased to approve of the award of the Meritorious Service Medal to the following Warrant Officers, Non-commissioned Officers and Men, in recognition of valuable services rendered with the Armies in France & Flanders:—   (628 names)

                                                   pages 12761–2

His Majesty the KING has been graciously pleased to approve of the award of the Meritorious Service Medal to the following Warrant Officers, Non-commissioned Officers and Man, in recognition of valuable services rendered with the British Forces in Italy:—   (9 names)

                                                   page 12762

His Majesty the KING has been graciously pleased to approve of the award of the Meritorious Service Medal to the following Warrant and Non-commissioned Officers in recognition of valuable services rendered with the British Forces in Egypt:—   (10 names)

1919 (Contd.)

16th October *(Contd.)*   page 12762

> His Majesty the KING has been graciously pleased to approve of the award of the Meritorious Service Medal to the following Warrant Officers, Non-commissioned Officers and Men, in recognition of valuable services rendered with the British Forces in the Balkans:—   (57 names)

page 12763

> His Majesty the KING has been graciously pleased to approve of the award of the Meritorious Service Medal to the following Warrant Officer, Non-commissioned Officer and Men, in recognition of valuable services rendered with the British Military Mission to Turkestan (Army of the Black Sea):—   (12 names)

> His Majesty the KING has been graciously pleased to approve of the award of the Meritorious Service Medal to the following Warrant Officers, Non-commissioned Officers and Men, in recognition of valuable services rendered with the British Forces in East Africa:—   (21 names)

> His Majesty the KING has been graciously pleased to approve of the award of the Meritorious Service Medal to the undermentioned Warrant and Non-commissioned Officers in recognition of valuable Service rendered with the Forces in South Persia:—   (6 names)

pages 12763–5

> His Majesty the KING has been graciously pleased to approve of the award of the Meritorious Service Medal to the undermentioned Warrant Officers, Non-commissioned Officers and Men, in recognition of valuable services rendered in connection with the war:—
> (99 names including 1 for Jamaica and 1 for Malta)

20th October   page 12875

> His Majesty the KING has been graciously pleased to approve of the award of the Meritorious Service Medal to the undermentioned Warrant Officer, Non-commissioned Officers and Men for gallantry in the performance of military duty:—   (20 names)

22nd November   page 14273

> His Majesty the KING has been graciously pleased to approve of the award of the Meritorious Service Medal to the following Non-commissioned Officer and Man for gallantry in the performance of military duty:—
> (2 names, 1 for France & Flanders and 1 Army of Black Sea)

> His Majesty the KING has been graciously pleased to approve of the award of the Meritorious Service Medal to the undermentioned Warrant and Non-commissioned Officers in recognition of valuable services rendered with the Armies in the Field:—   (2 names, 1 France & Flanders and 1 Army of the Black Sea)

1919 (Contd.)

28th November   page 14670

His Majesty the KING has been graciously pleased to approve of the award of the Meritorious Service Medal to the following Non-commissioned Officer and Men in recognition of their exceptional devotion in the performance of military duties:—   (5 names)

12th December   page 15439

His Majesty the KING has been graciously pleased to approve of the award of the Meritorious Service Medal to the undermentioned Warrant Officers, Non-commissioned Officers and Men in recognition of valuable services rendered with the Armies in France & Flanders:—   (77 names)

page 15443

His Majesty the KING has been graciously pleased to approve of the award of the Meritorious Service Medal to the following Warrant Officers, Non-commissioned Officers and Men in recognition of valuable services rendered with the British Force in Egypt and Palestine:—   (44 names)

pages 15447–8

His Majesty the KING has been graciously pleased to approve of the award of the Meritorious Service Medal to the following Warrant Officers, Non-commissioned Officers and Men in recognition of valuable services rendered with British Army of the Black Sea:—   (81 names)

page 15448

His Majesty the KING has been graciously pleased to approve of the award of the Meritorious Service Medal to the undermentioned Warrant Officers, Non-commissioned Officers and Men, in recognition of valuable services rendered with the British Forces in Mesopotamia:—   (13 names)

page 15449

His Majesty the KING has been graciously pleased to approve of the award of the Meritorious Service Medal to the undermentioned Warrant Officers and Non-commissioned Officers in recognition of valuable services rendered in connection with Military Operations with the Forces in East Africa:—

(4 names)

pages 15459–65

His Majesty the KING has been graciously pleased to approve the award of the Meritorious Service Medal to the undermentioned Warrant Officers, Non-commissioned Officers and Men in recognition of valuable services rendered in connection with the war:—   (412 names including 4 for Malta)

1919 (Contd.)

12th December *(Contd.)*   page 15465

His Majesty the KING has been graciously pleased to approve the award of the Meritorious Service Medal to the undermentioned Warrant Officers and Non-commissioned Officers in recognition of valuable services rendered in South Africa:—   (11 names)

YEAR 1920

3rd January   pages 160–1

His Majesty the KING has been graciously pleased to approve of the award of the Meritorious Service Medal to the undermentioned Warrant Officers, Non-commissioned Officers and Men, in recognition of valuable services rendered with the British Forces in North Russia—Murmansk Command:— (48 names)

pages 162–3

His Majesty the KING has been graciously pleased to approve of the award of the Meritorious Service Medal to the undermentioned Warrant Officers, Non-commissioned Officers and Man in recognition of valuable services rendered with the British Forces in Russia—Archangel Command:—   (27 names)

page 163

His Majesty the KING has been graciously pleased to approve of the award of the Meritorious Service Medal to the following Warrant Officers, Non-commissioned Officers and Men, in recognition of valuable services rendered with the British Forces in North Russia—Archangel Command:— (44 names)

pages 163–4

His Majesty the KING has been graciously pleased to approve of the award of the Meritorious Service Medal to the undermentioned Men in recognition of valuable service rendered with the British Force in Siberia:—   (10 names, of which at least two are for services in Northern Japan, supplying the Siberian Force)

15th January   page 683

His Majesty the KING has been graciously pleased to approve of the award of the Meritorious Service Medal to the undermentioned Non-commissioned Officer for gallantry in the performance of military duty with the British Force in India (Baluchistan Force):—   (1 name)

pages 683–4

His Majesty the KING has been graciously pleased to approve of the award of the Meritorious Service Medal to the undermentioned Warrant Officers and Men in recognition of valuable services rendered with the British Force in India (South Persia [Bushire Force]):—   (15 names)

1920 (Contd.)

22nd January   page 944

His Majesty the KING has been graciously pleased to approve of the award of the Meritorious Service Medal to the undermentioned Man for gallantry in the performance of military duty with the British Forces in North Russia—Archangel Command:—   (1 name)

pages 944–5

His Majesty the KING has been graciously pleased to approve of the award of the Meritorious Service Medal to the undermentioned Warrant Officers, Non-commissioned Officers and Man in recognition of valuable services rendered with the British Forces in North Russia—Archangel Command:—   (18 names)

pages 945–6

His Majesty the KING has been graciously pleased to approve of the award of the Meritorious Service Medal to the undermentioned Warrant Officers, Non-commissioned Officers and Men for valuable services rendered with the British Forces in Siberia:—   (63 names)

30th January   page 1223

His Majesty the KING has been graciously pleased to approve of the award of the Meritorious Service Medal to the undermentioned Warrant and Non-commissioned Officers in recognition of valuable services rendered in the Field, which have been brought to notice in accordance with the terms of Army Order 193 of 1919. To be dated 5th May 1919:—   (3 names)

pages 1225–7

His Majesty the KING has been graciously pleased to approve of the award of the Meritorious Service Medal to the undermentioned Warrant Officers, Non-commissioned Officers and Men, in recognition of devotion to duty and valuable services rendered whilst Prisoner of War or interned, which services have been brought to notice in accordance with the terms of Army Order 193 of 1919. To be dated 5th May 1919:—   (109 names)

3rd February   page 1378

His Majesty the KING has been graciously pleased to approve of the award of the Meritorious Service Medal to the undermentioned Non-commissioned Officers and Man, in recognition of valuable services rendered in connection with the operation in Finland and the Baltic States. Dated 11th November 1919:—

(4 names)

11th February   page 1784

His Majesty the KING has been graciously pleased to approve of the award of the Meritorious Service Medal to the undermentioned for gallantry in the performance of military duty with the British Troops in France & Flanders:—

(1 name)

1920 (Contd.)

11th February *(Contd.)* page 1784

His Majesty the KING has been graciously pleased to approve of the award of the Meritorious Service Medal to the undermentioned in recognition of his exceptional devotion in the performance of military duty:— (1 name)

12th February pages 1802–3

His Majesty the KING has been graciously pleased to approve of the award of the Meritorious Service Medal, on the recommendation of the General Commanding-in-Chief, Mesopotamian Expeditionary Force, to the undermentioned Non-commissioned Officers and Men, in recognition of valuable services rendered in connection with the operations in Southern and Central Kurdistan. Dated 15th November 1919:— (14 names)

24th February page 2262

His Majesty the KING has been graciously pleased to approve of the award of the Meritorious Service Medal to the undermentioned in recognition of valuable services rendered with the Army in Egypt. Dated 3rd June 1919:— (3 names)

4th March pages 2739–40

His Majesty the KING has been graciously pleased to approve of the award of the Meritorious Service Medal to the undermentioned Warrant Officers, Non-commissioned Officers and Men in recognition of valuable services rendered with the British Military Mission to South Russia:— (28 names)

page 2740

His Majesty the KING has been graciously pleased to approve of the award of the Meritorious Service Medal to the undermentioned in recognition of valuable services rendered with the Armies in the Field—Black Sea:— (1 name)

His Majesty the KING has been graciously pleased to approve of the award of the Meritorious Service Medal to the undermentioned in recognition of valuable services rendered with the Armies in the Field—Mesopotamia:— (3 names)

22nd March page 3517

His Majesty the KING has been graciously pleased to approve of the award of the Meritorious Service Medal to the undermentioned for Gallant conduct in the performance of military duty otherwise than in action:— (1 name)

1st April page 4016

His Majesty the KING has been graciously pleased to approve of the award of the Meritorious Service Medal to the undermentioned for gallantry in the performance of military duty otherwise than in action. To be dated 3rd June 1918—France & Flanders:— (4 names)

1920 (Contd.)

1st April *(Contd.)*   page 4016

> His Majesty the KING has been graciously pleased to approve of the award of the Meritorious Service Medal to the undermentioned Warrant Officers, in recognition of valuable services rendered in connection with the war. To be dated 3rd June, 1919:—   (7 names; 1 Aden, 1 Siberia, 1 France and 4 India)

20th April   page 4656

> His Majesty the KING has been graciously pleased to approve of the award of the Meritorious Service Medal to the undermentioned Warrant Officer for valuable services rendered in connection with the operation against the Northern Turkana and kindred tribes. Dated 3rd June 1919:—   (1 name)

23rd April   page 4694

> His Majesty the KING has been graciously pleased to approve of the award of the Meritorious Service Medal to the undermentioned in recognition of valuable services rendered with the British Forces in North Russia:—   (1 name)

12th May   page 5448

> His Majesty the KING has been graciously pleased to approve of the award of the Meritorious Service Medal to the undermentioned Non-commissioned Officers and Men in recognition of valuable services rendered with the British Military Mission in South Russia:—   (8 names)

> His Majesty the KING has been graciously pleased to approve of the award of the Meritorious Service Medal to the undermentioned Non-commissioned Officers in recognition of valuable services rendered while serving with the South Persia Rifles:—   (9 names)

14th May   pages 5476–7

> His Majesty the KING has been graciously pleased to approve of the award of the Meritorious Service Medal to the undermentioned Warrant Officers, Non-commissioned Officers and Men in recognition of valuable services rendered in connection with operations on the North West Frontier, India:—   (48 names)

26th May   pages 5911–2

> His Majesty the KING has been graciously pleased to approve of the award of the Meritorious Service Medal to the undermentioned Warrant Officers, Non-commissioned Officers and Men in recognition of valuable services rendered with the Baluchistan Force, North West Frontier, India:—   (24 names)

10th June   page 6437

> His Majesty the KING has been graciously pleased to approve of the award of the Meritorious Service Medal to the undermentioned in recognition of valuable services rendered in the Field, which have been brought to notice in accordance with the terms of Army Order 193 of 1919. To be dated 5th May, 1919:—

>   (1 name)

1920 (Contd.)

10th June *(Contd.)* pages 6437

His Majesty the KING has been graciously pleased to approve of the award of the Meritorious Service Medal to the undermentioned for valuable services rendered in connection with minor operations in Mesopotamia. To be dated 20th March 1920:— (1 name)

pages 6437–8

His Majesty the KING has been graciously pleased to approve of the award of the Meritorious Service Medal to the undermentioned Warrant Officers, Non-commissioned Officers and Men in recognition of devotion to duty and valuable services rendered whilst Prisoners of War or interned, which services have been brought to notice in accordance with the terms of Army Order 193 of 1919. To be dated 5th May 1919:— (12 names)

13th July page 7443

His Majesty the KING has been graciously pleased to approve of the award of the Meritorious Service Medal to the undermentioned Non-commissioned Officers and Men in recognition of valuable services rendered with the British Force in Siberia (Vladivostock):— (3 names)

His Majesty the KING has been graciously pleased to approve of the award of the Meritorious Service Medal to the undermentioned for gallantry in the performance of military duty:—
(8 names including 1 for India and 2 for France)

3rd August pages 8965–8

His Majesty the KING has been graciously pleased to approve of the award of the Meritorious Service Medal to the undermentioned Warrant Officers, Non-commissioned Officers and Men in recognition of valuable services rendered in India in connection with the war. Dated 3rd June 1919:— (193 names)

27th September page 9511

His Majesty the KING has been graciously pleased to approve of the award of the Meritorious Service Medal to the undermentioned Non-commissioned officer for gallantry in the performance of military duty with the British Force in Mesopotamia:— (1 name)

His Majesty the KING has been graciously pleased to approve of the award of the Meritorious Service Medal to the undermentioned Warrant Officers, Non-commissioned Officers and Men in recognition of valuable services rendered in connection with operations of the Waziristan Force on the North West Frontier— India:— (9 names)

1920 (Contd.)

20th October   page 10167

His Majesty the KING has been graciously pleased to approve of the undermentioned reward in recognition of Gallant conduct and determination displayed in escaping or attempting to escape from captivity, which services have been brought to notice in accordance with the terms of Army Order 193 of 1919. To be dated 5th May 1919:—   (1 name)

pages 10167–8

His Majesty the KING has been graciously pleased to approve of the award of the Meritorious Service Medal to the undermentioned Warrant Officers, Non-commissioned Officers and Men in recognition of valuable services in India in connection with the war:—   (52 names)

page 10168

His Majesty the KING has been graciously pleased to approve of the award of the Meritorious Service Medal to the undermentioned, in recognition of valuable services rendered in South Africa in connection with the war. Dated 3rd June 1919:—   (1 name)

28th October   page 10388

His Majesty the KING has been graciously pleased to approve of the award of the Meritorious Service Medal to the undermentioned Warrant Officer in recognition of valuable services rendered in connection with operations of the Baluchistan Force India:—   (1 name)

His Majesty the KING has been graciously pleased to approve of the award of the Meritorious Service Medal to the undermentioned Non-commissioned Officers and Men in recognition of valuable services rendered in connection with operations of the Waziristan Force India:—   (3 names)

His Majesty the KING has been graciously pleased to approve of the award of the Meritorious Service Medal to the undermentioned Warrant Officers in recognition of valuable services rendered with the North West Frontier Force, India:—   (2 names)

page 10389

His Majesty the KING has been graciously pleased to approve of the award of the Meritorious Service Medal to the undermentioned Warrant Officers and Non-commissioned Officers in recognition of valuable services rendered with North West Frontier Force in connection with operations against Afghanistan:—   (3 names)

His Majesty the KING has been graciously pleased to approve of the award of the Meritorious Service Medal to the undermentioned Warrant Officers, Non-commissioned Officers and Men in recognition of valuable services rendered with the British Military Mission—South Russia:—   (54 names)

YEAR 1921

14th January   page 368

His Majesty the KING has been graciously pleased to approve of the award of the Meritorious Service Medal to the undermentioned Non-commissioned Officers, on the recommendation of the General Officer Commanding-in-Chief, in recognition of valuable services rendered with the British Army of the Black Sea:—

(2 names)

21st January   page 558

His Majesty the KING has been graciously pleased to approve of the award of the Meritorious Service Medal to the undermentioned, on the recommendation of the Chief of the British Military Mission in Siberia, in recognition of valuable services rendered in Siberia. To be dated 16th October 1920:—   (1 name)

page 558

His Majesty the KING has been graciously pleased to approve of the award of the Meritorious Service Medal to the undermentioned Warrant Officer, on the recommendation of the General Officer Commanding-in-Chief, for valuable services rendered in connection with military operations in Mesopotamia and North West Persia:—

(1 name)

18th February   pages 1362–3

His Majesty the KING has been graciously pleased to approve of the award of the Meritorious Service Medal to the undermentioned Warrant Officers, Non-commissioned Officers and Men, in recognition of valuable services rendered in connection with operations of the Waziristan Force, India. To be dated 29th July 1920:—   (30 names)

15th March   page 2172

His Majesty the KING has been graciously pleased to approve of the award of the Meritorious Service Medal to the undermentioned in recognition of their gallantry:—   (2 names for India, 2 for Basra) (To be dated 3rd June 1919)

His Majesty the KING has been graciously pleased to approve of the award of the Meritorious Service Medal to the undermentioned in recognition of valuable services rendered in connection with the war:—

(2 names, including one for India).

29th July   page 6010

His Majesty the KING has been graciously pleased to approve of the award 1 of the Meritorious Service Medal to the undermentioned in recognition of valuable services rendered with the British Military Mission, South Russia. Date 28th October 1920:—   (1 name)

1921 (Contd.)

29th July *(Contd.)*   page 6010

> His Majesty the KING has been graciously pleased to approve of the award of
> the Meritorious Service Medal to the undermentioned in recognition of valuable
> services rendered in connection with operations of the Waziristan Force, India.
> To be dated 29th July 1920:—   (1 name)

> His Majesty the KING has been graciously pleased to approve of the award of
> the Meritorious Service Medal to the undermentioned for Gallant conduct in the
> performance of military duty—Egypt:—   (1 name)

9th September   pages 7195–6

> His Majesty the KING has been graciously pleased to approve of the award of
> the Meritorious Service Medal to the undermentioned Warrant Officers, Non-
> commissioned Officers and Men in recognition of valuable services rendered
> with the British Forces in Mesopotamia. To be dated 7th February 1921:—
> [These are also listed in Army Order 397 of 1921]   (20 names)

28th September   page 7641

> His Majesty the KING has been graciously pleased to approve of the award of
> the Meritorious Service Medal to the undermentioned for Gallant conduct in the
> performance in military duty:—   (1 name for Mesopotamia)

YEAR 1922

29th March   page 2583

> His Majesty the KING has been graciously pleased to approve of the award of
> the Meritorious Service Medal to the undermentioned Warrant Officers, Non-
> commissioned Officers and Men in recognition of valuable services rendered with
> the British Forces in Iraq:—   (8 names)

> His Majesty the KING has been graciously pleased to approve of the award of
> the Meritorious Service Medal to the undermentioned, in recognition of devotion
> to duty and valuable services while Prisoners of War (Eastern Anatolia):—
>   (8 Names)

8th May   page 3616

> His Majesty the KING has been graciously pleased to approve of the award of
> the Meritorious Service Medal to the undermentioned in recognition of valuable
> services rendered with the British Forces in North Persia:— (6 names)

                                                              page 3616

> His Majesty the KING has been graciously pleased to approve of the award of
> the Meritorious Service Medal to the undermentioned in recognition of valuable
> services rendered with the British Forces in North East Persia:— (1 name)

1922 (Contd.)

19th December   page 8956

His Majesty the KING has been graciously pleased to approve of the award of
the Meritorious Service Medal to the undermentioned in recognition of valuable
services in Iraq:—   (1 name)

26th December   page 9119

His Majesty the KING has been graciously pleased to approve of the award of
the Meritorious Service Medal to the undermentioned, in recognition of valuable
services rendered in connection with minor Military Operations undertaken by
the South Persia Rifles. To be dated 1st September 1922:—   (2 names)

YEAR 1923

25th May   page 3673

His Majesty the KING has been graciously pleased to approve of the award of
the Meritorious Service Medal to the undermentioned Warrant Officers, Non-
commissioned Officers and Men, in recognition of valuable services rendered
with the Waziristan Force 1920–21. To be dated 23rd October, 1921:—
                                                                            (16 names)

His Majesty the KING has been graciously pleased to approve of the award of
the Meritorious Service Medal to the undermentioned Non-commissioned Officers
and Men for bravery in the Field with the Waziristan Force 192–21. To be dated
23rd October 1921:—   (6 names)

12th June   page 4134

His Majesty the KING has been graciously pleased to approve of the award of
the Meritorious Service Medal to the undermentioned Warrant Officers, Non-
commissioned Officers and Men in recognition of valuable services rendered with
the Waziristan Force April 1921, to December, 1921. To be dated 24th May
1922:—   (12 names)

YEAR 1924

30th May   pages 4305–6

His Majesty the KING has been graciously pleased to approve of the
undermentioned rewards for valuable service rendered in the Field in connection
with Military Operations in Waziristan, January 1922 to April 1923:—
                                                                            (14 names)

                                                                                 page 4663

His Majesty the KING has been graciously pleased to approve of the award of
the Meritorious Service Medal to the undermentioned Non-commissioned Officer
and Men in recognition of valuable services rendered in connection with operations
in Kurdistan, 1923 to be dated 3rd June 1924:—   (4 names)

1924 (Contd.)

11th July   page 5321

His Majesty the KING has been graciously pleased to approve of the undermentioned rewards for gallant conduct in the performance of military duty:—   (1 name for Thrace)

YEAR 1925

13th March   page 1769

His Majesty the KING has been graciously pleased to approve of the award of the Meritorious Service Medal to the undermentioned Warrant Officers, Non-commissioned Officers and Men in recognition of valuable services rendered in connection with Military Operations in Waziristan, 21st April 1923 to 31st March 1924:—   (8 names)

YEAR 1926

28th May   page 3455

His Majesty the KING has been graciously pleased to approve of the award of the Meritorious Service Medal to No. 5763209 Serjeant Henry James Edwards, D.C.M., The Norfolk Regiment (Local Company Serjeant-Major, Iraq Levies) in recognition of valuable services rendered in connection with the operation in Iraq during the period September to November, 1924.   (1 name)

YEAR 1927

15th February   page 1046

His Majesty the KING has been graciously pleased to approve of the award of the Meritorious Service Medal to the undermentioned for gallant conduct in the performance of military duty:—   (1 name)

27th May   page 3447

The KING has been graciously pleased to approve of the award of the Meritorious Service Medal to the undermentioned for gallant conduct in the performance of military duty:—   (2 names for India)

YEAR 1928

13th April   page 2675

His Majesty the KING has been graciously pleased to approve of the undermentioned award which the General Officer Commanding-in-Chief, North Russian Expeditionary Force, conferred in pursuance of the powers then vested in him:—   (1 name for devotion to duty on 6th June, 1919)

APPENDIX K
Analysis of Awards by Regiment

In the analysis which follows, where the total exceeds the numbers awarded by theatre, the balance is made up of those awarded for home service, usually indicated in the *Gazette* by 'Valuable services in the War' or in unidentified theatres, indicated in the *Gazette* by 'Services in the present war with the Armies in the Field.' It should be noted that the seven bars are excluded.

Regiment	Gallantry	France & Flanders	France	Mesopotamia	Italy	E. Africa	Egypt	Balkans	Salonika	India
Royal Navy	1	22	15							
Royal Marines		37	3							
Royal Marine L.I.	1	1	6							
R.M. Artillery			6			2				
R.M.Maint. Unit			2							
Mercantile Marine Reserve										
Life Guards			7							
Royal Horse Guards		2	1							
Dragoon Guards		25	12	1 7th		1 2nd				2 1st
Dragoons		5	3						1 1st	1 6th
Hussars	3	31	18	27			2 8th 14th			
Lancers		6	12		2 12th 16th	1	3 17th			2 21st
R. Field Artillery	23+ 2FF 1Eg 1Mes	626	399	49	66		10	45	42	30
R. Horse Artillery		40	24	11	2		4			4
R. Garrison Artillery	15+ 3 Aden	380	207	13	28	9	6	18	21	20
Royal Artillery	*1	4	35	3	1					
Hon. Artillery Coy.	1	5	6		7					
Entrenching Battn.	1									
Volunteer Artillery					1					
Trench Mortar Bty	2									

Archangel	P.O.W.	Murmansk	Waziristan	S. Russia	Black Sea	Siberia	G.S.W.A.	NWF India	Egypt & Pal.	Others	Total
			1								44
		1									47
											11
											11
											2
										N Russia 1	1
											19
											9
	1 4th			1 5th							59
										NWF Afg 1 6th	15
7 20th 7th	1 14th		2 7th 4th	1 11th						A/O 193 1 14th; S Pers. 4 7th; Bal. 1 7th; Kurd. 1 7th; Turk. 1 7th; N Pers. 2	132
										S Pers. 2	41
8	3	5	4	8	13				2	Bal. 2; Aden 3; Turk. 1; NWF Afg 1	1566
									2		113
3	1	2	8	3				3		S. Pers. 1; N. Per. 1; Aden 6; U. of S.A. 1; Malta 2; Sing. 1; Turk. 4; China 1; Gib. 4; Russ. 2; Berm 1; Ceyl. 1; H.K. 2; W. Afr. 1; Jamaica 1	998
										*Mesopot. Iraq 3	62
1						1					28
											8
											1
											4

Regiment	Gallantry	France & Flanders	France	Mesopotamia	Italy	E. Africa	Egypt	Balkans	Salonika	India
Royal Engineers	47+ 4 Mes 1 Sal 1 Eg	1461	574	133	87	44	94	56	67	10
R. Anglian Engrs.										
R. Corps of Signals	*2									
Grenadier Guards		30	10		2					
Coldstream Guards		26	11		3	1				
Scots Guards		13	7		1					
Irish Guards		10	2				1			
Welsh Guards		5	2							
Guards M.G. Regt.		20	4							
Guards			1							
Guards Div. Sig. Coy.										
Royal Scots	3	52	23					3	3	1
Queen's (R.W.Surrey)	2	36	12	11	12					3
E. Kent (Buffs)	3	24	8	20	2			2	2	5
King's (R. Lancs.)	1	23	10	3		1	1	3	6	
Northumberland Fus.	4	59	42	16	15		1		1	1
Warwickshire Regt.	2	40	16	9	43		1			1
Royal Fusiliers	2	150	37		5	7	1		1	
Liverpool Regt.	3	80	56	2			1	1	5	4
Norfolk Regt.		21	7	10	4		2			2
Lincolnshire Regt.	1	30	20							4
Devonshire Regt.		17	2	12	12		3	2	5	7
Suffolk Regt.	1	30	13					5		
Somerset L.I.		27	9	11						12
W. Yorks. Regt.	5	58	34	1	8			·		
E. Yorks. Regt.	2	20	15					3	2	2
Beds. & Herts. Regt.		19	11	1	1		1			15
Leicestershire Regt.	1	32	24	3			2	1	1	2
R. Irish Regt.	4	15	3				3		1	

Archangel	P.O.W.	Murmansk	Waziristan	S. Russia	Black Sea	Siberia	G.S.W.A.	NWF India	Egypt & Pal.	Others	Total
31		26	6	18	22	4		3	7	S. Pers. 2; N. Russ 1; Baluch. 1; Jamaica 1; Kurd. 1; Gib. 3; U. of S.A. 3; H.K. 1; Aden 2; Sing. 2; Malta 2; China 1; Turk. 1; Medit. 1; Arabia 2; Vlad. 1; Bermuda 1; Japan 2	3375
											1
			6							*inc. 1 Waz. 1 Thrace	8
										Sing. 1	60
	1										66
	6										39
											20
											11
											27
											1
											1
10					1						111
1	1	7						1		Kurd. 1	109
		2						1		Baluch. 1; Sing. 1	93
	1										62
	1								1		164
1	1			1	1						137
3	5	1		1							242
8	1			1						China 1	184
		2							1	S. Persia 1; Bal. 1; Iraq 1	74
	1										70
1								1	1	Kurd. 1; Iraq 1	93
	1										64
								4		S. Pers. 1; Balk. 1; Vlad. 1	73
	2									Kurd. 1; Malta 1; Vlad. 1	137
		1								Berm. 1	56
	2	1								Baluch. 1; N. Persia 1	68
									1		78
	1										42

Regiment	Gallantry	France & Flanders	France	Mesopotamia	Italy	E. Africa	Egypt	Balkans	Salonika	India
Yorkshire Regt.	1	15	17		7		1			6
Lancashire Fus.		44	29					2	2	
R.Scots Fus.	1	31	14				1	2	3	1
Cheshire Regt.	3	29	11	11	2			9	4	
R.Welch Fus.	4	40	20	9	6		2	1	1	
S.W.B.		25	13	7				1	3	4
K.O.S.B.	1	23	6	1	2					
Cameronians (S. Rif.)	2	36	12					1		2
R. Inniskilling Fus.		30	8							
Gloucestershire Regt.		27	17	11	18	1		1	7	
Worcestershire Regt.	1	32	19	7	11			1	2	1
E. Lancs. Regt.		24	13	5				2	2	
E. Surrey Regt.	1	20	6	5	4				4	5
D.C.L.I.		13	8		1			6	4	4
W. Riding Regt.	2	41	17	2	5					7
Border Regt.	1	19	16	2	10			3	4	6
R. Sussex Regt.	2	34	15	2	10					16
R. Hampshire Regt.	1	18	9	30	3	1	1	2	8	15
S. Staffs. Regt.		20	18		12					4
Dorset Regt.	*3	13	7	11			1		1	2
S. Lancs. Regt.		22	12	9				3	2	6
Welsh Regt.		40	21	6				7	5	1
R. Highld. Regt.	*2	29	11	1		3		2	4	1
Ox. & Bucks. Regt.	*1	27	16	7	16			4	4	4
Essex Regt.		32	11				9			2
Notts. & Derbys. R.	2	57	3		4					
L.N. Lancs. Regt.	5	38		4			2			
Northants. Regt.		20	9							
Berkshire Regt.		30	12		8			4	1	
R.W. Kent Regt.	1	28	7	18	7			1		10
K.O.(Y.L.I.)	1	35	17		7				3	
K. Shropshire L.I.	1	16	9					6	4	
Middlesex Regt.	3	53	28	7	6			5	4	8
K.R.R.C.	2	51	24		6	1		4	3	
Wiltshire Regt.	1	17	10	11			1		2	8

Archangel	P.O.W.	Murmansk	Waziristan	S. Russia	Black Sea	Siberia	G.S.W.A.	NWF India	Egypt & Pal.	Others	Total
5		2								S. Pers. 3 (inc. 1 G/H.) Kurd. 1	69
	1		1								88
	3				2					Sierra L. 1	64
	8			1						Gib. 2	104
1	2									Gib. 1	110
1			1								64
	1									Bermuda 1	44
										Kurd. 2; Ex. Dev. 1 Malta 1	77
	1	.1									51
1					3						104
	1	1			1					Iraq 1; S. Pers. 1; Turkestan 1	95
					2			1			60
										Iraq 1	59
				1		1					49
	5	1								Turkestan 1 N. Persia 1	96
			2					1			78
1		6		1		1		1		S. Persia 2	100
2	3	4		2		25		1		Kurdistan 1; Aden 1 W. Afr. 1	149
	1			1						NWF. Afg. 1	68
	2							1		*inc. India 2 Baluch. 1	56
	1	2		1						S. Pers. 2; Bal. 2	77
			3								101
1		1			1					*inc. 1 F & F	85
3	1							1		*Mesopot Exc. Dev. 2	107
									1		71
1	1										108
	7									U. of S.A. 1; Bal. 1	88
	1										51
	1										78
		1						1		Baluch. 2	92
	2										78
						1				Sing. 2	54
2	3	4		2		12					176
	1	1						1		N. Persia 1; Baluch 1 Iraq 1	126
											61

Regiment	Gallantry	France & Flanders	France	Mesopotamia	Italy	E. Africa	Egypt	Balkans	Salonika	India
Manchester Regt.	1	59	35	5	24		1		3	
N. Staffs. Regt.	*1	27	17	7						1
Yorks. & Lancs.	4	38	15	7	8			6	1	
Durham L.I.	4	57	34		12			3	1	4
Highland L.I.	*2	43	22	9						
Seaforth Hldrs.	1	37	17	1		1	4	1	1	
Gordon Hldrs.	2	28	20	2	5					3
Cameron Hldrs.	1	21	10	1		1		1	3	2
R.I. Rifles (& R.U.R.)	5	25	23	*1						2
R. Irish Fus.		14	3	1			1	3	1	1
Connaught Rgrs.	2	1	3	8						
A.& S. Hldrs.		27	13		1	1		3	3	
Leinster Regt.	3	5	4							
Munster Regt.		8	3							
Dublin Regt.		9	8							
Rifle Brigade	3	37	24			1	2	1	2	8
Monmouth Regt.	1	8	7		1					
Cambridge Regt.		5	3							
London Regt.	3	189	64	1	2	2	2			1
Hertfordshire Regt.		7	3							
Herefordshire Regt.		3								
Yeomanry	*3	27	12	2	4		9	4	5	
N. Irish Horse		1	2							
S. Irish Horse		1	1							
K.Edward's Horse		4								
Res. Regt. of Cav.					1					
Kent Cyclist Bn.										1
North., Hunts. & Highland Cyc. B.										
Motor Machine Gun Service	*2	1								
Machine Gun Corps	9	209	104	34	32	1	2	8	6	3
Army Catering Corps		33	16	2	3		1	3	1	
Tank Corps	1	60	23							
Labour Corps	*13	826	112		20		18	19	7	
A. Supp. Corps			1							

Archangel	P.O.W.	Murmansk	Waziristan	S. Russia	Black Sea	Siberia	G.S.W.A.	NWF India	Egypt & Pal.	Others	Total
						1					157
					3			3		*Mesopot, Kurd. 2	76
										Kurdistan 2	93
4								1			131
										*Inc. India 1 S. Persia 1; Kurd. 1	106
			1								83
	8	1									87
	3		2		2						67
										*R.U.R. A.O.193–1919	61
	1										39
											23
	1										64
										Ex. Dev. 1	23
			1								23
	1										26
		2	1		2			2		S. Persia 2	120
											19
											9
2	5	2	1			1		3		Ex Dev. 2	363
											10
											3
	2				1					*inc. 1 F & F Hosp. Ship. 19	148
											4
											4
											6
											12
									1		2
											3
										*Mesopot	6
6	2		5	4	1	1				Kurd. 1; Turk. 1	466
				7							61
										Fin & B/States 2	101
					3				2	*inc. 4 F & F N. Russia 1	1114
											2

Regiment	Gallantry	France & Flanders	France	Mesopotamia	Italy	E. Africa	Egypt	Balkans	Salonika	India
Army Purchasing & Stores Dept. R.A.S.C.	21	1639	360	98	113	51	103	69	50	2
R.A.M.C.	9	432	178	55	31	31	61	35	44	7
M. Amb. Convoy. London Field Amb. R.A.V.C.		175	49	10	11		4	10	7	
Army Pay Corps		8	3			1	2	1		
C. of Military Police Mil. Prison Staff C.		12	1				2	1	1	
Mil. Mounted Police	1	95	31	4	3	2	15	1	4	
Mil Foot Police	5	78	23	9	2	4	5	9	3	
R.A.O.C.	*22	275	83	25	8	22	25	14	13	3
Army Gym. Staff R. Defence Corps		39	8		1		1		4	
C. of A.School Mstrs.	.			4						4
Royal Flying Corps	10	21		1						
Royal Air Force	2									
C. of School of Musketry		1								
Regt. of Militia of I. of Jersey		1								

Archangel	P.O.W.	Murmansk	Waziristan	S. Russia	Black Sea	Siberia	G.S.W.A.	NWF India	Egypt & Pal.	Others	Total
											1
23	3	19	3	18	6	6		5	1	S. Pers. 1; Kurd. 2; U. of S.A. 3; Malta 3; Turk. 2; Gib. 1; Berm. 1; H.K. 1; China 1; Medit. 1; Fin. & B/S. 2; Cey. 1; Arabia 1; N. Russ. 3	3551
8	6	12	1	11	8	1	1		1	Brav. (Murm.) 1; Dist. Serv. 1; S. Pers. 2; Bal. 1; Hosp. Ship 9; U. of S.A. 1; Malta 2; Gib. 1; Berm. 1; Sing. 1; Medit. 1	1222
											1
											1
1										Exc. Dev. 1	317
2		1			3	2				Malta 2; Gib. 1; Berm. 1; H.K. 1; Cey. 1; Jam. 1	81
				1							9
										Malta 2	35
				1	2				3		193
		1		1							173
9		9		6	6	10			5	*inc. 7 (F & F) 1 (Egy.) & 2 (Basra) Baluch. 1; U. of S.A. 2; Malta 1; Iraq 1; Gib. 1; China 1; Russ. 1; Cey. 1; N. Russia 2	744
											72
											54
										Malta 3; Gib. 1; Berm. 1	16
											141
											2
											12
											1

Regiment	Gallantry	France & Flanders	France	Mesopotamia	Italy	E. Africa	Egypt	Balkans	Salonika	India
G.H.Q.				1	1					
Remounts	1								1	
Canadians	*15	765	302							
R.N.W.M.Police										
Intelligence Corps			4							
Australian	*25	608	338	13			26			
New Zealand	4	123	76	1			5			
King's African Rifles	3					60				
E. African Forces	3		2			48				
Newfoundland		2								
Br. West Indies	2	2		3		2	3			
Aden Forces										
S. African Forces	1	36	16			115	1			
Indian Army	*2	6	4	121		15	17	2	1	22
Ex. Forces Cant.			3							
Staff Corps			1							
Trg. Res. Batt.	4									
Officers Trg. Corps										
Egypian Army							5			
Arab Levies				1						
Imp. Camel Corps							3			
Indian Tel. Corps										
W. African Forces	1			1		6				
B.S.A. Police						13				
N. Rhod. Police						12				
Rhodesia Regt.						1				
Nyasaland Forces						3				
Ch.Bu. & Nat. L.C.	7									
Maltese Troops								2		
TOTALS	380	10373	4254	938	732	471	471	413	398	332

Archangel	P.O.W.	Murmansk	Waziristan	S. Russia	Black Sea	Siberia	G.S.W.A.	NWF India	Egypt & Pal.	Others	Total
											8
											5
4	12	1				6				*inc. 1 (Fr.)	1344
										N. Russ. 1;	
										A.O.193 1	
						1					1
											5
	2								10	*inc. 1 (F & F)	1177
									1		335
											66
										N. Turk. 1	73
											17
											14
										Aden 3	3
							53			U. of S.A. 14; Medit 2	294
		23						12	2	*Ferozapore	523
										S. Pers. 8; Baluch. 7;	
										Kurd. 2; Aden 3;	
										Iraq 1; H.K. 1;	
										A/O 193 1; N. Pers. 1	
											3
											1
											5
1											1
											14
											1
											3
											1
							3				11
											13
											12
											1
											5
											7
				1							3
146	131	96	99	91	86	73	56	50	44		25670

APPENDIX L

Number Awarded by Theatre

The breakdown by theatre reflects, in the main, the size of any operation in WW1 and can be compared with casualty rolls or to battalions present. In the main the awards to 'remote' areas (Bermuda, Hong Kong etc.) are not likely to be 'action' awards but rather long and devoted service of an administrative nature, but are interesting in that they illustrate, as no other medals do, the part of the world a man served.

France & Flanders	10,373	Kurdistan	26
Unspecified	4.899	Union of South Africa	25
France	4,254	Aden	21
Service in War		Malta	18
(mainly in U.K.)	2,990	Gibraltar	16
Mespotamia	938	Turkestan	12
Italy	732	North Russia	10
East Africa	471	Iraq	9
Egypt	471	North & North East Persia	7
Balkans	413	Singapore	7
Salonika	398	Bermuda	6
India	332	Hong Kong	6
Archangel	146	China	5
P.O.W. A/O 193 of 1919 (escaped		Mediterranean	5
P.O.W.)	132	Finland & Baltic	4
Murmansk	96	Ceylon	4
Waziristan	99	Russia	3
South Russia	91	Arabia	3
Black Sea	86	N.W.F. Afghanistan	3
Siberia	73	Vladivostock	3
German South West Africa	56	Jamaica	2
N.W.F. India	50	West Africa	2
Egypt and Palestine	44	Thrace	1
South Persia	32	Northern Turkana	1
Hospital Ships	28	Sierra Leone	1
Baluchistan	26		

APPENDIX M

Number Awarded by Arm of the Service

Numbers of the Field Marshal obverse M.S.M. awarded to the various branches of the service:—

British Army	
Cavalry & Yeomanry	456
Artillery	2781
Engineers	3376
Guards (incl. Machine Gun Guards)	225
Infantry	6378
Other Corps (incl. R.A.M.C., R.A.S.C.)	8253
R.N., R.M.	116
R.A.F., R.F.C.	143
Dominions	3965
Indian Army	524
Colonies, Police, etc.	253

APPENDIX N

Awarded a Bar to Meritorious Service Medal

The Army Order No. 400 of 1916 dated 23rd November, 1916 authorised the award of a bar to the Meritorious Service Medal for acts of gallantry. Under this A.O. seven bars were awarded in the period 1916–1928, they are, in date order of the Gazelling of the bar:—

	M.S.M.	*Bar*
Sgt. J. Orr, R.A.M.C.	11.11.16	13.2.17
Sgt. A. Shenton, Manchester Regt. (M.S.M. to Y & L.)	26.5.17 (Gal.)	19.11.17
RQMS J. Elliott, Northumberland Huss. Yeo.	27.6.18 (F & F)	29.8.18 (for Val. Service)
2/Cpl A.M. T. J. Carmody, Aust. F. C.	21.8.17 (Gal.)	17.6.19
Cpl. J. Coxon, M.M.P.	18.1.19	20.10.19 (F & F)
Sgt. J. Berresford, 3/K.R.R.C.	14.5.20 (N.W.F. India)	18.2.21 (Waziristan)
Sgt. T. J. Coleman, R.A.S.C.	16.10.19 (Italy)	11.7.24 (Constantinople)

Citations appear in the L.G. for the bars of Beresford and Coleman and one has been traced in the Regimental History of Northumberland Hussars Yeomanry for Elliott's medal. These, and others traced, are in the footnotes.

APPENDIX O

Number Awarded by Year

The following table is quite explicit and will help identify the comparative rarity, or otherwise, of any year of issue. With such a large number of awards the figures cannot be other than approximate but they can only be marginally out, they are nett of all cancellations and forfeitures, and do not include the seven bars.

	Total
1916	605
1917	1,917
1918	6,356
1919	15,806
1920	842
1921	63
1922	21
1923	28
1924	19
1925	8
1926	1
1927	3
1928	1
	25,670

The Royal Air Force Meritorious Service Medal 1918–28

Twenty-three days after the first gazetting of 105 Royal Air Force M.S.M.s, the details of the Royal Warrant instituting the award appeared in the *London Gazette* of 26 June, 1918, as an Air Ministry instruction ('... for the recognition of valuable services rendered in the Field by Warrant Officers, Non-Commissioned Officers and Men, as distinct from actual flying duties ...'). The medal was, of course, introduced in order to ensure that members of the newly-formed Royal Air Force should not be disadvantaged compared with the two senior services, both of whom now had or soon would have immediate award M.S.M.s for gallantry or for valuable services not in the face of the enemy, the army since 18 November 1916 and the navy shortly to be available from 15 February 1919. Of course many members of the young Royal Air Force, ex-Royal Flying Corps, were wearing the Army Meritorious Service Medal ribbon earned before 1 April 1918. When both the Army and the Royal Navy Meritorious Service Medals (immediate awards) were discontinued in 1928, the Royal Air Force version was likewise abandoned and all three were replaced by the British Empire Medal.

The R.A.F. version of the M.S.M. bears the 'coinage head' of King George V on the obverse, has a standard reverse and floriated suspender, but unlike the Royal Naval award, whose ribbon was also standard, the Royal Air Force adopted a variation of their new Long Service and Good Conduct Medal ribbon, running a central white stripe down it. The naming is found in two distinct types, the first for medals awarded in the Great War and for service in Russia, which is similar to Distinguished Service Medals and 1914 Stars to the Royal Naval Division recipients. The later awards, for services in Iraq, Kurdistan, etc., are named in the thin sans serif capitals of the General Service Medals for these theatres. It should be noted that the Royal Air Force Meritorious Service Medal is worn before the R.A.F. Long Service and Good Conduct Medal.

The 873 awards traced in the *London Gazettes* from 1918 to 1924 (none were issued after June 1924, although the award was available until 1928) are included in the general tabulation in this volume and the page numbers are indicated against the names.

The following list of page numbers and dates, etc., will enable researchers to trace fuller details from the actual *Gazettes*.

Date	L.G. Page Numbers	Number Awarded	Theatre(s)
3.6.1918	6520–1	75	France
		10	Egypt
		8	Italy
		4	Salonika
		3	Adriatic
		4	Russia
2.7.1918	7745	1	Egypt
		3	Devotion to Duty, U.K., 'Fire in Govt. Establishment'
		1	East Africa
6.8.1918	9256	2	France, Gallantry
29.8.1918	10143	1	France, Gallantry
3.12.1912	14328–9	3	France
		1	Canada

1.1.1919	99–101	120	France
		25	Egypt
		11	Italy
		5	Salonika
		24	Independent Force, France
		4	N. Russia
		1	Vendome
		29	Dunkirk
		5	United Kingdom
		11	Aegean
		2	Mediterranean
8.2.1919	2050	2	France
		1	Egypt
		8	Mesopotamia
5.4.1919	4512	4	Mesopotamia
3.6.1919	7036–40	221	France
		42	Egypt
		6	Italy
		5	Salonika
		23	Independent Force, France
		1	Russia
		1	Vendome
		4	Dunkirk
		3	United Kingdom
		5	Mediterranean
		13	Mesopotamia
		4	Paris
		6	Flanders
		4	India
10.10.1919	12527	5	France
		8	Egypt
		3	S. Russia
22.12.1919	15840–1	25	N. Russia
		3	S. Russia
1.4.1920	4021	18	S. Russia
		10	Kurdistan
		4	N.W. Frontier India
		3	Afghanistan
12.7.1920	7424	27	S. Russia
		1	Mesopotamia
		1	N.W. Frontier India
		10	Somaliland
		5	Baltic
20.5.1921	4006	5	Waziristan
		2	Mesopotamia/Iraq (1920)
28.10.1921	8496	16	Mesopotamia/Iraq (1920)
10.10.1922	7134	8	Mesopotamia/Iraq (1920)
30.5.1924	4313	1	Waziristan
6.6.1924	4539	4	Mesopotamia/Iraq (1920)
11.6.1924	4664	8	Kurdistan

The totals for the various theatres can be further calculated thus:—

France	429	Aegean	11
Egypt	87	Mediterranean	7
Italy	25	Mesopotamia	26
Salonika	14	Paris	4
Adriatic	3	Flanders	6
'Fire in Govt. Establishment'	3	Kurdistan	18
East Africa	1	India	4
Canada	1	N.W. Frontier India	5
Independent Force, France	47	Afghanistan	3
Russia	5	Waziristan	6
N. Russia	29	Somaliland	10
S. Russia	51	Baltic	5
Vendôme	2	Mesopotamia/Iraq (1920)	30
Dunkirk	33		
United Kingdom	8	Total for Gazette	873

R.A.F. M.S.M. to Foreign Recipients

In addition to the above 873 medals Air Ministry Lists of 19 July and 10 December 1919 contain details of honorary awards as follows:—

France	7
Greece	4
Italy	1
U.S.A.	4
Slavo–British Aviation Corps	1
	17

Of these, four were for gallantry:—

Sgts. Dudley and Lewis, 11th American Aero Sqn., 'for gallant conduct & devotion to duty on 23rd March 1918, at Stamford Northamtonshire' [see Horse and Spike (Aust. F.C.) and Howard (R.F.C.) *ante*].

Acting Corporal Meckel, 163rd American Aero Sqn., 'for gallant conduct and devotion to duty on 12th June 1918, at Narborough, Norfolk'.

Seaman Mechanist (Stoker) Policisto, late Italian Royal Navy, 'for gallant conduct on 26th July 1919, at Albenga, Italy, in rescuing a British aviator who was in imminent danger of drowning'.

Only one hundred and twenty one R.A.F. M.S.M.s have been traced by the author. In view of the number of collectors of Royal Air Force medals this is a surprisingly low number.

APPENDIX Q

The Royal Naval M.S.M. (1919-1928)

On 14 January 1919 an Order in Council was published in which it was ordained that the Royal Naval Meritorious Service Medal could henceforth be awarded, but without any annuity or gratuity, to boys, men, petty officers and chief petty officers of the Royal Navy, to men, non-commissioned officers and warrant officers of the Royal Marines and to others of Auxiliary, Merchant and Commonwealth Naval Services who had performed arduous and specially meritorious service either afloat or ashore not in action with an enemy, or for a specific act of gallantry in the performance of his duty when not in the presence of an enemy.

One thousand and twenty-two of these medals appear from the *London Gazette* to have been awarded, these can be divided between the various services as follows (an additional seven were later withdrawn and are not included here):—

Royal Naval (R.N.)	601
Royal Naval Reserve (R.N.R.)	102
Royal Naval Volunteer Reserve (R.N.V.R.)	41
Royal Naval Volunteer Reserve (South Africa) (R.N.V.R. (S.A.)).	2
Royal Naval Air Service (R.N.A.S.)	28
Royal Naval Auxiliary Sick Berth Reserve (R.N.A.S.B.R.)	16
Royal Fleet Reserve (R.F.R.)	26
Mercantile Marine Reserve (M.M.R.)	17
Royal Canadian Navy (R.C.N.)	1
Royal New Zealand Navy (R.N.Z.N.)	4
Royal Navy (Newfoundland)	1
Royal Australian Navy (R.A.N.)	2
Nyasaland Volunteer Reserve	4
Royal Marines (R.M.)	3
Royal Marine Reserve (R.M.R.)	6
Royal Marine Artillery (R.M.A.)	35
Royal Marine Light Infantry (R.M.L.I.)	121
Royal Marine Labour Corps (R.M.L.C.)	5
Royal Marine Band (R.M.B.)	1
Royal Marine Artillery Reserve (R.M.A.R.)	1
School of Music	2
Coast Guard	3

In all cases this award can be easily identified by the Naval type George V Bust on the obverse (Admiral of the Fleet) and by the naming which is in large capitals with serifs (like that on the Distinguished Service Medal, and not at all like that of the Army M.S.M.s). Rather surprisingly the ribbon is that used on the Army issues from 1917 (red with three white stripes).

A list of awards of the R.N. M.S.M. is to be found in the *Navy Lists* of April, July and October of 1919 and of January 1920, but these are not found in any further issues. However, in these lists some Army awards are listed which can be found in the main section of this reference work.

The award of the R.N. M.S.M. was discontinued by another Order in Council of November 1928, although it will be noted that no gazettings were made after November 1923.

London Gazette Citation Headings and Dates

L.G. 15.2.1919 pp 2359-61   93
including
For Services in Cruisers employed on Escort, Convoy, and Patrol duties during 1917
    and 1918.   21
For Services in Vessels employed on Escort, Convoy, and Patrol duties between the
    1st January and the 30th June 1918.   3
For Services in Destroyers between the 1st January and the 30th June, 1918.   2
For Services on the Mediterranean Station between the 1st January and the 30th
    June, 1918.
        I Aegean   5
        II Adriatic   14
        III Malta   5
For services in mine laying vessels between 1st January and 30th June, 1918.   6

L.G. 17.3.1919 pp 3591-2   24
including
Honours for Services in Destroyers of the Grand Fleet Flotillas between the 1st July
    and 11th November, 1918.   23
Honours for Miscellaneous Services.
The KING has been graciously pleased to approve of the award of the following
    honours, decorations and medals to the undermentioned Officers and Men: 1

L.G. 24.3.1919 pp 3860-63   65
including
Honours for Services in Action with Enemy Submarines
The KING has been graciously pleased to approve of the award of the following
    decorations and medals to the undermentioned Officers and Men for
    services in action with enemy submarines.   1
Honours for Services in Minelaying Operations between the 1st July and 11th
    November, 1918.   15
Northern and Southern Patrol Forces. The following awards have been approved for
    services in the Northern and Southern Patrol Forces (submarine flotillas)
    between the 1st July and 11th November 1918:   7
Royal Naval Air Service.
The following awards have been approved for services in the Royal Naval Air Service
    between the 1st July and 31st December, 1917:   6
Honours for Services in Minesweeping Operations between the 1st July and 31st
    December 1918.   34

L.G. 1.4.1919, pp 4197-8   16

L.G. 11.4.1919, pp 4732-5   77
including
Honours for Services in the Auxiliary Patrol between the 1st July and 11th
    November, 1918.
The KING has been graciously pleased to approve of the award of the following
    honours, decorations and medals to the undermentioned Officers and Men:
    Services in Drifters, Trawlers and Yachts.   27
Services in Motor Launches.   4

Honours for Services in Sloops Employed on Convoy, Escort and Patrol Duties Between the 1st July and 11th November, 1918.	3
Honours for Services in Destroyers employed on Convoy, Escort and Patrol Duties between the 1st July and 11th November 1918.	30
Honours for Services in Local Defence Flotillas between the 1st July and 11th November, 1918.	5
Honours for Services on the Mediterranean Station between the 1st July and 11th November, 1918.	
Aegean	8

L.G. 22.4.1919 pp 5111–3   33
including
Honours for Services on the Mediterranean Station between the 1st July and 11th November, 1918.

I Adriatic	12
II Gibraltar	4
Honours for Services in Ocean Escorts between the 1st July and 11th November, 1918.	14
Honours for Miscellaneous Services.	3

L.G. 24.5.1919 p 6447   10
Honours for Services in the Auxiliary Patrol between the 1st July and 11th November, 1918.
Services in Yachts, Trawlers, and Drifters.

L.G. 24.5.1919 p 6448   5
Honours for Services in Minesweeping Operations between the 1st July and 31st December, 1918.

L.G. 24.5.1919 p 6448   2
Honours for Services in Ocean Escorts between the 1st July and 11th November, 1918.

L.G. 24.5.1919 p 6448   4
Honours for Miscellaneous Services

L.G. 24.5.1919 p 6504   9

L.G. 11.6.1919 pp 7511–2   50
The KING has been graciously pleased to approve of the award of the following honours, decorations and medals to the undermentioned Officers and Men:—

L.G. 21.6.1919 pp 7907–8   53
The KING has been graciously pleased to approve of the award of the following honours, decorations and medals to the undermentioned Officers and Men:

L.G. 27.6.1919 pp 8068–9   40
The KING has been graciously pleased to approve of the award of the following honours, decorations and medals in recognition of the services of the undermentioned Officers and Men during the War:—

L.G. 30.6.1919 pp 8202–3   23
including
The KING has been graciously pleased to approve of the award of the following
    honours, decorations and medals to the undermentioned Officers and Men: 19
Honours for Miscellaneous Services.   4

L.G. 4.7.1919 pp 8385–6   37
The following awards have also been approved for men of the Royal Naval Transport
    Service:—

L.G. 10.7.1919 pp 8737–8   13

L.G. 12.7.1919 p 8943   24

L.G. 17.7.1919 pp 9111–2   87
including
Honours for Services in Minesweeping Operations between the 1st July and 31st
    December, 1918.   2

L.G. 31.7.1919 pp 9833–4   23

L.G. 11.8.1919 p 10199   3

L.G. 16.9.1919 pp 11579-81   140

L.G. 17.10.1919 pp 12779-82   43
including
Honours for Services in Russia, 1919.   1
Honours for Services in Minesweeping Operations between the 1st July and 31st
    December, 1918.   5
Honours for Services in the Mine Clearance Force between the 1st January and 30th
    June, 1919.   5

L.G. 11.11.1919 p 13744   3

L.G. 11.11.1919 pp 13747–9   16
including
Services in the Caspian Sea 1918 & 1919.   7
Services in Mine Clearance Force subsequent to 30th June 1919.   7
Escaped P.O.W. at Yozgad (Turkey) in August 1918.   2

L.G. 12.12.1919 pp 15430–1   36
including
The following awards have also been approved for the undermentioned Men: 23
Honours for Services in Russia, 1918, 1919.   13

L.G. 22.1.1920 pp 948–9   10
including
Honours for Services in Russia, 1919.   4
Honours for Services in the Caspian Sea, 1919.   2
Honours for Services in the Mine Clearance Force (Final).   3

L.G. 8.3.1920 pp 2861–4	67
including	
Honours for Services in Siberia.	8
Honours for Services in N. Russia, 1919.	6
Honours for Services in the Baltic.	46
L.G. 7.9.1920 p 9055	1
Honours for Services in South Russia.	
L.G. 5.10.1920 p 9693	2
L.G. 12.11.1920 p 11002	5
Honours for Services in the Baltic.	
L.G. 24.12.1920 p 12600	2
L.G. 12.7.1921 p 5560	1
L.G. 18.11.1921 p 9150	1
In recognition of courage and promptitude displayed by him when a saluting gun misfired on HMS Hawkins on 19.8.21.	
L.G. 18.7.1922 p 5358	1
In recognition of his presence of mind and plucky action in dealing with a bomb at Shanghai.	
L.G. 30.11.1923 p 8327	3
Gallant Services in September last at the destruction by earthquake and fire of the R.N. Sick Quarters, Yokohama.	

'In addition, honorary awards (which were not gazetted) were made to eleven allied seamen in 1919 and 1920 (six Greek and five French)".

R.N. M.S.M.s differ from the R.A.F. and Army issues in that they include within the naming details of the service (or theatre) for (or in) which the award was made. This information is not always shown in the relevent *London Gazettes*. Where interesting awards have been traced as extant, the details found on the edge are included in the footnotes. As seen above the *L.G.* headings sometimes provide an indication. 419 of the 1022 are thus identifiable as follows:—

1. By Theatre	Baltic	51
	Adriatic	26
	Russia	18
	Aegean Sea	13
	Caspian Sea	9
	Siberia	8
	North Russia	6
	Malta	5
	Gibraltar	4
	Yokohama Japan	3
	Yozgad Turkey	2
	South Russia	1
	Shanghai	1

2. By Vessel	Destroyers	55
	Drifters, Trawlers, Yachts	37
	Motor Launches	4
	Submarine	1
3. By Function	Escort Patrols	50
	Minesweeping	46
	Mine Clearance	15
	Mine Laying	15
	Gun misfire	1
4. By Unit	R.N. Transport Service	37
	Land Defence Flotilla	5

APPENDIX R

Forfeitures

The following nine forteitures (of which one was subsequently restored) have been found. They have all been deducted from the numbers shown as issued by year, regiment, theatre, etc.

L.G.	Name, Unit etc	Authority or Reason	Original L.G.
22.8.22 (p6158)	Pte. L. J. Kent R.A.O.C.	R.W. Pay & Prom. 1914	1.1.19
22.8.22 (p6158)	Pte. H. Oldfield Lab. Corps	By sentence of Field G.C.M.	17.6.18
11.7.22 (p5961)	Pte. P. J. Maloney Lab. Corps	Art. 1236 R.W. Pay & Prom. 1914	16.10.19
11.7.22 (p5961)	T./Lieut. C. G. Dobbs R.A.S.C. (former Sgt. A.S.C.)	R.W. dated 6.11.20	18.10.16
11.7.22 (p5961)	Pte. W. N. Rowe R.A.S.C. (former Cpl./S./Sgt. A.S.C.) (This M.S.M. was restored under R.W. dated 6.11.20 in *L.G.* 2.10.25 p.6349)	R.W. dated 6.11.10	8.1.19
6.10.22 (p7049)	J. G. A. Forbes (late temp. Qr.M.S. & Lt.R.A.M.C.) (S./Sgt.)	Conviction by Civil Powers	1.1.18
25.5.23 (p3674)	Sgt. J. Hawkes 2/Devons	R.W. dated 6.11.20	18.12.22 (Iraq)
18.9.23 (p6275)	Spr. J. F. Moody R.E. (former Sgt.)	R.W. dated 6.11.20	18.1.19
21.11.24 (p8423)	Gdsm. A. Garnett Scots Guards	R.W. dated 6.11.20	22.2.19 (Q.M.S.)

C.P.O. H. Rickman, M.S.M.

Harry Rickman had an interesting, active, long and sometimes exciting career in the Royal Navy. He was awarded a group of five medals, 1914/15 Star trio, R.N. Long Service & Good Conduct Medal (Edward VII—H.M.S. *Victory*), and R.N. M.S.M. (H.M.S. *Torch*, 1 July to 11 November, 1918).

By good fortune his original service papers have survived and record the highlights, and, no doubt, the periods of mundane activities of his time in the Royal Navy. He was born at Lymington, Hampshire, on 30 January, 1875 and joined the navy proper on his eighteenth birthday on a twelve year engagement, having been a Boy 2nd class since 8 March 1890, aged only 15, when his occupation was a seaman. He was only 5 foot 2½ inches tall and he was paid 11 shillings recruit expenses.

He was rated Boy 1st class in March 1891. On his adult enlistment he was re-rated Ordinary Seaman, but only seven months later he found himself an A.B., a rate he held until March 1895 when he rose to Leading Seaman, quickly becoming P.O. 2nd class in April 1996 and P.O. 1st class in June that year, aged only 21 with 3½ years adult service. He was 31 in July 1906 when rated acting C.P.O., which was confirmed in September the following year. In March, 1908 he was awarded his Long Service & Good Conduct Medal.

He served on many ships during this period: *Excellent, Assistance, Volage, Raven, Caesar, Revenge, Duke of Wellington, Orion, Minotaur, Bramble, Hawke* and *Seahorse* amongst others. It would be possible to follow these ships around the world from surviving records, which would make a facinating research project.

We do know that he spent the early years of W.W.I ashore, in Portsmouth, being pensioned in January 1915 and transferred to the Royal Fleet Reserve. He then served for two months on board H.M.S. *Tipperary*, a destroyer lost at Jutland. He had by that time been transferred to H.M.S. *Opal* from March 1916. She had been launched in 1915 and was fitted out at Doxford's shipyard, Sunderland, in 1916. She was a 1,000 ton destroyer, 271.5 feet in length, capable of 34 knots and armed with three 4 inch guns and two smaller, plus four torpedo tubes.

Rickman was one of the complement of 80 aboard her during the Battle of Jutland, 31 May—1 June 1916, serving with the Grand Fleet Flotillas. He was still serving on this ship, in company with H.M.S. *Narbrough*, off Scapa Flow on 12 January, 1918 in a violant gale and snowstorm. Both vessels, sister ships, were wrecked.

On 17 April 1918, he was assigned to an 'S' class boat of the 'Yarrow' class—H.M.S. *Torch*, another Grand Fleet Flotilla destroyer which displaced 930 tons and was 260¼ feet in length, 25¾ feet in beam with a 9 feet draught. She too carried three 4 inch (Mk. IV 30° elevation) guns and one 2 pdr. pom-pom, with four 21 inch torpedo tubes. Designed to achieve 36 knots, she had a complement of 90.

Building began on her in April, 1917 and she was launched on 16 March, 1918, one month before Rickman joined her. She was completed the following month. On her trials she reached 39.19 knots.

It was for service with this ship that C.P.O. Rickman was awarded his R.N. M.S.M., gazetted on 17 March 1919, 'Honours for Services in Destroyers of the Grand Fleet Flotillas between 1st July and 11th November, 1918,' one of 23 men under this heading. Before the award was gazetted he had left *Torch*, on 21 February, 1919, returning to Portsmouth until his final demobilisation to pension on 3 February 1920, aged only 45.

(See Vol. I, 1919)

Leading Telegraphist J. B. Hutchinson, M.S.M.

James Bonthrone Hutchinson's medals are in the same New York Collection as Rickman's (see previous appendix). The group consists of 1914/15 Star trio and a R.N. M.S.M. This last was awarded for services in the Baltic Sea in 1919, one of 46 for this theatre in the *London Gazette* of 8 March 1920.

Unlike Rickman, very little is known of Hutchinson's W.W.I service, his papers not having survived. But it known that he was on H.M.S. *Voyager* in the Baltic Sea in 1918 and 1919. *'Voyager'* was one of nine destroyers in the 13th Flotilla, attached to the 6th Light Cruiser Squadron. Two of the nine were sunk during this period, *'Vittoria'* on 31 August, 1919 and *V'erulam'* in the following month. In all 238 R.N. Vessels were involved, including the Aircraft Carrier H.M.S. *Vintictive* and ten cruisers including H.M.S. *Curacao*, which was mined and severly damaged, and *'Cassandra,'* which was mined and sunk.

The fleet sailed for the Baltic on 22 November, 1918, eleven days after the men had no doubt celebrated the Armistice on 11 November. Their aim was to assist the White Russian Forces against the Bolsheviks and seek to contain the Red Navy. On 26 December, the Russia destroyer *'Spartak'* was forced to run aground and the next day the destroyer *'Arrotil'* was attacked and had to haul down her colours and surrender. Other Red Vessels destroyed or captured included the cruiser *'Oleg,'* sunk by Coastal Motor Boat No 4 (In this action her Captain, Lieut. A. N. Shilton-Agar won the Victoria Cross, Sub Lieut. J. W. Hampshire, R.N.R. was awarded the D.S.C. and C.M.Mech. Hugh Beeley R.N.V.R. the C.G.M.). The Reds also lost the dreadnoughts *'Pertopavloviek'* and *'Andrai Pervozvanni'* and the destroyers *'Svoboda,' 'Gavriil,' 'Konstantin'* and *'Azarl.'*

Besides the two British Destroyers and the cruiser, the Royal Navy lost two minesweepers, seven Coastal Motor Boats, a store carrier and H.M. Submarine L55, which was shelled and sunk with all hands. In all 127 officers and men were killed, died of wounds or were missing believed killed.

In addition to the 46 M.S.M.s for the Baltic in *L.G.* 8 March, 1920, a further five were awarded for this theatre in *L.G.* 12 November 1920. Of those 51 a further eight are known, two to the Cruiser H.M.S. *'Dragon,'* one to her sister ship *'Delhi'* and five to destroyers *'Viscount,' 'Wryneck,' 'Warwick,' 'Vanity'* and *'Velox'*. In addition two of the men awarded M.S.M.s for the Baltic had already won D.S.M.s during the War, C.E.R.A. W. W. Ford and P.O.Teleg. P. J. Olding.

One other R.N. M.S.M. for the Baltic is known and is found in the very first *L.G.* for this award, 15 February, 1919. A single piece, it is impressed *'Cassandra'* Baltic Sea 5 December, 1918.

(See Vol. I, 1920)

M.S.M.s to Yeomanry Regiments

M.S.M.s in the following numbers were awarded to individual Yeomanry Regiments as listed:—

Ayrshire Yeomanry	1	Middlesex Yeomanry	1
Bedfordshire Yeomanry	5	North Somerset Yeomanry	6
Berkshire Yeomanry	2	North Irish Horse	4
Buckinghamshire Yeomanry	1	Northamptonshire Yeomanry	9
County of London Yeomanry	7	Northumberland Hussars	5 (+ bar)
Denbighshire Yeomanry	1	Oxfordshire Yeomanry	6
Derbyshire Yeomanry	3	Royal North Devon Yeomanry	2
Dorset Yeomanry	1	Sherwood Rangers	1
Duke of Lancaster's Own Yeomanry	3	Staffordshire Yeomanry	1
Essex Yeomanry	3	Sussex Yeomanry	1
Fife & Forfar Yeomanry	1	Surrey Yeomanry	4
Glasgow Yeomanry	1	South Irish Horse	4
Glamorgan Yeomanry	2	Warwickshire Yeomanry	20
Hampshire Yeomanry	2	Westmorland & Cumberland Yeomanry	2
Hertfordshire Yeomanry	4	West Somerset Yeomanry	2
Imperial Camel Corps	3	Wiltshire Yeomanry	2
King Edward's Horse	6	Yorkshire Dragoons	3
Lanarkshire Yeomanry	1	Yorkshire Hussars	3
Leicestershire Yeomanry	3	Yeomanry (unspecified)	8
Lincolnshire Yeomanry	1	Attached to Yeomanry	2
Lothian & Border Horse	6		
Lovat's Scouts	5	Total	148 (+ 1 bar)

APPENDIX V

Royal Flying Corps M.S.M.s (an update)

In 1984, Picton Publishing issued *'The M.S.M. to Aerial Forces'* as a companion work to my previous book *'The M.S.M. to Naval Forces'* which they had produced in 1983.

In both I asked for details of any extant medals or groups. Only once or twice have items surfaced which were not listed as issued in the books. This was mainly because they were not indexed in the *London Gazette*, or became Admiralty or Army Orders were lost beyond retrieval. In the eight years which have followed publication, my store of knowledge has increased considerably, often thanks to members of the O.M.R.S., other collectors and readers of the various articles I have written, published by *Medal News* and other magazines.

Especially since I took on the task of researching the service record of the 1,400 pre-W.W.I N.C.O.s and men of the Royal Flying Corps, I have realised how ready for an up-date are some of the sections in the book. One section especially is that containing the Army M.S.M.s awarded to the R.F.C. When I had published the book, I knew of only 14 extant examples. I now know of 23. The biographical information to hand is now significantly increased, especially in respect of the 35 pre-war men listed amongst them. Fuller details of these and the other men have been included in a new book entitled *'A Contemptible Little Flying Corps'* published by The London Stamp Exchange. The following is the latest up-date, but, once again, I would be delighted to hear of any extent medals listed here, or details of earlier or later service known for any of the recipients. Remember, at this time the R.F.C. was a Corps of the Army, thus the George V Field Marshal version was automatically issued:—

KEY

No	L.G. Date	Page(s)
1	18.10.16	10042
2	11.11.16	10933–5
3	01.01.17	52–5
4	24.01.17	927
5	13.02.17	1575
6	12.03.17	2488 (Gallantry)
7	12.03.17	2487–8
8	04.06.17	5491–3 (France & Flanders)
9	18.06.17	6027–8
10	16.08.17	8431–3
11	29.08.17	9002
12	29.08.17	9003 (Mesopotamia)
13	19.11.17	11979 (Gallantry in France)
14	17.12.17	13202–4
15	17.12.17	13202 (Gallantry with Home Forces)
16	01.01.18	66-71
17	19.03.18	3473 (Gallantry with Home Forces)
18	11.04.18	4413 (Distinguished Services in Jerusalem)

8.   Anderson, 16796 F./Sgt. W.
18. Anthony, 403958 (formerly 51031) A.M.1 (A./Cpl.) H. (Lower Edmonton, N.)
8.   Aspinall, 266 F./Sgt. (A./Sgt. Maj.) J. A. Enlisted Coldstream Guards 1905. 1914 Star and bar in France with R.F.C. from October 1914. R.A.F. Long Service & Good Conduct Medal as S.M.1 in 1923
8.   Bates, 6682 Cpl. T. A.
9.   Batty, 2197 F./Sgt. F. Enlisted R.F.C. November 1914 as Aero Rigger. Entitled to 1914/15 trio, Army M.S.M. and Sudan (1910) Medal (with 17 Sqn. R.F.C.). Mentioned *L.G.* 25.10.1916 for Darfur.
2.   Bell, 4310 Cpl. G. D.
2.   Bethell, 348 F./Sgt. H. E. Enlisted 1912, a clerk. Awarded 1914 Star. Mentioned in 1916 and 1919. R.A.F. Long Service & Good Conduct Medal in 1930
3.   Bicknell, 5011 Sgt. G. N.
16. Booker, 11798 Sgt. G. A. (Wembley)
18. Bradwell 3206 Sgt.Maj. W. A. (Birdwell, Barnsley)
3.   Braine, 6217 Cpl. F. A. W.
8.   Brown, 1087 F./Sgt. (A./Sgt. Maj.) C. W. Formerly Grenadier Guards. France May 1916—September 1917. Commissioned 2/Lieut. R.F.C. that month. Trio known: British War and Victory Medals, M.S.M.
8.   Bunting, 950 A./Sgt. Major. Direct entrant November 1913. Served in Somaliland in 1920 and was mentioned in despatches in August. Africa General Service Medal and Army M.S.M. known. (His brother No 864 F./Sgt. R.A.F. was awarded an R.A.F. M.S.M.)
16. Carter, 2768 Cpl. G. W. (Swinton)
10. Chapman, 5046 Sgt. E. C.
4.   Childs, A.M.1 E. E.
16. Chirgwin, 13752 F./Sgt. G. E. (Streatham)
8.   Clarke, 291 Sgt. (A./Sgt./Maj.) J. F. Formerly Sapper, Air Battalion R.E. Cpl., 6 Sqn., France October, 1914. 2/Lieut. September 1917. Adjutant R.A.F. Hucknall in 1937. Sqn. Ldr. 1941
10. Coates, 1676 F./Sgt. W. A. H.
12. Colwill, 1859 Cpl. R.
16. Cook, 3472 Sgt. (A./Sgt. Maj.) A. J. (Newcastle-upon-Tyne)
8.   Cooper, 2131 F./Sgt. H. Born 1894. Enlisted November 1914. France February 1915. Flying Officer (C.E.O.) 1937. Retired 1948 as Wing Commander. Group was in McInnes collection:—1914/15 Star (A.M.1), British War and Victory Medals (S.M.1 R.A.F.), 1939/45 Star, Africa Star (N.A. 1942/3) Defence and War Medals, Jubilee 1935, Army M.S.M. and R.A.F. Long Service & Good Conduct Medal (Geo. V 1933)
3.   Cooper, 2570 Sgt. J. C.
16. Cummins, 632 Sgt. (A./Sgt.Maj.) T. Direct entrant August 1913. Group known: 1914 Star trio and Army M.S.M. Chief Master Mechanic 1918. 2/Lieut. 1920. From Bristol
16. Cundy, 1463 Sgt. (A./Sgt. Maj.) J. A. (St. John's Wood)
3.   Dandy, 6620 Cpl. (A./Sgt.) W. R.
14. Darke, Sgt. (A./F./Sgt.) F. F. W.
10. Davies, 213 Temp. S.M. C. T. Formerly Coldstream Guards. Served overseas from June, 1915. 2/Lieut. October 1917. Flight Lieut. 1927. Serving in 1931
10. Deacon, 77481 Sgt. H. Known, single
16. Dodd, 16530 F./Sgt. F. W. (Dalstone)
16. Duke, 4089 Sgt. (A./S.M.) R. W. (Folkstone)
6.   Dunn, 1847 Cpl. G. Enlisted September 1914. In France with 10 Sqn. at Chateau Warppe on 30 July 1916 when a phosphorus bomb fell from an aircraft in a hanger and the fuse ignited. He seized the bomb and ran 30 yds into the open. It exploded as he threw it away.

He prevented a most serious accident and loss of life. He was recommended for the Albert Medal but an Army M.S.M. for Gallantry was substituted. This is now in a significant collection in New York, together with the medals of Sweeting and Watson on this roll

3.   Durman, 3810 F./Sgt. C. W.

18.   Etheridge, 1669 F./Sgt. C. W. Enlisted September 1914, a fitter (Bishops Waltham)

18.   Evans, 403891 (formerly 50948) Sgt. T. (Merthyr). Group known: 1914/15 Star (Gunner R.F.A.), British War and Victory Medals (Chief Tech. R.A.F.) and Army M.S.M. (M.I.D. October, 1918)

2.   Felstead, 605 Sgt.Maj. G. Formerly Coldstream Guards. Entitled to 1914 Star trio. Awarded D.C.M. as S.M. 14 Sqn. in 1916. 2/Lieut. that year. Flying Officer (retired) 1921

1.   Foster, 2292 F./Sgt. R. G. Enlisted November 1914. Mentioned *L.G.* 11.10.16 with 11 Sqn. Devised machine gun mounting for Nieuport aircraft

3.   Fowles, 80 Sgt. (A./S.M.) E. A disciplinarian, enlisted August 1909 into Air Battalion R.E. Entitled to British War and Victory Medals. S.M.1 in 1918

7.   Frie, 3450 F./Sgt. L.

2.   Fulton, 1112 A./S.M. J. Enlisted into A.S.C. 1905. Entitled to 1914 Star trio. R.A.F. Long Service & Good Conduct Medal 1923 as S.M.1

2.   Gardiner, 178 F./Sgt. J. R. Formerly R.E. Royal Aero Club Aviator's Certificate December, 1913 as a Sergeant. Recommended for M.M. in July 1916. M.S.M. substituted. 2/Lieut. January 1918. Served in W.W.II as Wing Commander. Group known:— 1914/15 Star trio, 39/45 Star, Defence and War Medals and Army M.S.M.

18.   Gissing, 3090 F./Sgt. C. C. (Northampton). Flying Officer (Tech.) August 1919. Reserve of Air Force Officers 1926

2.   Goldthorpe, 498 F./Sgt. S. R. Enlisted in 1912 (Storeman), entitled to 1914 Star trio. R.A.F. Long Service & Good Conduct Medal, S.M.2, in 1930. Awarded 1935 Jubilee Medal, W.O.I, in 1938

18.   Golding, 1221 F./Sgt. W. J. F. (Kensington). Direct entrant, and electrician Entitled to 1914/15 Star trio

2.   Green, 1711 Cpl. G. Enlisted September 1914. Driver M.T. Sergeant in 1918

2.   Green, 136 F./Sgt. H. Enlisted 1909 Air Battalion R.E. D.C.M. in 1916 as F./Sgt. Chief Mechanic (Rigger Aero) in April 1918. Entitled to 1914 Star trio

18.   Hall, 9029 F./Sgt. F. S. (Sittingbourne)

8.   Hall, 1576 Sgt. G. H. Known: 1914 Star and bar trio and Army M.S.M. Aerial Gunner and photographer. 2/Lt. November 1917 K.I.A. December 1917

8.   Harrison, 39825 Sgt. (A./S.M.) R. W.

16.   Harvey, 5182 F./Sgt. W. (Wheathamstead)

2.   Hawley, 1025 F./Sgt. R. Entitled to 1914 Star. Retired 1920. Single M.S.M. known

3.   Hayward, 255 Sgt. (A./S.M.) W. C. Enlisted Grenadier Guards. 2/Lieut. February 1917. Group known: D.C.M. (June 1915), 1914 Star and bar trio (M.I.D.) and Army M.S.M.

2.   Hellyer, 718 F./Sgt. F. J. Direct entrant 1913. Entitled to 1914 Star trio. Awarded D.C.M. as a Pilot in Egypt 1916. Army M.S.M. and mention in despatches (1916), also for Egypt

3.   Hemming, 3724 Sgt. N. A. Entitled to 1914/15 Star trio (M.I.D. October 1916 for Darfur), Army M.S.M. and Sudan Medal (1910) with 17 Sqn. R.F.C.)

3.   Hepple, 780 Sgt. G. W. Direct entrant 1913. Fitter (aero engines). Group known: B.E.M. (Geo. V, 1927), 1914 Star and bar trio (M.I.D.), General Service Medal (Iraq, M.I.D.), India General Service Medal (N.W.F. 1935), Jubilee 1935, Army M.S.M. and R.A.F. Long Service & Good Conduct Medal (Geo. V, F./Sgt.). Awarded R.A.F. M.S.M. in 1921 for Mesopotamia but this was subsequently cancelled. Also served in W.W.II until 1944

16.   Hetton, 1647 F./Sgt. W. H. (Dover). Rigger Aero

14.   Holland, 1267 Sgt. R. J. H. (Branksome). Born 1894. Royal Aero Club Aviator's Certificate 1916. Commissioned 1917. Flying Officer in 1919. Flight Lieut. 1926. Retired 1934. Re-

called 1939-45. Sqn. Ldr. 1941. Alive in 1970. Group known: 1914/15 Star (Sgt.), British War and Victory Medals (Lieut. R.A.F., M.I.D.), Army M.S.M.

3.   Hooper, 3892 F./Sgt. H. I

3.   Horton, 3682 A.M.1 J. Entitled to 1914/15 Star trio (M.I.D. October 1916 for Darfur), Army M.S.M. and Sudan Medal (1910) (with 17 Sqn. R.F.C.)

14.   Horwood, 4384 Sgt. G. E. J. (Campden)

3.   Howard, 1416 F./Sgt. C. J. Enlisted 11 August 1914

9.   Huber, 3036 Tech.S.M. L. E.

2.   Hunt, 2057 Sgt. H. E. A. Clerk. Enlisted November 1914

18.   Hunt, 3552 F./Sgt. J. S. (Blandford). Commissioned and awarded Distinguished Flying Cross. A. photograph is known of his wearing D.F.C. and Army M.S.M. ribbons

18.   Huxter, 4256 S.M. T. J. (Barry Dock)

2.   Hyland, 607 Cpl. T. Enlisted 1913 directly into R.F.C. as a fitter. Awarded 1914 Star trio. Cpl. Mech. April 1918, later Sergeant 101 Sqn.

8.   Jappe, 1374 F./Sgt. G. Enlisted 8 August, 1914. Trio known: British War and Victory Medals and Army M.S.M. (Earned in 19 Sqn.). Chief Master Mech. April 1918

16.   Keane, 6281 Cpl. T. J. (Aberystwyth)

8.   Kellett, 4254 F./Sgt. J. W. Served in France from March 1916 in the fitting-shop

16.   King, 19497 Cpl. (A./Sgt.) E. W. (Harringay)

2.   Knight, 4999 (A./S.M. A. Pupil of Crypt Grammer School, Gloucester. Pilot Instructor pre-War at the Vickers Flying School. M.S.M. earned in France

8.   Lane, 10942 F./Sgt. E. A.

7.   Langfield, 106 F./Sgt. G. L. Enlisted 18 June 1912. In France from 9 August, 1914, the first R.F.C. O.R. traced as having landed. With the Aircraft Park. Disciplinarian S.M. in April 1918. R.A.F. Long Service & Good Conduct Medal 1930 as F./Sergeant

14.   Large Act F./Sgt. J. W. Single known

16.   Laughton, 11000 Sgt. E. (Conisbro)

16.   Leigh, 18014 Sgt. W. S. (Brighton)

14.   Leslie, 2021 Sgt. A. Group known: 1914/15 Star trio (all A.M.1 R.F.C.) and Army M.S.M.

7.   Lewis, 63 F./Sgt. E. A. Enlisted March 1907, served in the Air Battalion R.E. prior to the R.F.C. Awarded 1914 Star, then served in Egypt. Chief Master Mech. in April 1918

8.   Longhurst, 59 F./Sgt. J. Enlisted June 1911 into the Air Battalion R.E. Awarded 1914 Star trio. S.M.1 (Disciplinarian) April 1918

16.   Lyne, 4682 Sgt. C. (Chichester)

2.   Mantell, 3599 A./S.M. W. G.

14.   Medlam, 3396 Sgt. (A./F. Sgt.) H. H. (Nechells)

3.   Metz, 209 A./S.M. L. H. Enlisted 1910; formerly 57 Coy. R.G.A. Group known: 1914 Star and bar trio, Army M.S.M. and R.A.F. Long Service & Good Conduct Medal (last as S.M.1 in 1928). 7th Senior R.A.F. W.O. in 1931

2.   Meynell, 2988 A./S.M. E. Awarded D.C.M. Later Flight Lieutenant

2.   Millington, 8347 A./S.M. E. R.

8.   Moore, 16262 Cpl. T. H. Group known: British War and Victory Medals, 1935/45 Star, Defence and War Medals (M.I.D.), Army M.S.M., Air Efficiency Award (Flying Officer R.A.F.V.R.) and French Croix de Guerre

3.   Mullen, 64 A./S.M. C. Formerly 56 Coy. R.E. Royal Aero Club Aviator's Certificate 1913. Entitled to 1914 Star trio.Commissioned 1917

16.   Murton, 13795 F./Sgt. C. W. (Camberwell)

2.   Newton, 217 F./Sgt. D. H. Born 1891. Enlisted 1912. 1914 Star trio. Initially in the Aircaft Park from 16 August. R.A.F. Long Service & Good Conduct Medal July 1930 as S.M.1. Commissioned (C.E.O.) 1933. Awarded M.B.E. in 1937. Squadron Leader 1940. Wing Commander 1941. Retired 1947. Died 1978

13. Norris, 69380 AM2 A. H. 47th Balloon Section, France. Army M.S.M. for Gallantry
8. O'Connor, 1085 F./Sgt. (A./S.M.) M. Enlisted 1910. Trans into R.F.C. from Grenadier Guards. Awarded 1914 Star trio. S.M.1 (Disciplinarian) 1918
16. Orchard, 3862 F./Sgt. C. R. (Croydon)
15. Parke, 2546 Sgt. W. F. Army M.S.M. for Gallantry with the Home Forces
18. Payne, 11895 Sgt. A. L. (Blackheath)
8. Peters, 4234 F./Sgt. H.
18. Phillips, 404005 (formerly 51204) Cpl. C. H. (Cardiff)
12. Phillips, 78169 Cpl. P.
18. Pound, 3030 Sgt. F. W. (Liverpool)
14. Prickett, 5775 S.M. H. W. (Small Heath)
16. Ramsey, 22548 F./Sgt. F. (Snaith)
18. Rankin, 403905 (formerly 65382) A.M.1 J. (Kilmarnock). Group known: 1914/15 Star (Pte Ayrshire Yeo.), British War and Victory Medals (A.M.1 R.A.F.) and Army M.S.M.
2. Rapley, 1027 A./S.M. C. Born 1895. Awarded 1914 Star. 2/Lieut. R.F.C. 1917. Flight Lieut. 1927. Group Captain 1942 Air Commodore 1946 Awarded C.B.E. Retired 1950. Alive in 1977.
8. Ridley, 26950 Sgt. H. H.
10. Sharp, 120 A./S.M. W. Sgt. in 3 Sqn. in France August 1914. 2/Lt. October 1916
2. Shearing, 5853 A.M.1 S. Enlisted June 1915. Mentioned for work in Motor Pool at R.F.C. H.Q. Group known: 1914/15 Star (2A.M.), British War and Victory Medals (Sgt. R.A.F.) and M.S.M.
14. Simpson, 662 F./Sgt. W. (Sunderland). Direct entrant 1913. Awarded 1914 Star. S.M.1 (Discip.) in April 1918
3. Singleton, 7134 A.M.1 O. S.
3. Smith, 1498 F./Sgt. E. F.
16. Smyrk, 253 A./S.M. W. J. (Islington). Enlisted July 1912 directly into R.F.C. As Corporal in 6 Squadron, served in France from 7 October 1914. Serving with 60 Sqn. when awarded M.S.M. Chief Master Mech. in April 1918
3. Stringer, 3793 Sgt. H. B.
16. Sweeting, 1330 F./Sgt. W. H. (Cirencester). Enlisted in June 1914. Chief Master Mech. (Technical) in April 1918. Group known: 1914/15 Star trio and R.A.F. M.S.M. (in same collection as Dunne and Watson)
14. Swinburn, 11778 F./Sgt. W. (Sheffield)
3. Tallyn, 1428 F./Sgt. R. J.
8. Thomason, 5444 F./Sgt. W.
5. Todd, 3270 Sgt. J. W.
17. Treadaway, 77725 Cpl. E. M.S.M. for gallantry with the Home Forces
8. Trevett, 2507 F./Sgt. C.
7. Turner, 11181 Cpl. R. R. Pair known: British War Medal and Army M.S.M.
10. Vaile, 1651 F./Sgt. Enlisted September, 1914 as a Fitter
16. Wainwright, 1561 Sgt. (A./S.M.) J. (Caledonian Road, N.) Enlisted 14 August 1914 (Disciplinarian)
18. Walker, 1527 F./Sgt. R. O. (Chadleigh, Devon). Enlisted August 1914
2. Wansbury, 4865 Cpl. V. E.
3. Wardley, 2629 F./Sgt. L.
7. Watson, 20943 A.M.1 T. P. Pair known: British War Medal and Army M.S.M. See also Dunne and Sweeting. This M.S.M. was also gazetted 25 January, 1917. No cancellation has been traced.
2. Weaver, 2862 Cpl. R. S. Pair known: British War Medal and Army M.S.M.

16. Webb, 347 Sgt. (A./S.M.) H. (Finsbury Park, N.) Enlisted 1912 directly into R.F.C. Earned 1914 Star trio. Chief Master Mechanic (Technical) in 1918
16. Webber, 13802 F./Sgt. T. O. (Hawkhurst)
16. Weldon, 5082 A.M.1 J. G. (Sefton Park)
2. Whilton, 198 Sgt.Maj. E. Born 1887. Formerly Coldstream Guards. Central Flying School July 1912. Overseas as Sergeant in December 1915. Mentioned for Egypt in July 1916 (17 Sqn.). Awarded D.C.M. same month. Mentioned again in September, 1916 for Salonika. 2/ Lieut. October 1917. Again mentioned June 1919. Flight Lieut. 1924. Retired 1931. Served 1939/45 in R.A.F.V.R. Alive in 1969
16. White, 5949 F./Sgt. E. F. (Camberley)
11. Wilder, 8261 A.M.1 J. F.
16. Willis, 4996 Sgt. (T./S.M.) W. G. (Bristol)
18. Wilson, 7643 Cpl. F. E. (Great Yarmouth)
2. Wood, 1071 F./Sgt. E. R. A direct entrant in early 1914. Earned 1914 Star trio. 2/Lieut. February 1918. Sqn. Ldr. 1936. Wing Commander 1939, Group Captain 1941. Awarded C.B.E. Retired 1948. Alive 1977
3. Woodal, 7649 Sgt. F. A.
17. Woodford, 2190 A.M.1 C. J. Enlisted November 1914. Motor Cyclist. Promoted A.M.1 November 1917. M.S.M. for gallantry with the Home Forces
11. Wright, 2567 Sgt. H. H.

313303 W.O. James Robert Woollard, D.S.M.

Early in 1992, a very rare group appeared briefly on the market. With the medals were the original parchment discharge and service papers from the R.A.F. and the original Royal Naval certificate of Service.

The group is:—

> Distinguished Service Medal (Geo. V, *L.G.* 1 May, 1917, 'For Zeal and Devotion to Duty' during the period from 1 July to 31 December, 1917, K15829 P.O. (Mech.). R.N.A.S. (Mediterranean)),
>
> 1914/15 Star (K15829 A.M.1 R.N.A.S.),
>
> British War and Victory Medals (K15829 L.M. R.N.),
>
> India General Service Medal (Waziristan 1925, 313303 F./Sgt. R.A.F.),
>
> R.A.F. M.S.M. (313303 F./Sgt. R.A.F.) (For services in Kurdistan 1923 *L.G.* 11 June, 1924),
>
> R.A.F. Long Service & Good Conduct Medal (S.M.2 R.A.F.) (awarded with gratuity, A.M.W.O. 776/1930 *w.e.f.* 28 August, 1930.

This is a very unusual combination of medals. Firstly, the D.S.M. to R.N.A.S.—Abbott and Tamplin, in *'British Gallantry Awards,'* state that 4,052 D.S.M.s were awarded for services in the Great War, of which 53 were awarded to Allied (*i.e.* foreign) Seamen. No references have been traced to show the number awarded to P.O.s and ratings of the Royal Naval Air Service. However it is known that of the 1022 R.N. M.S.M.s issued 28 were to R.N.A.S. and of the 108 Conspicuous Gallantry Medals only four were to R.N.A.S. It may be acceptable to assume that between three and four per cent of D.S.M.s were likewise to R.N.A.S., perhaps 140 (?).

Secondly, the combination of D.S.M. and R.A.F. M.S.M.—only four such would appear to have been awarded:—

1. 204117 A./Chief Mech. W. S. Burville D.S.M., R.A.F. Formerly F4117 R.N.A.S. R.A.F. M.S.M. *L.G.* 1 January, 1919 (from East Cliff). Transferred to R.A.F. 1 April, 1918.

2. 3056 Chief Mech. Arthur Ernest Crispin, D.S.M., R.A.F. Formerly F2519 R.N.A.S. R.A.F. M.S.M. *L.G.* 3 June, 1919 (from Maidstone). Note: 3056 is an early 1915 R.F.C. number, indicating a transfer to R.N.A.S. later that year. The D.S.M. and R.A.F. M.S.M. are known, (D.S.M. as C.P.O. Mech. R.N.A.S. 1917) as a broken pair.

3. 200599 S.M.1 Samuel Percy Finch D.S.M., R.A.F. Formerly F599 R.N.A.S. R.A.F. M.S.M. *L.G.* 12 July, 1920 for services in South Russia. Transferred to R.A.F. 1 April, 1918.

4. Woollard, the subject of this appendix.

Thirdly, the India General Service Medal clasp Waziristan 1925, a bar almost exclusively awarded to the Royal Air Force—precise figures of the actual numbers issued varies, *'British Battles & Medals'* (Spink, 1988) suggests 47 Officers and 215 Men from 5, 27 and 60 Sqns. and Tank H.Q., plus one army officer and one civilian. Sqn. Ldr. Pickstock, in *O.M.R.S. Journal*, September 1968, suggests 75 Officers and 203 O.R.s and goes into great detail to explain why (and which) men chose to retain or claim Waziristan 1921/24 rather than Waziristan 1925. Remarkably, they were not allowed to claim both, even if so entitled. R. J. Malloch, in Hamilton's *Despatch No. 3*, 1978, whilst repeating the numbers of 47 Officers and 214 airmen, first recorded in Gordon, from the initial three Squadrons involved in March, than adds that 'At the end of March and early in April, further aircraft were brought into the area. One flight of No. 31 (A.C.) Sqn., one flight of No. 5 (A.C.) Sqn. and one flight of No. 20 (A.C.) Sqn. By the end of May the airborne force had increased to 35 aircraft, from the original 26.

The highest estimation of the number of personnel involved would appear to be 94 Officers and 369 O.R.s, but, as Wing Commdr. Routledge, in *O.M.R.S. Journal*, Winter 1990, explains, many of these would have retained or claimed the earlier clasp. However many were issued, one thing is certain, it wasn't many, and only three of these appear to be combined with an R.A.F. M.S.M.:—

1. 157159 A.C.1 Ernest William Braund, *L.G.* 12 July, 1920 for South Russia. He was entitled to British War and Victory Medals, India General Service Medal (Waziristan 1925, Sgt.), R.A.F. M.S.M., R.A.F. Long Service & Good Conduct Medal (as Flight Sergt..), and St. Stanislaus Medal. He joined the R.F.C. in May, 1917.
2. 651 Sergt. Mech. Frederick Ruben Joseph Cooper, from Bethnal Green, enlisted originally in June 1906, formerly 6812 3/Coldstream Guards. His M.S.M. was in *L.G.* 1 January, 1919. He was awarded 1914 Star trio, and later R.A.F. Long Service & Good Conduct Medal as Sergeant, *w.e.f.* 13 June, 1924.
3. Woollard, who therefore appears to have been awarded a unique group to the R.N. and the R.A.F.

James Robert Woollard was born 4 August, 1894, in Chelmsford, Essex, and was by trade a gardener. He joined the R.N. (Portsmouth Division) on 28 August, 1912, only 5′ 4½″ tall, as a Stoker 2nd class. Before W.W.I, he served on *'Renown,'* *'Bulwark'* *'Crescent'* and *'Audacious'* and appears to have spent most of his War Service in the Mediterranean Theatre (President II, E. Mediterranean). He was promoted to Stoker 1st class in August 1913, Air Mechanic in April 1915, Leading Mech. in August 1916 and P.O.M.(E.) in January, 1916.

He transferred to the Royal Air Force on its formation on 1 April, 1918 as Sergt. Mech. Reclassified F./Sergeant Fitter 4 November, 1918, he was promoted Sgt. Maj. 2nd class 1 November, 1928 and Warrant Officer (Engineer) 1 April 1933.

It was in November 1921, that, as part of Draft 30, 17 Sqn., he was posted to Iraq. There, he did not qualify for the General Service Medal (Iraq or Kurdistan) as his Squadron was not present in the relevant areas during the qualifying dates. However, it was for service in Kurdistan in 1923 that he was awarded the R.A.F. M.S.M.

In October, 1923 he was posted to 20 Sqn. at Karachi, India, and it was with the one eligible flight of that Squadron that he earned the Waziristan 1925 clasp.

1927 saw him back in the U.K., but from 1930 to 1932 he served on H.M.S. *Glorious*, finally taking his discharge in February, 1935.

His R.A.F. discharge states:—

This warrant officer has completed over 22 years service. He was transferred to the Royal Air Force on 1st April, 1918, having served with the Royal Navy and Royal Naval Air Service since 28th August, 1912. He is a very competent technical warrant officer with skill of hand as a mechanic and capable of supervising any normal workshop. He is recommended for any post where loyal and trustworthy attributes are essential qualifications.

His character and general conduct have at all times been 'Very Good.'

He has been awarded the Distinguished Service Medal, 1914/15 Star, British War and Victory Medals, India General Service Medal with Clasp 'Waziristan 1925,' Meritorious Service Medal, and the Long Service and Good Conduct Medal. He is also in possession of the Royal Air Force Swimming Certificate.

No R.A.F. M.S.M.s were gazetted after these eight for Kurdistan, 1923, in *L.G.* 11 June, 1924. In alphabetical order these were to:—

    755   Flight Sergeant William Gordon Bates
201227   Flight Sergeant Robert Leslie Bell
 14035   Sergeant Frederick Herbert Catton

      1905 Flight Sergeant William Dixon Fotheringham
      6475 Sergeant Sidney Hamblin
    206123 Flight Sergeant Sidney Walter Thomas
        23 Sergeant Major 1st Class John Wilkinson
    313303 Flight Sergeant James Robert Woollard

—making this not only a unique group, but also one containing effectively the last immediate R.A.F. M.S.M. awarded.

(See Vol. II, 1924)

APPENDIX X

L12448 Pte. A./Cpl. A. E. Funnell,
3/Royal Sussex Regt. (Mitchen)
ES50928 Pte. A./Sgt. W. Smith R.A.S.C. (Harrogate)

Naval Department
British Military Mission
Novorossisk
16th January 1920.

Sir,

I have the honour to forward a narrative account of my proceedings on board the Russian Ice Breaker *'Donskoi Gerla'* during the evacuation of the British Military Mission from Taganrog.

In accordance with your orders and by arrangements with the Chief of Russian General Staff, I boarded the Ice Breaker *'Donskoi Gerla'* at 5 a.m. on Thursday 1st January 1920, who was escorting to Yeisk a convoy of 8 ships. I took with me Corporal Smith R.A.S.C. and Private Funnell, Royal Sussex Regiment, as guard, and Victor Pintal (lent by Colonel Radcliffe of Tank Corps as Interpreter. My orders were to establish communication with a British destroyer that had been ordered to the 15 foot anchorage (about 25 miles from Taganrog) and on arrival of convoy at Yeisk to return to Taganrog in the icebreaker and take off any Russian or British personnel who had been unable to get away by rail or road.

A start was made at 8 a.m. the Ice Breaker first of all releasing the 8 ships, and then proceeding ahead to break a passage through the ice which was thick and solid.

Captain Podgourny of the Russian Navy was on board the *'Donskoi Gerla'* in charge of the convoy, and from the beginning he showed himself to be most obliging and ready to assist my plans.

The ships of the convoy were composed of four medium sized coasting steamers and four tugs. They were loaded with a certain quantity of military material, a few troops and a number of better class refugees with their belongings. I consider there was ample deck space remaining for a considerable quantity of stores and personnel, provided the draft of the ships and shallow water would permit of their being further loaded. The speed of advance of the convoy was about half a knot. About 6 p.m. in the evening a big fire was observed at Taganrog which was thought to be the Baltic Works.

During the night and following day thick ice was encountered and there was no sign of a destroyer at the 15 foot anchorage. Convoy arrived at Yeisk at 7 p.m. Friday 2nd January and I proceeded to the telephone office, and after getting into communication with Station Commandant at Raganrog I ascertained that all British and Russian Military Personnel had left Taganrog and that the town was being administered by a 'local government.' Therefore, in consultation with Captain Podgourny, I decided to proceed towards Mariupol in the hope of finding the destroyer in open water or of finding a second destroyer which had been ordered to Mariupol.

At 10 a.m. Saturday 3rd January, *'Donskoi Gerla'* proceeded, thick ice was encountered all the way and no destroyer was sighted. On arrival at Mariupol at midnight, what at first was thought to be a British Destroyer turned out to be another Russian Ice Breaker the *'Guidemac'* who informed us that the Bolsheviks had entered the town at 6 p.m. that day and that the ships around us were icebound and full of military stores, troops and refugees and he asked our assistance to free them. Owing however to a heavy fall of snow, the ice off Mariupol was of such a nature that *'Donskoi Gerla'* herself became icebound.

Daylight showed us to be in a position about 4 miles South East of Mariupol harbour and 11 ships of various sizes stuck fast in the ice in our vicinity. During Sunday efforts were made to reach the *'Violetta'* a large steamer crowded with refugees, but it was impossible to get closer than to a distance of 3 cables. In the afternoon I observed the people on board the two inshore ships were abandoning them and I later discovered that the soldiers and crews had looted these ships and then walked ashore across the ice to join the 'Reds.'

Meanwhile the whole ice flow was moving very slowly in a South Westerly direction, and the temperature rising above zero in the afternoon, the ice became penetrable and both icebreakers were able to continue freeing the ships. Work was continued all through the night the ships being freed, and a passage broken for them in a S.W. direction till open water was reached at a distance of approximately 12 miles from Mariupol.

At 8 a.m. it only remained to release and tow away the two inshore vessels that had been abandoned the previous day. While doing this the Bolshevik Artillery opened fire (probably from a armoured train) but owing to the morning mist, their shooting was very poor and both vessels were safely towed away, one ship contained two motor launches which may have belonged to the Volga Flotilla, and the other contained horses and stores.

On reaching open water, *'Guidemac'* took the vessels in tow and proceeded for Kertch, and *'Donskoi Gerla'* having completed with coal from one of the above mentioned vessels, shaped course for Yeisk.

On arrival at Yeisk on the morning of Tuesday 6th January 1920, I received information that Taganrog had fallen the previous day. I therefore decided to regain touch with Advanced Headquarters and left in the evening for Tichoretskaya.

On arrival at Tichoretskaya I fell in with Colonel Roch R.A.M.C. who was proceeding to Advanced Headquarters at Bataisk and he kindly offered me a passage in his coach. I therefore despatched Corporal Smith and Private Funnell to the Base in a Mission Coach and in due course arrived at Bataisk on Thursday 8th January 1920 and reported to Brigadier General Cotton. I then received information that you had left for Tichoretskaya the day previously, where I eventually joined you.

I should like to mention the great kindness and consideration I received from Captain Podgourny while I was on board *'Donskoi Gerla.'* Both he and the Captain of the *'Guidemac'* showed a commendable spirit of devotion to duty and seamanlike qualities in successfully freeing the steamers at Mariupol, as had they not remained standing by, these vessels, all the stores, troops and refugees on board would most certainly have been captured by the Bolsheviks.

Corporal Smith R.A.S.C. Private Funnell, Royal Sussex Regiment, and Interpreter Victor Pintal all carried out their duties in a most satisfactory manner under novel and trying conditions. I consider that their presence in the *'Donskoi Gerla'* had a considerable moral effect on the crew, some of whom were of doubtful temper.

I have the honour to be,
Sir,
Your Obedient Servant,
(Signed.) NORMAN B. F. PEPLOE.
Lieutenant R.N.

From. Naval Adviser, British Military Mission.

To.   Brigadier General A.S. Cotton, C.M.G. D.S.O. Royal Artillery.

Date.   22nd January 1920.

Lieutenant Norman B.F. Peploe's report of the proceedings of the Icebreaker *'Donskoi Gerla'* between dates of 1st and 6th January 1920 is forwarded to you for submission to the General Commanding British Military Mission in South Russia,

A copy of the report and of this minute has been sent to the Naval Commander-in-Chief, Mediterranean Station.

I consider that the operations of both Icebreakers were carried out with vigour and determination that the G.O.C. should be requested to bestow suitable decorations on Captain (First Rank) Pedgourmy, Russian Navy, of *'Donskoi Gerla'* and Captain (Second Rank), (name unknown) of the icebreaker *'Guidemac.'*

From Lieutenant Peploe's report it is clear that his presence in the icebreaker together with that of Corpl. Smith R.A.S.C. and Private Funnell, Royal Sussex Regiment, did much to support and encourage Captain Pedgourmy, especially on the 5th and 6th January, when the *'Donskoi Gerla'* lay icebound under the fire of Bolshevik Artillery, which might reasonable have been thought to be the commencement of a serious attack by 'Red' troops across the ice, and I consider that Lieutenant Norman B.F. Peploe and his men worthily upheld the best traditions of the British service.

Under these circumstances I wish to recommend Lieutenant Norman B. F. Peploe for a bar to his Distinguished Service Cross, and Corporal Smith and Private Funnell, and Interpreter Victor Pintal (attached Tank Corps) for suitable awards.

(Signed) G. D. FREEMANTLE
Constantinople.
Captain, Royal Navy.

22nd January 1920.

(See Vol II 1920)

APPENDIX Y

Faversham

M.S.M.s awarded following the Disastrous Explosion at the Explosive Loading Company's Works, Faversham, Kent, 2nd April, 1916.

[A much fuller account, from which this résumé is drawn, was published in the *O.M.R.S. Journal* of Summer, 1979. The author was Major J. D. Sainsbury, T.D.]

For several centuries Faversham had been recognised as one of the centres of explosives (particularly gunpowder) production in England. One of the Faversham firms devoted to war production was the Explosive Loading Company Ltd.; and it was at their works on Uplees Marshes that there occurred on 2 April 1916 one of the memorable disasters in the history of the British explosives industry.

At approximately 12.10 on 2 April 1916 it was noticed that sparks from a boiler house had set fire to some empty sacks which were piled against the matchboard wall of a shed being used as a T.N.T. store. The same building was also being used to store ammonium nitrate, which when mixed with T.N.T., produces a powerful and less stable explosive known as amatol. The store may have held as much as 200 tons, while the total distributed around the factory site may well have exceeded 500 tons. Very shortly afterwards, at approximately 1.20 p.m. the building blew up and there were two large sympathetic explosions in the nitro-glycerine washing plant some 150 yards away. Dead and injured lay everywhere, often covered in mud or debris and with their clothes alight.

Two further T.N.T. stores blew up. Two separate parties of troops who rushed to the scene, one from the Kent Royal Garrison Artillery and Kent Fortress Engineers from the anti-aircraft battery at Oare under Corporal C. T. Harris, and one from 2nd/13th Lancashire Battery, 2nd/3rd West Lancashire Brigade, R.F.A., under 2nd Lieutenant J. M. Stebbings.

Corporal Harris's Party

The first list of awards of the Meritorious Service Medal 'for gallantry in the performance of military duty' under the amending warrant of 3 January 1917 was gazetted on 12 March 1917 and corrected on 17 April 1917. It contained the following names:—

1105	Gunner C. P. Cotter	1st/1st Company, Kent R.G.A.
278	Bombardier A. F. Edwards	1st/1st Company, Kent R.G.A.
893	Gunner A. Pearce	1st/1st Company, Kent R.G.A.
1085	Gunner L. A. Beaney	2nd/1st Company, Kent R.G.A.
1175	Sapper S. G. Banester	1st/4th Company, Kent (Fortress) R.E.
982	Lance-Corporal H. W. Fever	1st/4th Company, Kent (Fortress) R.E.
587	Sergeant C. T. Harris	1st/4th Company, Kent (Fortress) R.E.
1366	Lance-Corporal S. Parker	1st/4th Company, Kent (Fortress) R.E.
1042	Corporal R. W. G. Rees	1st/4th Company, Kent (Fortress) R.E.
1153	2nd Corporal S. M. Williams	1st/4th Company, Kent (Fortress) R.E.

All ten soldiers were serving with the anti-aircraft battery at Oare, near Faversham. While the initial fire was still burning Corporal Harris was ordered to double the party to the scene and assist in any way possible. They arrived just as the explosion occurred but escaped injury even though they were only about 120 yards from the T.N.T. washing houses. They went at once to the scene of the main explosion and found a crater forty yards across and about twenty feet deep, surrounded by debris and dead and injured. Corporal Harris decided to concentrate on recovering the victims and depositing them across the ditch where they could be picked up by other helpers. In several cases the victims' clothing was on fire and had to be extinguished before they could be moved. The recommendation for all ten awards was in the following terms:

'While assisting in the rescue of the wounded at a fire which occurred at the Explosive Loading Company's works at Faversham on Sunday 2 April 1916, Corporal Harris and his party by their great courage, devotion to duty and self sacrifice, not only prevented further explosion, but by their gallant conduct set such a splendid example that others, who at first showed some diffidence at entering the danger area became willing helpers in the rescue. Explosions were constantly taking place making the work of rescuing the wounded particularly dangerous. A great crater measuring about forty yards in diameter and about twenty feet deep had been formed by the explosion of forty or fifty tons of T.N.T. and scenes around this crater were terrible. The fire was still raging and about 400 and 500 tons of explosives still remained in the vicinity. Sappers Parker and Williams actually entered a burning building full of loaded mines in their search for the wounded and they had just got clear when the mines in the building exploded. The first explosion took place at about 1.30 p.m. followed by numerous others. At 3.00 p.m. Corporal Harris reported to the O.C. Battery that plenty of assistance had then arrived and he was instructed to withdraw his party, which he did at 3.15 p.m. By their gallant conduct and devotion to duty Corporal Harris and his party not only showed a splendid example but were the means of preventing what promised to be a great disaster.'

2nd Lieutenant Stebbing's Party

A list of awards of the Meritorious Service Medal 'for gallantry' gazetted on 12 December 1917 contained the following names:—

685774	Bombardier C. Ashley	686271	Driver W. Neill
685900	Driver G. Critchley	685805	Gunner P. Roberts
685909	Gunner E. Comer	686377	Gunner G. E. Wright
688305	Driver B. Dugdale		

all of 3rd West Lancashire Brigade, R.F.A., and a full account of their involvement is in the form of a report by 2nd Lieutenant J. M. Stebbings, 2nd/3rd West Lancashire Brigade, R.F.A.

'.... on Sunday 2nd April at 1.20 p.m., on information received I commandeered a motor bus and proceeded with a detachment of men of the 2nd/3rd Lancashire Battery to the scene of a fire at Uplees. We arrived there between 1.30 and 1.35 p.m. and proceeded to remove injured men. At first I did not notice any other men present, but soon found 4–6 men whom I did not recognise; two men of the Royal Engineers I particularly noticed.

A second explosion occurred at about 1.40 p.m. besides many minor explosions. Each victim had to be dug out of the mud and debris by hand and in many cases it was necessary to extinguish their clothing or tear it off as many of the injured men were on fire. No hurdles were obtainable for use as stretchers and the casualties had to be dragged or carried through mud and ditches with their rescuers sometimes up to their necks in water.

The handful of rescuers worked heroically and were above all praise, especially during the explosion. Later more troops from this brigade arrived, passages were made across the ditches and hurdles procured. No fire fighting appliances were used until late in the afternoon.

I cannot speak too highly of the courage and endurance of these few men of the Engineers, Anti-Aircraft Battery and 2nd/13th Lancashire Battery who worked alone for the first 30–35 minutes and removed between 30 and 50 very badly injured men.'

Awards of the Edward Medal to Military Personnel

On 20 June 1917 the Secretary of State was able to write to A.G.10 as follows:—
'The Secretary of State considers that the soldiers whose conduct has been brought to his notice by the Army Council behaved with great bravery but he would not be able to recommend more than a limited number of medals as in the case of the fire brigade. He understands that two parties of soldiers took part in the work of rescue .... and he will be prepared to recommend the award of three (or at most four) Edward Medals of the Second Class to the men in these two parties who may be selected as most deserving of the medal.'

Although the way was now open for the Edward Medal to be awarded to the military personnel involved in rescue work following the explosion, it was not until 22 January 1918 that the *London Gazette* announced the award to Corporal Charles Ashley, Bombardier Bert Dugdale, Bombardier Arthur Frederick Edwards, Sergeant Charles Thomas Harris and Lieutenant John Morley Stebbings 'on account of their gallant conduct in assisting in the rescue work on the occasion of the explosion which occurred at Faversham on 2nd April 1916.' The Secretary of State's commitment to 'at the most four' medals was clearly extended. However no attempt seems to have been made to cancel awards of the Meritorious Service medal to the soldiers who later received the Edward Medal.

War Services of Recipients of Awards

Name	Faversham Award(s)	Great War Awards and others where known
C. P. Cotter	M.S.M.	British War and Victory Medals as 128457, R.G.A.
A. F. Edwards (1)	E.M./M.S.M.	British War and Victory Medals as 128452, R.G.A.
A. Pearce	M.S.M.	British War and Victory Medals as 128463, R.G.A.
L. A. Beaney (2)	M.S.M.	British War and Victory Medals as 1085, Gnr. R.A.
S. G. Banester	M.S.M.	No record of service abroad
H. W. Fever	M.S.M.	No record of service abroad
C. T. Harris (3)	E.M./M.S.M.	No record of service abroad, Territorial Force Efficiency Medal (A.O. 507/1920) as 540069, R.E.; First Clasp as 2201492, R.E. (A.O. 36/1931)
S. Parker	M.S.M.	No record of service abroad
R. W. G. Rees	M.S.M.	No record of service abroad
S. M. Williams	M.S.M.	No record of service abroad
C. Ashley	E.M./M.S.M.	British War and Victory Medals as 685774, R.F.A.
G. Critchley	M.S.M.	British War and Victory Medals as 685900, R.F.A.
E. Comer	M.S.M.	British War and Victory Medals as 685909, R.F.A.
B. Dugdale	E.M./M.S.M.	British War and Victory Medals as 686305, R.F.A.
W. Neill	M.S.M.	British War and Victory Medals as 686271, R.F.A.

P. Roberts	M.S.M.	British War and Victory Medals as 685805, R.F.A.
G. E. Wright	M.S.M.	British War and Victory Medals as 686377, R.F.A.
J. M. Stebbings (4)	E.M.	M.C. (*L.G.* 3 June 1919); M.I.D. (*L.G.* 21 May 1918); British War and Victory Medals; 1939/45, Africa and France & Germany Stars, Defence and War medals, M.I.D. (*L.G.* 16 April 1942), Coronation 1937, Coronation 1953, Efficiency Decoration (*L.G.* 13 Aug. 1935); Four Clasps (*L.G.* 16 March 1962).

As all the units involved were Home Defence or Second Line Territorial units, it is not surprising that there were no awards of the 1914 or 1914-15 Stars.

(1) Edward Medal exchanged for George Cross February 1973.
(2) Trio of medals known: British War and Victory Medals (1085 Gnr. R.A.) and M.S.M. (1085 Gnr. 2nd/1st Coy. Kent R.G.A. T.F.).
(3) Sergeant Harris's Edward Medal and M.S.M. are in the Royal Engineers Museum, Chatham, but without his Territorial Force Efficiency Medal.
(4) Lt.-Col. Stebbings served between the wars with 59th Field Brigade R.A. and was mobilised in 1939.

(See Vols. I & IV, 1917)

APPENDIX Z

Gallantry At Sea – Warwickshire Yeomanry

Built in 1903, the S.S. *Wayfarer* was a steel hulled four masted schooner of 9,599 gross tons, with twin screw steam reciprocating engines. She was built by Workman Clarke & Co. Ltd. of Belfast for the Charente Stream Ship Co. Ltd. and managed by T. & J. Harrison. Her length was 505 feet and Liverpool was her port of registration. During October 1914 the *'Wayfarer'* was placed under War Office control.

On the 10th April, 1915 the Transport *'Wayfarer'* sailed for Egypt, having on board, under the command of Major R. A. Richardson, five other officers; Capt. R. Lakin, Lieuts. H. R. Yorke, R. F. K. Gooch, R. B. Palmer (Vet. Officer, A.V.C.) and Capt. Wallace, R.A.M.C., with 189 N.C.O.s and men and 763 horses and mules. The following day, 11th April, when 60 miles W.N.W. of the Scilly Isles, the ship was struck by a torpedo, on the port side just forward of the engine room. Both the engine room and boilers were flooded.

All on board went to their boat stations and the boats with their occupants were safely got away with the exception of one, which capsized with the loss of Cpl. E. R. T. Powell, Pte. P. C. Kirby and Pte. W. H. Lawton of the Warwickshire Yeomanry and Pte. Phipps of the Army Service Corps. An hour later a small trading steamer, the S.S. *Framfield*, came to the rescue and all were transferred on board.

A few hours later the *'Wayfarer'* was still afloat and Major Richardson, after consultation with the Captain of the *'Wayfarer'*, Captain Cownie, decided to return to the ship and, fortunately was able to save the life of Pte. Birchley, who had been left behind and almost drowned under the bales of hay in one of the holds. Pte. G. A. Aston was unfortunately found drowned in the hay hold, having been on stable duty when the explosion took place (he was later buried with military honours at Queenstown, Ireland).

After working amongst the horses, Major Richardson decided to call for a fatigue party of twenty men from the *'Framfield'* to assist and Lieut. Yorke and Palmer arrived with 18 men, who in conjunction with the ships officers managed to carry on the work. Meanwhile H.M.T. *Newlyn* had come up and Lieut. Gooch and 115 men were taken on board for conveyance to Falmouth. The *'Framfield'* still with two officers and 53 men of the Warwickshire Yeomanry on board volunteered to take the *'Wayfarer'* in tow and headed for Queenstown. With six holds flooded out of nine and the horses up to their knees in water, progress was slow. On the morning of the 13th two Admiralty tugs relieved the *'Framfield'* and took the *'Wayfarer'* in tow, which was safely anchored in Queenstown Harbour later that afternoon. 760 animals were safely landed, only three horses having been lost, one of pneumonia and two by accident.

On the 29th April 1915 Major Richardson with Captain R.Lakin, Lieuts. Gooch and Yorke, and 130 N.C.O.s and men with 80 horses embarked on board H.M.T. *Lake Manitoba* and sailed for Egypt.

It was not until 1918 that the men received awards for their gallant and meritorious service in connection with the *'Wayfarer'* incident. The *'Wayfarer'* was repaired and survived the war, being broken up in 1926.

Of the horses, many were still in service at home and abroad up to the end of the war.

In 1918 re-organisation of the regiment took place for service in France, it was to form two companies (A and B) of a Machine Gun Battalion, eventually designated the 100 Warwick and S. Notts. Battalion, Machine Gun Corps. The command of this battalion was given to Lieut. Col H. Gray-Cheape and Major P. H. Warwick, S. Notts. Hussars, was appointed 2nd in Command. On 23rd May the battalion embarked on board H.M.T. *Leasowe Castle* at Alexandria. On 26th she sailed in a convoy of six transports and in the early hours of the 27th, about 100 miles from

Alexandria the *'Leasowe Castle'* was struck by a torpedo on the starboard side. The casualties included, Warwick Yeomanry: Lieut. Col. Gray-Cheape, O.C. Troops, Captain F. Drake, Ship's Adjutant and nine O.R.s; S. Notts. Hussars: eight officers and 44 O.R.s.

Honours and awards to the Warwickshire Yeomanry in connection with the 'Wayfarer' incident

Major R. Airth-Richardson. Officer Commanding.
The promotion of Major Richardson to the rank of Brevet Lieutenant Colonel was officially announced on 17th May 1915.

The following appear in the *London Gazette* of Friday 6th September, 1918.
His Majesty the King has been pleased to approve of the following awards for distinguished and gallant services rendered on the occasion of the destruction or damage by enemy action of Hospital Ships, transports and Storeships.

Military Cross;
    Captain (Acting Major) Robert Bacon Palmer. A.V.C. att. Yeomanry.
    Captain Henry Reginald Yorke. Yeomanry.

Meritorious Service Medal;

310446	Pte. Bennett, A.	310196	F.Q.M.Sjt. Jones, J. W.
310022	L./Cpl. Biddels, G.	311302	S./Smith Cpl. Newman, J.
310010	Pte. Bowen, A. J.	310255	Sgt. Pearson, J. E.
310725	Sjt Colley, C. H.	310307	Pte. Spencer, J. J. H.
1468	Sjt Cox, E. J.	310458	Cpl. Trenfield, E. G.
310106	L./Cpl. Daulman, H. H.	310354	Pte. Warner, T.
310104	Pte. Dixon, J.	2184	L./Cpl. Wilkes, J. A.
310120	Pte. Farndon, F.	310406	Pte. Woodward, A.
310181	Sjt Hough, B. M.M.	285970	Pte. Young, H. M.

The recipients of the Meritorious Service Medal were also mentioned as follows:—
'have been brought to the notice of the Secretary of State for War for valuable services rendered on the occasion of the sinking or damage by enemy action of Hospital Ships, Transports and Storeships' (*L.G.* 6.9.1918, page 10526).

Service notes of the Officers and men

R. A. Richardson	Major 1910. 2nd in Command August 1914. Brevet Lt. Col. 17th May 1915. M.I.D.
H. R. Yorke	Lieut. 21.9.1914. Captain 1.6.1916. Major 17.5.1916. Wounded in action Gallipoli 21.8.1915. M.C. Group sold 1985: M.C., 1914/15 Star (Lieut.), British War and Victory Medals (M.I.D. oakleaf)
R. E. Palmer	A.V. Corps attached Warwickshire Yeomanry. Lieut. 11.11.1913, Territorial Force. Captain 5.8.1915. M.C.
A. Bennett	Home town Leamington Spa, Warwickshire.
G. Biddells	Home town Rugby, Warwickshire.
A. J. Bowen	Enlisted Warwick. Later 201965 Tank Corps.
C. H. Colley	Enlisted Warwick. Later 2nd Lieut. Imp. Camel Corps.
E. J. Cox	Home town Knowle, Warwickshire. Died of disease, Alexandria 10.8.1915.

H. H. Daulman	Home town Nuneaton, Warwickshire. Wounded Gallipoli 21.8.1915. Killed in action, Romani, 5.8.1916.
J. Dixon	Home town Dunlavin, Wicklow, Ireland. Awarded Military Medal. Later commissioned Lieut.
F. Farndon	Enlisted Warwick. Later R./366615 A.S. Corps.
B. Hough	Home town Wolverhampton. Wounded in action, Romani, 5.8.1916. Took part in the charge of Huj, 8.11.1917. Military Medal.
J. W. Jones	Enlisted Warwick.
J. Newman	Home town Charlecote.
J. E. Pearson	Home town Swansea. Wounded Gallipoli 21.8.1915. Killed in action during the charge at Huj, 8.11.1917.
J. J. H. Spencer	Home town Elmdon, Warwickshire.
E. G. Trenfield	Home town Kineton, Warwickshire. Wounded, France. 20.9.1918.
T. Warner	Enlisted Warwick. Later 40343 1st Class A.M. R.A.F.
J. A. Wilkes	Enlisted Warwick. Later T./Lieut. M.G. Corps (Cav.).
A. Woodward	Enlisted Warwick.
H. M. Young	Home town Stow on the Wold, Gloucs.

(See Vol. III, 1918)

Printed in the United Kingdom
by Lightning Source UK Ltd.
121688UK00001B/13-14/A